Lecture Notes in Computer Science   9530

Commenced Publication in 1973
Founding and Former Series Editors:
Gerhard Goos, Juris Hartmanis, and Jan van Leeuwen

Editorial Board

More information about this series at http://www.springer.com/series/7407

Guojun Wang · Albert Zomaya
Gregorio Martinez Perez · Kenli Li (Eds.)

Algorithms and Architectures for Parallel Processing

15th International Conference, ICA3PP 2015
Zhangjiajie, China, November 18–20, 2015
Proceedings, Part III

 Springer

Editors
Guojun Wang
Central South University
Changsha
China

Gregorio Martinez Perez
University of Murcia
Murcia
Spain

Albert Zomaya
The University of Sydney
Sydney, NSW
Australia

Kenli Li
Hunan University
Changsha
China

ISSN 0302-9743   ISSN 1611-3349 (electronic)
Lecture Notes in Computer Science
ISBN 978-3-319-27136-1   ISBN 978-3-319-27137-8 (eBook)
DOI 10.1007/978-3-319-27137-8

Library of Congress Control Number: 2015955380

LNCS Sublibrary: SL1 – Theoretical Computer Science and General Issues

Springer International Publishing AG Switzerland is part of Springer Science+Business Media
(www.springer.com)

Welcome Message from the ICA3PP 2015 General Chairs

Welcome to the proceedings of the 15th International Conference on Algorithms and Architectures for Parallel Processing (ICA3PP 2015), which was organized by Central South University, Hunan University, National University of Defense Technology, and Jishou University.

It was our great pleasure to organize the ICA3PP 2015 conference in Zhangjiajie, China, during November 18–20, 2015. On behalf of the Organizing Committee of the conference, we would like to express our cordial gratitude to all participants who attended the conference.

ICA3PP 2015 was the 15th event in the series of conferences started in 1995 that is devoted to algorithms and architectures for parallel processing. ICA3PP is now recognized as the main regular event in the world that covers many dimensions of parallel algorithms and architectures, encompassing fundamental theoretical approaches, practical experimental projects, and commercial components and systems. The conference provides a forum for academics and practitioners from around the world to exchange ideas for improving the efficiency, performance, reliability, security, and interoperability of computing systems and applications.

ICA3PP 2015 attracted high-quality research papers highlighting the foundational work that strives to push beyond the limits of existing technologies, including experimental efforts, innovative systems, and investigations that identify weaknesses in existing parallel processing technology.

ICA3PP 2015 consisted of the main conference and six international symposia and workshops. Many individuals contributed to the success of the conference. We would like to express our special appreciation to Prof. Yang Xiang, Prof. Andrzej Goscinski, and Prof. Yi Pan, the Steering Committee chairs, for giving us the opportunity to host this prestigious conference and for their guidance with the conference organization. Special thanks to the program chairs, Prof. Albert Zomaya, Prof. Gregorio Martinez Perez, and Prof. Kenli Li, for their outstanding work on the technical program. Thanks also to the workshop chairs, Dr. Mianxiong Dong, Dr. Ryan K.L. Ko, and Dr. Md. Zakirul Alam Bhuiya, for their excellent work in organizing attractive symposia and workshops. Thanks also to the publicity chairs, Prof. Carlos Becker Westphall, Dr. Yulei Wu, Prof. Christian Callegari, Prof. Kuan-Ching Li, and Prof. James J. (Jong Hyuk) Park, for the great job in publicizing this event. We would like to give our thanks to all the members of the Organizing Committee and Program Committee as well as the external reviewers for their efforts and support. We would also like to give our thanks to the keynote speakers, Prof. John C.S. Lui, Prof. Jiannong Cao, Prof. Wanlei Zhou, and Prof. Hai Jin, for offering insightful and enlightening talks. Last but not least, we would like to thank all the authors who submitted their papers to the conference.

November 2015

Guojun Wang
Peter Mueller
Qingping Zhou

Welcome Message from the ICA3PP 2015 Program Chairs

On behalf of the Program Committee of the 15th International Conference on Algorithms and Architectures for Parallel Processing (ICA3PP 2015), we would like to welcome you to join the conference held in Zhangjiajie, China, during November 18–20, 2015.

The ICA3PP conference aims at bringing together researchers and practitioners from both academia and industry who are working on algorithms and architectures for parallel processing. The conference features keynote speeches, panel discussions, technical presentations, symposiums, and workshops, where the technical presentations from both the research community and industry cover various aspects including fundamental theoretical approaches, practical experimental projects, and commercial components and systems. ICA3PP 2015 was the next event in a series of highly successful international conferences on algorithms and architectures for parallel processing, previously held as ICA3PP 2014 (Dalian, China, August 2014), ICA3PP 2013 (Vietri sul Mare, Italy, December 2013), ICA3PP 2012 (Fukuoka, Japan, September 2012), ICA3PP 2011 (Melbourne, Australia, October 2011), ICA3PP 2010 (Busan, Korea, May 2010), ICA3PP 2009 (Taipei, Taiwan, June 2009), ICA3PP 2008 (Cyprus, June 2008), ICA3PP 2007 (Hangzhou, China, June 2007), ICA3PP 2005 (Melbourne, Australia, October 2005), ICA3PP 2002 (Beijing, China, October 2002), ICA3PP2000 (Hong Kong, China, December 2000), ICA3PP 1997 (Melbourne, Australia, December 1997), ICA3PP 1996 (Singapore, June 1996), and ICA3PP 1995 (Brisbane, Australia, April 1995).

The ICA3PP 2015 conference collected research papers on related research issues from all around the world. This year we received 602 submissions for the main conference. All submissions received at least three reviews during a high-quality review process. According to the review results, 219 papers were selected for oral presentation at the conference, giving an acceptance rate of 36.4 %.

We would like to offer our gratitude to Prof. Yang Xiang and Prof. Andrzej Goscinski from Deakin University, Australia, and Prof. Yi Pan from Georgia State University, USA, the Steering Committee chairs. Our thanks also go to the general chairs, Prof. Guojun Wang from Central South University, China, Dr. Peter Mueller from IBM Zurich Research, Switzerland, and Prof. Qingping Zhou from Jishou University, China, for their great support and good suggestions for a successful the final program. Special thanks to the workshop chairs, Dr. Mianxiong Dong from Muroran Institute of Technology, Japan, and Dr. Ryan K.L. Ko from the University of Waikato, New Zealand, and Dr. Md. Zakirul Alam Bhuiyan from Temple University, USA. In particular, we would like to give our thanks to all researchers and practitioners who submitted their manuscripts, and to the Program Committee and the external reviewers who contributed their valuable time and expertise to provide professional reviews working under a very tight schedule. Moreover, we are very grateful to our keynote speakers who kindly accepted our invitation to give insightful and prospective talks.

Finally, we believe that the conference provided a very good opportunity for participants to learn from each other. We hope you enjoy the conference proceedings.

Albert Zomaya
Gregorio Martinez Perez
Kenli Li

Welcome Message from the ICA3PP 2015 Workshop Chairs

Welcome to the proceedings of the 15th International Conference on Algorithms and Architectures for Parallel Processing (ICA3PP 2015) held in Zhangjiajie, China, during November 18–20, 2015. The program this year consisted of six symposiums/workshops covering a wide range of research topics on parallel processing technology:

(1) The 6th International Workshop on Trust, Security and Privacy for Big Data (TrustData 2015)
(2) The 5th International Symposium on Trust, Security and Privacy for Emerging Applications (TSP 2015)
(3) The Third International Workshop on Network Optimization and Performance Evaluation (NOPE 2015)
(4) The Second International Symposium on Sensor-Cloud Systems (SCS 2015)
(5) The Second International Workshop on Security and Privacy Protection in Computer and Network Systems (SPPCN 2015)
(6) The First International Symposium on Dependability in Sensor, Cloud, and Big Data Systems and Applications (DependSys 2015)

The aim of these symposiums/workshops is to provide a forum to bring together practitioners and researchers from academia and industry for discussion and presentations on the current research and future directions related to parallel processing technology. The themes and topics of these symposiums/workshops are a valuable complement to the overall scope of ICA3PP 2015 providing additional values and interests. We hope that all of the selected papers will have a good impact on future research in the respective field.

The ICA3PP 2015 workshops collected research papers on the related research issues from all around the world. This year we received 205 submissions for all workshops. All submissions received at least three reviews during a high-quality review process. According to the review results, 77 papers were selected for oral presentation at the conference, giving an acceptance rate of 37.6 %.

We offer our sincere gratitude to the workshop organizers for their hard work in designing the call for papers, assembling the Program Committee, managing the peer-review process for the selection of papers, and planning the workshop program. We are grateful to the workshop Program Committees, external reviewers, session chairs, contributing authors, and attendees. Our special thanks to the Organizing Committees of ICA3PP 2015 for their strong support, and especially to the program chairs, Prof. Albert Zomaya, Prof. Gregorio Martinez Perez, and Prof. Kenli Li, for their guidance.

Finally, we hope that you will find the proceedings interesting and stimulating.

Mianxiong Dong
Ryan K.L. Ko
Md. Zakirul Alam Bhuiyan

Welcome Message from the TrustData 2015 Program Chairs

The 6th International Workshop on Trust, Security and Privacy for Big Data (TrustData 2015) was held in Zhangjiajie, China.

TrustData aims at bringing together people from both academia and industry to present their most recent work related to trust, security, and privacy issues in big data, and to exchange ideas and thoughts in order to identify emerging research topics and define the future of big data.

TrustData 2015 was the next event in a series of highly successful international workshops, previously held as TrustData 2014 (Dalian, China, March 2012) and TrustData 2013 (Zhangjiajie, China, November, 2013).

This international workshop collected research papers on the aforementioned research issues from all around the world. Each paper was reviewed by at least three experts in the field. We feel very proud of the high participation, and although it was difficult to collect the best papers from all the submissions received, we feel we managed to have an amazing conference that was enjoyed by all participants.

We would like to offer our gratitude to the general chairs, Dr. Qin Liu and Dr. Muhammad Bashir Abdullahi, for their excellent support and invaluable suggestions for a successful final program. In particular, we would like to thank all researchers and practitioners who submitted their manuscripts, and the Program Committee members and additional reviewers for their tremendous efforts and timely reviews.

We hope you enjoy the proceedings of TrustData 2015.

Keqin Li
Avinash Srinivasan

Welcome Message from the TSP 2015 Program Chairs

On behalf of the Program Committee of the 5th International Symposium on Trust, Security and Privacy for Emerging Applications (TSP 2015), we would like to welcome you to the proceedings of the event, which was held in Zhangjiajie, China.

The symposium focuses on trust, security, and privacy issues in social networks, cloud computing, Internet of Things (IoT), wireless sensor networks, and other networking environments or system applications; it also provides a forum for presenting and discussing emerging ideas and trends in this highly challenging research area. The aim of this symposium is to provide a leading edge forum to foster interaction between researchers and developers with the trust, security, and privacy issues, and to give attendees an opportunity to network with experts in this area.

Following the success of TSP 2008 in Shanghai, China, during December 17–20, 2008, TSP 2009 in Macau SAR, China, during October 12–14, 2009, TSP 2010 in Bradford, UK, during June 29–July 1, 2010, and TSP 2013 in Zhangjiajie, China, during November 13–15, 2013, the 5th International Symposium on Trust, Security and Privacy for Emerging Applications (TSP 2015) was held in Zhangjiajie, China, during November 18–20, 2015, in conjunction with the 15th International Conference on Algorithms and Architectures for Parallel Processing (ICA3PP 2015).

The symposium collected research papers on the aforementioned research issues from all around the world. Each paper was reviewed by at least two experts in the field. We realized an amazing symposium that we hope was enjoyed by all the participants.

We would like to thank all researchers and practitioners who submitted their manuscripts, and the Program Committee members and additional reviewers for their tremendous efforts and timely reviews.

We hope you enjoy the proceedings of TSP 2015.

Imad Jawhar
Deqing Zou

Welcome Message from the NOPE 2015 Program Chair

Welcome to the proceedings of the 2015 International Workshop on Network Optimization and Performance Evaluation (NOPE 2015) held in Zhangjiajie, China, during November 18–20, 2015.

Network optimization and performance evaluation is a topic that attracts much attention in network/Internet and distributed systems. Due to the recent advances in Internet-based applications as well as WLANs, wireless home networks, wireless sensor networks, wireless mesh networks, and cloud computing, we are witnessing a variety of new technologies. However, these systems and networks are becoming very large and complex, and consuming a great amount of energy at the same time. System optimization and performance evaluation remain to be resolved before these systems become a commodity.

On behalf of the Organizing Committee, we would like to take this opportunity to express our gratitude to all reviewers who worked hard to finish reviews on time. Thanks to the publicity chairs for their efforts and support. Thanks also to all authors for their great support and contribution to the event. We would like to give our special thanks to the Organizing Committee, colleagues, and friends who worked hard behind the scenes. Without their unfailing cooperation, hard work, and dedication, this event would not have been successfully organized.

We are grateful to everyone for participating in NOPE 2015.

Gaocai Wang

Welcome Message from SCS 2015 Program Chairs

As the Program Chairs and on behalf of the Organizing Committee of the Second International Symposium on Sensor-Cloud Systems (SCS 2015), we would like to express our gratitude to all the participants who attended the symposium in Zhangjiajie, China, during November 18–20, 2015. This famous city is the location of China's first forest park (The Zhangjiajie National Forest Park) and a World Natural Heritage site (Wulingyuan Scenic Area).

The aim of SCS is to bring together researchers and practitioners working on sensor-cloud systems to present and discuss emerging ideas and trends in this highly challenging research field. It has attracted some high-quality research papers, which highlight the foundational work that strives to push beyond limits of existing technologies, including experimental efforts, innovative systems, and investigations that identify weaknesses in the existing technology services.

SCS 2015 was sponsored by the National Natural Science Foundation of China, Springer, the School of Information Science and Engineering at Central South University, and the School of Software at Central South University, and it was organized by Central South University, Hunan University, National University of Defense Technology, and Jishou University. SCS 2015 was held in conjunction with the 15th International Conference on Algorithms and Architectures for Parallel Processing (ICA3PP 2015), which highlights the latest research trends in various aspects of computer science and technology.

Many individuals contributed to the success of this international symposium. We would like to express our special appreciation to the general chairs of main conference, Prof. Guojun Wang, Prof. Peter Mueller, and Prof. Qingping Zhou, for giving us this opportunity to hold this symposium and for their guidance in the organization. Thanks also to the general chairs of this symposium, Prof. Jie Li and Prof. Dongqing Xie, for their excellent work in organizing the symposium. We would like to give our thanks to all the members of the Organizing Committee and Program Committee for their efforts and support.

Finally, we are grateful to the authors for submitting their fine work to SCS 2015 and all the participants for their attendance.

Xiaofei Xing
Md. Zakirul Alam Bhuiyan

Welcome Message from the SPPCN 2015 Program Chairs

On behalf of the Program Committee of the Second International Workshop on Security and Privacy Protection in Computer and Network Systems (SPPCN 2015), we would like to welcome you to join the proceedings of the workshop, which was held in Zhangjiajie, China.

The workshop focuses on security and privacy protection in computer and network systems, such as authentication, access control, availability, integrity, privacy, confidentiality, dependability, and sustainability issues of computer and network systems. The aim of the workshop is to provide a leading-edge forum to foster interaction between researchers and developers working on security and privacy protection in computer and network systems, and to give attendees an opportunity to network with experts in this area.

SPPCN 2015 was the next event in a series of highly successful international conferences on security and privacy protection in computer and network systems, previously held as SPPCN 2014 (Dalian, China, December 2014). The workshop collected research papers on the above research issues from all around the world. Each paper was reviewed by at least two experts in the field.

We would like to offer our gratitude to the general chair, Prof. Jian Weng, for his excellent support and contribution to the success of the final program. In particular, we would like to thank all researchers and practitioners who submitted their manuscripts, and the Program Committee members and additional reviewers for their tremendous efforts and timely reviews.

We hope all of you enjoy the proceedings of SPPCN 2015.

Mianxiong Dong
Hua Guo
Tieming Cheng
Kaimin Wei

Welcome Message from the DependSys 2015 Program Chairs

As the program chairs and on behalf of the Organizing Committee of the First International Symposium on Dependability in Sensor, Cloud, and Big Data Systems and Applications (DependSys2015), we would like to express our gratitude to all the participants attending the international symposium in Zhangjiajie, China, during November 18–20, 2015. This famous city is the location of China's first forest park (The Zhangjiajie National Forest Park) and a World Natural Heritage site (Wulingyuan Scenic Area).

DependSys is a timely event that brings together new ideas, techniques, and solutions for dependability and its issues in sensor, cloud, and big data systems and applications. As we are deep into the Information Age, we are witnessing the explosive growth of data available on the Internet. Human beings are producing quintillion bytes of data every day, which come from sensors, individual archives, social networks, Internet of Things, enterprises, and the Internet in all scales and formats. One of the most challenging issues we face is to achieve the designed system performance to an expected level, i.e., how to effectively provide dependability in sensor, cloud, and big data systems. These systems need to typically run continuously, which often tend to become inert, brittle, and vulnerable after a while.

This international symposium collected research papers on the aforementioned research issues from all around the world. Although it was the first event of DependSys, we received a large number of submissions in response to the call for papers. Each paper was reviewed by at least three experts in the field. After detailed discussions among the program chairs and general chairs, a set of quality papers was finally accepted. We are very proud of the high number of participations, and it was difficult to collect the best papers from all the submissions.

Many individuals contributed to the success of this high-caliber international symposium. We would like to express our special appreciation to the steering chairs, Prof. Jie Wu and Prof. Guojun Wang, for giving us the opportunity to hold this symposium and for their guidance in the symposium organization. In particular, we would like to give our thanks to the symposium chairs, Prof. Mohammed Atiquzzaman, Prof. Sheikh Iqbal Ahamed, and Dr. Md Zakirul Alam Bhuiyan, for their excellent support and invaluable suggestions for a successful final program. Thanks to all the Program Committee members and the additional reviewers for their tremendous efforts and timely reviews.

We hope you enjoy the proceedings of DependSys 2015.

Latifur Khan
Joarder Kamruzzaman
Al-Sakib Khan Pathan

Organization

ICA3PP 2015 Organizing and Program Committees

General Chairs

Guojun Wang   Central South University, China
Peter Mueller   IBM Zurich Research, Switzerland
Qingping Zhou   Jishou University, China

Program Chairs

Albert Zomaya   University of Sydney, Australia
Gregorio Martinez Perez   University of Murcia, Spain
Kenli Li   Hunan University, China

Steering Chairs

Andrzej Goscinski   Deakin University, Australia
Yi Pan   Georgia State University, USA
Yang Xiang   Deakin University, Australia

Workshop Chairs

Mianxiong Dong   Muroran Institute of Technology, Japan
Ryan K.L. Ko   The University of Waikato, New Zealand
Md. Zakirul Alam Bhuiyan   Central South University, China

Publicity Chairs

Carlos Becker Westphall   Federal University of Santa Catarina, Brazil
Yulei Wu   The University of Exeter, UK
Christian Callegari   University of Pisa, Italy
Kuan-Ching Li   Providence University, Taiwan
James J. (Jong Hyuk) Park   SeoulTech, Korea

Publication Chairs

Jin Zheng   Central South University, China
Wenjun Jiang   Hunan University, China

Finance Chairs

Pin Liu   Central South University, China
Wang Yang   Central South University, China

Local Arrangements Chairs

Fang Qi   Central South University, China
Qin Liu   Hunan University, China
Hongzhi Xu   Jishou University, China

Program Committee

1. Parallel and Distributed Architectures Track

Chairs

Stefano Giordano   Italian National Interuniversity Consortium
                           for Telecommunications, Italy
Xiaofei Liao   Huazhong University of Science and Technology,
                           China
Haikun Liu   Nanyang Technological University, Singapore

TPC Members

Marco Aldinucci   Universitá degli Studi di Torino, Italy
Yungang Bao   Chinese Academy of Sciences, China
Hui Chen   Auburn University, USA
Vladimir Getov   University of Westminster, UK
Jie Jia   Northeastern University, China
Yusen Li   Nanyang Technological University, Singapore
Zengxiang Li   Agency for Science, Technology and Research,
                           Singapore
Xue Liu   Northeastern University, China
Yongchao Liu   Georgia Institute of Technology, USA
Salvatore Orlando   Universitá Ca' Foscari Venezia, Italy
Nicola Tonellotto   ISTI-CNR, Italy
Zeke Wang   Nanyang Technological University, Singapore
Quanqing Xu   Agency for Science, Technology and Research
                           (A*STAR), Singapore
Ramin Yahyapour   University of Göttingen, Germany
Jidong Zhai   Tsinghua University, China
Jianlong Zhong   GraphSQL Inc., USA
Andrei Tchernykh   CICESE Research Center, Ensenada, Baja California,
                           Mexico

2. Software Systems and Programming Track

Chairs

Xinjun Mao   National University of Defense Technology, China
Sanaa Sharafeddine   Lebanese American University, Beirut, Lebanon

TPC Members

Surendra Byna   Lawrence Berkeley National Lab, USA
Yue-Shan Chang   National Taipei University, Taiwan
Massimo Coppola   ISTI-CNR, Italy
Marco Danelutto   University of Pisa, Italy
Jose Daniel Garcia   Carlos III of Madrid University, Spain
Peter Kilpatrick   Queen's University Belfast, UK
Soo-Kyun Kim   PaiChai University, Korea
Rajeev Raje   Indiana University-Purdue University Indianapolis,
                          USA
Salvatore Ruggieri   University of Pisa, Italy
Subhash Saini   NASA, USA
Peter Strazdins   The Australian National University, Australia
Domenico Talia   University of Calabria, Italy
Hiroyuki Tomiyama   Ritsumeikan University, Japan
Canqun Yang   National University of Defense Technology, China
Daniel Andresen   Kansas State University, USA
Sven-Bodo Scholz   Heriot-Watt University, UK
Salvatore Venticinque   Second University of Naples, Italy

3. Distributed and Network-Based Computing Track

Chairs

Casimer DeCusatis   Marist College, USA
Qi Wang   University of the West of Scotland, UK

TPC Members

Justin Baijian   Purdue University, USA
Aparicio Carranza   City University of New York, USA
Tzung-Shi Chen   National University of Tainan, Taiwan
Ciprian Dobre   University Politehnica of Bucharest, Romania
Longxiang Gao   Deakin University, Australia
Ansgar Gerlicher   Stuttgart Media University, Germany
Harald Gjermundrod   University of Nicosia, Cyprus
Christos Grecos   Independent Imaging Consultant, UK
Jia Hu   Liverpool Hope University, UK
Baback Izadi   State University of New York at New Paltz, USA
Morihiro Kuga   Kumamoto University, Japan
Mikolaj Leszczuk   AGH University of Science and Technology, Poland

Paul Lu	University of Alberta, Canada
Chunbo Luo	University of the West of Scotland, UK
Ioannis Papapanagiotou	Purdue University, USA
Michael Hobbs	Deakin University, Australia
Cosimo Anglano	Università del Piemonte Orientale, Italy
Md. ObaidurRahman	Dhaka University of Engineering and Technology, Bangladesh
Aniello Castiglione	University of Salerno, Italy
Shuhong Chen	Hunan Institute of Engineering, China

4. Big Data and Its Applications Track

Chairs

| Jose M. Alcaraz Calero | University of the West of Scotland, UK |
| Shui Yu | Deakin University, Australia |

TPC Members

Alba Amato	Second University of Naples, Italy
Tania Cerquitelli	Politecnico di Torino, Italy
Zizhong (Jeffrey) Chen	University of California at Riverside, USA
Alfredo Cuzzocrea	University of Calabria, Italy
Saptarshi Debroy	University of Missouri-Columbia, USA
Yacine Djemaiel	Communication Networks and Security, Res. Lab, Tunisia
Shadi Ibrahim	Inria, France
Hongwei Li	UESTC, China
William Liu	Auckland University of Technology, New Zealand
Xiao Liu	East China Normal University, China
Karampelas Panagiotis	Hellenic Air Force Academy, Greece
Florin Pop	University Politehnica of Bucharest, Romania
Genoveva Vargas Solar	CNRS-LIG-LAFMIA, France
Chen Wang	CSIRO ICT Centre, Australia
Chao-Tung Yang	Tunghai University, Taiwan
Peng Zhang	Stony Brook University, USA
Ling Zhen	Southeast University, China
Roger Zimmermann	National University of Singapore, Singapore
Francesco Palmieri	University of Salerno, Italy
Rajiv Ranjan	CSIRO, Canberra, Australia
Felix Cuadrado	Queen Mary University of London, UK
Nilimesh Halder	The University of Western Australia, Australia
Kuan-Chou Lai	National Taichung University of Education, Taiwan
Jaafar Gaber	UTBM, France
Eunok Paek	Hanyang University, Korea
You-Chiun Wang	National Sun Yat-sen University, Taiwan
Ke Gu	Changsha University of Technology, China

5. Parallel and Distributed Algorithms Track

Chairs

Dimitris A. Pados	The State University of New York at Buffalo, USA
Baoliu Ye	Nanjing University, China

TPC Members

George Bosilca	University of Tennessee, USA
Massimo Cafaro	University of Salento, Italy
Stefania Colonnese	Universitá degli Studi di Roma La Sapienza, Italy
Raphael Couturier	University of Franche Comte, France
Gregoire Danoy	University of Luxembourg, Luxembourg
Franco Frattolillo	Universitá del Sannio, Italy
Che-Rung Lee	National Tsing Hua University, Taiwan
Laurent Lefevre	Inria, ENS-Lyon, University of Lyon, France
Amit Majumdar	San Diego Supercomputer Center, USA
Susumu Matsumae	Saga University, Japan
George N. Karystinos	Technical University of Crete, Greece
Dana Petcu	West University of Timisoara, Romania
Francoise Sailhan	CNAM, France
Uwe Tangen	Ruhr-Universität Bochum, Germany
Wei Xue	Tsinghua University, China
Kalyan S. Perumalla	Oak Ridge National Laboratory, USA
Morris Riedel	University of Iceland, Germany
Gianluigi Folino	ICAR-CNR, Italy
Joanna Kolodziej	Cracow University of Technology, Poland
Luc Bougé	ENS Rennes, France
Hirotaka Ono	Kyushu University, Japan
Tansel Ozyer	TOBB Economics and Technology University, Turkey
Daniel Grosu	Wayne State University, USA
Tian Wang	Huaqiao University, China
Sancheng Peng	Zhaoqing University, China
Fang Qi	Central South University, China
Zhe Tang	Central South University, China
Jin Zheng	Central South University, China

6. Applications of Parallel and Distributed Computing Track

Chairs

Yu Chen	Binghamton University, State University of New York, USA
Michal Wozniak	Wroclaw University of Technology, Poland

TPC Members

Jose Alfredo F. Costa	Universidade Federal do Rio Grande do Norte, Brazil
Robert Burduk	Wroclaw University of Technology, Poland
Boguslaw Cyganek	AGH University of Science and Technology, Poland
Paolo Gasti	New York Institute of Technology, USA
Manuel Grana	University of the Basque Country, Spain
Houcine Hassan	Universidad Politecnica de Valencia, Spain
Alvaro Herrero	Universidad de Burgos, Spain
Jin Kocsis	University of Akron, USA
Esmond Ng	Lawrence Berkeley National Lab, USA
Dragan Simic	University of Novi Sad, Serbia
Ching-Lung Su	National Yunlin University of Science and Technology, Taiwan
Tomoaki Tsumura	Nagoya Institute of Technology, Japan
Krzysztof Walkowiak	Wroclaw University of Technology, Poland
Zi-Ang (John) Zhang	Binghamton University-SUNY, USA
Yunhui Zheng	IBM Research, USA
Hsi-Ya Chang	National Center for High-Performance Computing, Taiwan
Chun-Yu Lin	HTC Corp., Taiwan
Nikzad Babaii Rizvandi	The University of Sydney, Australia

7. Service Dependability and Security in Distributed and Parallel Systems Track

Chairs

Antonio Ruiz Martinez	University of Murcia, Spain
Jun Zhang	Deakin University, Australia

TPC Members

Jorge Bernal Bernabe	University of Murcia, Spain
Roberto Di Pietro	Universitá di Roma Tre, Italy
Massimo Ficco	Second University of Naples (SUN), Italy
Yonggang Huang	Beijing Institute of Technology, China
Georgios Kambourakis	University of the Aegean, Greece
Muhammad Khurram Khan	King Saud University, Saudi Arabia
Liang Luo	Southwest University, China
Barbara Masucci	Universitá di Salerno, Italy
Juan M. Marin	University of Murcia, Spain
Sabu M. Thampi	Indian Institute of Information Technology and Management – Kerala (IIITM-K), India
Fernando Pereniguez-Garcia	Catholic University of Murcia, Spain
Yongli Ren	RMIT University, Australia
Yu Wang	Deakin University, Australia
Sheng Wen	Deakin University, Australia

Mazdak Zamani	Universiti Teknologi Malaysia, Malaysia
Susan K. Donohue	University of Virginia, USA
Oana Boncalo	University Politehnica Timisoara, Romania
K.P. Lam	University of Keele, UK
George Loukas	University of Greenwich, UK
Ugo Fiore	Federico II University, Italy
Christian Esposito	University of Salerno, Italy
Arcangelo Castiglione	University of Salerno, Italy
Edward Jung	Kennesaw State University, USA
Md. Zakirul Alam Bhuiyan	Central South University, China
Xiaofei Xing	Guangzhou University, China
Qin Liu	Hunan University, China
Wenjun Jiang	Hunan University, China
Gaocai Wang	Guangxi University, China
Kaimin Wei	Jinan University, China

8. Web Services and Internet Computing Track

Chairs

Huansheng Ning	University of Science and Technology Beijing, China
Daqiang Zhang	Tongji University, China

TPC Members

Jing Chen	National Cheng Kung University, Taiwan
Eugen Dedu	University of Franche-Comte, France
Sotirios G. Ziavras	NJIT, USA
Luis Javier Garcia Villalba	Universidad Complutense de Madrid (UCM), Spain
Jaime Lloret	Universidad Politecnica de Valencia, Spain
Wei Lu	Keene University, USA
Stefano Marrone	Second University of Naples, Italy
Alejandro Masrur	Chemnitz University of Technology, Germany
Seungmin (Charlie) Rho	Sungkyul University, Korea
Giandomenico Spezzano	ICAR-CNR, Italy
Jiafu Wan	South China University of Technology, China
Yunsheng Wang	Kettering University, USA
Martine Wedlake	IBM, USA
Chung Wei-Ho	Research Center for Information Technology Innovation in Academia Sinica, Taiwan
Xingquan (Hill) Zhu	Florida Atlantic University, USA
Nikos Dimitriou	National Center for Scientific Research Demokritos, Greece
Choi Jaeho	CBNU, Chonju, Korea
Shi-Jinn Horng	National Taiwan University of Science and Technology, Taiwan

9. Performance Modeling and Evaluation Track

Chairs

Deze Zeng   China University of Geosciences, China
Bofeng Zhang   Shanghai University, China

TPC Members

Ladjel Bellatreche   ENSMA, France
Xiaoju Dong   Shanghai Jiao Tong University, China
Christian Engelman   Oak Ridge National Lab, USA
Javier Garcia Blas   University Carlos III, Spain
Mauro Iacono   Second University of Naples, Italy
Zhiyang Li   Dalian Maritime University, China
Tomas Margalef   Universitat Autonoma de Barcelona, Spain
Francesco Moscato   Second University of Naples, Italy
Heng Qi   Dalian University of Technology, China
Bing Shi   Wuhan University of Technology, China
Magdalena Szmajduch   Cracow University of Technology, Poland
Qian Wang   Wuhan University, China
Zhibo Wang   Wuhan University, China
Weigang Wu   Sun Yat-sen University, China
David E. Singh   University Carlos III of Madrid, Spain
Edmund Lai   Massey University, New Zealand
Robert J. Latham   Argonne National Laboratory, USA
Zafeirios Papazachos   Queen's University of Belfast, UK
Novella Bartolini   Sapienza University of Rome, Italy
Takeshi Nanri   Kyushu University, Japan
Mais Nijim   Texas A&M University – Kingsville, USA
Salvador Petit   Universitat Politècnica de València, Spain
Daisuke Takahashi   University of Tsukuba, Japan
Cathryn Peoples   Ulster University, Northern Ireland, UK
Hamid Sarbazi-Azad   Sharif University of Technology and IPM, Iran
Md. Abdur Razzaque   University of Dhaka, Bangladesh
Angelo Brayner   University of Fortaleza, Brazil
Sushil Prasad   Georgia State University, USA
Danilo Ardagna   Politecnico di Milano, Italy
Sun-Yuan Hsieh   National Cheng Kung University, Taiwan
Li Chaoliang   Hunan University of Commerce, China
Yongming Xie   Hunan Normal University, China
Guojun Wang   Central South University, China

Secretariats

Zhe Tang   Central South University, China
Feng Wang   Central South University, China

Webmaster

Xiangdong Lee   Central South University, China

TrustData 2015 Organizing and Program Committees

Steering Chairs

Guojun Wang	Central South University, China
Peter Mueller	IBM Zurich Research Laboratory, Switzerland

General Chairs

Qin Liu	Hunan University, China
Muhammad Bashir Abdullahi	Federal University of Technology, Minna, Nigeria

Program Chairs

Keqin Li	State University of New York at New Paltz, USA
Avinash Srinivasan	Temple University, USA

Publicity Chairs

Shui Yu	Deakin University, Australia
Weirong Liu	Central South University, China

Program Committee

Andrei Tchernykh	CICESE Research Center, Mexico
Baoliu Ye	Nanjing University, China
Bimal Roy	Indian Statistical Institute, India
Chang-Ai Sun	University of Science and Technology, China
Chao Song	University of Electronic Science and Technology of China, China
Christian Callegari	The University of Pisa, Italy
Chunhua Su	Japan Advanced Institute of Science and Technology, Japan
Franco Chiaraluce	Polytechnical University of Marche (UVPM), Italy
Hai Jiang	Arkansas State University, USA
Horacio Gonzalez-Velez	National College of Ireland, Ireland
Imed Romdhani	Edinburgh Napier University, UK
Jianguo Yao	Shanghai Jiao Tong University, China
Joon S. Park	Syracuse University, USA
Kevin Chan	US Army Research Laboratory, USA
Lizhe Wang	Rochester Institute of Technology, USA

TSP 2015 Organizing and Program Committees

Program Chairs

Imad Jawhar	United Arab Emirates University, UAE
Deqing Zou	Huazhong University of Science of Technology

Program Committee Members

Chao Song	University of Electronic Science and Technology, China
David Zheng	Frostburg State University, USA
Feng Li	Indiana University-Purdue University Indianapolis, USA
Haitao Lang	Beijing University of Chemical Technology, China
Huan Zhou	China Three Gorges University, China
Mingjun Xiao	University of Science and Technology of China, China
Mingwu Zhang	Hubei University of Technology, China
Shuhui Yang	Purdue University Calumet, USA
Xiaojun Hei	Huazhong University of Science and Technology, China
Xin Li	Nanjing University of Aeronautics and Astronautics, China
Xuanxia Yao	University of Science and Technology Beijing, China
Yaxiong Zhao	Google Inc., USA
Ying Dai	LinkedIn Corporation, USA
Yunsheng Wang	Kettering University, USA
Youwen Zhu	Nanjing University of Aeronautics and Astronautics, China
Yongming Xie	Changsha Medical University, China

Steering Committee

Wenjun Jiang	Hunan University, China (Chair)
Laurence T. Yang	St. Francis Xavier University, Canada
Guojun Wang	Central South University, China
Minyi Guo	Shanghai Jiao Tong University, China
Jie Li	University of Tsukuba, Japan
Jianhua Ma	Hosei University, Japan
Peter Mueller	IBM Zurich Research Laboratory, Switzerland
Indrakshi Ray	Colorado State University, USA

NOPE 2015 Organizing and Program Committees

Steering Committee Chairs

Wei Li	Texas Southern University, USA
Taoshen Li	Guangxi University, China

Program Chair

Gaocai Wang	Guangxi University, China

Program Committee Members

Dieter Fiems	Ghent University, Belgium
Shuqiang Huang	Jinan University, China
Juan F. Perez	Imperial College London, UK
Haoqian Wang	Tsinghua University, China
Yitian Peng	Southeast University, China
Hongbin Chen	Guilin University of Electronic Technology, China
Jin Ye	Guangxi University, China
Junbin Liang	Hong Kong Polytechnic University, Hong Kong, SAR China
Xianfeng Liu	Hunan Normal University, China
Hao Zhang	Central South University, China
Chuyuan Wei	Beijing University of Civil Engineering and Architecture, China
Hongyun Xu	South China University of Technology, China
Zhefu Shi	University of Missouri, USA
Songfeng Lu	Huazhong University of Science and Technology, China
Yihui Deng	Jinan University, China
Lei Zhang	Beijing University of Civil Engineering and Architecture, China
Xiaoheng Deng	Central South University, China
Mingxing Luo	Southwest Jiaotong University, China
Bin Sun	Beijing University of Posts and Telecommunications, China
Zhiwei Wang	Nanjing University of Posts and Telecommunications, China
Yousheng Zhou	Chongqing University of Posts and Telecommunications, China
Daofeng Li	Guangxi University, China

SCS 2015 Organizing and Program Committees

Steering Chairs

Jie Li   Tsukuba University, Japan
Dongqing Xie   Guangzhou University, China

Program Chairs

Xiaofei Xing   Guangzhou University, China
Md. Zakirul Alam Bhuiyan   Central South University, China
                                and Temple University, USA

Program Committee Members

Marco Aiello   University of Groningen, The Netherlands
David Chadwick   University of Kent, UK
Aparicio Carranza   City University of New York, USA
Mooi Choo Chuah   Lehigh University, USA
Yueming Deng   Hunan Normal University, China
Christos Grecos   Independent Imaging Consultant, UK
Dritan Kaleshi   University of Bristol, UK
Donghyun Kim   North Carolina Central University, USA
Santosh Kumar   University of Memphis, USA
Muthoni Masinde   University of Nairobi, Kenya
Satyjayant Mishra   New Mexico State University, USA
Nam Nguyen   Towson University, USA
Jean-Marc Seigneur   University of Geneva, Switzerland
Hamid Sharif   University of Nebraska, USA
Sheng Wen   Deakin University, Australia

Publicity Chairs

Zeyu Sun   Xi'an Jiaotong University, China
Yongming Xie   Hunan Normal University, China

SPPCN 2015 Organizing and Program Committees

General Chair

Jian Weng   Jinan University, China

Program Chairs

Mianxiong Dong   Muroran Institute of Technology, Japan
Hua Guo   Beihang University, China
Tieming Chen   Zhejiang University of Technology, China
Kaimin Wei   Jinan University, China

Program Committee

Fuchun Guo   University of Wollongong, Australia
Jianguang Han   Nanjing University of Finance and Economics,
                               Nanjing, China
Debiao He   Wuhan University, China
Xinyi Huang   Fujian Normal University, China
Xuanya Li   Chinese Academy of Sciences, China
Fengyong Li   Shanghai University of Electric Power, China
Changlu Lin   Fujian Normal University, China
Chang Xu   Beijing Institute of Technology, China
Tao Xu   University of Jinan, China
Yanjiang Yang   I2R, Singapore
Yang Tian   Beihang University, China
Shengbao Wang   Hangzhou Normal University, China
Wei Wu   Fujian Normal University, China
Xiyong Zhang   Information Engineering University, China
Lei Zhao   Wuhan University, China

DependSys 2015 Organizing and Program Committees

Steering Committee Chairs

Jie Wu	Temple University, USA
Guojun Wang	Central South University, China

General Chairs

Mohammed Atiquzzaman	University of Oklahoma, USA
Sheikh Iqbal Ahamed	Marquette University, USA
Md. Zakirul Alam Bhuiyan	Central South University, China and Temple University, USA

Program Chairs

Latifur Khan	The University of Texas at Dallas, USA
Joarder Kamruzzaman	Federation University and Monash University, Australia
Al-Sakib Khan Pathan	International Islamic University Malaysia, Malaysia

Program Committee Members

A.B.M Shawkat Ali	The University of Fiji, Fiji
A.B.M. Alim Al Islam	Bangladesh University of Engineering and Technology, Bangladesh
A. Sohel Ferdous	University of Western Australia, Australia
A.K.M. Najmul Islam	University of Turku, Finland
Abdul Azim Mohammad	Gyeongsang National University, South Korea
Abdur Rouf Mohammad	Dhaka University of Engineering and Technology, Bangladesh
Afrand Agah	West Chester University of Pennsylvania, USA
Andreas Pashalidis	Katholieke Universiteit Leuven – iMinds, Belgium
Asaduzzaman	Chittagong University of Engineering and Technology, Bangladesh
C. Chiu Tan	Temple University, USA
Changyu Dong	University of Strathclyde, UK
Dana Petcu	West University of Timisoara, Romania
Daqiang Zhang	Tongji University, China
Farzana Rahman	James Madison University, USA
Hugo Miranda	University of Lisbon, Portugal
Jaydip Sen	National Institute of Science and Technology, India
Jianfeng Yang	Wuhan University, China
Jinkyu Jeong	Sungkyunkwan University, South Korea

Kaoru Ota	Muroran Institute of Technology, Japan
Karampelas Panagiotis	Hellenic Air Force Academy, Greece
Lien-Wu Chen	Feng Chia University, Taiwan
Liu Jialin	Texas Tech University, USA
M.M.A. Hashem	Khulna University of Engineering and Technology, Bangladesh
M. Thampi Sabu	Indian Institute of Information Technology and Management, India
Mahbub Habib Sheikh	CASED/TU Darmstadt, Germany
Mahmuda Naznin	Bangladesh University of Engineering and Technology, Bangladesh
Mamoun Alazab	Australian National University, Australia
Manuel Mazzara	Innopolis University, Russia
Md. Abdur Razzaque	University of Dhaka, Bangladesh
Md. Arafatur Rahman	University Malaysia Pahang, Malaysia
Mohammad Asad Rehman Chaudhry	University of Toronto, Canada
Md. Obaidur Rahman	Dhaka University of Engineering and Technology, Bangladesh
Md. Rafiul Hassan	King Fahd University of Petroleum and Minerals, Saudi Arabia
Md. Saiful Azad	American International University, Bangladesh
Mehran Asadi	Lincoln University of Pennsylvania, USA
Mohamad Badra	Zayed University, UAE
Mohamed Guerroumi	University of Sciences and Technology Houari Boumediene, Algeria
Mohammad Asadul Hoque	East Tennessee State University, USA
Mohammad Mehedi Hassan	King Saud University, Saudi Arabia
Mohammad Shahriar Rahman	University of Asia Pacific, Bangladesh
Mohammed Shamsul Alam	International Islamic University Chittagong, Bangladesh
Morshed Chowdhury	Deakin University, Australia
Muhammad Mostafa Monowar	King AbdulAziz University, Saudi Arabia
N. Musau Felix	Kenyatta University, Kenya
Phan Cong	Vinh Nguyen Tat Thanh University, Vietnam
Qin Liu	Hunan University, China
Ragib Hasan	University of Alabama at Birmingham, USA
Raza Hasan	Middle East College, Oman
Reaz Ahmed	University of Waterloo, Canada
Risat Mahmud Pathan	Chalmers University of Technology, Sweden
S.M. Kamruzzaman	King Saud University, Saudi Arabia
Salvatore Distefano	Politecnico di Milano, Italy
Shan Lin	Stony Brook University, USA
Shao Jie Tang	University of Texas at Dallas, USA
Sheng Wen	Deakin University, Australia

Shigeng Zhang	Central South University, China
Sk. Md. Mizanur Rahman	King Saud University, Saudi Arabia
Subrota Mondal	Hong Kong University of Science and Technology, Hong Kong, SAR China
Syed Imran Ali	Middle East College, Oman
Tanveer Ahsan	International Islamic University Chittagong, Bangladesh
Tanzima Hashem	Bangladesh University of Engineering and Technology, Bangladesh
Tao Li	The Hong Kong Polytechnic University, Hong Kong, SAR China
Tarem Ahmed	BRAC University, Bangladesh
Tian Wang	Huaqiao University, China
Tzung-Shi Chen	National University of Tainan, Taiwan
Vaskar Raychoudhury	Indian Institute of Technology Roorkee, India
Wahid Khan	University of Saskatchewan, Canada
Weigang Li	University of Brasilia, Brazil
Weigang Wu	Sun Yat-sen University, China
William Liu	Auckland University of Technology, New Zealand
Xiaofei Xing	Guangzhou University, China
Xuefeng Liu	The Hong Kong Polytechnic University, Hong Kong, SAR China
Xuyun Zhang	University of Melbourne, Australia
Yacine Djemaiel	Communication Networks and Security, Res. Lab, Tunisia
Yifan Zhang	Binghamton University, USA
Yu Wang	Deakin University, Australia

Publication Chairs

Jin Zheng	Central South University, China
Wenjun Jiang	Hunan University, China

Local Arrangements Chairs

Fang Qi	Central South University, China
Qin Liu	Hunan University, China
Hongzhi Xu	Jishou University, China

Finance Chairs

Pin Liu	Central South University, China
Wang Yang	Central South University, China

Web Chair

Min Guo	Central South University, China

Contents – Part III

Applications of Parallel and Distributed Computing

Service Dependability and Security in Distributed and Parallel Systems

Applications of Parallel
and Distributed Computing

On Exploring a Virtual Agent Negotiation Inspired Approach for Route Guidance in Urban Traffic Networks

Wenbin Hu[✉], Liping Yan, Huan Wang, and Bo Du

School of Computer, Wuhan University, Wuhan 430072, China
{hwb, csyan}@whu.edu.cn, 694789758@qq.com,
gunspace@163.com

Abstract. The traditional route guidance system often provides the same shortest route to different drivers regardless of their different traffic conditions. As a result, many vehicles may rush into the same road segments at the same time that would lead to traffic congestion. Such uncontrolled dispersion of vehicles can be avoided by evenly distributing vehicles along the potential routes. This paper proposes a practical Virtual Agent Negotiation based Route Guidance Approach (VANRGA). In the proposed approach, vehicle agents (VAs) in the local vicinity communicate with each other before the intersections to achieve a real-time and dynamic route selection. Based on the route preference of the drivers and the traffic conditions, the vehicles are distributed on the routes equally, which can avoid the traffic congestion and maximize the utility of the road resources. After presenting the design and implementation methodology of VANRGA, this paper carries out extensive experiments on synthetic and real-world road networks. The experimental results show that compared to the shortest path algorithms, VANRGA offers a 22 %–37 % decrease in travel time (when traffic demand is below network capacity) and a 15 %–18 % decrease in travel time (when traffic demand exceeds network capacity).

Keywords: Dynamic route selection · Virtual negotiation · Congestion game · Nash equilibrium

1 Introduction

In recent years, with the rapid development of economy, the urban traffic congestion phenomenon is increasingly serious, especially in some big cities. In order to alleviate traffic congestion for vehicles and to reduce their travel time, many researchers have studied how to utilize the traffic resources effectively [1–3]. For example, reinforcement learning was used to adjust signal timing plans in real time in response to traffic fluctuations to minimize delay [1]. In [2] a multi-agent reinforcement learning (MARL) algorithm is proposed to solve vehicle delay problems by studying the weights of various components in road network environments to create a priority route plan for vehicles. However, the market diffusion of these technologies may not lead to the reduction of traffic congestion mainly due to the concentration of traffic into particular paths in the traffic networks. Yamada [4] proposed a hyperpath-based route

© Springer International Publishing Switzerland 2015
G. Wang et al. (Eds.): ICA3PP 2015, Part III, LNCS 9530, pp. 3–16, 2015.
DOI: 10.1007/978-3-319-27137-8_1

recommendation method to disperse the traffic through recommending a potential optimal set of paths instead of the shortest one to the vehicles. The simulation result indicated this method could contribute to the mitigation of traffic congestion in some aspects, but it was based on the static historical traffic data instead of the real-time and dynamic traffic data [5].

To alleviate traffic congestion in real-time and dynamic traffic conditions, vehicle agents needed to learn how to coordinate their actions with those of other agents, rather than learn a particular set of "good" actions [6–8]. This requires a vehicle to have knowledge of the route choices of the surrounding vehicles to make an informed decision about whether to take its intended route. This information exchange can be facilitated by intervehicular communication (IVC) [9] or by installing a roadside infrastructure unit for collecting and transmitting useful traffic information. However, given the vast expanse of road networks, it is impractical to have infrastructure units on every road segment/intersection due to prohibitive costs. IVC allows efficient and real-time information exchange where vehicles acting as mobile nodes form a wireless vehicular ad hoc network (VANET). Besides, because the routes are indivisible but sharable resources, the action of one vehicle agent would influence those of others [10]. How to allocate the routes for the vehicles based on their preferences [11] and the traffic conditions is a complex problem. Based on the MARA (Multi-Agent Resource Allocation) model proposed in [12] and the theory of vehicular communications, a congestion avoidance and route allocation using virtual agent negotiation (CAR-AVAN) model was proposed in [13]. CARAVAN was designed to achieve acceptable route allocation within a short time frame and with low communication overheads and alleviated the traffic congestion on a certain degree. But in this approach the vehicles were only allocated to one-way routes before junctions instead of intersections, which is the characteristic of urban traffic networks. One route is composed of several road segments, which are relative to the corresponding intersections. When the vehicle agents choose their preferred routes before intersections, the traffic conditions of the contained road segments will be influenced in the future that should be predicted, and the traffic congestion on them should be avoided. How to supply real-time and dynamic route guidance effectively for the driving vehicle agents in urban traffic networks is a significant problem.

Based on the above problems to be solved, this paper proposes a practical Virtual Agent Negotiation based Route Guidance Approach (VANRGA). In the proposed approach, the vehicles negotiate with each other in the vicinity based on their preferences for the optional routes in urban traffic networks, combined with the traffic conditions on these routes. To maximize the efficiency of the urban traffic networks, the vehicles are distributed on the optional routes equally.

The main contributions of this paper are (1) building a practical Virtual Agent Negotiation based Route Guidance Approach (VANRGA) model; (2) presenting a formula for computing the utilities of the optional routes for vehicle agents; (3) designing a dynamic route selection algorithm based on VANRGA model.

This paper is organized as follows. Section 2 introduces the design process of VANRGA model. Section 3 introduces the Traffic Flow Equilibrium Algorithm based on VANRGA model. Section 4 presents a detailed experimental evaluation of VANRGA solution. Section 5 concludes this paper with future research directions.

2 VANRGA Model

2.1 The Overall Structure of VANRGA Model

In this section, we discuss the overall structure of the VANRGA model, as is shown in Fig. 1. The detailed process is described as follows.

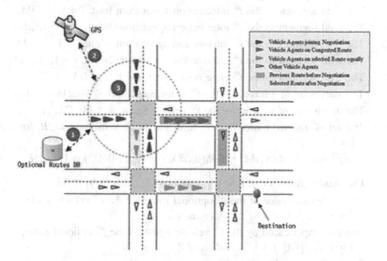

Fig. 1. The overall structure of VANRGA model

① When the vehicles are driving towards an intersection, the optional routes from their current positions to the destinations are obtained based on the dynamic route selection process, and stored in the database, which is detailed in Sect. 2.4. The first preferred route for each vehicle is chosen according to the preference values of the routes.

② Based on the information from GPS, the vehicle agents have full knowledge of the surrounding traffic conditions. Through communicating with the vehicles in the local vicinity, each vehicle obtains the traffic conditions of the road segments where it is to drive in the future, and the cost of the selected route can be calculated. The utility of the selected route can be calculated based on the preference value and the cost of the route. The calculation process is detailed in Sect. 2.5.

③ The vehicle agents in one area negotiate with each other based on the Traffic Flow Equilibrium Algorithm (TFEA), which is detailed in Sect. 3, and are distributed on the optional routes equally, which can make the vehicle agents avoid the traffic congestion and maximize the utility of the road resources.

2.2 Symbol Definition

The symbols used in the VANRGA model description are defined in Table 1.

Table 1. Definitions of the Symbols in VANRGA Model

Symbol	Description
VA	A set of vehicle agents in one area
SA	A set of road segment agents in one area
IA	A set of intersection agents in one area
DA	A set of edge node agents in one area
IA_ie	The road segment to the ith intersection agent from East, $i = 1, ..., |IA|$
IA_is	The road segment to the ith intersection agent from South, $i = 1, ..., |IA|$
IA_iw	The road segment to the ith intersection agent from West, $i = 1, ..., |IA|$
IA_in	The road segment to the ith intersection agent from North, $i = 1, ..., |IA|$
DA_ito	The road segment to the ith edge node agent, $i = 1, ..., |DA|$
o_i	The start point of a travel for the ith vehicle agent, $o_i \in IA \cup DA$, $i = 1, ..., |VA|$
d_i	The destination of a travel for the ith vehicle agent, $d_i \in IA \cup DA$, , $i = 1, ..., |VA|$
$R_i(o_i, d_i)$	The set of optional routes from o_i to d_i for the ith vehicle agent, R_i for short, $i = 1, ..., |VA|$
r_j	The jth route in $R_i(o_i, d_i)$, $r_j \in R_i(o_i, d_i)$, $i = 1, ..., |VA|$, $j = 1, ..., |R_i(o_i, d_i)|$
sa_k	One road segment of r_j, $r_j = \bigcup_{k=1}^{|r_j|} sa_k (k = 1, ..., |r_j|)$, $r_j \subset SA$
$p_{i,j}$	The preference value of the jth optional route for the ith vehicle agent, $i = 1, ..., |VA|$, $j = 1, ..., |R_i(o_i, d_i)|$
$c_{i,j}$	The cost experienced by the ith vehicle agent on the jth optional route, $i = 1, ..., |VA|$, $j = 1, ..., |R_i(o_i, d_i)|$
$p_{i,k}$	The preference value of the kth segment of the jth optional route for the ith vehicle agent, $i = 1, ..., |VA|$, $j = 1, ..., |R_i(o_i, d_i)|$, $k = 1, ..., |r_j|$
$c_{i,k}$	The cost experienced by the ith vehicle agent on the kth segment of the jth optional route, $i = 1, ..., |VA|$, $j = 1, ..., |R_i(o_i, d_i)|$, $k = 1, ..., |r_j|$
p	The multiplication factor for $p_{i,j}$, $i = 1, ..., |VA|$, $j = 1, ..., |R_i(o_i, d_i)|$
c	The multiplication factor for $c_{i,j}$, $i = 1, ..., |VA|$, $j = 1, ..., |R_i(o_i, d_i)|$
$u_{i,j}$	The utility of the jth optional route for the ith vehicle agent, $i = 1, ..., |VA|$, $|R_i(o_i, d_i)|$

2.3   VANRGA Model Description

According to the definition of Nash Equilibrium, the VANRGA model can be expressed as G = {A, I, S, U}, where A is the set of n vehicle agents, I represents the perception information on the surrounding environment of each vehicle agent that includes the set of optional routes and their utilities of the other vehicle agents, S is the set of optional routes from the origin to the destination. f each vehicle agent, and U is the utility of its chosen route for a vehicle agent when all vehicle agents have selected their preferred routes.

In order to avoid the traffic congestion on road segments, the vehicle agents communicate with each other to be distributed equally on their optional routes when they are approaching some intersection. Each vehicle agent chooses the preferred route from the set of its optional routes according to the information on route selection of the

others and negotiates with each other. They stop negotiation when their utilities reach
the Nash equilibrium, which means

$$u_i(r_i^*, r_{-i}^*) \geq u_i(r_i, r_{-i}^*), \forall r_i \in R_i \tag{1}$$

where r_i^* is the optimal route chosen by the ith vehicle agent, r_{-i}^* is the vector of the
routes chosen by the other vehicle agents except the ith one, u_i is the utility of its chosen
route for the ith vehicle agent, and R_i is the set of optional routes for the ith vehicle
agent.

The negotiations between vehicle agents can be divided into three levels. The lower
level is between the vehicles driving towards the same intersection. The middle level is
between the the vehicles driving towards the neighboring intersections. The upper level
is between the vehicles in a large area containing several intersections. The negotiation
levels are shown in Fig. 2.

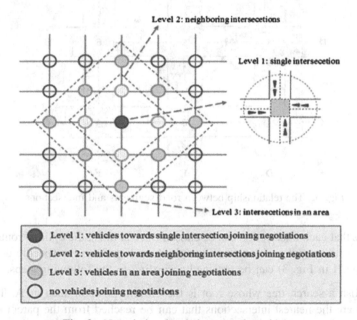

Fig. 2. Negotiation levels between the vehicles

2.4 Route Selection

When the vehicle agent is driving on the road, the routing table is used to store the set
of optional routes from its current position to all the destinations in one area. Each route
is composed of several road segment agents. Each road segment agent is responsible
for evaluating the road traffic service level (such as road congestion, road conditions),
setting up the routing table, releasing the traffic service level information, and providing the induced information for the vehicle agents. According to the driving
direction of the vehicle agent, the road segment agent is relevant to some interaction

agent. As is shown in Fig. 3, the serial number of one road segment agent consists of two parts, the first part of which is the number of the relevant intersection agent and the second one is the relationship to the intersection agent. The relationship is about the driving direction of the vehicle agent on the road segment, which is respectively from East, South, West and North and is represented by four characters 'e', 's', 'w' and 'n'. For example, '5e' represents the road segment agent on which the vehicle agent drives to the 5th intersection from East.

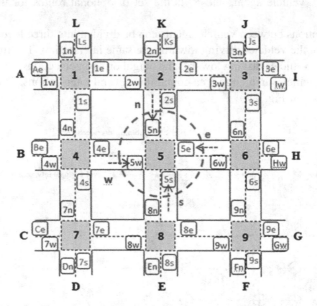

Fig. 3. The relationship between road segments and intersections

Assume that each intersection can be chosen once at most, the optimal route for one vehicle from its current position (for example A in Fig. 3) to the specific destination (for example H in Fig. 3) can be obtained according to the following steps.

(1) Establish a search tree whose root is the current position such as A. The child nodes are the nearest intersections that can be reached from the parent node.
(2) Traverse the search tree from the root to the node that corresponds to the specific destination such as H. The road segments between the traversed nodes consist of the optional routes from the current position A to the destination H, such as {1w, 4n, 5w, 6w, Hw}, {1w, 2w, 5n, 6w, Hw}, and {1w, 2w, 3w, 6n, Hw}.
(3) Evaluate the optional routes according to a assessment criteria and choose the optimal route, which is written in the corresponding table entry of the routing table for the vehicle. For example, {1w, 2w, 3w, 6n, Hw} is chosen as the optimal route from A to H and supplied to the vehicle as the first choice route.

2.5   Utility Calculation

Utility of One Route for One Vehicle. According to the routing table of each vehicle agent, the optional routes from the current position to the destination can be found. Before each vehicle reaches one intersection, the utility of each optional route for each vehicle can be calculated. One route is composed of several road segments and the utility of one route is the aggregate of the utilities of all contained segments, which depends on the preference value and the cost experienced by the vehicle on each contained segment.

Let $R_i(o_i, d_i)$ be the optional routes from the start point o_i to the destination d_i for the ith vehicle agent. $p_{i,j}$ is the preference value of the jth route for the ith vehicle agent. $c_{i,j}$ is the cost experienced by the ith vehicle agent on the jth route. $sa_k(k = 1, \ldots, |r_j|)$ is the contained road segment of the route r_j. $p_{i,k}$ is the preference value of the kth segment for the ith vehicle agent. $c_{i,k}$ is the cost experienced by the ith vehicle agent on the kth segment. The cost depends on the number of vehicles taking the route and the average travel time on that route, which is calculated below. p and c are the constant multipliers for $p_{i,j}$ and $c_{i,j}$ respectively. Hence, the utility $u_{i,j}$ of the jth route for the ith vehicle agent can be given as

$$u_{i,j} = p \times p_{i,j} - c \times c_{i,j}, p_{i,j} = \sum\nolimits_{k=1}^{|r_j|} p_{i,k}, c_{i,j} = \sum\nolimits_{k=1}^{|r_j|} c_{i,k}. \tag{2}$$

Preference Value of One Route by One Vehicle. Driver behavioral studies have shown that drivers do not always choose quicker routes, and route preference also depends on factors such as route familiarity, road conditions, road characteristics (e.g., toll roads and route complexity). Other than the preferred route, the most common criterion for acceptance of an alternate route is that it should not exceed the delay threshold, which is time limit to reach the destination. Road preference value is mainly calculated based on the combination weights of the parameters defined in Table 2.

According to the parameters described in Table 2, the preference value of the kth road segment of the jth optional route for the ith vehicle agent can be calculated as follows:

$$p_{i,k} = a_{i,k} \times w1 + c_{i,k} \times w2 + t_{i,k} \times w3 + d_{i,k} \times w4 + f_{i,k} \times w5 + r_{i,k} \times w6 \\ + s_{i,k} \times w7, k = 1, \ldots, |r_j| \tag{3}$$

where $a_{i,k}, c_{i,k}, t_{i,k}, d_{i,k}, f_{i,k}, r_{i,k}, s_{i,k}$ are the corresponding parameters of the kth road segment of the jth optional route for the ith vehicle agent, and $w1, \ldots, w7$ are the respective weight multiplying factors. The greater weight factor represents that the corresponding parameter is more important. The sum of weights $w1, \ldots, w7$ is 1. The preference value of one route is calculated as the aggregate of those of the contained road segment, as is shown in the following:

Table 2. Description of the parameters in preference calculation

Parameter	Value range	Description
a	{1, −1}	Choice of alternate route. If a = −1, none of the remaining parameter values are calculated and the preference value equals −1, indicating that the road segment is invalid for that vehicle as it does not lead to its destination
c	[0, 1]	Previous Compliance. The larger c is, the more compliant the driver is with the route guidance system
t	[0, 1]	Time tolerance. The larger t indicates the route is more similar with the "shortest time" route
d	[0, 1]	Distance tolerance. The larger d indicates the route is more similar with the "shortest distance" route
f	[0, 1]	Familiarity index. The larger f indicates the driver is more familiar with the route
r	{0, 1}	Lane type. If the route contains more than two lanes, r = 1; or else r = 0
s	{0, 1}	Sidewalk or not. If there is a sidewalk in the route, s = 0; or else s = 1

$$p_{i,j} = \sum\nolimits_{k=1}^{|r_j|} p_{i,k} \tag{4}$$

The higher the preference value is, the more preferable that route is.

Cost Experienced by One Vehicle on One Route. The cost experienced by the one vehicle on one road segment depends on the number of the vehicles choosing it, which is denoted by V_k and determines the traffic condition of the chosen segment. If the segment is more congested, the cost increases more rapidly. According to the different degrees of the congestion, we define different parameters to describe the traffic condition. *Threshold capacity* of a road segment is the number of vehicles that can traverse the road at free-flow speed per unit time, and beyond which congestion starts to build up, and which is denoted by Q_k. When the road segment is totally congested, the number of vehicles on it is denoted by T_k. According to the historical experience, we get that the cost experienced by one vehicle on one road segment $sa_k (k = 1, \ldots, |r_j|)$ contained in the route r_j can be calculated as the follows:

$$c_{i,k} = \begin{cases} 0, V_k \leq Q_k \\ V_k e^{-1}, Q_k < V_k \leq T_k, \quad k = 1, \ldots, |r_j| \\ Q_k e^{-T_k/V_k}, V_k > T_k \end{cases} \tag{5}$$

The cost experienced by one vehicle on the route r_j is calculated as the aggregate of those of the contained road segments:

$$c_{i,j} = \sum_{k=1}^{|r_j|} c_{i,k}. \tag{6}$$

3 Traffic Flow Equilibrium Algorithm

The Traffic Flow Equilibrium Algorithm (TFEA) is initiated when the vehicle agents detect the necessity of negotiation after the initial exchange of preference information on the road segments before the intersections, which is termed the *initiation criteria*.

Every vehicle agent starts with ranking the optional routes from its current position to the destination according to their priority. The ranking idea for different values of constants p and c in (2) is shown as follows: (1) $p = 0$ OR $c \neq 0, p \neq 0, c > p$, i.e., the routes are ranked in increasing order of travel time; (2) $c = 0$. OR $c \neq 0, p \neq 0, c < p$., i.e., the routes are ranked in decreasing order of preference utility value; and (3) ., i.e., the routes are ranked in decreasing order of preferences and increasing order of travel time.

Negotiations are started with the vehicle choosing the highest priority route, and the utility of the chosen route for each vehicle is calculated. All the vehicle agents driving towards the same intersection negotiate with each other to search for Nash Equilibrium. If Nash Equilibrium is not reached between the vehicles towards one intersection, the vehicles driving towards the neighboring intersections are included. If there is still no Nash Equilibrium in the negotiations between these vehicles, those in a larger area are included. The algorithm terminates if Nash Equilibrium is found before the preset number of negotiations or at a given distance before the intersection (based on the Global Positioning System location), which is termed the *termination criteria*. Here, we use 20 negotiations preset as the termination criteria (empirically found to be acceptable). At the end of all negotiations, the vehicle agents exchange the resulting route selection solution and its utility value. The best solution, obtained at Nash Equilibrium, is adopted by all the agents. The detailed process of the algorithm is shown in Table 3.

Table 3. The detailed process of TFEA

Step 1: Initialize the vehicles with their first optimal route respectively
Step 1.1: Search for the optional routes from their current position to the destination
Step 1.2: Rank the routes as per the initial values of p and c
Step 1.3: Assign vehicles to the routes as per the priority-based allocation
Step 2: Calculate the utility of the chosen route for each vehicle
Step 3: Start negotiation between the vehicles in the vicinity. If termination criteria is met, go to Step 5; else go to Step 4
Step 4: Choose other optional routes for the vehicles, go to Step 2
Step 5: Exchange the resulting route selection solution

4 Experiments

VANRGA was simulated using JADE as the agent simulator and VanetMobiSim as the mobility simulator. Various urban traffic networks were configured in VanetMobiSim using scenario Extensible Markup Language files, and agent behavior was simulated on JADE. VANRGA was tested in the following scenarios: (1) varying number of junctions and vehicles for a multijunction synthetic urban traffic network, and (2) scaling to a wider real urban traffic network in three scenarios, where the traffic conditions were free flow, mixed flow and block flow respectively.

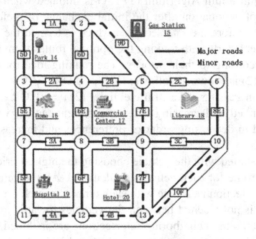

Fig. 4. A synthetic urban traffic network

4.1 Scenario 1: Synthetic Urban Traffic Networks

In this scenario a synthetic urban traffic network contains five major roads (labeled by solid lines) and four minor roads (labeled by dashed line), as is shown in Fig. 4. The seven spots respectively labeled by the No. 14 to 20 represent the starting points or destinations. Table 4 shows the capacities of the road segments.

In this scenario, we compare the performance of VANRGA with three no cooperative algorithms: *shortest path algorithm* (where $p = 0$), *preference-based algorithm* (where $c = 0$), and *preference-based shortest path algorithm* (where p and c are equal, and $p \neq 0$) and CARAVAN algorithm [13]. In these three algorithms traffic congestion cannot be avoided via cooperation as vehicles do not negotiate with each other. In the shortest path algorithm, all vehicles take the path with the least amount of travel time between the source and the destination, disregarding absolute road capacity. The utility of taking a route solely depends on the cost of traveling on it. In the preference-based allocation, routes are allocated to the vehicles according to the agent preferences. The vehicles take their best route choice, disregarding road capacity. The utility of taking a route solely depends on the preference utility of the route chosen by that agent. In preference-based shortest-path allocation, the vehicles take the shortest of their

Table 4. The capacities of road segments

Road segment	Threshold capacity	Congestion capacity	Road segment	Threshold capacity	Congestion capacity
1A	30	45	5E	30	45
2A	30	45	5F	40	60
2B	30	45	6D	30	45
2C	40	60	6E	30	45
3A	30	45	6F	40	60
3B	30	45	7E	30	45
3C	40	60	7F	30	45
4A	30	45	8E	30	45
4B	30	45	9D	40	60
5D	30	45	10F	50	70

preferred route choices, disregarding road capacity. The utility of the chosen routes in VANRGA is calculated using the formula (2).

In this scenario, the urban traffic network was scaled up to 1, 8, and 13 intersections to observe the performance of VANRGA on different scales. The roads in this network are two-direction roads, intersect with each other and have speed limits. The simulation was run with the nodes 14, 15, 16, and 17 as the starting points and the nodes 18, 19 and 20 as the destinations. The vehicles exchange information, negotiate with each other and choose the route before reaching each intersection. For this scenario, we assumed the traffic information was accurate by the aid of GPS (Global Position System), and vehicles were assumed to have full knowledge of the traffic joining at the forthcoming intersections.

Table 5. The performance of VANRGA in a synthetic urban traffic network

Decrease in % travel time over		Shortest path algorithm	Preference based algorithm	Preference based shortest path algorithm	CARAVAN algorithm
Number of intersections	Number of vehicles				
1	30	22.1	15.5	21.6	7.3
	60	14.9	11.4	13.7	6.2
8	240	26.3	21.7	25.9	9.6
	360	15.7	12.3	15.1	7.1
13	400	37.4	27.6	36.3	11.7
	500	18.2	13.4	16.9	9.3

Experimental Results: From the simulation results in Table 5, it can be seen that VANRGA against the three no cooperative algorithms and CARAVAN algorithm leads to decrease in the overall travel time and offers the highest percentages ranging from 22 % to 37 % when compared against the shortest path algorithm. In VANRGA, the vehicles communicate and cooperatively distribute themselves along the alternate routes to minimize travel time costs. All vehicles in the shortest path algorithm only select the shortest route (regardless of road capacity constraints), which is the main reason of traffic congestion. Preference-based and preference-based shortest path algorithms are driven by the preferences of drivers who may not always prefer one route. Therefore, in most cases, the decrease obtained against the shortest path algorithm is seen to be larger than the decrease obtained against the preference-based algorithm and the preference-based shortest path algorithm. Although CARAVAN algorithm alleviates the decrease in travel time, there is still reduction in travel time, because the vehicles in CARAVAN algorithm communicating with each other are only within those driving towards one intersection instead of several intersections in an area. Thus the vehicles in CARAVAN algorithm are distributed less equally than VANRGA and the travel time is therefore more.

The more intersections available for negotiation and route optimization, the more percentage in travel time decrease. This indicates that VANRGA's local decision-making at every intersection helps to reduce the overall travel time as it leads to a better distribution of vehicles along the urban traffic network.

4.2 Scenario 2: Real Urban Traffic Networks

To validate the stability and scalability of VANRGA, it was applied to a wider real urban traffic network. In this scenario, we applied VANRGA to the Wuchang District in Wuhan City, China, as is shown in Fig. 5. Three scenarios with a random variety of origin-destination pairs were simulated, where the traffic conditions were free flow, mixed flow and block flow respectively. Table 6 compares the performance of VANRGA with those of the three no cooperative algorithms and CARAVAN algorithm in terms of the travel time for these three simulation scenarios.

Fig. 5. The real urban traffic network of Wuchang District in Wuhan City

Experimental Results: As is seen in Table 6, even for a wider urban traffic network with a higher vehicle count, VANRGA consistently provides 8 %–36 % decrease in travel time over the three no cooperative algorithms and CARAVAN algorithm. It is also observed that the travel time reduction increases with the increase in total travel distance and the number of intersections encountered as the vehicles get more opportunities to negotiate and arrive at a better route selection.

Table 6. The performance of VANRGA in real urban traffic networks

Decrease in % travel time over Scenario No.	Shortest path algorithm	Preference based algorithm	Preference based shortest path algorithm	CARAVAN algorithm
1 (free flow)	36.1	25.3	32.8	10.6
2 (mixed flow)	24.3	16.4	22.5	8.3
3 (block flow)	17.5	12.6	15.4	7.9

5 Conclusions and Future Work

In order to reduce the travel time of the drivers, many researchers have studied how to utilize the traffic resources effectively to alleviate or avoid the traffic congestion for driving vehicles. However, the traditional route guidance system often provides the same shortest route to different drivers regardless of their different traffic conditions. As a result, many vehicles may rush into the same road segments at the same time that would lead to traffic congestion. Although CARAVAN allocated the routes for the vehicles before junctions based on virtual agent deals, this model didn't consider the characteristic of intersections in urban traffic networks. To improve this model this paper proposes a VANRGA model based on urban traffic networks. In the proposed approach, vehicle agents (VAs) in the local vicinity communicate with each other before the intersections to achieve a real-time and dynamic route selection. Based on the route preference of the drivers and the traffic conditions, the vehicles are distributed on the routes equally, which can avoid the traffic congestion, reduce the average travel time of the vehicles and maximize the utility of the road resources.

Through extensive experiments, we can draw the conclusions as follows.

(1) From the simulation results in a synthetic urban traffic network, it can be seen that VANRGA against the three no cooperative algorithms and CARAVAN algorithm leads to decrease in the overall travel time and offers the highest percentages ranging from 22 % to 37 % when compared against the shortest path algorithm.
(2) Even for a wider real urban traffic network with a higher vehicle count, VANRGA consistently provides 8 %–36 % decrease in travel time over the three no cooperative algorithms and CARAVAN algorithm.

In spite of the progress in this paper, there is still some work required to be further studied.

(1) In the VANRGA model, all vehicles are assumed to follow the route guidance system. In the reality, some drivers may not be obedient. In this case, the effect of varying the percentage of none quipped vehicles and noncompliant drivers on total travel time should be studied further.
(2) When the vehicles choose their preferred routes before intersections, the time intervals of traffic signals are ignored, which should be considered to make the VANRGA model closer to the real urban traffic scenarios.

Acknowledgments. This work is supported in part by the National Basic Research Program of China (973 Program) under Grant 2012CB719905, the National Natural Science Foundation of China under Grant 61572369 and 61471274, the National Natural Science Foundation of Hubei Province under Grant 2015CFB423, the Wuhan major science and technology program under Grant 2015010101010023.

References

1. El-Tantawy, S., Abdulhai, B.: Multi-agent reinforcement learning for integrated network of adaptive traffic signal controllers (MARLIN-ATSC). In: 2012 15th International IEEE Conference on Intelligent Transportation Systems (ITSC), pp. 319–326. IEEE (2012)
2. Zolfpour-Arokhlo, M., Selamat, A., Mohd Hashim, S.Z., et al.: Modeling of route planning system based on Q value-based dynamic programming with multi-agent reinforcement learning algorithms. Eng. Appl. Artif. Intell. **29**, 163–177 (2014)
3. Hu, W., Wang, H., Yan, L.: An actual urban traffic simulation model for predicting and avoiding traffic congestion. In: 17th International IEEE Conference on Intelligent Transportation Systems (ITSC 2014), pp. 2681–2686. Qingdao, China, 8–11 Oct 2014
4. Yamada, K., Ma, J., Fukuda, D.: Simulation analysis of the market diffusion effects of risk-averse route guidance on network traffic. Procedia Comput. Sci. **19**, 874–881 (2013)
5. Hu, W., Yan, L., Wang, H.: Traffic jams prediction method based on two-dimension cellular automata model. In: 17th International IEEE Conference on Intelligent Transportation Systems (ITSC 2014), pp. 2023–2028. Qingdao, China, 8–11 Oct 2014
6. Tumer, K., Proper, S.: Coordinating actions in congestion games: impact of top–down and bottom–up utilities. Auton. Agents Multi-agent Syst. **27**(3), 419–443 (2013)
7. Tumer, K., Agogino, A.K., Welch, Z., et al.: Traffic congestion management as a learning agent coordination problem. In: Multiagent Architectures for Traffic and Transportation Engineering. Springer, Berlin (2009)
8. Tumer, K., Welch, Z.T., Agogino, A.: Aligning social welfare and agent preferences to alleviate traffic congestion. In: Proceedings of the 7th International Joint Conference on Autonomous Agents and Multiagent Systems, vol. 2, pp. 655–662 (2008)
9. Lakas, A., Chaqfeh, M.: A novel method for reducing road traffic congestion using vehicular communication. In: Proceedings of the 6th International Wireless Communications and Mobile Computing Conference, pp. 16–20. ACM (2010)
10. Wenbin, Hu, Liang, Huanle, Peng, Chao, Bo, Du, Qi, Hu: A hybrid chaos-particle swarm optimization algorithm for the vehicle routing problem with time window. Entropy **15**, 1247–1270 (2013)
11. Adler, J.L., Satapathy, G., Manikonda, V., et al.: A multi-agent approach to cooperative traffic management and route guidance. Transp. Res. Part B Methodol. **39**(4), 297–318 (2005)
12. Airiau, S., Endriss, U.: Multiagent resource allocation with sharable items: simple protocols and Nash equilibria. In: Proceedings of the 9th International Conference on Autonomous Agents and Multiagent Systems, vol. 1, pp. 167–174 (2010)
13. Desai, P., Loke, S.W., Desai, A., et al.: CARAVAN: congestion avoidance and route allocation using virtual agent negotiation. IEEE Trans. Intell. Transp. Syst. **14**(3), 1197–1207 (2013)

Optimization of Binomial Option Pricing on Intel MIC Heterogeneous System

Weihao Liang$^{(\boxtimes)}$, Hong An, Feng Li, and Yichao Cheng$^{(\boxtimes)}$

School of Computer Science and Technology,
University of Science and Technology of China, Hefei 230026, China
{lwh1990,fli168,yichao}@mail.ustc.edu.cn, han@ustc.edu.cn

Abstract. In these years, computerization has been more and more important in the financial area. The computational intensity and real-time constraints of those financial models require high-throughput parallel architectures. In this paper, optimization of widely-used binomial option pricing model has been implemented on the worlds largest supercomputer, Tianhe-2. In our work, we employ several optimizing techniques to efficiently utilize the architecture of Intel MIC heterogeneous system to improve the performance. The experimental results show that, compared with the serial implementation, the optimized binomial option pricing achieves 33X speedup on one Intel Xeon CPU and 61X speedup on one Intel Xeon Phi coprocessor. Further experiments on Intel MIC heterogeneous system indicate that our implementation attains a speedup factor of 254 on one Tianhe-2 computing node.

Keywords: Binomial option pricing · MIC · Parallel process · Heterogeneous system · Optimization

1 Introduction

An option is a contract that gives right to the owner to buy or sell a financial asset or instrument at a specified strike price on or before the expiry date. Binomial option pricing is one of the most popular approaches that values an option using a time-step model [10]. With larger scale of financial problem, the number of option grows rapidly which makes the computation becomes very expensive. This issue often happens when a great number of real-time options need to be revaluated with live data. Hence, it is significant to improve the efficiency of binomial option pricing.

Related work mainly focuses on implementing the binomial option pricing on CPU. Previous researchers have presented parallel solution for binomial option pricing with low performance [17]. Gerbessiotis et al. [8] achieved high speedup with proposed algorithm on Intel Pentium CPU cluster. But it only achieves less than 2 % of peak performance of one single node and the performance decreases when scaling to multiple nodes. Zubair et al. [18] and John et al. [16] proposed another algorithm considering the memory hierarchy system to achieve 60 % of

© Springer International Publishing Switzerland 2015
G. Wang et al. (Eds.): ICA3PP 2015, Part III, LNCS 9530, pp. 17–29, 2015.
DOI: 10.1007/978-3-319-27137-8_2

the peak performance on 8 UltraSPARCIIIi processors. But it is not easy to optimize and extend to large CPU cluster. Other works deploy binomial option pricing on GPU. Matthew et al. [6] proposed a GPU-based market value-at-risk estimation algorithm which is suitable for Nvidia GPGPU. But it can only process small-scale Europe options. Although Qiwei et al. [12] and Mehmet et al. [9] also provided other GPU-based solutions for binomial option pricing, it does not get enough efficiency from the hardware.

In this paper, we implement and optimize the binomial option pricing on Intel MIC heterogeneous system which contains Intel Xeon CPU and Intel Phi coprocessor. Our method includes several optimizing techniques such as optimizing compiler options, OpenMP parallelization, vectorization by SIMD and modification of the serial algorithm to efficiently utilize Intel hardware's architecture to further improve the performance. The experimental results demonstrate that, compared with the CPU serial code, the optimized version of binomial option pricing achieves 33X speedup on one Intel Xeon CPU and 61X speedup on one Intel Xeon Phi. Further experiments on heterogeneous system of Tianhe-2 [7] indicate that our implementation attains a speedup of 254 times on one Tianhe-2 computing node.

The rest of the paper is organized as follows. We review the binomial option pricing model in Sect. 2 and introduce the architecture and programming model of Intel MIC heterogeneous system in Sect. 3. In Sect. 4, we present and implement several optimization strategies for binomial option pricing on Intel Xeon CPU and Intel Xeon Phi coprocessor. Detailed experimental results and analysis are provided in Sect. 5 and conclusions of our work is shown in Sect. 6.

2   The Binomial Option Pricing Model

2.1   Binomial Option Pricing Model Theory

The flowchart of the binomial option pricing is illustrated in Fig. 1. The binomial pricing model traces the evolution of the option's key underlying variables in discrete time which is done by a binomial tree [5]. Each node in the tree represents a possible price at a given point of time. The computation is performed iteratively, beginning at each of the leave nodes and then computing backwards through the tree towards the root node. The value of each node which depends on the values of its two child nodes is computed at each stage at that given point of time. In the end, the value of root node is the final result of binomial option pricing.

2.2   Serial Algorithm

Algorithm 1 presents the pseudocode of the serial kernel in binomial option pricing program. There are two main parts: the first one is a loop that initialize each leave node's value in the binomial tree (line 2 – 4); the second one is a nested loop (line 6 – 10). The outer loop is procedure of calculation following the time

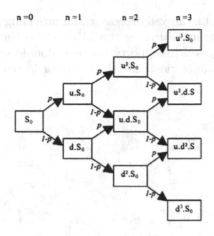

Fig. 1. The flowchart of the binomial option tree.

step from leave node to root node. The inter loop indicates that in each time step, all nodes of that stage will calculate its value by using its two child nodes' values. [13]

Algorithm 1. Serial algorithm of binomial option pricing

1: **for** all options **do**
2:    **for** all leave nodes **do**
3:        Initialize its value
4:    **end for**
5:
6:    **for** each time step **do**
7:        **for** nodes of each stage **do**
8:            Calculate its value
9:        **end for**
10:    **end for**
11: **end for**

---

3   Overview of Intel Many Integrated Core (MIC)

3.1   MIC Architecture

Figure 2 shows the microarchitecture of the Intel MIC. The main components of Intel Xeon Phi coprocessor are processing cores, caches, memory controllers, PCIe client logic, and a bidirectional ring interconnect with very high bandwidth. Each core directly connects with a private L2 cache. The memory controllers and the PCIe client logic respectively provide a direct interface to the GDDR memory on the coprocessor and the PCIe bus. In general, all these components are linked together by the ring interconnect [1]. Each core in the Intel Xeon Phi coprocessor is designed like an x86 processor and providing good programmability [11]. Another important feature of the MIC core is the 512 bit wide vector processing unit (VPU) which supports up to 8 double precision or 16 single precision floating point operations in a single vector instruction.

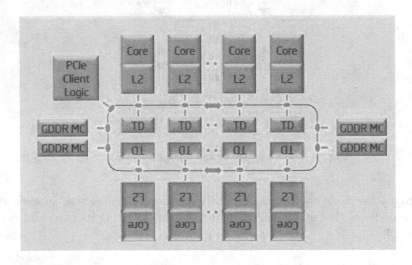

Fig. 2. The MIC microarchitecture.

3.2 MIC Programming Model

Execution of program normally begins on the host CPU and when it reaches some user-defined sections of the code, the corresponding parts are offloaded by the host CPU to the accelerators (MICs). The Intel MIC is based on x86 architecture and therefore standard parallel programming models like OpenMP [3] and MPI [2] can be seamlessly ported to MIC. There are three programming models in MIC: Native mode, symmetric mode and offload mode. Our work only use the offload mode [15]. In the MIC offload mode, the part of code which will be executed on the accelerators is following the offload pragma.

4   Optimizing Strategies

4.1   Optimization on Single CPU

In this section, we propose and implement several optimizing methods to efficiently utilize the features of Intel software and hardware environment.

Optimizing the Compiler Options. Because all the value in the binomial tree is float type or double type, large amount of floating-point data calculation will be performed during the runtime. For Intel CPU's architectures, compilation option *-fp-model* can allow the user to control the optimizations on floating-point data. When the option is turned on, the compiler optimizer removes redundant moves from the FPU registers to memory and back, leaving intermediary results in the FPU stack. With elaborately choosing the level of *-fp-model* option, it will always have good effect on compute-intensive applications' performance with guarantee of the values' safety [4].

Parallelization and SIMD. Because there is no data dependence between all the options. We can simply parallelize the outmost loop in the Algorithm 1 by using OpenMP parallel programming model. After that, we vectorize the inner loop by using AVX-256 SIMD instruction sets to overwrite the corresponding codes which aim at initialize the values of all leave nodes. Because the length of vector process unit (VPU) in Intel Xeon CPU is 256 bit, we can process 4 nodes (each node contains a double-precision floating point number) in one time by using SIMD instructions. In addition, some common factor which will be repeatedly computed in each iteration of the inner loop can be extracted out of the loop to be computed once instead. After the vectorization of the inner loop, we may further unroll the innermost loop. 8 is chosen as the unrolled factor based on some experiments.

Blocking Cache Memory. We can efficiently improve the reuse of data from cache by blocking the accessed data in the innermost loop. The core compute kernel of binomial option pricing is shown in Algorithm 2. The procedure of the core kernel begins from the leave nodes and moves backward in each time step which the values of *Call* array is updated by being computed at a previous step. Eventually, *Call*[0] contains the option price as the final result. Although the compiler is able to automatically vectorize and unroll the j loop of the reference code for Intel Xeon CPU, the resulting code still has troubles with unaligned load and loss of SIMD efficiency. Besides, frequently memory access of *Call* array may cause high miss rate in L1 cache which can be monitored from Intel Vtune [14].

Algorithm 2. Compute kernel of binomial option pricing

1: **for** $n = 0$ to N **do**
2:     **for** $i = TS$ to 1 **do**
3:         **for** $j = 0$ to $i - 1$ **do**
4:             $opt[n].Call[j] \leftarrow puByDf * opt[n].Call[j+1] + puByDf * opt[n].Call[j]$
5:         **end for**
6:     **end for**
7:     $opt[n].Result \leftarrow opt[n].Call[0]$
8: **end for**

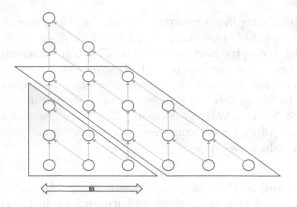

Fig. 3. Cache blocking algorithm.

In order to address the problem above, we present a auto-tuning cache blocking algorithm which shown in Algorithm 3 based on L1 cache size. The algorithm reduces both the working data set and instruction overhead of the computer kernel. First we chose a small or medium input size for this method in order to improve efficiency because we need to run the program more than one time. Then as shown in the outermost loop (line 2), we repeatedly run the compute kernel with increasing block size BS based on the size of a block array which can be allocated in a processors L1 cache. Figure 3 illustrates the key computing kernel (line 5 – 15), we separate the computation into two parts: in the first part (line 6), we read the first blocks values from the *Call* array and reduce it within the memory size of cache (see the lower triangular portion in Fig. 3). Time taken by this part is considered to be negligibly small; in the second part (line 7 – 16), the successive values are read and reduced by BS time steps from the *Call* array, then stored back to *Call*[i-BS] (the trapezoidal portion in Fig. 3). Some temporary variable like *b1, b2, b3* are used to improve reuse of data. So we read each value of *Call* array and store it back only once for every BS time step. In order to take advantage of Intel Xeon CPU's hardware features, we can use extra instructions to prefetch the data that we need during each iteration of inner loop which can further improve the cache's utilization. The entire computation during each BS time step occurs only within the cache which efficiently improves the arithmetic intensity of the code. At the end of each auto-tuning run, the computation time will be recorded and the minimum of all run (line 18 – 21) represents the corresponding best block size which will be chosen as the right parameter to run our compute kernel with normal input size. By applying the cache blocking algorithm with chosen best block size, the miss rate of L1 cache is lower than before which is monitored from Intel Vtune [14]. Overhead brought by this cache blocking algorithm is rather small compared to the benefit of its improvement of data reuse which we can see in further experiments shown in Sect. 5.

Algorithm 3. Auto-tuning cache blocking algorithm

```
 1: minTime = minBS = MAXINT, btime, etime
 2: for BS = 16, 32, 64... to CacheSize/ValueType do
 3:     VectorType Block[BS], b1, b2, b3
 4:     btime ← gettime()
 5:     for n = N, N - BS, ... to BS do
 6:         ...//Calculate lower triangular portion
 7:         for i = BS to n do
 8:             b1 ← Call[i]
 9:             for j = BS - 1 to 0 do
10:                 b2 ← puByDf * b1 + puByDf * Block[j]
11:                 Block[j] ← b1
12:                 b1 ← b2
13:             end for
14:             Call[i - BS] ← b1
15:         end for
16:     end for
17:     etime ← gettime()
18:     if etime - btime < minTime then
19:         minTime ← etime - btime
20:         minBS ← BS
21:     end if
22: end for
23: return  minBS
```

4.2   Porting to Single MIC

Because Intel Xeon Phi coprocessor (MIC) have more core and longer SIMD width than Intel Xeon CPU, it is obvious that the performance will be significantly improved by porting the computing codes to MIC. So we rewrite the corresponding AVX-256 instruction sets to AVX-512 instruction sets which fits the architecture of MIC. Additionally, MIC provide multiplication-subtraction operation instruction which can increase some degree of the arithmetic intensity of the code. We implement this part with the offload mode of MIC Programming Model.

4.3   Communication Optimization Between CPU and MIC

When the program is applied on the Intel MIC heterogeneous system, communication and cooperative problem between CPU and MIC cannot be neglected. Thanks to no data dependence between the options, the binomial option pricing model is highly scalable. The key communication problem becomes the task partition between CPU and MIC. If the task distribution is unbalanced, the synchronization problem will cause serious bottleneck in performance. To solve this problem, our solution is fine-grained tuning the task partition ratio between CPU and MIC by running the application multiple times with various task partition ratios. In the experiment, we set the ratio of the whole task for CPU from

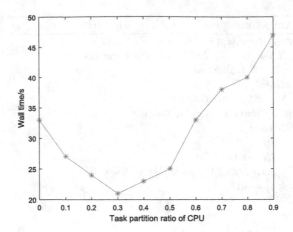

Fig. 4. Performances of different task partition ratio.

0.1 to 0.9 and run the program repeatedly. As we can see in Fig. 4, the optimal ratio is 0.3 when the wall time of whole application is the minimum.

When it comes to large heterogeneous system containing multiple CPUs and multiple MICs, we can deduce the optimal task partition ratio of each CPU and MIC based on the experimental result of Fig. 4. Let e denote the optimal partition ratio for CPU in the system containing one CPU and one MIC and e can be easily got through experiments above. If an Intel MIC heterogeneous system has M CPUs and N MICs, each CPU's best task ratio is r_c and each MIC's best task ratio is r_m. The relationship of r_c and r_m should be represented by:

$$Mr_c + Nr_m = 1 \tag{1}$$

Equation 1 indicates that all CPUs' ratio is the same and so does MICs. The sum of all ratio is 1. Equation 2 is based on the optimal task partition ratio of between one CPU and one MIC. In order to balance the work load between multiple CPUs and MICs, r_c and r_m must meet by:

$$\frac{r_c}{r_m} = \frac{e}{1-e} \tag{2}$$

We can get r_c and r_m after solving the linear equations containing Eqs. 1 and 2.

$$r_c = \frac{e}{Me + N(1-e)} \tag{3}$$

$$r_m = \frac{1-e}{Me + N(1-e)} \tag{4}$$

5   Experimental Results and Analysis

In this section, we first describe the configuration of our hardware platform. And then we present and analysis the performance of binomial option pricing on one single Intel Xeon CPU with different optimizing strategies. Furthermore, we show the performance on MIC heterogeneous system.

5.1 Hardware Platform Setup

We used one compute node of Tianhe-2 as the experimental hardware platform, which has two Intel Ivy Bridge E5-2692 CPUs and three Intel Xeon Phi 31S1P coprocessors. Each E5-2692 CPU has 12 cores and each 31S1P coprocessor has 57 cores. One compute node of Tianhe-2 can theoretically provide about 5.0 GFLOPs performance.

5.2 Single-CPU Performance

We test the single-CPU performance on the Intel Ivy Bridge CPU with different large problem size. We measure the speedup and Gflops rating of binomial option pricing with different optimizing strategies to the serial algorithm. In the experiment, each optimizing strategy is on the basis of the previous. The performance results are shown in Fig. 5.

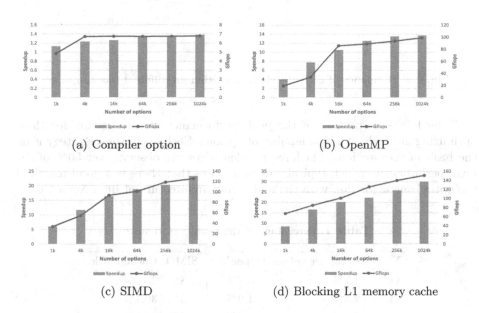

(a) Compiler option   (b) OpenMP

(c) SIMD   (d) Blocking L1 memory cache

Fig. 5. Speedup and Gflops rating of binomial option pricing with different optimizing strategies.

We can observe from the Fig. 5 that optimizing compiler options improves a little (about 10 %) in performance and parallelization with OpenMP can provide linear speedup (13X) corresponding to the number of cores in CPU. In addition, SIMD offers a very high performance which can achieve extra 10X speedup. As elaborated in Sect. 4, block size of the cache blocking algorithm has an impact upon the performance. To determine the optimal block size, we test performance of the proposed algorithm for different block sizes which can be seen in Fig. 6. We found the optimal block size to be 128 for N=4 K, 16 K, and 64 K which N is the number of options. By employing the auto-tuning cache blocking algorithm, we can obtain 33X speedup which surpasses previous version by over 10X. From Intel Vtune, we also monitor the L1 cache miss rate decreasing from 0.016 to 0.008, which demonstrates that the cache blocking optimization does really work.

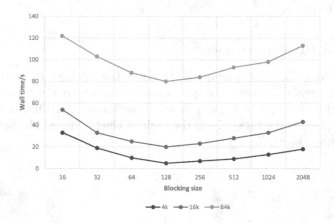

Fig. 6. Performance of cache blocking algorithm for different blocking sizes.

Table 1 lists percentage of the peak performance we are getting for these optimizing methods. N is the number of options. Each optimizing strategy is on the basis of the previous. For large problem sizes, we observe over 50 % of the peak performance, which typically demonstrates that there is a good match of the optimizing algorithm with the underlying architecture of Intel Xeon CPU.

Table 1. Percentage of the peak performance

N	Compiler options	OpenMP	SIMD	Cache block
1 k	1.7 %	6.7 %	11.8 %	23.7 %
4 k	2.3 %	11.9 %	19.3 %	30.1 %
16 k	2.3 %	30.4 %	33.2 %	35.7 %
64 k	2.3 %	31.5 %	35.8 %	44.5 %
256 k	2.4 %	33.3 %	42.1 %	49.6 %
1024 k	2.4 %	35.1 %	44.6 %	54.8 %

5.3   MIC Heterogeneous System Performance

We first conduct the performance on one single Intel Xeon Phi 31S1P coprocessor with MIC offload mode. When it comes to heterogeneous system, task distribution between host (CPU) and device (MIC) becomes important. Our solution is based on the fine-grained tuning the task partition ratio between CPU and MIC which is explained in Sect. 4. One compute node of Tianhe-2 contains two CPUs and three MICs and the optimal task partition ratio of one CPU is 0.11 and one MIC is 0.26 which is conducted by the conclusions of Eqs. 3 and 4 in Sect. 4.

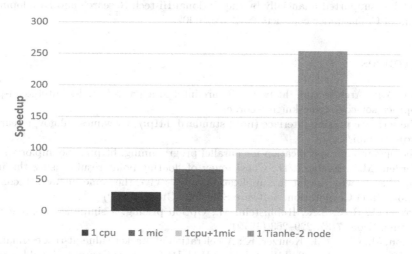

Fig. 7. Performance of Intel MIC heterogeneous system.

The experimental results is illustrated in Fig. 7 and we can explain something from it. The performance on one MIC is almost twice as that on one CPU (61X). Because of good scalability of binomial option pricing, it can get approximate linear performance improvement on multi-CPU or multi-MIC. When it comes to MIC heterogeneous system, the speedup is 93X for one CPU and one MIC, which cannot reach ideal performance provided by one CPU and one MIC because of the overhead caused by synchronization. In the end, we get 254X speedup on one compute node of Tianhe-2 containing two CPUs and three MICs.

6   Conclusion

In this paper, we have proposed a parallel implementation of binomial option pricing based on Intel MIC heterogeneous system. We have deployed several optimizing strategies including optimizing compiler options, paralleling with OpenMP and rewrite the key codes with SIMD instructions in order to make the best use of performance of Intel Xeon CPU and Intel Xeon Phi coprocessor. We also present a auto-tuning cache blocking algorithm to deal with the high L1 cache miss rate problem. The experimental results indicates that, our solution achieves 33X speedup on one Intel Xeon CPU and 61X speedup on one Intel Xeon Phi and on a compute node of Tianhe-2 our solution can achieve over 250-fold speedup compared with original serial algorithm.

In the future, we plan to extend our work to multiple compute nodes and find some ways to reduce the negative impact by the problem of synchronization and communication between CPUs and MICs.

Acknowledgments. We thank the anonymous reviewers for their valuable comments. This work is supported financially by the National Hi-tech Research and Development Program of China under contracts 2012AA010902.

References

1. Intel MIC Architecture. https://software.intel.com/en-us/articles/intel-xeon-phi-coprocessor-codename-knights-corner
2. The message passing interface (mpi) standard. http://www.mcs.anl.gov/research/projects/mpi/
3. The openmp api specification for parallel programming. http://openmp.org
4. Corden, M.J., Kreitzer, D.: Consistency of floating-point results using the intel compiler or why doesnt my application always give the same answer. Technical report, Intel Corporation, Software Solutions Group (2009)
5. Cox, J.C., Ross, S.A., Rubinstein, M.: Option pricing: a simplified approach. J. Financ. Econ. **7**(3), 229–263 (1979)
6. Dixon, M., Chong, J., Keutzer, K.: Acceleration of market value-at-risk estimation. In: Proceedings of the 2nd Workshop on High Performance Computational Finance, p. 5. ACM (2009)
7. Dongarra, J.: Visit to the National University for Defense Technology Changsha. University of Tennessee 199, China (2013). http://www.netlib.org/utk/people/JackDongarra/PAPERS/tianhe-2-dongarra-report.pdf
8. Gerbessiotis, A.V.: Architecture independent parallel binomial tree option price valuations. Parallel Comput. **30**(2), 301–316 (2004)
9. Horasanlı, M.: A comparison of lattice based option pricing models on the rate of convergence. Appl. Math. Comput. **184**(2), 649–658 (2007)
10. Hull, J.C.: Options, Futures, and Other Derivatives. Pearson Education, India (2006)
11. Jeffers, J., Reinders, J.: Intel Xeon Phi Coprocessor High-Performance Programming. Newnes, Boston (2013)
12. Jin, Q., Thomas, D.B., Luk, W., Cope, B.: Exploring reconfigurable architectures for tree-based option pricing models. ACM Trans. Reconfigurable Technol. Syst. (TRETS) **2**(4), 2586–2600 (2009). Article No. 21
13. Kwok, Y.K.: Mathematical Models of Financial Derivatives. Springer Science & Business Media, Heidelberg (2008)
14. Malladi, R.K.: Using intel vtune performance analyzer events/ratios optimizing applications (2009)

15. Newburn, C.J., Dmitriev, S., Narayanaswamy, R., Wiegert, J., Murty, R., Chinchilla, F., Deodhar, R., McGuire, R.: Offload compiler runtime for the intel xeon phi coprocessor. In: Parallel and Distributed Processing Symposium Workshops & Ph.D. Forum (IPDPSW), 2013 IEEE 27th International, pp. 1213–1225. IEEE (2013)
16. Savage, J.E., Zubair, M.: Cache-optimal algorithms for option pricing. ACM Trans. Math. Soft. (TOMS) **37**(1), 1–30 (2010). Article No. 7
17. Thulasiram, R.K., Dondarenko, D.: Performance evaluation of parallel algorithms for pricing multidimensional financial derivatives. In: International Conference on Parallel Processing Workshops, 2002, Proceedings, pp. 306–313. IEEE (2002)
18. Zubair, M., Mukkamala, R.: High performance implementation of binomial option pricing. In: Gervasi, O., Murgante, B., Laganà, A., Taniar, D., Mun, Y., Gavrilova, M.L. (eds.) ICCSA 2008, Part I. LNCS, vol. 5072, pp. 852–866. Springer, Heidelberg (2008)

Stencil Computations on HPC-oriented ARMv8 64-Bit Multi-Core Processor

Chunjiang Li[✉], Yushan Dong, and Kuan Li

School of Computer, National University of Defence Technology,
Changsha 410073, China
{chunjiang,likuan}@nudt.edu.cn, yushandong@hotmail.com

Abstract. The ARMv8 64-bit platform has been considered as an alternative for high performance computing (HPC). Stencil computations are a class of iterative kernels which update array elements according to a stencil. In this paper, we evaluate the performance and scalability of one ARMv8 64-bit Multi-Core Processor with 7-point 3D stencil code, and a series of optimization are devised for the stencil code. In the optimization, we mainly focus on how to parallelize the kernel and how to exploit data locality with loop tiling, also we improve the calculation of the block size in tiling. The achieved performance differs with the grid size of stencil, and the optimal performance is 24.4 % of the peak DP Flops for the grid size of 64^3. Comparing with Intel Xeon processor, the performance of the ARMv8 64-bit processor is about 40 % of that of Sandy Bridge for the stencil code with the grid size of 512^3, but this ARMv8 64-bit processor shows better scalability.

Keywords: Stencil computation · ARMv8 64-bit multi-core processor · Parallelization · Loop tiling

1 Introduction

Recently, ARM-based SoCs (system-on-a-chip) have a rapid evolution. Especially, the performance keeps improving and the overall power consumption is promising. While the power consumption has been one of the primary constraints on the development of large-scale High Performance Computing (HPC) system, ARM-based SoCs, the dominant platform in embedded and mobile computing, become the candidates for the next generation HPC system [1]. For instance, supported by the Mont-Blanc project [2], Barcelona Supercomputing Center built the world's first ARM-based HPC cluster–Tibidabo [3]. However, 32-bit ARMv7 has limitations for modern HPC: only 4GB of memory are supported per process [4], and the instruction set architecture (ISA) and hardware support for vector math is limited [5]. Recently, the new ARMv8 [6,7] has broken these limitations, and the ISA bears some important features, using 64-bit memory addresses, introducing double-precision floating point in the vector unit (NEON), increasing the number of registers, supporting fused multiply-add (FMA) instruction,

© Springer International Publishing Switzerland 2015
G. Wang et al. (Eds.): ICA3PP 2015, Part III, LNCS 9530, pp. 30–43, 2015.
DOI: 10.1007/978-3-319-27137-8_3

etc. Hence, it shows increasing interests to build HPC system with 64-bit ARMv8 based SoCs. However, it needs to be validated whether the ability of ARMv8 64-bit processor can deliver satisfactory performance to broad classes of HPC applications.

Stencil computations [8,9] are an important class of codes which are commonly found in a variety of applications ranging from image and video processing to computational science in several areas. Stencil computations describe a structured grid of points in N dimension. The values of the points in the grid are updated iteratively. The fixed set of neighboring points whose values are required to calculate the value of a point for each update is usually called a stencil. The stencil [10] defines how the value of a point should be computed from its value and its neighbors' value. But it can take many forms and can include points that are not directly adjacent to the current point.

In this paper, we evaluate the performance of one ARMv8 64-bit Multi-Core Processor with a typical 7-point 3D stencil which is the kernel of many HPC applications. With static program analysis, the behavior of the stencil is characterized, and a series of optimizations is applied, including parallelization and memory blocking. Simultaneously, we improve the method of calculating the block size for the given platform. As a comparison of performance, the stencil code with the same optimizations will be executed on the high-end Intel Sandy Bridge E5-2670, which is a popular platform among the largest modern supercomputers [11]. In summary, our work makes the following contributions:

1. Multi-level parallelism is leveraged to make used of the multi-core resource of the ARMv8 64-bit Multi-Core Processor. Loop tiling is used to exploit data locality of stencil code for further optimization. The optimal performance is 24.4% for the grid size of 64^3, 20.6% for the grid size of 128^3, 19.2% for the grid size of 256^3, and 7.4% for the grid size of 512^3 of the peak DP (double-precision) Flops of the ARMv8 64-bit processor respectively.
2. For the calculation of the block size in tiling, we improve the calculation based on multi-core multistage cache. The experiments show that our method achieves better performance than the traditional method.
3. Compared with Intel Xeon CPU, this ARMv8 64-bit multi-core processor only reached about 40% in the performance with grid size of 512^3. But it shows a better scalability for fetch-intensive stencil computations.

The rest of this paper is organized as follows. Section 2 introduces some related works. Section 3 presents the architecture of our platform. Section 4 analyzes the target stencils. Section 5 describes various performance optimization techniques we devised. Section 6 presents the performance evaluation. In Sect. 7, we summarize our work and give an outline of future work.

2 Related Work

This section summarizes the related literature in two areas that intersect with our work: ARM in HPC and stencil computations.

2.1   ARM in High Performance Computing

Before 2013, most of the research about ARM in HPC used the processor of ARMv7 microarchitecture [12,13], such as ARM Cortex-A8 processors and ARM Cortex-A9 processors. The focus of these research is the performance and energy efficiency of ARMv7 on a set of HPC kernels or benchmarks. On the other hand, comparison with Intel CPU on energy and cost efficiency [14,15] is another research point. All of these research concluded that ARMv7 has much more advantages on energy and cost efficiency. Recently, the ARMv8 64-bit processor, which has multiple cores and larger addressing space, has become a new platform for HPC research. Michael A. et al. [5] characterized the performance-energy tradeoff using HPC application performance modeling on ARMv7, ARMv8, and Sandy Bridge. Abdurachmanov, et al. [16] proposed a series of software porting results on one ARMv8 64-bit processor (X-Gene ARMv8 64-bit low-power server from Applied Micro) and Intel Xeon Phi coprocessor for scientific computing. But, evaluating the performance and scalability of the ARMv8 64-bit processor using fetch-intensive stencil computations has not been studied thoroughly.

2.2   Stencil Computations

As a class of iterative kernels in scientific and engineering computation, stencil computations have received considerable attention due to its importance. Since 2014, International Workshop on High-Performance Stencil Computations (HiStencils) [8] is convened in conjunction with HiPEAC in January each year. HiStencils focuses on the optimizations of stencil computations involving all fields. In recent years, with the development of multi-core and many-core architecture, efforts on stencils have a broad range: from exploiting data locality [17,18] to considering both locality and parallelism [19,20]. The target platforms have been changed from the traditional single core processor to symmetric multiprocessing on-a-chip, furthermore, accelerators are used, such as NVIDIA GPU [21,22] and Intel MIC [23]. Rahman [24] et al. modeled the relationship between performance improvements achieved by different optimizations and their efficiency of utilizing various hardware components on multi-core architectures, which can be used to guide the optimization of different stencil kernels. Schäfer A and Fey D [21] chose the Jacobi method to evaluate a set of algorithms on NVIDIA GPGPU. Maruyama N. and Aoki T. [22] evaluated the performance of a 7-point 3D stencil on NVIDIA Fermi GPU with a series of memory access optimizations, such as spatial blocking and temporal blocking with shared memory. Their approach effectively reduced the gap with the peak performance of the baseline kernel, and they also found that blocking with shared memory is unnecessary for Fermi GPU since the L1 cache of the Fermi GPU often works quite efficiently. Yang You et al. [23] accelerated the wave propagation forward modeling (a kind of stencil) on the CPU, GPU and MIC with various optimizations.

3   Overview of the ARMv8 64-Bit Processor

This section gives a brief overview of the architecture of the ARMv8 64-bit processor, which is the main target platform of our study. This processor introduces dual-core module design. Totally 4 modules are on the chip, and all the modules globally share the L3 Cache, system management controller, and peripheral bridge. All of these modules are interconnected with the high-speed network. Figure 1 illustrates the architecture of this ARMv8 64-bit processor.

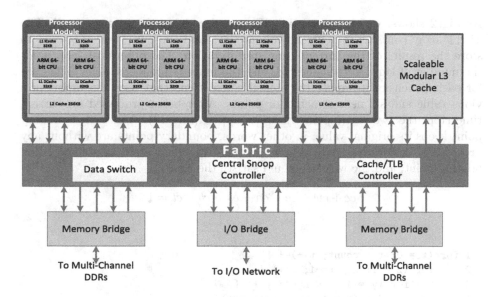

Fig. 1. Architecture of the ARMv8 64-bit Processor

The processor module contains two cores and a shared 256 KB L2-Cache. Each core has 32 KB L1 instruction cache and 32 KB L1 data cache, and the L2-Cache is inclusive of L1 write-through data caches. Moreover, 128-bit SIMD engine and 32 floating point vector registers are provided by each core. Besides, 4-width out-of-order superscalar pipelines are held, and hardware virtualization, hardware tablewalk and nested page tables are supported. Last-level globally shared L3 cache is connected with four processor modules by fabric. The fabric can afford bandwidth of 160 GB/s and delay of 15 ns. And the fabric can access multi-channel DDR memory and other IO devices by two memory bridges and an IO bridge.

As a high-performance low-power architecture, the four processor modules support high performance floating-point with the FMADD in the computing unit. And minimal instruction replay cases, separated smaller schedulers per pipe, a full set of power management features are also its outstanding features. At full load, the power usage is only 2 watts per core. When idling, the power usage is one fourth, 0.5 watts per core. For the 8-core chip at 3 GHz, the power usage works out to be 16 W, or 4 W when idling.

Our work aims to make the best of the advantage of the ARMv8 64-bit processor by optimizing the stencil codes, such that higher performance can be achieved. Optimization techniques used for stencil computations will be presented in detail in Sect. 5.

4   Target Stencils

As Fig. 2 shows, we choose 7-point 3D stencil code as the target stencil. The old[] array contains the current volume data and the cur[] array is used to store the results of the current time step iteration. The outermost loop is for the number of time steps requested, and the inner triple loops (lines 2–11) are for each dimension to apply the stencil calculations that uses the target previous value and six nearest neighbor points. After being processed for current time step, the two array pointers are swapped (line 12). And each boundary point keeps its original value, in other words, boundary points are without any processing. Besides, the data type of all the array elements is double-precision floating-point, and the weights should satisfy the Eq. (1).

$$cc + cw + ce + cn + cs + cb + ct = 1 \qquad (1)$$

```
1 for (t = 0; t < count; t++) {
2     for (z = 1; z < nz-1; z++) {
3         for (y = 1; y < ny-1; y++) {
4             for (x = 1; x < nx-1; x++) {
5                 cur[z,y,x] = cc * old[z,y,x] + cw * old[z,y,xC1] +
6                              ce * old[z,y,x+1] + cn * old[z,yC1,x] +
7                              cs * old[z,y+1,x] + cb * old[zC1,y,x] +
8                              ct * old[z+1,y,x] ;
9             }
10        }
11    }
12    swap (cur, old) ;
13 }
```

Fig. 2. 7-point 3D stencil code

From the stencil code shown in Fig. 2, that there is no data coherence for each iteration of time step, so the inner loops can be parallelized. On the other hand, no data dependency exists in the innermost loop, so the stencil code can be vectorized. Besides, every update of a signal point requires 13 double-precision float-point operations, so $(nx \times ny \times nz) \times 13 \times count$ operations are performed in all. Meanwhile, $(nx \times ny \times nz) \times sizeof(double) \times 3 \times count$ bytes data is loaded and stored. Hence, the computefetch ratio is calculated as Eq. (2).

$$\frac{(nx \times ny \times nz) \times 13}{(nx \times ny \times nz) \times sizeof(double) \times 3 \times count} = 0.54 Flops/B \qquad (2)$$

The ratio clearly indicates that the stencil computations are a class of memory-intensive applications. Hence, loop transformations based on the analysis of locality are necessary to optimize memory accesses in improving the performance of the stencil.

5   Optimizations

We take the code shown in Fig. 2 as the baseline for subsequent performance optimizations. In this section, a series of optimizations will be devised for the stencil code on the ARMv8 64-bit processor. Firstly, we parallelize the target stencil code. Then we apply memory blocking to exploit data locality.

5.1   Parallelization

As a shared memory multi-core processor, to enable the computation kernel to run on all cores is the first challenge. Fortunately, the simple and power-ful OpenMP [25,26], which is the prevalent standard API [27] and programming model for shared memory multiprocessing, brings our convenience. As the analysis in Sect. 3, the outer loop of the time steps can be parallelized. So an OpenMP parallel for loop "pragma" can be added before the z loop, so that its iterations can be evaluated by multiple threads, and all threads synchronize before entering the next iteration of the surrounding t loop. Line 2 of the code shown in Fig. 3 demonstrate the method of parallelization. Parameter "THNUM" is used to specify the number of threads in parallel. However, a class of kernels, such as the Gauss-Seidel kernel which uses a single grid instead of using the two grids old and cur in this paper cannot use this kind of parallelization scheme safely due to dependence constraints.

5.2   Memory Blocking

Previous optimizations mainly focus on using the multi-core resource of the ARMv8 64-bit processor. Another popular optimization is aiming to reduce DRAM pressure for fetch-intensive computations. A well-known technique is explicit blocking. To improve the performance of stencil codes, multi-level loop tiling [28] is applied to exploit data locality. This blocked variant is parallelized using single-sweep blocking parallelization.

In this scheme, a signal sweep of the grid is portioned into cuboid blocks (Fig. 4). Within a single iteration of the time-step loop t, it partitions the 3D domain of size $(nx \times ny \times nz)$ into blocks of size $(tx \times ty \times tz)$, so that grid

```
1 for (t = 0; t < count; t++) {
2 #pragma omp  parallel for num_threads(THNUM) private(x,y)
3     for (z = 1; z < nz-1; z++) {
4         for (y = 1; y < ny-1; y++) {
5             for (x = 1; x < nx-1; x++) {
6                 cur[z,y,x] = cc * old[z,y,x] + cw * old[z,y,xC1] +
7                             ce * old[z,y,x+1] + cn * old[z,yC1,x] +
8                             cs * old[z,y+1,x] + cb * old[zC1,y,x] +
9                             ct * old[z+1,y,x]  ;
10                }
11            }
12        }
13    swap (cur, old) ;
14 }
```

Fig. 3. 7-point 3D stencil code with parallelization

points which are close in space are grouped to be modified together. Each grid point in a block can remain in cache while being used to compute new values of points without fetching from memory frequently. And the size of the block should satisfy the Eq. (3).

$$(tx \times ty \times tz) \times sizeof(DType) \times T_p \times N_m < S_{cache} \tag{3}$$

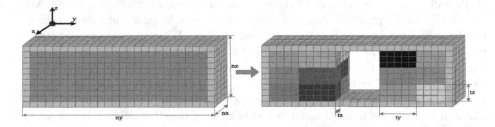

Fig. 4. 3D Grid with loop tiling

Where $DType$ represents the data type, T_p is the number of threads in each core, N_m is the amount of array read from memory, and S_{cache} represents the capacity of cache. For example, the capacity of L2 cache in each processor module of this ARMv8 processor is 256 KB. While the two cores of the processor module are working, the number of double-precision floating-point grid point in each block is 8K at most. Leopol [29] have found that when the 3D domain of size N^3 is tiled to achieve higher performance, the suggested size of block is $((N - 2), s, (s \times \frac{L}{2}))$. Where L is the size of cache line (64B), and s is the only parameter calculated to satisfy the target platform.

However, almost all the modern processors with multiple cores have larger globally shared LLC (Last Level Cache). While calculating the blocking size with Eq. (3), S_{cache} can use the capacity of LLC, and T_p is the number of logical computing cores in the processor. On the other hand, for reasonable parallelization of the inner loop and preferable vectorization of the stencil computing, we propose the size of block is calculated as $(N, min(s, \lfloor \frac{N}{T_p} \rfloor), min(s \times \frac{L}{2}, N))$. Corresponding to the Eq. (3), the size of block can be achieved easily (shown as Eq. (4)).

$$(N, min(\lfloor \sqrt{\frac{2S_{LLC}}{NLT_pN_m}} \rfloor, \lfloor \frac{N}{T_p} \rfloor), min(\lfloor \sqrt{\frac{LS_{LLC}}{2NT_pN_m}} \rfloor, N)) \qquad (4)$$

Figure 5 illustrates the result of applying conventional loop tiling to improve cache reuse of the 7-point 3D stencil code shown in Fig. 1, where the partitioned blocks with a single sweep of the grid are assigned to different threads to be evaluated simultaneously. As the analysis above, two-way blocking is applied.

```
1   for (t = 0; t < niter; t++) {
2   #pragma omp  parallel for num_threads(THNUM) private(xx, yy, x, y, z)
3
4     for (yy = 0; yy < ny; yy+=ty) {
5         for (zz = 0; zz < nz; zz+=tz) {
6
7           for (z = zz; z < zz+tz; z++) {
8               for (y = yy; y < yy+ty; y++) {
9                   for (x = 1; x < nx-1; x++) {
10                      cur[z,y,x] = cc * old[z,y,x] + cw * old[z,y,xC1] +
11                                   ce * old[z,y,x+1] + cn * old[z,yC1,x] +
12                                   cs * old[z,y+1,x] + cb * old[zC1,y,x] +
13                                   ct * old[z+1,y,x] ;
14                  }
15              }
16          }
17      }
18  }
19  swap (cur, old) ;
20 }
```

Fig. 5. 7-point 3D stencil code with loop tiling

6 Performance Evaluation and Analysis

6.1 Experiment Setup

We measure the performance of the 7-point 3D stencil kernel on the ARMv8 64-bit multi-core processor. In order to give a comparison of performance, the same test is done on Intel Xeon CPU. The basic specifications of the experimental platforms used in this paper are listed in Table 1. Furthermore, the hyper-threading of Intel Xeon CPU is shutdown in evaluation.

For the stencil kernel, we use the grid size of 64^3, 128^3, 256^3, and 512^3 with double-precision float-point data. The stencil code is compiled with gcc, using optimization level -O3 and vectorization support flags: -funsafe-math-optimizations -mavx on the Sandy Bridge and -funsafe-math-optimizations -mfpu=neon on ARMv8 systems. We measure execution time of 1000 time steps of each kernel for five times and use the fastest one to minimize system noise. About the size of tiling, Eqs. (3) and (4) have shown the method of calculation. When the size of grid is 512^3, for example, s is 4 for the evaluation on ARMv8 64-bit multi-core processor (based on L3-Cache). Our approach to measuring performance is to manually insert timing instrumentation around the stencil kernel loops, without the initialization and finalization code. Although the performance of these activities is important, they tend to be greatly over represented as a fraction of runtime relative to their runtime in full test code or application kernels.

6.2 Performance of Stencil Code

The performance comparisons between the serial algorithm and the optimization algorithm on ARMv8 64-bit multi-core processor with different grid sizes and optimization techniques are shown in Fig. 6.

We find that the significant improvements in performance over the baseline (serial code) are achieved after a series of optimization for different grid sizes. The optimal performance of each grid size is 24.4 %, 20.6 %, 19.2 %, and 7.4 % of the peak DP Flops of the ARMv8 processor respectively. With the parallelization, 7-point 3D stencil code achieves a performance of 7.7G Flops for the size of 64^3, 5.4G Flops for the size of 128^3, 5.1G Flops for the size of 256^3, and 2.5G Flops for the size of 512^3, and brings about speedup of 6.24, 4.96, 4.78, and 7.13 correspondingly. The loop tiling gives us a bit more of a boost and we ended up

Table 1. The specifications of experiment platform

	ARMv8 multi-core processor	Intel Xeon E5-2670 (Sandy Bridge)
Cores	8	8
SIMD Width (64-bit)	2	2 (SSE), 4 (AVX)
Clock Frequency	2.4 GHz	2.6 GHz
Memory Size/Type	16 GB/DDR3	128 GB/DDR3
Memory Speed	1333	1333
Peak DP/SP FLOPs	38.4/76.8 GFLOP/s	83.2/166.4 GFLOP/s
Cache	32 KB L1-D, 32 KB L1-I, 256 KB L2, 8 MB L3	32 KB L1-D, 32 KB L1-I, 256 KB L2, 20 MB L3
Host OS	Debian 3.16.7-2	Linux Redhat 4.4.5-6
Compiler	GCC Compiler, Version 4.9.0	

with another 21 %, 46 %, 47 %, and 12 % improvement over the parallelization. However, the performance achieved with different grid size is vary for 7-point 3D stencil code on the ARMv8 64-bit processor. And with the increase of the grid size, the performance is decreasing. The main reason may be that the grid with smaller size can take full advantage of the LLC of the processor to reduce the memory accessing delay for the memory-intensive stencil computations.

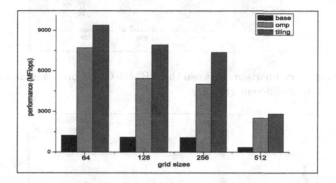

Fig. 6. Performance of the baseline and optimized versions on the ARMv8 64-bit processor with different grid size

6.3 Scalability

In order to investigate the scalability of the ARMv8 64-bit multi-core processor, we evaluate the performance of the stencil code with incrementally increasing the number of threads from 1 to 8. The performance of stencil code with different size of 3D domain is shown in Fig. 7. We can see that the performance of stencil computations increases proportionally along with the number of threads, and the speedup is 7.67 for the size of 64^3, 6.93 for the size of 128^3, 6.62 for the size of 256^3, and 7.18 for the size of 512^3 at most. Similarly, the larger the size of

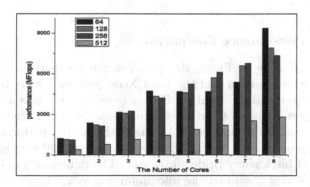

Fig. 7. Performance of stencil code on the ARMv8 64-bit Processor with different core counts

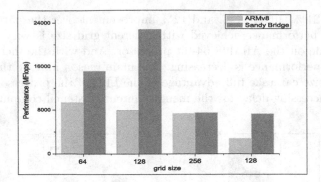

Fig. 8. Performance comparisons between the ARMv8 64-bit processor and Intel Sandy Bridge processor with different grid size

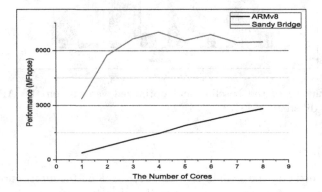

Fig. 9. Performance comparisons between the ARMv8 64-bit processor and Intel Sandy Bridge processor with different core counts

grid, the fewer the performance is increase. However, the speedup of our kernel demonstrate good scalability of performance on the ARMv8 64-bit multi-core processor.

6.4   Overall Performance Comparison

Using the stencil code in Fig. 5, the performance comparisons between the ARMv8 multi-core processor and the Intel Xeon processor with different optimization techniques and the number of cores is shown in Figs. 8 and 9. We can find that the performance of Intel Xeon processor is higher than that of the ARMv8 64-bit multi-core processor. As Fig. 8 shows, the performance of this ARMv8 64-bit processor for 7-point 3D stencil code with different grid size is all less than that of Intel Sandy Bridge processor. The minimum gap is 1.02 times when the grid size is 256^3, and the maximum gap is 2.9 times when the grid size is 128^3. Figure 9 shows the result of the performance of stencil code with grid size of 512^3 over increasing numbers of cores on both platforms. With the number of cores increasing, the gap of performance between Sandy Bridge and the ARMv8 64-bit processor is gradually narrowing from 8.6 times to 2.3 times. However, the performance of Sandy Bridge is not increasing from 4 cores due to the memory-bound nature of the kernel. Hence, the ARMv8 64-bit processor has better scalability than Sandy Bridge for such kind of stencil kernel.

7   Conclusions and Future Work

In this paper, we evaluated the performance and scalability of one HPC-oriented ARMv8 64-bit multi-core processor using the typical 7-point 3D stencil code with a series of optimizations applied, including parallelism and tiling. And we compared this ARMv8 processor with Intel Sandy Bridge processor using the same stencil code and the same optimizations. The results show that although the peak performance of this ARMv8 processor is one half of the Intel Sandy Bridge processor, the performance of the 7-point 3D stencil code with the same optimization on ARMv8 only takes 40 % of that on the Intel Sandy Bridge processor. But, taking the power consumption into consideration, the ARMv8 processor is still promising in the HPC world.

However, the stencil computations introduced in this paper could be further improved and more optimizations could be tried out in the future. For example, if we can deal with the data coherence within the t loop, the stencil code can be highly parallelized. And, as a fetch-intensive application, stencil computations may benefit from the data prefetch techniques.

Acknowledgements. The work in this paper is partially supported by the project of National Science Foundation of China under grant No.61170046, and the National High Technology Research and Development Program of China (863 Program) No.2012AA0 10903.

References

1. Rajovic, N., Carpenter, P.M., Gelado, I., Puzovic, N., Ramirez, A., Valero, M.: Supercomputing with commodity CPUs: are mobile SoCs ready for HPC? In: SC 2013: International Conference on High Performance Computing, Networking, Storage and Analysis, pp. 1–12. ACM, New York (2013)
2. Mont-Blanc. http://www.montblanc-project.eu/project/introduction
3. Rajovic, N., et al.: Building Supercomputers from Mobile Processors. In: EDA Work-shop13 Presentation, Dresden (2013)
4. Goodacre, J.: The evolution of the arm architecture towards big data and the data-center. In: VHPC 2013: Proceedings of the 8th Workshop on Virtualization in High-Performance Cloud Computing, pp. 1–10. ACM, New York (2013)
5. Laurenzano, M.A., Tiwari, A., Jundt, A., Peraza, J., Ward Jr., W.A., Campbell, R., Carrington, L.: Characterizing the performance-energy tradeoff of small ARM cores in HPC computation. In: Silva, F., Dutra, I., Santos Costa, V. (eds.) Euro-Par 2014 Parallel Processing. LNCS, vol. 8632, pp. 124–137. Springer, Heidelberg (2014)

6. ARMv8-A Architecture. http://www.arm.com/products/processors/instruction-set-architectures/armv8-architecture.php
7. ARM Infocenter. http://infocenter.arm.com/help/index.jsp
8. HiStencils. http://www.exastencils.org/histencils
9. Stencil code. http://en.wikipedia.org/wiki/Stencil_code
10. Mccool, M., Reinders, J., Robison, A.: Structured parallel programming: patterns for efficient computation. ACM SIGSOFT Softw. Eng. Notes **37**(6), 43 (2012)
11. The Top 500 list. http://www.top500.org
12. Edson, L.P., Daniel, A.G.O., Pedro, V., et al.: Scalability and energy efficiency of hpc cluster with arm mpsoc. In: Workshop of Parallel and Distributed Processing (2013)
13. Rajovic, N., Rico, A., Vipond, J., Gelado, I., Puzovic, N., Ramirez, A.: Experiences with mobile processors for energy efficient HPC. In: DATE 2013: Design, Automation and Test in Europe Conference and Exhibition, pp. 464–468. EDA Consortium, San Jose (2013)
14. Ou, Z., Pang, B., Deng, Y., Nurminen, J.K., Yla-Jaaski, A., Hui, P.: Energy- and cost-efficiency analysis of ARM-based clusters. In: 12th IEEE/ACM International Symposium on Cluster, Cloud and Grid Computing, pp. 115–123. IEEE, New York (2012)
15. Blem, E., Menon, J., Sankaralingam, K.: Power struggles: revisiting the RISC vs. CISC debate on contemporary ARM and x86 architectures. In: HPCA 2013: 19th IEEE International Symposium on High Performance Computer Architecture, pp. 1–12. IEEE Computer Society (2013)
16. Abdurachmanov, D., Bockelman, B., Elmer, P., Eulisse, G., Knight, R., Muzaffar, S.: Heterogeneous high throughput scientific computing with apm x-gene and intel xeon phi.CoRR.arXiv preprint arXiv:1410.3441 (2014)
17. Rivera, G., Tseng, C.W.: Tiling optimizations for 3D scientific computations. In: SC Conference, p. 32. IEEE Computer Society (2000)
18. Song, Y., Xu, R., Wang, C., Li, Z.: Data locality enhancement by memory reduction. In: Proceedings of the 15th International Conference on Supercomputing, pp. 50–64. ACM (2001)
19. Kamil, S., Datta, K., Williams, S., Oliker, L., Shalf, J., Yelick, K.: Implicit and explicit optimizations for stencil computations. In: MSPC 2006: Proceedings of the 2006 Workshop on Memory System Performance and Correctness, pp. 51–60. ACM (2006)
20. Krishnamoorthy, S., Baskaran, M.M., Bondhugula, U., Ramanujam, J., Rountev, A., Sadayappan, P.: Effective automatic parallelization of stencil computations. In: Proceedings of the ACM SIGPLAN 2007 Conference on Programming Language Design and Implementation, pp. 235–244. ACM (2007)
21. Schäfer, A., Fey, D.: High performance stencil code algorithms for gpgpus. Procedia Comput. Sci. **4**, 2027–2036 (2011)
22. Maruyama, N., Aoki, T.: Optimizing stencil computations for NVIDIA Kepler GPUs. In: Proceedings of the 1st International Workshop on High-Performance Stencil Computations, pp. 89–95 (2014)
23. Dehnavi, M.M., You, Y., Fu, H., Song, S.L., Gan, L., Huang, X., et al.: Evaluating multi-core and many-core architectures through accelerating the three-dimensional laxCwendroff correction stencil. Int. J. High Perform. Comput. Appl. **28**(3), 301–318 (2014)
24. Rahman, S.M.F., Yi, Q., Qasem, A.: Understanding stencil code performance on multicore architectures. In: Proceedings of the 8th ACM International Conference on Computing Frontiers, p. 30. ACM (2011)

25. Chapman, B., Jost, G., Van der Pas, R.: Using OpenMP: Portable Shared Memory Parallel Programming, vol. 10. MIT Press, Cambridge (2008)
26. Dagum, L., Enon, R.: Openmp: an industry-standard api for shared-memory programming. IEEE Comput. Sci. Eng. **5**(1), 46–55 (1998). IEEE
27. Board, O.A.R.: OpenMP application program interface. version 4.0. The OpenMP Forum, Technical report (2013)
28. Xue, J.: Loop Tiling for Parallelism. Springer Science & Business Media, US (2000)
29. Leopold, C.: Tight bounds on capacity misses for 3D stencil codes. In: Sloot, P.M.A., Tan, C.J.K., Dongarra, J., Hoekstra, A.G. (eds.) ICCS-ComputSci 2002, Part I. LNCS, vol. 2329, pp. 843–852. Springer, Heidelberg (2002)

A Particle Swarm Optimization Algorithm
for Controller Placement Problem
in Software Defined Network

Chuangen Gao, Hua Wang$^{(\boxtimes)}$, Fangjin Zhu,
Linbo Zhai, and Shanwen Yi

School of Computer Science and Technology,
Shandong University, Jinan 250101, China
gaochuangen@mail.sdu.edu.cn, wanghua@sdu.edu.cn

Abstract. Software defined network (SDN) decouples the control plane from packet processing device and introduces the controller placement problem. The previous methods only focus on propagation latency between controllers and switches but ignore either the latency from controllers to controllers or the capacities of controllers, both of which are critical factors in real networks. In this paper, we define a global latency controller placement problem with capacitated controllers, taking into consideration both the latency between controllers and the capacities of controllers. And this paper proposes a particle swarm optimization algorithm to solve the problem for the first time. Simulation results show that the algorithm has better performance in propagation latency, computation time, and convergence.

Keywords: Software defined network · Controller placement · Propagation latency · Particle swarm optimization

1 Introduction

Unlike traditional networks, where both control and forwarding planes are highly integrated on the same boxes, the Software Defined Network (SDN) architecture decouples control and forwarding planes. Such separation is realized by moving the network intelligence onto one or more external servers, called controllers, which make up a network-wide logically centralized control plane that oversees a set of dumb, and simply forwarding elements [1].

A particularly important task in SDN architectures is controller placement, i.e., the positioning of a limited number of controllers within a network to meet various requirements [2]. It is called the controller placement problem which is known to be NP-hard. These requirements range from latency constraints to failure tolerance and load balancing. We narrow our focus to latency constraints, because it places fundamental limits on availability and convergence time. Our goal is to find optimal minimum-latency placements, when the number of controllers is given. It has practical implications for software design, affecting whether controllers can respond to events in real-time, or whether they must push forwarding actions to forwarding elements in advance [3].

© Springer International Publishing Switzerland 2015
G. Wang et al. (Eds.): ICA3PP 2015, Part III, LNCS 9530, pp. 44–54, 2015.
DOI: 10.1007/978-3-319-27137-8_4

Previously, the solution only focused on propagation latency between controllers and switches but ignored the latency between controllers, which is a critical factor in real networks. If there is more than a single controller in a network, synchronization is necessary to maintain a consistent global state. Depending on the frequency of the inter-controller synchronization, the latency between the individual controllers plays an important role and thus should be considered during the controller placement [4]. Besides the propagation latency between controllers, the load of controllers is a critical factor in real networks too. Because of the constraints of possessor, memory, access bandwidth and other resources, a commodity server only has the capacity to manage a limited number of routers [6]. Whenever the load of a controller reaches a threshold, the message processing latency on the controller will increase substantially. In summary, we make the following contributions:

- To our best knowledge, this is the first work that proposes the Particle Swarm Optimization algorithm to solve the controller placement problem which is known to be NP-hard in SDN. By simulations, we show that the algorithm achieves better solutions than close-to-optimal ones obtained by the Integer Linear Program (ILP).
- We define the Global Latency Control Placement Problem with Capacitated Controllers (CGLCPP) which takes into consideration both the latency from controllers to controllers and the capabilities of controllers for the first time.

The rest of this paper is organized as follows. The related work is reported in Sect. 2. The Mathematical Model is depicted in Sect. 3. Section 4 briefs the particle warm optimization algorithm to solve the CGLCPP. The results of simulations and discussion of the performance are reported in Sect. 5. Finally, we conclude our work in Sect. 6.

2   Related Work

The controller placement problem in SDN was first proposed in [3]. The authors motivate the controller placement problem and present initial analysis of a fundamental design. This paper examines the impacts of placements on average and worst-case propagation latencies on real topologies. But its goal is not to find optimal minimum-latency placements and don't take into consideration the latency between controllers which is necessary in SDN with multiple controllers. This paper doesn't propose a useful algorithm to find the solution, and each optimal placement shown in this paper comes from directly measuring the metrics on all possible combinations of controllers. This method ensures accurate results, but at the cost of weeks of CPU time; the complexity is exponential for k, since brute force must enumerate every combination of controllers. The paper [4] discusses several aspects of the controller placement problem from the view of resilience and failure tolerance. The delay between controllers is only a small part of its multi-objective optimization considering and has not been studied in depth.

The paper [5] addresses the problem of placing controllers in SDN, so as to maximize the reliability of control networks. It presents a metric to characterize the reliability of SDN control networks, and further quantify the impact of controller number on the reliability of control networks. It proposes two heuristic algorithms to solve the problem, which are the greedy algorithm and Simulated Annealing algorithm respectively. In this letter [6], it focuses on the load of controllers and defined a capacitated controller placement problem, taking into account the capabilities of controllers. But it hasn't dealt with the latency between controllers.

The papers [4, 7] address the controller placement problem according to multiple objective functions. They argue a controller placement should also fulfill certain resilience constraints especially for the control plane. The model simultaneously determines the optimal number, location, and type of controller as well as the interconnections between all the network elements. The goal of the model is to minimize the cost of the network while considering different constraints.

3　Mathematical Model of the Global Latency Control Placement Problem

In SDNs, switches communicate with their controller via standard TLS or TCP connections. When multiple controllers are deployed, the latency between the individual controllers plays an important role, because communications between these controllers are also required to achieve global consistency of network state [8]. For example, the Google's B4 network provides connectivity among a modest number of data centers, e.g., for asynchronous data copies, index pushes for interactive serving systems, and end user data replication [9]. Thousands of internal application traffic runs across this network. And user data is the most latency sensitive, and is of the highest priority.

Besides the propagation latency between controllers, the load of controllers is a critical factor in real networks too. Because of the constraints of possessor, memory, access bandwidth and other resources, a commodity server only has the capacity to manage a limited number of routers [6]. Whenever the load of a controller reaches a threshold, the message processing latency on the controller will increase substantially. Heavy-load controllers always have higher failure probability, because they have little resources to handle various errors and are more likely to be attacked.

The latency between the individual controllers plays an important role, and the load of controllers is a critical factor in real networks too. Thus both them should be considered during the controller placement. We define the Global Latency Control Placement Problem with Capacitated Controllers (CGLCPP), which consists of both the latency from controllers to switches and the latency from controllers to controllers, and takes into consideration the capabilities of controllers.

For a network graph (V, E), where V is the set of nodes, E the set of links. Let n be the number of nodes. Let k denotes the number of controllers to be placed in the network, and n_c denotes the number of controller-to-controller paths. The edge weights represent propagation latencies, where $d(v, c)$ is the shortest path from node v to controller c, and $d(c_i, c_j)$ is the shortest path from controller c_i to controller c_j. Let $F(c)$ denote the forwarding switches controlled by the controller c. Each controller c has a capacity $L(c)$. The load of control attributed to switch v is denoted by $l(v)$.

In order to be applicable and universal, we compute the average delay. And the global average propagation latency for a placement of controllers S' is:

$$G(S') = \frac{1}{n}\sum_{v \in V} \min_{c \in S'} d(v, c) + \frac{1}{n_c} \sum_{c_i, c_j \in S'} d(c_i, c_j) \tag{1}$$

Definition:
Global Latency Control Placement Problem with Capacitated Controllers

$$Min \ G(S') \tag{2}$$

Subject to:

$$\sum_{v \in F(c)} l(v) \leq L(c) \quad \forall \, c \in S' \tag{3}$$

Given the number k of controllers to be deployed in SDN, our goal is to find the placement S' from the set of all possible controller placements S, such that $G(S')$ is minimum and $|S'| = k$.

4 Particle Swarm Optimization for GLCPP Algorithm

With the given input k, the number of controllers to place, the global latency control placement problem is an application example of the famous minimum k-median problem [10], which is proved to be NP-hard. To solve this problem, we propose particle swarm optimization algorithm that automate the controller placement decision for the first time, which has good performance in NP-hard problem optimization. Section 4.1 describes the PSO algorithm, and Sect. 4.2 explains PSO-CGLCPP algorithm.

4.1 PSO Algorithm

Particle swarm optimization algorithm (PSO) was proposed in 1995 by Eberhart and Kennedy [11]. It is a population-based stochastic optimization algorithm that originates from nature. PSO searches the optimum within a population called a swarm and benefits from two types of learning: cognitive learning based on an individual's history and social learning based on a swarm's history accumulated by sharing information among all particles in the swarm [12]. Successful applications of PSO have demonstrated that it is a promising and efficient optimization method.

The mathematical analysis of PSO is described as the following. There are n particles which represent potential solutions of the problem. The particle is defined as a d-dimensional vector. The current position of the particle in search space is $X_i = [x_{i1}, x_{i1}, \ldots, x_{id}]$, $i = 1, 2, \ldots, n$, and its current velocity vector is $V_i = [v_{i1}, v_{i2}, \ldots, v_{id}]$. We use P_i to stand for individual best position of the particle, $P_i = [p_{i1}, p_{i2}, \ldots, p_{id}]$.

And P_g is regarded as global best position vector which particle swarm have found, $P_g = [p_{g1}, p_{g2}, \ldots, p_{gd}]$. So, the position and velocity vector of the particles should adjust according to the following equations:

$$V_{id}^{t+1} = \omega V_{id}^t + c_1 r_1 (P_{id} - X_{id}^t) + c_2 r_2 (P_{gd} - X_{id}^t) \tag{4}$$

$$X_{id}^{t+1} = X_{id}^t + V_{id}^{t+1} \tag{5}$$

where ω expresses the inertia weight, r_1 and r_2 are elements from random sequences in the range of $(0, 1)$, which are mutually independent. The parameter c_1 controls the influence degree of a cognitive part of an individual, and c_2 determines the effect of a social part of the swarm.

The inertia weight ω lets the algorithm improve its performance in a series of applications. Paper [13] found that large inertia weight can help the global search, small inertia weight can improve local search ability. Therefore, adaptive adjustment of inertia weight is proposed. The inertia weight is not fixed value, but a function of linear reduction over time. The inertia weight function is shown as the following:

$$\omega = \omega_{max} - \frac{\omega_{max} - \omega_{min}}{t_{max}} \times t \tag{6}$$

ω_{max} is set as the initial weight, ω_{min} is set as the final weight. Variable t_{max} represents the maximum number of iteration, t is the number of current iteration. Usually ω_{max} is set as 0.9 and ω_{min} is set as 0.1.

The individual best position vector of each particle is computed using the following expression:

$$P_i(t+1) = \begin{cases} P_i(t) & \text{if } f(X_i(t+1)) \geq f(P_i(t)) \\ X_i(t+1) & \text{if } f(X_i(t+1)) \leq f(P_i(t)) \end{cases} \tag{7}$$

where f represents the fitness function.

Then, the global best position vector is found by

$$P_g(t+1) = \arg \min_{P_i(t+1)} f(P_i(t+1)). \tag{8}$$

4.2   PSO-CGLCPP Algorithm

In PSO, the position vector represents a solution to the optimized problem. For the global latency control placement problem, each particle represents one kind of placement for controllers to be deployed. With the given input k, the number of controllers to place, the particle is defined as a k-dimensional vector, and each dimension represents one of the controllers. So the position permutation of a particle i is defined as $X_i = [x_{i1}, x_{i1}, \ldots, x_{ik}]$. For we deploy each controller on one of the existing vertexes of the network, each dimension of position is a integer between 1 and n, i.e., $x_{ik} \in [1, n]$, where n is equal to the number of total vertexes in the network. Velocity works on the position sequence and it is rather crucial. A good velocity gives the particle a guidance and determines whether the particle can reach its destination and by how fast it could [14].

When the position of the particle is established, namely the controllers are in place, we compute the adaptive value of particle according to formula (1). Because the node is assigned to its nearest controller, the delay from node to corresponding controller is generally measured in that link length value. Then we compute load of controller according to formula (3). If it exceeds the load limitation of controller, assign the switch to the next nearest switch controller. And the delay between controllers and controllers is defined as the shortest link between them in the same way.

In this section, we propose Particle Swarm Optimization for CGLCPP Algorithm (PSO-CGLCPP). The basic idea is, by iteration, multiple particles search the optimal solution in parallel, and minimum total delay controller placement is located. And the overall procedure is about: initialize n particles randomly, with each particle representing a kind of placement of k controllers. Then set the particle with the highest fitness to be the current best solution whose latency value is smallest. According to the PSO algorithm, use the PSO velocity formulas (4) and (5) to merge the controller placement and determine the new particle position until this swarm obtains its longest lifetime or it converges. If PSO-CGLCPP converges, then the best solution can be obtained. The PSO-CGLCPP algorithm for global latency controller placement problem is described as follows.

Algorithm 1. Overall procedure of proposed*PSO-CGLCPP*

   Input: 1) Network topology graph (V, E);

            2) Objective function according to formula (1);

            3) The number of controllers k;

            4) The maximal generation T;

   Output: The minimum global latency controller placement S'

Initialization :

   1.   Randomly generate each particle's velocity and position;

   2.   Evaluate the fitness value of each particle;

   3.   Fill the P_i of each particle with its current position;

   4.   Fill the P_g with the optimal P_i;

Optimization :

   1.   **repeat**

   2.   **for** each particle

   3.   Update particle's velocity according to (4);

   4.   Update particle's position according to (5);

   5.   Evaluate the fitness value of the particle;

   6.   Update the P_i according to (7);

   7.   Update the P_g according to (8);

   8.   **end for**

   9.   **until** stopping criterion is satisfied

Algorithm 2. Procedure of evaluating the fitness of the particle

1.	**for** each particle
2.	**for** each node
3.	Find the shortest path to the each controller;
4.	Evaluate the longitude of the path;
5.	Assign the node to the controller nearest to it;
6.	Compute load of controller according to (3);
7.	**while** exceed load limitation of the controller **do**
8.	Assign the switch to the next nearest controller;
9.	**end for**
10.	**for** each controller
11.	Find the shortest path to other controllers;
12.	Evaluate the length of the path as controller-to-controller latency;
13.	**end for**
14.	Evaluate the global latency according to (1);
15.	**end for**

5 Simulation and Results Analysis

In this section, we generate network topologies randomly according to [15], which is almost closed to the real network. Controller's capability is a complex concept, including bandwidth, memory and computing resources and so on. In order to simplify the problem, we use a digital to denote it. The load of controller attributed to switch is processed in the same way. Our PSO-CGLCPP is written with C++ in VS2010, and runs on the machine equipped with Intel Core i5 4-Core processors and 4 GB RAM. We obtain the average solution by running the algorithm 100 times on every testing topology.

To evaluate the performance of our algorithm, we run the other two algorithms, along with the random placement algorithm (Random) for comparison purpose. The two algorithms are greedy algorithm (GL) proposed in [5] and integer linear programming algorithm (ILP) in [6] respectively. CPLEX is used to solve integer programming. For a NP-hard problem, it will be hard to find the solution based on the enumeration algorithm which ensures accurate results, but at the cost of weeks of CPU time. Linear programming algorithms are always used to solve the problems, and the solution is regarded as the optimal solution for a reference. So we mainly regard the ILP algorithm as a reference and compare with it. Since the random algorithm returns different results based on the locations selected, we execute random placements over 100 times, and select the placement that yields the best performance.

We evaluate the algorithms in two aspects, the first is the optimal latency solution, and the second aspect is computing time for algorithm to find the optimal solution.

And we further characterize both latency and computing time performance against the size of controllers. The results of the simulation are depicted in the following figures. PSO is abbreviated words of PSO-CGLCPP.

Figure 1 evaluates the optimal latency of four algorithms with increasing network nodes, given the same number of controllers. It shows that PSO and ILP get a better average delay. PSO's performance is slightly better than the ILP algorithms. Greedy algorithm and Random algorithm perform relatively poor, and the worst is random algorithm. Furthermore the Random and GL increase quickly along with increasing nodes while PSO and ILP provide an optimal solution more reliably. The greedy algorithm picks the next vertex that best minimizes latency, which always produces the best location currently, but local optimum does not represent a global optimum. Because of diversity of particles, PSO can search the entire space and jump out of local optimum through exchanging information with each other. Finally the particle will flight to a better global optimum after several iterations.

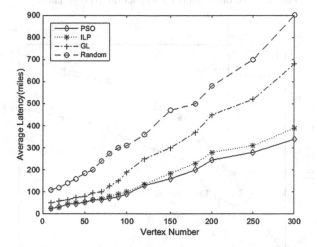

Fig. 1. Optimal latency solution of the algorithms

Figure 2 analyzes number of the controllers' impact on average latency under the same network topology. In the experiments, we gradually increase the number of controllers for each placement strategy. With the increase of controllers placed in, the average latency decreases. The average delay gained by PSO algorithm is always relatively stable, less volatile, compared with the greedy algorithm. This is because the particle swarm optimization through mutual learning and iteration between the particles can always find a better controllers' position to achieve better results. Furthermore, the diminishing returns that level off around 4–8 controllers, suggested by the literature [3], have been verified.

As can be seen from the Fig. 3, greedy algorithm consumes the shortest time, but the solution is far away from the optimal one, which is unacceptable in most environments. Processing time of both PSO and ILP are much more than GL algorithm,

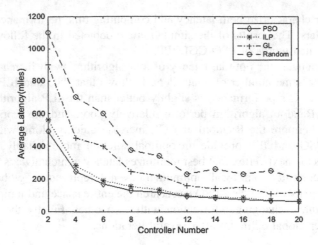

Fig. 2. Controller number's impact on average latency

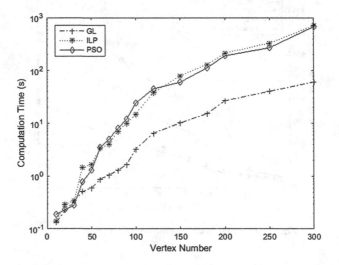

Fig. 3. Computing time of the algorithms

but produce a better solution. The time taken by the PSO and ILP algorithm are in almost close level. When network size is larger, PSO algorithm converges to the optimal solution slightly faster than ILP. PSO convergence must take advantages of the swarm intelligence, and achieve a more satisfactory solution within an acceptable timeframe, which can match with commercially available strategies. Although PSO takes much more time in the procedure of exploring the optimal placement than GL, the time is acceptable in lots real application scenarios in which the task has no real-time demand. Figure 4 evaluates calculation time with increasing controller nodes to be deployed, when the network size is the same. As can be seen, when the number of controllers deployed becomes bigger, the convergence of time becomes larger and

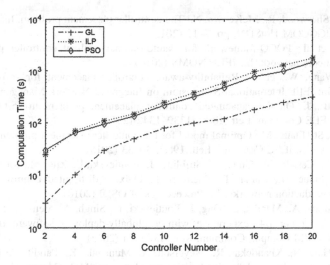

Fig. 4. Controller number's impact on computation time

larger. And the growth rate of computation time becomes bigger, because faster growth of number of links between controllers.

6 Conclusion

In this paper we investigate the controller placement problem in software defined network, and define the Global Latency Control Placement Problem with Capacitated Controllers (CGLCPP), taking into consideration both the latency between controllers and the capabilities of controllers. We then propose a PSO-CGLCPP algorithm based on particle swarm optimization to solve the problem for the first time. Our method could find an optimized solution for the given controllers while conforming to the constraints of controllers. Experimental results show that the algorithm performs rapidly and effectively.

Acknowledgments. The study is supported by the Natural Science Foundation of Shandong Province (Grant No. ZR2015FM008; ZR2013FM029), the Science and Technology Development Program of Jinan (Grant No. 201303010), the National Natural Science Foundation of China (NSFC No. 60773101), and the Fundamental Research Funds of Shandong University (Grant No. 2014JC037).

References

1. McKeown, N., et al.: Open flow: enabling innovation in campus networks. ACM SIGCOMM Comput. Commun. Rev. **38**(2), 69–74 (2008)
2. Lange, S., et al.: Heuristic approaches to the controller placement problem in large scale SDN networks. IEEE Trans. Netw. Serv. Manage. **12**(1), 4–17 (2015)

3. Heller, B., Sherwood, R., McKeown, N.: The controller placement problem. In: Proceedings of ACM SIGGCOM HotSDN, pp. 7–12 (2012)
4. Hock, D., et al.: POCO-framework for Pareto-optimal resilient controller placement in SDN-based core network. In: IEEE NOMS (2014)
5. Hu, Y., Wang, W., et al.: Reliability-aware controller placement for software-defined networks. In: IEEE International Symposium on Integrated Network Management (2013)
6. Yao, G., Bi, J.: On the capacitated controller placement problem in software defined networks. IEEE Commun. Lett. **18**(8), 1339–1342 (2014)
7. Sallahi, A., St-Hilaire, M.: Optimal model for the controller placement problem in software defined networks. IEEE Commun. Lett. **19**(1), 30–33 (2015)
8. Koponen, T., Casado, M., Gude, N., Stribling, J., Poutievski, L., Zhu, M., Ramanathan, R., Iwata, Y., Inoue, H., Hama, T., Shenker, S.: Onix: a distributed control platform for large-scale production networks. In: Proceedings of OSDI (2010)
9. Jain, S., Kumar, A., Mandal, S., Ong, J., Poutievski, L., Singh, A., Venkata, S., Wanderer, J., Zhou, J., et al.: B4: experience with a globally-deployed software defined wan. ACM SIGCOMM Comput. Commun. Rev. **43**, 3–14 (2013)
10. Arya, V., Garg, N., Khandekar, R., Meyerson, A., Munagala, K., Pandit, V.: Local search heuristics for k-median and facility location problems. SIAM J. Comput. **33**(3), 544–562 (2004)
11. Eberhart, R.C., Kennedy, J.: A new optimizer using particle swarm theory. In: Proceedings of the 6th International Symposium on Micromachine and Human Science, pp. 39–43 (1995)
12. Pehlivanoglu, Y.V.: A new particle swarm optimization method enhanced with a periodic mutation strategy and neural networks. IEEE Trans. Evol. Comput. **17**(3), 436–452 (2013)
13. Shi, Y., Eberhart, R.C.: A modified particle swarm optimizer. In: IEEE International Conference of Evolutionary Computation, Piscataway, vol. 8, no. 3, pp. 240–255 (1998)
14. Gong, M., Cai, Q., Chen, X., Ma, L.: Complex network clustering by multiobjective discrete particle swarm optimization based on decomposition. IEEE Trans. Evol. Comput. **18**(1), 82–97 (2014)
15. Naldi, M.: Connectivity of Waxman topology models. Comput. Commun. **29**, 24–31 (2005)

A Streaming Execution Method
for Multi-services in Mobile Cloud Computing

Lei Li[2], Yonghua Xiong[1(✉)], Shufan Guo[2], Keyuan Jiang[3],
and Yongbing Tang[3]

[1] School of Automation, China University of Geosciences, Wuhan 430074, China
xiongyh@cug.edu.cn
[2] School of Information Science and Engineering, Central South University,
Changsha 410083, China
csulilei@csu.edu.cn, guoshufan1990310@126.com
[3] Department of Computer Information Technology and Graphics,
Purdue University Calumet, Hammond 46323, USA
{Jiang,tang123}@purduecal.edu

Abstract. Commercially available mobile devices with various kinds of hardware and software platforms have resulted in a huge amount of mobile services. This has a new challenge in designing multiple services that are compatible with heterogeneous devices and operating systems (OSes). This paper presents a method of multi-services mobile cloud computing (MSMCC) for mobile device, which regards OS as a service to improve user experience. A multi-services pre-boot firmware (MSPF) is designed to stream multi-OS images and multi-application images to the mobile devices over wireless network. After that, we use the MSMCC method to run on the S3C6410 board equipped with MSPF, results illustrated that MSPF is able to support remote boot and streaming execution of multi-services with stable performance.

Keywords: Mobile cloud computing · Firmware · Multi-services · Streaming execution

1 Introduction

According to the expected statistical data released by Internet Data Center (IDC), the global smartphone shipments will reach 1.4 billion in 2015, and the growth rate of tablets and smartphone will reach 60 %. Thus it can be seen that huge numbers of mobile users will access the Internet via mobile devices. In recent years, with the massive growth of applications for OSes like Android, IOS, and Linux etc., users experience a rich and colorful mobile life via wireless network. In spite of advances in the performance of mobile devices and the multiplicity of applications, challenges will continue to exist with the conflict of high energy consumption and finite battery life, the requirements of abundant applications and some repeating problems such as software updating and bug-fixes. And the unreliable communication connection over wireless network makes

© Springer International Publishing Switzerland 2015
G. Wang et al. (Eds.): ICA3PP 2015, Part III, LNCS 9530, pp. 55–67, 2015.
DOI: 10.1007/978-3-319-27137-8_5

it more difficult for real-time communication. Wireless network environment is prone to some problems: such as, limited wireless bandwidth, traffic congestion, wireless failures, and the out-of-signal, and so on.

Much attention has been attracted to address these challenges. To use multiple OS and application services on single device, some schemes have been tried but with no special good effects as below:

- *Virtualization technology* just like the idea based Xen architecture in [1], designed and implemented a virtualization system for ARM CPU architecture based on Xen multiple operating system, but the virtual machine itself would generate a lot of energy consumption overhead.
- *Segmentation technology* to divide the processor core, memory blocks and I/O of hardware device in [2] that implemented *Mint* OS based on multiple instances of Linux.
- *Switcher technology* in [3], proposed a fast OS Switcher based ARM Consumer Electronics (CE) to enable users to utilize multiple OSes on single device, but there was no implementation result presentation.

Mobile cloud computing is also applied to the related research. Countering the service of multiple applications, distributed application processing frameworks (DAPFs) was discussed in [4] to state some challenges of the elastic mobile applications attributed with the features of runtime partitioning for Smart Mobile Devices (SMDs). A rendering adaptation technique [5], which can dynamically change the richness and complexity of graphic rendering, was proposed to enable rich mobile multimedia applications that need to be streamed back from the cloud to the mobile device.

Mobile transparent computing (MTC), as a new computing mode of mobile cloud computing and consisting of mobile computing and transparent computing, was introduced and implemented by S.Z. Huang et al. [6]. They transplanted and modified the TransOS mechanism in the heterogeneous mobile device, that the Linux and Android were successfully loaded to the tablet through wired network, even more depth in wireless environment in [7]. At present, as mentioned above, MTC has been partly implemented in mobile devices with loading two OSes.

Our work is primarily focused on applying the MCC concept to the multi-services of OS and application booting with streaming block, which not only enables mobile users to access alternative multi-OSes, but also provides rich applications neglecting their OS running environments. There are three main contributions of our work. First, we proposes the multi-services mobile cloud computing (MSMCC) method for mobile devices form underlying hardware to upper application layer. The second is MSPF firmware which can load required OSes and applications services through wireless network at runtime for mobile devices. The third is two scenarios implementations which are conducted with experiments: multi-OS services and multi-APP services, which test the feasibility and effectiveness of the MSPF.

The rest of the paper is organized as follows. The next section states the overview of MCC and the MSSE method. Section 3 describes the architecture of MSPF firmware and its key technologies. Section 4 details the MSPF implementation, evaluation and analysis of the results via real experiment platform of some pilot experiments. Finally, conclusion and future work are drawn in the last section.

2   Multi-Services Mobile Cloud Computing

This section presents some requirements of multiple service delivery in MCC environment.

It is well known that mobile software is tightly coupled with OS and the OS is highly dependent on hardware in mobile computing. So generally, one mobile device only supports only one mobile OS or even a particular version at normal condition due to the hardware or computation capacity constraints. Besides, each kind of OS has its own application development platform and application market. It means the application developers need to develop different version of application for each platform. Another challenge of mobile computing is the more unstable wireless connection and limited bandwidth compared with PC environment, especially the GPRS and 3G which are often extremely slower transmitting rate demand than that by NSAP.

The problems mentioned above influence the quality and stability of service. In this paper, OS is regarded as a service, just like applications. Therefore, this paper proposes a multi-services mobile cloud computing (MSMCC) method for mobile devices. MSMCC mainly runs in mobile devices, and the client always communicates with server via wireless network (e.g., Wi-Fi, 3G, WiMax).

In MSMCC mode, mobile devices are almost bare and not necessarily to install any OS and any applications. According to user demand, heterogeneous mobile OSes (e.g., android, iOS, Windows Mobile) can be loaded and launched on the mobile device, that makes full use of computing space and reduces the pressure of limited storage. A multi-services pre-boot firmware (MSPF) is designed to complete the process of remote boot over wireless network. The MSPF program, which is installed on the ROM of mobile devices, runs between the bare hardware and the upper layer OS. It supports multi-OSes and multi-APPs wireless booting and streaming execution. As the first program to be loaded and executed when powered, the MSPF is responsible for hardware initialization, the network interface drive, and the network protocol (such as DHCP, TFTP, SNP) stack installation. After these processes, it will broadcast the DHCP request and get the network parameters from server side to establish the network connection. In the next booting stage, the NFS service of the firmware is able to catch and parse clients local disk IO and redirect it to the server. Then the server reads the required data blocks from its local disk and streams them to the client.

Thus, the MSMCC has the following functionalities and characteristics:

- *Network storage and local computing.* To break through restriction of one mobile device one OS, MSMCC separates the storage and computation parameters of program. All resources are storaged in remote server, that can be dynamically streamed to execute on the mobile device based on user selections and demands. So that, multiple heterogeneous OSes can be booted at runtime without local storage.

- *Services streaming execution.* The MSPF embedded in the lower and the upper will catch the interrupt to fetch the related program instruction and network remote request services. Once the server receives the request, it gets the program instruction address through address mapping technology and send the data to client. The required blocks of program participating the execution process are streamed to client. With the same of user data, only needed parts take part in the streaming execution process.
- *Resources management and data security.* As mentioned above, the OS images, applications and user data are stored on remote server. All works of resources, user information, network and server itself, can be done on the sever side. So it is easy to implement the works of maintain and management on the client. And the republic OSes and applications are only read resources, that can avoid damages by any abnormal writing operation such as network virus and mis-operation.

3   MSPF

In this section, we discuss the MSPF in detail, its working process, and also provide some key technologies involved in, including multiple services supporting, net booting, and streaming execution.

3.1   Structure of MSPF

As a tentative solution to realize the MSMCC, the MSPF manages all the networked resources, dynamically schedules the centrally stored codes and all resources of OSes, applications and personal data, which supports multi-OS environment distributed loading and wireless booting, as well as local computing and remote storage. The structure is shown in Fig. 1. Generally speaking, the MSPF is a typical C/S mode that can be divided into two parts: the server side and the client side.

- *The server side* is mainly to complete two functions: start-up management and resources management. All OSes and APPs, either public or private, as well as the personal data, are central storage and management. Furthermore, it schedules some network resources (users, wireless network setting, server running monitoring, etc.) and respond the network interrupt control issued by client side.
- *The client side* lies in the mobile terminal, which only takes a very small percentage, but beneath the virtual running traditional OS and applications. It can support various hardware architectures, such as x86, ARM, MIPS, etc., through standardized BIOS interfaces (bootloader, UEFI, &BSP, for example). After completing mobile device initialization, especially wireless network

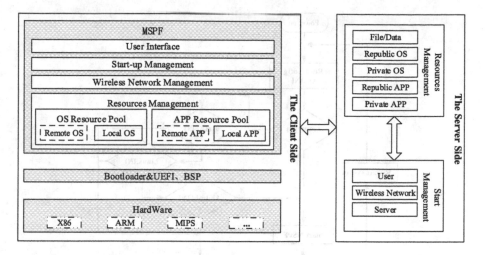

Fig. 1. Structure of MSPF

card (wireless NIC) driving, it contacts the server and lists the available OSes menu and APPs menu for a user to select. Then according to the choice of users, the corresponding OS images and applications will stream to execute on the client, otherwise the local OS will boot. The process contains management of resource pool, wireless network, start-up parameters and user interfaces.

3.2 Booting Process in MSPF

After in-depth research of network booting, we know that, in ARM architecture, the corresponding OS files, including u-boot, kernel and root filesystem (i.e. rootfs, including virtual file system (VFS) & real file system (RFS)), are usually stored and flashed in the concrete address of flash respectively. When powered on, a period of OS guide program called u-boot will run immediately to initiate the hardware, set the environment variables and prepare environment for kernel. Then, u-boot loads the kernel to RAM. When the kernel executes completely, it will find and mount the rootfs to complete the OS boot process.

Since OS is regard as generic resource service which can be accessed, streamed and boot via wireless network in MSPF system, this booting process may be different from previous booting. Our multi-OS and multi-APP loading rely on the MSPF loading selectively. Once the device powered on, MSPF will first initialize memory, network I/O, then read the configuration file of OS to load and start-up MSPF program which can display OS menu and APP menu to be chose by users. If users choose one OS in OS menu which provides diversified OSes booting via network, just like Android and Linux QT, and an optional other choice booting via local, just like WinCE, the MSPF will search for the relevant parameter of the selected OS whether has installed already from local storage, if not, will trigger an ordinary net boot process. This is a process of three

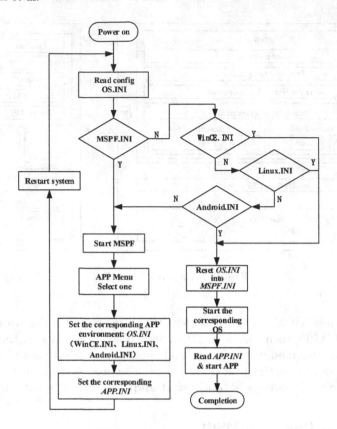

Fig. 2. Workflow of MSPF

steps: firstly appropriate boot parameters based on the OS selection are set up and push into the stack, secondly the boot interrupt request to the server can ask for the desired kernel and VFS (i.e. ramdisk) of OS, thirdly the requested rootfs is already searched to generate an acknowledge response back to the client side, and streamed to run on the mobile device at the same time. As for the personal data of users, the file system can be also mounted successfully in the form of NFS, otherwise, the MSPF will remind users of a required data not found error.

For example, illustrated as Fig. 2, all the *.INI* file can be regarded as a flag of u-boot. Once powered on, the *OS.INI* will retrieve to read *MetaOS.INI* which can estimate whether OS environment has existed according to the system detection situation. If the flag is *Yes*, that represents the device is bare without any OS, so MSPF will start up to provide user for an APP menu. Suppose that user chooses the *Browser* service on it, *OS.INI* will be reset into the parameters of the OS environment the *Browser* needed – *Android.INI*, and at the same time *APP.INI* stayed in the server side of MSPF will be reset. Then the system restarts. Since the *OS.INI* has reset, u-boot will trigger the change of flag, and send the boot interrupt request to the server to ask for the desired filesystem of the Android. Finally, the *Browser* will load completely and run normally while the Android has started up. The results of all modification can be saved in the server, and accessed by another device of one identification next time.

3.3 Key Technology

Multi-services Supporting. As we know, different OSes may use different bootloaders for the purpose of guiding OS kernel which is stored in the local Nand Flash, so reasonable storage partition of flash for kernel file is important. Generally speaking, the client side of MSPF is similar to a super bootloader which can support and load a variety of OSes from network, which also fully take charge of the design requirements of the flash partitioning with its number and size of different OSes.

Table 1. Multi-services boot image files

	RFS	Kernel	Ramdisk (VFS)
U-boot	–	256K	–
WinCE OS	nk.nb0 64M	–	–
MSPF	–	5M	34M
Linux	rootfs.yaffs 74.7M	5M	5M
Android	rootfs.yaffs 123M	5M	5M

In Table 1, the guidance code of u-boot, the central control program of MSPF and the OS rootfs of WinCE, Linux and Android are given. Among that, the *rootfs.yaffs* file of Linux and Android are what the MSPF should stream and load from server via wireless network to client according to the OS menu and the APP menu selection. Others locate in the local client. The startup mechanism of WinCE OS is entirely different with that of Android and Linux. As declared before, different OSes require different boot parameters and environment variables. MSPF, as the control center, sets the corresponding bootargs and environment variables through the boot program management mechanism. Afterwards, the rootfs are streamed to execute on client. After execution done, the RAM will be cleared and ready for the next service booting.

Figure 3 gives an example of flash partitioning in the client side of MSPF based on the Table 1. The u-boot can arbitrarily call and obtain the kernels as well as its ramdisk, all of which are separate storage and non-interfering. Some white and blank partitions are useful for the safety and independent between partitions. If one of kernels or ramdisks need to change or update, the blank partition is just the substantial room for expansion but do not affects other partitions, of which size is depending on the state of the former VFS. As noted before, different services need different boot parameters and environment variables. The related parameters and variables are set in MSPF while booting a

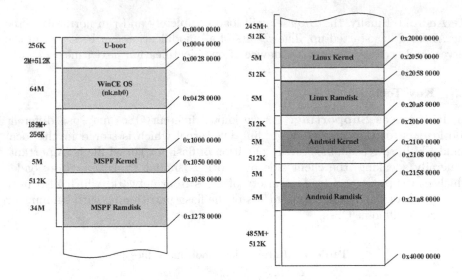

Fig. 3. Flash partition

service. When the *Browser* is chosen, the corresponding OS guidance code, kernel and ramdisk will run up at the specific partitions to set bootargs and environment variables. Then the client side of MSPF will get in touch with the server side of it. Afterwards, the Android RFS can be mounted to the mobile device in a form of streaming, and take over the main control right from the VFS to start up the corresponding OS. Follow on that, the Browser launches. It goes the same way with Linux and WinCE related service.

Wireless Booting. Multi-services has been realized by MSPF through wireless net boot, by means of loading the OS kernel and ramdisk to the corresponding flash partition. The implementation process claims that MSPF can connect to the server before OS, and send the wireless booting request to boot the VFS of OS. This includes the following three aspects:

– *Wireless NIC driver* in MSPF. To establish connection with the server before OS, MSPF adds the wireless activation function for Marvell 8686 NIC, which can be achieved conveniently by modifying part of device driver source code and transplanting it into the VFS. When the kernel needs to activate wireless NIC module, it will be dynamically load into RAM to run.
– *Remote boot protocol.* As mentioned before, filesystem, including OS rootfs and user data, is stored in the server as NFS, which can be accessed by all device equipped with MSPF client. In remote server, NFS provides the service to share the directory of filesystem that is able to be mounted to local client. As for the modifications to all resources will be updated to the server. To enable NFS access, TCP or UDP, as the underlying transport protocol, is

needed in MSPF. And the bootargs of mounting the NFS rather than local file system should be set by MSPF while powered on at the same time.

- *Permission of boot.* After the VFS starts, the information exchange of mobile device and the server will be successful using NFS and UDP protocol. Then the VFS, which later will be killed by MSPF, releases the control permission to RFS. Now the RFS starts up and is responsible for managing the wireless network device.

Fig. 4. Experimental environment

Streaming Execution. Traditionally, application software can start up and run normally only when it is stored in the local disk completely. But in this situation of remotely start-up over and over again, this will provide users for a bad experience on account of the long time consumption. The solution based on streaming loading on demand, that all these resources and services are presented to users as virtual disk file which is similar to the local disk file, may effectively reduce the waiting latency and improve user experience.

In this paper, only when a service is called, the related blocks can be transferred from wireless network and executed on the mobile device. This transferring process of different blocks is named streaming. Since MSPF is designed to run between the traditional OS and the local resources (including CPU, memory, and other hardware), which streams the needed execution blocks from the server side to mobile devices, thus, streaming execution leads to a service-oriented computing environment, in which users can enjoy the desired applications and services everywhere, regardless of restrictions of the heterogeneous mobile hardware.

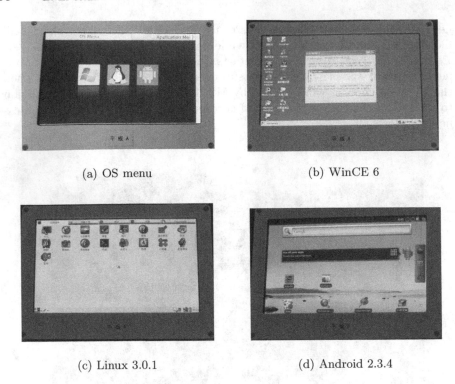

(a) OS menu   (b) WinCE 6

(c) Linux 3.0.1   (d) Android 2.3.4

Fig. 5. Multi-OS on-demand with MSPF

4   Implementation

The MSPF, as one implementation method of MSMCC, is suitable for SMDs with computing ability. We give an example below with field experiments. Figure 4 shows the real experimental environment. We use a demo tablet board-S3C6410 equipped with MSPF as the mobile client, with configurations of Samsung S3C6410A CPU (ARM1176JZF-S, 533 MHz), 256M DDR RAM, 1 GB Nand Flash, 800*480 LCD, I2C EEPROM, SDIO Interface. The server is an ordinary PC Lenovo E4430 (i7-4702MQ@2.20 GHz, 8 GB DDR3 1600 MHz, 1TB HDD) with Ubuntu 12.04.3, which can provide the NFS and FTFP services with the help of the server side of MSPF. The client and server are connected through a wireless module (Marvell 8686) and a wireless AP-TP-LINK WDR 4900.

4.1   Multi-service Implementation

Mobile users can choose one service in the mobile device and get required OS and APP services. We examine the function and performance of services booting in MSPF with the two scenarios: OS as a Service, APP as a Service.

Operating System as a Service. As we know, the OS in MSMCC is regarded as a service which is restored in remote server rather than directly installed in the mobile device. First, we confirmed that the OS as a service, implemented by MSPF for MSMCC. The tablet is equipped with our MSPF client side, through that the desired OS can be loaded from server via wireless network.

In order to verify the efficiency of OS as a Service, we implement the MSPF of selecting multi-OS as Fig. 5(a) shown, and are able to load the WinCE 6 (Fig. 5(b)), Linux 3.0.1 (Fig. 5(c))and Android 2.3.4 (Fig. 5(d)) successfully to the tablet with the help of MSPF mechanism.

Application as a Service. As stated earlier, applications as a service, needs additional runtime environments to allow it run normally. When using one application service, MSPF would generate an inquiry process to load the corresponding OS runtime environment in advance. An example of Application as a Service is provided for users to choose just illustrated as Fig. 6(a), in which the QQ (Fig. 6(b)) and Handwriting Board are WinCE applications, while the Browser and MusicPlayer (Fig. 6(c)) are programs that Android comes with, whereas the Minesweeper Game, Fifteen Game and SMPlayer (Fig. 6(d)) are Linux applications.

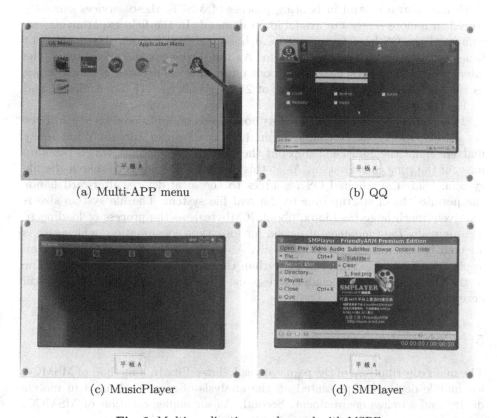

(a) Multi-APP menu   (b) QQ

(c) MusicPlayer   (d) SMPlayer

Fig. 6. Multi-application on-demand with MSPF

Table 2. Boot time contrast

	Local boot	wired boot	MSPF boot (wireless)
WinCE	23.0 s	–	24.5 s
Android	68.0 s	85.5 s	175.0 s
Linux	26.5 s	33.9 s	72.1 s

Table 3. Latency contrast of applications streaming execution process

	QQ	Music player	SMPlayer
MSPF booting	1.5 s	1.5 s	1.5 s
Kernel booting	0 s	18.5 s	14.6 s
Ramdisk mounting	0 s	3.9 s	3.9 s
Filesystem start-up	23.0 s	151.0 s	52.1 s
Application launch	3.5 s	6.7 s	3.8 s

4.2 Performance Analysis

With the central control in booting process of MSPF, these services centrally stored in remote server are available on demand. In the field experiments, we compared the OS booting time of local boot and MSPF boot. The local boot time of WinCE is 23.0 ss, and 68.0 s for Android, whereas 26.5 s for Linux. The latency (as shown in Table 2) of net boot under wireless network is almost twice as that of wired boot with the time of 24.5 s (WinCE), 175.0 s (Android) and 72.1 ss (Linux).

It is obviously that MSPF wireless boot needs an additional step, i.e., boot the MSPF, which can be completed in 1.5 s as shown in Table 3. What really matters is not the additional step but the subtask NFS mount, which takes up most of the time consumption. As at this stage, MSPF needs to search the file system, loads the required OS resources to the local device, afterward hands the permissions of startup over to the real file system. The file system size is relatively much large (as Linux, about 70Mbytes), so the process of loading to local is really the fundamental reason for long time consumption, which also is affected by the wireless condition easily. And the latency time of launching an application in Android is much more than that in WinCE and Linux likely due to the OS architecture. Though the response time is not that ideal, it is yet still acceptable.

5 Conclusion

The main contributions of the paper are as follows: Firstly, a method of MSMCC for mobile device was presented on the analysis of some challenges in mobile device and wireless environment. Second, As an implementation of MSMCC, the MSPF firmware, also as a control center, which can load required OSes and applications services over wireless network at runtime for mobile devices. Third, two scenarios are conducted with experiments: multi-OS services and multi-APP services, which test the feasibility and effectiveness of the MSPF. In addition, the latency comparison with our startup methods with traditional local methods indicated that the time cost of MSPF is normally because of the size of NFS influence, the network bandwidth limitation and network storage access protocol imperfection. We planned to investigate the following issues in the near future: how to find out a solution to supporting x86 architecture platform with the latest firmware technique: unified extensible firmware interface (UEFI).

Acknowledgments. This work was jointly supported by the National Nature Science Foundation of China under Grant No. 61202340, by the International Postdoctoral Exchange Fellowship Program under Grant No.20140011, and by and the Hubei Provincial Natural Science Foundation of China under Grant no. 2015CFA010.

References

1. Hwang, J.-Y., Suh, S.-B., Heo, S.-K., Park, C.-J., Ryu, J.-M., Park, S.-Y., Kim, C.-R.: Xen on ARM: system virtualization using Xen hypervisor for ARM-based secure mobile phones. In: 5th IEEE Consumer Communications and Networking Conference, 2008, CCNC 2008, pp. 257–261. IEEE (2008)
2. Madden, P.E., Pan, J.C., Raymond, R.S.: Managing multiple operating systems on a single computer. US Patent 6,178,503, 23 January 2001
3. Kim, C.-Y., Oh, S.-C., Kim, K., Ahn, C.-W., Kim, Y.-K.: Fast operating system switcher for mobile CE devices. In: 2013 IEEE International Conference on Consumer Electronics (ICCE), pp. 538–539. IEEE (2013)
4. Shiraz, M., Gani, A., Khokhar, R.H., Buyya, R.: A review on distributed application processing frameworks in smart mobile devices for mobile cloud computing. Commun. Surv. Tutorials **15**(3), 1294–1313 (2013)
5. Wang, S., Dey, S.: Adaptive mobile cloud computing to enable rich mobile multimedia applications. IEEE Trans. Multimedia **15**(4), 870–883 (2013)
6. Huang, S.-Z., Wu, M., Xiong, Y.: Mobile transparent computing to enable ubiquitous operating systems and applications. J. Adv. Comput. Intell. Intell. Inform. **18**(1), 32–39 (2014)
7. Xiong, Y., Huang, S., Wu, M., Zhang, Y., She, J.: A novel resource management method of providing operating system as a service for mobile transparent computing. Sci. World J. **2014**, 12 (2014)

Economy-Oriented Deadline Scheduling Policy for Render System Using IaaS Cloud

Qian Li[✉], Weiguo Wu, Zeyu Sun, Lei Wang, and Jianhang Huang

Department of Computer Science and Technology, Xi'an Jiaotong University,
Xi'an 710049, China
qian.l@stu.xjtu.edu.cn, wgwu@mail.xjtu.edu.cn,
{lylgszy,wangleihit09}@163.com, huangjhsx@gmail.com

Abstract. Along with the increase of demand for high definition animation film, when the render system with local computing resources cannot supply enough resources to satisfy the user requirement for time, acquiring additional resources is necessary. The Infrastructure as a service (IaaS) Cloud offers user with computing infrastructures on-demand to be used based on the paradigm of pay-per-use, which provides extra resources with fee to extending the capacity of render system with local cluster. Consequently, the scheduling policy under the hybrid render system should consider the constraints of deadline and budget and billing policy. In this paper, an economy-oriented deadline scheduling policy is proposed, which not only guarantees the deadline for user by the way of employing resources for rendering, but also offers an economic way to hire resources from IaaS Cloud provider reasonably. The experiment with single workload and multi workloads shows that the proposed policy can finish the user's rendering job before deadline as well as obtain approving cost efficient.

Keywords: Scheduling · Cluster rendering · IaaS cloud · Deadline · Budget

1 Introduction

High performance computing (HPC) is increasingly adopted by scientific organizations for settling the problems in intensive computation application. Rendering, as the key determinant for the visual effect of animation, is the process of creating an image from a model by means of computer programs and is actually a very complex and time consuming computation process [3]. With the characteristic of independence and nature parallelism among frames, rendering is very suitable for parallel processing in HPC environment. And along with the rapid development of animation industry, render farm is frequently used for film and television production.

Render farm is a cluster of interconnected computers which are used for rendering images in parallel [10]. Render farm provides users a way to submit and control the rendering jobs by web portal, and from the view of system it

© Springer International Publishing Switzerland 2015
G. Wang et al. (Eds.): ICA3PP 2015, Part III, LNCS 9530, pp. 68–78, 2015.
DOI: 10.1007/978-3-319-27137-8_6

is responsible for cluster management and parallel job scheduling. It is really a challenge to manage and schedule multiple different rendering jobs. Except that, with augment of frames scale and resolution ratio and improvement of texture quality for pictures, the time on rendering becomes longer. Actually, a render farm has the finite resources, due to limited computing infrastructure, the render farm could not completed the complex rendering job before deadline, which is the negative impact for user's Qos. The approach how to expand the ability for render farm is needed to finishing user's job on time.

With the promotion of the world's leading companies, Cloud computing is attracting more and more attention for providing a new type of information and services that broadens new vision of information technology (IT) services [4,17]. Commercial Cloud service providers offer computing facilities and resources to users in a manner of on-demand, pay-as-you-go model and in charge of fee, which is also known as Infrastructure as a Service (IaaS) providers [8,11].

Therefore, Cloud environment emerged as an alternate to provide the facility of parallel computations, and the render system can promote the computing ability with the help of IaaS Cloud to satisfy the user's requirement for deadline when the local resources are limited. Generally, the IaaS Cloud adopts a market-orient manner, i.e., there will incur cost when users hire the Cloud resources. For example, as a popular IaaS Cloud, Amazon EC2 supply different computing resources with various price in an hourly basis, which we call it billing cycle in this paper. Consequently, for the hybrid render system with free local resources and chargeable Cloud resources, it is a crucial to consider deadline and budget of users simultaneously from the view of economy when designing the rendering jobs scheduling policy.

In this paper, we propose an economy-oriented deadline scheduling policy which enlarges the ability of local render system by hiring the resources provided by IaaS Cloud and completes the user's rendering job by the given constraints of deadline and budget, and also offers an economic way to apply for Cloud resources.

The rest of this paper is organized as follows: related works are introduced in Sect. 2. In Sect. 3, we describe the hybrid render system. The proposed policy is introduced in Sect. 4. We present the experimental results in Sect. 5. And conclusion and future works are provided in Sect. 6.

2   Related Works

Cloud computing [2,7] is emerging as a disruptive paradigm that is giving users easy access to large numbers of leased infrastructure, software and platforms as services anywhere and anytime, especially, which adopts the market-oriented business model. Buyya et al. [7] define a Cloud as a type of parallel and distributed system consisting of a collection of interconnected and virtualized computers that are dynamically provisioned and presented as one or more unified computing resources based on service-level agreements. This definition puts

Cloud computing into a market oriented perspective and stresses the economic nature of this phenomenon [18].

The scheduling is a fundamental problem in order to optimize application execution and usage of necessary infrastructures. Traditional community based computing paradigms such as cluster and grid provide free resources for users to access, and the cost is not taken into account. Therefore, the scheduling policies only try to minimize the overall finish time. For example, many heuristic algorithms such as Minimum Execution Time, Minimum Completion Time, Min-min and Max-min are designed with different aims [5].

And along with the research spot from community to commercial model, Market-oriented cloud computing [6] in industry is getting real as evidenced by developments from companies such as Amazon. For example, Amazon EC2 started with flat pricing then moved to pricing based on service difference (http://aws.amazon.com/ec2). The design of a scheduling policy depends on various factors like the parameter to be optimized and quality of service to be provided. And the scheduling policies based on market-oriented business model in the cloud environments mainly consider to optimize performance with the way of minimize overall complete time as well as meet the user's specified QoS constraints [9,15], i.e. deadline and cost for hiring cloud resources.

Regarding the cloud market model, paper [8] describes some representative platforms for cloud computing covering the state-of-the-art, and provides the architecture for creating a general auction-based cloud market for trading cloud services and resource management. Buyya et al. [16] propose the DBC (Deadline Budget Constraint) scheduling strategy to address the time and cost minimization problem. The budget constrained genetic algorithm [19] is proposed to minimize the makespan while meeting a specified user budget. And a knowledge based ant colony optimization algorithm [13] minimizes execution cost while meeting the user's deadline.

Wu et al. [18] propose a market-oriented hierarchical scheduling strategy which consists of a service-level scheduling and a task-level scheduling. The service-level scheduling deals with the Task-to-Service assignment and the task-level scheduling deals with the optimization of the Task-to-VM assignment in local cloud data centers. A hybrid scheduling approach [14] was used to schedule workflow application in private clouds. In [12], the scheduling algorithm is implemented in ASKALON environment for Grid and Cloud Computing. It outperform as compared with bi-criteria heuristic and bi-criteria genetic algorithm. PCP algorithm [1] minimizes the execution time while meeting the user defined deadline, and two types of PCP is implemented in Cloud i.e. IC-PCP (IaaS Cloud Partial Critical Path) and IC-PCPD2 (IaaS Cloud Partial Critical Path with Deadline Distribution).

As an expanding render system which hiring resources from IaaS cloud, the scheduling policy should give consideration to deadline and user's budget while combining with the feature of rendering application and saving user's money as far as possible.

3   Overview of Render System

This section describe the hybrid render system which expands the computing ability of local render system by interacting with Amazon EC2 IaaS Cloud, which is shown in Fig. 1.

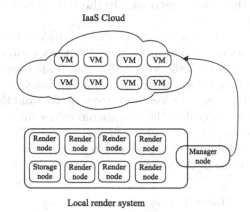

Fig. 1. The structure of hybrid render system

This work considers the case that the render system supply its users with free local resources and cloud resources hired from IaaS provider under deadline and budget constraints. The scenario, depicted in Fig. 1, can represent a hybrid render system that provision free and commercial computing resources with a way of combining to guarantee user's Qos while the local render nodes are insufficient.

The resources of the local render system, we call them render nodes, are supervise by manage node which includes a list of tasks and a list of render nodes. And the manage node also provides the user interface to manipulate the whole system, receives request of service from users and scheduling render jobs to corresponding render nodes. Furthermore, the manage node will interact with IaaS provider and take charge of applying and deploy virtual machines (VMs) as expanding resources from IaaS cloud according to special scheduling and provisioning policy, which are detailed in the next section. Except that, if the resources request is satisfied by IaaS cloud, manage node will add the accessible resources to the available resources and the render jobs can be submit to them. Meantime, manage node will handle the payment caused by hiring resources from IaaS cloud with the pricing model.

And the render node, which usually costs great deal of computations, receives the render task from manage node and start to render when it's idle and available. The storage node is used to store the input texture and materials files, output serial images files and other files which need to be shared, which requires strong I/O capabilities.

4   Proposed Policy

Scheduling rendering jobs with aim of satisfying user's Qos constraints such as deadline and computation cost is actually complex especially when the local resources of render system are insufficient. In this situation, scheduling policy should consider user's economic budget, i.e., pursuing the most cost-effective way, except meeting the above constraints. In this section, details of the proposed policy are described.

One of characteristics for rendering application is independence among frames and actually the frames are similar in a scene or camera, meantime the emphasis of this work is not coping with the workload estimation. Therefore, in this work we suppose that the frames have the same rendering time.

From the view of economy, the local resources are free and the cloud resources from IaaS provider are chargeable, the user should utilize fully the local resources and hiring legitimately cloud resources under budget. Therefore, the policy should consider the number of cloud resources with a saving way. And Table 1 summarizes the notations in the policy.

Table 1. Parameters in the policy.

Budget	Users budget
Deadline	Users deadline
Tfi	Rendering time of each frame
TF	Number of total frames
nl	Number of local resources
nc	Number of applied cloud resources
cc	Price of cloud resource (cent/hour)
Tl	Time of all frames by local render system
AR	Number of available resources
RB	Remaining budget

Here, the number of frames completed by local render system in one billing cycle is defined as $\left\lfloor \frac{nl}{Tf_i} \right\rfloor$.

And the available resources include the local resources and cloud resources hired from IaaS provider, i.e. $AR = nl + nc$. We suppose that the render system knows in advance the case of insufficient resources. When applying cloud resources the budget is not fully paid to the IaaS provider. We define α as the imprest factor $(0 < \alpha < 1)$. We use $\alpha * Budget$, defined as *pre-paid*, to applying resources for one billing cycle at the beginning and the number of cloud resources is *pre-paid/cc*. In our experiment we set $\alpha = 0.5$, and we will study the adaptive value for α in the future work.

And after one billing cycle we determine the use of remaining budget (RB) according to the remaining frames. In this way, the render system choose a relative economic manner to save user's money within the deadline. The pseudo code of proposed economy-oriented deadline scheduling policy is presented in Algorithm 1.

Algorithm 1. Economy-oriented deadline scheduling policy

Input: Deadline, Budget, cc
1: applying resources with pre-paid and charging
2: $RB = Budget - pre\text{-}paid$
3: calculating the number of cloud resources
4: $AR = pre\text{-}paid/cc + nl$
5: submitting frames to available resources with AR
6: estimating the time of remaining frames
7: **if** the time of remaining frames exceeds Deadline **then**
8:    applying resources with $\alpha * RB$ and charging
9: **else**
10:    submitting remaining frames to local resources
11: **end if**
12: terminating applying of cloud resources

In Algorithm 1, we use $Tf - \left\lfloor \frac{AR}{Tf_i} \right\rfloor$ to estimate remaining frames and then the time of remaining frames is calculated according to the time of each frame Tf_i. After the resources applied by the cost of *pre-paid* have been used, the remained budget will be determined to be use or not. If the time of remaining frames exceeds Deadline, the consuming with $\alpha * RB$ will be used to apply cloud resources and the charge will be deducted. The applied resources will be added to available resources and the remained frames are to be submitted. After the completion of all frames, the process of applying resources will be terminated. Results of our evaluation on the proposed policy in hybrid render system is presented in the next section.

5 Experimental Results

This section described the experiments to evaluate the proposed policy. The local system is constituted by local cluster and we choose Amazon EC2 as the IaaS Cloud provider. Amazon EC2 has three types of resources and the small computational unit is hired, which is similar to our local resources. The cost is 10 cents per hour. And we use Blender 2.49 as render engine. Next, we will test the single workload and multi workload, respectively.

5.1 The Single Workload

We use Blender to render 128 frames as the single workload to discuss the relationship between rendering time and the various budget supplied by user and two hours (120 min) as the deadline. The rendering time of these frames rendered in local render system is 130 min. Compared with the Cost Optimization policy (Cost-Opt) [16], the proposed policy is tested in the same situation, which is shown in Fig. 2.

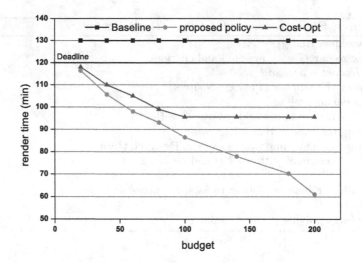

Fig. 2. The rendering time with different budget

As it can be seen from Fig. 2, along with the increase of budget, the rendering time is decreased with different velocity. The more available budget means more cloud resources and the render system can use these available resources to render more frames. In the proposed policy, the cost paid to IaaS provider is more than that of Cost-Opt, the rendering time is less. In Cost-Opt, the rendering time has not decrease after a certain budget (about 100 cents). The reason is that the core idea of Cost-Opt is saving user's money, and it just applies one resource over the time once the local resources are insufficient, then it has stopped applying even if there is still available budget. In fact, the proposed policy determines the number of cloud resources applied according to imprest factor. And along with the increase of available budget, there are enough available resources applied from IaaS provider for render system. Meanwhile, the proposed policy has not consume completely all the budget and adopts a evolutionary way to consume budget, therefore, the economic benefit of user can be guaranteed and the user can also obtain reasonable waiting time.

Here, we use cost efficiency to evaluate the relationship between the charge and performance improvement. The cost efficiency is defined as follows:

$$CF = \frac{Tl - TR}{\text{cost}} \tag{1}$$

Tl defined above means the rendering time of using local render system solely, TR means the rendering time of using hybrid render system and cost means the fee paid to IaaS provider. And the result is shown in Fig. 3.

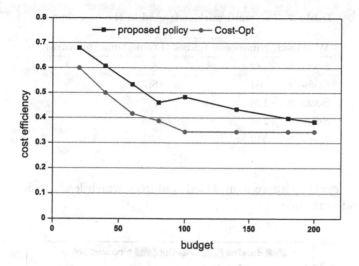

Fig. 3. Compassion of cost efficiency

In general, along with the increase of budget, the cost efficiency shows declining trend, which means that the cost has rapid cost efficiency increase speed in budget than that of rendering time reducing. In Cost-Opt policy, after 100 cents budget, cost efficiency tends to be uniform which is corresponding to the rendering time in Fig. 2 due to the constant cost. And in proposed policy, there is a little rise from 80 cents budget to 100 cents budget, which means the actual fee is decreased, i.e., the budget has not been consumed totally and there is just once applying resources according to estimation time. And after that, the cost efficiency declines due to the rise speed of budget has exceed that of rendering time reducing. Therefore, we can predict that the cost efficiency using our policy ultimately tends to be uniform once the budget is enough to complete all the frames in one frame time.

5.2   The Multi Workloads

In this part, the multi workloads will be used to test the proposed policy on rendering time. There are five types of workload [16] shown in Table 2. All the workloads have the same completion time using the local render system (150 min) and the same deadline and budget is used (2 h and 100 cents).

Figure 4 demonstrates the rendering time of proposed policy and Cost-Opt policy with different types of workloads. Except scene 1, for other scenes, two policies can finish rendering before deadline. For scene 1, the rendering time surpasses deadline using Cost-Opt policy due to less scheduling iteration, which means there are less resources request from IaaS Cloud. Cost-Opt policy request cloud resources over time which means the more extra overhead when connecting the IaaS provider. And compared with Cost-Opt policy, the proposed policy used

Table 2. The multi workloads used in the experiment

Workload	Number of frames	Frame time (minutes)
Scene 1	32	38
Scene 2	64	18.75
Scene 3	128	9.37
Scene 4	256	4.65
Scene 5	512	2.34

less charging cycle to apply more cloud resources which leads to less overhead and less rendering time.

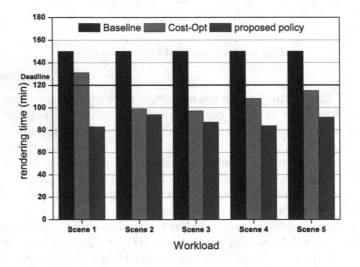

Fig. 4. The rendering time for different workloads

6   Conclusion and Future Work

In this paper, economy-oriented deadline scheduling policy is proposed to increase the capacity of local render system by hiring resources from IaaS Cloud. The proposed scheduling policy takes into account given constraints of deadline and budget. And also offers an economic way to apply Cloud resources. We evaluate the proposed policy using single workload and multi workloads comparing with Cost-Opt policy. For single workload, the proposed policy obtains less rendering time and higher cost efficient than Cost-Opt policy due to the economic budget for applying resources. For multi workloads, the proposed policy can finish the rendering frames before deadline with fixed budget. As a future work we plan to study the problem how to design scheduling policy for workloads with different rendering time.

Acknowledgments. This work is supported by National Natural Science Foundation of China (Grant No.61202041 and No.91330117) and National High-Tech Research and Development Program of China (Grant No.2012AA01A306 and No.2014AA01A302). Computational resources have been made available on Xi'an High Performance Computing Center.

References

1. Abrishami, S., Naghibzadeh, M., Epema, D.H.: Deadline-constrained workflow scheduling algorithms for infrastructure as a service clouds. Future Gener. Comput. Syst. **29**(1), 158–169 (2013)
2. Armbrust, M., Fox, A., Griffith, R., Joseph, A.D., Katz, R., Konwinski, A., Lee, G., Patterson, D., Rabkin, A., Stoica, I., et al.: A view of cloud computing. Commun. ACM **53**(4), 50–58 (2010)
3. Baharon, M.R., Shi, Q., Llewellyn-Jones, D., Merabti, M.: Secure rendering process in cloud computing. In: 2013 Eleventh Annual International Conference on Privacy, Security and Trust (PST), pp. 82–87. IEEE (2013)
4. Bala, A., Chana, I.: A survey of various workflow scheduling algorithms in cloud environment. In: 2nd National Conference on Information and Communication Technology (NCICT), pp. 26–30 (2011)
5. Braun, T.D., Siegel, H.J., Beck, N., Bölöni, L.L., Maheswaran, M., Reuther, A.I., Robertson, J.P., Theys, M.D., Yao, B., Hensgen, D., et al.: A comparison of eleven static heuristics for mapping a class of independent tasks onto heterogeneous distributed computing systems. J. Parallel Distrib. Comput. **61**(6), 810–837 (2001)
6. Buyya, R., Pandey, S., Vecchiola, C.: Cloudbus toolkit for market-oriented cloud computing. In: Jaatun, M.G., Zhao, G., Rong, C. (eds.) Cloud Computing. LNCS, vol. 5931, pp. 24–44. Springer, Heidelberg (2009)
7. Buyya, R., Yeo, C.S., Venugopal, S.: Market-oriented cloud computing: vision, hype, and reality for delivering it services as computing utilities. In: 10th IEEE International Conference on High Performance Computing and Communications, HPCC 2008, pp. 5–13. IEEE (2008)
8. Buyya, R., Yeo, C.S., Venugopal, S., Broberg, J., Brandic, I.: Cloud computing and emerging it platforms: vision, hype, and reality for delivering computing as the 5th utility. Future Gener. Comput. Syst. **25**(6), 599–616 (2009)
9. Chen, W.N., Zhang, J.: An ant colony optimization approach to a grid workflow scheduling problem with various QoS requirements. IEEE Trans. Syst. Man, Cybern. Part C: Appl. Rev. **39**(1), 29–43 (2009)
10. Chong, A., Sourin, A., Levinski, K.: Grid-based computer animation rendering. In: Proceedings of the 4th International Conference on Computer Graphics and Interactive Techniques in Australasia and Southeast Asia, pp. 39–47. ACM (2006)
11. Davia, C., Gowen, S., Ghezzo, G., Harris, R., Horne, M., Potter, C., Pitt, S.P., Vandenberg, A., Xiong, N.: Cloud computing services and architecture for education. Int. J. Cloud Comput. **2**(2), 213–236 (2013)
12. Fard, H.M., Prodan, R., Barrionuevo, J.J.D., Fahringer, T.: A multi-objective approach for workflow scheduling in heterogeneous environments. In: Proceedings of the 2012 12th IEEE/ACM International Symposium on Cluster, Cloud and Grid Computing (CCGrid 2012), pp. 300–309. IEEE Computer Society (2012)

13. Hu, Y., Xing, L., Zhang, W., Xiao, W., Tang, D.: A knowledge-based ant colony optimization for a grid workflow scheduling problem. In: Tan, Y., Shi, Y., Tan, K.C. (eds.) ICSI 2010, Part I. LNCS, vol. 6145, pp. 241–248. Springer, Heidelberg (2010)

14. Li, J., Peng, J., Lei, Z., Zhang, W.: An energy-efficient scheduling approach based on private clouds. J. Inf. Comput. Sci. **8**(4), 716–724 (2011)

15. Liu, X., Yang, Y., Jiang, Y., Chen, J.: Preventing temporal violations in scientific workflows: where and how. IEEE Trans. Softw. Eng. **37**(6), 805–825 (2011)

16. Salehi, M.A., Buyya, R.: Adapting market-oriented scheduling policies for cloud computing. In: Hsu, C.-H., Yang, L.T., Park, J.H., Yeo, S.-S. (eds.) ICA3PP 2010, Part I. LNCS, vol. 6081, pp. 351–362. Springer, Heidelberg (2010)

17. Whaiduzzaman, M., Haque, M.N., Chowdhury, M.R.K., Gani, A.: A study on strategic provisioning of cloud computing services. Sci. World J. **2014**, 1–16 (2014)

18. Wu, Z., Liu, X., Ni, Z., Yuan, D., Yang, Y.: A market-oriented hierarchical scheduling strategy in cloud workflow systems. J. Supercomput. **63**(1), 256–293 (2013)

19. Yu, J., Buyya, R.: A budget constrained scheduling of workflow applications on utility grids using genetic algorithms. In: Workshop on Workflows in Support of Large-Scale Science, WORKS 2006, pp. 1–10. IEEE (2006)

Towards Detailed Tissue-Scale 3D Simulations of Electrical Activity and Calcium Handling in the Human Cardiac Ventricle

Qiang Lan[1,2,3], Namit Gaur[2], Johannes Langguth[2(✉)], and Xing Cai[2,3]

[1] National University of Defense Technology, Changsha 410073, China
[2] Simula Research Laboratory, 1324 Fornebu, Norway
{lanqiang,ngaur,langguth,xingca}@simula.no
[3] Department of Informatics, University of Oslo, 0316 Oslo, Norway

Abstract. We adopt a detailed human cardiac cell model, which has 10000 calcium release units, in connection with simulating the electrical activity and calcium handling at the tissue scale. This is a computationally intensive problem requiring a combination of efficient numerical algorithms and parallel programming. To this end, we use a method that is based on binomial distributions to collectively study the stochastic state transitions of the 100 ryanodine receptors inside every calcium release unit, instead of individually following each ryanodine receptor. Moreover, the implementation of the parallel simulator has incorporated optimizations in form of code vectorization and removing redundant calculations. Numerical experiments show very good parallel performance of the 3D simulator and demonstrate that various physiological behaviors are correctly reproduced. This work thus paves way for high-fidelity 3D simulations of human ventricular tissues, with the ultimate goal of understanding the mechanisms of arrhythmia.

Keywords: Calcium handling · Multiscale cardiac tissue simulation · Supercomputing

1 Introduction

Calcium handling dysfunction is considered the likely cause of several cardiac pathological conditions such as heart failure [6,10], cardiac hypertrophy [2], cardiomyopathies [16], and inherited disorders of calcium release processes in the sarcoplasmic reticulum (SR) [7,17]. Many of these pathological conditions originate from dysfunctions of subcellular calcium release processes that occur at the microscopic and nanoscopic levels, ranging from dyadic disorganization by t-tubule malformation in heart failure [8,9,15] to single ryanodine receptor (RyR) dysfunction occurring in inherited cardiopathologies [5,7].

Over the last several years, advances in numerical methods and computing techniques have enabled the development of cardiac cell models of electrophysiology and calcium handling that take into account the discrete nature of subcellular stochastic calcium release processes [4,11,19,22]. This new generation of

© Springer International Publishing Switzerland 2015
G. Wang et al. (Eds.): ICA3PP 2015, Part III, LNCS 9530, pp. 79–92, 2015.
DOI: 10.1007/978-3-319-27137-8_7

models of calcium handling and action potential has been immensely useful in the study of causative and preventive mechanisms of arrhythmogenesis, which originates from the local nanoscopic level of channel and dyadic dysfunction to the subcellular and cellular levels of membrane potential abnormalities in the form of delayed afterdepolarizations, early afterdepolarizations [20], and cardiac alternans [12,13,19]. Despite this advancement in our understanding of how cardiac arrhythmogenesis can progress at different scales, ranging from single channel to whole-cell action potentials, several challenges remain.

For one, cardiac arrhythmias occur at the tissue and organ scale. Extrapolating the insights obtained from cell-level studies to understand how arrhythmias occur at the tissue and/or organ scale is often unclear and at times counterintuitive. Secondly, tissue-level studies have proven to be particularly difficult due to their huge computational demands. A typical human heart has around 2×10^9 cells [1], each of which has about 10^6 RyRs and roughly 10^5 L-type channels operating stochastically in response to membrane potentials and local calcium concentrations [3]. Realistic simulations at this level of detail require immense computational power of massively parallel computers, together with sophisticated algorithms, so that these cardiac excitation processes can be studied in reasonable time. Thus to date, to the best of our knowledge, arrhythmia mechanisms at the tissue level have not been investigated computationally with detailed cell models of calcium handling.

This paper reports our newly developed parallel 3D simulator of electrical activity and calcium handling in the cardiac ventricular tissue. We will start with describing the novel numerical and computational approaches that have enabled such simulations with a detailed model of calcium handling. Then we will examine the parallel performance of the 3D simulator, followed by presenting multiscale simulation results of cardiac activity, including single channel RyR stochastic behavior, local dyadic calcium dynamics, whole-cell action potential and calcium dynamics, as well as cardiac excitation activity in the 3D tissue.

2   Mathematical Models and Numerical Methods

2.1   At the Tissue Level

The cardiac tissue is modeled by the following partial differential equation, which is commonly called the monodomain model:

$$\frac{\partial V_m}{\partial t} = \frac{-I_{\text{ion}}}{C_m} + D_x \frac{\partial^2 V_m}{\partial x^2} + D_y \frac{\partial^2 V_m}{\partial y^2} + D_z \frac{\partial^2 V_m}{\partial z^2}, \tag{1}$$

where V_m is the membrane potential, I_{ion} the ionic current provided by the underlying multiscale cell model of calcium handling (see Sect. 2.2), $C_m = 1\mu\text{F cm}^{-2}$ the membrane capacitance of the cell, $D_x = D_y = D_z = 0.2 \text{ mm}^2/\text{ms}$ the voltage diffusion coefficients in three spatial directions. In this paper, we consider the 3D solution domain of (1) as a slab of tissue made up of cardiac cells. The finite difference method, combined with an operator-splitting approach [18], is used to discretize (1). This means that the diffusion terms are treated separately from the I_{ion} term, where the latter requires solving the following detailed cell model per cell.

2.2   At the Cell Level

Electrophysiology Component. The multiscale model of stochastic calcium handling in a ventricular myocyte [4] forms the basis of the cell model used in this work. The electrophysiological currents used in [4] were those of a guinea-pig. Therefore, to perform simulations of the human cardiac ventricular tissue, we replace the electrophysiological current formulation with the O'Hara-Rudy (ORd) model [14] of a healthy human cardiac ventricular action potential. The total ionic current I_{ion} needed in (1) is computed by summing up the total ionic currents obtained from solving the ordinary differential equations in the ORd model.

Calcium Handling Component. The cell model consists of 10000 calcium release units (CaRUs) or dyads arranged as an internal $100 \times 10 \times 10$ grid in each cell. Each CaRU consists of five calcium compartments: (1) myoplasm, (2) sub-membrane space, (3) network sarcoplasmic reticulum, (4) junctional sarcoplasmic reticulum, and (5) dyadic space. The reader is referred to [4] for the detailed equations and parameters. Of particular importance, however, is the dyadic space that contains 15 L-type calcium channels and 100 RyRs that operate stochastically. More specifically, each RyR can be in one of four states, denoted as C1, C2, C3, and O1, at any given time. Figure 1 shows the possible transitions between them, which occur stochastically with probabilities that are related to the local calcium concentrations. The number of open RyRs, i.e. those having state O1, is of principal interest due to the effect of calcium influx on a cell's interior voltage.

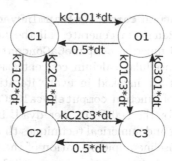

Fig. 1. The eight possible transitions between four states of a RyR, where the labels on the arrows indicate the probabilities of the transitions.

3   Implementation

3.1   Multi-level Parallelization

We adopt a multi-level parallelization strategy to facilitate our large scale tissue simulation. First, we divide the 3D tissue grid into a number of subgrids, each being handled by one MPI process that occupies a compute node of a cluster. Then, OpenMP threads are used within each MPI process to parallelize all the computations at the cell level. These together provide the value of I_{ion} per cell. MPI communication is only needed at the tissue level, due to calculating the diffusion terms in (1). The majority of the computing time is spent on the cell-level computations.

3.2   Cell-Level Computations

Among all the cell-level computations, the most time-consuming part concerns calcium handling. We therefore direct our attention to the following function, named `computeCalciumInDyad`, which implements the calcium handling component (see Sect. 2.2):

```
void computeCalciumInDyad()
{
    generateRandData();
    for(int i=0;i<Ndyads;i++) {
        computateLocalLtypeCurrent();
        computeLocalSRCaRelease();
        computeLocalCaConcentration();
    }
    computeCaConcentrationDiffusion();
}
```

Fig. 2. The function that implements calcium handling per cell.

It can be seen that function `computeCalciumInDyad` invokes five functions, where function `generateRandData` generates all the needed random numbers per cell per time step, and function `computeCaConcentrationDiffusion` computes the diffusion of intracellular calcium concentrations between the dyads. The other three functions are invoked in every iteration of the `for` loop. In particular, the main part of function `computeLocalSRCaRelease` addresses the random state transitions for the 100 RyRs per dyad. In the following, we will present three programming and numerical techniques that have a positive impact on the performance of a baseline implementation of the parallel simulator. Note that the computational cost of the entire `computeCalciumInDyad` function is directly proportional to the number of dyads Fig. 6.

Avoiding Redundant Calculations. s Many variables are involved in the computation of each dyad. Some of these variables vary from dyad to dyad, whereas others remain constant. Considering that the number of dyads in our detailed cell model is 10000, pre-calculating the constant variables outside the `for`-loop can yield substantial performance gains. The effort required is to identify these loop-constant variables among the complicated equations involved. Figure 5 clearly shows that the effect of this optimization is considerable.

Vectorizing Intracellular Diffusion Calculations. Intracellular diffusion in the 10000 dyads, which form an internal $100 \times 10 \times 10$ grid, is needed for three calcium concentrations. The code segment in Fig. 3 shows the actual implementation of one such 3D diffusion computation. In order to utilize the vectorization capability of modern CPUs, it is important to use a data structure where elements in x are contiguous in memory since the x loop is the innermost of the nested triple `for`-loops. In order to inform that the compiler that it is safe to vectorize this loop, we add the `ivdep`. Note that this pragma only asserts the data independency of the grid cells in the diffusion step. The actual vectorization is left to the compiler. However, even though the 256 bit vector length of our target machine suggests the possibility of a fourfold speeup, the fact that such stencil computations are generally memory bound implies that the actual performance gain will be far lower. Furthermore, the other parts of the computation are not vectorized manually and cannot be vectorized automatically by the compiler. The techniques required for efficient vectorization of such complex code are beyond the scope of this work.

Using Binomial Distribution. Recall from Sect. 2.2 that the dyadic space contains 100 RyRs, each of which can be in one of four states at any given time. Transitions between the states occur stochastically. To count the number of RyRs that have the open (O1) state, which determines the calcium influx on a cell's interior voltage, a straightforward approach is to individually simulate the random transition per RyR. In total 100 random numbers (lying uniformly between 0 and 1) are needed, one per RyR. Depending on the current state and on the corresponding transition probabilities, a RyR may change into another state. Such an approach is very computationally heavy, due to the need of generating many random numbers and the use of many `if`-tests in the implementation.

Therefore, it is computationally beneficial to collectively compute the number of RyRs in the four states, instead of individually tracing the transition of each RyR. We thus replace the 100 individual random experiments with eight random samples from a binomial distribution, one for each possible state transition, as shown in Fig. 1. The cumulative probability of having up to k successes in n trials with individual probabilities of success p is given as follows:

$$F(k, n, p) = Pr(X \leq k) = \sum_{i=0}^{k} \binom{n}{i} p^i (1-p)^{n-i}, \tag{2}$$

where

$$\binom{n}{i} = \frac{n!}{i!(n-i)!}$$

is the binomial coefficient.

As the number of RyRs in each state ranges from 0 to 100, we can precompute all the required binomial coefficients. This has a significant performance benefit. Using a random number r that is drawn from a uniform distribution in $[0, 1]$, we sample from the binomial distribution by finding the smallest k for

```
for(z=1;z<Nz_diff-1;z++)
    for(y=1;y<Ny_diff-1;y++) {
        int x,c,n,s,b,t;
        x=0;
        c=x+y*Nx_diff+z*Nx_diff*Ny_diff;
        n=c-Nx_diff;              s=c+Nx_diff;
        b=c-Nx_diff*Ny_diff;      t=c+Nx_diff*Ny_diff;

        U[c]=u[c]+fx*(2*u[c+1]-2*u[c])+fy*(u[n]+u[s]-2*u[c])
                +fz*(u[b]+u[t]-2*u[c]);
        #pragma ivdep
        for(x=1;x<Nx_diff-1;x++) {
            ++c; ++n; ++s; ++b; ++t;
            U[c]=u[c]+fx*(u[c-1]+u[c+1]-2*u[c])+fy*(u[n]+u[s]-2*u[c])
                    +fz*(u[b]+u[t]-2*u[c]);
        }
        U[c]=u[c]+fx*(2*u[c-1]-2*u[c])+fy*(u[n]+u[s]-2*u[c])
                    +fz*(u[b]+u[t]-2*u[c]);

}
```

Fig. 3. Pragma guided vectorization (in the x direciton) of one of three diffusion computations between the dyads in function computeCaConcentrationDiffusion.

which $r \leq F(k, n, p)$. While standard implementations of the binomial distribution incur a high computational cost, we use an efficient custom implementation which is shown in Fig. 4. Since the binomial coefficients are precomputed, we only need to multiply the base probability which starts at $(1 - p)^n$ by $p/(1 - p)$ in every round, store the result and multiply it by the binomial coefficient.

Let us denote the number of RyRs in the four states as x_1, x_2, x_3, x_4, and the number of RyRs which transition from state i to state j as x_{ij}. The values x_{ij} are obtained by sampling the binomial distribution as described above. Now, the number of RyRs in each state in the next time step is:

$$x_i = x_i - \sum_j x_{ij} + \sum_j x_{ji}. \tag{3}$$

Based on this, we add two optimizations according to the characteristics of the cell model. In our model, the transition probabilities from O1 to C1 and from C3 to C2 are constant at $p_c = 0.5 * dt$. Thus, we can pre-compute the entire cumulative probability function $F(k, n, p_c)$ in the same way that we pre-compute the binomial coefficient. In both cases, we need to store $101*100/2 = 5050$ values, which is no significant cost. In fact, storing a square table of 101^2 entries is more efficient and convenient.

In addition, we exploit a second property of the cell model. Most of time the RyRs are in state C2 and all the transition probabilities except the two constant ones mentioned above are close to 0. This means that it is quite likely that the result obtained by sampling from the binomial distribution is also 0. We make use of this by setting a small probability p_t as a threshold, and precompute

$F(0, n, p_t)$ for all $0 \leq n \leq 100$. Now, if $p \leq p_t$, for a given random number r we can simply check whether $r \leq F(0, n, p_t)$, and if that is the case, we obtain $k = 0$, i.e. no state transition happens, without computing the binomial distribution. Of course, if the number of RyRs in one state is 0, then the number of RyRs transitioning from that state is also 0. Figure 4 below shows our implementation of the optimized sampling from the binomial distribution.

Binomial distributions for modeling RyR transitions have been used in e.g. [19]. However, there the authors do not compute the actual binomial distribution. Instead, they approximate it using the normal and Poisson distributions, at the expense of accuracy.

4   Performance Results and Analysis

4.1   Hardware and Numerical Setup

Our test system is Abel [21], a supercomputer operated by the University of Oslo. The compute nodes on Abel are equipped with dual Intel Xeon E5-2670 (Sandy Bridge) processors. Each node has 16 physical compute cores running at 2.6 GHz. The interconnect is FDR (56 Gbps) Infiniband. We use Intel's *icc* compiler 15.1.0 for compilation and the Intel MPI 5.0.2 library for communication. Up to 128 compute nodes, i.e. 2048 CPU cores, have been used for the following numerical experiments.

For all the experiments, a fixed time step size of 0.05 ms is used at both the tissue level and the cell level. When doing tissue-scale simulations, we have chosen a fixed spatial mesh resolution of 0.5 mm to discretize the diffusion terms in (1).

4.2   Performance Optimization Experiment

The goal of our first numerical experiment is to test the improvement in performance obtained by our optimizations to the `compute_cell` function described in Sect. 3.2. To do so, we run 10000 time steps for a single cell with 10000 dyads. This is equivalent to simulating one cardiac beat of 500 ms. The cell is stimulated at $t = 50$ ms. Figure 5 shows the improvement in performance due to different optimizations. Removing redundant calculations yields a substantial improvement in three functions: `computateLocalLtypeCurrent` (by 37.5 %), `computeLocalSRCa Release` (by 24.4 %) and `computeCaConcentrationDiffusion` (by 12.4 %). The vectorization accelerates the diffusion further by 25 %. Finally, using binomial distributions has the highest impact, accelerating SRCaRelease by another 70 % and RandData by 79.9 %. The latter improvement is solely due to the reduced number of random values required by the binomial method. Overall, the combined effect of all three optimizations reduces the computation time by 50.7 %.

4.3   Scaling Experiment

We perform both weak scaling and strong scaling tests for a simulation of 1000 ms, and for each test we run two types of simulation, one uses 100 dyads per

```
int constant_p_binomial(n,randValue) {
    k=0;
    while(randValue>Table[n,k])
        k++;
    return k;
}

int binomial(n,p,randValue) {
        if n = 0
        return 0;
    if p < Threshold AND randValue < Precomp[n]
        return 0;
    k = 0;
    p_current =pow((1-p),n);
    p_step = p/(1-p);
    while(randValue > 0) {
        k++;
        randValue -= Binom[n,k]*p_current;
        p_current *= p_step;
    }
    return k;
}
```

Fig. 4. Implementation of Binomial Distribution Method. Function constant_p_binomial simply finds k by using the precomputed lookup table. In function binomial, we first test if the computation can be skipped, using the threshold p_t and the precomputed value $F(0, n, p_t)$. If this is not the case, the distribution function $F(k, n, p)$ is computed iteratively by subtracting from randValue using the precomputed binomial coefficients.

cell and the other uses 10000 dyads per cell. For weak scaling tests, the number of compute nodes we use ranges from 1 to 128. When using 100 dyads, the tissue size is $64 \times 64 \times 64$ per node for a total of $512 \times 256 \times 256$ cells at 128 nodes. For 10000 dyads, the tissue size is $16 \times 16 \times 16$ per node, which amounts to $128 \times 64 \times 64$ cells when using 128 compute nodes. We measure scalability via the number of cell computations performed for each wall-clock second of simulation time used. Here, a cell computation is defined as computing one cell for a single time step. We then plot this metric against the number of nodes used. Figure 6 shows that we obtain very good weak scaling.

For the strong scaling test, the tissue size is fixed at $256 \times 256 \times 256$ cells for the 100 dyad case and at $32 \times 32 \times 32$ cells when using 10000 dyads per cell. Due to memory requirements, at least 8 compute nodes are needed. The same cell computation metric as in the weak scaling case is used. Figure 6 shows the results of our experiments. Compared with the result of weak scaling, we achieve almost the same performance. The difference can be explained by the communication overhead, which is not hidden by computation in our current implementation.

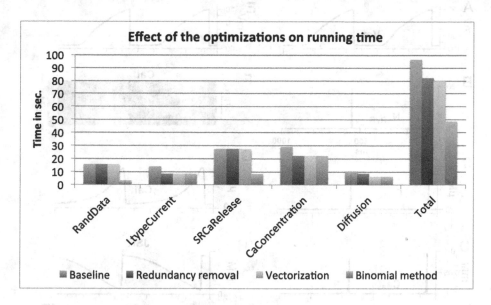

Fig. 5. Performance improvement of the individual functions in `computeCalciumInDyad` due to the different optimization techniques. The three optimizations are applied cumulatively. Thus, the values for the Binominal method reflect the sum of all improvements.

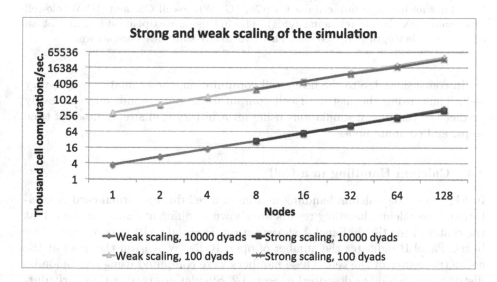

Fig. 6. Performance of weak and strong scaling tests of tissue simulations. The Y axis shows performance measured via the number of cell computations (i.e. time steps for a single cell) performed for each wall-clock second of simulation time used.

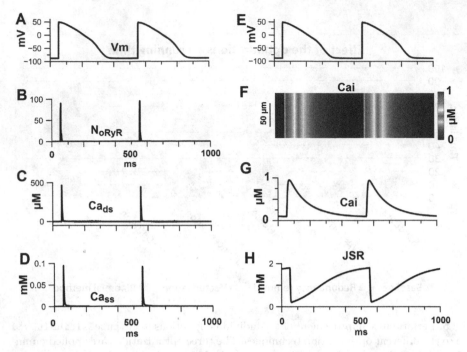

Fig. 7. Calcium handling in a cell in a human tissue during normal excitation. (A) Action Potential. (B) Number of open RyRs (N_oRyR) in the center dyad of the cell. (C) Dyadic space calcium (Ca_{ds}) (D) Submembrane space calcium (Ca_{ss}) (F) Simulated linescan image of intracellular Ca (Ca_i (G) Whole-cell Ca_i and (H) Whole-cell junctional sarcoplasmic reticulum (JSR). The 3D tissue was plane-stimulated at an edge at a cycle length (CL)=500 ms. Last two steady-state beats are shown.

In conclusion, due to the heavy cell computation, the simulation scales very well. Thus, using the metric of cell computations per second, one can easily predict the runtime of simulations using an arbitrary grid size, number of time steps, and compute nodes.

4.4   Calcium Handling in a Cell

In Fig. 7 we show calcium handling in a human cell during normal cardiac excitation. The calcium handling results are shown at different scales for the cell at the center of the tissue. Panel A shows action potential (AP) in two consecutive beats. Panel B indicates the number of open RyRs (N_{oRyR}) in the dyad at the geometric center of the cell. These numbers were computed using our binomial distribution method as described in Sect. 3.2. Simulations predict that early during the AP most of the RyRs are open. In response to these channel openings, Ca_{ds} (Panel C) in the dyad rises to a values as high as 500 μM and Ca_{ss} (panel D) to 0.1 mM. Within a dyad, the temporal profile of both Ca_{ds} and Ca_{ss} follow closely that of N_{oRyR}. At the subcellular scale, the simulated linescan image of

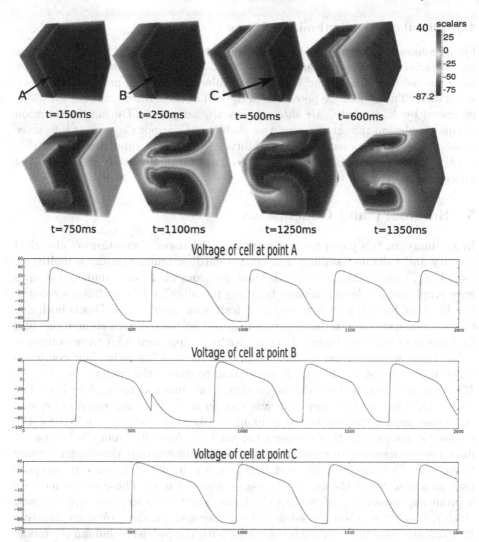

Fig. 8. Simulation of scroll waves in a 3D tissue. The top part shows voltage snapshots at different time points. The bottom section shows membrane potentials at three different locations in the tissue.

intracellular Ca (Ca_i) indicates that calcium release occurs synchronously across all the dyads (Panel F). The corresponding whole-cell Ca_i is indicated in Panel G. Panel H shows the whole-cell JSR. In summary, these results show calcium handling at different scales: dyad, subcell, and cell during tissue-simulations in a normal cardiac excitation process. The whole-cell values are consistent with [14].

4.5   Simulated Arrhythmia in Tissue

Figure 8 shows time snapshots of membrane potential in the 3D tissue. The tissue was stimulated at one edge at t = 0 ms. At t = 600 ms a portion of the tissue was cross field stimulated during the vulnerable window. This protocol initiates a scroll wave. The membrane potentials in the cell at three different tissue locations indicated by A, B, and C are shown below the snapshots. During the duration of this simulation the scroll waves were stable and did not degenerate into wave breaks. The simulations shows the ability of the tissue simulator to generate scroll waves which are commonly used to computationally study mechanisms of arrhythmia in cardiac tissue.

5   Summary and Conclusions

In summary, in this paper we report detailed 3D tissue simulations of electrical activity and calcium handling in a human cardiac ventricle using a multiscale model of calcium handling in a cell. Many previous 3D tissue simulation studies have employed whole-cell calcium handling models. To date multiscale calcium handling cell models have not been used for tissue simulations. This is both due to the immense computational power required to handle such simulations and limitations of current numerical and algorithmic approaches for these computations. Here, we have used optimizations such as avoiding redundant computations, vectorization and binomial distribution to reduce the computation time of 3D tissue simulations. Overall, the computation time was reduced by half. The most significant performance gain was due to using binomial distribution and the subsequent reduction in the random number generations required for the stochastic simulations that compute the SR Ca release flux and the L-type Ca flux. The weak scaling test indicates a near-constant compute time under varying tissue size. The strong scaling test indicates a near-linear decrease in compute time as a function of the number of compute nodes used. These results indicate a promising possibility of porting the tissue simulation to a massive compute cluster. Finally, we show the fidelity of our tissue simulations by demonstrating that calcium handling in a cell is consistent with the published human cell model [14]. We also show the ability to simulate reentrant arrhythmias in the 3D tissue.

To conclude, we have developed a detailed 3D tissue simulator of electrical activity and calcium handling in a human cardiac ventricle using algorithmic optimizations. The promising scalability suggests that whole-heart simulations are potentially within reach of the largest supercomputers available today. In future work, we intend to further improve the performance of our simulator and port it to hardware accelerator architectures. This will eventually open up the possibility of understanding the multiscale mechanisms of reentrant cardiac arrhythmias originating from calcium handling dysfunction.

Acknowledgements. The first author is supported by a mobility grant within UTFORSK project No. 2013-10091. The third and fourth authors are supported by FRINATEK project No. 214113. We gratefully acknowledge the computing time provided by NOTUR.

References

1. Adler, C., Costabel, U.: Cell number in human heart in atrophy, hypertrophy, and under the influence of cytostatics. Recent Adv. Stud. Card. Struc. Metab. **6**, 343–355 (1974)
2. Berridge, M.: Remodelling Ca2+ signalling systems and cardiac hypertrophy. Biochem. Soc. Trans. **34**(2), 228–231 (2006)
3. Cheng, H., Lederer, W., Cannell, M.B.: Calcium sparks: elementary events underlying excitation-contraction coupling in heart muscle. Science **262**(5134), 740–744 (1993)
4. Gaur, N., Rudy, Y.: Multiscale modeling of calcium cycling in cardiac ventricular myocyte: macroscopic consequences of microscopic dyadic function. Biophys. J. **100**(12), 2904–2912 (2011)
5. Jiang, D., Wang, R., Xiao, B., Kong, H., Hunt, D.J., Choi, P., Zhang, L., Chen, S.W.: Enhanced store overload-induced Ca2+ release and channel sensitivity to luminal Ca2+ activation are common defects of RyR2 mutations linked to ventricular tachycardia and sudden death. Circ. Res. **97**(11), 1173–1181 (2005)
6. Kubalova, Z., Terentyev, D., Viatchenko-Karpinski, S., Nishijima, Y., Györke, I., Terentyeva, R., da Cuñha, D.N., Sridhar, A., Feldman, D.S., Hamlin, R.L., et al.: Abnormal intrastore calcium signaling in chronic heart failure. Proc. Nat. Acad. Sci. USA **102**(39), 14104–14109 (2005)
7. Liu, N., Colombi, B., Memmi, M., Zissimopoulos, S., Rizzi, N., Negri, S., Imbriani, M., Napolitano, C., Lai, F.A., Priori, S.G.: Arrhythmogenesis in catecholaminergic polymorphic ventricular tachycardia insights from a RyR2 R4496C knock-in mouse model. Circ. Res. **99**(3), 292–298 (2006)
8. Louch, W.E., Bito, V., Heinzel, F.R., Macianskiene, R., Vanhaecke, J., Flameng, W., Mubagwa, K., Sipido, K.R.: Reduced synchrony of Ca2+ release with loss of T-tubulesa comparison to Ca2+ release in human failing cardiomyocytes. Cardiovasc. Res. **62**(1), 63–73 (2004)
9. Louch, W.E., Mørk, H.K., Sexton, J., Strømme, T.A., Laake, P., Sjaastad, I., Sejersted, O.M.: T-tubule disorganization and reduced synchrony of Ca2+ release in murine cardiomyocytes following myocardial infarction. J. Physiol. **574**(2), 519–533 (2006)
10. Marks, A.R., et al.: Calcium cycling proteins and heart failure: mechanisms and therapeutics. J. Clin. Investig. **123**(1), 46–52 (2013)
11. Nivala, M., de Lange, E., Rovetti, R., Qu, Z.: Computational modeling and numerical methods for spatiotemporal calcium cycling in ventricular myocytes. Front. Physiol. **3**, 114 (2012)
12. Nivala, M., Qu, Z.: Calcium alternans in a couplon network model of ventricular myocytes: role of sarcoplasmic reticulum load. Am. J. Physiol.-Heart Circulatory Physiol. **303**(3), H341–H352 (2012)
13. Nivala, M., Song, Z., Weiss, J.N., Qu, Z.: T-tubule disruption promotes calcium alternans in failing ventricular myocytes: mechanistic insights from computational modeling. J. Mol. Cell. Cardiol. **79**, 32–41 (2015)
14. O'Hara, T., Virág, L., Varró, A., Rudy, Y.: Simulation of the undiseased human cardiac ventricular action potential: model formulation and experimental validation. PLoS Comput. Biol. **7**(5), e1002061 (2011)
15. van Oort, R.J., Garbino, A., Wang, W., Dixit, S.S., Landstrom, A.P., Gaur, N., De Almeida, A.C., Skapura, D.G., Rudy, Y., Burns, A.R., et al.: Disrupted junctional membrane complexes and hyperactive ryanodine receptors after acute junctophilin knockdown in mice. Circulation **123**(9), 979–988 (2011)

16. Pieske, B., Kretschmann, B., Meyer, M., Holubarsch, C., Weirich, J., Posival, H., Minami, K., Just, H., Hasenfuss, G.: Alterations in intracellular calcium handling associated with the inverse force-frequency relation in human dilated cardiomyopathy. Circulation **92**(5), 1169–1178 (1995)

17. Priori, S.G., Chen, S.W.: Inherited dysfunction of sarcoplasmic reticulum Ca2+ handling and arrhythmogenesis. Circ. Res. **108**(7), 871–883 (2011)

18. Qu, Z., Garfinkel, A.: An advanced algorithm for solving partial differential equation in cardiac conduction. IEEE Trans. Biomed. Eng. **46**(9), 1166–1168 (1999)

19. Restrepo, J.G., Weiss, J.N., Karma, A.: Calsequestrin-mediated mechanism for cellular calcium transient alternans. Biophys. J. **95**(8), 3767–3789 (2008)

20. Song, Z., Ko, C.Y., Nivala, M., Weiss, J.N., Qu, Z.: Calcium-voltage coupling in the genesis of early and delayed afterdepolarizations in cardiac myocytes. Biophys. J. **108**(8), 1908–1921 (2015)

21. University of Oslo: Abel. http://www.uio.no/english/services/it/research/hpc/abel/

22. Williams, G.S., Chikando, A.C., Tuan, H.T.M., Sobie, E.A., Lederer, W., Jafri, M.S.: Dynamics of calcium sparks and calcium leak in the heart. Biophys. J. **101**(6), 1287–1296 (2011)

Task Parallel Implementation of Matrix Multiplication on Multi-socket Multi-core Architectures

Yizhuo Wang[✉], Weixing Ji, Xu Chen, and Sensen Hu

School of Computer Science and Technology, Beijing Institute of Technology,
Beijing 100081, China
{frankwyz,pass,xuchen,huss}@bit.edu.cn

Abstract. Matrix multiplication is a very important computation kernel in many science and engineering applications. This paper presents a parallel implementation framework for dense matrix multiplication on multi-socket multi-core architectures. Our framework first partitions the computation between the multi-core processors. Then a hybrid matrix multiplication algorithm is used on each processor, which combines the Winograd algorithm and the classical algorithm. In addition, a hierarchical work-stealing scheme is applied to achieve dynamic load balancing and enforce data locality in our framework. Performance experiments on two platforms show that our implementation gets significant performance gains compared with the state-of-the-art implementations.

Keywords: Matrix multiplications · Multi-socket · Fast algorithms · Winograd · Work-stealing

1 Introduction

Matrix multiplication is a fundamental routine in dense linear algebra, which is widely used by science and engineering applications. Therefore, a faster implementation of matrix multiplication immediately benefits a large range of applications.

Matrix multiplication algorithms and implementations have been studied for a long history. In the era of uniprocessor, the studies focus on two major objectives. The first is to improve the performance of matrix multiplication implementations by enforcing locality of memory accesses. Blocking, also known as tiling, is the most popular technique to enforce locality [1]. The second objective is to decrease the time complexity of matrix multiplication algorithm. The classical matrix multiplication algorithms have complexity $O(n^3)$. We use the term fast algorithms to refer to the algorithms that have asymptotic complexity less than $O(n^3)$. Strassen's algorithm [2] was the first fast algorithm. It uses 7 multiplications and 18 additions to perform 2×2 matrix multiplication, while the classical algorithm does 8 multiplications and 4 additions. By recursive application this yields an algorithm with the asymptotic complexity of $O(n^{2.807})$. Strassen's algorithm was improved by Winograd [3], which led to a highly practical algorithm requiring 7 multiplications and only 15 additions. After that, the fast algorithm researches achieve lower and lower complexity. But Winograd's algorithm is still the most practicable and widely used among the fast algorithms for matrix multiplication.

© Springer International Publishing Switzerland 2015
G. Wang et al. (Eds.): ICA3PP 2015, Part III, LNCS 9530, pp. 93–104, 2015.
DOI: 10.1007/978-3-319-27137-8_8

In the era of multiprocessor and multi-core, parallel implementation of matrix multiplication (MM) brings more challenges. The classical MM algorithms deal with regular computation pattern. They are normally implemented in parallel by partitioning the product matrix into blocks and distributing the computations of the blocks to the processing elements. Such implementations mainly exploit loop parallelism. The fast algorithms involve matrix multiplication, addition and subtraction. They can be represented with task DAGs. Therefore, it is applicable to exploit fine-grained task parallelism in their implementations. Because both the classical and fast algorithms are recursive algorithms and anyone of them can be used in a recursive step, more complicated algorithms can be developed such as 2D-Strassen and Strassen-2D [4]. In addition, communication cost and load balancing become the key issues in multiprocessor systems, besides locality which is the major concern of matrix multiplication in uniprocessor systems. Optimal design of parallel matrix multiplication requires that all the above factors are considered and highly depends on the platform being targeted.

Multi-socket multi-core (MSMC) architecture has become the mainstream in HPC systems. We study parallel matrix multiplication on shared memory MSMC computers and present a task-based parallel implementation framework in this paper. Our framework divides the matrix multiplication into three phases. In the first phase, blocked algorithm is used. The matrices are partitioned into blocks according to the number of the sockets. The blocks assigned to each socket are determined in this phase. During the second phase, the cores in each socket perform Winograd algorithm recursively until a *recursion point* is reached, at which the computation switches to the classical algorithm. The last phase refers to the classical matrix multiplication, in which the existing parallel BLAS library such as Intel MKL is used. The existing libraries have been carefully optimized, but they use blocked algorithms, not fast algorithms. Our framework combines the fast algorithms with the existing libraries to improve the performance. In addition, a hierarchical work-stealing scheme is applied to address load balancing and data locality issues in our framework.

The remainder of this paper is organized as follows. Section 2 provides relevant background information and related work. Section 3 describes our framework and its implementation. Section 4 presents the results of our experimental evaluation, and Sect. 5 gives the conclusions and further work.

2   Related Work

We group the related work into three categories: matrix multiplication algorithms, BLAS libraries and tasks scheduling schemes in parallel systems community.

2.1   Matrix Multiplication Algorithms

As discussed in the previous section, we classify matrix multiplication algorithms into three categories: classical, fast and hybrid. For classical MM algorithms, including blocked MM algorithms, performance improvements are normally achieved on the implementations, not on the algorithms. Data locality is a main consideration in optimizing implementations of them for performance. Loop tiling and data layout transformation [5] are two key techniques to improve both temporal and spatial locality in shared memory systems. Normally one level of tiling is used for each level of memory hierarchy to minimize data accesses at the all memory levels. By multiple levels of tiling, the matrices are partitioned into blocks in different sizes. To make the submatrices suited to the sizes of memory hierarchy, recursive array layout, such as Z-Morton [6], should be used in conjunction with tiling. Although the layout transformations bring extra overhead, they greatly benefit the locality and it is enough to offset the extra overhead.

Since Strassen's algorithm published in 1969 [2], the study on low-complexity matrix multiplication algorithms forms a new branch – fast matrix multiplication. In the history of fast MM study, Strassen and Coppersmith-Winograd (C-W) [7] are two most important algorithms. The other fast algorithms decrease algorithm complexity based on them. For instance, Pan extended Strassen's algorithm and showed an algorithm for multiplying $n \times n$ matrices in $O(n^{2.795})$ time in 1978 [8]. Coppersmith and Winograd broke $O(n^{2.5})$ complexity in 1981 [7]. After that, most studies of fast MM algorithms were based on C-W algorithm. The fastest algorithm achieved $O(n^{2.376})$ in 1990 [9]. Then the result was not broken until 2010s, when Stothers [10] and Williams [11] argue that $O(n^{2.3727})$ is a new bound of fast MM algorithms by extending C-W algorithm with group-theoretic approaches.

In practice, for small matrices, fast algorithm has a significant overhead and classical algorithm results in better performance. To overcome this, several authors have shown hybrid algorithms [12–14] in which fast algorithm is first recursively applied and switches to the classical implementations at a specific size of submatrices. Our algorithm is a hybrid of Winograd and the classical algorithm.

2.2 BLAS Libraries

Dense matrix multiplication is the most complex and fundamental routine in basic linear algebra subprograms (BLAS) which is a de facto application programming interface standard. There are many software libraries implementing BLAS, such as ATLAS [15], GotoBLAS [16], Intel MKL and AMD Core Math Library (ACML). None of these libraries uses fast MM algorithms. They provide efficient MM implementations by exploiting memory hierarchy of processors. Specifically, they use tiling with block data layout to exploit temporal and spatial locality in data caches. ATLAS addresses auto-tuning for most known architectures. The optimal block size is selected automatically at compile time by running several tests with different block sizes. GotoBLAS not only exploited the locality in data caches but also in TLB. It provides carefully hand-tuned kernels written directly in assembly for many current microprocessors. Therefore, it offers consistently better performance than ATLAS on recent machines. In contrast to GotoBLAS and ATLAS which are open-source libraries, MKL and ACML are commercial libraries and specifically optimized on the vendors' CPUs.

These libraries yield different performance on various hardware platforms. They are good candidates for the implementations of classical matrix multiplication algorithm. We use them in our framework introduced in the next section.

2.3 Task Scheduling

Task scheduling is a key problem for parallel programs. The main goal of task scheduling is to achieve optimal load balancing and therefore minimize the program completion time. Scheduling schemes can be classified as static and dynamic. Static scheduling is performed by the compiler or the programmer before the execution of the program. It is easy to implement and has minimal scheduling overhead. However, it suffers from load imbalance issue leading to severe performance loss in a volatile environment.

Dynamic scheduling can cope with the volatile execution environment. It is performed at runtime to achieve dynamic load balancing. Self-scheduling [17] and work-stealing [18] are two best-known dynamic scheduling schemes. Self-scheduling uses a centralized task queue. The processor/worker fetches a task from the queue to execute when it becomes idle. Self-scheduling is widely used in loop parallelization. For instance, chunk self-scheduling (CSS) with fixed chunk size and Guided self-scheduling (GSS) [19] with decreasing chunk sizes are typical loop scheduling schemes in OpenMP. The synchronization cost for access to the centralized queue is the major scheduling overhead in self-scheduling schemes. Work-stealing uses distributed tasks queues, that is, each worker maintains its own work queue. When a worker's task queue is empty, it attempts to steal a task from a victim worker's work queue. Work-stealing has been widely used in modern task-based parallel programing languages and tools, and been proven to be effective on shared memory systems. We adopt work-stealing in our framework.

3 Methodology

We first review Winograd algorithm, and setup the notations that will be used throughout the paper. Then we introduce our matrix multiplication framework and the scheduling scheme used in this framework.

3.1 Winograd Algorithm

The Winograd variant of the Strassen's Algorithm, uses the same number of multiplications as Strassen's Algorithm but reduces the number of additions from 18 to 15.

Let m, n and k be powers of 2. Let A and B be two matrices of dimension $m \times k$ and $k \times n$ and let $C = A \times B$. Consider the block decomposition:

$$\begin{bmatrix} C_{11} & C_{12} \\ C_{21} & C_{22} \end{bmatrix} = \begin{bmatrix} A_{11} & A_{12} \\ A_{21} & A_{22} \end{bmatrix} \begin{bmatrix} B_{11} & B_{12} \\ B_{21} & B_{22} \end{bmatrix} \tag{1}$$

where A_{11} and B_{11} respectively have dimensions $m/2 \times k/2$ and $k/2 \times n/2$. Winograd algorithm computes the matrix $C = A \times B$ with the 7 submatrix multiplications and 15 submatrix additions/subtractions. It runs recursively. The single level recursion of the algorithm is presented in Fig. 1(a) as in [13]. The task dependency graph, which is a directed acyclic graph (DAG), is presented in Fig. 1(b). We use Winograd for our implementation of fast matrix multiplication.

Pre-additions	Recursive calls	Post-additions
$T_1 = A_{21} + A_{22}$	$P_1 = A_{11} * B_{11}$	$U_1 = P_1 + P_4$
$T_2 = T_1 - A_{11}$	$P_2 = A_{12} * B_{21}$	$U_2 = U_1 + P_5$
$T_3 = A_{11} - A_{21}$	$P_3 = T_1 * T_5$	$U_3 = U_1 + P_3$
$T_4 = A_{12} - T_2$	$P_4 = T_2 * T_6$	$C_{11} = P_1 + P_2$
$T_5 = B_{12} - B_{11}$	$P_5 = T_3 * T_7$	$C_{12} = U_3 + P_6$
$T_6 = B_{22} - T_5$	$P_6 = T_4 * B_{22}$	$C_{21} = U_2 + P_7$
$T_7 = B_{22} - B_{12}$	$P_7 = A_{22} * T_8$	$C_{22} = U_2 + P_3$
$T_8 = B_{21} + T_6$		

(a) First level of recursion

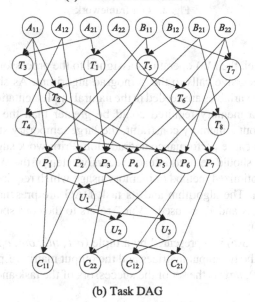

(b) Task DAG

Fig. 1. Winograd algorithm

Note that the padding or peeling methods [20] can be used to multiply matrices with odd dimensions.

3.2 Framework

Figure 2 depicts the framework of our matrix multiplication implementation. There are three levels separated by the dashed lines in the figure. In the top level, the computation is partitioned among the sockets (i.e. processors), and each processor does the computation of a block of the result matrix C. Because dual-socket and quad-socket are the major multi-socket architectures, we take them as examples. The matrices are blocked as in Eq. (1). For dual-socket architecture, one processor calculates C_{11} and C_{12}, and another calculates C_{21} and C_{22}. There are 4 MM operations and 2 MA (addition and subtraction) operations assigned to each processor. For quad-socket architecture, each processor calculates one block with 2 MM and 1 MA operations.

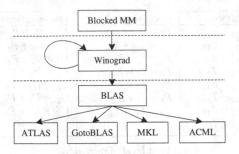

Fig. 2. Our framework

In the middle level, the MM operations assigned to the processors are implemented with one or more recursive calls to the Winograd algorithm. As shown in Fig. 1, 18 additional temporary variables are needed in the natural implementation of the Winograd algorithm. The extra memory required could be greater than the system's physical memory. Even without a memory constraint, the large temporary storage would harm the data locality and cause performance degradation. Prior work suggests two or three temporary variables should be used in each recursive step of the Winograd algorithm [21]. We adopt an optimized method of memory usage which requires only two temporaries in our system. The algorithm and its task DAG are presented in Fig. 3. Two temporary variables, X and Y, are used. "Var." refers to the corresponding algorithmic variables in Fig. 1(a).

Each task in Fig. 3(b) is represented by a tuple (*in1*, *in2*, *out*, *opt*, *next*, *cnt*) where *in1*, *in2* and *out* are the two input matrices and the output matrix respectively, *opt* is the operation (+, − or ×), *next* is the set of the successors of the task and *cnt* is the number of the predecessors.

For small matrices, the fast algorithm is slower than the classical algorithm because of the extra memory allocation and complicated cache blocking. Therefore, the Winograd algorithm needs to yield the computation to an efficient implementation of classical algorithm which is selected from ATLAS, GotoBLAS, MKL and ACML in the bottom lever of Fig. 2. Let r be the number of recursive steps. The extra memory requirement for multiplying $n \times n$ matrices with the Winograd algorithm in Fig. 3 is given by

$$E(n) = \frac{2n^2}{3}(1 - 0.25^r) < \frac{2n^2}{3}. \tag{2}$$

We determine the recursion point by an empirical study on the target machine. For instance, we use GotoBLAS as the implementation of classical MM. The number of worker threads is set to the number of cores in a single processor. We do two runs in a step. First, we multiply two square matrices of size n using DGEMM function of Goto-BLAS. Second, we perform the 22 matrix operations in Fig. 3(a) in the order. MM operations are still performed with GotoBLAS in parallel. Note that the matrix additions and subtractions are also implemented in parallel, which is described in the next subsection. Then we compare the two execution times. The size is increased when the first execution is faster, and vice versa, in the next step. The recursion point is the matrix size for which the above two execution times are similar.

Task	Operation	Var.
1	$X = A_{11} - A_{21}$	T_3
2	$Y = B_{22} - B_{12}$	T_7
3	$C_{21} = X * Y$	P_5
4	$X = A_{21} + A_{22}$	T_1
5	$Y = B_{12} - B_{11}$	T_5
6	$C_{22} = X * Y$	P_3
7	$X = X - A_{11}$	T_2
8	$Y = B_{22} - Y$	T_6
9	$C_{12} = X * Y$	P_4
10	$X = A_{12} - X$	T_4
11	$C_{11} = X * B_{22}$	P_6
12	$X = A_{11} * B_{11}$	P_1
13	$C_{12} = X + C_{12}$	U_1
14	$C_{21} = C_{12} + C_{21}$	U_2
15	$C_{12} = C_{12} + C_{22}$	U_3
16	$C_{22} = C_{21} + C_{22}$	C_{22}
17	$C_{12} = C_{12} + C_{11}$	C_{12}
18	$Y = Y - B_{21}$	T_8
19	$C_{11} = A_{22} * Y$	P_7
20	$C_{21} = C_{21} - C_{11}$	C_{21}
21	$C_{11} = A_{12} * B_{21}$	P_2
22	$C_{11} = C_{11} + X$	C_{11}

(a) First level of recursion   (b) Task DAG

Fig. 3. Memory efficient Winograd algorithm

Next, let's see the details of our implementation. Assume s processors (sockets) and p cores in each processor. Each processor maintains a task queue. Thus, there are s task queues in the system. Assume p threads $(T_1, T_2..., T_p)$ per processor and each thread is bound to a core. T_1 is a master thread and the others are worker threads. T_1 is responsible for task generation and scheduling, and also acts as a worker. To multiply two matrices on a processor, T_1 generates all the tasks by calling Winograd algorithm in Fig. 3 without performing real matrix operations, and pushes the tasks into the task queue at first. It is actually a depth first traversal of the recursion tree of Winograd algorithm, and will be quickly completed. Then T_1 fetches a task from the task queue each time and actives the worker threads to execute it in parallel.

The parallel MM or MA is performed according to *opt* of the task. T_1 directly calls DGEMM of the library used to invoke the parallel MM. The parallel MA is implemented by us. When the task is finished, the *cnt* elements of its successors, which are accessed through *next* of the task, are decreased by one. T_1 will attempt to steal a task of *cnt* 0 from a victim processor's task queue when the local task queue is empty.

3.3 Scheduling

Our framework incorporates static and dynamic scheduling. The top level of the frame-work does static scheduling by partitioning the matrices into blocks and evenly distrib-uting the blocks among the processors. Then dynamic scheduling works in the middle and bottom levels of our framework. As multi-socket multi-core architectures present two levels of parallelism, our dynamic scheduling scheme is designed as a hierarchical work-stealing scheme which has two levels. The upper level is the dynamic scheduling among the processors. The classical work-stealing is applied at this level. The steal rarely happens on a SMP system because the tasks (MM/MA) are not small here. Hence coarse-grained load balancing is achieved at this level. The lower level is the dynamic sched-uling among the cores of a processor. The multi-core processor executes a MM task in parallel by calling library routines. Because the libraries, such as GotoBLAS and MKL, have carefully considered load balancing, we need not to take care of fine-grained load balancing among the cores while performing MM tasks.

```
// w is the current thread index
v = (w+1)%p;    // victim thread index
while( g_flag[w] == 0 )
   sched_yield( );

for(; g_i[w] < g_u[w]; g_i[w]++)       Work
   for(j=0; j<n; j++)
      C[g_i[w]][j] = A[g_i[w]][j] + B[g_i[w]][j];

while(v != w){
   k = g_u[v] - g_i[v];
   if(k > T_h){
      g_u[w] = g_u[v];                 Steal
      g_u[v] = g_i[w] = g_i[v]+k/2;
      Work
   }
   v = (v+1)%p;
}
g_flag[w] = 0;
            (a) Worker thread
```

```
for(i=0; i<p; i++){
   g_i[i] = i*m/p;
   g_u[i] = (i+1)*m/p;
}
for(i=1; i<p; i++)
   g_flag[i] = 1;

Work (w=0)
Steal (w=0)

for(i=1; i<p; i++)
   while(g_flag[i])
      sched_yield( );

        (b) Master thread
```

Fig. 4. Pseudocode for parallel matrix addition implementation.

We focus on MA tasks and give an efficient implementation of parallel MA. Pseu-docode of the implementation is shown in Fig. 4. Assume p threads and m rows for the matrices. The "$g\_$" prefix denotes that the variable is accessible by all the threads. $g\_i[w]$ and $g\_u[w]$ are loop counter and loop bound of thread w respectively. $g\_flag[w]$ is a flag which is set to 1 for waking up the thread w. The array g_flag is initialized to zeroes. As shown in Fig. 4, the master thread makes even partitioning first. Then it wakes up the worker threads, do its own work and attempt to steal work from the other threads. Finally, it waits for the worker threads to finish by checking g_flag. Lock-free work-stealing with round-robin victim selection is used in Fig. 4. When the thread w finishes its work, it checks the remaining work (k) of the thread v. If k is greater than a predefined threshold T_h, the thread w steals half of the remaining work of the thread v by updating $g\_u[w]$, $g\_u[v]$ and $g\_i[w]$. The implementation is lock-free because the result will be correct even if the same $C = A + B$ statement is executed by two threads concurrently. Although there are data races on $g\_u[]$ and $g\_i[]$, they are benign data races whose existence does not affect the correctness of the program.

4   Experiments

4.1   Experimental Setup

To evaluate the performance of our MM implementation, we compare our implementation and GotoBLAS v2.1 on two multi-socket multi-core computers. One is equipped with two Intel Xeon E5-2650 processors. Each processor has 8 cores running at 2 GHz and 20 M LLC. Another is equipped with four AMD Opteron 8380 processors. Each processor has 4 cores running at 2.5 GHz and 6 M LLC. Both the computers are equipped with 32G memory.

We use DGEMM of GotoBLAS as the base case of the recursion in our implementation. The recursion point is found empirically for each platform. It is 1500 for the Intel platform and 1200 for the AMD platform. That is, the Winograd algorithm yields to GotoBLAS when the matrix size is smaller than 1500×1500 on the Intel platform and 1200×1200 on the AMD platform.

We compiled the programs using GNU GCC v4.5 and the optimization level $-O3$ enabled. Each performance result is the average of 10 runs of the considered program. We use GFLOPS as a measure. It is calculated as

$$\text{GFLOPS} = \frac{2n^3}{(\text{Execution time in seconds}) \times 10^9}. \tag{3}$$

4.2   Results

The results are reported in Fig. 5 for solo running the different MM implementations on the platforms without any interference from co-running. From the figure, we see that our implementation outperforms GotoBLAS on both the platforms. The performance gains increase with increasing the matrix size. Especially, our implementation achieves more than 20 % speedup over GotoBLAS when the matrix size is larger than 8000. The performance gains suggest that the fast algorithms, such as Winograd, should be used in the state-of-the-art BLAS libraries.

Our implementation partitions the matrices with respect to the multi-socket architecture before performing Winograd algorithm. That is different from the conventional implementations of the fast algorithms in which all the processing elements work on each subproblem (matrix operation) of a recursion step in parallel. We expect such initial partitioning enforces data locality and then improves performance. To test this, we run the conventional parallel implementation of the Winograd algorithm (denoted by ParFMM) on the platforms. The results are also shown in Fig. 5. To ensure a fair comparison, our implementation and ParFMM use the same recursion point on each platform. The figure shows our implementation outperforms ParFMM when the matrix size is large.

The hierarchical scheduling scheme is one of the key points distinguishing our technique from the others. It greatly ensures dynamic load balancing. To test this point, we run 4 interference threads on the Intel platform and 8 on the AMD platform to make load imbalance, while carrying out the experiments. The results are reported in Fig. 6. Our implementation gets more performance gains in this scenario than in the prior scenario. Moreover, the gains are greater in Fig. 6(b) which indicates our implementation outperforms the others more significantly when the load is more imbalancing.

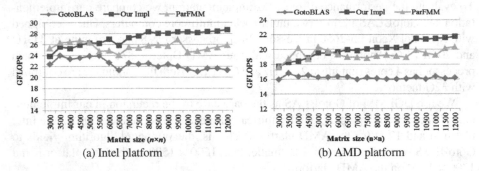

(a) Intel platform   (b) AMD platform

Fig. 5. Performance comparison of the implementations

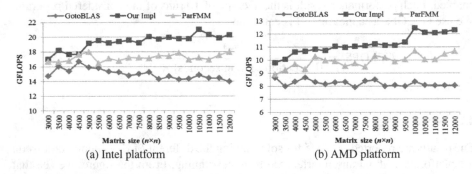

(a) Intel platform   (b) AMD platform

Fig. 6. Performance comparison of the implementations, with interference threads.

5   Conclusions

A practical implementation of parallel matrix multiplication on MSMC architectures is presented in this paper. Load balancing is addressed at two levels: multiple sockets and multiple cores by static partitioning and dynamic work-stealing. A memory efficient Winograd algorithm is used incorporating with the existing BLAS libraries in our implementation. The experimental results show that the fast algorithm provides significant performance benefit when the matrix size is large, and the scheduling scheme also contributes to the performance gain.

As future work, we would like to study the automatic tuning method of the recursion point, non-square partitioning of the matrices and the alternative Winograd algorithms using three temporary variables.

Acknowledgments. The authors thank Professor Alexandru Nicolau and Professor Feng Shi for their inputs during discussion sessions pertaining to the present study, and the anonymous reviewers for their valuable comments on the manuscript. This work was partially supported by the National Natural Science Foundation of China under grant NSFC- 61300011.

References

1. Wolf, M.E., Lam, M.S.: A data locality optimizing algorithm. In: PLDI, pp. 30–44, New York, NY, USA (1991)
2. Strassen, V.: Gaussian elimination is not optimal. Numer. Math. **14**(3), 354–356 (1969)
3. Winograd, S.: On the multiplication of 2×2 matrices. Linear Algebra Appl. **4**(4), 381–388 (1971)
4. Ballard, G., Demmel, J., et al.: Communication-optimal parallel algorithm for Strassen's matrix multiplication. In: SPAA, pp. 193–204, New York, NY, USA (2012)
5. Park, N., Hong, B., Prasanna, V.K.: Tiling, block data layout, and memory hierarchy performance. IEEE Trans. Parallel Distrib. Syst. **14**(7), 640–654 (2003)
6. Chatterjee, S., Lebeck, A.R., et al.: Recursive array layouts and fast matrix multiplication. IEEE Trans. Parallel Distrib. Syst. **13**(11), 1105–1123 (2002)
7. Coppersmith, D., Winograd, S.: On the asymptotic complexity of matrix multiplication. In: SFCS, pp. 82–90 (1981)
8. Pan, V.Y.: Strassen's algorithm is not optimal. FOCS **19**, 166–176 (1978)
9. Coppersmith, D., Winograd, S.: Matrix multiplication via arithmetic progressions. J. Symbolic Comput. **9**(3), 251–280 (1990)
10. Stothers, A.: On the complexity of matrix multiplication. Ph.D. Thesis, U. Edinburgh (2010)
11. Williams, V.V.: Multiplying matrices faster than Coppersmith-Winograd. In: STOC, pp. 887–898, New York (2012)
12. Hunold, S., Rauber, T., Rünger, G.: Combining building blocks for parallel multi-level matrix multiplication. Parallel Comput. **34**(6), 411–426 (2008)
13. Desprez, F., Suter, F.: Impact of mixed-parallelism on parallel implementations of the Strassen and Winograd matrix multiplication algorithms. Concurr. Comput. : Pract. Exper. **16**(8), 771–797 (2004)
14. Alberto, P.D., Nicolau, A.: Adaptive Winograd's matrix multiplications. ACM Trans. Math. Softw. **36**(1), 1–23 (2009)
15. Whaley, R.C., Dongarra, J.J.: Automatically tuned linear algebra software. Tech. Rep. UT-CS-97–366, University of Tennessee (1997)
16. Goto, K., Geijn, R.V.D.: High-performance implementation of the level-3 BLAS. ACM Trans. Math. Softw. **35**(1), 1–14 (2008)
17. Smith, B.J.: Architecture and application of the HEP multiprocessor computer system. Real Time Signal Process. IV **298**, 342–349 (1981)
18. Blumofe, R.D., Leiserson, C.E.: Scheduling multithreaded computations by work stealing. J. ACM **46**(5), 720–748 (1999)
19. Polychronopoulos, C.D., Kuck, D.J.: Guided self-scheduling: a practical scheduling scheme for parallel supercomputers. IEEE Trans. Comput. **36**(12), 1425–1439 (1987)

20. Huss-Lederman, S., Jacobson, E.M., et al.: Implementation of Strassen's algorithm for matrix multiplication. In: Supercomputing, article 32 (1996)
21. Boyer, B., Dumas, J.G., et al.: Memory efficient scheduling of Strassen-Winograd's matrix multiplication algorithm. In: ISSAC, pp. 55–62, New York, NY, USA (2009)

Refactoring for Separation of Concurrent Concerns

Yang Zhang[1]([⊠]), Dongwen Zhang[1], Weixing Ji[2], and Yizhuo Wang[2]

[1] School of Information Science and Engineering, Hebei University of Science and Technology, Shijiazhuang 050000, China
{zhangyang, zdwwtx}@hebust.edu.cn
[2] School of Computer, Beijing Institute of Technology, Beijing 100081, China
{jwx, frankwyz}@bit.edu.cn

Abstract. Concurrent concerns commonly scatter among multithreaded software and tangle with core functionalities, which will make the concurrent software difficult to be maintained. Separation of concurrent concerns will benefit to improve the design of concurrent software and to manage the concurrency uniformly. This paper presents a refactoring framework to separate concurrent concerns from core functionalities using aspect-oriented approach. The refactoring framework illustrates in detail how to transform thread-related operations including threads, synchronization, barriers, and thread communications, into aspects that are designed to be reused. The refactoring framework is evaluated on SPECjbb2005 benchmark and several benchmarks in JGF benchmark suite by presenting the detailed refactoring process. Experimental results show that the framework is effective to refactoring these benchmarks.

Keywords: Refactoring · Aspect-oriented programming · Concurrency · Separation of concerns · Thread-related operations

1 Introduction

Despite recent trends towards increasing concurrent programming on multi-core/many-core computers, software engineering practices are still far behind hardware. Concurrent programming different with the traditional programming lies in that it not only requires obeying the design principle of traditional software development, but also requires high performance, freedom of data race, and better modularity.

Separation of concerns is one of the most important principles in software engineering practices. Crosscutting concerns can be described as functionalities, such as logging, authentication, and exception handling, etc. It affects the whole application and should be centralized in one position when possible. Besides concerns mentioned above, concurrency is also a typical non-functional properties and should be separated from the software. Separation of concurrent concerns will make the structure of concurrent software clearer and make the software itself easier to maintain.

In the past decade, most of researchers worked on how to separate some concerns [1, 2, 3], such as logging and authentication etc. With the prevalence of concurrent programming on multi-core processors, some works start to concern about separation

© Springer International Publishing Switzerland 2015
G. Wang et al. (Eds.): ICA3PP 2015, Part III, LNCS 9530, pp. 105–118, 2015.
DOI: 10.1007/978-3-319-27137-8_9

of concurrent concerns [4, 5, 6]. However, separation of concurrent concerns is not trivial compared to separation of other concerns. Key challenges include: (1) how to separate the concurrent concerns from the concurrent software and encapsulate into the modularity as many concurrent classes are proposed in JDK and lots of classes could implement the same function; (2) how to refactor the software without sacrificing the performance; and (3) how to ensure the software safe when performing concurrent refactoring.

To meet the challenge, this paper proposes a refactoring approach to separation of concurrent concerns. Thread, synchronization, barrier, and thread communications operations are refactored into independent aspects based on aspect-oriented programming [7]. Therefore, the concurrency is centralized to be managed uniformly, will be reused at the code position where needed, and will not appear in the core function of the final software. Experimental results show that the framework is effective when refactoring some benchmarks including JGF benchmark suite [8] and SPECjbb2005 [9].

The main contributions of this paper are as follows.

- We present two motivating examples that use the different thread API to implement the same function, which illustrates that refactoring for separation of concurrent concerns is not trivial.
- We propose a refactoring framework to guide how to separate concurrent concerns, how to encapsulate them into aspects and how to reuse these aspects.
- Refactoring benchmarks in JGF benchmark suite and SPECjbb2005 benchmark to separate concurrent concerns, and comparing the refactored program with the original multithreaded program.

The rest of this paper is organized as follows. Section 2 presents some examples to motivate the refactoring. Section 3 presents the refactoring framework. Section 4 presents the evaluation results of our refactoring. Related literatures are examined in Sect. 5 and conclusions are drawn in Sect. 6.

2   Motivating Examples

To illustrate the difficulty of our refactoring, Fig. 1 presents two Java examples where programmers may use two kinds of behavior to program thread-related operations. Each example contains a class `Test` implementing the interface `Runnable` or extending the class `Thread`, which are common approaches to create worker threads. The class `Test` of both examples includes four methods: `Test()`, `run()`, `test-Meth()`, and `main()`.

In Fig. 1, part (a) shows that the method `run()` calls the method `testMeth()` in which surrounds with synchronized blocks by taken the current object this as its monitor. The method `main()` creates two threads, then starts them, and finally calls the method `join()` to wait for the end of worker threads. Part (b) shows the totally different way to implement the same function. The method main() firstly creates an instance `barrier` of the class `CyclicBarrier` with three parties, then creates and starts two threads by passing the argument `barrier`, and finally calls the method `await()` of the object `barrier` to wait for the end of worker threads. Another difference in part (b) from part (a) is the method `testMeth()` in that this method in part (b) is modified with the modifier `synchronized`, while this method in part (a) uses synchronized block. All thread-related codes are underlined in Fig. 1.

Although two examples have different forms apparently, they implement the same function. The refactoring operations will be totally different. The difficulties of refactoring are as follows.

- We need identifying the concurrent concerns (All underlined codes).
- When refactoring these concurrent concerns, much different refactoring operations could be applied to them. The thread-related operations, especially for those operations such as synchronization and barrier, must be considered to tune carefully. Taken the barrier operation as an example, when refactoring, part (a) needs registering all threads to a set and call join() on them, while part (b) requires defining new object `barrier` and call await() on the object `barrier`.
- We need refactoring them into an independent module to manage these concurrent concerns uniformly.

```
1      public class Test implements Runnable{        public class Test extends Thread{
2                                                     CyclicBarrier barrier;
3          public Test(){                             public Test(CyclicBarrier barrier){
4                                                        this.barrier = barrier;
5          }                                           }
6          public void run(){                         public void run(){
7             synchronized(this){                        testMeth();
8                testMeth();                             try {
9             }                                             barrier.await();
10         }                                           } catch (InterruptedException
11                                                             | BrokenBarrierException e) { }
12                                                     }
13         private void testMeth(){//...}             private synchronized void testMeth(){//...}
14         public static void main(String[] args){   public static void main(String[] args){
15            Test test1 = new Test();                  CyclicBarrier barrier = new CyclicBarrier(3);
16            Thread t1 = new Thread(test1);            Thread t1 = new Test(barrier);
17            t1.start();                               t1.start();
18            Test test2 = new Test();                  Thread t2 = new Test(barrier);
19            Thread t2 = new Thread(test2);            t2.start();
20            t2.start();
21            try {                                     try {
22               t1.join(); t2.join();                     barrier.await();
23            } catch (InterruptedException e) {        } catch (InterruptedException
24            }                                                 | BrokenBarrierException e) {    }
25            //...                                     //...
26         }                                           }
27      }                                            }
                        (a)                                              (b)
```

Fig. 1. Two examples where programmers may use two kinds of behaviors to program thread-related operations

3   Refactoring Framework

In this section, we propose a refactoring framework for separation of crosscutting concerns. Section 3.1 presents the overview of our framework. Sections 3.2 and 3.3 show how to refactor these concerns using aspect-oriented programming. Section 3.4 presents some limitations of our refactoring framework.

3.1   Overview

The aim of our refactoring is to separate concurrent concerns from concurrent software to make the concurrency centralized. Hence, the concurrent software will be easy to maintain, and concurrent concerns can be managed uniformly.

The overview of refactoring framework is presented in Fig. 2. Taking the concurrent software as the input, several concurrent concerns including thread, synchronization, barrier, thread communication, are identified firstly from the core function. Then all concurrent concerns are deleted from the codes of core function, and are refactored into aspect which is an aspect-oriented programming (AOP) mechanism [7] to encapsulate them. The detailed process of our refactoring is presented in Sect. 3.3.

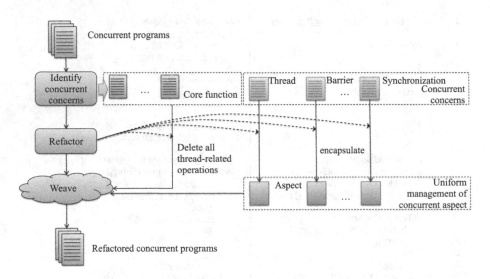

Fig. 2. The overview of refactoring framework

To make the aspect reusable, we refactor each kind of operations into a separated aspect. When applying an aspect to a class, we reuse the existing aspect by rewriting the pointcut while the advice is same. However, for synchronization operations, we handle with each pointcut case by case because the monitor of synchronization has many different usages. More details can be found in Sect. 3.3.2.

Aspects in refactoring framework are managed uniformly. The aspects handling with each kind of thread operations are centralized in a file. Some aspects could be applied to the same join points. The ordering of aspects is specified by the precedence of aspects. For example, a method run() is the entry point of thread, and it is also modified with synchronized modifier. We define two aspects at this join point, one named ThreadAspect is for thread operation, the other named LockAspect is for synchronized operation. LockAspect will be applied earlier than ThreadAspect by declaring precedence between them.

3.2 Identifying the Concurrent Concerns

Java has provided many classes and interfaces to support concurrent programming since the emergence of JDK. As shown in Sect. 2, implementing the same function may use different class and interfaces.

The kinds of concurrent concerns are shown as following.

- Thread operations. It includes create and run operations, such as start(), interrupt(), and join() etc.
- Synchronization operations. For synchronized lock, synchronized methods and blocks are commonly used, but they have different behaviors. Synchronized blocks use an explicit object lock to define the mutual exclusion region, while synchronized methods use the implicit object lock this or A.class where A represents for a class name.
- Thread communication and barrier operations, such as notify(), wait(), and barrier() etc.

3.3 Refactoring

3.3.1 Refactoring for Thread Operations

All concurrent software that written in Java are required to define threads by extending the class Thread or implementing the interface Runnable, then to start, or execute them in Executor or Fork/Join framework.

When performing the refactoring, we need to remove the extension of the class Thread or implementation the interface Runnable from the head part of the class, and then move the code of thread into an aspect. When creating the aspect, we take the head part of this method run() as the pointcut that are defined as follows:

```
pointcut pt_thread():call(public void run())&&within(A);
```

The pointcut will capture the method run() in class A, which is an option way to expose the join point. Another way to accurately expose the join point is to use annotation interface to annotate the specific method.

Advice around(), as shown in Fig. 3, is used to make the method at join point to be executed in a thread. We generate a new thread, and override the method run() (lines 5–9) in which call the method proceed()(line 7).

All created threads are required to execute a uniform action sometimes, for example, all threads arrive at some position and then go ahead together. To manage these threads, we record them in a list threads. The list adds new threads (line 11), clears all elements when the current number of threads is equal to the total number of threads (lines 2–3), or waits for their ending (lines 12–16).

```
1  void around() : pt_run(){
2    if(threads.size() == Config.NTHREAD){
3      threads.clear();
4    }
5    Thread thread = new Thread(new Runnable(){
6      public void run(){
7        proceed();
8      }
9    });
10   thread.start();
11   threads.add(thread);
12   if(threads.size() == Config.NTHREAD){
13     for(Thread t : threads){
14       try {t.join();} catch (InterruptedException e) {}
15     }
16   }
17 }
```

Fig. 3. Refactoring for thread operations

3.3.2 Refactoring for Synchronization Operations

Refactoring synchronization operations into an aspect is difficult in that synchronization in Java has two kinds of behaviors: synchronized methods and blocks. Synchronized methods put the modifier synchronized into the head part of the method, then the whole method is protected by the synchronized lock. Synchronized blocks usually start with the keyword synchronized followed by the monitor object, which can make the small part in the method to be protected by the synchronized lock. Synchronized method is easy to use and to find the monitor object, while synchronized blocks enable flexible synchronized control to small part of the whole method. When performing the refactoring, we provide two algorithms by distinguishing synchronized method with synchronized blocks.

For synchronized methods, the static one usually uses the A.class where A represents for a class as the monitor, while the non-static one uses the current object this as the monitor. When refactoring, we transform the synchronized methods into synchronized blocks. We firstly remove the modifier synchronized from the head part of the method, and then take this method as the join point to construct the aspect. The advice around() of the aspect returns the method proceed() surrounded with synchronized blocks. When refactoring the benchmarks listed in Sect. 4.2, some benchmarks have many synchronized methods to be refactored. To make the refactoring easy, we use annotation @Sync to all synchronized methods, and add it to the pointcut.

When refactoring synchronized blocks, we try to solve two key problems: (1) how to build the join point; (2) how to handle with all kinds of monitors. For problem (1), AOP cannot build join point in part of code, so we refactor each synchronized block into a method using the function Extract Method... in Eclipse, and then build the join point based on this method. For problem (2), the monitor of synchronized block has all kinds of usage. For example, we can use the current object this, local variant, parameter of the method, and reflection etc., which requires handling with them accordingly. Figure 4 presents three ways that we handle with the monitors. In advice `around()`, we firstly use the method `getTarget()` or `getArgs()` of the current join point `thisJoinPoint` to get the current object, and then obtain the monitor.

```
Object around() : pt_syncblk1() {
    Company company = (Company) thisJoinPoint.getTarget();
    synchronized(company.stopThreadsCountMonitor){
        proceed();
    }
}
```
(a)
```
void around() : pt_syncblk2() {
    Object[] objs = thisJoinPoint.getArgs();
    PrintStream out = (PrintStream) objs[0];
    synchronized(out){
        proceed();
    }
}
```
(b)
```
void around() : pt_syncblk3() {
    Object obj = thisJoinPoint.getTarget();
    synchronized(obj.getClass()){
        proceed();
    }
}
```
(c)

Fig. 4. Refactoring for synchronized operations

3.3.3   Refactoring for Other Thread-Related Operations

Other thread-related operations, such as barrier and thread communication, are refactored into a separated aspect. When refactoring barrier operations, we use a static method `barrier()` in which has no code to insert the position where the original barrier operation lies, take this method as the join point, then capture it as a pointcut, and finally call the method `await()` to implement the barrier in advice `around()`, as shown in Fig. 5.

When refactoring for the thread communication operations, the algorithm is similar to the algorithm of refactoring for synchronized blocks. We create a new method without any code, then capture it, and finally move all thread communication operations to the aspect.

```
1    pointcut pt_barrier() : call(public static void barrier()) && within(A);
2    CyclicBarrier cb = new CyclicBarrier(Config.NTHREAD);
3    void around() : pt_barrier() {
4        try {
5            cb.await();
6        } catch (InterruptedException | BrokenBarrierException e) {
7            e.printStackTrace();
8        }
9    }
```

Fig. 5. Refactoring for barrier operations

3.4 Limitations

To use the framework, refactoring is still needed to transform blocks into methods, and to apply AOP on these methods manually. We are currently working on an automatically solution to make the process automatically. Refactoring for synchronization operations still requires users to treat them case by case. Some cases may not be solved by AOP because our framework cannot cover all cases. Finally, our on-going work is trying to provide simplification solutions to apply these aspects.

4 Evaluation

In this section, we run measurements on JGF benchmark suite and SPECjbb2005 benchmark.

4.1 Setup

All evaluations are run on a Lenevo D30 workstation with two hexa-core 2.1 GHz Intel Xeon E5-2620 processors and 8 GB RAM. The CPU contains 12 cores, each of which supports two hardware threads. The total number of threads is 24. We use 64-bit linux operating system version 3.13 and JDK version 1.8.0_25. All benchmarks are run in Eclipse version 4.4.1 and its plugin ajdt version 1.8.5.

4.2 Benchmarks

To evaluate the impact of our refactoring, two benchmarks are selected to be refactored. One is JGF benchmark suits, the other is SPECjbb2005 benchmark.

JGF benchmark suit is composed of three sections: section 1, section 2 and section 3. We select several benchmarks from the section 2 and section 3. Benchmarks in the section 2 are small scientific applications, such as Crypt, Series, Sor, and Sparse-MatMulti. All benchmarks in the section 2 include three kinds of data size. According to the scale from small to large, data sizes are presented as Size-A, Size-B, and Size-C. Section 3 of JGF benchmark suit includes several large benchmarks, such as Moldyn,

Montecarlo, and Raytracer. Unlike the data sizes of benchmarks in the section 2, all benchmarks in the section 3 only have two kinds of data size: Size-A and Size-B. The detailed description of each benchmark and their data size are presented in Table 1. Note that multithreaded JGF benchmarks are used in our refactoring, so the data segmentation in each benchmark is not our work. We only refactor these benchmarks to separate concurrent concerns.

Table 1. The description and data size of JGF benchmarks

Benchmark	Description	Size-A	Size-B	Size-C
Crypt	International data encryption algorithm	3000000	20000000	50000000
Series	Fourier coefficients	10000	100000	1000000
Sor	successive over relaxation algorithm	1000	1500	2000
SparseMatMulti	Sparse matrix multiplication	250000	500000	2500000
Moldyn	N-body model	8	13	–
Montecarlo	Financial simulation application using Monte Carlo sampling techniques	10000	60000	–
Raytracer	3D ray tracer	150	500	–

SPECjbb2005 benchmark is a stand-alone Java application emulating a 3-tier system with emphasis on the middle tier. As shown in Table 2, 165 synchronized methods, 22 synchronized blocks, and 8 thread communication operations, are used in this benchmark.

Table 2. SPECjbb2005 benchmark

SPECjbb2005 concurrent components		#
Thread operations	Start	1
	Stop	1
Synchronized related operations	Methods	165
	Blocks	22
	Thread communication	8

4.3 Results

We firstly evaluate the refactoring framework on several benchmarks in JGF benchmark suite to check the effectiveness. As the framework starts with the concurrent software, we use its multi-threaded version. All benchmarks own a class implemented the interface Runnable, and encapsulate it into a thread array, the length of which is equal to the maximum number of hardware threads. We find this class, and refactor them using the approaches in Sect. 3.3.1. Nearly all benchmarks in JGF benchmarks need not synchronized operations, but benchmarks Moldyn and Raytracer use the barrier operations. We refactor them using the approaches in Sect. 3.3.3.

All benchmarks can be refactored successfully. Taken the crypt benchmark as an example, the refactoring result is shown in Fig. 6. Part (a) presents the original multi-threaded crypt benchmark. It generates thread arrays each of which owns a segment of datum and performs encrypt or decrypt operations. The join() operation is used to make the current thread to wait for the end of all worker threads. Part (b) shows the concurrent thread aspect which captures the call of method run() in class IDEATest. Part (c) presents the code of crypt benchmark after refactoring. All thread-related codes are removed to the aspect in part (b). The programmer only needs to concern about how to divide the datum and how to assign them to each potential multithreaded object. Consequently, the code after refactoring in part (c) is easier to understand and more clear than that in part (a). About 50~60 % of code length will be saved when comparing part (c) with part (a). Furthermore, thread aspect shown in part (b) can be reused in other benchmarks. All works that programmers need to refactor other benchmarks are to modify the pointcut which lies in the first line in part (b).

```
void Do() {
    Runnable thobjects[] = new Runnable[JGFCryptBench.nthreads];
    Thread th[] = new Thread[JGFCryptBench.nthreads];
    // Start the stopwatch.
    JGFInstrumentor.startTimer("Section2:Crypt:Kernel");
    // Encrypt plain1.
    for (int i = 1; i < JGFCryptBench.nthreads; i++) {
        thobjects[i] = new IDEARunner(i, plain1, crypt1, Z);
        th[i] = new Thread(thobjects[i]);
        th[i].start();
    }
    thobjects[0] = new IDEARunner(0, plain1, crypt1, Z);
    thobjects[0].run();
    for (int i = 1; i < JGFCryptBench.nthreads; i++) {
        try {
            th[i].join();
        } catch (InterruptedException e) {  }
    }
    // Decrypt.
    for (int i = 1; i < JGFCryptBench.nthreads; i++) {
        thobjects[i] = new IDEARunner(i, crypt1, plain2, DK);
        th[i] = new Thread(thobjects[i]);
        th[i].start();
    }
    thobjects[0] = new IDEARunner(0, crypt1, plain2, DK);
    thobjects[0].run();
    for (int i = 1; i < JGFCryptBench.nthreads; i++) {
        try {
            th[i].join();
        } catch (InterruptedException e) {      }
    }
    // Stop the stopwatch.
    JGFInstrumentor.stopTimer("Section2:Crypt:Kernel");
}
```

(a) Crypt benchmark before refactoring

```
void around() : call(public void run()) && within(IDEATest){
    if(threads.size() == Config.NTHREAD){
        threads.clear();
    }
    Thread thread = new Thread(new Runnable(){
        public void run(){
            proceed();
        }
    });
    thread.start();
    threads.add(thread);
    if(threads.size() == Config.NTHREAD){
        for(Thread t : threads){
            try {t.join();} catch (InterruptedException e) {  }
        }
    }
}
```

(b) Aspect

```
void Do() {
    IDEARunner thobjects[] = new IDEARunner[JGFCryptBench.nthreads];
    // Start the stopwatch.
    JGFInstrumentor.startTimer("Section2:Crypt:Kernel");
    // Encrypt plain1.
    for (int i = 0; i < JGFCryptBench.nthreads; i++) {
        thobjects[i] = new IDEARunner(i, plain1, crypt1, Z);
        thobjects[i].run();
    }
    // Decrypt.
    for (int i = 0; i < JGFCryptBench.nthreads; i++) {
        thobjects[i] = new IDEARunner(i, crypt1, plain2, DK);
        thobjects[i].run();
    }
    // Stop the stopwatch.
    JGFInstrumentor.stopTimer("Section2:Crypt:Kernel");
}
```

(c) Crypt benchmark after refactoring

Fig. 6. Refactoring for crypt benchmark

We also compare the performance of benchmarks after refactoring with the original multi-threaded benchmarks to check whether the refactoring operations have any impact on the software. We evaluate the execution time of each benchmark running on 24 threads by comparison benchmarks after refactoring with original benchmarks, as shown in Table 3. Due to the uncertain time of parallel execution, we execute each benchmark five times, and calculate the mean value.

The execution time of nearly all benchmarks after refactoring is a little more than those before refactoring. About $1 \sim 8$ % of execution time increase for almost all benchmarks except for Raytracer benchmark. This phenomenon will possibly be caused by the AOP mechanism compared to the original multithreaded implementation. We admit that the increase will be critical for some performance-critical software, but what we obtained is better modularity, more clear structure and less code length, which will improve the design of complex software. We should note that Moldyn and Raytracer benchmarks use different barrier operations before and after refactoring. Both benchmarks use self-defined barrier operations before refactoring, while they use `CyclicBarrier` in JDK after refactoring. It is the possible reason to make the execution time of Raytracer benchmark after refactoring becoming less than that before refactoring.

Table 3. The execution time of JGF benchmarks

Benchmarks	Data size	Execution time (s)	
		Refactored	Thread
Crypt	Size-A	0.14	0.13
	Size-B	0.19	0.18
	Size-C	0.34	0.32
Series	Size-A	0.46	0.43
	Size-B	2.63	2.63
	Size-C	48.19	47.26
Sor	Size-A	0.36	0.34
	Size-B	0.40	0.37
	Size-C	0.54	0.53
SparseMatMulti	Size-A	0.1	0.09
	Size-B	0.22	0.21
	Size-C	0.56	0.53
Moldyn	Size-A	0.64	0.64
	Size-B	3.31	3.26
Montecarlo	Size-A	0.58	0.53
	Size-B	2.12	1.98
Raytracer	Size-A	0.39	0.43
	Size-B	1.94	2.04

For SPECjbb2005 benchmark, we refactor thread-related methods `start()` and `stop()` into an aspect. Like the thread Aspect in JGF benchmarks, the new created thread is added to the list `threads`. Furthermore, the thread is removed from the list when stopping the thread. Besides the thread operations, this benchmark also includes 165 synchronized methods, 22 synchronized blocks, and 8 thread communication operations, using which we can evaluate how the framework handles with synchronization-related operations. We use the annotation `@Sync` to tag all synchronized methods, and remove `synchronized` from the method's modifiers. For synchronized blocks and thread communication operations, this benchmark adopts many kinds of objects as their monitors. We refactor synchronized blocks into methods and construct each pointcut case by case. Refactoring synchronized blocks into methods will not help the decrease of code length, but help to be handled with the aspects. All synchronized operations are refactored successfully.

5 Related Works

5.1 Refactoring for Concurrency

Recently, there are a lot of works on refactoring programs to enhance their concurrency. Dig et al. [10] presented a tool `concurrencer` that can refactor sequential Java code into concurrent code by converting int to `AtomicInteger`, converting `Hashmap` to `ConcurrentHashMap`, and converting recursion to `Fork/Join` framework. Dig also presented a summary about the refactoring approach to parallelism [11]. Schafer et al. [12] presented how correctly refactoring of concurrent Java code. They prove precise correctness results based on the Java memory model. Brown et al. [13] presented paraphrasing to guide how to generate parallel programs using refactoring. Some works are concerned about refactoring specific aspects, such as loop [14], synchronization [15], and flow-based application [16].

5.2 Separation of Concurrent Concern

Separation of concerns has long been a primary concern in the literature. It is one of the most important design rules in software engineering. AOP [7] is proposed by Kiczales to support the separation and the encapsulation to an aspect. In the past decades, most of works are concentrated on logging, exception handling, and safe etc. [17]. Concurrent concerns starts to be separated from the core code in recent years [5]. AOP not only benefits the design of software, but also helps improve the performance and facilitate the software development [18, 19]. Vidala and Marcosa [3] defined a process that assists the developer to transform an object-oriented system into an aspect-oriented one. They use association rules and Markov models to improve the assistance in accomplishing some of the tasks of this process. With the prevalence of multi- and many- core, how to separate of concurrent concerns are becoming the research hot spot. Soares et al. [20] proposed simple aspect software architecture as a guideline to modularize the synchronization. Difference from their works, we refactor not only synchronization operations, but also thread, barrier, and thread communication operations.

6 Conclusion

Concurrent concerns, as the main crosscutting concerns in multithreaded programs, should be separated from the core function. Separation of concurrent concerns will make the maintenance of concurrent software easy. This paper presents a framework for manually refactoring thread-related operations including thread, synchronization, barrier, and thread communication, based on aspect-oriented technologies. The refactoring framework is evaluated on several benchmarks in JGF benchmark suite and SPECjbb2005 benchmark. Experimental results show that the framework is effective to refactoring these benchmarks.

Future works will include that we will try to automatically transform concurrent concerns into aspects, and developing an aspect-oriented reuse library to support parallel programming.

Acknowledgments. This work is partially supported by National Nature Science Foundation of China under grant No. 61440012 and No. 61300120, the top-notch young talent Foundation of Hebei Province of China under Grant No. BJ2014023, and Nature Science Foundation of Hebei Province under Grant No. F2012208016. The authors also gratefully acknowledge the insightful comments and suggestions of the reviewers, which have improved the presentation.

References

1. Rashid, A.: Metalevel Architectures and Separation of Crosscutting Concerns, pp. 231–249. Springer, Berlin, Heidelberg (2001)
2. Ossher, H., Tarr, P.: Using multidimensional separation of concerns to (re)shape evolving software. Commun. ACM **44**(10), 43–50 (2001)
3. Vidala, S.A., Marcosa, C.A.: Toward automated refactoring of crosscutting concerns into aspects. J. Syst. Softw. **86**, 1482–1497 (2013)
4. Santosa, A.E., Ramirez, R.: A framework for separation of concerns in concurrent programming. In: International Computer Software and Applications Conference, pp. 619–628. IEEE Computer Society (2007)
5. Netinant, P.: Separation of concerns for multithreads object-oriented programming. In: 6th International Conference on Electrical Engineering/Electronics, Computer, Telecommunications and Information Technology, pp. 718–721 (2009)
6. Sobral, J.L.: Incrementally developing parallel applications with AspectJ. In: International Parallel and Distributed Processing Symposium, p. 95. IEEE Computer Society (2006)
7. Kiczales, G., Lamping, J., Mendhekar, A., et al.: Aspect-oriented programming. In: Ecoop97 — Object Oriented Programming (1997)
8. Smith, L.A., Bull, J.M., Obdrizalek, J.: A parallel Java grande benchmark suite. In: ACM/IEEE Conference of Supercomputing, p. 6. IEEE (2001)
9. Adamson, A., Dagastine, D., Sarne, S.: SPECjbb2005—ayear in the life of a benchmark. In: Proceedings of 2007 SPEC Benchmark Workshop, pp. 151–160. Austin, USA (2007)
10. Dig, D., Marrero, J., Ernst, M.D.: Refactoring sequential Java code for concurrency via concurrent libraries. In: Proceedings of IEEE 31st International Conference on Software Engineering, pp. 397–407 (2009)
11. Dig, D.: A refactoring approach to parallelism. Softw. IEEE **28**(1), 17–22 (2011)
12. Schafer, M., Dolby, J., Sridharan, M., Torlak, E., Tip, F.: Correct refactoring of concurrent Java code. In: Proceedings of 24th European Conference of Object-Oriented Programming, pp. 225–249. Maribor, Slovenia (2010)
13. Brown, C., Hammond, K., Danelutto, M., Kilpatrick, P., Schöner, H., Breddin, T.: Paraphrasing: generating parallel programs using refactoring. In: Boer, F.S., Bonsangue, M. M., Beckert, B., Damiani, F. (eds.) FMCO 2011. LNCS, vol. 7542, pp. 237–256. Springer, Heidelberg (2012)

14. Larsen, P., Ladelsky, R., Lidman, J., McKee, S.A., Karlsson, S., Zaks, A.: Parallelizing more loops with compiler guided refactoring. In: Proceedings of 42nd International Conference on Parallel Processing, pp. 410–419 (2012)
15. Tao, B.X., Qian, J.: Refactoring Java concurrent programs based on synchronization requirement analysis. In: IEEE International Conference on Software Maintenance and Evaluation, pp. 361–370. IEEE Computer Society (2014)
16. Chen, N., Johnson, R.E.: JFlow: Practical refactorings for flow-based parallelism. In: IEEE/ACM 28th International Conference on Automated Software Engineering (ASE), pp. 202–212, 11–15 November 2013
17. Tran, T., Steffen, M.: Design issues in concurrent object-oriented languages and observability. In: 2011 Third International Conference on Knowledge and Systems Engineering (2011)
18. Zhang, Y.: Java Parallel Programming. Tsinghua University Press, Beijing (2015)
19. Zhang, Y., Ji, W.: A scalable method-level parallel library and its improvement. J. Supercomputing **61**(3), 1154–1167 (2012)
20. Soares, S., Borba, P., Lima, R.: Concurrency control modularization with aspect-oriented programming. In: International Computer Software and Applications Conference, pp. 295–300. IEEE Computer Society (2007)

Exploiting Scalable Parallelism for Remote Sensing Analysis Models by Data Transformation Graph

Zhenchun Huang[1]([⊠]) and Guoqing Li[2]

[1] Department of Computer Science and Technology, Tsinghua University,
Beijing 100084, China
huangzc@tsinghua.edu.cn
[2] Institute of Remote Sensing and Digital Earth, CAS, Beijing 100094, China
ligq@radi.ac.cn

Abstract. According to the great hunger in performance capability and scalability for remote sensing analysis models, it is important to exploit scalable parallelism for remote sensing data analysis models. In this paper, a method named data transformation graph (shortly DTG) is introduced, which describes an analysis model by transformations among data items. DTG can be used to study the solvability and performance of analysis models. Taking global drought detection as an example, its execution and optimization are studied carefully by DTG, and some methods are proposed for accelerating remote sensing data analysis models. At last, a distributed data-intensive computing test system is built based on Robinia, and global drought detection application is implemented for performance evaluation. The test result shows that DTG based parallelization and optimization improves the performance with high efficiency evidently, and DTG is valuable to study and optimize remote sensing data analysis models for higher performance in distributed and parallel computing environments.

Keywords: Scalable parallelism · Remote sensing analysis models · Data transformation graph · Global drought detection · Data-intensive computing

1 Introduction

Remote sensing data are usually processed by analysis models for knowledge discovery. In the last decades, more satellites with higher resolution sensors were launched, and more data about the earth are captured every day. At the same time, more large-scale and high-temporal-resolution remote sensing data analysis models are proposed for great challenge applications such as inversion of global land surface parameters and emergency response for disaster. They cause great hunger in performance capability and scalability for spatial cyber-infrastructure to process and analyze remote sensing data. To run remote sensing data analysis models faster, parallelization is the best way.

© Springer International Publishing Switzerland 2015
G. Wang et al. (Eds.): ICA3PP 2015, Part III, LNCS 9530, pp. 119–133, 2015.
DOI: 10.1007/978-3-319-27137-8_10

Parallelism can be exploited in many ways. High Performance Fortran (HPF) [1] and OpenMP [2] exploit parallelism by employing many processors or processor cores to process different parts of a single array; MPMD programming with PVM [3] or MPI [4] extends the same idea to a local-area distributed setting such as a cluster. Supported by distributed infrastructures such as grid or cloud, data-intensive applications may exploit parallelism by running coarse-grain subtasks on geographically distributed computing nodes concurrently. In fact, most parallel methods decompose a data analysis job on tremendous amount of remote sensing data into many subtasks, which deal with a piece of data or a step of analysis model independently. The more subtasks can be processed concurrently, the higher performance and better scalability it can achieve.

Loosely coupled coarse-gain parallel applications are more extensible and scalable. Otherwise, remote sensing data are often geographically distributed in spatial agents around the world. To analyze these data from different agents by a universal model, distributed applications must execute on heterogeneous computing nodes for better performance. But, it is hard to create scalable applications for remote sensing data analysis models, especially for beginners who have not much knowledge and experiment in programming for distributed context. So, methods and toolkits which can help users study, develop and optimize distributed applications are very valuable.

The paper is organized as follows. After some related work about exploiting scalable parallelism for data analysis models are discussed in Sect. 2, Data transformation graph, which tries to describe and study scientific applications by their data dependency, is introduced in Sect. 3 first. Taking global drought detection application for example, Sect. 4 studies some problems in the parallelization and optimization of remote sensing analysis models. In Sects. 5 and 6, experiments of parallel implementations on distributed scientific computing framework named Robinia are reported, and test results are discussed. We conclude in Sect. 7 at last.

2   Related Work

There has already been a lot of work in the parallel community for data-intensive processing frameworks. Condor is an early example of such distributed systems which can schedule parallel jobs on computing nodes in a "Beowulf" cluster. [5] Grid infrastructures such as Data Grid/EGEE are built to enable individuals or groups of users the ability to access, transfer and process large amounts of geographically distributed data for research purposes. Based on grid computing, projects such as ESA G-POD [6] and GEO Gfarm [7] are proposed for users to store and process earth observation data more extensible and on-demand. In the recent years, more models and frameworks are proposed for parallel processing, such as Google's MapReduce [8].

MapReduce provides a good abstraction of group-by-aggregation operations over a cluster of machines. Programmer provides a map function for grouping and a reduce function for aggregation, and the run-time system achieves parallelism by partitioning the data and processing different partitions on multiple machines concurrently. Apache Hadoop [9], an open-source implementation for MapReduce, is widely used for delivering highly-available services for spatial applications which process remote sensing data parallel on top of a cluster of computers [10]. However, this model has its limitations. Developers are forced to map their analysis models to the map-reduce model, and this mapping is odd for most spatial applications.

Furthermore, there are more exploration projects on parallel processing models, services and infrastructures, such as Yahoo!'s PigLatin [11], Microsoft's Dryad [12] and SCOPE [13], Google's GFS [14], Big Table [15], Dremel [16], and Spanner [17]. More achievements are also introduced for parallel programming on remote sensing data, e.g. the Matsu Project which provide a cloud-based on-demand disaster assessment capability through satellite image comparisons [18], and parallel framework for processing massive spatial data with a Split-and-Merge paradigm proposed by Guan [19], and so on. The Global Earth Observation System of Systems(GEOSS), which is managed by the Group on Earth Observations (GEO), an international collaboration of many organizations that produce and consume Earth observation data, also deploys an international, federated infrastructure for sharing of Earth observation data products worldwide.

But, it is not enough for remote sensing data analysis applications. For example, data dependencies are too complex to be described by group-by-aggregation operations, so that developing parallel remote sensing data analysis applications in MapReduce model is often hard and causes performance loss. Furthermore, it is difficult to study, implement and optimize a remote sensing data analysis model because of the lack of domain-specific description and analysis toolkits. Hence, data transformation graph, a method which can describe and optimize scientific applications by data dependency analysis, is followed.

3   Data Transformation Graph

Discovering knowledge is the goal of most scientific applications, including remote sensing data analysis applications. Scientific applications often take mass observed data as input, process them by mathematic models, and get result data as output for further research. In the traditional way, applications usually adopt process-based description model, in which an application is regarded as a "process" assembled by process steps or activities, and a "control flow" describes the executing order among the process steps or activities.

Although the process-based description model is popular, there are still shortcomings for scientific applications. For example, scientist must describe data-centric scientific theories by process-based models first, and exploit the parallelism of analysis models manually. It is difficult for beginners in programming, and careless implementations may cause serious performance loss. For better description and analysis of scientific processing applications, Data Transformation Graph based description model is proposed. In this model, application is a graph which describes "whats the result" instead of "how to get the result". Following is the definition (suppose d_i is a data item):

Definition 1. *Application* $= < D, D_T, T, E >$
$D_T = \{d_i \mid d_i$ *is one of the result data items*$\}$
$D = \{d_i \mid d_i$ *is a data item used*$\}$
$T = \{t_i \mid t_i$ *is one of the data transformation elements*$\}$
$E = \{d_i \rightarrow t_j \mid d_i$ *is input of* $t_j\} \bigcup \{ t_j \rightarrow d_i \mid d_i$ *is output of* $t_j \}$

Regard d_i and t_i as vertices, and e_i as edges, an application can be plotted as a directed graph. To tell data vertices from transformation vertices, circles are used to identify data vertices, and blocks for transformation elements (shown in Fig. 1(a)). Data transformation vertices may vary greatly in their grain size. It may be anything from a fine-grained "add" instruction to a coarse-grained image converting task. Different from "variable" in the classical application descriptions, data vertices in DTG are data items with definite values, although these values are unknown before they are "solved" by their data dependencies. The followings are some propositions about data transformation graph.

Proposition 1. *If DTG of an application is a connected directed acyclic graph, and all transformation vertices can accomplish in limited time, it halts in limited time.*

If there is a cycle in the data transformation graph, at least one of the data items will depend on itself directly or indirectly, the data item will never be solved. So, if an application halts, its data dependency graph should be a directed acyclic graph with finite vertices. Supposing that all transformation vertices have at least one incoming edge (input data), then all vertices with no incoming edge are data vertices. They are called "original vertices" or "start-up data items" (the slash back-grounded nodes in Fig. 1(a), called D_O). If all original nodes are assigned, all nodes in D can be calculated by data transformations, the application will accomplish in limited time.

Proposition 2. *Supposing that* $f(t_i)$ *is the execution time for data transformation* t_i, *make the length of path between data vertices* $L_P = \sum f(t_i)$, *where* t_i *are data transformation vertices on the path* P *which connects data vertices. If* P_1, P_2, ..., P_n *are all paths connecting data vertices* d_i *and* d_j, *the distance between* d_i *and* d_j *is defined as* $g(d_i, d_j) = max(L_P)$, *which is the maximum length of all paths connecting data vertices* d_i *and* d_j. *As the result, the execution time of an application equals* $max(\{g \mid g = g(d_i, d_j), d_i \in D_O, d_j \in D_T\})$, *which is the maximum length of all paths among data vertices in DTG. This path is called* **key path.** *(the grey part in Fig. 1(b)).*

Ideally, execution time of an application depends on topology of DTG and execution time of data transformation vertices only. But, because data transformation vertices often have to compete for limited resources, concurrent execution among data transformation vertices is restrictive. By adding edges between vertex T_i and vertex T_j which runs just before T_i on the same computing resource (dashed line in Fig. 1(c)), enhanced DTG can be used to describe a definite scheduling scheme on a distributed application.

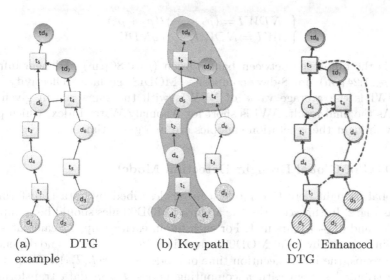

(a)   DTG example   (b) Key path   (c)   Enhanced DTG

Fig. 1. Data transformation graph

If execution time of each data transformation vertex on each computing node can be predicted, enhanced DTG can be used to minimize the execution time of a distributed application by traversing all possible scheduling schemes. But, when an application with n data transformation vertices runs on a distributed system with m computing nodes, there are n^m possible scheduling schemes to be traversed. It is impossible to optimize the execution of analysis models by this scheduling algorithm, unless there is a approximation algorithm which can find sub-optimal scheduling schemes in acceptable time.

Compared with the "data flow" or "information flow" based programming paradigms such as StreaMIT [20] or LUSTRE [21], DTG focuses on describing and optimizing scientific data analysis applications instead of streaming applications (StreaMIT) or reactive systems (LUSTRE). Furthermore, DTG can be used to describe and optimize applications in different levels. A data vertex in DTG can be a machine word, a matrix, a file, or a logical data item distributed on many hosts with a universal ID; a data transformation vertex also can be an instruction, a fragment of codes, or even a distributed task.

4   Remote Sensing Analysis Models and Global Drought Detection

Most remote sensing analysis models try to discover information and knowledge by processing archived remote sensing big data which are large scale in time and space. As an example, global drought detection application implemented by us processes the MODIS Surface-Reflectance Product (MOD09) for Normal Differential Water Index (shortly NDWI) brought up by Gao [22]:

$$\begin{cases} NDWI = (\rho_2 - \rho_5)/(\rho_2 + \rho_5) \\ AWI = NDWI_i - avgNDWI \end{cases}$$

NDWI is the difference between bands green ($\rho_2, 0.86\,\mu$m) and near-infra-red (NIR, $\rho_5, 1.24\,\mu$m) in 8-day composite MODIS surface reflectivity data. AvgNDWI is the average value of NDWIs with the same tile in given time scope. As the final result, AWI is short for Anomaly Water Index, which points out how drought the vegetation canopies are in a given time.

4.1 DTG of Global Drought Detection Model

The global drought detection model can be described by data transformation graph as Fig. 2. In this scenario, the archived MOD09 files should be grouped by their tiles and day-of-years first. For each file in each group, T_p calculates AWI files as final results by input MOD09 image files. Because there is no dependency among groups, the ideal execution time of model is $max(L(T_{pi}))$. When it runs on a distributed system with n computing nodes, $k * m$ data transformation vertices will compete for n computing resources. A possible enhanced DTG is shown in Fig. 3 as an example.

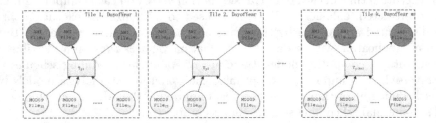

Fig. 2. DTG of global drought detection model

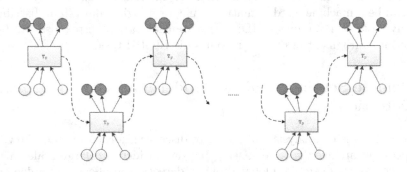

Fig. 3. Enhanced DTG of global drought detection model

In Fig. 3, the enhanced DTG are partitioned into n queues $(Q_1, Q_2, ..., Q_n)$ of data transformation vertices which are scheduled to the same computing node. Key path is the longest queue and execution time is $max(L(Q_i))$. Scheduler can balance load among computing nodes and shorten key path by Algorithm 1, an adaptive algorithm.

Algorithm 1. Adaptive schedule algorithm for global drought detection

---

1: **while** *readyTaskList* is not empty and *doingTaskList* is not empty **do**
2:   **if** *idelNodeList* is not empty **then**
3:     *readyNode* ← pop first node from *idleNodeList*
4:     **if** *readyTaskList* is not empty **then**
5:       schedule first task from *readyTaskList* to *readyNode*
6:     **else**
7:       **if** *doingTaskList* is not empty **then**
8:         schedule last task from *doingTaskList* to *readyNode*
9:       **end if**
10:    **end if**
11:   **end if**
12: **end while**

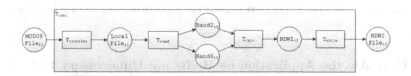

Fig. 4. Sub-graph of T_{ndwi} and T_{awi}

4.2   Optimizing by Nearby Computing and Smart Data Service

When we focus out interest on the detail of T_{ndwi} and T_{awi}, it is found that these vertices can be re-plotted as a detailed sub-graph shown in Fig. 4. In this graph, time cost of T_{ndwi} is:

$$f(T_{ndwi}) = f(T_{transfer}) + f(T_{read}) + f(T_{calc}) + f(T_{write})$$

$f(T_{transfer})$ is time cost for transferring MOD09 files, the main part of costs. Because the model codes are usually much smaller than data files, to migrate model codes towards where data files store should be a good idea for reducing $f(T_{transfer})$. If there are powerful computing resources "near" the storage nodes where remote sensing data files are archived, analysis models can be on-demand deployed on the "nearby" computing resources for higher performance. It is called **Nearby Computing**. Furthermore, if the data files are organized and distributed carefully, data files to be processed together are stored as close as possible, the time cost of data transfer will be much less. In extremity, when all data to be processed together are stored and processed in the same node, $f(T_{transfer})$ will be cut down to 0.

When something prevent the model codes from migrating to archived data, the time cost of data transfer must be reduced by less data transfer. Data transfer can be cut down by carefully studies on analysis models. For example, only 3 bands (ρ_2, ρ_5, and ρ_{state}) are useful for the global drought detection analysis model, about 75 % of the MOD09 data file transferred is unnecessary. But, we have to stand the 75 % waste in current remote sensing data infrastructure, in which image file is the atomic unit for remote sensing data service. If next generation remote sensing data infrastructure is smart enough to transfer data object such as band or block instead of data file as the atomic service unit, the unnecessary transfer can be prevented, and the data transfer time $f(T_{transfer})$ will be almost quartered. And the DTG in Fig. 4 will be re-constructed to that shown in Fig. 5.

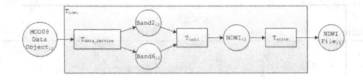

Fig. 5. T_{ndwi} and T_{awi} in the next generation remote sensing data infrastructure

4.3   Optimize the Application by Reducing Unnecessary I/O

Unnecessary I/O operations are wasting time, too. [23] shows that time for I/O is dozens of times than for calculating. We run a similar test which process 722 GB MOD09 data files on a computing node with Intel i3 3220 3.30 GHz CPU, 8 GB main memory and 1TB 7200 rpm SATA HDD. The experiment shows that time ratio between I/O and calculating is about 90:1. So, global drought detection application can run much faster if its I/O overhead can be reduced by careful optimization.

Considering the processing on MOD09 files with the same tile and Day-OfYear, DTG in Fig. 5 can be re-plotted as Fig. 6(a) in detail. In Fig. 6(a), data vertices named $NDWI_i$ and $avgNDWI$ need not be hibernated, the gray T_{read} and T_{write} vertices are unnecessary. These unnecessary I/O operations can be skipped by keeping data in main memory, so that the model can be optimized to DTG shown in Fig. 6(b). The same test shows that time ratio between I/O and calculating falls down to about 73:1, and run time is also reduced.

Furthermore, studies on data transformation vertices T_{ndwi}, T_{avg} and T_{awi} show that these vertices are point-to-point calculations. For data transformation vertices like T_{ndwi}, it is a good idea to accelerate the calculations by fine-grain data parallel frameworks such as CUDA.

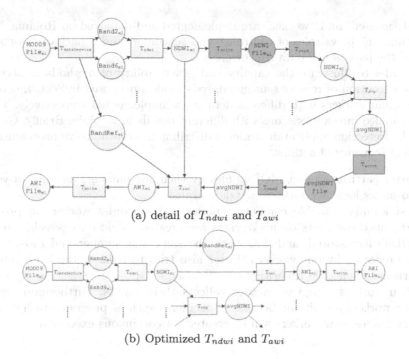

(a) detail of T_{ndwi} and T_{awi}

(b) Optimized T_{ndwi} and T_{awi}

Fig. 6. Reducing I/O from T_{ndwi} and T_{awi}

As a summary, some methods discovered from data transformation graph to accelerate execution of remote sensing analysis models are listed:

1. Nearby Computing and optimized remote sensing data storage for reducing time cost of data transfer;
2. Next generation data infrastructure which takes remote sensing data objects as atomic service unit for less unnecessary data transfer;
3. Careful optimization to cut down unnecessary I/O, data transfer, synchronous, and other operations;
4. Fine-grain parallelism in the model and implement it by high-performance processing units such as GPU or FPGA.

5   Implementations

According to discussions above, a Global Drought Detection application is implemented, optimized and evaluated based on Robinia, an open source distributed processing framework for data-intensive scientific computing. As a parallel processing framework for scientific applications, Robinia tries to exploits parallelism for processing remote sensing data distributed among institutes around the world. A center-less symmetric architecture is employed, in which nodes are independent and coequal for cooperation, no matter what they are desktop computers, high-performance clusters, or super computers. Two kinds of executors named "master" and "worker" are implemented and deployed on Robinia. The only "master" plays roles of controller and scheduler, and a pack of "workers" process the partitioned data concurrently.

In order to illustrate the validity and practicability of methods to accelerate the execution of remote sensing analysis models proposed in Sect. 4, several masters and workers with different details are implemented respectively. They are assembled into applications with different details in Robinia. Briefly, Global Drought Detection application achieves distributed data-intensive processing by following sequence of actions.

1. Master partitions input MOD09 files by their tile numbers and day-of-years into pieces logically without any data transfer.
2. Master finds available computing nodes and schedules workers to process partitioned data sets on it. Workers are created as close as possible to the MOD09 files stored, and data with the same tile number and day-of-year are processed by one worker. Master also tries to balance the loads among workers by schedule Algorithm 1.
3. When workers complete, master collects their results. Furthermore, when some workers are off-line because of accidents such as program crash or network failure, new workers will be created for continuous execution.

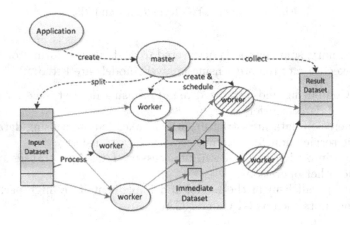

Fig. 7. Overview of implementation

Two different worker executors are implemented to process local or remote MOD09 data sets. One of the workers is based on the original algorithm shown in Fig. 6(a), and the other is optimized according to the analysis in Sect. 4. Both workers read and write MOD09 files by Java HDF Interface (JHI) produced by the HDF Group which can operate on local HDF files [24] (Fig. 7).

At the same time, two different master executors are implemented, one of them schedules worker executors on only one computing node, and the other schedules workers on all computing nodes in Robinia under the guidelines of data transformation graph for higher performance. Based on different masters, serial or parallel applications can be assembled. When "parallel master" schedules workers on all nodes, MOD09 data files are already stored on all nodes for "nearby computing", and the AWI files are left on nodes for future processing or visualization.

6   Experiments and Discussion

To make the test experiments closer to the reality, global drought detection applications are deployed and evaluated on a test system with four computing nodes connected by Gigabit ethernet, and the 4 PC nodes with different hardware and software configuration still provide other services such as database connection and HTTP service while the evaluation is running. These nodes are configured as Table 1.

Table 1. Configurations of nodes in test system

No	Processor	Memory	Disk	OS
1	i3 32203.30 GHz	8 GB	1 TB	Windows 7×64
2	i3 5302.93 GHz	4 GB	1 TB	Windows 7×86
3	Core2 94002.66 GHz	8 GB	2 TB	Windows 7×64
4	i5 45703.20 GHz	16 GB	4 TB	Windows 7×64

To benchmark performance and scalability of different implementations of the analysis model, an evaluation with 722 GB test data set which contains MOD09 data productions on the same four days in different seasons of 10 years is run serially on each node first.

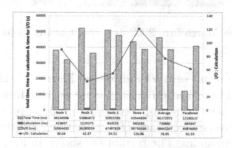

Fig. 8. Benchmark result of serial and parallel applications with original algorithm

In the result shown in Fig. 8, it can be found that node 1 and 4 accomplish the test much faster than node 2 and 3. It is in consonance with hardware configurations of the nodes. Furthermore, the not-so-good performance of node 4 is caused by collisions with more extra services deployed on node 4 such as database connections and file services.

Assuming that computation speed of nodes is stable; elapsed time for the evaluation of parallel application on 4 nodes should be the harmonic mean of elapsed times of serial application on all nodes, if overheads are ignored.

$$t = \frac{1}{\sum \frac{1}{t_i}} = 11361147.23(\text{ms}) \tag{1}$$

The result of evaluation on four nodes is also shown in Fig. 8 with tag paralleled. Comparing with the theoretical time of parallel application, the efficiency of parallelization is $11361147.23 \div 12190515 \approx 93.20\%$, and the equivalent speedup is about 3.728 for four computing nodes. The nearly linear speedup shows that parallel processing on multi computing nodes can accelerate remote sensing analysis models such as global drought detect very much, especially for those scenes that remote sensing data to be processed are distributed in advance. If some data files are not distributed well for nearby computing, the overhead of extra data transfer may slow down the execution.

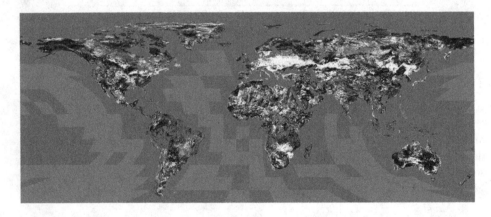

Fig. 9. AWI indexes on March 5th, 2002 as a result of the global drought detection

Figure 9 shows the result of AWI indexes on March 5th, 2002 as an example. All results from parallel application are the same as them from serial application.

For the optimized algorithm proposed in Sect. 4.3, more tests with optimized algorithm which reduces unnecessary I/O operations are run on the same test data set and computing nodes. The results are shown in Fig. 10(a), and comparisons between optimized and original algorithms are shown in Fig. 10(b). The results show that the ratio between I/O and calculating is lower obviously. For example, the ratio falls down from 120.86 to 86.94 on node 4, and leads to an outstanding performance improvement by about 17.49%. Even on average, the

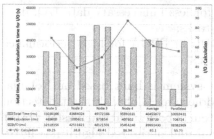

(a) Optimized analysis algorithm

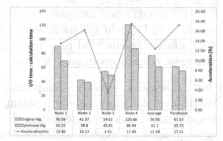

(b) Comparisons between optimized and original algorithms

Fig. 10. Benchmark results

elapsed time is also shortened for about 12.38 %. It is a powerful evidence for the optimized algorithm.

At last, the parallel application with optimized processing algorithm is evaluated on all four nodes, and the results are shown in Fig. 10(a), (b) with tag "paralleled". By the results in Fig. 10(b), the efficiency to the theoretical value calculated by elapsed times for serial applications on all nodes is 9868759 ÷ 10092431 ≈ 97.78 %, and the equivalent speedup is about 3.91 for four computing nodes. Compared with the parallel application with original algorithm shown in Fig. 10(b), the application with optimized algorithm is about 17.21 % faster than that with original algorithm. The execution time is reduced for 2098084 milliseconds, about 35 min are saved from 203 min. It illustrates the validity of optimized algorithm, nearby computing, and further, optimizations based on data transformation graph.

7 Conclusion

In order to study and optimize remote sensing data analysis models, data transformation graph is introduced first in this paper, which describes data analysis models by dependencies and transformations among their data items. If DTG of an analysis model is a directed acyclic graph with limited vertices, and all data transformation vertices finish in limited time, the analysis model can accomplish in limited time which equals the length of key path at the minimum.

Then, DTG is used to study global drought detection model as an example. The model is optimized by making the process parallel and reducing overheads. Due to the experiments from the example, some methods for accelerating the execution of remote sensing data analysis models are proposed below, which may be future work for better performance of remote sensing data analysis model.

1. On demand remote sensing data service with remote sensing data objects (such as a band or a polygon) as its atomic service unit instead of files;
2. Nearby processing, optimized remote sensing data storage pattern, and adaptive task scheduling for reducing overhead of data transfer;

3. Carefully optimized analysis algorithms for less unnecessary data I/O, data transfer and synchronization among sub-tasks;
4. Fine-grain data parallel processing by GPU or FPGA for high performance traversal operations in analysis models; etc.

At last, a scalable scientific computing test system is built based on Robinia, a distributed data-intensive computing middleware. Global drought detection applications are also implemented on the system in both serial and master-worker parallel processing models with both original and optimized algorithms introduced in Sect. 4. The result of tests on the four-node realistic test system shows that the performance of global drought detection model is improved about 10 % by the algorithm optimization, and parallel efficiencies of both parallel applications are 93 % at least. The experiments indicate that data transformation graph is valuable for study and optimization on remote sensing data analysis models for higher performance in distributed and parallel computing environments.

References

1. Loveman, D.B.: High performance fortran. IEEE Parallel Distrib. Technol.: Syst. Appl. **1**(1), 25–42 (1993)
2. Dagum, L., Menon, R.: OpenMP: an industry standard API for shared-memory programming. IEEE Comput. Sci. Eng. **5**(1), 46–55 (1998)
3. Geist, A. (ed.): PVM: Parallel Virtual Machine: A Users' Guide and Tutorial for Networked Parallel Computing. The MIT Press, Cambridge (1994)
4. Gropp, W., Lusk, E., Skjellum, A.: Using MPI: Portable Parallel Programming with the Message Passing Interface, vol. 1. MIT Press, Cambridge (1999)
5. Thain, D., Tannenbaum, T., Livny, M.: Distributed computing in practice: the condor experience. Concurr. Comput.: Prac. Exp. **17**(2–4), 323–356 (2005)
6. Cossu, R., Bally, P., Colin, O., Fusco, L.: ESA grid processing on demand for fast access to earth observation data and rapid mapping of flood events. European Geosciences Union General Assembly (2008)
7. Sekiguchi, S., Tanaka, Y., Kojima, I., Yamamoto, N., Yokoyama, S., Tanimura, Y., et al.: Design principles and IT overviews of the GEO Grid. IEEE Syst. J. **2**(3), 374–389 (2008)
8. Dean, J., Ghemawat, S.: MapReduce: simplified data processing on large clusters. In: Proceedings of the 6th Symposium on Operating Systems Design and Implementation (OSDI), pp. 137–150, December 2004
9. White, T.: Hadoop: The Definitive Guide. O'Reilly Media Inc., Sebastopol (2012)
10. Lee, C.A., Gasster, S.D., Plaza, A., Chang, C.I., Huang, B.: Recent developments in high performance computing for remote sensing: a review. IEEE J. Sel. Top. Appl. Earth Obs. Remote Sens. **4**(3), 508–527 (2011)
11. Olston, C., Reed, B., Srivastava, U., Kumar, R., Tomkins, A.: Pig latin: a not-so-foreign language for data. In: Proceedings of the 2008 ACM SIGMOD International Conference on Management of Data, pp. 1099–1110. ACM (2008)
12. Isard, M., Budiu, M., Yu, Y., Birrell, A., Fetterly, D.: Dryad: distributed data-parallel programs from sequential building blocks. ACM SIGOPS Oper. Syst. Rev. **41**(3), 59–72 (2007)

13. Chaiken, R., Jenkins, B., Larson, P.Å., Ramsey, B., Shakib, D., Weaver, S., Zhou, J.: SCOPE: easy and efficient parallel processing of massive data sets. Proc. VLDB Endow. **1**(2), 1265–1276 (2008)
14. Ghemawat, S., Gobioff, H., Leung, S.T.: The google file system. ACM SIGOPS Oper. Syst. Rev. **37**(5), 29–43 (2003)
15. Chang, F., et al.: Bigtable: a distributed storage system for structured data. In: OSDI 2006, pp. 205–218 (2006)
16. Melnik, S., Gubarev, A., Long, J.J., Romer, G., Shivakumar, S., Tolton, M., Vassilakis, T.: Dremel: interactive analysis of web-scale datasets. Proc. VLDB Endow. **3**(1–2), 330–339 (2010)
17. Corbett, J.C., Dean, J., Epstein, M., Fikes, A., Frost, C., Furman, J.J., et al.: Spanner: google's globally-distributed database. In: Proceedings of the 10th USENIX Symposium on Operating System Design and Implementation (OSDI 2012), pp. 251–264 (2012)
18. Mandl, D.: Matsu: an elastic cloud connected to a sensorweb for disaster response. In: Workshop on Cloud Computing for Spacecraft Operations, Ground System Architectures Workshop (GSAW), 2 March 2011
19. Guan, X., Wu, H., Li, L.: A parallel framework for processing massive spatial data with a SplitCandCMerge paradigm. Trans. GIS **16**(6), 829–843 (2012)
20. Thies, W., Karczmarek, M., Amarasinghe, S.: Streamit: a language for streaming applications. In: Nigel Horspool, R. (ed.) CC 2002. LNCS, vol. 2304, pp. 179–196. Springer, Heidelberg (2002)
21. Halbwachs, N., Caspi, P., Raymond, P., Pilaud, D.: The synchronous data flow programming language LUSTRE. Proc. IEEE **79**(9), 1305–1320 (1991)
22. Gao, B.C.: NDWI-a normalized difference water index for remote sensing of vegetation liquid water from space. Remote Sens. Environ. **58**(3), 257–266 (1996)
23. Wang, Q.S., Zhao, D., Huang, Z.C.: Research on the performance of virtualization-based remote sensing data processing platform. In: 2012 International Conference on Systems and Informatics (ICSAI 2012), Yantai, China, 19–21 May 2012
24. McGrath, R.E., Xinjian, L., Folk, M.: Java (TM) applications using NCSA HDF files. Concurr. Prac. Exp. **9**(11), 1113–1125 (1997)

Resource-Efficient Vibration Data Collection in Cyber-Physical Systems

Md Zakirul Alam Bhuiyan[1,2], Guojun Wang[2,3](✉), Jie Wu[1], Tian Wang[4], and Xiangyong Liu[2]

[1] Department of Computer and Information Sciences, Temple University, Philadelphia, PA 19122, USA
jiewu@temple.edu
[2] School of Information Science and Engineering, Central South University, Changsha 410083, Hunan, People's Republic of China
{zakirulalam,csgjwang}@gmail.com, xiangyongliu@163.com
[3] School of Computer Science and Educational Software, Guangzhou University, Guangzhou 510006, People's Republic of China
[4] College of Computer Science and Technology, Huaqiao University, Xiamen 361021, China
wangtian@hqu.edu.cn

Abstract. Cyber-physical systems (CPS) are becoming increasingly ubiquitous with applications in diverse domains, e.g., structural health monitoring (SHM). Wireless sensor networks (WSNs) are being explored for adoption to improve the performance of centralized wired-based SHM. Existing work often separates the functions and designs of WSNs and civil/structural engineering SHM algorithms. These algorithms usually requires high-resolution data collection for the health monitoring tasks. However, the task becomes difficult because of inherent limitations of WSNs, such as low-bandwidth, unreliable wireless communication, and energy-constraint. In this paper, we proposes a data collection algorithm, which shows that changes (e.g., damage) in a physical structure affect computations and communications in the CPS. To make use of WSNs for SHM tasks, we focus on low-complexity data acquisitions that help reduce the total amount of data transmission. We propose a sensor collaborative algorithm suitable for a wireless sensor in making a damage-sensitive parameter to ensure whether or not it should (i) continue data acquisition at a high frequency and (ii) transmit the acquired data, thus extending system lifetime. The effectiveness of our algorithms is evaluated via a proof-of-concept CPS system implementation.

Keywords: Cyber-Physical Systems · Wireless sensor networks · Structural health monitoring · Vibration data collection · Resource efficiency

1 Introduction

Wireless sensor network (WSN) are deployed to monitor and record physical conditions of environments or entities, and provide monitoring results. Examples include health care, emergency response, physical structure monitoring, intrusion

© Springer International Publishing Switzerland 2015
G. Wang et al. (Eds.): ICA3PP 2015, Part III, LNCS 9530, pp. 134–147, 2015.
DOI: 10.1007/978-3-319-27137-8_11

detection and tracking, and so on [1,7,26]. Applying WSNs (as cyber aspects) for monitoring engineering structural components (as physical aspects) is receiving significant attention recently because of their low-cost, highly scalable, and flexible deployment [1–3,18,20–22]. Traditional structural health monitoring (SHM) is based on wired sensor networks requiring extensive lengths of cables to transmit recorded data to a centralized data repository (a.k.a. the sink) [2]. However, the CPS co-design of SHM with WSNs is still under experimentation and exploration stage.

On the one hand, detection of structural damage through SHM algorithms used by civil, structural, or mechanical engineering is not as straightforward as event detection in other WSN applications [2,23]. These algorithms, such as detection, localization, and quantization of physical damage pose many challenges to WSNs, such as data acquisition at a high frequency, high time synchronization accuracy, storage, and transmission of large data sets, etc. They may also require the engineering domain specific knowledge, e.g., natural frequency, mode shape, finite element analysis [2,3]. In traditional event and target detection applications, each sensor node detects events/targets by comparing the received signal intensity, in terms of light, sound, etc., emitted by events or targets to a threshold. While in SHM, detection of event (i.e. structural damage) is through vibration characteristics. To accurately identify vibration characteristics, SHM algorithms work on the raw measured data of multiple sensor nodes, and the measured data from each sensor node involved is no longer a single value but a sequence of data with length generally more than hundreds of KB.

On the other hand, to date, most of the suggested WSN systems adopt centralized/global SHM , and rely on post experiment analysis for monitoring results at the sink [1–4,24]. It is practically infeasible for WSNs if all of the sensors transmit such a large amount of raw data to the sink. They incur huge communication overhead to the highly traffic-sensitive WSNs. As a result, WSNs may need to sacrifice their real-time performance, quality of monitoring, and lifetime.

The fundamental tool of vibration data collection is the fast Fourier transform (FFT). Existing SHM algorithms are usually based on the FFT [2,4,14, 15,17,24]. Transmitting a huge amount of data collected via FFT method is not potentially suitable for collaborative processing in WSNs, prior research in the field usually does not focus in a significant way on the design of collaborative damage-sensitivity indication (DPI). In this paper, we propose a low-complexity, lightweight solutions to data acquisition so as to overcome the limitations of FFT-based data collection in WSNs. We utilize quadrature amplitude modulation (QAM) [5] and Goertzel algorithm for this purpose [6,8]. Then, we present a simple collaborative data processing algorithm by which each sensor compare their signals and produces a DPI that helps identity damage-sensitive locations. When the DPI exceeds a certain threshold, the sensor requires transmitting their acquired data sets to the sink; otherwise, they do not transmit the data but only the DPI. The sink then analyzes the data and can know about a damage shortly.

Both the data acquisition and DPI reduce the volume of wireless vibration data transmission towards the sink. We present a proof-of-concept CPS implementation by using TinyOS [9] and Intel Imote2 [10]. Evaluation results

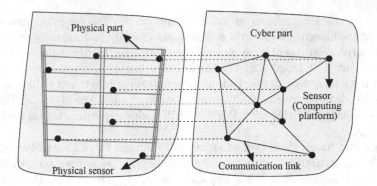

Fig. 1. A CPS model: finite element model (FEM) [3] of our designed structure and the sensor deployment on the physical structure; (b) the network deployed on the structure.

reveal that the overall capability of the WSN is functional enough to enable monitoring engineering structure with 40 % to 60 % of system lifetime extension compared to existing FFT-based approaches.

The rest of this paper is organized is as follows. Section 2 presents the CPS model. Sections 3 and 4 present the data acquisition and DPI identification, respectively. Section 5 provides an empirical analysis of the advantages of our CPS on a designed structure and on the Imote2 sensor platform. Finally, we conclude this paper in Sect. 6.

2 Cyber-Physical Co-design of SHM with WSNs

In this section, we present our CPS model and describe its different components, including WSN network model.

Definition 1 (Finite Element Model (FEM)). *A computer-based numerical model for calculating the behavior and strength of structural mechanics, such as vibration and displacement. Using FEM, a complex structural model is simplified by breaking it down into small elements. These elements are blocks that contain the information of the entire property of the structure [3, 19].*

Definition 2 (Damage). *Damage is a significant change to the geometric properties of a structure, such as changes to captured frequencies and mode shapes.*

Definition 3 (Mode Shape: Φ). *Each type of mechanical structure has a specific pattern of vibration at a specific frequency, called mode shape. It basically shows how a structure will vibrate, and in what pattern. Φ is the matrix of FEM target mode shapes, e.g., Mode1 (or Φ_1) : {2.56, 7.45, 10.56, 6.34} Hz [19].*

A major feature of a CPS is the tight combination and coordination of the computational resources and the physical elements [3]. We illustrate Fig. 1(a) as a representative model of the CPS. There are three major components.

- First, the underlying physical structure consists of a large set of elements. Civil or structural engineering domains use finite element model [2,3] to calibrate these structural elements (see Definition 1). Physical laws as specified by nature govern the physical elements.
- Second, there is a set of sensors or computing platforms that are capable of sensing as well as monitoring changes in the structural physical elements. The platforms may be systematically deployed by an engineering-driven method [3,19,25].
- Finally, a communication network connects these computing platforms. The platforms use a routing algorithm to forward their data to the sink [12]. The platforms and the network form the cyber-part of the system.

The central focus of SHM system is the detection and localization of damage event (changes in the elements) in a variety type of structures (see Definition 2). SHM techniques rely on measuring structural response to ambient vibrations or forced excitation. Changes in the structure produce an effect on vibrations data.

Taking into account a large scale CPS (both WSN and physical structure), the structural response may not be the same in the whole structure. It may vary in different parts of the structure in different time. It would be impractical to consider every sensor communicate to all others in such a CPS. We consider a link quality model regarding dynamic structural environments and interference. This adopts the idea of the log-normal path loss model [18], which is a popular radio propagation model, enabling us to have the formation of IEEE 802.15.4 links into three distinct reception regions: connected, transitional, and disconnected. Then, the strength of a radio signal decays with some power of distance.

Using the link model, sensors find the local topology if they need to exchange data each others. Consider R_M and R_m are the maximum and minimum communication ranges of a sensor, respectively. R_m is used to maintain local topology, where sensor within R_m can share their signals with their neighbors for DPI identification or other purposes. R_M is used when the sensors communicate to the sink directly. The intention of adopting adjustable communication range is to reduce energy consumption for communication.

3   Wireless Vibration Data Acquisition

In this section, we first describe our solutions to the vibration data acquisition. We then analyze the FFT performance with the QAM. Finally, we provide vibration data reduction method.

3.1   Our Solutions

The sensors deployed for SHM applications usually keep on sensing accelerations at a high-frequency in one period and produce a large amount of raw data. In the literature, fast Fourier transform (FFT) and wavelet transform have been a valuable tool for the analysis of vibration signals. FFT is used for the frequency domain analysis of signals. They require a relatively large buffer for storing the intermediate results since the whole spectrum is considered simultaneously. To achieve a frequency resolution below 1 Hz, one would need to use more than 256-point FFT when monitoring with sampling rate of 256 Hz. However, most of the existing WSN-based SHM systems are suggested data acquisition at 560 Hz or more. We assume that there is no memory space for performing, say, 512-point FFT on a sensor node. In fact, event of interest, e.g., damage, is concentrated on a relatively small portion of the vibration spectrum. In addition, we have observed that the changes in vibration frequencies are very small, thus requiring relatively accurate monitoring. Next, we present two solutions as second order infinite impulse response (IIR) based on Quadrature Amplitude Modulation (QAM) and Goertzel algorithm, respectively, which reduces amount data acquisition and transmission.

3.2   Fourier Analysis of QAM

In FFT, the wavelet transform induces greater computational complexity and does not investigate the high frequency range. Accuracy of FFT depends on the length of the considered time window, which also determines the memory requirements. We analyze FFT under quadrature amplitude modulation (QAM) to monitor only single frequency [5]. QAM, when used for digital transmission for radio communications applications, is able to carry higher data rates than ordinary amplitude modulated schemes and phase modulated schemes [5]. Radio receivers using QAM are based on monitoring a narrow frequency band and detecting changes in the amplitude and phase of the signal. Obviously, the application domain of digital radio communications is different in that the changes in the received signal are discrete and controlled by the transmitter. Currently, the monitored quantities are continuous and are expected to drift slowly.

The idea of monitoring on a single frequency f begins with correlating the acceleration measurements $x_s[n]$ with pure sine waves of orthogonal phases:

$$c_s(f) = \frac{1}{N} \sum_{n=1}^{N} x_s[n] \cdot \cos(2\pi(f/f_s)n + \phi_s) \tag{1}$$

$$s_s(f) = \frac{1}{N} \sum_{n=1}^{N} x_s[n] \cdot \sin(2\pi(f/f_s)n + \phi_s) \tag{2}$$

where f_s is the sampling frequency of interest and ϕ_s is the additional phase difference that indicate the fact that wireless sensors have independent clocks. The amplitude of vibration X_s can then be computed as:

$$X_s(f) = \sqrt{c_s(f)^2 + s_s(f)^2} \tag{3}$$

In order to make it more suitable for computing online, the following exponentially decaying window can be used, which can also be considered as the lowpass filter required in QAM:

$$\tilde{c}_s(f, 0) = 0 \tag{4}$$

$$\tilde{c}_s(f, n) = (1 - \kappa) \cdot \tilde{c}_s(f, n - 1) + \kappa \cdot x_s[n] \cdot \cos(2\pi(f/f_s)n) \tag{5}$$

where κ controls the effective window length of the method. There is a trade-off between accuracy (selectivity between adjacent frequencies) and the rate of convergence: small κ results in long windowing and slow response to changes, but also higher frequency resolution.

One important advantage is that $X_s(f)$ is insensitive to ϕ_s and also shows small time differences between sensor nodes. As in QAM, also the phase information can be computed from the intermediate values c_s and s_s. This method also resembles discrete cosine transformation (DCT) and discrete sine transformation (DST) [13], where

$$c_s[k] = \sqrt{\frac{2}{N}} \sum_{n=1}^{N} x_s[n] \cdot \cos(\frac{\pi k(2n + 1)}{2N}) \tag{6}$$

and

$$s_s[k] = \sqrt{\frac{2}{N + 1}} \sum_{n=1}^{N} x_s[n] \cdot \sin\left(\frac{\pi(k + 1)(n + 1)}{N + 1}\right) \tag{7}$$

The frequency bin k can be selected according to the monitoring frequency f as:

$$k \approx 2N\frac{f}{f_s} > 0. \tag{8}$$

3.3   Fourier Analysis Through Goertzel Algorithm

The algorithm derived above suffers from the burden of synthesizing cosine and sine signals. We use a method called the Goertzel algorithm [6,8] that is used to convert the raw accelerations into amplitude of vibrations, it can reduce the amount of transmitted data significantly, thus to reduce energy consumption. It is able to monitor a single narrow frequency band with even fewer requirements. More specificity, we calculate only specific bins instead of the entire frequency spectrum through the Goertzel algorithm, which can be thought of as a second order infinite impulse response (IIR) filter for each discrete Fourier transform (DFT) coefficient. The transfer function of the filter is omitted here for bravery. The Goertzel algorithm is a recursive implementation of the DFT.

Let f_i be the frequency of interest (or vector of frequencies of interest), and f_s be the sampling frequency. The key parameters of the Goertzel algorithm embedded in the sensor nodes are the sampling frequency f_s, the distance between two consecutive bins on the frequency axis (d_b), and the vector of frequencies of interest f_i. These parameters should be defined by the end-user operating at the sink and then broadcast to all of the sensor nodes in a WSN. During the data acquisition, in the algorithm, each sensor nodes iteratively execute the following equations:

$$y_k[0] = y_k[-1] = 0 \tag{9}$$

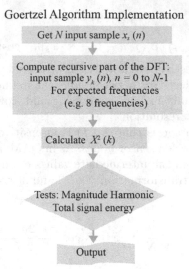

Fig. 2. Implementation steps of the Goertzel algorithm.

$$y_k[0] = x_n[n] + 2\cos(2\pi k/N) \cdot y_k[n-1] - y_k[n-2], \forall n \in [1, N\} \qquad (10)$$

$$|X_k[k]|^2 = y_k^2 + y_k^2[N-1] - 2\cos(2\pi k/N) \cdot y_k[N] \cdot y_k[N-2] \qquad (11)$$

where $y_k[n]$, $y_k[n-1]$, and $y_k[n-2]$ are the only intermediate results needed for computing the signal power $|X[k]|^2$ at frequency bin k. The sensor nodes calculate the number of samples N that must be collected to obtain the resolution $r = 1/d_b$ as:

$$N = \frac{f_s}{d_b} \qquad (12)$$

$$k \approx N\frac{f}{f_s} \qquad (13)$$

Due to the approximation in (13), the actual monitored frequencies could differ from the ones originally selected. This is not the case of a WSN since the frequencies of interest are chosen as integer multiple of the bins distance d_b. Figure 2 illustrates the implementation steps of data analysis utilizing the Goertzel algorithm, as described above.

The Goertzel algorithm has several advantages over the analysis of QAM and and original FFT. The cosine is computed only once and the following computation is in terms of simple multiplications and additions. It is more efficient when only few frequency bins are needed: for K bins, Goertzel requires $O(KN)$ operations while FFT takes $O(Nlog(N))$. For example, if $N = 512$, Goertzel is more (time) efficient if $K \approx 9$.

4   DPI: Damage-Sensitive Parameter Indication

Definition 4 (Finite Element Model (FEM)). *Every structure has a tendency to vibrate with much larger amplitude at some frequencies than others.*

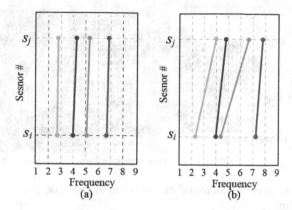

Fig. 3. Natural frequency sets f_i^k and f_j^k captured by sensor s_i and s_j, respectively, that are directly compared according to their orders: (a) comparable current natural frequency sets; (b) non-comparable.

Each such frequency is called a natural frequency denoted by f. f is internal vibration signal characteristic of structure and is different for different structures (such as from building to bridge, from indoor to outdoor).

We calculate a damage-sensitive parameter on the signal amplitude to represent the "damage"/"undamaged" and the area of damaged location (if any) of the structure. An important property of SHM is that the accurate identification of DPI requires data-level collaboration of multiple sensors. Data-level collaboration means that the collected data from multiple sensor nodes are processed simultaneously. If we allow all of the sensors share their data and transmit to the sink, it needs significant energy consumption, thus, the network lifetime reduces.

We allow sensors within R_m can share their data. Every sensor computes the DPI that can provide estimate of a possible physical change in a set of frequency contents. A sensor finds changes by computing a frequency specific *comparability function* as shown in Fig. 3. This requires a pair-wise comparison (i.e., a sensor s_i to another sensor s_j within R_m). After making comparison, each sensor is able to be aware of a possible "damage" in its vicinity of the structure. Its neighbors may also have the similar awareness. They can decide whether or not the set of acquired data is important, i.e., whether or not to transmit the set of acquired data to the sink.

The comparability function is defined as the ratio of acceleration amplitudes measured by any pair of sensors, s_i and s_j in its local area:

$$\frac{|f_{s_i}^{r-k} - f_{s_j}^{r-k}|}{|f_{s_i}^{r-k} + f_{s_j}^{r-k}|} \leqslant c(s_i, s_j, f)\% \tag{14}$$

where f is the monitoring frequency, r and k are the previous and current sets of frequencies of the sensor s_i and s_j, respectively. $c\%$ is a "threshold" defined by

(a) The sink location

(b) Test structure and sensor deployment on it

Fig. 4. A CPS system deployment: (a) the location of the sink; (b) sensor deployment on the test structure.

SHM system user, which is due to the measurement noise and generally ranges from 5 to 15.

This is related to the structure as a medium for vibrations traveling through it: *comparability function* describes how well an impulse travels from s_j to s_i. This point-of-view applies while considering a single impulse from a single sensor. The features can also be considered as properties of a "mode shape", i.e., certain resonance frequencies corresponding to standing waves or mode in a structure [3, 22]. Each sensor location status can be identified by analyzing each mode shape. Such shape mode contains several elements information around the location. The comparability function establishes a one-to-one mapping relationship between frequencies among different sensors since frequencies of the same sensor cannot be contained in the same set.

5 Performance Evaluation

We validate our approach by implementing a proof-of-concept CPS on top of the Imote2 [10] sensor platform using the TinyOS operating system [9]. We utilizes the ISHM services toolsuite [16] developed by the Illinois Structural Health Monitoring Project (ISHMP), which provides subsystems for reliable data transmission and time synchronization.

We evaluate both cyber and physical aspects of our system. The objective of this evaluation is in both aspects: (i) accuracy of mode shape identification; (ii) the network lifetime. We define the *network lifetime* to be the total rounds of data collection before any battery runs out of power [11,12]. This can be calculated by required energy for the rounds of monitoring to the energy reserve on each sensor. We calculate energy consumption for both data acquisition, computation, and transmission of each sensor. The *maximum* energy consumption by a node s_i to send data correctly to a node s_j is evaluated by a model [12]:

The Imote2 is an advanced wireless sensor platform. It consumes $382\mu A$ in its deep sleep state [10], plus $382\mu A$ for the accelerometer. Each Imote2 is deployed with a standard 3x AAA battery pack providing 2400 mAh of charge. We employ

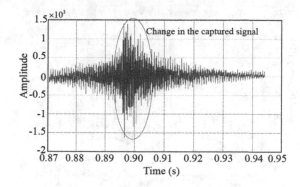

Fig. 5. Vibration signals in time domain captured by 5th sensor after forced excitation with a hammer on the first floor.

Table 1. Natural frequencies for the test structure

Mode	1	2	3	4	5
Analytical	1.2121	3.412	6.5911	11.211	15.2414
Identified	1.1822	3.331	6.5812	12.201	13.983

8 Imote2s on the different floors of the test structure as shown in Fig. 4. An additional Imote2 as the sink mote is located at 30 m located in the lab and a PC as a command center for the sink mote and data visualization. Each mote capture structure's horizontal accelerations and runs a program (implemented in the nesC language) to process the acceleration data acquired from on-board accelerometers. The accelerometer chip on the Imote2s ITS400 sensor board is programmed to acquire samples at 1120 Hz. Digital acceleration data, acquired within frames of 2048 points, is then stored in the local memory for each period of monitoring. Java and Matlab are used to calculate and visualize the whole structural health condition.

5.1 Results of Physical Aspects

We analyze the experiment results of the SHM system's physical performance, discussing the systems ability under reduced data collection while keeping monitoring performance similar to FFT based approaches [4,14,15,17,22,24] adopted by engineering domains. Sensors periodically sample vibration signals. An example of raw signals taken during the experiment is shown in Fig. 5.

In the first experiment, we vibrate the structure with a hammer when sensors involve in collecting the vibration data. We recover the mode shape of the structure offline, as shown Table 1. In our approach, after comparison of damage sensitive parameter (DPI), if there is a possible "change" appeared in the acquired set of signals with a single sensor only, the sensor may be faulty. If the change is present with multiple sensors, there is possibly "damage". In both

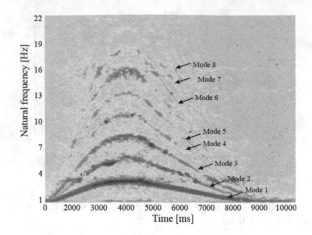

Fig. 6. Captured mode shapes considering different frequencies and time

cases, sensors transmit their data to the sink. We inject structural physical damage by removing the plate on the 5th floor and a side-beam between the 4th and 5th floor.

Figure 6 shows a set of the natural frequencies captured from the 5th sensor location that indicates the bending mode of the structure around the location (under damage injection). This implies that if there is a possible damage at some location of the structure, it can be seen by analyzing the mode shape information of the structure. We can see that, when we analyze the captured mode information (see Definition 3) of all of the locations of the structure, the damaged with its spreading area and intensity can be found. If there is no damage in the structure, some minor changes in the structure can be seen, that is also due to noise effect.

We present here only the first set of data, as shown in Fig. 7(a), under the damage injection and there is no DPI algorithm, meaning that all of the sensors send their data to the sink directly. In Fig. 7(b), the results is obtained when sensor are allowed to execute DPI algorithm. We can observe that the 1st, 2nd and 3rd sensors did not transmit any data to the sink since they did not find significant difference in the acquired vibration signals. This indicate that when there is no damage in the other part of the networks (particularity, in case of large scale WSN deployment), there is no need to transmit all of the data to the sink so as to prolong the network lifetime.

5.2 Results of Cyber Aspects

Here, we analyze the experiment results of the SHM system's cyber performance, discussing the system's ability to extend network lifetime. We allow all of the sensors to sleep after each monitoring period to perform power management. The TinyOS 2.0 drivers for the Imote2 supports to put all of the hardware to sleep when deactivated. Lifetime is calculated by the energy consumption

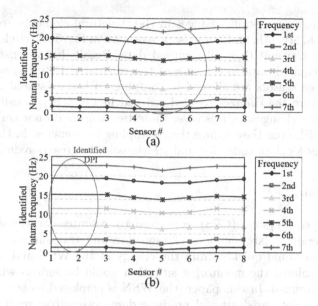

Fig. 7. Measured natural frequencies for the damaged structure

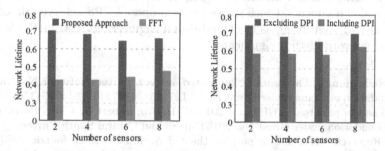

Fig. 8. Performance on network lifetime: (a) FFT-based vs. proposed approach; (b) excluding DIP vs. including DIP during data collection.

for computation, transmission, measurement, and overhead, where the overhead statistics with current consumption data for the radio, sensor, and CPU taken from the corresponding data sheets is combined [10].

After analyzing the results as shown in Fig. 8(a), we found that the FFT-based data collection consumes so much energy of each sensor, which results in a reduced network lifetime. This is because transmitting the raw data in each round, i.e., transmission of natural frequency sets and frequent retransmissions caused by packet losses require significant energy consumption. However, our approach achieves higher lifetime than the FFT-based solution. As shown in Fig. 8(b), the lifetime is further extended when we allow the sensors to compute DPI before transmitting the data. They do not transmit data if DPI does not exceed a given threshold.

Looking into more details, changes in the structural elements are only captured by the 4th, 5th, 6th, and 7th sensors, as shown in Fig. 5(a) (circled marked), but all sensors transmit their all acquired data. Recall that a sensor does not transmit its acquired data to the sink as the calculated DPI if lower than the threshold. When sensors are allowed to compute DPI, the 1st and 2nd sensors could not capture the changes (circled marked in Fig. 5(b)), possibly there is no impact of the changes. In this case, these two sensors do not transmit their all data but DPI, even they reduce their sampling frequencies. In this way, the required energy for data collection and transmission is greatly reduced.

6   Conclusion

In a cyber-physical system (CPS), considering a resource-constrained WSN to exchange generally a large amount of raw data and transmit to the sink for off-line analysis would quickly drain the energy of the WSN and reduce their lifetime. Particularly, the monitoring situation would be serious when a large-scale CPS is assumed. In this paper, the WSN is employed to acquire data by using two-order data analysis and produce damage-sensitive results (or parameters) utilizing sensor collaboration. The effectiveness of the CPS was evaluated via real experiments, which showed that proposed CPS achieves almost the same quality of monitoring as the tranditional engineering SHM methods while extending network lifetime significantly.

Acknowledgments. This work is supported in part by the National Natural Science Foundation of China under Grant Nos. 61272151, 61472451, 61402543, 61202468, 61572206 and in part by ISTCP grant 2013DFB10070, in part by China Postdoctoral Science Foundation under Grant No. 2015T80885 and Central South University Postdoctoral Research Fund, and in part by the US National Science foundation (NSF) under grants CNS 149860, CNS 1461932, CNS 1460971, CNS 1439672, CNS 1301774, ECCS 1231461, ECCS 1128209, and CNS 1138963.

References

1. Bhuiyan, M.Z.A., Wang, G., Cao, J., Wu, J.: Local monitoring and maintenance for operational wireless sensor networks. In: Proceedings of the IEEE ISPA, pp. 837–844 (2013)
2. Bhuiyan, M.Z.A., Wang, G., Wu, J., Cao, J., Liu, X., Wang, T.: Dependable structural health monitoring using wireless sensor networks. IEEE Trans. Dependable Secure Comput. (2015). doi:10.1109/TDSC.2015.2469655
3. Li, B., Wang, D., Wang, F., Ni, Y.Q.: High quality sensor placement for SHM systems: refocusing on application demands. In: Proceedings of IEEE INFOCOM, pp. 1–9 (2010)
4. Linderman, L., Mechitov, K., Spencer, F.: Real-Time Wireless Data Acquisition for Structural Health Monitoring. PhD thesis, University of Illinois at Urbana-Champaign, ISSN: 1940–9826 (2011)
5. Proakis, J.G., Salehi, M.: Digital Communications. McGraw-Hill, New York (2008)

6. Goertzel, G.: An algorithm for the evaluation of finite trigonomentric series. Am. Math. Mon. **65**, 34–35 (1958)
7. Bhuiyan, M.Z.A., Wang, G., Cao, J., Wu, J.: Energy and bandwidth-efficient wireless sensor networks for monitoring high-frequency events. In: Proceedings of IEEE SECON, pp. 194–202 (2013)
8. Wang, W., Gao, Z., Huang, L., Yao, Y.: Spectrum sensing based on Goertzel algorithm. In: Proceedings of IEEE WiCom, pp. 1–4 (2008)
9. http://www.tinyos.net
10. Crossbow Technology Inc., Imote2 Hardware Reference Manual (2007)
11. Olariu, S., Stojmenovic, I.: Design guidelines for maximizing lifetime and avoiding energy holes in sensor networks with uniform distribution and uniform reporting. In: Proceedings of IEEE INFOCOM (2006)
12. Sankar, A., Liu, Z.: Maximizing lifetime routing in wireless ad hoc neworks. In: Proceedings of IEEE INFOCOM (2004)
13. Theodoridis, S., Koutroumbas, K.: Pattern Recognition. Elsevier Academic Press, USA (2003)
14. Nagayama, T., Spencer Jr., B.F., Agha, G.A., Mechitov, K.A.: Model-based data aggregation for structural monitoring employing smart sensors. In: Proceedings of INSS, pp. 203–210 (2006)
15. Zimmerman, A., Shiraishi, M., Swartz, R., Lynch, J.: Automated modal parameter estimation by parallel processing within wireless monitoring systems. J. Struct. Syst. **14**(1), 102–113 (2008)
16. http://shm.cs.uiuc.edu/
17. Jiang, X.-D., Tang, Y.-L., Lei, Y.: Wireless sensor networks in structural health monitoring based on ZigBee technology. In: Proceedings of ASID (2009)
18. Chen, Y., Terzis, A.: On the implications of the log-normal path loss model: an efficient method to deploy and move sensor motes. In: Proceedings of ACM SenSys (2011)
19. Bhuiyan, M.Z.A., Wang, G., Cao, J., Wu, J.: Sensor placement with multiple objectives for structural health monitoring. ACM Trans. Sens. Netw. **10**(4), 1–45 (2014)
20. Hackmann, G., Guo, W., Yan, G., Sun, Z., Lu, C., Dyke, S.: Cyber-physical codesign of distributed structural health monitoring with wireless sensor networks. IEEE Trans. Parallel Distrib. Syst. **24**(1), 63–72 (2014)
21. Li, B., Sun, Z., Mechitov, K., Lu, C., Dyke, S.J., Agha, G., Spencer, B.F.: Realistic case studies of wireless structural control. In: Proceedings of ACM/IEEE ICCPS (2013)
22. Ko, J., Ni, Y., Zhou, H., Wang, J., Zhou, X.: Investigation concerning structural health monitoring of an instrumented cable-stayed bridge. Struct. Infrastruct. Eng. Maintenance Manag. Life-Cycle Des. Perform. **5**(6), 497–513 (2008)
23. Bhuiyan, M.Z.A., Wang, G., Cao, J., Wu, J.: Deploying wireless sensor networks with fault tolerance for structural health monitoring. IEEE Trans. Comput. **64**(2), 382–395 (2015)
24. Worden, K., Dulieu-Barton, J.: An overview of intelligent fault detection in systems and structures. Struct. Health Monit. **3**(1), 85–98 (2004)
25. Bhuiyan, M.Z.A., Wang, G., Cao, J., Wu, J.: Backup sensor placement with guaranteed fault tolerance for structural health monitoring. In: Proceedings of Sixth Beijing-Hong Kong International Doctoral Forum, pp. 1–4 (2011)
26. Bhuiyan, M.Z.A., Wang, G., Wu, J.: Target tracking with monitor and backup sensors in wireless sensor networks. In: Proceedings of IEEE ICCCN, pp. 1–9 (2009)

A New Approach for Vehicle Recognition and Tracking in Multi-camera Traffic System

Wenbin Jiang[✉], Zhiwei Lu, Hai Jin, and Ye Chi

Services Computing Technology and System Lab,
Cluster and Grid Computing Lab, School of Computer Science and Technology,
Huazhong University of Science and Technology, Wuhan 430074, China
wenbinjiang@hust.edu.cn

Abstract. In order to ensure recognition accuracy, intelligent traffic video tracking system usually requires various types of information. Therefore, multi-features fusion becomes a good choice. In this paper, a new recognition approach for vehicle types based multi-feature fusion is proposed, which is used for vehicle tracking in a multi-camera traffic system. An improved Canny operator is presented for edge detection. SURF (*Speeded Up Robust Features*) is used for local feature extraction. To improve the performance of distance calculation between features, a refined method based on Hellinger kernel is put forward. A position constraint rule is applied to reduce unnecessary fake matchings. Finally, the information of vehicle types combined with LBP (*Local Binary Pattern*), HOG (*Histogram of Oriented Gradients*) is used for a multi-camera vehicle tracking platform, which adopts Hadoop to realize the parallel computing of the system. Experimental results show that the proposed approach has good performance for the platform.

Keywords: Recognition · SURF · Distance calculation · Position constraint · Parallel computing

1 Introduction

In the past few years, traffic video surveillance technologies (mainly for vehicles) have gotten more and more attention. Applications based on these technologies have made rapid progress. Simultaneously, a large number of resources have been invested.

Intelligent traffic video surveillance is a new generation of monitoring technology, which uses cutting-edge computer vision technologies to analyze monitoring videos, does some forecasts, and identifies various abnormal conditions.

One of the key technologies for intelligent video surveillance is target recognition. Only after the target being identified from the surveillance video, further analysis about the behaviors and characteristics of the targets can be done.

Recently, multi-camera-based traffic video tracking systems become more and more popular, which track some targets among multiple cameras. The vehicle target recognition is also a very important beginning step for further tracking and other analysis.

© Springer International Publishing Switzerland 2015
G. Wang et al. (Eds.): ICA3PP 2015, Part III, LNCS 9530, pp. 148–161, 2015.
DOI: 10.1007/978-3-319-27137-8_12

The local feature extraction and matching of vehicle targets are very important for vehicle tracking, especially across different cameras. However, vehicle feature extraction and recognition still face many challenges:

- Feature diversity, such as shape, color, size, and fine differences between corresponding key points. Moreover, from different perspectives, the appearances of specific vehicle are usually different;
- Shield and interference, such as shields between vehicles and interference of the complex background. Especially in urban situations, backgrounds are generally complex;
- Computation and accuracy for feature extraction. More robust features and higher accuracy require more computation resources, which is a big bottleneck for real-time vehicle surveillance.

In this paper, we propose a new vehicle recognition approach based on multi-feature fusion. The front faces of vehicles are used for this task (allowing small inclination angles). Like faces of human being, the front faces of vehicles have abundant features to identify them. Considering the symmetry, only the left light of the vehicle is chosen for feature extraction.

In the proposed approach, the feature extraction has two steps. The first is to use an improved Canny [1] algorithm to extract the vehicle light shape from the image of the vehicle front face to get the profile image of the headlight. The second is to extract SURF (*Speeded Up Robust Features*) [2] features from the profile image of the headlight and the image of the vehicle face.

Some standard vehicle face images of different types of vehicles are selected as standard models. Their features are extracted by above approach and stored into a local standard feature database.

To identify a new vehicle, first, extract features from its face image by our proposed approach; then, compare them with the features of various vehicles stored in the standard feature database to find the type of the vehicle.

Finally, the information of vehicle types combined with other features of *Local Binary Pattern* (LBP) and *Histogram of Oriented Gradients* (HOG) is used for a multi-camera vehicle tracking system. Hadoop is used to realize the parallel computing of the system.

The remaining of this paper is organized as follows. Section 2 introduces related work on edge detection, extraction of local features, etc. Section 3 shows the architecture, algorithm and implementation of the proposed recognition system of vehicle, and some improvements in details. Section 4 gives the testing performance analysis. Finally, conclusion is drawn in Sect. 5.

2 Related Work

Anagnostopoulos et al. [4] presented a vehicle recognition system by automatic license plate recognition, vehicle manufacturer/model detection and under-vehicle inspection. Sivaraman et al. [5] proposed a novel active-learning approach to build vehicle-recognition and tracking systems. A passively trained recognition system was built using conventional supervised learning. A second round of learning was then performed to build an active-learning-based vehicle recognizer. Particle filter tracking was integrated to build a complete multiple-vehicle tracking system. Dlagnekov [6] presented a way to use SIFT (*Scale Invariant Feature Transform*) [7] feature of vehicle rear to recognize a specific vehicle. Petrovic et al. [8] presented an application of automatic recognition of vehicle type for secure access and traffic monitoring. It showed that a relatively simple set of features extracted from sections of front face images of cars can be used to obtain high performance verification and recognition of vehicle type (both car model and class). Euclidean distance is used to measure the similarity between the features from different objects.

Multiple features can help improve the effectiveness of the appearance matching and reduce the influence of environment changes, especially in multi-camera system. Tamrakar et al. [9] explored a way combining the features of shape and appearance for object recognition. Some ways were explored in which the geometric aspects of an object can be augmented with its appearance. The main idea is to construct a dense correspondence between the interior regions of two shapes based on a shape-based correspondence so that the intensity and gradient distributions can be compared. Wang et al. [10] employed multiple features such as color histogram, height, moving detection, travel time and speed to match objects across non-overlapping views.

In our proposed approach, SURF feature of vehicle front face image is combined with features of LBP and HOG to make vehicle tracking.

Edge detection is an important step for feature extraction. Existing edge detection algorithms can be roughly divided into five groups: gradient method [3], surface fitting method [11], second derivative method [12], multi-scale method [13] and morphological method [14]. Canny is a good practical edge detection algorithm. Its three performance criteria are: (1) good detection performance; (2) good localization performance; (3) only one response to a single edge. According to the above principles, Canny algorithm has a good intensity estimate of edges, which contains both edge gradient direction and edge intensity information. In our proposed approach, Canny is used for edge detection.

For feature extraction, SIFT [7] is a good image feature proposed by Lowe. It is invariant to rotation and scale, which is often used in image matching and connection. However, the complexity of computation for SIFT is usually high and the amount of data is large. SURF [2, 15] is a speedup and robust version of SIFT, which can offer better performance than SIFT. The calculation of SURF feature consists of keypoints detection, descriptor generation and keypoints matching. [16] gave the comparison of SIFT, *Principal Component Analysis* (PCA)-SIFT [17] and SURF.

For feature matching, there are some methods to compare the feature descriptors, such as L2 metric, Euclidean distance, *Earth Mover's Distance* (EMD) [18], EMD-L1 [19], diffusion distance [20], $\overline{EMD}$ [21] and Quadratic-Form distances [22]. SIFT and SURF are originally designed to be used with Euclidean distance [2, 7]. To improve the performance of feature matching, a refined distance calculation method based on Hellinger kernel is presented in our proposed approach.

3 Design and Implementation

3.1 Framework Architecture

The interactive traffic video tracking platform, which have been presented by our research group [23], consists of the following three parts: data storage layer, data analysis layer, data presentation layer. Figure 1 shows the hierarchical architecture of the interactive traffic video tracking system.

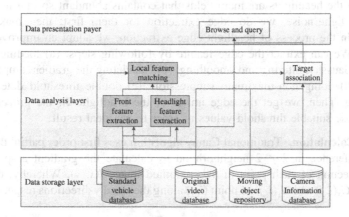

Fig. 1. The architecture of the interactive traffic video tracking system

In this architecture, data storage layer stores all data of the system (such as original video, multi-camera information, standard vehicle database). The data analysis layer includes several processes for traffic video, such as local feature extracting, local feature matching, and target association. The data presentation layer is the interface of the system to provide video browsing, object querying and so on.

In this paper, we focus on the recognition system of vehicle based on multi-feature fusion. The system is composed of two key steps: one is local feature extraction (including front feature and headlight feature extraction), and the other is local feature matching. The involved components are shown in Fig. 1 with gray color.

For vehicle type recognition, the input data are images of front faces of vehicles. The output data are types of the vehicles. The main procedure in the recognition system includes the following steps:

(a) Loading an image;
(b) Capturing the headlight area, and extracting the edges of the headlight;
(c) Extracting SURF feature of the front face of the vehicle;
(d) Calculating the distances between the features of headlight edge image as well as the front face image and ones in the model database respectively;
(e) Comparing the calculation results. The vehicle type which having the minimum distance is the most likely result.

Here, an improved Canny operator is presented for edge detection. To improve the performance of distance calculation between features, a refined distance calculation method based on Hellinger kernel is put forward. Moreover, a position constraint rule also is applied to reduce unnecessary fake matching. More details about them are shown below.

3.2 Edge Extraction

Considering the headlights are main fields that contains abundant special features but with much light noise, we do edge extraction for them first, then make feature extraction. In the process of headlight edge extraction, we adapt an improved Canny algorithm. We can extract the edge feature by following steps: (a) loading the gray image; (b) Gaussian filtering and smoothing; (c) calculating the gradient amplitude and direction; (d) doing non-maximum suppression; (e) double threshold detecting and edge tracing. Then, we get the edge image of the headlight. In the processing, we should choose suitable threshold values in order to get ideal result.

Gradient Calculation. Traditional Canny algorithm uses first order partial derivatives of finite difference in 2×2 neighborhood to calculate the gradient amplitude and gradient direction of each point in the smoothed image $I(x, y)$. Whereby, the partial derivatives $G_x(i, j)$ and $G_y(i, j)$ of point (i, j) along the x and y directions respectively are:

$$G_x(i,j) = [I(i,j+1) - I(i,j) + I(i+1,j+1) - I(i+1,j)]/2 \tag{1}$$

$$G_y(i,j) = [I(i,j) - I(i+1,j) + I(i,j+1) - I(i+1,j+1)]/2 \tag{2}$$

The gradient amplitude $M(i, j)$ and the gradient direction $\theta(i, j)$ of each pixel (i, j) in the image $I(x, y)$ are defined as follows respectively:

$$M(i,j) = \sqrt{G_x^2(i,j) + G_y^2(i,j)} \tag{3}$$

$$\theta(i,j) = \tan^{-1}(G_y(i,j)/G_x(i,j)) \tag{4}$$

Here, the gradient amplitude is calculated with the finite difference in 2×2 neighborhood, which is more sensitive to noise. Here, we make an improvement that calculates the gradient amplitude with 3×3 neighborhood to reduce the influence of noise. To save space, we just show the results of x direction in details. For y direction, it has a similar fashion to x direction.

The gradient amplitude of x direction is

$$G_x(i,j) = I(i+1,j) - I(i-1,j) \tag{5}$$

The gradient amplitudes of $\pi/4$ and $3\pi/4$ directions respectively are

$$G_{\pi/4}(i,j) = I(i-1,j+1) - I(i+1,j-1) \tag{6}$$

$$G_{3\pi/4}(i,j) = I(i+1,j+1) - I(i-1,j-1) \tag{7}$$

The difference of horizontal direction is

$$E_x(i,j) = G_x(i,j) + [G_{\pi/4}(i,j) + G_{3\pi/4}(i,j)]/2 \tag{8}$$

The gradient amplitudes and the gradient direction are

$$M(i,j) = \sqrt{G_x^2(i,j) + G_y^2(i,j) + G_{\pi/4}^2(i,j) + G_{3\pi/4}^2(i,j)} \tag{9}$$

$$\theta(i,j) = \tan^{-1}(E_y(i,j)/E_x(i,j)) \tag{10}$$

where G_y and E_y are similar to G_x and E_x respectively except different directions. Finally, formulas above can be turned into the templates as follows:

$$G_x(i,j) = \begin{vmatrix} -1 & 0 & 1 \\ -\sqrt{2} & 0 & \sqrt{2} \\ -1 & 0 & 1 \end{vmatrix}, G_y(i,j) = \begin{vmatrix} 1 & \sqrt{2} & 1 \\ 0 & 0 & 0 \\ -1 & -\sqrt{2} & -1 \end{vmatrix} \tag{11}$$

The improved method considers the diagonal direction of pixels, and draws it into the differential mean value calculation. The gradient amplitude of a pixel depends on the rest eight pixels in 3×3 neighborhood. Compared with the traditional way, the quantity of neighbor pixels of the proposed way is increased largely in our presented way. It enhances the gradient amplitude stability, reduces the impact of the single noise point, improves the edge localization accuracy, and effectively suppresses the noise.

Self-adaptive Double Threshold Detection. During the process of edge points detection, self-adaptive double threshold algorithm automatic reduces the influence of the pixels which have smaller gradient amplitude, further eliminates false edges. Higher threshold can eliminate most noise points, but cause the loss of some useful information; while lower threshold can save more image information. Therefore, we present a way for threshold decision based on higher threshold coupled with lower threshold as supplementary decision, which can effectively reduce false edges, and ensure the integrity of image edges greatly. The threshold is set automatically according to the gradient amplitudes of the image pixels, only depending on the initial selection proportion for threshold. No artificial operations are needed.

Noise Elimination. From the results of the image processed before, we know that, pixels in the image have not only the gradient amplitude information, but also the gradient direction information. If a point belongs to an edge, its gradient direction generally points to the normal direction of the edge. Isolated noise points often have not obvious gradient direction. Therefore, according to the difference of gradient direction characteristics between edge points and noise points, we can effectively distinguish edge points.

In the 3×3 neighborhood which centers on o, for a point t around o, if o and t are in the same edge, the line connecting point o and t has similar direction as the edge. Here, define $Angle_t$ as the absolute value of the angle between the normal direction of the line and the mean gradient direction of the edge. For a point on the edge, its gradient direction should have the similar direction as the normal direction of the line. So $Angle_t$ should be a very small value.

In the case of a noise point, because its gradient direction is generally different with its adjacent points, the corresponding $Angle_t$ is large usually. As a consequence, we can detect noise points and edge points in an image by this method effectively, and eliminate the noise points. At the same time, we can realize more precisely edge point detection and subsequent linking.

3.3   Local Feature Extraction

In image processing, there are many kinds of features for identifying and recognizing a target. In this paper, SURF is used for local feature extraction, which is scale-invariant and rotation-invariant. The main procedure to extract local features is: (a) loading the gray image and creating integral image; (b) computing interest points with Hessian matrix; (c) locating interest points precisely; (d) assigning dominant orientation; (e) creating interest point descriptors.

After these steps, we get hundreds of 64-length vectors for local features of the image. If the image is the front face image of a standard vehicle, we store the features into standard database.

The process to extract local feature is described briefly in the following sections.

Keypoints Detection. In SURF, the scale-space of the image (also called Gaussian pyramid) is mainly used to obtain interest points in different scales. It convolves the image iteratively with Gaussian kernel and sub-samples it repeatedly. This method results in each layer relying on the previous, and thus, high complexity. The sizes of kernels can be changed to create the Gaussian pyramid. Laplacian of Gaussian is approximated to a box filter. This allows multiple layers of the scale-space pyramid to be processed simultaneously without subsampling the image, which leads to better performance.

The matrix of Hessian is used for the interest point localization to determine whether a point is extremum. The integral image is used for the computation of the matrix of Hessian. Each extremum is compared with 26 adjacent points around it after they are picked out. If the value of an extremum point is above or below all of the 26 adjacent points, this extremum point becomes an interest point.

SURF Interest Point Descriptor. SURF interest point descriptor relies on the dominant orientations of all the interest points. The descriptor component is built based on the dominant orientations. Haar wavelet response is used for calculating the dominant orientation. The Haar responses are calculated in both x and y coordinates in the circle region centered at interest points with a radius of 6σ. The size of Haar wavelet is 4σ, and the sum of vectors is calculated in every 60 degrees in the circle. At last, the orientation with the largest sum of vectors is the dominant orientation.

After the dominant orientation is obtained, a square window with a side length of 20σ is constructed centered at each interest point. It is divided into 4 × 4 sub-regions. The wavelet response is calculated in both the dominant orientation and the direction vertical to it. The wavelets of x and y are defined as dx and dy. Four values $\sum dx$, $\sum dy$, $\sum |dx|$, $\sum |dy|$ are calculated. Then they are combined and normalized to a 64-length vector for each interest point, the SURF descriptor. The SURF descriptor is invariant to scale, rotation and translation of images.

3.4 Matching Local Features

Improvement in the Distance Calculation. For some tasks such as texture classification and image categorization, it is well known that using Euclidean distance to compare histograms often yields inferior performance compared with other measures [24]. SURF was originally designed to be used with Euclidean distance. However, since it is a histogram question, the question arises as to whether other histogram distance measures can work better with it. Here, we show that using Hellinger kernel does bring a great benefit indeed.

In the following, more details about how to use Hellinger kernel is shown. Suppose x and y are n-vectors with unit Euclidean norm ($\|x\| = 1$), then the Euclidean distance $d_E(x, y)$ between them is related to their similarity (kernel) $S_E(x, y)$:

$$d(x,y)^2 = \|x - y\|^2 = \|x\|^2 + \|y\|^2 - 2x^T y = 2 - 2x^T y$$

where $S_E(x, y) = x^T y$. Here, we intend to replace the Euclidean similarity/kernel with Hellinger kernel.

The Hellinger kernel (also known as the coefficient of Bhattacharyya) for two L1 normalized histograms x and y (i.e. $\sum_i^n x_i = 1$ and $x_i \geq 0$) is defined as

$$H(x,y) = \sum_{i=1}^{n} \sqrt{x_i y_i} \tag{12}$$

SURF vectors can be compared by a Hellinger kernel using a simple algebraic manipulation in two steps: (a) normalizing the SURF vector in L1 norm (originally it has unit L2 norm); (b) calculating the square root of each element

$$S_E(\sqrt{x}, \sqrt{y}) = \sqrt{x}^T \sqrt{y} = H(x,y)$$

and the obtained vectors are L2 normalized since

$$S_E(\sqrt{x}, \sqrt{x}) = \sum_i^n x_i = 1$$

Thus we use Hellinger kernel to compare the original SURF vectors:

$$d(\sqrt{x}, \sqrt{y})^2 = 2 - 2\sqrt{x}^T \sqrt{y} = 2 - H(x, y)$$

Constraints Between Matching Point Positions. For the situation in our system, the positions of matching points have some relationship. It means that a point in image A can only match with some points in image B which are close to the corresponding position of the former. In other words, we do not look for matching point from image B for the point in image A out of some areas centered at the point in A. This method can reduce considerable unnecessary fake matchings.

Suppose the threshold for the area is T. The judgment criteria for position constraints are shown as follow:

For the point A (x_1, y_1) in image I_1 with size (w_1, h_1) and the point B (x_2, y_2) in image I_2 with size (w_2, h_2), if the following conditions are met, the two points in image I_1 and I_2 are possible correct matching points.

$$\left| \frac{x_1}{w_1} - \frac{x_2}{w_2} \right| \leq T, \quad \left| \frac{y_1}{h_1} - \frac{y_2}{h_2} \right| \leq T \tag{13}$$

In the formulae above, T can be fixed according to practical requirements. In our system, T is usually less than 0.4, according to the experience.

3.5   Camera Network and Its Sub-graph Partitioning

Our proposed vehicle type recognition approach has been used in a non-overlapping multi-camera large surveillance platform that we presented in [23].

Generally, it is hard to track targets across multi-camera network. The burden of computation is often heavy. So can we divide the network into several independent sub-network (namely sub-graph) units so that some parallel strategies can be used?

In our multi-camera system, it is divided into some independent sub-networks according to the characteristics of its topology relationship. After this partitioning, target association algorithm can be run independently. The structure of the camera network should not be destroyed by the sub-network partition, which can make sure that the trajectory obtained in each sub-network can be easily merged to make the whole vehicle trajectory.

Two principles should be followed: completeness principle and minimization principle. The completeness principle assures that all nodes involved are within the sub-graph unit when calculating the associate relationship of the targets, and do not need exchange information with other units. The minimization principle makes the structure of each sub-graph unit as small as possible.

Our system uses Hadoop to parallelize the computation of all sub-graphs. First, different tasks from different sub-graphs are mapped to different MapReduce nodes for track analysis independently. Then, all information will be returned to central server to be reduced.

A minimum cost and maximum flow algorithm based on the relationship of the camera network topology is used for target association in our system.

One of the key parts of the target association is how to describe the similarity between objects from different objects. Here, assume target a and target b are two vehicles observed in camera C_i and C_j respectively, the similarity measure function S $(O_{i,a}, O_{j,b})$ is defined as:

$$S(O_{i,a}, O_{j,b}) = \omega_t T(t_{i,a}, t_{j,b}) \cdot \omega_l L(l_{i,a}, l_{j,b}) \cdot \omega_a A(a_{i,a}, a_{j,b}) \qquad (14)$$

where $T(t_{i,a}, t_{j,b})$ denotes the time relationship of the two objects; $L(l_{i,a}, l_{j,b})$ denotes their location relationship; and $A(a_{i,a}, a_{j,b})$ is for their appearances. Each weight ω is for each feature to control the reliability.

It is easy to construct the similarities of the parameters of time and location of the specific objects. They mainly depend on the object appearing time and the topology of the monitoring network. For appearances of the objects, vehicle types obtained by aforementioned proposed approach are main factors for them. Moreover, other features including LBP and HOG are combined together to make their appearance similarities. More details and experimental results about target association and MapReduce-based partitioning can be seen in [23].

4 Performance Evaluations

4.1 Test Environment

Test experiments are implemented on some Linux servers (Red Hat Enterprise Linux Server release 5.3) with OpenCV 2.4.3 [25]. One server has one eight-core CPU of Intel Xeon E5520 (2.27 GHz) with hyper-thread, and 16 GB memory. GCC 4.1.2 is used for compilation. For multi-camera tracking, a Hadoop cluster consisting of five aforementioned nodes is used.

4.2 Standard Model Database

For the standard model database in the system, 15 brands, amounting to 178 kinds of models, are built and recorded in the database. The information of model datasets is shown in Table 1.

Table 1. The Model Datasets

Brand	Amount	Brand	Amount	Brand	Amount
Audi	9	BMW	8	Honda	23
BYD	7	Peugeot	12	Buick	11
Volkswagen	37	Toyota	14	Ford	10
KIA	11	Nissan	8	Skoda	4
Hyundai	13	Chevrolet	4	Citroen	7

4.3   Evaluation of the Improvement in Distance Calculation

We use a square root (Hellinger) kernel instead of the standard Euclidean distance to measure the similarity between SURF descriptors, which leads to a dramatic performance improvement. This change can be implemented easily. It does not require any additional storage space for the distance calculation.

The time cost of distance calculations is shown in Fig. 2. The dramatic improvements in performance with the improvement method are shown in Fig. 3. These improvements come without additional cost, and additional storage since SURF features can be calculated with Hellinger online with a negligible processing overhead.

A standard image has 440 interest points. The line "Original" stands for the performance of non-modified SURF. The line "RefineD" stands for the performance of SURF with improvement in the distance calculation. The line "RefineDP" stands for the performance of SURF with improvements in the distance calculation and the position constraint. Figure 2 shows that RefineDP has obvious advantage in computation time cost.

From Fig. 3, we can see that the number of matched points in RefineDP method is improved significantly, since the improvement reduces the dependency between the feature descriptors and the points with extreme values, while improve the sensitivity of the feature descriptor to non-extreme points.

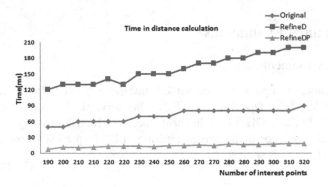

Fig. 2. Time cost of distance calculation

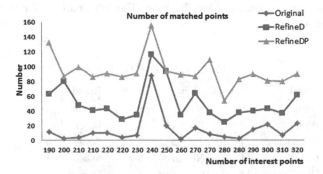

Fig. 3. Numbers of the matched points

4.4   Accuracy of Vehicle Recognition

This section shows the experimental results about the accuracy of vehicle recognition in different cases. The tested images not only include vehicle images downloaded from the Internet which are in good resolution, but also ones captured from some traffic videos which are in poor resolutions. In our system, clearer images can be extracted with more local features and get more precise result.

In Fig. 4, the x-axis stands for the numbers of feature points in the headlight edge images, and y-axis stands for the recognition accuracy. The lines with different legends stand for the numbers of feature points in front faces of vehicles. The numbers of feature points in headlight edge image and local features in front faces are in association with the image clarity. When the number of feature points in the headlight edge images is greater than 20, or the number of feature points in front faces is greater than 200, the accuracy is satisfactory.

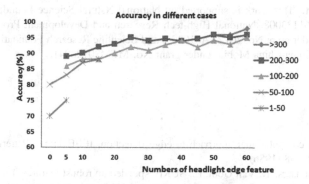

Fig. 4. The accuracy of vehicle recognition in different cases

4.5   Tracking Result of the Multi-camera Platform

To verify the effectiveness of the multi-camera platform, a batch of vehicle monitoring videos from 23 cameras in the real campus security monitoring system of Huazhong University of Science and Technology (HUST) are applied and analyzed (see Fig. 5(a)).

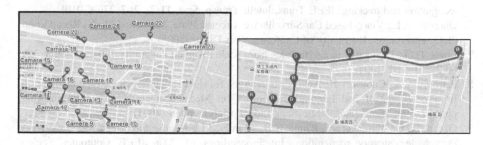

(a) The topology of multi-cameras   (b) The trajectory of one tracked vehicle

Fig. 5. Vehicle tracking of the multi-cameras platform

Figure 5(b) gives the trajectory of one tracked vehicle (white Honda SUV). It shows that the multi-camera platform based on Hadoop can track vehicle objects perfectly.

5 Conclusion

In this paper, a new recognition approach for vehicle types is designed and implemented. The vehicle type is distinguished by its front face image. The approach has been applied in a multi-camera traffic video monitoring platform, combining with LBP, HOG. The process of the whole camera network is parallelized based on sub-graph partitioning and Hadoop clustering. Experimental results indicate that the proposed modification in SURF can improve algorithm performance. The accuracy of the recognition can meet requirements of practical applications and the tracking result in the multi-camera system is satisfactory.

Acknowledgment. This work is supported by National Natural Science Foundation of China under grant No. 61133008, National High-tech Research and Development Program of China (863 Program) under grant No. 2012AA010905, and Scientific Research Foundation of Ministry of Education of China-China Mobile under grant No. MCM20122041.

References

1. Canny, J.: A computational approach to edge detection. IEEE Trans. Pattern Anal. Mach. Intell. **6**, 679–698 (1986)
2. Bay, H., Tuytelaars, T., Van Gool, L.: SURF: speeded up robust features. In: Leonardis, A., Bischof, H., Pinz, A. (eds.) ECCV 2006, Part I. LNCS, vol. 3951, pp. 404–417. Springer, Heidelberg (2006)
3. Sun, J., Gu, H.B.: Improved insensitivity to noise image edge detecting method based on the direction information. J. Chin. Comput. Syst. **27**(7), 1358–1361 (2006)
4. Anagnostopoulos, C.N., Giannoukos., I., Alexandropoulos, T., Psyllos, A., Loumos, V., Kayafas, E.: Integrated vehicle recognition and inspection system to improve security in restricted access areas. In: Proceedings of 13th International IEEE Conference on Intelligent Transportation Systems (ITSC 2010), pp. 1893–1898. IEEE Press, Piscataway (2010)
5. Sivaraman, S., Trivedi, M.M.: A general active-learning framework for on-road vehicle recognition and tracking. IEEE Trans. Intell. Transp. Syst. **11**(2), 267–276 (2010)
6. Dlagnekov, L.: Video-based Car Surveillance: License Plate, Make, and Model Recognition. Ph.D. dissertation, University of California, San Diego (2005)
7. Lowe, D.G.: Distinctive image features from scale-invariant keypoints. Int. J. Comput. Vis. **60**(2), 91–110 (2004)
8. Petrovic, V.S., Cootes, T.F.: Analysis of features for rigid structure vehicle type recognition. In: Proceedings of 2nd International Forum on Mechanical and Material Engineering, pp. 587–596, Trans Tech Publications Ltd., Zurich-Durnten (2004)
9. Ozcanli, O.C., Tamrakar, A., Kimia, B.B., Mundy, J.L.: Augmenting shape with appearance in vehicle category recognition. In: Proceedings of 2006 IEEE Computer Society Conference on Computer Vision and Pattern Recognition (CVPR 2006), pp. 935–942. IEEE Press, New York (2006)

10. Wang, Y., He, L., Velipasalar, S.: Real-time distributed tracking with non-overlapping cameras. In: Proceedings of IEEE Conference on Image Processing (ICIP 2010), pp. 697–700. IEEE Press, Piscataway (2010)
11. Archibald, R., Gelb, A., Yoon, J.: Polynomial fitting for edge detection in irregularly sampled signals and images. SIAM J. Numer. Anal. **43**(1), 250–279 (2005)
12. Sarkar, S., Boyer, K.L.: On optimal infinite impulse response edge detection filters. IEEE Trans. Pattern Anal. Mach. Intell. **13**(11), 1154–1171 (1991)
13. Yi, S., Labate, D., Easley, G., Krim, H.: A shearlet approach to edge analysis and detection. IEEE Trans. Image Process. **18**(5), 929–941 (2009)
14. Evans, A., Liu, X.: A morphological gradient approach to color edge detection. IEEE Trans. Image Process. **15**(6), 1454–1463 (2006)
15. Bay, H., Ess, A., Tuytelaars, T., Van Gool, L.: Speeded-up robust features (SURF). Comput. Vis. Image Underst. **110**(3), 346–359 (2008)
16. Juan, L., Gwun, O.: A comparison of SIFT, PCA-SIFT and SURF. Int. J. Image Process. **3** (4), 143–152 (2009)
17. Ke, Y., Sukthankar, R.: PCA-SIFT: a more distinctive representation for local image descriptors. In: Proceedings of 2004 IEEE Conference on Computer Vision and Pattern Recognition (CVPR 2004), vol. 2, pp. 511–517. IEEE Press, Los Alamitos (2004)
18. Rubner, Y., Tomasi, C., Guibas, L.J.: The earth mover's distance as a metric for image retrieval. Int. J. Comput. Vis. **40**(2), 99–121 (2000)
19. Ling, H., Okada, K.: An efficient earth mover's distance algorithm for robust histogram comparison. IEEE Trans. Pattern Anal. Mach. Intell. **29**(5), 840–853 (2007)
20. Ling, H., Okada, K.: Diffusion distance for histogram comparison. In: Proceedings of 2006 IEEE Conference on Computer Vision and Pattern Recognition (CVPR 2006), vol. 1, pp. 246–253. IEEE Press, New York (2006)
21. Pele, O., Werman, M.: A linear time histogram metric for improved SIFT matching. In: Forsyth, D., Torr, P., Zisserman, A. (eds.) ECCV 2008, Part III. LNCS, vol. 5304, pp. 495–508. Springer, Heidelberg (2008)
22. Pele, O., Werman, M.: The quadratic-chi histogram distance family. In: Daniilidis, K., Maragos, P., Paragios, N. (eds.) ECCV 2010, Part II. LNCS, vol. 6312, pp. 749–762. Springer, Heidelberg (2010)
23. Jiang, W., Xiao, C., Jin, H., Zhu, S., Lu, Z.: Vehicle tracking with non-overlapping views for multi-camera surveillance system. In: Proceedings of the 15th IEEE International Conference on High Performance Computing and Communications (HPCC 2013), pp. 1213–1220. IEEE Press, Los Alamitos (2013)
24. Arandjelovic, R., Zisserman, A.: Three things everyone should know to improve object retrieval. In: Proceedings of 2012 IEEE Conference on Computer Vision and Pattern Recognition (CVPR 2012), pp. 2911–2918. IEEE Press, Los Alamitos (2012)
25. Pulli, K., Baksheev, A., Kornyakov, K., Eruhimov, V.: Real-time computer vision with OpenCV. Commun. ACM **55**(6), 61–69 (2012)

DFIS: A Scalable Distributed Fingerprint Identification System

Yunxiang Zhao, Wanxin Zhang, Dongsheng Li$^{(\boxtimes)}$, and Zhen Huang

National Laboratory for Parallel and Distributed Processing College of Computer,
National University of Defence Technology,
Changsha 410073, Hunan, People's Republic of China
{zhaoyx1993,camu7s,lds1201,maths_www}@163.com

Abstract. Fingerprint has been widely used in a variety of biometric identification systems. However, with the rapid development of fingerprint identification systems, the amount of fingerprints information stored in systems has been rising sharply, making it challenging to process and store fingerprints efficiently and robustly with traditional stand-alone systems and relational databases. In this paper, we propose a scalable distributed fingerprint identification system, named DFIS. It combines the feature extraction procedure with HIPI library and optimizes the load balance strategy of MongoDB to construct a much more robust and stable system. Related experiments and simulations have been carried out and results show that DFIS can reduce the time expense by 70 % during the features extraction procedural. For load balance of MongoDB, DFIS can decrease the difference of access load to less than 5 % and meanwhile decrease 50 % data migration to gain more reasonable distribution of operation load and data load among shards compared with the default load balance strategy in MongoDB.

Keywords: Fingerprint identification · Distributed computing · HIPI · MongoDB

1 Introduction

Fingerprint identification [9] is one of the most well-known and publicized biometrics, which obtains fingerprints through specific devices and then processes fingerprint images to get corresponding features for the future match [4,14]. The processing of fingerprint involves complex techniques including optical sensor technology, image processing, etc. Now fingerprint identification is becoming more and more popular thanks to its high availability and ease of operation.

Existing fingerprint identification systems and related researches have been focused on how to increase single fingerprints processing speed, such as parallelizing the process of preprocessing and feature extraction [5]. However, with the popularity of fingerprint in biometric identification systems and the coming of big data, we have to consider the condition of massive users and concurrent access. Therefore, it is inevitable to take distributed computing and cluster computing into consideration.

© Springer International Publishing Switzerland 2015
G. Wang et al. (Eds.): ICA3PP 2015, Part III, LNCS 9530, pp. 162–175, 2015.
DOI: 10.1007/978-3-319-27137-8_13

Currently, researches in distributed fingerprint processing are still at their beginning as using multiple nodes to process one single fingerprint is costly (data transfer between nodes occupies plenty of time and resources of the whole procedure). Based on this background, researches are putting images one by one to computing nodes and decreasing the time consumption by the advantage of distributed systems on multitask. However, there are two shortcomings when processing fingerprints with distributed systems:

1. Fingerprint (approximately 40 KB per fingerprint) transfer between nodes is very time consuming.
2. Existing databases are only considering the volume of data among nodes to balance data storage without paying attention to the pressure difference of data accessing like query and insertion, which may cause breakdowns of nodes under high accessing pressure.

In doing so, we propose a fingerprint identification system based on HIPI [11] and MongoDB. HIPI is an image processing library used with Apache Hadoop MapReduce [2,12] parallel programming framework. By compressing images into a Hipi Image Bundle (HIB) to reduce small images transfer time, HIPI can reduce the time consumption heavily. MongoDB, which consists of front-end mongos, back-end data shards and config servers [10], is responsible for low time expense and robust storage and management of fingerprint information. The contribution of this work can be summarized as follows:

1. Combines the feature extraction procedural of fingerprints with Hadoop and HIPI consequently decreasing the time consumption of processing large scale fingerprints by about 70 %.
2. Proposes two load balancing algorithms that enhance the systems stability: one is for balancing access requests on front-end mongos nodes using consistent hashing, while the other is an optimization of MongoDBs default load balancing algorithm based on load of data operation of each shard.

2   Related Works

There have been many researches in distributed image processing using distributed development platforms inclusive of Hadoop and Spark [12,13], such as the large-scale graphics processing based on Spark proposed by Kevin Mader [8], and HIPI [11] which we recommended at the beginning of this paper. While these works did facilitate image processing in distributed systems, its still challenging and worth studying to process small images including those of fingerprints in a high performance manner.

Currently, in the field of fingerprint identification, researchers focus on cutting down the processing time of traditional stand-alone fingerprint identification systems [6,7]. Miguel Lastra [7] proposed a fingerprint identification algorithm using GPU acceleration and had testified that the algorithm can improve the process efficiency by about 15 times on average, and as much as 54 times when resources of GPU is sufficient. Indrawan, G.s algorithm [5], the basic idea of which is parallelizing the process of minutiae extraction, can shorten the total time by about 50 %. However, its still a fresh field that needs expanding to process large scale fingerprints in distributed development environment.

HIPI is an image processing library which is designed to be used with Apache Hadoop MapReduce. HIPI provides a solution for how to store a large collection of images on the Hadoop Distributed File System (HDFS) and make them available for efficient distributed processing. HIPI facilitates efficient and high-throughput image processing with MapReduce style parallel programs typically executed on a cluster. The primary input and output object to HIPI is a Hipi-ImageBundle (HIB) file, which can be generated by several tools.

MongoDB is one of the most popular and widely used databases nowadays. According to the database rank released by DB-engines in January 2015 [3], MongoDB ranked 4th in all databases and 1st in NoSQL databases. Moreover, thousands of companies including eBay, MTV Networks and Stripe use MongoDB as their data management tool to meet the requirements like distributed storage and real-time operations.

Although MongoDB itself supports technologies of automatic data sharding, dynamically adding nodes, and automatic fail-over and provides satisfying performance of balancing back-end data storage, it lacks control of front-end access request, and is incapable faced with some specific occasions. MongoDBs default load balance strategy, while guaranteeing the balance of storage amount, can easily lead to imbalance of data accessing pressure among shards as hot data do exist in real production environment. These problems can have different impacts on production efficiency and data security in different environment.

3   System Architecture

As shown in Fig. 1, this paper depicts a system that integrates the process of feature extraction of fingerprint with HIPI computing platform to reduce the time consumption, and uses MongoDB to store feature data of fingerprints obtained by feature extraction in an efficient and robust manner. Moreover, an optimized load balancing algorithm proposed by this paper is applied in MongoDB cluster to improve the performance of responding to users requests.

When faced with large scale fingerprints, the first step is to preprocess fingerprints and extract features based on HIPI and store the features into text files (each file corresponds to one fingerprint), and then the data of fingerprint features are read from the text files and inserted into MongoDB on the basis of both front-end and back-end load balancing algorithms proposed by this paper.

4   Distributed Processing of Fingerprint

4.1   Normalization of Fingerprints Based on HIPI

Unified format and size of images will definitely reduce the difficulty of programming while improving the overall performance as Hadoop processes data

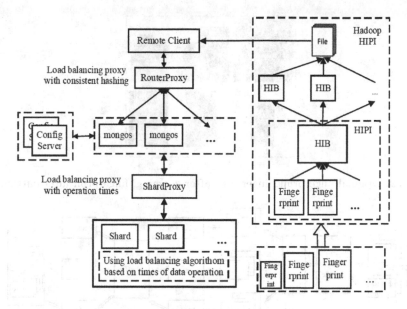

Fig. 1. System architecture of DFIS.

by blocks. Thus, we normalize fingerprint images of different sizes and scale collected by different fingerprint acquisition equipments at the beginning of the whole procedural by the following steps:

1. All the fingerprints downloaded from FCV database are zoomed by a predetermined height (580 pixels as default). As shown in Fig. 2, a_1 and b_1 are zoomed to a_2 and b_2.
2. Find the center of each fingerprints effective region; then use it as the standard point to cut the fingerprint processed after step 1 into a predetermined width (400 pixels as default).
   (a) If the width of a fingerprint is wider than 400 pixels, cut equal pixels from both left and right sides of the images while keeping the center point unchanged.
   (b) If the width of a fingerprint image is shorter than 400 pixels, we add equal solid colored pixels, which avoid influencing to recognition of effective region, to both sides of the images while keeping the center point unchanged.

As shown in Fig. 2, the height of a_1 is longer than the standard height and b_1 is shorter than the standard height. We first zoom them to the standard height at 580 pixels using bi-linear interpolation, which can keep the ridges shape stable and unchanged, and then get a_2 and b_2 in Fig. 2. After zooming, we cut fingerprint images according to the center of fingerprints effective region to get the final format a3 and b3 shown in Fig. 2.

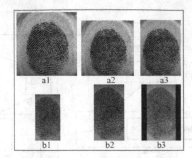

Fig. 2. Original fingerprint, fingerprint after zooming, fingerprint after cutting.

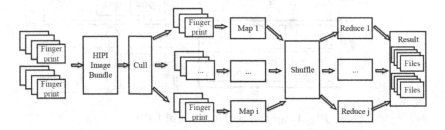

Fig. 3. Flow chart of fingerprint processing based on HIPI.

4.2 Fingerprint Processing Based on HIPI

To achieve low time expense of fingerprint processing, this paper combines the process with HIPI and the whole procedural is as shown in Fig. 3.

1. Transform all fingerprint images into a big HIB file using the APIs provided by HIPI to make the processing procedure much faster when dealing with big files.
2. The MapReduce program on Hadoop reads the HIB file and splits the big HIB file into several small HIB files for each mapper functions to process.
3. Complete the normalization described in Sect. 4.1 and then take the feature extraction step including segmentation, ridge orientation enhancement, average ridge distance calculation, minutiae detection, etc. All these jobs are executed in the map phase.
4. When the mappers complete their tasks successfully, the reducers combine the information of fingerprint and write the features information like average ridge distance and minutia to files.

5 Load Balance Optimization of MongoDB Cluster

Distributed system is outstanding to process big data and high concurrence. However, the imbalance of workloads among nodes or shards can easily cause unpredictable breakdown of a single node or even the whole system. Consequently, load balance in distributed systems has been the key point of related researches and also the first issue taken into consideration when constructing a distributed system.

However, researches focusing on solving the problem of load balance pay most of their attention to the balance of data volume, on the contrary neglecting the fact that operation load is the most important factor to evaluate the load balancing performance of a distributed system of high concurrency. This paper puts forward a load balance strategy for both the front-end mongos nodes and back-end data shards based on operation load.

The operation we mentioned here includes insertion, query, update and deletion. Previous research focus of load balance is data size, which can be represented by insertion because files which contain fingerprints information have similar sizes. Therefore, if the insertion times are balanced, then the data volume of shards will be in a balanced state too.

5.1   Load Balance Optimization of Front-End Mongos

As the only entrance from which clients can access MongoDB cluster, mongos plays an important role in the overall MongoDB architecture in terms of the clusters stability. However, MongoDB doesnt support load balancing and automatic fail-over of mongos nodes. Thus its a serious problem: Which mongos node should we choose to access and how can we react to an unpredictable breakdown?

To achieve the requirement of balancing the load of access to mongos nodes, we put a front-end Router Server in front of the MongoDB cluster to control the access from clients. When an access request comes, our router server distributes it to some mongos based on consistence hashing. By mapping all of the mongos nodes and data accessing requests to a circle space of hashed value and adding virtual nodes to each of them, the consistent hashing algorithm can distribute the data accessing requests evenly to mongos nodes. With consistence hashing algorithm shown in Algorithm 1, we can get the load balance of access requests among data shards while solving the problem of data shard breakdown.

5.2   Optimization of Load Balance on Back-End Data Shards

While MongoDB performs well distributing data among shards to reach a relative stable balanced state in terms of data size, in a fingerprint identification system where data are inserted once and then queried a lot, what we value most is the balance of data operation load. Operation load of a specific shard varies a lot and there are many factors count besides data size (for example, the users are located in one city mostly, and most people there have the fingerprint average ridge distance between 90 and 92; then the shards that store this range of fingerprint information might suffer obviously higher data accessing pressure). Therefore, load balance strategy based on data size among shards cannot balance the workloads among all shards indeed in a system that involves a large number of query operations.

Algorithm 1. Load balance of front-end mongos

```
Class Routers<Node> : {//data shard class
    nodes: mapping between virtual nodes to real mongos
    treeKey: mapping between key and real mongos
    routers: set of real mongos
}
init {//initialization
    add mongos to routers
    use mongos hostName+n as the input of hash() and map all the virtual nodes to
hash ring
}
connect {
    key: ip address of the access requirement
    hash(key): calculate the hash value of each access requirement and map them to
hash ring
    getMongosToConn(key)
    connectMongos()
}
getMongosToConn(String key) {
    find the mongos to connect by key
}
```

Based on the background introduced above, this paper proposes a load balance optimization strategy which can balance and migrate data chunks dynamically according to the operation load to reach a long term load balanced state both on data size and data operation load. We assume the size of each term of fingerprints information is in the same size, so we can use the amount of insertion operation to represent the data volume in shard.

Feature Analysis of Fingerprint. Average ridge distance is the most commonly used feature for fingerprint matching, and it is used as a reference feature by MongoDB to distribute items of fingerprint information among data shards. This paper aims at optimizing the default load balance strategy in MongoDB based on data operation load, and its essential to analyze the distribution feature of fingerprints based on average fingerprint ridge distance first on the basis of our optimization strategy.

This paper selects 5400 fingerprints form FCV2006 randomly and extracts their average ridge distance to analyze their distribution.

It is clearly shown in Fig. 4 that range $[67, 79)$ has about 70 percent of fingerprints even though the span is only a quarter. Another key observation is that the closer to 71 the average ridge distance is, the more intensive fingerprints distribution is.

The number of fingerprints is one of the most important reasons affecting the operation load, but not the only one, as hot data do exist in production environment, which leads to a different distribution of data operation load from that of the number of fingerprints. For example, as is shown by the dotted curve

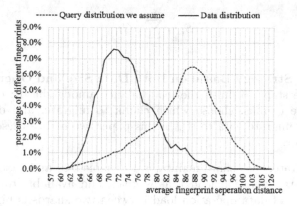

Fig. 4. The distribution of fingerprint based on average fingerprint ridge distance.

in Fig. 4, we assume a database stores fingerprints features of massive users, and operations on fingerprints occur most frequently when the average ridge distance is near 90. However, most fingerprints average ridge distance fall in the range of $[68, 72)$ according to the solid curve in Fig. 4. In this case, if we still shard data according to the data size, the nodes that store the fingerprints at average ridge distance of 90 will suffer much higher data operation workloads and are more likely to crash down.

Representation of Operation Load. Assuming that there are n chunks in a data shard, C_i represents chunk$[i]$, SC_j represents the operation load of Ci and SC represents the total operation load of this shard. There are four types of operation including insertion, deletion, update and query on the data in MongoDB cluster. We use I_i, Q_i, U_i, and D_i to represent the times of these four types of operation on C_i respectively. SC_i is calculated as follows:

$$S C_i = I_i + Q_i + U_i + D_i \tag{1}$$

It is obvious that four types of operation have different weights in different situations in terms of the difference in operating time and frequency. The fingerprint identification system proposed by this paper cares more about the performance of fingerprint matching, which corresponds to the query operation, so the weight for query operation is set to a number larger than 1 while weight of other operations are smaller than 1, and these weights can change with changing demand of different requests. Whats more, if the data size among shards is the most important feature when judging load balance, we can increase the value of Inc1 in formula 2 dynamically when we detect the importance of it during the time the system is running. Then we revise the formula as follows:

$$S C_j = Inc1 \times I_i + Inc2 \times R_i + Inc3 \times U_i + Inc4 \times D_i \tag{2}$$

The frequency of each shard SC_j is the sum of all the chunks frequency in that shard (assuming the chunk number of shard i is n), which can be represented as follows:

$$S_i = \sum_{i=1}^{n} SC_i. \tag{3}$$

Load Balance Strategy Based on Both Data Size and Operation Load.
There are three steps to finish the load balance among shards: determine the time to migrate chunks, choose which chunk to migrate, and determine the target shard to migrate data to [1]. In this paper, we realize these steps in the following manner:

1. Time to migrate: each shard maintains a variable SC_i and a global threshold based on data operation load that is given and available to all shards. If the difference of data operation load between two shards is bigger than the threshold, then the workloads on these shards are recognized as imbalanced and need balancing by migrating some number of chunks.
2. Choose the chunk to migrate: if the source shard from which chunks are migrated has more chunks, choose chunks in source shard with minimum SC_i to the target shard; else if the source shard has fewer chunks, choose chunks in source shard with maximum SC_i to the target shard; if the source shard and the target shard has the same number of chunks, choose chunks at the top of the source shard to gain the highest migration speed (the number of chunks we choose are related to the average chunk size of shards and the threshold we set. To make data operation load balanced between two shards, we need more chunks if we choose minimum SC_i and for the maximum chunks, we need fewer).
3. Migration: migrate the chunks selected form step 2 to the target shard and finish the migration. After these steps of two load balance strategies, we can reach a balanced state in terms of both data size and data operation load at the same time.

6   Evaluations

In this section we evaluate the performance of fingerprint image processing based on HIPI and load balancing optimization of MongoDB respectively.

After combining the process of fingerprint images feature extraction with HIPI, the time consumption is only about 30 % as that of using default Hadoop configuration. The load balancing strategy of mongos decreases the difference of access amount less than 5 % and the optimization of MongoDBs default load balancing strategy on data shards realizes the load balance of data amount and operation load at the same time.

6.1   Experiment Evaluation of Distributed Processing of Fingerprints

We first show that fingerprint images feature extraction based on HIPI gives a significant time-savings over Hadoop. Two experiments have been done with the

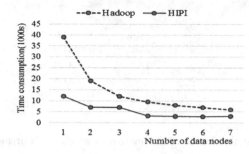

Fig. 5. Time consumption of Hadoop and HIPI.

FCV database (we select 12000 images in JPG format for simulation, while in practical application, the scale of images might be more than ten millions or even a billion). Experiment settings are as follows.

1. Using Hadoop platform, which contains one Name-node and several Data-nodes (1 to 7).
2. Using HIPI computing framework, which contains one Name-node and several Data-nodes (1 to 7).

Figure 5 shows that with the number of Data-nodes increasing, the time consumption decreases sharply. As we use the default size (64 MB) of HDFS block, the experiment fingerprint images will be grouped in 7 blocks in the HDFS. When there is only one Data-node, it has to process 7 chunks; for 2 and 3 Data-nodes, they have to process 3 and 4 chunks separately; for 4 to 7 Data-nodes, three of them have to process 2 chunks separately and one to process one chunk. So the Data-nodes number 1, 2 and 4 are what we should consider.

After the analysis of Fig. 5, we can conclude that fingerprint images feature exaction based on HIPI consumes only about 30 % time as that of using only MapReduce in Hadoop.

6.2 Experimental Evaluation of Load Balance on Front-End

We deploy a MongoDB cluster of one config server and four data nodes where each one runs a mongos at the same time and then use the MapReduce to count the number of requests processed on each mongos when faced with 1000 concurrent data accessing requests. Figure 6 shows the distribution of concurrent access from users among four mongos. Each mongos node located in a server machine undertakes 27 %, 25 %, 24 % and 24 % of 1000 concurrent requests respectively, indicating that this strategy can distribute the queries from clients evenly.

We get the conclusion that load balance of mongos based on consistent hashing can distribute the query requests evenly among mongos nodes. The difference of access amount is less than 5 % which can decrease the load of queries when the number of concurrent access is extremely high.

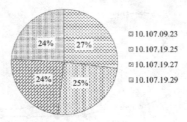

Fig. 6. Distribution of 1000 concurrent access on four mongos.

6.3   Analytical Evaluation of Load Balance on Back-End

We take the times of data migration as the standard to judge if our optimization strategy has better performance, for the reason that migrating data among shards consumes most of the time in the process of balancing the workloads on each shard. To make the result more intuitive, we make two simulation experiments selecting insertion and query as an example rather than all the four types of operation to compute frequency of data operation, and the weight of insertion and query are both set to 1. The assumptions are made as follows:

1. There are 4 shards to distribute.
2. Each size of an item inserted is 1M.
3. If a chunk is larger than 200M, then it will be split into several smaller chunks.
4. The thresholds that determine when to start load balance are set to 400MB for shard size and 400 times for operation (query) separately.
5. Since the chunk size is 200M and the thresholds are both 400(M or times), each time we will migrate chunks with the total size about 200M.
6. 10,000 insertion and 10,000 queries occur with the probability of 50 % for each.
7. We assume the weight of insertion and query are both 1.

According to the distribution of fingerprint based on average fingerprint distance in Fig. 4, we calculate the fitting formula of its distribution with gauss distribution as follows:

$$f(x) = 323 \times e^{(-(\frac{(x-70.86)}{5.087})^2)} + 175.3 \times e^{(-(\frac{(x-77.1)}{8.026})^2)} \qquad (4)$$

To evaluate our optimization strategy, we assume a formula of its query distribution based on the average ridge distance which is similar to the dotted curve in Fig. 4, and then the fitting result with gauss distribution of it is as follows:

$$f(x) = 289.4 \times e^{(-(\frac{(x-105.1)}{13.01})^2)} + 161.8 \times e^{(-(\frac{(x-89.17)}{29.21})^2)} \qquad (5)$$

Based on these assumptions, we carry out two experiments, each of which is repeated 20 times to obtain the average result. The experiments are constructed in different situations as follows:

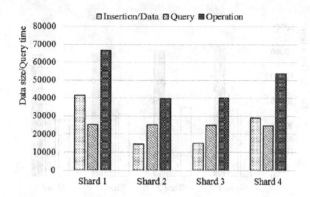

Fig. 7. Distribution of insertion and query with default strategy in MongoDB.

1. Default migration strategy in MongoDB, which migrates the chunks at the top of source shard if the number of chunks that the source shard has more than target shard is larger than a threshold.
2. Optimized migration strategy based on data operation load which migrates chunks according to the insertion (or data size) and query is explained in Sect. 5.2. After these experiments, we count the times of insertion and query on each shard and get the histograms which show the distribution of query, insertion with a weight for each and total operation load of these two experiments.

Figure 7 shows the distribution of data size and times of data query and insertion operation of each shard with the default strategy in MongoDB, and columns on each shard from left to right represent times of query, times of insertion at the same time the data size (MB), and times of total data operation including query and insertion respectively. We can observe that it takes 6.3 chunks migration to get the data balanced in average. Thus we can conclude from Fig. 8 that the MongoDBs default load balance strategy balances the load of each shard quite well in terms of data size. However the total operation load varies a lot among shards, as MongoDB lacks corresponding strategy.

Figure 8 shows the distribution of data size and times of data query and insertion operation of each shard with the optimization strategy, and columns on each shard from left to right represent times of query, times of insertion at the same time the data size (MB), and time of total data operation including query and insertion respectively. It can be computed by the results in the graph that it takes about 3.2 times migration in average to get the workloads on shards balanced. It is obviously that the optimized method reduces difference in both data size and amount of data operation among shards, even though the data distribution is not as good as the default strategy in MongoDB in terms of data size. However, the total operation load is much more balanced.

We can conclude from Figs. 7 and 8 that default load balance strategy in MongoDB can get the data balanced pretty well. In contrast, the optimization

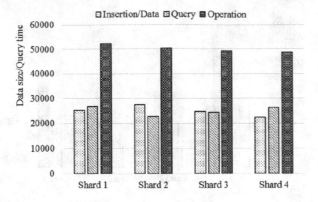

Fig. 8. Distribution of insertion and query with optimized strategy in MongoDB.

strategy proposed by this paper balances both the data storage and data operation load and at the same time migrate less chunks, even though the performance of data balance in terms of data size is not as good as MongoDBs default strategy. To explain whether our strategy is better, we choose another steeper formula of query distribution as formula 6 and the insertion distribution is unchanged.

$$f(x) = 520.3 \times e^{\left(-\left(\frac{(x-105)}{13.82}\right)^2\right)} + 188.8 \times e^{\left(-\left(\frac{(x-82.92)}{21.92}\right)^2\right)} \tag{6}$$

After the same experiment, we get that the average migration times of the steeper one is about 5.35 times using MongoDBs default strategy and 3 times using our optimization strategy. And because the insertion and query occur randomly, the result of our experiments can adapt to any occasions. We can get the conclusion that when the distribution of data operation load is different from that of data volume based on average ridge distance, our optimization strategy can get a much better performance no matter the curve is flat or steep.

7   Conclusion and Future Work

During the feature extraction of fingerprint images, this paper combines the traditional methods with HIPI to conquer the time consumption when dealing with massive fingerprint images using distributed computing systems. Compared with default Hadoop platform, the method we propose can decrease the time consumption by about 70 %. Using consistent hashing to distribute the concurrent queries can control the difference of access requests to less than 5 %, which improves the stability of the whole system effectively. We also proposed a load balance strategy based on both data size and operation load of insertion, query, update and deletion, which can use fewer migration times to gain more reasonable distribution of operation load and data size among data shards when the distribution of operation load is different from that of data size.

In the future, on the one hand, we will try to implement the load balance strategy of data shards in real MongoDB systems to make it available to all users. On the other hand, its worth working on to integrate MongoDB and HIPI, indicating that fingerprint features obtained by HIPI will be directly stored into MongoDB instead of storing them in HDFS first.

Acknowledgments. This work is supported by the National Basic Research Program of China (973) under Grant No.2014CB340303, the National Natural Science Foundation of China under Grant No.61222205, No.61402490, and No.61303064. This work is also supported by the Program for New Century Excellent Talents in University, the Fok Ying-Tong Education Foundation under Grant No. 141066, and Foundation of Distinguished PHD Thesis of Hunan Province.

References

1. Chodorow, K.: Scaling MongoDB. O'Reilly Media Inc, Sebastopol (2011)
2. Dean, J., Ghemawat, S.: Mapreduce: simplified data processing on large clusters. Commun. ACM **51**(1), 107–113 (2008)
3. Engines, D.: Db-engines ranking (2013)
4. Hong, L., Wan, Y., Jain, A.: Fingerprint image enhancement: algorithm and performance evaluation. IEEE Trans. Pattern Anal. Mach. Intell. **20**(8), 777–789 (1998)
5. Indrawan, G., Sitohang, B., Akbar, S.: Parallel processing for fingerprint feature extraction. In: 2011 International Conference on Electrical Engineering and Informatics (ICEEI), pp. 1–6. IEEE (2011)
6. Khanyile, N., Tapamo, J., Dube, E.: Distributed fingerprint enhancement on a multicore cluster (2012)
7. Lastra, M., Carabaño, J., Gutiérrez, P.D., Benítez, J.M., Herrera, F.: Fast fingerprint identification using gpus. Inf. Sci. **301**, 195–214 (2015)
8. Mader, K., Donahue, L.R., Müller, R., Stampanoni, M.: High-throughput, scalable, quantitative, cellular phenotyping using x-ray tomographic microscopy (2014)
9. Maltoni, D., Maio, D., Jain, A.K., Prabhakar, S.: Handbook of fingerprint recognition. Springer Science and Business Media, London (2009)
10. Membrey, P., Plugge, E., Hawkins, D.: The Definitive Guide to MongoDB: The noSQL Database for Cloud and Desktop Computing. Apress, Beijing (2010)
11. Sweeney, C., Liu, L., Arietta, S., Lawrence, J.: Hipi: A Hadoop Image Processing Interface for Image-based Mapreduce Tasks. University of Virginia, Chris (2011)
12. White, T.: Hadoop: The Definitive Guide. O'Reilly Media Inc, Sebastopol (2012)
13. Zaharia, M., Chowdhury, M., Franklin, M.J., Shenker, S., Stoica, I.: Spark: cluster computing with working sets. In: Proceedings of the 2nd USENIX Conference on Hot Topics in Cloud Computing, vol. 10, p. 10 (2010)
14. Zhu, E., Hancock, E., Yin, J., Zhang, J., An, H.: Fusion of multiple candidate orientations in fingerprints. In: Kamel, M., Campilho, A. (eds.) ICIAR 2011, Part II. LNCS, vol. 6754, pp. 89–100. Springer, Heidelberg (2011)

Energy Saving and Load Balancing for SDN Based on Multi-objective Particle Swarm Optimization

Runshui Zhu, Hua Wang[(⊠)], Yanqing Gao, Shanwen Yi,
and Fangjin Zhu

School of Computer Science and Technology,
Shandong University, Jinan 250101, China
zrs@mail.sdu.edu.cn, wanghua@sdu.edu.cn

Abstract. With the rapid development of cloud computing and large-scale data centers, the problem of network energy consumption is increasingly prominent. Most of the energy saving strategies on current IP network only aggregate traffic into a part of links. It leads to imbalance link utilization and seriously impacts the quality of service. With the emergence of the software defined network, the intelligent energy management becomes possible. In this paper, we take advantage of the centralized control and global vision of SDN to achieve the network energy saving and load balancing by dynamically aggregating and balancing of the traffic while ensuring QoS. We add actual QoS constrains to the basic maximum concurrent flow problem to formulate a multi-objective mixed integer programming model and we propose a multi-objective particle swarm optimization algorithm called MOPSO to solve this NP-hard problem. MOPSO distribute optimal paths for dynamic traffic demands and make idol switches and links into sleeping mode. Simulation results on real topologies and traffic demands show the effectiveness of our algorithm both on the objective of energy saving and load balancing compared with other algorithms.

Keywords: Software defined network · Multi-objective particle swarm optimization · Energy saving · Load balancing · Mixed integer programming

1 Introduction

In recent years, the power consumption problem in ICT industry is increasingly serious [1]. Reports indicate that the power consumption of ICT industry is 156 GWH, and the annual growth rate reached 12 % [2]. Servers, switches, cooling devices and other network devices consumed 868 billion KWH, accounting for 5.3 % of total global power consumption. Power consumption has become a great obstacle for sustainable development of network and information system [3]. Researches on network energy saving are of great importance in the current situation of global warming and energy shortage.

The network power consumption problem is largely caused by the current network architecture. There are two major problems: over-provisioning and redundancy [4]. Most of the network devices are running at full capacity in 7 * 24 h, but the utilization is quite low most of the time. Data shows that the current network link utilization is

© Springer International Publishing Switzerland 2015
G. Wang et al. (Eds.): ICA3PP 2015, Part III, LNCS 9530, pp. 176–189, 2015.
DOI: 10.1007/978-3-319-27137-8_14

very imbalance. The busiest link utilization can reach 80 %, while the average utilization is only 30 % to 50 % [5]. The current IP network can't fully understand the source and destination information of traffic demands, only routing to the shortest path according to the destination address. As a result, most QoS routing optimization algorithms cannot be achieved in actual networks. Although MPLS can be used for traffic engineering, explicit routing by establishing label switched paths costs too much.

Software defined network based on OpenFlow overcomes these shortcomings of the IP network. SDN supports well for source routing, flow splitting and multipath routing [6, 7]. The design and implementation of energy optimization algorithms in SDN is feasible and efficient. In this paper, we solve the imbalance utilization and power consumption problems based on the architecture of SDN through energy optimizing and load balancing. The main contributions of our paper are as follows. Firstly, we abstract this routing optimization problem and establish a multi-objective mixed integer programming model based on the maximum concurrent flow problem [8] by adding actual QoS constraints. Secondly, because the multi-objective mixed integer programming problem is NP-hard, we propose a multi-objective particle swarm optimization algorithm called MOPSO to solve it, optimizing the power consumption and link utilization at the same time. Finally, we do simulation experiments using topologies and traffic data from real networks and we compare our MOPSO algorithm with traditional OSPF, global greedy algorithm (GGA) and Multi-objective Evolutionary Algorithm (MOEA) in many respects.

The rest of this paper is organized as follows. Section 2 summarizes the study of network energy saving in recent years. Section 3 puts forward the definition and mathematical model of the energy efficiency and load balancing routing optimization problem. In Sect. 4 our multi-objective particle swarm optimization algorithm is proposed. Section 5 evaluates and analyzes the performance of the proposed algorithm through simulation experiments, and Sect. 6 concludes this paper.

2 Related Work

Early strategies of network energy saving simply consider routers as isolate hardware devices, and they save energy on hardware layer. They can be divided into two categories, one is the sleeping mode, and the other is adaptive link rate. Gupta et al. study the Sleeping Mode in [9, 10], and it achieves energy saving by putting network devices into Low-power mode. Gunaratne et al. discuss the adaptive link rate in [11, 12], and it decreases the link rate when links are idle.

Hardware level energy saving strategies are lack of overall collaboration between network devices, and the performance is unstable. Better energy saving effect can be obtained through the coordination between various devices on network level. The idea of energy aware routing is first proposed by Gupta et al. in [9]. He discusses the possibility of coordinating the sleeping timing of two routers. But it is difficult to be implemented subject to the architecture of IP network. Chiaraviglio et al. establish an Integer Linear Programming model for the energy aware routing problem in [13], and he uses greedy algorithm to turn off nodes and links gradually to solve the problem. Heller et al. propose elastic tree in [14]. It tries to satisfy the constantly changing traffic in data centers by adjusting the active links and switches, but it is not suitable for general network topologies. Chabarek et al. propose an energy aware network design method in [15], and it achieves energy saving by turning off low load links and nodes and transfers traffic to other links and nodes. IP networks do not support this routing method, and it is difficult to be deployed.

SDN gives the possibility of implementing more powerful routing optimization algorithms. Exploring the power management strategies of network based on SDN platform is feasible and is the trend of the present study. An energy aware routing algorithm called GGA in SDN is proposed in [16], and it reroutes traffic through different paths to adjust the workload of links when the network is relatively idle. The algorithm performance cannot be guaranteed using greedy algorithms and it does not take full advantage of SDN architecture. Tu et al. establishes an energy saving model for SDN in [17], and he tests the energy saving effect of the model under different traffic models and traffic load. But it only applies to data centers. The authors in [18] propose MOEA to optimize the energy performance in the whole network by utilizing a multi-objective evolutionary algorithm for route selection. MOEA can improve the energy performance of high priority traffic without degrading QoS, but its performance degrades on low priority traffic.

3   The Mathematical Model

3.1   Energy Model and Multiple Optimization Objectives

Through the experimental measurement, the power consumption of a switch is mainly composed of a chassis and several line cards. In this paper we use two-port line cards. A switch need to turn on a line card when connecting two new links. If a switch connects more than one link, its chassis must be kept on. So the energy model of the network can be described as Eq. (1) and the notation used is shown in Table 1.

Table 1. Notation used in this paper

Notation	Meaning
x_{ij}	1 if the link from i to j is used, 0 otherwise
x_{ij}^{st}	1 if the link from i to j is used by traffic demand from s to t, 0 otherwise
y_i	1 if the chassis on switch i is used, 0 otherwise
PN_{total}	Total power consumption of the network
PC	Power consumption of a chassis
PL	Power consumption of a line card
d^{st}	Traffic demand between source switch s and destination switch t
Del^{st}	Delay constrain of traffic demand between s and t
c_{ij}	Link capacity from i to j
θ	Maximum link utilization, ranges in [0,1]
λ	Maximum passing rate of traffic demands, ranges in [0,1]
f_{ij}^{st}	Capacity allocated to demand from s to t on link from i to j
f_{ij}	Total capacity allocated on link from i to j
del_{ij}	Delay of link from i to j

$$PN_{total} = \sum_{i=1}^{N} PCy_i + \sum_{i=1}^{N} \left[\sum_{j=1}^{N} (x_{ij} + x_{ji})/2 \right] PL \qquad (1)$$

Minimizing energy consumption PN_{total} is our first optimization objective, and we also optimize load balancing. The objective of load balancing is to minimize the maximum link utilization (MLU). We constrain the utilization θ of each link, then our second objective is to minimize θ.

3.2 MOMILP Formulation

The energy saving and load balancing routing optimization problem can be modeled based on the maximum concurrent flow problem. We add several actual QoS constraints to it and build a multi-objective mixed integer linear programming (MOMILP) to describe this problem. Servers are connected by switches and their traffic demands are transmitted through the switches between them. We model the network as a directed graph $G = (V, E)$, where V is the set of nodes (switches) and E is the set of links. The traffic demands of one moment can be represented by a *ST pair*. There are k traffic demands $STs = \{(s_i, t_i, d_i, Del_i), i = 1 \ldots k\}$, where s_i, t_i, d_i, Del_i represent the source, destination, demand and delay constrain of traffic demand i respectively. According to the description above, we can get the following MOMILP model.

$$\text{Minimize} \quad (PN_{total}, \theta) \qquad (2)$$

$$\text{Subject to:} \quad \sum_{j=1}^{N} f_{ij}^{st} - \sum_{j=1}^{N} f_{ji}^{st} = \begin{cases} \lambda d^{st} & \forall s, t, i = s \\ -\lambda d^{st} & \forall s, t, i = t \\ 0 & \forall s, t, i \neq s, t \end{cases} \qquad (3)$$

$$f_{ij} = \sum_{s=1}^{N} \sum_{t=1}^{N} f_{ij}^{st}, \quad \forall i, j, \forall s, t \qquad (4)$$

$$f_{ij} \leq \theta c_{ij} x_{ij}, \quad \forall i, j \qquad (5)$$

$$\sum_{i=1}^{N} \sum_{j=1}^{N} x_{ij}^{st} del_{ij} \leq Del^{st}, \forall i, j, \forall s, t \qquad (6)$$

$$\sum_{j=1}^{N} x_{ij} + \sum_{j=1}^{N} x_{ij} \leq My_i, \forall i \qquad (7)$$

$$f_{ij}^{st} \leq c_{ij} x_{ij}^{st}, \forall i, j, \forall s, t \qquad (8)$$

$$x_{ij} \in \{0, 1\}, x_{ij}^{st} \in \{0, 1\}, y_i \in \{0, 1\}, \ c_{ij} > 0, \ d^{st} > 0, \ f_{ij}^{st} > 0$$

Equation (3) states the classical flow conservation constraints. λ represents the passing rate defined as the rate that can be routed successfully of each demand. In order to ensure the QoS, we limit it to not less than 80 %. Equation (4) calculates the total flow routed on each link. Equation (5) is the load balance constraint and it limit the utilization of each link not to exceed θ. Equation (6) guarantees the QoS, and it constrains that the total delay of a routing path allocated to a demand cannot exceed the maximum delay it allows. Equation (7) ensures that the chassis of a switch can be turned off only if all line cards connected to it have been turned off. Equation (8) shows whether a link is used by a certain traffic demand. The big-M method is used to force the above two constraints, $M \geq 2N$.

On mathematics this model belongs to multi-objective mixed integer linear programming problem, and MOMILP is NP-hard that cannot be solved in polynomial time. It means that we will spend much time finding out a feasible routing solution in large-scale networks. It will seriously impact the efficiency of the network. Consequently, we must design a heuristic algorithms to tackle this problem.

4   Multi-objective Particle Swarm Optimization Algorithm

4.1   MOPSO Algorithm Description

Particle swarm optimization (PSO) algorithm is a kind of swarm intelligence algorithm, and it has a good convergence and optimization performance [19]. In this paper we extend standard PSO to multi-objective particle swarm optimization algorithm called MOPSO to solve the multi-objective optimization problem. Because multiple objectives may conflict with each other, we set up multiple populations and find out the optimal solution by cooperative coevolution between different populations.

The main ideas of MOPSO are as follows. We set up one population for every optimization objective. In each iteration, each population optimizes its own objective according to the standard PSO algorithm and each population's fitness is also determined by its own objective function. After each iteration, we select the Pareto solutions from each population and keep them in the external archive. By using the external archive we can guide the evolution of each population and realize information sharing between different populations.

4.2   MOPSO Algorithm Design

4.2.1   The Form of MOPSO Particles

Our routing optimization algorithm tries to find a subgraph that can satisfy all traffic demands as much as possible. The subgraph is composed of the paths allocated to each demand. In this paper, we first optimize the subgraph directly and a subgraph itself is a feasible solution, represented by a MOPSO particle. The evolution process of populations is the process of merging and optimizing subgraphs. A subgraph particle G is represented by a $N \times N$ adjacency matrix, and N is the number of nodes in the network topology. If $G[i][j] = 1$, the link between switch i and j is in this subgraph, otherwise not.

4.2.2   Initialization of MOPSO Particles

In order to guarantee the diversity of populations and avoid falling into local optimum, we first initialize all populations randomly. The random initialization steps are as follows.

Step1: Delete a link randomly from the topoology;
Step2: If this link connects a source node or destination node, cancel this deletion and go Step1;
Step3: If the subgraph after deletion is not a connected graph, cancel this deletion and go Step1;
Step4: If the number of deleted links is less than β, go Step1;
Step5: Cut off all terminal nodes that are not source nodes or destination nodes;
Step6: Output this subgraph;

β is the total number of links that allowed to be deleted, and we can adjust its value to change the random level. We need to compute optimal paths in this subgraph to route the flow of all traffic demands and cut off the links and nodes not involved in any path. We select links for each traffic demand based on the fitness of each link to compose a routing path. For different optimization objectives we design different fitness evaluation functions of links as follows.

$$Fitness(e)_{EC} = \begin{cases} 0, & if\ Bl(e) < Bl(d), \\ \alpha_1 e^{-Bl(e)/Bf(e)} + \alpha_2 e^{-Del(e)/AvgDel}, & otherwise, \end{cases} \quad (9)$$

$$Fitness(e)_{LB} = \begin{cases} 0, & if\ Bl(e) < Bl(d), \\ \alpha_1 e^{Bl(e)/Bf(e)} + \alpha_2 e^{-Del(e)/AvgDel}, & otherwise, \end{cases} \quad (10)$$

where $Bl(e)$ represents the remaining bandwidth of a link. $Bl(d)$ represents the traffic of a demand that has not been routed. $Del(e)$ represents the delay of a link. $AvgDel$ represents the average delay of the network. α_1 and α_2 are the weight values. $Fitness(e)_{LB}$ is the fitness function of the objective for load balancing, tending to choose links under low utilization. $Fitness(e)_{EC}$ is the fitness function of the objective for energy saving, tending to aggregate traffic into a part of links. We adopts the weighted value of exponential functions because an exponential function can reflect a slight change of variables more easily than linear function.

4.2.3   Fitness of MOPSO Particles

We calculate the fitness of a particle according to the property of the subgraph it represents. Fitness of a particle is equal to the fitness of its subgraph. For different optimization objectives we design different fitness evaluation functions of particles as follows.

$$Fitness(G)_{EC} = \alpha_1 e^{-PN(G)} + \alpha_2 e^{-Del(G)} \tag{11}$$

$$Fitness(G)_{LB} = \alpha_1 e^{-MLU(G)} + \alpha_2 e^{-Del(G)} \tag{12}$$

where $Fitness(G)_{EC}$ is the fitness function of the particles in the population of energy saving. $PN(G)$ represents the total power consumption of the subgraph and the subgraph with a lower power consumption gets a bigger fitness. $Fitness(G)_{LB}$ is the fitness function of the particles in the population of load balancing. $MLU(G)$ represents the maximum link utilization of the subgraph and the subgraph with a smaller MLU gets a bigger fitness. $Del(G)$ represents the maximum delay of paths in this subgraph.

4.2.4 Update of MOPSO Particles

The update of the particles of standard PSO is dictated by the following formula.

$$v_{id} = wv_{id} + c_1 r_1 (lb - x_{id}) + c_2 r_2 (gb - x_{id}) \tag{13}$$

$$x_{id} = x_{id} + v_{id} \tag{14}$$

where v_{id} indicates the particle speed, x_{id} refers to the current position of the particle, lb and gb represent this particle's local best position, and the global best position respectively. w is an inertia weight, c_1 and c_2 are acceleration coefficients. r_1 and r_2 are two random numbers within [0, 1]. Formula (13) calculates the current particle's velocity according to each particle's previous speed, the local best position and the global best position. Formula (14) updates every particle's position in the multi-dimensional space. In this paper we improve the standard update method based on the characteristics of the routing optimization problem and we first propose idea of subgraph merging and optimizing to update particles. We merge current particle's subgraph with the local best subgraph and global best subgraph and then optimize the merged subgraph. A subgraph is presented by its adjacency matrix, and we merge subgraphs by OR operation between their adjacency matrixes as follows.

$$G_{id}[i][j] = (w \cdot G_{id}[i][j]) \vee (c_1 r_1 \cdot G_{lb}[i][j]) \vee (c_2 r_2 \cdot G_{gb}[i][j]) \tag{15}$$

$$a \cdot G_{id}[i][j] = \begin{cases} 0, & if\ rand(0,1) > aG_{id}[i][j], \\ 1 & otherwise, \end{cases} \tag{16}$$

where a is any real number and $rand(0,1)$ is a random number between 0 and 1.

4.2.5 The External Archive

In multi-objective optimization problems each population evolves according to their own optimization objectives. Because multiple objectives may conflict with each other, we set up an external archive EA to coordinate different populations. Two optimal particles G_a and G_b will be generated by two populations after each iteration. If $G_a \prec G_b$ which means G_a dominants G_b, then G_a will be added to the external archive EA, otherwise G_b will be added. If they do not dominant each other, they both will be added to EA. We define $G_a \prec G_b$ as follows.

$$Fitness(G_a)_{EC} \geq Fitness(G_b)_{EC} \text{ and } Fitness(G_a)_{LB} > Fitness(G_b)_{LB} \quad or$$
$$Fitness(G_a)_{EC} > Fitness(G_b)_{EC} \text{ and } Fitness(G_a)_{LB} \geq Fitness(G_b)_{LB} \tag{17}$$

We merge all the particles in the external archive to realize information sharing between different populations. The merged particle is called the balance particle *Balancer*. Particles in different populations modify their evolution directions by emerging themselves with *Balancer*. Formulas (18) and (19) describe the two merging processes.

$$Balancer[i][j] = A_1[i][j] \vee A_2[i][j] \vee A_3[i][j] \vee \cdots A_n[i][j] \tag{18}$$

$$G_{id}[i][j] = b_1 \cdot G_{id}[i][j] \vee b_2 \cdot Balancer[i][j] \tag{19}$$

where A_{id} is a particle in the external archive, *Balancer* is the balance particle, b_1 and b_2 are acceleration coefficients.

4.2.6   Update of the External Archive

With the increase of the iteration number, the number of particles in the external archive increases. In order to ensure the convergence speed and computation efficiency of the algorithm, we limit the capacity of the external archive. When the particle number exceeds the maximum capacity C_{max}, a part of the particles will be eliminated. We sort all the particles based on their similarities between *Balancer* and then eliminate the particles with the highest similarities. The similarity of a particle Sim_{id} is defined as the proportion of the link number both in two graphs to the total link number as follows.

$$Sim_{id} = LinkNum(A_{id} \cap Balancer)/LinkNum(Balancer) \tag{20}$$

4.3   MOPSO Algorithm Implementation

Step1: Set two populations POP_{EC} and POP_{LB} for the objective of energy saving and load balancing respectively, randomly initialize n particles for each population according to algorithm 4.1.3. Each particle represents a subgraph G.

Step2: Select links for each traffic demand based on $Fitness(e)_{EC}$ and $Fitness(e)_{LB}$ to compose a routing path in each subgraph in POP_{EC} and POP_{LB}, cut off the links and nodes not involved in any path and get the new subgraph G'.

Step3: Calculate the fitness of each population's particles according to $Fitness(G)_{LB}$ and $Fitness(G)_{LB}$ and select the particle with the highest fitness as their local best particle l G_{lb} and global best particle G_{gb} respectively. If one population's G_{gb} dominate the other's G_{gb}, then we choose it as the Pareto best particle G_{pb}, otherwise we choose randomly.

Step4: Set the number of circulations m.

Step5: Save the two populations' G_{lb} into EA according to algorithm 4.1.6. Eliminate particles according to algorithm 4.1.7 and calculate *Balancer* according to formula (18).

Step6: Update all particles according to algorithm 4.1.5 and merge particles with *Balancer* according to formula (19). Optimize the merged subgraph according to Step2.

Step7: Calculate the fitness of all particles. Update G_{lb} and G_{gb}. If one population's G_{gb} dominate the other's G_{gb}, then we update G_{pb} by it.

Step8: Inspect the terminal condition. If the number of iterations reaches m or the Pareto best solution G_{pb} has not changed for some time, then go to Step 9. Otherwise, go to Step 5.

Step9: Output the optimal subgraph represented by G_{pb}.

5 Experiments and Evaluation

5.1 Simulation Environment

In the simulation experiment of this paper, the network topology and traffic demand information is from SNDLIB [19]. SNDLIB collects the topology and traffic model of real networks such as Abilen and GEANT. We assume that the network is equipped with the same 8-port switches. The power of the chassis is set as 100 W, and each line card is 20 W. The MOPSO algorithm we propose is implemented by C++ with Visual Studio 2013 and runs on an Intel Core i5-3470 with 4 GB memory running Windows 7. We also implement the MOEA, GGA algorithm in [16, 18] and traditional OSPF algorithm on the same platform. We will compare MOPSO with the other three algorithms in the following aspects. In the following figures, the network scale is represented by the number of nodes and the number of demands is set to 20 % of node numbers if there are no special instructions. Other detailed information about links and traffic demands is generated by the models from SNDLIB.

5.2 Power Consumption

According to Fig. 1, we can see that as the scale becomes larger, the power consumption of all algorithms increases. OSPF algorithm uses the shortest path routing, and it has no energy saving effect. GGA optimizes the single objective of energy saving based on greedy strategy and can really save some energy. MOEA saves much energy using genetic algorithm. Its performance is as good as MOPSO in small networks. When the topology becomes larger than 200 nodes, the superiority of MOPSO turns more obvious, because the crossover and mutation operation of chromosomes in MOEA costs too much time. MOPSO preforms better in large-scale topologies whose convergence has been proved. In general, MOPSO has the best energy saving performance and can save about 30 % more energy than OSPF in any network scales.

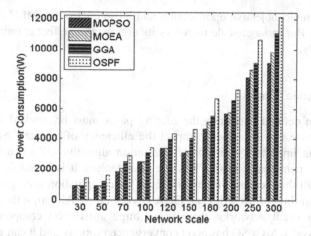

Fig. 1. Comparison of the power consumption of four algorithms in different network scales.

5.3 Maximum Link Utilization

To minimum MLU is the objective of traffic balancing. We can see from Fig. 2 that in small networks the MLU of traditional OSPF is already as high as 60 % and when the network scales is larger than 100 nodes its MLU keeps at 100 % without any Load balancing mechanism. GGA only aggregates traffic into a part of links, so its MLU is comparatively high. In the network scale up to 300 nodes, its MLU reaches 100 %. MOPSO is a multi-objective optimization algorithm, while minimizing power consumption it optimizes load balancing too. In MOPSO, the traffic is distributed equally to each path as far as possible. As a result, its MLU is the lowest in any network scale and is maintained between 30 % and 50 %. Obviously MOPSO realize the two objectives of energy saving and load balancing successfully at the same time. MOEA

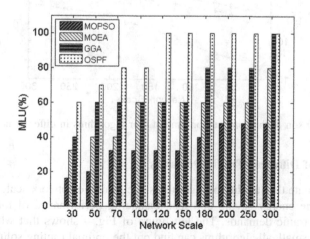

Fig. 2. Comparison of the MLU of four algorithms in different network scales.

also belongs to multi-objective optimization and it can control the MLU under 60 % in small networks. But in large-scale networks its optimization effect is much poorer due to its complexity.

5.4   Computation Time

In real software defined networks, the routing paths must be worked out as fast as possible, otherwise it will seriously impact the efficiency of network. So the computation time is an important indicator of evaluation algorithms. As can be seen from Fig. 3, the time complexity of OSPF is the best because it is based on shortest path routing. But with the increase of network scale, its computation time grows very fast. The computation time of MOPSO and GGA is very close. Although they spend much time routing in small networks, there is no huge growth on computation time in large-scale networks. MOPSO has good convergence property and it can get an optimal solution after a certain number of iterations no matter how large is the topology. The time is mostly spent on subgraph merging and optimizing. So MOPSO is an algorithm that can be actually deployed on software defined networks. The computation time of MOEA is much longer than other three algorithms, making it completely impractical in real networks. On one hand, it has slow convergence speed, on the other hand its basic operation of crossover and mutation costs too much time.

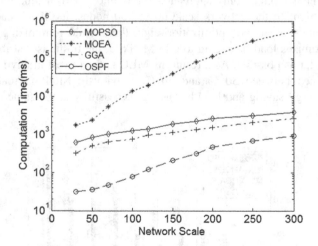

Fig. 3. Comparison of the computation time of four algorithms in different network scales.

5.5   Impact of Different Traffic Demands

In order to evaluate the stability of algorithms, we limit the network scale to 200 nodes and compare the energy saving and load balancing performance of four algorithms under different traffic demands. The left figure of Fig. 4 shows that when the traffic demand is very small, all algorithms can find out the optimal routing solution and have

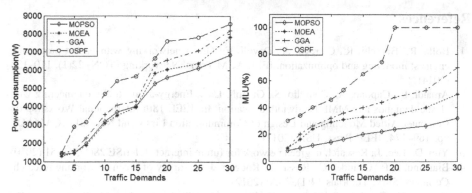

Fig. 4. Impact of traffic demands on power consumption and MLU

the same power consumption. With the increase of traffic demands, the power consumption of four algorithms increases. MOEA can save a little more energy than MOPSO in small networks, but its performance degrades when the network becomes larger. MOPSO algorithm can guarantee 30 % energy saving under various traffic demands and with the increase of traffic demands its energy saving effect is becoming more and more obvious. As can be seen from the right figure, with the increase of traffic demands, MLU of all algorithms increases too. When the number of traffic demands reaches 20, MLU of OSPF reaches 100 %. When the number of traffic demands reaches 20, MLU of GGA is close to 80 % too, which is not acceptable. Load balancing has the same priority as energy saving in MOPSO, but in MOEA it's the secondary optimization goal. As a result, they both greatly reduce the MLU and the optimization effect of MOPSO is better than MOEA.

6 Conclusion

In this paper, we consider how to solve the problem of power consumption and imbalance utilization in software defined networks. We optimize these two objectives at the same time and formulate a multi-objective mixed integer programming model. Then we propose a multi-objective particle swarm optimization algorithm called MOPSO to solve this NP-hard problem. MOPSO can work out optimal paths for dynamic traffic demands and make idol switches and links into sleeping mode. Simulation results on real topologies and traffic demands show the effectiveness of our algorithm both on energy saving and load balancing. The proposed MOPSO can save about 30 % energy and keep MLU under 50 % with acceptable computation time, which is a practical algorithm that can be actually deployed on real software defined networks.

Acknowledgments. The study is supported by the Natural Science Foundation of Shandong Province (Grant No. ZR2015FM008; ZR2013FM029), the Science and Technology Development Program of Jinan (Grant No. 201303010), the National Natural Science Foundation of China (NSFC No. 60773101), and the Fundamental Research Funds of Shandong University (Grant No. 2014JC037).

References

1. Bolla, R., Bruschi, R., Carrega, A., Davoli, F.: Green networking with packet processing engines: modeling and optimization. IEEE/ACM Trans. Networking (TON) **22**(1), 110–123 (2014)
2. Amaldi, E., Capone, A., Coniglio, S., Gianoli, L.G.: Energy-aware traffic engineering with elastic demands and MMF bandwidth allocation. In: IEEE 18th International Workshop on Computer Aided Modeling and Design of Communication Links and Networks (CAMAD), pp. 169–174. IEEE Press, USA (2013)
3. Yun, D., Lee, J.: Research in green network for future internet. J. KIISE **28**(1), 41–51 (2010)
4. Bianzino, A.P., Chaudet, C., Rossi, D., Rougier, J.: A survey of green networking research. Commun. Surv. Tutorials **14**(1), 3–20 (2012)
5. Hong, C.Y., Kandula, S., Mahajan, R., Zhang, M., Gill, V., Nanduri, M., Wattenhofer, R.: Achieving high utilization with software-driven WAN. SIGCOMM **43**(4), 15–26 (2013)
6. McKeown, N., Anderson, T., Balakrishnan, H., Parulkar, G., Peterson, L., Rexford, J., Shenker, S., Turner, J.: OpenFlow: enabling innovation in campus networks. SIGCOMM **38** (2), 69–74 (2008)
7. Nunes, B.A.A., Mendonca, M., Xuan-Nam, N., Obraczka, K., Turletti, T.: A survey of software-defined networking: past, present, and future of programmable networks. Commu. Surv. Tutorials **16**(3), 1617–1634 (2014)
8. Shahrokhi, F., Matula, D.W.: The maximum concurrent flow problem. J. Assoc. Comput. Mach. **37**(2), 318–334 (1990)
9. Gupta, M., Singh, S.: Greening of the Internet. In: Proceedings of the 2003 Conference on Applications, Technologies, Architectures, and Protocols for Computer Communications, pp. 19–26. ACM, USA (2003)
10. Gupta, M., Singh, S.: Using low-power modes for energy conservation in Ethernet LANs. In: INFOCOM, pp. 2451–2455. IEEE Press, USA (2007)
11. Gunaratne, C., Christensen, K., Suen, S.W.: Ethernet adaptive link rate (alr): analysis of a buffer threshold policy. In: Global Telecommunications Conference, 2006, GLOBECOM 2006, pp. 1–6. IEEE Press, USA (2006)
12. Gunaratne, C., Christensen, K., Nordman, B., Suen, S.: Reducing the energy consumption of Ethernet with adaptive link rate (ALR). IEEE Trans. Comput. **57**(4), 448–461 (2008)
13. Chiaraviglio, L., Mellia, M., Neri, F.: Reducing power consumption in backbone networks. In: IEEE International Conference on Communications ICC 2009, pp. 1–6. IEEE Press, USA (2009)
14. Heller, B., Seetharaman, S., Mahadevan, P., Yiakoumis, Y., Sharma, P., Banerjee, S., McKeown, N.: ElasticTree: saving energy in data center networks. In: NSDI, pp. 249–264. USENIX, USA (2010)
15. Chabarek, J., Sommers, J., Barford, P., Estan, C., Tsiang, D., Wright, S.: Power awareness in network design and routing. In: The 27th Conference on Computer Communications INFOCOM 2008, pp. 116–130. IEEE Press, USA (2008)
16. Rui, W., Zhipeng, J., Suixiang, G., Wenguo, Y., Yinben, X., Mingming, Z.: Energy-aware routing algorithms in software-defined networks. In: 2014 IEEE 15th International Symposium on A World of Wireless, Mobile and Multimedia Networks (WoWMoM), pp. 6–20. IEEE Press, USA (2014)
17. Tu, R.L., Wang, X., Yang, Y.: Energy-saving model for SDN data centers. J. Supercomput **70**(3), 1477–1495 (2014)

18. Wang, J., Chen, X., Phillips, C., Yan, Y.: Energy efficiency with QoS control in dynamic optical networks with SDN enabled integrated control plane. Comput. Netw. **78**(2), 57–67 (2015)
19. Orlowski, S., Wessäly, R., Pióro, M., Tomaszewski, A.: SNDlib 1.0—survivable network design library. Networks **55**(3), 276–286 (2010)

Pre-stack Kirchhoff Time Migration on Hadoop and Spark

Chen Yang, Jie Tang$^{(\boxtimes)}$, Heng Gao, and Gangshan Wu

State Key Laboratory for Novel Software Technology,
Department of Computer Science and Technology,
Nanjing University, Nanjing 210046, China
`tangjie@nju.edu.cn`

Abstract. Pre-stack Kirchhoff time migration (PKTM) is one of the most widely used migration algorithms in seismic imaging area. However, PKTM takes considerable time due to its high computational cost, which greatly affects the working efficiency of oil industry. Due to its high fault tolerance and scalability, Hadoop has become the most popular platform for big data processing. To overcome the shortcoming too much network traffic and disk I/O in Hadoop, there shows up a new distributed framework—Spark. However the behaviour and performance of those two systems when applied to high performance computing are still under investigation. In this paper, we proposed two parallel algorithms of the plre-stack Kirchhoff time migration based on Hadoop and Sark respectively. Experiments are carried out to compare the performances of them. The results show that both of implementations are efficient and scalable and our PKTM on Spark exhibits better performance than the one on Hadoop.

Keywords: Big Data · Hadoop · Spark · Kirchhoff · MapReduce · RDD

1 Introduction

Pre-stack Kirchhoff time migration (PKTM) [1] is one of the most popular migration technique in seismic imaging area because of its simplicity, efficiency, feasibility and target-orientated property. However, practical PKTM tasks for large 3D surveys are still computationally intensive and usually running on supercomputers or large PC-cluster systems with high cost for purchasing and maintaining.

Nowadays, cloud computing has received a lot of attention from both research and industry due to the deployment and growth of commercial cloud platforms. Compared to other parallel computing solutions such as MPI or GPU, cloud computing has advantages of automatically handling failures, hiding parallel programming caomplexity as well as better system scalability. Thus more and more geologists turn to finding seismic imaging solutions on Hadoop and Spark.

Hadoop is an Apache open source distributed computing framework for clusters with inexpensive hardware [2] and is widely used for many different classes of

© Springer International Publishing Switzerland 2015
G. Wang et al. (Eds.): ICA3PP 2015, Part III, LNCS 9530, pp. 190–202, 2015.
DOI: 10.1007/978-3-319-27137-8_15

data-intensive applications [3]. The core design of Apache Hadoop [4] is MapReduce and HDFS. MapReduce is a parallel computing framework to run on HDFS, it will abstract the user's program for two processes: Map and Reduce. A key benefit of MapReduce is that it automatically handles failures, hiding the complexity of fault-tolerance from the programmer [5].

Apache Spark, which is developed by UCBerkeley's AMP laboratory, is another fast and general-purpose cluster computing system. It provides high-level APIs in Java, Scala and Python, and an optimized engine that supports general execution graphs [6]. Spark is a MapReduce-like cluster computing framework [6–8]. However, unlike Hadoop, Spark enables memory distributed data sets, provides interactive query, optimize iterative workloads. Most importantly, Spark introduces the concept of memory computing (RDD) [3], i.e. data sets can be cached in the memory to shorten the access latency, which is very efficiency for some applications.

In this paper, we propose two parallel algorithms of the pre-stack Kirchhoff time migration based on Hadoop and Sark respectively. Experiments are carried out to compare the performances of them. The results show that both of implementations are efficient and scalable while PKTM on Spark exhibits better performance than the one on Hadoop.

2   Related Work

Several works exist in the literature with regards to implementation of Kirchhoff on MapReduce framework. Rizvandi [9] introduces an algorithm of PKTM on MapReduce framework, which splits data into traces, sends traces to Map function, then computes traces, shuffles data to Reduce function. The program use MapReduce parallel framework to realize parallelism of the PKTM, but the problem is that the shuffle data is very huge, and seriously affected the performance of the program.

Another kind of parallel PKTM uses GPUs to achieve parallelism. Shi [1] presents a PKTM algorithm on GPGPU [10], it uses multi-GPUs to compute the data and runs much faster than CPU implementation. However, the memory on GPUs are not large enough. Therefore, when the data gets bigger and bigger and cannot be hold in GPU memory, the data transfer between RAM and GPU memory will be the bottleneck of the program. Li [11] puts forward another PKTM on GPUs. It's 20 times faster than a pure CPU execution, still the data transfer between RAM and GPU memory as well as loop control are overloaded. Generally, Running PKTM on GPUs will have the problems of data transfer and synchronize between GPUs and CPU.

Gao [12] presents a solution utilizing the combination of the GPUs and MapReduce. It can greatly accelerate the execution time. However, it just abstract the Map function to a GPU implementation. If the Map function needs to change, the whole GPU codes must be modified, which is not flexible. So far, there is no Kirchhoff works on Spark.

3   Algorithms

Kirchhoff migration uses the Huygens-Fresnel principle to collapse all possible contributions to an image sample. Wherever this sum causes constructive interference, the image is heavily marked, remaining blank or loosely marked on destructive interference parts. A contribution to an image sample $T(z,x,y,o)$ is generated by an input sample $S(t,x,y,o)$ whenever the measured signal travel time t matches computed travel time from source to (z,x,y,o) subsurface point and back to receiver. The set of all possible input traces (x,y,o) that may contribute to an output trace (x,y,o) lie within an ellipsis of axis ax and ay (apertures) centered at (x,y,o). Input traces are filtered to attenuate spatial aliasing. Sample amplitudes are corrected to account for energy spreading during propagation. PKTM algorithm and program data flow structure shown in Fig. 1.

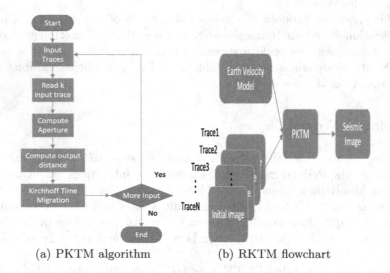

(a) PKTM algorithm   (b) RKTM flowchart

Fig. 1. PKTM flowchart

The schematic of the seismic imaging shown in Fig. 2.

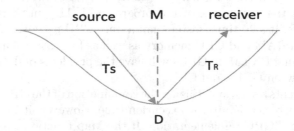

Fig. 2. Seismic imaging

The pseudocode of the Kirchhoff algorithm shown as below:

Algorithm 1. Kirchhoff Algorithm

1: **procedure** KIRCHHOFF(inputtraces)
2:     **for all** input traces **do**
3:         read input trace
4:         filter input trace
5:         **for all** output traces within aperture **do**
6:             **for all** output trace contributed samples **do**
7:                 compute travel time
8:                 compute amplitude correction
9:                 select input sample and filter
10:                accumulate input sample contribution into output sample
11:             **end for**
12:         **end for**
13:     **end for**
14:     dump output volume
15: **end procedure**

3.1   PKTM on Hadoop

We propose an algorithm to carry on PKTM on Hadoop framwork. The steps of the algorithm are as follows:

1. Acquiring cluster environment variables: As we all know, Hadoop framework is closely related to machine configuration. So in the first step, some system variables are detected and stored, including number of nodes n, memory of each node $M_1, M_2...M_n$, number of CPUs $cpus$, number of cores per CPU $cores$, threads per core $threads$.

2. Inputting data: In Hadoop, each input file block corresponds to a mapper. Also according to Hadoop [4] document, a node performs well when the number of mappers running on it are between 10 and 100. Therefore, in order to control the number of mappers, we override the $FileInputFormat$ class, which is in charge for how to logically split the input files. Each split will produce a mapper. Hadoop usually splits a file into default size. The size of the split is key to system efficiency. Hence, we need to re-split the whole file into splits with proper size. Firstly, we read in default splits lengths of the whole file $S_1, S_2, S_3...S_n$. Based on these lengths, we can calculate the total size of the input file as $\sum_{i=1}^{n} S_i$. The number of reduce tasks r_n is set by the user. Then to limit the number of mappers between 10~100, the size of a split is computed as follows:

$$f_{split} = \frac{\left(\sum_{i=1}^{n} S_i\right)}{k * min\left((cpus * cores + r_n), \left(\frac{\sum_{i=1}^{n} M_i}{M}\right)\right)}$$

where $k \in [1, \infty)$ is a controllable parameter that can be modified. f_{split} must be greater than 0. M is the memory size of a mapper. Finally we set the *mapreduce.input.fileinputformat.split.maxsize* as f_{split} which decides the split size. Through input split processing, we read in the samples of an input trace, producing $< key, value >$ pairs. *key* represents the offset of input trace in the input files, *value* represents the coordinate points of each input trace. One pair may combine many input traces. These pairs will be submitted to the mapper for execution.

3. Mapping: Since the input files are logically divided into E splits, each split data is submitted to a mapper, these mappers will be computing in parallel. Each mapper computes a lot of input traces, and each input trace will produce many output traces, so in order to achieve parallelism within the mapper, we use the multi-threads to process input traces. Each thread shares a data structure HashMap which is used to save the output trace with the same output key, so that the same output trace will be merge locally which greatly decrease the load of the data transmission. We detect the *Hyper-Threading* mode of the cluster system. If it is on, we set the number of threads of a mapper to $2 * (threads - 2)$, else we set it to $(threads - 2)$. Another strategy to decrease the load of data transmission is to write map values to the HDFS files, only send $< key, filename\#offset >$ pairs.

4. Combining: In this phase, we aggregate the output pairs which are generated by mappers with the same key on the same node and will reduce the network traffic across nodes, thus improve the efficiency of the program. Because in the same mapper and in the same node, there will be many output traces with the same key. This also largely decrease the load of data transmission.

5. Partitioning: The output $< key, value >$ pairs are mapped to reduce nodes with the key. Ensure that all keys are sorted in each reduce node according to its reduce task attempt id. The formula is as follows:

$$f_{hash} = \left[\frac{key}{\left(\frac{key_{max}}{reduce_{id}} \right)} \right]$$

In this way, the final large image data sort time will be reduced. We only need to sort the keys in each reduce task in parallel and this further reduces the application execution time.

6. Reducing: According to the output $< key, filename\#offset >$ pairs which are sent by map tasks, we read HDFS files according to *filename, offset* and aggregate them with the same key comes from different nodes. All the reduce tasks run in parallel. Besides, the number of the reduce tasks is set by the user, user can adjust this number to get the best performance.

7. Outputting: Each reduce task produces an output $< key, value >$ pairs, we sort these keys in each reduce task, then write them to a binary file, the file name contains the minimum key in each reduce task. All the sort operations are run in parallel.

8. Image Output: According to the reduce output files, we sort these file names with the minimum key, this only take a little time, then write them into only

one image binary file sequentially. This image file is the finally imaging file to show to the professionals.

The program's running architecture shown in Fig. 3.(a) and its flowchart shown in Fig. 3.(b). In the flowchart, the steps exact match the steps in the algorithm above.

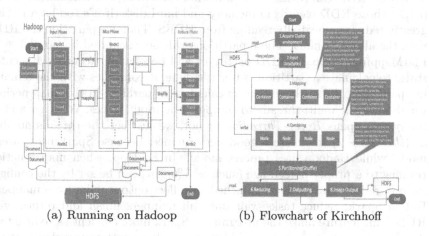

(a) Running on Hadoop   (b) Flowchart of Kirchhoff

Fig. 3. Kirchhoff implementation on Hadoop

3.2 PKTM on Spark

Spark provides RDD which shields a lot of interactions with the HDFS and achieve better efficiency for application with lots of iterations. Spark develops the ApplicationMaster which acts much more appropriate with Yarn. Hence we develop a new algorithm with Spark system on Yarn framework.

1. Acquiring cluster environment variables: The program on Spark need to read data from HDFS, we just simply read splits from HDFS using *newAPI-HadoopFile* with whatever splits, producing $< key, value >$ pairs as records of RDD. RDD can be partitioned according to user's wishes. One partition corresponds to an executor which is similar to mapper. In addition, Spark provides the command—"spark-submit" to submit an application. Users can set the number of task executors N, the memory of each executor and the CPU cores of each executor through the command line. This is very convenient compared to Hadoop. So we just read the environment variables from the command line, which is very convenience. Then the partitions of the RDD will be set as:

$$f_{pars} = k * min\left(N, \frac{\sum_{i=1}^{n} M_i}{M_{min}}\right)$$

2. Inputting data: Because we run the Spark on Yarn and HDFS framework, we need to read files from HDFS. Spark provides several functions to read input files from HDFS and return them in RDD model. Each RDD contains many records of $< key, value >$ pairs, key represents the offset of the input trace and $value$ represents the coordinate samples of the corresponding key. One record combines many traces.

   Moreover, RDD can persist data in memory after the first calculation, so we persist those RDD records in memory and hard disk (if it's too large). This greatly reduces repeatedly reading from HDFS. Then we partition the RDD with the above formula. These partitions will be calculated in parallel.

3. FlatMapping: In Spark, RDD partitions will be sent to executors. Executor starts to calculate a partition. After it's done, it continues with the remaining partitions. All of the executors calculate in parallel. In this map period, we also use the multi-threads to compute the input traces. Whether a cluster system opens *Hyper-Threading* or not, we just set the threads number as $(threads - 2)$ to ensure a good performance, because Spark uses thread model while Hadoop uses process model. In Hadoop, when map function running to a proper percentage (such as 5 %, this can be set by the configuration), reduce tasks will be launched to collect output pairs from mappers. But in Spark, reduce tasks wait until all mappers finish and return with RDD. This feature make the program on Spark more efficient as reduce task do not occupy the resources used by mappers. It's worth to mention that the partitions of RDD do not change until you invoke the *repartition* function.

4. Partitioning: Firstly, we get the total number of output trace onx. Then we divide these keys depending on the number of reduce partitions R_n. Smaller keys correspond to the smaller reduce task id. This helps the later sort operation. Each record in RDD applies a mapping operation to choose into which the reduce partition goes. The formula is as follows:

$$f_{partition} = \left[\frac{key}{\left(\frac{onx}{R_n}\right)}\right]$$

5. ReduceByKey: Spark ensures that the same key pairs will be sent to the same reduce task. According to this feature, the RDD datasets that come from a map operation are sent to the reduce tasks with the same key. So we aggregate the values by the same key in each reduce task. Each reduce task return an RDD partition which will be aggregated into a total RDD to the user, however, its partitions still exist. The important point of the *ReduceByKey* function is that the operation firstly merges map output pairs in the same node, then send pairs to the correspond reduce tasks. This feature greatly reduces the load of network traffic.

6. SortByKey: This function sorts the keys in each RDD partition which reduce tasks returned. The sort operation is also executed in parallel among different RDD partitions.

7. Image Output: According to the sorted keys, we write the corresponding values to a binary file to HDFS for permanent preservation.

The program's running architecture shown in Fig. 4.(a) and its flow chart shown in Fig. 4.(b). The steps of the flow chart corresponds to the steps of the algorithm above.

The program flowchart shown in Fig. 4.

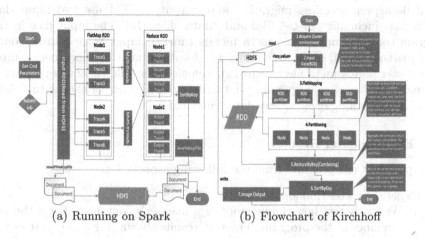

(a) Running on Spark   (b) Flowchart of Kirchhoff

Fig. 4. Kirchhoff implementation on Spark

4 Results and Analysis

We have run our two implementations on a cluster with six nodes, the details of which are shown in Table 1.

Table 1. Cluster Configuration

Name	CPUs	Cores per CPU	Thread per core	Memory(G)
Master	2	8	4	32
Slave1	2	6	4	32
Slave2	2	6	4	32
Slave3	2	6	4	32
Slave4	2	6	4	32
Slave5	2	6	4	32

4.1 Experiment Configuration

The node "Master" acts as the Hadoop Master node and the remaining nodes act as Hadoop Slave nodes. "Master" is not only the master of the HDFS framework (NameNode), but also the master of the Yarn framework (act as ResourceManager). Five nodes, "Slave1", "Slave2", "Slave3", "Slave4", "Slave5", are used as the DataNode and the NodeManager.

4.2   Data Preparation

We use Sigsbee2 Models to test our proposed PKTM methods on Hadoop and Spark. The model could be downloaded from http://www.reproducibility.org/ RSF/book/data/sigsbee/paper_html/. PKTM includes the following three main steps: data preprocessing, migration and output. PKTM use two input data file formats including "meta" files and "data" files [13]. The input files in this program contains input trace meta file(shot.meta), input trace seismic source meta file(fsxy.meta), input trace detector location meta file(fgxy.meta), input trace center points meta file(fcxy.meta), velocity meta file(rmsv.meta). Each of the meta file has a corresponding data file(*.data), such as shot.data (about 30 GB), fsxy.data, fgxy.data, fcxy.data, rmsv.data.

4.3   Experimental Results

We experiment our program from the following aspects:

(1). Experiments on Hadoop:
  a. We firstly test how the memory of a mapper's container affects the performance of the program. The test results shown in Fig. 5.(a). It can be seen that when the consumed memory exceeds over some threshold, the number of mappers reduces accordingly, which causes the execution time getting longer. The reason is that the number of active parallel tasks is constrained by the total memory of these mappers.
  b. Secondly, we test how the number of mappers affects the performance. The test results are shown in Fig. 5.(b). In the figure, it can be seen that the executing time is smallest when the mapper's number fits to the cluster's resources. If the number of mappers is small, the capacity of the cluster is not fully utilized, and results in a longer execution time. If the number of mappers is too large, the scheduling time usually will increase, which also results in a longer execution time.
  c. Finally, in Hadoop, the cluster will start Reduce tasks to receive map output files even when some Mappers still not finished. In this situation, the started Reduce tasks occupy the resources of memory and CPUs which affects other mappers' execution. Therefore, we try to test how reduce task numbers affects the performance. The results are shown in Fig. 5.(c). In the figure, it can be seen that when the numbers of reduce tasks match the number and output pairs of mappers, the best performance will be achieved.
(2). Experiments on Spark: in Spark, the contribution of two factors, memory of each execution (container) and number of RDD partitions, are investigated.
  a. We adjust the configuration of the container's memory and evaluate the performance of the system. The results are shown in Fig. 6.(a). Like Hadoop, if the memory of a container exceeds to a proper value, the execution time grows longer. Because the large memory affects the parallel number of tasks. When the number of parallel tasks is small, the execute time all the tasks also increases.

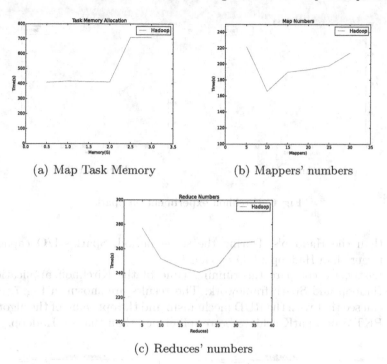

(a) Map Task Memory   (b) Mappers' numbers

(c) Reduces' numbers

Fig. 5. Kirchhoff experiment on Hadoop

b. In this part, we test the RDD partitions about the input traces, hope to find out the best partitions. The test results are shown in Fig. 6.(b). The figure indicates that when the number of RDD partitions is not enough to the cluster, it takes a longer time, but when partitions grows, it tends to a less and stable execution time. The reason of this phenomenon is that when RDD partition is more than the cluster resources can have, it makes the cluster run busy to handle RDDs with the same amount of time.

(3). Experiments of comparison between Hadoop and Spark: We mainly from three aspects to compare the Hadoop algorithm and Spark algorithm.

a. Firstly, we compare the yarn container memory between Hadoop and Spark. On Yarn, the tasks of Hadoop or Spark jobs are started in container, one task correspond to a container. The comparison figure is shown in Fig. 7.(a). As shown in the figure, we know that with the same memory of container, Spark shows a better performance, Because Spark use the RDDs to read input traces and persists data in memory, the computation of RDDs is in memory, so it runs fast.

b. Secondly, we compare the reading and writing time of Hadoop and Spark I/O capacity. The results are shown in Fig. 7.(b). We can see that when we access the same capacity of I/O data, the Spark algorithm runs faster

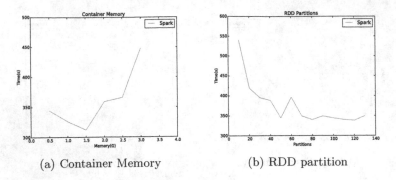

(a) Container Memory   (b) RDD partition

Fig. 6. Kirchhoff experiment on Spark

than the Hadoop's. During the same period, Spark's I/O capacity is larger than Hadoop's I/O capacity.

c. Lastly, we compare the running time of the Kirchhoff application on Hadoop and Spark framework. The results are shown in Fig. 7.(c). We can see that with the RDD mechanism and the optimum of the algorithm, PKTM on SparK achieve better efficiency than that on Hadoop.

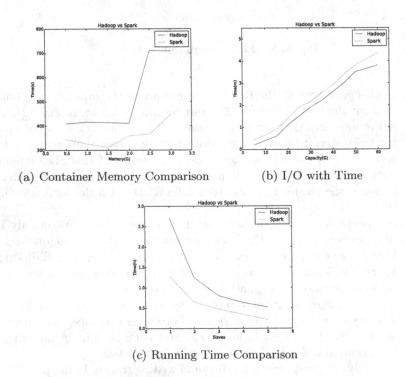

(a) Container Memory Comparison   (b) I/O with Time

(c) Running Time Comparison

Fig. 7. Kirchhoff Hadoop vs Spark

5   Conclusion

In this paper, we proposed two parallel algorithms of pre-stack Kirchhoff time migration based on Hadoop and Sark respectively. The results show that both of the implementations are efficient and scalable. And PKTM on Spark exhibits better performance than the one on Hadoop.

The future work includes how to improve the data transferring speed in both Hadoop and Spark, since the efficiency of these 2 programs are closely related to the data preparing speed. If the machine has a high throughput of the network and the high-speed hard disk I/O, the program will run faster. In Hadoop, we can apply RDMA (Remote Direct Memory Access) in HDFS through Infiniband [14]. This will greatly promote the acceleration of HDFS read and write time. We hope we can also apply Infiniband Network Interface Card to accelerate the network transfer in Spark.

Acknowledgments. We would like to thank the anonymous reviewers for helping us refine this paper. Their constructive comments and suggestions are very helpful. This paper is partly funded by National Science and Technology Major Project of the Ministry of Science and Technology of China under grant 2011ZX05035-004-004HZ. The corresponding author of this paper is Tang Jie.

References

1. Shi, X., Wang, X., Zhao, C. et al.: Practical pre-stack Kirchhoff time migration of seismic processing on general purpose GPU. In: World Congress on Computer Science and Information Engineering, pp. 461–465. IEEE (2009)
2. Xue-Qi, C., Xiao-Long, J., Yuan-Zhuo, W., et al.: Summary of the big data systems and analysis techniques in Chinese. Journal of Software, vol. 25(9) (2014)
3. Gu, L., Li, H.: Memory or time: performance evaluation for iterative operation on hadoop and spark. In: 2013 IEEE International Conference on High Performance Computing and Communications and 2013 IEEE 10th International Conference on Embedded and Ubiquitous Computing (HPCC_EUC), pp. 721–727. IEEE (2013)
4. Apache Hadoop. http://hadoop.apache.org
5. Zaharia, M., Konwinski, A., Joseph, A.D., et al.: Improving MapReduce performance in heterogeneous environments. In: OSDI, vol. 8(4), p. 7 (2008)
6. Apache Spark. http://spark.apache.org
7. Zaharia, M., Chowdhury, M., Franklin, M.J, et al.: Spark: cluster computing with working sets. In: Proceedings of the 2nd USENIX Conference on Hot Topics in Cloud Computing, p. 10 (2010)
8. Zaharia, M., Chowdhury, M., Das, T., et al.: Resilient distributed datasets: a fault-tolerant abstraction for in-memory cluster computing. In: Proceedings of the 9th USENIX Conference on Networked Systems Design and Implementation, p. 2. USENIX Association (2012)
9. Rizvandi, N.B., Boloori, A.J., Kamyabpour, N., et al.: MapReduce implementation of prestack Kirchhoff time migration (PKTM) on seismic data. In: 2011 12th International Conference on Parallel and Distributed Computing, Applications and Technologies (PDCAT), pp. 86–91. IEEE (2011)

10. De Verdiere, G.C.: Introduction to GPGPU, a hardware and software background. C. R. Mcanique **339**(2), 78–89 (2011)
11. Panetta, J., Teixeira, T., de Souza Filho, P.R.P.: Accelerating Kirchhoff migration by CPU and GPU cooperation. In: 21st International Symposium on Computer Architecture and High Performance Computing, SBAC-PAD 2009, pp. 26–32. IEEE (2009)
12. Gao, H., Tang, J., Wu, G.: A MapReduce computing framework based on GPU cluster. In: 2013 IEEE International Conference on High Performance Computing and Communications and 2013 IEEE 10th International Conference on Embedded Ubiquitous Computing (HPCC_EUC), pp. 1902–1907. IEEE (2013)
13. Gang, W., Jie, T., Gang-Shan, W.: GPU-based cluster framework in Chinese. Comput. Sci. Dev. **24**(1), 9–13 (2014)
14. Lu, X., Islam, N.S., Wasi-ur-Rahman, M., et al.: High-performance design of Hadoop RPC with RDMA over InfiniBand. In: 2013 42nd International Conference on Parallel Processing (ICPP), pp. 641–650. IEEE (2013)

A Cyber Physical System with GPU
for CNC Applications

Jen-Chieh Chang$^{(\boxtimes)}$, Ting-Hsuan Chien, and Rong-Guey Chang

Department of Computer Science and Information Engineering,
National Chung Cheng University, Chiayi 62102, Taiwan
{cjc99p,cth103p,rgchang}@cs.ccu.edu.tw

Abstract. In this paper, we parallelize the collision detection of five-axis machining as an example to show how to execute CNC applications on Graphics Processing Unit (GPU). We first design and implement an efficient collision detection tool, including the kinematics analyses for five-axis motions, separating axis method for collision detection, and computer simulation for verification. The machine structure is modeled as STL format in CAD software. The input to the detection system is the g-code part program, which describes the tool motions to produce the part surface. Then the g-code will be partitioned and be executed by our collision detection tool in parallel on Graphics Processing Unit (GPU). The system simulates the five-axis CNC motion for tool trajectory and detects any collisions according to the input g-codes. The result shows that our method can improve the performance of computational efficiency significantly when comparing to the conventional detection method.

Keywords: CNC · Five axis machining · Collision detection · GPU · Parallelization

1 Introduction

The Computer Numerically Controlled (CNC) machine has been widely used in mechanical engineering industry recently. In the past, although the performance is the key to CNC applications, however, how to parallelize them remains open. To understand how to parallelize CNC applications, we parallelize the collision detection of five-axis machining as an example to show how to execute CNC applications on GPU.

More advanced machining technologies use five-axis CNC machining for complicated part fabrication. Five-axis machine has two rotary tables that improve the machining capability and quality. However, five-axis machining has high chances of axial table colliding due to the coordinated motion for rotating and translating tables. If the machine tool collides during machining, it damages the machine itself and delays the productions. Therefore, how to prevent the axial table collisions during machining is very important for five-axis machining processes. Interference detection methods among objects have been presented

© Springer International Publishing Switzerland 2015
G. Wang et al. (Eds.): ICA3PP 2015, Part III, LNCS 9530, pp. 203–212, 2015.
DOI: 10.1007/978-3-319-27137-8_16

by many researchers. Palmer proposed bounding sphere method that detected any interference between two objects very quickly by checking the distance of two bounding spheres [1]. Bradshaw used Octree data structure to improve the bounding sphere method that made the object closer to the approximated spheres [2]. Instead of using bounding sphere, Cohen et al. used bounding box for collision detection [3]. Bergen improved the bounding box method by partitioning the object into smaller areas [4]. Gottschalk et al. proposed oriented bounding box method that made the collision detection more precise [5]. Chang et al. applied separating axis theorem on oriented bounding box method to speed up the detecting process [6]. However, with our knowledge, the five-axis machining collision detection has never been resolved with parallel optimization on GPUs.

The main goal for this paper is proposing an efficient algorithm for five-axis machining collision detections with compiler optimizations on GPU. This research uses a systematic approach for collision detection on GPU. The methodologies include the kinematics analyses for five-axis motions, separating axis method for collision detection, and computer simulation for detection verification. The collision detection process needs to construct the five-axis machine, according to the real machine configuration. To implement the collision detection process, the machine is modeled in terms of STL format, a triangular facet approximation. The input to the detection system is the g-code part program, which describes the tool motions to produce the part surface. Then the g-code will be partitioned and be executed by our collision detection tool in parallel on GPU. To further improve the performance, we deduce some optimization techniques to achieve this goal. The system simulates the CNC motion for tool trajectory. The axial table location are detected for any collisions according to the g-codes, using separation axis method. The machining simulation will stop and show the collided g-code block if any collision is detected. The improved efficiency for computation time is analyzed with demonstrated example in the end of this paper.

The rest of this paper is organized as follows. Section 2 presents the background and Sect. 3 shows our novel collision detection approach based on separate axis theorem. Section 4 presents the proposed parallel collision detection and its results are shown in Sect. 5. Section is the related work. Finally, we conclude this paper in Sect. 7.

2 Background

2.1 Five-Axis Machine Tools

The commonly used five-axis machine tools are table tilting type, spindle tilting type, and table/spindle tilting type. This research uses table tilting type five-axis machine for theorem derivation and explanation. However, the algorithm can be used for any types. A commercial available table tilting type five-axis machine is shown in Fig. 1.

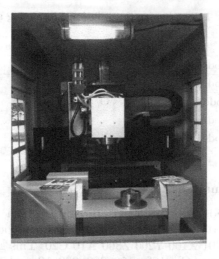

Fig. 1. The table tilting type five-axis machine.

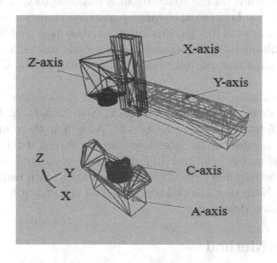

Fig. 2. The STL model of the machine.

2.2 CAD Model for Machine Tools

The machine design is usually modeled as STL format, which uses triangular facets to describe the designed object. Each triangular facet contains 3 vertices and a facial normal vector. Most of the commercial available Computer-Aided Design (CAD) softwares provide STL format for object deign output. Figure 1 shows the STL model for the machine shown in Fig. 2.

Table 1. The kinematics relationship among axes

	X axis	Y axis	Z axis	A axis	C axis
X code	O		O		
Y code	O	O	O		
Z code			O		
A code				O	O
C code					O

2.3   Kinematics Analyses

The machine tool reads the g-code part program, which controls the cutting tool to produce the part. The typical 5-axis machining g-code example for linear motion is shown as, G01 X100 Y200 Z300 A10 C20. This g-code moves X-axis, Y-axis, Z-axis, A-axis, and C-axis for 100, 200, 300, 10, and 20 units, respectively. The kinematics depends on the structure of a machine tool. Table 1 shows the kinematic relationship between axes for the machine structure shown in Fig. 1. The left column means reading g-codes for an axial motion that makes the other axial motion simultaneously. For example, if a g-code moves X axis, the Z-axis has to be moved simultaneous. Likewise, if A-axis moves, the C-axis has to be moved, too.

The typical collision detection process for a g-code motion on five-axis machine tools needs to detect 10 cases, X-to-Y, X-to-Z, X-to-A, X-to-C, Y-to-Z, Y-to-A, Y-to-C, Z-to-A, Z-to-C, and A-to-C. Although there are 10 detecting cases for fiveaxis motions, some detections can be waived if the axial structure is special arranged or the axial traveling distance is restricted. For the machine shown in Fig. 1, the required detections are z-axis table with respective to the A and C axes only. Note that the different machine structures have the different cases for the collision detection.

3   Detection Method

3.1   Separating Axis Theorem

Separating Axis Theorem for 2-D space states that two convex polygons do not intersect if and only if there exists a line such that the projections of the two polygons onto the line do not intersect. The line is called separating axis. In other words, it can be defined as two convex polygons do not intersect if and only if there exists a line that completely divides a polygon on one side of the line and the other polygon on the other side of the line. This line is called the separating line, which is perpendicular to the separating axis.

Separating Axis Theorem can apply to 3-D space for detecting if two objects interfered or not. Two objects do not intersect if and only if there exists a separating plane that completely separates these two objects. The separating plane is perpendicular to their corresponding separating axis.

3.2   Separating Axis Calculation

This research uses STL format for machine models, which uses triangular facets to describe the designed object. The collision detection process becomes to detect 2 triangular facets, which belongs to 2 different objects. Figure 3 shows two triangular facets. The first one has 3 vertices (P1, P2, P3) and facial normal. The second one has 3 vertices (Q1, Q2, Q3) and facial normal. There are 17 separating axes totally for 2 different triangular facets in 3-D space.

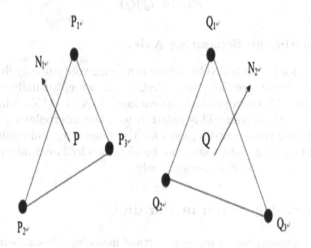

Fig. 3. Illustration for two triangular facets.

Separating axes for coplanar case are follows:

$$\vec{N1} \times \overrightarrow{P1P2} \tag{1}$$

$$\vec{N1} \times \overrightarrow{P2P3} \tag{2}$$

$$\vec{N1} \times \overrightarrow{P3P1} \tag{3}$$

$$\vec{N2} \times \overrightarrow{Q1Q2} \tag{4}$$

$$\vec{N2} \times \overrightarrow{Q2Q3} \tag{5}$$

$$\vec{N2} \times \overrightarrow{Q3Q1} \tag{6}$$

Separating axes for non-coplanar case are $\vec{N1}$, $\vec{N2}$ and follows:

$$\overrightarrow{P1P2} \times \overrightarrow{Q1Q2} \tag{7}$$

$$\overrightarrow{P1P2} \times \overrightarrow{Q2Q3} \tag{8}$$

$$\overrightarrow{P1P2} \times \overrightarrow{Q3Q1} \tag{9}$$

$$\overrightarrow{P2P3} \times \overrightarrow{Q1Q2} \tag{10}$$

$$\overrightarrow{P2P3} \times \overrightarrow{Q2Q3} \tag{11}$$

$$\overrightarrow{P2P3} \times \overrightarrow{Q3Q1} \tag{12}$$

$$\overrightarrow{P3P1} \times \overrightarrow{Q1Q2} \tag{13}$$

$$\overrightarrow{P3P1} \times \overrightarrow{Q2Q3} \tag{14}$$

$$\overrightarrow{P3P1} \times \overrightarrow{Q3Q1} \tag{15}$$

3.3 Interpolating for Separating Axis

Each axial table for five-axis CNC machine is moving continuously during machining. In order to detect precisely, each CNC motion step, usually $0.01\,\text{sec/step}$, needs to perform 15 cross-product operations, Eqs. (1)–(15), which are very heavy loaded in computation. This research uses the interpolating method that requires calculating the separating axes for the beginning and ending only. The separating axes for each motion step can be obtained by linear interpolating that reduces the computation time tremendously

4   Detection Algorithm in Parallel

The five-axis machining tool is more important nowadays. Because machine tools are expensive, the real time collision detection technique is a requirement. In fact, the developers need to confirm a g-code without collision by using software before the process of the five-axis machining tool. This is the off-line method, and because the execution time of the off-line method is very long, it must be executed before the process of the five-axis machining tool. Our purpose is to reduce the execution time of the off-line method so that it achieves a real time requirement.

In this work, we induce six separating axis in plan and 11 separating axis in non-plan between two triangle meshes. We also present the parallel method based on the characteristic of K20C GPU [7] to speed up the performance. We first apply loop unrolling technique and prefetching mechanism to applications. Then we follow K20C features to perform wrap-based execution of the hardware and avoid misaligned access pattern and non-strided accesses.

Additionally, using the bounding volume hierarchy technique with boxes developed by us reduces triangle meshes to find whether the separating axis exits or not.

Algorithm: Construct binary bounding volume hierarchies

```
Require: A set of triangles
1: Set n = number of triangles.
2: Compute each bounding volumes of triangles.
3: while n > 1 do
```

4: Find the two nearest bounding volumes pair.
5: Merge the two nearest bounding volumes pair to a new bounding volume.
6: Set n = n/2.
7: end while
8: return A bounding volume hierarchy.

To speed up overall performance while simulating G code in CNC machine tool system, we separate g-codes into several parts and let each part overlapping as shown in the algorithm above. G codes between each part can be regarded as independent of each other if we can know the positions of each axis in CNC tool machine.

Hence, we need to scan all g-codes and obtain the information of each axis position in the beginning of each part. It is quite easy since the g-code represented the position of each axis. Execution time of this collision detection can be improved significantly.

5   Result

This research uses the five-axis machine tool, as shown in Fig. 1, for collision detecting demonstration example. To implement the above collision detection algorithm, a simulation program was produced, using VB programming software. The computer used for this demonstration is 3.0 GHz AMD Athlon CPU. Figure 4 shows the solid model of the demonstrating example, which colors the STL model for clear visualization.

The testing g-code for five-axis motion is G01 X300 Y-200 Z-200 A-3 Z-3 F15000. The F15000 (mm/min) in the g-code means the feedrate that is the cutting tool moving velocity relative to the workpiece. The computation time for conventional method is shown in the top of Fig. 4 that the detecting

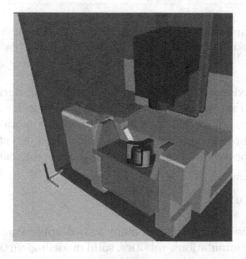

Fig. 4. The solid model for five-axis machine tool simulation.

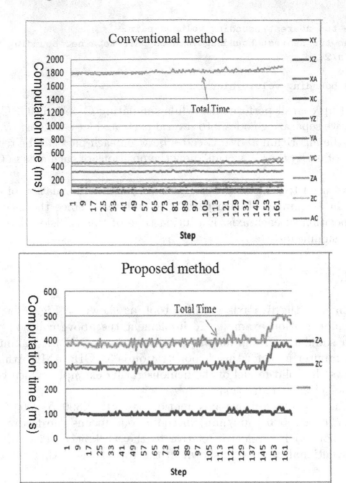

Fig. 5. The total computation time for each motion step, using conventional method and using the proposed method.

time for each five-axis motion is around 1800 msec. The horizontal axis is the CNC sampling step that is 0.01 sec/step. On the other hand, our approach, using interpolating method, takes 400 msec for each five-axis motion. The bottom of Fig. 5 shows the recorded computation time for collision detections. The computation efficiency improves 4.5 times, comparing to the conventional method.

6   Related Work

Collision detection is fundamental to many varied applications, including computer game, physical simulations, robotics, solid modeling, virtual reality and etc. The goal is to determine whether two objects in three dimension space intersect or not. Three dimension surface objects are modeled by triangle mesh for digital holography. That is triangles are the primitive elements of three dimension objects in computers. Hence, the intersection test for two triangles is basic.

In 1997, Moller designed a fast collision detection algorithm for two triangles, A Fast Triangle-Triangle Intersection Test [8]. And Held also designed a similar algorithm but in different way, A Collision of Efficient and Reliable Intersection Tests [9]. Both of them compute the signed distance of three vertices of triangle from the plane containing the other triangle. If all values are the same sign, they do not intersect. Otherwise they possibly intersect, and the problem is then reduced to an overlap test of two line segments lying on the same line of intersection between the two planes containing the triangles.

Moller computes a parametric equation of the line of intersection of the two planes, finds the intervals for which the line lies inside each triangle and performs a one-dimensional interval overlap test. Held reduces the problem to two-dimensional triangle/line-segment test after projecting to a convenient plane. In 2003, Guigue and Devillers follow Moller, Fast and Robust Triangle-Triangle Overlap Test Using Orientation Predicate [10]. They use an orientation predicate defined by a determinant of a 4×4 matrix and compute the signed distance of each vertex form orientation predicate. The intersection test is then reduced to checking the signs of orientation predicates. In 2006, Tropp et al. takes an algebraic approach, A Fast Triangle to Triangle Intersection Test for Collision Detection [10], while their basic framework is similar to that of Held. The key observation is that the set of equations are strongly related to each other. Using a technique based on linear algebra and reusing some computation results for certain variables, Thus, common elements of the different equations can be reused to speed up the solution, exploiting the linearity of the matrix operations involved. In 2009, Jung-Woo Chang and Myung-Soo Kim adopt the algorithm of Moller and improve it by using OBB-based collision detection Efficient TriangleTriangle Intersection Test for OBB-Based Collision Detection [12]. However, with our knowledge, the five-axis machining collision detection has never been resolved with parallel optimization on GPUs.

7   Conclusion

We first present an efficient method for axial table collision detection on five-axis machining. Then we aim at the parallelization of collision detection using compiler optimization on GPU. Our approach includes 1. the analysis for machine kinematics that eliminates the unnecessary collision detection; and 2. interpolating for separating axes that gets rid of complicated cross-product computation. The demonstrated example shows that it improves 4.5 time of computation efficiency, comparing to the conventional detection method.

Acknowledgments. The authors would like to acknowledge the financial support of the Ministry of Science and Technology, Taiwan, R. O. C. under the grant, 101-2221-E-194 -021 -MY3 and Hiwin Technology Corporation of R. O. C. under the Robot Language Compiler Project.

References

1. Palmer, I., Grimsdale, R.: Collision detection for animation using sphere-trees. Comput. Graph. Forum **14**(2), 105–116 (1995)
2. Bradshaw, G., O'Sullivan, C.: Adaptive medial-axis approximation for sphere-tree construction. ACM Translations Graph. **23**(1), 1–26 (2004)
3. Cohen, J.D., Lin, M.C., Manocha, D., Ponamgi, M.: I-COLLIDE: an interactive and exact collision detection system for large-scale environments. In: ACM Interactive 3D Graphics Conference, pp. 189–196 (1995)
4. Bergen, V.: Efficient collision detection of complex deformable models using AABB trees. J. Graph. Tools. **2**(4), 1–14 (1997)
5. Gottschalk, S., Lin, M., Manocha, D.: OBB-Tree: a hierarchical structure for rapid interference detection. In: Proceedings of the SIGGRAPH, pp. 171–180 (1996)
6. Chang, J., Wang, W., Kima, M.: Efficient collision detection using a dual OBB-Sphere bounding volume hierarchy. Comput. Aided Des. **42**, 50–57 (2010)
7. NVIDIA http://www.nvidia.com
8. Fan, L.M.: Study on improved collision detection algorithm. Adv. Comput. Sci. Inform. Eng. **2**, 589–594 (2012)
9. Cox, T.: Real-Time Collision Detection. 500 Sansome Street, Suite 400, San Francisco, pp. 94–111 (2005)
10. Guigue, P., Devillers, O.: Fast and robust triangle-triangle overlap test using orientation predicates. J. Graph. GPU Game Tools **8**(1), 25–42 (2003)
11. Oren Tropp, A.T., Shimshoni, I.: A fast triangle to triangle intersection test for collision detection. Vis. Comput. Graph. **17**(5), 527–535 (2006)
12. Chang, J.-W., Kim, M.-S.: Efficient triangletriangle intersection test for OBB-Based collision detection. Comput. Graph. **33**, 235–240 (2009)

NCPSO: A Solution of the Controller Placement Problem in Software Defined Networks

Shuai Liu, Hua Wang$^{(\boxtimes)}$, Shanwen Yi, and Fangjin Zhu

School of Computer Science and Technology, Shandong University,
Jinan 250101, Shandong, China
timeflyLS@mail.sdu.edu.cn, wanghua@sdu.edu.cn

Abstract. Controller placement is an important problem in software defined networks (SDN). Most of the placement strategies focused on propagation latency, but ignored the load of controllers, which is a critical factor in real networks. In this paper, we propose Network Clustering Particle Swarm Optimization Algorithm (NCPSO), which taking into consideration of the load of controllers, propagation latency and load balancing. By generating diverse individuals with high clustering efficiency and overcoming the disadvantages of PSO used in discrete problem, the NCPSO can solve the controller placement problem better than other algorithms. The evaluation shows that the new algorithm can significantly reduce the number of required controllers, reduce the load of the maximum-load controller, and have a good performance of load balance.

Keywords: Controller placement · Software defined networks · Clustering particle swarm optimization

1 Introduction

SDN architectures decouple network controllers and switches, a logically centralized controller manages switches by providing them with rules that dictate their packet handling behavior [1, 2]. To cover aspects like scalability and resilience, concepts like HyperFlow allow partitioning of OpenFlow [3] networks into multiple domains that are each handled by individual controllers. The complexity of generating forwarding rules are offloaded to the controllers. Mismatched packets will be buffered or discarded until the corresponding flow entries are installed by the controller. The propagation latency between the switches and the associated controller is a key point for the performance of SDNs, and the placement of controllers became a critical problem.

In [4], the SDN controller placement problem is raised for the first time. Thus, there is a guarantee for finding optima with respect to the latency. But most of the investigated topologies require only one controller to comply with realistic latency constraints. However as a controller only has the capacity to manage a limited number of routers, the latency of message processing and failure, loads of controllers must be taken into consideration whenever designing a placement strategy. There are some

© Springer International Publishing Switzerland 2015
G. Wang et al. (Eds.): ICA3PP 2015, Part III, LNCS 9530, pp. 213–225, 2015.
DOI: 10.1007/978-3-319-27137-8_17

references to the performance of SDN systems in the literature [5, 6]. For example, a study shows that a popular network controller handles around 35 k flow initiation events 1 per second while maintaining a sub-10 ms flow install time [5]. Unfortunately, recent measurements of some deployment environments suggests that these numbers are far from sufficient. The controller control capacity become a top priority on controller deployment. The basic case of optimizing the latency from nodes to their assigned controller is traced back to the facility location problem, which is known to be NP-hard [4]. Thus, finding a controller placement featuring an adequate trade-off between the goals that are relevant for a particular use case is crucial for an efficient operation. To cope with large scale networks, a computationally fast approach for the aforementioned placement problem is required.

2 Related Work

The controller placement problem in SDNs was first proposed by Heller et al. [4]. In many contexts compare the placement of controller with a facility location problem. In [4, 6], the controller placement was taken into consideration to minimize the propagation latency. The placement metrics use Average-case Latency and worst-case latency. Thus the placement problem was corresponding to the K-center (or K-median) problem [7, 8]. More surprisingly, one controller location is often sufficient to meet existing reaction-time requirements (though certainly not fault tolerance requirements) [4]. [7, 9] show that the controller load has become an important factor to consider when deployed. The placement of controller should try to minimize the propagation latency, while the load of each controller should not exceed its capacity. The capacitated controller placement problem (CCPP) mentioned in [7] considered the problem of load capacitated which is different from the well-known controller placement problem (CPP). CCPP is corresponding to the Capacitated K-center Problem. These algorithm for the deployment of the controller is set or estimate the number of the controller, can not be correctly estimated the number of controller based on the requirements. [6] assume that the mapping between a switch and a controller is configured dynamically, [10] has proposed an elastic distributed SDN controller. The dynamic allocation can improve the scalability and reliability when deploying the controller in LAN, but it is not suitable for Large-scale network. No paper can tell how many controllers we need through scientific computing in a given network.

Now we answer the question how many controllers are needed by our computing result. When we consider the question where in the topology should they go, we should make sure the load of each controller should not exceed its capacity. Propagation delay constraint from controller to switch should be satisfied. We also want to use the minimum number of controller to cover the having network topology. So we hope a controller can control the more switches.

Different from K-center algorithm and the other algorithm, for instance capacitated K-center, with the aid of a complex network of clustering algorithm [11] and in combination with PSO (Particle Swarm Optimization) which works with a population (i.e., swarm) of particles who can move in the search space to find optimal solutions, we propose Network Clustering Particle Swarm Optimization Algorithm (NCPSO) to solve the problem of controller placement. The clustering performances of the proposed algorithm have been validated on networks. Extensive experimental studies compared with other approaches have proved that the proposed algorithm is effective and promising.

3 The Mathematical Model and Formulation

Denote the network by (V, E), where $V = \{v_1, v_2, \ldots, v_n\}$ is the set of switches and $E = \{e_1, e_2, \ldots, e_n\}$ is the set of physical links between the switches. Assume network is divided into k partitions, each partition is handled by individual controller. Denote the set of k controllers by $\Theta = \{\theta_1, \ldots \theta_k\}$. $\phi(\theta_i)(i = 1, 2, \ldots, k)$ is used to denote all the switches which is under the individual controller θ_i. The network G is divided into k numbers of clusters: $\phi(\theta_1), \phi(\theta_2), \ldots, \phi(\theta_k)$. The clusters should to satisfy:

$$\phi(\theta_i) \neq \emptyset, \ i = 1, 2, \ldots, k \tag{1}$$

$$\cup_{i=1}^{k} \phi(\theta_i) = V \tag{2}$$

$$\phi(\theta_i) \cap \phi(\theta_j) = \emptyset, \quad i \neq j, \ i, j = 1, 2, \ldots, k \tag{3}$$

The formula $v \in \phi(\theta_i)$ represents the switch $v(v \in V)$ assign a controller θ_i. Each controller θ_i has the load capacity $C(\theta_i)$. $c(v_i)$ represents that the power spend which a controller controls the switch v_i. In a partition cluster we should make sure:

$$\sum\nolimits_{v_j \in \phi(\theta_i)} c(v_j) \leq C(\theta_i), \forall v_j \in \phi(\theta_i), \forall \theta_i \in \Theta \tag{4}$$

The formula (4) means that the total tasks which given by the switch should not exceed the power rating of the controller θ_i. These switch are directly controlled by the controller θ_i.

For a partition cluster, d_s^v is the shortest path from node v to node s. As we place the controller on a switch placement, d_θ^v represents the delay from a controller θ to a switch v, when $\theta \in \Theta$ and $v \in V$.

Due to one controller location is often sufficient to meet existing reaction-time requirements. For a partition cluster the propagation delay from a controller to a switch should not exceed constraint of the maximum controller-to-switch propagation delay. And the propagation delay of switches in a same propagation should not exceed constraint of the maximum switch-to switch propagation delay. We make propagation delay as a constraint. Under the constraint of propagation delay, we optimize the load of each controller. So we should make sure:

$$d_{\theta_i}^{v_j} \leq D(\theta_i), \forall v_j \in \phi(\theta_i), \forall \theta_i \in \Theta \tag{5}$$

$D(\theta_i)$ is the constraint of the controller θ_i maximum controller-to-switch propagation delay. At the same time the propagation delay between node to node should not exceed the maximum switch-to-switch propagation delay constraint $D(V)$. So we should make sure:

$$d_{v_n}^{v_m} \leq D(V), \forall v_m, v_n \in \phi(\theta_i), \forall \theta_i \in \Theta \tag{6}$$

We also hope can reduce the controller-to-switch propagation delay. According to the related work before, we can use the average-case latency (7) and worst-case latency (8) to represent it.

$$L_{avg}(\theta_i) = \frac{1}{n} \sum_{v_j \in \theta_i} \min \quad d_{\theta_i}^{v_j}, \ \forall \theta_i \in \Theta \tag{7}$$

$$L_{wc}(\theta_i) = \max_{(v_j \in \theta_i)} \min_{(\forall \theta_i \in \Theta)} d_{\theta_i}^{v_j} \tag{8}$$

In the formula (7), n is the numbers of switch control by the controller θ_i. The formulas (7) and (8) are measures in a partition cluster. According to the formula, we can choose a suitable place to set the controller in a certain partition cluster.

After consider these constraints, the objective of our controller placement problem is that every controller achieves its maximum utilization ratio. So we define objective function as follows:

$$max \, min_{\forall \theta_i \in \Theta} \sum_{v_j \in \phi(\theta_i)} c(v_j) \tag{9}$$

Load balance also need to be taken into account when a reliable network operation is desired. We consider load balance as a constraint. We get a constraint as follows:

$$(maxC'(\theta_i))^{\wedge}2 - (minC'(\theta_j))^{\wedge}2 \leq \pi_{balance}, \forall \theta_i, \theta_j \in \Theta \tag{10}$$

We hope the maximum load of controller in the network is not evident higher than the minimum load of controller. $C'(\theta)$ represents the real load of controller θ.

From the above, we get the mathematical model of controller placement problem.

4   NCPSO Algorithm

4.1   Introduction of NCPSO Algorithm

In this paper, a Network Clustering Particle Swarm Optimization Algorithm (NCPSO) is used for the solution of the Controller Placement Problem. PSO(particle swarm optimization) algorithm is inspired by the motion of a flock of birds searching for food. To find the optimal solution, initially a set of particles is created randomly where each particle corresponds to a possible solution. Each particle has a position in the space of solutions and moves with a given velocity. As same as PSO, in NCPSO, each particle adjust its search direction according to two factors, its own best previous experience (*Pbest*) and the best experience of all other members (*Gbest*). The particle search for an optimum is an iterative process that lies in the information between *Pbest* and *Gbest*.

This is similar to human behavior in making decisions where people consider their own best past experience and the best experience of how the other people around them have performed.

4.2   Definition of a Particle

In NCPSO algorithm, we use (11) to denote a solution of the controller placement problem p_i, the formula is:

$$p_i = (\theta_1, \phi(\theta_1)), (\theta_2, \phi(\theta_2)), \ldots, (\theta_k, \phi(\theta_k)) \tag{11}$$

From the formula (11) we can see, there are k-numbers of partitions cluster. Each partition cluster has a center controller θ_i. $\phi(\theta_i)$ is congregation of switch which all of them controlled by θ_i. A particle includes a solution of the controller placement problem. All of the particles move in the n dimensional search space according to given rules. Moreover, each individual particles has a memory unit that notes down at the optimal location it had arrived. Base on the optimal location which the individual particle had previously reached and the optimal location which his neighbor individuals had reached, the particle change his position and velocity. By adjusting their velocity and iterating search in the solution space NCPSO algorithm can find the optimal solution fast.

4.3   The Pseudo Codes of NCPSO Algorithm

4.3.1   The Pseudo Codes of NCPSO Algorithm as Follows

Algorithm. NCPSO Algorithm

Parameters: Swarm size: pop; Inertia weight: $\omega_{max}, \omega_{min}$; Cognitive factor: c_1; Social factor c_2; **Input:** The adjacent matrix A of a network. The maximum power C of a controller; The array of mission: $M = \{c(v_1), c(v_2), \ldots, c(v_i)\}$ for nodes which may consume the power of a switch. The maximum imbalance constraint: $\pi_{balance}$. The delay matrix of node to node: D. The maximum iteration times T_{max}.

Step 1. Initialization
   1.1)   **For each particle i do** // Initialize the velocity and position of particle.
   1.2)   Position initialization: $X_i = \{x_1, x_2, \ldots, x_j\}, x_k \in [1, j]$.
   1.3)   Velocity initialization: $V_i = \{v_1, v_2, \ldots, v_j\}, v_k = 1$.
   1.4)   Personal best position initialization:
             $Pbest_i = \{pbest_1, pbest_2, \ldots, pbest_j\}. \forall x_k \in X, pbest_k = x_k$.
   1.5)   **End For**
   1.6)   *Gbest*=rand (*particles*).
Step 2. Set $t = 0$. // the number of flight cycles
Step 3. Cycle
   3.1)   Particle Evolution

For the pseudo codes of particle evolution, the step 1 Initialization gets new initial partition. At the beginning, NCPSO Algorithm needs to initialize pop numbers of particles. For each particle i has j numbers of dimensions. j is equal to the numbers of nodes. Every particle has a best historical position *Pbest*. The initial value of *Pbest$_i$* is equal to X_i. The initial value of *Gbest* is equal to the best of *Pbest*. The process of NCPSO Algorithm is similar with PSO, it include initialization and cycle iteration. Cycle is the main body of NCPSO Algorithm.

4.3.2 Definition of Position and Position Initialization

Definition of position: In NCPSO algorithm, the position vector represents a solution of partition cluster. For the controller placement, the position permutation of a particle i is defined as $X_i = \{x_1, x_2, \ldots, x_n\} (x_j \epsilon [1, n])$. n is the total number of switch in network. We give each switch a sign x_j, If $x_i = x_j$, the switch i and j belong to the same partition cluster, else the switch i and j belong to different partition clusters. From the position permutation X_i, we can get partition clusters: $\phi(\theta_1), \phi(\theta_2), \ldots, \phi(\theta_k)$. The switches belong to the same $\phi(\theta_i)$ have a same sign x_j. We take an example of a partition cluster show like Fig. 1.

In the partition cluster, the nodes with same shape belong to the same cluster that have the same sign.

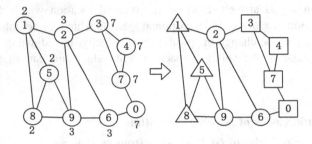

Fig. 1. An example of partition cluster for a network

4.3.3 Definition of Velocity and Velocity Initialization

Definition of velocity: The velocity gives the particle a guidance and determines whether the particle can reach its destination and by how fast it could. In NCPSO, velocity is define as $V_i = \{v_1, v_2, \ldots, v_n\} (v_j \epsilon [0, 1])$. If $v_j = 1$, the corresponding componential position element x_i will be changed, otherwise x_i keeps its original state. We set $v_j = 1$. This set means that we hope it can cover a comprehensive solve space at the very beginning.

4.4   The Node Cluster and Particle Status Updating

The movement of the particles for NCPSO algorithm is dictated by the following formula.

$$V_{i+1} = trans(\omega V_i + c_1 rand(0, 1)(pbest_i \oplus X_i) + c_2 rand(0, 1)(gbest \oplus X_i)) \quad (12)$$

$$X_{i+1} = X_i + V_i \quad (13)$$

ω is the inertia weight; c_1 is the cognitive component; c_2 is the social component; We set $\delta = c_1 + c_2$, δ is a constant. The ω is the influence degree which come from the last generation velocity. If the value of ω is larger, the ability of global search is better, otherwise the ability of partial search is better. We use dynamic inertia weight that the value of ω can linearly decreases.

$$\omega(t) = \omega_{max} - (\omega_{max} - \omega_{min}) \frac{t}{T_{max}} \tag{14}$$

ω_{max} is the initial maximum inertia weight, ω_{min} is the minimum inertia weight. T_{max} is the maximum iteration times.

$\oplus$ is defined as a Cluster XOR operator. Because of the random initialization, the sign system for each of particle is no unified. Different from XOR operator, the Cluster XOR operator should unify the sign of each constituent. For the position X_i, there is a partition cluster θ_i. According to θ_i, there is a set of constituent: $\{x_m, \ldots, x_l\}$ which have the same sign. At the same dimension of X_j, we obtain the maximum-same-sign. To calculate the value of $Y = X_i \oplus X_j$. If the dimension of X_j which is decided by X_i is equal to the maximum-same-sign, the value of the corresponding dimension y is equal to 0, else y is equal to 1.

The function $Y = trans(X)$ is defined as:

$$\begin{cases} y_i = 1 & rand(0,1) < transm(x_i) \\ y_i = 0 & rand(0,1) \geq transm(x_i) \end{cases} \forall x_i \in X, y_i \in Y \tag{15}$$

$$transm(x) = \frac{1}{1+e^{-x}} \tag{16}$$

We defined $X_{i+1} = X_i + V_i$ as:

$$\begin{cases} x_{i+1} = x_i & v_i = 0 \\ x_{i+1} = RMNS & v_i = 1 \end{cases}, \forall x_i \in X_i, x_{i+1} \in X_{i+1} \tag{17}$$

The operation of RMNS is actually a process of clustering. Each node in the graph attempts to chance its sign as the most appeared sign which is given by the direct adjacent nodes. We get the value of RMNS(random of max neighbor sign) by roulette. Suppose vertex i has a neighbor set: $N = \{n_1, n_2, \ldots, n_k\}$. According to N we get a neighbor sign set $X'_n = \{x_{n_1}, x_{n_2}, \ldots, x_{n_k}\}$. x_{i+1} is equal to one constituent of X'_n. According to the same sign number in X'_n, we get a probability ρ_{n_i}.

$$\rho_{n_i} = \frac{\sum_{n_j \in N} \varphi(x_{n_j}, x_{n_i})}{k} \tag{18}$$

If the random function is in the probability interval $\left[\rho_{n_i}, \rho_{n_j}\right]$, the value of x_{i+1} is x_{n_i}.

4.5 Algorithm Framework of Particle Evolution in the NCPSO

From above, the formulations (4)–(6) and (10) define the constraint of the placement problem. And the formulation (9) define the objective of the problem. The formulations (12) and (13) provide the most important evolvement method. In this section, we give a detail description. The particle evolution process include three parts: amend partitions according to delay constraint, amend partitions according to load constraint and update *Pbest* and *Gbest*.

4.5.1 The Pseudo Codes of Particle Evolution as Follows

Algorithm. Particle Evolution

1.   **For** $t < T_{max}$ **do**
2.   **For each particle do**
3.   Calculate V_{i+1} according to Eq. (12).
4.   Calculate X_{i+1} according to Eq. (13).
5.   Calculate deploy of controller by Dijkstra Algorithm according to Eq. (7)(8).
6.   **If** $\exists v_j, d^{v_j}_{\theta_i} > D(\theta_i)$ //Amend the position
7.   Put v_j out of the $\phi(\theta_i)$.
8.   Calculate min-load $\phi(\theta_j)$ according to Eq. (4) $\sum_{v_j \in \phi(\theta_i)} c(v_j)$ under the constraint of $C(\theta_i)$ and $D(\theta_i)$.
9.   **If** $\nexists \sum_{v_j \in \phi(\theta_i)} c(v_j) \leq C(\theta_i)$ && $d^{v_j}_{\theta_i} \leq D(\theta_i)$
10.   Give v_j a new sign.
11.   **End if**
12.   **End if**
13.   **If** $\exists \theta_i, \sum_{v_j \in \phi(\theta_i)} c(v_j) > C(\theta_i)$
14.   Put v_j out of the $\phi(\theta_i)$.
15.   Calculate min-load $\phi(\theta_j)$ according to Eq. (4) $\sum_{v_j \in \phi(\theta_i)} c(v_j)$ under the constraint of $C(\theta_i)$ and $D(\theta_i)$.
16.   **If** $\nexists \sum_{v_j \in \phi(\theta_i)} c(v_j) \leq C(\theta_i)$ && $d^{v_j}_{\theta_i} \leq D(\theta_i)$
17.   Give v_j a new sign.
18.   **End If**
19.   **End If**
20.   **End for**
21. $Gbest' = \max(particles)$
22.   **If** $Gbest \leq Gbest'$
23. $Gbest = Gbest'$
24.   Update *Pbest*.
25.   **End if**
26.   **End for**
27. Print the optimal solution.

4.5.2 The Particle Evolution Process Analysis

At the beginning of particle evolution, we get the original next generation particle by the method (12) and (13). The method of roulette make the tightly linked nodes gather to a group. Using Dijkstra algorithm calculate $L_{avg}(\theta_i)$ and $L_{wc}(\theta_i)$, we can find the controller placement position. Inevitably, we can't make sure the node which at the brink of a cluster or far from the center controller suffice the delay constraint. So the process of amend clusters is necessary.

Amend partitions according to delay constraint: From step 6 to step 12 is amending partitions according to delay constraint. If there is a node v_j which the delay from its center controller to it $d_{\theta_i}^{v_j}$ is exceed the max delay constraint $D(\theta_i)$. The node will be removed from the group and find the suitable group under the constraint of delay and load.

There may be not only one group satisfy the two constraint. In order to obtain a better load balance, we allocate the node to the current the minimum load controller. By this method, we increase the controller's minimum load, the evolution has the tendency to the load balance. At the same time, the method decreases the number of controllers.

Amend partitions according to load constraint: From step 13 to step 19 is amending partition according to load constraint. If there is a controller θ_j which the real power $\sum_{v_j \in \phi(\theta_i)} c(v_j)$ is exceed the load constraint $C(\theta_i)$. The node will be removed from the group and find the suitable group under the constraint of delay and load. Just as the above we allocate the node to the current the minimum load controller.

As the above introduction, nodes cluster according to the compactedness of contact with each other. The nodes may come under other directly adjacent cluster or become a new cluster. Then, we should adjust the clusters partitions according to load capacity.

In this way, the clusters will drift. They attempt to move to an optimality solution. We can effectually balance the load of controller and at the same time reducing the propagation delay from the controller to switch. After optimizing every particle, the *Pbest* is chose from a generation particle. We can get the *Gbest* in each cycle. According to the objective function (9), after repeated iteration the algorithm will obtain an optimal controllers placement strategy.

5 Simulation Result

It's impossible to evaluate all of variants of SDN in the real world. Thus, we evaluate the proposed placement strategy in the most common scenarios. We use the method mentioned in literature [12], randomly generated a number of different size of topology. We will contrast our algorithm with K-center algorithm and Capacitated K-center, which proposed in [4, 7]. We will compared the three algorithm from the number of controllers, the minimum utility ratio of controller power, the load balance and the propagation delay in different network scales.

5.1 Analysis of the Number of Controllers

Based on the experiments, we made the discovery: NCPSO strategy can reduce the number of controllers when every controller avoid overload.

In the experiments, we can get the number of controller directly by NCPSO and every controller under the constraint of avoid overload. When we use K-center algorithm and Capacitated K-center strategy, we gradually increase the number of controllers for each placement strategy until no overload happens. From Fig. 2, we can see

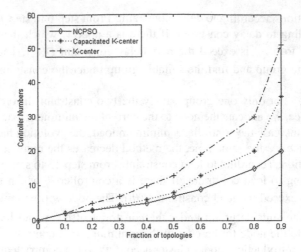

Fig. 2. Variation trend of controller numbers in different network

the numbers of controller obtained by NCPSO algorithm is better than the other two algorithm. In different network scales, the NCPSO can always obtains optimality solution. As the results illustrated in Fig. 2, to avoid overload, 6 controllers are required using NCPSO strategy for 50 % of topologies, and at most 20 controllers for all the topologies, whereas using Capacitated K-center strategy requires 8 and 36 controllers correspondingly.

K-center strategy is inferior to the other. Moreover, with the increasing of network topology, the variance ratio of NCPSO is less than capacitated K-center algorithm and K-center algorithm. Because of the intelligent cluster regulation, the particles can found the solution space based on the real network topology. At the same time, it avoids of the fault cause by artificially.

5.2 Analysis of the Minimum Utility Ratio of Controller Power in Different Network Scales

Based the NCPSO algorithm, it's a process of cluster. In the process of finding optimum solution, the switches which have closely relation will initiatively converge. As the mission converge, the minimum utility ratio of controller power increases, and the numbers of controller the networks should need declines.

According Fig. 3 we can see, in the partition cluster strategy obtained by NCPSO algorithm, the minimum utility ratio of controller power is obvious high than the other partition cluster strategy obtained by capacitated K-center algorithm and K-center algorithm. As the increase of network scales, the variation trend of minimum utility ratio obtained by NCPSO is gentle and it's always higher than 60 %. K-center algorithm ignore the power load, there is a gigantic downtrend of K-center curve.

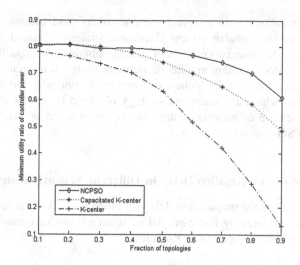

Fig. 3. The Minimum utility ratio of controller power

5.3   Analysis of the Load Balance in Different Network Scales

In our NCPSO analysis there are two master methods to make sure the placement has a good load balance. Frist, the minimum utility ratio of controller power increase as iteration. And every cluster center have a maximum utility ratio restrict. According to $X_{i+1} = X_i + V_i$ every cluster try to attract the more switch, every controller have tendency of get the max utility ratio. Then, when amending the particles, we try to assign the more switches to controllers which have a low utility ratio. By this two method, it has a good load balance.

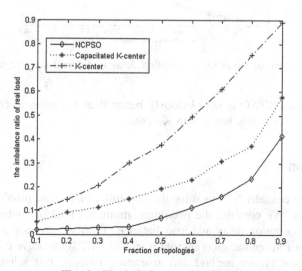

Fig. 4. The imbalance ratio of load

We use the imbalance ratio to reveal the controllers load balance. According to Fig. 4, we can see the imbalance ratio placement strategy obtained by NCPSO is obvious below than the other two placement strategy obtained by capacitated K-center algorithm and K-center algorithm in different network scales. It indicates that there is a small load's distance between the highest real power of controller and the lowest real power of controller which the placement strategy obtained by the NCPSO. From the curve with the increase of network scales, the variation trend of load balance ratio obtained by NCPSO is gentle.

5.4   Analysis of the Propagation Delay in Different Network Scales

From Fig. 5 we can see the propagation delay obtained by NCPSO is approximate the propagation delay obtained by K-center. All of them are obvious junior to the propagation delay obtained by capacitated K-center.

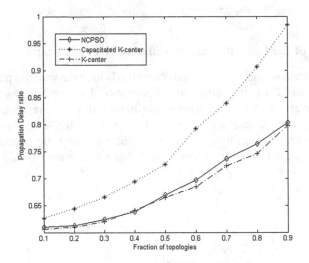

Fig. 5. Comparison of the propagation delay in different network scales

In spite of the NCPSO is not obviously better than K-center, to combine all the index, NCPSO is obviously better than K-center.

6   Conclusion

In this paper, we consider how to solve the controller placement problem in software defined networks. We optimize the maximum minimum-load of controller under the constraint of propagation delay and load balance. Then we propose a network clustering particle swarm optimization algorithm, called NCPSO to solve this problem. By the new intelligent cluster method and amending process, this scheme can ensure optimal n placement strategy. Simulation results on real topologies and load demands show the effectiveness of our algorithm on reduce the load of the maximum-load controller, and load balancing. It is a practical algorithm that can be actually deployed on real software defined networks.

Acknowledgments. The study is supported by the Natural Science Foundation of Shandong Province (Grant No. ZR2011FM021; ZR2013FM029), the Science and Technology Development Program of Jinan (Grant No. 201303010), the National Natural Science Foundation of China (NSFC No. 60773101), and the Fundamental Research Funds of Shandong University (Grant No. 2014JC037).

References

1. Kreutz, D., Ramos, F.M.V., Verissimo, P.E., Rothenberg, C.E., Azodolmolky, S., Uhlig, S.: Software-defined networking: a comprehensive survey. Proc. IEEE **103**, 14–76 (2015)
2. Feamster, N., Rexford, J., Zegura, E.: The road to SDN: an intellectual history of programmable networks. ACM SIGCOMM Comput. Commun. Rev. **44**, 87–98 (2014)
3. McKeown, N., Anderson, T., Balakrishnan, H., Parulkar, G., Peterson, L., Rexford, J., Shenker, S., Turner, J.: OpenFlow: enabling innovation in campus networks. ACM SIGCOMM Comput. Commun. Rev. **38**, 69–74 (2008)
4. Heller, B., Sherwood, R., McKeown, N.: The controller placement problem. ACM SIGCOMM Comput. Commun. Rev. **42**, 473–478 (2012)
5. Jain, S., Kumar, A., Mandal, S., Ong, J., Poutievski, L., Singh, A., Venkata, S., Wanderer, J., Zhou, J., Zhu, M., Zolla, J., Holzle, U., Stuart, S., Vahdat, A.: B4: experience with a globally-deployed software defined WAN. ACM SIGCOMM Comput. Commun. Rev. **43**, 3–14 (2013)
6. Dixit, A., Hao, F., Mukherjee, S., Lakshman, T.V., Kompella, R.: Towards an elastic distributed SDN controller. ACM SIGCOMM Comput. Commun. Rev. **43**, 7–12 (2013)
7. Guang, Y., Jun, B., Yuliang, L., Luyi, G.: On the capacitated controller placement problem in software defined networks. IEEE Commun. Lett. **18**, 1339–1342 (2014)
8. John, W., Kern, A., Kind, M., Skoldstrom, P., Staessens, D., Woesner, H.: SplitArchitecture: SDN for the carrier domain. IEEE Commun. Mag. **52**, 146–152 (2014)
9. Hock, D., Hartmann, M., Gebert, S., Jarschel, M., Zinner, T., Tran-Gia, P.: Pareto-optimal resilient controller placement in SDN-based core networks (2013)
10. Lange, S., Gebert, S., Zinner, T., Tran-Gia, P., Hock, D., Jarschel, M., Hoffmann, M.: Heuristic approaches to the controller placement problem in large scale SDN networks. IEEE Trans. Netw. Serv. Manage. **12**, 4–17 (2015)
11. Gong, M.G., Cai, Q., Chen, X.W., Ma, L.J.: Complex network clustering by multiobjective discrete particle swarm optimization based on decomposition. IEEE Trans. Evol. Comput. **18**, 82–97 (2014)
12. Naldi, M.: Connectivity of Waxman topology models. Comput. Commun. **29**, 24–31 (2005)
13. Shah, S.A., Faiz, J., Farooq, M., Shafi, A., Mehdi, S.A., C.: An architectural evaluation of SDN controllers. In: 2013 IEEE International Conference on Communications, pp. 3504–3508. IEEE (2013)

Parallel Column Subset Selection of Kernel Matrix for Scaling up Support Vector Machines

Jiangang Wu, Chang Feng, Peihuan Gao, and Shizhong Liao[✉]

School of Computer Science and Technology, Tianjin University,
Tianjin 300072, China
szliao@tju.edu.cn

Abstract. Nyström method and low-rank linearized Support Vector Machines (SVMs) are two widely used methods for scaling up kernel SVMs, both of which need to sample part of columns of the kernel matrix to reduce the size. However, existing non-uniform sampling methods suffer from at least quadratic time complexity in the number of training data, limiting the scalability of kernel SVMs. In this paper, we propose a parallel sampling method called parallel column subset selection (PCSS) based on the divide-and-conquer strategy, which divides the kernel matrix into several small submatrices and then selects columns in parallel. We prove that PCSS has a $(1+\epsilon)$ relative-error upper bound with respect to the kernel matrix. Further, we present two approaches to scaling up kernel SVMs by combining PCSS with Nyström method and low-rank linearized SVMs. The results of comparison experiments demonstrate the effectiveness, efficiency and scalability of our approaches.

Keywords: Support Vector Machines (SVMs) · Nyström method · Low-rank linearized SVMs · Column subset selection · Parallel sampling

1 Introduction

The Support Vector Machines (SVMs) is one of the most popular classification tools, which is based on statistical learning theory and delivers excellent results for non-linear classification in machine learning and data mining [14,18]. Such methods project data points into a high-dimensional or even infinite-dimensional feature space and find the optimal hyperplane in that feature space with strong generalization performance. They typically suffer from at least quadratic running-time complexity in the number of observations n, as this is the complexity of computing the kernel matrix. In large-scale settings where n may be large, this is usually not acceptable [17].

In order to scale up kernel SVMs to large-scale problems, a lot of approximation methods of kernel matrix have been proposed, such as sparse greedy matrix approximation [15], Nyström approximations [19] and low rank Cholesky decomposition [8], among which the Nyström method is the most popular and has been well studied theoretically and experimentally. The basic idea of Nyström

© Springer International Publishing Switzerland 2015
G. Wang et al. (Eds.): ICA3PP 2015, Part III, LNCS 9530, pp. 226–239, 2015.
DOI: 10.1007/978-3-319-27137-8_18

method lies that one samples a few columns from the original symmetric positive semidefinite (SPSD) kernel matrix and uses the sampled columns to generate a low-rank approximation to the original kernel matrix. In this way, one can speed up some operations on kernel matrix for large-scale datasets, for instance, computing the inverse or eigenvalue decomposition of the kernel matrix. Initially the Nyström method was used to speed up Gaussian process regression [19] and now its applications have been extended to many different fields, such as kernel SVM [3], spectral clustering [9]. Recently Zhang et al. [20] propose low-rank linearized SVMs. They uses low-rank approximation of kernel matrix with Nyström method to linearize the non-linear kernel SVMs, which can also be used to address the scalability problem of kernel SVMs.

The sampling process plays an important role in Nyström method because it determines which columns of the kernel matrix to be chosen and the selected columns will affect the result of low-rank approximation. Therefore, there has been a lot of work on the sampling process in Nyström method theoretically and empirically. Williams and Seeger [19] use the uniform sampling without replacement to sample columns of the kernel matrix, the most commonly used sampling method in practice, which cannot make full use of the information of kernel matrix and leads to poor low-rank approximation. In order to boost the precision of approximation, some non-uniform sampling methods using the information of kernel matrix have been proposed, column-norm sampling [4], leverage score sampling [13], adaptive sampling method [2], k-means based sampling [21]. Unfortunately, such sampling methods suffer from at least quadratic time complexity, which prevents themselves from scaling up to large-scale problems.

Column subset selection (CSS) [5] is an effective method to analyze and interpret data, which represents a matrix using a small number of informative actual columns of the matrix. As existing CSS algorithms are time-consuming, in this paper, we present a parallelized approach to CSS, called PCSS, to speed up kernel SVMs. It consists of three stages:

(1) Dividing the original kernel matrix into several small submatrices;
(2) Performing column subset selection to select columns on each submatrix in parallel;
(3) Combining those selected columns.

We prove that PCSS has a $(1 + \epsilon)$ relative-error bound of the kernel matrix without losing any precision with respect to that of CSS. By combining PCSS with Nyström method and low-rank linearized SVMs, we propose two new methods to scale up kernel SVMs: PCSS-Nyström and PCSS-LLSVM. Experiments results show that our methods have low running time and preserve good prediction accuracy.

The rest of the paper is organized as follows: Sect. 2 introduces the notation and some preliminary algorithms. Section 3 gives a detailed description and theoretical analysis about our PCSS method. Section 4 introduces PCSS into Nyström method and low-rank linearized SVMs. Section 5 conducts experiments to illustrate the advantages of our method. Finally, a short conclusion follows in Sect. 6.

2   Preliminaries

In this section, we will introduce some notational conventions, best rank-k approximation, Nyström method and linearization of kernel SVMs.

2.1   Notation

Let $\|\cdot\|_2$ and $\|\cdot\|_F$ denote the spectral norm and Frobenius norm respectively and $\|\cdot\|_\xi$ denotes either $\|\cdot\|_2$ or $\|\cdot\|_F$. For a matrix $\mathbf{M} \in \mathbb{R}^{m \times n}$, let $r = \text{rank}(\mathbf{M})$ denote its rank. We write the compact singular value decomposition of $\mathbf{M}$ as $\mathbf{U}_M \mathbf{\Sigma}_M \mathbf{V}_M^T$. $\mathbf{\Sigma}_M$ is a diagonal matrix containing r non-zero singular values of $\mathbf{M}$ in decreasing order, denoted as $\sigma_1(\mathbf{M}) \geq \sigma_2(\mathbf{M}) \geq \cdots \geq \sigma_r(\mathbf{M}) > 0$. $\mathbf{U}_M \in \mathbb{R}^{m \times r}$ and $\mathbf{V}_M \in \mathbb{R}^{n \times r}$ are the corresponding left and right singular vectors of $\mathbf{M}$ and we let $\mathbf{u}_i(\mathbf{M})$ and $\mathbf{v}_i(\mathbf{M})$ denote the i-th left and right singular vector. $\mathbf{M}^+ = \mathbf{U}_M \mathbf{\Sigma}_M^{-1} \mathbf{V}_M^T$ denotes the Moore-Penrose pseudoinverse of $\mathbf{M}$ and $\mathbf{P}_M = \mathbf{M}\mathbf{M}^+$ represents the orthogonal projection onto the column space of $\mathbf{M}$.

2.2   Best Rank-k Approximation

For a matrix $\mathbf{M} \in \mathbb{R}^{m \times n}$ and $k \leq \min\{m, n\}$, we let $\mathbf{M}_k$ denote its best rank-k approximation which is defined in the following way:

$$\mathbf{M}_k = \sum_{i=1}^{k} \sigma_i(\mathbf{M}) \mathbf{u}_i(\mathbf{M}) \mathbf{v}_i(\mathbf{M})^T,$$

which satisfies $\|\mathbf{M} - \mathbf{M}_k\|_\xi = \min_{\text{rank}(\mathbf{A}) \leq k} \|\mathbf{M} - \mathbf{A}\|_\xi$. The most straightforward way to get $\mathbf{M}_k$ is to truncate the full SVD and remain the top k singular values and singular vectors, thus the running time is $O(mn \min\{m, n\})$ for this method. There is also an $O(mnk)$ time complexity algorithm to calculate $\mathbf{M}_k$ [10].

2.3   Nyström Method

Let $\mathbf{K} \in \mathbb{R}^{n \times n}$ denote a symmetric positive semi-definite kernel matrix. Supposed that we have obtained l columns, generally $l \ll n$, from the kernel matrix using certain sampling method. Let $\mathbf{C}$ denote the $n \times l$ matrix formed by the l columns and $\mathbf{W}$ denote the $l \times l$ matrix formed by the intersection entries of the l columns with corresponding l rows. After rearranging columns and rows $\mathbf{K}$ and $\mathbf{C}$ can be written as:

$$\mathbf{K} = \begin{bmatrix} \mathbf{W} & \mathbf{K}_{21}^T \\ \mathbf{K}_{21} & \mathbf{K}_{22} \end{bmatrix} \quad \text{and} \quad \mathbf{C} = \begin{bmatrix} \mathbf{W} \\ \mathbf{K}_{21} \end{bmatrix}. \tag{1}$$

With matrix $\mathbf{K}$ and $\mathbf{C}$, Nyström method constructs a rank-k approximate matrix as follows:

$$\widetilde{\mathbf{K}}_k = \mathbf{C}\mathbf{W}_k^+ \mathbf{C}^T, \tag{2}$$

where $\mathbf{W}_k^+$ denotes the Moore-Penrose inverse of the best rank-k approximation to $\mathbf{W}$. The time complexity of Nyström method is $O(kln + l^3)$.

From Eq. (2) we can see that the approximate matrix $\tilde{\mathbf{K}}_k$ is mainly determined by $\mathbf{C}$ and $\mathbf{W}$, when parameter k is given, so the l sampled columns will directly influence the accuracy of Nyström approximation. Thus the sampling method plays an important role in Nyström method.

A lot of work has been proposed to analyze the sampling method. Uniform sampling is the most basic sampling method. Some non-uniform sampling methods aim to select more informative columns via a precalculated sampling probability distribution, such as diagonal sampling, column-norm sampling, leverage score sampling and so on.

Different from the sampling methods abovementioned, adaptive sampling method selects columns iteratively, which is first proposed by Deshpande et al. [2] in matrix projection. In each iteration the sampling probability distribution is updated and the s ($s < l$) columns are sampled according to the new updated probability distribution. This iteration is repeated until all the l columns are sampled. It aims to make the deviation between $\mathbf{K}$ and $\mathbf{CC}^+\mathbf{K}$ as small as possible, whose time complexity is $O(ln^2)$. Kumar et al. [12] improve the adaptive sampling method in computational and storage burdens.

2.4 Linearization of Kernel SVMs

Zhang et al. [20] present a way to linearization of kernel SVMs and use linear SVM on the derived explicit features. Suppose we are given a set of training pairs $(\mathbf{x}_i, y_i)$, where $\mathbf{x}_i \in \mathbb{R}^{d \times 1}$ are concatenated as rows in the $n \times d$ training data matrix $\mathbf{X}_r$ and $y_i \in \{-1, +1\}$ are stored in the training label $\mathbf{y}_r \in \mathbb{R}^{n \times 1}$. Similarly we have m testing samples in $\mathbf{X}_e \in \mathbb{R}^{m \times d}$. Assume we use a positive semi-definite (PSD) kernel function $k(\mathbf{x}_i, \mathbf{x}_j) = \langle \phi(\cdot), \phi(\cdot) \rangle : \mathbb{R}^d \times \mathbb{R}^d \to \mathbb{R}$, and define the kernel matrix on the training and testing data in blocks as

$$\mathbf{K} = \begin{bmatrix} \mathbf{K}_{rr} & \mathbf{K}_{re} \\ \mathbf{K}_{er} & \mathbf{K}_{ee} \end{bmatrix},$$

where $\mathbf{K}_{rr} \in \mathbb{R}^{n \times n}$ is the kernel matrix defined on $\mathbf{X}_r$, $\mathbf{K}_{ee} \in \mathbb{R}^{m \times m}$ is defined on $\mathbf{X}_e$, and $\mathbf{K}_{er} \in \mathbb{R}^{m \times n}$ is defined on $\mathbf{X}_e$ and $\mathbf{X}_r$. A kernel SVM trained on $\mathbf{X}_r$, $\mathbf{y}_r$, and tested on $\mathbf{X}_e$ is equivalent to a linear SVM trained on $\mathbf{F}_r$, $\mathbf{y}_r$ and tested on $\mathbf{F}_e$, where

$$\mathbf{K} = \begin{bmatrix} \mathbf{F}_r \\ \mathbf{F}_e \end{bmatrix} \begin{bmatrix} \mathbf{F}_r^{\mathrm{T}} & \mathbf{F}_e^{\mathrm{T}} \end{bmatrix}$$

is any decomposition of the PSD kernel matrix $\mathbf{K}$ evaluated on $(\mathbf{X}_r, \mathbf{X}_e)$, and the factor $\mathbf{F}_r \in \mathbb{R}^{n \times p}$ and $\mathbf{F}_e \in \mathbb{R}^{m \times p}$ can be seen as the explicit features of training data in feature space.

3   Parallel Column Subset Selection

In this section, we will introduce column subset selection (CSS) and propose a new parallel framework to CSS based on divide-and-conquer strategy. Then we will present a theoretical analysis about the parallel method.

3.1   Column Subset Selection

We consider the problem of selecting the best set of exactly l columns from a matrix, which is called column subset selection (CSS) problem:

Definition 1. *Given a matrix $\mathbf{M} \in \mathbb{R}^{m \times n}$ and a positive integer l, pick l columns of $\mathbf{M}$ forming a matrix $\mathbf{C} \in \mathbb{R}^{m \times l}$ such that the residual $\|\mathbf{M} - \mathbf{P}_C\mathbf{M}\|_\xi$ is minimized over all possible $\binom{n}{l}$ choices for the matrix $\mathbf{C}$.*

CSS is also called column-based matrix approximation. The goal of this problem is to find a subset of exactly l columns of $\mathbf{M}$ that captures as much of $\mathbf{M}$ as possible, with respect to the spectral norm and/or Frobenius norm, in a projection sense.

In general case we have $l \ll n$, and we can treat l as a constant. From the above definition we can see that CSS expresses each of the columns of $\mathbf{M}$ in terms of a linear combination of $\mathbf{C}$, which are actual columns of $\mathbf{M}$.

Many CSS algorithms, both deterministic and randomized, can give a relative-error upper bound, that is $\|\mathbf{M} - \mathbf{C}\mathbf{C}^+\mathbf{M}\|_\xi \leq \Delta\|\mathbf{M} - \mathbf{M}_k\|_\xi$ with $\Delta \geq 1$. In this paper we mainly consider the relative-error bound in Frobenius norm. Guruswami and Sinop [11] have summarized some CSS algorithms with $(1 + \epsilon)$ relative-error bound. Here, we adopt a typical CSS algorithm in [6], as shown in Algorithm 1.

Algorithm 1. A Column Subset Selection Algorithm

Input: Matrix $\mathbf{M} \in \mathbb{R}^{m \times n}$,
    the number of selected columns l and rank parameter k.
Output: Selected columns $\mathbf{C} \in \mathbb{R}^{m \times l}$.
1: Compute sampling probabilities $p_i = \frac{1}{k}\|\mathbf{v}_{i,k}(\mathbf{M})\|_2^2$ for all $i \in [n]$
   where $\mathbf{v}_{i,k}(\mathbf{M})$ denotes the first k elements of $\mathbf{v}_i(\mathbf{M})$.
2: Initialize a sampling matrix $\mathbf{S} \in \mathbb{R}^{n \times l}$ and
   a diagonal rescaling matrix $\mathbf{D} \in \mathbb{R}^{l \times l}$ to all zeros matrices.
3: **for** $i \in [1 \ldots l]$ **do**
4:    Pick $j \in [n]$, where $\mathbf{Pr}(j = t) = p_t$.
5:    $\mathbf{S}_{ji} = 1$.
6:    $\mathbf{D}_{ii} = 1/\sqrt{(lp_j)}$.
7: **end for**
8: Construct and return the matrix $\mathbf{C} = \mathbf{MSD}$.

The existing CSS algorithms are not scalable when dealing with large-scale data because of the quadratic time complexity. In this paper, we present a parallelized CSS to scale up such an algorithm.

3.2 Divide-and-Conquer Strategy

Given a kernel matrix $\mathbf{K} \in \mathbb{R}^{n \times n}$, $r = \mathrm{rank}(\mathbf{K})$. We want to select l columns of $\mathbf{K}$, denoted as $\mathbf{C}$, in order to make $\|\mathbf{K} - \mathbf{C}\mathbf{C}^+\mathbf{K}\|_\xi$ close to $\|\mathbf{K} - \mathbf{K}_k\|_\xi$ for a given number k, where $k \leq r$ and $k \leq l \leq n$. Next we propose our parallel framework for CSS which consists of the following three stages:

Divide Matrix into Submatrices: Let t be the number of parallel nodes, we divide $\mathbf{K}$ into t submatrices in the following way $\mathbf{K} = [\mathbf{K}^{(1)}, \ldots, \mathbf{K}^{(t)}]$, where $\mathbf{K}^{(i)}$ contains n/t columns [1] , $i = 1, 2, \ldots, t$.

Perform CSS Algorithm in Parallel: We perform CSS algorithm on $\{\mathbf{K}^{(1)}, \ldots, \mathbf{K}^{(t)}\}$ in parallel, then from each submatrix we can obtain l/t columns[2]. It yields t results $\{\mathbf{C}^{(1)}, \ldots, \mathbf{C}^{(t)}\}$.

Merge Selected Columns: We merge the selected columns in last stage to form the final output $\mathbf{C} = [\mathbf{C}^{(1)}, \ldots, \mathbf{C}^{(t)}] \in \mathbb{R}^{n \times l}$.

We summarize the above stages into Algorithm 2, which is called parallel column subset selection (PCSS). Note that we do not specify the CSS algorithm, and we can use any CSS algorithm in our framework, in this paper we use Algorithm 1. Let $\mathrm{T}(n, n)$ denote the running time of the base CSS algorithm on a $n \times n$ matrix. As the running time of Step 1 and Step 5 is trivial, the bottleneck of Algorithm 2 is Step 3. To sum up, the time complexity of Algorithm 2 is $\mathrm{T}(n, n/t)$.

3.3 Theoretical Analysis

Our PCSS method is accuracy-preserving, that is it has exactly the same relative-error bound as that of the base CSS algorithm.

Theorem 1. *Given a matrix* $\mathbf{K} \in \mathbb{R}^{n \times n}$, $r = \mathrm{rank}(\mathbf{K})$ *and* $\mathbf{K}_k$ *is the best rank-k approximation to* $\mathbf{K}$, *where* $k \leq r$. *Given constants* t *and* l, *where* $k \leq l \leq n$. *If the base column subset selection algorithm yields*

$$\|\mathbf{K}^{(i)} - \mathbf{C}^{(i)}\mathbf{C}^{(i)+}\mathbf{K}^{(i)}\|_F \leq \Delta \|\mathbf{K}^{(i)} - \mathbf{K}_k^{(i)}\|_F$$

for $\Delta \geq 1$ *by choosing* l/t *columns* $\mathbf{C}^{(i)}$ *from* $\mathbf{K}^{(i)}$. *Then perform Algorithm 2 on* $\mathbf{K}$ *we can get*

$$\|\mathbf{K} - \mathbf{C}\mathbf{C}^+\mathbf{K}\|_F \leq \Delta \|\mathbf{K} - \mathbf{K}_k\|_F.$$

---

[1] We assume $n \bmod t = 0$ for simplicity, then each submatrix contains n/t columns. In a general case we can also partition $\mathbf{K}$ into t submatrices and each contains $\lfloor n/t \rfloor$ or $\lceil n/t \rceil$ columns.

[2] Here we also assume $l \bmod t = 0$ for simplicity. In a general case we can select $\lfloor l/t \rfloor$ or $\lceil l/t \rceil$ columns from each submatrix in order to insure that the number of entire selected columns is l.

Algorithm 2. Parallel column subset selection (PCSS)

Input: Kernel matrix $\mathbf{K} \in \mathbb{R}^{n \times n}$,
    number of parallel nodes t,
    number of selected columns l and rank parameter k.
Output: Selected columns $\mathbf{C} \in \mathbb{R}^{n \times l}$.
1: Divide matrix $\mathbf{K} = [\mathbf{K}^{(1)}, \dots, \mathbf{K}^{(t)}]$.
2: **do in parallel**
3:    $\mathbf{C}^{(i)} =$ CSS-Algorithm$(\mathbf{K}^{(i)})$.
4: **end do**
5: $\mathbf{C} = [\mathbf{C}^{(1)}, \dots, \mathbf{C}^{(t)}]$.
6: **return** $\mathbf{C}$.

Proof. We consider the upper bound of

$$\|\mathbf{K} - \mathbf{C}\mathbf{C}^+\mathbf{K}\|_F^2. \tag{3}$$

According to the definition of Frobenius norm, we can represent (3) in terms of the deviation of submatrices:

$$\|\mathbf{K} - \mathbf{C}\mathbf{C}^+\mathbf{K}\|_F^2 = \sum_{i=1}^{t} \|\mathbf{K}^{(i)} - \mathbf{C}\mathbf{C}^+\mathbf{K}^{(i)}\|_F^2.$$

Note that $\mathbf{C}\mathbf{C}^+\mathbf{K}^{(i)}$ means projecting $\mathbf{K}^{(i)}$ onto the column space of $\mathbf{C}$, where $\mathbf{C} = [\mathbf{C}^{(1)}, \dots, \mathbf{C}^{(t)}]$.

Since the column space of $\mathbf{C}^{(i)}$ is the subspace of that of $\mathbf{C}$, projecting $\mathbf{K}^{(i)}$ onto the column space of $\mathbf{C}^{(i)}$ instead of the column space of $\mathbf{C}$ will increase the deviation between $\mathbf{K}^{(i)}$. Thus we have

$$\sum_{i=1}^{t} \|\mathbf{K}^{(i)} - \mathbf{C}\mathbf{C}^+\mathbf{K}^{(i)}\|_F^2 \leq \sum_{i=1}^{t} \|\mathbf{K}^{(i)} - \mathbf{C}^{(i)}\mathbf{C}^{(i)+}\mathbf{K}^{(i)}\|_F^2.$$

Then we can apply the assumption in Theorem 1:

$$\sum_{i=1}^{t} \|\mathbf{K}^{(i)} - \mathbf{C}^{(i)}\mathbf{C}^{(i)+}\mathbf{K}^{(i)}\|_F^2 \leq \sum_{i=1}^{t} \Delta^2 \|\mathbf{K}^{(i)} - \mathbf{K}_k^{(i)}\|_F^2$$

$$= \Delta^2 \sum_{i=1}^{t} \|\mathbf{K}^{(i)} - \mathbf{K}_k^{(i)}\|_F^2.$$

Divide $\mathbf{K}_k = [\mathbf{N}^{(1)}, \dots, \mathbf{N}^{(t)}]$ according to $\mathbf{K} = [\mathbf{K}^{(1)}, \dots, \mathbf{K}^{(t)}]$.
Since rank$(\mathbf{N}^{(i)}) \leq$ rank$(\mathbf{K}_k) = k =$ rank$(\mathbf{K}_k^{(i)})$, we have

$$\sum_{i=1}^{t} \|\mathbf{K}^{(i)} - \mathbf{K}_k^{(i)}\|_F^2 \leq \sum_{i=1}^{t} \|\mathbf{K}^{(i)} - \mathbf{N}^{(i)}\|_F^2$$

$$= \|\mathbf{K} - \mathbf{K}_k\|_F^2.$$

Combining the above results, we have

$$\|\mathbf{K} - \mathbf{C}\mathbf{C}^+\mathbf{K}\|_F^2 \leq \Delta^2 \|\mathbf{K} - \mathbf{K}_k\|_F^2,$$

and therefore

$$\|\mathbf{K} - \mathbf{C}\mathbf{C}^+\mathbf{K}\|_F \leq \Delta \|\mathbf{K} - \mathbf{K}_k\|_F. \qquad \square$$

From Theorem 1 we can see that PCSS has a $(1 + \epsilon)$ relative-error bound as long as the base CSS algorithm gives a $(1 + \epsilon)$ relative-error bound. Note that in Algorithm 2 we can divide the matrix into more than t submatrices without violating Theorem 1, which may lead to faster speed and worse performance, thus the choice of the number of submatrices is a balance of performance and speed.

4   Two Approaches to Scaling up Kernel SVMs

Next we will introduce PCSS into Nyström method and low-rank linearized SVMs as sampling method, to make kernel SVMs scalable.

Common CSS algorithms cannot easily deal with large-scale data due to at least quadratic time complexity. Our PCSS method can be implemented easily and fitted into distributed environment. In Algorithm 3, we summarize Nyström method with PCSS.

Algorithm 3. PCSS-Nyström

Input: Kernel matrix $\mathbf{K} \in \mathbb{R}^{n \times n}$,
  number of selected columns l and rank parameter k.
Output: Approximate matrix $\widetilde{\mathbf{K}}_k$.
1: Obtain columns' indices R of $\mathbf{K}$ using Algorithm 2.
2: Select corresponding matrix $\mathbf{C}, \mathbf{W}$ from $\mathbf{K}$ using R.
3: Construct approximate matrix $\widetilde{\mathbf{K}}_k = \mathbf{C}\mathbf{W}_k^+\mathbf{C}^T$ via Nyström method.
4: **return** $\widetilde{\mathbf{K}}_k$.

Transforming non-linear SVM into linear SVM needs to select a small number of informative columns of kernel matrix, and then construct explicit features using matrix decomposition methods, which is called low-rank linearized SVM (LLSVM). In the following, we introduce PCSS into LLSVM:

5   Empirical Evaluation

Our experiments consist of two parts: Firstly we compare the matrix approximation error, prediction accuracy and running time of our PCSS-Nyström with that of some existing Nyström sampling methods. Secondly we compare prediction accuracy and running time of our PCSS-LLSVM with that of kernel SVM.

Algorithm 4. PCSS-LLSVM

    Input: Kernel matrix $\mathbf{K}_{rr} \in \mathbb{R}^{n \times n}$,
       $\mathbf{K}_{er} \in \mathbb{R}^{m \times n}$,
       number of selected columns l and rank parameter k.
    Output: Predicted labels $\hat{\mathbf{y}}_e$.
    1: Select l columns from $\mathbf{K}_{rr}$ using Algorithm 2 and let $\mathcal{Z}$ denote the indices.
    2: Compute eigendecomposition of $\mathbf{K}_{zz}$: $\mathbf{U}_z \mathbf{\Lambda}_z \mathbf{U}_z^\mathsf{T}$.
    3: Compute $\mathbf{M} = \mathbf{U}_z \mathbf{\Lambda}_z^{-1/2}$.
    4: Train linear SVM on $\mathbf{K}_{rz}\mathbf{M}$ to get model $\hat{\mathbf{w}}$.
    5: Predicted labels $\hat{\mathbf{y}}_e = \hat{\mathbf{w}}^\mathsf{T} \mathbf{K}_{ez} \mathbf{M}$.
    6: **return** $\hat{\mathbf{y}}_e$.

5.1   General Settings

We use 5 classification datasets from LIBSVM[3] [1] which are summarized in Table 1. We divided each dataset into two halves randomly, one for training set and another for test set. In experiment, we use Gaussian kernel $k(x_i, x_j) = \exp(-\gamma \|x_i - x_j\|_2^2)$ with $\gamma = 2^{-3}$. We adopt the least square support vector machine (LSSVM) algorithm [16] to train kernel SVM and LIBLINEAR [7] library to train linear SVM. We select the regularization parameters through 5-fold cross validation. We use Algorithm 1 proposed by [6] in our PCSS method as base CSS algorithm. All the experiments are implemented in R and on a public SUSE Linux enterprise server 10 SP2 platform with 2.2 GHz AMD Opteron Processor 6174 CPU and 48GB RAM. Average results of 20 repeated experiments are reported.

Table 1. Information of datasets used in experiment.

Dataset	#Instances	#Features
mushrooms	8124	112
a7a	16100	123
w6a	17188	300
ijcnn1	49990	22
cod-rna	59535	8

5.2   Evaluation of PCSS-Nyström

In the first experiment, we empirically evaluate different sampling methods of Nyström approximation. We include 5 methods:

(1) Original: Original kernel matrix without approximation;
(2) ColNorm: Nyström approximation with column norm sampling;

---

[3] http://www.csie.ntu.edu.tw/~cjlin/libsvmtools/datasets/.

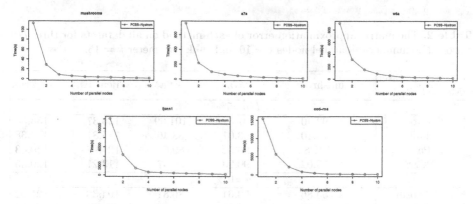

Fig. 1. The evolution of running time of PCSS-Nyström. The number of parallel nodes $t = 1, 2, \ldots, 10$, the sampling ratios $l/n = 10\%$ and rank parameter $k = 15$.

(3) Full: Nyström approximation with adaptive sampling method Full proposed by [2];

(4) Part: Nyström approximation with adaptive sampling method Part proposed by [12];

(5) PCSS: Our Nyström approximation with parallel column subset selection sampling method.

We first compare the matrix approximation error of each method, which is defined as $\|\mathbf{K} - \mathbf{C}\mathbf{W}_k^+\mathbf{C}^{\mathrm{T}}\|_F$. The results are shown in Table 2. Our method PCSS aims to select the columns that capture the column space of kernel matrix as much as possible, which turns out to be more accurate in terms of matrix approximation error than other methods.

Then we compare the prediction accuracy of each method. The results are shown in Table 3. In general case, lower matrix approximation error will lead to higher prediction accuracy, and we can notice this phenomenon from Tables 2 and 3. Our method preserves the best prediction accuracy because it recovers the most information of the kernel matrix.

The running time results are shown in Table 4. Note that we set the number of parallel nodes $t = 10$ and obtain the lowest running time. We can further reduce the running time of our method by assigning a larger number to t.

Next we test the scalability of our method on different number of parallel nodes. The results are shown in Fig. 1. Note that the running time drops rapidly as the number of parallel nodes increase. Because the time complexity of CSS algorithm is at least quadratic in the size of kernel matrix, the decrease of kernel matrix's size will bring considerable improvement in terms of computational efficiency. Figure 1 shows the super-linear speed-up of our method.

5.3 Evaluation of PCSS-LLSVM

In the second experiment, we empirically compare LSSVM with our PCSS-LLSVM. We use PCSS to select a small part of kernel matrix, thus we can

Table 2. The matrix approximation error of each method on all datasets for three l/n ratios. The number of parallel nodes $t = 10$ and rank parameter $k = 15$.

Dataset / Method	mushrooms	a7a	w6a	ijcnn1	cod-rna
l/n=5%					
ColNorm	93.40	91.52	101.69	135.37	154.56
Full	76.10	93.01	88.46	115.81	134.38
Part	131.83	96.52	89.61	125.92	140.43
PCSS	73.02	90.23	86.57	113.21	129.35
l/n=10%					
ColNorm	58.86	59.61	86.81	104.38	121.92
Full	43.02	58.35	69.23	88.10	104.58
Part	77.37	61.59	72.05	95.27	109.35
PCSS	40.83	53.48	65.29	83.96	98.71
l/n=15%					
ColNorm	43.06	46.83	77.93	84.36	103.39
Full	24.58	43.19	59.44	71.40	84.79
Part	56.20	46.20	64.45	79.29	94.63
PCSS	19.96	41.12	52.98	68.47	75.36

Table 3. The prediction accuracy of each method on all datasets for three l/n ratios. The number of parallel nodes $t = 10$ and rank parameter $k = 15$.

Dataset / Method	mushrooms	a7a	w6a	ijcnn1	cod-rna
l/n=5%					
Original	99.80%	82.74%	96.95%	90.01%	88.90%
ColNorm	99.14%	82.49%	95.66%	88.57%	87.45%
Full	99.20%	82.51%	95.70%	88.66%	88.01%
Part	99.05%	82.47%	95.67%	88.60%	87.78%
PCSS	99.24%	82.53%	95.73%	88.77%	88.12%
l/n=10%					
Original	99.80%	82.74%	96.95%	90.01%	88.90%
ColNorm	99.17%	82.50%	95.87%	88.73%	87.83%
Full	99.23%	82.58%	95.95%	88.87%	88.21%
Part	99.08%	82.49%	95.89%	88.82%	88.02%
PCSS	99.31%	82.61%	96.04%	88.97%	88.35%
l/n=15%					
Original	99.80%	82.74%	96.95%	90.01%	88.90%
ColNorm	99.23%	82.53%	95.90%	88.90%	88.27%
Full	99.31%	82.61%	96.06%	89.13%	88.57%
Part	99.14%	82.50%	95.98%	89.03%	88.38%
PCSS	99.36%	82.70%	96.20%	89.25%	88.65%

Table 4. The running time (seconds) of each method on all datasets for three l/n ratios. The number of parallel nodes $t = 10$ and rank parameter $k = 15$.

Dataset / Method	mushrooms	a7a	w6a	ijcnn1	cod-rna
$l/n=5\%$					
Original	25.01	119.28	135.81	3103.51	5281.35
ColNorm	0.61	2.73	3.14	48.41	62.39
Full	2.12	8.74	13.73	168.91	192.94
Part	0.86	5.23	7.61	128.18	142.34
PCSS	0.56	2.74	3.13	46.42	59.26
$l/n=10\%$					
Original	25.01	119.28	135.81	3103.51	5281.35
ColNorm	1.59	10.98	12.76	97.16	132.16
Full	3.89	25.85	26.46	256.62	295.08
Part	2.68	19.28	20.54	198.22	237.34
PCSS	1.44	10.41	12.05	96.64	126.38
$l/n=15\%$					
Original	25.01	119.28	135.81	3103.51	5281.35
ColNorm	3.49	29.02	29.43	179.90	236.58
Full	7.65	44.87	46.17	396.20	440.08
Part	5.12	37.01	37.54	317.26	387.42
PCSS	3.10	27.84	28.56	174.71	225.20

Table 5. Comparison of the prediction accuracy and running time (seconds) of LSSVM and PCSS-LLSVM. The sampling ratio $l/n = 5\%, 10\%, 15\%$, the number of parallel nodes $t = 10$ and rank parameter $k = 15$.

Dataset	LSSVM		PCSS(5 %)		PCSS(10 %)		PCSS(15 %)	
	Accuracy	Time	Accuracy	Time	Accuracy	Time	Accuracy	Time
mushrooms	99.80 %	25.01	98.60 %	0.42	98.83 %	1.28	99.20 %	2.74
a7a	82.74 %	119.28	82.20 %	2.13	82.53 %	8.78	82.63 %	16.31
w6a	96.95 %	135.81	95.62 %	2.87	95.98 %	9.30	96.15 %	19.78
ijcnn1	90.01 %	3103.51	88.63 %	39.47	88.91 %	87.18	89.19 %	142.68
cod-rna	88.90 %	5281.35	88.03 %	54.38	88.28 %	102.94	88.55 %	176.46

reduce the size. The prediction accuracy and running time are shown in Table 5. We can see that our PCSS-LLSVM method tremendously reduces the running time, and meanwhile preserves good prediction accuracy.

The scalability results of our PCSS-LLSVM method on different number of parallel nodes are shown in Fig. 2. Similarly the increasing number of parallel nodes will make running time drop rapidly, which shows super-linear speed-up. To sum up, our proposed approaches to kernel SVM are effective, efficient and scalable.

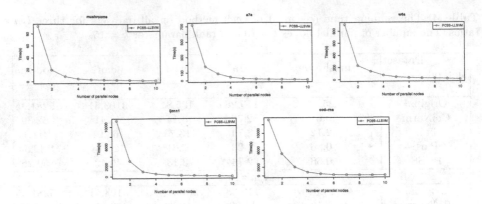

Fig. 2. The evolution of running time of PCSS-LLSVM. The number of parallel nodes $t = 1, 2, \ldots, 10$, the sampling ratios $l/n = 10\%$ and rank parameter $k = 15$.

6   Conclusion

In this paper, we propose the parallel column subset selection (PCSS) method for Nyström approximation and low-rank linearized kernel SVMs to scale up the kernel SVMs on large-scale problems. We prove that PCSS has a $(1+\epsilon)$ relative-error upper bound with respect to the kernel matrix. Empirical results illustrate that our proposed methods exhibit good prediction accuracy, low running time and super-linear speed-up.

Acknowledgements. This work was supported in part by Natural Science Foundation of China under Grant No. 61170019.

References

1. Chang, C.C., Lin, C.J.: LIBSVM: a library for support vector machines. ACM Trans. Intell. Syst. Technol. **2**, 1–27 (2011)
2. Deshpande, A., Rademacher, L., Vempala, S., Wang, G.: Matrix approximation and projective clustering via volume sampling. Theor. Comput. **2**, 225–247 (2006)
3. Ding, L., Liao, S.: Nyström approximate model selection for LSSVM. In: Advances in Knowledge Discovery and Data Mining - 16th Pacific-Asia Conference (PAKDD 2012), pp. 282–293 (2012)
4. Drineas, P., Kannan, R., Mahoney, M.W.: Fast monte carlo algorithms for matrices II: computing a low-rank approximation to a matrix. SIAM J. Comput. **36**(1), 158–183 (2006)
5. Drineas, P., Mahoney, M.W., Muthukrishnan, S.: Subspace sampling and relative-error matrix approximation: column-based methods. In: Díaz, J., Jansen, K., Rolim, J.D.P., Zwick, U. (eds.) APPROX 2006 and RANDOM 2006. LNCS, vol. 4110, pp. 316–326. Springer, Heidelberg (2006)
6. Drineas, P., Mahoney, M.W., Muthukrishnan, S.: Relative-error CUR matrix decompositions. SIAM J. Matrix Anal. Appl. **30**(2), 844–881 (2008)

7. Fan, R.E., Chang, K.W., Hsieh, C.J., Wang, X.R., Lin, C.J.: LIBLINEAR: a library for large linear classification. J. Mach. Learn. Res. **9**, 1871–1874 (2008)
8. Fine, S., Scheinberg, K.: Efficient svm training using low-rank kernel representations. J. Mach. Learn. Res. **2**, 243–264 (2002)
9. Fowlkes, C., Belongie, S., Chung, F., Malik, J.: Spectral grouping using the Nyström method. IEEE Trans. Pattern Anal. Mach. Intell. **26**(2), 214–225 (2004)
10. Golub, G., Van Loan, C.: Matrix Comput. Johns Hopkins University Press, Baltimore (1996)
11. Guruswami, V., Sinop, A.K.: Optimal column-based low-rank matrix reconstruction. In: Proceedings of the Twenty-Third Annual ACM-SIAM Symposium on Discrete Algorithms, pp. 1207–1214 (2012)
12. Kumar, S., Mohri, M., Talwalkar, A.: Sampling methods for the Nyström method. J. Mach. Learn. Res. **13**, 981–1006 (2012)
13. Mahoney, M.W., Drineas, P.: CUR matrix decompositions for improved data analysis. Proc. Natl. Acad. Sci. **106**(3), 697–702 (2009)
14. Schölkopf, B., Smola, A.J.: Learning with Kernels: Support Vector Machines, Regularization, Optimization, and Beyond. MIT Press, Cambridge (2002)
15. Smola, A.J., Schökopf, B.: Sparse greedy matrix approximation for machine learning. In: Proceedings of the Seventeenth International Conference on Machine Learning, pp. 911–918 (2000)
16. Suykens, J., Vandewalle, J.: Least squares support vector machine classifiers. Neural Process. Lett. **9**(3), 293–300 (1999)
17. Tsang, I.W., Kwok, J.T., Cheung, P.M., Cristianini, N.: Core vector machines: fast SVM training on very large data sets. J. Mach. Learn. Res. **6**(4), 363–392 (2005)
18. Vapnik, V.N.: Statistical Learning Theory. Wiley, New York (1998)
19. Williams, C., Seeger, M.: Using the Nyström method to speed up kernel machines. In: Advances in Neural Information Processing Systems 13 (NIPS 2001), pp. 682–688 (2001)
20. Zhang, K., Lan, L., Wang, Z., Moerchen, F.: Scaling up kernel SVM on limited resources: a low-rank linearization approach. In: Proceedings of the 15th International Conference on Artificial Intelligence and Statistics (AISTATS), pp. 1425–1434 (2012)
21. Zhang, K., Tsang, I.W., Kwok, J.T.: Improved Nyström low-rank approximation and error analysis. In: Proceedings of the 25th International Conference on Machine Learning (ICML 2008), pp. 1232–1239 (2008)

Real-Time Deconvolution with GPU and Spark for Big Imaging Data Analysis

Lianyu Cao[1(✉)], Penghui Juan[2], and Yinghua Zhang[1]

[1] School of Computer and Communication Engineering, University of Science and Technology Beijing, Beijing 100083, China
{caoly,zhangyh}@sugon.com
[2] Institute of Computing Technology, Chinese Academy of Sciences, Beijing 100190, China
juanpenghui@ict.ac.cn

Abstract. Light sheet fluorescence microscopy (LSFM) led researchers to get optical sections of large samples, virtually without toxicity and light bleaching and with high temporal resolution, and to record the development of large, living samples with exceptionally high information content. And images observed by LSFM with high signal to noise ratio are very suited for three-dimensional reconstruction. Deconvolution reduces blurring from out-of-focus light to improve the contrast and sharpness of image, but commercial deconvolution software is slow and expensive which cannot meet the current demand. GPU is the new many-core processor with powerful floating point performance, so we parallelized the Richardson Lucy Deconvolution on the GPU. Under ensuring image quality, the implementation on the GPU runs ~30 times faster than the implementation on the CPU. For an image of size $1024 \times 1024 \times 25$, the deconvolved time of 50 iterations on the GPU is no more than 2 s.

Keywords: Deconvolution · GPU · Spark · Manycore · Imaging

1 Introduction

LSFM is a selective light sheet illumination microscopy that uses a layer of light beam from the side of sample to illuminate the sample and collect photons by CCD [1], with low damage, virtually no toxicity or light bleaching, is very suited to keep track of the development of large, living samples. With its unique sheet illumination technology, weakening the impact of non-focal plane of light, LSFM have a higher signal to noise ratio, the images produced by LSFM are more suitable for digital image processing. Limited by the wave nature of light, standard microscopy optical resolution is determined by the wavelength of excitation light and the numerical aperture of microscopy objective [2], so the limited microscopy resolution makes the observed image blurry. Blurring is modeled in software as a point spread function (PSF), deconvolution removes blurring and reduces the effect of noise by applying some mathematical algorithm. Because blurring influences the downstream processing, deconvolution facilitates the image registration and fusion to make images better visualization. Since deconvolution is a computing-intensive algorithm [3] and the biological data is very huge, traditional

© Springer International Publishing Switzerland 2015
G. Wang et al. (Eds.): ICA3PP 2015, Part III, LNCS 9530, pp. 240–250, 2015.
DOI: 10.1007/978-3-319-27137-8_19

commercial deconvolution software is slow and expensive which cannot meet the growing demand.

In this paper, we parallelized the Richardson Lucy algorithm on the platform of CUDA and Spark [4, 5, 17], compared with the implementation on the CPU, a speedup of 30 is achieved. The parallelized implementation in this paper not only can deconvolve the images produced by LSFM, but also can achieve excellent results for wide-field and confocal microscopy by choosing right PSF.

In this paper, we not only optimized the algorithm for one picture, but also presented the batch optimization implementation for a batch of pictures by using the batch feature of cuFFT, and parallelized the algorithm on the multiple GPU. And Apache Spark is a newly fast and general-purpose cluster computing system which is suitable for the iterative algorithm [6], because Richardson Lucy is iterative algorithm [18], we offer an optimized implementation in Spark. To our knowledge, ours is the first implementation to optimize deconvolution in Spark and to use the batch feature of cuFFT in deconvolution optimization implementation.

2 Background

The Richardson Lucy is a iterative deconvolution algorithm for reconstructing a true image that has been independently put forward by William Richardson in 1972 and Leon Lucy in 1974 [7, 8, 19]. Currently Richardson Lucy is widely used in the field of deblurring and image reconstruction, and employs the most likely method to correct the observed images.

When an image is acquired on a detector such as CCD camera, it is generally slightly blurred by out-of-focus light, with an ideal point source not appearing as a point but being spread out into light spot which can model as point spread function. Non-point sources are ideally the sum of many individual point sources, and pixels in an observed image can be represented in the terms of true images and point spread function as [9]:

$$d_i = \sum_j p_{ij} u_j \tag{1}$$

Where p_{ij} is the point spread function (PSF), u_i is the pixel gray value at location j in the latent image, and d_i is the observed gray value at location i. The statistics are performed under the assumption that u_j are Poisson distributed.

Given the observed d_i and p_{ij}, the basic idea to calculate the u_j in the latent image is calculate the most likely u_j. This leads to an equation for computing u_j which can be solved iteratively according to:

$$u_j^{(t+1)} = u_j^{(t)} \sum_i \frac{d_i}{c_i} p_{ij} \tag{2}$$

Where

$$c_i = \sum_j p_{ij} u_j^{(t)} \tag{3}$$

It has been shown empirically that if this iteration converges, it converges to the maximum likelihood solution. Figure 1 is the flow of Richardson Lucy algorithm.

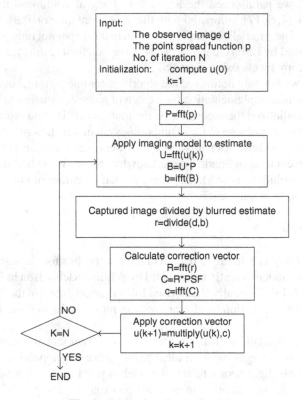

Fig. 1. Richardson Lucy algorithm

From Fig. 1, we know that the algorithm computes twice fourier transformation and inverse transformation to accelerate the convolution computation. Because Richardson Lucy is an iterative and computing-intensive algorithm which is slow, with the coming of the GB, TB biological image data, it is not possible to deconvolve all image data, so we need to parallelize the Richardson Lucy algorithm.

3   Parallel Implementation

Richardson Lucy is computing-intensive algorithm. We will describe our implementation on the platform of CUDA and Spark that not only uses the common optimization strategies, but also uses the optimization methods related to the algorithms.

According to the analysis of Richardson Lucy, we know the computational bottle-neck of Richardson Lucy is the calculation of Fourier Transform. The cuFFT provides a simple interface for computing FFTs up to $10 \times$ faster than CPU FFT implementation. By using hundreds of processor cores inside NVIDIA GPUs, cuFFT delivers the floating-point performance of a GPU without having to develop our custom GPU FFT implementation [21], we have accelerated the Richardson Lucy on the GPU by involving cuFFT [10, 11, 20].

From the existing parallel optimization on the GPU, we know the communication between CPU and GPU is often the computational bottleneck [12], the implementation of Richardson Lucy on the GPU is not exception. In order to optimize the communication, we attempt to reduce the data transmission between GPU and CPU by implementing the iteration computation on the GPU which doesn't have data transmission during iteration, and we implement the wise divide and multiply on the GPU to further accelerate the program execution. Figure 2 is the basic optimization on the GPU.

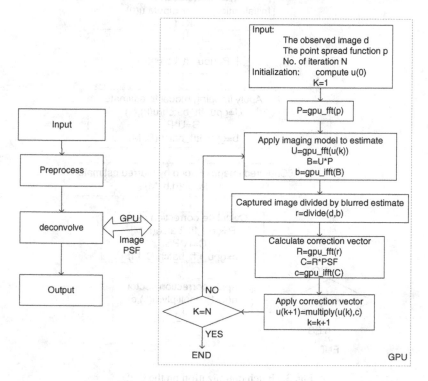

Fig. 2. Basic optimization on the GPU

3.1 GPU Optimization

The batch feature of cuFFT is execution of multiple FFT transforms simultaneously, and the batched transforms have higher performance than single transforms, so we try to parallelize the algorithm on the GPU with the batched computation of cuFFT.

Firstly, we scan the input noise images to produce the path of output images, and save the path of input and output image in a text file. Then CPU reads all noise images from the text file to memory, and transfers all images to video-memory. The noise images are deconvolved simultaneously rather than one by one. The usage of cuFFT batch is described as follows.

cufftResult cufftPlanMany (cufftHandle *plan, int rank, int *n, int *inembed, int istride, int idist, int *onembed, int ostride, int odist, cufftType type, int batch)

Figure 3 is the batch optimization on the GPU. We not only employ the batch feature of cuFFT to optimize program, but also implement the batch of wise divide and multiply on the GPU to further accelerate algorithm execution.

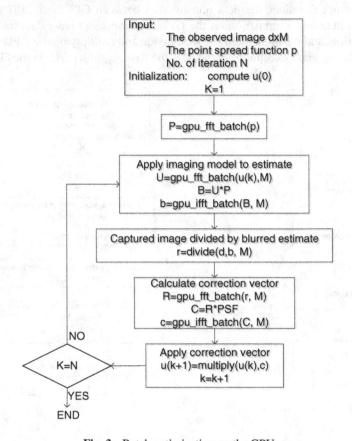

Fig. 3. Batch optimization on the GPU

Limited by the size of video-memory, all noise images are not possible to deconvolve simultaneously, so we need to partition the uncorrelated images suited for video-memory. And how to partition the images can be adjusted by the parameter batch of cufftPlanMany.

In order to further accelerate deconvolution, we will optimize the deconvolution on multiple GPUs. As GPU cards almost always connect via the PCIe slot to CPU, they share the data of compute nodes, so we don't communication between GPU cards. We will partition the images averagely to every GPUs, and GPU deconvolve the images independently.

3.2   Spark Optimization

Apache Spark is a newly fast and general-purpose cluster computing system which exchanges data in memory, and has a higher efficiency for the iterative computation [13]. Richardson Lucy is an iterative and computation-intensive algorithm. Because subsequent images are processed in spark, it is necessary to parallelize deconvolution in Spark.

The process in Spark: building the context of spark driver SparkContext, creating the RDD via SparkContext, applying a series of transformations to data (stored in the RDD), finally performing an action to get an answer. In order to deconvolve the noise images in spark, we create the RDD from noise images, and apply the transformation of deconvolution to RDD to get the deconvolved RDD.

For the images in HDFS, because the file system don't support reading the format of TIFF directly, we create the binary RDD of images via SparkContext. binaryFiles, then transform to the gray value RDD from binary RDD of images. Figure 4 is how to read images to spark.

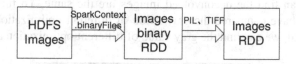

Fig. 4. Read images from HDFS

Spark has local, yarn, mesos, and standalone mode. Standalone is the master-slave architecture that have one master process and many slave processes. In this paper, we have implemented the standalone mode of Richardson Lucy deconvolution. Figure 5 is our standalone implement of Richardson Lucy.

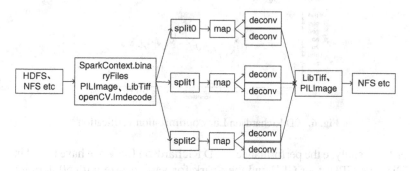

Fig. 5. Optimization in Spark

4   Experiment

4.1   Experiment Environment and Data

We have test our implementation in Dawn nebula high performance computing nodes with two six-core Intel Xeon E5-2620 CPU and four Tesla K40, and blade servers with

10 compute nodes with two six-core Intel Xeon X5675 CPU. Software environment is for the Spark1.2, hadoop2.4, CUDA6.5 and GCC4.47.To analyze the performance of our optimization versus CPU-based implementation, we replace all CUFFT calls with multi-threaded FFTW [14].

We have tested with standard data set Synthetic hollow bars and mouse embryo produced by LSFM. Synthetic hollow bars have been blurred using the theoretical microscope PSF, and corrupted by Gaussian noise and Possion noise with several signal to noise (SNR = 15) [15]. Mouse embryo data have been produced by LSFM to record the development of living, large mouse embryo cell from real biological experiment.

4.2 2D Richardson Lucy

To verify our correctness of 2D Richardson Lucy optimization, we deconvolve real data from biological experiment. Figure 6 is the test result. We have a noise data (Noise) which have be deconvolved by origin JAVA, multi-cores CPU and many-core CPU. From eye, we can find the deconvolved images are the same, To further verify the correctness, we have compared the gray value of different optimization drawing line using ImageJ [16], we can find the gray value of different optimization are an overlap.

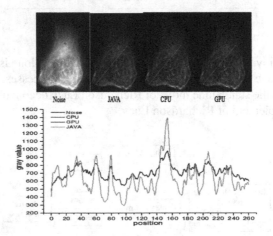

Fig. 6. 2D Richardson Lucy optimization verification

In order to analyze the performance of 2D Richardson Lucy, we have tested in multi-core CPU, one GPU, four GPU and the Spark for various size with 50 iterations. The 256 × 256 × 100 means 100 images of size of 256 × 256. Figure 7 is the test result.

Spark with 4 computing nodes with CPU clock speed 3.1 GHz, the other with CPU clock speed 2.1 GHz.

Multicore CPU program refers to the deconvolution program which replace cuFFT with multi-threaded FFTW, 1-GPU, 4-GPU refer to the optimization with 1 GPU or 4 GPU in batch optimization. Spark 4-Nodes refer to the standalone mode with one master node and four slave nodes which call multi-threaded FFTW to optimize convolution. We can find the performance of GPU overwhelms the performance of multi-threaded

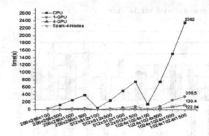

Fig. 7. Different 2D Richardson Lucy optimization result

CPU with the increase of data, and the performance of Spark is almost the same with the performance of GPU in 50 iterations, because they are tested in different computing platforms.

We have parallelled the Richardson Lucy on the GPU with involving cuFFT, but it is not possible to transfer all images to the GPU because of limited of video-memory size, we will adjust the batch parameter of cuFFT to control. Figure 8 is the run-time for various batch size and various image size in 50 iterations.

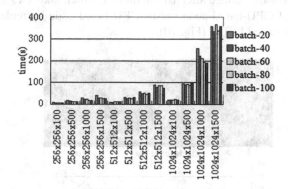

Fig. 8. Performance with different batch parameter

The batch size of cufftPlanMany affect the batch of computing FFT simultaneously, the setting of batch is determined by the size of images and capacity of video-memory. We found the performance of program is improved with increase with batch size when the batch is greater than 20.

Because it is not related between frames in 2d deconvolution, we parallelize deconvolution in multiple GPU to deal with huge amount of images as quickly as possible. We have test the deconvolution for various image size with 50 iterations on one, two and four GPU (Fig. 9).

We found the speedup is not obvious because of the small data and the GPU initialization overhead and speedup is increased with the increase of data in multi-GPU to parallelize deconvolution.

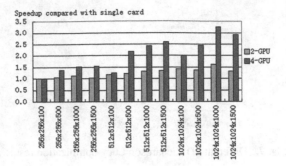

Fig. 9. Mult-GPUs scale

4.3 3D Richardson Lucy

To analyze the performance of 3d Richardson Lucy, we tested with the standard data set of Synthetic hollow bars. Our implementation was able to produce an excellent reconstruction of the true image after 100 iterations, which take 1.19 s. We compared the performance of GPU-based code versus CPU-based code by replacing all cuFFT calls with multi-threaded FFTW (Fig. 10).

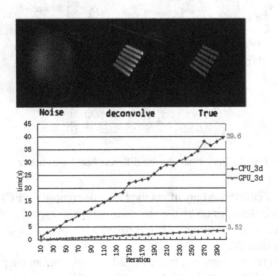

Fig. 10. 3D Richardson Lucy optimization verification

In order to further analyze the performance of ours, we tested 3d Richardson Lucy with various image size and various iterations (Fig. 11). We found the deconvolution time linearly increased with the increase of the number of iterations for the given image size, and the run-time is no more than 5 s for common image size within 100 iterations.

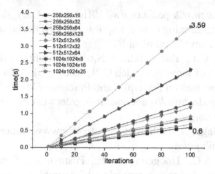

Fig. 11. Different 3D Richardson Lucy optimization result

5 Conclusion

Deconvolution plays a very important role in deblurring and image reconstruction, but the feature of computation-intensive algorithm bring about a consequence that image processing time is too long to limit its use. With the growing bio-image data, the existing software which is slow and expensive cannot meet the current demand. We have optimized the deconvolution on the platform of GPU and Spark. Our parallel implementation can improve the efficiency of biological experts to analyze the experiment data, especially for huge amount of fluorescence image data, ours are able to quickly deconvolve to noise data; Spark is a new type of large data processing framework, our optimization implementation on the platform of Spark achieve a excellent speedup, and will offer help to the other developers for their image processing optimization in Spark. We believe our parallel optimization of Richardson Lucy will be widely used.

References

1. Santi, P.A.: Light Sheet fluorescence microscopy a review. J Histochem Cytochem **59**(2), 129–138 (2011). doi:10.1369/0022155410394857
2. Reynaud, E.G., Krzic, U., Greger, K., Stelzer, E.H.K.: Light sheet-based fluorescence microscopy: more dimensions, more photons, and less photodamage. HFSF J **2**(5), 266–275 (2008)
3. Shaw, P.J.: Comparison of wide-field/deconvolution and confocal microscopy for 3D imaging. In: Pawley, J.B. (ed.) Handbook of Biological Confocal Microscopy, pp. 373–387. Springer, Heidelberg (1995)
4. Apache Spark. https://spark.apache.org/
5. NVIDIA CUDA. http://www.nvidia.com/object/cuda_home_new.html
6. Zaharia, M., Chowdhury, M., Franklin, M.J.: Spark: cluster computing with working sets (2010)
7. Richardson, W.H.: Bayesian-base iterative method of image restoration. JOSA **62**(1), 55–59 (1972)
8. Lucy, L.B.: An iterative technique for the rectification of observed distributions. Astron. J. **79**, 745–754 (1974)

9. Richardson Lucy: http://en.wikipedia.org/wiki/RichardsonLucy_deconvolution
10. NVIDIA CUDA C Programming Guide. http://www.NVIDIA.com/cuda
11. cuFFT. https://developer.nvidia.com/cuFFT
12. Ryoo, S., Rodrigues, C.I., Baghsorkhi, S.S.: Optimization principles and application performance evaluation of a multithreaded GPU using CUDA. In: Proceedings of the 13th ACM SIGPLAN Symposium on Principles and Practice of Parallel Programming (2008)
13. Spark Programming Guide. http://spark.apache.org/docs/latest/programming-guide.html
14. FFTW. http://www.fftw.org
15. Griffa, A., Garin, N., Sage, D.: Hollow Bars. http://bigwww.epfl.ch/deconvolution/?p=bars
16. ImageJ. http://imagej.nih.gov/ij/
17. Ingaramo, M., York, A.G., Hoogendoorn, E., Postma, M., Shroff, H., Patterson, G.H.: Richardson-Lucy deconvolution as a general tool for combining images with complementary strengths. ChemPhySchem 15(4), 794–800 (2014)
18. Liu, H., Zhang, Z., Liu, S., Liu, T., Yan, L., Zhang, T.: Richardson-Lucy blind deconvolution of spectroscopic data with wavelet regularization. Appl. Optics 54(7), 1770–1775 (2015)
19. Stohl, F., Kaminski, C.F.: A joint Richardson—Lucy deconvolution algorithm for the reconstruction of multifocal structured illumination microscopy data. Methods Appl. Fluoresc. 3(1), 014002 (2015)
20. Zhu, J., Chen, L., Chen, A., Luo, G., Deng, X., Liu, X.: Fast 3D dosimetric verifications based on an electronic portal imaging device using a GPU calculation engine (2015)
21. Sherry, M., Shearer, A.: IMPAIR: massively parallel deconvolution on the GPU. In: Proceedings of SPIE - The International Society for Optical Engineering (2013)

Parallel Kirchhoff Pre-Stack Depth Migration on Large High Performance Clusters

Chao Li[1][✉], Yida Wang[1], Changhai Zhao[2],
Haihua Yan[1], and Jianlei Zhang[2]

[1] School of Computer Science and Engineering,
Beihang University, Beijing 100191, China
casesense@163.com
[2] Research and Development Center, BGP Inc.,
CNPC, Zhuozhou 072751, Hebei, China

Abstract. Kirchhoff Pre-Stack Depth Migration (KPSDM) is a widely used algorithm for seismic imaging in petroleum industry. To provide higher FLOPS, modern high performance clusters are equipped with more computing nodes and more cores for each node. The evolution style of clusters leads to two problems for upper layer applications such as KPSDM: (1) the increasing disparity of the I/O capacity and computing performance is becoming a bottleneck for higher scalability; (2) the decreasing Mean Time Between Failures (MTBF) limits the availability of the applications. In this paper, we present an optimized parallel implementation of KPSDM to adapt to modern clusters. First, we convert the KPSDM into a clear and simple task-based parallel application by decomposing the computation along two dimensions: the imaging space and seismic data. Then, those tasks are mapped to computing nodes that are organized using a two-level master/worker architecture to reduce the I/O workloads. And each task is further parallelized using multi-cores to fully utilize the computing resources. Finally, fault tolerance and checkpoint are implemented to meet the availability requirement in production environments. Experimental results with practical seismic data show that our parallel implementation of KPSDM can scale smoothly from 51 nodes (816 cores) to 211 nodes (3376 cores) with low I/O workloads on the I/O sub-system and multiple process failures can be tolerated efficiently.

Keywords: High performance computing · Parallel computing · Kirchhoff Pre-Stack depth migration · Seismic imaging · Parallel algorithms

1 Introduction

Seismic exploration is widely used to locate the oil and gas reservoir area and estimate potential reserves in petroleum industry because of its ability to provide the images of earth interior geologic structures. Seismic exploration can be divided into three stages: acquisition, processing and interpretation. Seismic data is collected from fields in the first stage and processed in the second stage using various seismic imaging algorithms such as Kirchhoff Pre-Stack Depth Migration (KPSDM) to translate the unknown

© Springer International Publishing Switzerland 2015
G. Wang et al. (Eds.): ICA3PP 2015, Part III, LNCS 9530, pp. 251–266, 2015.
DOI: 10.1007/978-3-319-27137-8_20

geologic structures into visual images that can be understood and analyzed by geophysicists and geologists in the interpretation stage.

KPSDM is one of the most important and popular depth-domain imaging algorithms [4, 8] for its computation efficiency and support for irregular seismic data as well as target migration. As the survey target is becoming increasingly complex in recent years, e.g., deep sea explorations, the seismic data size of some 3D survey areas can achieve hundreds of Terabytes. The explosive growth of seismic data size leads to the processing time becoming undesirably long.

Clusters with higher FLOPS are deployed to shorten the processing time. This demands the parallel algorithms and applications can scale well so that more nodes can be utilized. However, the increasing scale and performance of the clusters lead to two severe problems that may limit the scalability and availability of the applications. First, since the improvement of I/O capacity cannot compete with the improvement of computing performance [9, 10], the increasing gap between I/O and FLOPS is becoming a hinder for achieving higher scalability. For example, to balance the I/O capacity and computing performance, traditional computing platforms need to provide at least 2 byte/sec for each 1000 float operations [14]. However, the state of art clusters, especially those equipped with GPU accelerators, I/O/flops is usually 1 or 2 orders of magnitude lower than the value recommended for traditional computers. [1, 2] have reported that the I/O sub-system has become the bottleneck of Reverse Time Migration (RTM), a more compute-intensive seismic algorithm. Second, an observation in [15] shows that the Mean Time Between Failures (MTBF) of large clusters consisted by hundreds of computing nodes ranges from 6 to 13 h. Parallel applications deployed on large clusters should tolerate the node failures to ensure the availability.

The parallel implementation of KPSDM proposed in this paper can overcome these problems. First, we convert the KPSDM into a simple task-based parallel application by decomposing data along the dimensions of imaging space and seismic data according to the hardware resource capacity of one computing node. Then, the tasks are scheduled to the computing nodes which are organized by a two-level master/worker architecture. The seismic data is first broadcast by a I/O proxy node to each worker in one process group to reduce the I/O workloads on the parallel file system. Then the data will be buffered by the local disks of computing nodes so that a large amount of remaining tasks can obtain seismic data directly from local disks. Thus, the I/O workloads on the I/O subsystem of clusters can be significantly reduced. Finally, the task-based parallel pattern and two-level master/worker architecture guarantee the independence of computations and processes, which greatly facilitates the implementation of fault tolerance and checkpoint.

Experiments are carried out using practical data on a high performance production cluster. Our implementation of KPSDM can scale smoothly from 51 nodes (816 cores) to 211 nodes (3376 cores). I/O throughput monitoring tests during the run show that our implementation of KPSDM can keep the I/O workloads at a low level, which suggests that higher scalability can be achieved if more computing nodes are added. Failure injection tests show that multiple processes failures can be tolerated and the overhead incurred by those failures is neglectable.

The rest of the paper is organized as follows. Seismic imaging and the theory of KPSDM are introduced in Sect. 2. In Sect. 3, we describe the design and implementation of parallel KPSDM in details. Section 4 presents the experimental results. We give comparisons to related work in Sect. 5 and conclude the paper in Sect. 6.

2 Background

2.1 Seismic Imaging

Figure 1 describes how the seismic data is collected. First, seismic waves are generated by an artificial seismic source at a shot point (also called source point). During the trip of propagating through the subsurface, those waves will be reflected and refracted by the interfaces between rock stratums. Then the waves will travel back to the surface and be recorded by the geophones deployed on the surface. The term trace refers to the seismic waves recorded by one geophone. A trace is composed of a series of float numbers that represent energy amplitude of the seismic wave. The float number is called sample. Each trace is associated with three key position coordinates: the shot point **S**, the receiver point **R** and the middle point of **S** and **R**. The term gather refers to a collection of traces that have a common attribute. For example, a collection of traces that share a same shot point is called common shot gather (CSG). The term offset refers to the distance between the shot point and receiver point.

Fig. 1. Seismic data acquisition

2.2 A Brief Introduction of KPSDM

In the processing stage, the survey area of surface is divided by two-dimensional grid as shown in Fig. 2. The dimensions are called inline and crossline respectively. We define the intersection points of inline and crossline as imaging cells. And the points of an imaging cell along the depth direction are defined as imaging points. From the view of surface, the imaging space is a two-dimensional grid consisted by imaging cells. And from the view of subsurface, the imaging space is a three-dimensional grid

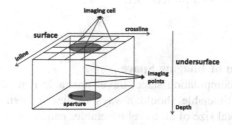

Fig. 2. Seismic data processing

consisted by imaging points of all imaging cells. The KPSDM algorithm aims to calculate the energy value of each imaging point based on the seismic data and travel timetable information of seismic waves.

Each imaging cell can delimit an valid range in a shape of ellipse based on aperture parameters, as shown in Fig. 2. Any trace whose shot point and receiver point located in the ellipse should perform the migration computation to the imaging cell, i.e. to each imaging point of the imaging cell. Let ξ denote the imaging point, $I(\xi)$ denote the imaging result of ξ, T denote the input trace, D denote the valid range. First, we need to get time cost by the seismic wave from the shot point to the imaging point t_s and the time cost from the receiver point to the imaging point t_r. Then, energy amplitude A of imaging point ξ can be calculated with t_r, t_s and discrete energy amplitudes of T. Finally, we add the amplitude A to $I(\xi)$, so the energy contribution of T to imaging point ξ is stacked. The final imaging result of ξ is the summation of contributed amplitudes of all valid traces located in the valid range as shown by Eq. 1.

$$I(\xi) = \sum_{T \in D} f(t_s, t_r, T). \tag{1}$$

2.3   I/O Workload of KPSDM

A KPSDM job can impose huge I/O workloads on the I/O sub-system for several reasons. First, comparing with wave equation-based algorithms such as Reverse Time Migration (RTM), summation operations of integral involve less computations. Second, during the running of KPSDM, travel timetables need to be read from storage system iteratively. For a medium 3D migration job, the data size of travel timetables can achieve dozens or hundreds of Terabytes. While the RTM method has no need of travel timetable data. Third, as the size of travel timetable is large, only a few imaging cells can reside in the memory, KPSDM needs to acquire more seismic traces from I/O sub-system to fully utilize the computation resources.

3   Design and Implementation

For a KPSDM job, before the migration computation starts, there are extra two steps: building travel timetables and pre-processing seismic data. The decomposition of the imaging space and seismic data are done in first two steps. More details on the decomposition are introduced in Sect. 3.1.

3.1   Decomposition

3.1.1   Decomposition of Imaging Space

During the migration computation stage, travel timetable is used for the lookup of t_s and t_r, so the travel timetable should always resides in memory. However, for a medium 3D job, the total size of all travel timetables can achieve dozens of Terabytes.

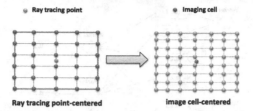

Fig. 3. Ray tracing point-centered travel timetable and imaging cell-centered travel timetable

The decomposition of imaging space is to divide the travel timetable in the principle that the travel timetable of one imaging space can be loaded into memory.

The travel timetable of each ray tracing point (also called shot point) is calculated based on ray tracing theory. Ray tracing points are arranged by a two-dimensional grid on the surface. And ray tracing grid and the imaging cell grid are two independent grids.

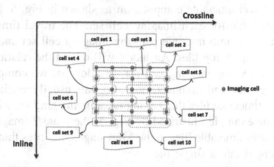

Fig. 4. Decomposition of imaging cells

We propose a data structure called imaging cell-centered travel timetable to organize the travel timetable data. For each ray tracing point, from view of the surface, the travel timetable calculated by ray tracing is a two-dimensional array of which elements are the time cost from the position of ray tracing point to the positions of different imaging cells. While the aim of imaging cell-centered travel timetable is to construct a two-dimensional array of which elements are the time cost from the position of the imaging cell to position of different ray tracing points. Figure 3 contrast these two different organization structures. The benefit of the imaging cell-centered travel timetable structure is that any valid trace for the imaging cell can obtain corresponding t_s and t_r in the time complexity of $O(1)$.

The decomposition of travel timetables is based on the data structure of imaging cell-centered travel timetable. According to the size of memory and the maximum travel timetable size of one imaging cell, the maximum number of imaging cells L can be calculated. Then, total imaging cells are divided into imaging cell sets based on L. Figure 4 illustrates a decomposition example, in which there are 30 imaging cells and the L is 3. The imaging cells are divided into 10 imaging cell sets.

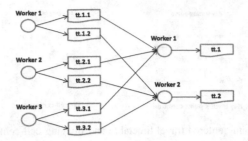

Fig. 5. MapReduce-like travel timetable computation architecture

To accelerate the loading speed of travel timetable, all travel timetables of one imaging cell set are stored in only one file, i.e., each imaging cell set corresponds to a travel timetable file. Note that the travel timetable of each ray tracing point may contain the data that belongs to different imaging cell sets. To reorganize the travel timetable data into files based on imaging cell sets, a MapReduce-like computation pattern is used in the step of travel timetable computation as shown in Fig. 5. In the Map stage, each process creates a file for each imaging cell set. The travel timetable of one ray tracing point will be split into multiple parts by imaging cell set and then these parts will be output to corresponding files. An index will record the relation information of the ray tracing point and the imaging cell set. In addition, we compressed the travel timetable data using zlib and compression ratio can usually achieve $6 \sim 8$. In the Reduce stage, travel timetable files that belong to same imaging set will be merged into one single file. In the example illustrated by Fig. 5, there are 2 imaging sets and each process outputs 2 travel timetable files in the Map stage. And files that share a common imaging set are merged into a single file.

3.1.2   Decomposition of Seismic Data

In our implementation, each migration job can have multiple seismic data files. The input files are first split into sub-files and then reorganized by common offset range. Let F denote the set of input files, F_i denote i-th seismic file. In one migration job, the offset parameter can be set as $[O_1, O_2, O_3]$, in which O_1 is the minimum offset, O_2 is the maximum offset and O_3 is the offset interval. Let O denote the number of offset range, O_i denote i-th offset range. O can be calculated by Eq. 2.

$$O = \frac{(O_2 - O_1)}{O_3} \tag{2}$$

Each seismic file F_i is spilt into O sub-files. Let matrix D denote the sub-files of all input files. D_{ij} is the j-th sub-file of i-th input seismic file. In matrix D, the first dimension is input file and the second dimension is offset range. Sub-files of matrix D that share common offset range are divided into multiple segments according to the available space size of local disks. For example, there are 6 input files and 6 offset range in Fig. 6. All sub-files of offset range 0 and the first two sub-files of offset range 1 are grouped into a seismic data segment. With this decomposition approach, the seismic data that has same offset range is aggregated. Note that the imaging results are organized by offset range. After all the seismic data of one offset range finishes the migration computations to an imaging cell set, the imaging results of the offset range and the imaging cell set can be output into database.

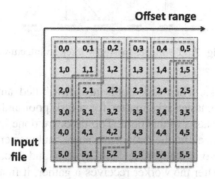

Fig. 6. Decomposition of seismic data

3.1.3 Task-Based Parallel KPSDM

In conclusion, imaging space is divided by the size of memory and seismic data is divided by the available size of local disks. Let N denote the number of imaging cell sets, M denote the number of seismic data segments. The total tasks of one migration job is M*N. The sequential version of KPSDM can be summarized as Algorithm 1. For each seismic data segment, there are N imaging cell sets to be migrated. As to one task, the travel timetable file is always first loaded into memory for the lookup of t_s and t_r during the migration. Then the seismic data is read as gathers for the migration computations. Now, we have convert the KPSDM algorithm into a task-based parallel application.

Algorithm 1. Single node KPSDM

1:   for i = 1 to M
2:     for j = 1 to N
3:       load the travel timetable file of **j-th** imaging cell set
4:       foreach **gather** in **i-th** seismic data segment
5:         perform migration computation with **gather** and travel timetables

---

3.2 Cluster-Level Parallelism

All processes are organized by a two-level master/worker architecture as shown in Fig. 7. Process 0 acts as the master and remaining processes are divided into groups with 4 processes in one group. All the processes in one group are workers and the worker with least rank also acts as submaster.

Figure 8 presents the flowchart of parallel KPSDM. Once the migration computation starts, master builds M task pools. Each pool corresponds to a seismic data

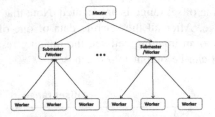

Fig. 7. Two-level master/worker architecture

segment and has N tasks. Then task pools are distributed among different process groups. Specifically, submaster asks master for a task pool and the group are responsible for finishing all the tasks of this pool. The tasks are done in two stages: broadcast stage and autonomy stage. In the broadcast stage, submaster reads gathers of the seismic data segment from the parallel file system and broadcasts the gathers to workers in this group. After the worker receives a gather, it first writes the gather into local disk and then migrates this gather to current imaging cell set. In the autonomy stage, all workers will finish the remaining N-4 tasks and read seismic gathers directly from local disks.

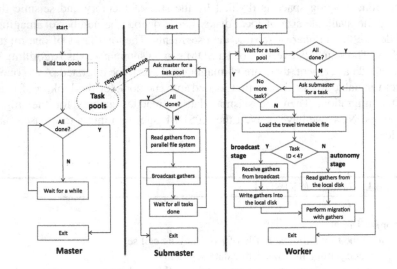

Fig. 8. Flowchart of the parallel KPSDM

The architecture and design can greatly reduce the I/O workloads on the I/O sub-system for several reasons listed as follows.

- Since each group has a submaster acting as the I/O proxy, it is not necessary for all workers to read seismic data from the parallel file system.
- All the seismic data for tasks in autonomy stage can be obtained from local disks, so one seismic data segment needs to be read from the parallel file system for only once and N tasks of the segment can be done.

- By building index information for buffered seismic data on local disks, each task can choose valid seismic data for current imaging cell set in the autonomy stage. Unnecessary I/O workloads caused by invalid seismic data are filtered.
- Local disk buffering mechanism allows part of the buffered seismic data to be cached by the memory. As the seismic data will be read iteratively for different imaging cell sets, memory caching of the local file system can reduce the number of actual disk operations.

Note that in the broadcast stage, performance degrades because of the synchronization side effects and invalid input seismic data. In the autonomy stage, these problems can be avoided. For a medium or large 3D migration job, there are thousands or hundreds of thousands of imaging cell sets. Thus, the overhead caused in the broadcast stage when performing the first four tasks can be ignored. The saved bandwidth of the parallel file systems are conserved for reading travel timetable files.

In addition, a simple work-stealing mechanism are employed to achieve better load balance. When there are no more task pool for a submaster, it first checks current unfinished task pools of other process groups. Submaster will join the group whose task pool has maximum number of unfinished tasks.

3.3   Node-Level Parallelism

Figure 9 illustrates the parallel migration architecture of a single node. After a worker gets a new imaging set from master, the corresponding compressed travel timetable file is first loaded from parallel file system into memory. Then the data structures of imaging cell-centered travel timetable are built based on the index and compressed data of the file. When the building process finishes, each imaging cell corresponds to a three-dimensional grid which enables any valid trace to obtain t_s and t_r in constant time. Then gathers from broadcast or local disks are loaded into a gather queue continuously. Each gather contains 1000 traces in default and all the traces in the gather share a common offset range due to the decomposition design of seismic data. Traces of the gather popped from the gather queue are distributed among multi-threads.

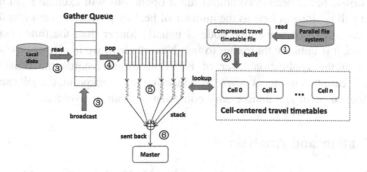

Fig. 9. Parallel architecture of one computing node

Algorithm 2 describes the migration process of one thread. Note that each trace fetched from the gather needs to perform the migration computation for all imaging cells of current cell set. For one imaging cell C, t_s vector and t_r vector are first obtained from the cell-centered travel timetable of C. Then, imaging result of < T, C > is calculated with t_s vector and t_r vector.

Algorithm 2. Migration process of one thread

1: fetch one trace **T** from the gather **G**
2: foreach imaging cell **C** in current cell set:
3:      lookup for t_s vector from cell-centered travel timetable of **C**
4:      lookup for t_r vector from cell-centered travel timetable of **C**
5:      computing imaging result of <**T**, **C**> with t_s vector and t_r vector

---

To avoid the writing contention, each thread is equipped with an imaging buffer for storing the imaging results. After all the gathers of one offset range are migrated, the results of all threads are stacked. The final results are then sent back to master. If the whole data of one offset range is contained in only one seismic data segment, master can directly output the imaging results into database. Otherwise, master needs to further stack the imaging results from different groups and then writes the results into database.

3.4   High Availability

We implement fault tolerance at the application layer to guarantee that the migration job can still progress to finish even multiple process failures happen. Specifically, master monitors the health states of all processes. When a process failure happens, master first marks the node and then broadcasts the information of the failed node to every healthy process. And the failed task of will be re-scheduled to a healthy worker. In our implementation, the failed tasks will be re-processed after all normal tasks finish. Processes located in the same group with the failed node will start fault tolerance processing. For example, if submaster is down, a new submaster will be elected. If a worker is down, the collective communication operations will exclude it. In this way, the job can still be done as long as the number of healthy processes is not less than two.

Since the MTTF of one single node is usually longer than the time cost by one migration job, it is unlikely for master to fail. Nevertheless, we implement a checkpoint mechanism at the application layer of KPSDM which records the finished tasks cyclically. In case that master is down, by analyzing the checkpoint, the job can recover from the broken point and unnecessary computations can be avoided.

4   Evaluation and Analysis

All experiments are performed on a cluster called IBM2 which contains 220 computing nodes. Each node is equipped with two 2.6 GHz, 8 cores, 64-bit Intel Xeon E5-2670 processors and 128 GB DRAM. Thus, each node has 16 physical cores. The operating system of each computing node is Red Hat Enterprise Linux Server release 6.4 (Santiago). The parallel file system deployed on IBM2 is GPFS [3]. The total storage space of the parallel file system is 683 TB.

4.1 Cluster-Level Migration Scalability

Practical seismic data set named Jinyao collected in a field located in western China is used for tests. The field covers an area of 2760 square kilometers and the depth of the survey area is 8.75 km. The number of samples in each trace is 1750. We choose part of the data for the experiments, in which inline ranges from 1686 to 1986 and crossline ranges from 1231 to 2548. And the total size of the test data is 427.58 GB.

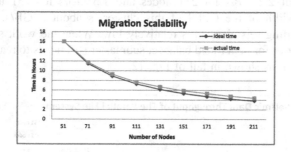

Fig. 10. Cluster-level migration scalability

Figure 10 shows the scalability of our parallel implementation of KPSDM by increasing the number of computing node from 51 to 211. The increment of nodes number between two adjacent tests is 20. The ideal time is calculated proportionally based on the time cost using 51 nodes and the number of nodes in other tests. From Fig. 10, we can conclude that our implementation can achieve high scalability since the actual time cost is nearly close with the ideal time when more computing nodes are added to accelerate the migration computations.

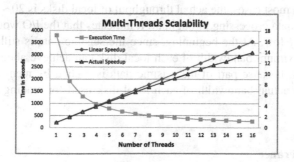

Fig. 11. Node-level migration scalability

4.2   Node-Level Migration Scalability

A small migration job is used for the multi-threads scalability test. The experimental results in Fig. 11 illustrate that our implementation of KPSDM can maintain a near-linear speedup when the number of threads ranges from 1 to 16. Thus, a good scalability for a multi-threads computing node is also achieved.

4.3   Seismic Data Throughput Monitoring

A migration job with Jinyao dataset is used for the tests in this experiment. Figure 12 shows the seismic data throughput of 151 and 211 computing nodes, respectively. In both cases, the throughput only refers to the seismic data that is read from the parallel file system. The average bandwidth during the broadcast stage after the migration starts can achieve about 2.2 GB/s for 211 nodes and 1.5 GB/s for 151 nodes. And the maximum bandwidth of the GPFS of this cluster is about 5 GB/s. Thus, the I/O workloads of reading seismic data is relatively low. When the work stealing mechanism begins to work for better load balance, submaster still needs to read data from the parallel file system as shown in tail of Fig. 12.

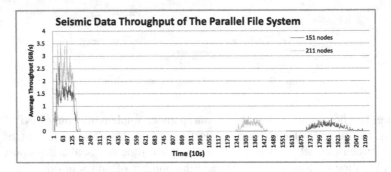

Fig. 12. Seismic data throughput of parallel file system

Figure 13 contrasts the seismic data processing throughput and actual seismic data throughput from local disks. In this test, 211 computing nodes are used for the migration job. In most cases, the actual throughput of local disks is $20 \sim 40$ times lower than the seismic data processing throughput. It indicates that the I/O workloads on each local disk is very low. At the beginning, since the seismic data is still not cached by memory, the maximum bandwidth of each local disk can achieve about 15 MB/s. For subsequent tasks, because part of the seismic data is cached by memory of the computing node, the actual bandwidth of each local disk used for reading seismic data is very low.

4.4   Fault Tolerance

A medium migration job using Jinyao dataset is used for this experiment with 33 computing nodes, i.e., 8 process groups. We compare the seismic data processing

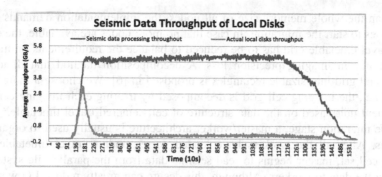

Fig. 13. Seismic data throughput of local disks

throughput of all workers in four tests. In the first test, no process is killed. In the second test, four submaster from four groups are killed. In the third test, four submasters from four groups and four workers from other four groups are killed. In the last test, two workers for each group are killed, i.e. 16 workers are killed. In all the tests, the faults are injected after the KPSDM has been running for about 1500 s. Figure 14 presents the throughput changes when faults happen. First, Fig. 14 shows that multiple process failures can be tolerated. The migration job can still be done even half of the workers fail. Second, Fig. 14 illustrates that the faults almost have no side effects on the healthy processes since the throughput drops proportionally. Thus, our implementation of KPSDM can recover from failures with very low overhead.

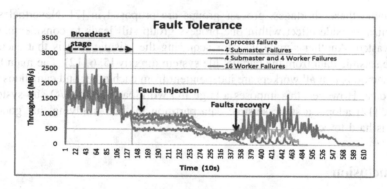

Fig. 14. I/O throughput of KPSDM when multiple process failures happen

5   Related Work

As noted in [11], due to trade secrets, there are only a few literatures on the parallel implementation of KPSDM. One method is to divide the migration computation by inline just as the method proposed in [11] for Kirchhoff Pre-Stack Time Migration (KPSTM) based on the assumption that the memory of all computing nodes can usually hold the travel timetables of all imaging cells of one inline. However, the method cannot scale in problem domain. When the total size of travel timetables of one inline is larger than the whole memory size of all nodes, the implementation demands adding more nodes to start the migration. In case that no more nodes are available, the density of the travel timetable grid has to be reduced to balance the requirements on memory, which results in imaging precision loss. A decomposition method that divides the imaging cell grid into sizable rectangles is proposed in [6]. We choose a more simple method, i.e., the imaging cell grid is decomposed by treating each imaging cell as an independent unit based on the data structure of cell-centered travel timetable.

In the migration stage, a master/worker architecture is usually used to organize all processes. After all the workers have loaded corresponding travel timetable of an imaging cell set, master begins to read seismic data from the parallel file system and broadcast the data to workers. Although, this design can greatly reduce I/O workloads on the I/O sub-system, it has several shortcomings as follows.

- Poor scalability. For small migration jobs, with the increasing number of computing nodes, the number of imaging cells distributed to each node is decreasing. Master needs to achieve higher read and broadcast bandwidth, which makes the master become the I/O bottleneck. The execution time cannot be shortened even if more nodes are added when master achieves the bandwidth bottleneck.
- Poor performance. Broadcast mechanism makes all workers process the same input seismic data. Note that each computing node progresses at a different pace since the seismic data could be invalid for some nodes when the received data is not in the valid range delimited by current imaging cells. Because of the synchronization side effect caused by broadcast, all other computing nodes need to wait for the slowest node. Thus, a great amount of CPU cycles is wasted.

To avoid these shortages, process groups are proposed in [7]. Nevertheless, the synchronization side effect within one process group still leads to considerable CPU cycles wasted. Another simple way for acquiring the seismic data is that each node reads the seismic data from the parallel file system directly [5, 6, 12]. The main benefit of this method is that all workers are independent from each other and can choose valid seismic data. However, this imposes a huge I/O workloads on the I/O sub-system. In addition, [12] adopts a static seismic data partition method implying that good load balance is hard to achieve.

6   Conclusion

In this paper, we present a highly optimized parallel implementation of KPSDM which achieves four goals:

- **Simple and clear.** We present a simple and clear task-based parallel implementation of KPSDM, which also facilitates the goal of scalability and availability.
- **Low I/O workloads.** The combination of I/O proxy in a process group, local disk buffering, invalid seismic data filtering and memory caching can dramatically reduce the I/O workloads on I/O sub-system of clusters.
- **High scalability.** The design of task-based parallel pattern as well as the balance between I/O capacity and computing performance enables our implementation to

scale out on large high performance clusters. In addition, our implementation of KPSDM also has a near-linear scalability for a multi-cores computing node.

- **High availability.** When the scale of the clusters continues to expand, it becomes failure prone for upper layer applications. The availability of KPSDM is guaranteed by fault tolerance and checkpoint mechanism.

References

1. Perrone, M. P., Zhou, H., Fossum, G., Todd, R.: Practical VTI RTM. In: 72nd EAGE Conference and Exhibition, June 2010
2. Perrone, M., Liu, L. K., Lu, L., Magerlein, K., Kim, C., Fedulova, I., Semenikhin, A.: Reducing data movement costs: scalable seismic imaging on blue gene. In: 2012 IEEE 26th International Parallel & Distributed Processing Symposium (IPDPS), pp. 320–329. IEEE May 2012
3. Schmuck, F.B., Haskin, R.L.: GPFS: A shared-disk file system for large computing clusters. In: Proceedings of FAST 2002, vol. 2, p. 19 January 2002
4. Yilmaz, Ö., Doherty, S.M.: Seismic Data Processing, vol. 2. Society of Exploration Geophysicists, Tulsa (1987)
5. Chang, H., VanDyke, J.P., Solano, M., McMechan, G.A., Epili, D.: 3D pre-stack Kirchhoff depth migration: from prototype to production in a massively parallel processor environment. Geophys. **63**(2), 546–556 (1998)
6. Panetta, J., de Souza Filho, P.R., da Cunha Filho, C.A., da Motta, F.M.R., Pinheiro, S.S., Pedrosa, I., de Albrecht, C.H.: Computational characteristics of production seismic migration and its performance on novel processor architectures. In: 19th International Symposium on Computer Architecture and High Performance Computing, SBAC-PAD 2007. pp. 11–18. IEEE October 2007
7. Li, J., Hei, D., Yan, L.: Partitioning algorithm of 3D pre-stack parallel Kirchhoff depth migration for imaging spaces. In: Eighth International Conference on Grid and Cooperative Computing, GCC 2009. pp. 276–280. IEEE August 2009
8. Bevc, D.: Imaging complex structures with semi-recursive Kirchhoff migration. Geophys. **62**(2), 577–588 (1997)
9. Yin, Y., Byna, S., Song, H., Sun, X.H., Thakur, R.: Boosting application-specific parallel i/o optimization using IOSIG. In: 2012 12th IEEE/ACM International Symposium on Cluster, Cloud and Grid Computing (CCGrid), pp. 196–203. IEEE May 2012
10. Yu, H., Sahoo, R.K., Howson, C., Almasi, G., Castanos, J.G., Gupta, M., Gropp, W.D.: High performance file i/o for the blue Gene/L supercomputer. In: The Twelfth International Symposium on High-Performance Computer Architecture, pp. 187–196. IEEE February 2006
11. Dai, H.: Parallel processing of pre-stack Kirchhoff time migration on a PC cluster. Comput. Geosci. **31**(7), 891–899 (2005)
12. Sen, V., Sen, M.K., Stoffa, P.L.: PVM based 3-D Kirchhoff depth migration using dynamically computed travel-times: an application in seismic data processing. Parallel Comput. **25**(3), 231–248 (1999)
13. Marr, D.T., Binns, F., Hill, D.L., et al.: Hyper-threading technology architecture and microarchitecture. Intel. Technol. J. **6**(1), 4–15 (2002)

14. Nowak, D.A., Seagar, M.: ASCI tera-scale simulation: requirements and deployments. http://www.ornl.gov/sci/optical/docs/Tutorial19991108Nowak.pdf
15. Heien, E., Kondo, D., Gainaru, A., LaPine, D., Kramer, B., Cappello, F.: Modeling and tolerating heterogeneous failures in large parallel systems. In: 2011 International Conference for High Performance Computing, Networking, Storage and Analysis (SC), pp. 1–11. IEEE November 2011

MrBayes for Phylogenetic Inference Using Protein Data on a GPU Cluster

Shuai Pang, Rebecca J. Stones, Ming-ming Ren[✉], Gang Wang,
and Xiaoguang Liu

College of Computer and Control Engineering, Nankai University, Tianjin, China
{pangshuai,rebecca.stones82,renmingming,wgzwp,liuxg}@nbjl.nankai.edu.cn

Abstract. MrBayes is a widely used software for Bayesian phylogenetic inference: we input biological sequence data from various taxonomic groups, and MrBayes returns its estimate of the phylogenetic tree which gave rise to those taxa. This paper presents ta(MC)^3, based on its predecessor a(MC)^3, which, for protein datasets, improves computational efficiency and overcomes major obstacles in analyzing larger datasets on HPCs with multiple Graphics Processing Units (GPUs). The major improvements are (a) a new task mapping strategy, (b) the use of Kahan summation to resolve non-convergence issues, and (c) the introduction of 64-bit variables. We evaluate ta(MC)^3 on real-world protein datasets both on a desktop server and the Tianhe-1A supercomputer. With a single GPU, ta(MC)^3 is nearly 90 times faster compared with the serial version of MrBayes, up to around 9 times faster than MrBayes utilizing a GPU via the BEAGLE library, and up to 2.5 times faster than a(MC)^3. On larger datasets with 64 nodes (GPUs) on Tianhe-1A, ta(MC)^3 is capable of obtaining 1000+ speedup vs. serial MrBayes.

Keywords: MrBayes · GPU · Protein · Task mapping strategy

1 Introduction

In biology, "phylogeny" refers to the evolutionary relationships between species or taxonomic groups, and can be inferred from the pattern of states at homologous characters in biological sequences; it is typically formulated as a phylogenetic tree. A number of numerical methods have been presented for using DNA or protein sequence data to infer phylogenetic trees, including parsimony methods [17], distance matrix methods [13], maximum probability methods [14], and the Bayesian method [7,8,12]. The Bayesian method outperforms other methods in terms of easy interpretation of results, the capability to incorporate prior information, and several computational advantages [6,16]. MrBayes is a popular program that implements the Metropolis Coupled Markov Chain Monte Carlo ((MC)^3 for short) sampling method for Bayesian phylogenetic inference.

MrBayes typically runs multiple Markov chains simultaneously, and since each chain runs almost independently, MrBayes is well-suited to parallel implementation on multi-core systems. To speed up Bayesian phylogenetic inference,

© Springer International Publishing Switzerland 2015
G. Wang et al. (Eds.): ICA3PP 2015, Part III, LNCS 9530, pp. 267–280, 2015.
DOI: 10.1007/978-3-319-27137-8_21

some parallel algorithms have been presented [1,15]. To our knowledge, $g(MC)^3$, by Pratas et al. [11], was the first attempt at parallelizing MrBayes on a GPU. The disadvantage of $g(MC)^3$ is that the transfer of transition probability matrices between the CPU and GPU is so frequent that it results in a large transfer overhead. Zhou et al. [18] subsequently presented $n(MC)^3$, an improved parallel version of MrBayes for the GPU. The authors decreased the frequency of transition probability matrix uploads and made both the CPU and GPU perform computations in parallel. This improvement results in overlap in CPU-GPU data communication and computation. A modified version of this GPU parallel algorithm, $a(MC)^3$ by Bao et al. [2] is a CPU-GPU cooperative algorithm which improves on $n(MC)^3$ such as by using dynamic task decomposition and mapping and a node-by-node scheduling model. Furthermore, BEAGLE, an open API library, has been designed to speed up probability calculations using the GPU. The BEAGLE library is now supported in MrBayes 3.2.1.

A GPU is a programmable many-core co-processor and has strong computational power and high memory bandwidth. Aside from graphics processing, many applications have been accelerated by using GPU, e.g. general signal processing, physics simulation, computational finance, and computational biology [3]. NVIDIA GPUs, for example, have a large number of cores grouped into *stream multiprocessors* (SMs, for short) which can run thousands of threads concurrently. CUDA, introduced by NVIDIA, is a general purpose parallel computing architecture and a parallel programming model. It allows developers to program NVIDIA GPUs using a minimally-extended version of the C language in a fashion very similar to CPU programming. The high-level unit of computation running on the GPU is called *kernel*, and is executed by potentially thousands of threads organized into *thread-blocks*, with all blocks able to be executed concurrently. A stream multiprocessor creates, manages, schedules, and executes threads in groups of 32 parallel threads called *warps*; the threads in a block are divided into warps. A warp is the basic scheduling unit on GPU, and the threads in a warp must run synchronously on a SM. An important consideration of CUDA programming is memory hierarchy, there are three kinds of memory in NVIDIA GPUs: *global memory* is the largest memory space but the slowest; *shared memory* is much faster but much smaller; *registers* are the fastest, but smallest memory. Consequently, loading repeatedly accessed data into shared memory or registers is a common strategy to improve performance of GPU-based software.

To our knowledge, to date, $a(MC)^3$ obtains the greatest speedup among all GPU versions for MrBayes. Although originally focused on analyzing DNA data, $a(MC)^3$ has subsequently been extended to be capable of analyzing protein data. This paper presents an improvement upon $a(MC)^3$, which we call $ta(MC)^3$, which overcomes several obstacles to analyzing large protein datasets, particularly on high-performance computuational platforms:

– To improve computational efficiency when analyzing large protein datasets, $ta(MC)^3$ adopts an efficient task mapping strategy which makes better use of GPU cores and GPU memory and reduces redundant operations.

- When analyzing large datasets, due to the long inference process, MrBayes (and its parallel variants) might encounter non-convergence problems caused by large accumulating errors. To address this issue, we reformulate MrBayes's core computing flow by adopting the Kahan summation algorithm.
- We modify some data structures and processing logic to overcome inherent memory allocation limitations in MrBayes. With this improvement, ta(MC)^3 is capable of analyzing larger datasets than its predecessors.

2   Methods and Implementation

2.1   Optimizable Part of (MC)^3

The (MC)^3 procedure is outlined below (the details can be found in [1]). MrBayes runs H Markov chain simultaneously, and we let ψ_i denote the current tree for Markov chain i. Each is initialized randomly. For practical reasons, MrBayes also approximates the gamma distribution into several *categories*.

1. For each chain $i \in \{1, 2, \ldots, H\}$, we propose a new tree ψ_i' by randomly perturbing ψ_i, and replace ψ_i by ψ_i' with probability

$$R_i := \min \left[1, \left(\frac{f(X|\psi_i')}{f(X|\psi_i)} \times \frac{f(\psi_i')}{f(\psi_i)} \right)^{\beta_i} \times \frac{q(\psi_i)}{q(\psi_i')} \right].$$

   Here: (a) X denotes the input protein data, (b) $f(X|\psi_i)$ is the likelihood of data X occurring given tree ψ_i, (c) $f(\psi_i)$ is the probability of tree ψ_i, (d) $q(\psi_i')$ is the probability of proposing the new state, (e) the probability of proposing the old state starting from the new state is $q(\psi_i)$, and (f) β_i is the *heat* of chain i; for the cold chain, $\beta_i = 1$.
2. After all chains have advanced a given number of iterations, we randomly choose two chains (j and k) to swap states. We swap these states with probability

$$\min \left[1, \frac{f(\psi_k|X)^{\beta_j} f(\psi_j|X)^{\beta_k}}{f(\psi_j|X)^{\beta_j} f(\psi_k|X)^{\beta_k}} \right].$$

3. Go to Step 1.

A *transition probability matrix* gives the probabilities of transitioning from one amino acid to another. At a given site, the *conditional likelihood* is the likelihood of a node having a specific amino acid conditioned on its child nodes having their specific amino acids with their conditional likelihoods. Terminal-node conditional likelihoods are determined from the protein data. To calculate an acceptance probability R_i, we

1. calculate the transition probability matrices for every node according to the instantaneous transition probability matrix Q, then
2. traverse the tree in post order and compute the conditional likelihoods for each internal node according to its child nodes' conditional likelihoods.

The conditional likelihoods of the root node are used to calculate the local likelihoods of the tree (the likelihood at a given site), which combine to give the global likelihood. These computations are the most frequently called and time-consuming components of MrBayes.

The computation is performed as described in Algorithm 1, which implements Felsenstein's algorithm [4]. The 20×20 array TM_n denotes the transition probability matrix of an internal node n (in MrBayes, there are 20 possible amino acids). The vectors CL_n of length 20 are used to store the conditional likelihoods of node n.

Algorithm 1. Computing the conditional likelihoods in MrBayes.

1: **for each** internal node n, with child nodes l and r **do**
2:     **for each** site (or character) **do**
3:         **for each** Γ category **do**
4:             **for each** amino acid $k = 0, 1, \ldots, 19$ **do**
5:                 $T_l \leftarrow 0$
6:                 $T_r \leftarrow 0$
7:                 **for** $m = 0, 1, \ldots, 19$ **do**
8:                     $T_l \leftarrow TM_l[k][m] \times CL_l[m]$
9:                     $T_r \leftarrow TM_r[k][m] \times CL_r[m]$
10:                 **end for**
11:                 $CL_n[k] \leftarrow T_l \times T_r$
12:             **end for**
13:         **end for**
14:     **end for**
15: **end for**

From a computational point of view, the main difference between DNA and protein data is the number of possible characters at a given site (4 nucleotides vs. 20 amino acids). Consequently, analyzing protein data on a GPU requires a different strategy than analyzing DNA data.

2.2   Task Mapping Strategy of a(MC)^3

In this section, we review a(MC)^3's method for computing conditional likelihoods on the GPU, described in Algorithm 2 and illustrated in Fig. 1. The data transfer method and chain scheduling method remain the same in ta(MC)^3, so we omit discussion of these components.

In a(MC)^3, each CUDA block is two dimensional with dimensions 4×20, and is responsible for computing the conditional likelihoods for an individual site in a non-terminal node. The threads (x, y), where threadIdx.$x \in \{0, 1, 2, 3\}$, together compute the conditional likelihood that the node has amino acid $k = $ threadIdx.y at that site. An individual thread (x, y) is responsible for the computation of 5 elements in this conditional likelihood for amino acid k. In a(MC)^3, a grid is

---

Algorithm 2. The contribution of thread (x, y) to the computation of the conditional likelihood $CL_n[k]$ for non-terminal node n and amino acid k in a(MC)^3; the node has child nodes l and r

1: $t_x \leftarrow$ threadIdx.x // we will have $t_x \in \{0, 1, 2, 3\}$
2: $t_y \leftarrow$ threadIdx.y // by design, $t_y = k$
3: Load TM_l, TM_r, CL_l, and CL_r into shared memory
4: Synchronize all threads
5: $T_l^{(x)}[t_y] \leftarrow 0$
6: $T_r^{(x)}[t_y] \leftarrow 0$
7: **for** $i = 0, 1, \ldots, 4$ **do**
8:     $T_l^{(x)}[t_y] \leftarrow T_l^{(x)}[t_y] + TM_l[t_y][5t_x + i] \times CL_l[5t_x + i]$
9:     $T_r^{(x)}[t_y] \leftarrow T_r^{(x)}[t_y] + TM_r[t_y][5t_x + i] \times CL_r[5t_x + i]$
10: **end for**
11: $T_l[t_y] \leftarrow \sum_{i=0}^{3} T_l^{(i)}[t_y]$
12: $T_r[t_y] \leftarrow \sum_{i=0}^{3} T_r^{(i)}[t_y]$
13: Synchronize all threads
14: **if** $t_x = 0$ **then**
15:     $CL_n[t_y] \leftarrow T_l[t_y] \times T_r[t_y]$
16: **end if**

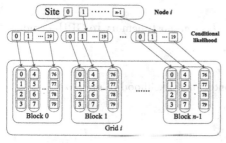

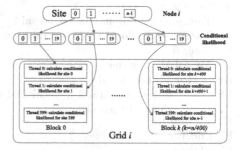

Fig. 1. Task mapping strategies for a(MC)^3.

Fig. 2. Task mapping strategies for ta(MC)^3.

responsible for the computation of the conditional likelihoods over all sites of each non-terminal node, as indicated in Fig. 1.

We highlight two drawbacks in this algorithm:

- Since groups of four consecutive threads cooperatively compute a conditional probability, we require intermediate storage and calculation. In turn, this requires thread synchronization to ensure correct results are calculated.
- For large datasets, fine-grained task mapping results in a large number of small tasks. Therefore, the number of blocks may exceed the limits of NVIDIA Fermi architecture (i.e., at most $2^{16} - 1 = 65535$ blocks in a grid).
- Assigning small tasks results in each thread having low *arithmetic intensity*, defined as the ratio of the number of arithmetic instructions executed to the

number of memory accesses. Having low arithmetic intensity results in sub-optimal GPU utilization.

2.3 Proposed Task Mapping Strategy: $ta(MC)^3$

To address the aforementioned drawbacks of $a(MC)^3$, we design a coarse-grained task mapping strategy for $ta(MC)^3$, given in Algorithm 3 and illustrated in Fig. 2. In Algorithm 3, conditional likelihood vectors are stored in a matrix called the conditional likelihood table. Algorithm 4 gives the kernel function.

Algorithm 3. Outline of $ta(MC)^3$

1: *Stage 1*
2: **for all** Markov chains i **do**
3:     propose a new tree ψ_i' by randomly perturbing ψ_i
4:     **for** non-root nodes n **do**
5:         Calculate transition probability matrix TM_n
6:     **end for**
7: **end for**
8: *Stage 2*
9: Transpose conditional likelihood table
10: Transfer conditional likelihood table and TM_n from host memory to GPU memory
11: *Stage 3*
12: **for all** Markov chains i **do**
13:     **for all** nodes n **do**
14:         Call kernel function to calculate conditional likelihood of node n in
            chain i in parallel
15:     **end for**
16: **end for**
17: *Stage 4*
18: **for all** Markov chains i **do**
19:     Call kernel function to calculate the local likelihoods L_u for ψ_i' in parallel
20: **end for**
21: *Stage 5*
22: Transpose conditional likelihood table
23: Transfer conditional likelihood table from GPU memory to host memory
24: Transfer local likelihoods from GPU to CPU
25: *Stage 6*
26: **for all** Markov chains i **do**
27:     Synchronize corresponding GPU stream
28:     Calculate acceptance probability for ψ_i' using global likelihood
        $\prod_{\text{site } u} L_u$
29: **end for**

The proposed $ta(MC)^3$ utilizes the GPU memory hierarchy in two significant ways:

- We first make each block transfer the transition probability matrices TM_l and TM_r from global memory to shared memory. At a given node, the TMs are repeatedly used over all sites when calculating conditional likelihoods. Consequently, since each thread in ta(MC)^3 computes the conditional likelihoods for an individual site, TM is repeatedly accessed from shared memory by all threads in the same block.
- We use registers to store the conditional likelihoods of the current node's children and for the intermediate calculation as indicated in Algorithm 4.

In the end, the final result is written back to global memory.

Algorithm 4. The kernel function of ta(MC)^3 for computing conditional likelihoods

---

1: load TM_l and TM_r into shared memory
2: Synchronize all threads
3: **for** amino acid $k = 0, 1, \ldots, 19$ **do**
4:     register_var $c_l \leftarrow CL_l[k]$
5:     register_var $c_r \leftarrow CL_r[k]$
6:     register_var $t_l \leftarrow 0$
7:     register_var $t_r \leftarrow 0$
8:     **for** amino acid $m = 0, 1, \ldots, 19$ **do**
9:         $t_l \leftarrow t_l + TM_l[m][k] \times c_l$
10:         $t_r \leftarrow t_r + TM_r[m][k] \times c_r$
11:     **end for**
12:     $CL_n[k] \leftarrow t_l \times t_r$
13: **end for**

We also coalesce global memory accesses by transposing the conditional likelihood table, as indicated in lines 9 and 22 in Algorithm 3. This has the benefit of aligning 32 consecutive 4-byte words into 128 bytes, which can be fetched from global memory in a single transaction. Without transposing this matrix, the threads in a warp load multiple discontinuous words from global memory.

Additionally, GPU utilization is linked to the number of simultaneously active warps. The time a warp needs to reach the next ready state is the *latency*. *Full utilization* occurs when latency is "hidden" by other warps. From the algorithm specifications, we can compute that about 40 warps are required to hide the latency under ta(MC)^3, whereas 240 warps are required under a(MC)^3. However, CUDA devices of compute capability 3.× allow no more than 64 simultaneous warps on a multiprocessor [9]. This implies that ta(MC)^3 is capable of achieving full utilization, whereas a(MC)^3 is incapable.

We set the block size in ta(MC)^3 to 400, which has the following benefits:

- The number of registers used by a kernel has a significant impact on the number of resident warps. In a CUDA device of compute capability 3.×, each multiprocessor has $65,536$ registers. Since each thread uses up to 36 registers (using the -maxrregcount compiler option to control register usage)

in ta(MC)^3 and only very little shared memory are needed, the number of actual resident warps is determined by the number of registers used by kernel. When we set the block size to 400, each block consequently occupies $400 \times 36 = 14,400$ registers. Consequently, each multiprocessor can accommodate at most 4 blocks and there are 13 warps in a block, that is, 52 warps totally which is more than 40 warps needed to hide latency. This satisfies the requirement of full utilization.

- A block size of 400 matches the size of transition probability matrix, i.e., $20 \times 20 = 400$ cells, resulting in coalesced memory accesses and avoiding idle threads.

Experimental results agree with 400 being a good choice of block size; see Fig. 5.

2.4 Precision Optimization

Non-convergence problems can occur in MrBayes when we analyze protein data with too many taxa or amino acid sites (characters). The root cause of non-convergence is large truncation errors accumulating when analyzing larger datasets. Summation of a sequence of floating-point values is required in MrBayes. If we perform such summations naively, eventually non-negligible truncation errors will accumulate. In ta(MC)^3, we adopt the Kahan summation algorithm [5] to improve the precision. This is implemented on the GPU side when computing conditional likelihoods. Specifically, in Algorithm 4, we (a) declare new registers y, e_l, e_r, and t after Line 7, initializing e_l and e_r to zero, and (b) replace Line 9 with:

1: $y \leftarrow TM_l[m][k] \times c_l - e_l$
2: $t \leftarrow t_l + y$
3: $e_l \leftarrow (t - t_l) - y$
4: $t_l \leftarrow t$

A similar modification is made for Line 10.

Kahan summation minimizes truncation error by keeping a variable to account for truncation errors, which are corrected in the next iteration. Summing a sequence of n numbers naively has a worst-case error that grows proportional to n, whereas, with Kahan summation, the worst-case error is independent of n, depending on the floating-point precision of the machine.

2.5 A Memory Allocation Limitation

The length of real-world amino acid sequences can have tens of thousands or even hundreds of thousands of amino acids, which, along with the number of taxa studied, results in increased system memory requirements. Since the serial version of MrBayes and its parallel versions are still use 32-bit variables, they are incapable of analyzing datasets of this size even if there is enough memory in the GPU devices. More specifically, if the dataset requires more than 4 GB memory per GPU to be analyzed, these versions of MrBayes will crash. To solve this problem, we use 64-bit variables in ta(MC)^3. The program component responsible for memory management is redesigned to deal with 64-bit addresses and manage large memory space. The specific variables changed are listed in Table 1.

Table 1. Variables changed to 64-bit.

Variable	Description
numCompressedChars	number of sites
condLikeRowSize	row size of CPT
globaloneMatSize	size of CPT
offsetclP, offsetclL, offsetclR, offsetclA	offset in CPT

As a specific example of this limitation, we include a real-world dataset in our experiments (dataset 7), which has 31 taxa and 360031 sites. At least 12.8 GB is required to store its conditional likelihood table, which is far beyond what a 32-bit variable can represent.

3   Experimental Results and Discussion

We evaluate the performance of ta(MC)^3 with eight real-world datasets. These datasets are used in phylogenetics research by Prof. Qiang Xie's research group and can be found in TreeBASE repository (both the datasets and source code are available from http://sourceforge.net/projects/mrbayes-gpu/). The dataset statistics are listed in Table 2.

The larger datasets (7 and 8) require substantially more memory and processing time. We use eight NVIDIA Titan cards in a GPU cluster to test the performance of ta(MC)^3 on these larger datasets. We test ta(MC)^3 both on a desktop server and the Tianhe-1A heterogeneous multi-core supercomputer. Each execution uses the same substitution model and lasts 100000 generations for datasets 1 to 6 and 10000 generations for datasets 7 and 8.

Table 2. Real-world protein datasets used in experiments

Dataset	1	2	3	4	5	6	7	8
No. taxa	32	85	8	48	59	39	31	14
No. characters	9377	13087	10088	11949	12428	11445	360031	407604

We compare run-times vs. MrBayes running in serial, and this is how we define "speedup" throughout. The most appropriate choice of baseline is not obvious: $a(MC)^3$ (which is the fastest known software prior to $ta(MC)^3$) was also developed by our research laboratory, and consequently cannot provide an independent baseline. Also, $a(MC)^3$ does not have the popularity of official versions of MrBayes.

In several experiments, the numerical value of the speedup is not important (e.g., to test scalability, or for block size optimization), and the speedup could, in principle, be normalized to the interval $(0, 1]$ without affecting the conclusions. Where the numerical value of the speedup is relevant, if the reader's preferred baseline differs from that used, they can readily divide through by its corresponding speedups (be that of $a(MC)^3$ or MrBayes + BEAGLE).

Desktop Server. We first test $ta(MC)^3$ on a desktop server with the following specifications: CentOS 6.2; 1× Intel Xeon E5645 (6 cores; 2.4 GHz); 6× 4 GB DDR3 1333 RAM; 8× NVIDIA GeForce GTX Titan. We compare its performance against $a(MC)^3$ and MrBayes 3.2.1 (the GPU parallel version of MrBayes which utilizes the BEAGLE library), and the serial version of MrBayes 3.1.2 is chosen as the baseline serial algorithm. Table 3 shows the experimental run-times on a desktop server on a single NVIDIA GeForce GTX Titan graphics card.

Table 3. Run-times of MrBayes 3.1.2, MrBayes 3.2.1, $a(MC)^3$, and $ta(MC)^3$ on datasets 1–6 in Table 2

Dataset	Execution time (sec.)				Speedup		
	MrBayes 3.1.2	MrBayes 3.2.1	$a(MC)^3$	$ta(MC)^3$	MrBayes 3.2.1	$a(MC)^3$	$ta(MC)^3$
1	40216	3212	1183	535	12	34	75
2	253953	17663	6194	2919	14	41	87
3	3744	401	267	117	9	14	32
4	57025	4320	1840	738	13	31	77
5	123656	8721	3171	1508	14	39	82
6	52650	4113	1423	675	13	37	78

Multi-GPU Hardware. Figure 3 shows the speedups on artificial datasets of $ta(MC)^3$ and $a(MC)^3$ on multiple GPUs on the desktop server. In this experiment, both algorithms distribute the eight Markov chains evenly between the GPUs as eight almost-independent processes.

Multi-GPU Hardware: Larger Datasets. Due to the use of 64-bit variables, we can analyze larger datasets using $ta(MC)^3$ than its 32-bit predecessors. The original MrBayes and its parallel variants will crash if set to analyze one of these larger datasets. To test $ta(MC)^3$ on these datasets, we compare its performance against modified versions of MrBayes 3.1.2 and $a(MC)^3$ in which 64-bit variables have

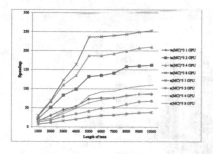

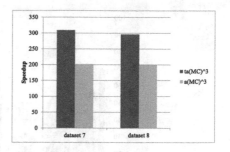

Fig. 3. Speedup on the multi-GPU desktop server.

Fig. 4. Speedup of larger datasets on multi-GPUs.

been introduced. We use double precision floating point data type to reduce errors and improve precision. We also use eight NVIDIA GeForce GTX Titan graphics cards to analyze these datasets, since these datasets require more than 30 GB memory under double-precision. The results are plotted in Fig. 4.

Tianhe-1A Supercomputer. The Tianhe-1A (TH-1A) supercomputer was chosen as our experimental platform for testing ta(MC)^3 on a GPU cluster. TH-1A is one of the few petascale supercomputers in the world, located at the National Supercomputing Center in Tianjin, China. It once became the world's fastest supercomputer[1] with a peak performance of 2.507 petaflops in October 2010. TH-1A is now equipped with 2,048 NUDT FT1000 heterogeneous processors, 14,336 Xeon X5670 processors and 7,168 NVIDIA Tesla M2050 GPU cards. We conduct our experiments on 64 nodes of TH-1A, each of which is equipped with one NVIDIA Tesla M2050 GPU card. Here we use NVIDIA CUDA Toolkit Version 4.0 and GCC version 4.12.

Table 4. Speedup of ta(MC)^3 vs. MrBayes 3.1.2 on the Tianhe-1A supercomputer on datasets 1–8 in Table 2

Dataset	4 nodes	8 nodes	16 nodes	32 nodes	64 nodes
1	117	165	264	361	424
2	139	186	290	381	451
3	50	69	108	188	288
4	123	168	269	333	425
5	128	177	283	359	451
6	122	169	271	334	425
7	–	201	378	672	1067
8	–	191	366	657	1039

---

[1] http://www.top500.org/lists/2010/11/.

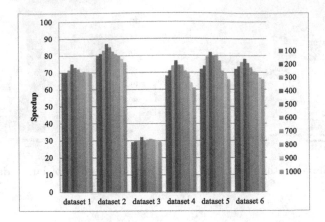

Fig. 5. Performance with various block sizes.

Table 5. Convergence speed (no. generations and run-time) with and without Kahan algorithm; the datasets are ordered as in the main text.

Dataset	With Kahan summation		Without Kahan summation	
	No. generations	Run-time (sec.)	No. generations	Run-time (sec.)
1	9156000	45000	9866000	50000
2	14581000	390000	15730000	410000
3	1997000	1900	2486000	2500
4	12235000	84000	14009000	100000
5	12142000	180000	12975000	190000
6	17067000	120000	18424000	130000

Experimental results on TH-1A are shown in Table 4 under single precision. The baselines are the runtimes of the modified version of MrBayes 3.1.2 with 64-bit variables on a single CPU of TH-1A. Since datasets 7 and 8 require more than 15GB memory under single precision and each GPU on TH-1A has 2G memory, we cannot analyze them with 4 nodes.

Block Size. We evaluate the impact of block size on performance of ta(MC)^3. The speedup vs. MrBayes 3.1.2 under varying block sizes is given in Fig. 5.

Kahan Summation. To evaluate the effectiveness of Kahan summation algorithm, we compare the convergence speed of ta(MC)^3 with and without Kahan summation algorithm. The convergence speed is measured in the generations and time spent in making the average standard deviation of split frequencies below 0.01. The results on datasets 1 to 6 are shown in Table 5.

4 Discussion

It is obvious from these experiments that GPU parallel algorithms significantly accelerate inference MrBayes. We further observe from Table 3 that ta(MC)^3 is around twice as fast as a(MC)^3 on single-GPU hardware. On multi-GPU hardware, we can see that ta(MC)^3 continues to outperform a(MC)^3, achieving, for example, up to 253 speedup vs. the serial algorithm on a quad-GPU configuration compared with 110 speedup of a(MC)^3. For the larger datasets, 7 and 8, ta(MC)^3 achieves around 300 speedup, while it would not be possible to analyze these data without modifying MrBayes or a(MC)^3.

On the Tianhe-1A supercomputer, Table 4 shows ta(MC)^3 is capable of achieving over 1000 speedup with 64 nodes on the larger datasets. The speedup of datasets 7 and 8 continues to increase as the number of GPU nodes grows to 64, whereas for the smaller datasets (datasets 1–6) the speedup tended to converge. For datasets 7 and 8, we can see that the efficiency (the ratio of speedup to the number of processors) is a relatively stable value (around 20). This result indicates that ta(MC)^3 is scalable and is capable of efficiently analyzing larger protein datasets on larger parallel systems.

In Fig. 5, we see that when ta(MC)^3 is assigned small increasing block sizes, the speedup increases, which we attribute to the arithmetic intensity increasing. However, once block size exceeds a certain value, the speedup curve goes down, which we attribute to the concurrency then dominating the performance and decreasing gradually. We can see that the peak speedup happens around when the block size is set to 400, which agrees with the theoretical analysis.

The introduction of Kahan summation had a surprisingly large impact (see Table 5); this results in the same quality of results in far fewer iterations compared with ta(MC)^3 without Kahan summation.

5 Conclusion

In this paper, we present a modified parallel version of MrBayes, called ta(MC)^3, designed to analyze large protein datasets efficiently on GPUs. The major improvements are: (a) a new task mapping strategy that can reduce intermediate computations and storage, (b) the introduction of Kahan summation to eliminate accumulating roundoff error, and (c) the introduction of 64-bit variables to make analyzing larger datasets possible.

In comparison to other GPU-accelerated versions of MrBayes, we see a runtime improvement of around 9 times faster than MrBayes + BEAGLE, and 2.5 times faster than a(MC)^3 (the predecessor of ta(MC)^3). With eight GTX Titan cards, ta(MC)^3 is nearly 300 times faster than serial MrBayes, and on a 64-node GPU cluster, it achieves over 1000 speedup vs. serial MrBayes.

Acknowledgements. A biology-focused version of this paper has been published [10]. This work is partially supported by NSF of China (grant numbers: 61373018, 11301288), Program for New Century Excellent Talents in University (grant number:

NCET130301) and the Fundamental Research Funds for the Central Universities (grant number: 65141021). Stones was supported by her NSF China Research Fellowship for International Young Scientists (grant number: 11450110409). We would also like to thank Hongju Xia, Jianfu Zhou, Jie Bao and Prof. Qiang Xie for their valuable input.

References

1. Altekar, G., Dwarkadas, S., Huelsenbeck, F., Ronquist, J.P.: Parallel metropolis coupled markov chain monte carlo for bayesian phylogenetic inference. Bioinformatics **20**, 407–415 (2004)
2. Bao, J., Xia, J., Zhou, J., Liu, X.G., Wang, G.: Efficient implementation of MrBayes on multi-GPU. Mol. Biol. Evol. **30**, 1471–1479 (2013)
3. Farber, R.: CUDA Application Design and Development. Morgan Kaufmann, San Francisco (2011)
4. Felsenstein, J.: Evolutionary trees from DNA sequences: a maximum likelihood approach. J. Mol. Evol. **17**, 368–376 (1981)
5. Kahan, W.: Pracniques: further remarks on reducing truncation errors. Commun. ACM **8**(1), 40 (1965). http://doi.acm.org/10.1145/363707.363723
6. Larget, B., Simon, D.L.: Markov chain monte carlo algorithms for the bayesian analysis of phylogenetic trees. Mol. Biol. Evol. **16**, 750–759 (1999)
7. Li, S., Pearl, D.K., Doss, H.: Phylogenetic tree construction using markov chain monte carlo. J. Am. Statist. Assoc. **95**, 493–508 (2000)
8. Mau, B., Newton, M.A.: Phylogenetic inference for binary data on dendrograms using markov chain monte carlo. J. Comp. Graph. Stat. **6**, 122–131 (1997)
9. NVIDIA: CUDA C Programming Guide (2013)
10. Pang, S., Stones, R.J., Ren, M.M., Liu, X.G., Wang, G., Xia, H., Wu, H.Y., Liu, Y., Xie, Q.: GPU MrBayes v3.1: GPU MrBayes on graphics processing units for protein sequence data. Mol. Biol. Evol. **32**(9), 2496–2497 (2015)
11. Pratas, F., Trancoso, P., Stamatakis, A., Sousa, L.: Fine-grain parallelism using multi-core, Cell/BE, and GPU systems: accelerating the phylogenetic likelihood function. In: 42nd International Conference on Parallel Processing, pp. 9–17 (2009)
12. Rannala, B., Yang, Z.: Probability distribution of molecular evolutionary trees: a new method of phylogenetic inference. J. Mol. Evol. **43**, 304–311 (1996)
13. Saitou, N., Nei, M.: The neighbor-joining method: a new method for reconstructing phylogenetic trees. Mol. Biol. Evol. **4**, 406–425 (1987)
14. Schmidt, H., Strimmer, K., Vingron, M., Haeseler, A.: Tree-puzzle: maximum likelihood phylogenetic analysis using quartets and parallel computing. Bioinformatics **18**, 502–504 (2002)
15. Thuiller, W., Lavergne, S., Roquet, C., Boulangeat, I., Lafourcade, B., Araujo, M.B.: Parallel algorithms for bayesian phylogenetic inference. J. Parallel Distrib. Comput. **63**, 707–718 (2003)
16. Xie, Q., Bu, W., Zheng, L.: The bayesian phylogenetic analysis of the 18s RNA sequences from the main lineages of trichophora (insecta: Heteroptera:pentatomomorpha). Mol. Biol. Evol. **34**, 448–451 (2005)
17. Yang, Z.: Phylogenetic analysis using parsimony and likelihood methods. J. Mol. Evol. **42**(2), 294–307 (1996)
18. Zhou, J., Liu, X.G., Stones, D.S., Xie, Q., Wang, G.: MrBayes on a graphics processing unit. Bioinformatics **27**, 1255–1261 (2011)

Paralleled Continuous Tabu Search Algorithm with Sine Maps and Staged Strategy for Solving CNOP

Shijin Yuan$^{(\boxtimes)}$, Yiwen Qian, and Bin Mu

School of Software Engineering,
Tongji University, Shanghai 201804, China
yuanshijin@tongji.edu.cn

Abstract. Intelligent algorithms have been extensively applied in scientific computing. Recently, some researchers apply variable intelligent algorithms to solve conditional nonlinear optimal perturbation (CNOP) which is proposed to study the predictability of numerical weather and climate prediction. Among all the methods that have been studied, the principal components-based great deluge method (PCGD) showed remarkable effect and achieved the best result from the perspectives of CNOP magnitudes and patterns and efficiency. However, compared with adjoint-based method which is referred to as a benchmark, PCGD gets the smaller CNOP magnitude and cannot always get stable solutions. This paper proposes continuous tabu search algorithm with sine map and staged strategy (CTS-SS) to solve CNOP, then parallels CTS-SS with MPI. Based on continuous tabu search algorithm, CTS-SS uses sine chaotic maps to generate the initial candidates to avoid trapping in local optimum and then uses staged search strategy to accelerate the solving speed. To demonstrate the validity of CTS-SS, we take Zebiak-Cane model as a case to compare CTS-SS with the adjoint-based method and PCGD. Experimental results show that CTS-SS can efficiently obtain a satisfactory CNOP magnitude which is more close to the one computed with the adjoint-based method and larger than PCGD. Besides, CTS-SS can get more stable result than PCGD. In Addition, CTS-SS consumes similar time to PCGD and the adjoint-based method with 15 initial guess fields.

Keywords: Continuous tabu search algorithm · Sine chaotic maps · Staged strategy · Parallelization · CNOP · Zebiak-Cane model

1 Introduction

Conditional nonlinear optimal perturbation (CNOP) [1] is an initial perturbation evolving into the largest nonlinear evolution at the prediction time. It has played an important role in predictability and sensitivity studies of meteorology and oceanography [2–4]. The common method for solving the CNOP is the adjoint-based method which is always referred to as the benchmark [5]. However, using the adjoint-based method to compute CNOP requires the gradient information while many modern numerical models have no corresponding gradient information. To avoid that, some researchers have made attempts to apply intelligent algorithms to solve CNOP.

© Springer International Publishing Switzerland 2015
G. Wang et al. (Eds.): ICA3PP 2015, Part III, LNCS 9530, pp. 281–294, 2015.
DOI: 10.1007/978-3-319-27137-8_22

The key issue on applying intelligent algorithms to solve CNOP is to raise efficiency because modern numerical models usually contain tens of thousands dimensions in solution space. For better efficiency, some researchers use feature extraction methods to reduce dimensions and transfer original solution space to lower dimensions and then apply intelligent algorithms in it. Zhang [6] proposed a genetic algorithm based on principal components analysis (PCAGA) in which the principal components analysis (PCA) was used to reduce the dimensions of original solution space and then the genetic algorithm (GA) was applied. Later Wen [7] proposed a principal components-based great deluge method (PCGD) and parallelized PCGD with MPI. The great deluge algorithm with regeneration strategy was applied in an 80-dimension feature space reduced by PCA. Each method could obtain the similar result as the adjoint-based method, which means they are both valid methods for solving CNOP. Among the two methods, PCGD obtained the better result and efficiency. However, the PCGD method still has two disadvantages: the CNOP magnitude still has quite smaller values than the adjoint-based method and the magnitude results are not always stable.

To overcome those disadvantages, we carry out our research on Continuous Tabu Search algorithms (CTS), which has an advantage on stability. However, from experiments we found that CTS consumes quite a lot of time on convergence and sometimes would be trapped into local optimum. To improve that, in this paper we propose a continuous tabu search algorithm with sine maps and staged strategy (CTS-SS) for solving CNOP. We apply sine chaotic maps to generate initial solutions [8] instead of the random initialization to achieve larger CNOP magnitude. Then in order to accelerate the convergence speed, we design a staged search strategy to divide the whole calculation process into two stages and in each stage we select a different set of parameters for computing. Firstly we apply the principal component analysis (PCA) method to reduce the dimensions of original solution space to an 80-dimension feature space, and then in the feature space we apply the CTS-SS algorithm. Finally we parallel the CTS-SS method with message passing interface (MPI) technology.

To demonstrate the validity of CTS-SS for solving CNOP, we take Zebiak-Cane (ZC) model as a case and compare CTS-SS with adjoint-based method [9] and PCGD. Experimental results show CNOP results from CTS-SS is more close to the adjoint-based method compared to PCGD. Besides, CTS-SS can obtain more stable CNOP results than PCGD. From the perspective of efficiency, CTS-SS consumes similar time to the adjoint-based method with 15 initial guess fields. The paralleled CTS-SS costs similar time to the paralleled PCGD, much less than the adjoint-based method. The paralleled CTS-SS reaches the speedup of 8.7 times with 9 cores.

The paper is structured as follows. Section 2 introduces the related work. The concept of CNOP and ZC model will be described. Section 3 describes continuous tabu search first and then gives a detailed definition to CTS-SS. Then the framework of solving CNOP with CTS-SS is depicted in Sect. 4. The experiments and result analysis among CTS-SS, adjoint-based method and PCGD is given in Sect. 5. This paper ends with the conclusion and future work in Sect. 6.

2   Related Works

2.1   CNOP

According to the definition, the perturbation $u_{0\delta}^*$, which makes the objective function $J(x_0)$ achieve the maximum at the prediction time τ under the constraint of $\|u_0\|_\delta \leq \delta$, is CNOP. CNOP is computed as follows:

$$J(u_{0\delta}^*) = \max_{\|u_0\|_\delta \leq \delta} J(u_0) = \max_{\|u_0\|_\delta \leq \delta} \|M_\tau(U_0 + u_0) - M_\tau(U_0)\|_\delta \tag{1}$$

where M_τ means the propagator of a nonlinear model from the initial time to the prediction time τ, $J(u_0)$ the nonlinear evolution of the initial perturbation, u_0 the initial perturbation, and δ the magnitude of uncertainty. Here, $\|\cdot\|_\delta$ denotes the L^2 norm. For convenient computing, Eq. (1) can be converted into a minimum problem:

$$J(u_{0\delta}^*) = \min_{\|u_0\|_\delta \leq \delta} -J(u_0). \tag{2}$$

2.2   Zebiak-Cane Model

The ZC model [10] is a mesoscale air-sea coupled model for the Tropical Pacific. Since ZC model successfully forecasted the El Nino event of 1986–1987, it has been widely applied to the research of the predictability and dynamics of ENSO [11].

In ZC model, an annual mean state or seasonal cycle of both ocean and atmosphere is obtained from data and the evolution of anomalies with respect to this reference state is computed with the model. This coupled model produces recurring warm events that are irregular in both amplitude and spacing, but favor a 3–4 year periods. Analysis of these results indicated that ENSO is a basin wide oscillation in the coupled ocean-atmosphere system. The ZC model consists of three sub-models: the atmospheric model, ocean model and coupled model.

3   CTS and CTS-SS

Through a mass of experiments, we find that solving CNOP with CTS has drawbacks mentioned above. To overcome these, we apply sine chaotic maps to explore the whole solution space in a traversal way. Then we take staged searching strategy to search for global best value. The two improvements added in CTS forms CTS-SS algorithm.

In this section, firstly we introduce basic concepts of continuous tabu search, then introduce two improvements, at last pseudo code of CTS-SS is given.

3.1   Continuous Tabu Search

Hu [12] proposed the idea of Continuous Tabu Search (CTS). The method was later enhanced by Chelouah and Siarry [13]. CTS algorithm is described as follows:

1. Initialize the *current point* C and generate m neighbors $(S_1, S_2, ..., S_m)$ in n-dimensional space by Eq. (3). $S_{i,j}$ is the value of j-th dimension of i-th neighbor. The radius of the neighborhood is r.

$$C_j = rand(-1, 1)$$
$$S_{i,j} = rand(-1, 1), \quad j = 1, 2...n; \quad i = 1, 2...m \tag{3}$$

2. Use Eq. (4) to keep every neighbor in the neighborhood hypersphere.

$$S_{i,j} = \begin{cases} S_{i,j}, & \|C - S_i\| < = r \\ C_j - \frac{r}{\|C - S_i\|} \times (C_j - S_{i,j}), \|C - S_i\| > r \end{cases}, j = 1, 2, ...n; i = 1, 2, ..., m \tag{4}$$

3. Compute the adaptive values of C and copy it to the best solution $f(S_{best})$.
4. Compute every neighbor and select the neighbor with the best adaptive value to update the C according to the Tabu Criterion. A tabu neighbor can be accepted as a next move if it outperforms the S_{best}.
5. The process of generating random neighbors and selecting the best ones is continued until it reaches the max iteration number *maxcycle*.

3.2   CTS-SS

In order to escape from local optimum, we use sine maps to replace random initialization. To accelerate the convergence speed and raise the efficiency, we design staged search strategy. In the next three subsections we are about to describe the two improvements and utilize the pseudo code to demonstrate the whole process of CTS-SS.

The Initialization with Sine Chaos Maps. As is shown above, the Eq. (3) is used for initialization of the CTS algorithm. Through many experiments we find that sometimes the random function cannot get good initial solutions. So we use sine chaotic maps based initialization to replace the random initialization. Here, sine map equation is defined as follows:

$$x_{0,j} = rand(-1, 1), \quad j = 1, 2, ..., n \tag{5}$$

$$x_{k+1,j} = \sin(\pi x_{k,j}), \quad x_{k,j} \in (-1, 1), \quad k = 0, 1, 2...K \tag{6}$$

$$C_{i,j} = x_{k+1,j}, \quad i = 1, 2, \ldots, pop \tag{7}$$

$$C = \min\{C_1, C_2, \ldots, C_{pop}\} \quad i = 1, 2, \ldots, pop \tag{8}$$

where k is the iteration counter, while K is the preset maximum number of chaotic iterations and C_i is a certain individual. Compared with Eq. (3), the Eq. (5) use random function to initialize the chaotic operator x and then Eqs. (6, 7) add sine function to improve the ergodicity of every neighbor. The initialization of CTS is to directly generate a random point while the CTS-SS is different. As depicted in Eq. (7), CTS-SS randomly select pop points and disperse them in a widespread way by sine map. Then in Eq. (8), the one with the best adaptive value is selected as the current point.

Staged Searching Strategy. In CTS, a fixed set of parameters are utilized in Eq. (4) through the whole searching period, which makes the efficiency degraded. Considering that the more space has been explored, the less the rest of the search space is. We don't have to keep the same parameters setting through the whole process.

Based on this idea, we proposed a staged searching strategy to divide the whole searching process into two stages. We can choose the most suitable parameters in Eq. (4) for each stage. In Stage 1 the iteration-number and the neighbor-number in every iteration step can be a bit large to locate the minimum area. In Stage 2 since the search range has been reduced, both iteration-number and neighbor-number should be modified either in a right way. In stage 1, we change the radius in Eq. (4) to be R_1 and the neighbor-number to be m_1. In Stage 2, we replace r by R_2 and m by m_2. Thus the original Eq. (4) should be converted into Eqs. (9) and (10) respectively:

$$S_{i,j} = \begin{cases} S_{i,j}, & \|C - S_i\| <= R_1 \\ C_j - \frac{R_1}{\|C - S_i\|} \times (C_j - S_{i,j}), & \|C - S_i\| > R_1 \end{cases} \quad j = 1, 2, \ldots n; \ i = 1, 2, \ldots, m \tag{9}$$

$$S_{i,j} = \begin{cases} S_{i,j}, & \|C - S_i\| <= R_2 \\ C_j - \frac{R_2}{\|C - S_i\|} \times (C_j - S_{i,j}), & \|C - S_i\| > R_2 \end{cases} \quad j = 1, 2, \ldots n; \ i = 1, 2, \ldots, m \tag{10}$$

where the Eq. (9) is used for the computing in Stage 1 and the Eq. (10) in Stage 2. Besides, the *maxcycle* is replaced by *maxcycle1* and *maxcycle2*. The number *maxcycle1* and *maxcycle2* represent the max loop number of each stages.

The Algorithm of CTS-SS. In this subsection, the complete algorithm of CTS-SS is demonstrated as follows.

Algorithm 1. CTS-SS

```
Setting parameters:
Stage1:  neighbor-number: m₁; neighborhood-radius: R₁;
         max iteration number: maxcycle1;
Stage2:  neighbor-number: m₂; neighborhood-radius: R₂;
         max iteration number: maxcycle2;
Others:  the objective function f();
         Dimension number n; Chaotic iteration number: K;
         i=i1=i2=0,j=0; iter1=iter2=0; k=0
         Initial individuals number: pop;
Initialization with Sine Maps:
1:  for i=1 to pop do
2:         for j=1 to n do
3:             for k=1 to K do
4:                 use Eq. (7,8,9) to generate Cᵢ,ⱼ;
5:             end for
6:         end for
7:  end for
8:  use Eq. (10) to obtain current point C.
Loop of Stage I:
9:  for iter1=1 to maxcycle1 do
10:       for i1=1 to m1 do
11:           for j=1 to n do
12:           Generate Sᵢ,ⱼ by Eq. (5) and Eq. (11), set r =R₁
13:               end for
14:           Calculate f(Sᵢ)
15:           if Sᵢ is in not tabu list then
16:                  if f(Sᵢ)≤best_value then
17:               set C in tabu list, best_value=f(Sᵢ); C=Sᵢ
18:                  end if
19:               end if
20:       end for
21:  end for
Loop of Stage II:
22:  for iter2=1 to maxcycle2 do
23:         for i2=1 to m₂ do
24:             for j=1 to n do
25:           Generate Sᵢ,ⱼ by Eq.(5) and Eq.(12); set r=R₂
26:               end for
27:           Calculate f(Sᵢ)
28:           if Sᵢ is not in tabu list then
29:                  if f(Sᵢ)≤best_value then
30:               set C in tabu list, best_value=f(Sᵢ); C=Sᵢ
31:                  end if
32:               end if
33:           end for
34:  end for
Output: Current point C, best_value
```

---

4 The Framework of Solving CNOP with CTS-SS

There are two physical variables in ZC model which named sea surface temperature anomalies (SSTA) and thermocline height anomalies (THA). And generally we pick 30*34 grids when study ENSO event. So the optimization object u_0, refer to Eq. (1), is a vector which is composed of SSTA and THA.

So original solution space is a high-dimension space with $30 \times 34 \times 2$ (2040) dimensions. Even we remove the unused marginal area, there are still $20 \times 27 \times 2$ (1080) dimensions [14]. Therefore, if we use CTS-SS algorithm directly, the high dimension in ZC model will result in the high complexity of computing the neighborhood hyper-sphere. According to [6, 7], we select Principal Components Analysis (PCA) method to reduce dimensions in this paper. The framework of solving CNOP with intelligent algorithms is demonstrated in Fig. 1.

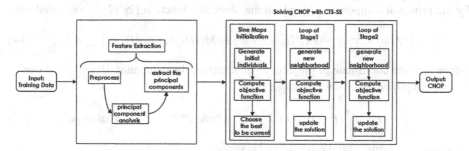

Fig. 1. The framework of solving CNOP with CTS-SS

As is shown in Fig. 1, the whole process contains 4 steps: Input training data, Feature extraction, Solving CNOP with CTS-SS and Output the CNOP results.

In this section, we first introduce feature extraction method, then we demonstrate the algorithm of solving CNOP with CTS-SS. At last we introduce the parallel strategy.

4.1 Feature Extraction

At the beginning, we run the numerical model to export the training dataset, $X = \{x_1, x_2, \cdots x_n\}$, $x_i \in R^D (i = 1, 2 \cdots n)$. Then we use Eqs. (11) and (12) to pre-process the dataset, according to [7]. In Eq. (11) a is a positive coefficient.

$$x_i = x_i/a \ (i = 1, 2 \cdots n) \tag{11}$$

$$x'_i = x_i - \bar{x} \ (i = 1, 2 \cdots n), \bar{x} = \frac{1}{n} \sum x_i \tag{12}$$

Then we put the data into PCA program to convert the original high dimension space to lower dimension feature space. Then we search the solution in the new feature space and map the final result back to the original space with the singular vectors. The principal components can be acquired by the Eigen-decomposition:

$$XX^T P = P\Sigma \qquad (13)$$

where Σ is a diagonal matrix whose diagonal entries are the corresponding eigenvalues. Since the matrix, XX^T is a positive definite matrix, the columns of the eigenvectors matrix P are mutually orthogonal. Then the n ($n \ll D$) eigenvectors corresponding to the top n biggest eigenvalues are taken as the principal components.

4.2   Solving CNOP with CTS-SS

In order to solve CNOP with CTS-SS, we need to set the objective function. As is shown in Eqs. (1, 2), the perturbation u_0 needs to be projected onto the space expanded by the principal components, by which the objective function Eq. (2) is converted into:

$$J(\omega) = \min - \|M_\tau(U_0 + P \cdot \omega) - M_\tau(U_0)\|, s.t. \|P \cdot \omega\|_\delta \leq \delta \qquad (14)$$

where ω is the coordinate of projection. In addition, the constraint $\|P \cdot \omega\|_\delta \leq \delta$ can be further simplified as follows:

$$\|P \cdot \omega\| = (P \cdot \omega)^T (P \cdot \omega) = \omega^T P^T P\omega \text{ (where } P^T P = I) = \omega^T \omega = \|\omega\|. \qquad (15)$$

as a result, the final optimal objective becomes:

$$J(\omega) = \min - \|M_\tau(U_0 + P \cdot \omega) - M_\tau(U_0)\|, s.t. \|\omega\|_\delta \leq \delta \qquad (16)$$

here, the argument for the objective function has been changed into the coefficient ω rather than u_0. As the coefficient ω locate in a space with the dimension n ($n \ll D$), it can be obtained by CTS-SS. The algorithm 2 denotes the process of CTS-SS:

Algorithm 2. The Algorithm of solving CNOP with CTS-SS

```
Input: training dataset X
Feature extraction:
1:   Make the eigen-decomposition of XX^T by Eq. (13)~(15);
2:   Take the top n eigenvectors as principal components;
Setting Parameters:
     Stage1: m₁, R₁, maxcycle1;(defined in algorithm 1)
     Stage2: m₂, R₂, maxcycle2;(defined in algorithm 1)
     Others: the objective function J(ω), shown as Eq.(18);
             n, pop, K; (defined in algorithm 1)
             i=i1=i2=0,j=0;iter1=iter2=0;k=0
CTS-SS:
3:   ω is treated as S and C;J(ω) as f(S);(see algorithm 1)
Output: ω= C, J(ω)=best_value, return back to Eq.(18)
```

4.3   The Parallelization of CTS-SS

During the computation of the CNOP with CTS-SS, the time consumption increases with the rise of times of invoking objective function. In order to reduce the time consumption, we take MPI to parallelize CTS-SS.

When we use MPI technology, we need to set the number of processes first. Supposing that we set N as the processes number, when the MPI program runs, one process will be treated as the main process called master and other N-1 are created as slave process. Master allocates sub-tasks to each slave process. As one slave process has received the sub-task, it will begin to work and send the results back to master.

In the CTS-SS method, we follow the rule to divide sub-tasks: We divide the m neighbors equally into N-1 groups. When the computing begins, the master process split each group of neighbors to each slave process. Then in each iteration step, each slave process will receive m/(N-1) neighbors and compute their adaptive values in parallel. When the computation is finished, they send the results back to master.

5   Experiments and Results Analysis

All the experiments run on an HP Z800 workstation server with Intel Xeon CPU E5645, 24 cores and 8G RAM and operating system is CentOS 6.5. All the codes are written in FORTRAN language and complied by GFortran Compiler.

In this paper we adopt the Zebiak-Cane model (ZC model) as a case study. We analyze the validity of CTS-SS from the perspective of CNOP magnitude and pattern. Besides, we make the analyses on stability and efficiency. Then a comparison is performed with the PCGD and adjoint-based method [9] (ADJ-method). After that we parallelize the CTS-SS and compare it with the paralleled PCGD.

5.1   Parameter Settings

After many experiments, the parameters are set in Table 1.

Table 1. Parameter Settings of CTS-SS in experiments

Name	Meaning	Value
n	Dimension number of the feature space	80
pop	Initial individuals number	60
K	Chaotic iteration number	160
ε	Tabu coefficient	0.01
m_1	number of neighbors in each step in stage 1	24
R_1	Radius of neighborhood in stage 1	0.1
$maxcycle1$	Max iteration number in stage 1	70
m_2	Number of neighbors in each step in stage 2	32
R_2	Radius of neighborhood in stage 2	0.05
$maxcycle2$	Max iteration number in stage 2	40

5.2   Validity Analysis

In this subsection we analyze the validity on solving CNOP with CTS-SS from the perspective of CNOP magnitude and patterns, which is generally used to judge whether the result is good or not. In the experiments we set the dimension number of the feature space as 80, which is the same as [7].

For the CNOP magnitude, our inspection standard is the larger the better. What's more, the magnitude of 12 months in a year should show up the same tendency with ADJ-method and PCGD method.

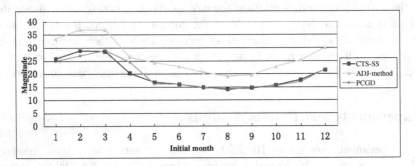

Fig. 2. The magnitude of the CNOP at each initial month. The x-axis represents the each initial month. The y-axis represents the magnitude of the CNOP. The ADJ-method is represented in the yellow line with triangles; The PCGD in green line with '*'s and the CTS-SS in the pink line with squares. (Color figure online)

As is shown in Fig. 2, we can see the magnitude of CNOP each initial month, in which we set each month as the initial month and optimization time span as 9 months. The yellow line represents the magnitude of CNOP generated by adjoint-based method; CTS-SS generates the pink line; the green line is generated by PCGD.

From the Fig. 2, we can observe that both of CTS-SS and PCGD have the same tendency with results of the adjoint-based method. The results of CTS-SS are a bit larger than that of PCGD except March and April.

It's obvious that the ADJ-method has larger magnitudes than the other two. The reason is that both CTS-SS and PCGD takes the same number of principal components, which is only 80. Despite the dimension reducing causes a little information loss, we consider it acceptable because the difference is not large and it can capture the correct CNOP spatial feature in the pattern.

As there are 12 groups of results from each initial month, it is not wise to list all of their patterns. Furthermore, if the patterns in the months with the largest gap between CTS-SS and the adjoint-based method look similar, the other patterns must be similar as well. From Fig. 2 we can see that the CNOP in January has the largest difference of magnitudes between CTS-SS and the adjoint-based method. So we choose the results and the related CNOP patterns of January to demonstrate the effectiveness of the proposed method. As is shown in Fig. 3, the initial month is January and the blue and red colors denote negative and positive. Figure 3 represents the patterns produced by

CTS-SS method, the adjoint-based method and PCGD method. In each figure, the first row is the SSTA, while the second is the THA and the third is the evolution of the SSTA. In ZC model the positive and negative number are used as the symbol to describe the El-Nino event.

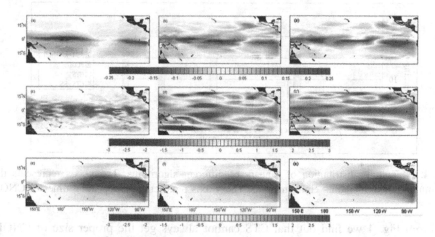

Fig. 3. CNOP pattern in January. Three columns from left to right are respectively the patterns of ADJ-method, PCGD and CTS-SS. Three rows of each sub-figure are the patterns of SSTA, THA and the evolution of SSTA, respectively. (Red color represents positive and blue color represents negative) (Color figure online)

From the pattern showed in Fig. 3 can we learn that all the three methods have the same physical meanings and the characters that the negative area is on the left while the positive area on the right are the same as well. Since the number of principal components of the adjoint-based method is different from that of the other two, it's a normal phenomenon that the THA, which is described in the second row, also looks different from the others. However, they all have the same characters that the middle areas are positive while both sides of the positive area are negative. In the third row, the patterns of SSTA evolution from each method look quite similar except that the red area in the adjoint-based method and CTS-SS are larger than that in PCGD. So we can make the conclusion that the results of the CTS-SS method are close to the adjoint-based method, while better than the PCGD method.

Since the gap of CNOP magnitude is not so large, and the spatial features on CNOP patterns are similar too, the CTS-SS can be regarded as an approximate solution to the adjoint-based method.

5.3 Stability Analysis

As Intelligence algorithms are all stochastic, even the same inputs could obtain different outputs. In CTS-SS, we use sine maps to improve the initialization, so it is meaningful to analyze and compare the stability of CTS-SS with the CTS method. In the stability experiments we compared the CTS-SS method with the adjoint-based method, the CTS method and the PCGD method. We conducted 30 times of experiments for each method, the initial month is still January. Figure 4 shows the distribution of CNOP magnitudes from each method.

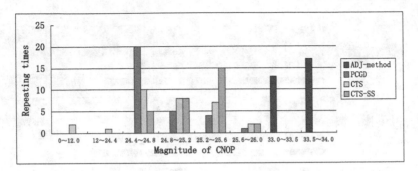

Fig. 4. Magnitude distribution of January of different algorithms. The x-axis represents the magnitude range, including eight intervals. The y-axis represents the repeating times of CNOP

From Fig. 4 we find out that CTS cannot always get the proper size of CNOP. It runs 3 times into the 0–24.4 area and the data is uniformly distributed, which means sometimes the initial solutions generated by the random initialization are quite close to each other so that the computation is trapped into local optimal position. The results of the adjoint-based method are all in the 33–34 area, which shows an outstanding stability. The results of PCGD represented by the red columns are mostly gathered from 24.4 to 24.8. The results of CTS-SS represented by the green columns are mostly gathered from 24.8 to 25.6, which are more close to the right correct solution than that of PCGD. Compared with PCGD, it's obvious that CTS-SS is more stable.

5.4 Efficiency Analysis

In order to improve the efficiency of solving CNOP with CTS-SS and observe how fast its speedup can reach, we have achieved the parallelization of the CTS-SS method with MPI technology. In this experiment we follow the rule mentioned in Sect. 4.3 to parallel the CTS-SS method.

To demonstrate the efficiency of the paralleled CTS-SS, we compare it with the paralleled PCGD (pPCGD) and the adjoint-based method with 15 initial guess fields. We have also made the comparison between CTS and CTS-SS to reveal the advantage the staged searching strategy, which accelerates the convergence speed. In this experiment, we choose number 1, 2, 4, 5, 7, 9, 12 as the process number respectively. Figure 5 shows the time consuming of several different methods.

As the consuming time of methods is demonstrated in Fig. 5, the adjoint-based method with 15 initial guess fields consumes about 432 s while the PCGD method and CTS consumes about 332 s and 459 s respectively. The CTS-SS costs 393 s, which depicts that the staged searching method actually has an apparent effect on the convergence speed. It is obvious that the PCGD method is the fastest in serial computation.

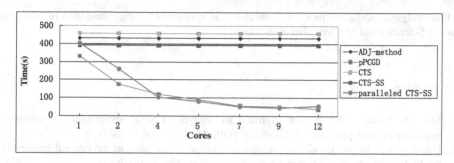

Fig. 5. The time consuming. The x-axis is the number of cores and the y-axis is the consuming time of every methods. ADJ-method is in dark blue line with diamonds; CTS in pink line with squares; CTS-SS in blue line with squares; the paralleled PCGD in red line and the paralleled CTS-SS in green line. (Color figure online)

In Fig. 5, the x-axis is the number of cores and the y-axis is the consuming time of different methods. From the pattern can we learn that when cores increase, both pPCGD and paralleled CTS-SS consumes less time. More importantly, the paralleled CTS-SS runs a bit faster than the pPCGD method when the number of cores ranges from 4 to 9. When the number of cores is 9, the paralleled CTS-SS and costs 46 s and its speed reaches 8.7 times, which is its upper limit. However, when 12 cores are set, the consuming time of the PCGD is about 37 s whose speedup can reach 9.7. Although the paralleled CTS-SS cannot be as fast as the pPCGD, it's quite close to that and according to the Figs. 2 and 4 it has better results most of the time.

6 Conclusion

In order to develop a more stable method for solving CNOP, we made our study on the CTS method. Then use sine maps and the staged searching strategy on CTS to overcome its drawbacks. Based on the two improvements, we propose a CTS-SS method and then implement the parallel version by MPI technology.

In this paper we use ZC model as a case and analyze the validity of solving CNOP with CTS-SS from the perspective of the CNOP magnitude and patterns. After that we make the comparison with the adjoint-based method and the PCGD method. In this paper we have also analyzed the stability and efficiency of solving CNOP with several different methods. The experiment results show that the CTS-SS method can obtain a satisfactory result and the CNOP magnitude is more close to the adjoint-based method. The time consuming of CTS-SS is quite similar to that of the adjoint-based method with 15 initial guess fields. In addition, the time consuming of the paralleled CTS-SS is similar to the paralleled PCGD. Compared with PCGD, the CTS-SS method not only can achieve satisfactory results and time efficiency but also has a better stability. When 9 cores are set, the speedup of the paralleled CTS-SS can reach 8.7 times.

Our future work is trying to apply the CTS-SS method on the other complex numerical models for solving CNOP, such as the MM5 model and the WRF model, the solution space of which is no less than 30,000 dimensions. To achieve that goal, the key issue is how to rise up the efficiency. It's a main task of our future works.

Acknowledgments. In this paper, the research was sponsored by the Foundation of National Natural Science Fund of China (No. 41405097).

References

1. Mu, M., Duan, W.S.: A new approach to studying ENSO predictability: conditional nonlinear optimal perturbation. Chin. Sci. Bull. **48**, 1045–1047 (2003)
2. Duan, W.S., Mu, M.: Conditional nonlinear optimal perturbation as the optimal precursors for El Niño-Southern oscillation events. Geogr. Res. **109**, 1–12 (2004)
3. Mu, M., Sun, L., Dijkstra, H.: The sensitivity and stability of the ocean's thermocline circulation to finite amplitude freshwater perturbations. J. Phys. Oceanogr. **34**, 2305–2315 (2004)
4. Wu, X.G., Mu, M.: Impact of horizontal diffusion on the nonlinear stability of thermohaline circulation in a modified box model. J. Phys. Oceanogr. **39**, 798–805 (2009)
5. Birgin, E.G., Martinez, J.E.M., Raydan, M.: No monotone spectral projected gradient methods on convex sets. Soc. Ind. Appl. Math. J. Optim. **10**, 1196–1211 (2000)
6. Mu, B., Zhang, L.L.: PCAGA: principal component analysis based genetic algorithm for solving conditional nonlinear optimal perturbation. In: International Joint Conference on Neural Networks (2015)
7. Wen, S.C., Mu, B., Yuan, S.J., Li, H.Y., Ren, J.H.: PCGD: principal components based great deluge method for solving CNOP. In: 2015 IEEE Congress on Evolutionary Computation
8. Gao, W., Liu, S.: A modified artificial bee colony algorithm. Comput. Oper. Res. **39**(3), 687–697 (2012)
9. Xu, H., Duan, W.S., Wang, J.C.: The tangent linear model and adjoint of a coupled ocean-atmosphere model and its application to the predictability of ENSO. In: Proceedings of IEEE International Conference on Geoscience and Remote Sensing Symposium, pp. 640–643 (2006)
10. Zebiak, S.E., Cane, M.A.: A model El Niño-Southern oscillation. Mon. Weather Rev. **115** (10), 2262–2278 (1987)
11. Yu, Y.S., Duan, W.S., Xu, H., Mu, M.: Dynamics of nonlinear error growth and season-dependent predictability of El Niño events in the ZebiakCane model. Q. J. Roy. Meteorol. Soc. **135**(645), 2146–2160 (2009)
12. Hu, N.: Tabu search method with random moves for globally optimal design. Int. J. Numer. Meth. Eng. **35**(5), 1055–1070 (1992)
13. Chelouah, R., Siarry, P.: Enhanced continuous tabu search: an algorithm for the global optimization of multiminima functions. In: Voss, S., Martello, S., Osman, I.H., Roucairol, C. (eds.) Meta-heuristics, Advances and Trends in Local Search Paradigms for Optimization, pp. 49–61. Kluwer Academic Publishers, Dordrecht (1999)
14. Chen, L., Duan, W.S., Xu, H.: A SVD-based ensemble projection algorithm for calculating conditional nonlinear optimal perturbation. Sci. Chin. Earth Sci. **58**, 385–394 (2015)

Service Dependability
and Security in Distributed
and Parallel Systems

VCLT: An Accurate Trajectory Tracking Attack Based on Crowdsourcing in VANETs

Chi Lin[1,2](✉), Kun Liu[1,2], Bo Xu[1,2], Jing Deng[3], Chang Wu Yu[4],
and Guowei Wu[1,2]

[1] School of Software, Dalian University of Technology, Dalian 116621, China
c.lin@dlut.edu.cn
[2] Key Laboratory for Ubiquitous Network and Service Software of Liaoning Province,
Dalian 116621, China
[3] Department of Computer Science, University of North Carolina at Greensboro,
Greensboro, NC 27412, USA
[4] Department of Computer Science and Information Engineering,
Chung Hua University, Hsinchu, Taiwan

Abstract. We investigate trajectory tracking in Vehicular Ad hoc Networks (VANETs) in this work. Previous tracking methods suffer from low accuracy, large overhead, and big error. In this paper, we propose a Vehicular Crowdsourcing Localization and Tracking (VCLT) scheme for mounting a trajectory tracking attack. In our scheme, crowdsourcing technique is applied to sample the location information of certain users. Then matrix completion algorithm is used to generate our predictions of the users' trajectories. To alleviate the error disturbance of the recovered location data, Kalman filter technique is implemented and the trajectories of certain users are recovered with accuracy. At last, extensive simulations are conducted to show the performance of our scheme. Simulations results reveal that the proposed approach is able to accurately track the trajectories of certain users.

Keywords: Trajectory tracking · Crowdsourcing · Matrix completion · Kalman filter · VANETs

1 Introduction

In recent years, there have been growing interests and research efforts in the area of Vehicular Ad-hoc Networks (VANETs) [1]. VANETs can provide users with various kinds of services, such as safety information delivery, entertainment, commercial recommendation, and location based services (LBS). Location and trajectory, the sorted list of locations through which a user travels, are fundamental to most of these services. Therefore, it is critical to provide efficient trajectory tracking. Most of prior arts used the methods of Variable-order Markov model [2], Probabilistic model [3] and Dirichlet-multinomial model [4]. These techniques suffer from the following drawbacks:

© Springer International Publishing Switzerland 2015
G. Wang et al. (Eds.): ICA3PP 2015, Part III, LNCS 9530, pp. 297–310, 2015.
DOI: 10.1007/978-3-319-27137-8_23

1. Complicated and costly architecture. Many tracking methods require complex system architecture to track user's trajectory. For example, an on-board tracking device would require speed/GPS sensors and information from Road Side Units (RSUs) to collect surrounding geospatial information and then transmit these data to location server for computation [5].
2. Low accuracy and big error. In general, GPS can only provide an accuracy within 5~30 meters in a dense urban city environment. Recovered targets are usually represented by a matrix. In addition, it often has the problem of missing data or noise pollution [6].

Motivated by the aforementioned drawbacks and to enhance attacking accuracy, we propose a scheme that uses a unique Matrix Completion technique in trajectory tracking or recovering area. Our scheme utilizes the concept of crowdsourcing to sample the location information of a target user. Then matrix completion technique is used to recover the location information matrix, which accurately describes the timely location information of a target user. In addition, we employ Kalman filter to further improve accuracy. Generally, the contributions of this paper can be summarized as follows.

1. We propose a trajectory tracking scheme called VCLT that takes advantages of crowdsourcing in sampling vehicles' location information.
2. To recover the trajectory of mobile users, matrix completion mechanism is used. In the matrix completion calculation process, a target's location history is sampled by crowdsourcing, then a complete trajectory will be restored.
3. To enhance the accuracy of the recovered trajectory data, we use Kalman filter to reduce the errors generated in matrix completion stage.

The rest of the paper is organized as follows. We reviewed related literatures in Sect. 2, and present the preliminary techniques in Sect. 3. The crowdsourcing based localization and tracking scheme is introduced in Sect. 4. We report our extensive simulation results in Sect. 5 and discuss and conclude the paper in Sect. 6.

2   Literature Review

Vehicle tracking systems [7] can be used in theft prevention, retrieval of lost vehicles, providing traffic oriented services on lanes. There are two main categories for trajectory tracking attack in VANETs: Dynamic Position-aware method and Static Position-aware method. They are just corresponding to two different ways of dedicated short-range communication (DSRC) [8] that is exchanging information either vehicle-to-vehicle (V2V) or vehicle-to-infrastructure (V2I). In the Static Position-aware method, it relies on the fixed-location Road Side Units (RSU) and cellular base stations. Hidden Markov Model is proposed in [10] to recover trajectory sequence by analyzing trace histories of mobile nodes and the spatial correlation between the base station and the mobile station. It has a stable trajectory recovering ability under the rigid assumption that there is a high state transmission chance between the nodes. However, V2V communication is a more viable solution for the near future [11] and Dynamic Position-aware method is well adapted to the ever-changing traffic flows. For the tracking purpose, each vehicle is assumed to be equipped with a DSRC radio and a GPS receiver. As shown in the Fig. 1, each vehicle is designed to continuously report its own status by broadcasting safety messages. At the same time, each vehicle also tracks movements of neighboring vehicles based on information received from them over the shared channel [12]. Probabilistic model [3] shows its great application value in solving long-term trajectory tracking by using a small amount of mobile observation data, but the exact success probability is difficult to be measured.

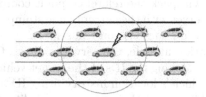

Fig. 1. Tracking the position of neighboring vehicles

Besides trajectory tracking, crowdsourcing can also play an important assistant role in the position-aware process. In general, crowdsourcing is the approach of obtaining needed content by soliciting contributions from a large group of users. Based on crowd-generated data, we can extract the information to optimize localization and tracking. In the field of indoor location [13], a hot research trend is to incorporate crowdsourcing model and built-in sensors in today's smartphone. In parallel, we are being witness of a fast growing needs for improving driving experience based on crowdsourcing like road traffic aware trip planning [14], alert broadcasting [15] or car-pooling services [16].

3   Preliminary

We present preliminary on crowdsourcing, matrix completion, and Kalman filter in this section.

3.1   Crowdsourcing Computation Model

The Crowdsourcing Computation Model is proposed to get the target vehicle's information by gathering the efforts of the vehicles during a specific period. Our model is divided into three sub-module: position-aware module, online localization module and self-learning module, as shown in Fig. 2.

In the position-aware module, we randomly select some nodes as the detectors. The detectors' responsibility is to collect IDs from the surrounding nodes. The ID is mapped to the Media Access Control Address of the vehicle, which is unique.

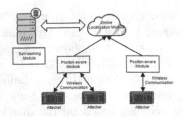

Fig. 2. Mobile vehicle tracking system

We neglect the weak signal connection, which can ensure the accuracy of the location. The detectors will pack the reference point coordinate and the ID set and upload them to the server with the current time stamp. All these information is stored in dynamic location database on the server.

In the online localization module, the server analyzes the location data and extract the information matching the IDs of the target vehicles. We create a map to store the individual vehicle's location history using ID as the key. Each entry combines the source position and the sampling time like (x, y, t). The map is left to generate sparse matrix for further trajectory recovery.

In the self-learning module, we accept feedback from the comparison between the output and the observation and handle the subtle deviation. Based on the large amount of history location data, we can figure out habitual traveling route of the targeted vehicle. Dynamic location database will be continuously updated during operation, so that it can adapt to the dynamic VANETs environment.

3.2 Matrix Completion Method

Method Overview. Matrix Completion (MC) [17] is an extension of Compressive Sensing [18,19], which has become a popular research direction in the fields of Signal Processing, Machine Learning, Artificial Intelligence and so on in recent years. MC is the process of recovering a sparse matrix $M \in R^{m \times t}$ with rank r, with some unknown or missing values. It is mainly under the assumptions that the matrix is low-rank, i.e., $r \ll m$ or t. In other words, MC enables us to obtain the predicted traveling route and we compare it to the real trajectory.

We design Vehicle Trajectory Recovery based on Matrix Completion (VTRMC) to take advantage of space and time correlation between each source node and reduce the sampling frequency. The method acquires the result from the online localization module of the Crowdsourcing Computation Model, and recover the locations of target with tolerable deviation based on Low-rank MC.

In the online localization module, we have selected detector vehicle randomly, and denote their reference point as $P_i(x_i, y_i)$ and the time as t. We generate an original map constructed by these source vehicle ID, location vectors and the sampling time. Based on these information, we supplement the missing location vector according to timetable, that is to say the size of the original map is expanded to N ($N > \max(n_i)$). Using the map, we construct the sparse matrix including the original and missing location vectors.

In this paper, we mainly use matrix completion to solve the problem of missing information recovery. Because we have got a complete location list at every determinate time, it can help us recover the trajectory more efficiently. We adopt a high performance linear operation to get the result and the reconstruction will be addressed by solving the following optimization problem [20]:

$$\min \text{rank}(X) \text{ s.t. } A(X) = B. \tag{1}$$

Here, X presents an observation matrix containing complete information, and it is also $m \times n$ order low-rank matrix. A is a linear map from X to B and B is a sparse matrix.

However, the reconstruction problem in (1) is NP-hard. The time required to solve the problem increases exponentially with the growth of the matrix size. So for the mass matrix, rank minimization method is almost unsolvable.

But for the reason that the rank r of a matrix is as same as the number of non-zero singular values of it, we use the sum of the singular values, which is nuclear norm, approximating for rank of the matrix.

Thus, problem in (1) can be converted into the problem as follows:

$$\|X\|_* \text{ s.t. } A(X) = B. \tag{2}$$

Here, we define $\|X\|_*$ as a nuclear norm of the matrix X meeting the following condition:

$$\|X\|_* = \sum_{i=1}^{n} \sigma_i(X). \tag{3}$$

Nuclear norm corresponds to l_1 norm of the vector composed of the matrix singular value, and the rank corresponds to l_0 norm of the vector.

Sparse Matrix Completion. In the session, an observation matrix is builded, and the rows of the matrix represent the x(y) coordinate of single source vehicle at every determinate time, while the columns represent the time. The time interval between each columns is even.

With more vehicles involved in sampling, we have a greater opportunity of capturing the source information from the target vehicle. As a result, the accuracy of the positioning result will be higher. In our scheme, for vehicles' movement is a continuous process, our observation matrix X can be considered to have a low rank characteristics. Based on the actual situation, a vehicle's location information usually has strong association with the continuity of the route.

We donate $A_{N \times T}(X) = B$ indicate the sampling process. X is an observation matrix, and each element in the matrix represents the sampling x(y) position of vehicle i at time j. For a better expression, $A(X)$ can be defined as a matrix $Q_{N \times T}(t)$ as below:

$$Q(i, j) = \begin{cases} 1 & \text{if vehicle } i \text{ at time } j \text{ is sampled,} \\ 0 & \text{otherwise.} \end{cases} \tag{4}$$

We can compute by this formula

$$A_{N \times T}(X) = Q_{N \times T}(t) \cdot X(t) = B, \tag{5}$$

where $\cdot$ represents a dot product of two matrix.

As illustrated before, we can solve the following optimization problem to reconstruct the observation matrix:

$$\min \|X(t)\|_* \text{ s.t. } A_{N \times T}(X) = B. \tag{6}$$

3.3 Kalman Filtering

We find that there are some errors in the restored matrix after VTRMC. We need efficient ways to filter noise out of original data. So, we choose to suppress the sampling data noise by Kalman filtering.

Kalman filter [21] is the optimal filter with a minimum mean-square error. It was first used to estimate the parameters of stochastic processes, and soon gained wide application in the problems of the filtering and optimal control.

The starting point of the Kalman filter is based on the dynamic model of the system:

$$x(n) = \Phi(n, n - 1)x(n - 1) + \Delta(n)u(n) + \omega(n - 1), \tag{7}$$

$$z(n) = H(n) \times n + v(n). \tag{8}$$

Here, we donate $x(n)$ as M-dimensional state vector of the system. The purpose of the Kalman filtering is in accordance with the best estimation of the state vector. The other symbols are defined in Table 1 below:

Table 1. Variable definition of Kalman Filter

$u(n)$	S-dimensional system input vector
$z(n)$	L-dimensional measurement vector
$\omega(n)$	M-dimensional system noise vector
$v(n)$	L-dimensional measurement noise vector
$\Phi(n, n - 1)$	$M \times M$ system transition matrix
$\Delta(n)$	$M \times S$ system input matrix
$H(n)$	$L \times M$ measurement matrix

Additionally, noise vectors $\omega(n)$ and $v(n)$ are white noise vectors with the following properties:

$$E\{\omega(n)\} = 0, E\{v(n)\} = 0, \tag{9}$$

$$E\{\omega(n)\omega^T(n)\} = R, E\{v(n)v^T(n)\} = S. \tag{10}$$

Suppose the estimate of the location vector at time n is $\hat{x}(n)$. Thus, we define error estimation vector as

$$e(n) = x(n) - \hat{x}(n). \tag{11}$$

Estimation error covariance matrix is

$$P(n) = E\{e(n)e^T(n)\} = E\{[x(n) - \hat{x}(n)][x(n) - \hat{x}(n)]^T\}. \tag{12}$$

We can get the estimation error variance:

$$\xi(n) = \sum_{i=1}^{M} E\{e_i^2\}, \tag{13}$$

or

$$\xi(n) = T_r p(n). \tag{14}$$

Kalman Filter is the system described by the above formulas (Φ, Δ, H, R, S are known). According to the input vector $u(n)$ and measurement vector $z(n)$, we can find out the best estimate $\hat{x}(n)$ of the state vector making the estimation error variance $\xi(n)$ minimum.

We assume that it is known the best estimate at the time $(n - 1)$ and the corresponding covariance matrix

$$P(n - 1) = E\{[x(x - 1) - \hat{x}(x - 1)][x(n - 1) - \hat{x}(n - 1)]^T\}. \tag{15}$$

Kalman Filtering Algorithm get the best estimate $\hat{x}(n)$ at time n in two steps:

Step 1: Prediction. Based on $\hat{x}(n-1)$ at time (n-1), we can get the best estimate $\hat{x}(n, n - 1)$ at time n according to formula (7):

$$\hat{x}(n, n - 1) = \Phi(n, n - 1)\hat{x}(n - 1) + \Delta(n)u(n - 1). \tag{16}$$

The corresponding prediction variance matrix is

$$P(n, n - 1) = \Phi(n, n - 1)P(n - 1)\Phi^T(n, n - 1) + R. \tag{17}$$

On the basis of $\hat{x}(n, n - 1)$ and the regulation of the vehicle movement, we can get the predicted value:

$$z(n) = H(n)\hat{x}(n, n - 1). \tag{18}$$

Step 2: Filtering. According to the actual measured value, we can get the predicted value:

$$\hat{x}(n) = \hat{x}(n, n - 1) + K(n)[z(n) - H(n)\hat{x}(n, n - 1)]. \tag{19}$$

Here, K represents the gain matrix.

It can be proved that the best treatment is showed as follows:

$$K(n) = P(n.n - 1)H^T(n)[H(n)P(n - 1)H^T(n) + R]^{-1}, \tag{20}$$

$$P(n) = [I - K(n)H(n)]P(n, n - 1). \tag{21}$$

Generally speaking, the dynamic system represented by the formula (7), and its Kalman filter equations include formula (16–21).

According to the initial value of the state vector $\hat{x}(0)$ and error variance $P(0)$, we can receive the best estimate of the locations of target vehicles at each time with these equations.

4   Crowdsourcing Localization and Tracking

4.1   Problem Statement

Crowdsourcing-based Localization and Tracking scheme encourages the vehicle users to participate to improve the accuracy of the estimated position of the targeted vehicle. Figure 3 shows our thoughts in designing the scheme.

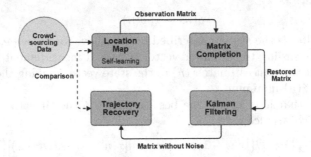

Fig. 3. Vehicle tracking setup

As illustrated before, we consider a vehicle network composed of a set of N vehicles including detectors and target vehicles. A detector is capable of tracking the neighboring vehicles based on information (e.g., ID, position, time) received from them, recorded as (id, x, y, t). The duty of the detectors is tracking and reporting to the control center timely the location information of any vehicle including the target one in VANETs. After the original information is processed with Matrix Completion and Kalman Filtering, we extract the information of the target vehicles like $G_t(ID) = \{P_0, P_1, P_2, \cdots, P_{t-1}\}$, which can generate the estimated trajectory.

4.2   Trajectory Recovering

The original data is shown in the map as discrete points. We use VTRMC method to recover the undetected location information and adopt Kalman filtering to eliminate these errors in the recovered matrix. Algorithm 1 shows the operational details of the Crowdsourcing Tracking and Recovery algorithm.

Algorithm 1 proceeds as follows: Firstly, we import the VANET map along with scenarios in which we set the initial state of the vehicles and the street. We also input some attacking parameters, such as vehicle communication interval, the amount of vehicles and sampling frequency. After the initialization of VANETs, the vehicles are driven towards the destination. Meanwhile, the tracking attack process begins.

The detectors report the received information to the control center. The crowdsourcing computation model and will first record the location list over time for each vehicles in a map, and then generate the observation matrix $X_{N \times T}$

Algorithm 1. Crowdsourcing Tracking and Recovery

1: **Input:** VANET Map, Scenarios, Tracking parameters
2: **Output:** Reconstruction matrix $\hat{B}_{N \times T}$
3: VANET Initialization
4: Crowdsourcing Computation Model Initialization
5: Record the target vehicles location list over time within a map
6: Generate observation matrix $X_{N \times T}$, corresponding two-valued matrix Q
7: Compute the estimate location matrix $B_{N \times T}$ in accordance with Eq. 2
8: Generate the prediction location matrix based on the state of vehicles
9: Kalman filtering noise out of $B_{N \times T}$ according to the prediction matrix C_l

---

according to the map. Matrix completion method will be performed to generate $B_{N \times T}$ as recovery matrix of original matrix. At last, it handles noise out base on Kalman Filter and work out the reconstruction matrix $\hat{B}_{N \times T}$. The algorithm will finally return $\hat{B}_{N \times T}$ as the output, which can be treated as the recovered coordination matrix of all the vehicles running in the sampling region.

5   Simulations

We conduct the simulations to evaluate the performance of VCLT in realistic settings. Our data is generated from VANETsim [22], a simulator for security and privacy concepts in VANETs.

5.1   Simulation Setup

For vehicles' movement in simulation, we use trajectories produced by VANET-sim. This scenario corresponds to a medium speed of 30 km/h. Upon receiving information from other cars, each vehicle uploads its communication records with neighboring vehicles. We choose Crowdsourcing-based Localization and Tracking scheme for tracking attacked vehicles. The street maps of three different cities in China, Dalian, Changsha, and Wuhan, have been chosen from

Table 2. Simulation parameters

Parameters	Values
Sampling interval	60 s
Average speed	30 km/h
Max communication distance	100 m
Simulation time	6 h
Number of vehicles	200
Map size	10 km by 7 km (Dalian)
	10 km by 10 km (Changsha)
	10 km by 8 km (Wuhan)

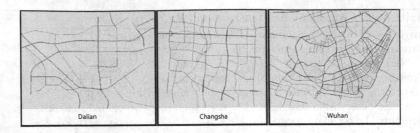

Fig. 4. Road maps of Dalian, Changsha & Wuhan

the OpenStreetMap (OSM) project [23]. We use only a small region in each city to simulate our scheme. Related simulation parameters are listed in Table 2.

5.2 Vehicle Network Establishment

The construction of road network data for Vehicle Network is based on OSM, which provides us with original geographic data which improve our attack mechanism's credibility. We reconstruct the road network data by removing unnecessary geographic elements, as shown in Fig. 4.

We create the scenarios by randomly sampling locations and destination of the vehicles. In order to simulate the real situation of the vehicle, we set the speed, communication distance, braking rate and acceleration rate and so on. We assure that Wi-Fi connection is available to each vehicle. The tracked vehicle is selected randomly during simulation, and its real trajectory will be recorded.

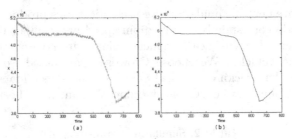

Fig. 5. A contrast between trajectory recovering (a) The position curve with noise, and (b) The position curve after filtering

5.3 Matrix Completion and Filtering

To illustrate the accuracy and energy-saving features of our scheme, we extract 100 vehicles experiments data to construct the original sampling matrix. Matrix completion make trajectory tracking more efficient by abandoning extra communication cost in VANETs.

We capture the location information of the target from the restored matrix. The diagrams show the performance of VCLT test. The left Fig. 5(a) shows

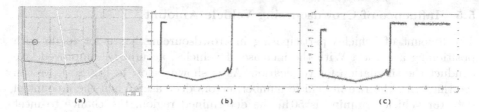

Fig. 6. A trajectory tracking example: (a) The position curve with noise, (b) The position curve after filtering and (c) Contrast of before and after filtering (Color figure online)

the curve of the position of vehicle on the x-axis coordinates over time. After removing the noise included in the restored information, we get an ideal curve in Fig. 5(b) that displays the position change process of the vehicle.

Citing Dalian as an example, Fig. 6(a) shows the real trajectory of a vehicle user in a period of time, as the blue line shows. The circle marks its starting point, and the cross represents the ending point. The medium Fig. 6(b) reflects the recovered trajectory and the red points stand for the sampling points during the crowdsourcing period. From right Fig. 6(c), the effect of trajectory recovery is in the continuing optimization, as the recovery route (green) and the filtered route (blue) show.

5.4   Recovered Trajectory

To illustrate that VCLT is capable of multi-vehicle tracking, we randomly select 3 vehicles in tracking region and recover their locations and trajectory. Based on the restored information without noise, we can determine a rough trajectory of the target vehicle. Based on the road network map, we use the estimated position to restore a credible traveling route. The Fig. 7 shows the intermediate achievement of three target attacked vehicle after the Trajectory Recovering.

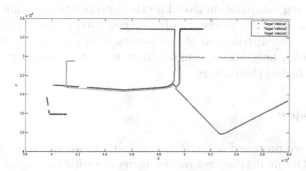

Fig. 7. The recovered tracking results

5.5 Influence of Crowdsourcing Vehicle Amount

The amount of vehicles participating in crowdsourcing has a lot to do with positioning accuracy. With the increase of vehicles, accuracy is improved. We conduct the simulation for verification. As is shown below in Fig. 8(a), we can see that with the rise in vehicle number, errors decrease. When the amount of detector vehicles running is 50 in the determined region, the chance to meet and communicate with the target vehicles is greatly reduced. In addition, we notice that the relative error of Wuhan is the highest. It is for the reason that the number of intersections and complexity of road network will also influence the accuracy. In short, vehicle amount needs to match the sampling area, and adapt to road network capacity in the reality. According to our road network in simulation, we set the number of vehicle is 200, which lets VCLT scheme run efficiently with the appropriate data that it requires.

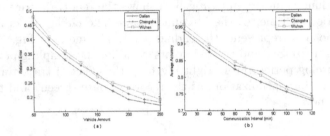

Fig. 8. Comparisons with different (a) Vehicle amount and (b) Comm. interval

5.6 Influence of Vehicle Communication Interval

In this session, we mainly discuss the influence of the vehicle communication interval which is related to the sampling frequency. As shown in Fig. 8(b), the shorter time interval will lead to the lower average tracking accuracy. It means our crowdsourcing computation model needs appropriate sampling frequency to reduce the error and improve the tracking success rate. From Fig. 8(b), we notice that the denser the distribution of the streets is, it's of the greater chance to communicate with neighboring vehicles, that is why the accuracy of Wuhan is comparatively higher than others.

6   Conclusion

In this paper, we proposed a VANET localization and tracking crowdsourcing model VCLT. Our model does not require using the additional sensors, except for the availability of Wi-Fi wireless connection. We believe that crowdsourcing is an ideal way for tracking that benefits from the mass participation and effective network connection. An innovative and practical method VTRMC was proposed to accurately estimate the position and restore missing information based on the continuity of the trajectory. We filter noise out of restored data. We built the vehicle network and simulate the process. Our extensive evaluation results indicate that our crowdsourcing model successfully handles complex city road network structure and simultaneously provides good performance in localization cost and trajectory recovering.

Acknowledgments. This research is sponsored in part by the National Natural Science Foundation of China (No.61173179, No.61402078 and No.61502071). This research is also sponsored in part supported by the Fundamental Research Funds for the Central Universities (DUT14RC(3)106, No.DUT14RC(3)090).

References

1. Zeadally, S., Hunt, R., Chen, Y., et al.: Vehicular ad hoc networks (VANETS): status, results, and challenges. Telecommun. Syst. **50**(4), 217–241 (2012)
2. Reza, T.A., Barbeau, M., Lamothe, G., et al.: Non-cooperating vehicle tracking in VANETs using the conditional logit model. In: International IEEE Conference on Intelligent Transportation Systems, pp. 626–633. IEEE (2013)
3. Hao, P., Boriboonsomsin, K., Wu, G., et al.: Probabilistic model for estimating vehicle trajectories using sparse mobile sensor data. In: IEEE International Conference on Intelligent Transportation Systems, pp. 1363–1368. IEEE (2014)
4. Xue, G., Luo, Y., Yu, J., et al.: A novel vehicular location prediction based on mobility patterns for routing in urban VANET. EURASIP J. Wireless Commun. Networking **2012**(1), 1–14 (2012)
5. Shafiee, K., Leung, V.C.M.: Connectivity-aware minimum-delay geographic routing with vehicle tracking in VANETs. Ad Hoc Netw. **9**(2), 131–141 (2011)
6. Tsai, M., Wang, P., Shieh, C., et al.: Improving positioning accuracy for VANET in real city environments. J. Supercomput., 1–21 (2014)
7. Thangavelul, A., Bhuvaneswari, K., Kumar, K., et al.: Location Identification and Vehicle Tracking using VANET (VETRAC) (2007)
8. Cheng, L., Henty, B.E., Stancil, D.D., et al.: Mobile vehicle-to-vehicle narrowband channel measurement and characterization of the 5.9 GHz dedicated short range communication (DSRC) frequency band. IEEE J. Sel. Areas Commun. **25**(8), 1501–1516 (2007)
9. Jiang, D., Delgrossi, L.: IEEE 802.11p: Towards an international standard for wireless access in vehicular environments. In: IEEE Vehicular Technol Conference, pp. 2036–2040 (2008)
10. Vasquez, D., Fraichard, T., Laugier, C.: Growing hidden markov models: an incremental tool for learning and predicting human and vehicle motion. Int. J. Robot. Res. **28**, 1486–1506 (2009)
11. Fallah, C.H., Sengupta, Y.P., Krishnan, R., et al.: Adaptive intervehicle communication control for cooperative safety systems. Netw. IEEE **24**(1), 6–13 (2010)
12. Rezaei, S., Sengupta, R., Krishnan, H., et al.: Tracking the position of neighboring vehicles using wireless communications. Transp. Res. Part C Emerg. Technol. **18**(3), 335–350 (2010)
13. Jiang, Z., Zhao, J., Li, X., et al.: Communicating is crowdsourcing: Wi-Fi indoor localization with CSI-based speed estimation. J. Comput. Sci. Technol. **29**(4), 589–604 (2014)

14. Artikis, A., Weidlich, M.: Heterogeneous stream processing and crowdsourcing for urban traffic management. In: Edbt (2014)
15. Suriyapaibonwattana, K., Pomavalai, C.: An effective safety alert broadcast algorithm for VANET. In: International Symposium on Communications & Information Technologies, pp. 247–250. IEEE (2008)
16. Corporation, H.P.: Mobility crowdsourcing: toward zero-effort carpooling on individual smartphone. Int. J. Distrib. Sens. Netw. **12**(3), 188–192 (2013)
17. Cands, E.J., Recht, B.: Exact matrix completion via convex optimization. Found. Comput. Math. **9**(6), 717–772 (2009)
18. Wang, J., Tang, S., Yin, B., et al.: Data gathering in wireless sensor networks through intelligent compressive sensing. In: Infocom, IEEE, pp. 603–611. IEEE (2012)
19. Wang, H., Zhu, Y., Zhang, Q.: Compressive sensing based monitoring with vehicular networks. In: Infocom, IEEE, pp. 2823–2831. IEEE (2013)
20. Lin, Z., Chen, M., Ma, Y.: The augmented lagrange multiplier method for exact recovery of corrupted low-rank matrices. Eprint Arxiv (2010)
21. Welch, G., Bishop, G.: An Introduction to the Kalman Filter. University of North Carolina at Chapel Hill (1995)
22. VANET Simulator. http://svs.informatik.uni-hamburg.de/vanet/
23. OpenStreetMap. http://www.openstreetmap.org

A Novel Search Engine-Based Method
for Discovering Command and Control Server

Xiaojun Guo[1,2,3,4]($\boxtimes$), Guang Cheng[1,2], Wubin Pan[1,2],
Truong Dinhtu[1,2], and Yixin Liang[1,2]

[1] School of Computer Science and Engineering,
Southeast University, Nanjing 211189, China
xjguo@njnet.edu.cn
[2] Key Laboratory of Computer Network and Information Integration,
Southeast University, Nanjing 211189, China
[3] School of Information Engineering, Xizang Minzu University,
Xianyang 712082, China
[4] XiZang Key Laboratory of Optical Information Processing and Visualization
Technology, Xizang Minzu University, Xianyang 712082, China

Abstract. To solve the problem of getting command and control (C&C) server
address covertly for malware of Botnet or advanced persistent threats, we
propose a novel C&C-server address discovery scheme via search engine. This
scheme is com-posed of five modules. The botmaster uses publish module to
issue C&C-server IPs in diaries of several free blogs on Internet firstly. Then
these diaries could be indexed by search engine (SE). When the infected terminal becomes a bot, it uses keyword production module to produce search
keyword and submits some or all these keywords to SEs to obtain the search
engine result pages (SERPs). For items in SERPs, the bot uses filtering algorithm to remove noise items and leave valid items whose abstract contain
C&C-server IPs. Lastly the bot utilizes extraction and conversion module to
extract these C&C-server IPs and translates them into binary format. The
experimental results show that our proposed scheme is fully able to discover and
obtain C&C-server IPs via various search engines. Furthermore, if we set proper
threshold value for SE, it can extract C&C-server IPs accurately and efficiently.

Keywords: Top-K algorithm · Search engine · Command and control server ·
Botnet · Advanced persistent threat (APT)

1 Introduction

Botnets have become one of the biggest threats to Internet security. A typical botnet [1]
is a highly controlled platform which consists of many compromised terminals (called
bots) like smartphone, tablet, or personal computer etc.

The controller of botnet (called *botmaster*) can send commands to these bots
through command and control (C&C) servers to launch various of network attacks,
such as Phishing fraud, E-mail bombing Session Hijacking and DDoS attack [2–4].

Therefore, these C&C servers are the rendezvous points of bots and botmaster.
Only if the bots find C&C-server address information (eg. IP address, domain name,

© Springer International Publishing Switzerland 2015
G. Wang et al. (Eds.): ICA3PP 2015, Part III, LNCS 9530, pp. 311–322, 2015.
DOI: 10.1007/978-3-319-27137-8_24

URL) can they be controlled and managed by botmaster. Otherwise, these bots have no threat and practical value [5]. So how to find and get C&C-server addresses for bots is the first step to ensure the whole botnet to work correctly.

There already exist several finding C&C-server address methods. The most com-mon method is to directly hardcode C&C server address (i.e. static IP/domain name) into malware binary code of botnet [6]. But these hardcoded C&C server address will be easily analyzed through reverse analysis, sandbox, etc. The stealthy of this meth-od will become worse as the time goes on. For further improving stealthy, another finding C&C-server address method by means of dynamic DNS service is introduced, such as Domain-Flux [7] and Fast-Flux [11]. The genuine C&C-servers address can be shield by mixed into many seemingly legal but nonexistent domain names or IPs. Unfortunately, the procedure of accessing C&C-servers address will produce a lot of failure DNS queries which seriously expose the bot behavior and cause the detection of C&C domains easily.

Finding C&C-server address method is so critical for botnet that a more stealthy and secure finding scheme is really needed for botmaster. In this paper, inspired by the item structure in search engine result pages (SERP) as shown in Fig. 1, we propose a novel C&C-server address finding scheme based on search engine, named CAFSE, to satisfy the latency and stealth of C&C-servers address finding process. CAFSE is mainly composed of publish module (PM), keyword production module (KPM), search module (SM), noise item filter module (NIFM) and extraction and conversion module (ECM). This paper will describe the mechanism of CAFSE in detail and present the simulation test results.

Fig. 1. The valid item and noise item in Google's SERP

The remainder of this paper is organized as follows: Sect. 2 presents the mechanism of CAFSE. In Sect. 3, we present the simulation test results of our proposed scheme. Finally, Sect. 5 draws the conclusion.

2 The Proposed Scheme

The proposed CAFSE scheme is depicted in Fig. 2. The botmaster firstly uses PM to issue some C&C-server IP addresses as the text-format content in diaries of several Internet free blogs. These diaries can be indexed by search engine. When the infected terminal becomes a bot, it uses KPM to produce the keyword list and submits some or all keywords in this list to search engines to obtain the SERPs. Then the NIFM removes the noise items and leaves the valid items whose abstract part contain C&C-server IP addresses. Lastly the ECM extracts these C&C-server IP addresses and translates them into binary format. Thus, the bots can directly communicates with C&C-servers indicated by these binary-format IP addresses.

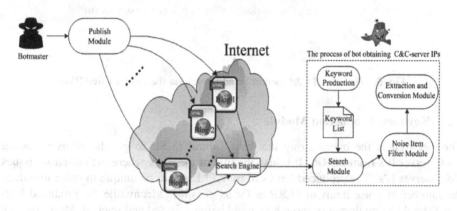

Fig. 2. The mechanism of CAFSE

2.1 Publish Module

In order to provide C&C-server IP addresses for bots, the botmaster uses this module to issue the newest C&C-server IP addresses on the webpage indexed by SE. So how to achieve this function is the main task of PM.

Here we utilize blog, the most common thing on Internet, to implement the publish module. The botmaster can use one account name to register N (here, $N = 10$) different free blogs on internet in advance. When needing to update the C&C-server IP addresses, the botmaster will issue new IPs on the diaries of these registered N Blogs. There are three points that need to be noticed as follows:

Point 1: For the convenience of bots to get the C&C-server IPs via SE, the botmaster uses keyword and new C&C-server IP addresses as the title and content of the diary respectively when publishing these new C&C-server IPs in blog, as shown in Fig. 3.

Point 2: The number of C&C-server IPs in content part of the diary should be limited, because the abstract of valid item in SERP only can display a small section of the content text of the corresponding diary, not all of it (see Fig. 1). This is decided by the abstract generation algorithm of SE. Here, the number is set less than 10.

Point 3: If there are a lot of C&C-server IPs (≥ 10) to be published, the botmaster can divide these IPs into several groups, each of which only contains less than 10 IPs, and then issue each group in one of Blog1–BlogN via the method described in Point 1.

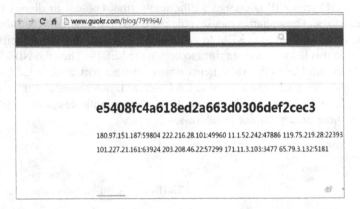

Fig. 3. The issued C&C-server IP addresses via the diary of free Blog

2.2 Keyword Production Module

The keyword is the query string that bots submit to SE to get the items including C&C-server IPs from SERPs. It is also the title of the diary where the botmaster issues C&C-server IPs. The produced keyword by KPM should be unique in order to reduce the number of noise items in SERP as far as possible. Meanwhile the produced keyword should be randomness enough to avoid being detected and tracked. Moreover, the time-space cost of KPM should be low enough to do execution because of the limited resource for bots. Here, we employ the Message-Digest Algorithm 5 (MD5) [24] as the KPM and use the MD5 value of date (YYYY-M-D, e.g. "2014-12-6" as the keyword, as shown in Algorithm 1.

Algorithm 1. KeywordProduction ( )

1: **String** *Klist*[13];　//Keyword List
2: **String Year**, *Day*, *DataStr*;
3: *Year*←get the year of current date of victim system;
4: *Day* ← get the day of current date of victim system;
5: **for** (int *i*=1 ; *i* <13; *i* ++)
6: 　*DateStr* ← *Year*+"-"+itoa(*i*)+ "-"+*Day*;
　　　// date format is: YYYY-M-D
7: 　*Klist*[i] ← **MD5**(*DataStr*);
8: **end for**

In order to avoid producing overmany keywords in a short time, KPM only produces 12 keywords for each day. When bots need to search, they will submit the entire MD5 value of date (i.e. keyword) to SE not a part of it (see Sect. 3.2).

2.3 Search Module

For different SEs, Search Module constructs retrieval URL (uniform resource locator) with each keyword in keyword list *Klist*[]. Then it submits these URLs to corresponding SE to get the SERPs and extracts each item in SERPs to form item dataset Ω.

Although the retrieval URL (rURL) may include many various parameters for different SEs, the basic format of rURL is nearly the same except the slight difference in parameters name [25]. For example, the Google's basic rURL is "http://www.google.com/search?q=Keyword&num=20", while which of Baidu is "http://www.baidu.com/s?word=Keyword&rn=20". From the comparison of these two rURLs, we can see that the parameters *"search"*, *"q"* in Google's rURL, *"s"*, *"word"* in Baidu rURL have the same meanings. They both represent using text search function of Google and Baidu with query entry *"Keyword"*. The rURL for other SEs also has the same basic format. In addition, after getting SERPs from SEs, the extraction of each item can be achieved by Jsoup Library [26].

2.4 Noise Item Filter Module

The item in Ω obtained from Search Module can be classified into two types: valid item and noise item, as seen in Fig. 1. The valid item is the item whose abstract includes C&C-server IPs. The noise items means the rest items in Ω except valid items. For example in Fig. 1, the first and fourth item are valid items, while the rest items are noise items.

In SERPs, the valid items and noise items appear randomly without any regularity in order. So the NIFM should eliminate the noise items and gather valid items together as much as possible, which can help bots extract C&C-server IPs effectively. Here we use the Top-K query algorithm [27] to implement NIFM to deal with item dataset Ω. The process is as follows:

Firstly, compute the score for each item in Ω. Given set $R = \{I_i : 1 \leq i \leq n\}$, where I_i is score vector for i-th item in Ω and $I_i = (s_1, s_2, s_3)$, n is the amount of item in Ω. Because each item is composed of 3 parts: title, link and abstract (see Fig. 1), here s_1, s_2, s_3 indicates the score of title, link and abstract of i-th item respectively. As shown in Fig. 1, we can find that in the valid item, the keyword may appear in both title and abstract, while the string *"blog"* may appear mostly in link. This feature is obvious for valid item, but not for noise item. Therefore, the score s_1 is the length of keyword included by title, s_2 is the length of string *"blog"* included by link and s_3 is the length of keyword included by abstract.

$$\sum_{e=1}^{v} w_e = 1 \tag{1}$$

Secondly, set the weight vector w. Here, $w = (w_1, w_2,...,w_v)$, $w_e \in [0,1]$, $1 \le e \le v$, v is dimension of I_i, and $v = 3$. According to the observation of the items in SERPs, we found that the number of times that keyword and string "*blog*" appears in abstract and link part of valid item is more than that keyword appears in title. Hence the relation for the corresponding weight of s_1, s_2, s_3 is satisfied $w_1 < w_2 = w_3$.

Lastly, execute the Top-K query procedure on R. For any $e(1 \le e \le v)$, if $I_i[e] \ge I_j[e]$, the query function f must be satisfied $f(I_i) \ge f(I_j)$. Thus it can be conclude that f should be a monotone increasing function. Here we let f be a weighted-sum function, as shown in formula (2):

$$f(I_i) = \sum_{e=1}^{v} w_e \cdot I_i[e] \tag{2}$$

When executing Top-K query algorithm on R, the top k values among $f(I_1)$–$f(I_n)$ will be returned. So the k items corresponded with these top k values have higher possibility of being the valid items. And the noise items can be filtered through this Top-K query procedure.

2.5   Extraction and Conversion Module

This module uses pattern matching algorithm to find and extract the IP pattern strings from the abstract part of the selected top k items by Top-K query procedure. Then it verifies if IP pattern strings are right or not.

The right IP pattern strings will be converted into binary format IPs in order to facilitate bots to directly access the C&C-servers represented by these IPs.

3   Simulation Results and Discussion

In this section, we present some simulations to evaluate the performance of proposed CAFSE scheme.

We firstly register 10 free blogs on Internet, as shown in Table 1. To implement the function of publish module, we utilizes the Chrome-v39.0.2171.95 m and Plug-in Tab-Snap-v1.2.9 [28] to open and login on these 10 free registered blogs, then use the MD5 values of three dates as the diary's titles, several C&C-server IP addresses (each address format is "IP:Port Number" and separated by space) as the diary's content and publishes these diaries on 10 Blogs listed in Table 1 respectively.

The KPM, SM, NIFM and ECM are implemented in Java language and tested on a PC with an Intel Pentium G640 CPU of 2.8 GHz, DDR3 SDRAM of 4 GB and Windows 7 (32 bit).

3.1   Indexing Time and Quantity

Indexing time (IT) is period which starts from C&C-server IPs issued by publish module until the first valid item appears in SERPs. Indexing quantity (IQ) denotes the

Table 1. 10 free blogs used to issue C&C-server IPs

Number	Blog URL
1	http://blog.163.com/gxjjxg_0617/
2	http://gxjjxg0617.blog.sohu.com/
3	http://blog.csdn.net/gxjjxg_0617
4	http://www.guokr.com/i/0977717367/
5	http://hexun.com/gxjjxg0617/default.html
6	http://blog.tianya.cn/blog-5204529-1.shtml
7	http://gxjjxg0617.blog.51cto.com/
8	http://my.oschina.net/u/2254035/blog
9	http://bbs.chinabyte.com/space-uid-469064.html
10	http://blog.chinaunix.net/uid-29961317-id-4702765.html

number of valid items in SERPs of one SE. Here we use this two metrics to evaluate the search results generated by the SEs for the 10 Blogs in Table 1 which contain the issued C&C-server IPs.

For each MD5 value of three dates, we use search module to search in Google, Baidu, Bing and Haosou respectively and record the number of valid items in their SERPs at a fixed time in a day. This record process lasts 30 days. The IQ here was the average value of the number of valid items for this 30 days, as shown in Fig. 4.

From Fig. 4, we can find that the IT of Haosou is 0 day, i.e. the first valid item containing C&C-server IPs is successfully indexed as the same day as when C&C-server IPs were published. The IT of Haosou is the shortest one of 4 SEs. The IT of Google and Baidu is 1day, the worst is Bing whose IT is 6 day. This 4 SEs have big difference in indexing time, but most of them cost more than 1 day. Compared with the four existing C&C-server IP finding schemes for bots (see Sect. 1), in our proposed method the appearance of C&C-server IPs in SERPs of 4 SEs is so slow that bots can't find and obtain the issued C&C-server IPs immediately through SEs. Therefore, this feature is consistent with the requirement that APT [29] and Botnet need malware to possess latency in order to increase their covertness.

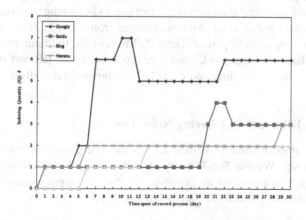

Fig. 4. Valid item number in SERPs of 4 SEs varies with time

In Fig. 4, we can also see that the IQ of 4 SEs increase overall as time goes on, especially for Google and Baidu. And the IQ of 4 SEs is tending towards stability. At the time when C&C-server IPs are issued 30 days, the IQ of Google is stable at 6, which means Google presents better indexing effects. By contrast, the IQ of the other three SEs, i.e. Baidu, Haosou and Bing, decreases fewer. The indexing effect of this three SEs is worse, but the bot still can get the C&C-server IPs from the these few valid items.

3.2   Keyword Length and Direction Impact on Search Effect

We select the first d characters of each keyword as the new keywords to do search test in 4 SEs, record IQs for these new keywords and compute corresponding average value of IQs for the same length new keywords, as shown in left part of Table 2. Note that this test is conducted at the time when C&C-server IPs were issued 30 days.

It can been found that, as the new keyword length d increasing, the IQ of 4 SEs is also increasing. When using entire length of keyword, the IQ achieves the maxi-mum. Therefore, only using the whole MD5 value of date as search keyword can the best search result be presented.

Table 2. Selected direction and different length of new keyword impact on search effect

Search engines	From beginning to end				From end to beginning			
	$d = 8$	$d = 16$	$d = 24$	$d = 32$	$d = 8$	$d = 16$	$d = 24$	$d = 32$
Google	0	0	0	6	0	0	0	6
Baidu	0	1	1	3	1	1	0	3
Bing	0	0	0	1	0	0	0	1
Haosou	1	3	4	3	2	4	1	3

In addition, changing selection direction of new keyword can't improve the search result. The right part of Table 2 presents test result for different length new keywords which are selected in reverse direction (i.e. from end to beginning). Obviously, if d is 8, 16 and 24, the total number of valid items obtained from Google, Baidu and Bing is 2, which is the same as in right part of Table 2. Meanwhile, the number of valid items obtained from Haosou is decreased. Therefore, compared with left part of Table 2, the keyword selected in reverse direction can't help improve search effect.

3.3   Different K Impact on Filtering Noise Item

Although the number of valid items increases as the time goes on, the number of noise items also increases. We use Top-K query algorithm to make valid items to appear in the first ranking k items as far as possible, so that the noise items can be filtered efficiently, which is convenient for bots to extract C&C-server IPs.

Figure 5 presents different k values impact on the accuracy achieved by using Top-K algorithm on the SERPs of 4 SEs ($w = (w_1, w_2, w_3) = (0.2, 0.4, 0.4)$). Here, accuracy means the percentage of valid items that appear in the top k items obtained from using Top-K algorithm on SERPs. We can find that the accuracy is rather sensitive to the variation of k values. For example, the range of k for Google varies in $1 \leq k \leq 6$, which for other SEs is $k \leq 3$. As a whole, the accuracy for 4 SEs shows a decreased tendency along with increment of k, which means that the percentage of noise items in the selected top k items becomes higher. Therefore, different k values should be set for different SEs due to their difference in search ability and indexing mechanism.

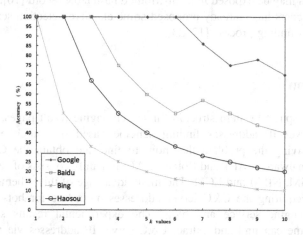

Fig. 5. Different K values impact on filtering noise items

4 Related Work

From the currently published literatures about this topic, the existing methods for finding C&C-server address can be grouped into four categories:

- Static IPs/domain name: The IPs/domain names of C&C-servers are hardcoded into malware beforehand. When the terminal is infected by this malware and become a bot, it directly communicates with C&C-servers represented by these IPs/domain names and joins into corresponding botnet. The typical malwares are Merga-D and Rustock [6]. The big disadvantage of this approach is that the hardcoded IPs or domain names in malware can be obtained by reverse engineering analysis. So that the corresponding C&C-servers are easy to be tracked and shut down.
- Domain-flux: Bots use a special domain name generation (DGA) algorithm to produce a number of bogus domain names but some of which represent real C&C-servers. Then the bots attempt to send DNS query for each bogus domain name, try to find out those ones who receive successful DNS response, and communicate directly with them. The typical malwares are Conficker, Pushdo and Bobax [7]. Although domain-flux method is more invisible and robust, the DNS

query packets still present obvious features which can provide a way to detect and block this method in local network [8–10].

- Fast-flux: Some of bots who own public IP addresses have been disguised "proxy", other bots can communicate with C&C-servers only via these proxy bots [11]. To enhance the flexibility and invisibility, the IP addresses of proxy bots are always changing. But there already exist some detection schemes against fast-flux method and achieve good effect [12, 13].
- P2P-based method: P2P bots (e.g. Phatbot, Nugache [14]) utilize some inherent dynamic discovery mechanism of P2P protocol to find C&C-servers [15], such as Chord, Symphony, Kelips and so on. Once the bot of this type is identified, the C&C-servers may be exposed in its distributed hash table record [16]. Based on this point, researchers have already proposed some effective detection schemes for this C&C-servers finding process [17–23].

5   Conclusion

In this paper, inspired by item structure in search engine result pages, we provide a novel C&C-server IP addresses finding scheme based on search engine, named CAFSE, for solving the problem that how to find and obtain the C&C-server IP ad-dresses for malware in APT and Botnet. CAFSE mainly consists of several modules as PM, KPM, SM, NIFM and ECM. The main advantage of this scheme is enhancing the stealth of acquiring the C&C-server addresses procedure for bots, due to using public search engine service and blog. The experimental results show that our pro-posed scheme can find and extract C&C-server IP addresses via various search en-gines accurately. The future research work will be launched in the following aspects: (1) how to increase the amount of valid item in SERPs. (2) for keeping better security, consider how to issue the C&C-server IP addresses in covert ways rather than issuing the plaintext of C&C-server IP addresses directly in abstract part of valid item. (3) further improve the Top-K algorithm to filter noise items as far as possible.

Acknowledgments. This work is completed under the support of the Scientific Research Innovation Projects for General University Graduate of Jiangsu province (KYLX_0141); the Fundamental Research Funds for the Central Universities; the National High Technology Research and Development Program ("863" Program) of China (2015AA015603); Jiangsu Future Networks Innovation Institute: Prospective Research Project on Future Networks (BY2013095-5-03); Six talent peaks of high level Talents Project of Jiangsu province (2011-DZ024); Natural Science Foundation of Tibet Autonomous Region of China (2015ZR-13-17, 2015ZR-14-18).

References

1. Khattak, S., Ramay, N.R., Khan, K.R., et al.: A taxonomy of botnet behavior, detection, and defense. IEEE Commun. Surv. Tutorials **16**(2), 898–924 (2014)

2. Chen, P., Desmet, L., Huygens, C.: A study on advanced persistent threats. In: De Decker, B., Zúquete, A. (eds.) CMS 2014. LNCS, vol. 8735, pp. 63–72. Springer, Heidelberg (2014)
3. Juels, A., Yen, T.F.: Sherlock Holmes and the case of the advanced persistent threat. In: Proceedings of the 5th USENIX Conference on Large-Scale Exploits and Emergent Threats, San Jose, CA, USA, pp. 63–72 (2012)
4. Rafael, A.R.G., Gabriel, M.F., Pedro, G.T.: Survey and taxonomy of botnet research through life-cycle. ACM Comput. Surv. 45(4), 1–33 (2013)
5. Zand, A., Vigna, G., Yan, X., et al.: Extracting probable command and control signatures for detecting botnets. In: Proceedings of the 29th Annual ACM Symposium on Applied Computing, pp. 1657–1662. ACM (2014)
6. Ken, C., Levi, L.: A case study of the rustock rootkit and spam bot. In: Proceedings of the 1st Workshop on Hot Topics in Understanding Botnets (2007)
7. Damballa. Top-5 most prevalent DGA-based crimeware families. https://www.damballa.com/downloads/r_pubs/WP_DGAs-in-the-Hands-of-Cyber-Criminals.pdf
8. Yadav, S., Reddy, A.K.K., Reddy, A.L.N., et al.: Detecting algorithmically generated domain-flux attacks with DNS traffic analysis. IEEE/ACM Trans. Netw. 20(5), 1663–1677 (2012)
9. Antonakakis, M., Perdisci, R., Nadji, Y., et al.: From throw-away traffic to bots: detecting the rise of DGA-based malware. In: Proceedings of the 21st USENIX Security Symposium (2012)
10. Bilge, L., Kirda, E., Kruegel, C., et al.: EXPOSURE: finding malicious domains using passive DNS analysis. In: Proceedings of the 2011 Symposium on Network and Distributed System Security (2011)
11. Riden, J.: Know your enemy: fast-flux service networks, the honeynet project. http://www.honeynet.org/book/export/html/130
12. Holz, T., Gorecki, C., Rieck, K., Freiling, F.C.: Measuring and detecting fast-flux service networks. In: Proceedings of the 15th Annual Network and Distributed System Security Symposium (2008)
13. Nazario, J., Holz, T.: As the net churns: fast-flux botnet observations. In: Proceedings of the 3rd International Conference on Malicious and Unwanted Software, pp. 24–31 (2008)
14. Stover, S., Dittrich, D., Hemandez, J., et al.: Analysis of the storm and nugache trojans: P2P is here. In: Proceedings of USENIX, pp. 8–27 (2007)
15. Dittrich, D., Dietrich, S.: P2P as botnet command and control: a deeper insight. In: Proceedings of the 3rd International Conference on Malicious and Unwanted Software, pp. 41–48 (2008)
16. Thorsten, H., Moritz, S., Frederic, D., et al.: Measurements and mitigation of peer-to-peer-based botnets: a case study on storm worm. In: Proceedings of the 1st USENIX Workshop on Large-Scale Exploits and Emergent Threats, pp. 1–9 (2008)
17. Chang, S., Daniels, T.E.: P2P botnet detection using behavior clustering and statistical tests. In: Proceedings of the 2nd ACM Workshop on Security and Artificial Intelligence, pp. 23–30 (2009)
18. Zhang, J.J., Perdisci, R., Lee, W.K., et al.: Detecting stealthy P2P botnets using statistical traffic fingerprints. In: Proceedings of the 2011 IEEE/IFIP 41st International Conference on Dependable Systems and Networks, pp. 121–132 (2011)
19. Zhao, D., Traore, I., Ghorbani, A., et al.: Peer to peer botnet detection based on flow intervals. Inf. Secur. Privacy Res. 376, 87–102 (2012)
20. Singh., K., Guntuku, S.C., Thakur, A., et al.: Big data analytics framework for peer-to-peer botnet detection using random forests. Inf. Sci., (Online Press) (2014)
21. Zhao, D., Traore, I., Sayed, B., et al.: Botnet detection based on traffic behavior analysis and flow intervals. Comput. Secur. 39, 2–16 (2013)

22. Stevanovic, M., Pedersen, J.M.: An efficient flow-based botnet detection using supervised machine learning. In: Proceeding of the 2014 IEEE International Conference on Computing, Networking and Communications, pp. 797–801 (2014)

23. Garg, S., Sarje, A.K., Peddoju, S.K.: Improved detection of P2P botnets through network behavior analysis. In: Martínez Pérez, G., Thampi, S.M., Ko, R., Shu, L. (eds.) SNDS 2014, CCIS, vol. 420, pp. 334–345. Springer, Heidelberg (2014)

24. The MD5 Message-Digest algorithm. https://tools.ietf.org/html/rfc1321

25. Oh, J., Lee, S., Lee, S.: Advanced evidence collection and analysis of web browser activity. In: Proceedings of 11th Annual Digital Forensics Research Conference, pp. S62–S67. New Orleans, USA (2011)

26. Hedley, J.: Jsoup HTML parser. http://jsoup.org/

27. He, Z., Lo, E.: Answering why-not questions on top-k queries. IEEE Trans. Knowl. Data Eng. **26**(6), 300–1315 (2014)

28. Jones, T.: Tab-Snap. https://github.com/tdj28?tab=repositories

29. Brewer, R.: Advanced persistent threats: minimising the damage. Netw. Secur. **4**, 5–9 (2014)

Leveraging Behavior Diversity to Detect Spammers in Online Social Networks

Jian Cao, Qiang Fu, Qiang Li$^{(\boxtimes)}$, and Dong Guo

College of Computer Science and Technology, Jilin University,
Changchun 130012, China
{caojian13,fuqiang2111}@mails.jlu.edu.cn,
{li_qiang,guodong}@jlu.edu.cn

Abstract. Online social networks have become very popular and convenient for communication. However, spammers often take control of accounts to create and propagate attacks using messages and URLs. Most existing studies to detect spammers are based on machine learning methods. Features are the key factors considered in these methods, and most documented features in existing studies can be evaded by spammers. In this study, we propose behavior features, which are based on behavior diversity when sending messages, combined with existing effective features, to build a detection system. We leverage entropy to present differences in behavior diversity between spammers and normal accounts. In the cases of evasion by periodically changing a behavior model in the sending of messages by spammers, we also introduce conditional entropy, which is calculated based on the Markov model. To achieve our goal, we have collected information from approximately 489,451 accounts including 108,168,675 corresponding messages from Sina Weibo. Through evaluation of our detection methods, the accuracy rate of this system is approximately 91.5 %, and the false positive rate is approximately 3.4 %.

Keywords: Online social network · Spammer detection · Behavior diversity · Entropy · Conditional entropy

1 Introduction

The online social networks (OSNs) such as Google+, Facebook, Twitter, and Sina Weibo have become very popular in recent years. Information in an online social network is proposed in almost real-time and discussion published by people in cyberspace is beneficial for presenting current facts. Sina Weibo is one of the largest microblogs in China. According to the studies from Sina Weibo Reports of Third Query 2014 [1], the monthly active users (MAUs) have reached 167 million, and daily active users (DAUs) were 76.6 million. These numbers show that any information shared on Sina Weibo has a high probability to propagate and may have a huge impact.

Spammers take a ride on OSNs to create and spread spam information far and wide. Spam information has no real significance in social communication and also

© Springer International Publishing Switzerland 2015
G. Wang et al. (Eds.): ICA3PP 2015, Part III, LNCS 9530, pp. 323–336, 2015.
DOI: 10.1007/978-3-319-27137-8_25

confuses and annoys people who while scanning information are interrupted by different kinds of irrelevant advertisements. People are tired of spam information. More urgently, some URLs contained in spam information may be a threat to privacy and security in OSNs. Attacks from spammers may include a drive-by-download, injection, phishing, etc. If people clicks on suspicious URLs and are attacked, personal information may be sent to spammers, then the suspicious URLs will be forwarded from the targets accounts, which will in turn, threaten their friends because of trust that exists among them.

Due to the grim situation for combating spammers and protecting privacy of people in OSNs, several studies have been proposed by researchers from schools, engineers from enterprises, and professionals from security companies. Most of these studies are based on machine learning. The key factor in machine learning is the feature. Existing studies focus on features from message content, accounts, URLs, etc. Although these features cover several kinds of spam information and spammers, spammers still have tactics to evade detection [2]. Most features in previous studies are static and can be easily disguised if they have been detected by spammers, such as the length of URLs, the length of message, etc.

In this paper, we focus on the difference in behavioral diversity in messages sent by spammers and normal accounts in OSNs. When normal accounts send messages, they just send what they want to. Contents of sending lists of normal accounts have huge differences. There is no deliberately typical template for normal accounts to send messages. All of information from messages is intended for sharing and communication with others. However, spammers have a different performance in sending messages than normal accounts. Behavioral diversity of spammers sending messages is weak. As most messages from spammers are send by a robot, several consequent messages in a period usually present same type, such as the message comprises a sentence, a picture, and a URL.

We propose to utilize entropy and conditional entropy, which is based on Markov model, to present behavioral diversity in messages sent by accounts. We then identify these values as behavior features, and train for a robust and effective classifier with several existing effective feature sets, to identify spammers in OSNs. In order to achieve our goal in detection of spammers in OSNs, we have collected about 489,451 account information sets and about 108,168,675 corresponding messages from Sina Weibo. When we have extracted the necessary features and after several rounds of training, we have attained a classifier with an accuracy rate of approximately 91.5 %, and a false positive rate of about 3.4 %.

In summary, we have made three contributions as follows:

– We have proposed utilizing entropy and conditional entropy to present the behavior diversity in messages sent by spammers and normal accounts. Entropy can clearly reveal the behavioral diversity of normal accounts in sending messages.
– We combine Markov model with the machine learning method to train for an effective classifier. We utilize Markov model to calculate conditional entropy in order to reveal the single type and cyclical change of spammers in sending messages.

- We have designed behavior features that are based on entropy and conditional entropy. Through combining these features with existing features in building a classifier, the accuracy rate is 91.5 % and the false positive rate is 3.4 %.

The rest of our paper is organized as follows: We first provide necessary related work in Sect. 2. Then we present a background overview, which is related to detection methods, and the dataset in Sect. 3. Design and analysis of the detection system is presented in Sect. 4. Next we illustrate existing effective features and design our behavior features in detail in Sect. 5. We evaluate our detection system and the effectiveness of our behavior features in Sect. 6. Finally, we talk about limitations of our methods and future work in Sect. 7, and conclude the whole paper in Sect. 8.

2   Related Work

Due to the ubiquity of spammers in Online Social Network, researchers have paid increasing attention to the investigation of spammers in recent year.

A part of previous works focus on characterizing spammers in various aspects. Most of them analyzed the how the profiles and behaviors of spammers differ from normal users. Stringhini et al. [3] investigated how spammers are using social network to spread spam, they found that spamers show different behaviors strategies to deliver spam and distinguish four categories of spammers based on their spam strategy. Grier et al. [4] analyzed the accounts that send spam and find evidence that it originate from previously legitimate accounts that have been compromised. Thomas et al. [5] use their dataset to characterize the behavior and lifetime of spam account, including campaigns they execute, and the wide-spread abuse of legitimate web services. Almaatouq et al. [6] also present a analysis of spammers in OSNs viewed through the lens of their behavioral characteristics and show that there exist two behaviorally distinct categories of spammers. Some existing works foucus on the network structure of spammers in Online Social Network, Yang et al. [7] through analyzing inner and outer social relationships in the spamm account community, they find that spammer accounts tend to be socially connected to form a small-world network and reveal three categories of accounts that have close friendships with spammers accounts. In Online Social Network, spammers often execute campaigns to spread a massive spam messages in a short time, Zhang et al. [8] present a study on revealing features that spammers behave to dominate the information diffusion in a campaign, they further inspect to what extent these features can help to weed out spammer accounts.

Many existing works addressed the problem of spammer detection in Online Social Network. Those works try to solve the problem by two method: The one is identify the spammers themselves [9,10], and another one is identify the spam messages send by spammers and identify the spammers through it [11]. Prior works using first method mainly make use of the features that spammers behave differ from normal users, including account properties, behaviors, and message content. Chu et al. [10] observe the difference among human, bot, and cyborg in term of tweeting behavior, tweet content, and account properties and propose a classification system based on machine learning to determine a user's likelihood of being a human, bot, or cyborg. Egele et al. [9] present a novel approach to detect compromised user accounts in social network, they build a statistical model based on behavior and message, and use a anomaly detection system to identify accounts that experience a sudden change in behavior. Some works using first method exploit the network structure of spammers in Online Social Network, and propose some graph-based algorithms to identify spammers. Tan et al. [12] first propose a sybil defense based spammer detection scheme SD2 by taking the social network relationship into consideration, and further design an unsupervised spam detection scheme called UNIK in order to make it highly robust in facing an increasing level of spam attacks. However, Social Network spammers are evolving to existing detection features, Yang et al. [2] make a comprehensive and empirical analysis of the evasion tactics utilized by Twitter spammers and further design several new detection features to detect more Twitter spammers. The other existing works using second method utilized text-based features of spam messages. Gao et al. [13] presented an online spam filtering system, they propose to reconstruct spam messages into campaigns of classification. Martinez-Romo et al. [14] presented the first work tries to detect spam tweets in real-time using language as the primary tool, they proposed several new feature based on Statistics Language models.

Different from previous works, we proposed using behavior diversity when sending messages in online social network. Our work focuses on behavior in different type of messages. We have proposed entropy and conditional entropy to present the diversity. Through analysis of these measurements, we demonstrate that behavior diversity is highly effective in detection of spammers in OSNs.

3   Background and Dataset

In this section, we first present a background to get a broader view of the detection method, which includes discussing Sina Weibo, forwarding, topics ("#"), and replying someone ("@") in messages, etc. Then we introduce our dataset, which is the basis for achieving our goal. We will discuss the dataset in two subchapters, dataset collection and identifying.

3.1   Background Overview

In order to analyze behavior in sending messages on accounts, we need to present basic information related to our methods. As our method focuses on sending messages in Sina Weibo, we introduce Sina Weibo and some typical features in that ONS's messages.

Sina Weibo: Sina Weibo is one of the largest micro-websites in China. It provides an online community that is open for the public to talk about the latest news. As it has more than 70 million daily active users, each topic or current news item may have a huge response in different areas. Because of characters limitation in

Sina Weibo, messages are short for people reading anytime from anywhere. However, there still exist security issues as spammers try to hide attacks in suspicious URLs in sent messages. Sina Weibo was attacked by Cross Site Scripting (XSS) in 2011, creating a lot of confusion for people. Ensuring privacy and security in Sina Weibo is necessary.

Forward: There exists a behavior named "forward" in Sina Weibo, which is almost the same as the function called "retweet" in Twitter. However, forward in Sina Weibo contains the original message, and this is different from retweet in Twitter. If a message has been forwarded, people can easily look at the original message. Message forwarded in same cycle can be seen as power-law distribution. However, even with the convenience and wider extent of forwarding messages, unfortunately, spammers also focus on this mechanism. Spammers utilize it to propagate advertisements or suspicious URLs in hot topic messages.

Topic("#"): Topic in Sina Weibo is very popular as it provides a platform for people, who have the same interest, to discuss the topic with each other. If a message begins with the character "#", it means this message is related to this topic, which is described between the two "#". There are many hot topics every day that identify the latest news for people to talk about. However, these topics also give spammers a new way to lure people to search and click on suspicious URLs. Spammers usually utilize comments after the hot topics. Comments usually contains a few enticing characters and one suspicious URL. Of course, the URL is not actually related to the enticing characters, it is just a door to the spam contents.

Reply Someone("@"): Replying to someone in a message or private message can make person notice the message. This character ("@") is often used among friends who are in the same interest cycle or are real friends in real life. This mechanism has made it convenience for people to communicate with a target person and share opinion. However, utilizing this reply character ("@") also gives spammers a powerful cheating method based on users trust. Spammers often utilize this character to randomly point out people in the current pages to get them to read and click on suspicious URLs of spam information.

3.2 Dataset

To achieve our goal in detection of spammers in OSNs, we need to collect real-time data before analysis. Because Sina Weibo is one of the largest micro-websites in China, it has many spammers in it, we used Sina Weibo as our source of real-time data. After collection, we still needed to identify spammers from among the millions of accounts in order to have a comparison for subsequent data analysis.

Data Collection: Sina Weibo has already provided free API [15] for researchers to collect information on accounts and messages. We have built a collection crawler based on python to collect a real-time dataset. First, we took several account seeds randomly, from different cycles, in order to replicate close to natural distribution. Then we use the resultant list of account seeds as new seeds to spread by crawling. Not only user information, but also messages that they have sent will be collected concurrently. Both features from accounts information and corresponding messages together are needed to train a classifier. Preliminary data collection from online social networks is currently difficult. Because of privacy and protection of personal information, it is hard for researchers to crawl for as much data as they want, especially for big data. So after a long time, we collected approximately 489,451 accounts, and about 108,168,675 corresponding messages.

Labeling: In order to have an effective analysis on spammers and normal accounts, we need to first distinguish and label them. We transfer URLs extracted from corresponding messages to Google safe browsing API [16] and Virustotal [17] to create official labels. If URLs from one account have been labeled by these two websites more than five times, we will consider this account as a spammer. After this step, we still need to independently judge strange accounts. Our team labeled these accounts by random selection. Eventually, we labeled approximately 2,000 spammers, and 2,000 normal accounts.

4 System Overview

In this section, we plan to introduce every part of our detection system in detail in an online social network. We have built a detection system which is based on machine learning methods, which can be viewed in Fig. 1. This system has about seven main parts. The flow of data in the models is similar to other system parts which are based on machine learning. However, we included our own elements based on our behavior features and we plan to introduce these elements into the system one by one.

Feature Extraction: This part is the first part encountered when a messages stream comes from OSN server. We need to extract features by kinds and prepare for further handling. In this part, we utilize multi-process and Sina Weibo API to extract the basic features that we need to handle. As features in our methods are not simple ones, we still need to treat these basic features for calculation in next few parts. Features about behavior will be sent to entropy parts, which can calculate the value of entropy and conditional entropy based on Markov model. Of course, accounts and URLs in messages will first be sent to the Blacklist Dataset. After normal judgment, features will be sent to the Classifier part together, to identify spammers in messages.

URLs Transforming: This is an accessorial part of Feature Extraction. Because of the 140 characters limitation for messages in Sina Weibo, URLs in each message have been shorted by an official server. Short URLs in Sina Weibo consist of two parts, one is the short domain "t.cn", and the other one is a combination of random numbers. The length of these short URLs are similar, so cannot be analyzed as features. Attempts are made to transform these short URLs back to the original ones based on Sina Weibo URLs API. Once an URL has been

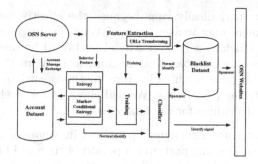

Fig. 1. System overview

sent from Feature Extraction part, the URLs Transforming part will call for a transformation through a given API and send back it.

Blacklist Dataset: This part is set for saving time in detection existing spammers and suspicious URLs. We have built a blacklist based on an existing blacklist from official sources. This dataset has two main indexes, one is spam account id, and the other is URLs in blacklist. If an URL has been identified as a suspicious one, we will put its corresponding sending accounts into this dataset. Then, accounts from where messages containing these URLs sent immediately will be identified as spammers. Also, if an account is matched with one in this dataset, this account will be identified as a spammer. If none of accounts or URLs has been matched in this part, features should be calculated and transferred to the classifier.

Behavior Features Model: This part is based on our behavior features. We have proposed utilizing entropy and conditional entropy to present behavioral diversity in sending messages in online social networks. We get features, which are needed to calculate the value of entropy and conditional entropy, from Feature Extraction parts. The values will be seen as behavior features for further training and identifying. In building the Markov model process, we still need to take several messages from the sending list of corresponding sending accounts. Actually, the features may easily identify spammers but since spammers have methods to evade a static model, we would like to calculate a value of conditional entropy for future identification based on machine learning.

Account Dataset: This is anapriori part for building the Markov model in order to calculate the value of conditional entropy. Account Dataset first concludes all vectors from the Feature Extraction part. Meanwhile, building this dataset can be used as a cache dataset for getting existing information regarding accounts from Sina Weibo server through API. As multi accounts need to be identified at the same time, we need to use a cache vector to collect corresponding information on the target accounts. When the collection step has finished, features on each message and account will be sent to Behavior Feature Model for future calculation. Meanwhile, information about this account will be cleared in this dataset for privacy.

Training: This part periodically runs because the effectiveness of the system in detecting spammers may weaken over of time. Features vectors from Feature Extraction and Behavior Feature Model parts will be sent to this part for training an effective classifier, based on machine learning methods. In this part, we utilized several effective machine learning methods, such as Random Forest, Support Vector Machine (SVM), etc. We will choose a relatively balanced value from among these algorithms for the final classifier.

Classifier: This part is for identifying spammers in a normal messages stream. Classifier built in the Training part over a period of time will be updated in this part. Features for identifying them will be sent to this part through the Feature Extraction part and our Behavior Feature Model part. If accounts have been identified as spammers, a spam signal will be labeled in the message and sent to Blacklist Dataset for subsequent identification. If not, the normal signal will be labeled as safe.

Overall, our system needs to be deployed on the server side to identify and stop spammers in online social networks. Our Behavior Feature Model part is the key part for detection of spammers, and we would like to see it constitute an exhaustive prevention for privacy and security in online social network.

5 Features Illustration

In this section, we illustrate the behavior features that we originally proposed. Then we plan to introduce several effective features that have been used in previous studies. These existing features will be combined to build an effective classifier, together with our behavior features.

5.1 Behavior Features

In this part, we are going to illustrate our proposed behavior features. We have introduced utilizing entropy and conditional entropy to present behavior diversity when sending messages in online social networks. Normal accounts and spammers have different behavior models in sending messages. The behavior model of normal accounts is much more diverse, while spammers have a simple model in sending messages. First, for preliminary calculation purposes, we plan to introduce entropy and some basic items in sending messages. Then, we need to build a Markov model to calculate conditional entropy. The values of entropy and conditional entropy are the behavior features we have proposed.

Entropy: This item is the typical one to measure the degree of confusion in statistics. We have introduced it to present the behavior diversity when sending messages in online social networks. The bigger this value, the more diverse the behavior. In order to calculate this value, we need to make sure sending messages' category. We have variously chosen from five items, such as the URL, Picture, Hashtag, Forward, Reply, etc. We take an 5-bits integer to represent the category of each message, which can be seen in Fig. 2, every bit maps to corresponding item. If the sending message contains any behavioral item, the corresponding bit of it will be set to 1, otherwise, it will remain at 0 at the initial stage. Then, the category of all sending message can be seen in this integer. We calculated entropy of a user's behavior based on Formula 1, in which the p_i represent the ratio of messages belong to category i.

$$H(X) = -\sum_{i=1}^{n} p_i \log_2 p_i \qquad (1)$$

According to the Formula 1, we have calculated the value of entropy on normal accounts and spam accounts. Then we have counted the number of different values and drawn a CDF, which can be seen in Fig. 3. Observing this figure, we determine that the value of entropy based on behavior can easily distinguish spammers from normal accounts. First, more than 65 % of normal accounts have a higher value than 2.5. However, value of entropy on spammers are almost always lower than 2.5. This is an obvious threshold in entropy between spammers and normal accounts. Further, about 22 % in normal accounts, have a value of entropy lower than 2.0. We analyzed the reason, and we determined that most of them are sending by cyborg. Most of them have the same behavior model in sending messages. Finally, we also determined that more than half of spammers have a value of entropy is between 1.5 and 2.5. After analyzing samples, whose value of entropy is in this interval, we have found that most of these spammers are trying to change their behavior model periodically in order to evade detection.

Behavior	URL	Hashtag	Picture	Forward	Reply
Statement	1	0	0	1	0

Fig. 2. Sample of items in sending messages

In summary, we still need to consider behavior features more carefully, considering the evasion tactics of spammers. Then, we introduce conditional entropy to prevent periodically changing behavior models from spammers.

Conditional Entropy: We introduced conditional entropy to deal with the shortfall of entropy because of periodically changes in sending behavior by spammers. Conditional entropy is a typical measure in information theory. If the value of conditional entropy has been higher, it means that the behavior model in sending messages is simpler. Otherwise, it means the behavior model in sending messages is more diverse. In order to get this value, we used Markov model for calculation. At first, we need to introduce Formula 2, which is utilized for calculation.

$$H(Y|X) = H(X,Y) - H(X) \qquad (2)$$

According to the Formula 2, we need to determine joint entropy $H(X,Y)$ in order to calculate conditional entropy. We have introduced transition probabilities in Markov model to deal with this problem. After transferring our dataset samples into the Markov model, we determine the final value of conditional entropy. We have drawn a figure based on the values, which can be seen in Fig. 4.

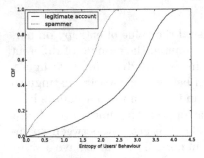 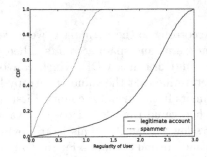

Fig. 3. Entropy of users' behavior   **Fig. 4.** Conditional entropy of users' behavior

Observing from this figure, we can see that values of conditional entropy in most spammers are lower than 1.0. However, for normal accounts, no more than 10 % has a value lower than 1.0. Of course, this result is based on the same entropy value for spammers and normal accounts. This compared result clearly proves that spammers have a much simpler model in sending messages than normal users. Through this conditional entropy, we can identify disguised spammers who are good at changing their behavior model in sending messages in online social networks.

Both of these features are good at distinguishing behavior models in sending messages in online social networks. We will put them together with existing effective features to build a classifier in detection of spammers.

5.2   Existing Features

We also made use of other seven features, which are based on accounts and messages. These features have been effective in previous studies and will be combined with our behavior methods to train for a classifier.

We can see those existing Features in Table 1, along with Behavior Feature. Although there are several other features, we integrate only these effective features in the current work. Then we transfer the value of these features from labeled dataset to train for a classifier. Evaluation and performance of these features to build a detection system will be introduced in the next section.

Table 1. Feature sets

Behavior feature	Entropy	Behavior diverse in sending messages by normal accounts
	Conditional entropy	Behavior simple in sending messages by spammers
Without behavior feature	Number of fans	Friends in following list of accounts
	Account reputation	Ratio between number of fans and sum of related friends
	Age	Age of accounts
	URL ratio	Ratio between number of URLs in sending messages of latest one week by accounts and sum of number of messages
	Hashtag (#) ratio	Ratio between number of hashtags (#) in sent messages of latest one week by accounts and sum of number of messages
	Reply (@) ratio	Ratio between number of reply (@) characters in sent messages of latest one week by accounts and sum of number of messages
	Forward ratio	Ratio between number of forward in sending messages of latest one week by accounts to sum of number of messages

6   Evaluation

In this section, we plan to prove the effectiveness of our detection system in online social networks, including the effectiveness of the behavior features model that has been proposed. Finally, we compare effectiveness of the system with and without the proposed behavior feature model.

6.1   Evaluation on Detection System

In this section, we plan to evaluate our detection system based on data from Sina Weibo, which we have collected and labeled. First, utilize several machine learning methods to train for an effective classifier. Then we put our test samples into the classifier for evaluation.

As labeled beforehand, we have about 2,000 normal accounts and 2,000 spam accounts. Next we conduct ten-fold cross-validation in Weka on different machine learning methods, such as J48, Random Forest, and Support Vector Machine (SVM). Accuracy rate and false positive rate can be seen in Table 2, which is based on Table 1 and Formula 8, and we will take an average of these to be the final value. Ultimately, the accuracy rate of the detection system is about 91.5 %, and false positive rate is about 3.4 %.

Table 2. Accuracy rate and false positive rate

	Accuracy rate	False positive rate
J48	89.6 %	4.9 %
Random forest	93.7 %	2.1 %
SVM	91.2 %	3.3 %

According to the labeled samples, we have analyzed the reason for these values. After we have observed the part of false positive labels and false negative labels, we found that labeled samples cannot be assured of complete label accuracy. Labels based on the blacklist need to be re-labeled to deliver a higher accuracy rate and lower false positive rate.

6.2 Evaluation on Effective of Behavior Feature Model

In this section, we plan to evaluate effectiveness of our proposed behavior feature model. First, we divide value of features that have been extracted by us previously, according to Table 3. Then we use features sets with and without behavior features to re-train and evaluate. We still use ten-fold cross-validation based on machine learning methods, such as J48, Random Forest, and SVM. The accuracy rate value and false positive rate can be seen in Table 3.

Table 3. Evaluation on effective of behavior features

	Accuracy rate	False positive rate
Without behavior feature	85.4 %	7.2 %
With behavior feature	91.5 %	3.4 %

According to the results in Table 3, the behavior model is much more effective in detection of spammers in OSNs. As we have proposed above, behavior features are very important for presenting behavior diversity when sending messages. Although there exist some ups and downs in these machine learning methods, based on these behavior features, detection systems can achieve a higher accuracy rate and a lower false positive rate. This is enough for proving the effectiveness of the proposed behavior features model.

7   Limitation and Future Work

This section discusses limitations of our detection system, first objective conditions, and then we present future work planned to complete the detection system.

Comparison with previous research is challenging. We cannot reproduce existing methods in detail because of differences in datasets and source code. We needed to take a completely different approach for using work to prove the effectiveness of our detection system and proposed behavior features. Finally, additional features on behavior still need to be added as we only proposed several features. There exist several other features, which can communicate with and augment the detection system.

For future work, we first need to collect much more data from different OSNs. We will communicate with officials and cooperate with them to acquire more data. Meanwhile, we install our detection methods on different OSNs to ascertain the optimum balance of detection system. Then, we will communicate with authors of prior research to get their samples and source code for comparison. It is essential to compare with existing studies in order to complete our detection system. In other hand, we will consummate our detection system by optimize the system's procedure, such as feedback training. Finally, we will try to re-analyze the dataset to identify other features that are related to behavior features. We hope we can complete our behavior model and whole detection system, and present a more effective detection system for use in online social networks.

8 Conclusion

In OSNs, thinking about privacy and security is essential for protecting people from attack. Spammers usually hide spam information and even attack in messages sent across OSNs. This spam information includes injection, phishing, irrelevant advertisement, etc. In this paper, we have proposed behavior features, combined with several effective features in existing studies, to build a detection system. From results of evaluation, we can conclude that behavior features proposed by us have a significant effect in detection and improve performance for detection of spammers in OSNs. Consideration of behavior features in sending messages is necessary. We hope to complete our work gradually and we would sincerely like to communicate with other researchers working in this area.

Acknowledgements. This work is supported by the National Natural Science Foundation of China under Grant No. 61170265 and Grant No.61472162.

References

1. Ciw team: Weibo had 167m monthly active users in q3 (2014). http://www.chinainternetwatch.com/10735/weibo-q3-2014
2. Yang, C., Harkreader, R., Guofei, G.: Empirical evaluation and new design for fighting evolving twitter spammers. IEEE Trans. Inf. Forensics Secur. **8**(8), 1280–1293 (2013)
3. Stringhini, G., Kruegel, C., Vigna, G.: Detecting spammers on social networks. In: Proceedings of the 26th Annual Computer Security Applications Conference, pp. 1–9. ACM (2010)

4. Grier, C., Thomas, K., Paxson, V., Zhang, M.: @ spam: the underground on 140 characters or less. In: Proceedings of the 17th ACM Conference on Computer and Communications Security, pp. 27–37. ACM (2010)

5. Thomas, K., Grier, C., Song, D., Paxson, V.: Suspended accounts in retrospect: an analysis of twitter spam. In: Proceedings of the 2011 ACM SIGCOMM Conference on Internet Measurement Conference, pp. 243–258. ACM (2011)

6. Almaatouq, A., Alabdulkareem, A., Nouh, M., Shmueli, E., Alsaleh, M., Singh, V.K., Alarifi, A., Alfaris, A., Pentland, A.S.: Twitter: who gets caught? observed trends in social micro-blogging spam. In: Proceedings of the 2014 ACM Conference on Web Science, pp. 33–41. ACM (2014)

7. Yang, C., Harkreader, R., Zhang, J., Shin, S., Gu, G.: Analyzing spammers' social networks for fun and profit: a case study of cyber criminal ecosystem on twitter. In: Proceedings of the 21st International Conference on World Wide Web, pp. 71–80. ACM (2012)

8. Zhang, Y., Ruan, X., Wang, H., Wang, H.: What scale of audience a campaign can reach in what price on twitter? In: INFOCOM, 2014 Proceedings IEEE, pp. 1168–1176. IEEE (2014)

9. Egele, M., Stringhini, G., Kruegel, C., Vigna, G.: COMPA: detecting compromised accounts on social networks. In: NDSS (2013)

10. Chu, Z., Gianvecchio, S., Wang, H., Jajodia, S.: Detecting automation of twitter accounts: are you a human, bot, or cyborg? IEEE Trans. Dependable Secure Comput. 9(6), 811–824 (2012)

11. Gao, H., Hu, J., J., Wilson, J., Li, Z., Chen, Y., Zhao, B.Y.: Detecting and characterizing social spam campaigns. In: Proceedings of the 10th ACM SIGCOMM Conference on Internet Measurement, pp. 35–47. ACM (2010)

12. Tan, E., Guo, L., Chen, S., Zhang, X., Zhao, Y.: Unik: unsupervised social network spam detection. In: Proceedings of the 22nd ACM International Conference on Conference on Information and Knowledge Management, pp. 479–488. ACM (2013)

13. Gao, H., Chen, Y., Lee, K., Palsetia, D., Choudhary, A.N.: Towards online spam filtering in social networks. In: NDSS (2012)

14. Martinez-Romo, J., Araujo, L.: Detecting malicious tweets in trending topics using a statistical analysis of language. Expert Syst. Appl. 40(8), 2992–3000 (2013)

15. Sina weibo api. http://open.weibo.com/

16. Google safe browsing api. https://developers.google.com/safe-browsing/?hl=zh-CN

17. Virustotal. https://www.virustotal.com/

A Proactive Fault Tolerance Scheme for Large Scale Storage Systems

Xinpu Ji, Yuxiang Ma, Rui Ma, Peng Li, Jingwei Ma, Gang Wang,
Xiaoguang Liu$^{(\boxtimes)}$, and Zhongwei Li$^{(\boxtimes)}$

College of Computer and Control Engineering, Nankai University,
Tianjin 300350, China
{jixinpu,mayuxiang,marui,lipeng,mjwtom,wgzwp,liuxg,
lizhongwei}@nbjl.nankai.edu.cn

Abstract. Facing increasingly high failure rate of drives in data centers, reactive fault tolerance mechanisms alone can hardly guarantee high reliability. Therefore, some hard drive failure prediction models that can predict soon-to-fail drives in advance have been raised. But few researchers applied these models to distributed systems to improve the reliability.

This paper proposes SSM (Self-Scheduling Migration) which can monitor drives' health status and reasonably migrate data from the soon-to-fail drives to others in advance using the results produced by the prediction models. We adopt a self-scheduling migration algorithm into distributed systems to transfer the data from soon-to-fail drives. This algorithm can dynamically adjust the migration rates according to drives' severity level, which is generated from the realtime prediction results. Moreover, the algorithm can make full use of the resources and balance the load when selecting migration source and destination drives. On the premise of minimizing the side effects of migration to system services, the migration bandwidth is reasonably allocated. We implement a prototype based on Sheepdog distributed system. The system only sees respectively 8 % and 13 % performance drops on read and write operations caused by migration. Compared with reactive fault tolerance, SSM significantly improves system reliability and availability.

Keywords: Proactive fault tolerance · Distributed storage system · Priority scheduling · Data migration · Resource allocation

1 Introduction

With the development of information technology, the scale of the storage system is increasing explosively. Drives are the most commonly replaced hardware component in the data centers [1]. For example, 78 % of all hardware replacements were caused by hard drives in data centers of Microsoft [1]. Moreover, block and sector level failures, such as latent sector errors [2] and silent data corruption [3], cannot be avoidable when the capacity of the whole system becomes larger and larger.

© Springer International Publishing Switzerland 2015
G. Wang et al. (Eds.): ICA3PP 2015, Part III, LNCS 9530, pp. 337–350, 2015.
DOI: 10.1007/978-3-319-27137-8_26

Since drive failures have become a serious problem, lots of studies have been focusing on designing erasure codes or replication strategies to improve storage system reliability. They are typical reactive fault tolerance methods used to reconstruct data after failures occur. However, due to the high cost, these methods cannot meet the demands of the high service quality in data centers.

To reduce the reconstruction overhead and improve the system reliability, proactive fault tolerance was proposed, which enables the actions to be taken before failures happen. Hard drive failure prediction models are proposed firstly as a typical proactive fault tolerance strategy. These models use some statistical or machine learning methods to build prediction models based on the SMART attributes [4]. Some of them have reached a good prediction performance. For example, a model using classification Tree (CT) could predict over 95 % of failures at a FAR under 0.1 % on a real-world dataset containing 25,792 drives [5].

Although failure prediction is of great significance, the ultimate goal of prediction is to adopt some reasonable strategies to handle the failure prediction results. Recently, some studies applied failure prediction models to distributed systems, such as Fatman [6] and IDO [7], but they simply migrated dangerous data by using prediction results without taking priority and the migration impact on the system performance into consideration.

In this paper, we develop SSM (self-scheduling migration), which collects drives' status to determine their severity levels and uses a pre-warning handling algorithm to protect the in danger data. There are several issues needed to be addressed by the algorithm. How to fully use the system resources to migrate the data as soon as possible. How to dispose the drives in different severity levels differently. How to reduce the impact on the normal service. More importantly, the algorithm also balances the migration load evenly to each drive, which guarantees a stable quality of service when data is scattered evenly.

In summary, our main contributions are:

- Design *Monitor* and *Predictor* module which can monitor drives' health status in distributed systems using prediction models and then determine drives' severity levels.
- Propose an pre-warning handling algorithm to achieve high availability and reliability.
- Apply SSM to Sheepdog and evaluate the benefit.

The rest parts of this paper are organized as follows. Section 2 surveys related work of fault tolerance in storage systems. Section 3 illustrates the design of SSM. We will present the experimental results in Sect. 4. Section 5 concludes the paper.

2   Related Work

Storage is a critical component in data centers and how to ensure their reliability becomes a popular topic in the storage community. In the late 1980s, RAID technologies, such as RAID-1 and RAID-5, were firstly proposed as a fault tolerance mechanism and have been widely used in the disk array [8]. Blaum et al. [9] proposed EVENODD which is the first double-erasure-correcting parity array code based on exclusive-OR operations. The computational complexity of this kind of codes is far lower than that of RS code.

With the development of cloud storage, hard drive failures are common which need to be handled. So the data recovery performance becomes increasingly important. In cloud storage systems, network and disk I/O, have a great influence on the service. Consequently, recent research on reliability focused on how to reduce I/O overhead incurred by data recovery. For example, Cidon et al. proposed Copyset [10], which limits the data replicas within node groups rather than over all storage nodes. This strategy reduces the data loss probability and the recovery overhead effectively. Quite a few methods [11] are also proposed to improve the recovery performance for cloud storage systems using erasure codes. Weaver code [12] and Regenerating code [13] all reach a balance between space utilization and disk/network I/O overhead.

Either replication or erasure coding are typical reactive fault tolerant techniques. Even with aforementioned methods, they hardly can provide satisfactory reliability and availability with low cost. On the contrary, proactive fault tolerance can predict drive failures in advance and therefore provide enough time for the operator to take actions before failures really occur. At present, Self-Monitoring, Analysis and Reporting Technology (SMART) is implemented inside of most hard drives [4]. The threshold-based method can only obtain a failure detection rate (FDR) of 3–10 % with a low false alarm rate on the order of 0.1 % [14]. So researchers have proposed some statistical and machine learning methods to improve the prediction performance. Especially in [5], Li et al. presented hard drive failure prediction models based on Classification and Regression Trees, which perform better in prediction performance as well as stability and interpretability.

Hard drive prediction models are intended to be used in real-world storage systems to improve reliability and availability. However, only a few researchers focused on how to use the predictions (pre-warnings) to improve the reliability of the real storage systems. IDO can find the soon-to-fail disk, migrate proactively data of hot zones to surrogate RAID set [7]. Once a disk fails, it reconstructs hot data with surrogate set and recovers cold data with RAID mechanism on the failed disk. However, IDO is not designed for distributed storage systems and locality implementation needs information from the superior file system. RAID-SHIELD [15] uses the threshold-based algorithm to predict single drive failures and prioritizes the most dangerous RAID groups according to joint probability.

In this paper, we present SSM, which is an comprehensive system, employing pre-warning handling algorithm combined with drive prediction models. Moreover, we apply the mechanism into Sheepdog to evaluate the effectiveness.

3   Architecture and Design

Figure 1 depicts the architecture of our proactive fault tolerant system, namely SSM. It consists of five functional modules: *Monitor*, *Collectors*, *Predictor*,

Trainer and *Scheduler*. *Monitor* is used to monitor the status of individual drives. *Collectors* are responsible for collecting SMART information from *Monitor*. *Predictor* assesses drives' severity levels based on failure prediction models. The function of *Trainer* is updating prediction models periodically to prevent them from aging. *Scheduler* as the kernel module in SSM, manages and schedules data migration tasks with different severity levels. It is composed of three parts: priority-based scheduling, multi-source migration and bandwidth allocation.

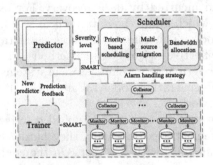

Fig. 1. The architecture of SSM.

In order to achieve portability, *Monitor*, *Collectors*, *Trainer* and *Predictor* are designed as four independent modules. They expose several interfaces (as Table 1 shows) that can be used by other modules in the system. Due to their independence, the interfaces also can be used in other distributed systems to implement their own migration algorithm.

Table 1. The interfaces exposed by *Monitors* and *Predictor*.

Interface name	Input	Output
smart	None	SMART dataset
predict	SMART dataset	Severity level
feedback	Prediction result	Sample weight
predictor_upd	SMART samples	New predictor

3.1   Monitor

Monitors are implemented to gather the SMART attributes from the drives in SSM, which are required by *Predictor* to predict the health status of the drives. Also, this information is used by *Trainer* to improve the prediction model (build a new model). We employ multi-level *Collectors* to gather SMART samples. The *Collectors* at the bottom use *smart* to gather information directly from *Monitors*, then send it to the upper level *Collectors* regularly after necessary pre-processing such as adding drive identification information and data normalization. *Collectors* of each layer are selected according to the topological structure of the storage system. If one *Collector* fails, a new *Collector* will be elected to ensure the availability of SSM. Because the collection job is executed per hour, it has little impact on system services. Once the root *Collector* has accumulated enough samples, *Predictor* and *Trainer* will call the *smart* interface to get SMART dataset.

3.2   Predictor

In general, hard drives deteriorate gradually rather than suddenly. Most previous works simply output a binary classification result which can not accurately describe drives' health status. On the contrary, the Regression tree (RT) model proposed by [5] does not simply output good or failed, but a deterioration degree which can be regarded as the health degree. This model can achieve a detection rate above 96 % and therefore most data from soon-to-fail drives can be protected by SSM.

We want to deal with pre-warnings according to the level of urgency so that the limited system resources can be effectively used to migrating dangerous data. For this, a coarse gained severity level evaluation is enough. For example, considering a drive predicted to be failed 250 h later, we do not have to distinguish it from the other one with a predicted remaining life of 249 h, but make sure to prioritize the other one predicted to be failed within 150 h over it. Thus, we can define k severity levels by dividing the domain of RT output values into k ranges. In our prototype system, we use 5 equal length ranges. Level 5 represents the healthy status and level 1 means the most urgent status. *Predictor* is responsible for converting a continuous value output by the prediction model into a discrete severity level. To verify how good our method evaluate the level of urgency, we apply it to two real-world datasets. Dataset A is from [5] and dataset B is collected from another data center. Figures 2 and 3 show the predicted results of failed drives in the test sets, which are very close to the ground truth. There are respectively 95 % and 96 % predicted results that are exactly equal to or one level away from the ground truth on A and B. It is can concluded that our method assesses the level of urgency effectively and can be used to prioritize migration tasks (Table 2).

Table 2. Two dataset details.

Dateset name	Good drive	Failed drive (training/test)
A	22,790	434 (302/132)
B	98,060	243 (169/74)

The SMART attribute values of drives change over time, and failure reasons vary as the environment changes. As a result, *Predictor* will become ineffective as time goes by, and therefore *Trainer* updates the model periodically. It uses

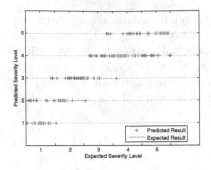
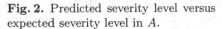
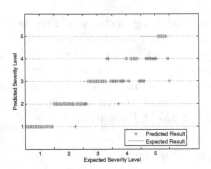

Fig. 2. Predicted severity level versus expected severity level in A.

Fig. 3. Predicted severity level versus expected severity level in B.

the updating strategies proposed in [5] to build new models using the old and/or the new SMART samples. The *predictor_upd* interface is invoked to replace the old model by the new one, and then *Predictor* will use the new model so that the good prediction performance is maintained. Though systems always try to avoid missed alarms and false alarms, they are generally inevitable. When they arise unfortunately, the system will catch them and send the wrong predicted SMART samples to *Trainer* as the *feedback*. These samples will be used in model updating to improve the accuracy of the model.

3.3   Self-Scheduling Migration

When an alarm arises in the system, the data on the soon-to-fail drive should be effectively protected. A handling strategy can reasonably process multiple pre-warnings according to the current health status and the redundancy layout of the storage system. We design a self-scheduling migration algorithm, which migrates data on the soon-to-fail drive as soon as possible. The migration algorithm has three distinguished features. First, it uses a dynamic priority scheduling rather than the traditional first come first service discipline when migrating data. Different levels of priority (severity) possess different migration rates. We also have a good strategy to handle the priority changing with time. Second, we do not simply use the soon-to-fail drive as the migration source. The healthy drives containing the replicas of a dangerous data block may be selected as the source to slow the deterioration of the soon-to-fail drive. Third, we try to reduce the overhead of migration as much as possible. We measure the bandwidth required by the normal service and then set a migration bandwidth to ensure the migration has a low impact on the system. As Fig. 1 shows, we design three modules, priority based scheduling, multi-source migration and bandwidth allocation, in *Scheduler* to implement these features. The detailed self-scheduling migration algorithm is shown in Algorithm 1.

Algorithm 1. self-scheduling migration

Input: New soon-to-fail drives set W', current soon-to-fail drives set W
Output: none
1: **Begin**
2: $W \leftarrow W \cup W'$
3: $q \leftarrow NULL$ ▷ q: priority queue
4: **for** each drive d in W **do**
5:    calculate $score(d)$ using Eq. 1
6:    **for** each unmigrated block b on d **do**
7:     $t_b \leftarrow$create a migration task for b
8:     $t_b.prio \leftarrow (score(d), dr(b))$ ▷ dr: the number of dangerous replicas
9:     q.insert(t_b)
10:    **end for**
11: **end for**
12: calculate the total relative severity score by a reduction operation
13: **for** each drive d in W **do**
14:    calculate $bt(d)$ using Eq. 2
15:    $c(d) \leftarrow 0$ ▷ $c(d)$: bandwidth usage
16: **end for**
17: **while** q is not empty **do**
18:    q.deletemax(t_b)
19:    select the source drive S and the destination drive D for b
20:    **if** $c(S) + m(b) < bt(S)$ **then**   ▷ $m(b)$: bandwidth required to migrate b
21:     copy b from S to D ▷ perform migration
22:     update b's metadata and mark it as migrated
23:     **if** all blocks on the same drive d have been migrated **then**
24:      remove d from W
25:     **end if**
26:    **end if**
27: **end while**

Alarm Handling Mechanism. We introduce a drive alarm daemon (DAD) to implement self-scheduling migration. When *Predictor* reports pre-warnings (generally periodically), DAD will receive the alarms and perform the following steps as Algorithm 1 shows: firstly, scan all the unmigrated blocks on the soon-to-fail drives (line 4–12) and create a migration task for every block (line 7); secondly, allocate migration bandwidth for every drive (line 13–16); thirdly, select the source and destination drives for each migration task (line 19); and finally, perform migration tasks if there is enough migration bandwidth available and update metadata (line 20–26).

Data consistency is a critical problem. When a block is being migrated, users may update its content, where data inconsistency may occur. To address this issue, we adopt a fine-grained locking mechanism. While a data block is being migrated to a new drive, the system blocks write operations to it. Read operations are served as usual. Writes are unblocked after this migration task is accomplished. Since the locking granularity is just a block, it will not cause great impact on the system service.

Priority-Based Scheduling. It is not rare that multiple drive failures occur simultaneously in a large data center. Consequently, how to allocate reasonably migration bandwidth to multiple pre-warnings is the key problem. A reasonable strategy is to give more resources to the drives in higher severity levels. We introduce a *relative severity score* as the priority to control bandwidth allocation. It takes both severity level s and migration progress p into account. The migration progress is measured by the ratio of the number of migrated blocks to the total number of ones on the soon-to-fail drive. Drives with higher severity levels and lower migration ratios will be given a higher *relative severity score* which implies a larger share of migration bandwidth. The *relative severity score* of the ith drive is calculated as

$$score(i) = \frac{1 - p(i)}{s} \tag{1}$$

Line 5 in Algorithm 1 calculates the *relative severity score* for every block and line 8 uses the score as the priority of a block.

Multi-source Migration Algorithm. The fundamental difference between pre-warning handling and failure handling is that the soon-to-fail drives are still in operation. So an intuitive idea is to migrate data only from soon-to-fail drives. However, it will be bound to put more pressure on the soon-to-fail drives, which may accelerate their deterioration. SSM instead selects the source drive for a block D to be migrated from all of the drives having D's replicas, which fully uses the bandwidth and balances the load. More specifically, SSM selects the source drive by taking both load and health status of drives into account: firstly, prefer drives with lower load. Secondly, when the soon-to-fail drive deteriorates faster than ever, choose another source. Finally, when a source drive is being offline, choose another one. Then the destination drive is selected in the same way as normal replica creation except that the soon-to-fail drives are not considered as candidates. This ensures good system reliability. By using this multi-source strategy, we can achieve a better migration performance compared with traditional reactive systems.

Migration Bandwidth Allocation. To reduce the impact of migration on system service, we only allocate a proportion of available bandwidth to migration tasks and reserve the rest to serve normal service. Let α denote the percentage of allocated migration bandwidth in the total bandwidth and B denote the total bandwidth. Migration task is executed on the basis of what migration bandwidth is below αB. If the overload of migration tasks is below αB, they will be scheduled normally.

A drive with a higher *relative severity score* should be allocated a higher migration bandwidth on the basis of the same total migration bandwidth. We set a migration threshold $b(i)$ for every soon-to-fail drive i. The migration bandwidth is allocated according to Eq. 2. For a block b on the drive i, the migration task is performed if the migration rate of b's source drive S does not exceed its migration threshold $b(S)$.

$$b(i) = \alpha B * \frac{score(i)}{\sum_{i=1}^{n} score(i)} \qquad (2)$$

where n is the total number of soon-to-fail drives and $score(i)$ is i's current relative severity score. Line 14 in Algorithm 1 calculates the migration threshold for every soon-to-fail drive.

3.4 Reliability Analysis

Related researches [5] show that accurate detection rates of prediction models can help increase the Mean Time To Data Loss (MTTDL) and thus improve the reliability of storage systems greatly. However, the building of prediction models is just the first step and far from enough. Our ultimate goal is to put these models into practice by guiding system's pre-warning process. Once the *Scheduler* receives pre-warnings, it will trigger the recover process to migrate the data on soon-to-fail drives in advance. As a result, by deploying the proactive fault tolerance mechanism, we can shorten the system reconstruction time and reduce the Mean Time To Repair (MTTR) as much as possible, which enhances the reliability of system significantly. On the other hand, given plenty of time for data migration, *Scheduler* can utilize system resources more efficiently. That is, while the system is heavy loaded, a low bandwidth will be limited in the migration process, whereas a high one can be adopted, which means side effects to normal read and write performance are minimized dramatically while compared with the original system without SSM.

4 Evaluation

In this section, we present the experimental results of SSM. We implement SSM as a modified instance of Sheepdog which is an open source project of a distributed storage system. Sheepdog provides a high available block level storage volumes and adopts a completely symmetrical architecture, which implies no central control node. The nodes and data blocks are addressed by Distributed Hash Table (DHT).

We set up a cluster comprising of 12 nodes to simulate a local part of a large scale distributed storage system. Since a Sheepdog system is completely symmetrical, experimental results on this local part can reflect the overall performance. Each machine runs CentOS 6.3 on a quad-core Intel(R) Xeon(TM) CPUs @ 2.80 GHz with 1 GB memory and a RAID-0 consisting of six 80 GB SATA disks. The machines are connected by Gigabit Ethernet. SSM in Sheepdog takes three replicas as the redundancy strategy and uses the default 4 MB block size. Through the experiments, we try to show that (1) SSM is superior than reactive fault tolerance and (2) migration scheduling algorithm is effective in reducing the impact on system service.

4.1   Proactive Fault Tolerance Versus Reactive Fault Tolerance

An important advantage of SSM over traditional reactive fault tolerant technologies is that it can achieve good reliability while remaining the quality of service. In a reactive fault tolerant system, once a hard drive failure occurs, the system must recover it as soon as possible. This "best effort" strategy implies that the repair process will occupy a large part of the system resources which will affect the performance of users' read and write requests significantly. On the other hand, the system certainly can guarantee QoS by limiting the resources used by the repair process. However, that will lead to a much longer MTTR which is detrimental to the reliability. In other words, a reactive fault tolerant system cannot obtain both the reliability and QoS. In contrast, SSM can predict drive failures several days even several weeks in advance. Therefore, even though it only allocates a small share of disk and network bandwidth to the migration process, it still can complete the migration before the failure actually occurs. Since the state-of-art drive failure prediction method [5] maintains good prediction accuracy, few missed failures will not defer SSM from obtaining both good reliability and minimal impact on reading and writing service.

Table 3 compares degraded read and write throughput and MTTR (migration time) of SSM and RFT (reactive fault tolerance). SSM adopts multi-source migration and bandwidth limitation to evaluate its performance. We assume that 8 TB (typical per-node data volume in modern cloud storage systems) data needs to be recovered (migrated). As expected, RFT with "best effort" repair impacts normal read and write throughput (118 MB/s and 25 MB/s respectively) seriously although it guarantee a short MTTR. Limiting repair bandwidth (10 MB/s) in RFT (RFT(BL)) alleviates impact on QoS effectively but leads to an unacceptable MTTR. In contrast, SSM remains good QoS and achieves a short migration time (compared with the prediction time in advance). Moreover, we have enough space to further reduce migration bandwidth limitation to obtain better QoS because there still a wide gap between the migration time and the prediction time in advance.

Table 3. Reactive versus Proactive

Strategy	Read (MB/s)	Write (MB/s)	MTTR (hours)
RFT	80	15	14.56
RFT (BL)	100	22	58.24
SSM	110	23	66.58

4.2   Evaluating Migration Performance

We manually simulated a drive with 20 GB data that is going to fail to trigger the pre-warning and then the migration. The throughput of single-source migration (SS), about 28 MB/s, is 16 % slower than that of multi-source. Multi-source migration (MS) dose not only improve the migration rate, but also achieves a more balanced load by diverting the pressure to multiple drives. Replicas are scattered well by the consistent hash algorithm.

Migration also affects the data access performance. We test the write performances with migration using the following steps. First, we start a sequential write job, then simulate a pre-warning to trigger the migration, and record the running state trace of the system when write and migration exist simultaneously. The test lasts 350 s which is long enough to reflect the correlativity between data access and migration. Also, we evaluate the read performance by a similar method. A pre-warning is triggered when the user requires a read service. Moreover, we implement MS to evaluate the read and write performance. In Fig. 4, write throughout is about 26 MB/s without any migration, while it is reduced by more than 80 % with migration not limiting the bandwidth. Quality of normal service drops down heavily when migration occupies lots of resources. We should make effects to decrease the drops. DHT constructs a ring and each node covers a part of the ring. Neighbors in the ring always have a higher similarity in data and resource. We allocate migration bandwidth based on a concept of locality. The ring are divided into many parts, and every part has their allocation bandwidth. In the part consisting of 12 nodes, 10 % (α) of the total bandwidth (B), about 10 MB, is allocated to the migration job. With bandwidth limitation (BL), the write throughout is only reduced by 13 %. From Fig. 5, read throughout is around 120 MB/s in normal condition through simulation of a disk drive failure. It is decreased by 8 %, namely about 110 MB/s in migration with bandwidth limitation. While without bandwidth limitation, read rate is as low as 95 MB/s. Since the system blocks write operations when the block is being migrated, write rate decreased more than that of read. The degradation of write and read performance are all acceptable for the system with bandwidth limitation.

We also explore read and write performance under four different strategies and the results are shown in Fig. 6. Except for the fault-free configuration which means no alarms nor migrations, SSM with BLMS has the best performance in all other cases, which has the minimal impact on the users' operations. Compared

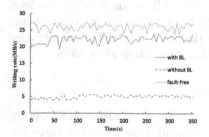

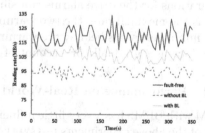

Fig. 4. Write rate in fault-free, bandwidth with limitation and without bandwidth limitation. Migration job has an great influence on write services. The writing operation with BL performs well.

Fig. 5. Read rate in fault-free, bandwidth limitation and without bandwidth limitation conditions. Migration job has an light influence on read services. The reading operation with BL performs well.

with MS, the read throughput of BLSS is higher, which means BLSS can reduce the impact on system performance more effective than MS. When using MS without BLSS, there is a higher possibility that a write should wait for the lock acquired by the migration process as more drives participate in the migration. So the write performance of MS is worse than that of BLSS. In Subsects. 4.3 and 4.4, we all adopt BLMS and allocate 10 MB as the migration bandwidth.

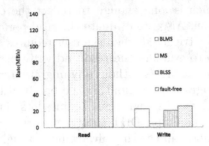

Fig. 6. Read rate and write rate of fault-free, BLSS, MS and BLMS.

4.3   Evaluating Priority-Based Scheduling

Our system migrates data according to the priority making drives with different severity levels treated differently. We simulate a process with multiple warnings in different severity levels. In Figs. 2 and 3, our proposed method that converts health degrees to severity levels is proven to be reasonable. We trigger a pre-warning with level 1 first, and the migration rate is about 30 MB/s. After 90 s, a level 2 alarm arrives with a lower priority. At the same time, the migration rate of the drive in level 1 decreases. Another pre-warning with the same severity level appears at the 150th second and its migration rate is almost equal to the first 2 warnings. At the 210th second, an alarm with severity level 4 was raised. From the 210th second to the 630th second, as is detailed in Fig. 7, the four migrations for the drive alarms run simultaneously. Migration for drives in level 1 has the maximal rate, the two warnings with level 2 have the middle rate and the minimum rate is held by the warning with the drive in level 4. The migration rate increases gradually on account of migration completing after 630 s.

4.4   Performance on Real-World Traces

SSM with BLMS has a very little influence on the normal operations in Sheepdog. All of the above experiments use synthesized workload. Now we choose three real traces (fileserver, webserver and netsfs) of Filebench to test our system. Figure 8 illustrates the throughout (Y-axis, IO/second) of the system. Compared with the fault-free condition, the throughput of fileserver is decreased by 15 %, that of webserver is decreased by 10 % and for the case of netsfs it decreases the least for only 1 %. SSM performs well with all the three cases.

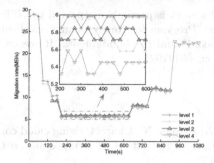

Fig. 7. The change of migration rates as four alarms with different severity levels are raised at different times.

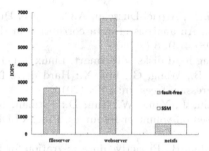

Fig. 8. IOPS of fault-free and pre-warning condition in the real workloads fileserver, webserver and netsfs.

5 Conclusion

This paper provides a proactive fault tolerance mechanism for a typical distributed system, Sheepdog. In our method, we migrate data on the soon-to-fail drives before disk failures really occur. By increasing the number of replicas for the blocks on these soon-to-fail drives, the reliability of storage system gets improved. When a failure happens, data reconstruction overhead will be significantly reduced. Different severity levels are proposed for the health degree. We introduce a *relative severity score* to evaluate the severity level. For a higher *relative severity score*, data on this drive will be migrated as soon as possible thus is given a high processing rate. On account of every block having several replicas, we take some conditions into consideration to choose a proper source. By combining fully multi-source migration and bandwidth limitation, SSM has a little influence on the original distributed system.

Adding SSM to the distributed system, we handle threatened data before failure, which will influence the original service. Migration rate is restricted to reduce the impact on system. Every soon-to-fail drive has their own migration mechanism to allocate migration bandwidth. As a result, the system only causes respectively 8 % and 13 % performance drops on read and write operations. Compared with traditional reactive fault tolerance, SSM significantly improves system reliability and availability.

Acknowledgments. This work is partially supported by NSF of China (grant numbers: 61373018, 11301288), Program for New Century Excellent Talents in University (grant number: NCET130301) and the Fundamental Research Funds for the Central Universities (grant number: 65141021).

References

1. Vishwanath, K.V., Nagappan, N.: Characterizing cloud computing hardware reliability. In: Proceedings of the 1st ACM Symposium on Cloud Computing, pp. 193–204. ACM (2010)
2. Bairavasundaram, L.N., Goodson, G.R., Pasupathy, S., Schindler, J.: An analysis of latent sector errors in disk drives. ACM SIGMETRICS Perform. Eval. Rev. **35**, 289–300 (2007)
3. Bairavasundaram, L.N., Arpaci-Dusseau, A.C., Arpaci-Dusseau, R.H., Goodson, G.R., Schroeder, B.: An analysis of data corruption in the storage stack. ACM Trans. Storage (TOS) **4**(3), 8 (2008)
4. Allen, B.: Monitoring hard disks with smart. Linux J. (117), 74–77 (2004)
5. Li, J., Ji, X., Zhu, B., Wang, G., Liu, X.: Hard drive failure prediction using classication and regression trees. In: DSN (2014)
6. Qin, A., Hu, D., Liu, J., Yang, W., Tan, D.: Fatman: cost-saving and reliable archival storage based on volunteer resources. Proc. VLDB Endow. **7**(13), 1748–1753 (2014)
7. Wu, S., Jiang, H., Mao, B.: Proactive data migration for improved storage availability in large-scale data centers (2014)
8. Patterson, D.A., Gibson, G., Katz, R.H.: A case for redundant arrays of inexpensive disks (RAID) **17**(3), 109–116 (1988)
9. Blaum, M., Brady, J., Bruck, J., Menon, J.: Evenodd: an effcient scheme for tolerating double disk failures in raid architectures. IEEE Trans. Comput. **44**(2), 192–202 (1995)
10. Cidon, A., Rumble, S.M., Stutsman, R., Katti, S., Ousterhout, J.K., Rosenblum, M.: Copysets: reducing the frequency of data loss in cloud storage. In: USENIX Annual Technical Conference, pp. 37–48. Citeseer (2013)
11. Ford, D., Labelle, F., Popovici, F.I., Stokely, M., Truong, V.A., Barroso, L., Grimes, C., Quinlan, S.: Availability in globally distributed storage systems. In: OSDI, pp. 61–74 (2010)
12. Hafner, J.L.: Weaver codes: highly fault tolerant erasure codes for storage systems. In: FAST, vol. 5, pp. 16–16 (2005)
13. Papailiopoulos, D.S., Luo, J., Dimakis, A.G., Huang, C., Li, J.: Simple regenerating codes: network coding for cloud storage. In: INFOCOM, 2012 Proceedings IEEE, pp. 2801–2805. IEEE (2012)
14. Murray, J.F., Hughes, G.F., Kreutz-Delgado, K.: Machine learning methods for predicting failures in hard drives: a multiple-instance application. J. Mach. Learn. Res. **6**, 783–816 (2005)
15. Ma, A., Douglis, F., Lu, G., Sawyer, D., Chandra, S., Hsu, W.: Raidshield: characterizing, monitoring, and proactively protecting against disk failures. In: Proceedings of the 13th USENIX Conference on File and Storage Technologies, pp. 241–256. USENIX Association (2015)

When Software Defined Networks Meet Fault Tolerance: A Survey

Jue Chen, Jinbang Chen$^{(\boxtimes)}$, Fei Xu$^{(\boxtimes)}$, Min Yin, and Wei Zhang

School of Computer Science and Software Engineering,
East China Normal University, Shanghai 200062, China
jue0428@126.com, {jbchen,fxu}@cs.ecnu.edu.cn

Abstract. Software Defined Network (SDN) is emerging as a novel network architecture which decouples the control plane from the data plane. However, SDN is unable to survive when facing failure, in particular in large scale data-center networks. Due to the programmability of SDN, mechanism could be designed to achieve fault tolerance. In this survey, we broadly discuss the fault tolerance issue and systematically review the existing methods proposed so far for SDN. Our representation starts from the significant components that OpenFlow and SDN brings – which are useful for the purpose of failure recovery, and is then further expanded to the discussion of fault tolerance in data plane and control plane, in which two phases – detection and recovery – are both needed. In particular, as the important part of this paper, we have highlighted the comparison between two main methods – restoration and protection – for failure recovery. Moreover, future research issues are discussed as well.

Keywords: Software defined network · Fault tolerance · OpenFlow · Failure detection · Recovery · Restoration · Protection

1 Introduction

When the Internet was stretched even though continuous efforts were made to upgrade devices or protocols, an innovative network architecture – Software Defined Network (SDN), has gained much attention in both academia and industry. With the ability to decouple the data plane from the control plane, SDN brings much benefit to commercial enterprises [13,20]. For instance, Google's B4 – a globally-deployed software defined WAN [15], has successfully improved the utilization of network links up to nearly 100 percent, which is threefold as before. As for any network systems, including Google's geo-distributed data-centers B4, network faults are prevalent, which can inevitably cause catastrophic effects to user applications. Therefore, to consider and further to solve every possible malfunction becomes a need for all network systems. Accordingly, one of the urgent needs for SDN is to provide the ability of failure recovery. For this issue, we focus ourselves on the breakdown of network components in this article,

© Springer International Publishing Switzerland 2015
G. Wang et al. (Eds.): ICA3PP 2015, Part III, LNCS 9530, pp. 351–368, 2015.
DOI: 10.1007/978-3-319-27137-8_27

while excluding the discussion of network update [44] such as forwarding loop and forwarding black hole.

In traditional networks, such as the Internet, routing protocols can help convergence of the whole network automatically. However, as the "brain" of SDN, a controller does not have the ability of self-healing when initially designed and introduced, and it must be equipped with the capacity of fault tolerance. In SDN, the fault tolerance issue covers across two different levels – the data plane and the control plane.

On one hand, if a link breaks or a switch meets an outage in the forwarding plane, a controller needs to help to find another valid routing path to continuously deliver packets as there is almost no intelligence on network devices – which is called the failure recovery of data plane. Chronologically, this procedure consists of two phases – failure detection and failure recovery. Furthermore, two typical methods – restoration and protection [43] are commonly used in the recovery process. With restoration, switches must alert the controller to the fault, then the controller will generate certain commands to direct data plane to update their forwarding tables. On the contrary, with protection, switches would establish table entries for two paths – the working path and the backup path before the fault occurs. If the switch detects the malfunction, it can switch over to the protection path automatically without the participation of the controller. At the moment, most papers in this area are focusing on solving a single link failure. As a result, the solutions for multiple link failures and the outage of a switch remain a challenge.

On the other hand, the fault tolerance of control plane is of much concern as well. Controllers need to take charge of the whole network all the time. As a result, the diagram of multiple controllers have been proposed to ensure the reliability of the control plane [25]. In addition, the OpenFlow channel between controllers and switches may also meet fault. If a switch loses connection with the controller, another path is needed which may walk through other neighbours to reach the controller [38]. Nearly no papers are focusing on solving the failure of the OpenFlow channel and it could be regarded as a future research direction. In summary, both devices and links need to be provided with redundancy to cope with a variety of failures in the context of SDN.

The rest of this survey is organized as follows. Section 2 presents some preparatory work for fault tolerance in SDN, which is based on the main idea of evolution from the traditional networks to SDN, including existing strategies (mostly heuristic) of failure recovery in traditional networks, and essential structures in OpenFlow [27] protocol which are used for fault tolerance of SDN. The existing methods as well as comparison, summaries and future research issues are then discussed in the following three sections. We review the failure detection of data plane in Sect. 3, and then discuss the failure recovery of data plane and control plane in Sects. 4 and 5 respectively. Finally, a conclusion is given in Sect. 6.

2   Prerequisites for Fault Tolerance in SDN

There are preparatory works related to the fault tolerance in SDN. In this section, we first summarize the experience of failure recovery in traditional networks, and

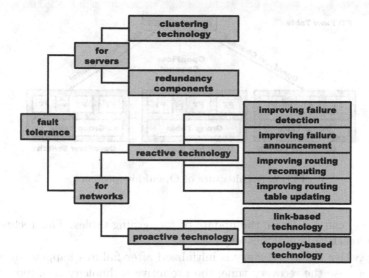

Fig. 1. Classification of fault tolerance methods in traditional networks

then provide the concepts of flow table and group table which are the bases of the OpenFlow protocol.

2.1 A Review of Fault Tolerance in Traditional Networks

In general, each network component may face a failure. Here we mainly discuss fault tolerance on servers and links for traditional networks [35], which are summarized and classified in Fig. 1.

Based on the difference with respect to the number of nodes (servers), the fault tolerance on servers can be separated into two parts. When using the clustering technology, multiple computers cooperate with each other. As long as at least one of them works correctly, the whole system can provide services to users. On the other hand, in the situation that only one server is in use, equipping each component (including CPU, memory, disk, network card and even power supply, *etc.*) with a backup is effective.

Traditional routing protocols (such as OSPF [28]) may need tens of seconds to converge. However, in the carrier grade networks, the recovery time is required to be within millseconds. Considering the fault tolerance which consists of four steps – failure detection, failure announcement, route recomputing and routing table updating, efforts have been made to decrease the running time of each procedure to reduce the whole recovery time. Firstly, methods such as reducing the transmit interval of probing packets [8] or combining with other detection methods (Bidirectional Forwarding Detection [17]) can be used to cut down the failure detection time. Secondly, when considering the transient failure, a self-adapting timer [9], for example, can be adopted to avoid announcement of this fault. Thirdly, routing algorithms can be improved. Finally, the batch update,

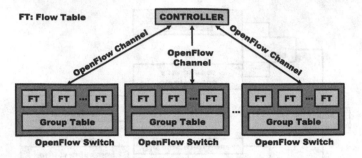

Fig. 2. Architecture of OpenFlow protocol

for instance, can accelerate the update of forwarding tables. This technology is called the reactive failure recovery.

The reactive failure recovery is initialized after failures happen. In order to further decrease the recovery time, the proactive technology is proposed. With this method, resources have been preserved and backup paths have been worked out [21] before the failure happens, leading to the benefit that protection paths could come into use immediately once the faults are detected. According to the difference in the scale of malfunction, the proactive mechanism can be classified into link-based and topology-based technology, aiming at a single failure or multiple failures respectively. The former mainly focuses on protecting certain links or devices, such as Loop-Free Alternates (LFA) algorithm [7] and Not-Via algorithm [11]; while the latter will calculate a few logical backup topologies which can help to protect the whole network [31,32,45]. In comparison, the proactive technology performs better on recovery time as a few preparatory works have been done before failures happen. However, these works will spend extra network resources which can not be neglected especially in the overloaded networks.

2.2   What Does OpenFlow Bring for Fault Tolerance

The architecture of SDN can be divided into two parts: the control plane and data plane. The control plane is composed of the controller and the channels between the controller and network elements; while the data plane contains switches and hosts [18]. Besides, the OpenFlow protocol (Fig. 2 shows the architecture of this protocol) is widely used for communicating between the two planes, and most of the methods mentioned in this paper are based on this *de facto* southbound protocol. In SDN, switches can only forward packets according to the forwarding rules established and updated by the controller.

This paper mainly focuses on how to use the OpenFlow protocol to solve the fault tolerance problem in SDN. At first a few concepts of this new protocol are introduced, including the flow table and group table. Each flow table contains a set of table entries, and each table entry consists of match fields, counters, and a set of instructions which are deployed for packets matching [4]. Firstly, each match field is composed of tuples, consisting of ingress port, source/destination

MAC address, source/destination IP address, port numbers, *etc.* Moreover, a flow can be defined according to arbitrary combinations of these elements, unlike the traditional routing protocols which are based on the destination IP address only. Secondly, the counters are used to count the number of packets/bytes of a flow. Finally, the instructions describe how to process these packets such as forwarding, dropping, redirecting to the group table and so on.

When a flow table entry points to a group, the concept of group table needs to be described. A group table consists of several group table entries, and each entry contains: group identifier, group type, counters and action buckets. Firstly, the group identifier uniquely identifies each group. Secondly, the group type determines the group semantics, including the following types: "all", "select", "indirect" and "fast fail over". Thirdly, the counters are used to count the number of packets/bytes. Finally, the action buckets contain a set of actions and associated parameters. The principle of the "fast fail over" group type is to execute the first live bucket every time which can be applied in the fault tolerance. Multiple paths of an identical flow can be preserved into the same group table entry with the working path in the first bucket. When the working path fails, the following buckets of protection paths (if alive) can be used, enabling the switch to automatically change forwarding route without informing the controller [5].

3 Fault Tolerance on Data Plane: Phase 1-Detecting Link Failures

To guarantee the availability of the data plane, the source host is required to communicate with the destination even though link failures happen. When referring to the fault tolerance on this plane, the two steps – detecting and recovering from failures, are needed which will be described in the following two sections, respectively.

3.1 Methods

Loss Of Signal (LOS, as shown in Fig. 3(a)), which is widely used to detect link failures in carrier-grade networks [39], can be utilized by switches to perceive the status change of each port. In SDN, this warning message need to be transferred to the controller for further processing. Similarly, the method proposed in [22] (as shown in Fig. 3(c)) is also applied to detect link failures. The main idea of this approach is using a circle which starts and terminates at the controller to monitor the status of a few links. Under normal circumstances, the control packet is transmitted along the loop, and finally return to the controller. However, if there is a failure inside the circle (which means a link breaks), the second stage initiates where each switch in the loop is required not only to deliver the packet to the next hop, but also send back to the controller. As the result, the link failure can be located.

Sometimes detecting path failures is needed where a path is composed of multiple links. Bidirectional Forwarding Detection (BFD) [17] (as shown in Fig. 3(b))

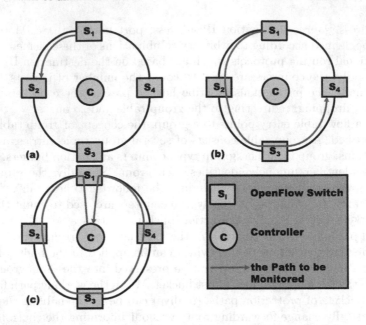

Fig. 3. Detection methods (a) LOS through monitoring a link (b) BFD through monitoring a path (c) two methods through monitoring a circle

is designed for this purpose. It is a Hello protocol and the two end nodes of a BFD session transmit echo packets periodically. If a system stops receiving the packet from the monitored connection, the path may be assumed to be broken [39].

With the number of devices increases, multiple controllers are needed to cooperate to control the whole network. In this situation, each controller has its own control domain. However, considering packets can pass through arbitrary links, the controller may need to be informed of a failure outside of its region. [19] (as shown in Fig. 3(c)) suggests using a circle to help locating link failures which is similar to the approach proposed in [22], but the difference is when a fault is detected, the binary search is adopted so that the hunting zone decreases until a single broken link is figured out. Moreover, the two methods by using a circle need extra flow table entries to return packets to the controller, or change the walking direction.

3.2 Comparison and Summaries

A comparison is summarized in Table 1 with some extended discussion. As the methods mentioned before are executed in different experimental environment, the detection time doesn't have comparability, but the factors affecting the detection time can be discussed. It can be concluded that each method is related to the length of the monitoring path, and the LOS is relatively stable as its granularity is a link.

Table 1. Comparison of failure detection methods

Approaches	LOS [40]	BFD [39]	[22]	[19]
Factors affecting detection time	X	Length of path	Length of circle	Length of circle
Location of a single link failure	✓	X	✓	✓
Location of multiple link failures	✓	X	X	X
Number of failure detection messages	0	1 packet from each switch in each time interval	The number of rounds	$1 + \lceil log_2(L_{opt}) \rceil$
Using in-band connection	X	✓	✓	✓
Requirement of extra flow table entries	X	X	✓	✓
Applying to multiple controllers	X	X	X	✓

Location of failures means finding out the specific broken link or links, more than just detecting failures in the data plane. Firstly, BFD can only judge whether the whole path is normal or not. Secondly, the two methods by the use of a circle can only locate the first failed link near the controller. Finally, by using LOS, each switch will generate port status message to the controller independently when its link has broken, then each link can be located separately. As the result, only the LOS can locate multiple link failures.

Summaries. When choosing an appropriate failure detection method, the recovery technology (restoration or protection) to be used in combination can be considered. If the restoration mechanism is adopted which means informing the controller after the link breaks, the LOS which will generate port status message to the controller is a good choice. If the protection is in use, the BFD can be applied to protect each path without the involvement of the controller. Specifically in the situation where a number of hosts want to communicate with each other, multiple paths must be established and observed for all the pairs when adopting BFD. In order to reduce the number of BFD sessions as well as the detection time, establishing BFD sessions for per link can be a choice as the number of links is relatively less and more stable compared to the number of paths when BFD sessions are set up for each path.

4   Fault Tolerance on Data Plane: Phase 2-Recovering from Link Failures

The recovery methods are divided into restoration and protection, respectively. In this section, these two technologies are introduced firstly, and next open research issues will be discussed.

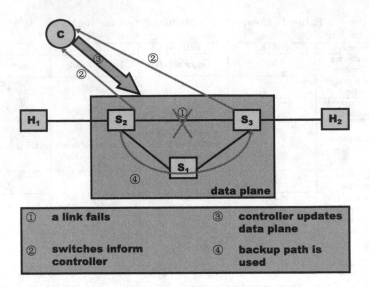

Fig. 4. Restoration technology

4.1 Restoration

Considering the situation where a working path is broken, the restoration technology is a choice which can be used to recover from link failures. Generally speaking, This technology can be divided into three steps (shown in Fig. 4): 1. The relevant switches inform the controller about the change of a port's status. 2. The controller can either work out another path after the link failure [40], or has calculated the protection path along with the working path before the failure. In the latter situation, the protection path can be saved in switches' flow tables [29], or stored inside the controller [24]. Regardless of the methods adopted, the controller must send packets out to update switches' flow tables. 3. Data flows will go through the protection path.

In detail, the method proposed in [40] uses the shortest path algorithm to calculate route before the link failure. It can be integrated with the LOS. When the "port down" event arrived at the controller, the controller can find the flows affected by the failed link, and recompute paths for these flows. Similar with the failure detection algorithms described in the previous section, there is a recovery approach based on cycle structure [29]. This approach firstly computes a tree for the topology, then assigns a tie-set (in fact a circle) for each remaining link (which is not contained in the tree). As the result, if a link is broken, the algorithm can find and use the responding tie-set to repair.

The paper [24] puts forward a method to recover from link failures in the fat-tree topology where only two switches belonging to different layers can have a connection. If they have a directly connected link, there will going to be at least another detour path consisting of three links to connect them as well. This

Table 2. Comparison of restoration methods

Approaches	[40]	[29]	[24]
Algorithm of computing routes	Shortest path algorithm	Tie-set graph	According to the fat-tree topology
The stability of control messages when recovering	✗	✓	✗
Controllers job (initialization)	Update flow tables for working paths	Update flow tables for working paths and each tie-set	Update flow tables for working paths
Applying to failures of multiple links	✓	✗	✓
Applying to failure of switch	✓	✗	✓
Limitation	✗	✗	Fat tree topology
Consideration of traffic	✗	✗	✓

is the main idea of this approach, and the controller records the load of each link to help decide the protection paths.

At the end of this subsection, a comparison is summarized in Table 2. The controller's job before and after the link failure is discussed. For the second method, as flow table entries for each working path and each tie-set has been worked out before the fault, few packets are needed to change the path from the primary one to the appropriate tie-set, which is contrary to other two approaches.

Next, the scalability problem is explained. For the first and the last method, as long as there is a path available, they can find it for recovering. However, for the second approach, each link only belongs to limited tie-sets, and each tie-set can only deal with a single link failure. As the result, the second approach has drawbacks in expansibility.

4.2 Protection

After the working path is broken, the protection technology can be used which contains two steps (shown in Fig. 5): 1. The controller has worked out the backup path along with the working path, and stored the information into switches' forwarding tables [37], [39] or packet headers [33]. When the failure happens, the switches can detect this fault, and change the route to the backup path without the participation of the controller. 2. Data flows will go through the protection path.

According to the difference in the version of OpenFlow protocol adopted, the methods based on the protection mechanism can be divided into two categories: approaches based on OpenFlow 1.0 and OpenFlow 1.1, respectively. When adopting OpenFlow 1.0, [37] suggests that the working path and backup path can be preserved into two kinds of flow tables which are different in priorities. When the working path breaks, only if its corresponding flow table entries are deleted,

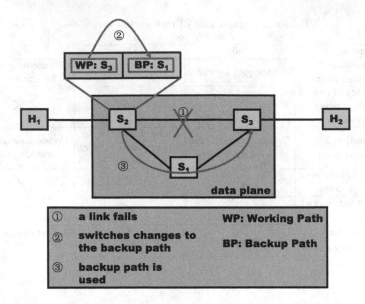

Fig. 5. Protection technology

the protection path which is lower in priority can be used. As the result, this method will generate OFP_FLOW_RESTORE packet to inform the controller to recompute route if the primary one recovers. While [33] proposes the two paths can be coded into the headers of packets. Moreover, a label is assigned for each port of each switch to save space. Nevertheless, the length of route is restricted by the size of the header without doubt.

From OpenFlow 1.1, the concept of group table is proposed, and the method proposed in [39] uses the "fast fail over" group type to save working path and protection path in multiple action buckets.

At the end of this subsection, a comparison is summarized in Table 3. The granularity of protection is discussed which can be divided into two categories: for each link, or for each path. The first two methods compute a backup path for each link contained in the working route. By contrast, the approach based on the group table uses BFD to monitor the whole path periodically. As long as any link of the working path breaks, the whole route is announced to be failed, and the protection path can be activated immediately.

Similar with the restoration, the scalability problem needs to be explained as well. As long as both the working path and the protection path face a failure, data flows can't find another route to deliver packets any more even though there are other routes available.

4.3   Comparisons, Summaries and Open Research Issues

We conducted the simulation experiments on fault tolerance of the data plane. In detail, we implemented a restoration and protection method both using the

Table 3. Comparison of protection methods

Approaches	[37]	[33]	[39]
Method to save routes	Two flow table entries with different priorities	Reuse the packet header	Group table
Method to return to the working path	OFP_FLOW_RESTORE packet	automatically	automatically
Granularity	Each link of the working path	Each link of the working path	The whole working path
Applying to failures of multiple links	✗	✗	✗
Applying to failure of switch	✓	✓	✓
Limitation on the length of each route	✗	✓	✗
Version of OpenFlow	1.0	1.0	1.1

shortest path algorithm to calculate routes. These two fault tolerance applications were developed on Ryu – a python-based controller [3]. When referring to the topologies, the 4-ary and 6-ary fat-trees [6], and two real-world network scenarios – basic reference topology of the COST 266 action project [26] and a topology from the Topology Zoo [1] – were used for experiments. Specifically, we implemented the protection method by calculating a backup path for each link instead of for each path as the number of links is relatively less and more stable.

When referring to the simulation and emulation tools for SDN, Mininet adopted in our experiments is the most popular one. Besides, [14,36] are especially designed for the distributed experimental environments. By using Mininet [2], we measured three metrics – the number of total table entries, the average number of hops for backup paths, and the recovery time – on each topology. Firstly, as for the recovery time, the protection was much less than the restoration. Moreover, the recovery time of the former was stable as backup paths were calculated in advance and could be activated as soon as links fail. Secondly, the number of table entries was discussed. The ratio between the protection and the restoration was in the range of 2.78 to 3.90. Thirdly, the average number of hops was compared. The backup path calculated by the protection needed 1.23 to 2.53 more hops than the restoration. Specifically, in the fat-tree topology, all the connections have inherent rules. For example, each two hosts have at least two paths of the same length to reach each other, which is proven by the restoration. As the result, a few protection paths for an identical flow can be calculated rapidly according to the inherent rules, and can be stored into the group tables for failure recovery. The benefit is that the recovery time is less than the restoration, and the calculation of protection paths is easy to realize than the algorithms to find disjoint alternative paths (such as Suurballe's algorithm [41]).

Besides the conclusions inferred from the experiments, the comparisons between the two mechanisms can be analyzed in theory. In general, the restoration has the advantage of flexibility. For example, as the size limit of the group table, it is hard to exhaust all the backup paths before the failures. By contrast, provided that at least one path is available, the restoration can be used for fault tolerance in any case. When considering the metric of length, only the restoration can always compute a shortest path after the failure. Moreover, there are other factors (such as the load of each link) need to be considered except for "the distance of each path" when choosing a backup path. In this situation, the real-time data of each link's load is required, and the restoration can be adopted while the protection cannot satisfy the demand.

As for future research directions, the idea of combination is considered at first. Routing methods in traditional networks can be combined with SDN. As described in [47], the method uses routing tables and flow tables to forward packets before and after link failures, respectively. Another situation is when the controller functions normally, flow tables are used to route messages. Once the controller breaks, all the switches can use traditional routing protocols to calculate paths which looks like a reversion of the former approach. Similarly, there is an idea combining the restoration with protection which aim to take advantages of both.

In the second place, the scalability is of concern as well. Most methods introduced in this paper are focusing on the failure of a single link especially for the protection mechanism, then it can be extended to solve failures of multiple links. As for multiple links, the problem of failure recovery can be further classified according to the properties of these broken links. On one hand, if all the failed links belong to the working path, most existing methods can solve it. In [40], each link is managed by the controller independently. While in [39], no matter how many links are broken in the same working path, the protection path can be active as long as the primary route fails. On the other hand, some failed links belong to the working path, and others are part of the protection path. In this situation, the failure recovery may not be achieved if 1:1 protection is adopted. To solve the limitation, For example, maybe non-intersect paths can be calculated as many as possible. The scalability problem can be extended further to solve the failure of a switch. As this is different from the failure of a link, the difference need to be caught and a more appropriate approach for this situation can be found out. For example, if a switch fails, the controller can judge whether this is a normal fault where just several links break or this is a outage of a switch, then a different solution is given based on different judgment. More specifically, if a port status message of a switch is transmitted to the controller, the controller can probe the other end of this failed link (as the controller knows two switches and their corresponding ports of each link) to confirm whether the opposite switch goes wrong. If so, the controller needs to update the topology and recompute relevant flow table entries.

Moreover, if no backup path is available, the controller can inform the relevant switches to stop transmitting messages walking through these broken links. The problem can be divided into two parts according the types of these links. On one hand, for the link between switches using in-band connection, only a few switches directly connect to the controller. If a node discovers the failure of a link, it may require a long time to inform the controller. To avoid this phenomena, [12] proposes the switch can inform the affected nodes, other than the controller. The switch on the failed link can use the ingress port to help informing upstream nodes. On the other hand, the link between host and switch is considered. If such a connection breaks, the relevant host can't be reached any more. Therefore the controller need to be informed and relative flow table entries targeting the destination host can be deleted.

There are some papers discussing the problem of fault tolerance from different angles. [34] proposes a declarative language for network administrators to specify working paths as well as backup paths. Based on the syntax and the normalization rules of this language called FatTire, a program can be generated and a compiler is used for translating into configurations of switches. [46] discusses the topic of multicast in SDN, but the fault tolerance problem has been left out which needs to be considered as well.

5   Fault Tolerance on Control Plane

To guarantee the resiliency of the control plane, there are two aspects need to be considered. Firstly, the controller must function properly, which means that the failure of the controller is not allowed. Secondly, switches can communicate with the controller even though the OpenFlow channel breaks. In this section, these two aspects are introduced respectively.

On one hand, considering the situation where the controller is down, the OpenFlow channels are useless, and the underlying switches are out of control. A general solution (as shown in Fig. 6) is using multiple controllers to provide

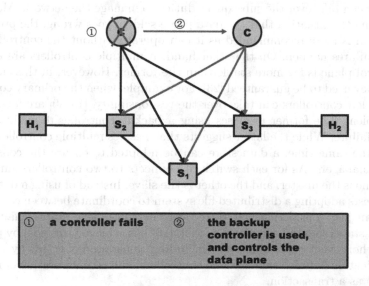

Fig. 6. Deal with the failure of controller

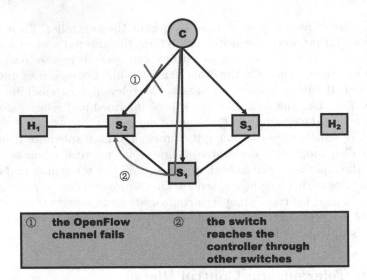

Fig. 7. Deal with the failure of OpenFlow channel

resiliency. When the primary one is wrong, the backup controller can take over the whole data plane.

The problem mentioned above can be further divided into two parts – whether one controller or multiple controllers are in use. On one hand, if only one controller is adopted, its failure is catastrophic. As long as the network changes after the controller fails, there is going to be inconsistency between the data plane and control plane. To solve this problem, for example, traditional routing protocols can take over the subsequent duties to manage the network. Moreover, considering the situation that the data plane seldom goes wrong, the protection mechanism is more recommended as it can operate without the controller even though failures happen. On the other hand, if multiple controllers are applied, the control plane is far more stable than the former. However, in this situation, consistency need to be guaranteed [23]. For example, when the primary controller fails, the left controllers can take over the responsibility. [10,30] are focusing on this problem. The former proposes using a backup controller to avoid a single point of failure. While the latter suggests that besides multiple controllers being used at the same time, a data store can be adopted to ensure the consistency of these managers. As for each switch, it connects to two controllers simultaneously – one is the master, and the other is the slave. Instead of using a data store, [42] suggests adopting a distributed file system to coordinate between controllers. More than just considering how to recover the controllers' states, maintaining switches' states should be involved as well. [16] has achieved this goal by processing the whole event-processing cycle (including: generation of events by switches, communication between switches and controllers, and reconfiguration of relevant switches) as a transaction.

On the other hand, considering the situation where the OpenFlow channel breaks with other network elements operating normally. In general, the out-band and in-band control can be adopted before and after failures, respectively (as shown in Fig. 7). When the control traffic goes through the same path as the data flow does, the fault tolerance methods on the data plane mentioned before can be used for reference [38].

6 Conclusion

SDN is a novel network architecture which decouples the data plane from the control plane. However, SDN is not able to recover from failures automatically. Therefore mechanisms need to be designed for fast failover via the coordination between controller and switches. In this paper, we broadly discuss the fault tolerance issue and systematically review the existing methods proposed so far for SDN. Our representation starts from the significant components that OpenFlow and SDN brings – which are useful for the purpose of failure recovery, and is then further expanded to the discussion of fault tolerance in data plane and control plane, in which two phases – detection and recovery – are both needed. In particular, as the important part of this paper, we have highlighted the comparison between two main methods – restoration and protection – for failure recovery. So far, the recovery for multiple link failure remains an open issue and could be our future research direction. As one of the first few authors, we have shed a light in this paper on the issue of fault tolerance for software defined networks. We expect that our work could attract more researchers' attention, and encourage them to deliver more contributions in this issue.

Acknowledgments. Corresponding authors: Jinbang Chen and Fei Xu. They are with Shanghai Key Laboratory of Multidimensional Information Processing & Department of Computer Science and Technology, East China Normal University, China. This work was supported by the Science and Technology Commission of Shanghai Municipality under research grant no. 14DZ2260800, and China Postdoctoral Science Foundation under grant no. 2014M561438.

References

1. The internet topology zoo. http://www.topology-zoo.org/
2. Mininet. http://mininet.org/
3. Ryu. http://osrg.github.io/ryu/
4. Openflow switch specification: version 1.0.0, December 2009
5. Openflow switch specification: version 1.1.0, Feburuary 2011. http://archive.openflow.org/documents/openflow-spec-v1.0.0.pdf
6. Al-Fares, M., Loukissas, A., Vahdat, A.: A scalable, commodity data center network architecture. In: 2008 ACM International Conference on Special Interest Group on Data Communication (SIGCOMM), pp. 63–74, August 2008

7. Atlas, A.K., Zinin, A., Torvi, R., Choudhury, G., Martin, C., Imhoff, B., Fedyk, D.: Basic specification for IP fast reroute: loop-free alternates. In: RFC-5286, September 2008. https://tools.ietf.org/html/rfc5286

8. Basu, A., Riecke, J.: Stability issues in OSPF routing. In: 2001 ACM International Conference on Special Interest Group on Data Communication (SIGCOMM), pp. 225–236, August 2001

9. Bonaventure, O., Filsfils, C., Francois, P.: Achieving Sub-50 milliseconds recovery upon BGP peering link failures. IEEE/ACM Trans. Netw. 15(5), 1123–1135 (2007)

10. Botelho, F.A., Ramos, F.M.V., Kreutz, D., Bessani, A.N.: On the feasibility of a consistent and fault-tolerant data store for sdns. In: 2013 2nd European Workshop on Software Defined Networks (EWSDN), pp. 38–43, October 2013. http://dx.doi.org/10.1109/EWSDN.2013.13

11. Bryant, S., Previdi, S., Shand, M.: A framework for IP and MPLS fast reroute using not-via addresses. In: RFC-6981, August 2013

12. Desai, M., Nandagopal, T.: Coping with link failures in centralized control plane architectures. In: 2010 2nd International Conference on Communication Systems and NETworks (COMSNETS), pp. 79–88, January 2010. http://dl.acm.org/citation.cfm?id=1831443.1831452

13. Farhady, H., Lee, H., Nakao, A.: Software-defined networking: a survey. Comput. Netw. 81, 79–95 (2015)

14. Ficco, M., Avolio, G., Palmieri, F., Castiglione, A.: An HLA-based framework for simulation of large-scale critical systems. Concurr. Comput.: Prac. Exp. (2015). doi:10.1002/cpe.3472

15. Jain, S., Kumar, A., Mandal, S., Ong, J., Poutievski, L., Singh, A., Venkata, S., Wanderer, J., Zhou, J., Zhu, M., Zolla, J., Hölzle, U., Stuart, S., Vahdat, A.: B4: experience with a globally-deployed software defined wan. In: 2013 ACM International Conference on Special Interest Group on Data Communication (SIGCOMM), pp. 3–14, August 2013

16. Katta, N., Zhang, H., Freedman, M., Rexford, J.: Ravana: controller fault-tolerance in software-defined networking. In: 2015 1st ACM SIGCOMM Symposium on Software Defined Networking Research, pp. 4:1–4:12, June 2015

17. Katz, D., Ward, D.: Bidirectional forwarding detection. In: RFC-5880, June 2010

18. Kim, H., Santos, J.R., Turner, Y., Schlansker, M., Tourrihes, J., Feamster, N.: Coronet: fault tolerance for software defined networks. In: 2012 20th IEEE International Conference on Network Protocols (ICNP), pp. 1–2, October 2012

19. Kozat, U.C., Liang, G., Kokten, K.: On diagnosis of forwarding plane via static forwarding rules in software defined networks. In: 2014 33rd IEEE Conference on Computer Communications (INFOCOM), pp. 1716–1724, April 2013. http://arxiv.org/abs/1308.4465

20. Kreutz, D., Ramos, F., Esteve Rothenberg, P., Esteve Rothenberg, C., Azodolmolky, S., Uhlig, S.: Software-defined networking: a comprehensive survey. Proc. IEEE 103(1), 14–76 (2015)

21. Lee, S., Yu, Y., Nelakuditi, S., Zhang, Z.L., Chuah, C.N.: Proactive vs. reactive approaches to failure resilient routing. In: 2004 23rd IEEE Conference on Computer Communications (INFOCOM), pp. 176–186, March 2004. http://arxiv.org/abs/1308.4465

22. Lee, S., Li, K.Y., Chan, K.Y., Lai, G.H., Chung, Y.C.: Path layout planning and software based fast failure detection in survivable openflow networks. In: 2014 10th International Conference on the Design of Reliable Communication Networks (DRCN), pp. 1–8, April 2014

23. Levin, D., Wundsam, A., Heller, B., Handigol, N., Feldmann, A.: Logically central-ized? state distribution tradeoffs in software defined networks. In: 2014 Proceedings of 3rd Workshop on Hot Topics in Software Defined Networking (HotSDN), pp. 1–6, January 2012

24. Li, J., Hyun, J., Yoo, J.H., Baik, S., Hong, J.K.: Scalable failover method for data center networks using openflow. In: 2014 14th IEEE Network Operations and Management Symposium (NOMS), pp. 1–6, May 2014

25. Liu, Z., Li, Y., Su, L., Jin, D., Zeng, L.: M2cloud: software defined multi-site data center network control framework for multi-tenant. In: 2013 ACM International Conference on Special Interest Group on Data Communication (SIGCOMM), pp. 517–518, August 2013

26. Maesschalck, S., Colle, D., Lievens, I., Pickavet, M., Demeester, P., Mauz, C., Jaeger, M., Inkret, R., Mikac, B., Derkacz, J.: Pan-european optical transport networks: an availability-based comparison. Photonic Netw. Commun. **5**(3), 203–225 (2003). http://dx.doi.org/10.1023/A%3A1023088418684

27. McKeown, N., Anderson, T., Balakrishnan, H., Parulkar, G., Peterson, L., Rexford, J., Shenker, S., Turner, J.: Openflow: enabling innovation in campus networks. ACM Comput. Commun. Rev. **38**(2), 69–74 (2008)

28. Moy, J.: OSPF version 2. In: RFC-2328, April 1998

29. Nagano, J., Shinomiya, N.: A failure recovery method based on cycle structure and its verification by openflow. In: 2013 IEEE 27th International Conference on Advanced Information Networking and Applications (AINA), pp. 298–303, March 2013

30. Fonseca, P., Bennesby, R., Mota, E., Passito, A.: A replication component for resilient openflow-based networking. In: 2012 IEEE 13th Network Operations and Management Symposium (NOMS), pp. 933–939, April 2012

31. Przygienda, T., Shen, N., Sheth, N.: M-ISIS: multi topology (MT) routing in inter-mediate system to intermediate systems (IS-ISs). In: RFC-5120, February 2008

32. Psenak, P., Mirtorabi, S., Roy, A., Nguyen, L., Pillay-Esnault, P.: Multi-topology (MT) routing in OSPF. In: RFC-4915, June 2007

33. Ramos, R.M., Rothenberg, C.E.: Slickflow: resilient source routing in data center networks unlocked by openflow. In: 2013 IEEE 38th Conference on Local Computer Networks (LCN), pp. 606–613, October 2013

34. Reitblatt, M., Canini, M., Guha, A., Foster, N.: Fattire: declarative fault tolerance for software-defined networks. In: 2013 Proceedings of 2nd Workshop on Hot Topics in Software Defined Networking (HotSDN), pp. 109–114, August 2013

35. Rongqing, C.: Research on the fast failure recovery technologies of IP networks. Master's thesis, Hangzhou Dianzi University, March 2012

36. Roy, A.R., Bari, M.F., Zhani, M.F., Ahmed, R., Boutaba, R.: Dot: distributed openflow testbed. In: 2014 ACM International Conference on Special Interest Group on Data Communication (SIGCOMM), pp. 367–368, August 2014

37. Sgambelluri, A., Giorgetti, A., Cugini, F., Paolucci, F., Castoldi, P.: Openflow-based segment protection in ethernet networks. IEEE/OSA J. Opt. Commun. Netw. **5**(9), 1066–1075 (2013)

38. Sharma, S., Staessens, D., Colle, D., Pickavet, M., Demeester, P.: Fast failure recovery for in-band openflow networks. In: 2013 9th International Conference on the Design of Reliable Communication Networks (DRCN), pp. 52–59, March 2013

39. Sharma, S., Staessens, D., Colle, D., Pickavet, M., Demeester, P.: Openflow: meet-ing carrier-grade recovery requirements. Comput. Commun. **36**(6), 656–665 (2013). http://www.sciencedirect.com/science/article/pii/S0140366412003349

40. Staessens, D., Sharma, S., Colle, D., Pickavet, M., Demeester, P.: Software defined networking: meeting carrier grade requirements. In: 2011 18th IEEE Workshop on Local Metropolitan Area Networks (LANMAN), pp. 1–6, October 2011
41. Suurballe, J.W.: Disjoint paths in a network. Networks 4(2), 125–145 (1974)
42. Tootoonchian, A., Ganjali, Y.: Hyperflow: a distributed control plane for openflow. In: 2010 7th Internet Network Management Conference on Research on Enterprise Networking (INM/WREN), p. 3, April 2010
43. Vasseur, J.P., Pickavet, M., Demeester, P.: Network Recovery: Protection and Restoration of Optical, SONET-SDH, IP, and MPLS. Morgan Kaufmann, San Francisco (2004)
44. Wang, S., Li, D., Xia, S.: The problems and solutions of network update in SDN: a survey. In: 2015 IEEE Conference on Computer Communications Workshops (INFOCOM WKSHPS), pp. 474–479, April 2015
45. Wei, T., Mishra, P., Wu, K., Zhou, J.: Quasi-static fault-tolerant scheduling schemes for energy-efficient hard real-time systems. J. Syst. Softw. 85(6), 1386–1399 (2012)
46. Gu, W., Zhang, X., Gong, B., Wang, L.: A survey of multicast in software-defined networking. In: 2015 5th International Conference on Information Engineering for Mechanics and Materials (ICIMM), July 2015
47. Yu, Y., Shanzhi, C., Xin, L., Yan, W.: A framework of using openflow to handle transient link failure. In: 2011 1st International Conference on Transportation, Mechanical, and Electrical Engineering (TMEE), pp. 2050–2053, December 2011

A Novel Signature Generation Approach for Polymorphic Worms

Jie Wang[✉] and Xiaoxian He

School of Information Science and Engineering, Central South University,
Changsha 410083, China
jwang@csu.edu.cn

Abstract. Because of complex polymorphism in worms and the disturbance of crafted noises, it becomes more difficult to generate signatures quickly and accurately. This paper proposes a neighbor relation signature (NRS) for polymorphic worms,which is a collection of distance frequency distributions between neighbor byte. Moreover, we propose a signature generation algorithm (NRS-CC) by combing NRS and color coding technique. NRS-CC selects sequences randomly from suspicious flow pool to generate neighbor relation signatures, and then uses color coding technique to get rid of noise disturbance. Extensive experiments are carried out to demonstrate the validity of our approach. The experiment results show that our approach can generate polymorphic signature more quickly compared with existing signature generate approaches when the suspicious flow pool contains noise sequences.

Keywords: Signature generation · Polymorphic worm · Worm detection · Intrusion detection · Worm signature

1 Introduction

Polymorphic worms have self-replicating and rapid-spreading characteristics which transforms the detection problem into a much harder one [1, 2]. Because polymorphic worm pattern changes at each copy of the same worm while spreading on networks, detection of polymorphic worm becomes more and more difficult [3]. Existing recent research works on detecting and defending against polymorphic worm attacks are mainly based on signature-based detection techniques [4,5]. Their efficiency of defending against worms depends on the quality of generated worm signatures. Generating high quality and accurate signatures based on the characteristics of polymorphic worm remains an open problem.

Moreover, noise injecting attacks are proposed to disturb signature generation for polymorphic worm [6]. Noise flow is the fake anomalous flow that does not exploit the vulnerability. Noise flow can be crafted in a very flexible manner so that they appear like the real worm everywhere except for the invariant parts. For example, a fake anomalous flow can be crafted so that it contains the same protocol framework as the worm, but not contains the real worm's invariants.

© Springer International Publishing Switzerland 2015
G. Wang et al. (Eds.): ICA3PP 2015, Part III, LNCS 9530, pp. 369–382, 2015.
DOI: 10.1007/978-3-319-27137-8_28

After the fake anomalous flow is injected into suspicious flow pool, it will be difficult to generate accurate worm signature.

Existing work for defending against polymorphic worms and generating their signatures have shortcomings because they can not generate quickly high quality signature for polymorphic worm in the noisy environment. In this work, we propose a neighborhood-relation signatures (NRS). NRS is a collection of distance frequency distributions between adjacent bytes. Moreover, we select sequences from suspicious flow pool to generate NRS. In order to make our approach effective in noisy environments, color coding technique is applied. This process is called NRS-CC. NRS-CC can generate NRS more quickly from suspicious flow pool with noise sequences. NRS generated can obtain lower positive ratio and lower negative ratio than other worm signatures.

The rest of the paper is organized as follows. Related works are introduced in Sect. 2. Section 3 describes neighborhood-relation signatures (NRS) and the process of generating NRS. NRS-CC algorithm is proposed in Sect. 4. Experimental results are illustrated in Sect. 5. Section 6 draws the conclusions.

2   Related Work

Polymorphism techniques include instructions rearrangement, garbage-code insertion, encryption and register-reassignment techniques. Instructions rearrangement technique products a polymorphic worm by rearranging the order of instructions and using jump instructions to keep the instruction flow intact. Garbage codes are some garbage instructions or non-meaningful instructions. Polymorphic worms can be obtained by inserting non-meaningful instructions into the copies of a worm. For example, no-operation (NOP) instructions can be inserted into different places of the worm body, which makes it more difficult to compare the byte sequences of two instances of the same worm. Encryption techniques with the same decoding routine can encrypt the worm's payload using a variable key [7]. When a worm replicates, the worm chooses a key and encrypts the new copy before sending the copy to a victim machine. The key and the decryption routine are usually sent together with a copy of the worm. When the worm executes on the target machine, the decryption routine uses the key to obtain the worm code and begins the next round of propagation. Because polymorphic worms have the same decoding engine, the decoding engine can be considered as a worm signatures. Encryption technology with several decryption routines changes the decryption routine each time when a copy of worm is sent to another victim host. When the worm tries to make a copy, one routine is randomly selected and other routines are encrypted together with the worm body. Because the total length of the worm is limited, encryption can use only some simple techniques, such as INC, DEC, and XOR encryption. The register-reassignment techniques can alter appearance of a worm by changing the registers which are used in the worm code, but it only causes "minor" changes in the code sequence. Instruction-substitution [8] technique can also produce polymorphic worms by replacing meaningful sequences of instructions with different sequences which have the same functions. For instance, the instruction "**add eax, 2**" can be substituted with two instruction "**inc eax**". When polymorphic engine uses instruction-substitution, unless the substitution is done over the entire code without compromising the code integrity (which is a great challenge by itself), it is likely that there exists shorter constant byte sequences in the stationary portion of the worm.

From above analysis we can know that most of polymorphism techniques keep the worm containing common subsequences. These invariant have the same neighbor distance distribution. When there are no common between polymorphic worm, neighbor distance distribution frequency of all mutation copies can be treated as worm signatures.

Recently, there have been many research efforts on generating signature for worms [9]. Some of them only can detect single worms. For example, S. Ranjan et al. [10] presented DoWicher, which extracts the worm content signature via a LCS algorithm applied over the flow payload content of isolated flows. M. Cai et al. developed a collaborative worm signature generation system (WormShield) [11] that employs distributed fingerprint filtering. In these systems, a worm is assumed to have a long invariant substring, which is used as a signature to detect the worm. However, different instances of polymorphic worms do not contain a long enough common substring, so signatures generated by the above systems are not applicable for detecting polymorphic worms.

Some methods generating worm signatures are more complicated than that based on LCS algorithm. For example, J. Newsome et al. [12] presented Polygraph, which is a signature generation system. Polygraph extracted multiple invariant substrings in all worm variants as worm signature. Z. Li et al. [13] developed the Hamsa, an improved system over Polygraph in terms of both speed and attack resilience. Hamsa takes the number of occurrences of a substring token into a part of signature. Lorenzo Cavallaro et al. [14] proposed LISABETH, an improved version of Hamsa, an automated content-based signature generation system for polymorphic worms that uses invariant bytes analysis of network traffic content. Burak Bayogle et al. [15] proposed Token-Pair Conjunction and Token-Pair Subsequence signature for detecting polymorphic worm threats. Y. Tang [16] et al. proposed Simplified Regular Expression (SRE) signature, and used multiple sequence alignment techniques to generate exploit-based signatures. Above methods assumed that multiple invariant substrings must often be present in all variants of a worm payload. However, these methods will suffer when there are no same byte sequences exist among different copies of polymorphic worms. Moreover, noise injection attack can mislead these methods to generate useless signatures. In some methods, hierarchical clustering algorithm is applied for isolating the worm flows from the noise. However, when suspicious flow pool contains some crafted noise flows,the signature produced by hierarchical clustering algorithm will likely produce high false positive ratio [13].

Y. Tang et al. [17] proposed automating approach based on PADS (position-aware distribution signature) to defend polymorphic worms. However, PADS generated in noisy environments will also misjudge polymorphic worms.

CCSF [18] proposed an algorithm based on color coding which can generate worm signatures. However, worm signatures generated by CCSF is also based on invariant substrings of worm sequences. It will also suffer when there are no common byte sequence among different copies of polymorphic worms.

In this paper, we propose NRS to detect polymorphic worms. NRS is the collection of distance frequencies between adjacent bytes. From polymorphic techniques it can be seen that some polymorphic worms have invariant bytes which have the same distance frequencies between adjacent bytes. Others generated by applying some simple encryption routines also have the same distance frequencies between adjacent bytes. Even complicated encryption algorithm is used, a limited number of decryption routines can be looked as the key subsequences to generate NRS after obtaining enough worm samples.

As mentioned above, no existing work can generate high quality worm signature from the suspicious flow pool with noise disturbance. To address this issue, we propose a signature generation algorithm (NRS-CC) by combing NRS and color coding technique. Firstly, NRS-CC selects randomly sequences from suspicious flow pool to generate NRS for polymorphic, and then uses color coding in the process of solving noise disturbance. Experiment results show that our algorithm can generate polymorphic worm signature more quickly. NRS generated by NRS-CC has the lower false positive ratio compared with other existing approaches. They can be applied in practice to detecting polymorphic worms.

3   Neighbor Relationship Signature (NRS)

Given a string $c_1 c_2 \cdots c_m$, c_i is a byte.

Definition 1. Neighbor distance of position i in string $c_1 c_2 \cdots c_m$ is difference between c_i and c_{i+1}, and is denoted as $d_{i,i+1}$

$$d_{i,i+1} = |c_{i+1} - c_i|$$

Consider a set of strings $\{t_1, t_2, \cdots, t_n\}$, where $t_i = c_1 c_2 \cdots c_w$ and the length of every string is w. Let $count(p, d)$ denote the occurrence number of every neighbor distance d in every position p of string, where $p = 1, 2, ..., w - 1$ and $d \in [0...255]$.

Definition 2. Neighbor distance distribution $f(p, d)$ is the occurrence frequency of every byte distance d in every position p of string, where $p \in [1, w - 1]$ and $d \in [0...255]$.

$$f(p, d) = \begin{cases} \frac{b}{n+e} & \text{if } count(p, d) = 0 \\ \frac{count(p,d)}{n} & \text{otherwise} \end{cases}$$

where b, e is a small enough real number. All values of $f(p, d)$ in the domain constitute NRS. Table 1 gives NRS with signature length $w = 9$.

Assuming that Q is a byte sequence and l is the length of Q. Let $d_{1,2}, d_{2,3}, \cdots$, $d_{l-1,l}$ denote the neighbor distances of position $1, 2, ..., l - 1$ in Q, respectively.

Table 1. An example of a SNS with $w = 10$

d	$p = 1$	$p = 2$	...	$p = 9$
0	f(1,0)	f(2,0)	...	f(9,0)
1	f(1,1)	f(2,1)	...	f(9,1)
...	...	...	...	
255	f(1,255)	f(2,255)	...	f(9,255)

Definition 3. Let t be the substring of Q with the starting position a and the length w, the matching score $R(Q, a, w)$ of t is expressed as

$$R(Q, a, w) = \frac{1}{w-1} \sum_{p=1}^{w-1} log \frac{f(p, d_{a+p,a+p+1})}{f},$$

There exists a substring t of sequence Q that maximizes $R(Q, a, w)$. The matching score of sequence Q is defined as

$$\Theta = \max_{a=1}^{l-w+1} R(Q, a, w) = \max_{a=1}^{l-w+1} \frac{1}{w-1} \sum_{p=1}^{w-1} log \frac{f(p, d_{a+p,a+p+1})}{f} \tag{1}$$

where f can be set $\frac{1}{255}$. However, in order to distinguish worm sequence and normal flow, we set f be the neighbor distance distribution of normal traffic. $f(d)$ denote occurrence frequency of neighbor distance d. Occurrence frequency of every neighbor distance is computed and it composes $f(d)$.

3.1 Process of Computing NRS

Consider a set S of worm sequences $S_1, S_2, \cdots, S_n$, and a set T of strings $t_1, t_2, \cdots, t_n$. The starting positions $a_1(0), a_2(0), \cdots, a_n(0)$ of $t_1, t_2, \cdots, t_n$ are chosen randomly from worm sequences $S_1, S_2, \cdots, S_n$, respectively. The length of t_i is w. Next we use Gibbs sampling to generate iteratively SNS.

Firstly, NRS is generated from $T - t_1$ based on Definition 2. The matching score Θ_1 of S_1 is computed based on Equation (1), and $a_1(0)$ of the string t_1 is replaced with $a_1(1)$ which maximizes $R(S_1, a, w)$. That is, $a_1(1)$ is drawn from the $T - t_1$, given $a_2(0), a_3(0), \cdots, a_n(0)$. Then we make the following drawings on the first iteration of Gibbs sampling.

$a_2(1)$ is drawn from the $T - t_2$, given $a_1(1), a_3(0), \cdots, a_n(0)$.

$\cdots$

$a_k(1)$ is drawn from the $T - t_k$, given $a_1(1), \cdots, a_{k-1}(1), a_{k+1}(0), \cdots, a_n(0)$.

$\cdots$

$a_n(1)$ is drawn from the $T - t_n$, given $a_1(1), a_2(1), \cdots, a_{n-1}(1)$.

We proceed in the same manner on the second iteration and every other iteration of the sampling scheme. At last, NRS is generated based on $a_1(m), a_2(m), \cdots,$

$a_n(m)$ after m times iteration. We call above process NRS signature generation algorithm (GNRS).

GNRS terminates if the average value of matching score between the all worm sequences and the signature NRS is within $(1 \pm \varepsilon)$ of that of previous k iterations, where ε is a small predefined percentage. n strings in the last set T are considered as significant regions of n sequences in set S. The pseudo code of GNRS is shown in Fig. 1.

Algorithm GNRS(S,w)
Input:$S = \{S_1, S_2, ..., S_n\}$; length=$w$;
Output:NRS; {Randomly choosing the start position $a_1(0), a_2(0), \cdots, a_n(0)$ of strings $t_1, t_2, ..., t_n$ from sequences $S_1, S_2, ..., S_n$ to construct a string set T;
$j = 1$;
Flag=false;
while(Flag==false)
    $\{j = (j \mod n)$;
    NRS are generated based on $T - t_j$;
    The matching score Θ_j of S_j is computed and a_j are replaced;
    $j + +$;
    If the average value of matching score between sequences in set S and the
NRS is within $(1 \pm \varepsilon)$ of that of previous k iterations
    then Flag=true;}
NRS=SNS}
Return NRS;

Fig. 1. Algorithm GNRS

4   NRS-CC Algorithm

Consider an n-size suspicious flow pool with k worm sequences, NRS-CC is designed to generate worm signature from the pool. The suspicious flow pool comprises of worm sequences and noise sequences. Worm sequences are generated artificially based on polymorphic technique. Noise sequences contain normal flow sequences from real network, sequences generated by using special methods discussed in [6] or contain both of them.

Color coding is a family of perfect hash functions from $\{1, 2, ..., |V|\}$ to $\{1,2,...,k\}$. Basic principle for designing color coding is to use as few as possible the number of colorings to cover all u-combinations of g. In this paper, a coloring scheme based partition is adopted to color g nodes in u colors. We describe how to apply color coding in the process of generating worm signature in reference [18]. Getting 20 sequences from suspicious flow pool, a sequence equal a point in a 20-size graph. The graph can be colored by using 19, 18,..., 11 colors. Sequences with the same color compose a cluster. When 20 sequences contain $m(m > 10)$ worm sequences, there must be a m'-color scheme $(11 \le m' \le m)$, which makes every sequence cluster contain at least one worm sequence. Then sequences with the same color are merged. Therefore, combined sequences will contain worm variant. We can further extract worm signature from these combined sequences.

We choose randomly 20 sequences from a n-size suspicious flow pool with k worm sequences. The probability that the number of worm sequences in 20 sequences is greater than m is

$$P_m = (\frac{C_{n-k}^{20-m}C_k^m}{C_n^{20}} + \frac{C_{n-k}^{20-m-1}C_k^{m+1}}{C_n^{20}} + \cdots + \frac{C_{n-k}^{20-20}C_k^{20}}{C_n^{20}}) \qquad (2)$$

When the number of suspicious flow pool n is 1000, the value of probability P_m is showed in Table 2.

Table 2. The value of probability P_m

Worm number k	$m = 20$	$m = 19$	$m = 18$	$m = 17$	$m = 16$	$m = 15$	$m = 14$	$m = 13$	$m = 12$	$m = 11$
1000	1	1	1	1	1	1	1	1	1	1
900	0.119	0.38915	0.67722	0.86905	0.95851	0.98957	0.99789	0.99965	0.99995	0.99999
800	0.01099	0.06726	0.20329	0.40968	0.6301	0.8062	0.91543	0.96928	0.99071	0.99766
700	7.34562E-4	0.00721	0.03416	0.10473	0.23495	0.41501	0.6086	0.77428	0.88894	0.95374
600	3.21397E-5	4.74683E-4	0.00336	0.01516	0.04927	0.12316	0.24766	0.4148	0.59633	0.75741
500	7.85665E-7	1.71197E-5	1.77766E-4	0.00117	0.00551	0.0197	0.05584	0.12917	0.24953	0.41101
400	8.21356E-9	2.66908E-7	4.12058E-6	4.02223E-5	2.78762E-4	0.00146	0.00601	0.01999	0.05471	0.12516
300	2.2093E-11	1.12285E-9	2.70433E-8	4.10629E-7	4.4116E-6	3.56781E-5	2.25628E-4	0.00114	0.00474	0.0162
200	4.753E-15	4.2491E-13	1.79481E-11	4.7642E-10	8.91653E-9	1.25125E-7	1.36687E-6	1.19118E-5	8.41905E-5	4.88034E-4
100	1.5788E-21	3.5242E-19	3.6894E-17	2.4090E-15	1.1006E-13	3.7415E-12	9.8222E-11	2.03998E-9	3.40596E-8	4.61947E-7

From Table 2, when worm number in suspicious flow pool is greater than 500, the probability that more than 11 worm sequences is obtained from randomly choosing 20 sequences is greater. For example, when suspicious flow pool contains 600 worm sequences, the probability of containing 11 worm sequences from 20 sequences is 0.75741. Therefore, in order to get greater probability, we apply (20,11)-coloring scheme when we identify worm sequences from 20 sequences.

Algorithm NRS-CC aims to generate worm signature from the suspicious flow pool with noise sequences. Firstly, m groups of sequences $G_1, G_2, ..., G_m$ are randomly selected, and every group contains 20 sequences. Then algorithm identify worm sequences from every group. The process of identification is as follows: 20 sequences are treated as 20 nodes. (20,11)-coloring scheme is built to color 20 nodes. Assuming f is the coloring number of (20,11)-coloring scheme. For each (20, 11)-coloring, sequences with the same color are merged. So 20 sequences are converted to 11 sequences. Then GNRS generates NRS_i signature for the 11 sequences. After NRS_i is generated, it is evaluated in one filter flow pool, which contains n normal sequences. We compute the matching score Θ_j of the jth sequence in the filter flow pool with NRS_i based on equation (1). If $\Theta_j > 0 (1 \leq j \leq n)$, p_i adds 1. If $p_i/n < \varepsilon$, the 11 sequences used to generate NRS_i is considered as 11 worm sequences in the suspicious flow pool, where ε is a small predefined percentage. If all $NRS_i (1 \leq i \leq f)$ are not satisfied, 11 worm sequences are not identified. We call the process IdenWS.

For group G_i, if 11 worm sequences are identified, they are put into a set S'. Finally, if the set S' is not null, GNRS is used to generate NRS for S. Algorithm NRS-CC is illustrated in Fig. 2. As shown in Fig. 2, if there is at least one group which obtains the set of worm sequences, NRS-CC can generate worm signature with probability 1.

Algorithm NRS-CC(S, N, w)
Input: l sequences $S = \{x_1, \cdots, x_l\}$, n normal sequences $N = N_1, N_2, \cdots, N_n$, the width of signature w;
Output: worm signature NRS;
$S \rightarrow S_1, S_2, \cdots, S_m$;
Build (20,11)-coloring scheme;
For $i = 1$ to m
   For each $(20, 11)$-*coloring*
      \{20 sequences of S_i are colored with the $(20, 11)$-*coloring*;
      $S'_i = \{x_1, \cdots, x_{11}\}$ is generated by merging sequences with the same color in S_u;
      $NRS_i \leftarrow GNRS(S'_i, w)$;
      For $j = 1$ to n
         Computing the matching score Θ_j of N_j with NRS_i;
         If $(\Theta_j > 0)$ then $p_i ++$;
      If $p_i/n < \varepsilon$
         Combing the set of sequences S' and S'_i; break;\}\}
If S' is not null, then
   \{$NRS \leftarrow GNRS(S', w)$;
   return (NRS);\}
Else return ("not generating signature");

Fig. 2. Algorithm NRS-CC

When one group sequence is selected randomly from suspicious flow, the probability that worm sequences can be identified from this group is denoted as P_t. When 10 group sequences are randomly selected from suspicious flow pool containing 1000 sequences, the probability that algorithm NRS-CC identifies worm sequences from more than 1 group is denoted as P_1. $P_1 = 1 - (1 - P_t)^{10}$. The probability P_3 that NRS-CC identifies worm sequences from more than 3 groups is

$$P_3 = 1 - (1 - P_t)^8 (P_t)^2 - (1 - P_t)^9 (P_t) - (1 - P_t)^{10}.$$

The values of P_1 and P_3 are showed in Table 3. From the Table 3, when the number of worm sequences is larger than the number of noise sequences in the suspicious flow pool, the probability that algorithm NRS-CC identifies worm sequences from over 1 group and over 3 group sequences in selecting randomly 10 group sequences.

Table 3. The probability that NRS-CC identifies worm sequences from suspicious flow and generates worm signature

The number of noise sequences	P_1	P_3
0	1	1
100	1	1
200	1	1
300	1	1
400	0.999999	0.99999
500	0.994976	0.989023
600	0.737405	0.694462
700	0.150686	0.13647
800	0.00486964	0.0043835
900	4.61946E-6	4.15752E-6

5 Experiments and Results

MS Blaster worm and SQL Slammer worm are used in the experiments. The MS Blaster worm exploits a vulnerability in Microsoft's DCOM RPC interface. Upon successful execution, the MS Blaster worm retrieves a copy of the file msblast.exe from a previously infected host. In our experiments, we artificially generate polymorphic worms based on polymorphism techniques mentioned in Sect. 2.

Firstly, 1000 Blaster worm sequences and 1000 SQL Slammer worm sequences are generated. Suspicious flow pool includes 1000 worm sequences. Then worm sequences are gradually replaced with noise sequences. Noise sequences is generated by method discussed in [6].We generate 3 class NRS, NRS_1, NRS_2, NRS_3, from the suspicious flow. Firstly, 10 group sequences are selected randomly from the suspicious flow pool. When IdenWS identifies 11 worm sequences for the first time, NRS_1 is generated from the 11 worm sequences. NRS_2 is generated by running NRS-CC in the end. Moreover, we use the same group strategy with CCSF [18] to generate NRS_3 signature. We divide suspicious flow pool into 50 groups and every group include 20 sequences. Then IdenWS identifies worm sequences for every group. NRS_3 is generated by merging all worm sequences identified. The process is called CCSF'. Finally, we use these NRS and PADS [17]

Table 4. The false negative ratio of different Blaster worm signatures

The number of noise sequences	NRS_1	NRS_2	NRS_3	PADS
0	0	0	0	0
100	0.6624	0	0	0
200	0	0	0	0
300	0.6662	0	0	0
400	0.6646	0	0	0
500	0	0	0	0
600	none	none	0	0
700	none	none	0	0
800	none	none	0	0
900	none	none	0	0

to detect 10000 worm sequences and 10000 normal flow sequences. The results are showed in Tables 4, 5, 6 and 7.

From the Tables 4 and 6, we can see that NRS_1 and NRS_2 can not be generated when the suspicious flow pool includes more than 600 noise sequences. It is mainly because a great number of noises leads to 20 sequences selected randomly include more than 9 noise sequences. Color coding method can not be used to generate signature from 20 sequences with more than 9 noise sequences. The false negative ratio of three class worm signature expect for NRS_1 is 0. In Table 4, when the suspicious flow pool includes 200 and 500 noise sequences, the false negative ratio for NRS_1 is 0. However, when the suspicious flow pool includes 100, 300 and 400 noise sequences, the false negative ratio for NRS_1 is high. NRS_1 is generated only from 11 worm sequences. Because the number

Table 5. The false positive ratio of different Blaster worm signatures

The number of noise sequences	NRS_1	NRS_2	NRS_3	PADS
0	0	0	0	0.2933
100	0	0	0	0.4655
200	0	0	0	0.5072
300	0	0	0	0.7086
400	0.0001	0	0	0.8404
500	0	0	0	0.9329
600	none	none	0.0085	0.9798
700	none	none	0.0113	0.9815
800	none	none	0.0235	0.991
900	none	none	0.0594	0.9998

Table 6. The false negative ratio of different SQL Slammer worm signatures

The number of noise sequences	NRS_1	NRS_2	NRS_3	PADS
0	0.3315	0	0	0
100	0.3333	0	0	0
200	0.3333	0	0	0
300	0.3313	0	0	0
400	0.3333	0	0	0
500	0.3317	0	0	0
600	none	none	0	0
700	none	none	0	0
800	none	none	0	0
900	none	none	0	0.0244

Table 7. The false positive ratio of different SQL Slammer worm signatures

The number of noise sequences	NRS_1	NRS_2	NRS_3	PADS
0	0	0	0	0.2015
100	0	0	0	0.2931
200	0	0	0	0.3541
300	0	0	0	0.5067
400	0	0	0	0.6852
500	0	0	0	0.8034
600	none	none	0.0011	0.9032
700	none	none	0.0046	0.9433
800	none	none	0.0111	0.9716
900	none	none	0.0213	0.9923

of worm sequences which are used to generate worm signature is few, worm signatures only have characteristics of these worm sequences, and they can not detect effectively all worm mutation. Due to 11 sequences are selected randomly, randomness causes that NRS_1 can detect well worm sequences occasionally.

From the Tables 5 and 7, it can be seen that the false positive ratio of NRS_1, NRS_2 and NRS_3 is lower than that of PADS. Because color coding is used in the process of generating the NRS_1, NRS_2 and NRS_3, noise disturbance is removed and these signatures do not classify non worm sequences as worm sequences. PADS has characteristics both worm sequences and noise sequences due to noise disturbance. Therefore, PADS obtains the high false positive ratio.

Furthermore, we compare NRS_2 and NRS_3. When the suspicious flow pool includes 1000 sequences, coloring number of (20,i)-coloring scheme is denoted in C_i. Maximum coloring number in running algorithm NRS-CC for generating

Table 8. Comparing running time of NRS-CC and CCSF'

The number of noise sequences	Time for NRS-CC	CCSF'
0	8.06 s	120.04 s
100	39.16 s	2807.22 s
200	66.01 s	19375.1 s
300	78.48 s	41356.4 s
400	1526.23 s	60798.6 s
500	6857.64 s	79459.3 s

NRS_2 is $T_1 = 10 * C_{11}$. Maximum coloring number in running CCSF' for generating NRS_3 is $T_2 = 50 * \sum_{i=20}^{11} C_i$. Based on the coloring number of color coding,

$$T_1 = 10 * C_{11} = 10 * 3250 = 32500$$
$$T_2 = 50 * \sum_{i=20}^{11} C_i = 50 * (1 + 10 + 50 + 170 + 403 + 862 + 1220 + 2036$$
$$+ 2085 + 3250) = 504350$$

We use 1000 Blaster sequences as test variants. In the same environment, NRS-CC and CCSF' are running to generate worm signature. We compare them with running time. When the suspicious flow includes different noise number, the running time is showed in Table 8.

From Table 8, when there are fewer noise sequences in the suspicious flow pool, for example noise number is 100, both NRS-CC and CCSF' can generate worm signature quickly. But when noise number increases, NRS-CC is more quicker than CCSF'.

6   Conclusion

In order to generate effective polymorphic worm signatures in noisy environments, in this paper an approach NRS-CC is proposeed to generate neighbor relation signatures. NRS-CC applies color coding to solve noise disturbance problem. Compared with PADS, NRS generated by NRS-CC has lower false positive ratio. When the number of noise is less than worm number, NRS-CC can generate worm signature more quickly than CCSF which simply uses color coding. In the future, we will apply the NRS-CC in real environment to generate worm signature.

Acknowledgment. This work is supported by National Natural Science Foundation of China under Grant No.61202495 and No.61402542.

References

1. Kaur, R., Singh, M.: A survey on zero-day polymorphic worm detection techniques. IEEE Commun. Surv. Tutorials 16(3), 1520–1549 (2014)
2. Bayoglu, B., Sogukpinar, L.: Graph based signature classes for detecting polymorphic worms via content analysis. Comput. Netw. 56(2), 832–844 (2012)
3. Mohammed, M.M.Z.E., Chan, H.A., Ventura, N., Pathan, A.S.K.: An automated signature generation method for zero-day polymorphic worms based on multilayer perceptron model. In: Proceedings of 2013 International Conference on Advanced Computer Science Applications and Technologies (ACSAT), Kuching, pp. 450–455, December 2013
4. Comar, P.M., Liu, L., Saha, S., Tan, P.N., Nucci, A.: Combining supervised and unsupervised learning for zero-day malware detection. In: Proceedings of 32nd Annual IEEE International Conference on Computer Communications (INFOCOM 2013), Turin, Italy, pp. 2022–2030, April 2013
5. Kaur, R., Singh, M.: Efficient hybrid technique for detecting zero-day polymorphic worms. In: Proceedings of 2014 IEEE International on Advance Computing Conference (IACC), pp. 95–100, February 2014
6. Perdisci, R., Dagon, D., Lee, W., Fogla, P., Sharif, M.: Misleading worm signature generators using deliberate noise injection. In: Proceedings of 2006 IEEE Symposium on Security and Privacy, Atlanta, GA, USA, pp. 17–31 (2006)
7. Stephenson, B., Sikdar, B.: A quasi-species model for the propagation and containment of polymorphic worms. IEEE Trans. Comput. 58(9), 1289–1296 (2009)
8. Talbi, M., Mejri, M., Bouhoula, A.: Specification and evaluation of polymorphic shellcode properties using a new temporal logic. J. Comput. Virol. 5(3), 171–186 (2009)
9. Codi, M., Patel, D., Borisaniya, B., Patel, H., Patel, A., Rajarajan, M.: A survey of intrusion detection techniques in cloud. J. Netw. Comput. Appl. 36(1), 42–57 (2013)
10. Ranjan, S., Shah, S., Nucci, A., Munafo, M., Cruz, R., Muthukrishnan, S.: DoWitcher: effective worm detection and containment in the internet core. In: IEEE Infocom, Anchorage, Alaska, pp. 2541–2545 (2007)
11. Cai, M., Hwang, K., Pan, J., Christos, P.: WormShield: fast worm signature generation with distributed fingerprint aggregation. IEEE Trans. Dependable Secure Comput. 5(2), 88–104 (2007)
12. Newsome, J., Karp, B., Song, D.: Polygraph: automatically generation signatures for polymorphic worms. In: Proceedings of 2005 IEEE Symposium on Security and Privacy Symposium, Oakland, California, pp. 226–241 (2005)
13. Li, Z., Sanghi, M., Chen, Y., Kao, M., Chavez, B.: Hamsa: fast signature generation for zero-day polymorphic worms with provable attack resilience. In: Proceedings of IEEE Symposium on Security and Privacy, Washington, DC, pp. 32–47 (2006)
14. Cavallaro, L., Lanzi, A., Mayer, L., Monga, M.: LISABETH: automated content-based signature generator for zero-day polymorphic worms. In: Proceedings of the Fourth International Workshop on Software Engineering for Secure Systems, Leipzig, Germany, pp. 41–48 (2008)
15. Bayoglu, B., Sogukpinar, L.: Polymorphic worm detection using token-pair signatures. In: Proceedings of the 4th International Workshop on Security, Privacy and Trust in Pervasive and Ubiquitous Computing, Sorrento, Italy, pp. 7–12 (2008)

16. Tang, Y., Xiao, B., Lu, X.: Signature tree generation for polymorphic worms. IEEE Trans. Comput. **60**(4), 565–579 (2011)
17. Tang, Y., Chen, S.: An automated signature-based approach against polymorphic internet worms. IEEE Trans. Parallel Distrib. Syst. **18**, 879–892 (2007)
18. Wang, J., Wang, J.X., Chen, J.E., Zhang, X.: An automated signature generation approach for polymorphic worm based on color coding. In: IEEE ICC 2009, Dresden, Germany, pp. 1–6 (2009)

Scalable Access Policy for Attribute Based Encryption in Cloud Storage

Jing Wang[1,2], Chuanhe Huang[1,2(✉)], and Jinhai Wang[1,2]

[1] Computer School, Wuhan University, Wuhan 430072, China
{wjing,huangch,wangjinhai}@whu.edu.cn
[2] Collaborative Innovation Center of Geospatial Technology, Wuhan University, Wuhan 430072, China

Abstract. Cloud storage provides outsourced storage services in a cost-effective manner. A key challenge in cloud storage is the security and integrity of outsourced data. A security mechanism known as Attribute-Based Encryption (ABE) represents the state-of-the-art in providing fine-grained access control for cloud storage. A critical issue in ABE is the managing of access policy. Policy managing may incur substantial computation and communication overhead in the ABE scheme with unscalable access policy. In this work, we propose a form of access policy named block Linear Secret Sharing Scheme (LSSS) matrix. The scalability of block LSSS matrix provides an efficient policy managing interface for ABE schemes. Thus, the ABE schemes use block LSSS matrix as access policy are light weight in computation and communication, as compared with other schemes during access policy managing. Furthermore, the block LSSS matrix enjoys advantages of efficiency, flexibility and security, bringing a number of improvements in various aspects of ABE.

Keywords: Cloud · Data security · Access control · Attribute-based encryption · Access policy management

1 Introduction

Cloud data storage offers a number of advantages over traditional storage, in terms of availability, scalability, performance, portability and functional requirements. It develops a national strategy to collect, preserve and make available digital content for current and future generations based on cloud storage. Though the advantages of cloud storage are clear, a critical concern in the present data outsourcing scenario is the enforcement of strong data security mechanisms [11]. Ensuring privacy and security of such data is important for users to trust the service providers. Along that direction, adequate access control techniques are to be deployed, ensuring services are only provided to legitimate users. Attribute Based Encryption (ABE) is a novel cryptographic tool that can provide fine-grained ciphertext access control for cloud storage. The core properties of such a cryptographic storage service include: (1) access control of the data is maintained by the customer instead of the service provider; (2) the security properties are

© Springer International Publishing Switzerland 2015
G. Wang et al. (Eds.): ICA3PP 2015, Part III, LNCS 9530, pp. 383–402, 2015.
DOI: 10.1007/978-3-319-27137-8_29

derived from cryptography, as opposed to traditional access control. Therefore, such a service provides several compelling advantages over other storage services based on public cloud infrastructures.

A crucial concept in ABE is known as the access policy/access structure. The data owner can manage the access privilege of his data through manipulating its access policy. In fact, the performance of ABE schemes depends significantly on their access policy. For example, the scale of access policy decides the size of ciphertext and the computation of encrypting, the expression of access policy decides the flexibility of the access control mechanism. Many researchers focus on optimizing ABE via optimizing the access policy. However, scalability, as an important property of access policy, was often ignored. In many scenarios, access policy are dynamically and frequently updated for various reasons. Thus, the data owner needs to re-encrypt the data with the new policy and upload new ciphertext to the cloud during policy updating in such ABE schemes without scalable access policy. Heavy computation and communication overhead are incurred by such processing.

The grand challenge of policy updating in ABE based access control mechanism is to jointly guarantee correctness, completeness and security [17]. At the same time, efficiency is further considered as an important requirement in this paper. The policy updating issue has been discussed in a few ABE schemes [15–17]; yet there are still weaknesses in terms of fulling meeting the above requirements. In [15,16], the updated access policy should be more restrictive than the previous one, because the scalability of the access policy is limited. Although [17] has improved the completeness of policy updating method, the updating process of this scheme is still not efficiency enough. In some cases, the access policy is required to re-construct (especially, the processing of threshold updating is cumbersome).

Focusing on scalability, we propose a new access policy called block LSSS matrix. Block LSSS matrix comes with an efficient managing interface that greatly improves the manageability of ABE schemes. The advantages of describing access policy as a block LSSS matrix are two fold. First, the computation and communication of policy updating are both light weight via processing in block. Because each block of the matrix is independent, block updates are co-relation free. Second, the computational complexity of decryption is reduced for the ABE scheme. Because the decryption operation can be decomposed into blocks, lowering the computation scale. Besides, a feature of block matrix lies in the following intuition: the logical construction of access policy is intuitively presented in a matrix. In order to hide the structure of access policy and extend the space of LSSS matrix, the mask matrix is provided. Mask matrix is an available tool to improve the security and flexibility of block LSSS matrix; it eliminates the intuition of block LSSS matrix yet retainss its logic structure.

The contributions of this paper are summarized as follows.

(1) For optimizing the performance of ABE, we provide a generalized method to describe the access policy in ABE as a block LSSS matrix, which enables high scalability;

(2) In order to improve the flexibility and security of block LSSS matrix, we introduce the concept of mask matrix. The mask matrix can expand the policy and hide the policy structure;

(3) We provide four kinds of managing function for bock LSSS matrix. The functions are convenient and efficient, they can process any type of policy updates.

2   Related Work

Cloud computing is a new architecture that is envisioned as the next generation computing paradigm [8]. It introduces a major change in data storage and application execution, with everything now hosted in the cloud — a nebulous assemblage of computers and servers accessible via the Internet [9]. As a successful case, the United States Library of Congress moved its digitized content to the cloud in 2009 [10]. It develops a national strategy to collect, preserve and make available digital content for current and future generations based on cloud storage.

Many researchers focus on the security in cloud storage systems [23–26]. ABE provides a smart way to construct a fined-grained access control for cloud storage [15, 20–22, 27]. Access privileges described by access policy in ABE are more flexible and expressive than in traditional coarse-grained access control mechanisms. The access policy is derived from a Secret Sharing Scheme (SSS) which shares a secret among a group of participants [12]. In such a way, the secret can be reconstructed only by a specified group of shares. A wide range of general approaches for designing secret sharing schemes are known, e.g., Shamir [6], Benaloh [2], Bertilsson [3], Brickell [4], Massey [5], Blakley [1], Simonis [7], Ventzislav [13] and Svetla [14]. Thus, access policy is often described in various forms, such as monotonic Boolean formula, access tree or Linear Secret Sharing Scheme (LSSS) matrix. All these forms of access policy are poor in scalability and the policy updates of ABE is limited or inefficient.

Table 1. Comparison of ABE schemes

Scheme	Goyal [15]	Sahai [16]	Yang [17]	Proposed
Limit of updating	Y	Y	N	N
Form of policy	Access tree	LSSS matrix	Boolean formula Access tree LSSS matrix	Boolean formula Access tree LSSS matrix
Re-construct SSS	N	Y	Y	N
Update unit	Node	Row	Node/Row	Sub-tree/matrix

Recently, only a few ABE schemes have considered policy updating and provided solutions. Table 1 shows the comparison of existing ABE schemes that support access policy updating. Compared with Goyal, Sahai and Yang's scheme, our scalable ABE scheme is optimized for SSS updating. Different from [15,16], the updating of policy in our scheme is more flexible without any restrictions. Compared with the other three schemes, our updating method is processed in sub-tree/matrix instead of in node/row. Consequently, the proposed scheme is more efficient. Specifically, our scheme is more streamlined and intuitive than [17] in dealing with threshold. Thus, the block LSSS matrix as a scalable access policy can improve the ABE scheme in policy managing.

3   Scalable Access Policy

3.1   Definitions and Symbols

Access Policy. The access policy in ABE is usually defined as monotonous access structures.

Definition 1 (Monotonous Access Structures). *Let* $P = \{P_1, P_2, \ldots, P_N\}$ *be a set of parties. A collection* $\mathbb{A} \subset 2^{\{P_1, P_2, \ldots, P_N\}}$ *is monotone if*

$$\forall B, C \subset P, B \in \mathbb{A} \land B \subset C \rightarrow C \in \mathbb{A}$$

Specially, $A \in \mathbb{A}$ is called authorized set, and $A \notin \mathbb{A}$ is called unauthorized set. In the ABE context, the role of the parties are taken by the attributes. Thus, an access policy $\mathbb{A}$ is a collection of attribute sets. In fact, an access policy can be realized by a Secret Sharing Scheme which decomposes a secret s into a share set $S = \{s_i, \ldots, s_n\}$. Let ρ be a map form S to P, S' be a subset of S and $P' = \{\rho(s_i) | s_i \in S'\}$. Secret s can be recovered by S' iff P' is authorized.

Furthermore, an access policy can be viewed as a circuit which consists of a set of gates (AND, OR, threshold) and inputs, as shown in Fig. 1. The circuit takes a set of shares S' as inputs and outputs the secret s iff P', the image set of S', is authorized.

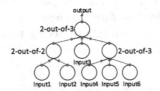

Fig. 1. An access policy described as tree-circuit

The block LSSS matrix proposed in this paper is generated by the tree-circuit and its node matrices[1]. We formalize the processing of block LSSS matrix generation in Fig. 2. Firstly, each non-leaf node is defined a node matrix which is generated by a Vandermonde matrix and a mask matrix. Secondly, a block LSSS matrix is generated by all of these node matrices. Finally, the block LSSS matrix is masked with a full rank matrix.

Matrix Notations and Operations. Unless otherwise indicated, a boldface lowercase letter denotes a vector, an uppercase letter denotes a matrix in this paper. Key notations are summarized in Table 2 for ease of reference.

---

[1] The detailed describing of node matrix is given in Sect. 3.2.

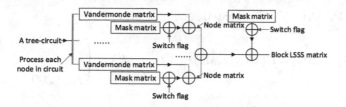

Fig. 2. Tree-circuit to Block LSSS Matrix

Table 2. Key notations

Notation	Description
I_k	The unit matrix with order k
$O_{m \times n}$	The null matrix with m row and n column
$R(*)$	The rank of the matrix $*$
ε	A binary vector in $\{0,1\}^n$, ε_i denotes the ith entry of ε
$\mathbf{e_i}$	A unit vector whose i^{th} entry is 1 and other entries are all 0
M^ε	A sub-matrix of M, each row of M^ε is the ith row of M where $\varepsilon_i = 1$
$* \approx **$	Matrix $*$ and matrix $**$ can describe the same access policy
$\lVert * \rVert_0$	The standard zero-norm of the vector $*$

We further define a few matrices with specific structure:

$$I'_k = \begin{pmatrix} O \\ I_{k-1} \end{pmatrix} \tag{1}$$

where $O_{1 \times (k-1)}$ is simplified to O. For simplicity, we shall omit the subscript in some cases.

$$F(V, k) = \begin{pmatrix} V \\ O_{(k-1) \times l} \end{pmatrix} \tag{2}$$

where $V \in Z^l$.

$$E(A, k_1, \ldots, k_n) = \begin{pmatrix} F(A_1, k_1) & I'_{k_1} & \ldots & O \\ \vdots & \vdots & \ddots & \vdots \\ F(A_n, k_n) & O & \ldots & I'_{k_n} \end{pmatrix} \tag{3}$$

where $A \in Z^{n \times l}$ and A_i denotes the ith row of A.

$$U(M_1, \ldots, M_n) = \begin{pmatrix} M_1 & \ldots & O \\ \vdots & \ddots & \vdots \\ O & \ldots & M_n \end{pmatrix} \tag{4}$$

Let $M_i = (\bar{M}_i, \hat{M}_i) \in Z^{k_i \times l_i}$ where $\bar{M}_i \in Z^{k_i \times 1}$, $\hat{M}_i \in Z^{k_i \times (l_i - 1)}$,

$$U^*(A, M_1, \ldots, M_n) = U(M_1, \ldots, M_n)E(A, l_1, \ldots, l_n) = \begin{pmatrix} \bar{M}_1 A_1 & \hat{M}_1 & \ldots & O \\ \vdots & \vdots & \ddots & \vdots \\ \bar{M}_n A_n & O & \ldots & \hat{M}_n \end{pmatrix} \quad (5)$$

Specifically,

$$U^\dagger(A, k, M) = \begin{pmatrix} A_1 & O \\ \vdots & \vdots \\ A_k \bar{M} & \hat{M} \\ \vdots & \vdots \\ A_n & O \end{pmatrix}. \quad (6)$$

3.2   Node Matrix

Node matrix is a special LSSS matrix[2] which can describe a node in the tree-circuit. Generally, a t-out-of-n node (as a general gate node) can be described by a matrix $M \in Z^{n \times t}$, where M^ε is full rank, $\forall \varepsilon \in \{0,1\}^n$ and $||\varepsilon||_0 = t$.

Transformation. In order to make the scalable access policy more general, we present a method to transform various gate forms into node matrices. The node matrix must keep the same inputs and output as the gate does. This implies that, the share set generated by the node matrix and by the gate are equal.

In a monotonic Boolean expression, there are two gate forms: AND($\wedge$) and OR($\vee$) [18]. Threshold(t-out-of-n, $Thr_{t,n}(a_1, \ldots, a_n)$) can be represented by a combination of AND and OR. For example, $Thr_{2,3}(a_1, a_2, a_3) \Longleftrightarrow (a_1 \wedge a_2) \vee (a_2 \wedge a_3) \vee (a_1 \wedge a_3)$. AND gate is a specific threshold, n-out-of-n. Let the original share set be $S = \{s_1, \ldots, s_n\}$ and the secret $s = \sum s_i$. The node matrix and vector are defined as follows:

$$M_A = \begin{pmatrix} 1 & -1 & \ldots & 0 \\ 0 & 1 & \ddots & \vdots \\ \vdots & \vdots & \ddots & -1 \\ 0 & 0 & \ldots & 1 \end{pmatrix}, V_A = \begin{pmatrix} s & v_2 & \ldots & v_n \end{pmatrix}$$

where $v_i = \sum_{j=i}^n s_j$. Let M_i denote the ith row vector of M_A. As a result, $\forall i, s_i = M_i V_A^T$, OR gate is also a specific threshold, 1-out-of-n. Let the secret set be $s \in Z$. The OR-node matrix and vector are defined as $M_O = (1, \ldots, 1)^T$ and $V_O = (s)$.

In an access tree, each threshold node can be described as a Vandermonde matrix [19]. A t-out-of-n node can be described as a $n \times t$ Vandermonde matrix $V_{n \times t}$ and a node vector V_t:

$$V_{n,t} = \begin{pmatrix} 1 & x_1 & \ldots & x_1^{t-1} \\ \vdots & \vdots & & \vdots \\ 1 & x_n & \ldots & x_n^{t-1} \end{pmatrix}, V_t = \begin{pmatrix} s & a_1 & \ldots & a_{t-1} \end{pmatrix}$$

---

[2] The detailed definition of LSSS matrix is given in [16].

where x_i denotes the interpolation of its ith child, a_j denotes the coefficient of x_i^j in the node polynomial $f(x)$ and s denotes the constant term of $f(x)$. Furthermore, $\forall i, M_i V_t^T = f(x_i) = s_i$.

Scalable Node Matrix. A generalized method to define scalable node matrix is given in this section. Let $V_{t,n} \in Z^{n \times t}$ be a Vandermonde matrix, $T_t \in Z^{t \times t}$ be an upper triangular matrix and $R(T_t) = t$. Thus, the matrix $M_{n,t}$ is calculated as $M_{n,t} = V_{n,t} T_t$. Significantly, $M_{n,t} \approx V_{n,t}$ and $M_{n't}^\varepsilon \approx V_{n,t}^\varepsilon, \forall \varepsilon \in \{0,1\}^n$. T_t is called mask matrix and the space of the node matrix can be extended via the mask matrix. Finally, a secret s is chosen at random and node vector is generated as $V_t = (s, v_2, \ldots, v_t)$, where $v_i \in Z$ is chosen randomly. The node matrix generated by this method is expressiveness and scalable. There are four scaling functions of node matrix defined as follows.

$Node_n^+(node, \Delta n)$: The function modifies the node matrix M_n, into $M_{n+\Delta n, t}$. Let $M_{n,t} = V_{n,t} T_t$ and $\Delta M_{\Delta n, t} = V_{\Delta n, t} T_t$ where $V_{n,t}, V_{\Delta n, t}$ are two Vandermonde matrices and T_t is a full rank upper triangular matrix. Thus,

$$M_{n+\Delta n, t} = \begin{pmatrix} V_{n,t} \\ V_{\Delta n, t} \end{pmatrix} T_t = \begin{pmatrix} M_{n,t} \\ \Delta M_{\Delta n, t} \end{pmatrix} \tag{7}$$

As a result, Δn more rows are inserted into $M_{n,t}$ and the node vector V_t is kept intact.

$Node_n^-(node, \varepsilon)$: The function removes the rows assigned by binary vector ε. Let $M_{n,t} = V_{n,t} T_t$ be the original node matrix. $M_{n,t}^\varepsilon$ can describe the modified node because $M_{n,t}^\varepsilon \approx V_{n,t}^\varepsilon$. Besides, the node vector V_t remains intact with this function.

$Node_t^+(node, \Delta t)$: The node threshold t is changed into $t + \Delta t$ and node matrix $M_{n,t}$ is changed into $M_{n, t+\Delta t}$. Let $M_{n,t} = V_{n,t} T_t$ and $\Delta V_{n, \Delta t}$ be the increment matrix of $V_{n,t}$ defined as follows:

$$\Delta V_{n, \Delta t} = \begin{pmatrix} x_1^t & \cdots & x_1^{t+\Delta t} \\ \vdots & & \vdots \\ x_n^t & \cdots & x_n^{t+\Delta t} \end{pmatrix} \tag{8}$$

Let $V_{n, t+\Delta t} = (V_{n,t}, \Delta V_{n, \Delta t})$ and $T_{\Delta t} \in Z_{\Delta t \times \Delta t}$ be an upper triangular matrix, $P \in Z^{t \times \Delta t}$ is a non-zero matrix. The mask matrix is modified as follows:

$$T_{t+\Delta t} = \begin{pmatrix} T_t & P \\ O & T_{\Delta t} \end{pmatrix} \tag{9}$$

Thus, $M_{n, t+\Delta t} = V_{n, t+\Delta t} T_{t+\Delta t} = (M_{n,t}, \Delta M_{n, \Delta t})$ where $\Delta M_{n, \Delta t} = V_{n,t} P + \Delta V_{n, \Delta t} T_{\Delta t}$. Finally, the node vector V_t is changed into $V_{t+\Delta t} = (V_t, v_{t+1}, \ldots, v_{t+\Delta t})$ where $v_{t+1}, \ldots, v_{t+\Delta t}$ are chosen at random.

$Node_t^-(node, \Delta t)$: The function changes the node threshold t into $t - \Delta t$. Let $M_{n,t} = V_{n,t} T_t$ be the node matrix. Similar to $Node_t^+(node, \Delta t)$, we define

$$M_{n,t} = (M_{n, t-\Delta t}, \Delta M_{n, \Delta t}), V_{n,t} = (V_{n, t-\Delta t}, \Delta V_{n, \Delta t}), T_t = \begin{pmatrix} T_{t-\Delta t} & P \\ O & T_{\Delta t} \end{pmatrix}$$

Thus, $M_{n, t-\Delta t} = V_{n, t-\Delta t} T_{t-\Delta t}$ can be obtain by removing the last Δt columns from $M_{n,t}$ directly. Finally, node vector $V_{t-\Delta t}$ is obtain by removing the last Δt entries from original node vector V_t.

3.3   Block LSSS Matrix

The matrix can describe not only a node but also a complete tree-circuit. A theorem in [13] provides an efficient way to construct block LSSS matrix — a *compound matrix* of a set of node matrices.

Theorem 1. *Let $M_1 \in Z^{m_1 \times n_1}, \ldots, M_l \in Z^{m_l \times n_l}$ be a set of LSSS matrices described access policy $\mathbb{A}_1, \ldots, \mathbb{A}_l$, $A \in Z^{l \times k}$ is a LSSS matrix described access policy $\mathbb{A}'$ and $P_1, \ldots, P_l$ be the parties of $\mathbb{T}$. Access policy $(\mathbb{A}_1 \mapsto P_1) \ldots (\mathbb{A}_l \mapsto P_l)\mathbb{A}'$ can be described by matrix $M = U^*(A, M_1, \ldots, M_l)$.*

Proof. The detailed proof is shown in [13].

Following Theorem 1, Algorithm 1, an iterative algorithm, is proposed to generate *compound LSSS matrix*. Let $\mathbb{T}$ be an access policy/tree-circuit and *root* be the root of $\mathbb{T}$. $TreeToLSSS(\mathbb{T}, root)$ performs a depth-first traversal of $\mathbb{T}$ and generates a matrix M by its node matrices $M_k, 1 \leq k \leq n$. The matrix M is called block LSSS matrix, which is a sparse block matrix and an effective LSSS matrix.

Algorithm 1. $TreeToLSSS(\mathbb{T}, node)$

Input: A matrix-tree: $\mathbb{T}$; A node of matrix: *node*;
Output: LSSS matrix: M; Vector: V;
1: **if** *node* is a leaf **then**
2:     $M \leftarrow (1)$;
3:     $V \leftarrow (1)$;
4: **else**
5:     **for** each child c_i of *node* **do**
6:         $(M_i, V_i) \leftarrow TreeToLSSS(\mathbb{T}, c_i)$;
7:     **end for**
8:     $M \leftarrow U^*(M(node), M_1, \ldots, M_n)$;//$M(node)$ is the node matrix of *node*, n is the total number of children of *node*
9:     $V \leftarrow (V(node), \hat{V}_1, \ldots, \hat{V}_n)$;//$V(node)$ is the node vector of *node*
10: **end if**
11: **return** (M, V);

To facilitate discussions, we introduce the following notations.
$\varphi : \{1, 2, \ldots, n\} \rightarrow N(\mathbb{T})$, where $N(\mathbb{T})$ denotes the set of non-leaf nodes in $\mathbb{T}$ (ψ denotes the inverse of φ).
$\delta : \{1, 2, \ldots, l\} \rightarrow L(\mathbb{T})$, where $L(\mathbb{T})$ denotes the set of leaves in $\mathbb{T}$ (σ denotes the inverse of δ).
$Anc(\delta(i))$ or $Anc(\varphi(i))$: the set of ancestors of $\delta(i)$ or $\varphi(i)$.
$I(j, i)$: a function returning the index of the subtree of $\varphi(j)$ which include node $\delta(i)$ or $\varphi(i)$.

Performances of Block LSSS Matrix. $\forall \mathbb{T}$ with l leaves and n non-leaf nodes can be viewed as a block matrix M generated by Algorithm 1:

$$M = \begin{pmatrix} c_{1,1} & \mathbf{m}_{1,1} & \ldots & \mathbf{m}_{1,n} \\ \vdots & \vdots & & \vdots \\ c_{1,l} & \mathbf{m}_{l,1} & \ldots & \mathbf{m}_{l,n} \end{pmatrix} \tag{10}$$

where

$$
\mathbf{m_{i,j}} = \begin{cases} \mathbf{o} & \varphi(j) \notin Anc(\delta(i)) \\ c_{i,j}\hat{M}(\varphi(j))_k & \varphi(j) \in Anc(\delta(i)), k = I(j,i) \end{cases} \tag{11}
$$

$c_{i,j} = \sum_{node \in Anc(\delta(i)) - Anc(\varphi(j))} M(node)_{1,k}$. $\forall node \in T$, we set $\bar{M}(node) = (1,1,\ldots,1)^T$.
That implies every node-mask matrix is an upper triangular matrix with the first column e_1. As a result, $\forall i,j, c_{i,j} = 1$ and Eq. (10) can be simplified:

$$
\mathbf{m_{i,j}} = \begin{cases} \mathbf{o} & \varphi(j) \notin Anc(\delta(i)) \\ \hat{M}(\varphi(j))_k & \varphi(j) \in Anc(\delta(i)), k = I(j,i) \end{cases} \tag{12}
$$

It is important that, the sorting of the column blocks does not affect the expression of access policy.

Theorem 2. *Let $s(n)$ be a sorting of $\{1,2,\ldots,n\}$ and described as $\{j_1, j_2,\ldots,j_n\}$. Assume that, M is a block LSSS matrix as shown in Eq. (10) and $M_{s(n)}$ is defined as follows:*

$$
M_{s(n)} = \begin{pmatrix} 1 & \mathbf{m_{1,j_1}} & \cdots & \mathbf{m_{l,j_n}} \\ \vdots & \vdots & & \vdots \\ 1 & \mathbf{m_{l,j_1}} & \cdots & \mathbf{m_{l,j_n}} \end{pmatrix} \tag{13}
$$

Then, $M_{s(n)} \approx M$.

Proof. $M_{s(n)}$ can be obtained by executing a series of elementary column transformations of M. Thus, there must be a full rank column transformation matrix T which make $M_{s(n)} = MT$. In another words, $M_{s(n)} \approx M$.

At the same time, the solution of the block LSSS matrix can be computed by *compounding* the solutions of its node matrices.

Theorem 3. *Let $M = U^*(A, M_1, \ldots, M_n)$, where $A \in Z^{l \times k}, M_1 \in Z^{l_1 \times k_n},\ldots, M_n \in Z^{l_n \times k_n}$ is a set of LSSS matrixes, $e_{1,i} \in \{0,1\}^i$ denote a unit vector whose first entry is 1 and sum $= \sum_{j=1}^n l_i$. Assume that $\mathbf{x}, \mathbf{x_1}, \ldots, \mathbf{x_n}$ are the solutions of $A^T X = e_{1,1}^T, M_1^T X = e_{1,l_1}^T, \ldots, M_n^T X = e_{1,l_n}^T$, respectively. Let $\mathbf{x^*} = U^*(\mathbf{x}, \mathbf{x_1}, \ldots, \mathbf{x_n})$. As a result, $(M)^T \mathbf{x^*} = e_{1,sum}$.*

Proof.

$$
M^T \mathbf{x^*} = (U^*(A, M_1, \ldots, M_n))^T U^*(\mathbf{x}, \mathbf{x_1}, \ldots, \mathbf{x_n})
$$
$$
= (E(A, l_1, \ldots, l_n))^T (U(M_1, \ldots, M_n))^T U(\mathbf{x_1}, \ldots, \mathbf{x_n}) E(\mathbf{x}, l_1, \ldots, l_n)
$$
$$
= (E(A, l_1, \ldots, l_n))^T U(e_{1,l_1}, \ldots, e_{1,l_n}) E(\mathbf{x}, l_1, \ldots, l_n)
$$
$$
= \begin{pmatrix} A^T \\ O \end{pmatrix} E(\mathbf{x}, l_1, \ldots, l_n)
$$
$$
= e_{1,sum}
$$

On the other hand, the block LSSS matrix is sparse. That makes block LSSS matrix weak in security, revealing the structure of access policy. To eliminate zero blocks, the block LSSS matrix can be masked by a full rank matrix when strong security is desired. At the same time, the mask matrix can expand the space of LSSS matrix and make the LSSS matrix more flexible. Let $M \in Z^{l \times m}$ be a block LSSS matrix, $T \in Z^{m \times m}$ be a full rank matrix chosen as mask matrix and $M' = MT$. As a result, $M' \approx M$ and M' is eliminated zeros. In fact, an upper triangular matrix is easy to generate and scale. Thus, upper triangular matrices are chosen as mask matrices to keep the scalability of block LSSS matrices.

Dynamic Updates of Block LSSS Matrices.
The block LSSS matrix is scalable. Each pair of blocks are mutual independent. Modifying one block has no effect on other blocks. We will give the scalable functions of block LSSS matrix in this section, arbitrary updates of block matrix can be achieved by these functions.

Firstly, we define four scalable functions that apply to the LSSS matrix without mask. The functions output non-zero adding blocks, modifying blocks and removing blocks of LSSS matrix. Note that, we omit the repeated rows of each block to save computation and communication cost.

$Thr(\mathbb{T}, \alpha, \Delta t)$: Let $\varphi(\alpha)$ be a t-out-of-n node. The threshold of $\varphi(\alpha)$ is changed to $t + \Delta t$ via this function. The function is discussed in two cases:

(1) Δt is positive. $Node_t^+(node, \Delta t)$ is run to add columns of node matrix $M_{\varphi(\alpha)}$ and node vector $V_{\varphi(\alpha)}$, each block $\mathbf{m}_{i,\alpha}$ and $V_{\varphi(\alpha)}$ are modified to a $t + \Delta t$ dimension vector. The non-zero adding block $\Delta M_{n, \Delta t}$ is generated by $Node_t^+(node, \Delta t)$.
(2) Δt is negative. $Node_t^-(node, |\Delta t|)$ is run to remove the last $|\Delta t|$ column vectors of node matrix $M_{\varphi(\alpha)}$ and node vector $V_{\varphi(\alpha)}$, each block $\mathbf{m}_{i,\alpha}$ and $V_{\varphi(\alpha)}$ are removed with the last $|\Delta t|$ entries. The removed blocks are denoted as $\Delta M_{n, \Delta t}$.

$Path(\mathbb{T}, \alpha, \gamma)$: A sub-tree of $\mathbb{T}$ with root $\varphi(\alpha)$ is moved to be a sub-tree of node $\varphi(\gamma)$. Let $M(\gamma) \in Z^{n' \times t'}$ be the node matrix of $\varphi(\gamma)$, $Node_n^+ \varphi(\gamma, 1)$ is run to insert a row vector $M(\gamma)_{n'+1}$ into $M(\gamma)$. Then, we set the block node vectors $V_\alpha = (1, \mathbf{v}_{\alpha,1}, \dots, \mathbf{v}_{\alpha,n})$ and $V_\gamma = (1, \mathbf{v}_{\gamma,1}, \dots, \mathbf{v}_{\gamma,n})$ where

$$\mathbf{v}_{\alpha,j} = \begin{cases} \hat{M}(\varphi(j))_k & \text{if } \varphi(j) \in Anc(\varphi(\alpha)) \text{ and } k = I(j, \alpha) \\ \mathbf{o} & \text{if } \varphi(j) \notin Anc(\varphi(\alpha)) \end{cases} \tag{14}$$

$$\mathbf{v}_{\gamma,j} = \begin{cases} \hat{M}(\gamma)_{n'+1} & \text{if } j = \gamma \\ \hat{M}(\varphi(j))_k & \text{if } \varphi(j) \in Anc(\varphi(\gamma)) \text{ and } k = I(j, \gamma) \\ \mathbf{o} & \text{Otherwise} \end{cases} \tag{15}$$

Let $\Delta V = V_\gamma - V_\alpha$ be the modifying block. Finally, $\forall \delta(i) \in L(\alpha), M_i \leftarrow M_i + \Delta V$, where $L(\alpha)$ denotes the set of leaves in the subtree with root $\varphi(\alpha)$.

$Add(\mathbb{T}, \alpha, subT)$: A subtree $subT$ is inserted into the tree $\mathbb{T}$ with the inserted node $\varphi(\alpha)$ or $\delta(\alpha)$. Let $\mathbb{T}$ be described by matrix M, $subT$ be described by matrix ΔM and The random vector of $\mathbb{T}$ and $subT$ be expressed as V and ΔV respectively. The function is processed in two case:

(1) The inserted node is a leaf $\delta(\alpha)$ associated with the insertion vector M_α. Then we calculate the updating LSSS matrix and random vector as follows:

$$M \leftarrow U\dagger(M, \alpha, \Delta M), V \leftarrow (V, \Delta \hat{V})$$

The adding blocks are $\Delta \hat{M}$ and M_α in this case.

(2) The inserted node is a non-leaf node $\varphi(\alpha)$. Function $Node_n^+(\varphi(\alpha), 1)$ is run to insert a row vector $M(\varphi(\alpha))_{n'+1}$ into $M(\varphi(\alpha))$. The inserted vector is defined as $V_{add} = (1, \mathbf{v}_{add,1}, \ldots, \mathbf{v}_{add,n})$ where

$$\mathbf{v}_{add,j} = \begin{cases} \hat{M}(\varphi(\alpha))_{n'+1} & \text{if } j = \alpha \\ \hat{M}(\varphi(j))_k & \text{if } \varphi(j) \in Anc(\varphi(\alpha)) \text{ and } k = I(j, \alpha) \\ \mathbf{o} & \text{Otherwise} \end{cases} \quad (16)$$

Then,

$$M \leftarrow \begin{pmatrix} M \\ V_{add} \end{pmatrix}$$

Finally, the updating LSSS matrix and random vector are calculated as follows:

$$M \leftarrow U^\dagger(M, n+1, \Delta M), V \leftarrow (V, \Delta \hat{V})$$

where n denotes the number of row of the original matrix M. The adding blocks are V_{add} and $\Delta \bar{M}$.

Remove$(\mathbb{T}, \gamma)$: A subtree $\mathbb{T}_\gamma$ with root $\varphi(\gamma)$ is removed from $\mathbb{T}$. $\forall M_\alpha$ is removed from the block LSSS matrix M where $\delta(\alpha) \in L(\varphi(\gamma))$, $\forall \mathbf{m}_{i,j}$, $\varphi(j) \in N(\mathbb{T}_\gamma)$ are removed, which are all zero-block in the rest rows. Thus, there is no non-zero removing block generated by this function. Finally, the random vector V is removed of all the node vector V_j, $\varphi(j) \in N(\varphi(\gamma)$.

Similarly, we define four scalable functions for the block matrix with mask.

Thr$_M(\mathbb{T}, \alpha, \Delta t)$: Let access policy $\mathbb{T}$ be described by matrix $M' = MT$ where M is a LSSS matrix generated by Algorithm 1 and T is a mask matrix. This function is also discussed in two cases.

(1) $\Delta t > 0$. Let M, T and M' be viewed as a block matrixes

$$M = \begin{pmatrix} M_{u_1} & M_{u_2} \\ M_{\alpha_1} & M_{\alpha_2} \\ M_{d_1} & M_{d_2} \end{pmatrix}, T = \begin{pmatrix} T_1 & P \\ O & T_2 \end{pmatrix}, M' = \begin{pmatrix} M'_{u_1} & M'_{u_2} \\ M'_{\alpha_1} & M'_{\alpha_2} \\ M'_{d_1} & M'_{d_2} \end{pmatrix}$$

where $(M_{\alpha_1}, M_{\alpha_2})$ is the block with non-zero blocks $\mathbf{m}_{i,\alpha}$ and $M_{u_1}, M_{\alpha_1}, M_{d_1}$ are the blocks with $\mathbf{m}_{i,\alpha}$ as the last columns. *Thr*$(\mathbb{T}, \alpha, \Delta t)$ is run, M and T are modified into M_{Thr} and T_{Thr}:

$$M_{thr} = \begin{pmatrix} M_{u_1} & O & M_{u_2} \\ M_{\alpha_1} & \Delta M_\alpha & M_{\alpha_2} \\ M_{d_1} & O & M_{d_2} \end{pmatrix}, T_{thr} = \begin{pmatrix} T_1 & \Delta P_1 & P \\ O & \Delta T & \Delta P_2 \\ O & O & T_2 \end{pmatrix}$$

where $\Delta T \in Z^{\Delta t \times \Delta t}$ is a full rank upper triangular matrix and ΔP_1, ΔP_2 are random matrix without zero elements. As a result, we get the matrix:

$$M'_{thr} = M_{thr} T_{thr} = \begin{pmatrix} M'_{u_1} & M_{u_1} \Delta P_1 & M'_{u_2} \\ M'_{\alpha_1} & M_{\alpha_1} \Delta P_1 + \Delta M \Delta T & M'_{\alpha_2} + \Delta M \Delta P_2 \\ M'_{d_1} & M_{d_1} \Delta P_1 & M'_{d_2} \end{pmatrix} \quad (17)$$

There are one adding block A and one modifying block B:

$$A = \begin{pmatrix} M'_{u_1} \Delta P_1 \\ M_{\alpha_1} \Delta P_1 + \Delta M \Delta T \\ M_{d_1} \Delta P_1 \end{pmatrix}, B = \Delta M \Delta P_2$$

(2) $\Delta t < 0$. Similarly, original matrix M and T are expressed as follows

$$M = \begin{pmatrix} M_{u_1} & O & M_{u_2} \\ M_{\alpha_1} & \Delta M_\alpha & M_{\alpha_2} \\ M_{d_1} & O & M_{d_2} \end{pmatrix}, T = \begin{pmatrix} T_1 & \Delta P_1 & P \\ O & \Delta T & \Delta P_2 \\ O & O & T_2 \end{pmatrix}$$

Then, we get

$$M' = MT = \begin{pmatrix} M'_{u_1} & \Delta M'_u & M'_{u_2} \\ M'_{\alpha_1} & \Delta M'_\alpha & M'_{\alpha_2} \\ M'_{d_1} & \Delta M'_d & M'_{d_2} \end{pmatrix} \tag{18}$$

Firstly, $Thr(\mathbb{T}, \alpha, \Delta t)$ is run to modify matrix M and vector V. Thus,

$$M_{thr} = \begin{pmatrix} M_{u_1} & M_{u_2} \\ M_{\alpha_1} & M_{\alpha_2} \\ M_{d_1} & M_{d_2} \end{pmatrix}, T_{thr} = \begin{pmatrix} T_1 & P \\ O & T_2 \end{pmatrix}$$

The modified matrix is:

$$M'_{thr} = \begin{pmatrix} M'_{u_1} & M'_{u_2} \\ M'_{\alpha_1} & M'_{\alpha_2} - \Delta M \Delta P_2 \\ M'_{d_1} & M'_{d_2} \end{pmatrix} \tag{19}$$

There are one modifying block $\Delta M \Delta P_2$ and three removing blocks ΔM_u, ΔM_α, ΔM_d.

$Path_M(\mathbb{T}, \alpha, \gamma)$: Let access policy $\mathbb{T}$ be described by matrix $M' = MT$. $Path(\mathbb{T}, \alpha, \gamma)$ is run to modify matrix M. Vector ΔV is generated as shown in $Path(\mathbb{T}, \alpha, \gamma)$ and $\Delta V'$ is set to be ΔVT. Finally, $\forall \rho(i) \in L(\alpha)$, $M'_i \leftarrow M'_i + \Delta V'$. $\Delta V'$ is the only modifying block generated by this function.

$Add_M(\mathbb{T}, \alpha, sub\mathbb{T})$: Let access policy $\mathbb{T}$ be described by matrix $M' = MT \in Z^{l \times m}$ and $\Delta M' = \Delta M \Delta T \in Z^{\Delta l \times \Delta m}$ denote the submatrix describes $sub\mathbb{T}$. The function is discussed in two cases.

(1) $\rho(\alpha) \in L(\mathbb{T})$. Let M, M' be described as block matrices

$$M = \begin{pmatrix} M_u \\ M_\alpha \\ M_d \end{pmatrix}, M' = \begin{pmatrix} M'_u \\ M'_\alpha \\ M'_d \end{pmatrix} = \begin{pmatrix} M_u T \\ M_\alpha T \\ M_d T \end{pmatrix}$$

where M_α, M'_α denote the vector representative node $\varphi(\alpha)$ in M and M', T is the mask matrix. $Add(\mathbb{T}, \alpha, sub\mathbb{T})$ is run to modify M and V. Then, we obtain

$$M_{add} = \begin{pmatrix} M_u & O \\ \varepsilon M_\alpha & \Delta \hat{M} \\ M_d & O \end{pmatrix}, V_{Add} = (V, sub\hat{V}), T_{add} = \begin{pmatrix} T & P \\ O & \Delta \tilde{T} \end{pmatrix}$$

where $\varepsilon = (1, \ldots, 1)^T$ and $\tilde{T}$ denotes the matirx T removed the first column and first row. As a result,

$$M'_{add} = M_{add} T_{add} = \begin{pmatrix} M'_u & M_u P \\ \varepsilon M'_\alpha & \varepsilon M_\alpha P + \Delta \hat{M} \Delta \tilde{T} \\ M'_d & M_d P \end{pmatrix} \tag{20}$$

$\varepsilon M_\alpha P + \Delta\hat{M}\Delta\tilde{T}$, M_α are the adding blocks. It is important that, $\Delta\hat{M}\Delta\tilde{T} = \Delta\hat{M}' - sub\bar{M}\Delta\dot{T}$ where $\Delta\dot{T}$ denotes the first row of T removed of the first entity. Following the definition of our scalable LSSS matrix, $\Delta\bar{M} = (1,1,\ldots,1)^T$. Thus, $\Delta\hat{M}\Delta\tilde{T} = \Delta\hat{M}' - \varepsilon\Delta\dot{T}$. That is an efficient way to calculate adding blocks.

(2) $\varphi(\alpha) \in N(\mathbb{T})$. Then,

$$M_{add} \leftarrow U^\dagger(\begin{pmatrix} M \\ V_{add} \end{pmatrix}, n'+1, \Delta M), V_{add} \leftarrow (V, sub\bar{V})$$

where V_{add} is generated by $Add(\mathbb{T}, \alpha, sub\mathbb{T})$. Similarly, we get

$$M_{add} = \begin{pmatrix} M & O \\ \varepsilon V_{add} & \Delta\hat{M} \end{pmatrix}, T_{add} = \begin{pmatrix} T & P \\ O & \Delta\tilde{T} \end{pmatrix}$$

where $P \in Z^{l\times\Delta l}$ is generated at random. Thus,

$$M'_{add} = \begin{pmatrix} MT & MP \\ \varepsilon V_{add}T & \varepsilon V_{add}P + \Delta\hat{M}\Delta\tilde{T} \end{pmatrix} \tag{21}$$

There are two adding blocks generated in this case:

$$(V_{add}T, V_{add}P), \begin{pmatrix} MP \\ \Delta\hat{M}\Delta\tilde{T} \end{pmatrix}.$$

$Remove_M(\mathbb{T}, \gamma)$: Let access policy $\mathbb{T}$ be described by LSSS matrix $M' = MT$ and $\phi(\gamma)$ be the root of the removed subtree. M, T can be expressed as follows

$$M = \begin{pmatrix} M_u & O & subM_u \\ M_\gamma & subM_\gamma & O \\ M_d & O & subM_d \end{pmatrix}, T = \begin{pmatrix} T_u & P_{u_1} & P_{u_2} \\ O & T_\gamma & P_\gamma \\ O & O & T_d \end{pmatrix}$$

where $subM_\gamma$ is the block of M which can describe the removed subtree. We get

$$M' = \begin{pmatrix} M_uT_u & M_uP_{u_1} & M_uP_{u_2} + subM_uT_d \\ M_\gamma T_u & M_\gamma P_{u_1} + subM_\gamma T_\gamma & M_\gamma P_{u_2} + subM_\gamma P_\gamma \\ M_dT_u & M_dP_{u_1} & M_dP_{u_2} + subM_dT_d \end{pmatrix} = \begin{pmatrix} M'_{u_1} & M'_{u_2} & M'_{u_3} \\ M'_{\gamma_1} & M'_{\gamma_2} & M'_{\gamma_3} \\ M'_{d_1} & M'_{d_2} & M'_{d_3} \end{pmatrix} \tag{22}$$

$Remove(\mathbb{T}, \gamma)$ is run to get

$$M_{rmv} = \begin{pmatrix} M_u & subM_u \\ M_d & subM_d \end{pmatrix}, T_{rmv} = \begin{pmatrix} T_u & P_{u_2} \\ O & T_d \end{pmatrix}$$

As a result

$$M'_{rmv} = M_{rmv}T_{rmv} = \begin{pmatrix} M'_{u_1} & M'_{u_3} \\ M'_{d_1} & M'_{d_3} \end{pmatrix} \tag{23}$$

At the same time, the random vector V is removed from the blocks $V_j, \varphi(j) \in N(\gamma)$. $((M'^T_{u_2})^T, (M'^T_{d_2})^T)^T$ is the removing block generated by this function.

4   Scalable Attribute-Based Encryption Scheme with Block LSSS Matrix

As shown in Fig. 3, the system model of scalable ABE scheme consists of the following entities:

Authority: Authority is global trusted in the system and is responsible for managing public key(PK), secret key(SK) and master key(MK). Additionally, Authority is responsible for dealing with intermediate set $\{\Delta C_t'\}$ and generating ciphertext increments $\{\Delta C_t, \Delta \bar{C}_t\}$ during policy updating.

Cloud: cloud provides data storage and access server to clients. The other important role of the cloud is the updating agent, it is responsible for most computation during policy updating.

Owner: owners upload ciphertext CT to the cloud and generate parameter set $\{\Delta_i, \Theta_i\}$ to the cloud during policy updating.

User: users access ciphertext CT stored in cloud.

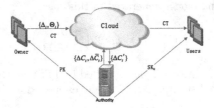

Fig. 3. System model.

4.1   Bilinear Map

Bilinear maps, as defined below, play a crucial role in ABE.

Definition 2 (Bilinear Map). *Assume G_0, G_T are two multiplicative cyclic groups with prime order p, and g is a generator of G_0. A function $e : G_0 \times G_0 \to G_T$ is a bilinear map if it satisfies three criteria:*

(1) bilinearity: $\forall u, v \in G_0$ and $a, b \in Z_p$, $e(u^a, v^b) = e(u, v)^{ab}$;
(2) non-degeneracy: $\forall u, v \neq g^0, e(u, v) \neq 1$;
(3) computability: e can be computed efficiently.

Additionally, we defined some matrix and vector operations in bilinear map group G_0. Let $g \in G_0$ and $M = (m_{i,j})_{m \times n}$, g^M denotes a matrix in G_0 is shown as follows:

$$g^M = \begin{pmatrix} g^{m_{1,1}} & \cdots & g^{m_{1,n}} \\ \vdots & & \vdots \\ g^{m_{m,1}} & \cdots & g^{m_{m,n}} \end{pmatrix} \tag{24}$$

Assume that, $\mathbf{v} = (v_1, \ldots, v_n) \in Z^n$ and $\mathbf{g} = (g_1, \ldots, g_n) \in G_0^n$. we define $\mathbf{g}^{\mathbf{v}} = \prod_{i=1}^n g_i^{v_i}$.

4.2 Functional Modules

The scheme includes five functional modules: *Setup, KeyGen, Encrypt, Decrypt* and *Updata*.

Setup(1^l): Authority generates a tuple $\{p, G_0, G_T, e\}$ as public parameters where $p \in Z$, G_0, G_T are groups with order p and $e : G_0 \times G_0 \to G_T$ is a bilinear map. Then, it picks $g_1, g_2 \in G_0$, and $\gamma_1, \gamma_2 \in Z_p$ at random and sets $\gamma = \gamma_1\gamma_2$. Let $S = \{A_1, \ldots, A_n\}$ be a set of attributes defined by authority and $s = \{a_1, \ldots, a_n\}$ be the image set of S in Z_p. PK and MK are calculated as follows:

$$PK = \{Y = e(g_1, g_2)^w, g_2, P' = g_1, P'' = g_1^\gamma, P_r = g_1^{\gamma_1}, P_c = g_1^{\gamma_2}, P_i = g^{\gamma a_i}, 1 \leq i \leq n\}$$

$$MK = \{w, \gamma_1, \gamma_2, \gamma, a_i, 1 \leq i \leq n\}$$

KeyGen(U_s, MK): Let $U_s \subset S$ be the attribute set of user. Authority picks $p_u \in G_0$ randomly and calculates SK:

$$SK_u = \{D' = g_2^\omega p_u^{-\gamma}, D'' = p_u, D_i = p_u^{\gamma a_i}, A_i \in U_s\}$$

Encrypt$(M, M(\mathbb{T}), \rho, PK)$: Let M be the plaintext and $M(\mathbb{T}) \in Z_p^{l \times m}$ be the block LSSS matrix describing access policy $\mathbb{T}$. Owner calculates $C_0 = MY^s$ and $C' = P'^s$ where $s \in Z_p$ is chosen at random. Then, he picks a vector $V = (s, v_2, \ldots, v_m)$ and calculates $C_k = P_{\rho(k)}^{r_k} P''^{s_k}, \bar{C}_k = P'^{r_k}$ where $s_k = VM(\mathbb{T})_k$ and $r_k \in Z_p$. Finally, the ciphertext is:

$$CT = \{C_0, C', C_k, \bar{C}_k, 1 \leq i \leq l\} \tag{25}$$

Decrypt$(C, M(\mathbb{T}), SK)$: Let $\sum_{\rho(k) \in I_u} u_k M(\mathbb{T})_k = \mathbf{e_1}$ where $I_u \subset U_s$ and $u_k \in Z$. The plaintext is recovered as follows:

$$M = \frac{C_0}{e(C', D')} \prod_{\rho(k) \in I_u} \left(\frac{e(\bar{C}_k, D_{\rho(k)})}{e(C_k, D'')}\right)^{u_k} \tag{26}$$

In fact, $e(\bar{C}_k, D_{\rho(k)})/e(C_k, D'') = e(g_1, g_u)^{-\gamma s_k}$. Furthermore,

$$\prod_{\rho(k) \in I_u} \left(\frac{e(\bar{C}_k, D_{\rho(k)})}{e(C_k, D'')}\right)^{u_k} = e(g_1, g_u)^{-\gamma V \sum_{\rho(k) \in I_u} u_k M(\mathbb{T})_k} = e(g_1, g_u)^{-\gamma s}$$

Thus, Eq. (26) holds.

Update$(\mathbb{B}_1, \mathbb{B}_2)$: Let $\mathbb{B}_1 = \{M_1, \ldots, M_{n_1}\}, \mathbb{B}_2 = \{R_1, \ldots, R_{n_2}\}$ be the non-zero adding/ modifying block set and removing block set generated by scaling functions, $\mathbb{V}_1 = \{\mathbf{v}_1, \ldots, \mathbf{v}_{n_1}\}, \mathbb{V}_2 = \{\mathbf{w}_1, \ldots, \mathbf{w}_{n_2}\}$ denote the corresponding blocks in random vector V. Let $M_i \in Z^{l_i \times m_i}$ and $R_i \in Z^{l'_i \times m'_i}$. Then, owner calculates

$$\Delta_i = \begin{cases} P_c^{\mathbf{v}_i} & l_i \geq m_i \\ P_r^{\mathbf{v}_i M_i} & \text{Otherwise} \end{cases}, \Theta_i = \begin{cases} (P'')^{\mathbf{w}_i} & l'_i \geq m'_i \\ (P'')^{\mathbf{w}_i R_i} & \text{Otherwise} \end{cases}$$

where Δ_i, Θ_i are vectors in G_0. $\mathbb{B}_1, \mathbb{B}_2, \Delta = \{\Delta_i, 1 \leq i \leq n_1\}, \Theta = \{\Theta_i, 1 \leq i \leq n_2\}$ are sent to cloud. Let κ_i, μ_i denote the map from row label of M_i and R_i to the row label of the final LSSS matrix, respectively. For the adding/modifying blocks, the cloud calculates

$$\Delta C'_t = \begin{cases} \Delta_i^{M_{i,j}} (P_k)^{r_{i,j}} & l_i \geq m_i \\ \Delta_{i,j} (P_k)^{r_{i,j}} & \text{Otherwise} \end{cases}, \Delta \bar{C}'_t = (P')^{r_{i,j}}$$

where $t = \kappa_i(j)$, $A_k = \rho(t)$, $M_{i,j}$ denotes the jth row of M_i, $\Delta_{i,j}$ denotes the jth entity of Δ_i and $r_{i,j} \in Z$ is chosen randomly. Then, all C'_t is sent to the authority, who computes:

$$\Delta C_t = \begin{cases} (\Delta C'_t)^{\gamma_2} & l_i \geq m_i \\ (\Delta C'_t)^{\gamma_1} & \text{Otherwise} \end{cases}, \Delta \bar{C}_t = \begin{cases} (\Delta \bar{C}'_t)^{\gamma_2} & l_i \geq m_i \\ (\Delta \bar{C}'_t)^{\gamma_1} & \text{Otherwise} \end{cases}$$

Then, the ciphertext is updated as follows

$$C_t \leftarrow C_t \Delta C_t, \bar{C}_t \leftarrow \bar{C}_t \Delta \bar{C}_t$$

If C_t and $\bar{C}_t$ are non-existence, they were initialed as $C_t = \bar{C}_t = 1$. For the removing blocks, the cloud calculates

$$\Theta C'_t = \begin{cases} \Theta_i^{R_{i,j}}(P_k)^{r_{i,j}} & l'_i \geq m'_i \\ \Theta_{i,j}(P_k)^{r_{i,j}} & \text{Otherwise} \end{cases}, \Theta \bar{C}'_t = (P')^{r_{i,j}}$$

where $t = \mu_i(j)$, $A_k = \rho(j)$, $R_{i,j}$ denotes the jth row of R_i, $\Theta_{i,j}$ denote the jth entity of Θ_i and $r_{i,j} \in Z$ is chosen randomly. Then,

$$C_t \leftarrow C_t(\Theta C_t)^{-1}, \bar{C}_t \leftarrow \bar{C}_t \Theta(\bar{C}_t)^{-1}.$$

5 Performance Evaluation

5.1 Performance Analysis of Block LSSS Matrix

Block LSSS matrix is intuitive and easy to compute. In certain scenarios, the block LSSS matrix needs to sacrifice its readability to increase the security or extend the matrix space via multiplying a full rank mask matrix. Choosing an upper triangular matrix as the mask matrix is an effective way to maintain the scalability of block LSSS matrix. These mask matrices require moderate computation during matrix generation and scaling. We simulate the operation time for each type of matrix functions proposed in this paper. The simulation is run on a PC with an Intel Core 2 Duo CPU at 3.14 GHz and 8.00 GB RAM. The code is written in MATLAB and simulate the generating and managing of block LSSS matrix. The simulation results are shown in Figs. 4 and 5.

Figure 4 describes the efficiency of generation of block LSSS matrix. Let $\mathbb{T}$ be an access tree must be transformed into Matrix, n be the number of non-leaf $node_i$ of $\mathbb{T}$ and $node_i$ be a t_i-out-of-n_i node. We set all t_i equal and all n_i equal in the simulations. As shown in Fig. 4, the generation time increases with n_i, t_i and n. But, the mask of block LSSS matrix only costs a little time that is much less than the total generation time.

Figure 5 shows the operation time of the scaling functions. Let $M \in Z^{l \times m}$ and $subM \in Z^{subl \times subm}$ denote the LSSS matrix and modifying/adding/removing sub-matrix, respectively. Figure 5(a) describes the runtime of Thr and Thr_M increases with threshold increment $|\Delta t|$. Figure 5(b), (c) and (d) show the increase of runtime of scaling functions $Path$ and $Path_M$, Add and Add_M, $Remove$ and $Remove_M$ incurred by the size increasing of $subM$ respectively. Similarly, Fig. 5(e), (f), (g) and (h) describe the runtime of the above scaling functions increase with the size increase of M. All the scaling functions are efficient and cost less time than the generation function. Figure 5 is also shows that, the additional computation time of scaling functions caused by mask matrix is limited and acceptable.

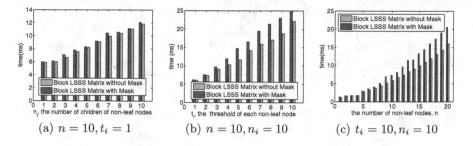

(a) $n = 10, t_i = 1$　　　　(b) $n = 10, n_i = 10$　　　　(c) $t_i = 10, n_i = 10$

Fig. 4. Generation time of Block LSSS Matrix

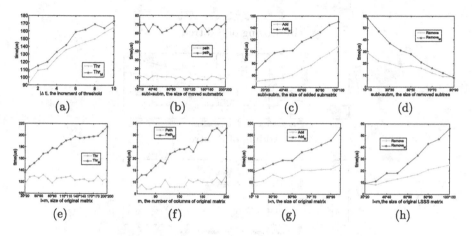

(a)　　　　　(b)　　　　　(c)　　　　　(d)

(e)　　　　　(f)　　　　　(g)　　　　　(h)

Fig. 5. Computation time of Scaling Functions

5.2　Performance Analysis of Scalable ABE Scheme

The most advantage of our scalable ABE scheme is efficiency and low-overhead. Comparing with [15–17], our scheme is more efficient on various types of updating operations for access policy. We also give the simulation of these schemes. The simulation is run on a Linux virtual machine with a CPU at 3.16 GHz and 1.00 GB RAM. It uses PBC lab to simulate the bilinear group operation. In fact, the policy managing operations of scheme [16] is too complex to evaluate. In order to compare, we only consider the optimum case of scheme [16] in the simulation.

Figure 6 describes the operation time of policy updating of various schemes for the data owner. Figure 6(a) shows the computation time of modifying the threshold of a node n_j where the x axis represent $subl$, the number of leaves in the subtree with root n_j. In this situation, the operation time of our scheme is incurred by the increment/decrement of threshold $|\Delta D|$ while the time of others are all incurred by $subl$. Clearly, our scheme is more efficient than others because $|\Delta D|$ is much less than $subl$. As shown in Fig. 6(b), our scheme takes only a little time to move a subtree. Different from other schemes, the runtime of this our scheme is not really effected by the size of modified subtree but close a small constant. That implies, our scheme cost the lowest computation in this case. From Fig. 6(c), we can see that the computation time of adding a subtree of our scheme is minimum. Because the access policy of our

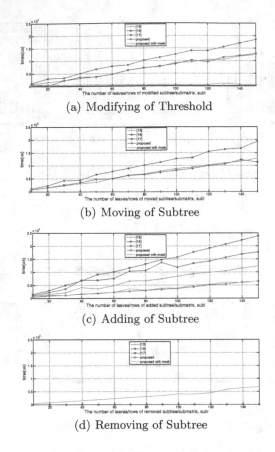

(a) Modifying of Threshold

(b) Moving of Subtree

(c) Adding of Subtree

(d) Removing of Subtree

Fig. 6. Simulation of policy updating operations

scheme is scalable, it can process the adding part of access policy only and do not need to reconstruct other parts. That make our scheme more efficient than others. As show in Fig. 6(d), removing a subtree costs little time can be ignored in all of these schemes except of masked case of our scheme. Actually, only the masked block LSSS matrix generates increment of attribute ciphertexts in this case. In other schemes, the access policies are updated via removing the invalid attribute ciphertexts immediately. In summary, the ABE scheme with block LSSS matrix, the scaling policy, is more efficient in access policy managing than others.

6   Conclusion

We provided a scalable access policy, block LSSS matrix, which is constructed by a set of node matrixes. The block matrix is efficient to generate and update. Eight scaling functions are given to update the block LSSS matrix, each being efficient and intuitive. We construct a scalable ABE scheme which describes the access policy by block LSSS matrix. In the scheme, data own updates access policy by scaling functions and generates minimum increment set Δ and Θ. Authority and cloud update ciphertext stored in the cloud via Δ and Θ. In the updating process, most computation is done by the authority and the cloud. The data owner faces rather low computational complexity to manage access privilege of data stored in cloud. In brief, the ABE scheme with scaling access policy is great improved of policy manageability.

Acknowledgments. This work is supported by the National Science Foundation of China (No.61373040, No.61173137), The Ph.D. Programs Foundation of Ministry of Education of China (20120141110073), Key Project of Natural Science Foundation of Hubei Province (No. 2010CDA004).

References

1. Blakley, G.R., Kabatianskii, G.A.: Linear algebra approach to secret sharing schemes. In: Chmora, A., Wicker, S.B. (eds.) Information Protection 1993. LNCS, vol. 829. Springer, Heidelberg (1994)
2. Benaloh, J., Leichter, J.: Generalized secret sharing and monotone functions. In: Goldwasser, (ed.) Advances in Cryptology – CRYPTO 1988. LNCS, vol. 403, pp. 27–35. Springer, New York (1990)
3. Bertilsson, M., Ingemarsson, I.: A construction of practical secret sharing schemes using linear block codes. In: Zheng, Y., Seberry, J. (eds.) AUSCRYPT 1992. LNCS, vol. 718, pp. 27–35. Springer, Heidelberg (1993)
4. Brickell, E.F.: Some ideal secret sharing schemes. In: Quisquater, J.-J., Vandewalle, J. (eds.) EUROCRYPT 1989. LNCS, vol. 434, pp. 468–475. Springer, Heidelberg (1990)
5. Massey, J.L.: Minimal codewords and secret sharing. In: Proceedings of the 6th Joint Swedish-Russian International Workshop on Information Theory, pp. 276–279 (1993)
6. Shamir, A.: How to share a secret. Commun. ACM **22**(11), 612–613 (1979)
7. Simonis, J., Ashikhmin, A.: Almost affine codes. Des. Codes Crypt. **14**(2), 179–197 (1998)
8. Chellappa, R.: Intermediaries in Cloud-Computing: A New Computing Paradigm. INFORMS Annual Meeting, Dallas (1997)
9. Wu, J., et al.: Cloud storage as the infrastructure of cloud computing. In: International Conference on Intelligent Computing and Cognitive Informatics, pp. 380–383. IEEE (2010)
10. Abu-Libdeh, H., Princehouse, L., Weatherspoon, H.: RACS: a case for cloud storage diversity. In: Proceedings of the 1st ACM Symposium on Cloud Computing, pp. 229–240. ACM (2010)
11. Kamara, S., Lauter, K.: Cryptographic cloud storage. In: Sion, R., Curtmola, R., Dietrich, S., Kiayias, A., Miret, J.M., Sako, K., Sebé, F. (eds.) RLCPS, WECSR, and WLC 2010. LNCS, vol. 6054, pp. 136–149. Springer, Heidelberg (2010)
12. Stadler, M.A.: Publicly verifiable secret sharing. In: Maurer, U.M. (ed.) EUROCRYPT 1996. LNCS, vol. 1070, pp. 190–199. Springer, Heidelberg (1996)
13. Nikov, V., Nikova, S.: New monotone span programs from old. IACR Cryptology ePrint Archive 2004, p. 282 (2004)
14. Karchmer, M., Wigderson, A.: On span programs. In: Structure in Complexity Theory Conference, pp. 102–111 (1993)

15. Goyal, V., et al.: Attribute-based encryption for fine-grained access control of encrypted data. In: Proceedings of the 13th ACM Conference on Computer and Communications Security, pp. 89–98. ACM (2006)

16. Sahai, A., Seyalioglu, H., Waters, B.: Dynamic credentials and ciphertext delegation for attribute-based encryption. In: Safavi-Naini, R., Canetti, R. (eds.) CRYPTO 2012. LNCS, vol. 7417, pp. 199–217. Springer, Heidelberg (2012)

17. Yang, K., et al.: Enabling efficient access control with dynamic policy updating for big data in the cloud. In: Proceedings of the IEEE Conference on INFOCOM 2014, pp. 2013–2021. IEEE (2014)

18. Lewko, A., Waters, B.: Decentralizing attribute-based encryption. In: Paterson, K.G. (ed.) EUROCRYPT 2011. LNCS, vol. 6632, pp. 568–588. Springer, Heidelberg (2011)

19. Zhen, L., Cao, Z., Wong, D.S.: Efficient generation of linear secret sharing scheme matrices from threshold access trees. Cryptology ePrint Archive, Report 2010/374. http://eprint.iacr.org/2010/374

20. Xavier, N., Chandrasekar, V.: Cloud computing data security for personal health record by using attribute based encryption. Bus. Manag. $7(1)$, 209–214 (2015)

21. Xhafa, F., et al.: Designing cloud-based electronic health record system with attribute-based encryption. Multimedia Tools Appl. $74(10)$, 3441–3458 (2015)

22. Horváth, M.: Attribute-based encryption optimized for cloud computing. In: Italiano, G.F., Margaria-Steffen, T., Pokorný, J., Quisquater, J.-J., Wattenhofer, R. (eds.) SOFSEM 2015-Testing. LNCS, vol. 8939, pp. 566–577. Springer, Heidelberg (2015)

23. Khedkar, S.V., Gawande, A.D.: Data partitioning technique to improve cloud data storage security. Int. J. Comput. Sci. Inf. Technol. $5(3)$, 3347–3350 (2014)

24. Wei, L., et al.: Security and privacy for storage and computation in cloud computing. Inf. Sci. 258, 371–386 (2014)

25. Meenakshi, I.K., George, S.: Cloud server storage security using TPA. Int. J. Adv. Res. Comput. Sci. Technol. $2(1)$, 295–299 (2014)

26. Shetty, J., Anala, M.R., Shobha, G.: An approach to secure access to cloud storage service. Int. J. Res. $2(1)$, 364–368 (2015)

27. Hohenberger, S., Waters, B.: Online/Offline attribute-based encryption. In: Krawczyk, H. (ed.) PKC 2014. LNCS, vol. 8383, pp. 293–310. Springer, Heidelberg (2014)

Minimizing Resource Expenditure While Maximizing Destructiveness for Node Capture Attacks

Chi Lin[1,2]([✉]), Guowei Wu[1,2], Xiaochen Lai[1,2], and Tie Qiu[1,2]

[1] School of Software, Dalian University of Technology, Dalian 116621, China
c.lin@dlut.edu.cn
[2] Key Laboratory for Ubiquitous Network and Service Software of Liaoning Province, Dalian University of Technology, Dalian 116621, China

Abstract. In node capture attacks, an attacker intellectually captures nodes and extracts cryptographic keys from their memories to wreck security, reliability and confidentiality of wireless sensor networks. Previous methods suffered from low attacking efficiency and neglected resource expenditure. A novel method of modeling the node capture attack is proposed aiming at maximizing destructiveness while minimizing resource expenditure. We convert routing paths into abstracted vertexes and formalize hybrid graph model for the network. A property called destructive value is defined for expressing the destructiveness of attacking a node. We develop a Greedy AttaCking algoRithm named GACR on the hybrid graph. An attacker is able to maximize the destructiveness of the attack while constructing the shortest Hamiltonian cycle to reduce resource expenditure. At last, extensive simulations are conducted to show the advantages of our scheme. Simulation results demonstrate that, GACR can reduce the attacking times, enhance the attacking efficiencies and save energy cost in compromising the network.

Keywords: Node capture attack · Wireless sensor networks · Resource expenditure · Destructiveness · Hybrid graph

1 Introduction

A Wireless sensor network (WSN) typically consists of small, low-cost, battery-powered nodes, which are deployed in thousands over a target area for sensing data processing and communicating with other sensors or sinks. However, due to limited computing and storage capacity, WSNs are prone to various attacks.

As a special kind of attacks, *node capture attacks* [1] destroy the network by physically accessing to the cryptographic keys which are stored in memories of nodes. By recovering of cryptographic keys, the adversary can eavesdrop on the message exchanging process of applied links, which pose potential threats for the security, reliability and confidentiality of the network.

© Springer International Publishing Switzerland 2015
G. Wang et al. (Eds.): ICA3PP 2015, Part III, LNCS 9530, pp. 403–416, 2015.
DOI: 10.1007/978-3-319-27137-8_30

In literature, previous methods [2,3] have focused on mitigating node capture attack by implementing key pre-distribution against random node capture attack, which ensures the authenticity, integrity, and confidentiality of the exchanged messages between neighboring sensor nodes. Nevertheless, only designing a mechanism of distributing encryption keys is not sufficient. In [4], Tague et al. stated that the adversary can compromise a node intelligently to improve the efficiency of node capture attack with publicly available information, which is learned by eavesdropping on insecure message exchange throughout the network.

However, there has been little research that demonstrates how to design an efficient node capture attack algorithm in wireless sensor network [1,5–8]. In [4,9,10], Tague et al. proposed a formal method to formalize the vulnerability of the network by using circuit theoretic analysis. They devised a Greedy Node capture Approximation using Vulnerability Evaluation (GNAVE) to approximate the minimum cost. In our latest works [1,5–8], we have proposed several attacking algorithms for enhancing the efficiency of the node capture attacks. GNRMK [1] mapped the network as a flow network and calculated the route minimum key set based on the maximum flow of the network. We developed a node capture attack algorithm which destroys the node with the maximum overlapping value. As GNRMK neglected analyzing destructiveness from the point view of key sharing between nodes and paths, we used a matrix to express such relations [5], we also took the energy cost into consideration when mounting an attack. However, MA [5] still suffers from limitations, it pays little attention to the relationship between the attacking efficiency and the attacking cost. Therefore, in [6,7], we proposed a way of evaluating the destructiveness in the mobile networks. Moreover, we constructed the connected dominating set and weakly-connected dominating set as the backbones of networks for mounting the node capture attack. Unfortunately, the energy cost issue is neglected to discuss in these work [6,7].

To overcome the limitations above, in this paper, we focus on designing a novel way of modeling the node capture attack. We abstract the routing paths into abstracted vertexes and convert the network into a *hybrid graph* model. We propose a metric named destructive value for each node to express its destructiveness after it is attacked. Finally we develop a Greedy AttaCking node capture attack algoRithm (GACR) on the *hybrid graph* which aims at maximizing destructiveness while minimizing resource expenditure. At last, we implement our algorithms and put forward some experiments to show the advantages of the proposed algorithms.

1.1   Our Contributions

The contributions can be summarized as follows.

1. We abstract routing paths into *abstracted vertexes* and devise the *destructive value* metric for sensor nodes to express the destructiveness and cost after they are compromised.

2. We establish a *hybrid graph* to describe the key sharing relationship between abstracted vertexes and sensor nodes. We design *GACR* in which the adversary seeks for the minimum number of nodes to compromise the network.
3. To save resource expenditure, we construct the shortest Hamiltonian cycle for expressing resource expenditure in attacking candidates, which guides the moving manner for the attacker.

The rest of this paper is organized as follows: Sect. 2 introduces relevant preliminaries in this paper. Section 3 illustrates the method of modeling node capture attack and proposes a *GACR* algorithm. Simulations and experimental results are shown in Sect. 4. At last, we conclude our paper in Sect. 5.

2   Preliminaries

2.1   Network Model

The network consists of a set of wireless sensor nodes N. The network topology is represented as a directed network graph $G = (N, L)$. The link set L represents the set of one hop neighbors. A pair of nodes $i, j \in N$ within each other's transmission range is able to securely communicate if and only if they share at least one common key, i.e. $K_i \bigcap K_j \neq \emptyset$. A link (i, j) indicates a reliable and secure link in which messages can be transmitted directly without relaying to other intermediate nodes between i and j.

2.2   Key Assignment Model

In our scenario, the key pre-distribution model is applied. Each node i is assigned a subset keys K_i of the key pool K and the corresponding label subset L_i. The shared keys between node i and j can be expressed as $K_{i,j} = K_i \bigcap K_j$. i and j can communicate with each other iff $K_{i,j} \neq \emptyset$ and they both locate in each other's communication range. When communicating, i and j utilize the whole set of $K_{i,j}$ to encrypt the messages transmitted between i and j. Therefore, the safety of a secure link (i, j) is directly related to the number of keys in $K_{i,j}$ (i.e. $|K_{i,j}|$). Bigger $|K_{i,j}|$ provides safer protection for the link. We assume that each node i publicly broadcasts the label set L_i, allowing each neighboring node j to determine the set $K_{i,j}$ of shared keys [11].

2.3   Routing Model

We denote S and D as the sets of sources and destinations respectively, which are the subset of $N (S \subseteq N, D \subseteq N)$. Determined by the routing protocol, routes from sources to destinations are established, the set of routes is denoted as $R = \{r_{s,d} | s \in S, d \in D\}$.

The routing protocols fall into three kinds [4,9,10]: the single path routing protocol, the multiple independent path routing protocol and the multiple dependent path routing protocol. The single path routing protocol requires routes consisting of a single, fixed path, such as the AODV [12] routing protocol. The multiple independent path routing protocol requires messages are forwarded in different paths such as the GBR [13]. In multiple dependent path routing protocol, each message is fragmented into multiple packets which are sent in a disjoint path, such as [14]. From the perspective of providing end-to-end security, a route, which ensures a message additionally encrypted by the keys shared between the source node and the destination node as [4], is called an end-to-end safe route.

2.4 Adversary Model

We consider the adversary has the ability and resources to **physically** eavesdrop on messages throughout the network, capture nodes, and extract cryptographic keys from the memories of the captured nodes in polynomial-time. We also assume that the adversary has the knowledge of the key assignment (i.e. he only knows the assignment of key labels) and routing protocols, including all the parameters of the network and the protocol.

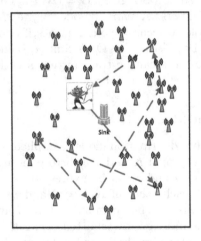

Fig. 1. Formalization of GACR (Color figure online)

The energy cost of compromising is not easy to formulate, because cost in attacking process includes energy consumed in compromising and traveling. For ease of modeling, in this paper, we regard the resource expenditure of the attacker as the energy spent in traveling from one attacking candidate to another.

The main objective for the adversary is to compromise the network, meanwhile, consume minimum resource expenditure (i.e. costs in traveling from one attacking candidate to another physically). As it is difficult to model how much resource are consumed in compromising a node, here, we just omit such cost and pay close attention to the energy consumption spent in traveling. To intuitively show the process of attacking, we depict an overview in Fig. 1. Obviously, in the example, the path scheduling of the attacker is not of high efficiency. The constructed cycle is not the shortest. Therefore, to enhance the effectiveness, it is necessary to establish the shortest Hamiltonian cycle as a solution to the Traveling Salesman Problem (TSP) for attacking candidates (i.e. green nodes). Hence, we formalize the node capture attack with minimum cost in Algorithm 1.

Algorithm 1. Node Capture Attack Formalization

1: **Input:** $G(N, L)$, K
2: **Find:** $C_n \subseteq N$
3: such that $\sum_{i=0}^{n} \sum_{j \neq i, j=0}^{n} c_{ij} x_{ij}$ is minimized
4: and $\forall s \in S, d \in D$, $r_{s,d}$ is compromised.

Where:

$$x_{ij} = \begin{cases} 1 & \text{the path goes from node } i \text{ to node } j \\ 0 & \text{otherwise} \end{cases} \tag{1}$$

For $i = 0, ..., n$, let u_i be an artificial variable, and finally take c_{ij} to be the distance from node i to node j. Then TSP can be written as the following integer linear programming problem:

$$\min \sum_{i=0}^{n} \sum_{j \neq i, j=0}^{n} c_{ij} x_{ij} \tag{2}$$

Subject to:

$$0 \leq x_{ij} \leq 1 \qquad i, j = 0, \cdots, n$$
$$u_i \in \mathbf{Z} \qquad i = 0, \cdots, n$$
$$\sum_{i=0, i \neq j}^{n} x_{ij} = 1 \quad j = 0, \cdots, n$$
$$\sum_{j=0, j \neq i}^{n} x_{ij} = 1 \quad i = 0, \cdots, n$$

Therefore, to mount a minimum cost node capture attack, it is necessary to (1) choose attacking candidates, and (2) construct a shortest Hamiltonian cycle to guide for the attacker's movement.

3   Our Scheme

In this section, we present a novel method to model the node capture attack. Firstly, we propose some definitions of compromise of link, path and route due to capturing of a set of node C_n. We denote C_k as the set of compromised keys (i.e. $C_k = \bigcup_{i \in C_n} K_i$). If a message traversed in a link, path or route which is secured by C_k, the security of the message will be eavesdropped. Above all, we propose the definition of the compromised links.

A link $(i,j) \in L$ is compromised iff $K_{i,j} \subseteq C_k$.

Then we further define the compromise of the paths and the routes. Commonly, a path contains multiple nodes and links. A node i which stays in a path p can be expressed as $i \lhd p$. Similarly, a link which belongs to a path is denoted as $(i,j) \sqsubset p(i \lhd p, j \lhd p)$.

A path $p \in P$ is compromised iff there exist a compromised link (i,j) in which $K_{i,j} \subseteq C_k$.

Since a route is composed of multiple paths. Next we propose the definition of the compromised route.

A route $r \in R$ is compromised iff all paths in the route are compromised.

Similarly, when paths or routes are implemented with end-to-end safe mechanism. To compromise such paths or routes, the attacker needs to additionally compromise the keys shared by the source node and the destination node.

An end-to-end safe path $p_{s,d}$ is compromised if and only if there exist a compromised link (i,j) meets $K_{i,j} \subseteq C_k$ meanwhile $K^E(p_{s,d}) \subseteq C_k$.

An end-to-end safe route $r_{s,d}$ is compromised if every path in the route is compromised and $K^E(r_{s,d}) \subseteq C_k$.

To compromise a network, it is necessary to compromise every route $r_{s,d} \in R$ in the network. More precisely, to compromise a route, the attacker needs to capture a set of nodes, that can compromise all the paths in the routes. Thus, the node capture attack problem can be turned into compromising all the paths in the network with minimum compromised node set. This information is extremely useful in modeling the node capture attack. We abstract each path in the network graph as a vertex called *path vertex* and define PV as the set of abstracted vertexes of all the paths.

If capturing node i leads to the compromise of a path corresponding to the path vertex $pv_t (pv_t \in PV)$, we express $i \rightharpoonup pv_t$. We propose a function $Cp(i, pv_t)$: $N \times PV \rightarrow \mathbb{R}^{\{0,1\}}$ for representing if capturing node i can compromise pv_t, which is defined as follows.

$$Cp(i, pv_t) = \begin{cases} 1 & i \rightharpoonup pv_t \\ 0 & \text{otherwise} \end{cases} \tag{3}$$

Then we develop two kinds of edges named *direct edge* and *indirect edge* respectively to represent the relationships between the sensor nodes and the path vertex nodes.

A sensor node i has a direct edge linking with a path vertex pv if capturing node i yields to the compromise of the path p which is corresponding to a path vertex pv. We say that i has a direct relationship with pv.

A sensor node i has an indirect edge connecting with a path vertex pv if capturing node i yields to partially compromising a set of links within the path p which is corresponding to pv. We say i has an indirect relationship with pv.

We devise a function $Ip(i, pv_t)$ which is formalized as $N \times PV \rightarrow \mathbb{R}^{[0,+\infty)}$ to express the indirect value of node i to path vertex pv_t. The indirect value is computed as:

$$Ip(i, pv_t) = \sum_{(i,j) \sqsubseteq p_{s,d}} \frac{1}{|pv_t|} \frac{|K_{i,j} \cap C_k|}{|K_{i,j}|}. \tag{4}$$

3.1 Establishment of Hybrid Graph

A *hybrid graph* is defined as $G^h = (N, PV, E^d, E^i)$, where N is the set of nodes in the network, PV stands for the set of the abstracted vertexes. E^d and E^i stand for the sets of the direct edges and the indirect edges between sensor nodes and abstracted vertexes.

After establishing the *hybrid graph*, we propose a method to manifest the destructiveness of a sensor node after it is attacked. We develop three kinds of metrics, the direct value $D(i)$, the indirect value $I(i)$ and the destructive value $R(i)$. $D(i)$ and $I(i)$ can be calculated as follows.

$$D(i) = \sum_{i \in N, pv_t \in PV} Cp(i, pv_t) \tag{5}$$

Direct value expresses how many paths will be compromised if i is captured whereas indirect value manifests the influences of shared keys in the links of other paths. We proposed a way of calculating the indirect value which is similar to page rank algorithm [15,16] in searching engine field. The indirect value can be calculated as follows.

$$I(i) = \sum_{i \in N, pv_t \in PV} Ip(i, pv_t) \tag{6}$$

Next we propose the definition of destructive value $R(i)$ which evaluates the destructiveness of a node after it is attacked based on $D(i)$ and $I(i)$. The destructive value can only be used to compare between two nodes.

The destructive value of i is higher than j, which can be expressed as $R(i) > R(j)$, iff $D(i) > D(j)$ or $D(i) = D(j), I(i) > I(j)$.

3.2 GACR

The aforementioned definitions and equations lay good foundations for designing a node capture attack in the *hybrid graph*. We devise a scheme in which the attacker captures the node with the highest destructive value aiming at maximizing the destructiveness to the network. We name our method Minimum Destructive Attack (MDA), which is illustrated in Algorithm 2.

Algorithm 2 illustrates the process of the *MDA*. Initially, the network initialization starts (line 3–9). Each sensor node acquires the set of keys and establishes the secure links with neighboring nodes locally. Then the source nodes set up the routing paths to the destination nodes by means of implementing certain routing protocols such as the single path routing protocol, the multiple independent path routing protocol or the multiple dependent path routing protocol. Once the initialization process finished, each node $i \in N$ calculates the values of $D(i)$ and $I(i)$ of every path vertex $pv_t \in PV$. After that, the attack process

---

Algorithm 2. $C_n = \mathrm{MDA}(G, K)$

1: **Input:** $G = (N, L)$, K
2: **Output:** C_n
3: Network initialization
4: Generate PV
5: **for all** $i \in N$ **do**
6:     **for all** $pv_t \in PV$ **do**
7:         Calculate $D(i)$ and $I(i)$
8:     **end for**
9: **end for**
10: **while** Network is not compromised **do**
11:     Find $m = \underset{i \in N}{\mathrm{argmax}}\, R(i)$
12:     Attack node m, $C_n = C_n \bigcup m$
13:     Adjust G^h
14: **end while**
15: Return C_n

---

starts (line 10–14). In each round, the attacker selects the node with the highest $R(i)$ and attacks it.

The attacking process repeats when the network is compromised. Algorithm 2 returns the set of the compromised nodes C_n as the output.

Algorithm 3. $L_l = \mathrm{GACR}(C_n)$

1: **Input:** C_n
2: **Output:** A Location list L_l
3: Calculate C_n using Algorithm 2
4: Compute L_l to form a shortest Hamiltonian cycle using [17]
5: Return L_l

To minimize the resource expenditure, the Hamiltonian cycle should be constructed. We made further improvements for MDA to solve the resource expenditure problem and propose a Greedy Attacking node capture attack AlgoRithm (GACR), which is shown in Algorithm 3. For ease of application, we utilize Concorde [17] (see Algorithm 3), which is a tool for calculating the shortest Hamiltonian cycle to guide the movement manner for the attacker.

4   Simulations and Analysis

4.1   Experiment Setup

To observe the performance of the node capture attacks, we simulate the node capture attack under different routing protocols: the single path routing protocol, the multiple independent path routing protocol and the multiple dependent path routing protocol. To guarantee the confidentiality and security of routing, some of the simulations are implemented with end-to-end safe mechanisms.

In the network, $|N| = 500$ nodes with randomly selected keys are deployed as reference [3,18,19] ($|K| = 10000$). 100 source nodes and 10 destination nodes are randomly selected to establish the routing paths. To avoid loops in setting up the network topology, the hop count [20] is applied. In the single path routing protocol, the next hop is chosen as the neighbor closer to the destination with equal hop count or smaller hop count in the neighborhood, while for the multiple path routing protocol, three such neighbors are selected. Other experimental parameters are identical with reference [9].

In our simulation, we assume that the attacker of GNAVE is capable for utilizing Concorde to generate the shortest Hamiltonian cycle.

4.2 Case Study

First, we propose an example to show the attacking results of GACR. As shown in Fig. 2, in a 100 m × 100 m WSN, 500 nodes are deployed. After executing, C_n is obtained with 12 attacking candidates (i.e. red dots). Then the attacker constructs shortest Hamilton cycle (i.e. blue cycle) using Algorithm 3 and performs the attack. In the whole process, the attacker needs to travel 353 m.

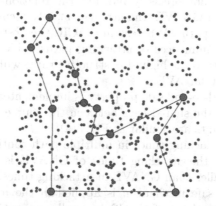

Fig. 2. A case study: 100 m × 100 m area, $|N| = 500$, $C_n = 12$, $|K_i| = 60$, cycle length 353 m (Color figure online)

4.3 Attacking Times

In this simulation, we compare the number of nodes each algorithm needs to capture to compromise the network. The x-coordinate indicates how many keys are assigned to each node. The y-coordinate shows how many nodes the attacker needs to capture to compromise the network.

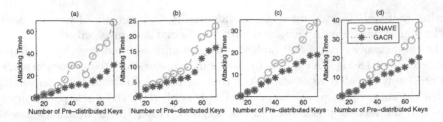

Fig. 3. The number of nodes the attacker needs to capture are illustrated for (a) single path routing protocol, (b) multiple path routing protocol, (c) single path routing protocol with end-to-end safe mechanism and (d) multiple path routing protocol with end-to-end safe mechanism

From Fig. 3(a), we note that, the attacking times of GNAVE and GACR are nearly the same. We note that, GNAVE attacks more nodes than GACR. The reason is quite simple, GNAVE maps the vulnerability of a route into a real number within the interval [0,1]. Then each node calculates the route vulnerability, which indicates that removing that node will cause how much damage to each route. Finally, the sum of route vulnerability of all routes is computed. A node with the highest incremental node value [4] will be captured by the attacker. Although GNAVE can enhance the efficiency of the node capture attack, the vulnerability value cannot precisely indicate the relationship between a node and a path. Because in GNAVE, the attacker mainly focuses on compromising the routes but not the paths. Whereas in GACR, the destructiveness is mainly evaluated in terms of influences of attacking paths, which is more precise. In each round, the node with the highest destructive value will be captured. GACR is 35.68 % smaller than GNAVE.

In Fig. 3(c), the end-to-end safe property is implemented. Messages are additionally encrypted by the shared keys between the source nodes and the destination nodes. The results are similar as Fig. 3(a).

In Fig. 3(b), the attacking times in multiple path routing protocol are presented. We note that the attacking times of GNAVE is bigger than GACR. GACR is 36.04 % smaller than GNAVE in attacking times.

When end-to-end safe mechanism is applied in the multiple path routing protocol, the attacking times of GACR is smaller than GNAVE. In Fig. 3(d), GACR is 12.33 % smaller GNAVE.

Therefore, we conclude that, GACR attacks fewer nodes than GNAVE in both single path routing protocol and multiple path routing protocol whether the end-to-end safe mechanism is implemented or not. Moreover, in the end-to-end safe routing protocols, the attacker needs to capture more nodes than the protocols which do not ensure end-to-end safe mechanism.

4.4 Fraction of Compromised Traffic

The fraction of the compromised traffic can express the efficiency of node capture attack. It can also indicate how many nodes the attacker needs to compromise.

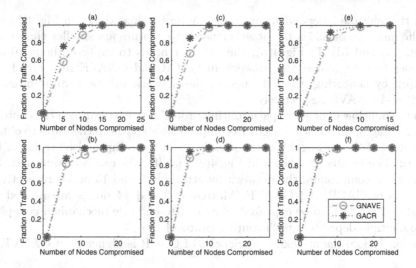

Fig. 4. The fraction of compromised traffic is illustrated for (a) single path routing protocol, (b) multiple independent path routing protocol, (c) multiple dependent path routing protocol, (d) single path routing protocol with end-to-end safe mechanism, (e) multiple independent path routing protocol with end-to-end safe mechanism and (f) multiple dependent path routing protocol with end-to-end safe mechanism

The smaller number of nodes the attacker needs to capture to compromise the network, the higher attacking efficiency the attacker holds. To analyze the fraction of the traffic compromised by the attacker, the following experiment is implemented. In the multiple path routing protocols, we implement the multiple independent path routing protocol and the multiple dependent path routing protocol to analyze the influence of the compromised nodes to the fraction of the compromised traffic.

In Fig. 4, the x-coordinate stands for how many nodes are compromised by the attacker. The y-coordinate indicates how many fractions of the traffic are compromised. In GNAVE, the route vulnerability metric is developed to express the significance of nodes in node capture attack. But it also emphasizes the relationships between the nodes and the routes, though the qualification method cannot manifest the destructiveness of nodes appropriately. In GACR, all the paths are abstracted into the abstracted vertexes. The destructive value is calculated to show the destructiveness of a node after it is attacked. The node with the highest destructive value will be chosen by the attacker. The comparisons of the fractions of compromised traffic are shown in Fig. 4.

In Fig. 4(a), we note that, the attacker needs to attack 15 and 17 nodes to compromise the network using GACR and GNAVE respectively.

From Fig. 4(d), we note that, the attacker needs to compromise 16 and 21 nodes by applying GACR and GNAVE respectively in the single path routing protocol with end-to-end safe mechanism.

In the multiple independent path routing protocol, as shown in Fig. 4(b) and (e), the numbers of nodes the attacker needs to capture are smaller than those in Fig. 4(a) and (d). In Fig. 4(b), the attacker needs to capture about 10 and 15 nodes to compromise the network in GACR and GNAVE respectively. In Fig. 4(e), by capturing 9 and 15 nodes, the network will be compromised by GACR and GNAVE respectively.

In the multiple dependent path routing protocol, to eavesdrop on the contents of the messages, the attacker needs to compromise all paths in the route to obtain the content of the message. We statistically count the compromised traffic of the network. The results are shown in Fig. 4(c) and (f). We can conclude that, the attacker can compromise the network by attacking 9 and 15 nodes respectively by means of GACR and GNAVE. Moreover, 9 and 14 nodes are needed for GACR and GNAVE to be captured when end-to-end safe mechanism is applied in the multiple dependent path routing protocol.

In conclusion, the attacking efficiencies of GACR is higher than GANVE.

4.5 Resource Expenditure

In this experiment, we measure the distance that an attacker needs to travel to compromise the network. The x-coordinate indicates how many keys are assigned to each node. The y-coordinate stands for the length in meters.

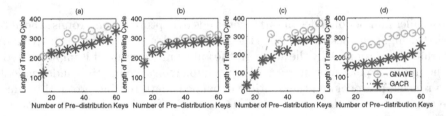

Fig. 5. The time for compromising a network for each algorithm is illustrated for (a) single path routing protocol, (b) multiple path routing protocol, (c) single path routing protocol with end-to-end safe mechanism and (d) multiple path routing protocol with end-to-end safe mechanism

As shown in Fig. 5, since GACR concentrates on resource expenditure in traveling, the shortest Hamiltonian cycle will be established when attacking candidate set is established. Therefore, the resource expenditure is much smaller than GNAVE, that pays no attention to resource cost.

Therefore, we can conclude that GACR can save resource expenditure in the attacking process.

5   Conclusion and Future Works

In this paper, a novel method of modeling the node capture attack in wireless sensor networks is proposed. We abstract the routing paths in the network into the abstracted vertexes and convert the network into the *hybrid graph*. We develop a metric called destructive value to indicate the destructiveness of a node after it is attacked. After that, GACR is proposed which focuses on minimizing resource expenditure while making maximum destructiveness. Finally, simulations have been implemented to prove the efficiency of the proposed algorithms. We can conclude that GACR can reduce the attacking times in compromising the network. The attacking efficiency is higher than GNAVE.

In the future, we will put forward theories for minimizing the resource expenditure while maximizing destructiveness in attacks.

Acknowledgments. This research is sponsored in part by the National Natural Science Foundation of China (No.61173179, No.61202443 and No.61402078), Major National Science and Technology Special Projects High-Nuclear-Based Project of China under Grant (No. 2012ZX01039-004-21 and No. 2012ZX01039-004-44) and Program for New Century Excellent Talents in University (NCET-13-0083). This research is also sponsored in part supported by the Fundamental Research Funds for the Central Universities (No.DUT14RC(3)090) and Major State Basic Research Development Program of China (973 Program), No.201300185.

References

1. Wu, G., Chen, X., Obaidat, M.S., Lin, C.: A high efficient node capture attack algorithm in wireless sensor network based on route minimum key set. Secur. Commun. Netw. **6**(2), 230–238 (2013)

2. Tague, P., Lee, J., Poovendran, R.: A set-covering approach for modeling attacks on key predistribution in wireless sensor networks. In: Third International Conference on Intelligent Sensing and Information Processing, ICISIP 2005, pp. 254–259. IEEE (2005)

3. Tague, P., Poovendran, R.: A canonical seed assignment model for key predistribution in wireless sensor networks. ACM Trans. Sens. Netw. (TOSN) **3**(4), 19-es (2007)

4. Tague, P.: Identifying, modeling, and mitigating attacks in wireless ad-hoc and sensor networks. PhD thesis, University of Washington (2009)

5. Lin, C., Wu, G.: Enhancing the attacking efficiency of the node capture attack in WSN: a matrix approach. J. Supercomputing **66**(2), 989–1007 (2013)

6. Lin, C., Wu, G., Xia, F., Yao, L.: Enhancing efficiency of node compromise attacks in vehicular ad-hoc networks using connected dominating set. Mob. Netw. Appl. **18**(6), 908–922 (2013)

7. Lin, C., Wu, G., Yim, K., Yao, L., Hou, G.: Compromising ad-hoc networks by attacking weakly connected dominating set. In: The 9-th International Conference on Innovative Mobile and Internet Services in Ubiquitous Computing (IMIS 2015). IEEE (2015) (to appear)

8. Lin, C., Wu, G., Yu, C.W., Yao, L.: Maximizing destructiveness of node capture attack in wireless sensor networks. J. Supercomputing (2015) (to appear) doi:10. 1007/s11227-015-1435-7

9. Tague, P., Slater, D., Rogers, J., Poovendran, R.: Vulnerability of network traffic under node capture attacks using circuit theoretic analysis. In: The 27th Conference on Computer Communications, INFOCOM 2008, IEEE, pp. 161–165. IEEE (2008)

10. Tague, P., Slater, D., Rogers, J., Poovendran, R.: Evaluating the vulnerability of network traffic using joint security and routing analysis. IEEE Trans. Dependable Secure Comput. **6**, 111–123 (2008)
11. Liu, D., Ning, P., Li, R.: Establishing pairwise keys in distributed sensor networks. ACM Trans. Inf. Syst. Secur. (TISSEC) **8**(1), 41–77 (2005)
12. Perkins, C., Belding-Royer, E., Das, S., et al.: Ad hoc on-demand distance vector (AODV) routing (2003)
13. Schurgers, C., Srivastava, M.: Energy efficient routing in wireless sensor networks. In: Military Communications Conference on Communications for Network-Centric Operations: Creating the Information Force, IEEE, MILCOM 2001, vol. 1, pp. 357–361. IEEE (2001)
14. Jain, K.: Security based on network topology against the wiretapping attack. IEEE Wirel. Commun. **11**(1), 68–71 (2004)
15. Brin, S., Page, L.: The anatomy of a large-scale hypertextual web search engine* 1. Comput. Netw. ISDN Syst. **30**(1–7), 107–117 (1998)
16. Langville, A., Meyer, C.: Google Page Rank and Beyond. Princeton University Press, Princeton (2006)
17. http://www.math.uwaterloo.ca/tsp/concorde.html
18. Chan, H., Perrig, A., Song, D.: Random key predistribution schemes for sensor-networks (2003)
19. Eschenauer, L., Gligor, V.: A key-management scheme for distributed sensor networks. In: Proceedings of the 9th ACM Conference on Computer and Communications Security, pp. 41–47. ACM (2002)
20. Akkaya, K., Younis, M.: A survey on routing protocols for wireless sensor networks. Ad hoc Netw. **3**(3), 325–349 (2005)

Deviation-Based Location Switching Protocol for Trajectory Privacy Protection

Shaobo Zhang[1,3], Qin Liu[2], and Guojun Wang[1,4(✉)]

[1] School of Information Science and Engineering, Central South University,
Changsha 410083, China
{shaobozhang,csgjwang}@csu.edu.cn
[2] School of Information Science and Engineering, Hunan University,
Changsha 410082, China
gracelq628@hnu.edu.cn
[3] School of Computer Science and Engineering,
Hunan University of Science and Technology, Xiangtan 411201, China
[4] School of Computer Science and Educational Software,
Guangzhou University, Guangzhou 510006, China

Abstract. With the development of trajectory data mining, personal privacy information is facing a great threaten. To address the problems, some trajectory privacy-preserving methods are proposed. The trajectory k-anonymous is the mainstream of the current trajectory privacy protection, which trys to anonymize k location together in a cloaked region at every sample location. However, the user's trajectory can be easily disclosed by tracking all the cloaked regions. In this paper, we propose a deviation-based location switching (DLS) protocol to break the correlation between user's real trajectory identity and the LBS server in order to achieve user's trajectory privacy. When a service user needs LBS, he first will build a mobile social network (MSN) and select a best matching user (BMU) to switch query, then send the query to LBS server. By virtue of the efficient weight-based private matching technique, the DLS protocol allows the user to enjoy LBS while preserving privacy from the BMU and LBS server. The analysis results prove that our proposal can protect trajectories privacy effectively and can get the results of the query without redundancy.

Keywords: Trajectory privacy-preserving · Deviation-based · Switching · Mobile Social Network (MSN) · Best Matching User (BMU)

1 Introduction

With the development of wireless communication technologies and personal mobile devices with global positioning functionality (e.g., GPS), Location-Based Services (LBS) develop fast and have been obtaining extensive concerns in recent years [1–3]. In LBS, user can obtain his current location by his Smartphone with GPS builting in, then sends a query with his location to LBS server. With the

© Springer International Publishing Switzerland 2015
G. Wang et al. (Eds.): ICA3PP 2015, Part III, LNCS 9530, pp. 417–428, 2015.
DOI: 10.1007/978-3-319-27137-8_31

help of LBS server, he can find Point Of Interests (POIs) nearby, for example, the nearest restaurant, hospital, shopping mall. Even if the user is always in a state of continuous movement, the location query services are available in every position in reality LBS. When a service user issues a continuous LBS queries, where continuous position information will form the trajectory, it can be used in our daily lives, such as business analysis, city planning. However, when users enjoy the great convenience and entertainment from LBS, they may confront privacy risks of sensitive information leakage. According to the user's continuous LBS queries, adversary can analyze the characteristics of trajectory and then collect sensitive things including corresponding working place, home address, even behavior patterns and living habits to a pointed person. What's worse, LBS servers may disclose users' private information to third parties for pecuniary advantage, which may become the serious threat. As a result, many users tend to hold reserved attitude to LBS, concerning about the leakage and abuse of their sensitive private information. Therefore, the privacy problem on the trajectory has been becoming increasingly prominent and needs to be solved.

To reduce the risk of privacy disclosure, many methods are proposed to protect users' trajectory privacy. Generally, they can be classified into three main types: the dummy trajectory method, the suppression method and the generalized method. The dummy trajectory method is by producing some dummy trajectory for each trajectory to reduce the risk of disclosure [4,5]. The more the dummy trajectory produces, the less the risk will disclosure. This dummy trajectory method is simple and has small computational overhead, but it has some shortcomings, such as large data storage capacity and data availability reduce. The suppression method in which the sensitive position of trajectory according to specific circumstances to the user could not released to the LBS server, which protected the position of some sensitive or frequently accessed [6,7]. This suppression method is easy, but if the sensitive locations on trajectories are suppressed too much, it might cause lots of information loss. The generalized method was to generalize the sampling points of trajectory to corresponding anonymous area, so that the user's position cannot be accurately determined [8]. This generalized method can ensure that data is true, but it has high computational cost. Among these methods, the trajectory k-anonymity of generalized method is a most widely used metric for location anonymization, which attempts to make a user's location indistinguishable from a certain number of others [9–12]. But this techniques also has certain privacy disclosure risk. Although each individual is protected based on the k-anonymity paradigm, the user trajectory can be easily disclosed by the following circumstances. (1) When the service user issues LBS requests in each point, it always formed a cloaked region. If the adversary connect the cloaked region, the user's trajectory will be exposed. (2) If the adversary compares the users of each cloaked region at a different time, it also can pinpoint the real user. (3) When the cloaking region is in a small region, their positions are almost identical, then the position information of each member can be easily revealed.

To overcome the defects above, we propose a DLS protocol in MSN. The MSN is a kind of new emerging social network, and the service users can utilize their location information to access some LBS nearby [13]. In our protocol when a service user needs LBS, he first will build a MSN and select a best matching user (BMU) who is the maximum location deviation and have different moving direction of the service user to switch the LBS query. The content of query will not disclose to each other by the symmetric encryption. Meanwhile, we utilize the efficient weight-based private matching technique to achieve privacy preserving between the service user and the matching user, which will not reveal sensitive information to each other. Because the service user sends the query to other users who possess the maximum location deviation every time, the LBS server cannot deduce the relationship between them. Furthermore, the LBS server records the identity of the BMU in query, so it is impossible to infer the user's real identity through the LBS servers, and the adversary can not identify the users' real trajectory. At the same time, the location of service user which the BMU send to LBS server is accurate, and it also will get the results of the query without redundancy. The main contributions of this paper are shown as follows.

(1) We propose a DLS protocol in MSN. In our protocol we first form a MSN at query point on the trajectory and find a BMU to switch query with the service user and send to the LBS server, which can effectively protect the identity of the service users.
(2) In the process which finds the BMU in MSN, we utilize the efficient weight-based private matching technique to achieve a secure and efficient matching, which can ensure the privacy between the service user and matching users.
(3) In MSN we find a user with the maximum location deviation and have different moving direction of the service user as the BMU, so the LBS server cannot deduce the relationship between them.
(4) We thoroughly analyze the security of the DLS protocol in MSN. Our protocol can protect trajectories privacy effectively.

The rest of this paper is organized as follows. In Sect. 2, we provide an overview of our system architecture and definition. In Sect. 3, we describe our privacy protocol in detail for trajectory privacy protection. Then, the security analysis is provided in Sect. 4. Finally, we conclude our work in Sect. 5.

2   The System Model and Definition

In this section, we first depict the DLS protocol in MSN for the trajectory privacy-preserving framework, then we formulate the problem for this work and provide the attacker model. Finally, we define some basic notions.

2.1   System Architecture

In this paper, we propose a novel DLS protocol in MSN, which introduces the MSN and finds a BMU in it to switch query with the service user, then send

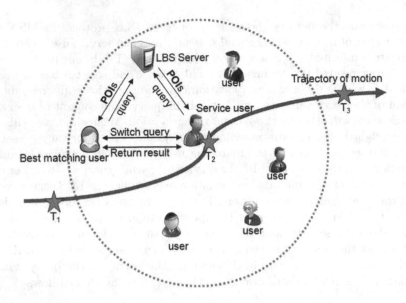

Fig. 1. The Architecture of DLS in MSN

the query to LBS server. Before the query sent to the LBS server, they achieved the ID transformation between the service user and the BMU, so that the LBS server has no knowledge of a real identity of the service user. The protocol is shown (see Fig. 1) and works as follows: the stars on the trajectory represents a sequence of point queries issued by service user at a different time from T_1 to T_3, and the circle represents the range covered by MSN. We take the time point T_2 as example, the service user should first build a MSN at the point issued query at the time T_2 on the trajectory, then select a BMU and switch the query, then they send the query to LBS server, respectively. For the BMU forward the query of the service user. After the LBS server received a query request, it can find out the POIs of the service user, and return the query result to the BMU. Then the BMU recovered the service user's ID and return the result to the service user. Similarly, the service user can forward the query of BMU to LBS service. The main merits of our protocol are preserving trajectory privacy effectively relative to k-anonymity model. According to the different roles of function characteristics, the main components of the protocol are made up of the three entities: service user, BMU and LBS Server.

2.2 Problem Statement

For LBS provider, the LBS server stored the spatial-temporal information of service user, and it is considered as an honest but curious entity in our system architecture. If the LBS server be compromised, the adversary is able to collect all LBS data which a sequence of continuous LBS query issued by service user. The adversary which may conduct trajectory correlation attacks has a high chance of successfully inferring the trajectory from a continuous query and the service user who is travelling on the trajectory. Then the analysis of trajectories over the data information of LBS server may help adversary to reveal users' identities. Additionally, it will exploit the frequently visited locations, for example, adversary can use the frequent information which arrives at a specific location from a fixed location everyday to deduce the location of his home and the work place. Consequently, the user's privacy would suffer a huge threat if the service user send a request directly to the LBS server. In our protocol the query point information of trajectory is forward by BMU which finds in MSN. However, the BMU, which is an intermediate tier between the service user and the LBS server, it may also reveal the forward information to adversary. Furthermore, in the matching process the users' attributes may include some sensitive information, if the initiator broadcasts its attributes to nearby users directly, it will reveal their attributes to strangers and result in the matching user's privacy breach. Therefore, with users' growing privacy concerns, private matching is also very important in MSN.

2.3   The Attack Model

In this paper the main goal of adversary is to identify the users' trajectory associated with the true identity. In our threat model, the communication channels in MSN are assumed to be secured when the query information is switch between service user and BMU and send to LBS server. The existing security schemes [e.g., secure sockets layer (SSL)] and conventional solutions (e.g., cryptography and hashing) can be used to protect the secrecy and integrity of the information through network [14,15]. A common adversary can be an entity that eavesdrops on wireless channel between BMU and LBS server, or an attacker who has compromised the LBS servers, or the BMU can be considered malicious. Then based on the sensitive information which an adversary can get, we define two types of adversary in this paper: internal adversary and external adversary [16].

Internal Adversary. The LBS server and BMU are considered as internal adversary. The LBS is capable to be a global, long-term and active observer, it manages all the queries for users' server and collects all LBS data. It may be compromised by the adversary or may leak information for making profits. The BMU forwards the query messages as an intermediate tier between the service user and the LBS server, it may also reveal the forward messages to adversary.

External Adversary. It is only an adversary that can wiretap the insecure wireless channel. Eavesdroppers are usually local, short-term and passive because of their status features and limited resources. he tries to infer some sensitive information of user from the eavesdropped information, such as sensitive locations of the user, user's identity and interest.

2.4 Definitions

The definitions and symbols we use throughout the following sections are defined as follows.

Definition 1: (Best Matching). The best matching is the similarity of some attributes between users in mobile social network. The higher it is similar, the more it will match.

Definition 2: (Location). The location L is a two-tuple (x, y) which represents the latitude and longitude of the location.

Definition 3: (Distance). $A(x_1, y_1)$ and $B(x_2, y_2)$ is the two location point of two-dimensional plane, between which the Euclidean distance is D_{AB}.

$$D_{AB} = \sqrt{(x_1 - x_2)^2 + (y_1 - y_2)^2} \tag{1}$$

Definition 4: (Trajectory). For a moving object Q, its trajectory T is a set of discrete locations at sampling time, which be represented as:

$$T = \{ID_Q, (x_1, y_1, t_1), (x_2, y_2, t_2), ..., (x_n, y_n, t_n)\}, t_1 < t_2 < ... < t_n \tag{2}$$

here ID_Q represents the trajectory identity of moving object Q, (x_i, y_i, t_i) represents the sample location of moving object Q at time t_i on the trajectory.

3 The DLS Protocol for Trajectory Privacy Protection

In this section, we present the DLS protocol for trajectory privacy in LBS. we first provide an overview of it, and then describe concrete working processes of this protocol, finally we describe in details on the matching process.

3.1 Overview

Our basic idea is to introduce the MSN and find a BMU in it to switch query with the service user, then send the query to LBS server. As illustrated previously, the main reason for switching query is to prevent the LSP from having the service users' actual identity information, so that the LSP cannot infer the information of the trajectory. The system consists of the service user, the BMU and the LBS server.

We formalize the information request by service user U as:

$$MSG_{U2B} = \{ID_U, E_{PK_S}(T_i, L_i, Q, K_{AES})\} \tag{3}$$

where ID_U represents the service user identity of U, T_i and L_i is the spatial-temporal information tagged by queries issued location point at the time t_i on the trajectory, Q is the content of query which sends to LBS server. E is an asymmetric encryption function, while PK_S is a public key which is issued by the LBS server. K_{AES} is a key of symmetric encryption between the LBS server and the service user, which can be encapsulated in asymmetric encryption function in MSG_{U2B}. The service user should first find the BMU in MSN. The main task of the BMU is to switch query with the service user, which can construct the ID transformation between them and to forward the information request to the LBS server. Since the LSP does not have any knowledge of the service user, it cannot deduce the real identity information about the service user. The protocol mainly consists of five steps:

Step 1: Matching. After forming the MSN based on the service user as center, the service user runs Algorithm 1 (details in Sect. 3.2) to find the BMU, who satisfied the maximum location deviation and movement direction of the difference with the service user, which can ensure that finding the BMU in MSN with the service user have the biggest difference of the trajectory. In order to find the BMU in MSN, service users may need to compute the similarity of their attributes. Since users' attributes may include some sensitive information, the matching must be done privately. Therefore, privacy matching schemes between users are needed. We utilize the efficient weight-based private matching technique which can not only ensure a privacy of users' sensitive information, but also can greatly improve the efficiency of the matching process [17,18].

Step 2: ID Transformation. After receiving the forward request of the service user, the BMU first gets the information parameter ID_U from MSG_{U2B}, and stores it in the file list. Then the BMU transforms the service user's real ID (ID_U) into the BMU's pseudo-ID (ID_{B_i}), finally the forward information of the BMU to LBS server is MSG_{B2S}.

$$MSG_{B2S} = \{ID_{B_i}, E_{PK_S}(T_i, L_i, Q, K_{AES})\} \qquad (4)$$

Where ID_{B_i} is the ID of BMU which find in MSN at the time t_i, he is also the pseudo-ID of service user ID_U. the BMU doesn't know the content of query of the service user, because he doesn't have private key SK_S, only the LBS server can decrypt.

Step 3: Search. Before the LBS server searches the POIs for a service user, it needs to decrypt the information with the private key SK_S of the server when it receives the query request from the BMU, and it obtains the information which is the location of request point and the query of the service user. Then the LBS server searches in the service data and gets the result MSG according to the parameter of request information. At the same time the LBS server records the BMU's ID and relates query record in the server.

$$MSG = \{service\ user's\ POIs\} \qquad (5)$$

After getting the result MSG, the LBS server need encrypt the MSG in symmetric encryption function En with K_{AES}, which can get the $En_{K_{AES}}(MSG)$, only the service user and LBS server have the key K_{AES}. Then the messages MSG_{S2B} from the LBS server to the BMU is

$$MSG_{S2B} = \{ID_{B_i}, En_{K_{AES}}(MSG)\}. \qquad (6)$$

Step 4: ID Recovery. The BMU gets the query result information MSG_{S2B} which returns from the LBS server, it recovers the identity of the service user ID_U from the file list of the BMU, and then forwards the result information to the service user. The messages MSG_{B2U} from the BMU to the service user is

$$MSG_{B2U} = \{ID_U, En_{K_{AES}}(MSG)\}. \tag{7}$$

Step 5: Result. The service user gets the query result information MSG_{B2U} which forwards from the BMU, but the information is encrypted, then we need to decrypt the information parameter $En_{K_{AES}}(MSG)$ with the user's key K_{AES}. Therefore, the user can easily get the exact result MSG.

3.2   Matching

To find the BMU and achieve privacy preserving in MSN, we utilize an efficient weight-based private matching technique to achieve a secure and efficient matching, which uses a realistic matching approach considering both the number of common attribute and the corresponding weights on them. This method is effectively compared with the traditional homomorphic and commutative encryption. But if the service user broadcasts to every one for matching in MSN, it will produce a large amount of the computation and communication overhead. To solve this problem, we can randomly select the k user for matching in MSN.

In the matching process we define two matching properties: distance (D) and angle difference (θ). D denotes the distance between the service user and the matching user, $D \in [0, D_{larger}]$, D_{larger} denotes the maximum radius range of the MSN coverage. θ denotes the angle difference between the service user and the matching user, $\theta \in [0, 180^0]$. We created the attribute matrix $M_{L \times 2}$ according to user's two common attributes and their weights, which the row vectors L indicates the weight of attribute and the column vectors 2 means the two common attribute. Suppose the maximum radius range of the MSN is H meters, we take every H/L meters as a unit of distance, and every angle of $180/L$ degrees as one unit angle, then the weights of the two attributes can be divided into L levels, we select a corresponding integer i, $i \in [1, L]$, which indicates the weight of an attribute. In order to resist continuous tracing attack by BMU, we choose a user as BMU which is farthest away from the service user and the angle difference with it, then the attribute matrix $M_{L \times 2}$ of the service user can be defined as $A_{L \times 2}$, which $m_{Lj} = 1$ and where $i \neq L$, $m_{Lj} = 0$, $m_{ij} \in A_{L \times 2}$.

$$M_{L \times 2} = \begin{bmatrix} m_{11} & m_{12} \\ m_{21} & m_{22} \\ \dots & \dots \\ m_{L1} & m_{L2} \end{bmatrix} \qquad A_{L \times 2} = \begin{bmatrix} 0 & 0 \\ 0 & 0 \\ \dots & \dots \\ 1 & 1 \end{bmatrix}$$

The weight matrix $W_{L \times L}$ to indicate different attention degree for the attributes. The greater the similarity attribute value is, the bigger the weight will be, and the generation of the element $(W_{ij})_{L \times L}$ according to the Formula-8:

$$(W_{ij})_{L\times L} = \begin{cases} i; & i = j; \\ i - |i - j|; & (i - |i - j|) > 1; \\ 1; & (i - |i - j|) \leq 1; \end{cases} \tag{8}$$

Algorithm 1. The Calculation Process of Matching

Input:

The initiator's attribute matrix $A_{L\times 2}$,

two large prime α, β,where $|\alpha| = 256, \beta > 3L^2\alpha^2$.

Output:

the match value φ.

1: Randomly generate two matrixes $P_{L\times 2}, R_{L\times 2}$, for $\forall p_{ij} \in P_{L\times 2}, \forall r_{ij} \in R_{L\times 2}$,

  have $\sum_{i=1}^{L} \sum_{j=1}^{2} p_{ij} < (\alpha - 2L), |r_{ij}\beta| \approx 1024; 1 \leqslant i \leqslant L, 1 \leqslant j \leqslant 2$;

2: Calculate $\begin{cases} a^*_{ij} = \alpha + p_{ij} + r_{ij}\beta; & (a_{ij} = 1) \\ a^*_{ij} = p_{ij} + r_{ij}\beta; & (a_{ij} = 0) \end{cases}$,

  the initiator can get the encrypted matrix $A^*_{L\times 2}$;

3: The candidate computer $D = (d_{ij})_{L\times L} = A^*_{L\times 2} * B^T_{L\times 2}$;

4: The initiator makes a further transformation $T^* = \frac{t_{ij} - (t_{ij} \bmod \alpha^2)}{\alpha^2}$,

  $t_{ij} = (d_{ij} + k_i) \bmod \beta, d_{ij} \in D_{L\times L}, k_i \in \vec{K}$;

5: The initiator considers the corresponding weights and computes

  $H_{L\times L} = (h_{ij})_{L\times L} = T^*_{L\times L} \bullet W_{L\times L}$;

6: We can get the match value $\varphi = \sum_{i=1}^{L} \sum_{j=1}^{L} h_{ij}$;

7: **return** φ

In the matching process the user in MSN can be defined as the initiator (the service user), the candidate and the best matcher (BMU), and each user in the MSN has the attributes $M_{L\times 2}$. To find the BMU with private, we define three operations: confusion matrix transformation, matrix multiplication and similarity calculation. In confusion matrix transformation operation the initiator encrypted matrix $A_{L\times 2}$ by matrix confusion, which is used for hiding personal information. We randomly generate two matrixes $P_{L\times 2}$ and $R_{L\times 2}$, and choose two large prime α, β, where $|\alpha| = 256$, $\beta > 3L^2\alpha^2$. $\vec{K}$ is the secret key to help us get our original results. By Algorithm 1, we can get the encrypted matrix $A^*_{L\times 2}$, then broadcast her best matching discovery request to other k candidates in MSN. Since the candidate does not have any knowledge of confusion matrix, it cannot deduce the real attribute information about the initiator. When the candidate matrix $B_{L\times 2}$ receives the request from the initiator, it can execute matrix multiplication operator $D_{L\times L} = A^*_{L\times 2} \times B^T_{L\times 2}$, $B^T_{L\times 2}$ is the transpose matrix of the candidate matrix $B_{L\times 2}$. The candidate sends computing result $D_{L\times L}$ to the initiator, then the initiator makes a further transformation to get T^*. The similarity calculation operation considers the corresponding weights and computes $H_{L\times L} = T^*_{L\times L} \bullet W_{L\times L}$, '$\bullet$' means dot production, $W_{L\times L}$ is the weight matrix which can indicate the different attention degree for the attributes. Then we can get the match value $\varphi = \sum_{i=1}^{l} \sum_{j=1}^{l} h_{ij}$, it means the weighted average similarity value between the initiator and candidate where a bigger φ means a better matching. The process of matching is shown in Algorithm 1.

4   Security Analysis

Our security analysis will focus on how the DLS protocol achieve the user's trajectory privacy preservation and resist the possible privacy attack from internal adversary, external adversary and other attacks, the threat model in Sect. 2.3 has been discussed. The security of the proposed protocol against all kinds of attacks will be analyzed in the following respectively.

4.1   Resistance Against Internal Adversary

From the LBS Side. The LBS server masters all the queries information from the service user and he can perform inference attack with this information, which aims to disclose the real identity of the user's trajectory. In our protocol, we switch the query information between the service user and BMU, then send to LBS server for query. Since the BMU is different at different query point, it is dynamically changing and there is no relationship between them, the LBS server cannot identify the user's real identity from arbitrary BMU-IDs. Moreover, it is almost impossible that the same user is repeatedly found in MSN. So the LBS server can't link the queries through the BMU-ID identifying the real identity of trajectory.

From the BMU Side. The BMU forwards the message that is encrypted with the asymmetric and symmetric encryption. The BMU doesn't have the key, it cannot decrypt the message. For example, when the service user sends the query message $\{ID_U, E_{PK_S}(T_i, L_i, Q, K_{AES})\}$ to the BMU, the BMU doesn't have the public key PK_S of the asymmetric encryption function E, and it can not get any information except for ID_U. So the BMU is impossible to get the effective forward messages.

4.2   Resistance Against External Adversary

To avoid the passive attack like eavesdropping, all the messages transmitted in the wireless channel are encrypted with the asymmetric and symmetric encryption. For example, in the phase of the forward message MSG_{B2S} from BMU to LBS server, the adversary can only get the BMU's identify ID_{B_i} from the message $\{ID_{B_i}, E_{PK_S}(T_i, L_i, Q, K_{AES})\}$. Because the other information is encrypted by asymmetric encryption with the public key PK_S, the adversary cannot get the secret private key SK_S from the LBS server. Similarly, in the phase of the query result returning, the result MSG is encrypted by symmetric encryption function with the key PK_{AES}. If the adversary cannot get the secret key PK_{AES}, it will not get the effective message from the $En_{K_{AES}}(MSG)$. So the eavesdroppers cannot understand the obtained information without knowing the related secret key.

4.3 Resistance Against Other Attacks

In our protocol we match the user in MSN who satisfied the maximum location deviation and movement direction of the difference with the service user as BMU, which can ensure that finding the BMU in MSN with the service user has the biggest difference of the trajectory. In the process of the service user moving, the formed MSN is different at the different query point, so the BMU is found to be different, and it is from the service user whose location has maximum deviation, which can effectively resist continuous tracing attack by BMU. At the same time, we utilize the efficient weight-based private matching technique to find the BMU in MSN, which can effectively achieve privacy preserving and guarantee the user's information which is not leaked.

5   Conclusion

In this paper, we propose a DLS protocol in MSN for the protection of user's trajectory privacy. A key feature of the protocol is that we break the correlation between a user's real trajectory identity and the LBS server by the BMU in MSN to switch the query with the service user. The BMU who are the maximum location deviation and have different moving direction of the service user in MSN. Moreover, we utilize the efficient weight-based private matching technique to achieve privacy preserving for matching user in MSN. Security analysis demonstrates that our protocol can achieve the user's trajectory privacy protection and resist the possible privacy attack from internal adversary, external adversary and other attacks. In our future work, we will implement our scheme into real smartphones to test its performance and make further improvements.

Acknowledgments. This work is supported in part by the National Natural Science Foundation of China under Grant Numbers 61272151, 61472451 and 61402161, the International Science & Technology Cooperation Program of China under Grant Number 2013DFB10070, the China Hunan Provincial Science & Technology Program under Grant Number 2012GK4106 and 2013FJ4046, and the "Mobile Health" Ministry of Education - China Mobile Joint Laboratory (MOE-DST No. [2012]311).

References

1. Lu, R., Lin, X., Liang, X., Shen, X.: A dynamic privacy-preserving key management scheme for location-based services in vanets. IEEE Trans. Intell. Transp. Syst. **13**(1), 127–139 (2012)

2. Shin, K.G., Ju, X., Chen, Z., Hu, X.: Privacy protection for users of location-based services. IEEE Wirel. Commun. **19**(1), 30–39 (2012)

3. Peng, T., Liu, Q., Wang, G.: Privacy preserving for location-based services using location transformation. In: Wang, G., Ray, I., Feng, D., Rajarajan, M. (eds.) CSS 2013. LNCS, vol. 8300, pp. 14–28. Springer, Heidelberg (2013)

4. Lei, P.R., Peng, W.C., Su, I.J., Chang, C.P.: Dummy-based schemes for protecting movement trajectories. J. Inf. Sci. Eng. **28**(2), 335–350 (2012)

5. You, T.H., Peng, W.C., Lee, W.C.: Protecting moving trajectories with dummies. In: 2007 International Conference on Mobile Data Management, pp. 278–282. IEEE (2007)

6. Terrovitis, M., Mamoulis, N.: Privacy preservation in the publication of trajectories. In: The 9th International Conference on Mobile Data Management (MDM08), pp. 65–72. IEEE (2008)

7. Gruteser, M., Bredin, J., Grunwald, D.: Path privacy in location-aware computing (2004)

8. Nergiz, M.E., Atzori, M., Saygin, Y.: Towards trajectory anonymization: a generalization-based approach. In: Proceedings of the SIGSPATIAL ACM GIS 2008 International Workshop on Security and Privacy in GIS and LBS, pp. 52–61. ACM (2008)

9. Xu, T., Cai, Y.: Exploring historical location data for anonymity preservation in location-based services. In: The 27th Conference on Computer Communications (INFOCOM 2008). IEEE (2008)

10. Gruteser, M., Grunwald, D.: Anonymous usage of location-based services through spatial and temporal cloaking. In: Proceedings of the 1st International Conference on Mobile Systems, Applications and Services, pp. 31–42. ACM (2003)

11. Gedik, B., Liu, L.: Protecting location privacy with personalized k-anonymity: architecture and algorithms. IEEE Trans. Mob. Comput. **7**(1), 1–18 (2008)

12. Hwang, R.H., Hsueh, Y.L., Chung, H.W.: A novel time-obfuscated algorithm for trajectory privacy protection. IEEE Trans. Serv. Comput. **7**(2), 126–139 (2014)

13. Lu, R., Lin, X., Shi, Z., Shao, J.: Plam: a privacy-preserving framework for localarea mobile social networks. In: 2014 IEEE INFOCOM, pp. 763–771. IEEE (2014)

14. Wang, G., Yue, F., Liu, Q.: A secure self-destructing scheme for electronic data. J. Comput. Syst. Sci. **79**(2), 279–290 (2013)

15. Wang, G., Du, Q., Zhou, W., Liu, Q.: A scalable encryption scheme for multiprivileged group communications. J. Supercomput. **64**(3), 1075–1091 (2013)

16. Zhu, X., Chi, H., Jiang, S., Lei, X., Li, H.: Using dynamic pseudo-IDs to protect privacy in location-based services. In: 2014 IEEE International Conference on Communications (ICC), pp. 2307–2312. IEEE (2014)

17. Zhu, X., Liu, J., Jiang, S., Chen, Z., Li, H.: Efficient weight-based private matching for proximity-based mobile social networks. In: 2014 IEEE International Conference on Communications (ICC), pp. 4114–4119. IEEE (2014)

18. Lu, R., Lin, X., Shen, X.: SPOC: a secure and privacy-preserving opportunistic computing framework for mobile-healthcare emergency. IEEE Trans. Parallel Distrib. Syst. **24**(3), 614–624 (2013)

Exploring Efficient and Robust Virtual Machine Introspection Techniques

Chonghua Wang[1,2], Xiaochun Yun[1], Zhiyu Hao[1(✉)], Lei Cui[1],
Yandong Han[1,2], and Qingxin Zou[1]

[1] Institute of Information Engineering,
Chinese Academy of Sciences, Beijing 100093, China
haozhiyu@iie.ac.cn
[2] School of Computer and Control Engineering,
University of Chinese Academy of Sciences, Beijing 100049, China

Abstract. Upon practical implementation of virtual machine introspection (VMI), administrators may be overwhelmed by dozens of research works. Specifically, the adopted introspection mechanism perform differently with regard to various performance and security requirements. Besides, most of previous works do not clarify the boundary between Trusted Computing Base (TCB) and attacks towards introspection. This paper aims to help administrators to determine the appropriate introspection approach. Firstly, we summarize current VMI technologies, and present a classification method mainly depending on whether hardware assistance is required, how it solves the semantic gap problem and how introspection is triggered. Secondly, we discuss how to achieve a good trade-off between the two metrics of performance and security. Thirdly, we propose a TCB threat model to employ VMI along with other enhancing mechanism to tackle attacks in different levels of TCB. Finally, we discuss some future trends related to VMI for further improving security.

Keywords: Cloud security · Virtualization · VM introspection · Interception · Snapshot

1 Introduction

Virtualization significantly improves the utilization of computing resources by sharing the resource of a single physical server to multiple virtual machines (VMs) and migrating the running state of the VMs among servers, and thus becomes the key in cloud infrastructures. To ensure the cloud security in face of various attacks, virtual machine introspection (VMI) is proposed [1] and employed in a variety of security fields including intrusion detection, malware detection, virtual firewalls, memory forensics, OS integrity protection, etc. Taking malware detection as an example, even though malware can hide itself from the guest's perspective, the traces can still be detected in bytes from memory which can be captured by hypervisor[1]. The key of introspection is to acquire the detailed view of guest within the

---

[1] Hypervisor is also referred to "Virtual Machine Monitor" (VMM), we do not differentiate them in this paper.

© Springer International Publishing Switzerland 2015
G. Wang et al. (Eds.): ICA3PP 2015, Part III, LNCS 9530, pp. 429–448, 2015.
DOI: 10.1007/978-3-319-27137-8_32

hypervisor, so that the hypervisor is able to detect the anomalies and then handle the attacks in real time.

However, the VMI does not come for free. The difficulty of extracting high level semantic information from low level bits and bytes is known as semantic gap. To reconstruct the internal view of the monitored VM, the hypervisor can obtain memory pages from a snapshot or registers by tracking specific events (e.g., context switches). Different ways of tackling the semantic gap problem bring great differences in performance and security. In addition, the VMI tool can be placed in the hypervisor, a sibling security VM, the hardware, or the guest OS itself to monitor the VM, and thus it would be misguided by malware if not properly handled well. Even worse, many previous works encompass guest kernel into Trusted Computing Base (TCB) so that there is no clear boundary between TCB and attacks towards introspection. Many works are based on the assumption that guest OS is benign, but the guest OS is often compromised in read world scenarios. If the kernel data structures are not completed or changed, the view reconstruction would be misguided by still using the compromised data structure template. Therefore, the VMI itself may be not robust. These factors bring confusions to an administrator upon practical implementation of introspection in cloud infrastructures. Firstly, which introspection method should be adopted to meet a specific requirement, i.e., an administrator prefers performance to security, or prefers security to performance, or even favors a simple design and implementation. Secondly, should the introspection tool be trusted in face of different levels of TCB, if not, how to enhance the VMI mechanism.

This paper aims to answer the above questions. Firstly, this paper summarizes the state-of-the-art techniques related to VMI for providing a brief overview to researchers. Then, we present a classification method on the basis of three key aspects: whether hardware assistance is required, how it solves the semantic gap problem, and how it is triggered. Meanwhile, we analyze the pros and cons of each kind of VMI techniques, and provide several guidelines to help researchers to determine a preferable mechanism in a specific scenario.

Secondly, we explore two key metrics of VMI: performance and security. While current VMI techniques concentrate on how to achieve a good trade-off between performance and security, our work aims to present three critical issues upon balancing the two metrics: transient attacks, passive and active introspection, hardware invariants and OS invariants. We not only discuss why balance is important for these issues but also discuss how to achieve a good trade-off between them.

Thirdly, we formulate a Trusted Computing Base (TCB) threat model with the aim to acquire trustworthy introspection results. Then we discuss the attacks that would abate the introspection technique, and present several related protecting mechanisms that help to improve the security level of TCB.

Finally, we outline some further search directions related to VMI, which would contribute to security improvement in cloud computing.

The rest of this paper is organized as follows. Section 2 introduces the taxonomy of current VMI techniques and describes the specific categories along with related techniques in detail. Section 3 explores analysis of the trade-off between performance and security. Section 4 discusses the TCB threat model. Section 5 prospects on the future trends of VMI and Sect. 6 concludes this work.

2   Taxonomy of Virtual Machine Introspection

We characterize the current VMI techniques based on three orthogonal dimensions: (1) *Whether hardware assistance is required.* A technique is **hardware-assisted** if it requires the involvement of hardware, otherwise is *software-based.* (2) *How it solves the semantic gap problem.* If it solves the semantic gap problem through directly reconstructing the guest semantics, it is classified into *semantics reconstruction.* Or else, it avoids the semantic gap problem in an indirect way, and thus is regarded as **semantic gap avoiding**. (3) *How introspection is triggered.* The technique can introspect the full snapshot of guest memory, so it is called **snapshot-triggered**. Or it can intercept specific events during normal execution for acquiring the semantics, and is classified into **event-triggered**. It is worth noting that there exist a lot of works combining two or more dimensions, we leave the discussion as our future work. Figure 1 presents the taxonomy of current VMI techniques and following sections will describe the related techniques in detail. They are organized in sequence based on the terminal node of the classification tree in Fig. 1.

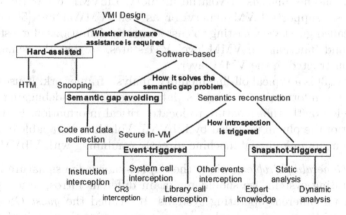

Fig. 1. Taxonomy of VMI techniques

2.1   Snapshot-Triggered Approach

Snapshot-triggered method means that the VMM introspects a full snapshot of guest memory. The introspection can be conducted on-line or off-line. In on-line way, the VMM introspects the memory using copy-on-write method during the guest's suspending interval [2]. In off-line way, the VMM introspects a dumped file of memory instead of the volatile memory [3].

The whole introspection process can be divided into two phases: signing and mapping. The signing phase extracts useful information related to kernel data structures based on some kernel invariants, and generates a data structure signature. With the signature, we can identify several data structure entities such as process list, module list, etc. The state-of-the-art signing technologies include expert-knowledge signature, static analysis signature and dynamic learning signature. The mapping phase is responsible for reconstructing high level semantics based on the signature generated in the signing phase. If the signature is robust, the mapping phase can remove false positives and false negatives as possible. An attempt to evade the signature will lead to crash of the guest OS and the functionality associated with the entity. Considering that the mapping phase is easy to implement, the rest of this section will focus on signing techniques.

Expert-Knowledge Signature. Expert-knowledge signature is generated by a manual process based on the internal knowledge of guest OS. For example, the *System.map* file in Linux kernel, which maps the symbol names into memory addresses and vice versa, acts as the expert knowledge. Likewise, Windows has its own symbol table as the expert knowledge. A lot of works have been proposed to perform introspection with expert-knowledge signature [1–6].

XenAccess [2] provides a useful application programming interface for reading (writing) data from (to) a virtual machine's memory on Xen platform, which is suitable for on-line analysis of volatile memory. LibVMI [6], as the extension of XenAccess, supports KVM hypervisor as well. VMWatcher [5] proposes a technique called guest view casting to cast semantic definitions of guest OS data structures and functions on VMM-level VM states, so that the semantic view can be reconstructed in the VMM layer.

Volatility [3] is a typical off-line memory analysis framework. It uses a profile containing the information of kernel's data structure and debugging symbols. The profile is exactly the signature to locate critical information. Further, with the support of the plugin provided by LibVMI, Volatility is capable of accessing memory on a running virtual machine directly combining with LibVMI.

Guest OS-Generality Problem: Since the expert-knowledge signature is specific to the operating system, we should maintain different introspection programs customized for different operating systems. It's called the *guest OS-generality problem*. Considering that a cloud platform may provide thousands of VMs that differ in operating systems, kernel versions and patches, thus the kernel data structure layout and invariants are different accordingly. Managing a diversity of signatures for various OSes is extremely complex, so that administrators tend to seek for a dynamic introspection tool. VMDriver [8] encapsulates the OS-related information of a guest VM within a monitoring driver. The monitoring driver which holds various expert-knowledge signatures is dynamically loaded when the corresponding guest VM is launched. The driver can provide a uniform interface for VMI tools. VMDriver is an attracting method to address the *guest OS-generality problem*, but the "generality" is limited since the driver just maintain finite types of mainstream OSes. As a result, the administrators still have to update the driver when a newer guest OS is required. Therefore, many works try to develop automated techniques that do not rely on expert-knowledge, as will be described in the followings.

Static Analysis Signature. Static analysis signature is an automated technique in some degree to solve the OS-generality problem. It relies on source code analysis and some source invariants to identify all the kernel object entities. To locate a kernel object entity, a reference to it should be found, usually in the form of a pointer. Meanwhile, the pointer could be located in another kernel object entity. Leveraging points-to analysis [9,10] to identify the graph of kernel object entities is a fundamental approach to obtain static analysis signature. Current techniques such as SigGraph [11], MAS [12], KOP [13], SIGPATH [14], DeepScanner [15] employ static analysis to generate this kind of signature.

The use of points-to method [9,10] to identify the graph of kernel object entities is a compelling approach to obtain the static analysis signature. KOP [13] starts with deriving a points-to graph based on the kernel source code analysis. Some modifications are done to generate an extended type graph not only containing type definitions and global variables but also candidate target types for generic pointers whose target type cannot be extracted from definition. KOP is capable of distinguishing the fields inside an object and calling contexts, as well as resolving type ambiguities (e.g., unions and generic pointers have multiple candidate target types) in memory traversal. Instead of using points-to analysis, Christian et al. [16] put forward a method to establish used-as relations between structure and union field, as well as global variables and data types. The used-as analysis not only identifies all types that a pointer or an integer type is used as, but also records all static pointer arithmetic that is applied in situations to retrieve the target address from a source pointer.

Dynamic Analysis Signature. Dynamic analysis signature does not require source code, debugging symbols, or any API in the target operating system. It launches the OS instance, traces the execution, monitors which fields are read and written in the OS kernel structure, aggregates and analyzes runtime information, and finally recovers syntax and semantics of data structures during the normal execution. Moreover, it forks a program acted as stimuli running concurrently to monitor certain interested data which would be manipulated.

Brendan et al. [17] profile target data structure to determine which fields are most commonly accessed by guest OS. A field can be modified without adversely affecting OS functionality if it has never been accessed during the normal execution of OS. The field that is frequently accessed is regarded as a stronger signature candidate than the one never accessed. However, it is insufficient to be treated as a robust signature since some fields are not important for correct execution of OS even though they have been updated frequently. Fuzzing is designed to test these stronger signatures to determine which one can be modified without causing a crash or violating its intended functionality.

2.2 Event-Triggered Approach

Different from snapshot-triggered introspection systems which follow static and fixed scheduling, event-triggered introspection suffers dynamical and unpredicted strike due to the arbitrary occurrence of various events (e.g., context switch, system call, interrupt). Event-triggered approach intercepts specific events and inserts codes into the routines which handle those events. Upon the occurrence of a specific event, a corresponding trap will be notified to hypervisor, so that the inserted codes can be executed. Based on the position where interception is placed, the commonly used event-triggered VMI techniques fall into several categories: instruction interception, *CR3* interception, system call interception, library interception, *I/O* interception, network interception and control flow interception. Beyond that, memory access interception is also employed in some scenarios with specific requirements. To obtain a more comprehensive view, the combination of several interceptions can be employed. Typically, HyperTap [18] leverages instruction interception, *CR3* interception, system call interception and *I/O* interception in a hypervisor-level framework to provide reliable and secure monitoring. The followings will discuss these issues in detail.

Instruction Interception. Instruction interception monitors detailed execution process of instructions in the guest VM. A basic approach is to set single-stepping mode for performing instruction-level tracing. Generally speaking, achieving this kind of functionalities requires the assistance of certain CPU features such as the *trap flag* in *EFLAGS* register or the *int 3* breakpoint instruction. Instruction interception achieves monitoring at a fine-grained level. XenProbes [19] is a typical debugger-based approach to probe the guest kernel of Xen VM. It is capable of monitoring real-time status of guest OS, analysing performance bottleneck, logging specific events and tracing anomalies. Ether [20] and MAVMM [21] guarantee the occurrence of a debug exception after every instruction by setting *trap flag* in the analysis target.

However, single-stepping for instruction-level trapping will trigger a transition between hypervisor and guest upon execution of each guest instruction. Since each transition will suspend the guest for hundreds to thousands cycles (multiple times than an instruction execution), it will impose significant performance loss. Moreover, it is required to monitor each instruction even if we are only interested in several specific execution points, and thus lacks of flexibility. Sebastian et al. [22] employ the *Performance Monitoring Counters (PMCs)* which are available on most mainstream processors, to trap hardware performance events. It only traps certain types of instructions, such as call, ret and conditional branches. In addition, Ralf at el. [23] leverage a processor feature called *Branch Tracing* to keep track of all branches taken during code execution. Each conditional or unconditional branch, such as jump, call, and exception will be intercepted by [23]. The interception granularity of [22,23] are more moderate than intercepting the whole instructions, thus is more flexible.

V2E [24], a malware analysis platform, records malware execution using hardware virtualization for transparency and replays them using dynamic binary translation for efficiency. SPIDER [25] introduces the idea of invisible breakpoint to trap the execution of target program at any desired instruction and data access at any memory address, meanwhile guaranteeing flexibility. To achieve transparency, SPIDER [25] uses the *monitor trap flag (MTF)* which is a flag specifically designed for single-stepping in hardware virtualization instead of *trap flag*. Once *MTF* is set, the guest will trigger a VM Exit after executing each instruction, so that the trapping is transparent to the guest.

***CR3* Interception.** *CR3* stores the page directory address of current tasks and each task has a unique *CR3* value for identification. Since *CR3* is a privileged register, the modification to it will be notified to VMM. As a result, by intercepting *CR3*, the VMM is able to accurately perceive when a guest operating system creates processes, destroys them, or switches context between them.

Antfarm [26] is a VMM component that implicitly obtains information of guest operating system events like process creations and exits by observing closely related events like virtual address space creation and destruction. It achieves this by intercepting the *CR3* value, a VMM-visible value, which is called *address space identifier (ASID)* by Antfarm. In addition, it also provides estimations for other process-related entities such as CPU execution time, working set size, and context switch counts by observing virtual address space analogues. Lycosid [27] adopts the idea of Antfarm to acquire trusted view of guest processes, and then detects the hidden process through cross-view validation.

System Call Interception. In most mainstream operating systems, system call is a very important interface to access kernel services. It is used by a user process to perform privileged operations. During normal execution, an application might issue millions of system calls in a short period, which can be regarded as a sufficient signature to distinguish between normal behaviour and malicious attacks [28]. Therefore, system call interception is a powerful technique for obtaining enrich semantics. Current system call mechanisms fall into three categories: software interrupt based, *SYSENTER*-based and *SYSCALL*-based.

In order to monitor the events of process creating, hard disk writing, and process communication, Lares [32] inserts many hooks into the guest VM. These hooks can actively intercept the sequences of system calls of the monitored events (e.g., *NtCreateSection*, hook for monitoring process creation). However, in order to make use of hardware virtualization for system call interception, some mechanisms should be explored to cause a trap into hypervisor when system call happens. A lot of works [7,8,20,21,31,33–35] are proposed to cause a trap into hypervisor for intercepting system calls.

For software interrupt based, AMD's hardware virtualization provides a direct means to cause VMExit [30], whereas an indirect way for trapping should be found with Intel *VT*. Changing the interrupt descriptor table entry of interrupt (*INT 80* for Linux and *INT 2E* for windows) to point to a non-present page is a common solution. The non-present page will generate a page fault (*#PG*) and then cause a VMExit. Ether [20] and HyperSleuth [34] both take this method for system call interception. For *SYSENTER*-based, Ether [20] and HyperSleuth [34] trap to hypervisor by setting the value of $SYSENTER\_EIP\_MSR$ to an address of a non-existent memory which will also generate a page fault. Differently, MAVMM [21] and Nitro [33] copy the value of $SYSENTER\_CS\_MSR$ into the CS register when $SYSENTER$ is executed and attempt to load the CS register with a null value, which will results in a general protection exception trapping into the hypervisor. For $SYSCALL$-based, only Nitro [33] supports this kind of system call interception so far. Typically, $SYSCALL$-based system calls can be turned on and off easily by setting and unset the SCE flag. Unsetting SCE will cause an invalid *op-code* exception for trapping.

Library Call Interception. In some cases, malware does not invoke any system calls, so that system call interception fail to detect. Library calls are able to provide more abundant information than system calls. Specifically, commodity operating systems, such as Linux and Windows, own thousands of library functions but only hundreds of system calls (e.g., Linux-2.6.15 has 289 system calls whereas libc.so.6 has 2016 library functions [36]). As a result, user-level library call interception allows for understanding which library functions are being called by running process, as well as the value of parameters. The big weakness is that library call interception can not be easily trapped into hypervisor.

IntroLib [37] performs library call interception by tracking and logging the sequence of user-level library calls made by malware. To trap library calls into hypervisor, IntroLib utilizes *Shadow Page Table* to set a transparent barrier in memory between malware and the called library functions. Malware have different privileges on the memory isolated by the barrier. Any control flow transition crossing the isolated memory will be intercepted by IntroLib, and then a VMExit will be triggered.

Other Events Interception. Besides basic events interception, other approaches attempt to exploit more complicated interception for retrieving richer semantic information. In particular, since processors with Intel VT provide a bitmap to determine whether I/O access is captured or not, BitVisor [38] uses the bitmap to intercept I/O access to specific port address. BitVisor also captures other types of events, such as execution of some privileged instructions, exceptions and hardware interrupts, and inter-processor interrupts. BareCloud [39] is capable of intercepting all network communications during the malware execution. Another useful event to be intercepted is control path. IntroLib [37] and GateWay [40] both generate two memory spaces and insert a barrier between them. Any control flow switches between kernel and drivers (GateWay), or between malware and library functions (IntroLib) will be captured by hypervisor.

2.3 Semantic Gap Avoiding Approach

The above two introspection techniques, either snapshot-triggered or event-triggered, require to reconstruct semantics of guest to fill the semantic gap. In contrast, semantic gap avoiding approach attempts to avoid semantic gap problem indirectly, rather than solve it. It can be achieved by *(i)* redirecting the code and data related to introspection from monitoring VM to guest VM, named as *code and data redirection,* or *(ii)* performing introspection by the guest itself by means of moving the introspection back to the guest VM, meanwhile guaranteeing the security of the introspection tools, named as *secure in-VM.*

Code and Data Redirection. By redirecting the relative code and data that are kernel-dependent (mainly for system call), Process out-grafting [41] and ShadowContext [42] achieve to support existing user-mode process monitoring tools (e.g. *strace, ltrace and gdb*), running in the monitoring VM without modifying them and making them introspection-aware. These tools are logically running inside the guest VM, but physically running inside the monitoring VM. In this way, the semantic gap is effectively removed and the monitor can now directly intercept and analyse the process execution without hypervisor's intervention. Rather than redirecting system call, Process implanting [43] implants whole process to the guest VM and executes it under the cover of an existing running process to avoid the semantic gap. At function granularity, SYRINGE [44] uses a technique known as *function-call injection* to implant functions of the monitor to the guest VM and another technique known as *localized shepherding* to guarantee the secure execution of the invoked guest OS code.

VIRTUOSO [45] makes first step to reuse the legacy binary code to automatically create introspection tools. The key idea of VIRTUOSO is to train a particular system call or an entire utilities (e.g., *ps,lsmod*) inside the guest VM, record multiple executions, and analyse the resulting instruction traces. Then it translates the trained traces (essentially slices) into an independent introspection program that can be deployed in the monitoring VM. The generated introspection program contains all the low-level instructions that are necessary to implement guest OS's API in monitoring VM. It is another form of code and data redirection to avoid semantic gap. The code and data of introspection tool that are OS API-dependent are all translated into instruction traces.

VMST [46] identifies only system call execution context relevant to introspection and ensures that kernel data redirection only redirects data in the context of interest. While Process out-grafting [41] aims to monitor an untrusted process by intercepting kernel executions at system call granularity, VMST aims to inspect the whole OS at finer granularity. EXTERIOR [47] extends VMST to enable an out-of-VM shell with guest-OS writable and executable capabilities. Compared to VMST, ShadowContext [42] is capable of dealing with OS that can page out memory in kernel space and focuses on system call execution redirection instead of system call data redirection as VMST does. Another recent work HyperShell [64] is also based on the concept of system call redirection, mainly designed for cloud in-VM management, whereas ShadowContext is mainly for security.

Secure In-VM. SIM [48] is the first system that leverages hardware memory protection and hardware virtualization features available in contemporary processors to create a hypervisor protected address space to enable introspection tools execute and access data in native speed. By forwarding introspection tool back to guest VM within the protected address space, SIM achieves both efficiency and security. In specific, SIM creates another virtual address space called SIM virtual address space along with the system address space. The permissions of these two address space are set differently and any malware codes attempt to execute in SIM virtual address space will be denied. For efficiency, SIM leverages the *CR3_TARGET_LIST* feature maintained by the hypervisor to switch between the system address space and SIM without trapping into hypervisor.

Gateway [40] is another *secure in-VM* method, which is designed for detecting kernel malware by monitoring kernel APIs invoked by device drivers. Gateway creates distinct virtual memory regions for commodity kernels and their drivers. Any control flows between kernel and drivers will result in page faults trapped into hypervisor. The main idea of Gateway is similar to SIM, both forwards the introspection tools back to guest VM to avoid the semantic gap. IntroLib [37] maintains two mutually exclusive *SPT*s for each guest, worked as a barrier. When control flow transitions between malware and library functions happen, it will trigger events that could be captured by hypervisor.

2.4   Hardware-Assisted Approach

More and more researches focus on leveraging existing hardware [22,23,49] or customized hardware [50,51] to assist introspection in order to race with malware. Meanwhile, hardware-assisted introspection helps to achieve higher performance than software-based approach. For example, [22] makes use of *Performance Monitoring Counters* to complete *PMCs*-based trapping and [23] leverages *Branch Tracing* to keep track of all branches taken during code execution. In addition, HyperSentry [52], HyperCheck [57] and SPECTRE [66] introspect with the assistance of *System Management Mode (SMM)*. We present two most common techniques of hardware-assisted introspection: transactional memory used to support concurrent introspection, and snoop mechanism employed for cache granularity monitoring.

Hardware Transactional Memory. *Hardware Transactional Memory (HTM)* attempts to simplify concurrent programming by allowing a group of load and store instructions to execute in an atomic way. TxIntro [49] leverages HTM to support concurrent, timely and consistent introspection of guest VM. Since many VMI tools (e.g., LibVMI, Volatility) need to suspend the guest VM in order to get a consistent state of guest VM. The suspended time suffers a strong intrusiveness of guest VM and may cause services disruption. Worse still, some pending updates to data structures to be monitored may result in an inconsistent introspection. Transient attacks may also arise during two introspection cycles due to the suspending. To make introspection concurrent and consistent, TxIntro starts a transaction and adds the addresses of critical kernel data structures to the read set of the CPU core running VMI tools. Any updates to the monitored data will result in transaction abort of VMI tools. The abort handler will notify VMI daemon in another core to retry VMI to get a consistent state.

Snooping Mechanism. Snooping systems can monitor guest OS at cache granularity. Vigilare [50] pioneers to implement snooping capability of the bus traffic to perform integrity analysis of the guest by adding newly designed *Snooper* hardware connections module to the monitored system. Since all the processor instructions and data transfers among memory, processor and I/O have to go through system bus, Vigilare [50] can observe all the monitored system activities by monitoring the critical path of instructions and data transfers. It makes Vigilare completely independent from potential compromise or attacks, especially for transient attacks. Ki-Mon [51] is capable of monitoring address and value pair of memory modifications with a bus traffic monitoring module called *Value Table Management Unit (VTMU)* and a DMA module. Overall, snooping makes a great advance both in monitoring performance and defending transient attacks.

2.5 Summary

Figure 2 gives a brief summary of VMI techniques, it reports the main approaches, basic idea as well as the key issues of each VMI category. Further, it summarizes several typical systems using these introspection approaches for security improvement.

3 Performance and Security

Performance and security are two key metrics to characterize virtual machine introspection. Performance is measured in terms of response latency, while security copes with malicious attacks. It is impossible to achieve high performance and security at the same time since an attempt to enhance security will always degrade performance, and vice versa. As a result, current VMI techniques tend to trade off the two metrics. This section aims to present three critical issues upon balancing the two metrics: transient attacks, passive and active introspection, hardware invariants and OS invariants. We not only discuss why balance is important for these issues but also discuss how to achieve a good trade-off.

3.1 Transient Attacks

Transient attacks often perform malware activities without incurring persistent changes to the victim's system, which is the main obstruction when dealing with performance and security. Since the evidence of malicious modification with monitored system is visible for a short period, detecting such modification becomes difficult. In detail, for snapshot-triggered approaches, if attackers have a sense of monitor existence and know exactly the interval of snapshot polling, stealthy malware can be completed during the interval and restore the modification to normal before next snapshot polling. In such scenario, snapshot-triggered approaches might raise the rate of snapshot polling to increase the probability of detection for lower false negatives. However, frequent snapshot polling would

VMI Taxonomy	Main Approaches	Basic Idea	Key Issues	Typical Systems
Snapshot-triggered	Expert-knowledge signature	Traverse kernel data structure	Guest OS-generality problem; Transient attacks	[2,3,4,5,8]
	Static analysis signature	Employ code analysis	Not supported by closed-source OS	[11,12,13,15,16]
	Dynamic learning signature	Train OS instance to find robust signature	False positives and false negatives	[14,17]
Event-triggered	Instruction interception	Debug in single-step mode	Frequent traps lead to significant overheads	[18-25]
	CR3 interception	Trap the CR3 register	Monitor process create, destroy and context-switch	[18,26,27]
	System call interception	Software interrupt based, SYSENTER-based, SYSCALL-based	Find suitable hardware invariants to trap into hypervisor for system call	[7,8,19,32, 33,34,35]
	Library interception	Leverage control flow transition between two isolated memory region	Alternative for those malware don't invoke system call	[37]
	Other events interception	I/O, Network traffic, control flow and customized events such as memory modification	Obtain information on demand according to different customized events	[38,39,40]
Semantic gap avoiding	Code and data redirection	Redirect the introspection-related code and data into guest VM for continuous executing	Support existing security tools naturally	[41,42,43,44,45 ,46,47,48,67]
	Secure In-VM	Transfer the introspection tools back into guest VM	Access data in native speeds without sacrificing security	[40,49]
Hardware-assisted	Hardware Transaction Memory	Leverage the atomicity of HTM	Concurrent, timely and consistent introspection	[50]
	Snooping mechanism	Snoop the bus traffic	Cache granularity monitoring	[51,52]

Fig. 2. Summary of virtual machine introspection techniques

inevitably introduce higher overheads for bad performance. HyperSentry [52] tries to meet both higher performance and security by confusing attackers to predict the snapshot polling time exactly impossible. Leveraging the knowledge of probability to randomizing the snapshot interval might be an assistant method to minimize the false negatives as possible. It seems attractive, but if malware leaves the traces as minimal as possible for a passing-by period, there is still a chance that it can avoid being detected by the snapshot. However, event-triggered approaches avoid transient attacks by intercepting specific events and trapping into hypervisor. Without the overheads of frequent snapshot polling, but other form of overheads is arising (e.g., trapping into hypervisor consumes several CPU cycles). Fortunately, Vigilare [50] and Ki-Mon [51] can monitor all system activities by snooping bus traffic of the monitored system, which are capable of detecting all transient attacks without significant performance degradation.

3.2 Trade-Off Between Passive and Active

The monitoring manners are also the critical determinants when making a trade-off between performance and security. Active monitoring is consuming more overheads than passive monitoring, but more secure and more informative relatively.

Passive monitoring performs VMI by external scanning or in a polling manner, whereas active monitoring achieves goals in an event-triggered manner (e.g., placing a hook inside the system being monitored or intercepting specific events). Snapshot-based approaches (e.g., XenAccess [2]) are always performing VMI in a passive manner by extracting knowledge from the internal data structures of guest OS. Passive monitoring makes transient attacks escape easily, which performs malware activities between snapshot polling phases. Given all that, passive monitoring is more suitable for persistent failures and attacks supposing that the corrupted or compromised state remains even longer than the polling interval.

To some degree, active monitoring is supposed to perform better than passive monitoring since the former can not only capture system's state but also operational events. When execution reaches the corresponding event, it will be trapped and pass control to VMI tools timely. Event-triggered feature results in no time dependence that can be exploited. Active monitoring plays an important role in VMI design due to the event-triggered nature and potential for real-time attack prevention, which can complement passive monitoring. Lares [32], for example, is an active monitoring architecture that places hooks in guest VM with no intrusiveness and intercepts critical events. However, active monitoring is not fool proof since it may still suffer from event bypass attacks (e.g., attack can prevent or avoid generation of event that will trigger).

3.3   Trade-Off Between Hardware Invariants and OS Invariants

An OS invariant is a property defined and enforced by the design and implementation of a specific OS, so that the specific value of the critical data structure can be mapped correctly. Several snapshot-based VMI tools, as demonstrated in [2,5] make use of previously delivered symbol table of the guest OS kernel to determine the position of the key data structures. In other words, OS variants allow the internal state of guest VM to be monitored by mapping the VM's memory with VMI tools. An hardware invariant is a property defined and enforced by the hardware architecture (e.g., x86, x64). For example, OS should use $CR3$ register to locate the page directory entry address of a process and $IDTR$ to find the address of interrupt descriptor table.

Compared to those VMI approaches relying on hardware invariants, OS invariant based systems are more vulnerable to attacks, such as [53,54]. Worse still, approaches relying on OS invariants are lack of OS-generality as demonstrated in Sect. 2.1. However, hardware invariants can build more robust VMI tools against those do not rely on any hardware knowledge since any adversaries can hardly circumvent at a lower level. More attractive, hardware invariants do not rely on the specific OS kernel and they are suitable for coping with the OS-generality problem. On the other hand, the semantic gap will be widen if only considering hardware invariants without relying on any guest OS invariants and thus inevitably resulting in worse performance.

4   Robust Virtual Machine Introspection

Virtual machine introspection is proposed to obtain trustworthy monitoring results in out-of-VM manner so as to guarantee security transparently. Since the security of VMI itself is related to the specific definition of TCB, VMI techniques may be vulnerable to malicious attacks, such as DKSM [53], KOH [67] and DKOM [55] for a loose TCB. Several works tend to minimize the size of TCB for robust introspection. Essentially, how to define a minimized TCB while campaigning against attacks is a trade-off problem, this section will attempt to clarify the relations between TCB and relative attacks, and also present several related protecting mechanisms that help to improve the security level of TCB.

4.1   Trusted Computing Base

Bare metal, hypervisor, monitoring VM, guest OS and applications are main considering determinants when deciding TCB of the whole system. Within these determinants, applications are concerns of high level. Monitoring VM is acting as a security VM and bare metal is not easy to attack. Therefore, this paper mainly talks about hypervisor and guest OS level which are more related to VMI field, others are out of scope. Currently, most VMI approaches encompass hypervisor into TCB. In these works, an implicit assumption is that since hypervisor enforces security, it must be trustworthy and reliable, otherwise there is no guarantee that security functionalities will be effectively enforced. However, even though the code size of hypervisors (e.g., Xen, KVM) is smaller than traditional OS, there still exists many vulnerabilities to be exploited by attackers. Many approaches for protecting the hypervisor have been arisen in recently years including HyperSentry [52], HyperSafe [56], HyperLock [58], and HyperCheck [57]. For example, HyperSafe [56] is a lightweight approach that endows existing bare-metal hypervisors with a unique self-protection capability to provide lifetime control-flow integrity. Further, many works develop customized hypervisors for secure monitoring, such as Bitvisor [38] and CloudVisor [59].

We build a TCB threat model, which depicts the relationship between TCB and the relative robustness level in Fig. 3. If TCB only includes the last level (bare metal), the system can achieve strongest robustness. By adding hypervisor to TCB, robustness decreases just like a pyramid and relative measures should be taken to achieve equal robustness (e.g., self-protection capabilities of hypervisor or customizing a secure hypervisor). Likewise, if other level is going to be added into TCB, some mechanisms should be taken to guarantee security of the relative level. Except for the hypervisor, guest OS integrity is another implicit assumption by most works. Unfortunately, the guest OS kernel could be compromised. Once compromised, the assumption on the kernel respecting its own data structures becomes seriously questionable. Introspection by following these data structure templates may lead to wrong results.

Jain et al. [65] defines strong semantic gap problem as that systems would not make any assumptions about the guest OS being benign. The strong semantic gap problem is still unsolved, declared by paper [65]. However, researchers could find effective ways to protect the guest OS integrity rather than adding it to TCB with no consideration of threat. SecVisor [60] and NICKLE [62] are customized hypervisors that can guarantee only authenticated kernel code will be executed based on W⊕X principle to ensure guest OS intergrity. In addition, Patagonix [61], Lares [32], OSCK [63] and Hooksafe [67] also have made much contribution to protect guest OS integrity.

Some approaches trade robustness for usefulness and performance or other needs by expanding the TCB. ShadowContext's [42] TCB incorporates not only the hypervisor and the monitoring VM, but also the dummy process and the system call code of the guest VM. In this scenario, the dummy process could be easily subverted by in-guest user-space malwares or kernel rootkits, which cannot guarantee the robustness of entire monitoring system.

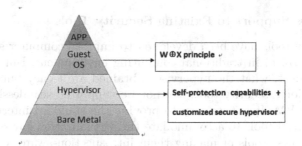

Fig. 3. The TCB threat model

4.2   Attacks Towards Introspection

DKSM: Direct Kernel Structure Manipulation (DKSM) [53] attacks foil existing VMI techniques by breaking the basic assumption that guest OS are trusted. DKSM [53] presents three ways, syntax-based manipulation, semantic-based manipulation and multifaceted combo manipulation, to modify the data structures of guest kernel. Unfortunately, Many VMI tools depend on the guest memory state and expect the untrusted guest to present a trusted data kernel structure.

Kernel Rootkits: Kernel rootkits can be roughly classified into Kernel Object Hooking (KOH) [67] and Dynamic Kernel Object Manipulation (DKOM) [55]. KOH rootkits hijack kernel control flow by modifying function pointers located in kernel text or data sections, while DKOM rootkits subvert kernel by directly modifying dynamic data objects. These attacks can lead to deceptive results when administrator still trust the guest OS kernel. KOH rootkits can gain the control of kernel execution after hijacking the control flow. Even though systems such as SecVisor [60], NICKLE [62], Patagonix [61] have been developed to preserve kernel code integrity by preventing malicious rootkit code from being executed, some KOH rootkits such as return-oriented rootkits [13] can bypass it. These rootkits first subvert kernel control flow and then launch the attack by only utilizing legitimate kernel code snippets. For DKOM, given that an attacker has privilege to use the direct memory access devices (e.g., /dev/kmem), then the attacker can modify any kernel data including data structures and kernel function pointers. The main challenge to defend is that the attacker does not attempt to execute new code violating the code integrity, but instead only change the data value and data structure.

5 Future Trends of VMI

This section discusses several future trends in the field of VMI technique, which would help to improve cloud security.

5.1 Seamless Support to Existing Security Tools

Various security tools have been developed to improve computer security (e.g., *ltrace, ptrace, strace*) in traditional computing environment. But in the virtualized environment, what the hypervisor obtained are legacy binary code and thus the traditional security tools can not be supported seamlessly running in the monitoring VM. It is necessary to provide the standard interface to apply traditional security tools to accommodate the virtualization environment without modifying these tools or making them introspection-aware. *Code and data redirection* method such as Process-out-grafting [41], ShadowContext [42] try to avoid semantic gap to satisfy the requirements, but there are still many limitations. For example, Process-out-grafting only support out-grafting of a single process, whereas multiple processes support for simultaneous out-grafting is imperative. ShadowContext [42] can go beyond simply collecting guest's information, but incapable of guest's configuration management. Researchers should find a more general and effective way to support existing security tools seamlessly.

5.2 Effective Accommodation with Cloud Platforms

A cloud service provider allocates resources and configure environment according to cloud users' demand. The system environment differ in thousand ways, such as various types or even versions of guest OS, which increases the complexity of monitoring for security administrators. On one hand, most of the state-of-the-art VMI techniques require customizing monitoring VMs and introspection tools for different system environment, which brings the *guest OS-generality problem*. On the other hand, monitoring thousands of guest VMs will introduce non-trivial overhead, which might be unacceptable by end-users. Applying VMI to accommodate cloud computing environment effectively is actually a problem of both guest OS-generality and overheads.

5.3 Digging the Newest Features on Demand

Compared to software features, hardware sometimes brings qualitative leap if researchers can exploit it well. For example, TxIntro [49] retrofits hardware transactional memory for concurrent, timely and consistent introspection. Restricted transaction memory is a concrete embodiment of Intel transactional synchronization extensions, but it is not released to the mass market until the middle of 2013. Researchers could track the newest development of hardware closely to decide if there are some useful features to be exploited. Besides exploiting existing features of hardware, customizing hardware on demand Vigilare [50] and

Ki-Mon [51] might be a more flexible but complex way. Overall, both digging the newest features of existing hardware and customizing hardware for efficient and robust VMI are still in their infancy.

5.4   Safe Modification of Guest State

Given that malicious processes and kernel modules hide from in-VM system monitoring tools (e.g., ps, lsmod), even though the VMI tools can detect them in the monitoring VM, prevention could not be done. Administrators need to kill these hidden processes to update kernel state in case of advanced malicious activities. It is especially important for cloud environment which should give a timely response. Recent achievement EXTERIOR [47] can be used in a timely, trusted manner for guest OS administration, including but not limited to system introspection, (re)configuration and recovery of kernel intrusions. Unfortunately, most of the VMI techniques discussed in this paper are incapable of writable operations to recover. It can also be a worthy researching in-depth point.

5.5   Security Improvement of Hypervisor

Recently, attacks aiming at hypervisors arise mainly through breaking the isolation feature so as to perform a VM escape, namely the process of breaking out of a virtual machine and interacting with the host OS. HyperSentry [52] and HyperCheck [57] both exploit the *System Management Mode (SMM)* of CPU to scan the hypervisor periodically for security. Except for protecting hypervisor itself, minimizing the code base for a customized hypervisor like BitVisor [38] is an alternative way. The relationship between attack and defence is always a mutual chasing problem, as long as VMI techniques are still valuable, research on the security of the virtualization environment itself can not be ceased.

6   Conclusion

This paper aims to provide researchers with guidelines on how to determine an efficient and robust virtual machine introspection technique for cloud security improvement. We firstly propose the taxonomy of current VMI techniques and present a brief overview of each categories and the related techniques. Then, we introduce two key metrics of introspection: performance and security, and discuss how to trade off these two metrics. In addition, we explore the security of introspection techniques themselves, report some attacks that may invalidate introspection, and discuss how to define a minimized TCB to provide a trustworthy and robust introspection in face of various attacks. Finally, we present several future trends related to introspection techniques. We believe that our work would provide researchers and administrators with a thorough understanding on VMI.

Acknowledgement. We would like to thank the anonymous reviewers for their valuable comments and help in improving this paper. This work is supported by China National Key Technology Support Program (2012BAH46B02).

References

1. Garfinkel, T., Rosenblum, M.: A virtual machine introspection based architecture for intrusion detection. In: NDSS 2003, pp.191–206 (2003)
2. Payne, B., Carbone, M., Lee, W.: Secure and flexible monitoring of virtual machines. In: ACSAC 2007, pp. 385–397 (2007)
3. The volatility framework. https://github.com/volatilityfoundation/volatility
4. Volatilitux. https://code.google.com/p/volatilitux/
5. Jiang, X., Wang, X., Xu, D.: Stealthy malware detection through VMM-based "out-of-the-box" semantic view reconstruction. In: CCS 2007, pp. 128–138 (2007)
6. LibVMI library. https://github.com/libvmi/libvmi
7. Jiang, X., Wang, X.: "Out-of-the-Box" monitoring of VM-based high-interaction honeypots. In: RAID 2007, pp. 198–218 (2007)
8. Xiang, G., Jin, H., Zou, D., Zhang, X., Wen, S., Zhao, F.: VMDriver: a driver-based monitoring mechanism for virtualization. In: SRDS 2010, pp. 72–81 (2010)
9. Andersen, L.O.: Program analysis and specialization for the C programming language. Ph.D. thesis, DIKU, University of Copenhagen (1994)
10. Heintze, N., Tardieu, O.: Ultra-fast aliasing analysis using CLA: a million lines of C code in a second. In: PLDI 2001, pp. 254–263 (2001)
11. Lin, Z., Rhee, J., Zhang, X., Xu, D., Jiang, X.: SigGraph: brute force scanning of kernel data structureinstances using graph-based signatures. In: NDSS 2011 (2011)
12. Cui, W., Peinado, M., Xu, Z., Chan, E.: Tracking rootkit footprints with a practical memory analysis system. In: USENIX Security 2012, p. 42 (2012)
13. Carbone, M., Cui, W., Lu, L., Lee, W., Peinado, M., Jiang, X.: Mapping kernel objects to enable systematic integrity checking. In: CCS 2009, pp. 555–565 (2009)
14. Xu, Z., Zhang, J., Gu, G., Lin, Z.: SigPath: a memory graph based approach for program data introspection and modification. In: Vaidya, J., Kutyłowski, M. (eds.) ESORICS 2014. LNCS, vol. 8713, pp. 237–256. Springer, Heidelberg (2014)
15. Liang, B., You, W., Shi, W., Liang, Z.: Detecting stealthy malware with interstructure and imported signatures. In: ASICCS 2011, pp. 217–227 (2011)
16. Schneider, C., Pfoh, J., Eckert, C.: Bridging the semantic gap through static code analysis. In: EuroSec 2012 (2012)
17. Dolan-Gavitt, B., Srivastava, A., Traynor, P., Giffin, J.: Robust signatures for kernel data structures. In: CCS 2009, pp. 566–577 (2009)
18. Pham, C., Estrada, Z., Cao, P., et al.: Reliability and security monitoring of virtual machines using hardware architectural invariants. In: DSN 2014, pp. 13–24 (2014)
19. Quynh, N.A., Suzaki, K.: Xenprobe: a lightweight user-space probing framework for xen virtual machine. In: USENIX ATC 2007 (2007)
20. Dinaburg, A., Royal, P., Sharif, M., Lee, W.: Ether: malware analysis via hardware virtualization extensions. In: CCS 2008, pp. 51–62 (2008)
21. Nguyen, A.M., Schear, N., Jung, H., Godiyal, A., King, S.T., Nguyen, H.D.: MAVMM: lightweight and purpose built VMM for malware analysis. In: ACSAC 2009, pp. 441–450 (2009)
22. Vogl, S., Eckert, C.: Using hardware performance events for instruction-level monitoring on the x86 architecture. In: EuroSec 2012 (2012)
23. Willems, C., et al.: Down to the bare metal: using processor features for binary analysis. In: ACSAC 2012, pp. 189–198 (2012)
24. Yan, L., Jayachandra, M., Zhang, M., Heng, Y.: V2E: combining hardware virtualization and softwareemulation for transparent and extensible malware analysis. In: ACM SIGPLAN Notices, pp. 227–238 (2012)

25. Deng, Z., Zhang, X., Xu, D.: SPIDER: stealthy binary program instrumentation and debugging via hardware virtualization. In: ACSAC 2013, pp. 289–298 (2013)
26. Jones, S.T., Arpaci-Dusseau, A.C., Arpaci-Dusseau, R.H.:. Antfarm: tracking processes in a virtual machine environment. In: USENIX ATC 2006, pp. 1–14 (2006)
27. Jones, S.T., Arpaci-Dusseau, A.C., ArpaciDusseau, R.H.: VMM-based hidden process detection and identification using lycosid. In: VEE 2008, pp. 91–100 (2008)
28. Forrest, S., Hofmeyr, S., Somayaji, A.: The evolution of system-call monitoring. In: ACSAC 2008, pp. 418–430 (2008)
29. Intel corp. Intel 64 and IA-32 Architectures Developer's Manual, vol. 3B (2013)
30. AMD64 Architecture Programmer's Manual. Volume 2: System Programming. AMD Inc. (2013)
31. Li, B., et al.: A VMM-based system call interposition framework for program monitoring. In: ICPADS 2010, pp. 706–711 (2010)
32. Payne, B., Carbone, M., Sharif, M., Lee, W.: Lares: anarchitecture for secure active monitoring using virtualization. In: SP 2008, pp. 233–247 (2008)
33. Pfoh, J., Schneider, C., Eckert, C.: Nitro: hardware-based system call tracing for virtual machines. In: AICS 2011, pp. 96–112 (2011)
34. Martignoni, L., Fattori, A., Paleari, R., Cavallaro, L.: Live and trustworthy forensic analysis of commodity production systems. In: Jha, S., Sommer, R., Kreibich, C. (eds.) RAID 2010. LNCS, vol. 6307, pp. 297–316. Springer, Heidelberg (2010)
35. Sebek. http://www.honeynet.org/tools/sebek/
36. Lin, Z., Zhang, X., Xu, D.: Automatic reverse engineering of data structures from binary execution. In: NDSS 2010 (2010)
37. Deng, Z., Xu, D., Zhang, X., Jiang, X.: Introlib: efficient and transparent library call introspection for malware forensics. In: DFRW 2012, pp.13–23 (2012)
38. Shinagawa, T., et al.: BitVisor: a thin hypervisor for enforcing I/O device security. In: VEE 2009, pp. 121–130 (2009)
39. Kirat, D., Vigna, G., Kruegel, C.: Barecloud: bare-metal analysis-based evasive malware detection. In: USENIX Security 2014, pp. 287–301 (2014)
40. Srivastava, A., Giffin, J.: Efficient monitoring of untrusted kernel-mode execution. In: NDSS 2011 (2011)
41. Srinivasan, D., Wang, Z., Jiang, X., Xu, D.: Process out-grafting: an efficient "out-of-VM" approach for fine-grained process execution monitoring. In: CCS 2011, pp. 363–374 (2011)
42. Wu, R., Chen, P., Liu, P., Andmao, B.: System call redirection: a practical approach to meeting real-world VMI needs. In: DSN 2014, pp. 574–585 (2014)
43. Gu, Z., Deng, Z., Xu, D., Jiang, X.: Process implanting: a new active introspection framework for virtualization. In: SRDS 2011, pp. 147–156 (2011)
44. Carbone, M., Conover, M., Montague, B., Lee, W.: Secure and robust monitoring of virtual machines through guest-assisted introspection. In: RAID 2012, pp. 22–41 (2012)
45. Dolan-Gavitt, B., Leek, T., Zhivich, M., Giffin, J., Lee, W.: Virtuoso: narrowing the semantic gap in virtual machine introspection. In: S&P 2011, pp. 297–312 (2011)
46. Fu, Y., Lin, Z.: Space traveling across VM: Automatically bridging the semantic gap in virtual machine introspection via online kernel data redirection. In: S&P 2012, pp. 586–600 (2012)
47. Fu, Y., Lin, Z.: Exterior: using a dual-VM based external shell for guest-OS introspection, configuration, and recovery. In: VEE 2013, pp. 97–110 (2013)
48. Sharif, M.I., Lee, W., Cui, W., Lanzi, A.: Secure in VM monitoring using hardware virtualization. In: CCS 2009, pp. 477–487 (2009)

49. Liu, Y., Xia, Y., Guan, H., Zang, B., Chen, H.: Concurrent and consistent virtual machine introspection with hardware transactional memory. In: HPCA 2014, pp. 416–427 (2014)

50. Moon, H., Lee, H., Lee, J., Kim, K., Paek, Y., Kang, B.B.: Vigilare: toward snoop-based kernel integrity monitor. In: CCS 2012, pp. 28–37 (2012)

51. Moon, H., Lee, H., Lee, J., Kim, K., Paek, Y., Kang, B.B.: Vigilare: toward snoop-based kernel integrity monitor. In: CCS 2012, pp. 28–37 (2012)

52. Azab, A.M., Ning, P., Wang, Z., Jiang, X., Zhang, X., Skalsky, N.C.: Hypersentry: enabling stealthy incontext measurement of hypervisor integrity. In: CCS 2010, pp. 38–49 (2010)

53. Bahram, S., Jiang, X., Wang, Z., Grace, M., Li, J., Srinivasan, D., Rhee, J., Xu, D.: DKSM: subverting virtual machine introspection for fun and profit. In: SRDS 2010, pp. 82–91 (2010)

54. Hund, R., Holz, T., Freiling, F.C.: Return-oriented rootkits: bypassing kernel code integrity protection mechanisms. In: USENIX Security 2009, pp. 383–398 (2009)

55. Butler, J., Hoglund, G.: Vice - catch the hookers!. In: Black Hat USA (2004)

56. Wang, Z., Jiang, X.: Hypersafe: a lightweight approach to provide lifetime hypervisor control-flow integrity. In: S&P 2010, pp. 380–395 (2010)

57. Wang, J., Stavrou, A., Ghosh, A.: Hypercheck: a hardware-assisted integrity monitor. In: Jha, S., Sommer, R., Kreibich, C. (eds.) RAID 2010. LNCS, vol. 6307, pp. 158–177. Springer, Heidelberg (2010)

58. Wang, Z., Wu, C., Grace, M., Jiang, X.: Isolating commodity hosted hypervisors with hyperlock. In: EuroSys 2012, pp. 127–140 (2012)

59. Zhang, F., Chen, J., Chen, H., Zang, B.: CloudVisor: retrofitting protection of virtual machines in multi-tenant cloud with nested virtualization. In: SOSP 2011, pp. 203–216 (2011)

60. Seshadri, A., Luk, M., Qu, N., Perring, A.: SecVisor: a tiny hypervisor to provide lifetime kernel code integrity for commodity OSes. In: SOSP 2007, pp. 335–350 (2007)

61. Litty, L., Lagar-Cavilla, H., Lie, D.: Hypervisor support for identifying covertly executing binaries. In: USENIX Security 2008, pp. 243–258 (2008)

62. Riley, R., Jiang, X., Xu, D.: Guest-transparent prevention of kernel rootkits with VMM-based memory shadowing. In: RAID 2008, pp. 1–20 (2008)

63. Hofmann, O.S., Dunn, A.M., Kim, S., Roy, I., Witchel, E.: Ensuring operating system kernel integrity with OSck. In: ASPLOS 2011, pp. 279–290 (2011)

64. Fu, Y., Zeng, J., Lin, Z.: HYPERSHELL: a practical hypervisor layer guest OS shell for automated in-VM management. In: USENIX ATC 2014, pp. 85–96 (2014)

65. Jain, B., Baig, M.B., Zhang, D., Porter, D.E., Sion, R.: SoK: introspections on trust and the semantic gap. In: S&P 2014, pp. 605–620 (2014)

66. Zhang, F., Leach, K., Sun, K., Stavrou, A.: SPECTRE: a dependable introspection framework via system management mode. In: DSN 2013, pp. 1–12 (2013)

67. Wang, Z., Jiang, X., Cui, W., Ning, P.: Countering kernel rootkits with lightweight hook protection. In: CCS 2009, pp. 545–554 (2009)

CRVad: Confidential Reasoning and Verification Towards Secure Routing in Ad Hoc Networks

Teng Li$^{(\boxtimes)}$, Jianfeng Ma, and Cong Sun

School of Cyber Engineering, Xidian University, Xi'an 710071, China
litengxidian@gmail.com

Abstract. Routing security plays an important role in the security of the entire Mobile Ad hoc Network (MANET). In this paper we discuss the issue of private-preserving verification and detection of active attack and passive attack among the peers in MANET. Due to the variability of MANET, attack detection is difficult and usually needs to expose some private data from each node. Attackers can attempt to rewrite, discard the packets or tamper their own log against the expected security requirement to confidentially forwarding the messages. The routers can be easily attacked because of the lack of checking on the message transmission. In this paper, we present CRVad, a method detecting both active and passive attacks in ad hoc network while preserving the privacy of each node. Without introducing any third party to assist this approach, CRVad can be conducted using the information we already know in the MANET and it can detect attacks of multi-hops. CRVad consists of two phases, a reasoning phase with the known confidential information to infer the expected log information of the peers, and a verification phase using Merkle Hash Tree to verify the derived information without revealing any private information of the router. To show our approach can be used to detect the attacks, we conduct our experiment in NS3, and we report the experimental results on the correctness, and efficiency of our approach.

Keywords: Ad hoc networks · Private preserving · Attack detection · Routing security · Confidential verification

1 Introduction

Different from the traditional wired network, Mobile Ad hoc Network (MANET) transports data via interconnected mobile nodes in the limited transporting area without depending on any fixed infrastructure or management center [1]. Besides, ad hoc network is lean to be attacked by some malicious routers and it needs complicated mechanisms to guarantee the security of the network. Security has become an important concern in order to provide protected communication between mobile nodes in ad hoc network environment. But the traditional security solutions for wired networks cannot be directly applied to ad hoc network

© Springer International Publishing Switzerland 2015
G. Wang et al. (Eds.): ICA3PP 2015, Part III, LNCS 9530, pp. 449–462, 2015.
DOI: 10.1007/978-3-319-27137-8_33

due to its own characteristics. The routing security of the MANET relies on the following features.

1. Self-configurable. The MANET is more likely to be attacked by malicious nodes because it is more difficult to distinguish the normal nodes from the attackers compared with wired networks. So we need a decentralized method to handle the attacks.

2. Changeable in network topology. Nodes are free to move arbitrarily, thus, the network topology, which is typically multi-hop, may change randomly and rapidly at unpredictable moments, and may consist of both bidirectional and unidirectional links. This feature leads to more obstacles to embed the security mechanism into the routing protocols of MANET, and consequently many kinds of attacks in MANET [1].

3. Various attack behaviors. Due to the mobility and the absence of centralized management nodes, the MANET is more vulnerable to attacks than wired networks. Generally, there are two different kinds of attacks, passive attacks and active attacks [2]. As for passive attacks, the attackers try to listen to the channel but do not create new packets or disrupt the regular communications. However, active attacks are designed to modify or discard the packets and attempt to influence the quality and performance of the whole network. Recent efforts have mainly focused on detecting passive attacks that just tamper the router's own log [3]. Because different kinds of attacks may be combined to vulnerate the network together, the new detection approach should be able to distinguish these two kinds of attacks and to detect both ones conjunctively.

4. Privacy preserving. Privacy should draw intensive attention in ad hoc networks. If we want to conduct the attack detection through verifications on the log of nodes in MANET, we should globally know some aspects of the nodes. This global knowledge may reveal some private data and violate potential privacy policy. For instance, PeerReview [4] collects all information of the nodes to detect faults, but it violates the privacy of each node. It seems that verification and privacy preserving are two conflict goals. But we need to achieve both goals in MANET.

With a consideration on the above features, we propose CRVad (Confidential Reasoning and Verification in Ad hoc Network) to secure the communication, detect passive and active attacks in MANET without revealing any privacy of the nodes. First, CRVad meets the self-configurability criteria and can be used in changeable environments. It can make out the malicious nodes and distinguish which attack it is. Second, considering the changeability of the network topology in MANET, CRVad takes a topology-insensitive manner. It works while the nodes are transmitting data. Third, CRVad can be used to combat both the active and passive attacks. It combines the reasoning and verification to find malicious nodes without revealing the router's privacy. Considering that the malicious nodes may affect the forwarding information, our reasoning and verification only rely on the information what we have already known and confirmed to be correct.

The rest of paper is organized as follows. Section 2 introduces the framework of CRVad. In Sect. 3, we elaborate the phases of CRVad. Experiment results and the limitations are presented in Sect. 4. We review previous related work in Sect. 5 and conclude the paper in Sect. 6.

2 Related Work

Reasoning proof. There has been a great deal of work on the reasoning, most of which uses the declarative networking [5]. The declarative networking programming language has absorbed the experience of database management system's success and divided the network into logical level and physical level. The network protocol designers only need to use the high-level programming abstraction provided by declarative networking. However, its application is mainly on the network protocol designing. On the contrary, we mainly use it as the deductive method in our paper. In recent work [3], Papadimitriou et al. also use the reasoning method, but trust the MOS as confidential information. Because of the malicious nodes in ad hoc network, we cannot trust any other node except the sender at first. The information of other nodes can only be used after they have been proved to be correct.

Passive and active attacks. In the context of ad hoc networks, there are a lot of work focusing on the attack prevention, such as [6]. But most of these work focus on secure network protocols which is a security issue before the link is built. On the contrary, our approach detects malicious behavior during the message transmission. AODV [7] and DSR [8] are efficient in terms of network performance, but they allow attackers to easily advertise falsified route information, to redirect routes, and to launch denial-of-service attacks. Several secure protocols [9,10] have been proposed to guarantee the security of the log. These protocols require that all nodes meet a certain criteria and share a common secret key. Meanwhile they only focus on either passive or active attacks but cannot handle both of them.

Privacy preserving. Initiated by NetReview [11], privacy preserving routing uses the hash-chain to preserve the privacy. PVR [12] proposes to use Merkle Hash Tree to verify BGP routing decisions. Privacy preserving is also very important in vehicular communications (VC). Li et al. propose a lightweight authenticated key establishment scheme with privacy preservation to secure the communications between mobile vehicles and roadside infrastructure in VANET [13]. They focus on the vehicular networks and our work has different background from theirs.

3 Overview and Roadmap

We consider an ad hoc network in which the connections between nodes are configured randomly. In this network, the sender finds the routes for the messages to the receiver. We trust the sender at first and get the information of it, then we use this information to verify the nodes on the routing path.

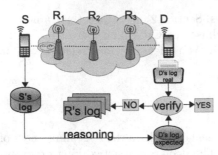
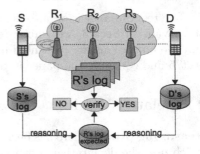

(a) The Procedure of Active Attack Detection

(b) The Procedure of Passive Attack Detection

Fig. 1. The procedure of CRVad

Considering the possibility of malicious medial routers in the network, we introduce the overview architecture of CRVad. Figure 1 shows the procedure of CRVad. It has two steps, active attack detection and passive attack detection. For each detection there are also two phases, reasoning and verification.

First, we use the confidential information in the log of message sender S to infer the log information that message receiver D should have. The log of D may be poisoned by the forwarding node R_i which may be a malicious router along the path. Therefore the receivers expected information should be deduced first using the confidential log information of the sender. Then, the validation of receiver's log should be verified from the deduced information using Merkle Hash Tree, see Fig. 1(a).

If the result is true, it means the receiver gets the correct messages. In this case, we can exclude the active attacks because the nodes R_i didn't temper or discard the forwarded messages to the receiver D. Then we know the faults during this phase in R_i may be caused by passive attacks. Detecting whether D is under passive attack requires further verifications. In order to achieve this purpose, we will use the log from both S and D to reason the log of the forwarding nodes R_i, see Fig. 1(b).

If the result is false, it means receiver D gets the wrong messages, In this case, we know there must be some forwarding nodes violating their promise to forward the messages confidentially. There may be some active attack from the forwarding nodes. We will move to the step to verify the forwarding nodes directly from the evidences of the trusted sender, i.e., using the log information from the sender S to infer and verify the nodes R_i.

After these two phases, we will know which kind of attack ad hoc network suffered and we will find the malicious nodes causing these attacks. Different from the MOS (Minimum observer sets) [3] which trust both-end nodes to deduce conclusion about the direct middle routers, in this paper we allow to trust only senders and focus on malicious forwarding by vulnerable routers. Take a simple instance to see this difference, for a MOS$\{C_1, C_2\}$, the confidential information of C_1 and C_2 are used to derive conclusions about the router S between C_1 and C_2. But actually, the information on C_2 may be faulty because of the malicious forwarding of S. In this scenario, the MOS cannot be used.

During the phases of the reasoning and the verification, CRVad may detect the faults of some nodes and our security mechanism meets the following requirements.

1. Verifiability. If a node is malicious or its behavior is abnormal, our method will find it and report this abnormality to other nodes.
2. Accuracy. If a node's behavior is normal, our method should not report any false negative to decide it to be a malicious node.
3. Self-detection. The whole reasoning and verification phases should be accomplished by ad hoc nodes themselves and the third party should be forbidden.
4. Privacy. In the verification phase, the neighbor nodes should not infer more knowledge of the verified node than what they have already learned during the message delivering.

4   Confidential Reasoning and Verification

In this section, we elaborate the method of confidential reasoning and verification of CRVad. We use the NDlog language in the reasoning phase and Merkle Hash Tree in the verification phase. An NDlog program is basically a set of rules that describe how tuples can be derived from other tuples. NDlog is a natural and compact way to implement a variety of routing protocols and describe the communication process briefly. The Merkle Hash Tree is mainly for the purpose of the privacy and verification. We check the hash value instead of searching the original data of the nodes. We demonstrate our approach under a running scenario, sending and receiving messages in ad hoc network. After the routing path setting up, the sender will know the path to the destination. The sender initializes a one-round handshaking before the sequential messages are sent to the receiver along this routing path.

4.1   NDlog and Its Syntax

NDlog is based on the Datalog. A Datalog program includes a set of declarative rules [5]. Every rule has the form p :- q_1, q_2, q_3, ..., q_n ..., which means as "q_1 and q_2 and q_3 and q_n implies p". The left side of :- is called the head of the rule and corresponds to the output or result of the query. The right side of :- is the body of the rule. It consists of a list of literals q_1, q_2, q_3, ..., q_n. A Literal is either a predicate or a function applied to fields (constants or variables). Commas separating the predicates in the right side represents logical conjunctions (AND). Then the right parts can derive the left head. Datalog rules can refer to one another in a recursive fashion. NDlog supports location specifier as a store of information in each rule. The specifier is represented as an @ symbol followed by an attribute. We illustrate NDlog using the following two simple examples:

```
ancestor(@S,X,Y) :- parent(@S,X,Y).
ancestor(@S,X,Y) :- parent(@S,X,Z), ancestor(@S,Z,Y).
```

The first rule means that if X is the parent of the Y, then X is the ancestor of Y. Both of the messages are stored in the place S. The second rule means that if

X is the parent of Z, and Z is the ancestor of Y, then X is the ancestor of Y. We can interpret the above rules as the following sentences:

```
parent(@S,X,Y) → ancestor(@S,X,Y)
parent(@S,X,Z) ∧ ancestor(@S,Z,Y) → ancestor(@S,X,Y)
```

All the messages are store in the place S.

4.2 The Deduction Rules for CRVad

First we present the rules of the messages sending and receiving, and we use the following rules to conduct the deduction.

In these rules, C means the sender's storage place, R means receiver's storage place, S means the sender, D means the receiver or the destination. M is the medial router, and MSG is the messages that sender wants to send. STAUS in sendReply' means it agrees or disagrees the previous sendRequest. STAUS in linkBuild means that whether the link between two nodes build or not. The predicate sendRequest and sendRequest have the identical semantics, the literal difference is only for the convenience of tool-supported reasoning. For instance, both sendRequest(@X,S,D) and sendRequest'(@X,S,D) have a meaning that the message request sent from S to D is logged at node X, where X = C, R or M. Similar cases can be found for the predicates sendReply, sendReply', msgAck, msgAck' and so on. When a sender performs a message sending, first it sends the request, sendRequest'(@C,S,D), to the receiver and waits for the reply from it. The request means S requests a message sending to the destination D and this request is logged at C. If the receiver is free to answer, it will send the reply sendReply'(@R,S,D,STAUS). The reply means that D replies the sender S with an answer STATUS, and D itself will log this reply at R. If the medial routers deliver the request and reply straightforwardly, i.e. Rule 1–3, the link between

Table 1. The deduction rules for CRVad

```
1.  sendRequest(@M, S, D)          :- sendRequest'(@C, S, D)
2.  sendReply(@M, S, D, STAUS)     :- sendReply'(@R, S, D, STAUS),
                                       STAUS=YES/NO
3.  linkBuild(@M, S, D, STAUS)     :- sendRequest(@M, S, D),
                                       sendReply(@M, S, D, STAUS), STAUS=YES/NO
4.  authSend(@C, S, D, STAUS)      :- linkBuild(@M, S, D, STAUS),
                                       sendRequest'(@C, S, D), STAUS=YES/NO
5.  msgForward(@M, S, D, MSG)      :- sendMsg(@C, S, D, MSG),
                                       authSend(@C, S, D, 'YES')
6.  msgRecv(@R, S, D, MSG)         :- msgForward(@M, S, D, MSG)
7.  msgAck'(@C, S, D, MSG)         :- msgRecv(@R, S, D, MSG)
8.  msgAck(@M, S, D, MSG)          :- msgAck'(@C, S, D, MSG)
9.  msgAck''(@R, S, D, MSG)        :- msgAck(@M, S, D, MSG)
10. sendMsg(@C, S, D, MSG)         :- msgRecv(@R, S, D, MSG),
                                       authSend(@C, S, D, 'YES')
```

the sender and receiver is built. If the link has been correctly built, and the sender issued a message sending request, the sender can be authorized to send the message, see Rule 4. The medial router should log the forwarded message `msgForward(@M,S,D,MSG)`, see Rule 5. If all the routers behave well, the destination will receive the messages (Rule 6) and then send the ACK to the sender (Rule 7–9). If the sender wants to send the next message, it should be authenticated and get the ACK from the destination. After that it can continue sending the messages (Rule 10). Then, the rules can go to the rule 5 and go through the above mentioned phases again.

Except for the primary rules presented in Table 1, there are still auxiliary NDlog rules to support the correct running of our whole reasoning process. For instance, due to Rule 4, Rule 5–9 and Rule 1 in Table 1, we know the following auxiliary rules hold:

```
linkBuild(@M, S, D, STAUS) :- authSend(@C, S, D, STAUS),
                                 sendRequest'(@C,S,D),STATUS=YES/NO
msgAck''(@R, S, D, MSG)     :- sendMsg(@C, S, D, MSG),
                                 authSend(@C, S, D,'YES')
sendRequest'(@C, S, D)      :- sendRequest(@M, S, D)
```

These rules proposed in Table 1 in our NDlog program can support the correct running of our whole reasoning phase.

4.3 CRVad Reasoning and Verification

CRVad Reasoning. First we use the sender's information to infer the log of the receiver. This process is denoted by $S \rightarrow D$, which consists of the reasoning of the following propositions:

$$\text{authSend(@C,S,D,'YES')} \land \text{sendRequest'(@C,S,D)} \rightarrow \text{sendReply'(@R,S,D,'YES')} \quad (1)$$

$$\text{authSend(@C,S,D,'NO')} \land \text{sendRequest'(@C,S,D)} \rightarrow \text{sendReply'(@R,S,D,'NO')} \quad (2)$$

$$\text{sendMsg(@C,S,D,MSG)} \land \text{authSend(@C,S,D,'YES')} \mapsto \text{msgRecv(@R,S,D,MSG)} \quad (3)$$

We can use the information of S to deduce the information of D according to our rules. Using these rules, we can infer whether D is normal or malicious from D's log. There are several choices on deducing whether D is valid. One choice is to collect all information of D, then deduce whether the derived messages belong to the whole log. But this approach violates our security goal on privacy. We have to learn all the private information in D's log before we can verify the derived message. So how can we achieve a privacy-preserving verification which protects the privacy of individual log at the same time? Next, we will use the Merkle Hash Trees to conduct this phase of verification.

Privacy-Preserving Verification. In this section, we introduce how can we use the derived information to conduct the privacy-preserving verification. The purpose of verification is to ensure the expected actions or messages derived in the reasoning phase do exist in the log of related nodes.

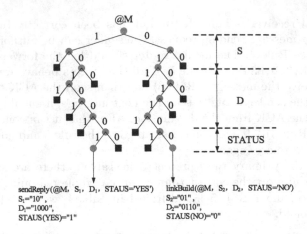

Fig. 2. Merkle Hash Tree

We use the Merkle Hash Tree [14] (MHT) as the mechanism to preserve the privacy during the verification. MHT is a tree in which every non-leaf node is labeled with the hash value of the labels of its children nodes, and every leaf node is labeled with the hash value of real data. As a kind of binary tree, the edges of MHT from every parent's node to its two children are tagged with 0 and 1 respectively, see Fig. 2.

Before we build the tree, we should first encode our information. Take the following message encoding for example, sendReply(@M,S_1,D_1,STAUS='YES') can be encoded by specifying S_1="10", D_1="1000", STAUS(YES)="1". The message linkBuild(@M,S_2,D_2,STAUS='NO') can be encoded by specifying S_2="01", D_2="0110", STAUS(NO)="0".

How many bits does the variables, such as S_1 and S_2, cost for the message encoding will depend on the number of the nodes and number of the variables. Our goal is to distinguish each message on different nodes.

After we encode the message sendReply(@M,S_1,D_1,STAUS='YES') as a string "1010001", we use it to build the tree. Each router will build a Merkle Hash Tree using its log information. We label the node's left child as 1 right child as 0. With the string, we can build up a tree, which is stored as an array.

Now we can calculate the hash value of each node: H_i=(H(node_num$\|$ bit_data $\|$parent_num$\|$parent_bit_data)$\|$ $H_{\text{left\_child}}\|$ $H_{\text{right\_child}}$). As an index of node array, node_num specifies the array element w.r.t the current node. Similarly, parent_num specifies the array element w.r.t the parent of current node. Also bit_data and parent_bit_data are respectively the value of current node and parent node, which can be either 0 or 1. When a node is the root of MHT, we define parent_bit_data of this node as 'X'. $H_{\text{left\_child}}$ and $H_{\text{right\_child}}$ are respectively the hash value of the left child and right child. They will be empty if the current node is leaf node. We can calculate the hash value from the leaf node to the root, and this value will be published. That means every node may know the root hash value of any other nodes.

In the verification phase, the router S_1 infer the information `sendReply'` (`@R,S_1,D_1,STAUS='YES'`) of D_1, then S_1 will ask D_1 whether you have such information. D_1 use the string `"1010001"` to find the leaf node in its own hash tree and then provide the leaf's brother hash value and the `node_num`, `parent_num`, `parent_bit_data` of the leaf. Then S_1 can use these values to calculate the root hash of the tree. If the latter equals to the published value, the verification result is true.

4.4 CRVad Algorithm

First we define S as the sender and D as the receiver, R_i represents the medial routers $(R_1, R_2, \ldots R_n)$. Algorithm 1 shows the whole algorithm.

1. We use the log of S to deduce the prospective results about the log of D, and use the results to verify the D's real log with the Merkle Hash Tree. If the correctness of D's log is verified, it means there is no active attack between S and D, then we just go to the step 3 to detect passive attacks; otherwise go to the step 2 to detect active attacks.
2. We use the log of S to deduce the prospective results about the log of the medial routers R_i, where i ranges from n to 0. Then we use the results to verify the real log of R_i with the Merkle Hash Tree. If we find any violation, there exists some active attack between S and R_i. We reduce i to i-1 to find the exact malicious node that performs active attack. Otherwise we know the active attack occurs between R_{i+1} and R_n, and R_{i+1} must be malicious.
3. We use the log of S and D to reason the prospective results about the log of the medial routers R_i and use the results to verify the real log of R_i with the Merkle Hash Tree. If a violation is found, there exists some passive attack and the router R_i had the malicious behavior.

4.5 Active and Passive Attack Detection

The predicate ActiveAttackDetected() and PassiveAttackDetected() in Algorithm 1 are used to detect the active and passive attacks. In these detections, we have both the reasoning phase and the privacy-preserving verification phase.

Active Attack Reasoning and Verification. If there are some errors in $S \Rightarrow D$, that means the medial routers didn't keep their promise to confidentially forward the messages, and we know D's errors are caused by the active tempering of the medial routers. Then we can move to the step of checking the forwarding router R. First we should conduct the process $S \Rightarrow R$. In this process we should reason the following proposition:

$$\text{sendRequest'}(@C, S, D) \rightarrow \text{sendRequest}(@M, S, D) \tag{4}$$

$$\text{authSend}(@C, S, D, 'YES') \wedge \text{sendRequest'}(@C, S, D) \rightarrow \text{linkBuild}(@M, S, D, 'YES') \tag{5}$$

$$\text{sendMsg}(@C, S, D, MSG) \wedge \text{authSend}(@C, S, D, 'YES') \rightarrow \text{msgForward}(@M, S, D, MSG) \tag{6}$$

Algorithm 1. CRVad Algorithm

1: n = medial routers number
2: $S \Rightarrow D$
3: **if** !ActiveAttackDetected($S \Rightarrow D$) **then**
4:    **for** $i = 0$ to n **do**
5:       ▷ Check the passive attack ;
6:       **if** PassiveAttackDetected($S + D \Rightarrow R_i$) **then**
7:          **return** "R_i has passive attack."
8:       **end if**
9:    **end for**
10:    **return** "No attack found."
11: **else**
12:    **for** $i = n$ to 0 **do**
13:       ▷ Check the active attack ;
14:       **if** ActiveAttackDetected($S \Rightarrow R_i$) **then**
15:          continue;
16:       **end if**
17:       **if** $i == n$ **then**
18:          **return** "D itself changes the log."
19:       **else**
20:          **return** "R_{i+1} has active attack, and R_{i+2} to R_n might have active attack."
21:       **end if**
22:    **end for**
23: **end if**

In most cases, the route path often has more than one hop to the destination. For example, N_1-N_2-N_5-N_7-N_{10}, the medial routers are N_2, N_5, N_7. So we should check them one by one from the farmost router to the nearest router. The derived messages are expected to be existing on each medial router. For instance, the derived message `sendRequest(@M,S,D)` means that we expect the message `sendRequest(@N2,S,D)`, `sendRequest(@N5,S,D)`, and `sendRequest(@N7,S,D)` exist on the node N_2, N_5, and N_7 respectively. Then we can use the Merkle Hash Tree to verify the real log of these routers.

Passive Attack Reasoning and Verification. If the active attacks are not detected in $S \Rightarrow D$ and $S \Rightarrow R$, this indicates the routers just truly transmit the messages. But they may temper their own log data. Here we can use the real log of D, because we have proved the correctness of D's log. We call this process as $S+D \Rightarrow R$. In this process we should reason the following proposition:

$$\texttt{sendRequest'(@C, S, D)} \rightarrow \texttt{sendRequest(@M, S, D)} \tag{7}$$

$$\texttt{sendRequest'(@C, S, D)} \wedge \texttt{sendReply'(@R, S, D,'YES')} \rightarrow \texttt{linkBuild(@M, S, D,'YES')} \tag{8}$$

$$\texttt{sendMsg(@C, S, D, MSG)} \wedge \texttt{authSend(@C, S, D,'YES')} \rightarrow \texttt{msgForward(@M, S, D, MSG)} \tag{9}$$

$$\texttt{msgAck'(@C, S, D, MSG)} \rightarrow \texttt{msgAck(@M, S, D, MSG)} \tag{10}$$

Then we use the Mekle Hash Tree to verify that the real log of medial routers comply with the expected log information, e.g. `linkBuild(@M, S, D, STAUS)`.

5   Evaluation

In this section, we evaluate CRVad through our experiment results. Specifically, our goal is to answer the following high-level research questions.

RQ1. How can the reasoning process run automatically and correctly?

RQ1. Can CRVad detect the mistakes of the router in the network?

5.1   Experiment Setup

We use the tool IRIS (Integrated Rule Inference System), an open source tool, to conduct our reasoning process, and prove the conclusions we inferred are correct. All the reasoning results we use has been wrote in NDlog and verified on IRIS. We use NS3 to conduct our sending and receiving experiment. First is the one hop topology and then we increase it to two hops. Finally is the multi-hop topology. We let one node send messages to other nodes of different areas or with different network address through the medial nodes. We use the tracing system in NS3 to get the content of the log. Then each node can use these kinds of information to build up the Merkle Hash Tree.

5.2   Experimental Results

In this part we show our experimental results to answer the research questions mentioned above.

RQ1. We use the IRIS to conduct our reasoning process. We first extract the sending and receiving rules from the logs. According to these rules, we write the NDlog program and run it in IRIS. The time and spatial cost of the reasoning of each rule are given in Figs. 3 and 4.

From Fig. 3 we can see that the less the steps and variables needed for the conduction, the less the time costs. The memory cost is mainly affected by the variety of the variables. To make sure the correctness of the reasoning results, we also conduct the whole deduction phase manually. We can get the same results we receive from the IRIS.

RQ2. We use NS3 to simulate ad hoc network environment and let the nodes send and receive packets. At the same time, the log file for each node will be created as .pcap file. Each node reads the file and uses the information to build up the Merkle Hash Tree and conducts the verification phase. The time and spatial cost of the tree-build and verification phase are respectively given in Figs. 5 and 6. *Msg Code Len* denotes the length of bit string which encodes the messages. We can see both the time and spatial cost roughly increase along with

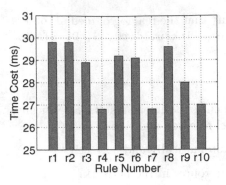

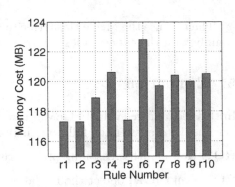

Fig. 3. Time cost of the reasoning

Fig. 4. Memory cost of the reasoning

the increase on the number of logs. But the overall cost is limited and the results show that our approach is practical for use on real network logs.

Take the message `sendReply(@M,S₁,D₁,STAUS='YES')`, whose string code is `"1010001"` for example, if we verify this message, we can find it from the MHT. The whole root hash is `"56cf61dc988c9e1873f10d9ba8db91611f1a60e56bd53a5ed2d14d95cdea6b45"`. We calculate the hash from the leaf node, and finally we will work out the same value. If the router deliberately changes the message and the bit string will turn to, such as `"0011101"`, which is not expected to be the correct log message. We will get the value of `"3f89e081cf9b97df1cdc5c3218ea4ab457318a81725bba9667a2556428c9bcfc"`. It is not equal to the root value from

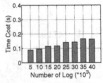 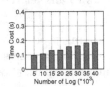 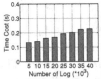 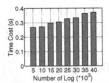

(a) Msg Code Len=4   (b) Msg Code Len=6   (c) Msg Code Len=8   (d) Msg Code Len=10

Fig. 5. Time cost of tree-build and verification

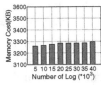 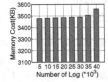 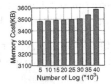

(a) Msg Code Len=4   (b) Msg Code Len=6   (c) Msg Code Len=8   (d) Msg Code Len=10

Fig. 6. Memory cost of tree-build and verification

the result. We can detect the change of the information and then determine that the owner of the information has the malicious behavior.

5.3   Limitation

In this section, we discuss some of the limitations and the prospective future work.

Focusing on the first malicious node. CRVad always detects the first malicious node in the routing path. If the link has more than one malicious nodes, we can just detect the first malicious node. The next malicious node can only be detected after fixing the previous one. Because CRVad depends on the confidential information, if the malicious nodes hide in downstream behind the first malicious node, CRVad cannot distinguish it and we treat all the downstream nodes as poisoned by the first malicious node. We should eliminate this malicious node from the route path and then run the next round reasoning and verification phases to detect the other malicious nodes. In the future, we plan to expand our approach to detect multiple nodes at the same time.

Focusing on message transmission established routing path. CRVad can only be used when the routing path has been determined and has some messages transported. It cannot detect the malicious nodes before the path is established, because we should know which nodes are involved in the messages sending and receiving from the log of nodes and the malicious nodes behave abnormally only during the message transmission phase.

6   Conclusion

In this paper, we propose an approach, CRVad, to automatically detect attacks by reasoning and verifying the nodes in ad hoc network. We use NDlog in reasoning expected log information and Merkle Hash Tree in the verification to imply the privacy-preserving detection of the active and passive attacks. Given the sender's confidential log, we first perform the reasoning, and decide whether the expected log information is matched with the fact from the real log of the receiver and medial routers. According to the algorithm of CRVad, we can detect which router is malicious and what kind of attack it meets without revealing any private information of each node. Our approach is scalable and practical for use on real ad hoc network.

Acknowledgments. This work was supported by the Key Program of NSFC-Guangdong Union Foundation (No. U1135002), The Key Program of NSFC (No. U1405 255), the National High Technology Research and Development Program (863 Program) of China (No. 2015AA011102, 2015AA011704), the National Natural Science Foundation of China (No. 61303033), and the Aviation Science Foundation of China (No. 2013ZC31003, 20141931001).

References

1. Abusalah, L., Khokhar, A., Guizani, M.: A survey of secure mobile ad hoc routing protocols. IEEE Commun. Surv. Tutorials **10**(4), 78–93 (2008)
2. Pirzada, A.A., McDonald, C.: Establishing trust in pure ad-hoc networks. In: Proceedings of the 27th Australasian Conference on Computer Science, vol. 26, pp. 47–54. Australian Computer Society, Inc. (2004)
3. Papadimitriou, A., Zhao, M., Haeberlen, A.: Towards privacy-preserving fault detection. In: Proceedings of the 9th Workshop on Hot Topics in Dependable Systems, Article no. 6. ACM (2013)
4. Haeberlen, A., Kouznetsov, P., Druschel, P.: Peerreview: practical accountability for distributed systems. In: ACM SIGOPS Operating Systems Review, vol. 41, pp. 175–188. ACM (2007)
5. Loo, B.T., Condie, T., Garofalakis, M., Gay, D.E., Hellerstein, J.M., Maniatis, P., Ramakrishnan, R., Roscoe, T., Stoica, I.: Declarative networking. Commun. ACM **52**(11), 87–95 (2009)
6. Hauser, R., Przygienda, T., Tsudik, G.: Lowering security overhead in link state routing. Comput. Netw. **31**(8), 885–894 (1999)
7. Perkins, C., Belding-Royer, E., Das, S.: Ad hoc on-demand distance vector (AODV) routing. Technical report (2003)
8. Johnson, D.B., Maltz, D.A., Hu, Y.C., Jetcheva, J.: The dynamic source routing (DSR) protocol for mobile ad hoc networks. IETF Draft, draft-ietf-manet-dsr-009. txt (2003)
9. Yi, S., Naldurg, P., Kravets, R.: Security-aware ad hoc routing for wireless networks. In: Proceedings of the 2nd ACM International Symposium on Mobile Ad Hoc Networking and Computing, pp. 299–302. ACM (2001)
10. Venkatraman, L., Agrawal, D.P.: Strategies for enhancing routing security in protocols for mobile ad hoc networks. J. Parallel Distrib. Comput. **63**(2), 214–227 (2003)
11. Haeberlen, A., Avramopoulos, I.C., Rexford, J., Druschel, P.: Netreview: detecting when interdomain routing goes wrong. In: NSDI, pp. 437–452 (2009)
12. Zhao, M., Zhou, W., Gurney, A.J., Haeberlen, A., Sherr, M., Loo, B.T.: Private and verifiable interdomain routing decisions. In: Proceedings of the ACM SIGCOMM 2012 Conference on Applications, Technologies, Architectures, and Protocols for Computer Communication, pp. 383–394. ACM (2012)
13. Li, C.T., Hwang, M.S., Chu, Y.P.: A secure and efficient communication scheme with authenticated key establishment and privacy preserving for vehicular ad hoc networks. Comput. Commun. **31**(12), 2803–2814 (2008)
14. Merkle, R.C.: Protocols for public key cryptosystems. In: null, p. 122. IEEE (1980)

NMHP: A Privacy Preserving Profile Matching Protocol in Multi-hop Proximity Mobile Social Networks

Entao Luo[1,3], Qin Liu[2], and Guojun Wang[1,4]($\boxtimes$)

[1] School of Information Science and Engineering, Central South University,
Changsha 410083, China
{cs_entaoluo,csgjwang}@csu.edu.cn
[2] School of Information Science and Engineering, Hunan University,
Changsha 410082, China
gracelq628@hnu.edu.cn
[3] School of Electronics and Information Engineering,
Hunan University of Science and Engineering, Yongzhou 425199, China
[4] School of Computer Science and Educational Software,
Guangzhou University, Guangzhou 510006, China

Abstract. With the rapid development of mobile devices and online social networks, users in Proximity-based Mobile Social Networks (PMSNs) can easily discover and make new social interactions with others by profile matching. The profiles usually contain sensitive personal information, while the emerging requirement of profile matching in proximity mobile social networks may occasionally leak the sensitive information and hence violate people's privacy. In this paper, we propose a multi-hop profile matching protocol (NMHP) in PMSNs. By using our protocol, users can customize the matching matrices to involve their own matching preference and to make the matching results more precise. In addition, to achieve a secure and efficient matching, we utilize the confusion matrix transformation and the idea of multi-hop, which means we make profile matching within several hops instead one. Security analysis shows that our proposed protocol can realize privacy-preserving friend discovery with higher efficiency.

Keywords: Profile matching · Friend discovery · Trusted third party · Confusion matrix · Dot production

1 Introduction

With the increasing popularity of mobile devices (e.g., smart phones) and the great advancement of online social networking, Mobile Social Networks (MSN) have become a vital part in our daily life [20]. Especially, the explosive growth of mobile-connected and location-aware devices makes it possible and meaningful to do MSN in proximity (PMSNs) [16,17]. Proximity-based Mobile Social Networks

© Springer International Publishing Switzerland 2015
G. Wang et al. (Eds.): ICA3PP 2015, Part III, LNCS 9530, pp. 463–474, 2015.
DOI: 10.1007/978-3-319-27137-8_34

(PMSNs) is one of the fastest-growing activities among mobile users. Nowadays, users can discover and make new social interactions easily with physical-proximate mobile users through Wi-Fi or Bluetooth interfaces embedded in their Smartphone or Tablet.

Fig. 1. Profile matching in friend discovery

In PMSNs, in order to join and enjoy the social activities, users usually begin by creating a profile, then interact with other users. In the process, it is necessary to disclose some personal and private information, it is clearly that, the user's privacy may be revealed during such process. However, users' profile may include some sensitive information, so it is dangerous to leak them to nearby strangers.

In order to solve this problem, a group of private matching protocols have been proposed recently, among which these protocols, some protect users' privacy with reliance on a TTP (Trusted Third Party) [3,8,10,12]. In TTP-based approaches, TTP is the bottleneck from both the security and system performance points of view. The reason is that the TTP needs to know all the users' interests to perform the matching process, so it is quite dangerous when the TTP is compromised.

In the other TTP-free schemes, there are two mainstreams of approaches to solve this problem. The first category treats a user's profile as a set of attributes and provides private attributes matching based on private set intersection (PSI) and private cardinality of set intersection (PCSI) [7,15]. The second category considers a user's profile as a vector and measures the social proximity by private vector dot production [5,19].

Although the above mentioned protocols can provide private matching, most of them use complicated cryptographic computation to ensure the privacy, which are not efficient enough for the resource-restricted mobile devices. For example, homomorphic encryption and decryption are used in [4,6,13], introducing more computation overhead due to modulus exponentiation and modulus multiplication. BGN cryptosystem [1] is employed in [2,14], which also requires a large amount of computation resource. Commutative Encryption Function [18] is used in [20], which also needs a lot time to do the encryption. In addition, Zhu et al. adopted the confusion matrix model, however, she only considered the friends that can be matched within 1-hop range, which may not be the best match.

To reduce the computation cost in existing protocols and not rely on TTP, according to nonhomomorphic encryption-based privacy-preserving scalar product computation [9], we propose a novel multi-hop protocol (NMHP) by employing confusion matrix transformation algorithm instead of complex computations. The main contributions of this paper are shown as follows.

(1) We propose TTP-free protocol (NMHP), in our protocol, we protect users' profile item details during the matching.

(2) We use the lightweight confusion matrix transformation algorithm instead of public-key cryptosystem and homomorphic encryption in NMHP.

(3) We consider profile matching in multi-hop instead of one hop, in this way, we can find the better match within a wider range.

The rest of this paper is organized as follows. Section 2 shows some preliminaries in our work. Following in Sect. 3, we describe the details of our proposed protocol and prove the correctness of our protocol. Sections 4 and 5 give the security analysis and performance evaluation. Finally, we draw the conclusions in Sect. 6.

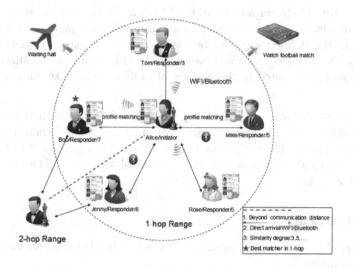

Fig. 2. Multi-hop profile matching process

2   Relate Definition

2.1   System Model

The whole process can be divided into two phases, illustrated by Figs. 1 and 2.

(1) The 1-Hop Friend Discovery Matching Phase. When user joins social networks, they usually begin by creating a profile, and then interact with other users. He/She will broadcast his/her personality profile in the list of neighbors within the 1-hop range. In the process, we mainly use the dot product and matrix confusion algorithm to obtain the degree of similarity between two users. In this way, we can find the *initiator*'s best matcher user in the 1-hop range.

(2) The Multi-hop Friend Discovery Matching Phase. Actually, there is often no suitable friend in 1-hop, so we need to use the multi-hop ideas in our protocol. We use *responder* as an agent to forward the *initiator*'s personality profile and calculate the degree of similarity between the next hop or multi-hop user.

2.2   Adversary Model

In the profile matching phase, if a party obtains one or more users (partial or full) attribute sets without their explicit consents, it is said to conduct user profiling attacks [9]. In this paper, we consider two types of user profiling attacks.

(1) Honest but Curious Adversaries Model. The honest but-curious (HBC) adversary is a legitimate participant in a communication protocol who will not deviate from the defined protocol but will attempt to learn all possible information from legitimately received messages. In this paper, we assume that the attacker is more interested in the privacy of mobile social network actors.

(2) Malicious Adversaries Model. A user who may launch some active attacks do not honestly follows the protocol but tries to learn more information than allowed. These adversaries may behave arbitrarily and are not bound in any way to follow a specified protocol. Such as denial-of-service (DoS) and continuous fake-profile attacks.

2.3   Design Goal

Our main goal is to achieve a secure private matching between an *initiator* and several *responders*.

(1) Definition 1. Level-I Privacy. When the protocol process ends, the *initiator* and each *responder* should only know the size of the intersection set of their attributes (the attribute degree of similarity) set mutually. Any other attribute information should not be known by any other party.

(2) Definition 2. Level-II Privacy. When the protocol process ends, it is assumed that the outside attacker can intercept the user's interaction information, but the outside attacker can not decrypt or recover the user's details.

3   Friend Discovery Privacy Preserving Profile Matching

In this section, we propose our profile matching protocol in privacy-preserving proximity-based mobile social networks. As shown in Fig. 2. Firstly, we will introduce the basic idea behind the proposed protocol. Then, we will introduce the

Table 1. Summary of notations

Notation	Description
$MA_{l\times n}$, $MA^*_{l\times n}$	The *initiator* profile matrix and confusion profile matrix
$MC_{l\times n}$, $MD_{l\times n}$	Randomly generate two matrixes
α, β	Two large prime
$E()$	Asymmetric encryption function
PK, SK	Public key and private key
$H()$	Hash function
$\overrightarrow{K}$	The secret key to help get original results
$MB_{l\times n}$, $MB^T_{l\times n}$	The *responder* profile matrix, the transpose of $MB_{l\times n}$
D	The product of matrix MA^* and MB^T
$(W_{ij})_{l\times l}$	The weight degree between *initiator* and *responder*
λ_{max}	The similarity between the *initiator* and *responder*
λ'_{max}	The similarity between the *initiator* and *responder* in n-hop
MSG_{I2R}	MSG from the *initiator* to the *responder*
MSG_{R2I}	MSG from the *responder* to the *initiator*
MSG_{A2R}	MSG from the *agent* to the *responder*

protocol in details. It mainly consists of the following three phases: system initialization, the 1-hop friend discovery matching phase, and the multi-hop friend discovery matching phase. The summary of notations used in our protocol is shown in Table 1.

3.1 The System Initialization Phase

During this stage *Alice* and other users who are willing to participate in social activities will start installing applications on their Smartphone or Tablet, in our designed mechanism, this application includes a number of functional modules each functional module will correspond to an actual application scenario and a user list. In a scenario, social users can choose their own interests and preferences for variety of presetting options, thus forming a property of profile, then *Alice* broadcast the profile to the her own user list, to start with interesting social activities. Specific friend discovery profile matching process see Sect. 3.2.

3.2 The 1-hop Friend Discovery Matching Phase

Alice first runs the following steps to start the preparation of the matching (see Fig. 3).

Step 1-Matrix-Confusion. In our protocol, we assume the PMSNs application developers define a public attribute set in advance, which consists of n attributes

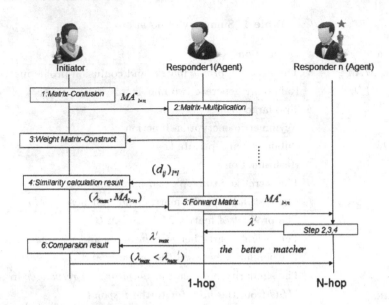

Fig. 3. Working processes of NMHP

$I = \{I_1, I_2, ...I_n\}$, when a user first joins the application, he/she will select a corresponding integer $i \in [1, l]$, (l called as the weight of an attribute) for each attribute to indicates the level of interest. l could be a small integer, say 2–10, which may be sufficient to differentiate user's interest level. Given n user attribute and l kinds of user interest level weight, we can organize the set of rating scores as a $n - by - l$ rating matrix $MA_{l \times n}$, this matrix can completely describe an user's profile, in which the row vectors indicate the weight of interest and column vectors mean the public attribute.

Alice first chooses a subset of $I_{Alice} = \{I_{ai1}, I_{ai2}, ...I_{aij}\}$ to indicate the profile items she wants to match with *Bob*, i.e., $MA_{l \times n}$, where a_{ij} denotes the user's interest level of the $j'th$ attribute in the public attribute set is i, $a_{ij} \in [0, 1]$. For example, if the *Alice*'s interest level of the $5'th$ attribute in the public attribute set is 3, he set $a_{35} = 1$ and $a_{n5} = 0$.

$$MA_{l \times n} = \begin{bmatrix} a_{11} & a_{12} & ... & a_{1n} \\ a_{21} & a_{22} & ... & a_{2n} \\ ... & ... & ... & ... \\ a_{l1} & a_{l2} & ... & a_{ln} \end{bmatrix}$$

Secondly, she choose two large prime α, β, where $|\alpha| = 256, \beta > (n+1)l^2\alpha^2$. Meanwhile, *Alice* randomly generate two matrixes $MC_{l \times n}$ and $MD_{l \times n}$, used for hiding personal information, computes the two large prime with $MA_{l \times n}$ and gets $MA^*_{l \times n}$. After that, *Alice* sends Msg_{I2R} as a matching query to *Bob* through her mobile device. The messages from *initiator* to the *responder* are:

$$Msg_{I2R} = \{MA^*_{l \times n}, ID_i, H(D_i), Q, t\} \tag{1}$$

where $MA^*_{l \times n}$ is a confusion matrix, which contains the weight of interest and public attribute of *initiator*. ID_i is the identity of the *initiator* (e.g., IP address), $H(ID_i)$ stands for the hash value of ID_i. Q denotes friend discovery query, and t refers to the time point at which the user gets the result from the *responder*. If beyond t, this information will be abandoned or relaunched.

Step 2-Matrix-Multiplication. After receiving *Alice*'s matching query Msg_{I2R}, *Bob* dose the following: Firstly, *Bob* will use the public hash function $H()$ to check the correctness of *Alice*'s identity information. i.e., $H()+ID_i = H(ID_i)$. Secondly, if *Bob* (or other *responders*) is also interested in profile matching, then he/she will choose a subset of $I_{Bob} = \{I_{bi1}, I_{bi2}, ...I_{bin}\}$ to indicate the profile items and construct a *responder* matrix that he wants to match with *Alice*, i.e., $MB_{l \times n}$, and computes the intersection of $MA_{l \times n}{}^*$ and $MB^T_{l \times n}$. If they have same interest, the value will be 1, or will be 0. When the process ends, *Bob* gets a matrix $D = MA^*_{l \times n} * MB^T_{l \times n} = (d_{ij})_{l*l}$. Lastly, *Bob* sends Msg_{R2I} as a reply of the matching to *Alice* through his mobile device. The messages from the *responder* to *initiator* are:

$$Msg_{R2I} = \{D, H(D), ID_R, H(ID_r), PK_{Bob}, t\} \tag{2}$$

where ID_r is the identity of the *responder*, The public key is the groundwork for the following task. $H(ID_r)$, $H(D)$ are ID_r's, D's hash value, mainly used to verify the value of ID_r and D whether being modified by the external attackers in the transmission process.

Step 3-Weight Matrix-Construct. When *Alice* receives *Bob* message Msg_{R2I}, she will verity the message. After verifying, *Alice* will construct a weight matrix $(W_{ij})_{l \times l}$, the weight matrix can indicate the different attention (interest) degree for the attributes between *initiator* and *responder*, we describe the generation of the element $(W_{ij})_{l \times l}$ according to the Formula-3:

$$(W_{ij})_{l \times l} = \begin{cases} i; & i = j; \\ i - |i - j|; & (i - |i - j|) > 1; \\ 1; & (i - |i - j|) \leq 1; \end{cases} \tag{3}$$

Step 4-Similarity Calculation Results. In this step, *Alice* runs Algorithm 1 to get T^*. Meanwhile, *Alice* uses T^* and $(W_{ij})_{l \times l}$ to make dot production. Up to now, *Alice* can get the match value λ_{Bob}, then she knows the similarity with *Bob*. And so on, *Alice* can knows the similarity value with the other *responder* in 1-hop. i.e., $\lambda = [\lambda_1 \lambda_2 ... \lambda_n]$. Until now, *Alice* can choose the user who has the largest similarity value λ_{max} in the 1-hop region as the best matcher.

We assume *Bob* is the best match user, he also wants to make friends with *Alice*, so *Alice* will start a session process and send a message to *Bob*.

$$Msg_{I2R} = \{PK_{Alice}, E_{PK_{Bob}}(C)\} \tag{4}$$

where $E_{PK_{Bob}}(C)$ is cipher text which is encrypted by *Bob*'s public key, C is a specific session content (plain text).

Algorithm 1. Similarity Calculation Results Algorithm

Input:

   Alice received *Bob* computer results $D = (d_{ij})_{l*l}$;

Output:

   Generate similarity value λ by *Alice* and *Bob*'s matrix dot production;

1: *Alice* computer $T = (t_{ij})_{l*l}$, $t_{ij} = (d_{ij} + k_i) \bmod \alpha$, $for\, d_{ij} \in D_{l \times l}$;

2: *Alice* makes a further transformation to get $T^* = \frac{t_{ij} - (t_{ij} \bmod \alpha^2)}{\alpha^2}$;

3: *Alice* considers the corresponding weights and computes $H_{l \times l} = T^*_{l \times l} \circ (W_{ij})_{l \times l}$, "$\circ$" is dot production;

4: Up to now,we can get the match (similarity) value $\lambda = \sum\limits_{i=1}^{l} \sum\limits_{j=1}^{l} h_{ij}$;

5: **return** λ.

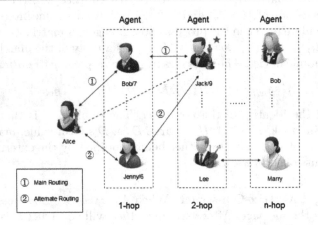

Fig. 4. Multi-hop friend discovery profile matching process

3.3   The Multi-hop Friend Discovery Matching Phase

Step 5-Forward the Initiator Profile Matrix. In the actual scenario, in 1-hop range the chances of finding a friend who has the similar interests and hobbies are usually limited, so we use the idea of multi-hop in the network, use a responder as a agent to forward the initiator profile to find the better match user, then we may find the largest similarity degree friend with *Alice* in a wider range (see Fig. 4).

In this section, in order to simply describe the process, we set the routing as two hops, *Alice* as a initiator, *Bob* and *Jenny* are *Alice*'s neighbors in 1-hop range, *Alice* can not directly through the Wi-Fi and Bluetooth communicate with *Jack* (beyond the range of communication), *Bob*, *Jenny*, and *Jack* can communicate directly (they are neighbors in a hop range); Firstly, in order to expand the range of friend discovery, *Alice* will randomly select a user (we assume the user is *Bob*) from her user list as a agent for forwarding her profile ($MA^*_{l \times n}$) and the max similarity value (λ_{max}); Secondly, *Jack* receives this profile, he will carry out matrix calculation; Lastly, *Bob* will calculate the similarity result with dot product. This process is the same as *Step 2, 3, 4*, the messages from the agent (*Bob*) to *responder* (*Jack*) are:

$$Msg_{A2R} = \{\lambda_{max}, MA^*_{l \times n}, ID_{agent}, t\}. \tag{5}$$

Step 6-Comparison of Results. Via calculation *Bob* can get the match value λ_{Jack}, then *Bob* knows the similarity with *Jack*, and he will compare λ_{Jack} with λ_{max}, when $\lambda_{jack} > \lambda_{max}$, *Bob* will forward the result to *Alice*. So far, *Alice* decides whether or not to build up a communication relationship with *Jack*.

Otherwise *Alice* knows that the search for a matching user has failed in the 2-round. And she will choose the best match user in the first round or continue to search for matching users in the next hop.

4 Security Analysis

4.1 Resistance to Attacks from HBC Model

(1) Privacy of the *Initiator*. In our protocol, *Alice* does not directly send her interested profile to *Bob*, The *initiator* reveals his/her personal profile matrix $MA^*_{l \times n}$ to the potential *responder*s in vicinity, all the elements in this transition matrix $MA^*_{l \times n}$ are randomly generated by two large prime α, β, meanwhile, we use the random matrix $MC_{l \times n}, MD_{l \times n}$ to make a confusion about the original matrix, and each of random number in the matrix is used only once in the interactive process. So it is very difficult for the *responder* to recover the *initiator* profile. This method is proved to be secure in [9]. Therefore, except for the profile items *Alice* and *Bob* are both interested in, the names of other unnecessary items are all protected.

(2) Privacy of the *Responder*. In our protocol, elements in matrix $MB_{l \times n}$ is also privacy-preserving using the large prime β and matrix multiplication, obviously, the unknown a^*_{ix} will hide the operation on each $D = (d_{ij})_{l*l}$, although *Alice* can decrypt the data *Bob* sends to him, say Msg_{R2I}, because of the determined operation properties of the matrix, *Alice* will not monitor the matching process and decrypt the intermediate results to get the original results of $MA_{l \times n} * MB^T_{l \times n}$, so *Alice* learns nothing about the *responder* other than the matching value. The privacy of the *responder* can be protected too. Moreover, any other sensitive information (e.g., *responder* attributes, interest level etc.) cannot be inferred from the exponentiated values they receive.

4.2 Defense Against Outside Adversary

If external adversary would like to use the background knowledge to build attack dictionary to attack on the user, then this dictionary will be very large to make the dictionary profiling. This is due to the attribute could be the user's personal information including profession, interest, favorite song, etc. So in most cases, it is very difficult for the external adversary trying to get the user's attribute information to get through the brute force.

In our protocol, all the delivered important information will be processed by a hash function H() to get a hash value, this value is also included in the message, when users get the message, they can check if the information is modified or not by comparing the hash value. Furthermore, we assume that an attacker intercepts information through an insecure channel. However, because we use asymmetric encryption algorithm, the external attacker does not know the user's private key, so he has no way to recover the information. Hence, our protocol can resist external attackers.

5   Performance Evaluation

In this section, we evaluate the performance of the proposed protocol in terms of computation complexity and communication overhead in the mobile social networks. At the same time, we compare our protocol's privacy preserving degree.

Table 2. Comparison of related work

Protocol	Offline		Online		Communication.(bits)	
	Initiator	Responder	Initiator	Responder	Initiator	Responder
NMHP	$l \cdot n \cdot mul1 + 2l \cdot n \cdot add$	$\sim$	$2l \cdot l \cdot mul1 + 3l \cdot l \cdot n \cdot add$	$2l \cdot l \cdot mul1 + 3l \cdot l \cdot n \cdot add + l.n.mul1 + l.n.add$	$(l.+2) \cdot 1024$	$2(l \cdot l) \cdot 1024$
WAS [11]	$n \cdot exp1 + n \cdot h$	$n \cdot exp1 + n \cdot h$	$n \cdot exp1$	$n \cdot exp1$	$2n \cdot 1024$	$(n+2) \cdot 1024$
Fine-grained [19]	$2l \cdot n \cdot exp1 + l \cdot n \cdot mul2$	$\sim$	$1 \cdot exp2$	$1 \cdot exp1 + 1 \cdot exp2 + n \cdot mul2$	$l \cdot n \cdot 2048$	$l \cdot 2048$

We make an analysis about the complexity of our protocol and some existing work in this section. The offline, online computation cost as well as the communication overhead are used to measure the complexity of our protocol. The number of the multiplication and exponentiation operations is used to evaluate the computation cost, since these operations are always resource-consuming in mobile devices. The communication overhead is evaluated by counting the transferred and received bits.

In our paper $exp1$ means 1024-bit exponentiation operation, $exp2$ means 2048-bit exponentiation operation, add indicates modular addition, and $mul1$, $mul2$ represent 1024-bit and 2048-bit multiplication operation, respectively. We assume that each user in our protocol has n interests and the highest corresponding weight value is l. From Table 2, we can learn that our protocol decreases computation and communication costs significantly, especially the online computation cost which has a direct impact on system performance.

6   Conclusion

In this paper, we have proposed a multi-hop profile matching protocol for privacy preserving in mobile social networks. By computation of profile similarity, users can find out potential friends with similar interests, skills, age, location, etc., through a privacy preserving way. Our protocol uses confusion matrix technology, dot product, weight of interest level to get the similarity value, in which the weights and threshold are both chosen by users themselves. Detailed security analysis shows that the privacy of both names and values of users' profile items is well protected by our protocol.

Acknowledgments. This work is supported in part by the National Natural Science Foundation of China under Grant Numbers 61272151, 61472451 and 61402161, the International Science & Technology Cooperation Program of China under Grant Number 2013DFB10070, the China Hunan Provincial Science & Technology Program under Grant Number 2012GK4106, the Hunan Provincial Education Department of China under grant number 2015C0589. and the "Mobile Health" Ministry of Education - China Mobile Joint Laboratory (MOE-DST No. [2012]311).

References

1. Boneh, D., Goh, E.-J., Nissim, K.: Evaluating 2-DNF formulas on ciphertexts. In: Kilian, J. (ed.) TCC 2005. LNCS, vol. 3378, pp. 325–341. Springer, Heidelberg (2005)
2. De Cristofaro, E., Kim, J., Tsudik, G.: Linear-complexity private set intersection protocols secure in malicious model. In: Abe, M. (ed.) ASIACRYPT 2010. LNCS, vol. 6477, pp. 213–231. Springer, Heidelberg (2010)
3. Dong, W., Dave, V., Qiu, L., Zhang, Y.: Secure friend discovery in mobile social networks. In: 2011 IEEE INFOCOM, pp. 1647–1655. IEEE (2011)
4. Freedman, M.J., Nissim, K., Pinkas, B.: Efficient private matching and set intersection. In: Cachin, C., Camenisch, J.L. (eds.) EUROCRYPT 2004. LNCS, vol. 3027, pp. 1–19. Springer, Heidelberg (2004)
5. Ioannidis, I., Grama, A., Atallah, M.J.: A secure protocol for computing dotproducts in clustered and distributed environments. In: Proceedings of the 2002 International Conference on Parallel Processing, pp. 379–384. IEEE (2002)
6. Kissner, L., Song, D.: Privacy-preserving set operations. In: Shoup, V. (ed.) CRYPTO 2005. LNCS, vol. 3621, pp. 241–257. Springer, Heidelberg (2005)
7. Li, M., Cao, N., Yu, S., Lou, W.: Findu: privacy-preserving personal profile matching in mobile social networks. In: 2011 IEEE INFOCOM, pp. 2435–2443. IEEE (2011)
8. Lu, R., Lin, X., Liang, X., Shen, X.: A secure handshake scheme with symptoms-matching for mhealthcare social network. Mob. Netw. Appl. **16**(6), 683–694 (2011)
9. Lu, R., Lin, X., Shen, X.: Spoc: a secure and privacy-preserving opportunistic computing framework for mobile-healthcare emergency. IEEE Trans. Parallel Distrib. Syst. **24**(3), 614–624 (2013)
10. Manweiler, J., Scudellari, R., Cox, L.P.: Smile: encounter-based trust for mobile social services. In: Proceedings of the 16th ACM Conference on Computer and Communications Security, pp. 246–255. ACM (2009)

11. Niu, B., Zhu, X., Liu, J., Li, Z., Li, H.: Weight-aware private matching scheme for proximity-based mobile social networks. In: 2013 IEEE Global Communications Conference (GLOBECOM), pp. 3170–3175. IEEE (2013)

12. Pietiläinen, A.K., Oliver, E., LeBrun, J., Varghese, G., Diot, C.: Mobiclique: middleware for mobile social networking. In: Proceedings of the 2nd ACM Workshop on Online Social Networks, pp. 49–54. ACM (2009)

13. Rane, S., Sun, W., Vetro, A.: Privacy-preserving approximation of l1 distance for multimedia applications. In: 2010 IEEE International Conference on Multimedia and Expo (ICME), pp. 492–497. IEEE (2010)

14. Sang, Y., Shen, H.: Efficient and secure protocols for privacy-preserving set operations. ACM Trans. Inf. Syst. Secur. (TISSEC) 13(1), 9 (2009)

15. Von Arb, M., Bader, M., Kuhn, M., Wattenhofer, R.: Veneta: serverless friend-of-friend detection in mobile social networking. In: 2008 IEEE International Conference on Wireless Communications, Networking and Mobile Computing, pp. 184–189. IEEE (2008)

16. Wang, Y., Vasilakos, A.V., Jin, Q., Ma, J.: Survey on mobile social networking in proximity (msnp): approaches, challenges and architecture. Wireless Netw. 20(6), 1295–1311 (2014)

17. Wang, Y., Xu, J.: Overview on privacy-preserving profile-matching mechanisms in mobile social networks in proximity (msnp). In: 2014 Ninth Asia Joint Conference on Information Security (ASIA JCIS), pp. 133–140. IEEE (2014)

18. Xie, Q., Hengartner, U.: Privacy-preserving matchmaking for mobile social networking secure against malicious users. In: 2011 Ninth Annual International Conference on Privacy, Security and Trust (PST), pp. 252–259. IEEE (2011)

19. Zhang, R., Zhang, J., Zhang, Y., Sun, J., Yan, G.: Privacy-preserving profile matching for proximity-based mobile social networking. IEEE J. Sel. Areas Commun. 31(9), 656–668 (2013)

20. Zhu, X., Liu, J., Jiang, S., Chen, Z., Li, H.: Efficient weight-based private matching for proximity-based mobile social networks. In: 2014 IEEE International Conference on Communications (ICC), pp. 4114–4119. IEEE (2014)

A New Data Replication Scheme for PVFS2

Nianyuan Bao, Jie Tang(✉), Xiaoyu Zhang, and Gangshan Wu

State Key Laboratory for Novel Software Technology,
Department of Computer Science and Technology,
Nanjing University, Nanjing 210046, China
tangjie@nju.edu.cn

Abstract. PVFS is one of the most popular distributed file systems with parallelism, which is still widely used today. Now PVFS is in its version 2, called PVFS2. PVFS2 has a leading performance on I/O operations, but the reliability and stability are not as good. One of the reasons is the lack of data replication. This paper presents a new data replication scheme in PVFS2. In our approach, the backup operation is done on the servers, therefore the user experience is not affected while creating copies of files. In addition, we optimized the read operation of PVFS2. With copies, we can choose the servers to read from, so we can maintain parallelism of read operation under complex conditions such as a server is down or the load of some servers are obviously higher than others. Experimental results verify the effectiveness and efficiency of our method.

Keywords: PVFS2 · Distributed file system · Parallel file system · Data replication · Read optimization

1 Introduction

With the rapid growth of data size in scientific computing, High Performance Computing (HPC) has received wide concern. While the computing performance is the most influential factor in a HPC cluster, the storage module is also important [1]. Typically, the storage module is a distributed file system, such as Parallel Virtual File System (PVFS).

PVFS is a widely used distributed file system that works well in Linux, now in its 2nd version [3]. The original PVFS was built by Ross R B and Thakur R in 2000, which was designed to have a high parallelism [2]. In fact, the performance of parallel I/O operations of PVFS is in the leading level [4,5]. Now PVFS is widely used in computing clusters, distributed databases and Storage Area Networks (SANs).

However, PVFS has no data replication [6]. As we know, PVFS slices files into stripes and store them evenly on all data servers. This manner of file storage ensures the high parallelism of PVFS, but it raises the risk of data corruption without data replication. Data has been stored on all servers without a copy, so any server crash will lead to collapse of the whole system. Thus the robustness has been in a great influence. So the data replication of PVFS is essential.

© Springer International Publishing Switzerland 2015
G. Wang et al. (Eds.): ICA3PP 2015, Part III, LNCS 9530, pp. 475–491, 2015.
DOI: 10.1007/978-3-319-27137-8_35

To improve the robustness of PVFS, we managed to achieve a method of data replication. We store the redundant copies in different servers, so that when any server is down, there are always at least one copy stored on another server. In order to maintain the efficiency of PVFS, backup operations are executed by data servers after the users write operation. So the users would not notice the time spend on data replication.

Furthermore, we optimized the read performance of PVFS with data replication. When reading data, PVFS will first find the stripes of the data, then read them. The data layout scheme of PVFS ensures that these stripes would be stored evenly on each data server. So when data servers are in the very balanced state, PVFS can have a nice read performance. But when any server crash happened, or when the server load is badly imbalanced, the parallelism of PVFS would be partly broken, so the performance of the original read operation can no longer meet the expectation. In this condition, redundant copies can be used to rebalance the read time on every data server, so we optimized the read performance in this way.

2   Relative Works

Despite the high performance on I/O operations, the original PVFS has some vital disadvantages on its stability. It has Single Point of Failure (SPoF) along with the lack of data replication [6].

In order to make improvements to the stability and robustness of PVFS, the developers of PVFS have tried to make lots of optimization since 2004 [10], and finally released Parallel Virtual File System, version 2 (PVFS2) in 2006 [3]. PVFS2 inherited the high parallelism, and improved the stability [11–13]. In this approach, the server architecture of PVFS has been changed. All servers in PVFS2 play the same role. They use the same resource to do the same job, and are under unified management. Thus PVFS2 solved the SPoF problem of PVFS. But still, PVFS2 has a lack of data replication [8,14].

A cost-effective, fault-tolerant parallel virtual file system (CEFT-PVFS, CEFT in short) [6] has been proposed by Zhu Y and Jiang H in 2006. They borrowed some ideas from Google File System (GFS), made some complement and extension for the function of PVFS, and enhanced its fault-tolerant level to RAID10 [6,15]. They used mirror disks to backup data so that they managed to increase the fault tolerance of PVFS at the cost of decreasing the write performance. However, CEFT is based on the original PVFS, which means it hasn't solve the SPoF problem. Further more, as we mentioned, PVFS2 has been released just in 2006 and has made lots of changes in PVFS to improve its performance and reliability, so CEFT has been out of time.

A fault tolerant PVFS2 based on data replication was made by Nieto E, Camacho H.E. and Anguita M. [8] in 2010. In their approach, they made some changes to the creation state machine so the client will create the copy after the original data. In this method, the client has to write twice or more before it gives the return to the user, so the performance of create and write is severely affected. In their experiment, a one-copy write operation in their approach costs almost twice as much time as in PVFS2 [8].

Our work is based on PVFS2. We made full use of the storage structure in PVFS2 and made some small changes for data replication. In our approach, the replicate operation is not done by clients, but servers. When creating or writing data, the client just do the same job as if there's no data replication, then gives the return user immediately. After that, the server will create the copies when it is idle. In this way, we can provide data replication with little impairment in write performance. In addition, we used our data replication to optimize the reading performance on several conditions. We managed to increase the reading performance when servers have imbalance load or some of the servers are lost.

3 Overview on PVFS2

PVFS was released in 2000. It is coded in C and works in Linux. PVFS is known for its high parallelism in I/O operation which ensures its I/O performance [2]. The original PVFS had some vital problems such as SPoF or the lack of data replication, so its development team did lots of changes in the coding and architecture, and finally released PVFS2 in 2006 [3,10].

In PVFS2, all servers do the same job. There are no master server, and all servers in PVFS2 can play the role of either data server all metadata server or both. Thus PVFS2 solved the SPoF problem PVFS had. But still, PVFS2 has no data replication, so our job is to achieve data replication in PVFS2.

In this section we will introduce the features in PVFS2, so that we can explain our approach in the following sections.

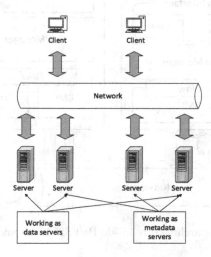

Fig. 1. The structure of PVFS2

3.1 Server Architecture

PVFS2 uses the typical Client-Server Model (C/S Model). There are three logical parts in a PVFS2 cluster, known as the clients, the metadata servers, and the data servers, as shown in Fig. 1.

A client is working on a user's terminal. It listens to the user's instructions and executes them. Also, a client is responsible for the access to servers during the execution of instructions.

A metadata server stores the metadata of the files stored in PVFS2. The metadata are needed in almost all the operations in PVFS2, so once a client receives a instruction, it will always have to access the metadata server to get some metadata.

A data server is in charge of data storage. When executing I/O instructions, a client will first get the metadata of the target, then access the data server to transmit data.

The metadata servers and the data servers are set up on the same devices in general. We collectively call them servers. Furthermore, in a server, the metadata server and the data server use the same process. A client uses the same interface to access the metadata and data. So we say, all servers in PVFS2 do the same job.

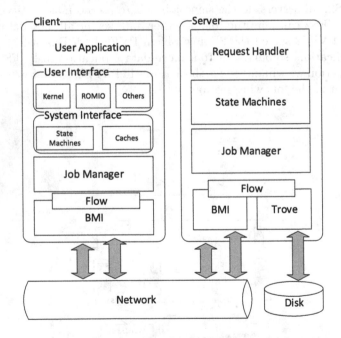

Fig. 2. The architecture inside PVFS2 clients and servers

Figure 2 shows the architecture inside a client or server. In PVFS2, the execution of instructions are in the unit of jobs, which is managed by the Job module.

The Job module exists both on the clients and the servers. They work in coordination to accomplish the whole instruction. When we need to transmit data between devices, we use the Buffered Message Interface (BMI) module. The BMI module also exists both on the clients and the servers. Not only the transmission between clients and servers, but also the transmission between servers and servers will be achieved in it. The BMI module can use different communication protocols such as TCP/IP or Infiniband. In the servers, a Trove module is used for data and metadata storage. Data and metadata are stored in the same form, and a handle is used to access everything stored in Trove.

3.2   Storage Structure

As we all know, PVFS split files into stripes, which ensures the parallelism of I/O operations so that the system would have a nice I/O performance. As a matter of fact, the stripes is only a logical unit. When a file is split into stripes and stored in servers, all the stripes of the file in a single server will be stored in a single file, called datafile, as shown in Fig. 3.

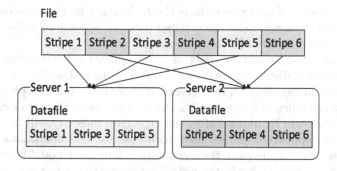

Fig. 3. The storage structure of PVFS2

In PVFS2, files are stored in the form of datafiles. When we need to access a specific stripe of a file, we should get the location of the datafile the stripe stored in as well as the offset of the stripe. The information is stored in metadata. Both datafiles and metadata are stored in Trove. Everything stored in Trove must have a handle, so that we can access it. We can treat a handle as a unique ID. So when accessing datafiles or metadata, we need to get the handle of them first.

The handles of datafiles are stored in metadata, while the handle of metadata are obtained from a hash algorithm. Within the metadata, there stored not only file information and handles of datafiles, but also the position of the stripes, including which datafile a stripe is in and the offset of a stripe inside the datafile. When accessing data in a file, the client first obtains the handle of its metadata with the hash algorithm, then get the metadata from the servers. After that, the client will get the handles of datafiles and positions of the target stripes from the metadata, then finally get the target stripes from the servers. The process is shown in Fig. 4.

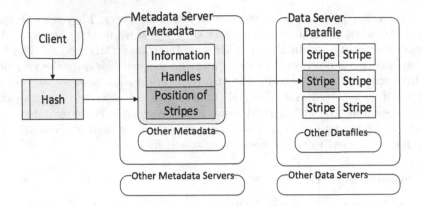

Fig. 4. Process of the I/O operation in PVFS2

4 Data Replication

Generally speaking, data replication is the technology to replicate one or more copies on other devices besides the original data [7]. Specific to a distributed file system, it brings two sort of advancements.

Firstly, the most important effect of data replication is the enhancement of the reliability of a distributed file system [6,8,9]. In a distributed file system, files are stored in the disks on the servers. If there are no data replication, each file will have no copies. When a server is down or a disk on the server crashes, the data on the disk will be unreachable, thus the data integrity will be damaged.

Also, data replication can be used to accelerate I/O operations [7,15–17]. When we have data replication, the same data will be stored on different devices. So we can choose to access a faster and closer device to get the data, so that the I/O cost can be reduced. Furthermore, when more than one client is reading the same data, they can read different copies at the same time without waiting for each other. So the parallelism of the system can be further improved.

There are two major methods to achieve data replication. One of them is using mirror servers [6,18,19], the other is storing the copies in the existing servers [8,20,21].

Mirror servers are servers that only store copies. Generally, there is a one-to-one correspondence between the mirror servers and original servers. A mirror server simply copies the same data in the corresponding server. When data in a server change, the corresponding mirror server should be synchronized. The method using mirror servers can be easily achieved, and the process is simple. But the cost of this method is too much. Even if we want to store only one copy, the number of servers in the cluster should be doubled.

The other method is to store the copies in the existing servers. In this method, either the client or the server should be in charge of the backup operation, and the information of copies should be stored in somewhere, usually in metadata. This method is much more flexible. We can set different redundant strategies for each file, and don't need to add new servers until disks are full or nearly full. But in this method, the system should do some extra work such as deciding the position of the copies or maintaining the replication information. The operations will be more complicated.

In our approach, we use the second method. Different with others, in our approach the backup operation is not executed on clients, but servers. When copying backups on clients, the backup operation would spend more time on network transmission or disk reading before the operation on clients is complete. In our approach, we move the time cost of the backup operation onto servers. Clients only take care of the writing operation, and the backup operation will be done on servers while clients doing other operations. When the users create a new file or write something in a existing file, our system will first complete the operations on the original file. Once these operations complete, the users will be given the result so they can continue to do other works. After that, the servers will execute the backup operation later. Thus we achieved data replication with little reduction on user experience.

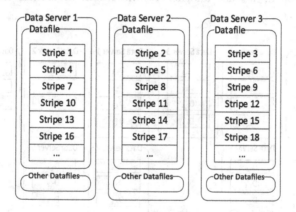

Fig. 5. The PVFS2 Round-Robin Layout

4.1   Backup Distribution

In PVFS2, a Round-Robin Layout is used to decide the distribution of data, which means all stripes are stored in the servers according to the sequence in turn, as Fig. 5 shows. For example, if a file is stored in 3 servers and the 1st stripe is stored in Server 1, so the 2nd stripe will be stored in Server 2, and then the 3rd in Server 3, the 4th in Server 1, the 5th in Server 2, etc. This feature shows us two things. The stripes are stored evenly in the datafiles, and the datafiles of a file are almost the same in size. Thus, when creating copies, we can backup data in the unit of datafiles. Here we have three principles:

1. All datafiles and their copies should be stored evenly on all servers. As we all know, PVFS2 doesn't have dynamic load balance, so when we create or write data, we should make the best we can to balance the load of servers.

2. A datafile or its copies should not be stored in the same server. For our major target, the data replication is used to improve the reliability of the system. Specifically, we hope the data can be maintained after servers are down or disks crash. So the datafile or its copies must be on different servers, otherwise a single crash of disk would make two or more copies unreachable, which we don't want to happen.

3. All datafiles of a single backup should not be stored in the same server. This principle is for our backup operation. When creating copies, by default, we primarily copy all datafiles of the first backup, and then the second backup, the third backup, etc. If there are two or more datafiles of a single backup are stored in the same server, the parallelism of the backup operation will be reduced. So we make this principle to avoid this situation.

When a new file is created, we can't predict how large it will grow, so we just consider the number of datafiles stored in a server. After our backup operation, the datafiles and their copies should be evenly allocated to the servers in number. So in our approach, we use another Round-Robin algorithm for the backup distribution.

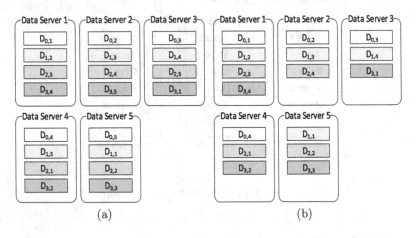

Fig. 6. Examples of backup distribution

Firstly we should get the number of datafiles D, the number of backups B (including the original data), and the number of servers N. On one hand, when $D = N$, which means the number of datafiles is equal to the number of servers. So the datafiles of each single backup will be stored in all of the servers. On the other hand, when $B = N$, which means the number of backups is equal to the number of servers. So every datafile and its copies will be stored in all of the servers. In these two conditions, we can simply store the copies on a next server. So we always backup the datafiles in the Xth server to the $((X+1)\bmod N)$th, $((X+2)\bmod N)$th, ..., $((X+B)\bmod N)$th server. For example, a datafile is stored in the third of five servers, so the first copy will be stored in the forth server, the second copy will be stored in the fifth server, the third copy will be stored in the first server, etc. Another example of the storage of a file with five datafiles and three copies in a cluster with five servers is shown in Fig. 6a. In the figure, $D_{i,j}$ means the jth datafile of the ith copy, while $D_{0,j}$ means the jth datafile of the original file.

When B and D are both less than N, we first get S = (B * D)mod N, which means there are S servers that need to store more datafiles than others. We choose S servers that have the lightest load, so now we know the number of datafiles or their copies to be stored in each server. Then we use a Greedy algorithm to allocate the datafiles and their copies into the servers, following the three principles. A example of the storage of a file with four datafiles and three copies in a cluster with five servers is shown in Fig. 6b.

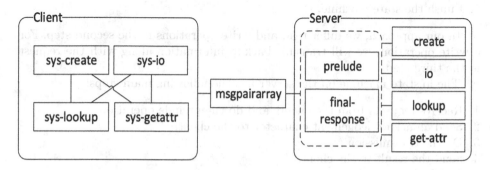

Fig. 7. Some major state machines about I/O operation

4.2 State Machines

State machines are an important part of PVFS2. All the instructions and operations in PVFS2 are executed through state machines. Figure 7 shows some of the major state machines about I/O operation in PVFS2 and some of their relationship.

Due to the modification in the metadata we made, almost all the state machines are updated. In this chapter we only focus on the major changes we made in state machines. We mainly made some changes in the create state machine on the server, the sys-io state machine on the client and the io state machine on the server. Furthermore, we added a new state machine on the server called backup.

The create state machine on the server has the following main steps:

1. Create metadata for the new file.
2. Allocate servers for the datafiles.
3. Create local datafile.
4. Create handles.

5. Send the request to other servers for creating datafiles on them.
6. Save the handles of datafiles into the metadata.
7. Finish the state machine.

In our approach, we allocate servers for the copies in the second step in the create state machine. In the following steps, we create datafiles and handles for the copy along with the same work done for the original file. The creation doesn't take much time, so it can be done on the client.

The sys-io state machine on the client has the following main steps:

1. Obtain the information of the file.
2. Find the target stripes in the datafiles.
3. Send the request to the servers the datafiles are on for data transmission.
4. Transmit data.
5. Finish the state machine.

In our approach, we differ read and write operations in the second step. For a write operation, we will transmit backup information along with the request in the third step.

The io state machine on the server has the following main steps:

1. Receive requests from the clients and do the prelude operation.
2. Send an acknowledgement character to the client.
3. Do the transmission.
4. Send the result to the client.
5. Finish the state machine.

In our approach, if the request contains backup information, the io state machine will jump to the backup state machine when finished.

The backup state machine on the server is a new state machine added in our approach, which takes charge of the backup operation. It has the following main steps:

1. Analyze the backup information.
2. Obtain the metadata.
3. Change the backup status in the metadata.
4. Wait until the server is in a rest.
5. Send a request to the target servers for backup.
6. Transmit copies.
7. Refresh the backup status in the metadata.
8. Finish the state machine.

5   Reading Optimization

With data replication, most data will have one or more copies, so we can optimize the reading performance of PVFS2 now.

As shown in the previous chapters, data replication can be used to accelerate I/O operations [7,15–17]. Specific to PVFS2, the parallelism will be improved with data replication. For instance, when a file with three datafiles is stored in a PVFS2 cluster of five servers, we can read data from no more than three servers at the same time. After data replication, the datafiles and their copies will be stored in all five servers, so we can read data from up to five servers at the same time, which means the reading speed can be increased by up to 66 %.

Moreover, with data replication, the target to read can be chosen wisely to accelerate I/O operations. Without data replication, every single stripe of a file is only saved on one server, so we have no other choice when we want to access this stripe. But the situation has been changed because of data replication. Now datafiles have their copies stored in other servers, so there are more than one choice to access a stripe. We can choose to access a stripe on a server with a lightest load. When accessing more than one stripes at once, we can adjust the data scale of the targets on each server, so that we can access less data from a server with a lighter load and more data from a server with a heavier load.

In the extreme case, when some servers are down, we have to read data from other servers. In our approach we can still read data evenly from the rest of the servers, so the parallelism is maintained.

5.1   Hotspot Detection

The load of servers will not be always the same. In actual operations, there will always be some servers with a higher load, while some others with a lower one. A server is called a hotspot when the load of it becomes so high that its operating or I/O efficiency is badly influenced.

There are some ways to detect hotspot. Most of them use a percentage to show how high the load of the server is. In our approach, we'd rather use a expected transmission speed (ETS) to show this, so that when reading, we can use the ETS to work out a best allocation of the targets.

We consider of the read speed of the disk first. There are always a standard read speed of a disk, and we call it S. We define X as the current read speed of the disk, N as the network speed, and E as the ETS. When the load of the server is extremely low, we consider E = S. If some accident happens that the network speed becomes so slow, we consider E = N. In general case, X will have some effect on E, but in our practice we notice that the effect is not linear. When the value of X is small, it has little effect on E, while when the value of X is big, it will have a greater effect than we expect. The RAM and CPU occupancy rate can also affect the ETS, but the case only happens when the RAM or CPU occupancy rate grows so high that the server process has no response, in this case we assume E = 0. We temporarily use the following formula to calculate the value of E:

$$E = min(S - aX^b/S^c, N)$$

While the value of a, b and c still need to be adjusted. In our practice, we found a = 3, b = 2, c = 1 is a simple answer that has a fair performance.

5.2 Target Selection

Because of the data replication, we can choose the datafiles or their copies to read, so we can read more data from servers with lower load and read less data from servers with higher load. To achieve this theory, we have to decide which server do we read each stripe from.

First we can obtain the ETS of the servers. Considering the load of the server is a real-time attribute, the client should send an additional request to get the ETS. Once we got the ETS of the servers, we can obtain a allocation of servers to read stripes from so that the transmission time in every server can be the same. Thus we can get the optimistic plan that has the least read time. For example, if we have to read 1000 stripes from two servers A and B. After the first step we get the ETS of A and B to be 200 MB/s and 300 MB/s, so we can read 400 stripes from A and 600 stripes from B, so that the expected transmission time of A and B can be the same, and the read time can be the shortest. Besides, a server should be selected for each stipe we read. In the selection, we prefer to read the stripes continuously stored in a datafile from one server, so we use a depth-first search. Figure 8 shows a simple example of target selection.

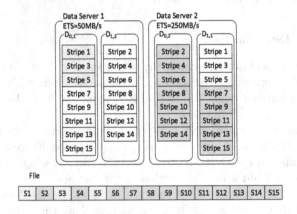

Fig. 8. A simple example of target selection

6 Experimental Results

First we verified the effectiveness of our data replication. We used a number of servers as data servers, and another server as the metadata server to do the experiment. Thus, the influence of the lost of metadata has been prevented. As Table 1 shows, we used different files that have different sizes, different number of datafiles, different number of copies stored in different number of servers. Then we shut one of the servers down, and check if the data stored in the rest of the servers are complete. The table shows under the correct settings, a file with copies stored in other servers can maintain complete when a server is down. As a result, the fault tolerance of PVFS2 has been improved.

Table 1. The efficiency of data replication

File size/MB	1	16	1024	1024	1024	1024
Datafile number	1	3	3	1	1	1
Backup number	1	2	2	0	2	0
Server number	3	3	3	1	3	3
If passed validation	Yes	Yes	Yes	No	Yes	No

Then we did some experiments to test the write performance of our approach. Figure 9a shows the write performance of PVFS2 with and without data
replication. In the experiment, we separately wrote different files into a PVFS2
cluster with four servers with and without data replication. We recorded the
write time on the client side, which shows how long the users have to wait until
they can do their next works. In the figure, we can find the PVFS2 with data
replication is a little slower than the original PVFS2. This is because we have
to spend more time on creating metadata and allocating servers for copies. The
time we do these jobs are almost regular, so when the data size grows large, the
time gap between the two systems will be shorten. As shown in the figure, when
the size of the file grows larger than 64MB, the two systems have almost the
same performance.

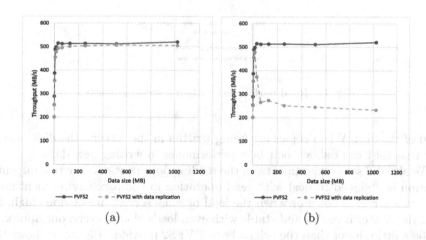

(a)   (b)

Fig. 9. Write performance of PVFS2 with data replication

Figure 9b shows the write performance a short period after the previous write
operation. We can find the write performance of our approach is badly affected
in this experiment. In our approach, the backup operation is done by the servers
when they are free, which brings us a shortcoming. When the user wants to
do some write operation just when the servers are doing backup operation, the
write performance can be badly endangered. This is because of the limit of write

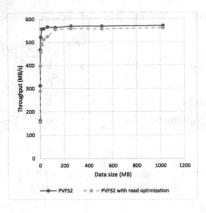

Fig. 10. Read performance

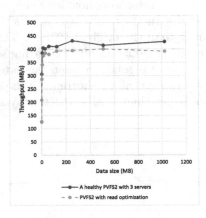

Fig. 11. Read performance when a server crashed

speed of the disk. When copies are being written in the servers, the disks are so busy that they can't show their best performance in writing new data.

We also did some experiments on the reading optimization. The reading optimization is designed to deal with read operation in complex environment such as when a server is down or when the load of some servers are obvious high. So when the cluster is health and stable with even loads of all servers, our approach will be a little slower than the original one PVFS2 provides. Figure 10 shows the contrast reading files from a cluster with four servers. Though the difference is very small, our approach is slower indeed. So we allow users to use the original read operation PVFS2 provides. Figure 11 shows the read performance when a server crashed. In the experiment, we store the file and three copies in a cluster with four servers, then we shut one server down. As we can see, the read performance of the rest three servers is almost the same as which in a healthy cluster with three servers. So in our approach, we can ensure the parallelism even in the extreme case that a server is down.

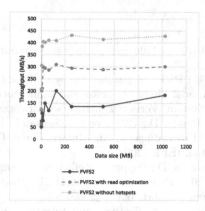

Fig. 12. Read performance when the load of servers is imbalance

At last we tested the read performance of a cluster with three servers when one of the servers has a very high load. As we can see in Fig. 12, the read performance is obviously better than the one before reading optimization. This is because in our method, the size of data read from the server with the high load is less.

7 Conclusion

In our approach, we achieved data replication in PVFS2. We placed the backup operation on the server, so that the user experience will not be affected while the stability of the system is improved. The result of our experiment shows the reliability of our approach, and the speed is nearly the same with the original PVFS2. In additional, we optimized the read performance using copies. As a result, our system managed to maintain parallelism when the cluster is not in a perfect situation.

Still there are some points for us to improve. We are going to find some way to avoid the conflict between backup operation and the following write operation. Also we can try to use the buffer to accelerate the backup operation. Besides, we can improve PVFS2 in other ways. For example, we can achieve a dynamic load balance for PVFS2.

Acknowledgments. We would like to thank the anonymous reviewers for helping us refine this paper. Their constructive comments and suggestions are very helpful. This paper is partly funded by National Science and Technology Major Project of the Ministry of Science and Technology of China under grant 2011ZX05035-004-004HZ. The corresponding author of this paper is Jie Tang.

References

1. Zhao, D., Raicu, I.: Distributed file systems for exascale computing. Doctoral Showcase, SC, 12 (2012)
2. Ross, R.B., Thakur, R.: PVFS: a parallel file system for Linux clusters. In: Proceedings of the 4th Annual Linux Showcase and Conference, pp. 391–430 (2000)
3. Parallel Virtual File System, Version 2. http://www.pvfs.org/
4. Wu, J., Wyckoff, P., Panda, D.: PVFS over InfiniBand: design and performance evaluation. In: 2003 Proceedings of the International Conference on Parallel Processing, pp. 125–132. IEEE (2003)
5. Wu, J., Wyckoff. P., Panda, D.: Supporting efficient noncontiguous access in PVFS over InfiniBand. In: 2003 Proceedings of the IEEE International Conference on Cluster Computing, pp. 344–351. IEEE (2003)
6. Zhu, Y., Jiang, H.: Ceft: a cost-effective, fault-tolerant parallel virtual file system. J. Parallel Distrib. Comput. **66**(2), 291–306 (2006)
7. Bell, W.H., Cameron, D.G., Millar, A.P., et al.: Optorsim: a grid simulator for studying dynamic data replication strategies. Int. J. High Perform. Comput. Appl. **17**(4), 403–416 (2003)
8. Nieto, E., Camacho, H.E., Anguita, M., et al.: Fault tolerant PVFS2 based on data replication. In: 2010 1st International Conference on Parallel Distributed and Grid Computing (PDGC), pp. 107–112. IEEE (2010)
9. Satyanarayanan, M.: A survey of distributed file systems. Annu. Rev. Comput. Sci. **4**(1), 73–104 (1990)
10. Latham, R., Miller, N., Ross, R., et al.: A next-generation parallel file system for Linux cluster. LinuxWorld Mag. 2 (ANL/MCS/JA-48544) (2004)
11. Zhang, X., Jiang, S., Davis, K.: Making resonance a common case: a high-performance implementation of collective I/O on parallel file systems. In: IEEE International Symposium on Parallel & Distributed Processing, 2009, IPDPS 2009, pp. 1–12. IEEE (2009)
12. Kunkel, J.M., Ludwig, T.: Performance evaluation of the PVFS2 architecture. In: 15th EUROMICRO International Conference on Parallel, Distributed and Network-Based Processing, 2007, PDP 2007, pp. 509–516. IEEE (2007)
13. Chai, L., Ouyang, X., Noronha, R., et al.: pNFS/PVFS2 over InfiniBand: early experiences. In: Proceedings of the 2nd International Workshop on Petascale Data Storage: Held in Conjunction with Supercomputing 2007, pp. 5–11. ACM (2007)
14. Choi, Y.H., Cho, W.H., Eom, H., et al.: A study of the fault-tolerant PVFS2. In: 2011 6th International Conference on Computer Sciences and Convergence Information Technology (ICCIT), pp. 482–485. IEEE (2011)
15. Zhu, Y., Jiang, H., Qin, X., et al.: Improved read performance in a cost-effective, faulttolerant parallel virtual file system (CEFT-PVFS). In: 2003 Proceedings of the 3rd IEEE/ACM International Symposium on Cluster Computing and the Grid, CCGrid 2003, pp. 730–735. IEEE (2003)
16. Wolfson, O., Jajodia, S., Huang, Y.: An adaptive data replication algorithm. ACM Trans. Database Syst. (TODS) **22**(2), 255–314 (1997)
17. Saadat, N., Rahmani, A.M.: PDDRA: a new pre-fetching based dynamic data replication algorithm in data grids. Future Gener. Comput. Syst. **28**(4), 666–681 (2012)
18. Cachin, C., Junker, B., Sorniotti, A.: On limitations of using cloud storage for data replication. In: 2012 IEEE/IFIP 42nd International Conference on Dependable Systems and Networks Workshops (DSN-W), pp. 1–6. IEEE (2012)

19. Lustre. http://lustre.org/
20. Ghemawat, S., Gobioff, H., Leung, S.T.: The Google file system. In: SIGOPS Operating Systems Review, vol. 37(5), pp. 29–43. ACM (2003)
21. Shvachko, K., Kuang, H., Radia, S., et al.: The hadoop distributed file system. In: 2010 IEEE 26th Symposium on Mass Storage Systems and Technologies (MSST), pp. 1–10. IEEE (2010)

Efficient Private Matching Scheme for Friend Information Exchange

Fang Qi and Wenbo Wang$^{(\boxtimes)}$

School of Information Science and Engineering,
Central South University, Changsha 410083, China
{csuqifang,wb_wang}@csu.edu.cn

Abstract. In the recent years, with the rapid development of social networks and mobile devices, mobile users can exchange the information and find the potential friends in vicinity through comparing the similarity degree between their personal attributes and make a connection via Wi-Fi/Bluetooth. The personal attributes, however, usually contain some private information, and users are not willing to reveal these to others in the process of friend discovery. In this paper, we proposed a novel efficient private matching scheme, which adopts an asymmetric scalar-preserving encryption according to the idea of k-nearest neighbor (kNN) queries. The personal profile of users will be processed in different ways, which is not recoverable. Moreover, our scheme relies on no Trusted Third Party (TTP). Detailed security and performance analysis demonstrate that our scheme can protect users' private information and resist outside attack during the matching process.

Keywords: Profile matching · Privacy-preserving · Information exchange · Asymmetric scalar-preserving encryption · PMSNs

1 Introduction

Nowadays, with the explosive growth of mobile devices and the increasing popularity of mobile devices, the proximity-based mobile social networks (PMSNs) has become an essential part in our daily life [8]. Comparing to traditional web-based online social networks, PMSNs provides users more opportunities to make new social interaction with their neighbors.

To enjoy these activities, the first step of users is to reveal their personal information to nearby strangers to find out potential friends. However, the personal information can be sensitive, for it may contain private information such as location, interests, name, etc., and the disclosure of which may lead to some unexpected problems [16].

To handle this problem, many private matching schemes have been proposed in recent years. Some schemes protect users' privacy with reliance on a TTP [9,11,12,17]. In this kind of scheme, users submit their interests to the TTP. In some TTP-free schemes, there are two mainstreams of methods to solve this problem. One is to treat a user's profile as a set of attributes and provide attributes

© Springer International Publishing Switzerland 2015
G. Wang et al. (Eds.): ICA3PP 2015, Part III, LNCS 9530, pp. 492–503, 2015.
DOI: 10.1007/978-3-319-27137-8_36

matching based on private set intersection and private cardinality of set intersection (PCSI) [3,5,7,15]. The other is to consider a user's profile as a vector and measures the social proximity by private vector dot production [13,19].

Though the above schemes can get the similarity value, but they fail in two main problems: (1) many approaches realize the profile matching through a third party, which has a bottleneck that the security cannot be guaranteed; (2) the cryptographic techniques used in the schemes are too complicated to be efficient enough. For example, homomorphic encryption and decryption are used in [1,3,4,6,15]. BGN cryptosystem is employed in [2,10,14,18], which also requires a large amount of computation resource.

From the former analysis, it is obvious that the existing works either relies on the third party or fails in high efficiency. In this paper, we formulate an efficient friend discovery scheme which relies on no third party and can guarantee the security. Our proposed scheme is based on the idea of kNN query. The kNN query is an important database analysis operation. In the common situation of kNN problem, there is a point p and we first find out k nearest points in vicinity. Then the point p will be classified into the classification of the majority among the k points. Based on this idea, we consider a special situation. The k is set to be 1, and the location attributes are replaced by the personal attributes. After computation, we can get the most similarity one. In our scheme, we adopt an asymmetric scalar-preserving kNN based encryption. The profiles of *initiator* and *responder* are encrypted in different way which is not recoverable. The new kNN based asymmetric encryption is easy to access and possesses high efficiency, and at the same time it captures the execution and security requirements.

The remainder of this paper is organized as follow: Sect. 2 shows the preliminaries in our scheme. In Sect. 3, we depict our profile matching scheme in detail. We provide security in Sect. 4. Finally, Sect. 5 concludes this paper.

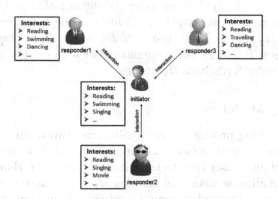

Fig. 1. Interest based friend discovery.

2   Preliminaries

In this section, we first briefly formalize the problem about profile matching in mobile social networks. Then present the adversary models as well as design goal. With our scheme, two users can compare their interests without revealing any private information.

2.1   Problem Statement

We consider a typical mobile social network scenario, where each user carries a portable mobile device such as smart phone or a tablet and all of them installed the same friend finding application. This application allows users to choose their interests which had been preseted. Each user has a profile which includes the information of use's interests, as shown in Fig. 1. The information is sensitive and private, so the users expect to get the satisfied result without revealing any private information.

In this paper, we proposed a secure and efficient scheme, which relies on no Trusted Third Party and can be applied to proximity-based mobile social networks. Suppose each user has an interests vector denoted as $I_{id} = (i_1, i_2, \ldots, i_n)$. The items, $i_1, i_2, \ldots, i_n$, represent different interest choices preseted in the application. For example, i_1 stands for movies, i_2 represents reading. Each item has a value 0 or 1, 1 means I have this interest, 0 means not.

First, the *initiator* sends a friend matching request to the *responder*. Once the *responder* receives the request, his/her profile will expand to $n + 1$ dimensions, and the scheme will generate a $n + 1$ dimensions dividing vector S and two $(n + 1) \times (n + 1)$ dimensions invertible matrices M_1, M_2 randomly. The *responder*'s profile I_r can be divided into two vectors I_{r1} and I_{r2} according to S, and then be encrypted into $A = \{M_1^T I_{r1}{}^*, M_2^T I_{r2}{}^*\}$ by M_1^T, M_2^T. Next *responder* sends S, M_1^{-1} and M_2^{-1} to *initiator*. When *initiator* gets these, does the same thing like responder, at last, the *initiator*'s profile I_i can be encrypted into $B = \{M_1^{-1} I_{i1}{}^*, M_2^{-1} I_{i2}{}^*\}$. Then, the *initiator* sends B to *responder*, the dot calculation between B and A will come into process to get the similarity value. Finally, the *responder* feeds back the value.

2.2   Adversary Model

In the profile matching process, there usually exist two main adversary model: honest but curious adversaries model and malicious model. In honest but curious adversaries model, each user tries to learn more information than allowed about other users. In a malicious model, an attacker will learn more profile information using the background knowledge beyond received information or deviating from the scheme. Such as denial-of-service (DoS) and continuous fake-profile attacks.

In this paper, we assume that each user in our scheme is an honest-but-curious user, which means that a user will honestly follow the protocol but at the same time tries to get more information than allowed in our model. Since the information can be sensitive, e.g., it may include users' interests, location and gender. We can presume that the *responder* is legal or honest-but-curious, for the identity of the responder can be easily authorized and our scheme can be reversed to achieve a dual matching. Moreover, the unmatched *responders* will get nothing about *initiators*. For *initiator*, he/she can also be an attacker, since he/she may choose the interests deliberately to gain more information about nearby users. For example, the *initiator* may be an advertiser and wants to deliver ads to those who are interested in the appointed hobbies.

2.3   Design Goal

Our main goal and great challenge of our scheme is to develop a secure, efficient and privacy-preserving matching between an *initiator* and several *responders*. Once the friend making request has been accepted, our scheme will generate the unique identity sign of *initiator* and *responder*. According to the identity sign, our scheme can be reversed to achieve a dual matching during the communication. When protocol ends, the *initiator* gets the similarity value between he/she and each *responder*, that is to say, after running out protocol, the *initiator* can find the best matcher safely and efficiently. At the same time, we also established a secure communication channel against outside attack. Without any trusted third party, our scheme, in mobile social networks, are designed to be lightweight and practical, since it only needs low communication cost and low computation.

Furthermore, based on the adversary model, we defined two privacy levels.

Definition 1. Level-I Privacy. When the protocol ends, the *initiator* and *responder* know nothing about each other's concrete private information.

Definition 2. Level-II Privacy. When the protocol ends, the external attacker knows nothing about the *initiator* and *responder*'s private information.

3   Interest Based Friendship Discovery Scheme

In this section, we first propose the overview of our scheme in proximity-based mobile social networks without any trusted third party. Then we describe our scheme in details, it mainly consists of the following parts: system initialization, matching preparation, profile matching, similarity calculation and feedback.

3.1   Scheme Overview

Our main idea is to develop a secure and practical scheme to achieve the goal of effective friends finding. According to a lot of surveys and analysis of many social networking systems (SNS), most people have a unique profile which can be used to do friends finding and identity authority. But it is very dangerous to reveal these information to strangers. In most social networks, there are usually two steps to make friends: profile matching and communication, which cause some privacy problems (Table 1).

Table 1. Summary of notations

Notation	Description
I_{id}	The initiator profile matrix
S	Dividing vector
M_1, M_2	Random invertible matrix
M_1^T, M_2^T	Transpose of M_1^T, M_2^T
M_1^{-1}, M_2^{-1}	Inverse matrix $M_1^{-1} M_2^{-1}$
$H()$	The Hash function
B	Encrypted profile of initiator
A	Encrypted profile of responder
v	Similarity value
Δt	Threshold of response time

(1) Profile Privacy. The profiles of all the users should not be exposed without their permission. For all users, protecting their information is necessary and can decrease the hostage to take part in mobile social networks.

(2) Communication Privacy. The message between users should be transmitted via a secure channel. In practice, privacy and profile information can be exposed via communication through insecure channels (e.g., public Wi-Fi).

Base on their different roles, mobile users can be classified into two categories: *initiator* and *responder*. An *initiator* is a user who wants to make friends with nearby users, so he/she initiates a friend discovery request. A *responder* is a user who may reply the request he/she received.

In our scheme, in order to get the same attribute matrix if the users have the same interests, is it necessary to unify the choice of interests. Considering that if users type in their own interests, it can cause some problems. For example, both Alice and Bob like swimming, but Alice inputs "swim" while Bob inputs "I like swimming". It will take a lot of time to extract key words and if someone deliberately inputs some illegal words, it may cause chaos. Hence, we consider checkboxes instead of typing in the interests items.

Moreover, we preset a hash function in the application to check whether the message is correct or not.

Step 1 - System Initialization. In the system initialization phase, the installed application first sets up system parameters and registers users. Users choose their interests among n choices. And then the *initiator* broadcasts his/her friend making request.

$$M_{request} = \{ID_i, q, H(ID_i), t_1\} \tag{1}$$

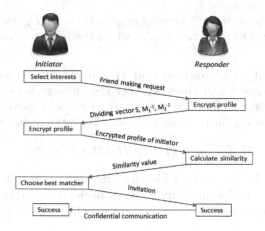

Fig. 2. Matching process.

Where ID_i is the *initiator*'s identity information. q denotes the friend making request. $H(ID_i)$ stands for the hash value of ID_i. t_1 refers to the time point at which the *initiator* sends this request (Fig. 2).

Step 2 - Matching Preparation. When *responder* gets the request message $M_{request}$ at t_2 time point, he/she first will check whether $t_2 - t_1 < \Delta t$, if so, this information will be abandoned or relaunched. Then *responder* will use the hash function $H()$ to check the correctness of *initiator*'s identity information. When both response time and *initiator*'s id are verified, the scheme expands *responder*'s interests set I_r into $n + 1$ dimensions, we denotes it as I_r^*. Then the scheme will generate a $(n + 1)$ dimensions dividing vector S and two $(n + 1) * (n + 1)$ dimensions invertible matrices M_1, M_2 randomly, all of them are binary. Next I_r^* will be divided into I_{r1}^* and I_{r2}^* by Algorithm 1. Finally, the *responder*'s interests will be encrypted as $A = \{M_1^T I_{r1}^*, M_2^T I_{r2}^*\}$. After finishing above operations, *responder* will send a message to *initiator*.

$$M_{prepare} = \{ID_r, S, M_1^{-1}, M_2^{-1}, H(ID_r), H(S), H(M_1^{-1}), H(M_2^{-1}), t_3\} \quad (2)$$

Where ID_r is the *responder*'s identity information. S is the dividing vector and M_1^{-1}, M_2^{-1} are the inverse matrix of M_1, M_2. Each of them has a hash value respectively. t_3 refers to the time point at which the responder sends this message.

Step 3 - Profile Matching. When *initiator* receives the $M_{prepare}$, he/she will first check whether the message is out of the response time, and then verify the message. After verifying, *initiator* will use the S, M_1^{-1} and M_2^{-1} to divide his/her interests vector I_i, and encrypt it into $B = \{M_1^{-1} I_{i1}^*, M_2^{-1} I_{i2}^*\}$ according to Algorithm 2. Finally, the *initiator* sends back the message.

$$M_{profile} = \{ID_i, B, H(ID_i), t_4\} \quad (3)$$

Where ID_i is the *initiator*'s identity information. $H(ID_i)$ stands for the hash value of ID_i. t_4 refers to the time point at which the *initiator* sends this message.

Step 4 - Similarity Calculation and Feedback. When *responder* receives the $M_{profile}$, he/she will first check whether the message is out of the response time, and then verify the message. After verifying, the *responder* will run Algorithm 3 to calculate similarity value and sends back the result.

$$M_{similarity} = \{ID_r, v, H(ID_r), H(v), t_5\} \tag{4}$$

Where ID_r is the *responder*'s identity information. $H(ID_r)$ stands for the hash value of ID_r. v is the similarity between *initiator* and *responder*, and $H(v)$ is its hash value. t_5 refers to the time point at which the *responder* sends this message.

Finally, when *initiator* receives the $M_{similarity}$, he/she will first check whether the message is out of the response time, and then verify the message. After that, the *initiator* will sort the similarity values which come from different *responder*. According to the principle that the bigger the values is, the more similar they are, and the *initiator* can find the best matcher.

3.2 System Initialization

To begin with, all the users get registered and we assume that there are total n interests considered in our scheme, and each use's interests situation can be represented through his/her personal profile, a binary vector $I_{id} = (i_1, i_2, \ldots, i_n)$ in the n-dimensional space, where i_n in I_{id} indicates an interest, e.g., swimming. At first the value of $i_1, i_2, \ldots, i_n$ will be set to 0. Then, according to security requirement, the scheme will publish a hash function $H()$. Next, each registered user chooses the interests according to his/her own situation. For those items which are chosen by users, the value of them will be set to 1. Finally, the *initiator* will broadcasts his/her friend making request.

3.3 Matching Preparation

In the matching preparation phase, two users, *initiator* and *responder*, would interact with each other and prepare for the profile matching.

Once received $M_{request} = \{ID_i, q, H(ID_i), t_1\}$, the *responder* will check whether it is a legal message. Using the published $H()$, if $H(ID_i) = H(ID_i)$ (the latter $H(ID_i)$ is brought by the message), it means that the message is legal; if not, the message will be discarded. After that, the *responder* will check if it is instant. Suppose that the *responder* gets the message at time point, if $t_2 - t_1 > \Delta t$, this request is out of response time, and will be discarded or relaunched. If not, the responder will continue next steps. According to Euclidean norm, the I_r will be expanded into I_r^*. The I_r^* can be defined as

$$I_r^* = (I_r, -0.5||I_r||^2) \tag{5}$$

The $||I_r||^2$ can be represented by $I_r \cdot I_r$, or $(\sqrt{I_r[1]^2 + I_r[2]^2 + \cdots + I_r[n]^2})^2$.

Next, the scheme will generate a $n+1$ dimensions dividing vector S and two $(n+1)*(n+1)$ dimensions invertible matrices M_1, M_2 randomly, all of them are binary. According to the S, I_r^* will be divided into two vectors. The process is shown in Algorithm 1.

Algorithm 1. Vector Dividing of Responder

Input:

The expanded interests vector of initiator I_r^* and dividing vector S

Output:

The divided set I_{r1}^* and I_{r1}^*;

1: The initiator executes the following operations:

2: For each item i in S $(1, 2, \ldots, n, n+1)$ do:

3: According to the value of $S[j]$ generate new vectors:

$$\begin{cases} I_{r1}^*[j] = I_{r2}^*[j] = I_r^*[j]; S[j] = 0 \\ I_{r1}^*[j] + I_{r2}^*[j] = I_r^*[j]; S[j] = 1 \end{cases}$$

4: End for

5: **return** I_{r1}^* and I_{r1}^*;

Using M_1^T and M_2^T, I_{r1}^* and I_{r1}^* will be encrypted into $A = \{M_1^T I_{r1}^*, M_2^T I_{r2}^*\}$.

3.4 Profile Matching

When *initiator* receives the $M_{prepare}$, he/she will first check whether the message is out of the response time, and then verify the message. Next, I_i will be expanded into I_i^*. First, simply set the $n+1$ dimension's value of I_i to 1, denotes as $(I_i, 1)$, then the $(I_i, 1)$ is multiplied by a random number r. The I_i^* can be defined as

$$I_i^* = r(I_i, 1) \tag{6}$$

According to S, I_i^* will be divided into two vectors. The process is shown in Algorithm 2. Different from Algorithm 1, the Algorithm 2 operates the opposite process.

Using M_1^{-1} and M_2^{-1} in the received message, I_{i1}^* and I_{i1}^* will be encrypted into $B = \{M_1^{-1} I_{i1}^*, M_2^{-1} I_{i2}^*\}$.

3.5 Similarity Calculation and Feedback

In this step, the *responder* runs Algorithm 3 to calculate the similarity value and then give a feedback. The process is shown in Algorithm 3.

When the similarity value is calculated, the *responder* will send it to *initiator*. Until now, *initiator* received all the similarity values, our scheme will find the greatest one, and inform the *initiator*. Therefore, the user can easily find the one who is most likely to be a potential friend.

Algorithm 2. Vector Dividing of Initiator

Input:
  The expanded interests vector of initiator I_i^* and dividing vector S
Output:
  The divided set I_{i1}^* and I_{i1}^*;
1: The initiator executes the following operations:
2: For each item i in $S[1, 2, \ldots, n, n+1]$ do:
3: According to the value of $S[j]$ generate new vectors:

$$\begin{cases} I_{i1}^*[j] + I_{i2}^*[j] = I_i^*[j]; S[j] = 0 \\ I_{i1}^*[j] = I_{i2}^*[j] = I_i^*[j]; S[j] = 1 \end{cases}$$

4: End for
5: **return** I_{i1}^* and I_{i1}^*;

Algorithm 3. Similarity Calculation

Input:
  The encrypted profile of responder $A = \{M_1^T I_{r1}^*, M_2^T I_{r2}^*\}$ and the encrypted
  profile of initiator $B = \{M_1^{-1} I_{i1}^*, M_2^{-1} I_{i2}^*\}$
Output:
  Similarity value v;
1: The responder executes the following calculation:

$$\begin{aligned} v &= A \cdot B \\ &= \{M_1^T I_{r1}^*, M_2^T I_{r2}^*\} \cdot \{M_1^{-1} I_{i1}^*, M_2^{-1} I_{i2}^*\} \\ &= \{M_1^T I_{r1}^*, M_2^T I_{r2}^*\}^T \cdot \{M_1^{-1} I_{i1}^*, M_2^{-1} I_{i2}^*\} \\ &= (M_1^T I_{r1}^*)^T \cdot M_1^{-1} I_{i1}^* + (M_2^T I_{r2}^*)^T \cdot M_2^{-1} I_{i2}^* \\ &= I_{r1}^{*T} \cdot I_{i1}^* + I_{r2}^{*T} \cdot I_{r2}^* \\ &= I_r^* \cdot I_i^* \\ &= r(I_r \cdot I_i - 0.5\|I_r\|^2) \end{aligned}$$

2: Up to now, the responder calculated the similarity value v;
3: **return** v;

---

4   Security Analysis

In this section, we discuss the security issues involved in the proposed scheme
and provide some security proofs according to our adversary model, including
the communication security and protection for the users' profile.

(1) Communication Security. In order to guarantee communication security,
it is necessary to resist the attack from external adversary. Any entity can be an
external adversary if he/she tries to modify or eavesdrop on the wireless channel between entities. Our scheme, however, can realize the secure information

exchange between users. In our scheme, all the users need to register and get certificates ID, and they can check other entities by verifying the certificates. Moreover, all the delivered important information will be processed by a hash function $H()$ to get a hash value, this value is also included in the message, when users get the message, they can check if the information is modified or not by comparing the hash value. In addition, the delivered profile is encrypted by M_1^{-1} and M_2^{-1}. Through this way, users can verify message easily and external adversaries can get nothing of users' information. Besides, we set a threshold of response time, Δt, to resist the replaying attack. We assume the message is sent at t time point, and received at t^* time point. If $t^* - t < \Delta t$, users accept the message, and rejects otherwise.

(2) Profile Security. In our scheme, the *initiator*'s interest information is encrypted by two random matrices which is very difficult to decipher by brute force, and other transmitting message between *initiator* and *responder* only includes randomly generated vector and matrices as well as similarity value v. Therefore, it is impossible to infer any useful information from the delivered message.

Theorem 1. We can realize the Level-I privacy if the initiator's information is secure when it has been processed.

Proof: the message from *responder* to *initiator* contains nothing that has a correlation with the *responder*'s private information, so the *initiator* cannot infer anything. As for *initiator*'s information, it is expanded and multiplied by r which is generated randomly and the number in different time periods may not be the same, it is hard to guess the specific number. As the *responder* is honest-but-curious user, he/she will not monitor the exact process when initiator expands his/her interests vector and runs the Algorithm 2. Without knowing the operation process, it is difficult to attain the exact profile of *initiator*.

Theorem 2. We can realize the Level-II privacy if the users' information is protected based on Algorithm 2.

Proof: on the *responder*'s side, the context in the delivered message has no correlation with *responder*'s private information. Even though the message has been captured by external adversary, there is no possibility to infer the *responder*'s information. On the *initiator*'s side, according to Algorithm 2, finally the *initiator*'s interests profile is encrypted into $B = \{M_1^{-1}I_{i1}^*, M_2^{-1}I_{i2}^*\}$. The dividing vector S as well as matrices M_1^{-1} and M_2^{-1} is generated randomly and individually used for only one time, in different time periods they are certainly not the same. Even the external adversary captured the message which contain the M_1^{-1} and M_2^{-1}, it is very difficult to guess and not to mention getting the exact information about *initiator*.

From the above analysis, the security of profile can be guaranteed.

5   Conclusion

In this paper, we proposed a secure and effective friend finding scheme to satisfy the requirements of privacy preserving in proximity mobile social networks without any trusted third party. We adopt a novel kNN based encryption, asymmetric scalar-preserving encryption, which is not recoverable. The profile of users will be processed in different ways using binary random vector and matrices. Our scheme avoids possible attacks from both the users and external adversaries. The analysis shows that our scheme can realize a secure fine-grained matching.

Acknowledgements. This work is supported by the National Natural Science Foundation of China under Grant No. 61103035 and the Science and Technology Program of Hunan Province under Grant No. 2014GK3029.

References

1. Boneh, D., Goh, E.-J., Nissim, K.: Evaluating 2-DNF formulas on ciphertexts. In: Kilian, J. (ed.) TCC 2005. LNCS, vol. 3378, pp. 325–341. Springer, Heidelberg (2005)
2. De Cristofaro, E., Kim, J., Tsudik, G.: Linear-complexity private set intersection protocols secure in malicious model. In: Abe, M. (ed.) ASIACRYPT 2010. LNCS, vol. 6477, pp. 213–231. Springer, Heidelberg (2010)
3. Dong, W., Dave, V., Qiu, L., Zhang, Y.: Secure friend discovery in mobile social networks. In: 2011 IEEE INFOCOM, pp. 1647–1655. IEEE (2011)
4. Freedman, M.J., Nissim, K., Pinkas, B.: Efficient private matching and set intersection. In: Cachin, C., Camenisch, J.L. (eds.) EUROCRYPT 2004. LNCS, vol. 3027, pp. 1–19. Springer, Heidelberg (2004)
5. Ioannidis, I., Grama, A., Atallah, M.J.: A secure protocol for computing dotproducts in clustered and distributed environments. In: Proceedings of 2002 International Conference on Parallel Processing, pp. 379–384. IEEE (2002)
6. Kissner, L., Song, D.: Privacy-preserving set operations. In: Shoup, V. (ed.) CRYPTO 2005. LNCS, vol. 3621, pp. 241–257. Springer, Heidelberg (2005)
7. Li, M., Cao, N., Yu, S., Lou, W.: FindU: privacy-preserving personal profile matching in mobile social networks. In: 2011 IEEE INFOCOM, pp. 2435–2443. IEEE (2011)
8. Liu, Q., Wang, G., Wu, J.: Time-based proxy re-encryption scheme for secure data sharing in a cloud environment. Inf. Sci. **258**, 355–370 (2014)
9. Lu, R., Lin, X., Liang, X., Shen, X.: A secure handshake scheme with symptoms matching for mHealthcare social network. Mob. Netw. Appl. **16**(6), 683–694 (2011)
10. Lu, R., Lin, X., Shen, X.: SPOC: a secure and privacy-preserving opportunistic computing framework for mobile-healthcare emergency. IEEE Trans. Parallel Distrib. Syst. **24**(3), 614–624 (2013)
11. Manweiler, J., Scudellari, R., Cox, L.P.: Smile: encounter-based trust for mobile social services. In: Proceedings of the 16th ACM Conference on Computer and Communications Security, pp. 246–255. ACM (2009)
12. Pietiläinen, A.K., Oliver, E., LeBrun, J., Varghese, G., Diot, C.: MobiClique: middleware for mobile social networking. In: Proceedings of the 2nd ACM Workshop on Online Social Networks, pp. 49–54. ACM (2009)

13. Rane, S., Sun, W., Vetro, A.: Privacy-preserving approximation of L1 distance for multimedia applications. In: 2010 IEEE International Conference on Multimedia and Expo (ICME), pp. 492–497 (2010)
14. Sang, Y., Shen, H.: Efficient and secure protocols for privacy-preserving set operations. ACM Trans. Inf. Syst. Secur. (TISSEC) **13**(1), 9 (2009)
15. Von Arb, M., Bader, M., Kuhn, M., Wattenhofer, R.: VENETA: serverless friend-of-friend detection in mobile social networking. In: IEEE International Conference on Wireless and Mobile Computing Networking and Communications (WIMOB 08), pp. 184–189. IEEE (2008)
16. Wang, G., Musau, F., Guo, S., Abdullahi, M.B.: Neighbor similarity trust against sybil attack in P2P e-commerce. IEEE Trans. Parallel Distrib. Syst. **26**(3), 824–833 (2015)
17. Wang, Y., Xu, J.: Overview on privacy-preserving profile-matching mechanisms in mobile social networks in proximity (MSNP). In: 2014 Ninth Asia Joint Conference on Information Security (ASIA JCIS), pp. 133–140. IEEE (2014)
18. Xie, Q., Hengartner, U.: Privacy-preserving matchmaking for mobile social networking secure against malicious users. In: 2011 Ninth Annual International Conference on Privacy, Security and Trust (PST), pp. 252–259. IEEE (2011)
19. Zhang, R., Zhang, J., Zhang, Y., Sun, J., Yan, G.: Privacy-preserving profile matching for proximity-based mobile social networking. IEEE J. Sel. Areas Commun. **31**(9), 656–668 (2013)

A Real-time Android Malware Detection System Based on Network Traffic Analysis

Hongbo Han[1], Zhenxiang Chen[1(✉)], Qiben Yan[2], Lizhi Peng[1], and Lei Zhang[1]

[1] School of Information Science and Engineering, University of Jinan,
Jinan 250022, China
czx@ujn.edu.cn
[2] Shape Security, Mountain View, CA 94040, USA

Abstract. Mobile devices are everywhere nowadays, such as mobile phone, mobile tablets. Meanwhile, various malwares on mobile terminals are emerging one after another, especially on the open-source Android system. Traditional detection schemes are based on static method or dynamic method. In recent years, industry and academia have paid close attention to the detection mechanisms using network behaviors to identify the malware. In this paper, we design a real-time Android malware detection system based on network traffic analysis, which includes a training model and a real-time detection model. By training over the malware traffic using the training model, we find that 76.33 % DNS queries and 45.39 % HTTP requests are all malicious. We set up a real-time scanning service based on the malicious URLs that are captured in the training model, which is the core of the real-time detection model. By performing malware detection using the established real-time detection model, we show that the detection rate using the real-time scanning service is much higher than the integrated service. Meanwhile, the detection rate will further improve by integrating more third-party scanning services into our system.

Keywords: Android malware · Network traffic · Real-time detection system · DNS traffic · Integrated service · Training model

1 Introduction

The usage of mobile terminals makes us step into the era of mobile, various applications make our life richer and more colorful, but what followed is the proliferation of malicious software. It has attracted more researchers in this field and made a large number of significant efforts [1,2]. The traditional detection scheme is the static method, it gets source codes and analyzes the malicious program segments. But this method lacks of real-time analysis, and couldn't detect the malware variants. Unlike static technique, dynamic technique is based on behavior analysis, it monitors the system calls, access to the sensitive data and so on, distinguish between normal and abnormal behavior to reach the purpose

© Springer International Publishing Switzerland 2015
G. Wang et al. (Eds.): ICA3PP 2015, Part III, LNCS 9530, pp. 504–516, 2015.
DOI: 10.1007/978-3-319-27137-8_37

of identifying, but to provide real time analysis of application behaviors are too resource consuming to be deployed on smart phones.

Some works that are based on network behavior features to identify the malware have attracted more researches gradually in recent years, currently implemented modules but due to the lack of a large-scale malware repository and a systematic analysis of network traffic features, the existing researches mostly remain in theory. Our previous work was based on the Drebin dataset [3] which included 5560 malware samples, captured the first 5 min traffic, had a systematic analysis about the compositions of the traffic data and some features on the application layer, it verified that more than 70 % DNS queries are all malicious in the first 5 min, DNS query and HTTP request could be used to identify the malware.

Based on our previous work, we designed a real-time Android malware detection method. The innovations of this paper lie in the following two aspects:

- Try to use the network traffic to identify the malware.
- Design the distributed third-party scanning services into our system and a method of setting up our real-time scanning service.

This paper is organized as follows: in Sect. 3 we give some backgrounds about the malware network behaviors and the principle of DNS that we most focused on in this paper; readers familiar with this may skip to Sect. 4, which is the system architecture, we describe details about our system in this section; in Sect. 5, we have a presentation about the detection results on our system; in Sect. 7, we make a summary and give our conclusions; in Sect. 6, we discuss the limitations in our system and the future work we need to do.

2 Related Work

Mobile devices such as smart phones, tablets, and mobile broadband cards, are important to users with the widespread popularity of the network, especially on Android OS. The analysis and detection of Android malware have been an active area of research in recent years.

Numerous studies have highlighted the weaknesses and potential for misuse of various aspects of the Android security model [4]. These researches are mostly based on static analysis, and open-source tools [5] are used to decompile and disassemble the source code. Recent studies focus on the malicious behaviors [6], these researches all analyze the malware at run-time dynamically. Meanwhile, several works have examined mobile device network traffic to learn about their general network characteristics [7].

Network level analysis of malware behavior offers a complementary means of characterizing and mitigating malware. Cheng et al. [8] designed SmartSiren to collect the communication activity information from the smart phones. But it's impractical to run a agent on each smart phone. Tenenboim-Chekina et al. [9] described and analyzed a new type of mobile malware applications with self-updating capabilities, and then presented a network-based behavioral analysis for detecting this type of malware, their work has shown that there was a huge difference in network features between the malicious and the benign, for instance, inbound and outbound bytes, inbound and outbound data, inner and outer time intervals. Furthermore, based on the applications' network traffic patterns, Shabtai et al. [10] designed a system that followed the hybrid In trusion Detection Systems (IDS) approach and in the client-server architecture. But their work only focused on the several malicious types, which is not scalable. Recently, Jin et al. [11] presented a SDN (Software Defined Network) based mobile malware detection system and proposed several mobile malware detection algorithms that are implemented using SDN. It detects mobile malware by identifying suspicious network activities through real-time traffic analysis, which only requires connection establishment packets. Their detection framework is advanced, but it is difficult to deploy the system on the existing computer network architecture.

Furthermore, recent work has shown that detection of malicious domains can also be accomplished by passively monitoring DNS at the upper levels of the DNS hierarchy, this allows DNS operators to independently detect malicious domains without relying on local recursive DNS servers [12]. Ultimately, these systems allow network operators to assemble DNS blacklists of malicious and suspicious domains in order to detect and prevent malicious activities on the network. Leyla et al. [13] detect malicious domains through the use of passive DNS monitoring and machine learning. Lever et al. [14] analyzed malicious traffic in cellular carriers and verified the malicious existing in real mobile network through empirical results. KANEI et al. [15] proposed a method to observe these DNS communication of Android malware using sandbox analysis.

Through summarizing the existing research works above, we knew that although there were some studies focusing on network behaviors about the Android malware, lacked of some detection methods using the Android malware network traffic, especially for real-time detection method. In this paper, for the basic two points: to identify the Android malware using network traffic and the real-time detection, we proposed an Android malware detection system including training model and real-time detection model.

3   Background

3.1   Malware Network Behavior

During the analysists examine the remote control functionality among the malware payloads, most of the samples will turn the infected phones into bots for remote control [1]. As we know, the C&C channel utilizes some communication protocols to distribute the instructions (commands) from the C&C servers to the bots. As this coordination empowers the botnet, the communication channel plays the vital role in the existence of the botnet and the effectiveness of the botnet's attacks. A botnet's communication channel can either be a pushor pull channel: in the push channel, the bots wait for the C&C servers to actively contact them with instructions; while in the pull channel, the bots periodically contact one of the C&C servers for instructions. The encrypted IRC protocol was widely used by early botnets for their communication. This protocol is still used by many current botnets. However, as IRC becomes a less common protocol and as defenders pay increasing attention to detection of botnets based upon their communication signatures botnets are shifting to more sophisticated and agile communication methods. For example, the communication can be disguised as common and legitimate network traffic using HyperText Transfer Protocol (HTTP) or Peer-to-Peer (P2P) protocols especially for the mobile botnets controlling. Additionally, some botnets hide instructions in postings on social network sites. There is also increasing use of public key cryptography to authenticate the C&C servers and their instructions, thus making it hard for others to take control of a given botnet. Specifically, the malware that use the HTTP-based web traffic to receive bot commands from their C&C servers. We also observe that some malware families attempt to be stealthy by encrypting the URLs of remote C&C servers as well as their communication with C&C servers.

3.2 DNS Query and Response

The domain name space is structured like a tree. A domain name identifies a node in the tree. For example, the domain name F.D.B.A. identifies the path from the root to a node F in the tree (see Fig. 1(a)). The set of resource information associated with a particular name is composed of resource records (RRs) [16,17]. The depth of a node in the tree is sometimes referred to as domain level. For example, A. is a top-level domain (TLD), C.A. is a second-level domain (2LD), F.C.A. is a third-level domain (3LD), and so on. DNS queries are usually initiated by a stub resolver on a user's machine, which relies on a recursive DNS resolver (RDNS) for obtaining a set of RRs owned by a given domain name. The RDNS is responsible for directly contacting the AuthNSs on behalf of the stub resolver to obtain the requested information, and return it to the stub resolver. The RDNS is also responsible for caching the obtained information up to a certain period of time, called the Time To Live (TTL), so that if the same or another stub resolver queries again for the same information within the TTL time window, the RDNS will not need to contact the authoritative name servers (thus improving efficiency). Figure 1(b) enumerates the steps involved in a typical query resolution process, assuming an empty cache. During some study [1], they found that most C&C servers were registered in domains controlled by attackers themselves. In this paper, DNS is one kind of the traffic that we most focused on.

4 Methodology

Zhou et al. [1] examined the remote control functionality of the malware payloads. Specifically, almost all of these samples that used the HTTP based web traffic to receive bot commands from their C&C servers. Furthermore, they also found that most C&C servers were registered in domains controlled by attackers themselves. Based on this, our detection method is based on the DNS query and HTTP request, uses these two network behavior features to identify the malware.

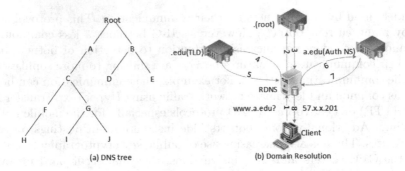

Fig. 1. Example of the domain space and resolution process

4.1 Dataset

The dataset comes from Drebin project [3], which was collected from the Google-Play Store, different alternative Chinese Markets, alternative Russian Markets and other Android websites, malware forums and security blogs during August 2010 to October 2012. Additionally, it includes all samples from the Android Malware Genome Project [1]. After the adware samples having been removed, the final dataset contains 5,560 malware samples. To the best of our knowledge, this is one of the largest malware datasets that has been used to evaluate a malware detection method on Android. An overview of the top 24 malware families (malware number exceed 20) in the dataset is provided in Table 1 including several families that are currently actively distributed in application markets. Note that only the top 24 families are shown and our dataset contains 927 further malicious samples.

Table 1. Top 24 families in our dataset (number ≥ 25)

ID	FamilyName	Num	ID	FamilyName	Num
1	FakeInstaller	925	13	ExploitLinuxLotoor	70
2	DroidKungFu	667	14	Glodream	69
3	Plankton	625	15	MobileTx	69
4	Opfake	613	16	FakeRun	61
5	GinMaster	339	17	SendPay	59
6	BaseBridge	330	18	Gappusin	58
7	Iconosys	152	19	Imlog	44
8	Kmin	147	20	SMSreg	41
9	FakeDoc	132	21	Yzhc	37
10	Geinimi	92	22	Jifake	29
11	Adrd	91	23	Hamob	28
12	DroidDream	81	24	Boxer	27

4.2   System Architecture

Overview. Our system is an anti-malware system for Android, and it has two models: the training model (showed in Fig. 2(a)) and the real-time detection model (showed in Fig. 2(b)). The former is designed to train the malware samples to set up the real-time scanning service, which is the core matter of the latter. The training model uses existing third-party malware scanning services to detect the malicious URLs that extract from the malware traffic data. It is an modular, extensible, distributed and has been tested with freely available online services such as URLVoid [18], VirusTotal [19] and Trend Micro [20].

As shown in Fig. 2, our system consists of three main modules: (1) detection center, which provides scanning services; (2) traffic collector, which collects the network traffic data; (3) notifier, which mainly sends detection result to the user. Next, we will give more details about these three modules.

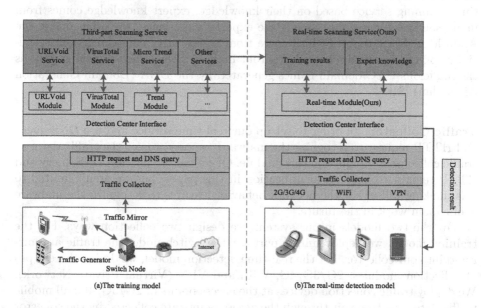

(a)The training model   (b)The real-time detection model

Fig. 2. System architecture

Detection Center. Detection center use malware scanning service with a public API or web interface to provide service for the system. At present, the third-party malware scanning services in our training model include URLVoid, Virus-Total and Trend Micro.

The currently implemented modules and their descriptions in the training model:

– URLVoid: It integrates more than 40 kinds online URL scanning service, which includes MyWOT, SpyEye Tracker, DrWeb, BitDefender, AVGThreatLabs and so on. Its detection result is more accurate than the single scanning engine.

- VirusTotal: Like URLVoid, VirusTotal is an information aggregator from Google, website/domain scanning engines includes Alexa from Amazon, Baidu-International from baidu, Kaspersky URL advisor from Kaspersky and so on.
- Trend Micro: Site Safety Center, one of the biggest domain credit database in the world. Relative to the integration scanning services, Trend Micro could provide more specific details about the website, such as the site type, it helps block the pornographic website, which may be considered as safety.

Third-party scanning services are provided by the third-party safety monitoring service providers, these services are distributed on the web, as an extensible architecture, any verified and public third-party service who provides malicious URL detection service could serve for our system. In the real-time detection model, the real-time service is mainly set up by the malicious URLs detected by the training model, on the other hand, for some suspicious URLs, which have some malicious features, security experts could put them into the real-time scanning service based on their knowledge, expert knowledge comes from many sources, for instance, one is the experts' experience, the other one is the Android malware reports which come from the security companies daily, especially for the newly discovered Android malware, the other typical sample is the malicious C&C domain names generated by the DGA (Domain Generation Algorithm) [21].

Traffic Collector. In order to set up our real-time service and use DNS query and HTTP request to recognize the malware, we need to get the traffic data, so traffic collector is designed in this module. Of course, we just use DNS query and HTTP request to have an identification in this paper, but we aren't limited to this, making full use of the network behavior features to recognize the malware is our main work in the future.

For the two models in our system, we design two collection ways. For the training model, we deploy mirror ports at the switch node, the traffic are mirrored into our collector. For the real-time detection model, we design three types of collection modules: 2G/3G/4G, WiFi and VPN (Virtual Private Network). We deploy traffic collection devices at the access points of 2G/3G/4G, all mobile traffic data that transmit through the access points are collected by the collector server; a WiFi collection module is designed in this connectivity mode, firstly, we deploy port mirrors at the router nodes, when user's device connects to the Internet through the router, the traffic data are mirrored into our collector server via the port mirrors; our system also provides the other type of traffic collection service, it collects users' mobile traffic who use VPN, we set up mirror ports at the gateway nodes, these traffic data are also mirrored into our collector server.

Last but not least, it should accomplish the extraction of DNS query and HTTP request information from the traffic data in this module, at this point, we have special python program to deal with it, after getting the DNS queries and HTTP requests from traffic data, they are sent to the detection center.

Notifier. Once find an app connecting to a malicious site, the user needs to get warning message from the detection center. In our system we design an app called Notifier which installed in the user's mobile terminal, it connects to the detection center, and any malicious connection detected by third-party scanning services could be notified to the user.

5 Evaluation

5.1 The Training Model

In order to set up our real-time scanning service, firstly, we sample 3500 malware samples in our 4546 samples (all in the first 24 malware families showed in Table 1) randomly, then import the emulator to capture their traffic in the first 5 min based on the automated collection platform we designed in our previous work. After detecting the DNS query and HTTP request that extracted from the traffic data, we found that at least 69.55 % DNS and 40.89 % HTTP traffic data were malicious using the method of detecting the traffic data packets on the URLVoid. Furthermore, we use the other third-party scanning services VirusTotal and Trend Micro in our system to detect the DNS queries and HTTP requests, the results are showed in Fig. 3.

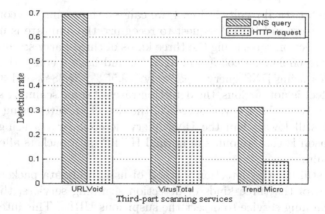

Fig. 3. The percentage of malicious DNS queries and HTTP requests detected by the three third-party scanning services

From Fig. 3, we know that the Trend Micro performs the worst, the detection rate using DNS query is about 30 % and the detection rate using HTTP request is even lower than 10 %; moreover, the integrated detection scanning services URLVoid and VirusTotal perform better than the single scanning service Trend Micro; the effect using DNS query is better than HTTP request.

In addition, considering some malwares only have DNS queries, which indicates that the malwares have begun to show a tendency to the malicious sites, but have not begun to transmit data to the C&C servers; also, some malwares directly set up HTTP connection to the C&C server and have no DNS queries. So we use the combined feature of DNS query and HTTP request to recognize the malware, and then have a detection, the results are shown in Fig. 4.

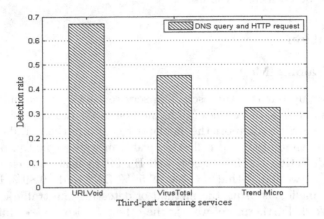

Fig. 4. The detection results using the combined feature of DNS query and HTTP request

From our statistical results in Fig. 4, we can see that using the combined feature of DNS query and HTTP request to recognize the malware is not so satisfactory, the detection rates using the three kinds of third-party scanning services respectively are 66.93 %, 45.63 % and 32.52 %, and have a comparison with the detection rates using DNS query separately: 69.55 %, 52.38 % and 31.34 %, the promotion effect is not obvious, the detection rates of some scanning services like URLVoid and Trend Micro even decrease, the detection rates using VirusTotal increase, but still lower than the DNS query detection rates using URLvoid. The main reason is that amounts of normal HTTP data packets affect the final detection results.

Next, we still use the detection method of using the data packets, but have an integration of the three kinds of detection scanning services, then use this integrated scanning service to detect the suspicious URLs. This integrated way includes three steps: first, use the URLVoid to have a detection with the selected 3500 malware samples; then for the rest samples that cannot be detected, use the VirusTotal to have a detection; finally for the rest samples that couldn't be detected by URLVoid and VirusTotal, use the Trend Micro service to detect them. The detection results are showed in Fig. 5. It shows that the detection result of the integrated scanning service is better than any of the three third-party scanning services, the DNS query detection rate could reach 76.33 % and the HTTP request detection rate could reach 45.39 %. It indicates that integrating the third-party scanning services could improve the detection rate, and the more third-party scanning services integrated into our system, the more accurate detection results will be.

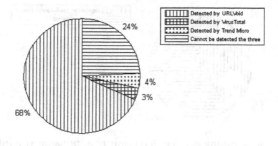

(a) The percentage of malicious DNS queries

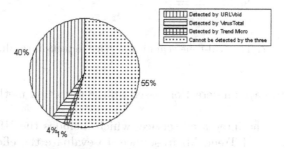

(b) The percentage of malicious HTTP requests

Fig. 5. The detection results using the integrated scanning service

5.2 The Real-time Detection Model

After detecting the 3500 malware samples, we have got the malicious URLs from
their traffic data, and use these malicious URLs to set up our real-time scanning
service, then for the rest of the 1046 samples, we have a detection in our real-time
detection model. To detect how many malwares could be identified, we adopt
an intuitive and pellucid detection method that is based on malware number, it
means if one app whose traffic data contains malicious DNS query or malicious
HTTP request, we consider it as a malware. But according to experiments above,
we know the detection rate using HTTP request is worse than the DNS query,
even nor the combined feature of DNS query and HTTP request, so we just use

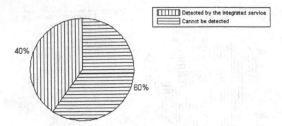

Fig. 6. The real-time scanning service detection results using the integrated scanning service

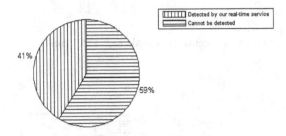

Fig. 7. The real-time scanning service detection results

the DNS query to have an detection based on the detection method of malware number.

Firstly, we use the integrated service, which includes the URLVoid service, VirusTotal service and Trend Micro service, to evaluate the effect in the real-time detection model, the result is showed in Fig. 6. We can see that about 421 samples (40.28 % of all 1046 malware samples) could be detected by this integrated scanning service.

Secondly, to have a comparison with our real-time scanning service, we detect the 1046 malware samples in the real-time detection model, the result is showed in Fig. 7, about 41.18 % malware samples (about 431 samples) could be identified by our real-time scanning service, comparing with the detection rate 40.28 % by the integrated service according to the first step, the real-time scanning service could improve the detection rate in some extent. It mainly because that the experts domain knowledge plays a vital role.

6   Limitations

By our experiments, we have validated the performance of our designed system, as a real-time Android malware detection method using the network traffic, its final detection rate could reach 41.18 %, which is a low detection rate, but we need to realize that we just use the DNS query feature to have an identification, more features need us to discover in our future work, meanwhile, due to only having three third-party scanning services provided in the training model, as we integrate more third-party scanning services training the malware samples, the real-time detection rate would increase more. Besides, the energy consumption problem, especially how to solve the high demands on the computing resource, is not described in this paper.

7   Conclusion

In this paper, we designed a real-time Android malware detection method, which is based on distributed third-party scanning services, and our system is based on the starting point of using network traffic to identify the malware.

Two models (the training model and the real-time detection model) were designed in our system. For the training model, we capture malware samples traffic on our automated collection platform, then use the distributed third-party scanning services to get malicious URLs from the malware samples' traffic data, finally set up the real-time scanning service, which could be used in the real-time detection model. We found that 76.33 % DNS queries and 45.39 % HTTP requests were all malicious; through comparing the detection rate of the integrated scanning service with the real-time service in the real-time detection model, we validated that our real-time scanning service was better than the integrated scanning service, besides, its detection rate would be more higher with more third-party scanning services integrated into our system.

Acknowledgments. This work was supported by the National Natural Science Foundation of China under Grants No.61472164 and No.61203105,the Natural Science Foundation of Shandong Province under Grants No.ZR2014JL042 and No.ZR2012FM010.

References

1. Yajin, Z., Xuxian, J.: Dissecting android malware: characterization and evolution. In: 2012 IEEE Symposium on Security and Privacy (SP), pp. 95–109. IEEE (2012)
2. Becher, M., Freiling, F.C., Hoffmann, J., Holz T., Uellenbeck, S., Wolf, C.: Mobile security catching up? revealing the nuts and bolts of the security of mobile devices. In: 2011 IEEE Symposium on Security and Privacy (SP), pp. 96–111. IEEE (2011)
3. Daniel, A., Michael, S., Malte, H., Hugo, G., Konrad, R., Cert, S.: Effective and Explainable Detection of Android Malware in Your Pocket, DREBIN (2014)
4. Fang, Z., Han, W., Li, Y.: Permission based android security: issues and countermeasures. Comput. Secur. **43**, 205–218 (2014)
5. Jesus, F.: Smali: An Assembler/Disassembler For Androids Dex Format, Google Project Hosting (2013). http://code.google.com/p/smali
6. Lok-Kwong, Y., Yin, H.: DroidScope: seamlessly reconstructing the OS and Dalvik semantic views for dynamic android malware analysis. In: Usenix Security Symposium, pp. 569–584 (2012)
7. Falaki, H., Lymberopoulos, D., Mahajan, R., Kandula, S., Estrin, D.: A first look at traffic on smartphones. In: Proceedings of the 10th ACM SIGCOMM Conference on Internet Measurement, pp. 281–287. ACM, November 2010

8. Cheng, J., Wong, S.H.Y., Yang, H., Lu S.: Smartsiren: virus detection and alert for smartphones. In: Proceedings of the 5th International Conference on Mobile Systems, Applications and Services, pp. 258–271. ACM (2007)

9. Tenenboim-Chekina, L., Barad, O., Shabtai, A., Mimran, D., Shapira, B., Elovici, Y.: Detecting application update attack on mobile devices through network features. In: INFOCOM (2013)

10. Shabtai, A., Tenenboim-Chekina, L., Mimran, D., Rokach, L., Shapira, B., Elovici, Y.: Mobile malware detection through analysis of deviations in application network behavior. Comput. Secur. **43**, 1–18 (2014)

11. Jin, R., Wang, B.: Malware detection for mobile devices using software-defined networking. In: 2013 Second GENI Research and Educational Experiment Workshop (GREE), pp. 81–88. IEEE (2013)

12. Antonakakis, M., Perdisci, R., Lee, W., Vasiloglou, N., Dagon, D.: Detecting malware domains at the upper DNS hierarchy. In: USENIX Security Symposium (2011)

13. Bilge, L., Kirda, E., Kruegel, C., Balduzzi, M., Antipolis, S.: EXPOSURE: Finding Malicious Domains Using Passive DNS Analysis, NDSS (2011)

14. Charles, L., Manos, A., Bradley, R., Patrick, T., Wenke, L.: The core of the matter: analyzing malicious traffic in cellular carriers. In: NDSS (2013)

15. Kanei, F., Yoshioka, K., Matsumoto, T.: Observing DNS Communication of Android Malware using Sandbox Analysis, Ieice Technical report Information and Communication System Security, 112 (2013)

16. Mockapetris, P.: Domain Names-Concepts andFacilities. RFC 1034. X.509 Internet Public Key Infrastructure Online Certificate Status Protocol-OCSP. RFC 2560 (1987)

17. Mockapetris, P.: Domain names-implementation and specification, request for comments 1035. Usc Inf. Sci. Inst. Mar. **19**(6), 697 (1987)

18. URLVoid. https://www.urlvoid.com

19. VirusTotal. https://www.virustotal.com

20. Micro, T.: http://global.sitesafety.trendmicro.com

21. Schiavoni, S., Maggi, F., Cavallaro, L., Zanero, S.: Phoenix: DGA-based botnet tracking and intelligence. In: Dietrich, S. (ed.) DIMVA 2014. LNCS, vol. 8550, pp. 192–211. Springer, Heidelberg (2014)

Sky: Opinion Dynamics Based Consensus for P2P Network with Trust Relationships

Houwu Chen and Jiwu Shu$^{(\boxtimes)}$

Department of Computer Science and Technology, Tsinghua University,
Beijing 100084, China
chenhw11@mails.tsinghua.edu.cn, shujw@tsinghua.edu.cn

Abstract. Traditional Byzantine consensus does not work in P2P network due to Sybil attack while the most prevalent Sybil-proof consensus at present can't resist adversary with dominant compute power. This paper proposed opinion dynamics based consensus consisting of a framework and a model. With the framework, opinion dynamics can be applied in P2P network for consensus which is Sybil-proof and emerges from local interactions of each node with its direct contacts without topology, global information or even sample of the network involved. The model has better performance of convergence than existing opinion dynamics models, and its lower bound of fault tolerance performance is also analyzed and proved. Simulations show that our approach can tolerate failures by at least 13 % random nodes or 2 % top influential nodes while over 96 % correct nodes still make correct decision within 70 s on the SNAP Wikipedia who-votes-on-whom network for initial configuration of convergence >0.5 with reasonable latencies. Comparing to compute power based consensus, our approach can resist any faulty or malicious nodes by unfollowing them. To the best of our knowledge, it's the first work to bring opinion dynamics to P2P network for consensus.

Keywords: Opinion dynamics · P2P · Byzantine consensus · Sybil attack

1 Introduction

Emerging cryptocurrencies (e.g., Bitcoin) demonstrate the demand of consensus over P2P network [19]. However, to keep decentralization, no logically central and trusted authority vouches for a one-to-one correspondence between entity and identity, thus makes it difficult to resist Sybil attack, wherein a adversary creates a large number of pseudonymous identities to gain a disproportionately large influence [13]. Traditional Byzantine consensus algorithms that tolerate only a fixed fraction faulty nodes are not useful in P2P network with the presence of Sybil attack [3]. Existing consensus based on compute power can be Sybil-proof but can't resist adversary with dominant compute power [11].

Opinion dynamics is a field where mathematical-and-physical models and computational tools are utilized to explore the dynamical processes of the diffusion and evolution of opinions in human population. Based on observations of

© Springer International Publishing Switzerland 2015
G. Wang et al. (Eds.): ICA3PP 2015, Part III, LNCS 9530, pp. 517–531, 2015.
DOI: 10.1007/978-3-319-27137-8_38

existing studies that opinion might converge when nodes only take local interactions [7], we proposed the *sky* framework to apply opinion dynamics in P2P network for consensus, as well as the *sky* model to maximize performance. In the framework each node identified by a public key follows nodes they trust, during consensus process each node broadcasts opinion to its followers and decides new opinions from the opinions of its followees following rules of the sky model. The model has better performance of convergence than existing models including MR, voter and Sznajd, and its lower bound of fault tolerance performance is also analyzed and proved. Comparing to compute power based approach, ours enables disarming faulty or potentially malicious nodes by unfollowing them. Theoretic analysis and simulations both show that it can tolerate failures by at least 13 % random nodes while over 96 % correct nodes still make correct decision for initial configuration with convergence $\geq$50 %. Simulations also show that on the SNAP dataset of the Wikipedia who-votes-on-whom network [18] with reasonable latencies, it can reach almost-everywhere consensus within 70 s and tolerate failures committed by 2 % top influential nodes. To the best of our knowledge, it's the first work to bring opinion dynamics to P2P network for consensus.

2   Related Work

Sybil Attack Resistance. One approach to resisting Sybil attack is relying on a certifying authority to perform admission control, which will break decentralization [8]. Another approach is remotely issuing anonymous certification of identity by identifying distinct property of a node, e.g., utilizing geometric techniques to establish location information, but it's unreliable in a network with changing environment [5]. Puzzle computing is also introduced to increase the cost of Sybil attack [6], however, there's no way to resist Sybil attack if the adversary has dominant computing resources. Sybil prevention techniques based on the connectivity characteristics of social graphs is another direction, because of the difficulty to engineer social connections between attack nodes and honest nodes, this approach is considered to be more robust over other ones [2]. Those approaches don't target at the consensus problem directly.

Cryptocurrency. Bitcoin provides Sybil-proof consensus mechanism through an ongoing chain of hash-based proof-of-work (PoW) [19], which is actually a puzzle computing based approach. However, one has dominant compute power can control the network while the rest of the network has no means to resist it, and the proliferation of ASIC miner and mining pools already leads to the monopoly of compute power [9,11]. Ripple [21] also use a relationship based solution to resist Sybil attack similar to ours, however, their algorithm has a major defect that it relies on the assumption that for a node, if 80 % of its followees agree on a opinion, then 80 % of all nodes agrees on the same opinion, but the assumption only stands when a node follows an overwhelming majority of all nodes. As reported, Ripple and other existing solutions like PoS have problem even bigger than PoW [17,20].

3   The Problem and Evaluation Datasets

In traditional definition of consensus, specifically binary consensus, each node has a initial value $v_i \in \{0,1\}$, the consensus problem is to decide upon a common value among all nodes. A node is *correct* if it behaves honestly and without error. Conversely, a node is *faulty*. In a P2P network under an eclipse attack [22], an adversary can always isolate some number of correct nodes hence *almost-everywhere consensus* is the best one can hope for in such networks [14]. Similar to existing definition [4], *almost-everywhere consensus* is defined that up to εn correct nodes in a P2P network agreed on the *wrong* value, where n is the network size, and $\varepsilon > 0$ is sufficiently small, the wrong value is 1 if initially 0 is the majority among all correct nodes, and vise versa. We use the term *opinion* instead of *value* in later sections following the convention of opinion dynamics.

We evaluate our approach on the SNAP dataset of Wikipedia who-votes-on-whom [18] called as the *wiki* dataset in this paper. We also impose a constraint which can be enforced in P2P client of each correct node that *indegree* $>= 10$, thus all nodes with followees less than 10 are removed. Parameters of the result network is shown in Table 1, and the cumulative distributions of indegrees and outdegrees are shown in Fig. 1.

Table 1. Datasets parameters

Name	Wiki
Nodes counts	998
Average degree	33.33
Diameter	5
Average path length	2.34
Density	0.033
Average clustering coefficient	0.183
Eigenvector centrality sum change	0.029

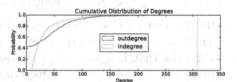

Fig. 1. Degree distribution of the wiki dataset

To facilitate comparing the impact of network size, we also run simulations upon three uniform networks with size of 100, 1000, 5000 nodes, where each node has the same degree and connect to each other randomly. Those dataset are named as *uniform-less*, *uniform* and *uniform-more* respectively.

4   The Sky Opinion Dynamics Framework

4.1   Network Constructing

In our framework, each node in the P2P network is owned by somebody and identified by a public key. When the owner of node A trusts the owner of node B, owner of A can set A to follow B in the P2P client, and B is called as *followee* while A is called as *follower*. The network can be abstracted to a directed graph where each peer is a node, and each trust relationship is a directed edge. To ensure connectivity and safety, each correct node is constrained by the P2P client to have at least a minimum number of followees.

4.2 Consensus Process

Nodes in our framework are equally privileged and equipotent participants in the consensus process in any time as ordinary opinion dynamics. However, we introduced the concept of *round* into the consensus process which is commonly used in existing Byzantine consensus but not in opinion dynamics. Starting from a initial state as the first round, each correct node determines when to finish its current round and decides its new value following a common rule according to its current value and the values of its followees, and then enters the next round. The common rule used here shapes *the opinion dynamics model* which will be introduced in Sect. 5. Note here to avoid centralization no global clock or coordinator is used, each node decides how and when to enter next round separately, thus each node may enter the same round in different time.

A node makes its final decision when enough rounds (e.g., 40) passed. A node is *deciding* before making final decision. If a node finally agrees at 0 or 1, then it's *decided*. A node is *confused* if it's considered to be safe at neither 0 nor 1. For each node, by denoting the count of 0 and 1 in its current value and the values of its followees respectively, the final decision follows the following rules:

1. If $n0 > (n0 + n1) * T$ then agree at 0 and the criteria to agree 1 is similar. The T constant controls the strategy to be aggressive or conservative. Greater T results that less nodes to agree at wrong opinion but more nodes to be confused. We use $T = 2/3$ in experiments.
2. If can't agree at 0 or 1, then it's *confused*.

4.3 Message Passing

A followee unidirectional broadcasts signed messages to all its followers. We allow a faulty node's signature to be forged by an adversary, thereby permitting collusion among the faulty nodes. Broadcast is implemented by DHT and asymmetric cryptography. For a node as followee, all its followers and itself form a sharing group (known as a "swarm") identified by the followee's public key. Each broadcasted message is signed with the private key of the followee, and the followers can check the identity and integrity against the followee's public key.

Each message broadcasted by $node_i$ is a tuple of (*nodeid*, *round*, *opinion*, *state*), where *nodeid* is the id of $node_i$, *round* and *opinion* is its current round and opinion, and *state* $\in$ {*deciding*, *decided*, *confused*}.

4.4 Message Handling

According to the well known FLP impossibility [15], consensus cannot be solved deterministically with even a single crash failure in an asynchronous system, because of the inherent difficulty of determining whether a process has actually crashed or is only "very slow" [10]. We use a *message filter* and a *failure detector* which can make mistakes by erroneously adding nodes to its list of suspects [10].

For a *node*, the message filter will refuse to accept any new messages if it has already made its final decision, and it will always keep at most one message from a followee with the largest round denoted as $round_{max}$ while $round_{max} \geq node.round$. The filter is applied when a node receiving a new message as well as when a node finish a round after broadcasting opinion to its followees.

The key idea of the failure detector is that each node maintains a followee nodes list as well as a suspect nodes list. A message is a *valid message* for a node marked as *node* if $msg.round \geq node.round$ or $msg.state \in \{decided, confused\}$. For each node, initially all followees are in the followee nodes list, in each round, a followee is moved to the suspect nodes list for the followee nodes list if no valid message from it in message buffer for a long time (failure detector time out), while a node is moved from the suspect nodes list to the followee nodes list when a new valid message from it is received.

With the help of message filter and failure detector, a node can apply the common rule which shapes the opinion dynamics model in the following way:

1. If a node received a message passed through the message filter, then it should check whether to apply the common rule or not.
2. On failure detector timeout event for each round, it should check whether to apply the common rule or not.
3. A node apply the common rule only when its message buffer has messages from all nodes in its followee nodes list.

5   The Sky Opinion Dynamics Model

At time t, a node receives all the messages broadcasted by its followees at $t - dt$, then finishes processing the received messages and broadcast its new opinion at t. By designating the opinion of $node_i$ at time t to be $v_i(t)$, the model can be expressed as a function $\mathcal{F}$:

$$v_i(t + dt) = \mathcal{F}(v_i(t), V_i(t)) \qquad (1)$$

where $V_i(t) = [v_{f_1}(t), v_{f_2}(t), \ldots, v_{f_n}(t)]$ and $f_1, f_2, \ldots, j_n$ are followees of $node_i$. In later sections we designate the count of 0 and 1 in $\{V_i(t), v_i(t)\}$ to be $n0_i(t)$, $n1_i(t)$ respectively.

However, due to the difficulty to directly analyze the stochastic process of the interactions between every nodes described in Eq. (1), we analyze our opinion dynamics model using *mean field theory (MFT)* [1] which is widely used in opinion dynamics as an effective modeling method [7]. By MFT, the opinion dynamics model shaped by the common rule can be expressed by a continuous differential equation, and the *round* can be regarded as $dt = 1$ in the corresponding equation shown in Eq. (2).

We denote the densities of correct nodes to be $c = c_0 + c_1$ where c_0 and c_1 are the densities of correct nodes with opinion of 0 and 1, and densities of faulty nodes to be $f = f_0 + f_1 + f_s$ where f_0 and f_1 are the density of faulty nodes with opinion of 0 and 1 and f_s are the density of faulty nodes without opinions broadcasted. So we have $c + f = 1$. We also denote densities of all nodes (including correct and faulty nodes) with opinion 0 and 1 to be a_0 and a_1 respectively, thus we have $a_0 = (c_0 + f_0)/(1 - f_s)$ and $a_1 = (c_1 + f_1)/(1 - f_s)$.

By designating the derivative of c_0 on t to be dc_0/dt which is actually the change speed of c_0, we can have Eq. (2) where s_1 is the probability that a node flips from opinion 1 to opinion 0, and s_0 is the contrary.

$$\frac{dc_0}{dt} = -\frac{dc_1}{dt} = c_1 s_1 - c_0 s_0 \tag{2}$$

We adapt the paradigmatic majority rule (MR) model, and then proposed the *sky* model by incorporating the MR model with a simulated annealing (SA) model we proposed.

5.1   Majority Rule Model

Traditional *majority rule (MR)* model needs to select a group each time and then make all of the nodes in the group conform the majority opinion of the group, however, there's no such group in the sky framework. We adapt the MR model by regarding each node and all of its followees as a group, but instead of making all of the nodes inside the group to have the majority opinion, we just let the node itself to have that opinion without its followees changed. The rule is shown as following:

1. If $n0_i(t) > n1_i(t)$, then set new opinion to 0, and vise versa.
2. If $n0_i(t) = n1_i(t)$, then select from $\{0, 1\}$ randomly.

We specify the mean indegree and outdegree of a node to be D. According to the first rule, a node flips from opinion 1 to opinion 0 only when the count of its followees with opinion of 1 is less than $D/2$, and vice versa, and according to the second rule, when the count of its followees with opinion of 1 equals to $D/2$, it has probability of 1/2 to flip, thus for Eq. (2), we can have the following equation:

$$\begin{cases} s_1 = F(\frac{D}{2} - 1; D, a_1) + \frac{1}{2} d(\frac{D}{2}; D, a_1) \\ s_0 = F(\frac{D}{2} - 1; D, a_0) + \frac{1}{2} d(\frac{D}{2}; D, a_0) \end{cases} \tag{3}$$

where $F(k; n, p)$ is the *cumulative distribution function* and $d(k; n, p)$ is the *probability mass function* for k successes in binomial distribution of n trials with probability p.

5.2 Simulated Annealing Model

The *simulated annealing (SA)* model we proposed provides nodes the ability to escape from their current opinion at some probability while keep stable if $n1_i(t)/n0_i(t)$ or $n0_i(t)/n1_i(t)$ is big enough for a node, as shown in the following:

1. If $n0_i(t) > 4 * n1_i(t)$ then set new opinion to 0, while if $n1_i(t) > 4 * n0_i(t)$ then set new opinion to 1.
2. Otherwise set new opinion to 0 with probability of $n0_i(t)/(n0_i(t) + n1_i(t))$ and set new opinion to 1 with probability of $n1_i(t)/(n0_i(t) + n1_i(t))$.

With the notations same as the previous section, for Eq. (2), we can have the following equation:

$$\begin{cases} s_1 = F(0.2D; D, a_1) + \sum_{i=0.2D}^{0.8D} d(i; D, a_1)(\frac{D-i}{D} + \frac{1}{2D}) \\ s_0 = F(0.2D; D, a_0) + \sum_{i=0.2D}^{0.8D} d(i; D, a_0)(\frac{D-i}{D} + \frac{1}{2D}). \end{cases} \tag{4}$$

5.3 Sky Model

For each node, the *sky* model randomly selects a rule from the rules corresponding to the *MR* model and the *SA* model, thus dc_0/dt is a linear combination of that of the MR and the SA model as the following equation, where $d_g c_0/dt$ is Eq. (2) with Eq. (3) and $d_s c_0/dt$ is Eq. (2) with Eq. (4):

$$\frac{dc_0}{dt} = \frac{d_g c_0}{dt} * ratio + \frac{d_s c_0}{dt} * (1 - ratio) = \frac{1}{2}(\frac{d_g c_0}{dt} + \frac{d_s c_0}{dt}). \tag{5}$$

6 Convergence of the Sky Model

Under the assumption that all nodes are correct, we can have $a_0 = c_0$ and $a_1 = c_1$. Because the model is symmetric on binary opinion 0 and 1, and $c_0 + c_1 = 1$, it's **sufficient to only track c_0 and consider** $c_0 \geq 0.5$. According to the mean field equations, dc_0/dt (a.k.a. the change speed of c_0) and $\int \frac{dc_0}{dt} dt$ (a.k.a c_0) are demonstrated in Fig. 2a and b respectively. From Fig. 2a we can see that $\forall c_0 \in (0.5, 1)$ and $\forall D > 0$, change speed of c_0 is always positive, i.e., sky c_0 strictly increases with time t. This conclusion can also be proved mathematically, but it won't be presented here due to lack of space in this paper. From Fig. 2b we can see that network with greater degree D will converge more quickly. We can also see that with a tiny deviation of c_0 from 0.5, even when $D = 5$, c_0 can still converge to 1 in about 10 rounds.

We simulate the sky model on the wiki dataset for 1000 runs starting with $c_0 = c_1 = 0.5$, where *convergence* is defined as $cvg = |c_0 - c_1|/(c_0 + c_1)$, note here the network may also agree at 1 instead of 0. Some of other existing opinion

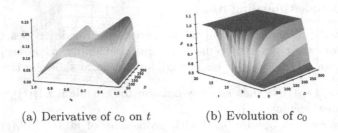

(a) Derivative of c_0 on t (b) Evolution of c_0

Fig. 2. Numeric analysis of the sky model

dynamic models besides the MR model can also be adapted to our framework, the *voter* model can be adapted by that for each node the opinion of a random selected node from all of its followees is chosen, and the *Sznajd* model can be adapted by that for each node if two randomly chosen followees have the same opinion, then the node set its opinion to that opinion otherwise nothing happens. The convergence and rounds to converge for all the models on the wiki dataset are show in Fig. 3. Note **round 41 means the network failed to reach consensus within 40 rounds in that run**, and also each bin of the histogram is 2.

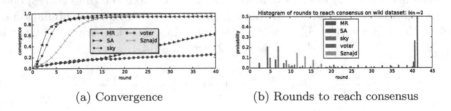

(a) Convergence   (b) Rounds to reach consensus

Fig. 3. Simulation of all the models on the wiki dataset

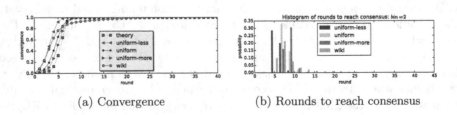

(a) Convergence   (b) Rounds to reach consensus

Fig. 4. Simulation of the sky model on different datasets

From Fig. 3b, we can see that for the sky model, probability of rounds needed to reach consensus decrease asymptotically when greater than 10, and all of the runs can reach consensus within 40 rounds. In contract, all of the other models have some runs can't reach consensus within 40 rounds. Some of runs of the MR model can never reach consensus, and simulation shows the network may stuck in a stable state where both the nodes with opinion of 0 and 1 exist, but they never change in later rounds. Majority of the runs of the SA model will not reach consensus in 40 rounds, simulations shows that the network may vastly change in each round without steady change direction of convergence, and escape in a tiny probability from the state to the track with convergence steadily increased in each round.

The sky model on all the datasets are show in Fig. 4. From Fig. 4a, we can see that for the sky model on each dataset, simulation result of the sky model approximately fits theoretical analysis. Rounds to converge grows with nodes count (denoted as N), and approaches more closely to theoretical result when N is larger, that's because mean field equation works best when $N \rightarrow \infty$, thus $\forall N$ the theoretical result is in fact the theoretical lower bound. From Fig. 4b, we can see that for the sky model, all the runs on all datasets can reach consensus within 40 rounds. Most of the runs can reach consensus quickly in about 10 rounds.

7 Fault Tolerance of the Sky Model

7.1 Sybil Attack

Sybil attack resistance analysis is straightforward. See Fig. 5, where node marked by A is the current node deciding its new opinion, and A decide its opinions according to opinions broadcasted by its followees including correct nodes C and faulty nodes F while nodes S are Sybil nodes. Because of the difficulty for S to make A trust S which is actually **controlled by A rather than** S, there are no directed links from S to A, so Sybil nodes take no effect when A is deciding its new opinion. Collusion among F and S does not help the attack, because the contribution to the decision of A is still the same with F without S.

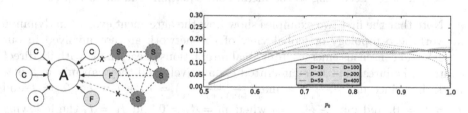

Fig. 5. Sybil attack   **Fig. 6.** Critical points

To compromise the network, creating new Sybil nodes or relationships between them are useless, instead, the adversary should attract more correct nodes to follow the nodes controlled by him. Experiments presented in later sections even show that for the same number of trust relationships from correct nodes to faulty nodes, the smaller the faulty nodes number is, the stronger the attack is.

7.2   Lower Bound

Because the model is symmetric on binary opinion 0 and 1, **it's sufficient to only track the case that** $c_0 \geq c_1$.

According to our definition of *almost-everywhere consensus*, a successful consensus process should fulfill the following requirements:

1. If c_0 is far greater than c_1 (e.g., $c_0 \geq 2c_1$), then at least $(1 - \epsilon)$ proportion of correct nodes should agree at 0.
2. Else at least $(1 - \epsilon)$ proportion of correct nodes should agree at the same opinion which is either 0 or 1.

Under Byzantine failures, a faulty node can behave arbitrarily or even collude with other nodes. Different behavior of faulty nodes contributes differently to the evolution of c_0 in the mean field equations. Here are some scenarios:

1. All faulty nodes left the network at $t - dt$, then at t we have $a_0 = c_0/(1 - f)$ and $a_1 = c_1/(1 - f)$.
2. This scenario is not about failure, but about the dynamic characteristic of P2P network. Same number of correct nodes with opinion 0 joins the network at $t - dt$, then at then at t we have new c_0 denoted as c_0' with $c_0' = 2c_0/(1 + c_0)$ together with the corresponding $c_1' = c_1/(1 + c_0)$, $a_0' = 2c_0/(1 + c_0)$ and $a_1' = c_1/(1 + c_0)$.
3. All faulty nodes always broadcast 1 at $t - dt$, then at t we have $a_0 = c_0$ and $a_1 = c_1 + f$.
4. All faulty nodes broadcast 1 to half of their followees and 0 to the other half at $t - dt$, then at t we have $a_0 = c_0 + f/2$ and $a_1 = c_1 + f/2$.
5. Faulty nodes broadcast opinion randomly chosen from 0 and 1 at $t - dt$, then at t we also have $a_0 = c_0 + f/2$ and $a_1 = c_1 + f/2$.
6. Faulty nodes broadcast 1 when they should broadcast 0 and vise versa at $t - dt$, then at t we have $a_0 = c_0 + f_0'$ and $a_1 = c_1 + f_1'$, where f_0' and f_1' can be calculated according to the mean field equations similar to Eq. (2).

Note that the first two examples show how the agreement evolves in dynamic network, also topology or global view of the network are not involved in our model, and consensus emerges from local interactions of each node with its direct contacts. Failures can't be enumerated exhaustively and they can mix in a network, but since $\max(\frac{c_0+f_0}{1-f_s}) = \max(\frac{c_0+f_0}{c_0+c_1+f_0+f_1}) = c_0 + f$ when $f_0 = f$ and $f_1 = f_s = 0$, and $\min \frac{c_0+f_0}{1-f_s} = c_0$ when $f_0 = f_s = 0$ and $f_1 = f$, the following constraint always stands:

$$\begin{cases} a_0 \in [c_0, c_0 + f] \\ a_0 + a_1 = 1. \end{cases} \tag{6}$$

Lemma 1 (If the network can tolerate any failures committed by given faulty nodes, it must agree at 0). *For a network with c_0, c_1 and f given at time t to be $c_0(t)$, $c_1(t)$ and $f(t)$, if it can tolerate **any** failures committed by faulty nodes, then it must agree at 0.*

Proof. For the case that $c_0(t)$ that is far greater than $c_1(t)$, it stands according to the almost-everywhere consensus requirements stated above. For the else case, if some failures can stop it to agree at 0, then according to the requirements it must agree at 1, s.t. $\exists$ time $t' > t$ and $c_0(t') \leq \varepsilon(1 - f)$. Because of the continuity of c_0 on t, must $\exists t''$, s.t $t' > t'' > t$, $c_0'' \in [c_0(t'), c_0(t)]$, $c_0(t'') = c_1(t) < c_0(t)$ and $c_1(t'') = 1 - f - c_0(t'') = c_0(t'')$. But according to the symmetric property of the model, the failures must also be able to stop it to agree at 1 from time t'', thus leads to contradiction.

Lemma 2 (For given f, greater c_0 tolerate failures equally or better). *For a network with given f, if at two times t' and t'' (no relationship between t' and t'' assumed), s.t $c_0(t') < c_0(t'')$, and for $t > t'$, network can tolerate any failures, then it can also tolerate any failures for $t > t''$.*

Proof. If for $t > t'$ and the network can tolerate any failures, then according to Lemma 1, it must agree at 0. We then discuss in two cases. For $c_0(t'') \leq \varepsilon(1 - f)$, because of the continuity of c_0 on t, $\exists t'''$ s.t. $c_0(t''') = c_0(t'') \in [c_0(t'), \varepsilon(1 - f)]$ and $c_1(t''') = 1 - f - c_0(t''') = c_1(t'')$, thus the network can tolerate any failures for $t > t'''$, we can then conclude the network can also tolerate any failures for $t > t''$. For $c_0(t'') > \varepsilon(1 - f)$, if it can't reach consensus successfully, then must $\exists t''' > t''$ s.t $c_0(t''') \in [c_0(t'), \varepsilon(1 - f)]$, but it's already known that for $t > t'$ s.t $c_0(t) \in [c_0(t'), \varepsilon(1 - f)]$ it can tolerate any failures, thus leads to contradiction.

Lemma 3 (If tolerate smaller a_0, then tolerate greater a_0). *For a network with given f, c_0 and c_1, if at two times t' and t'' (no relationship between t' and t'' assumed), s.t $a_0(t') < a_0(t'')$, and for $t > t'$, network can tolerate any failures, then it can also tolerate any failures for $t > t''$.*

Proof. From Eq. (5) we can see that given other parameters, dc_0/dt strictly increases with a_0 (note that $a_1 = 1 - a_0$), then $c_0(t' + dt) < c_0(t'' + dt)$. According to Lemma 2, it can also tolerate any failures for $t > t''$.

Theorem 1 (Lower bound of fault tolerance). *For any network with known faulty nodes and initial states of correct nodes, thus c_0, c_1 and f are given, if the network can tolerate the failure that all the faulty nodes always output 1, it can tolerate any other failures.*

Proof. According to Lemma 3, and Eq. (6), if a network can tolerate failure with $a_0 = c_0$ together with $a_1 = c_1 + f$, then it can tolerate any other failures. And $a_0 = c_0$ together with $a_1 = c_1 + f$ is exactly the case all the faulty nodes always output 1, thus the theorem stands.

7.3   Fault Tolerance Performance

Because of the constraint that $c_0 + c_1 + f = 1$, it's not convenience to study the performance threshold of fault tolerance on C_0 directly. However, we can translated the threshold question to a new one: if at time t a network with

$c_0 = p$ has no faulty nodes, then uniformly choose f proportion of all the nodes (including opinion with 0 and 1) to be faulty, what's the max value of f the network can tolerate?

$f_{critical}$ is the *critical point* for p if $f_{critical}$ fulfill the following two requirements:

1. $\forall f < f_{critical}$, when $t \to \infty$ and under any failures, $c_0/(1 - f) \geq 1 - \varepsilon$.
2. $\nexists f'$ such that f' fulfill the previous requirement while $f' > f_{critical}$.

Following the definition of *critical point*, according to Theorem 1 for $\varepsilon = 0.05$, by iterating on the mean field equation, critical points can be plotted in Fig. 6, where solid lines are critical points. There are also dotted lines where at each point $dc_0/d_t = 0$. From the figure we can see that $\forall D \in [10, 400]$, as long as $p \geq 0.75$, the network can tolerate any failure with $f \leq 0.13$.

8   Experiment

According to existing studies, latency between peers in DHT is mostly between 50 and 1000 ms [12]. In our experiment, we employ a simply latency model that the time for each message to be delivered conforms gauss distribution of ($\mu = 500$, $\sigma = 500$) with lower cutoff of 50 and no upper cutoff which means a message may never be lost in a small probability even if the node broadcasts it is correct, we also set $timeout = 2000$ for the failure detector.

Since for a network with c_0 far greater than c_1 (e.g., $c_0 \geq 2c_1$), reaching consensus at 0 is successful, but that at 1 is failed, we define *signed convergence* as the Eq. (7), thus only if a network survive from failures, *signed convergence* will equal to *convergence* defined earlier.

$$cvg = (c_0 - c_1)/(c_0 + c_1) \tag{7}$$

To measure final decision of correct nodes, we also define *decision* as the following equation:

$$decision = |d_0 - d_1|/(d_0 + d_1) \tag{8}$$

where d_0 and d_1 is the count of correct nodes which have final decision on opinion 0 and 1 respectively.

We experiment on network started with $cvg = 0.5$ and $f = 13\%$ while faulty nodes always output 1, then in all decided correct nodes (agree at 0 or 1), for all dataset correct deciding (agree at 0) is about 96 %, and uniform datasets have almost the same performance regardless their network scale, as shown in Fig. 7a.

But for the wiki datasets, we also concern the tolerance of failures by collusion of *top $n\%$ influential nodes*, defined as the first $n\%$ nodes by sorting all nodes in descendant order on the count of a node's followees. Simulation shows that for the target $\varepsilon < 5\%$, the algorithm can tolerate failures by 2 % top nodes on the wiki dataset, as shown in Fig. 7b, where the red dotted lines are the case of failed to reach the goal under failures committed by 3 % top nodes. In all decided correct nodes (agree at 0 or 1), correct deciding (agree at 0) is about 96.8 %.

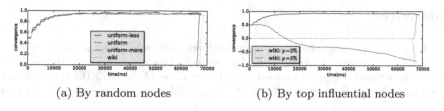

(a) By random nodes   (b) By top influential nodes

Fig. 7. Convergence under failures

Comparing failures committed by random nodes and top influential nodes, we also find that **more centralized trust relationships is easier to compromise the network** even when the total trust relationships participated in the collusion are the same. For the wiki dataset, the total trust relationships is 33256, and for 13 % random nodes, the trust relationships involved is about 4323, while for top 3 % nodes, the trust relationships involved is only 2155, in contrast that the network can survive in the former but no in the later. Even excluding the factor that lots of trust relationships are among the faulty nodes which has no effect for correct nodes in the 13 % random node case, the result also supports the finding.

9 Future Work and Conclusion

Although our approach can successfully runs over the wiki dataset, it also shows the consensus speed degrades comparing to the uniform dataset, as existing studies show that community strength impacts the performance [16]. The relationships between our model and community strength need to be studied further. Fault tolerance performance will degenerate when starting with convergence ≤ 0.5 as we can see from Fig. 6. However, layered on this work, hash value consensus has been developed by us which can tolerate failures well in any case utilizing the premise that hash collision is impossible when hash size is big enough.

Sybil-proof consensus is still an open problem, and even the most prevalent Sybil-proof consensus at present still can't resist adversary with dominant compute power. Opinion dynamics based approach is a new attempt to circumvent problems in existing solutions. Theoretical and experimental result reveals that it has acceptable performance and the ability to resist any faulty or malicious nodes by unfollowing them. To the best of our knowledge, it's the first work to bring opinion dynamics to P2P network for consensus.

Acknowledgments. The authors would like to greatly appreciate the anonymous reviewers for their insightful comments. This work was supported by the National Natural Science Foundation of China (Grant No. 61433008), the National High Technology Research and Development Program of China (Grant No. 2013AA013201), and Project of science and technology of Beijing City (Grant No. D151100000815003).

References

1. Mean Field Theory (2005). http://en.wikipedia.org/wiki/Mean_field_theory
2. Alvisi, L., Clement, A., Epasto, A., Lattanzi, S., Panconesi, A.: SoK: the evolution of sybil defense via social networks. In: Proceedings of the 2013 IEEE Symposium on Security and Privacy, SP'13, pp. 382–396. IEEE Computer Society, Washington, DC (2013)
3. Aspnes, J., Jackson, C., Krishnamurthy, A.: Exposing computationally-challenged Byzantine impostors. Technical report YALEU/DCS/TR-1332, Yale University, Department of Computer Science (2005)
4. Augustine, J., Pandurangan, G., Robinson, P.: Fast Byzantine agreement in dynamic networks. In: Proceedings of the 2013 ACM Symposium on Principles of Distributed Computing, PODC 2013, pp. 74–83. ACM, New York (2013)
5. Bazzi, R.A., Konjevod, G.: On the establishment of distinct identities in overlay networks. In: Proceedings of the Twenty-fourth Annual ACM Symposium on Principles of Distributed Computing, PODC 2005, pp. 312–320. ACM, New York (2005)
6. Borisov, N.: Computational puzzles as sybil defenses. In: Proceedings of the Sixth IEEE International Conference on Peer-to-Peer Computing, P2P 2006, pp. 171–176. IEEE Computer Society, Washington, DC (2006)
7. Castellano, C., Fortunato, S., Loreto, V.: Statistical physics of social dynamics. Rev. Mod. Phys. **81**(2), 591–646 (2009)
8. Castro, M., Druschel, P., Ganesh, A., Rowstron, A., Wallach, D.S.: Secure routing for structured peer-to-peer overlay networks. SIGOPS Oper. Syst. Rev. **36**(SI), 299–314 (2002)
9. Cawrey, D.: Are 51 % attacks a real threat to bitcoin? 20 June 2014. http://www.coindesk.com/51-attacks-real-threat-bitcoin/
10. Chandra, T.D., Toueg, S.: Unreliable failure detectors for reliable distributed systems. J. ACM **43**(2), 225–267 (1996)
11. Courtois, N.T., Bahack, L.: On subversive miner strategies and block withholding attack in bitcoin digital currency. CoRR abs/1402.1718 (2014)
12. Dabek, F., Li, J., Sit, E., Robertson, J., Kaashoek, M.F., Morris, R.: Designing a DHT for low latency and high throughput. In: Proceedings of the 1st Conference on Symposium on Networked Systems Design and Implementation, NSDI 2004, vol. 1, pp. 7–7. USENIX Association, Berkeley (2004)
13. Douceur, J.R.: The sybil attack. In: Druschel, P., Kaashoek, M.F., Rowstron, A. (eds.) IPTPS 2002. LNCS, vol. 2429, pp. 251–260. Springer, Heidelberg (2002)
14. Dwork, C., Peleg, D., Pippenger, N., Upfal, E.: Fault tolerance in networks of bounded degree. In: Proceedings of the Eighteenth Annual ACM Symposium on Theory of Computing, STOC 1986, pp. 370–379. ACM, New York (1986)
15. Fischer, M.J., Lynch, N.A., Paterson, M.S.: Impossibility of distributed consensus with one faulty process. J. ACM **32**(2), 374–382 (1985)
16. Gargiulo, F., Huet, S.: Opinion dynamics in a group-based society. EPL (Europhys. Lett.) **91**(5), 58004 (2010)
17. Kim, J.: Safety, liveness and fault tolerance—the consensus choices stellar (2014). https://www.stellar.org/blog/safety_liveness_and_fault_tolerance_consensus_choice/
18. Leskovec, J., Krevl, A.: SNAP Datasets: Stanford large network dataset collection (2014). http://snap.stanford.edu/data
19. Nakamoto, S.: Bitcoin: a peer-to-peer electronic cash system (2009). http://www.bitcoin.org/bitcoin.pdf

20. Poelstra, A.: A treatise on altcoins (2014). https://download.wpsoftware.net/bitcoin/alts.pdf
21. Schwartz, D., Youngs, N., Britto, A.: The Ripple protocol consensus algorithm (2014). https://ripple.com/files/ripple_consensus_whitepaper.pdf
22. Singh, A., Castro, M., Druschel, P., Rowstron, A.: Defending against eclipse attacks on overlay networks. In: Proceedings of the 11th Workshop on ACM SIGOPS European Workshop, EW 2011. ACM, New York (2004)

Adopting Multi-mode Access Control for Secure Data Sharing in Cloud

Chunhua Li[✉], Ronglei Wei, Zebang Wu, Ke Zhou, Cheng Lei, and Hao Jin

Wuhan National Lab for Optoelectronics, Huazhong University of Science and Technology,
Wuhan 430074, China
{li.chunhua,hust_wrl}@hust.edu.cn

Abstract. Cloud data sharing introduces a new challenge to the enforcement of security controls. The existing approaches are not flexible and low efficiency while performing access control. In this paper, we propose a multi-mode access control scheme, which can support multiple access strategies for data distributed at different areas in cloud. Meanwhile, we introduce the concept of dynamic attribute into the access policy to adjust user's access privileges timely according to his changeable characteristics. Specifically, we present an efficient revocation method which uses confusion token to process the ciphertext at the server. We apply these techniques to design a muti-mode access control system and implement the prototype based on the Openstack platform. Furthermore, we devise a Uniform Access Control Markup Language (UACML) based on XACML, which greatly improves the expressiveness of our multi-mode access control policies. The experimental results show that our scheme has low computational overhead for revocation as well as good flexibility.

Keywords: Cloud · Access control · Dynamic attribute · Revocation

1 Introduction

Data sharing is becoming an important application of cloud storage service [1, 2], which offers service for data owners to conveniently share their data with other users within the cloud. Many cloud service providers, such as Dropbox, Amazon and Aliyun, provide this kind of service. However, this new paradigm of data sharing and access service introduces a great challenge to data access control. First, the means of shared data in cloud is usually diverse, different ways of data sharing should adopt different access control policies. Second, a user may be added into or withdrawn from the cloud frequently, so his access permissions to data should be changed accordingly, thus yielding great performance overhead.

According to ways of data sharing, the space of storage in cloud servers can be logically divided into three categories: private area, group area and public area. In private area, only a data owner has rights to access his/her data at any geographical location or on any terminals, while other users are not allowed to access private data. In group area, users in the same group usually have many common characteristics like interests, research field and educational background, so every user in the same group has identical

G. Wang et al. (Eds.): ICA3PP 2015, Part III, LNCS 9530, pp. 532–546, 2015.
DOI: 10.1007/978-3-319-27137-8_39

permissions to data shared by group users, while other users cannot access these data. Thus all the shared resources can be downloaded by group users with no strict limitation. This access control scheme for group is popular adopted by current cloud storage systems. Let's consider a practical scenario: an assistant wants to share a notice with all the party members and class leaders who are only part of users in the grade group. It is obviously that using the same access privilege for all the members in the group cannot meet such kinds of fine-gained access requirement. In public area, no effective security solution is taken in the existing clouds, all users have free access to public resources as long as they log into the system legally, which is obviously not conducive to encouraging users to share valuable resources. What' more, some users may want to dominate the usage of their data shared in the public environment. For example, Bob hopes that his contributed resources only be read by those who frequently access the similar resources. To meet the demand of such kind of situation, we need to capture the user's access behavior, and then to adjust his access privilege dynamically. Therefore, the dynamic characteristics of user should be taken into account in order to encourage them to share more interesting resources. Similarly, the access to group resources should also be treated discriminatorily for different members in the same group.

Three types of access control system are commonly suggested for cloud environment, that is, Role Based Access Control (RBAC), Attribute Based Access Control (ABAC), Attribute and Role Based Access Control (ARBAC). Sirisha and G. Kumari have proposed RBAC at API level in cloud [3], which follows the least privilege principle by assigning rights according to role specification and user attributes. Data can be accessed by users who have matching roles. RBAC is mostly used for commercial organizations and enterprises. In RBAC, roles are defined in a static manner and cannot be modified dynamically according to the change of organization security requirements. Privacy aware access control system (ARBAC) is proposed for cloud which is composed of two models: RBAC and ABAC [4]. In ARBAC, user needs to provide corresponding subject, resource and environment attributes that are required for the service when he requests to access data. Cloud service provider verifies the given attributes according to defined privacy policy. User and data classification levels are defined according to which privacy preferences and access policies are formulated. Hence complexity of defining policies becomes high with the increase of user classification levels.

To provide fine grained access control in cloud, attribute based encryption (ABE) has been suggested in [5–7]. There are two kinds of ABE: key-policy ABE (KP-ABE) and cipher-text policy ABE (CP-ABE). In KP-ABE, access policy is defined in private key which is assigned to users and can decrypt only those files whose attributes match with this policy. On the other hand, in CP-ABE, access policy is given in cipher text with each file and each user is issued a secret key associated with its attributes, where access structure is defined over attributes assigned to each file. Only users that his attributes' list matches with the structure can access the data. This system requires to define access structure for each user which may become complex because of their varying access requirements. Data owner defines the threshold value in policy specification that represents the number of attributes to be matched for each user request. Therefore, ABE systems introduce large overhead in terms of mathematical operations and algorithms which affect performance of enforcement mechanism. Although CP-ABE is regarded as one of the most desirable technologies for data access control in cloud environment, existing CP-ABE schemes [8–10] are still inefficient for coping with the privilege revocation and inflexible for expression of access control policies.

In this paper, we address aforementioned issues and present a multi-mode access control scheme which combines the advantages of IBAC (Identity-Based Access Control), RBAC and ABAC. Meanwhile, we extend the connotation of attribute by introducing the dynamic characteristic into the ABAC to fulfill the dynamical access control. Besides, an efficient revocation method is proposed to solve the privilege revocation problem in the system. We apply our proposed techniques to construct a prototype of multi-mode access control system based on the Openstack platform, and express the corresponding polices with our defined uniform access control markup language.

2   Notations and Concepts

In this section we mainly define some notations involved in this paper.

Definition 1. In this paper, **attribute** is specified as the user's characteristics. It is represented with a two-tuple consisting of attribute name and its value, and categorized as two kinds of types: static attribute and dynamic attribute.

Static attribute, refers to the attributes whose value are relatively fixed or rarely changed within a period of time. For instance, user's identification number is generally unchangeable, user' email address is usually stable, and user's name rarely alters, so these attributes can be regarded as static attributes. A static attribute set can be represented as

$$S_{static\_attr} = \{attr_{name}{:}attr_{value}\},$$

here, $attr_{name}$ is a set of user's stable characteristics, $attr_{value}$ is the corresponding value, they are one-to-one relationship.

Dynamic attribute, refers to the attribute whose value often changes or cannot be quantified within a certain time range. For example, it is difficult to quantify the user's skill level, which varies along with user's experience. Other similar characteristics like user's activity level and location information are often considered as dynamic attributes. In some situations, dynamic attribute cannot be ignored. For instance, location information is a very important decision factor in the system of geographic information service. A dynamic attribute set can be represented as:

$$S_{dynamic\_attr} = \{attr_{name}{:}attr_{value1}, attr_{value2}, \ldots\},$$

here, $attr_{name}$ is a set of user's variable characteristics, $attr_{value1}$, $attr_{value2}$, …, is the possible value, they are one-to-many relationship.

We can set the user's attribute according to the specific requirements. Supposed the following actual scenario.

A mall is offering online discount, getting coupons must satisfy the following rules: (1) super member of the mall (2) at the specified areas (3) online user registered with his phone number.

From above description, we can extract the following set of user attributes:

{memberlevel, geographic information, phone number}

Here, *phone number* can be regarded as a static attribute because its value doesn't change within a period of time, *geographic information* is a distinct dynamic attribute, *member level* is a non-quantitative feature which corresponds to consumption range, and it will be adjusted with user's consumption.

Therefore, it is obviously inappropriate that only static attribute is considered while formulating access control policy.

Definition 2. UACML (Uniform Access Control Markup Language), a kind of access control policy description language, is designed to uniformly describe different kinds of access control policies such as identity-based access control (IBAC), static attribute-based access control (ABAC) and dynamic attribute-based access control (DABAC). It can express and enforce complex access control policy in a simple and flexible way. Table 1 gives a concrete instance of policy description.

Table 1. An example of access policy description

```
<DACML>
<method value="DABAC" /> <!-- one of in [ IBAC | ABAC | DABAC | NONE] -->
<white list="Bob, Jim, Lucy" />
<black list="Lily, Sally" />
<rule>
    <item name="item1" attr="programming language" value="one in {android, object-c,
c#}" weight=1/>
    <item name="item2" attr="job" value="client developer" weight =1 />
    <item name="item3" attr="skill" value="junior" weight =1 />
    <item name="item4" attr="work years" value=">3" weight =2 />
    <item name="item5" attr="os" value="linux" weight =1 />
    <item name="item6" attr="job" value="server developer" weight =1 />
</rule>
<policy
    value="(weight >2=in {item1,item2,item3})or(weight>2=in{item4,item5,item6})">
</policy>
</DACML>
```

The meanings of labels in Table 1 are described below.

method, used to set the mode of access control, it can be one of the *IBAC, ABAC, DABAC* and *NONE*. If method is set to *NONE, it will* mean that the resource is open for all users.

white, used to set users in the whitelist. Users in the whitelist has priority access to the data, even if his attributes do not satisfy the access policy.

black, used to set users in the blacklist. Users in the blacklist cannot access the data, no matter whether his attributes meet the access policy.

rule, used to describe all kinds of atom-unit of access policy. Each atom-unit is expressed with *item* label which indicates attribute's name and value.

policy, used to describe the logical expression of access policy. If *method* is set to DABAC, *item* label within *rule* label will represent the dynamic attribute, at this moment it will not be a simple 'yes' or 'no' decision while matching the logical expressions (detailed decision processes will be shown in Sect. 3.2).

***Definition 3.* Auth_Token**, a kind of data structure for privilege decision. It is generated by system and returned to the user after a user logs into the system legally. **Auth_Token** has a life cycle, it includes two kinds of types: Basic_Auth_Token and Extend_ Auth_Token. Basic_Auth_Token only contains user's identity, Extend_Auth_Token is an extension to the Basic_Auth_Token, it includes user's identity, static attributes set and dynamic attributes set.

***Definition 4.* Confusion Token**, a kind of data structure for privilege revocation. It describes the rules to create, insert and delete the confusion block, and we use these rules to scramble the ciphertext whose access permissions need to be updated.

3   Our Multi-mode Access Control

Figure 1 gives the model of our multi-mode access control for data sharing in cloud. According to the figure, IBAC scheme is used to quickly verify user's identity in private area, ABAC scheme is chiefly adopted in group area for its flexible and fine-gained access control, and DABAC scheme is considered for uncertain users in public area.

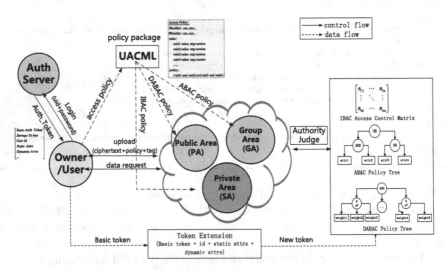

Fig. 1. Multi-mode access control model for data sharing

From Fig. 1 we can find that the process of access control mainly involves four parts: authentication, access policy expression, privilege decision and privilege revocation.

Authentication is used to determine whether the user's request is valid when he logs in the system. Every user should register to the *Auth Server* during the system initialization. If the user is a legal user, *Auth Server* will assign a global unique user's identity (UID) to the user. We use the structure Auth_Token to describe UID which is unique and timeliness. When Auth_Token comes to its end of life, the system will reassign a new Token to the user. UID is used for IBAC scheme to verify the validity of access. User's static attributes set in the structure Extend_Auth_Token is associated with his group characteristics, which means that the element in a user's S_{static_attr} comes from his multiple different groups. User's dynamic attributes set in the structure Extend_Auth_Token is only associated with user's behavior and environment, which means that the element in a user's $S_{dynamic\_attr}$ may be changed with the user's access trace.

3.1 Access Policy Formulation

We have given a general description on the access policy with our UACML and illustrated the meanings of all tags and labels in Sect. 2. Here, we give the corresponding structure schematic about the policies of IBAC, ABAC and DABAC (shown in Fig. 2).

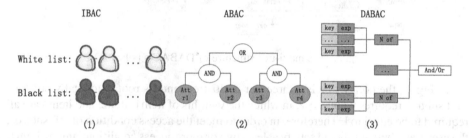

Fig. 2. Structure schematic for different policies

According to the rule of UACML, data owner only need to define the whitelist or blacklist when formulates the access policy for data stored in private area, and to write the valid users' identities into ACL. In our system, the priority of blacklist's decision is higher than whitelist's, namely, if a user is both in whitelist and blacklist, he still has no access to the data.

A binary tree is usually used to represent the policy of ABAC, where the leaf nodes indicate the static attributes, while the non-leaf nodes are logical operators, such as *and*, *or*, *not*, etc. The main work of policy formulation is to set the atom-unit of *rule* labels in UACML, each *item* in rule label implies a static attribute, the policy can be finally formulated through the logical combination of the *item* based on logical operators, e.g.

Policy = ((developer and java) or (designer and max *3d)) and work_years > 2*

The policy of DABAC is also represented in a form of tree structure, but it is different from ABAC's because the policy tree of DABAC is a multi-tree, its leaf nodes are generally expressed with the conditional expressions that the dynamic attributes should meet, and the non-leaf nodes are logical operators or weight value, etc. Generally, the *item* is a conditional expression of dynamic attributes attached a weight options, more detailed description can be seen in Sect. 3.3.

3.2 Privilege Decision

The process of decision is related to the access control policies. In this section we will describe the processes of policy matching by taking an example of DABAC. Due to the limitation of space, the decision processes of IBAC and ABAC are not discussed. Figure 3 shows the multi-tree structure of DABAC's policy which is corresponding to the policy formulation given in Table 1.

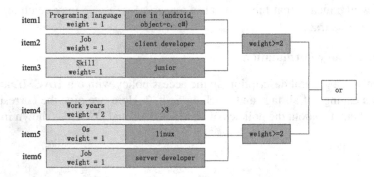

Fig. 3. The multi-tree structure of DABAC's policy

In Fig. 3, the policy tree is a three-tier multi-tree, and its root is logical word 'or'. Left subtree requires weight ≥ 2, in which the weights of item1, item2 and item3 are all required to be equal to 1. Therefore, in order to meet the access condition of left subtree, the user's attribute set should satisfy at least two or more access conditions among item1, item2, and item3. The expression of item1 requires that user's programming language must be object-c or android or c#, so if a user's attribute value of programming language is in this range, he will meet this condition. The expression of item2 requires that the user's job is a client developer, so if the values of a user's working attributes contain 'client developer', he will also meet this condition. The expression of item3 requires that the user's skill proficiency should be at least junior, here junior is a range rather than an exact value, thus if the value of a user's skill attribute is not under the lower limitation of junior, he will meet the access requirements. The decision processes of the right subtree are similar to the left subtree.

After the authority judgment, the system will send feedback to the user attached with his dynamic attributes value. It is generally required that TAG labels in UACML should be set for DABAC scheme, and the value of TAG labels combines dynamic attribute with correction value. After a user accesses the data, the system should not only respond to his request, but also return the TAG labels to the user, and then the user updates his dynamic attribute value according to the TAG label value.

As shown in Fig. 4, the user Job has an uncertain attribute 'dev' in his $S_{dynamic\_attr}$, its original value is 126 and its correction value is 2. So after Job accesses the certain object, the value of attribute 'dev' will be added 2 and become to 128 according to the returned result of TAG label. When the value of attribute 'dev' is added to be greater than the threshold (here, assumed to be 127), uncertain attribute 'dev' will become the user's official attribute and thus affect the authority decision.

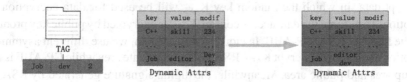

Fig. 4. The processes of dynamic attribute's change

3.3 Privilege Revocation

Most revocation methods need to re-encrypt the data and update the access keys of valid users. Therefore, for user's frequent entrance or revocation in cloud, it always confronts the dilemma of low efficiency. To solve this problem, we present a new data retreatment solution instead of re-encrypting the data. Figure 5 shows the process of data retreatment with confusion token for revocation.

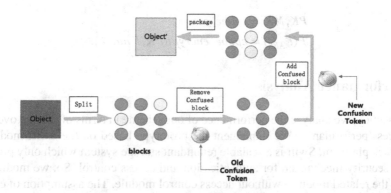

Fig. 5. The process of data re-procession

As described in Sect. 2, confusion token is a structure which defines the rules to create, insert or delete the confused block. When a user's privilege is revoked, an old token and a new token will be send to the cloud server by authorization center, the cloud server then utilizes the old confusion token to scramble the split blocks (insert some new blocks or delete the shuffled blocks) in ciphertext, and the new confusion token is used to recover the structure of scrambled blocks. In the end, only valid users receive the new token, he can access the data with the new token and the secret key. Whereas, the revoked users will be unable to access the raw data because they don't have the new token to recover the structure of scrambled ciphertext even if they own the secret keys. Since the ciphertext needn't be decrypted and re-encrypted, the overhead of revocation is greatly reduced.

3.4 Data Encryption

Data encryption is a basic method to protect data confidentiality. In order to ensure system performance and practicability, we adopt symmetric encryption algorithm AES to encrypt data, in which the random key K_{AES} will be used for data encryption and decryption. To enforce the data access control, K_{AES} is encrypted by public key produced from the PKI, i.e. RSA, CP-ABE. In cloud storage system, we use different asymmetric encryption algorithm to encrypt K_{AES}. RSA is used in private area while CP-ABE is used in group area and public area. Meanwhile, the digital signature generated by RSA will be used in our system to make sure the integrity of data stored in untrusted cloud servers. The process of data encryption is as follows:

$$K_{AES} = rand()^\wedge rand()$$
$$E(Data) = aes\_encrypt(Data, K_{AES})$$

if private area:

$$PK, SK = rsa\_key\_generate()$$
$$E(K_{AES}) = rsa\_pk\_encrypt(K_{AES}, PK)$$

else:

$$PK, MK = cpabe\_setup()$$
$$E(K_{AES}) = cpabe\_encrypt(PK, Data, T).$$

4 Performance Analysis

In this section, we analyze the performance of our scheme in terms of storage overhead and access performance. We implement the prototype based on the Swift module of OpenStack platform. Swift is a scalable redundant storage system which only provides a basic security mechanism for authentication and access control. So, we modify and replace the related modules with our access control module. The assumption of experiment is as follows: the size of user's UID is 8 bytes, each attribute (including attribute name and its value) is 16 bytes, weight value is 2 bytes and logical operator is 4 bytes.

4.1 Storage Overhead

Figures 6 and 7 show the storage overhead of IBAC, ABAC and DABAC. From them we can see the storage overhead of IBAC has a linear relationship with the number of UID, while the overhead of ABAC and DABAC is mainly associated with the access tree structure. Because of the structural characteristics of the binary tree, the number of access policies that a n-layer binary tree can represent is $2^{n-1} - 1$ (not considering the sort of the leaf nodes). In contrast, access matrix of IBAC needs $2^{n-1} - 1$ ACLs to represent the same number of access policies. We take a 5-layer full binary tree as an example for discussion.

The number of access policies that a 5-layer full binary tree can represent is $2^4 - 1 = 15$, the number of associated attributes is 16, and its storage overhead is $16 * 8 + 15 * 4 = 188$ bytes, while the storage overhead of IBAC is $16 * 15 * 8 = 1920$ bytes under the same circumstances. Hence we can conclude that the larger the number of user is, the more complicate the access policy is, and the better ABAC and DABAC are.

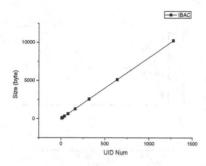

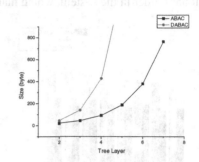

Fig. 6. Storage overhead of IBAC

Fig. 7. Storage overhead of ABAC and DABAC

4.2 Performance Evaluation

The two principal factors that affect the security performance are privilege decision and data encryption and decryption. Since our work mainly focuses on the performance analysis of different access control scheme, we utilize the access time to evaluate the performance. It's necessary to emphasize that access time in our experiments is calculated from positioning the object at Server to getting the object at Client which includes the cost of judging a user's permission and network communication.

Figure 8 shows that the access cost of IBAC grows linearly as the number of user increases. That is because the volume of ACL is becoming larger and larger as the number of user grows, so the additional overhead of reading access policy increases accordingly.

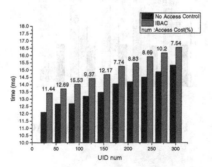

Fig. 8. Access cost of IBAC

Figure 9 shows the access cost of ABAC under two different situations, in which the significant factors are the depth of the access tree and the number of the user's static attribute. As shown in the figure, the access cost becomes larger as the depth of the access tree increases, while the number of user's static attribute has little influence on the cost of decision-making. The reason is that user attributes are organized in a dictionary order in the system, which makes little influence on the query efficiency.

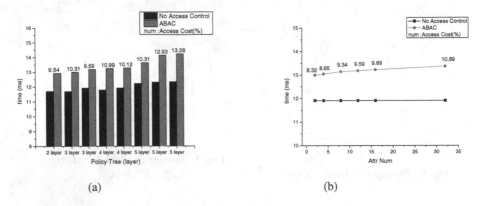

(a)   (b)

Fig. 9. Access cost of ABAC

DABAC has a similar impact factors with ABAC's, but DABAC has higher access cost than ABAC (shown in Fig. 10). The reasons that cause the difference mainly lie in two aspects. (1) The algorithm that DABAC used to judge the user permission is much more complicated than ABAC's. (2) After authorization, some callback functions will revise the values of a user's dynamic attributes which incurs extra performance overhead. So, DABAC's access cost is higher than ABAC's, but it can execute dynamic access control.

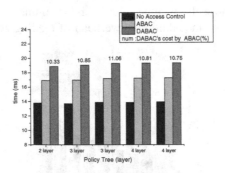

Fig. 10. Access cost of DABAC

As shown in the test results, the net cost of the user authorization is in millisecond level (<10 ms), and when there is no access control, the time from locating the object at Server to getting the object at Client is generally between 10 ms and 20 ms. Contrasting to the time cost (often in second level) of network transmission and data encryption and decryption, our system maintains high performance.

4.3 Revocation Efficiency

From Figs. 11, 12 and 13, we show the time cost of revocation using AES re-encryption and our token scheme respectively. Here, the process of re-encryption contains two steps: to decrypt the ciphertext and then to encrypt the raw data using the new keys. In our test, the delay of network transmission is ignored, and 128-bit keys are adopted in re-encryption scheme, the size of plaintext is from 4 KB to 128 MB, and the ciphertext is divided into twenty pieces of data blocks.

Figure 11 shows that the scheme of re-encryption costs about 25 ms for each MB data when enforcing the revocation, while our token scheme only costs about 6 ms for inserting confused blocks and less than 1 ms for reordering blocks. Hence it is very obvious that the computational overhead of our revocation scheme is far less than that of re-encryption scheme, even though the network transmission overhead is not taken into consideration.

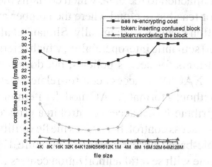

Fig. 11. Time cost per MB data   **Fig. 12.** Time cost for 20 blocks

Figure 12 shows that when the size of file is bigger than 4 MB, the time cost increases sharply for the scheme of re-encryption, and the reordering token scheme almost keeps stable. For example, the time cost for 128 MB-size file of our reordering token scheme is 92.80 ms, while the re-encryption scheme costs 3913.14 ms, and the confused block scheme needs 2047.03 ms. So our revocation scheme is much more efficient than the re-encryption scheme.

From Figs. 11 and 12, we can find the different rules of token has also influence on the efficiency of revocation. We shows the effects of block number on revocation time using two kinds of basic rules, that is inserting the confused blocks into the ciphertext and scrambling the ciphertext (seen in Fig. 13, given 4 MB-size data). From Fig. 13 we can see, with the increase of block number, the time cost of confused blocks shows a linear growth trend, while that of reordering blocks moves in a tight range. That is because the rules of confusion block are much more complicated than that of reordering block, and the former algorithm is also robust enough against attacks, so has better security than the latter.

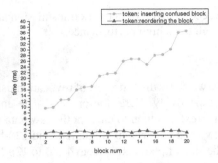

Fig. 13. Time cost vs block number (for 4 MB data)

5 Related Work

Ferraiolo, D.F. and Sandhu, R. provided a kind of RBAC [11], where roles are system-atically defined. An access control list (ACL) is attached to the data, which contains the list of users authorized to access data. This is not feasible in cloud where the number of users is enormous and the status of users also often changes dynamically. Slimani et al. [12] expanded the description of access policy and semantic interoperability, which refers to the idea of XACML to set formalized constraints for access policies, but does not consider the change of attribute. What's more, XACML s access control-related web services standards which language is designed without a formal ABAC model. Literature [13] combines role-based access control and attribute-based access control in a private cloud to achieve the mandatory and discretionary access control, but it loses the flexibility of ABAC because of its combination with role-based access control. Literature [7] proposes an attribute-based access control scheme with several authorization centers to deal with the performance bottleneck caused by a single authorization center, however it causes attribute conflict between different authorization centers when recovering attribute, and it also does not give the sound solution to the revocation. In order to solve the problem of revocation, Hur and Noh [14] proposes a lazy permission revocation scheme from key refreshing with the combination of attribute encryption algorithm, but the security problem caused by the uncertainty of writing time is still potential in the scheme, and it does not discuss the way of revocation for read-only data. G. Wang, Q. Liu and J. Wu presented a hybrid access control model in [15] involving attribute based encryption (ABE), proxy re-encryption and lazy encryption, where complexity and overhead for policy specification increases with the number of attributes and steps required to execute mathematical operations.

6 Conclusions

In this paper, we built a multi-mode access control system for data sharing in cloud that enables only the authorized users to decrypt a ciphertext. Our proposed construction is efficient for revocation and supports both backward and forward security because it is based on the CP-ABE scheme. Specially, our system can support dynamic access control which is very suitable for frequent changeable cloud environment. Our token revocation scheme is a promising technique, which can be applied in any remote storage systems and online social networks etc. In the next phase of the research, we will focus on the algorithm of scrambling confusion blocks to further improve our performance and security.

Acknowledgments. Firstly, the authors would like to thank the anonymous referees of ICA3PP 2015 for their reviews and suggestions to improve this paper. Secondly, the work is supported by the National High Technology Research and Development Program (863 Program) of China under Grant No. 2013AA013203, and also supported by the National Natural Science Foundation of China under Grant No. 61232004.

References

1. Masood, R., Shibli, M.A.: Comparative analysis of access control systems on cloud. In: 13th ACIS International Conference on Software Engineering, Artificial Intelligence, Networking and Parallel and Distributed Computing (SNPD), pp. 41–46. IEEE (2012)
2. Ruj, S.: Attribute based access control in clouds: a survey. In: Signal Processing and Communications (SPCOM), pp. 1–6 (2014)
3. Sirisha, A., Kumari, G.: API access control in cloud using role based access control model. In: Trendz in Information Sciences and Computing (2010)
4. Sanka, S., Hota, C., Rajarajan, M.: Secure data access in cloud computing. In: International Conference on Internet Multimedia Services Architecture and Application (2010)
5. Lee, C.-C., Chung, P.-S., Hwang, M.-S.: A survey on attribute-based encryption schemes of access control in cloud environments. IJ Netw. Secur. 15(4), 231–240 (2013)
6. Yu, S., Wang, C., Ren, K., Lou, W.: Achieving secure, scalable, and fine-grained data access control in cloud computing. In: IEEE INFOCOM, pp. 534–542 (2010)
7. Chase, M., Chow, S.S.M.: Improving privacy and security in multi-authority attribute-based encryption. In: Proceedings of the 16th ACM Conference on Computer and Communications Security (CCS 2009), pp. 121–130 (2009)
8. Yu, S., Wang, C., Ren, K., Lou, W.: Attribute based data sharing with attribute revocation. In: Proceedings of the 5th ACM Symposium Information, Computer and Comm. Security (ASIACCS 2010), pp. 261–270 (2010)
9. Hur, J., Noh, D.K.: Attribute-based access control with efficient revocation in data outsourcing systems. IEEE Trans. Parallel Distrib. Syst. 22(7), 1214–1221 (2011)
10. Xu, Z., Martin, K.M.: Dynamic user revocation and key refreshing for attribute-based encryption in cloud storage. In: 2012 IEEE 11th International Conference on Trust, Security and Privacy in Computing and Communications (TrustCom), pp. 844–849 (2012)
11. Ferraiolo, D.F., Sandhu, R., Gavrila, S.: Proposed NIST standard for role based access control. ACM Trans. Inf. Syst. Secur. 4, 224–274 (2001)
12. Slimani, N., Khambhammettu, H., Adi, K., et al.: UACML: unified access control modeling language. In: 2011 4th IFIP International Conference on New Technologies, Mobility and Security (NTMS), pp. 1–8 (2011)
13. Mon, E.E., Naing, T.T.: The privacy-aware access control system using attribute-and role-based access control in private cloud. In: 2011 4th IEEE International Conference on Broadband Network and Multimedia Technology (IC-BNMT), pp. 447–451 (2011)

14. Hur, J., Noh, D.K.: Attribute-based access control with efficient revocation in data outsourcing systems. IEEE Trans. Parallel Distrib. Syst. **22**(7), 1214–1221 (2011)
15. Wang, G., Liu, Q., Wu, J.: Achieving secure, scalable, and fine-grained data access control in cloud computing. In: IEEE Proceedings of INFOCOM (2010)

A Scheme to Manage Encrypted Data Storage with Deduplication in Cloud

Zheng Yan[1,2(✉)], Wenxiu Ding[1], and Haiqi Zhu[1]

[1] State Key Lab on Integrated Services Networks,
Xidian University, Xi'an 710071, China
zyan@xidian.edu.cn, wenxiuding_1989@126.com,
zhuhaiqi_xdu@163.com
[2] Department of Communications and Networking,
Aalto University, 02150 Espoo, Finland

Abstract. Cloud computing offers a new way of service provision by re-arranging various resources and IT structures over the Internet. Private user data are often stored in cloud in an encrypted form in order to preserve the privacy of data owners. Encrypted data sharing introduces new challenges for cloud data deduplication. We found that existing solutions of deduplication suffer from high computation complexity and cost and therefore few of them can be really deployed in practice. In this paper, we propose a scheme to deduplicate encrypted data stored in cloud based on proxy re-encryption. We evaluate its performance and advantages based on extensive analysis and implementation. The results show the efficiency and effectiveness of the scheme for potential practical deployment.

Keywords: Cloud computing · Data deduplication · Proxy Re-encryption

1 Introduction

Cloud computing offers a new way of Information Technology services by rearranging various resources (e.g., storage, computing) and providing them to users based on their demands. Cloud computing provides a big resource pool by linking network resources together. It has desirable properties, such as scalability, elasticity, fault-tolerance, and pay-per-use. Thus, it becomes a promising service platform.

The most important and typical cloud service is data storage service. The cloud users upload personal data to a Cloud Service Provider (CSP) and allow it to maintain these data. Rather than fully trusting the CSP, existing research proposed to only outsource encrypted data to the cloud in order to ensure data privacy. But duplicated data in an encrypted form could be stored by the same or different users, especially for shared data. Although cloud storage space is huge, this kind of duplication greatly wastes networking resources, consumes a lot of power energy, and makes data management complicated. Deduplication has proved to achieve high space and cost savings, which can reduce up to 90–95 % storage needs for backup applications [9] and up to 68 % in standard file systems [10]. Saving storage is becoming a crucial task of CSP. Obviously, the savings, which can be passed back directly or indirectly to cloud

© Springer International Publishing Switzerland 2015
G. Wang et al. (Eds.): ICA3PP 2015, Part III, LNCS 9530, pp. 547–561, 2015.
DOI: 10.1007/978-3-319-27137-8_40

users, are significant to the economics of cloud business. How to manage encrypted data storage with deduplication in an efficient way is a practical issue. However, current industrial deduplication solutions cannot handle encrypted data. Existing solutions for deduplication suffers from brute-force attacks [7, 11–14]. They cannot flexibly support data access control and revocation [16, 18–20]. Most existing solutions cannot ensure reliability, security and privacy with sound performance [23–25].

In real practice, it is hard to allow data holders to manage deduplication due to a number of reasons. First, the data holder may not be always online or available for such a management, which could cause a big storage delay. Second, the designed system for deduplication could be very complicated in terms of communications and computations. Third, it may intrude the privacy of data holder in the process of discovering the duplicated data by the CSP. Forth, the data holder has no idea how to issue access rights or deduplication keys to a user in some situations when he/she does not know other data holders due to data super-distribution. Therefore, CSP cannot cooperate with the data holder on data storage deduplication in many situations.

In this paper, we propose a scheme based on Proxy Re-Encryption (PRE) to manage encrypted data storage with deduplication. We aim to solve the issue of deduplication in the situation where the data holder is not available or hard to be involved. Specifically, the contributions of this paper can be summarized as below:

- We motivate to save the storage of cloud and preserve the privacy of data owners by proposing a scheme to manage encrypted data storage with deduplication. Our scheme can flexibly support data update and sharing with deduplication even when the data holder is offline. And it does not intrude the privacy of data owners.
- We prove the security and justify the performance of our scheme through analysis and implementation.

The rest of the paper is organized as follows. Section 2 gives a brief overview of related work. Section 3 introduces a system model and preliminaries. Section 4 gives the detailed description of our schemes, followed by security analysis and performance evaluation in Sect. 5. Finally, a conclusion is presented in the last section.

2 Related Work

Reconciling deduplication and client-side encryption is an active research topic [1]. Cloud storage service providers such as Dropbox [2], Google Drive [3], Mozy [4], and others perform deduplication to save space by only storing one copy of each file uploaded. However, if clients conventionally encrypt their data, storage savings by deduplication are totally lost. This is because the encrypted data are saved as different contents by applying different encryption keys. Existing industrial solutions fail in encrypted data deduplication. DeDu [17] is an efficient deduplication system but it cannot handle encrypted data.

Message-Locked Encryption (MLE) intends to solve this problem [5]. The most prominent manifestation of MLE is Convergent Encryption (CE), introduced by Wallace et al. [6] and others [7, 11, 12]. CE was used within a wide variety of commercial and research storage service systems. Letting M be a file's contents, hereafter called the message, the client first computes a key $K \leftarrow H(M)$ by applying a cryptographic hash function H to the message, and then computes the ciphertext $C \leftarrow E(K, M)$ via a deterministic symmetric encryption scheme. A second client B encrypting the same file M will produce the same C, enabling deduplication. However, CE is subject to an inherent security limitation, namely, susceptibility to offline brute-force dictionary attacks [13, 14]. Knowing that the target message M underlying a target ciphertext C is drawn from a dictionary $S = \{M_1, \ldots, M_n\}$ of size n, the attacker can recover M in the time for $n = |S|$ off-line encryptions: for each $i = 1, \ldots, n$, it simply CE-encrypts M_i to get a ciphertext denoted as C_i and returns the M_i such that $C = C_i$. (This works because CE is deterministic and keyless.) The security of CE is only possible when the target message is drawn from a space too large to exhaust.

Another problem of CE is that it is not flexible to support data access control by data holders, especially for data revocation process, since it is impossible for data holders to generate the same new key for data re-encryption [18, 19]. An image deduplication scheme adopts two servers to achieve verifiability of deduplication [18]. The CE-based scheme described in [19] combines file content and user privilege to obtain a file token, which achieves token unforgeability. However, both schemes directly encrypt data with a CE key, thus hold the problem as described above. To resist the attack of manipulation of data identifier, Meye et al. proposed to adopt two servers for intra-user deduplication and inter-deduplication [20]. The ciphertext C of CE is further encrypted with a user key and transferred to the servers. However, it does not deal with data sharing after deduplication among different users. ClouDedup [16] also aims to cope with the inherent security exposures of CE, but it cannot solve the issue caused by data deletion. A data holder that removes the data from the cloud can still access the same data since it still knows the data encryption key if the data is not completely removed from the cloud.

Bellare et al. [1] proposed DupLESS that provides secure deduplicated storage to resist brute-force attacks. In DupLESS, a group of affiliated clients (e.g., company employees) encrypt their data with the aid of a Key Server (KS) that is separate from a Storage Service (SS). Clients authenticate themselves to the KS, but do not leak any information about their data to it. As long as the KS remains inaccessible to attackers, high security can be ensured. Obviously, DupLESS cannot control data access of other data users in a flexible way. Alternatively, a policy-based deduplication proxy scheme [15] was proposed but it did not consider duplicated data management (e.g., deletion, owner change, etc.) and evaluated scheme performance.

As stated in [21], reliability, security and privacy should be taken into consideration when designing a deduplication system. The strict latency requirements of primary storage lead to the focus on offline deduplication systems [22]. Recent studies propose techniques to improve their performances, especially restore performance [23–25]. Fu et al. [23] proposed History-Aware Rewriting (HAR) algorithm to accurately identify and rewrite fragmented chunks, which improved the restore performance. Kaczmar-czyk et al. [24] focused on inter-version duplication and proposed Context-Based Rewriting (CBR) to improve the restore performance for latest backups by shifting fragmentation to older backups. Some other work [25] even proposed to forfeit deduplication to reduce the chunk fragmentation by container capping.

In this paper, we apply PRE and symmetric encryption to deduplicate encrypted data. Our scheme can resist the attacks mentioned above and achieve good performance with no need to keep data owners online all the time. Meanwhile, it also ensures the confidentiality of stored data and supports digital rights management. We aim to achieve the mandatory requirements of encrypted cloud data deduplication.

3 Problem Statements

3.1 System Model and Security Model

We propose a scheme to deduplicate encrypted data at CSP by applying PRE to issue

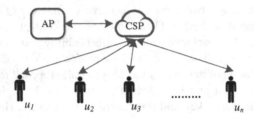

Fig. 1. System model

the keys to different authorized data holders. It is applied into the scenario that the data holder is not available to be involved into deduplication control.

As shown in Fig. 1 the system contains three types of entities: (1) CPS that offers storage services and cannot be fully trusted since it is curious about the contents of stored data, but should perform honestly on data storage in order to gain commercial profits; (2) data holder (u_i) that uploads and saves its data at CSP. In the system, it is possible to have a number of eligible data holders $(u_i, i = 1, \ldots, n)$ that could save the same encrypted raw data; (3) an authorized party (AP) that does not collude with CSP and is fully trusted by the data holders to handle data deduplication. AP cannot know the raw data stored in CSP and CSP should not know the plain user data in its storage.

Additional assumptions include: the hash code of data M is applied as its indicator, which is used to check the duplication of data during data uploading and storage. We assume that the data holder signs the right hash code honestly for the origin verification at CSP. This hash code is protected and cannot be obtained by system attackers. In another line of our work, we improve the security of data origin verification based on hash chain challenge. We further assume that the first data uploader (holder) has the highest priority. A valid proof should be provided by a data holder in order to request a special treatment. Users, CSP and AP communicate through a secure channel with each other.

3.2 Preliminary and Notations

Preliminary. A PRE scheme is represented as a tuple of (possibly probabilistic) polynomial time algorithms $(KG; RG; E; R; D)$:

- $(KG; E; D)$ are the standard key generation, encryption, and decryption algorithms. On input the security parameter 1^k, KG outputs a public and private key pair $(pk_A; sk_A)$ for entity A. On input pk_A and data m, E outputs a ciphertext $C_A = E(pk_A; m)$. On input sk_A and ciphertext C_A, D outputs the plain data $m = D(sk_A; C_A)$. On input $(pk_A; sk_A; pk_B)$, the re-encryption key generation algorithm RG, outputs a re-encryption key $rk_{A \to B}$ for a proxy.
- On input $rk_{A \to B}$ and ciphertext C_A, the re-encryption function R, outputs $R(rk_{A \to B}; C_A) = E(pk_B; m) = C_B$ which can be decrypted with private key sk_B.

Notations. Table 1 summarizes the notations used in the proposed scheme.

Table 1. System notations

Key	Description
(pk_u, sk_u)	The public key and secret key of user u for PRE
(PK_u, SK_u)	The public key and secret key of user u for public-key cryptographic operations
DEK_u	The symmetric key of u
$H()$	The hash function
CT	The ciphertext
CK	The cipherkey
M	The sser data
$Encrypt(DEK, M)$	The symmetric encryption function on M with DEK
$Decrypt(DEK, CT)$	The symmetric decryption function on CT with DEK

During system setup, every data holder u generates pk_u and sk_u for PRE. Meanwhile, it also generates a key pair PK_u and SK_u for Public-Key Cryptosystem (PKC), e.g., signature generation and verification. Generation of the above keys is the task of u. The keys $(pk_u; sk_u)$ and $(PK_u; SK_u)$ of u are bound to the unique identity of the user (It can be a pseudonym of user u). This binding is crucial for the verification of the user identity. At system setup, pk_u and PK_u are certified by an authorized third party as $Cert(pk_u)$ and $Cert(PK_u)$, which can be verified by CSP, AP, and any CSP users. AP independently generates pk_{AP} and sk_{AP} for PRE and broadcast pk_{AP} to CSP users.

4 Scheme Design and Algorithms

Our scheme contains the following main aspects:

(1) Data holder encrypts its data using a randomly selected symmetric key DEK and stores the encrypted data at CSP together with the signed hash code of the data;

(2) Data duplication occurs at the time when another data holder tries to store the same raw data at CSP. The CSP cooperates with AP to perform deduplication;

(3) When a data holder deletes data from CSP, CSP updates the records of duplicated data holders to forbid this holder to access the data later on;

(4) In case that a real data owner uploads the data later than the data holder, the CSP can update the records and keys to transfer the ownership to the real owner;

(5) In case that DEK is updated by a data owner and the new encrypted raw data is provided to CSP for the reason of achieving better security, CSP can decide to issue the new re-encrypted DEK' to all data holders with the support of AP.

4.1 Schemes

Each entity in the system has a public and private key pair under the PRE scheme. Let $(pk_{AP}; sk_{AP})$ denote the key pair of the AP and $(pk_u; sk_u)$ the key pair of data holder u. A data holder u encrypts its secret key DEK with $E(pk_{AP}, DEK)$ and publishes it along with its encrypted data $Encrypt(DEK, M)$ to the CSP. If another data holder u' uploads the same raw data encrypted using a different key, then CSP contacts AP to grant DEK to the eligible duplicated data holder u' as follows.

Algorithm: Grant access to duplicated data - grant (u')
Input: $pk_{u'}$, $Policy(u)$, $Policy(AP)$

- CSP requests AP to grant access to duplicated data for u' by providing $pk_{u'}$.
  - AP checks $Policy(AP)$ and issues CSP $rk_{AP \to u'} = RG(pk_{AP}; sk_{AP}; pk_{u'})$ if the check is positive.
  - CSP transforms $E(pk_{AP}; DEK)$ into $E(pk_{u'}; DEK)$ if $Policy(u)$ authorizes u' to share the same data storage of M encrypted by DEK: $R(rk_{AP \to u'}; E(pk_{AP}; DEK)) = E(pk_{u'}; DEK)$.
    Note: $rk_{RC \to u'}$ calculation can be skipped if it has been executed already and the value of $(pk_{u'}; sk_{u'})$ and $(pk_{AP}; sk_{AP})$ remain unchanged.
  - Data holder u' obtains DEK by decrypting $E(pk_{u'}; DEK)$ with $sk_{u'}$: $DEK = D(sk_{u'}; E(pk_{u'}; DEK))$, and then it can access data M at CSP.

In this scheme, CSP operates as the proxy in PRE scheme. It indirectly distributes DEK for data decryption to duplicated data holders without learning anything about these secrets (e.g., DEK and raw data stored at CSP). Note that AP itself is not allowed by the CSP to access the user's personal data due to business reasons and incentives.

4.2 Procedures

Data Deduplication. Figure 2 illustrates the procedure of data deduplication at CSP with the support of AP based on the proposed scheme. We suppose that user $u1$ saves its sensitive personal data M at CSP with protection using DEK_1, while user $u2$ is a data holder who tries to save the same data at CSP.

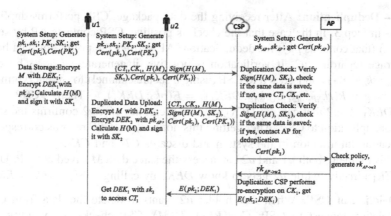

Fig. 2. A procedure of data deduplication

Step 1 – System setup: each user of CSP generates personal credentials and two key pairs $(pk_i; sk_i)$ for PRE and $(PK_i; SK_i)$ for PKC, $(i = 1, 2, \ldots n)$. Meanwhile, each user gets the certificate of its public keys $Cert(pk_i)$ and $Cert(PK_i)$. AP independently generates its public key pair (pk_{AP}, sk_{AP}) and publishes pk_{AP} publically.

Step 2 – Data storage: user $u1$ saves data M at CSP. In this step, $u1$ encrypts data M for privacy and security protection with a randomly selected symmetric key DEK_1 to get $CT_1 = Encrypt(DEK_1, M)$. It then encrypts DEK_1 with pk_{AP} to get CK_1 by calling $E(pk_{AP}, DEK_1)$. User $u1$ calculates $H(M)$ and signs it with SK_1 as $Sign(H(M), SK_1)$. Then $u1$ sends the data package $DP1$ to CSP where $DP1 = \{CT_1, CK_1, H(M), Sign(H(M), SK_1), Cert(pk_1), Cert(PK_1)\}$.

Step 3 – Duplication check: After receiving the data package, CSP verifies $Cert(pk_1)$ and $Cert(PK_1)$, checks if the duplicated data is stored as below: it verifies $Sign(H(M), SK_1)$, checks if the same data is saved by finding if there is the same $H(M)$ in stored records. If the check is negative, it saves CT_1, CK_1 and $H(M)$, as well as other related information such as $Cert(pk_1)$, $Cert(PK_1)$. If the check is positive and the pre-stored data is from the same user, it informs the user about this situation. If the same data is from a different user, refer to Step 5 for deduplication.

Step 4 – Duplicated data upload: user $u2$ later on saves the same data M at CSP following the same procedure of Step 2. That is, $u2$ sends the data package $DP2$ to CSP where $DP2 = \{CT_2, CK_2, H(M), Sign(H(M), SK_2), Cert(pk_2), Cert(PK_2)\}$.

The scheme can support a large number of data storage at CSP. In this case, the data holder sends $DP2 = \{H(M), Sign(H(M), SK_2), Cert(pk_2), Cert(PK_2)\}$ for duplication check before real encrypted data uploading. If duplication happens, $u2$ only needs to get $E(pk_2, DEK_1)$ from CSP through re-encryption with the support of AP.

Step 5 – Deduplication: After receiving the data package, CSP performs duplication check as in Step 3. In the case that the check is positive, CSP contacts AP by sending $Cert(pk_2)$ (that contains pk_2) for deduplication. AP verifies the policy for data holding and storage regarding $u2$. If verification is positive, it generates $rk_{AP \to u2}$ by calling $RG(pk_{AP}; sk_{AP}; pk_2)$ and issues it to CSP (using a secure channel) for re-encrypting CK_1 by calling $R(rk_{AP \to u2}; E(pk_{AP}; DEK_1)) = E(pk_2; DEK_1)$. Then CSP sends $E(pk_2; DEK_1)$ to $u2$ that can get DEK_1 with its secret key sk_2. $u2$ confirms the success of data deduplication to CSP. After getting this notification, CSP records corresponding deduplication information in the system and discards CT_2 and CK_2.

At this moment, both $u1$ and $u2$ can access the same data M saved at CSP. User $u1$ uses DEK_1 directly, while $u2$ gets to know DEK_1 by calling $D(sk_2; E(pk_2; DEK_1))$.

Data Deletion at CSP. When data holder $u2$ wants to delete the data from CSP, it sends deletion request to CSP: $Cert(PK_2)$, $H(M)$. CSP checks the validity of the request, then removes deduplication record of $u2$, block $u2$'s later access to M. CSP further checks if the deduplication record is empty. If yes, it deletes encrypted data CT and related records.

Data Owner Management. In case that the real data owner $u1$ uploads the data later than the data holder $u2$, the CSP can manage to save the real data owner encrypted data at the cloud and allow it to share the storage. In this case, the CSP contacts AP and provides all data holders' pk_u (e.g., pk_2) if CSP does not know its corresponding re-encryption key $rk_{AP \to u}$ (e.g., $rk_{AP \to u2}$). AP issues $rk_{AP \to u}$ (e.g., $rk_{AP \to u2}$) to CSP if validity check is positive. CSP performs re-encryption on CK_1, gets $E(pk_2, DEK_1)$ and sends re-encrypted DEK_1 to all related data holders (e.g., $u2$), deletes CT_2 and CK_2 by replacing it with $u1$'s encrypted copy CT_1 and CK_1, and updates corresponding deduplication records.

Encrypted Data Update. In some cases, a data holder could update encrypted data stored at CSP by generating a new DEK' and upload the new encrypted data with DEK' to CSP.

As illustrated in Fig. 2, $u1$ uploads its data and the CSP manages the encrypted data with deduplication. User $u2$ shares the data with $u1$. Suppose $u1$ wants to update encrypted data stored at CSP with new symmetric key DEK'_1. Figure 3 shows the procedure of encrypted data update. User $u1$ sends an update request as below:

$$DP1' = \{CT'_1, CK'_1, H(M), Sign(H(M), SK_1), Cert(pk_1), Cert(PK_1), updateCT_1\}.$$

The CSP verifies $Sign(H(M), SK_1)$ and contacts AP for updating re-encryption keys. AP checks its policy for generating and sending corresponding re-encryption keys (e.g., $rk_{AP \to u2}$), which are used by the CSP to perform re-encryption on CK'_1 for generating encrypted keys that can be decrypted by all eligible data holders (e.g., $E(pk_2, DEK'_1)$). The re-encrypted keys (e.g., $E(pk_2, DEK'_1)$) are sent back to the eligible data holders for future access on data M.

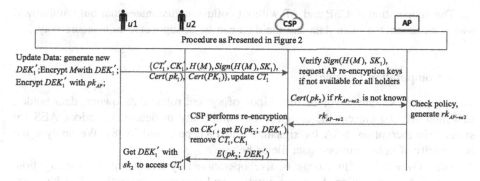

Fig. 3. A procedure of encrypted data update

Any data holder can perform the encrypted data update. Based on storage policy and service agreement between the data holder and CSP, CSP decides if such an update can be performed.

5 Security Analysis and Performance Evaluation

5.1 Security Analysis

Our scheme realizes a secure way to protect and deduplicate the data stored in cloud by concealing plaintext from both CSP and AP. The security of the proposed scheme is ensured by the PRE theory, symmetric key encryption and PKC theory. CSP has no way to know the raw data since it is always in an encryption status. CSP knows the encrypted DEK with pk_{AP}, but AP won't share its own secret key sk_{AP} with CSP. Thus CSP cannot know DEK and then the raw or plain data. AP has no way to access the data since this is blocked by CSP although AP can obtain DEK. In addition, we apply proper management protocols to support data storage management and data owner management at the same time when deduplication is achieved.

Data confidentiality is achieved by symmetric key encryption (e.g., AES) and PRE. The user data is presented in two different ways. One is $H(M)$. The hash function is assumed to be secure, i.e., it is difficult to find collision attack. The raw data is impossible to be obtained through the hash code. Another is the ciphertext of symmetric key encryption $CT = Encrypt(DEK, M)$. We assume that the symmetric key encryption is secure. Therefore, DEK becomes the key point. In the proposed scheme, we adopt PRE to protect DEK. First, DEK is encrypted with pk_{AP} through PRE to obtain the cipherkey $E(pk_{AP}, DEK)$. We assume that CSP and AP would not collude with each other. Although CSP can obtain the ciphertext, it cannot gain DEK because it knows nothing about the secret key of AP. The re-encryption with key $pk_{AP \to u}$ transforms the cipherkey under pk_{AP} into the cipherkey under sk_u. Similarly, the CSP can get nothing from the cipherkey for knowing nothing about sk_u. The authorized user u can obtain the data M by decrypting $E(pk_u, DEK)$ with its own secret key sk_u, which can guarantee that the raw data is secure and can be shared by eligible users.

The cooperation of CSP and AP without collusion guarantees that only authorized users can access the plain data and the data can be deduplicated in a secure way.

5.2   Computation Complexity

The proposed scheme involves four kinds of system roles: data owner, data holder, CSP and AP. To present the computation complexity in details, we adopt AES for symmetric encryption, RSA for signature and PRE proposed in [8]. We analyze the complexity of uploading one data file as below.

Data Owner: It is in charge of five operations: system setup, data encryption, symmetric key encryption, hash computation and signature generation. The key generation of PRE includes 1 exponentiation. The RSA key generation needs 1 modular inversion. The computation complexity of encrypting data using *DEK* depends on the size of data, which is inevitable in any cryptographic methods for protecting the data. Likewise, the computation complexity of hash depends on the size of data, but it is very fast. The sign requires 1 exponentiation and the encryption of *DEK* using PRE needs 2 exponentiations. Thus, the computation complexity of data owner is $\mathcal{O}(1)$. In addition, the burden of system setup can be amortized over all data storage operations.

CSP: Each user uploads its data to CSP. CSP should first check the signature and choose to save the appropriate copy of the data. This needs 1 exponentiation. If the data holder uploads the same data, the CSP contacts the AP for gaining a re-encryption key. In this case, CSP has to finish the re-encryption operation of PRE, which requires 1 pairing.

If the same data is uploaded by n data holders, the computational complexity results to be $\mathcal{O}(n)$. CSP is responsible for allowing the access to the same data for all data holders by avoiding storing the same data in the cloud.

Data Holder: When it uploads the same data that has been stored in the CSP, data holder does the same as the data owner has done. In addition, the data holder has to do one more decryption for accessing the data, which involves 1 exponentiation. The computational complexity of PRE decryption for data holder is $\mathcal{O}(1)$.

AP: It is responsible for the re-encryption key management. It checks the policy and issues key for authorized user. The re-encryption key generation needs 1 exponentiation. It needs to issue keys for all authorized data holders who upload the same data. The computational complexity of this is $\mathcal{O}(n)$.

It is noted that the computational burden of system setup, especially the generation of key pairs, can be amortized over the lifetime of entities. Thus, our scheme is very efficient. Table 2 lists the computation operations and complexity of different roles.

5.3   Performance Analysis

Implementation and Testing Environment. We implemented the proposed scheme and tested its performance. Table 3 describes our implementation and testing environment. We cannot test our scheme directly in the cloud. Instead, we applied a MySQL database to store data files and related information. In our test, we did not take

Table 2. Computation complexity of system entities

	Algorithm	Computations	Complexity
Data owner	Setup	1*ModInv + 1*Exp	$\mathcal{O}(1)$
	Data upload	3*Exp	
CSP	Re-encryption	1*Pair	$\mathcal{O}(n)$
Data Holder	System Setup	1*ModInv + 1*Exp	$\mathcal{O}(1)$
	Data upload	3*Exp	
	Decryption for access	1*Exp	
AP	System Setup	1*Exp	$\mathcal{O}(n)$
	Re-encryption key generation	1*Exp	

Notes: Pair: Bilinear Pairing; Exp: Exponentiation; n: Number of data holders who share the same data; ModInv: Modular Inversion

Table 3. Test environment

Hardware environment	CPU: Intel Core 2 Quad CPU Q9400 2.66GHZ
	Memory: 4 GB SDRAM
Software environment	Operating system: Ubuntu v14.04, Windows Home Ultimate editions 64bit
	Programming environment: Eclipse Luna CDT, Java
	Secure protocol: OpenSSL
	Library: Pairing based cryptography (http://crypto.stanford.edu/pbc/)
	Database: MySQL v5.5.41

into account the time of data uploading and downloading. We focused on testing the performance of the deduplication procedure and algorithms designed in our scheme.

Experiments. We set up two users (User 1: *zhq*; User 2: *cyl*) in the system for testing purpose in order to illustrate that the designed scheme works.

Correctness of Scheme Implementation

Case 1: User *zhq* uploads a new file named *chandelier.txt*.

User *zhq* encrypts a encryption key *DEK* with pk_{AP} and generates key file named as *key_zhq_chandelier.txt*, As the cloud has not yet stored this file, the file is encrypted and successfully uploaded to the cloud as an encrypted file *C_chandelier.txt*, shown in Fig. 4. When user *zhq* tried to access the data, it obtains the plaintext file *M_chandelier.txt*.

Case 2: User *cyl* uploads the same file chandelier.txt.

As shown in Fig. 5, the CSP found that the file has been uploaded by user *zhq* through duplication check. Notice that no matter what the file name is, the CSP can detect duplication if the file content is the same as a file saved already. The CSP would not save the file but ask AP to issue a re-encryption key to user *cyl* for accessing the

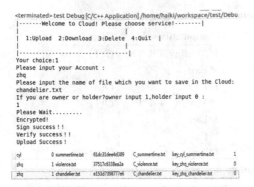

```
<terminated> test Debug [C/C++ Application] /home/haiki/workspace/test/Debu
|------Welcome to Cloud! Please choose service!------|
|                                                     |
|  1:Upload  2:Download  3:Delete  4:Quit  |
|                                                     |
|-----------------------------------|
Your choice:1
Please input your Account :
zhq
Please input the name of file which you want to save in the Cloud:
chandelier.txt
If you are owner or holder?owner input 1,holder input 0 :
1
Please Wait.........
Encrypted!
Sign success!!
Verify success!!
Upload Success!
```

cyl	0 summertime.txt	61dc31dee4d389	C_summertime.txt	key_cyl_summertime.txt	1
zhq	1 violence.txt	37517c6338ea2a	C_violence.txt	key_zhq_violence.txt	0
zhq	1 chandelier.txt	e153d7398777e6	C_chandelier.txt	key_zhq_chandelier.txt	0

Fig. 4. New file upload process

```
<terminated> test Debug [C/C++ Application] /home/haiki/workspace/test/Debı
|------Welcome to Cloud! Please choose service!------|
|                                                     |
|  1:Upload  2:Download  3:Delete  4:Quit  |
|                                                     |
|-----------------------------------|
Your choice:1
Please input your Account :
cyl
Please input the name of file which you want to save in the Cloud:
chandelier.txt
If you are owner or holder?owner input 1,holder input 0 :
0
Please Wait.........
Encrypted!
Sign success!!
Verify success!!
set share success!
File has been saved by other users!
```

cyl	1 young.txt	f729dd74cebc5c	C_young.txt	key_cyl_young.txt	0
cyl	0 summertime.txt	61dc31dee4d389	C_summertime.txt	key_cyl_summertime.txt	1
zhq	1 violence.txt	37517c6338ea2a	C_violence.txt	key_zhq_violence.txt	0
zhq	1 chandelier.txt	e153d7398777e6	C_chandelier.txt	key_zhq_chandelier.txt	1

Fig. 5. Reject duplicated saving

```
<terminated> test Debug [C/C++ Application] /home/haiki/workspace/test/De|
|------Welcome to Cloud! Please choose service!------|
|                                                     |
|  1:Upload  2:Download  3:Delete  4:Quit  |
|                                                     |
|-----------------------------------|
Your choice:2
Please input your Account :
cyl
Please input the name of file which you want download from Cloud:
chandelier.txt
Decryption! Download Success!
```

Fig. 6. Access shared duplicated data

cyl	1 young.txt	f729dd74cebc5c	C_young.txt	key_cyl_young.txt	0
cyl	0 summertime.txt	61dc31dee4d389	C_summertime.txt	key_cyl_summertime.txt	0
zhq	1 violence.txt	37517c6338ea2a	C_violence.txt	key_zhq_violence.txt	0

↓

cyl	1 young.txt	f729dd74cebc5c	C_young.txt	key_cyl_young.txt	0
zhq	1 violence.txt	37517c6338ea2a	C_violence.txt	key_zhq_violence.txt	0
zhq	1 chandelier.txt	e153d7398777e6	C_chandelier.txt	key_zhq_chandelier.txt	1
zhq	1 summertime.txt	61dc31dee4d389	C_summertime.txt	key_zhq_summertime.txt	1

Fig. 7. Data owner management

same file. Finally, the AP issues a re-encryption key $rk_{1 \to 2}$ to allow user cyl to share the file chandelier.txt that has been stored already.

Case 3: User *cyl* accesses the shared file chandelier.txt

User *zhq* uploaded chandelier.txt and denoted as data owner. User *cyl* uploaded the same file. Now it tried to access this shared file. As shown in Fig. 6, the CSP and AP allow *cyl* to access the pre-uploaded file. User *cyl* can download the file and obtain the data successfully.

Case 4: Data owner management

User *cyl* has uploaded file summertime.txt as a data holder. When the data owner *zhq* uploads this file, CSP removes the data record of *cyl* and replaces it with the corresponding record of *zhq*, as shown in Fig. 7.

Case 5: Data deletion

User *zhq* is the data owner of the file chandelier.txt. If user *cyl* as a data holder wants to delete the file, CSP just blocks the access of *cyl*, as shown in Fig. 8 But if the data owner *zhq* wants to delete the file, CSP needs to delete the record of *zhq* but keep the record of *cyl*. CSP blocks the access of *zhq* to the file, as shown in Fig. 9.

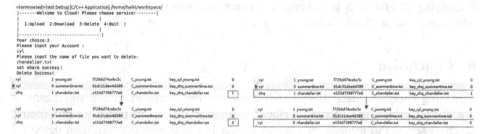

Fig. 8. Data deletion by a data holder   **Fig. 9.** Data deletion by a data owner

Efficiency Test

Test 1: Efficiency of PRE

We test the efficiency of each operation of PRE with different sizes of AES symmetric keys (128 bits, 196 bits and 256 bits). Figure 10 shows the operation time. We observe that our scheme is very efficient. The time spent for PRE key pair generation (KeyGen), re-encryption key generation (ReKeyGen), encryption (Enc), re-encryption (ReEnc) and decryption (Dec) is not related to the length of input. For the tested three AES key sizes, the encryption time is less than 6 ms. The decryption time is trivial, which implies that our scheme does not introduce heavy processing load to data holders. We also observe that the computation time of each operation does not vary too much with the different length of AES key size. Therefore, our scheme can be efficiently adapted to various security requirements in various scenarios.

Test 2: Efficiency of file encryption and decryption

In this experiment, we tested the operation time of file encryption and decryption with AES by applying different AES key sizes (128 bits, 196 bits and 256 bits) and different file size (from 10 megabytes to 600 megabytes). We observe from Fig. 11 that even when the file is as big as 600 MB, the encryption/decryption time is less than 30 s

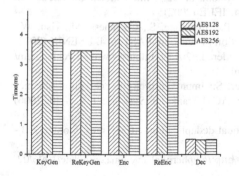

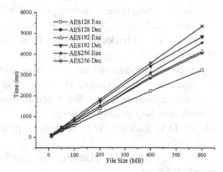

Fig. 10. The execution time of PRE operations

Fig. 11. Operation time of file encryption and decryption with AES

if applying 256-bit AES key. Applying symmetric encryption for data protection is a reasonable and practical choice.

6   Conclusion

Managing encrypted data storage with deduplication is important and significant in practice for achieving a successful cloud storage service. In this paper, we proposed a practical scheme to manage the encrypted data in cloud with deduplication based on PRE. Our proposed scheme can flexibly support data update and sharing with deduplication even when the data holder is offline. The encrypted data can be securely accessed because only authorized data holders can obtain the symmetric key used for data decryption. Extensive performance analysis and test show that our scheme is secure and efficient under the described security model. The implementation further shows the practicability of our scheme. Future work includes further optimizing the current implementation for practical deployment and usage.

Acknowledgement. This work is sponsored by the PhD grant (JY0300130104) of Chinese Educational Ministry, the "111 project" (B08038), the initial grant of Chinese Educational Ministry for researchers from abroad (JY0600132901), and the grant of Shaanxi Province for excellent researchers from abroad (680F1303), as well as Aalto University.

References

1. Bellare, M., Keelveedhi, S., Ristenpart, T.: Dupless: Server-aided encryption for deduplicated storage. In: 22nd USENIX Conference on Security, pp. 179–194. USENIX (2013)
2. A file-storage and sharing service. http://www.dropbox.com/
3. Google Drive. http://drive.google.com
4. Mozy: A file-storage and sharing service.http://mozy.com/
5. Douceur, J.R., Adya, A., Bolosky, W.J., Simon, D., Theimer, M.: Reclaiming space from duplicate files in a serverless distributed file system. In: 22nd International Conference on Distributed Computing Systems, pp. 617–624. IEEE (2002)
6. Wallace, G., Douglis, F., Qian, H., Shilane, P., Smaldone, S., Chamness, M., Hsu, W.: Characteristics of backup workloads in production systems. In: FAST, p. 4. USENIX (2012)
7. Wilcox Z.O.: Convergent encryption reconsidered (2011). http://www.mailarchive.com/cryptography@metzdowd.com/msg08949.html
8. Ateniese, G., Fu, K., Green, M., Hohenberger, S.: Improved proxy re-encryption schemes with applications to secure distributed storage. ACM Trans. Inf. Syst. Secur. **9**, 1–30 (2006)
9. Opendedup. http://opendedup.org/
10. Meyer, D.T., Bolosky, W.J.: A study of practical deduplication. ACM Trans. Storage **7**, 1–20 (2012)
11. Pettitt, J.: Hash of plaintext as key? http://cypherpunks.venona.com/date/1996/02/msg02013.html
12. The Freenet Project. Freenet. https://freenetproject.org/

13. Bellare, M., Keelveedhi, S., Ristenpart, T.: Message-locked encryption and secure deduplication. In: Johansson, T., Nguyen, P.Q. (eds.) EUROCRYPT 2013. LNCS, vol. 7881, pp. 296–312. Springer, Heidelberg (2013)
14. Perttula: Attacks on convergent encryption. http://bit.ly/yQxyvl
15. Liu, C., Liu, X., Wan, L.: Policy-based de-duplication in secure cloud storage. In: Yuan, Y., Wu, X., Lu, Y. (eds.) ISCTCS 2012. CCIS, vol. 320, pp. 250–262. Springer, Heidelberg (2013)
16. Puzio, P., Molva, R., Onen, M., Loureiro, S.: ClouDedup: Secure deduplication with encrypted data for cloud storage. In: 5th International Conference on Cloud Computing Technology and Science, pp. 363–370. IEEE (2013)
17. Sun, Z., Shen, J., Yong, J.M.: DeDu: Building a deduplication storage system over cloud computing. In: 15th International Conference on Computer Supported Cooperative Work in Design, pp. 348–355. IEEE (2011)
18. Wen, Z.C., Luo, J.M., Chen, H.J., Meng, J.X., Li X., Li J.: A verifiable data deduplication scheme in cloud computing. In: 2014 International Conference on Intelligent Networking and Collaborative Systems, pp. 85–90. IEEE (2014)
19. Li, J., Li, Y.K., Chen, X.F., Lee, P.P.C., Lou, W.J.: A hybrid cloud approach for secure authorized deduplication. IEEE Trans. Parallel Distrib. Syst. **26**, 1206–1216 (2015)
20. Meye, P., Raipin, P., Tronel, F., Anceaume, E.: A secure two-phase data deduplication scheme. In: HPCC/CSS/ICESS 2014, pp. 802–809. IEEE (2014)
21. Paulo, J., Pereira, J.: A survey and classification of storage deduplication systems. ACM Comput. Surv. **47**, 1–30 (2014)
22. Li, Y.-K., Xu, M., Ng, C.-H., Lee, P.P.C.: Efficient hybrid inline and out-of-line deduplication for backup storage. ACM Trans. Storage **11**, 2:1–2:21 (2014)
23. Fu, M., Feng, D., Hua, Y., He, X., Chen, Z.N., Xia, W., Huang, F., Liu, Q.: Accelerating restore and garbage collection in deduplication-based backup systems via exploiting historical information. In: 2014 USENIX Annual Technical Conference, pp. 181–192. USENIX Association (2014)
24. Kaczmarczyk, M., Barczynski, M., Kilian, W., Dubnicki, C.: Reducing impact of data fragmentation caused by in-line deduplication. In: 5th Annual International Systems and Storage Conference, pp. 15:1–15:12. ACM (2012)
25. Lillibridge, M., Eshghi, K., Bhagwat, D.: Improving restore speed for backup systems that use inline chunk-based deduplication. In: FAST, pp. 183–198. USENIX (2013)

HCBE: Achieving Fine-Grained Access Control in Cloud-Based PHR Systems

Xuhui Liu[1], Qin Liu[1(✉)], Tao Peng[2], and Jie Wu[3]

[1] College of Computer Science and Electronic Engineering,
Hunan University, Changsha 410082, People's Republic of China
gracelq628@hnu.edu.cn
[2] School of Information Science and Engineering, Central South University,
Changsha 410083, People's Republic of China
[3] Department of Computer and Information Sciences, Temple University,
Philadelphia, PA 19122, USA

Abstract. With the development of cloud computing, more and more users employ cloud-based personal health record (PHR) systems. The PHR is correlated with patient privacy, and thus research suggested to encrypt PHRs before outsourcing. Comparison-based encryption (CBE) was the first to realize time comparison in attribute-based access policy by means of the forward/backward derivation functions. However, the cost for encryption is linearly with the number of attributes in the access policy. To efficiently realize a fine-grained access control for PHRs in clouds, we propose a hierarchical comparison-based encryption (HCBE) scheme by incorporating an attribute hierarchy into CBE. Specifically, we construct an attribute tree, where the ancestor node is the generalization of the descendant nodes. The HCBE scheme encrypts a ciphertext with a small amount of generalized attributes at a higher level, other than lots of specific attributes at a lower level, largely improving the encryption performance. Furthermore, we encode each attribute node with the positive-negative depth-first (PNDF) coding. By virtue of the backward derivation function of the CBE scheme, the users associated with the specific attributes can decrypt the ciphertext encrypted with the generalized attributes, within the specified time. The experiment results show that the HCBE scheme has better performance in terms of the encryption cost, compared with the CBE scheme.

Keywords: Personal health record · Cloud computing · Comparison-based encryption · Fine-grained access control · Attribute hierarchy

1 Introduction

In recent years, personal health record (PHR) [1] as a patient-centric model of health information exchange has become popular with more and more users due to its convenience to access a patient's centralized profile by merging a wide range of health information sources. PHR allows medical practitioners to online

© Springer International Publishing Switzerland 2015
G. Wang et al. (Eds.): ICA3PP 2015, Part III, LNCS 9530, pp. 562–576, 2015.
DOI: 10.1007/978-3-319-27137-8_41

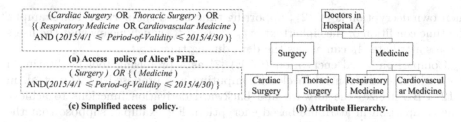

Fig. 1. Application scenario.

access a complete and accurate summary of a patient's medical history, thereby making the healthcare processes much more efficient and accurate [2].

Cloud computing is a model for enabling ubiquitous and convenient network access to data resources [3]. Due to its overwhelming advantages, e.g., rapid elasticity, high availability, and low cost, more and more patients decide to outsource their PHRs to the cloud for flexibility and convenience. The most popular cloud-based PHR systems include Google Health [4] and Microsoft HealthVault [5], which promise the users to access the PHR services anytime and anywhere using any devices connected to the Internet.

However, a PHR which includes patient-centric health data, such as allergies and adverse drug reactions, family history, imaging reports (e.g. X-ray) and so on, is closely related to patient privacy. Allowing a cloud service provider (CSP), like Amazon, Google, and Microsoft, to take care of sensitive medical data, may raise potential issues. For instance, an untrustworthy CSP may intentionally leak PHRs to medical companies or medical instrument companies for making a profit. To preserve the patients's privacy while using the cloud-based PHR systems, research suggested to encrypt PHR before outsourcing [6].

Let us consider the following application scenario: Alice was hospitalized in Hospital A, requiring heart surgery. Unfortunately, the surgery may face high risk, since Alice also suffered from hypertension and asthma. The related attending doctors in Hospital A needed to hold a consultation to decide surgery program after carefully studying Alice's PHR. For convenience and flexibility, Alice uploaded her encrypted PHR to Google Health, specifying an access control policy, as shown in Fig. 1(a).

The access policy can be viewed as a description of attributes and time condition, specifying that only the users whose attributes satisfying the access policy can decrypt the ciphertext within the specified time. For instance, Fig. 1(a) stipulates that the cardiologists and the respiratory physicians, can view Alice's PHR during the consultation (April 1, 2015 – April 30, 2015), as well as the cardiac surgeons and the cardiothoracic surgeons can view it anytime.

To ensure fine-grained access control in above application scenario, the adopted encryption scheme needs meeting the following requirements: (1) Supporting attribute-based access policy. For example, for a given ciphertext associated with access policy $[(A_1 \wedge A_2) \vee A_3]$, only the users who possess both attributes A_1 and A_2 or those who possess attribute A_3 can recover it using their own decryption keys. (2) Supporting time-based comparison. For example, the time condition of the ciphertext is $t_x \leq A_k \leq t_y$, which means that the users possess attribute A_k can access the data during time $[t_x, t_y]$.

Comparison-based encryption (CBE) [7] as a promising tool facilitating a fine-grained access control in cloud computing was proposed by Zhu et al. in 2012. CBE utilizes the forward and backward derivation functions to achieve time comparison in attribute-based encryption. For example, suppose that the access policy of the ciphertext is $A_t \wedge [t_x, t_y]$, and the authorization time of the user with attribute A_t is $[t_a, t_b]$. Then, the user can decrypt the ciphertext only when the current time $(t_c \in [t_x, t_y]) \wedge (t_c \in [t_a, t_b])$. Meanwhile, the key delegation mechanism was applied to assign a majority of decryption cost to the cloud, so as to take full advantage of cloud resources.

However, the main drawback of CBE is that the encryption cost grows linearly with the number of attributes in the access policy. For a system of a large number of attributes, the cost for encryption may be extensive. To solve this problem, we propose a hierarchical comparison-based encryption (HCBE) scheme for efficiently achieving a fine-grained access control in cloud-based PHR systems. The main idea of the HCBE scheme is building a hierarchical structure for attributes, where the attribute at a higher level is a generalization of the attributes at lower levels. Specifically, we encrypt the ciphertext with a small amount of generalized attributes at the higher level, other than lots of specific attributes at the lower level. For example, if we construct an attribute tree as shown in Fig. 1(b), the access policy can be simplified as shown in Fig. 1(c), with which the computation cost for encryption may be largely reduced compared to that in Fig. 1(a).

To realize the attribute hierarchy, we encode each node in an attribute tree with the positive-negative depth-first (PNDF) coding. Then, we apply the backward derivation function of CBE to allow the descendant attribute node to deduce the secrets associating with its ancestor attribute nodes. Therefore, the users with the specific attributes can decrypt the ciphertext encrypted with the generalized attributes. For example, when the ciphertext is encrypted with access policy $(medicine) \wedge [2015 - 4 - 1, 2015 - 4 - 30]$, only the cardiologists and the respiratory physicians can decrypt it during April 1, 2015 – April 30, 2015. Our main contributions in this work are summarized as follows:

1. We proposed a hierarchical comparison-based encryption (HCBE) scheme, by incorporating attribute hierarchy into CBE, so as to efficiently achieve a fine-grained access control in cloud-based PHR systems.
2. We constructed an attribute hierarchy tree, and encode each attribute node with the PNDF coding. By applying the backward derivation function, the users with the specific attributes can decrypt the ciphertext encrypted with the generalized attributes.
3. We analyze the security of the proposed scheme, and conduct experiments to validate its effectiveness and efficiency.

The rest of this paper is organized as follows. In Sect. 2, we introduce our models, design goals, and technical preliminaries. Then, we overview our HCBE scheme in Sect. 3 and provide its construction in Sect. 4. We analyze the security of our scheme in Sect. 5 and conduct experiments in Sect. 6. Finally, we introduce the related work in Sect. 7, and conclude this paper in Sect. 8.

2 Preliminaries

2.1 System Model

The system consists of the following parties: the cloud service provider (CSP), the data owner, and the data users. The CSP operates the cloud-based PHR system, which locates on a large number of interconnected cloud servers with abundant hardware resources. The data owner is the individual patient who employs the cloud-based PHR system to manage her PHR. The data users are the entities who is authorized by the data owner to access the cloud-based PHR system. Take the scenario in Fig. 1 as an example, Alice is the data owner, Google is the CSP, and Alice's lead doctors in Hospital A are the data users. Specially, when all the data users located in the same trusted domain, a proxy server responsible for part of the decryption operation can be deployed inside.

Suppose that the universal attribute set $\mathcal{A} = \{A_1, \ldots, A_m\}$, from which an attribute hierarchy $\widehat{\mathcal{A}}$ of L levels is built. In the tree structure, each attribute A_k contains two hierarchy codes, $\{Pcode_k, Ncode_k\}$, s.t. the descendant node's codes are larger than those of its ancestors. To efficiently achieve a fine-grained access control while using the cloud-based PHR services, our HCBE scheme will be employed as follows. We describe each user with an attribute-based access privilege $\widehat{\mathcal{L}}$, where each attribute $A_k \in \widehat{\mathcal{L}}$, denoted as $A_k(t_a, t_b, Pcode_k, Ncode_k)$, is associated with the authorization time $[t_a, t_b]$ and hierarchy codes $\{Pcode_k, Ncode_k\}$.

The PHR is encrypted with an attribute-based access policy, $\widehat{AP}$, where each attribute $A_l \in \widehat{AP}$, denoted as $A_l(t_i, t_j, Pcode_l, Ncode_l)$, is also associated with the time condition $[t_i, t_j]$ and hierarchy codes $\{Pcode_l, Ncode_l\}$. The data user can decrypt the PHR only when the following conditions are simultaneously satisfied: (1) user attributes satisfy the access policy, denoted $\widehat{\mathcal{L}} \subseteq \widehat{AP}$; (2) the current time $(t_c \in [t_x, t_y]) \wedge (t_c \in [t_a, t_b])$; (3) the attributes in $\widehat{\mathcal{L}}$ are either the same as or more specific than those in $\widehat{AP}$, denoted as $Pcode_k \geq Pcode_l$ and $Ncode_k \geq Ncode_l$.

2.2 Adversary Model

Our design goal is to preserve privacy for the data owner while using the cloud-based PHR services. There are two main attacks under such a circumstance, i.e., *external attacks* initiated by unauthorized outsiders, and *internal attacks* initiated by an *honest but curious* CSP and the untrusted data users. The communication channels are assumed to be secured under existing security protocols such as SSL and SSH, thus we only consider the internal attacks. We assume that the honest but curious CSP will always correctly execute a given protocol, but may try to learn some additional information about the stored data. The untrusted data users may collude to access the PHRs outside their permissions.

The HCBE scheme is considered fail if the following cases happens:

- **CASE 1.** The data user uk of access privilege $\widehat{\mathcal{L}}$ can access the PHR of access policy $\widehat{AP}$ while (1) $\widehat{\mathcal{L}} \not\subseteq \widehat{AP}$; or for attribute $A_k[t_a, t_b, Pcode_k, Ncode_k] \in \widehat{\mathcal{L}}$ and $A_l[t_i, t_j, Pcode_l, Ncode_l] \in \widehat{AP}$ (2) the intersection of the authorization time $[t_a, t_b]$ in $\widehat{\mathcal{L}}$ and the time condition $[t_i, t_j]$ in $\widehat{AP}$ is empty; or (3) $Pcode_k < Pcode_l \vee Ncode_k < Ncode_l$.
- **CASE 2.** The CSP can access the PHR without permission.

2.3 Composite Order Bilinear Map

Let p, q be two large primes, and $N = pq$ be the RSA-modulus. Following the work in [8], we define a bilinear map group system $S_N = (N, \mathbb{G}, \mathbb{G}_T, e)$, where $\mathbb{G}$ and $\mathbb{G}_T$ are cyclic groups of prime order $n = sp'q'^1$, and $e : \mathbb{G} \times \mathbb{G} \to \mathbb{G}_T$ is a bilinear map with the following properties:

- **Bilinearity**: for $a, b \in \mathbb{Z}_n$ and $g_1, g_2 \in \mathbb{G}$, it holds that $e(g_1^a, g_2^b) = e(g_1, g_2)^{ab}$;
- **Non-degeneracy**: $e(g_1, g_2) \neq 1$, where g_1, g_2 are the generators of group $\mathbb{G}$;
- **Computability**: $e(g_1, g_2)$ is efficiently computable.

As the work in [7], we make N public and keep n, s, p', q' secret in this system. Let $\mathbb{G}_s$ and $\mathbb{G}_{n'}$ denote the subgroups of order s and $n' = p'q'$ in $\mathbb{G}$, respectively. We have $e(g, h) = 1$, when $g \in \mathbb{G}_s$ and $h \in \mathbb{G}_{n'}$.

2.4 Comparison-Based Encryption (CBE)

In CBE, time is denoted as a set of discrete values $U = \{t_1, t_2, \ldots, t_T\}$, with total ordering $0 \leq t_1 \leq t_2 \leq \ldots, \leq t_T \leq Z$, where Z is the maximal integer. Let $\varphi, \overline{\varphi}$ be two random generators in $\mathbb{G}_{n'}$, where $n' = p'q'$ and p' and q' are two large primes. The functions $(\psi(\cdot), \overline{\psi}(\cdot))$ mapping from integer set $U = \{t_1, t_2, \ldots, t_T\}$ to $V = \{v_{t_1}, \ldots, v_{t_T}\} \in \mathbb{G}_{n'}$ and $\overline{V} = \{\overline{v}_{t_1}, \ldots, \overline{v}_{t_T}\} \in \mathbb{G}_{n'}$ are defined as follows:

$$v_{t_i} \leftarrow \psi(t_i) = \varphi^{\lambda^{t_i}}, \qquad \overline{v}_{t_i} \leftarrow \overline{\psi}(t_i) = \overline{\varphi}^{\mu^{Z-t_i}} \tag{1}$$

where λ, μ are randomly chosen from $\mathbb{Z}_{n'}^*$.

Based on Eq. 1, the forward derivation function (FDF), $f(\cdot)$, and the backward derivation function (BDF), $\overline{f}$, are defined as follows:

$$\begin{aligned} v_{t_j} \leftarrow f(v_{t_i}) = (v_{t_i})^{\lambda^{t_j-t_i}}, \quad t_i \leq t_j \\ \overline{v}_{t_j} \leftarrow \overline{f}(\overline{v}_{t_i}) = (\overline{v}_{t_i})^{\mu^{t_i-t_j}}, \quad t_i \geq t_j \end{aligned} \tag{2}$$

FDF and BDF have the *one-way* property, under the RSA assumption that λ^{-1} and φ^{-1} cannot be efficiently computed based on the secrecy of n'. That is,

---

[1] Let s_1, s_2 be two secret large primes. We have $n = sn' = s_1 s_2 p'q'|lcm(p+1, q+1)$, where $n' = p'q'|n$, $s = s_1 s_2$, $p = 2p's_1 - 1$, and $q = 2q's_2 - 1$.

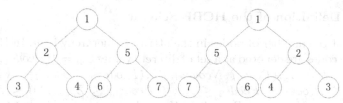

(a) Positive depth-first coding (b) Negative depth-first coding

Fig. 2. Sample PNDF coding.

Eq. 2 is efficiently computable; However, it is intractable to obtain v_{t_j} from v_{t_i} while $t_i > t_j$, and obtain $\overline{v}_{t_j}$ from $\overline{v}_{t_i}$ while $t_i < t_j$.

For a given set of attributes $\mathcal{A} = \{A_1, \ldots, A_m\}$, CBE consists of the following algorithms: *Setup, GenKey, Encrypt, Delegate, Decrypt1,* and *Decrypt2.* For improving the efficiency, the output of the *Encrypt* algorithm is a random session key ek, which can be used to encrypt files using symmetrical-key cryptosystem.

3 Overview of the HCBE Scheme

3.1 Positive-Negative Depth-First Coding

From the attribute set $\mathcal{A} = \{A_1, \ldots, A_m\}$, we build an attribute hierarchy $\widehat{A}$ of L levels. In attribute tree, the attribute at a higher level is a generalization of the attributes at lower levels. We associate each node with two hierarchical codes, i.e., the positive depth-first code (Pcode) and the negative depth-first code (Ncode). Suppose that each node has four fields: *Pcode, Ncode, rchild* describing the right subtree, and *lchild* describing the left subtree. First, we push the root node R to two stacks, *PStack* and *NStack.* For the *PStack,* the right subtree of each node will be first pushed in, thus the left subtree's Pcodes will be larger than those of right subtree. In contrast, the left subtree of each node will be first pushed in the *NStack,* thus the right subtree's Ncodes will be larger than those of left subtree. Take the attribute tree shown in Fig. 1(b) as an example. The PNDF coding is shown in Fig. 2.

Let $Pcode_i$ and $Ncode_i$ denote the Pcode and Ncode of node i, respectively. The PNDF coding has the property that $Pcode_i > Pcode_j$ and $Ncode_i > Ncode_j$, if i is the descendant node of j. For example, the $Pcode$ and $Ncode$ of attribute *Surgery* are 2 and 5, respectively; the $Pcode$ and $Ncode$ of attribute *Cardiac Surgery* are 3 and 7, respectively; the $Pcode$ and $Ncode$ of attribute *Respiratory Medicine* are 6 and 4, respectively. *Cardiac Surgery* as the descendant of *Surgery*, with both $Pcode$ and $Ncode$ larger than those of *Surgery. Respiratory Medicine* is not the descendant of *Surgery*, and its $Ncode$ is smaller than that of *Surgery.*

3.2   The Definition of the HCBE Scheme

Suppose that the number of nodes in the attribute hierarchy is m. In HCBE, the hierarchical codes are denoted as a set of discrete values $U_m = \{(Pcode_1, Ncode_1),$ $(Pcode_2, Ncode_2), \ldots, (Pcode_k, Ncode_k), \ldots, (Pcode_m, Ncode_m)\}$, with total ordering $0 \leq Pcode_1 \leq Pcode_2 \leq \ldots, \leq Pcode_m \leq Z_m$ and $0 \leq Ncode_1 \leq Ncode_2 \leq \ldots, \leq Ncode_m \leq Z_m$, where Z_m is the maximal integer.

We apply the BDF to accomplish the attribute hierarchy. Let $\mathbb{G}_{n'}$ be a multiplicative group of RSA-type composite order $n' = p'q'$, where p', q' are two large primes. First, we choose random generators φ_1, φ_2 in $\mathbb{G}_{n'}$ and random numbers θ_1, θ_2 in $\mathbb{Z}_{n'}^*$, where the order of θ_1, θ_2 are sufficiently large in $\mathbb{Z}_{n'}^*$. Next, we define mapping functions $\psi_1(.), \psi_2(.)$ from an integer set $U_m = \{(Pcode_1, Ncode_1), \ldots, (Pcode_k, Ncode_k), \ldots, (Pcode_m, Ncode_m)\}$ into $V_m = \{(v_{Pcode_1}, v_{Ncode_1}), \ldots, (v_{Pcode_k}, v_{Ncode_k}), \ldots, (v_{Pcode_m}, v_{Ncode_m})\}$ as follows:

$$v_{Pcode_k} = \varphi_1^{\theta_1^{Z_m - Pcode_k}}, \qquad v_{Ncode_k} = \varphi_2^{\theta_2^{Z_m - Ncode_k}} \tag{3}$$

According to the definitions of $\psi_1(.), \psi_2(.)$, it is easy to define BDFs $f_1(.), f_2(.)$ as follows:

$$v_{Pcode_j} \leftarrow f_1(v_{Pcode_k}) = (v_{Pcode_k})^{\theta_1^{Pcode_k - Pcode_j}}, \quad Pcode_k \geq Pcode_j$$
$$v_{Ncode_j} \leftarrow f_2(v_{Ncode_k}) = (v_{Ncode_k})^{\theta_2^{Ncode_k - Ncode_j}}, \quad Ncode_k \geq Ncode_j \tag{4}$$

The definition of the HCBE scheme consists of the following algorithms:

- $Setup(1^\kappa, \widehat{\mathcal{A}}) \rightarrow (MK, PK_{\widehat{\mathcal{A}}})$: The data owner takes a security parameter κ and the attribute hierarchy $\widehat{\mathcal{A}}$ as inputs, and outputs the master key MK and the system public key $PK_{\widehat{\mathcal{A}}}$;
- $GenKey(MK, uk, \widehat{\mathcal{L}}) \rightarrow SK_{\widehat{\mathcal{L}}}$: The data owner utilizes her master key MK to generate a private key $SK_{\widehat{\mathcal{L}}}$ on an access privilege $\widehat{\mathcal{L}}$ for user uk, where each attribute $A_k \in \widehat{\mathcal{L}}$, denoted as $A_k(t_a, t_b, Pcode_k, Ncode_k)$, is associated with the authorization time $[t_a, t_b]$ and hierarchy codes $\{Pcode_k, Ncode_k\}$.
- $Encrypt(PK_{\widehat{\mathcal{A}}}, \widehat{AP}) \rightarrow (\widehat{\mathcal{H}_\mathcal{P}}, ek)$: The data owner takes the public key $PK_{\widehat{\mathcal{A}}}$ and an access policy $\widehat{AP}$ as inputs to generate a session key ek and a ciphertext header $\widehat{\mathcal{H}_\mathcal{P}}$, where each attribute $A_l \in \widehat{AP}$, denoted as $A_l(t_i, t_j, Pcode_l, Ncode_l)$, is associated with the time condition $[t_i, t_j]$ and hierarchy codes $\{Pcode_l, Ncode_l\}$.
- $Delegate(SK_{\widehat{\mathcal{L}}}, \widehat{\mathcal{L}'}) \rightarrow SK_{\widehat{\mathcal{L}'}}$: The data user takes the private key $SK_{\widehat{\mathcal{L}}}$ and an access privilege $\widehat{\mathcal{L}'}$ as inputs to generate a derived private key $SK_{\widehat{\mathcal{L}'}}$ for the proxy server if $\widehat{\mathcal{L}'} \preceq \widehat{\mathcal{L}}^2$.

---

[2] Let S and S' denote the set of attributes in $\widehat{\mathcal{L}}$ and $\widehat{\mathcal{L}'}$, respectively. $\widehat{\mathcal{L}'} \preceq \widehat{\mathcal{L}}$ iff $S' \subseteq S$, and for each attribute $A_k[t_a, t_b, Pcode_k, Ncode_k] \in \widehat{\mathcal{L}}$ and $A_l[t_i, t_j, Pcode_l, Ncode_l] \in \widehat{\mathcal{L}'}$, $t_a \leq t_i$, $t_b \geq t_j$, $Pcode_k \geq Pcode_l$, and $Ncode_k \geq Ncode_l$.

- $Decrypt1(SK_{\widehat{\mathcal{L}'}}, \widehat{\mathcal{H_P}}) \rightarrow \widehat{\mathcal{H'_P}}$: The proxy server takes the derived private key $SK_{\widehat{\mathcal{L}'}}$ and a ciphertext header $\widehat{\mathcal{H_P}}$ as inputs, and outputs a new ciphertext header $\widehat{\mathcal{H'_P}}$ if $\widehat{\mathcal{L}'}$ satisfies $\widehat{AP}$.
- $Decrypt2(SK_{\widehat{\mathcal{L}}}, \widehat{\mathcal{H'_P}}) \rightarrow ek$: The data user takes the private key $SK_{\widehat{\mathcal{L}}}$ and the new ciphertext header $\widehat{\mathcal{H'_P}}$ as inputs, and outputs a session key ek, which can be used to decrypt the stored data.

4   Our Construction

$Setup(1^{\kappa}, \widehat{\mathcal{A}}) \rightarrow (MK, PK_{\widehat{\mathcal{A}}})$: Given a bilinear map system $S_N = (N = pq, \mathbb{G}, \mathbb{G}_T, e)$, where $\mathbb{G}, \mathbb{G}_T$ are cyclic groups of composite order $n = sn'$, and $e : \mathbb{G} \times \mathbb{G} \rightarrow \mathbb{G}_T$, this algorithm first chooses the random generators $\omega \in \mathbb{G}, g \in \mathbb{G}_s$, and $\varphi, \overline{\varphi}, \varphi_1, \varphi_2 \in \mathbb{G}_{n'}$, where $\mathbb{G}_s$ and $\mathbb{G}_{n'}$ are two subgroups of $\mathbb{G}$. Thus, we have $e(g, \varphi) = e(g, \overline{\varphi}) = e(g, \varphi_1,) = e(g, \varphi_2) = 1$, but $e(g, \omega) \neq 1$.

Then, it chooses four random numbers $\lambda, \mu, \theta_1, \theta_2 \in \mathbb{Z}_n^*$, and employs a hash function $H : \{0,1\}^* \rightarrow \mathbb{G}$, mapping the root attribute, R, described as a binary string to a random group element. Next, it chooses two random exponents $\alpha, \beta \in \mathbb{Z}_n^*$ and sets $h = \omega^\beta, \eta = g^{1/\beta}, \zeta = e(g, \omega)^\alpha$. The master key is set as $MK = (g^\alpha, \beta, p, q, n')$, and the public key is set as:

$$PK_{\widehat{\mathcal{A}}} = (S_N, \omega, g, \varphi, \overline{\varphi}, \varphi_1, \varphi_2, h, \eta, \zeta, \lambda, \mu, \theta_1, \theta_2, H). \tag{5}$$

$GenKey(MK, uk, \widehat{\mathcal{L}}) \rightarrow SK_{\widehat{\mathcal{L}}}$: Given a user uk with license $\widehat{\mathcal{L}}$, this algorithm chooses two random numbers $\tau_{uk}, r \in \mathbb{Z}$, and then for each attribute $A_k[t_a, t_b, Pcode_k, Ncode_k] \in \widehat{\mathcal{L}}$, it calculates:

$$\begin{aligned} D_{A_k} &= (D_t, D'_{t_a}, \overline{D'}_{t_b}, D''_t, D_{K_1}, D_{K_2}) \\ &= (g^{\tau_{uk}} H_{A_k}{}^r, (v_{t_a})^r, (\overline{v}_{t_b})^r, \omega^r, (v_{Pcode_k})^r, (v_{Ncode_k})^r). \end{aligned} \tag{6}$$

where $H_{A_k} = H(R) \cdot v_{Pcode_k} \cdot v_{Ncode_k}$, $v_{t_a} = \varphi^{\lambda^{t_a}}$, $\overline{v}_{t_b} = \overline{\varphi}^{\mu^{-t_b}}$, $v_{Pcode_k} = \varphi_1^{\theta_1^{Z_m - Pcode_k}}$ and $v_{Ncode_k} = \varphi_2^{\theta_2^{Z_m - Ncode_k}}$. Then, uk's private key is set as:

$$SK_{\widehat{\mathcal{L}}} = (D = g^{(\alpha + \tau_{uk})/\beta}, \{D_{A_k}\}_{A_k \in \widehat{\mathcal{L}}}). \tag{7}$$

$Encrypt(PK_{\widehat{\mathcal{A}}}, \widehat{AP}) \rightarrow (\widehat{\mathcal{H_P}}, ek)$: Given an access policy tree $\mathcal{T}$ over access policy $\widehat{AP}$, the ciphertext header $\widehat{\mathcal{H_P}}$ can be calculated with:

$$\begin{aligned} \widehat{\mathcal{H_P}} = (\mathcal{T}, C = h^\sigma, \{(\bar{E}_{t_i}, E'_{t_i}), (E_{t_j}, E'_{t_j}), \\ (E_{Pcode_l}, E'_{Pcode_l}), (E_{Ncode_l}, E'_{Ncode_l})\}_{A_l[t_i, t_j, Pcode_l, Ncode_l] \in \mathcal{T}}). \end{aligned} \tag{8}$$

Here, each component is set as follows:

$$\begin{aligned} (\bar{E}_{t_i}, E'_{t_i}) &= (\bar{v}_{t_i}\omega)^x, H_{A_l}^x), (E_{t_j}, E'_{t_j}) = ((v_{t_j}\omega)^y, H_{A_l}^y), \\ (E_{Pcode_l}, E'_{Pcode_l}) &= ((v_{Pcode_l} \cdot \omega)^{z_1}, H_{A_l}^{z_1}), \\ (E_{Ncode_l}, E'_{Ncode_l})) &= ((v_{Ncode_l} \cdot \omega)^{z_2}, H_{A_l}^{z_2}). \end{aligned} \tag{9}$$

where $H_{A_l} = H(R) \cdot v_{Pcode_l} \cdot v_{Ncode_l}$. The session key ek is set as $\zeta^\sigma = e(g^\alpha, \omega)^\sigma$ where σ is a main secret in $\mathbb{Z}_n$ for tree $\mathcal{T}$, and $\triangle_\sigma(A_l) = x + y + z_1 + z_2$ is the secret share of σ in the tree $\mathcal{T}$ for an attribute A_l (see [9]).

$Delegate(SK_{\widehat{\mathcal{L}}}, \widehat{\mathcal{L}}') \rightarrow SK_{\widehat{\mathcal{L}'}}$: Given a specified access privilege $\widehat{\mathcal{L}}'$, and the private key $SK_{\widehat{\mathcal{L}}} = (D, \{(D_t, D'_{t_a}, \overline{D}'_{t_b}, D''_t, D_{K_1}, D_{K_1})\}_{A_k[t_a, t_b, Pcode_k, Ncode_k] \in \widehat{\mathcal{L}}})$, this algorithm checks for each attribute $A_l[t_i, t_j, Pcode_l, Ncode_l] \in \widehat{\mathcal{L}}'$ whether A_l is a generalized attribute of A_k, $t_a \le t_j$ and $t_b \ge t_i$. If so, this algorithm uses Eqs. 2 and 4 to compute:

$$
\begin{aligned}
D'_t &\leftarrow g^{\tau uk} H_{A_k}{}^r \cdot \frac{f_1(D_{K_1}) \cdot f_2(D_{K_2})}{(v_{Pcode_k})^r \cdot (v_{Pcode_k})^r} \\
&= g^{\tau uk} (H(R) \cdot v_{Pcode_k} \cdot v_{Ncode_k})^r \cdot \frac{f_1((v_{Pcode_k})^r) \cdot f_2(f_1((v_{Ncode_k})^r))}{(v_{Pcode_k})^r \cdot (v_{Pcode_k})^r} \\
&= g^{\tau uk} H(R)^r \cdot v_{Pcode_l}{}^r \cdot v_{Ncode_l}{}^r = g^{\tau uk} H_{A_l}^r \\
D'_{t_j} &\leftarrow f(D'_{t_a}) \cdot D''_t = f((v_{t_a})^r) \cdot \omega^r = (v_{t_j})^r \cdot \omega^r, \qquad (10) \\
\overline{D}'_{t_i} &\leftarrow \overline{f}(\overline{D}'_{t_b}) \cdot D''_t = \overline{f}((\overline{v}_{t_b})^r) \cdot \omega^r = (\overline{v}_{t_i})^r \cdot \omega^r, \\
D'_{Pcode_l} &\leftarrow f_1(D_{K_1}) \cdot D''_t = f_1((v_{Pcode_k})^r) \cdot \omega^r = (v_{Pcode_l})^r \cdot \omega^r, \\
D'_{Ncode_l} &\leftarrow f_2(D_{K_2}) \cdot D''_t = f_2((v_{Ncode_k})^r) \cdot \omega^r = (v_{Ncode_l})^r \cdot \omega^r,
\end{aligned}
$$

where

$$
\begin{aligned}
f((v_{t_a})^r) &= (\varphi^{r\lambda^{t_a}})^{\lambda^{t_j - t_a}} = \varphi^{r\lambda^{t_j}} = (v_{t_j})^r, \\
\overline{f}((\overline{v}_{t_b})^r) &= (\overline{\varphi}^{r\mu^{Z-t_b}})^{\mu^{t_b - t_i}} = \overline{\varphi}^{r\mu^{Z-t_i}} = (\overline{v}_{t_i})^r, \\
f_1((v_{Pcode_k})^r) &= (\varphi_1^{r\theta_1^{Z_m - Pcode_k}})^{\theta_1^{Pcode_k - Pcode_l}} = \varphi_1^{r\theta_1^{Z_m - Pcode_l}} = (v_{Pcode_l})^r, \\
f_2((v_{Ncode_k})^r) &= (\varphi_2^{r\theta_2^{Z_m - Ncode_k}})^{\theta_2^{Ncode_k - Ncode_l}} = \varphi_2^{r\theta_2^{Z_m - Ncode_l}} = (v_{Ncode_l})^r.
\end{aligned}
\tag{11}
$$

Next, it chooses a random $\delta \in \mathbb{Z}$ and computes:

$$
\begin{aligned}
\widetilde{D}_t &= D'_t \cdot (gH_{A_l})^\delta = g^{\tau uk} H_{A_l}{}^r \cdot (gH_{A_l})^\delta = g^{\tau uk + \delta} H_{A_l}^{r+\delta} = g^{\tau'_k} H_{A_l}^{r'}, \\
\widetilde{D}'_{t_j} &= D'_{t_j} \cdot (v_{t_j}\omega)^\delta = (v_{t_j}\omega)^{r+\delta} = (v_{t_j}\omega)^{r'}, \\
\widetilde{\overline{D}}'_{t_i} &= \overline{D}'_{t_i} \cdot (\overline{v}_{t_i}\omega)^\delta = (\overline{v}_{t_i}\omega)^{r+\delta} = (\overline{v}_{t_i}\omega)^{r'}, \qquad (12) \\
\widetilde{D}'_{Pcode_l} &= D'_{Pcode_l} \cdot (v_{Pcode_l}\omega)^\delta = (v_{Pcode_l}\omega)^{r+\delta} = (v_{Pcode_l}\omega)^{r'}, \\
\widetilde{D}'_{Ncode_l} &= D'_{Ncode_l} \cdot (v_{Ncode_l}\omega)^\delta = (v_{Ncode_l}\omega)^{r+\delta} = (v_{Ncode_l}\omega)^{r'},
\end{aligned}
$$

where $H_{A_l} = H(R) \cdot v_{Pcode_l} \cdot v_{Ncode_l}$, and $\tau'_k = \tau_{uk} + \delta, r' = r + \delta$. Finally, the derivation privacy key is set as $SK_{\widehat{\mathcal{L}'}} = \{\widetilde{D}_t, \widetilde{D}'_{t_j}, \widetilde{\overline{D}}'_{t_i}, \widetilde{D}'_{Pcode_l}, \widetilde{D}'_{Ncode_l}\}_{A_l \in \mathcal{L}'}$.

$Decrypt1(SK_{\widehat{\mathcal{L}'}}, \widehat{\mathcal{H_P}}) \rightarrow \widehat{\mathcal{H'_P}}$: Given the private key $SK_{\widehat{\mathcal{L}'}}$ and a ciphertext header $\widehat{\mathcal{H_P}}$, we check whether each attribute $A_l[t_i, t_j, Pcode_l, Ncode_l] \in \widehat{\mathcal{L}}'$ is consistent with $A_l[t_i, t_j, Pcode_l, Ncode_l] \in \widehat{AP}$. If true, the secret share $\triangle_\sigma(A_l)$ of σ over $\mathbb{G}_T$ is reconstructed by using

$$
\begin{aligned}
F_1 &\leftarrow \frac{e(\widetilde{D}_t, E_{t_j})}{e(\widetilde{D}'_{t_j}, E'_{t_j})} = \frac{e(g^{\tau'_k} H_{A_l}^{r'}, (v_{t_j}\omega)^x)}{e((v_{t_j}\omega)^{r'}, H_{A_l}^x)} \\
&= e(g^{\tau'_k}, v_{t_j}^x) \cdot e(g^{\tau'_k}, \omega^x) = e(g^{\tau'_k}, \omega)^x
\end{aligned}
\tag{13}
$$

$$F_2 \leftarrow \frac{e(\widetilde{D}_t, \overline{E}_{t_i})}{e(\overline{D}'_{t_i}, E'_{t_j})} = \frac{e(g^{\tau'_k} H^{r'}_{A_l}, (\overline{v}_{t_i} \omega)^y)}{e((\overline{v}_{t_i} \omega)^{r'}, H^y_{A_l})}$$
$$= e(g^{\tau'_k}, \overline{v}^y_{t_i}) \cdot e(g^{\tau'_k}, \omega^y) = e(g^{\tau'_k}, \omega)^y \tag{14}$$

$$F_3 \leftarrow \frac{e(\widetilde{D}_t, E_{Pcode_l})}{e(\overline{D}'_{Pcode_l}, E'_{t_j})} = \frac{e(g^{\tau'_k} H^{r'}_{A_l}, (v_{Pcode_l} \omega)^{z_1})}{e((v_{Pcode_l} \omega)^{r'}, H^{z_1}_{A_l})}$$
$$= e(g^{\tau'_k}, v^{z_1}_{Pcode_l}) \cdot e(g^{\tau'_k}, \omega^{z_1}) = e(g^{\tau'_k}, \omega)^{z_1} \tag{15}$$

$$F_4 \leftarrow \frac{e(\widetilde{D}_t, E_{Ncode_l})}{e(\overline{D}'_{Ncode_l}, E'_{t_j})} = \frac{e(g^{\tau'_k} H^{r'}_{A_l}, (v_{Ncode_l} \omega)^{z_2})}{e((v_{Ncode_l} \omega)^{r'}, H^{z_2}_{A_l})}$$
$$= e(g^{\tau'_k}, v^{z_2}_{Ncode_l}) \cdot e(g^{\tau'_k}, \omega^{z_2}) = e(g^{\tau'_k}, \omega)^{z_2} \tag{16}$$

$$F_t = F_1 \cdot F_2 \cdot F_3 \cdot F_4 = e(g^{\tau'_k}, \omega)^{\Delta_\sigma(A_l)} \tag{17}$$

where $H_{A_l} = H(R) \cdot v_{Pcode_l} \cdot v_{Ncode_l}$. We have $e(g^{\tau'_k}, v^x_{t_j}) = e(g^{\tau'_k}, \overline{v}^y_{t_i}) = e(g^{\tau'_k}, v^{z_1}_{Pcode_l}) = e(g^{\tau'_k}, v^{z_2}_{Ncode_l}) = 1$ due to $g^{\tau'_k} \in \mathbb{G}_s$ and $v^x_{t_j}, \overline{v}^y_{t_i}, v^{z_1}_{Pcode_l}, v^{z_2}_{Ncode_l} \in \mathbb{G}_{n'}$. Next, the value $C_2 = e(g^{\tau'_k}, \omega)^\sigma$ is computed from $\{e(g^{\tau'_k}, \omega)^{\Delta_\sigma(A_l)}\}_{A_l \in \mathcal{T}}$ by using the aggregation algorithm (see [9]). Finally, the new ciphertext header $\widehat{\mathcal{H}'_\mathcal{P}} = (C = h^\sigma, C_2)$ is returned.

$Decrypt2(SK_{\widehat{\mathcal{L}}}, \widehat{\mathcal{H}'_\mathcal{P}}) \rightarrow ek$: After receiving $\widehat{\mathcal{H}'_\mathcal{P}} = (C, C_2) = (\omega^{\beta\sigma}, e(g^{\tau'_k}, \omega)^\sigma)$, the data user uses the secret δ to compute

$$D' = D \cdot \eta^\delta = g^{(\alpha + \tau_{uk})/\beta} g^{\delta/\beta} = g^{(\alpha + \tau_{uk} + \delta)/\beta} = g^{(\alpha + \tau'_k)/\beta}. \tag{18}$$

Next, the session key is computed by

$$ek = \frac{e(C, D')}{C_2} = \frac{e(g^{(\alpha + \tau'_k)/\beta}, (\omega^\beta)^\sigma)}{e(g^{\tau'_k}, \omega)^\sigma} = e(g^\alpha, \omega)^\sigma. \tag{19}$$

5 Security Analysis

As described in Sect. 2, the HCBE scheme is considered failed if either CASE 1 or CASE 2 happens. In this section, we will sketch the security of our scheme as follows:

The data file stored in the cloud is in the encrypted with a session key $ek = e(g^\alpha, \omega)^\sigma$. For ease of illustration, we assume that ek is encrypted with the access policy $\widehat{AP} = A_l[t_i, t_j, Pcode_l, Ncode_l] \wedge A_x[t_i, t_j, Pcode_x, Ncode_x]$. We consider the first condition in CASE 1 is true, if user uk_1, whose access privilege $\widehat{\mathcal{L}}_1 = A_l[t_i, t_j, Pcode_l, Ncode_l]$, can recover ek, by colluding with uk_2, whose access privilege $\widehat{\mathcal{L}}_2 = A_x[t_i, t_j, Pcode_x, Ncode_x]$. The construction of the HCBE scheme allows them to recover $F_{t1} = e(g^{\tau'_{k1}}, \omega)^{\Delta_\sigma(A_l)}$ and $F_{t2} = e(g^{\tau'_{k2}}, \omega)^{\Delta_\sigma(A_x)}$, with private keys $SK_{\widehat{\mathcal{L}}_1}$ and $SK_{\widehat{\mathcal{L}}_2}$, respectively. However, τ'_{k1}, τ'_{k2} are uniquely chosen to distinguish different users. Therefore, with F_{t1}, F_{t2}, they cannot obtain either $T1 = e(g^{\tau'_{k1}}, \omega)^\sigma$ or $T2 = e(g^{\tau'_{k2}}, \omega)^\sigma$, to recover ek, and the first condition in CASE 1 is false.

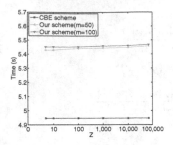
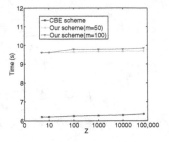

Fig. 3. Computation cost of *Setup*.   **Fig. 4.** Computation cost of *Genkey*.

Next, we assume that ek is simply encrypted with the access policy $\widehat{AP} = A_l[t_i, t_j, Pcode_l, Ncode_l]$. We consider the second condition in CASE 1 is true, if user uk_1, whose access privilege $\widehat{\mathcal{L}_1} = A_l[t_a, t_b, Pcode_l, Ncode_l]$ can recover ek while $t_j < t_a$ (or $t_i > t_b$). Note that, due to the one-way property of the FDF and BDF in CBE, uk_1 cannot derive D'_{t_j} and $\overline{D}'_{t_i}$ from D'_{t_a} and $\overline{D}'_{t_b}$ while $t_j < t_a$ (or $t_i > t_b$). Therefore, uk_1 cannot obtain F_1 and F_2 to recover ek, and the second condition in CASE 1 is false.

Finally, we consider the third condition in CASE 1 is true, if user uk_1, whose access privilege $\widehat{\mathcal{L}_1} = A_l[t_a, t_b, Pcode_l, Ncode_l]$ can recover ek while access policy $\widehat{AP} = A_x[t_a, t_b, Pcode_x, Ncode_x]$, while $Pcode_x > Pcode_l$ or $Ncode_x > Ncode_l$. Note that, due to the one-way property of the BDF in CBE, uk_1 cannot derive D'_{Pcode_x} from D'_{Pcode_l} while $Pcode_x > Pcode_l$. The same situation holds for $Ncode_x > Ncode_l$. Therefore, the third condition in CASE 1 is false, and CASE 1 will not happen. ∎

The proof of CASE 2 is similar with that of CASE 1. To obtain ek, the CSP needs to calculate $F_1 \cdot F_2 \cdot F_3 \cdot F_4$ to obtain $e(g^{\tau'_k}, \omega)^{\triangle_\sigma(A_l)}$ for sufficient attributes $A_l \in \mathcal{T}$. Since the CSP is not allowed to access the PHR system, it cannot obtain sufficient private keys. As proved in CASE 1, the entities that do not meet the access policy cannot recover ek. Therefore, CASE 2 will not happen. ∎

6   Experimental Results

In this section, we will compare our proposed scheme with the CBE scheme in terms of computation cost. Our experiments are conducted with Java programming language. We implement our scheme on an stand-alone mode, on a PC with Intel Core i3 CPU running at 2.3 GHz and 2 G memory. The practical computational costs of algorithms *Setup*, *Genkey*, *Encrypt*, *Delegate*, *Decrypt1*, and *Decrypt2* in both schemes are shown in Figs. 3 and 8.

The parameter settings in the experiments are as follows: N_A is the number of specific attributes in the access policy, m indicates the number of attribute nodes in an attribute hierarchy tree. Here, we take $m = 50, N_A = 10$ and $m = 100$, respectively. In our experiments, we generate a private key with privilege $[t_1, t_2]$, where $t_1 \in_R [1, Z/4]$ and $t_2 \in_R [3Z/4, Z]$, for a certain comparison range $[1, Z]$.

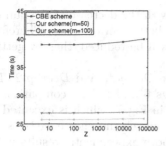

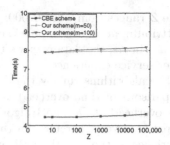

Fig. 5. Computation cost of *Encrypt*.   **Fig. 6.** Computation cost of *Delegate*.

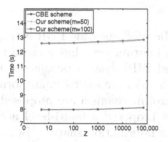

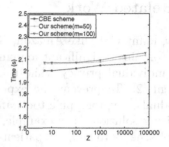

Fig. 7. Computation cost of *Decrypt1*.   **Fig. 8.** Computation cost of *Decrypt2*.

Furthermore, the message is encrypted by the time condition $t \in_R [Z/4, 3Z/4]$ to ensure that $\max(t - t_1, t_2 - t) \geq Z/4$.

Our experimental results are shown in Figs. 3 and 8. We observe that the growth of time overhead is not significant as the value of Z increases in terms of the HCBE scheme and the CBE scheme. Meanwhile, in our scheme, the growth of time overhead is not significant while m grows from 50 to 100. Due to the introduction of attribute hierarchy in our scheme, the computational overhead of *Setup* and *GenKey* algorithms in our scheme is larger than that of the CBE scheme. However, the difference is minor. For example, as shown in Fig. 3, the computation time of our *Setup* algorithm grows from 5.43 s to 5.46 s under the setting of $m = 50$, and the computation time of the *Setup* algorithm of the CBE scheme grows from 4.94 s to 4.95 s, while Z ranges from 7 to 70,000; as shown in Fig. 4, the computation time of our *Genkey* algorithm grows from 9.62 s to 9.85 s under the setting of $m = 100$, and the computation time of the *Genkey* algorithm of the CBE scheme grows from 6.20 s to 6.36 s, while Z ranges from 7 to 70,000.

In the experiment, in order to get better comparison results between our scheme and CBE scheme, we use $N_A = 10$ specific attributes for CBE encryption. As shown in Fig. 5, the encryption time of our scheme is much smaller than that of the CBE scheme. For example, the computation time of our *Encrypt* algorithm grows from 25.75 s to 25.98 s under the setting of $m = 50$, and the computation time of the *Encrypt* algorithm of the CBE scheme grows from 38.95 s to 40.00 s, while Z ranges from 7 to 70,000; Furthermore, with the decrease of the number of attribute, m, in access policy, our scheme has better performance. Therefore, in our scheme, the data owner's time overhead will be reduced, thereby getting better service experience.

The algorithms run by the data user include *Delegate* and *Decrypt2*. The comparisons of time overhead are shown in Figs. 6 and 8. The comparison of time overhead of *Decrypt1* algorithm is shown in Fig. 7, which is executed by the proxy server. Therefore, for the data users in our scheme, they have the same experience as those in the CBE scheme. The above experimental results verify our theoretical analysis in Sect. 5.

7   Related Work

Today, many CSP, like Amazon, Google, and Microsoft, provide PHR services. PHR contains a significant amount of sensitive information, thus how to preserve individual privacy while using cloud-based PHR system becomes a key problem [2]. To prevent the exposure of health information to unauthorized individuals, cryptographic tools and access control mechanism are proposed as promising solutions. For example, Jin et al. [10] proposed a multi-level access control scheme to support patient-centric health information sharing. Benaloh et al. [11] designed a Patient Controlled Encryption (PCE) system to secure the storage of patients' medical records. With the PCE system, patients can share partial access rights with others, and to perform searches over their records in a secure way. Li et al. [12] proposed a novel framework for scalable and efficient access control to PHRs in cloud computing environment. Yao et al. [13] utilized order preserving symmetric encryption (OPSE) [14] for preserving data privacy in multi-source personal health record clouds. Li et al. [15] utilized predicate encryption [16] to achieve authorized search on PHRs in cloud computing.

Most existing work adopted Attribute Based Encryption (ABE) [9,17] as the cryptographic tool to achieve fine-grained access control in cloud-based PHR systems. The original ABE systems only support monotone access policy and assume the existence of a single private key generator (PKG). A lot of research has been done to achieve more expressive access policy [18], and distributed key management [19]. To achieve dynamic access control in cloud computing, Yu et al. [20] applied the proxy re-encryption (PRE) technique [21] to ABE. Wang et al. [6] proposed a hierarchical ABE scheme to achieve key delegation in cloud environment. On the basis of ABE scheme, Zhu et al. [7] proposed the CBE scheme by making use of the forward/backward derivation functions, and applied CBE to the cloud environment. However, the encryption cost of the CBE scheme will grow linearly with the number of attributes in the access policy. To solve this problem, we proposed the HCBE scheme by incorporating the attribute hierarchy to the CBE scheme.

8 Conclusion and Future Work

In this paper, we proposed a HCBE scheme for achieving a fine-grained access control in cloud-based PHR systems. Our scheme supports time comparison in attribute-based encryption in an efficient way, by incorporating attribute hierarchy into CBE. However, due to the limited space, we only sketch the security of the proposed scheme. In our future work, we will try to prove that the HCBE scheme has key security under chosen derivation-key attacks (KS-CDA) and semantical security under chosen derivation-key attacks (SS-CDA).

Acknowledgments. This work was supported in part by NSFC grants 61402161, 614721 3161272546; NSF grants CNS 149860, CNS 1461932, CNS 1460971, CNS 1439672,CNS 1301774, ECCS 1231461, ECCS 1128209, and CNS 1138963.

References

1. Tang, P., Ash, J., Bates, D., et al.: Personal health records: definitions, benefits, and strategies for overcoming barriers to adoption. J. Am. Med. Inf. Assoc. **13**(2), 121–126 (2006)
2. Guo, L., Zhang, C., Sun, J., et al.: PAAS: A privacy-preserving attribute-based authentication system for ehealth networks. In: Proceedings of IEEE ICDCS, pp. 224–233 (2012)
3. Armbrust, M., Fox, A., Griffith, R., et al.: A view of cloud computing. Commun. ACM **53**(4), 50–58 (2010)
4. Googlehealth. https://www.google.com/health/
5. Healthvault. http://www.healthvault.com/
6. Wang, G., Liu, Q., Wu, J.: Hierarchical attribute-based encryption for fine-grained access control in cloud storage services. In: Proceedings of ACM CCS, pp. 735–737 (2010)
7. Zhu, Y., Hu, H., Ahn, G., et al.: Comparison-based encryption for fine-grained access control in clouds. In: Proceedings of ACM CODASPY, pp. 105–116 (2012)
8. Boneh, D., Franklin, M.: Identity-based encryption from the weil pairing. In: Kilian, J. (ed.) CRYPTO 2001. LNCS, vol. 2139, pp. 213–229. Springer, Heidelberg (2001)
9. Bethencourt, J., Sahai, A., Waters, B.: Ciphertext-policy attribute based encryption. In: Proceedings of IEEE S&P, pp. 321–349 (2007)
10. Jin, J., Ahn, G.-J., Hu, H.: Patient-centric authorization framework for sharing electronic health records. In: Proceedings of ACM SACMAT, pp. 125–134 (2009)
11. Benaloh, J., Chase, M., Horvitz, E., Lauter, K.: Patient controlled encryption: ensuring privacy of electronic medical records. In: Proceedings of ACM CCSW, pp. 103–114 (2009)
12. Li, M., Yu, S., Ren, K., Lou, W.: Securing personal health records in cloud computing: patient-centric and fine-grained data access control in multi-owner settings. In: Jajodia, S., Zhou, J. (eds.) SecureComm 2010. LNICST, vol. 50, pp. 89–106. Springer, Heidelberg (2010)
13. Yao, X., Lin, Y., Liu, Q., et al.: Efficient and privacy-preserving search in multi-source personal health record clouds. In: Proceedings of IEEE ISCC (2015, accepted to appear)

14. Boldyreva, A., Chenette, N., O'Neill, A.: Order-preserving encryption revisited: improved security analysis and alternative solutions. In: Rogaway, P. (ed.) CRYPTO 2011. LNCS, vol. 6841, pp. 578–595. Springer, Heidelberg (2011)

15. Li, M., Yu, S., Cao, N., et al: Authorized private keyword search over encrypted data in cloud computing. In: Proceedings of IEEE ICDCS, pp. 383–392 (2011)

16. Okamoto, T., Takashima, K.: Hierarchical predicate encryption for inner-products. In: Matsui, M. (ed.) ASIACRYPT 2009. LNCS, vol. 5912, pp. 214–231. Springer, Heidelberg (2009)

17. Goyal, V., Pandey, O., Sahai, A., Waters, B.: Attribute-based encryption for fine-grained access control of encrypted data. In: Proceedings of ACM CCS, pp. 89–98 (2006)

18. Waters, B.: Ciphertext-policy attribute-based encryption: an expressive, efficient, and provably secure realization. In: Catalano, D., Fazio, N., Gennaro, R., Nicolosi, A. (eds.) PKC 2011. LNCS, vol. 6571, pp. 53–70. Springer, Heidelberg (2011)

19. Lewko, A., Waters, B.: Decentralizing attribute-based encryption. In: Paterson, K.G. (ed.) EUROCRYPT 2011. LNCS, vol. 6632, pp. 568–588. Springer, Heidelberg (2011)

20. Yu, S., Wang, C., Ren, K., Lou, W.: Achieving secure, scalable, and fine-grained data access control in cloud computing. In: Proceedings of IEEE INFOCOM, pp. 534–542 (2010)

21. Libert, B., Vergnaud, D.: Unidirectional chosen-ciphertext secure proxy re-encryption. In: Cramer, R. (ed.) PKC 2008. LNCS, vol. 4939, pp. 360–379. Springer, Heidelberg (2008)

Lightweight Virtual Machine Checkpoint and Rollback for Long-running Applications

Lei Cui[1], Zhiyu Hao[1]($\boxtimes$), Lun Li[1], Haiqiang Fei[1], Zhenquan Ding[1], Bo Li[2], and Peng Liu[2]

[1] Institute of Information Engineering, Chinese Academy of Sciences,
Beijing 100093, China
{cuilei,haozhiyu}@iie.ac.cn
[2] School of Computer Science and Engineering, Beihang University,
Beijing 100191, China
{libo,liupeng}@act.buaa.edu.cn

Abstract. Checkpoint/rollback is an effective approach to guarantee that the long-running applications can be completed in the face of failures. However, it does not come for free. The application suffers from long downtime and performance penalty when it is being checkpointed or rolled back, which result in extra overhead on application execution time. This problem would get worse in virtualized environment mainly due to the heavyweight of virtual machine. This paper proposes warmCR, a lightweight checkpoint/rollback system for virtual machine, which aims to reduce its own extra overhead on application execution time. First, warmCR employs the redirect-on-write approach to create disk checkpoint and leverages the copy-on-write method to lively create memory checkpoint, so that both the downtime and checkpoint duration are reduced. Second, we propose a working set based rollback approach to provide short downtime without compromising application performance. Third, workload-aware batched processing is proposed to achieve trade-off between downtime and performance loss. In addition to presenting warmCR, we detail its implementation, and provide extensive experimental results to prove its efficiency and effectiveness.

Keywords: Checkpoint · Rollback · Virtual machine · Reliability · Long-running application

1 Introduction

Machine virtualization is now used widely in data centers, the applications are now encapsulated into virtual machine (VM) which provides an isolated computing paradigm, rather than physical machine. For example, popular web servers such as Raddit, Netflix, Airbnb are running on VMs provided by Amazon EC2 [1]; Emulab provides scalable platform for scientific computing applications [22]. However, nowadays data centers always utilize unreliable commodity devices, so

G. Wang et al. (Eds.): ICA3PP 2015, Part III, LNCS 9530, pp. 577–596, 2015.
DOI: 10.1007/978-3-319-27137-8_42

that failures become norm rather than exception [4]. The unpredictable underlying failures, such as server crash, network interruption and software hang, may cause the VM crash, and further lead to application disruption. What's worse, the long time running applications, such as scientific computing or image processing, may not be completed due to the loss of intermediate results upon frequent failures.

Checkpoint/rollback [5] is one well known technique to enhance system availability. It periodically saves the running state of the applications to persistent storage during failure-free execution. Upon a failure, the system can be restored from the previously recorded state, and continues to execute from that intermediate state rather than the initial state, thereby reducing the amount of lost computation. This ability is especially valuable for long-running applications, because it prevents the loss of intermediate results in the face of failures and thus guarantees that the applications can be completed within a certain period. Several works [23,24] provide checkpoint/rollback ability for HPC applications.

However, checkpoint/rollback itself introduces extra overhead on application execution time. Downtime and duration are two key metrics used to characterize the overhead. Downtime is the overhead that the VM must be suspended when it is checkpointed or rolled back, it directly increases the application execution time. Duration is related to the time required to save or retrieve the entire VM state. The application in this stage experiences performance degradation, it therefore requires more time to finish a task. Since the VM is heavy in memory state, it would take more IO resources and longer time to save (retrieve) the entire memory image, so that both downtime and duration are significant. For example, the nowadays VMs are always equipped with dozens of GB RAM, therefore, the downtime and duration may reach several minutes for 1 Gbps network bandwidth [21]. Consider that the checkpoint interval has to be set to be hours or even minutes to ensure the successful completion of long-running applications [7], the downtime and duration of several minutes for each checkpoint are obviously non-trivial. Although lots of approaches have been proposed to reduce the downtime [18,19], the attempt to reduce the downtime always results in the increase in duration. Therefore, the actual execution time may increase due to the cumulative performance loss in longer duration [7].

This paper proposes warmCR, a lightweight checkpoint and rollback system, which aims to guarantee the completion of long term applications while minimizing its own overhead on execution time. On one hand, warmCR employs redirect-on-write (ROW) approach to create disk checkpoint, and leverages copy-on-write (COW) technique to create memory checkpoint, thereby reducing the checkpoint downtime and duration. Meanwhile, it estimates the working set through tracing the memory operations during checkpoint stage, and loads the working set instead of the entire memory state upon rollback, thereby reducing the rollback downtime without comprising application performance. On the other hand, a two-phase page saving/loading policy is proposed to save the memory pages in a workload-aware manner, this approach achieves a trade-off between downtime and duration while preserving the overall performance, and consequently reduces the overhead on application execution time.

We implement warmCR on QEMU/KVM platform to justify its efficiency and effectiveness, and evaluate warmCR under several workloads. Compared to the native checkpoint/rollback approach (coldCR) in QEMU/KVM, warmCR reduces the downtime of checkpoint and rollback by 96.6 % and 94.3 % respectively. Compared to the live migration based checkpoint/rollback approach (liveCR), warmCR reduces the duration by 41.4 % and 40.5 % respectively. Further more, the numerical results show that warmCR reduces the expected application completion time by 18.2 % compared to coldCR, and 6.96 % compared to liveCR.

The rest of the paper is organized as follows. The next section introduces the background and reviews the current checkpoint and rollback techniques. Section 3 presents the design of warmCR, and Sect. 4 describes implementation specific details on QEMU/KVM platform. The experimental and numerical results are shown in Sect. 5. Finally we conclude our work in Sect. 6.

2 Background and Problem Analysis

2.1 System Model

A VM is checkpointed periodically in the predefined interval, and the checkpoint images are stored into the stable storage. Upon VM crash, the latest created checkpoint image will be retrieved to roll back the VM, as shown in Fig. 1.

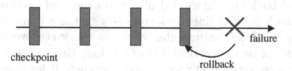

Fig. 1. System execution model.

The stable storage is assumed to be failure-free, this is reasonable since the storage system always provides high availability through replication or erasure coding technique and hence hides failures to the upper systems. We only consider the simple fail-stop model for VMs and the underlying physical servers, so that we can detect the failure immediately [16] and then recover the system. The VM is subject to both transient and permanent failures, and the root cause may come from software bug, hardware error or human misbehavior. The failure finally leads to the crash of the applications along with the VM. The failures of VMs are independent of each other, so are the failures of the physical servers. However, obviously, the failure of physical server would lead to the crash of all the VMs running on the server.

If the VM fails due to the failure of applications or guest OS, the VM can stay in the same host after rollback-recovery. If it is the crash of host OS or underlying hardware which results in the failure of VM, the VM would be resumed on

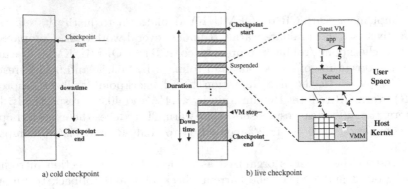

Fig. 2. Checkpoint approaches.

another failure-free host. We assume that no failure occurs when the VM is being checkpointed or rolled back. This is reasonable because the checkpoint or rollback duration is always minor compared to the mean time to failure (MTTF) of the system.

2.2   Virtual Machine Checkpoint/Rollback

The most simple checkpoint/rollback approach is coldCR, also known as sequential checkpointing, which suspends the VM while the VM is being checkpointed or rolled back [3]. Figure 2(a) illustrates the cold checkpoint approach. The downtime with coldCR linearly increases with the amount of VM memory size, and it may reach several minutes as the memory size would be dozens of GB, making coldCR be impractical due to the long time service disruption.

liveCR is an alternative and widely used approach, it leverages the pre-copy approach to checkpoint the VM [18]. Specifically, it sets write-protect flag of memory pages to trace the write operation. Once the application accesses the write-protected page, the following steps (shown in Fig. 2(b)) will be executed: (1) the application exits to guest kernel, (2) guest exits to VMM, (3) VMM sets the associated bit in the dirty bitmap, (4) VMM resumes the VM, (5) application is allowed to access the page. The forked checkpoint thread scans the dirty bitmap, saves the pages that are dirtied, and then sets the write-protect flag again to trace the subsequent write operations. This procedure would continue iteratively until certain condition is satisfied, e.g., the amount of remaining pages is little enough, or a certain number of iterations is reached. Finally, liveCR stops the VM, flushes the remaining pages into checkpoint image, saves the CPU and other devices' state, creates disk snapshot, and then resumes the VM. At this moment live checkpoint is completed. The drawback of pre-copy checkpoint is that it iteratively saves the dirtied memory pages, therefore a large amount of pages are required to be saved, resulting in long duration and performance loss due to IO contention. Moreover, the downtime is directly related to the amount of remaining pages in the final iteration which may reach hundreds of MB, so that the downtime would be up to several seconds [9]. As a result, the application execution time with liveCR is actually much longer. Sun et al. [19] propose a copy-on-write approach to checkpoint the VM on Xen platform, which achieves checkpoint duration reduction. Our warmCR approach also adopts the COW method, but is different in that we estimate the working set during checkpoint and propose two-phase page saving/loading policy to eliminate performance loss.

Several optimizations are proposed to reduce the checkpoint duration, and the key is to reduce the saved amount of memory pages. QEMU/KVM uses one byte to represent the entire zero page whose bytes are identical. Jin el al. [26] compress the VM in-memory state based on strong data regularities. Hines et al. [27] leverage balloon mechanism to reclaim memory pages, and then compress the reclaimed page into one byte. Park et al. [28] track IO operation to find the duplicate pages that are resident in both memory and disk blocks, and discard these pages upon snapshot. Chiang et al. [29] introspect the guest kernel to acquire the free pages, and remove them from snapshot. We make no attempt to optimize the snapshot size, however, we believe these approaches can be used as supplement to our work.

VM rollback also attracts attention recently. Garg el al. [21] start the VM immediately when rollback-recovery is required, leaving the memory state to be loaded in an on-demand manner. Zhang et al. [8] propose working set based rollback to reduce the downtime without compromising performance loss after rollback. Our rollback approach is inspired by Zhang's work, but we adopt a different estimation method both on working set pages selection and size determination (Sect. 3.2).

In addition to checkpoint and rollback technologies, checkpoint interval also plays an important role in reducing the execution time for long running applications [12–15, 17]. A long interval reduces the overhead but may loss more computation upon failures. A small interval, on the contrary, saves more computation but incurs larger checkpoint overhead. Our work does not focus on checkpoint interval, instead, we attempt to reduce the overhead incurred by the checkpoint and rollback approaches. However, we believe these work can be complemented with warmCR to reduce the application execution time further.

3   System Design

warmCR decreases the application execution time through lightweight checkpoint and rollback. VM checkpoint is light because the downtime is minimized and duration is reduced by saving each memory page once. VM rollback is light in that the VM can execute soon after a small fraction of memory state is loaded. The following subsections will describe the design of warmCR along with optimizations in details.

3.1   Copy-on-write Memory Checkpoint

The copy-on-write (COW) idea is not new, it has been widely used to take the checkpoint of data, software or the whole system. A recent work [19] employed

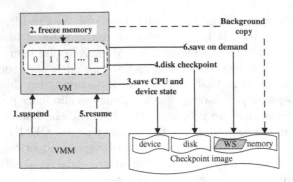

Fig. 3. Copy-on-write checkpoint.

COW to create memory checkpoint on XEN platform. Our method is similar to that work. The main difference is that we estimate the working set (WS) during checkpoint stage for fast rollback. We present how to checkpoint the memory in this part, and will describe working set estimation in the next section.

Figure 3 demonstrates the COW manner to create memory checkpoint. The VMM firstly suspends the VM, freezes the memory through setting write-protect flag to the page table entries of all memory pages, saves the CPU state and devices' state, and then creates the disk checkpoint. After that, the VM is resumed and continues to execute, and the memory pages are to be saved on demand. Since the memory pages are now write-protected, the memory write operation issued by application will trigger page fault and force the VM exit to VMM. VMM handles the page fault by the following steps: (1) save the page content to the checkpoint image, (2) clear the write-protect flag to allow the page to be written by subsequent operations without triggering page fault again, (3) resume the VM. The applications after the VM is resumed can continue to execute until another page fault is triggered. Meanwhile, a background thread is forked to save the memory pages concurrently with the VM execution, with the aim to ensure that the checkpoint procedure terminates within a limited period.

warmCR is expected to outperform liveCR in two aspects on checkpoint. First, warmCR takes less downtime. Generally, the downtime mainly involves four parts: (1) save CPU state and other devices' state, (2) create disk checkpoint, (3) set write-protect flags and (4) save memory pages. The amount of CPU state and devices' state is always small, e.g., it is 526 KB for a VM with default configuration in QEMU/KVM platform. Our iROW approach takes less time to create disk checkpoint than the default qcow2 format in QEMU/KVM, because it does not require block or cluster indexing. Setting write-protect flags only involves bit operations, so that the time cost is short too. In addition, warmCR does not require to save memory pages. Consequentially, the entire downtime of warmCR checkpoint is short and almost constant for fixed size of disk and memory. In contrast, liveCR approach tends to flush the remaining pages in the final iteration, and the downtime would be up to several seconds for memory intensive workloads.

Second, the duration of warmCR checkpoint is short too. As mentioned before, the liveCR approach iteratively saves the pages that are dirtied in the last iteration until certain condition is satisfied. This suggests that one page would be saved repeatedly once it is dirtied iteratively. Due to the memory access locality, lots of pages tend to be saved repeatedly, making the memory checkpoint size be much larger than the VM memory size, meanwhile resulting in longer duration. COW memory checkpoint reduces the duration by saving each page only once. Specifically, the memory page that has ever been saved will not trigger page fault again because the associated write-protect flag is removed, it therefore won't be saved. Meanwhile, a background thread is forked to save memory pages concurrently to speed up the checkpoint procedure.

Compared to coldCR which suspends the VM during the whole checkpoint stage, warmCR only suspends the VM for a few milliseconds. Since warmCR saves the memory pages on demand, the VM will exit from and re-enter VMM frequently due to the page fault, so that the duration of warmCR is longer than that of coldCR. Fortunately, the experimental results demonstrate that the extra time overhead is minor compared to the benefit of reduction on downtime.

3.2 Working Set Based Rollback

warmCR adopts a working set based rollback approach to reduce the rollback downtime. Rather than resume the VM lazily [21] or eagerly [20], warmCR tends to load the working set pages first and then starts the VM. This approach brings several benefits to reduce application execution time. On one hand, it directly reduces the rollback downtime. The working set always takes a small fraction of the entire memory image due to memory access locality, so that the downtime is within only a few seconds. On the other hand, the working set represents the latest recently used pages, therefore lots of memory operations after rollback-recovery will touch the pages in the working set. As a result, the performance loss after VM starts is insignificant. To achieve this, warmCR needs to solve two key problems: working set estimation and partial rollback.

One classical method is to trace the memory read/write operations during normal application execution and then select the pages based on statistical method [25]. Unfortunately, it causes performance penalties due to heavy tracing overhead. warmCR adopts an efficient approach to estimate working set, specifically, it determines the working set from the pages that are saved on-demand during post checkpoint stage. This is motivated by two observations under the assumption of deterministic VM execution. First, the pages saved in COW manner are touched by application during post-checkpoint, so they are latest recently used pages and thus are candidates for the working set. Second, the VM after being rolled back to the checkpoint time point will re-execute the instructions and touch the same memory area. This implies that the memory pages accessed during post-checkpoint will be touched again after the VM resumes. So far the candidate memory pages for the working set are known. We employ a simple method to determine the working set size. We set a threshold, which is ten percents of the memory size. If the amount of accessed pages is less than the

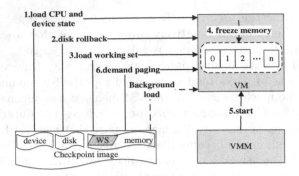

Fig. 4. Working set based rollback.

threshold, all these pages are filled into the working set. Otherwise, only the pages that are accessed prior are selected as the working set pages.

The name "partial rollback" comes from the fact that the VM resumes after only a fraction of memory pages are loaded. Figure 4 illustrates the rollback steps. The VMM firstly loads the CPU state and devices' state, rolls back the disk state, prefetches the working set pages into memory, freezes the pages that are not in the working set through setting non-present flag to associated page table entries, and finally starts the VM. The VM after it starts may trigger page fault when accessing non-present pages. The VMM handles the page fault by: (1) loading the corresponding page content from checkpoint image into memory, (2) clearing the non-present flag, (3) resuming the VM. Similar to checkpoint, a background thread is forked to load memory pages actively to speed up rollback procedure and alleviate performance loss.

3.3   Two-Phase Workload Aware Page Saving/Loading

warmCR achieves lightweight checkpoint/rollback by overlapping the VM execution with checkpoint/rollback, but at the cost of handling a number of page faults. The VM is paused when the VMM handles page fault. The pause time involves three parts: (i) switch between the application and guest kernel, (ii) switch between guest and VMM, and (iii) save/load page. Although the pause time to handle one page fault is only a few microseconds, the cumulative time for handling thousands of page faults would reach dozens of seconds, and consequently increase the application execution time. The pause time can be diminished by a specific syscall [10], however, it requires modification of both guest OS and application. To reduce the cumulative pause time, we tend to reduce the count of page faults rather than the pause time for each page fault.

Memory access locality reflects that the application always touch a limited range of memory area in a short period. This feature gives us a hint that the neighbor pages are always touched together, therefore, saving or retrieving multiple pages instead of only one page for each page fault would reduce the possibility of page faults. Determining the page count is critical, a large page count will lead to long pause time to write (read) pages into (from) storage, while a small one saves the time but at the cost of more page faults.

We propose a two-phase saving/loading policy, On-demand Phase and Background Phase, to reduce the count of page faults. For clarity, we only describe the approach on checkpoint, which shares the similar method to rollback. The VM is hung in the On-demand Phase and resumes in Background Phase. Once a page fault occurs, saving page firstly experiences the On-demand Phase. In this phase, α neighbor pages that are not saved and are adjacent to the touched page are saved together with the touched page. Then the VM is resumed. After that the Background Phase starts, a lightweight thread is forked to save β pages that are not saved and are adjacent to the touched page. Compared to the naive background thread which scans the pages sequentially and blindly, this lightweight thread saves the pages that are neighbour to the touched page. As a result, this policy is aware of the page access pattern of the workloads and thus is more effective than the native one.

Note that the so called "neighbor" pages that are to be saved together may be unexpectedly far, i.e., they are not physically adjacent. This is because the touched pages may scatter in the memory, and the pages after being saved are no longer saved again. As more pages are saved during the checkpoint procedure, searching α or β neighbor unsaved pages may take longer and longer time. This inspires us to set a upper bound T to restrict the search scope. Once T neighbor pages have been scanned, the searching stage would be terminated even if the count of saved page is less than α or β. The value of α, β and T are empirically set, in our platform, we set α to be 4, β to be 12 and T to be 100, which achieves an exciting effect. The pseudo-code below describes the procedure for search α pages in On-demand Phase.

Listing 1.1. Saving pages in On-demand Phase.

```
save_pages(page_gfn)
{
  save(page_gfn)
  page_shift = saved_page_cnt = 0
  while(saved_page_cnt < alpha)
    gfn = page_gfn + page_shift
    if(page_not_saved(gfn))
      save(gfn)
      saved_page_cnt++
    page_shift++
    if(page_shift == T)
      break
}
```

3.4   Expected Application Execution Time

In this section, we analyze the expected application execution time when coldCR, liveCR and warmCR are employed respectively, and discuss how warmCR reduces the execution time. The execution time can be determined by the sum of original execution time and extra time incurred by checkpoint and rollback, so the key is to calculate the extra time overhead on checkpoint and rollback.

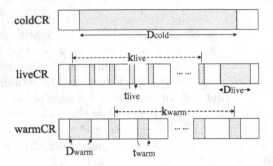

Fig. 5. Application execution time during checkpoint procedure.

Extra Time Overhead on Checkpoint. The application is completely suspended when the VM is being checkpointed with coldCR approach, while it keeps running during the checkpoint procedure of warmCR and liveCR. At the macroscopic level, the application experiences performance degradation because it is paused for a short while by VMM to handle page fault. The performance degradation is hard to calculate due to varieties of workloads. Therefore, we resort to calculate the extra time overhead from the microscopic perspective, specifically, we approximate the extra time with the cumulative pause time during checkpoint procedure. Figure 5 illustrates the idea of computation on extra time. The downtime of coldCR, liveCR and warmCR are denoted by D_{cold}, D_{live} and D_{warm} respectively. Let t_{warm} and t_{live} be the pause time for handling one page fault, k_{warm} and k_{live} are referred to as the count of page faults during checkpoint procedure of warmCR and liveCR. Apparently, the extra execution time introduced by coldCR, which is denoted by T_{cold}, is equal to D_{cold}. For liveCR, the cumulative pause time is the product of pause time t_{live} and the count k_{live}, therefore we can get $T_{live} = D_{live} + k_{live} * t_{live}$. Similarly, $T_{warm} = D_{warm} + k_{warm} * t_{warm}$.

As mentioned before, warmCR takes the minimum downtime since no memory page is saved, so that $D_{warm} < D_{live} < D_{cold}$. In addition, warmCR reduces the count of page faults by employing COW method and two-phase saving policy while liveCR iteratively triggers page faults, therefore, $k_{warm} < k_{live}$. The only issue is that the time to handle page fault in warmCR is larger than that of liveCR, i.e., $t_{warm} > t_{live}$. This is because liveCR only sets the associated bit of the dirtied page in dirty bitmap, while warmCR needs to save page content. Fortunately, the time can be diminished by firstly saving the pages into a temporarily buffer and then flushing into disk in an asynchronous manner. As a result, the difference between t_{warm} and t_{live} can be eliminated, so that the cumulative pause time T_{warm} is less than T_{live}. The detailed results will be demonstrated in Sect. 5.3.

Extra Time Overhead on Rollback. We denote DR_{cold}, DR_{live} and DR_{warm} to the downtime of the three rollback approaches. coldCR and liveCR load the entire memory state before resuming the VM, while warmCR resumes the VM

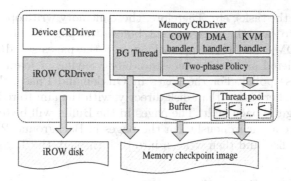

Fig. 6. Architecture of warmCR.

after the working set pages are loaded, so that $DR_{warm} < DR_{live} = DR_{cold}$. Let tr_{warm} be the pause time for handling each page fault, and kr_{warm} be the count of page faults during rollback, the cumulative pause time during rollback recovery TR_{warm} is denoted by $DR_{cold} + tr_{warm} * kr_{warm}$. Since the two-phase loading policy and the background thread reduce the occurrences of page faults, the pages required to be loaded take only a small fraction of the entire memory. Consequently, we can conclude that warmCR incurs much less extra time than coldCR and liveCR. We will report the results in Sect. 5.3.

4 Implementation Issues

4.1 Architecture of WarmCR

We implement warmCR on QEMU/KVM. QEMU takes charge of disk checkpoint and memory checkpoint. KVM module is modified to set write-protect flag or non-present flag of page table entries during checkpoint or rollback, for triggering page fault upon subsequent page access operations.

The architecture of warmCR is illustrated in Fig. 6. The checkpoint consists of three kinds of state: disk state, devices' state and memory state. warmCR leverages the default method in QEMU/KVM to save or load the devices' state. To save disk state, warmCR employs our previous iROW (improved redirect-on-write) approach [6]. iROW CRDriver (checkpoint/rollback driver) creates a *btmp file* and a *irvd file* as the new state. The *btmp file* is used to index the block in the *irvd file* which is regarded as the new disk file. All the disk operations after checkpoint will be directed to the blocks in the new created *irvd file*. Meanwhile, the previous *irvd file* is reserved as the disk checkpoint file.

Memory CRDriver takes charge of memory checkpoint and rollback. It would lead to incompleteness of memory state if we only save the pages on page fault and in background. This because the simulated DMA device would write the guest memory pages directly without triggering page fault. In addition, the KVM kernel also writes pages for specific purposes, such as setting the guest clock, switching the tasks, etc. Therefore, these memory write operations should be intercepted to save the page content before the page is dirtied. The pages intercepted in DMA and KVM operations, and the pages saved on write page fault, are considered as working set candidates. Saving or loading these pages adopts two phase policy. For the pages in On-demand Phase, they are firstly written into a Buffer rather than disk directly, with the aim to reduce the pause time for handing the page fault. The pages in the Buffer will be flushed into the checkpoint image asynchronously. For the pages in Background Phase, they are enqueued into a list, and then written into disk through the Thread Pool.

4.2 Working Set Estimation

We create memory checkpoint in copy-on-write manner, which means that we set write-protect flag for tracing the memory write operations. However, the simply COW approach cannot capture an accurate working set, because the memory read operations are bypassed. As a result, massive memory read operations after rollback will cause hit miss in loaded working set and then trigger page faults, and consequently lead to performance degradation. Apart from setting write-protect flag, we also set read-protect flag for all memory pages to record which pages are accessed during checkpoint (i.e., record-on-access), and treat these pages as working set candidates. Upon the page fault triggered by read operation, we only record the frame number of the page and its neighbour pages through the On-demand Phase policy described in Sect. 3.3, and then resume the VM. The responsibility to save the page into checkpoint image is taken by the COW Handler, DMA Handler or the BG Thread. This copy-on-write combined with record-on-access method help warmCR to create memory checkpoint efficiently while capturing the working set accurately.

The working set requirement makes the BG Thread be different from COW Handler or DMA Handler when saving the page. Specifically, BG Thread reserves the read/write-protect flag after the page is saved during checkpoint, so that the later access operation on the page can be traced and the touched page can be regarded as candidate of the working set.

5 Evaluation

We try to answer how much the key aspects are improved with warmCR compared to coldCR or liveCR. We calculate the downtime and duration of checkpoint and rollback under several workloads, and measure the performance loss on both macro-level and micro-level. Then, we calculate the numerical expected application execution time in the face of failures.

5.1 Experiment Setup

We conduct experiments on four physical servers equipped with 2 GHz 16 core Intel processor and 32 GB of RAM. The servers are connected via 1 Gbps switch.

All the checkpoint files are stored into a local 7,200 RPM Seagate 1T disk. We configure the VM with 2 GB RAM and 20 GB disk. The operating system on physical server and VM is debian6.0 with Linux kernel 2.6.32-5. We evaluate warmCR under several workloads: (1) Compilation represents a development workload which involves memory and disk I/O operations. We compile the Linux 2.6.32 kernel along with all modules. (2) Mplayer is a movie player, it prefetches a fraction of movie file in the buffer for performance when playing movie. We play a HD video whose size is 4 GB. (3) Elasticsearch is a distributed, de-centralized search server to search documents [2]. We fill 5000,000 mircoblogs into the sever, and request microblogs with different keywords continuously. The server will return the top 40 results for each request. (4) Gzip is a compression utility. We compress the /home directory whose size is 2.1 GB.

5.2 Key Metrics on Checkpoint and Rollback

We firstly profile the checkpoint metrics to show the introduced overhead. We conduct the experiments ten times and report the average value, the results of downtime and duration are shown in Table 1. As we can see, the downtime of coldCR is large, it reaches about 49.6 s on average for the four workloads. As expected, the downtime of warmCR is minor and almost constant, i.e., it keeps at 70 ms; this is because wamCR only conducts lightweight operations and involves a small constant amount of state. The downtime of liveCR is also minor, it is about 137 ms on average.

Table 1. Checkpoint downtime and duration (seconds).

Metrics	Checkpoint downtime			Checkpoint duration		
Workloads	warmCR	liveCR	coldCR	warmCR	liveCR	coldCR
Mplayer	0.072	0.147	52.4	53.6	110.2	52.4
Elasticsearch	0.074	0.070	48.7	52.3	86.4	48.7
Compilation	0.062	0.215	47.1	51.7	79.5	47.1
Gzip	0.081	0.118	50.3	52.7	83.1	50.3

We further count the downtime to create disk checkpoint, save devices' state and save memory state (only for liveCR). We write a memory intensive program (Mem) which requests a memory region and fills it with randomly generated data in the rate ranged from 20 MB/s to 80 MB/s, this helps us to understand the association between downtime and memory write speed. Then we create disk checkpoint for various disk sizes to analyze the relationship between downtime and disk size. Figure 7(a) compares the time to save devices' state and memory state of warmCR and liveCR (note that the y-axis is log scaled). As we can see, warmCR takes almost constant time regardless of the memory speed. However, the downtime of liveCR rises with the increase of memory speed. It is up to 1.9 s

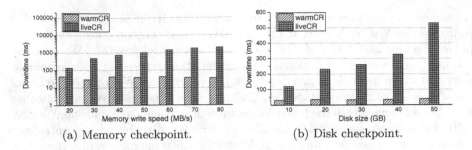

(a) Memory checkpoint.   (b) Disk checkpoint.

Fig. 7. Downtime to create memory and disk checkpoint.

when the speed reaches 80 MB/s. Figure 7(b) depicts the downtime to create disk checkpoint. The results show that the proposed iROW disk format introduces minor downtime, that is, dozens of milliseconds. Moreover, it keeps constant regardless of the disk size. In contrast, liveCR, which adopts the qcow2 disk format, takes gradually incremental time to complete the disk checkpoint as the size increases.

The duration of warmCR keeps almost constant too, as illustrated in Table 1. This is because each page is saved only once so that the checkpoint image size is equivalent to the memory size. liveCR iteratively saves the dirtied pages, therefore it generates a much larger size checkpoint image, and thus results in longer duration. On average, warmCR achieve a 41.4 % reduction of duration compared to liveCR.

We then measure the rollback metrics and report the results in Table 2, the duration is equal to downtime for coldCR and liveCR. Compared to coldCR and liveCR which take dozens of seconds to boot up the VM, warmCR can resume the VM within 3 s since the VM is resumed after the working set pages are loaded, which takes a few fraction of the entire memory space. The downtime of liveCR is the largest due to the large checkpoint image size. Similarly, the rollback duration of warmCR is shorter; on average, warmCR reduces the duration by 40.5 % compared to liveCR.

Table 2. Rollback downtime and duration (seconds).

Metrics	Rollback downtime			Rollback duration		
Workloads	warmCR	liveCR	coldCR	warmCR	liveCR	coldCR
Mplayer	2.96	90.6	43.9	44.2	90.6	43.9
Elasticsearch	2.86	73.2	42.1	45.2	73.2	42.1
Compilation	2.82	67.1	41.5	43.1	67.1	41.5
Gzip	1.07	68.8	42.6	45.9	68.8	42.6

5.3   Performance Overhead

As mentioned earlier, the application experiences performance degradation when warmCR or liveCR is employed since it will be frequently paused. We firstly present the count of page faults during checkpoint and rollback, and report the cumulative pause time to handle page faults, to profile the detailed performance loss (micro-level). Then, we profile the performance loss under Elasticsearch workload when the VM is being checkpointed and rolled back, to demonstrate the macro-level performance degradation. The results of coldCR are not reported because the application is completely suspended during checkpoint or rollback.

Micro-level Performance Overhead. Overhead During Checkpoint. The application when accessing the protected page will firstly exit to guest kernel, and then exit to VMM layer. As a result, it is difficult to count the actual pause time in VMM layer unless modifying the guest OS. We use the time difference between VM exit and VM re-entry to approximate the actual value.

Table 3 reports the count of triggered page fault as well as the cumulative pause time during checkpoint procedure. Compared to liveCR which triggers several hundred thousands of page faults, warmCR only triggers a few thousands. This is because warmCR never triggers fault twice for the same page by clearing the protect flag. Moreover, the proposed two-phase policy saves the neighbor pages together, and therefore helps to reduce the count of page faults a lot. On the contrary, liveCR after one dirtied page is recorded will set write-protect flag again, and may incur hundreds of page faults on the same page. Although warmCR takes more time for handling each page fault (about 30us) than liveCR (about 2us), it incurs much less page faults, so that the cumulative pause time of warmCR is less as well. Table 3 show that warmCR reduces the total pause time by about 36.5 % on average compared to liveCR.

It is worth noting that the practical pause time to handle page fault is actually longer than our approximated value calculated in VMM layer, due to the time cost on switch between application and guest kernel. Therefore, the cumulative pause time for liveCR which incurs more page faults would be much longer than that of warmCR, this implies that warmCR actually reduces much more time than the results in Table 3.

Table 3. Overhead during checkpoint.

Metrics	Page fault count		Total pause time (s)	
Benchmarks	warmCR	liveCR	warmCR	liveCR
Mplayer	18210	486432	1.68	3.34
Elasticsearch	6837	351752	2.10	1.97
Compilation	5920	276631	1.71	2.92
Gzip	4372	298168	1.06	2.07

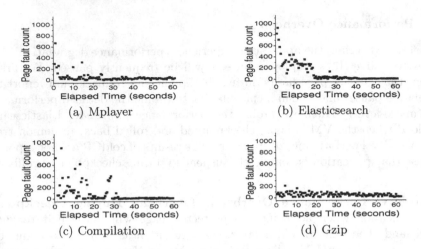

Fig. 8. Count of page faults during rollback.

Overhead During Rollback. We count the page faults during rollback stage in 0.5 s interval under four workloads, and report the results in Fig. 8. As we can see, the count is high at the beginning after the VM starts, e.g., it reaches 672, 923, 726 and 90 respectively in the first interval. The count decreases as the VM runs, because most of the subsequent memory operations would hit the page that has been loaded either on-demand or by the background thread. As we can see, the count drops to a few dozens since the 20th second. The count under Mplayer is less than that under Compilation, implying that execution of Mplayer is more deterministic so that the estimated working set is more accurate. The results of Gzip show some difference in two aspects: (i) the count is not as high as that of the other workloads, (ii) the count keeps almost steady during the entire rollback procedure. This is because Gzip involves IO intensive operations and dirties the page via DMA directly, meanwhile, it reads file consecutively and hence touches the pages sequentially. Overall, the total amount of page faults is minor as expected, and the cumulative pause time to handle page faults is within only a few seconds.

Macro-Level Performance Overhead. We profile the performance overhead on Elasticsearch in term of requests per second (RPS). Figure 9 depicts the RPS during normal execution, checkpoint procedure and rollback procedure.

At the start of the trace, the Elasticsearch server achieves a constant RPS which approximates 6,250. After warmCR checkpoint starts at the 10th second, the RPS firstly suffers a sharp drop to 2,265 because the VM is suspended for a few milliseconds. Then the RPS arises to 3,254 and keeps the value for about 39 s. Finally the Elasticsearch server regains the full capacity after checkpoint is completed at the 49th second. The RPS during checkpoint with liveCR is higher than that of warmCR, e.g., the average RPS is 4,540 while it is 3,441

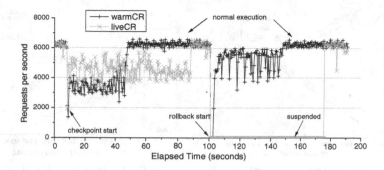

Fig. 9. Requests per second during checkpoint and rollback.

with warmCR. This is because warmCR incurs longer pause time upon each page fault. Fortunately, although warmCR suffers lower rate RPS than liveCR, the checkpoint duration of warmCR is much shorter, it is about 40 s while it reaches up to 79 s with liveCR. During the 79 s execution, Elasticsearch server with warmCR serves 390,384 requests in all, while it serves 361,007 requests with liveCR. This result implies that warmCR outperforms liveCR in terms of overall performance.

During rollback procedure, warmCR performs much better. The Elasticsearch server with liveCR is completely suspended for 74 s, however, with warmCR it starts to serve requests after 2 s downtime. The RPS gradually increases to 1,967 and 3,994 in the first two seconds after VM resumes. During the whole rollback stage, the RPS is 5,221 on average, and regains the full capacity after rollback is completed at the 151th second. During the 74 s duration, Elasticsearch server serves 388,058 requests with warmCR, while it is completely unavailable with liveCR.

5.4 Application Execution Time

We evaluate warmCR in terms of the expected application execution time in the face of failures. There may exist several kinds of faults that lead to system crash, e.g., network interruption, disk failure and power outages [30]. Moreover, the dynamic change of network and IO bandwidth may also affect the application performance. As a result, rather than compute the practical execution time in read-world scenarios, we employ the model (shown in Eq. 1) described by Arunagiri [11] to calculate the numerical results.

$$E(T) = Me^{(R/M)}(e^{(\tau+\gamma)/M} - 1)\frac{T_s}{\tau} \qquad (1)$$

T is the failure free application execution time without experiencing checkpoint or rollback. τ is referred to as the checkpoint interval. We denote the mean time to failure (MTTF) by M. γ is the time overhead on checkpoint, and R is the time overhead on rollback.

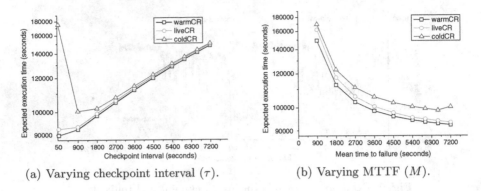

(a) Varying checkpoint interval (τ).   (b) Varying MTTF (M).

Fig. 10. Expected execution time with varying parameters.

In the numerical simulations, we assign the variables above with the following values. The execution time T is 86400 s. Checkpoint overhead γ and rollback overhead R adopt the results shown in Table 4, which are the average value from Tables 1, 2, and 3. The actual value of τ and M are unknown, therefore we take varying values. The value of M ranges from 900 to 7200 s, and the checkpoint interval τ takes value ranged from 50 to 7200 s.

Table 4. Time overhead (seconds).

	warmCR	liveCR	coldCR
Checkpoint overhead	1.71	2.71	49.63
Rollback overhead	2.43	74.93	42.53

Figure 10(a) plots the expected execution time with varying checkpoint intervals when M is fixedly 7200 s. The execution time with coldCR approach is extremely high when τ is 50 s, because coldCR incurs heavy downtime on each checkpoint. Such a large time implies that coldCR is impractical when checkpoints are required to be taken frequently. The execution time with coldCR drops to the optimal result when τ is 900 s, and then increases gradually as the interval grows. The increase is mainly due to the fact that larger τ leads to more computation loss upon failures. liveCR achieves less execution time than coldCR when τ is 50 s, because it brings only a few seconds downtime during checkpoint. warmCR performs much better, it reduces the execution time by 2552 s compared to liveCR when τ is 900 s. The reduction comes from the decrease of time overhead both on checkpoint and rollback.

Figure 10(b) compares the expected execution time for different M when τ is fixedly set 900 s. As we can see from the picture, all the three lines show a global decrease trend, this is mainly attributed to less failures as M grows. First, the number of rollback is less, so that the total time overhead on rollback decreases. Second, the computation loss due to failures is reduced accordingly. The time difference between warmCR and liveCR is large when M is small, and gradually disappears as M grows. For example, the time difference is 12810 s when M is 900 s, and drops to 1040 s when M is 7200 s. For small M, the time difference mainly lies in the large rollback overhead, because the VM is rolled back frequently due to more failures. Once M is large, implying that failures occur less, the checkpoint overhead becomes the key factor on execution time. Consider that the downtime as well as cumulative pause time of warmCR and liveCR are both a few seconds, therefore the execution time difference between two approaches is slight. These results demonstrate that warmCR is effective particularly in scenarios which suffer frequent failures.

On average, warmCR achieves 18.2 % reduction on expected execution time compared to coldCR, and 6.96 % reduction compared to liveCR.

6   Conclusion and Future Work

Long running applications may never be completed in the face of failures, unless fault tolerance technique is provided. In this paper, we propose warmCR, a lightweight checkpoint and rollback technique, with the aim to reduce the extra execution time incurred by checkpoint and rollback technique themselves for long running applications. We employ copy-on-write technique to reduce the checkpoint downtime and duration, and leverage working set based rollback to reduce the rollback downtime without compromising performance after the VM is resumed. Moreover, we propose two-phase workload aware saving/loading policy to reduce the performance loss. We have implemented warmCR on QEMU/KVM, and conducted a set of experiments to prove its effectiveness.

Our future work tends to improve warmCR further. Observed that the application always experiences phase change during the whole execution lifetime, for example, it becomes active for a while and then turns to be steady, we plan to estimate the phase change and then create checkpoint when the application is inactive with the aim to reduce the amount of page faults during checkpoint, for eventually reducing performance loss.

Acknowledgement. We would like to thank the anonymous reviewers for their valuable comments and help in improving this paper. This work is supported by National Key Technology Support Program under grant No. 2012BAH46B02.

References

1. Amazon EC2. http://aws.amazon.com/ec2/
2. ElasticSearch. http://www.elasticsearch.org/
3. Vallee, G., Naughton, T., Ong, H., et al.: Checkpoint/restart of virtual machines based on Xen. In: HAPCW (2006)
4. Ford, D., Labelle, F., Popovici, F.I., et al.: Availability in globally distributed storage systems. In: OSDI, pp. 1–14 (2010)

5. Plank, J.S., Beck, M., Kingsley, G., et al.: Libckpt: transparent checkpointing under Unix. Computer Science Department (1994)
6. Li, J., Liu, H., Cui, L., Li, B., Wo, T.: iROW: an efficient live snapshot system for virtual machine disk. In: ICPADS, pp. 376–383 (2012)
7. Vaidya, N.H.: Impact of checkpoint latency on overhead ratio of a checkpointing scheme. TOC **46**(8), 942–947 (1997)
8. Zhang, I., Garthwaite, A., Baskakov, Y., et al.: Fast restore of checkpointed memory using working set estimation. In: VEE, pp. 87–98 (2011)
9. Song, X., Shi, J., Liu, R., et al.: Parallelizing live migration of virtual machines. In: VEE, pp. 85–96 (2013)
10. Lee, M., Krishnakumar, A.S., Krishnan, P., et al.: Hypervisor-assisted application checkpointing in virtualized environments. In: DSN, pp. 371–382 (2011)
11. Arunagiri, S., Seelam, S., Oldfield, R.A., et al.: Impact of checkpoint latency on the optimal checkpoint interval and execution time (2008)
12. Young, J.M.: A first order approximation to the optimal checkpoint interval. Comm. ACM **17**(9), 530–531 (1974)
13. Tantawi, A.N., Ruschitzka, M.: Performance analysis of checkpointing strategies. TOC **2**(2), 123–144 (1984)
14. Duda, A.: The effects of checkpointing on program execution time. Inf. Process. Lett. **16**(5), 221–229 (1983)
15. Kourai, K., Chiba, S.: Fast software rejuvenation of virtual machine monitors. TDSC **8**(6), 839–851 (2011)
16. Leners, J.B., Wu, H., Hung, W.L., et al.: Detecting failures in distributed systems with the FALCON spy network. In: SOSP, pp. 279–294 (2011)
17. Garg, S., et al.: Minimizing completion time of a program by checkpointing and rejuvenation. In: SIGMETRICS, pp. 252–261 (1996)
18. Kangarlou, A., Eugster, P., Xu, D.: VNsnap: taking snapshots of virtual networked environments with minimal downtime. In: DSN, pp. 524–533 (2009)
19. Sun, M.H., Blough, D.M.: Fast, Lightweight Virtual Machine Checkpointing (2010)
20. Liu, H.K., Jin, H., Liao, X.F., et al.: VMckpt: lightweight and live virtual machine checkpointing. Sci. China Inf. Sci. **55**(12), 2865–2880 (2012)
21. Garg, R., Sodha, K., Cooperman, G.: A generic checkpoint-restart mechanism for virtual machines (2012). arXiv preprint. arXiv:1212.1787
22. Hibler, M., Ricci, R., Stoller, L., Duerig, J., et al.: Large-scale virtualization in the emulab network testbed. In: ATC, pp. 113–128 (2008)
23. Liu, Y., Nassar, R., Leangsuksun, C.B., Naksinehaboon, N., Paun, M., Scott, S.L.: An optimal checkpoint/restart model for a large scale high performance computing system. In: Symposium on Parallel and Distributed Processing, pp. 1–9 (2008)
24. Maoz, T., Barak, A., Amar, L.: Combining virtual machine migration with process migration for HPC on multi-clusters and grids. In: Cluster, pp. 89–98 (2008)
25. Waldspurger, C.A.: Memory resource management in VMware ESX server. In: OSDI, pp. 181–194 (2002)
26. Jin, H., Deng, L., Wu, S.: Live virtual machine migration with adaptive memory compression. In: CLUSTER, pp. 1–10 (2009)
27. Hines, M.R., Gopalan, K.: Post-copy based live virtual machine migration using adaptive pre-paging and dynamic self-ballooning. In: VEE, pp. 51–60 (2009)
28. Park, E., Egger, B., Lee, J.: Fast and space-efficient virtual machine checkpointing. In: VEE, pp. 75–85 (2011)
29. Chiang, J.-H., Li, H.-L., Chiueh, T.-C.: Introspection-based memory de-duplication and migration. In: VEE, pp. 51–62 (2013)
30. Gray, J.: Why do computers stop and what can be done about it? In: German Association for Computing Machinery Conference on Office Automation (1985)

Fast and Scalable Regular Expressions Matching with Multi-Stride Index NFA

Sheng Huo, Dafang Zhang$^{(\boxtimes)}$, and Yanbiao Li

College of Computer Science and Electronic Engineering,
Hunan University, Changsha 410082, China
ed3200@163.com, {dfzhang,lybmath_cs}@hnu.edu.cn

Abstract. Regular expression matching plays an important role in modern Deep Packet Inspection (DPI) engines, to classify or filter packets by matching their payloads toward a series of pre-defined rules represented as regular expressions. Generally, finite automaton-based approaches are utilized to perform fast and scalable regular expression matching. Among those approaches, Deterministic Finite Automaton (DFA) has the fastest speed yet suffers from the state space explosion problem. By contrast, Nondeterministic Finite Automaton (NFA) can achieve the highest memory efficiency at the cost of complicated and thus low-speed matching process.Instead of seeking for a reasonable trade-off between memory efficiency and processing throughput from DFA, this paper chooses the NFA as the start point for optimization. Based on two important observations, a Multi-Stride Index (MSI) table is designed for pre-processing before going into the NFA. As the MSI table can filter most of unsuccessful matchings and thus significantly reduce the chance of processing on the NFA, the proposed MSI-NFA approach achieves a fast speed approximate to the DFA when processing real-world HTTP packets. As demonstrated in the experimental results, its speed is at most 10 % lower than that of DFA. Moreover, the additional memory cost is as low as 20 KB compared with NFA.

Keywords: Regular expression matching · Deep packet inspection · Multi-stride

1 Introduction

Network Intrusion Detection and Prevention System (NIDS/NIPS) is one of the most important network component to protect network security [15]. As a core function of NIDS/NIPS, Deep Packet Inspection (DPI) not only checks packet headers, but also goes deep into the packet payloads. It usually works by matching packet contents against a series of pre-defined rules to identify unexpected and harmful traffics [16,18]. Further, DPI is also proved to be valuable in other content-filter based applications, such as packet classification on application-layer and contextual traffic accounting [14,17], to name only a few.

© Springer International Publishing Switzerland 2015
G. Wang et al. (Eds.): ICA3PP 2015, Part III, LNCS 9530, pp. 597–610, 2015.
DOI: 10.1007/978-3-319-27137-8_43

In the past, DPI always utilized string matching to match packet payloads with pre-defined rules which have already been described as strings. But now, Regular Expression (RE) matching plays more important role in DPI. In this schema, all pre-defined rules are specified as regular expressions which are more efficient and flexible. Most modern DPI engines, such as Snort [3], Bro [16], TippingPoint IPS [4], Cisco IOS IPS [1], all utilize RE to describe signature rules.

1.1 Technical Challenges

There are two basic challenges in achieving fast and scalable regular expressions matching to our work.

1. For each input character, only one memory accesses is required to move forward the matching process (e.g. Deterministic Finite Automaton). It's the key point to ensure fast and low-cost matching.
2. Total memory footprint increases linearly with the scale of the rule table (e.g. Non-deterministic Finite Automaton). It's the key point to enhance system scalability.

To explain that more detailedly, the Deterministic Finite Automaton(DFA) is considered to be processing efficient with the worse case processing complexity of $O(1)$ for each input character, as compare to Non-deterministic Finite Automaton(NFA) which has $O(n)$ worse case complexity - n being the length of the regular expression [24]. On the other hand, NFA is considered to be more space efficient with the worse case storage cost of $O(n)$, as compared to DFA which has $O(2^n)$ worse case storage cost. Over the years, the big trouble of the trade-off between DFA and NFA - namely the matching speed and space usage, which have been disturbed the researchers. In this paper, we present a approach that try to fix this problem.

1.2 Our Approach

In this paper, we present an improvement of NFA that can achieve a matching speed as fast as DFA in most cases, while the total memory usage just increase a bit in comparison to NFA and the additional memory consumption is consistent and acceptable.

Our approach is based on two important key observations: **Low Matching Ratio** and **High State Locality**. More specifically, when performing DPI on real-world network traffics, a successful matching occurs very rarely. According to our experiment result, only 0.39 % of 400 K real-world HTTP packets result in successful matching against 500 Snort rules, according to other researcher [13] is 0.27 %. This means, in normal cases, there are very less unexpected packets that will match pre-defined rules. On the other hand, we measured all encountered transitions during the matching process and found that 91 % of these transitions only relate to top-10 "hot" states. Furthermore, top-20 "hot" states cover 99 % of these transitions. In another word, during the matching process, most encountered transitions are transferred between some "hot" states. Besides, these "hot" states always have very low depth in the FA-tree. Actually, the **High State Locality** is always resulted by **Low Matching Ratio**. Since states in deep levels of the FA-tree will only be traversed in successful matchings, they have very less chances to be traversed due to the low matching ratio.

In our approach, we propose a Multi-Stride Index (MSI) table that generated from some low-depth states of NFA for fast pre-processing. Only the matching succeeds in MSI will be performed in the NFA then. As most matching will fail in MSI (due to above observations), NFA will rarely be involved in the matching process. Thus, our MSI-NFA schema operates RE matchings as fast as DFA when processing real world Internet traffic. Meanwhile, although our approach consumes more memory resources due to MSI, the additional memory consumption is low, consistent, and controllable, ensuring that MSI can be stored on high-speed cache to further enhance the matching performance.

The rest of this paper is organized as follows. We firstly introduce some related works in Sect. 2. Then, we present the MSI on Sect. 3 and discuss system architecture of MSI-NFA schema along with core algorithms and theory analysis in Sect. 4. At last, we demonstrate our experiment results on Sect. 5 and conclude the whole paper in Sect. 6.

2 Related Work

Generally, Finite Automaton (FA) is always adopted to perform Regular Expression (RE) matching. Among these approaches, DFA has the fastest matching speed at the cost of high memory consumption, while, by contrast, NFA employs the most compact structure but requires a more complicated matching logic with large per-flow states thus it is slow. According to the traditional knowledge, it's impossible to acquire both advantages of DFA and NFA at the same time. Many great efforts have been made to seek for reasonable trade-off between those two schemas.

As the challenge of improving processing throughput to meet the high-speed link rate is more serious than memory efficiency, DFA is always chosen as the start point for optimization due to its fast and stable matching speed. For instance, mDFA [24] divides RE rules into groups and then constructs DFA for each of group to reduce memory usage. The cost is all these DFAs should be involved in one matching. Fortunately, matching on these independent DFAs can be processed in parallel with the cost of more compute resources and memory bandwidth. Moreover, mDFA can be optimized by recursively grouping to CODFA-tree [13] to gain further memory cost reduction with more groups while sacrifice a little speed on average condition. Grouping the rules still may lead to lower whole matching speed as the power of parallelism is limited. With the help of auxiliary variables and additional operations, XFA [20,21] successfully eliminates the state space explosion of DFA. However, it costs more time to process RE matching on XFA than on DFA. Another optimization of DFA is to compress the transitions. The proposed approach D^{2}FA [11] can even reduce 90 % of transitions. But it consumes more time when processing each transition to handler explicit error. In a word, they optimize the memory efficiency of DFA at the loss of matching speed to achieve reasonable trade-off.

On the other hand, the matching speed can also be improved on basis of some specific hardwares, such as FPGA [6–8,19], ASIC [23], TCAM [22,25], and GPU [26,27]. The mutli-striding method [5,9,10,12] that two or more characters are processed together in each step enhances the throughput of string matching, but is difficult to be utilized in RE matching due to the complex semantics.

Instead of DFA, we chose NFA as the start point, and then optimize the matching speed based on our observations of RE matching with real-world Internet traffics, achieving a fast speed as DFA in practice with only a little increment of memory cost than NFA.

3   Multi-Stride Index Table

Generally, in each step of processing packet payload on the NFA one byte is consumed and used as the input character to trigger all possible state transitions from all active states, generating a series of active states for next step. Thus, multiple memory accesses are required in each step of performing RE matching on NFA.

According to our observations, most RE matching of real-world Internet traffics will fail after processing first several characters. A natural idea of optimization is to reduce the chance of processing bytes on NFA by filtering the packets that will not lead to successful matching outside the NFA. This is our basic motivation to design a Multi-Stride Index (MSI) table to filter those matching who will fail finally.

To accelerate the process of finding unsuccessful matching, we employ the multi-striding technical that consuming two or more characters in each step. Given a stride n, we extract all possible n-combinations[1] of all RE rules to construct the MSI table. In this way, as long as one of the n-combinations of the input content does not exist in the MSI table, it can be deduced that this content will not match any of pre-defined rules. In another word, the MSI table is used to select candidate matches after filtering obvious-unsuccessful ones.

3.1   Complete *N-Combination* Set

We try to extract all possible *n-combinations* to make the deduction of unsuccessful matching trustable. There are different policies to extract complete *n-combination* sets for different type of RE rules.

String Expressions. This is the easiest case, in which we can simply extract consequent combination of characters. For example, when $n = 2$, we can get 3 *2-combinations*, $\{ab, bc, cd\}$, from the rule *abcd*.

---

[1] A group of n continuous characters.

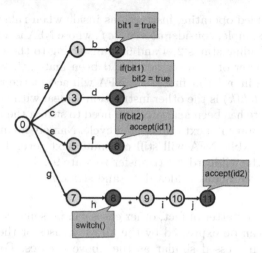

Fig. 1. Instructions have been added in NFA to handle the splitting problem of rule

Meta-Character ?. The meta-character ? matches the preceding character zero or one time. If one rule contains this meta-character, we can firstly expand it to two rules containing zero or one preceding character respectively and then process them separately to extract all possible *n-combinations*. For example, to process the rule *ab?cd* when $n = 2$, we can firstly expand it to *acd* and *abcd* respectively and then extract 4 *2-combinations* $\{ac, cd, ab, bc\}$ in total.

Meta-Character +. The meta-character + matches the preceding character one or more times. If one rule contains this meta-character, we can expand it to unlimited number of rules in theory. However, given that the stride is also pre-specified as n, we can only expand such rule to $n - 1$ or n rules according to whether the next character is the same as the preceding character or not. No more *n-combination* can be generated if more rules are expanded to. For example, to process the rule *ab + cd* when $n = 2$, we can firstly expand it to 2 rules, *abcd* and *abbcd*, respectively, and get 4 *2-combinations* $\{ab, bc, cd, bb\}$ in total. Even by expanding the original rule to *abbbcd*, no more *2-combinations* will be generated. While for the rule *ab + bd*, we should only expand it to 1 rule *abbd*, leading to 3 *2-combinations* $\{ab, bb, bd\}$.

Wildcard .* and . The wildcard "." matches any single character while the wildcard ".*" matches any number of any character. If a RE rule contains any such wildcard, we can firstly split it into segments at the position of these wildcards and then process them separately with all *n-combinations*. For example, to process the rule *ab.cd* when $n = 2$, we first split it into *ab* and *cd*, and then obtain 2 *2-combinations* $\{ab, cd\}$.

Moreover, in order to match correctly, we add some instructions inside states in NFA to handle these two wildcards. Figure 1 shows the corresponding NFA which had been added operating instructions inside when rule set is $\{ab.*cd.*ef, gh.ij\}$. As an example, consider $ab.*cd.*ef$, whose NFA is added instructions inside the corresponding states 2, 4 and 6, transferring to these states represent that the last character of each segments had been matched. Only if ab and cd have been matched in order at first, then NFA will accept the rule when ef had been matched. $switch(k)$ is the other instruction to deal with the wildcard".", it means once the state has been activated, we need to switch the matching process by MSI-NFA temporary in next k matching cycle. Namely no matter what is the retrieving result in MSI, NFA will still consume next several input characters directly to match the wildcard "." (transfer to state 9). The value of k depends on the number of continuous wildcard "." and stride n.

Other Cases. As a matter of fact, other cases can be some combination of the above 4 cases, or can be expressed by the above 4 cases or their combinations, or can be simply processed similar as the above 4 cases. For examples, rule $ab + cd.*ef$ is a combination of meta-character $+$ and wildcard $.*$. Rule $ab*cd$ can be expressed by $ab?cd$ and $ab+cd$. Rule $ab|cd$ can be expanded to ab and cd. Rule $[ab]cd$ can be expanded to acd and bcd. Rule $ab\{4,6\}cd$ can be expanded based on the similar policy applied for $ab + cd$. To name only a few.

3.2 Structure Design of the MSI Table

To enhance the processing speed, the first design principle is to ensure each matching step requires only one memory access to the MSI table. Besides, it's important to keep the MSI table as small as possible to control the total memory footprint. Moreover, if the MSI table is small enough to be kept in the cache, the processing speed will also be enhanced.

Accordingly, we design the MSI table as a n-dimensional array aligned to the cache line. Each array entry is composed of two bits, indicating whether it is a valid n-combination and whether it's a $tail$ part respectively. While the size of each dimensional is just the size of the alphabet $\|\Sigma\|$. Thus, the total bits the MSI table consumes is $2 \times \|\Sigma\|^n$, which is 16 KB and 4 MB when $n = 2$ and $n = 3$ respectively (suppose the alphabet is ASCII, namely $\|\Sigma\| = 256$). According to our experimental evaluation, $n = 2$ or $n = 3$ can already filter most of unsuccessful matches. Such small MSI tables can fit into most modern caches.

Figure 2 shows an example of the MSI table when $n = 2$ and the alphabet is $\Sigma = \{a, b, c, d\}$. Only one rule $abcd$ is expressed. 3 2-combinations $\{ab, bc, cd\}$ are extracted, among which cd is flagged as $tail$.

4 MSI-NFA

4.1 The Matching Process of MSI-NFA

The matching process of MSI-NFA is composed of the pre-processing in MSI and the matching phase in NFA. The pre-processing in MSI is responsible for

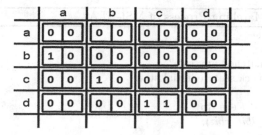

	a		b		c		d	
a	0	0	0	0	0	0	0	0
b	1	0	0	0	0	0	0	0
c	0	0	1	0	0	0	0	0
d	0	0	0	0	1	1	0	0

Fig. 2. The MSI table for rule $abcd$, $\Sigma = \{a, b, c, d\}$, n = 2

answering whether the *n-combination* extracted from the input content exists in the MSI table. This step requires only one simple memory access since MSI table is a *n*-dimensional array, in which the indexing key of each dimension is just the ASCII code of a character. Such a fast indexing in MSI is the key point to achieve a matching speed approximately equal to that of DFA in the low matching ratio case. According to the pre-processing result (the value of L-bit and R-bit of the hit entry in the MSI table), the algorithm will then decide whether it's required to apply next step and how to do that. NFA is a traditional automaton structure and has been used many years for multi-pattern matching. In our approach, we just utilize the original NFA with some instruction added just like XFA [20,21], so the matching process of NFA is unnecessary to illustrate specificly here. Algorithm 1 is the pseudo-code that describes the matching process of MSI-NFA.

In Algorithm 1, the input is the packet payload w and stride n, while the output is whether payload w matches any of pre-defined rules. We use $F[i-1]$ to denote the ith character of fragment F. The matching process can be described as follows:

- Initialize variables. *current_state* is the active state set of NFA, *check_state* stores active states during tail-matching process (when R-bit is 1). (As shown by step 1-2)
- Read the payload w by n consecutive characters to form a *n-combination* fragment, which is then used to retrieve a entry from the MSI table. (As shown by steps 3-4 in Algorithm 1)
- If the value of L-bit of the retrieved MSI entry is 0, it indicates current fragment is not any of available *n-combinations* of rules. Then we end this step by resetting the *current_state* to the initial value. Otherwise, we go into the NFA for regular expression matching. (As shown by steps 5-6 in Algorithm 1)
- If the L-bit's value is 1, we then check the R-bit of the retrieved MSI entry and process the corresponding matching steps. (As shown by steps 8-11 and 13-14 in Algorithm 1)
- Execute the instructions inside *check_state* set at each end of tail-matching. (As shown by steps 12 in Algorithm 1)

Algorithm 1. Matching Process of MSI-NFA

Data: Payload w
Input: Stride n
Output: Is w matched any rule?
1 current_state=check_state =initial_state;
2 lbit=rbir=0;
3 **foreach** *fragment* $F \in w$ **do**
4 | msiIndex(F, *lbit*, *rbit*);
5 | **if** *!lbit* **then**
6 | | current_state=initial_state;
7 | **else**
8 | | **if** *rbit* **then**
9 | | | check_state=nfaMatch(current_state,$F[1]$);
10 | | | **foreach** *character* $F[i] \in F$ *(1<i<n)* **do**
11 | | | | check_state=nfaMatch(check_state,$F[i]$);
12 | | | **end**
13 | | | execInstrs(check_state);
14 | | **else**
15 | | | current_state=nfaMatch(current_state, $F[0]$);
16 | | **end**
17 | **end**
18 **end**

The reason why we match all characters of the current *n-combination* extracted from the payload rather than the its first character on the NFA is to avoid missing match due to the tail-matching issue. Generally, the head-matching and tail-matching issue is very common in multi-stride string matching. Actually, it's possible to miss the right match in both head-matching or tail-matching when processing two or more characters together in FA.

MSI-NFA will only suffer the similar issue during the tail-matching, because the matching process is pushed forward character by character even though we processing MSI matching with a combination of characters. For instance, we match the payload *abcde* on the 2-stride MSI-NFA constructed from the rule *abcd*. As the *2-combinations ab*, *bc*, *cd* exists in the MSI table, the input payload will retrieve them from the MSI table consequently. Since *cd* is flagged as *tail*, we must processing both characters of it on the NFA to get the final matching. Otherwise, we can only get a sub-matching *abc* while fail on the next step for *de* as it does not exit in the MSI table.

The *accept*() instruction will output the rule ID which be matched successfully in NFA. Moreover, if the instruction in *check_state* include any *switch(k)* instruction, the matching process will be switched temporary in the next k cycle as shown in Algorithm 2. Meanwhile, the value of k inside each state depends on the number of continuous wildcard "." and stride n, more specifically, $k = n+t-1$ while t is the number of continuous wildcard ".". In special circumstances, if the *check_state* set include more than one *switch(k)* instruction, the *switch(k)* process will take the maximum value of k. To illustrate at last, as shown by step 10 in Algorithm 2, if $execInstrs(check\_state)$ also include any $switch(k)$ instruction, the current $switch(k)$ process will be broken while the new value of k greater than or equal to the old, then the new $switch(k)$ process will be restarted.

Algorithm 2. switch(k)

Input: k
Input: current_state
1 **while** $k>0$ **do**
2 $\quad$ get the corresponding input n-combination fragment $F \in w$;
3 $\quad$ msiIndex(F, $lbit$, $rbit$);
4 $\quad$ current_state=nfaMatch(current_state, $F[0]$);
5 $\quad$ **if** $rbit$ **then**
6 $\quad\quad$ check_state=nfaMatch(current_state,$F[1]$);
7 $\quad\quad$ **foreach** *character* $F[i] \in F$ $(1<i<n)$ **do**
8 $\quad\quad\quad$ check_state=nfaMatch(check_state,$F[i]$);
9 $\quad\quad$ **end**
10 $\quad\quad$ execInstrs(check_state);
11 $\quad$ **end**
12 $\quad$ $k--$;
13 **end**

4.2 Theoretical Analysis

The Correctness of Matching with MSI-NFA. Now we prove that MSI-NFA will correctly match the payload with the rules. Assume S is the signature rules, then $L(S)$ is the language accepted by NFA. The string in payload $c_1c_2...c_k \in L(S)(k \geq n)$ is splited into *n-combinations* $\{F_1,F_2...F_{k-n+1}\}$. $\{T_1,T_2...T_p\}$ are $L(S)$'s *n-combinations*. Obviously, $\{F_1,F_2...F_{k-n+1}\} \subseteq \{T_1,T_2...T_p\}$ since $c_1c_2...c_k \in L(S)$. Thus each element in $\{F_1,F_2...F_{k-n+1}\}$ will get a successful matching on MSI consequently and should be further matched with NFA later. Defining $c_i=F_i$ if c_i is the first character to F_i. Then, NFA will match the string $c_1c_2...F_{k-n+1}$ after the pre-processing. Finally, NFA can match the string $c_1c_2...c_k$ correctly since the tail-fragment $F_{k-n+1}=c_{k-n+1}...c_k$.

The Filtration Ratio of MSI. The MSI table can filter part of unsuccessful matchings but not all of them. It's possible that all *n-combinations* of some input payload exists in the MSI table, but it can not match any of predefined rules. For example, the MSI table for rules *ab.cd* and *bc.de* contains 4 *2-combinations* $\{ab, cd, bc, de\}$. Although all *2-combinations* of the payload *abcd* (namely $\{ab, bc, cd\}$) exist in the MSI table, it can match neither *ab.cd* nor *bc.de*.

To measure the filteration ratio of MSI approximately, we present the Filtration Ration in Theory (FRT) that is calculated as E/P where E and P are the number of empty entries (whose L-bit is 0) and the total number of entries of the MSI table. The FRT can represent the power of MSI to filter unsuccessful matchings to some extent. That's because if some *n-combination* of the input payload does not exist in the MSI table it must be a unsuccessful matching.

Misjudgment. If MSI makes a mistake by matching a wrong *n-combinations*, namely a *n-combinations* from payload is not a real matching part but should be further matched in NFA according to the indexing result with MSI, we called it as a misjudgment. Fortunately, it is not too bad for MSI-NFA because of the matching mechanism. With the increase of matching character number, NFA needs more time to consume a input character, because multiple states may be active at the same time and they do not exhibit deterministic computation and memory bandwidth guarantees. But in the most case to our approach, NFA matches the character as the first cycle when a misjudgment has occurred, since MSI-NFA will reset the NFA to initial when MSI filter a *n-combinations* successfully. It means only the condition of MSI matching succeed occur continuously lead to the increment of matching time for NFA in a single cycle, but actually, except for real matching traffic, this possibility is very small since it decrease exponentially along with the increasing of matching succeed times from MSI. In additional, we can also increase the stride n in order to decrease the occurring chance of misjudgment while pay more memory space for MSI table.

5   Evaluation Experiments

Based on the software of regular expression processing [2], we implement MSI-NFA using C/C++ and then evaluate its performance, in terms of filtration ratio, matching speed and memory usage, by matching real-world Internet traffics toward 500 Snort [16] rules.

5.1   Filtration Ratio of MSI

Those 500 Snort rules are divided into 5 groups, each containing $100 \sim 500$ rules.

Table 1 demonstrates Filtration Ratio (FR), Filtration Ratio in Theory (FRT) and Misjudgment (Mis) by MSI when processing 400 K real-world packets. FRT is calculated as E/P where P and E are the total number of entries and the number of empty entries in the MSI table respectively. FR is calculated as $(M-N)/M$ where M and N denote the number of matching steps processed on the MSI and NFA respectively, and are both measured through the experiments. Mis express the ratio that MSI table perform a misjudgment.

As shown in Table 1, FR decrease significantly with the increasing of the number of rules for 2-stride MSI. While the FR of the 3-stride MSI can even keep above 99 %, which is extremely close to the real matching ratio. This means increasing the stride has significant effect on improving the filteration ratio.

Table 1. The filtration efficiency of MSI

Rule num	Matching ratio	n = 2			n = 3		
		FR%	FRT%	Mis%	FR%	FRT%	Mis%
100	0.11%	96.82	96.95	3.16	99.87	99.99	0.10
200	0.24%	91.57	93.69	8.38	99.78	99.97	0.17
300	0.22%	85.93	89.10	14.01	99.75	99.95	0.19
400	0.28%	80.17	85.75	19.75	99.59	99.94	0.33
500	0.39%	75.43	82.50	24.46	99.45	99.93	0.43

Table 2. The parametric statistics of rule set

Rule set	States (NFA)	States (DFA)	Edges (NFA)	Edges (DFA)	Matching ratio
Snort-24	848	13,886	217,088	3,445,816	0.06%
Snort-27	731	106,452	187,136	27,251,712	0.03%
Snort-34	1,236	13,825	316,416	3,539,200	0.14%
Snort-36	979	190,951	250,624	48,883,456	0.09%
Snort-51	1,498	157,150	383,488	40,230,400	0.18%

However, the memory cost of MSI increases exponentially with the stride. Fortunately, 3-stride MSI is enough to achieve a desirable filteration even there are in total 500 rules combined.

5.2 Matching Speed and Memory Usage

We randomly select 5 groups of rules from 500 Snort rules, whose specifications are collected in Table 2. Each state include 256 transition edges since using alignment 2-dimensional table to store. The number of rules in each group is expressed as a suffix of its name. Then we process 2000 K real-world HTTP packets on 2-stride MSI-NFA, 3-stride MSI-NFA, DFA and NFA respectively, and measure their matching speed and memory usage in each case for comparison.

Figure 3 presents the memory usage of MSI-NFA and NFA, in which MSI-NFA(2) and MSI-NFA(3) represent the 2-stride and 3-stride MSI-NFA respectively. In comparison of NFA, MSI-NFA consumes additional memory resources for the MSI table and other use during the matching process. As demonstrated, such additional memory cost of the 2-stride MSI-NFA is as small as 20 KB, which of the 3-stride MSI-NFA is almost 4 MB. In another word, in both cases, the MSI table can benefit much from the high-speed cache.

Then, we divide those 2000 K packets into 5 groups, each group contains 400 K packets. We measure the average processing time of these 5 groups of packets on MSI-NFA and DFA respectively to indicate their matching speed indirectly. As shown in Fig. 4, the matching speed of MSI-NFA is only a bit lower (the difference is only up to 10%) than that of DFA. In some cases, processing

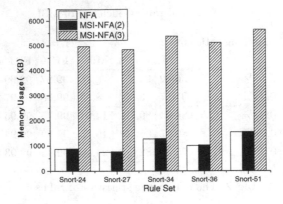

Fig. 3. Memory Usage with MSI-NFA and NFA.

speed of the MSI-NFA is even faster than that of DFA due to the cache hitting problem with more larger transition table by corresponding DFA.

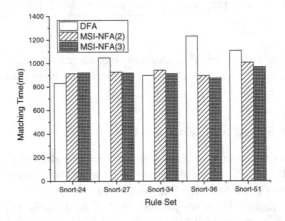

Fig. 4. Matching speed of MSI-NFA and DFA.

6   Conclusion

In this paper, we presented a fast and scalable approach named MSI-NFA to perform regular expression matching. In view that most matching toward real-world Internet traffics will fail at the first several states of finite automate, we proposed the MSI table for efficient pre-processing that is constructed by complete *n-combination* sets extracted from all pre-defined rules. The MSI table works in cooperation with the NFA and reduces sharply the chance of matching on NFA by filtering parts of unsuccessful matchings in directly in the pre-precessing step.

According to our experimental evaluation on matching real-world HTTP packets against the Snort rules, the matching speed of MSI-NFA is only 10 % lower than that of DFA, while all additional memory cost resulted by the MSI table and some required operations is only 20 KB when the stride is 2.

Acknowledgments. This work is supported by the National Science Foundation of China under Grant 61173167, 61472130, the National Basic Research Program of China (973) under Grant 2012CB315805, the Prospective Research Project on Future Networks of Jiangsu Future Networks Innovation Institute under Grant BY2013095-1-05, and the Hunan Provincial Innovation Foundation For Postgraduate under Grant CX2014B150.

References

1. Cisco IOS IPS (2015). http://www.cisco.com/
2. Regular Expression Pocessor (2015). http://regex.wustl.edu
3. Snort Website (2015). http://www.snort.org/
4. TippingPoint IPS (2015). http://www.tippingpoint.com/
5. Alicherry, M., Muthuprasanna, M., Kumar, V.: High speed pattern matching for network ids/ips. In: Proceedings of the 2006 14th IEEE International Conference on Network Protocols, 2006, ICNP 2006, pp. 187–196, November 2006
6. Brodie, B., Cytron, R., Taylor, D.: A scalable architecture for high-throughput regular-expression pattern matching. In: 33rd International Symposium on Computer Architecture, 2006, ISCA 2006, pp. 191–202, April 2006
7. Clark, C.R., Schimmel, D.E.: Efficient reconfigurable logic circuits for matching complex network intrusion detection patterns. In: Cheung, Peter Y.K., Constantinides, George A. (eds.) FPL 2003. LNCS, vol. 2778, pp. 956–959. Springer, Heidelberg (2003)
8. Clark, C., Schimmel, D.: Scalable pattern matching for high speed networks. In: 12th Annual IEEE Symposium on Field-Programmable Custom Computing Machines, 2004, FCCM 2004, pp. 249–257, April 2004
9. Dharmapurikar, S., Lockwood, J.: Fast and scalable pattern matching for content filtering. In: Proceedings of the 2005 ACM Symposium on Architecture for Networking and Communications Systems, ANCS 2005, pp. 183–192. ACM (2005)
10. Hua, N., Song, H., Lakshman, T.: Variable-stride multi-pattern matching for scalable deep packet inspection. In: INFOCOM 2009. IEEE, April 2009
11. Kumar, S., Dharmapurikar, S., Yu, F., Crowley, P., Turner, J.: Algorithms to accelerate multiple regular expressions matching for deep packet inspection. In: Proceedings of the 2006 Conference on Applications, Technologies, Architectures, and Protocols for Computer Communications, SIGCOMM 2006. ACM (2006)
12. Lu, H., Zheng, K., Liu, B., Zhang, X., Liu, Y.: A memory-efficient parallel string matching architecture for high-speed intrusion detection. IEEE J. Sel. Areas Commun. **24**(10), 1793–1804 (2006)
13. Luchaup, D., De Carli, L., Jha, S., Bach, E.: Deep packet inspection with dfa-trees and parametrized language overapproximation. In: INFOCOM, 2014 Proceedings IEEE, pp. 531–539, April 2014
14. Paxson, V.: Application Layer Packet Classifier for Linux (2008). http://l7-filter.sourceforge.net/. Accessed 19 July 2008

15. Paxson, V., Asanović, K., Dharmapurikar, S., Lockwood, J., Pang, R., Sommer, R., Weaver, N.: Rethinking hardware support for network analysis and intrusion prevention. In: Proceedings of the 1st USENIX Workshop on Hot Topics in Security, p. 11 (2006)
16. Paxson, V.: Bro: A system for detecting network intruders in real-time. Comput. Netw. **31**(23–24), 2435–2463 (1999)
17. Sen, S., Spatscheck, O., Wang, D.: Accurate, scalable in-network identification of P2P traffic using application signatures. In: Proceedings of WWW.Manhantan. ACM (2004)
18. Roesch, M.: Snort - lightweight intrusion detection for networks. In: Proceedings of the 13th USENIX Conference on System Administration (1999)
19. Sidhu, R., Prasanna, V.: Fast regular expression matching using fpgas. In: The 9th Annual IEEE Symposium on Field-Programmable Custom Computing Machines, 2001, FCCM 2001, pp. 227–238, March 2001
20. Smith, R., Estan, C., Jha, S.: Xfa: Faster signature matching with extended automata. In: IEEE Symposium on Security and Privacy, 2008, SP 2008, May 2008
21. Smith, R., Estan, C., Jha, S.: Deflating the big bang: fast and scalable deep packet inspection with extended finite automata. In: Proceedings of the ACM SIGCOMM 2008 Conference on Data Communication, SIGCOMM 2008. ACM (2008)
22. Sourdis, I., Pnevmatikatos, D.: Pre-decoded cams for efficient and high-speed nids pattern matching. In: 12th Annual IEEE Symposium on Field-Programmable Custom Computing Machines, 2004, FCCM 2004, pp. 258–267, April 2004
23. Tan, L., Brotherton, B., Sherwood, T.: Bit-split string-matching engines for intrusion detection and prevention. ACM Trans. Archit. Code Optim. **3**(1), 3–34 (2006)
24. Yu, F., Chen, Z., Diao, Y., Lakshman, T., Katz, R.: Fast and memory-efficient regular expression matching for deep packet inspection. In: ACM/IEEE Symposium on Architecture for Networking and Communications systems, 2006, ANCS 2006, pp. 93–102, December 2006
25. Yu, F., Katz, R., Lakshman, T.: Gigabit rate packet pattern-matching using tcam. In: Proceedings of the 12th IEEE International Conference on Network Protocols, 2004, ICNP 2004, pp. 174–183 October 2004
26. Yu, X., Becchi, M.: Gpu acceleration of regular expression matching for large datasets: exploring the implementation space. In: Proceedings of the ACM International Conference on Computing Frontiers, CF 2013. ACM (2013)
27. Zu, Y., Yang, M., Xu, Z., Wang, L., Tian, X., Peng, K., Dong, Q.: Gpu-based nfa implementation for memory efficient high speed regular expression matching. In: Proceedings of the 17th ACM SIGPLAN Symposium on Principles and Practice of Parallel Programming, PPoPP 2012, pp. 129–140. ACM (2012)

A Robust and Efficient Detection Model of DDoS Attack for Cloud Services

Jian Zhang, Ya-Wei Zhang, Jian-Biao He[✉], and Ou Jin

School of Information Science and Engineering, Central South University,
Changsha 410083, China
jbhe@csu.edu.cn

Abstract. Recently, DDoS attacks have become a major security threat
to cloud services. How to detect and defend against DDoS attacks is currently a hot topic in both industry and academia. In this paper, we
propose a novel model to detect DDoS attacks and identify attack packets for abnormal traffic filtering. The novelties of the model are that:
(1) combined with the characteristics of three types of IP spoofing-based
attacks and temporal correlation of transport layer connection state, a
set of accurate check rules for abnormal packets are designed; (2) by
improving the Bloom Filter algorithm, the efficient mapping mechanism
of TCP2HC/UDP2HC and the reliable two-way checking mechanism of
abnormal data packet are implemented; (3) DDoS attacks detection and
filtering are realized by using non-parameter CUSUM algorithm to model
the growth scale of abnormal packets. Experiments show that no matter
what type of IP spoofing technology and the attack traffic scale, detection model can accurately detect the DDoS attacks as early as possible.

Keywords: DDoS · IP spoofing · HOP COUNT · Check · CUSUM

1 Introduction

With the development and application of cloud computing, the main goal of
DDoS attacks turns to cloud node [1,2], the specific performance for the limited
computing resources (such as CPU, memory and network bandwidth, protocol
stack, etc.), relies on exhausting the damaged cloud nodes resources to achieve
the effect of attack. Since cloud computing has strong service resources, DDoS
needs to launch large-scale attack to be effective.

In view of research on DDoS attack detection for cloud services, it is necessary
to satisfy three major goals: one is the timeliness of detection, that is, as far as
possible to detect aggressive behavior in the early time, because it is meaningless
to detect aggressive behavior after large-scale attack outbreaks and it has caused
damage to the availability of the target; secondly, it is the sensitivity of attack
traffic, detection features can be used to distinguish between normal traffic and
abnormal traffic effectively, which improve the accuracy of attack detection and
filtering; the third one is the adaptability of attack scale, that is, whether it is a

© Springer International Publishing Switzerland 2015
G. Wang et al. (Eds.): ICA3PP 2015, Part III, LNCS 9530, pp. 611–624, 2015.
DOI: 10.1007/978-3-319-27137-8_44

high-rate attack or low-rate one, the method of detection can detect aggressive behavior accurately. At present, most of the DDoS attack detection methods in academia [3–8] are proposed by the target of the sensitivity of abnormal traffic. These methods emphasize the ability of detection feature to distinguish between normal and abnormal traffic, present many complicated machine learning algorithm to detect, and obtain good detection precision. However, with the application layer based on DDoS attacks of low-rate rampant, a few DDoS detection methods [16,17] begin to focus on the adaptability of attack scale, but also because of the high complexity of detection algorithm, these methods can't satisfy the goal of the timeliness of detection. The contradiction between the complexity of detection methods and the timeliness of detection caused that the current detection method can not meet all the requirements of three goals, how to achieve a good tradeoff is the urgent problem need to solve.

There are many destructive and strong DDoS attacks [9–11], such as SYN flooding, ACK flooding and RST/FIN flooding in the transport layer, the DNS flooding, HTTP flooding and Mail flooding in the application layer. These attacks are threatening the dependability of cloud computing with varying degrees. In addition, their common features mainly exist in two aspects: first of all, they are based on transport layer protocol such as TCP or UDP transport layer protocol; secondly, all of the attacks use IP spoofing technology, and the transport layer connection state of attack traffic exists abnormal. Therefore, we can judge in a timely and effective manner whether the cloud node is under DDoS attack or not through the cumulative calculation based on both the check results of abnormal transport layer connection state and the authenticity of transport layer data segments source. Compared to IP flow, the HOPCOUNT value calculated by TTL values in TCP segment has better stability, which helps to reduce the occurrence of judging the legal packets to be IP spoofing packets due to update delay of HOPCOUNT, and can better solve the problem of false positives. This paper presents a DDoS attack detection model for traffic filtering. The core idea is that through analysis on the characteristics of HOPCOUNT value calculated from the packets with different types of IP spoofing, the preliminary checks of the abnormal packets from inbound and outbound traffic are accomplished by temporal correlation features of transport layer connection state; on this basis, a non parameter CUSUM algorithm is used to achieve accurate DDoS attack detection and filtering. The experiment results show that detection model can divide packets into the normal and the abnormal accurately. And aggressive behavior can be found at the beginning of the attack, which makes a best opportunity for cleaning the attack traffic. In addition, our detection model is not only sensitive to DDoS attack with high-rate, but also to low-rate one such as HTTP asymmetric attack, the data of ROC curves indicate that our detection model has better performance.

The rest of the paper is organized as follows. In Sect. 2, we briefly overview the related work. Section 3 presents our framework of DDoS attacks detection model designed in this paper. In Sect. 4, we propose a set of check rules and relevant check algorithm for abnormal packets. Section 5 presents the DDoS attacks detection algorithm based on non-parameter CUSUM. In Sect. 6, we introduce the evaluation and analysis results of experimental scheme and data used in this paper by deploying model in actual network architecture, and the summary of the paper and the future research work are given in the last section.

2   Related Work

In this section, we scan related work on the three goals above-mentioned.

For the first goal of the timeliness of detection, Peng et al. [12] proposed the method of monitoring the number of new IP addresses to achieve DDoS attack detection, and it decreased false alarm due to flash crowd to some extent. This method uses a simple database to store the legitimate IP address set, and realizes judging the new IP address by simple search algorithm, and can detect the aggressive behavior earlier. However, the method for the judgment of new IP address is only based on the source IP address of packets, and the source of packets is not authenticated, so it is susceptible to IP Spoofing attack. Tao and Yu [13] proposed a feature independent DDoS flooding detection method, which can detect the attack behavior in the early detection. The simulation results prove the validity of the method, but the method is limited to the detection of the high strength flood. FireCol [14] is a distributed cooperative detection system deployed in multiple ISP overlay networks. The early attack behavior can be detected accurately and reliably by monitoring the network traffic between target host and attack source. However, the system can only be used for the detection of high strength flooding type DDoS attack.

For the second goal of the sensitivity of the abnormal traffic, Vikas et al. [15] proposed the thought that using packets hop count to judge the authenticity of the source of packets, they analyzed and demonstrated the feasibility, stability, the diversity of distribution of the authenticity of the source of the IP address by using HOPCOUNT, and based on this, they realized the filtering of DDoS attack packets by the mapping table between IP and hop count. For the aggressive behavior of IP spoofing, the detection accuracy rate can reach 90 %, with good effect, and easy deployment. However, the method itself is vulnerable to distributed attacks. In addition, if the IP2HCs update is not timely, the legitimate packets will be mistaken for attack traffic and cause false alarm. Based on chaos modeling, Chonka et al. [16] exploited the self similarity theory to distinguish DDoS attack traffic and normal traffic. The method can accurately filter abnormal traffic, but the computational complexity caused by this method make it hard to detect the attack behavior timely. By mining the correlation features of attributes in both IP header and TCP header, Dou et al. [17] proposed a method to DDoS attack detection for cloud computing environment which is based on Credible Filtering (CBF). This method has high detection accuracy for the trained DDoS aggressive behavior, but for the unknown aggressive behavior, both false negatives and false positives are higher because of the weight of relevant characteristics cannot be measured.

For the third goal of the adaptability of attack scale, Wang et al. [18] divide the attack detection into three stages, including NTS (network traffic state) forecasting, fine-grained singularity detection and malicious address extraction engine, and proposed a multistage detection method. The method can accurately detect multiple types of DDoS attacks including subtle DDoS attacks, but due to the complexity of the method, it causes bad real-time performance of the attack detection, and it cant detect the aggressive behavior in the early outbreak of attacks. Through empirical evaluation of the ability to detect high-rate and low-rate based DDoS attacks respectively, Monowar et al. [19] put forward a effective detection model. They use several information metrics to detect different kinds of attacks such as the Hartley entropy, Shannon entropy, Renyi entropy, generalized entropy, Kullback-Leibler divergence distance and generalized information distance. Although the model can be applied to detect any traffic scale, the capability of detecting early attacks is relatively weak.

3   Overall Architecture of the Model

Figure 1 shows the overall architecture of the model. The abnormal check component monitors IP flow and TCP/UDP segment. This component monitors the packets through the inbound and outbound, checks the authenticity of the source of data segment and the abnormality of the packets. Caching the source IP address in the data segment and corresponding TTL values by the IP flow monitoring, and preliminary checks the authenticity of the IP flow's source by

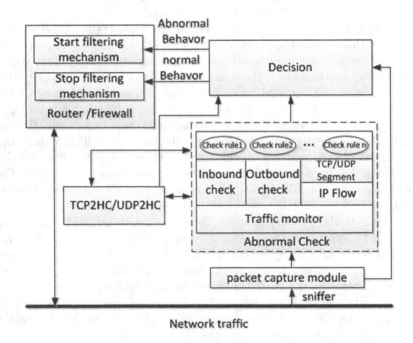

Fig. 1. The architecture of the defensive model

HOPCOUNT. The packets which are judged as IP source forging and related to abnormal connection state of the transport layer are called abnormal packets. They include TCP based abnormal packets, such as SYN and SYN/ACK, ACK, and UDP based abnormal packets, such as DNS, NTP, and common packets. Their quantity indicates the growth of abnormal traffic. All check results are submitted to the decision component. The decision component judges whether the network service is under DDoS attack. Finally, the decision is sent to response components (router or firewall). This paper focuses on the traffic abnormal check component and decision component which are related to DDoS attack detection.

4 Abnormal Check Component of Network Traffic

The traffic abnormal check component contains two main functions. After the authentication of network traffic source, the first check judges the authentication of source of data segments in transport layer by searching data segment address. The second check is based on the abnormal connection state of the transport layer. They provide important information for the decision component. This component is a part of packet parsing process, therefore, it must be efficient. Efficient mapping data structure and corresponding search algorithm are required.

4.1 Data Structure of Check Algorithm

Definition 1. *Key of Transport Layer Connection State*. *Supposed the transport layer connection address is represent as TCA, where TCA = <SIP, SPort, DIP, DPort>, $\overline{TCA}$ = <DIP, DPort, SIP, SPort>. If the connection state of transport layer is represented as KEY, where KEY = <TCA, FLAG>, we can classify KEY into requestKEY and replyKEY according to the finite state machine in the transport layer. For example, if requestKEY = <TCA, SYN>, then its replyKEY = <$\overline{TCA}$, SYN/ACK>; While if requestKEY = <SYN/ACK>, then its replyKEY = <TCA, ACK>.*

The TCP2HC database keeps the records of legitimate TCP connections within a certain survival period. Each record contains the Key of TCP connection state, source IP address, HOPCOUNT, and timestamp. Every record in the database have a unified survival period T_1, which is related to the maximum length of TCP timeout retransmission. When the difference between the current time and the timestamp exceeds the survival period, the corresponding record will be delete automatically from the database. If UDP protocol is used, the UDP2HC database is adopted to save the legitimate UDP connection records, and the lifetime of UDP2HC record is set to be T_2, which is different from T_1.

In order to realize an efficient lookup and storage of transport layer connection state, we propose an improved data structure for bloom filter algorithm [20]. As shown in Fig. 2, a 2-Bits array is adopted. The first bit is the same as the bloom filter, and the second bit groups stores the first pointer to the linear linked list which is composed of different nodes corresponding to the same KEY. Once the second bit is assigned, it can't be re-assigned to avoid the conflict of the hash function and the damage to the first pointer of the linear linked list. Nodes of linear list include the Source IP, the corresponding HOPCOUNT value and the time stamp. If the KEY search conflict occurs, the information in the nodes can help to avoid misjudgment. The improved bloom filter provides an efficient data structure for both TCP2HC and UDP2HC. Efficient key searching and robust HOPCOUNT abnormal check are supported, which is helpful to improve the overall performance of the check component.

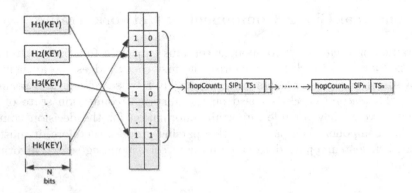

Fig. 2. The improved data structure of bloom filter algorithm

4.2   Check Algorithm

The core of our check algorithm includes new TCA check and abnormal data packet check. Because most of the DDoS attacks use IP spoofing, it is necessary to authenticate the source of connection before the connection checking. To check the abnormal data packet, we must check if there is connection state abnormity in transport layer first.

In this research, 3 assumptions are followed:

Assumption 1. *The router of ISP communication network is not controlled by attackers;*

Assumption 2. *All the DDoS attacks use IP spoofing technical;*

Assumption 3. *The attacker and the faked IP are not in the same LAN;*

Assumptions 1 and 2 are general assumptions and widely accepted. For Assumption 3, the attacker can be easily exposed if the attacker and the faked IP are in the same LAN.

According to Assumption 1, it is feasible to authenticate the source of connection by hop count. The hop count of a packet is determined by the structure of communication network and relatively stable [21], especially for the packet in the transport layer. Whether the attacker can pass the checking system depends on if it can set a proper initial TTL value for each cheating packet. In order to set a proper initial TTL value, the attacker should get the h_s which is the hop number between the host of cheating IP to the target machine. However, it is difficult to get h_s when the attacker randomly select cheating source IP for each packet. The attacker must have a mapping table from the IP addresses in all the random IP space to their corresponding h_s. The attacker must break through at least one host in each subnet of every random address space to get the h_s by traceroute.

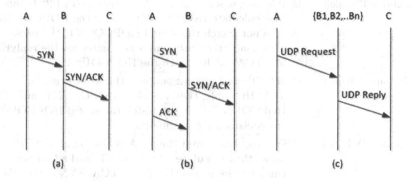

Fig. 3. Illegal connection form based on IP spoofing

According to Assumption 2, we focus on the abnormal packet checking of DDoS attacks with IP spoofing. In the transport layer, IP spoofing can be characterized into three types according to the types of attacks. Figure 3 shows the 3 main types of IP spoofing. Figure 3a shows the IP spoofing of half-open connection form. A fakes the address of C and requests connection to B. B sends a response to C to accept this connection and then waits for the response from C until timeout. We use timeout to represent highest tolerance time for the first timeout, regardless of different settings of different systems. Figure 3b shows that A gets a successful guess by RTT and ISN, sends response to B, and establishes a cheating 'legal' connection. It shows that it is inaccurate to judge the authenticity of source IP only by whether the connection is established. In this case, we can judge the authenticity of unknown source IP address by the difference of the TTL value of SYN packet and subsequent packets. The SYN/ACK packets are from A and the subsequent packets are from C. According to Assumption 3, A and C are in different LANs, there are obvious difference between the TTL value of them. Figure 3c shows the IP spoofing of indirect form. A masquerades the IP address of C and requests connections to a group of IP nodes. By rebound protocol, this group of IP nodes sends responses to C simultaneously. Because the IP addresses of received packets are real, we should check if corresponding request packets have been sent out before receiving.

Table 1. Abnormal connection state check rules

Coding of the rule	Contents of the rule
TCP_InboundCRule1	If SYN flag is not set and TCA exists in TCP2HC table, then calculate the packets HOPCOUNT. Check if the HOPCOUNT matches with the stored HOPCOUNT, if not, then the source of the packet is forged, and the packet is abnormal;
TCP_InboundCRule2	If SYN flag is not set and the TCA is not found in TCP2HC table, then the packet is abnormal;
TCP_InboundCRule3	If ACK flag is set and the TCA exists in TCP2CH table, then calculate HOPCOUNT, and if the HOPCOUNT does not match the stored HOPCOUNT, the packet is abnormal; otherwise, add a new entry for the replyKEY of <TCA, ACK> with the HOPCOUNT;
TCP_InboundCRule4	If all TCP flags are not set, and the TCA exists in TCP2HC table, then calculate HOPCOUNT, and if this HOPCOUNT does not match the stored HOPCOUNT, the packets are abnormal;
TCP_InboundMRule1	If SYN flag is set, and the TCA is not found in TCP2HC table, then calculate HOPCOUNT, and add a new entry for the requestKEY of <TCA, SYN> with the HOPCOUNT;
TCP_InboundMRule2	If SYN flag is set, and the TCA exists in TCP2HC table, then calculate HOPCOUNT, but if the packets SIP is not found in table, it indicates that Bloomfilter conflicts, then add a new node including the SIP, HOPCOUNT and time stamp in linear linked list; otherwise, if calculated HOPCOUNT does not match the stored HOPCOUNT, then update the HOPCOUNT and timestamp field of node;
TCP_OutboundCRule1	If both SYN flag and ACK flag are set, then search the entry for the requestKEY of <TCA, SYN> in TCP2HC table, if it does not exist, then the packet is abnormal;
TCP_OutboundCRule2	If both SYN flag and ACK flag are set, and TCA exists in TCP2HC table, start the timeout retransmission timer. When the timer overflow,query the entry with replyKEY of <TCA, ACK> in TCP2HC table, if it does not exist, then the packet is abnormal;
UDP_InboundCRule1	If the TCA of UDP request packet does not exist in UDP2HC table during the lifetime, then the packet is abnormal;
UDP_OutboundMRule1	If the TCA is not found in UDP2HC table, then add a new entry for the KEY of <TCA, SYN> in UDP2HC table.

In order to guarantee that a real TCP packet with ACK flag can be queried in TCP2HC database after the overflow of retransmission timeout, $T_1 > RTO + RTT + a$ should be satisfied, where RTO is the maximum time of time-out retransmission timer, T_1 is the maximum time of life cycle of each record in the TCP2HC database, RTT is the round time of transmission between the TCP endpoints, and a is the reliable boundary coefficient for safety. According to $RTO = RTT + 4* MDEV$, we have $T_1 > 2*RTT + 4*MDEV$, where MDEV is the average deviation of RTT which can measure the RTT jitter. For UDP2HC database, we set $T_2 > RTT + a$, where T_2 is the maximum time of life cycle of each record in the UDP2HC database.

According to the analysis on new TCA check and abnormal data packet check, we propose two categories of check rules: Inbound and Outbound. The main rules are shows in Table 1.

5 Decision Component

The check algorithm in Sect. 4 is only to authenticate each single packet. Although the check result of single packet cannot directly judge if the network is being attacked, it affords necessary information for further decision. A sudden increase of abnormal packet indicates that there is DDoS attack or scanning to the network [22]. Therefore, the DDoS attack decision algorithm can be based on the cumulative check results in a certain period of time.

5.1 The Selection of Detection Feature

In normal state, the accumulated number of abnormal packets is small and stable. When DDoS attack occurs, those abnormal events increase fast. Because there are a small number of errors and misses in the check component, we choose the accumulated number of abnormal packets as the detection feature in the decision component. We set counters for the number of packets and abnormal packets in the decision component, θ_n denotes the count of the collected packets at the end of period Δt, and ϕ_n denotes the count of the abnormal packets at the end of the period Δt. We use the following metric to describe the growth of abnormal packets in different time periods of Δt:

$$C_n = \frac{\Phi_n}{\Theta_n}. \tag{1}$$

5.2 Non-parametric CUSUM Based Decision Algorithm

Network traffic on the internet is considered as a complex stochastic model. Any abnormal traffic leads to changes of the model. In order to achieve real-time detection at the early stage of attack, The sequence C(n, Δt) is convert into a form of continuous function:

$$C_n = b + \xi_n I(n < m) + (h + \eta_n)I(n \geq m) \tag{2}$$

where $E(C_n) = b$, $\xi = \{\xi_n\}_{n=1}^{\infty}$ and $\eta = \{\eta_n\}_{n=1}^{\infty}$ are two stochastic sequences satisfying $E(\xi_n) = E(\eta_n) \equiv 0$, $h \neq 0$. $I(H)$ is an indicator function. The function value equals 1 if H is true, 0 otherwise. For sequence C(n, Δt), if the mean value exists a step change from b to b+h at the point m, it indicates that there is a sudden change in the sequence value. We adopt non-parametric CUSUM algorithm to continuously detect the sequence change and the change point m. It can monitor the sequence in real-time with low false-alarm rate and thus detect DDoS attacks immediately.

In case the network traffic is in normal state, the mean value of C(n, Δt) is close to 0, i.e., $E(C_n) \ll 1$. We denote $F(n) = C_n - \lambda$, when $b' = b - \lambda$, $h \gg \lambda$. λ is the offset determined for each specific network environment. The mean value of sequence F_n in normal state is offset to negative and turns positive when a attack occurs. Consequently, the offset sequence is applicable to the non-parametric CUSUM algorithm:

$$F_n = b' + \xi_n I(n < m) + (h + \eta_n)I(n \geq m) \tag{3}$$

where $b' < 0$, $-b' < h < 1$. According to the non-parametric CUSUM algorithm, the stochastic sequence F_n produces negative mean value φ. When the attack occurs, F_n jump to positive ($h + b' > 0$, h is the minimum growth of the sequence F_n when attack occurs). We accumulate the positive value and ignore the negative value. If the accumulation exceeds the threshold at a certain moment, the system determined that DDoS attack occurs. In normal state, the value of sequence F_n is either negative or non-continuous small positive. The accumulation will not exceed the threshold. Furthermore, the algorithm is converted into a problem of calculating formula 4. It is worth noting that h is the smallest increment when attack occurs, it is not the threshold for attack detection in the algorithm.

$$\gamma_n = T_n - \min_{1 \leq k \leq n} T^k, \; where \; T^k = \sum_{i=1}^{k} F^i, T_0 = 0 \tag{4}$$

γ_n is the statistical feature of our detection method, in order to reduce the complexity of the implementation, a nested non-parametric CUSUM algorithm is used, as follows:

$$\gamma_n = (\gamma_{n-1} + F_n)^+ \tag{5}$$

Where x^+ expresses $x^+ = x$ when $x > 0$; $x^+ = 0$, when $x \leq 0$.

A greater value γ_n (exceeds the corresponding threshold) means that attack exists in the network. γ_n represents the sum of the positive sequence. When $\gamma_{t_N} \geq N$, it shows that the statistic is mutated at the time of t_N, and the network is suffering from distributed denial of service attack. The decision function based on the number of abnormal packets is described as:

$$W_N(\gamma_n) = \{_0^1 \; {}_{\gamma_n \leq N}^{\gamma_n > N} \tag{6}$$

Where N is the threshold of attack detection, $W_N(\gamma_n) = 1$, if and only if $\gamma_n > N$ means the occurrence of attack behavior $W_N(\gamma_n) = 0$, if and only if $\gamma_n < N$ means the network traffic is normal.

6   Performance Evaluation

In order to evaluate the detection performance of the model, we conduct attack experiment in the MAN network of Changsha National Software industry base. Exploiting BOT network, we launch SYN flooding attacks by (a) type of IP spoofing, HTTP flooding attacks by (b) type of IP spoofing and DNS flooding attacks by (c) types of IP spoofing. Table 2 gives the statistical data of different types of attacks, where K is the number of abnormal packets of SYN flooding attack, Σ is the number of abnormal packets of Http flooding attack and Ω is the number of abnormal packets of DNS flooding attack. Δt is set as 10 s. Figure 4 shows the detection results of 3 types of attack. The result shows that SYN flooding attack (Fig. 3a) can be detected in 23.7 s with accurate rate of 100 % when the K is equal to 53. False negative exists only if $K < 53$. The HTTP flooding attack (Fig. 3b) can be detected in 83.6 s with accurate rate of 100 % when Σ is equal to 19. The detection miss occurs only if $\Sigma < 19$. The DNS flooding attack (Fig. 3c) can be detected in 68.4 s with accurate rate of 100 % when Ω is equal to 32. The detection miss occurs only if $\Omega < 32$.

Table 2. DDoS traces statistics.

TestBed type	Experiment times	Average size of each traces (MB)	Average packet size (bytes)
SYN flooding	6	120	65
DNS flooding	6	54	1050
HTTP flooding	6	60	420

Table 3 list out the average accuracy and delay of detection with different K, Σ and Ω values. The result shows that the proposed model has a high accuracy and can satisfy the demand of detect attack in early stage.

To test the adaptability of the detection model to different attack scale, we give the ROC curves of SYN flooding attack detection, HTTP flooding attack detection and DNS flooding attack detection respectively. As shown in Fig. 5, the result demonstrates that the abnormal detection rate of high distribution SYN flooding attack reached almost 100 % while the false alarm rate is less than 2 %; for the high intensity DNS flooding attack, the abnormal detection rate is more than 90 % when the false alarm rate is 2.5 %; for the lower distribution of HTTP flooding attacks, the abnormal detection rate is more than 90 % when the false alarm rate is 9 %. It can be seen that the model has a superior performance against the high distribution of DDoS. Although the performance of low distribution and small-rate DDoS attack detection is decreased slightly, the overall performance is relatively stable and effective. So we can say that the detection model has a good adaptability for different scale of DDoS attack.

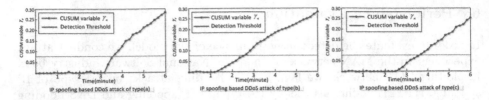

Fig. 4. Three critical values of different attack in the detection

Table 3. The results of performance test

(a) DDoS attack			(b) HTTP flooding attack			(c) DNS flooding attack		
K	Accuracy (%)	Test time	Σ	Accuracy (%)	Test time	Ω	Accuracy (%)	Test time
30	98.9	45.3	14	92.1	115.8	25	94.6	86.4
53	100	23.7	19	100	83.6	32	100	68.4
68	100	11.2	35	100	17.3	45	100	14.5
89	100	6.7	50	100	8.7	60	100	7.1
120	100	5.1	85	100	8.3	75	100	6.3

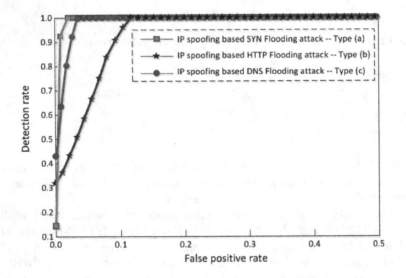

Fig. 5. The ROC curve of three different types of attack

7   Conclusions and Future Work

This paper proposed a robust and efficient detection model of DDoS attack for cloud services. First, we give a set of rules on IP address authenticity, transport layer connection address authenticity and transport layer abnormal connection state to check the abnormal packet in the communication process in the transport layer. In detail, we use hop-count based filtering for IP address authentication.

For transport layer connection address authentication, we use hop-count based filtering and connection address aggregation. The improved bloom-filter algorithm is used to achieve efficient address query and data storage. The transport layer abnormality check uses TCP state diagram and UDP reflection protocol characteristics based on the former authentication. Second, we analysis the increase of the number of abnormal packets by non-parameter CUSUM algorithm to detect DDoS attacks. The experiments demonstrate that the detection model shows strong advantages in the immediacy of detection, the sensitivity to attack traffic and the adaptability of attack scale.

Acknowledgment. This work is partially supported by the Planned Science and Technology Project of Hunan Province, China (NO.2015JC3044), and the National Natural Science Foundation of China (NO.61272147).

References

1. Sumter, R.L.Q.: Cloud Computing: Security Risk Classification. ACMSE, Oxford (2010)
2. Jansen, W., et al.: Cloud hooks: security and privacy issues in cloud computing. In: 44th Hawaii International Conference on System Sciences (HICSS), pp. 1–10. IEEE (2011)
3. Bhuyan, M.H., Kashyap, H.J., Bhattacharyya, D.K., Kalita, J.K.: Detecting distributed denial of service attacks: methods, tools and future directions. Comput. J. bxt031 (2013)
4. Patel, K.: Security survey for cloud computing: threats and existing IDS/IPS techniques. In: 24th International Conference on Control, Communication and Computer Technology, pp. 88–92. IEEE (2013)
5. Zargar, S.T., Joshi, J., Tipper, D.: A survey of defense mechanisms against distributed denial of service (DDoS) flooding attacks. IEEE Commun. Surv. Tutor. **15**(4), 2046–2069 (2013)
6. Gupta, S., Kumar, P., Abraham, A.: A profile based network intrusion detection and prevention system for securing cloud environment. Int. J. Distrib. Sens. Netw. (2013)
7. Yi, F., Yu, S., Zhou, W., Hai, J., Bonti, A.: Source-based filtering scheme against DDoS attacks. Int. J. Database Theory Appl. **1**(1), 9–20 (2008)
8. Gavaskar, S., Surendiran, R., Ramaraj, D.E.: Three counter defense mechanism for TCP SYN flooding attacks. Int. J. Comput. Appl. **6**(6), 0975–8887 (2010)
9. Gulshan, S., Kavita, S., Swarnlata, R.: A technical overview DoS and DDoS attack. Proc. Int. Conf. Comput. **2010**, 274–282 (2010)
10. Bogdanoski, M., Suminoski, T., Risteski, A.: Analysis of the SYN flood DoS attack. Int. J. Comput. Netw. Inf. Secur. (IJCNIS) **5**(8), 1–11 (2013)
11. Bhandari, N.H.: Survey on DDoS attacks and its detection and defence approaches. Int. J. Sci. Mod. Eng. (IJISME) **1**(3), 2319–6386 (2013)
12. Peng, T., Leckie, C., Ramamohanarao, K.: Protection from distributed denial of service attacks using history-based IP filtering. In: IEEE International Conference on Communications, pp. 482–486 (2003)
13. Tao, Y., Yu, S.: DDoS attack detection at local area networks using information theoretical metrics. In: 12th IEEE International Conference on Trust, Security and Privacy in Computing and Communications (TrustCom), pp. 233–240 (2013)

14. François, J., Aib, I., Boutaba, R.: Firecol: a collaborative protection network for the detection of flooding DDoS attacks. IEEE/ACM Trans. Netw. (TON) **20**(6), 1828–1841 (2012)
15. Chouhan, V., Peddoju, S.K.: Packet monitoring approach to prevent DDoS attack in cloud computing. Int. J. Comput. Sci. Electr. Eng. (IJCSEE) **1**(2), 2315–4209 (2013)
16. Chonka, A., Singh, J., Zhou, W.: Chaos theory based detection against network mimicking DDoS attacks. IEEE Commun. Lett. **13**(9), 717–719 (2009)
17. Dou, W., Chen, Q., Chen, J.: A confidence-based filtering method for DDoS attack defense in cloud environment. Future Gener. Comput. Syst. **29**(7), 1838–1850 (2013)
18. Wang, F., Wang, H., Wang, X., Su, J.: A new multistage approach to detect subtle DDoS attacks. Math. Comput. Model. **55**(1), 198–213 (2012)
19. Bhuyan, M.H., Bhattacharyya, D., Kalita, J.: An empirical evaluation of information metrics for low-rate and high-rate DDoS attack detection. Pattern Recognit. Lett. **51**, 1–7 (2015)
20. Broder, A., Mitzenmacher, M.: Network applications of bloom filters: a survey. Internet Math. **1**(4), 485–509 (2004)
21. Paxson, V.: End-to-end routing behavior in the internet. IEEE/ACM Trans. Netw. **5**(5), 601–615 (1997)
22. Jung, J., Krishnamurthy, B., Rabinovich, M.: Flash crowds and denial of service attacks: characterization and implications for cdns and web sites. In: Proceedings of the 11th International Conference on World WideWeb, pp. 293–304. ACM (2002)

Secure Bisimulation for Interactive Systems

Guanjun Liu[1][(✉)] and Changjun Jiang[2]

[1] Department of Computer Science, Tongji University, Shanghai 201804, China
liuguanjun@tongji.edu.cn
[2] Key Lab of the Ministry of Education for Embedded Systems and Services
Computing, Tongji University, Shanghai 201804, China
cjjiang@tongji.edu.cn

Abstract. In real applications, many systems have the same functions
but their securities are different due to different security policies. We
find that different security policies can affect the interacting behavior of
a system, which exactly is the reason why a good policy can strengthen
the security. In other words, two interactive systems with different security policies are not of an equivalent behavior although their functions
are identical. However, the classic (weak) bisimulation theory draws an
opposite conclusion that their behaviors are equivalent. The notion of
(weak) bisimulation is not suitable for these security-oriented interactive
systems since it does not consider a security policy while the security
policy can affect their interacting behaviors. This paper proposes the
concept of *secure bisimulation* in order to solve the above problem. Based
on secure bisimulation, we furthermore define a binary relation $\geq_{SL}$ to
compare the levels of different security policies. We prove that $\geq_{SL}$ is a
partial order but not a total one.

Keywords: Interactive systems · Labelled petri nets · Labelled transition systems · Bisimulation · Security

1 Introduction

In the classic theory of formal languages and automata, two systems are thought
of having an equivalent behavior if two automata modeling them recognize the
same language [4]. Roughly speaking, two automata recognize the same language if and only if they have the same set of action sequences. Later, Milner found that this classic notion of language equivalence is not reasonable to
explain some real applications. The famous example given by him is about two
tea/coffee-vending machines [6]: one is deterministic and another is nondeterministic. In other words, those classic automata models like Turing machines,
register machines, and the lambda calculus are concerned with *computational
behavior* but not *interactional behavior*. A basic action of an interactive system is to communicate across an interface with a handshake. He found that
the determinism/nondeterminism of the internal actions of a system can affect
the interacting behavior while the notion of language equivalence does not consider the difference between determinism and nondeterminism. He thus proposed

© Springer International Publishing Switzerland 2015
G. Wang et al. (Eds.): ICA3PP 2015, Part III, LNCS 9530, pp. 625–639, 2015.
DOI: 10.1007/978-3-319-27137-8_45

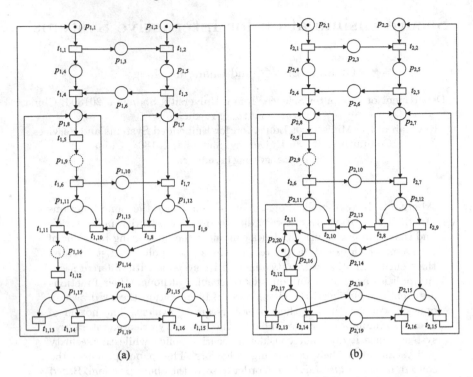

Fig. 1. Two Petri nets modeling bank transfer systems: (a) logging in the system and receiving the verification information are operated in the same terminal device, (b) in two different ones.

the notion of (weak) bisimulation equivalence [5,6]. If two systems are (weakly) bisimular, they recognize the same language, but not vice versa. The (weak) bisimulation equivalence takes account of a more detailed relationship of states than the language equivalence does.

With the development of the internet, an increasing number of interactive systems have occurred, e.g., electronic trading system. Security is one of the most important topics for most of these networked systems. Engineers can design and develop such two systems that accomplish the same functions but take two different security policies. We find that different security policies can affect the interacting behaviors of a system. A good policy can ensure a system securer by these affections. When we try to use the (weak) bisimulation to explain the reason, we find that it is not suitable. To the interactional behaviors, the (weak) bisimulation considers the affections of the (non)determinism of the internal actions of a system but not considers the affections of the external events. A security policy enhances the security of a system just by avoiding the affections taken by these external events. We first use an example of two versions of a bank transfer system to illustrate this. The two systems are sketched as shown in Fig. 1(a), (b) and they run as follows:

First, a user logs in her/his account by using her/his networked PC. This login process is modeled by transitions $t_{1,1}$–$t_{1,4}$ in Fig. 1(a) or $t_{2,1}$–$t_{2,4}$ in Fig. 1(b). Then the user submits a request for transferring money (transition $t_{1,5}$ in Fig. 1(a), or $t_{2,5}$ in Fig. 1(b)). Notice that the submitted information is first packaged and encrypted in the PC and then is sent from the PC to the bank system located in the bank. The process of packaging and encrypting the information is modelled by place $p_{1,9}$ in Fig. 1(a) or $p_{2,9}$ in Fig. 1(b). Firing transition $t_{1,6}$ in Fig. 1(a) or $t_{2,6}$ in Fig. 1(b) represents that the packaged request is sent from the PC to the bank system. After receiving the request ($t_{1,7}$ in Fig. 1(a) or $t_{2,7}$ in Fig. 1(b)), the bank system checks if the request is legal. If it is illegal, the bank system sends ($t_{1,8}$ in Fig. 1(a) or $t_{2,8}$ in Fig. 1(b)) an information of canceling this request. If it is legal, then the bank system sends ($t_{1,9}$ in Fig. 1(a) or $t_{2,9}$ in Fig. 1(b)) a verification information. When the user receives ($t_{1,10}$ in Fig. 1(a) or $t_{2,10}$ in Fig. 1(b)) the information of canceling the request, (s)he returns back to refill a request. When the user receives ($t_{1,11}$ in Fig. 1(a) or $t_{2,11}$ in Fig. 1(b)) the verification information, (s)he will decide if (s)he agrees this transfer or not. Notice that, place $p_{1,16}$ in Fig. 1(a) or $p_{2,16}$ in Fig. 1(b) represents the state that the verification information has been received but not yet shown to the user. Firing transition $t_{1,12}$ in Fig. 1(a) or $t_{2,12}$ in Fig. 1(b) means that the verification information is shown to the user. Transition $t_{1,13}$ in Fig. 1(a) or $t_{2,13}$ in Fig. 1(b) means that the user disagrees this transfer, while transition $t_{1,14}$ in Fig. 1(a) or $t_{2,14}$ in Fig. 1(b) means agreement.

The two systems are of the same functions and business processes. They are equivalent according to the bisimulation equivalence theory. The distinction between them is that the system in Fig. 1(a) sends the verification information to the PC itself while the one in Fig. 1(b) sends the verification information to another independent device (e.g., the user's cell phone). In other words, Fig. 1(a) means that the devices of logging in the bank transfer system and receiving the verification information are the same but Fig. 1(b) means that the two devices are different. At present, banks do not think that they are equivalent. They usually use the system in Fig. 1(b) rather than the one in Fig. 1(a) because they believe that the former is much securer[1] than the latter. For the system in Fig. 1(a), a Trojan program can transfer the user's money from her/his account into an account that is not the user wants.

For example, a Trojan program is implanted into the user's PC. The Trojan program can tamper with the data in her/his transfer request during the period of packaging the request, and can also tamper with the verification information before it is shown to the user. After the user submits a request for transferring money from Account 1 to Account 2, the Trojan changes this request into the one of transferring money from Account 1 to Account 3. Thus, the tampered request is sent to the bank system. The bank system finds that Accounts 1 and 3 are both legal and then sends a verification information in which the bank

---

[1] The security of a system is related to many factors including cryptosystems, rights of accessing data, and other supporting policies like the one of separating "verification" from "login" in Fig. 1(b). The security in this paper is about those supporting policies rather than cryptosystems.

tells the user that money will be transferred into Account 3 and gives the user a verification code. When the PC has received the verification information but not yet shown it to the user, the Trojan changes Account 3 in this verification information into Account 2. Finally, the user finds that all are correct and then inputs the verification code to agree on this transfer. Unfortunately, the money is actually transferred into Account 3 rather than Account 2. It is almost impossible for the system in Fig. 1(b) that a Trojan program is simultaneously implanted into both the PC and cell phone of a user and thus the above case does not occur. Therefore, the two systems are not *equivalent*: they produce different results for the same input. Different security policies can lead to different interacting behaviors between the system and its users since they handle the external nondeterministic events through different measures. This is exactly the reason that the policy in Fig. 1(b) can enhance the security. Therefore, the bisimulation notion is not suitable for this case. Later, we will give another example to show that the notion of weak bisimulation is not suitable for some security-oriented interactive systems.

The questions are: how to use a formal method to declare the (non-) equivalence of two given systems with different security policies and to compare their secure levels. This paper focuses on these questions and obtains the following results:

1. We define *labelled Petri net with insecure places* (LPNIP). The only difference between LPNIP and PN (the classic Petri nets) is that some places of the former are labelled *insecure*, but these labels do not affect the rules of enabling and firing transitions. By using the reachability graph of an LPNIP, a *labelled transition system with insecure states* (LTSIS) is yielded. Based on LTSIS, we propose the concept of *secure bisimulation* that is an extension to *weak bisimulation*.

2. Based on secure bisimulation, we furthermore define a binary relation $\geq_{SL}$ to compare the levels of different security policies. We prove that $\geq_{SL}$ is a partial order but not a total order. This means that for a system and two different security policies we cannot always assert which policy makes the system more securer.

The remainder of this paper is organized as follows: Sect. 2 reviews the classic (weak) bisimulation. Section 3 defines LTSIS and proposes secure bisimulation based on LTSIS. Section 4 defines LPNIP and transplants the concept of secure bisimulation onto LPNIP. Section 5 defines the binary relation $\geq_{SL}$ and proves that it is a partial order. Section 6 concludes this paper.

2   Labelled Transition Systems and (Weak) Bisimulation

In this section, we first recall the concepts of *labelled transition system* (LTS) and (weak) bisimulation. For more details, one may refer to [6]. For readability, Table 1 lists the main symbols often used in this paper.

Definition 1 (LTS [6]**).** *An LTS is a 3-tuple* $\Gamma = (Q, Act, Tr)$, *where*

1. *Q is a set of* states;
2. *Act is a set of* actions *including* unobservable action ε; *and*
3. *Tr* $\subseteq (Q \times Act \times Q)$ *is a set of* transitions.

Transition (q, a, q') is also denoted as $q \xrightarrow{a} q'$. It is denoted as $q \rightarrow q'$ if $a = \varepsilon$.

Definition 2 (Bisimulation [6]**).** *Let* (Q, Act, Tr) *be an LTS such that there is no transition with* ε. *Binary relation* $B \subseteq (Q \times Q)$ *is a* bisimulation *if*

1. *B is symmetric; and*
2. *If* $(q, r) \in B$ *and* $q \xrightarrow{a} q'$, *then there exists* r' *such that* $r \xrightarrow{a} r'$ *and* $(q', r') \in B$.

Given two states q and r in Q, q is *bisimular* to r, written as $q \approx r$, if there is a bisimulation B such that $(q, r) \in B$. $q_1 \rightarrow q_2 \rightarrow \cdots \rightarrow q_n$ is denoted as $q_1 \rightsquigarrow q_n$. We assume that $\rightsquigarrow$ is reflexive, i.e., $q \rightsquigarrow q$. $q_1 \rightsquigarrow q_n \xrightarrow{a} q_{n+1}$ is denoted as $q_1 \xrightarrow{a}{\rightsquigarrow} q_{n+1}$.

Definition 3 (Weak Bisimulation [6]**).** *Let* (Q, Act, Tr) *be an LTS. Binary relation* $B \subseteq (Q \times Q)$ *is a* weak bisimulation *(or* observational equivalence*) if*

1. *R is symmetric;*
2. *If* $(q, r) \in B$ *and* $q \rightarrow q'$, *then there exists* r' *such that* $r \rightsquigarrow r'$ *and* $(q', r') \in B$; *and*
3. *If* $(q, r) \in B$ *and* $q \xrightarrow{a} q'$, *then there exists* r' *such that* $r \xrightarrow{a}{\rightsquigarrow} r'$ *and* $(q', r') \in B$.

Given two states q and r in Q, q is *weakly bisimular* to r, written as $q \approxeq r$, if there is a weak bisimulation B such that $(q, r) \in B$.

Table 1. Symbols often used in this paper.

Q	the set of states of an LTS	$^\bullet x$	the pre-set of a node $x \in P \cup T$
Act	the set of actions of an LTS	$x^\bullet$	the post-set of a node $x \in P \cup T$
Tr	the set of transitions of an LTS	$M[t\rangle$	transition t is enabled at marking M
Q_S	the set of secure states of an LTSIS	$M[t\rangle M'$	M' is reached by firing t at M
Q_U	the set of insecure states of an LTSIS	$R(M)$	the set of markings reachable from M
P	the set of places of an LPN	$q \approx r$	q is bisimular to r
T	the set of transitions of an LPN	$q \approxeq r$	q is weakly bisimular to r
F	the set of arcs of an LPN	$q \widetilde{\approx} r$	q is securely bisimular to r
E	the set of actions of an LPN	$\Sigma_1 \bowtie \Sigma_2$	Σ_1 is bisimular to Σ_2
M	a marking of an LPN	$\Sigma_1 \bowtie \Sigma_2$	Σ_1 is weakly bisimular to Σ_2
λ	the label function of transitions in LPN	$\Sigma_1 \boxtimes \Sigma_2$	Σ_1 is securely bisimular to Σ_2
P_S	the set of secure places of an LTSIS	$\Sigma_1 =_{SL} \Sigma_2$	Σ_1 is as secure as Σ_2
P_U	the set of insecure places of an LTSIS	$\Sigma_1 >_{SL} \Sigma_2$	Σ_1 is securer than Σ_2
$q \xrightarrow{a} q'$	a transition in an LTS, i.e., state q' is reached from state q by executing action a		
$q \rightarrow q'$	q' is reached from q by executing the unobservable action ε		
$q \rightsquigarrow q'$	q' is reached from q by executing a sequence of unobservable actions		
$q \xrightarrow{a}{\rightsquigarrow} q'$	q' is reached from q by executing a sequence of unobservable actions followed by an observable action a		

3   Secure Bisimulation Over LTSIS

Let (Q, Act, Tr) be an LTS. Denote $Q_U \subseteq Q$ as the set of *insecure states* and $Q_S = Q \setminus Q_U$ as the set of *secure states*. Here, we do not give a concrete explanation for each insecure/secure state. An insecure state may be the one leaded to by an illegal user or the one attacked by a Trojan. From the aspect of functions of two systems, insecure states are not different from secure ones, i.e., they do not influence the executions of the two systems. From the aspect of securities of two systems, they are crucial since we can utilize them to distinguish the behaviors of the two systems. For convenience, we use $(Q_S \cup Q_U, Act, Tr)$ to represent a *labelled transition system with insecure state* (LTSIS).

Definition 4 (Secure Bisimulation). *Let $(Q_S \cup Q_U, Act, Tr)$ be an LTSIS. Binary relation $B \subseteq ((Q_S \cup Q_U) \times (Q_S \cup Q_U))$ is a secure bisimulation if*

1. *B is symmetric;*
2. *If $(q, r) \in B$ and $q \to q'$, then there exists r' such that $r \rightsquigarrow r'$ and $(q', r') \in B$;*
3. *If $(q, r) \in B$ and $q \xrightarrow{a} q'$, then there exists r' such that $r \overset{a}{\rightsquigarrow} r'$ and $(q', r') \in B$; and*
4. *If $(q, r) \in B$ and $q \in Q_U$, then $r \in Q_U$.*

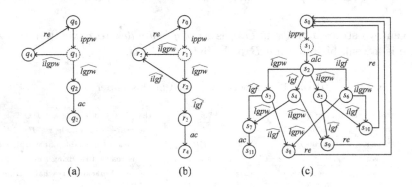

(a)   (b)   (c)

Fig. 2. Login a smartphone system: (a) single verification policy, (b) double verifications policy, and (c) double verifications policy executed in parallel.

Given two states q and r in $Q_S \cup Q_U$, q is *securely bisimular* to r, written as $q \approxeq r$, if there is a secure bisimulation B such that $(q, r) \in B$. By the definitions of weak bisimulation and secure bisimulation, we know that each secure bisimulation is a weak bisimulation, i.e., B is a secure bisimulation iff B is a weak bisimulation such that $\forall (q, r) \in B$: $q \in Q_U \Leftrightarrow r \in Q_U$. If the set of insecure states is empty in the definition of secure bisimulation, then the definition is weak bisimulation. Furthermore, if no unobservable action occurs in its transitions, then it is bisimulation. In a diagram of LTSIS, an insecure state is depicted with a dotted circle/ellipse (e.g., q_1 in Fig. 2(a)).

Now, we consider an example of smartphone. At present, when some smartphone systems are accessed, it verifies not only the input password but also the user's behavioral features of inputting the password (such as the pressure of clicking the keyboard, the writing trajectory, and so on) [9,12,13]. This policy of double verifications is securer than that of single verification. Figure 2(a) shows the process of verifying the user's identity by using the single verification policy. At the initial state (this state is represented by q_0), a user inputs a password (this action is represented by $ippw$). Then, the system checks if the password is legal or not. If the password is illegal (this unobservable action is represented by $\widehat{ilgpw}$), then the system returns to the initial state (re represents this action). If the password is legal ($\widehat{lgpw}$), then the user may access the system (ac). Figure 2(b) shows the process of executing the double verifications. When the password is legal, the system continues to verify whether the captured behavioral feature matches with the legal user's. If they match ($\widehat{lgf}$), then the system is opened (ac), or else ($\widehat{ilgf}$), it also returns to the initial state. Notice that an action with a hat (e.g., $\widehat{lgf}$) means that it is unobservable, i.e., it is equal to ε.

We know that $\{(q_0, r_0), (r_0, q_0), (q_1, r_1), (r_1, q_1), (q_1, r_2), (r_2, q_1), (q_2, r_3),$
$(r_3, q_2), (q_3, r_4), (r_4, q_3), (q_4, r_5), (r_5, q_4)\}$ is a weak bisimulation in Fig. 2(a), (b). Therefore, $q_0 \approx r_0$, i.e., the two systems are observationally equivalent (weakly bisimular) by the weak bisimulation theory [6]. However, even from the perspective of the observers (e.g., a legal user and an illegal user), the two systems are not observationally equivalent because the legal user can log in it after (s)he inputs the correct password, but the illegal one can not log in it after (s)he inputs the correct password. If we use the concept of secure bisimulation, we can distinguish the two systems since there exists no secure bisimulation B such that $(q_0, r_0) \in B$. Here, q_1 and r_1 are two insecure states because anyone (an illegal or legal user) can make the system reach them.

We assume that a system with the double verification policy supports parallel processes, i.e., after a user inputs her/his password, the system can verify the password and behavioral feature in parallel. Figure 2(c) shows the related LTSIS. Notice that this LTSIS actually demonstrates the interleaving semantics of such a concurrent system and later we will show its Petri net model that can characterize its concurrent process. $\widehat{alc}$ is an unobservable action that allocates the task of verifying the password and the task of verifying the behavioral feature to a related subsystem, respectively. From the perspective of observers, the two LTSISs in Fig. 2(b), (c) are equivalent because there exists a secure bisimulation B such that $r_0 \approx s_0$, where r_1 and s_1 are two insecure states and $B = \{(r_0, s_0),$
$(s_0, r_0), (r_1, s_1), (s_1, r_1), (r_2, s_2), (s_2, r_2), (r_2, s_3), (s_3, r_2), (r_2, s_4), (s_4, r_2),$
$(r_2, s_5), (s_5, r_2), (r_2, s_6), (s_6, r_2), (r_3, s_7), (s_7, r_3), (r_4, s_{11}), (s_{11}, r_4), (r_5, s_8),$
$(s_8, r_5), (r_5, s_9), (s_9, r_5), (r_5, s_{10}), (s_{10}, r_5)\}$.

As said in Sect. 1, the determinism/nondeterminism of the internal actions of a system can affect the interaction between the system and its user and thus Milner proposed the notion of (weak) bisimulation. In fact, some external events (especially those unobservable and nondeterministic events that themselves do not belong to the system) can also affect the interaction when they happen in some states of the system (e.g., tampering with a data). These states are defined as *insecure*. Usually, a security policy is taken for these insecure states, e.g., encrypting the data in an insecure state or separating two insecure states into two independent devices. Therefore, it is reasonable to partition the states of a system into two parts.

Milner [6] has shown that $\approx$ (resp. $\approx$) is an equivalence relation and itself is a (resp. weak) bisimulation. The same conclusion holds for $\widetilde{\approx}$.

Proposition 1. $\widetilde{\approx}$ *is an equivalence relation and itself is a secure bisimulation.*

4   Secure Bisimulation Over LPNIP

We first recall *labelled Petri nets* (LPN). For more details one can refer to [10,11].

Definition 5 (LPN [10]**).** *An LPN is a 6-tuple* $\Sigma = (P, T, F, M_0, E, \lambda)$, *where*

1. *P is a set of* places *and T is a set of* transitions *such that* $P \cap T = \emptyset$;
2. $F \subseteq (P \times T) \cup (T \times P)$ *is a* flow relation;
3. $M_0 \colon P \to \{0, 1, 2, \cdots\}$ *is the* initial marking;
4. *E is a set of* actions *including* unobservable action ε; *and*
5. $\lambda \colon T \to E$ *is a* label function.

Denote $^\bullet t = \{p \in P \mid (p, t) \in F\}$ and $t^\bullet = \{p \in P \mid (t, p) \in F\}$ as the *pre-* and *post-sets* of transition t, respectively. Let $M \colon P \to \{0, 1, 2, \cdots\}$ be a *marking* of an LPN and t be a transition. Then, t is *enabled* at M if $\forall p \in^\bullet t \colon M(p) > 0$. This is denoted as $M[t\rangle$. *Firing* an enabled transition t at M yields a new marking M' such that $\forall p \in P \colon M'(p) = M(p) - 1$ if $p \in{}^\bullet t \backslash t^\bullet, M'(p) = M(p) + 1$ if $p \in t^\bullet \backslash^\bullet t$, or $M'(p) = M(p)$ otherwise. This is denoted as $M[t\rangle M'$.

Definition 6 (Reachable Marking Set [10]**).** *The set* $R(M_0)$ *of all* reachable marking *of an LPN* $(P, T, F, M_0, E, \lambda)$ *is recursively defined as follows:*

1. $M_0 \in R(M_0)$.
2. *Let* $M \in R(M_0)$. *Then* $M' \in R(M_0)$ *if* $\exists t \in T$ *such that* $M[t\rangle M'$.

Based on the reachable marking set of an LPN, we can construct an LTS as follows:

Definition 7 (LTS Generated by LPN). *LTS* (Q, Act, Tr) *is generated by LPN* $(P, T, F, M_0, E, \lambda)$ *if*

1. $Q = R(M_0)$;
2. $Act = E$; *and*
3. $M \xrightarrow{a} M' \in Tr$ *iff* $\exists t \in T \colon M[t\rangle M' \wedge \lambda(t) = a$.

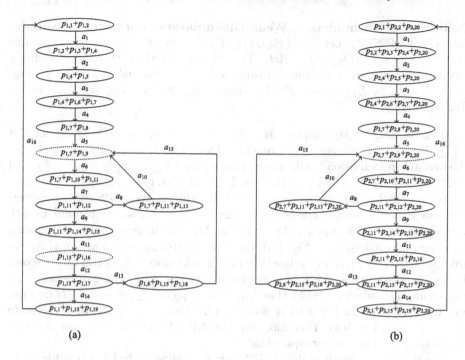

Fig. 3. LTSs generated by LPNs in Fig. 1(a), (b), respectively.

For example, Fig. 3(a), (b) are the LTSs generated by the LPNs in Fig. 1(a), (b), respectively. Action a_i in Fig. 3 is the label of transitions $t_{1,i}$ and $t_{2,i}$ in Fig. 1, where $i \in \{1..16\}$. Obviously, the LTS generated by a given LPN is unique.

Let $\Sigma = (P, T, F, M_0, E, \lambda)$ be an LPN. Similar to the insecure states of an LTSIS, $P_U \subseteq P$ is the set of *insecure places* of Σ and $P_S = P \backslash P_U$ is the set of *secure places*. In the diagram of an LPN, an insecure place is depicted with a dotted circle (e.g., $p_{1,9}$ in Fig. 1(a)). For convenience, we use $(P_S \cup P_U, T, F, M_0, E, \lambda)$ to represent a *labelled Petri net with insecure places* (LPNIP). Let $\Gamma = (Q, Act, Tr)$ be the LTS generated by an LPNIP Σ. Then, $M \in Q$ is an *insecure state* of Γ if $\exists p \in P_U : M(p) > 0$. We still use $(Q_S \cup Q_U, Act, Tr)$ to represent the LTSIS generated by an LPNIP. Consequently, we can define *secure bisimulation* over LPNIPs based on the definition over LTSISs.

Definition 8 (Union of Two LTSISs). *Let* $\Gamma_i = (Q_{S_i} \cup Q_{U_i}, Act_i, Tr_i)$, $i \in \{1, 2\}$, *be two LTSISs.* $\Gamma = \Gamma_1 \uplus \Gamma_2 = (Q_S \cup Q_U, Act, Tr)$ *is the* union *of* Γ_1 *and* Γ_2 *if*

1. $Q_S = Q_{S_1} \cup Q_{S_2}$;
2. $Q_U = Q_{U_1} \cup Q_{U_2}$;
3. $Act = Act_1 \cup Act_2$; and
4. $Tr = Tr_1 \cup Tr_2$.

Definition 9 (Bisimulation, Weak Bisimulation, and Secure Bisimulation Over LPNIP). Let $\Sigma_i = (P_{S_i} \cup P_{U_i}, T_i, F_i, M_{0_i}, E_i, \lambda_i)$, $i \in \{1, 2\}$, be two LPNIPs, and $\Gamma_i = (Q_{S_i} \cup Q_{U_i}, Act_i, Tr_i)$ be their LTSISs. Then Σ_1 is securely bisimular (resp. weakly bisimular, bisimular) to Σ_2, denoted as $\Sigma_1 \boxtimes \Sigma_2$ (resp. $\Sigma_1 \bowtie \Sigma_2$, $\Sigma_1 \bowtie \Sigma_2$), if $M_{0_1} \approxeq M_{0_2}$ (resp. $M_{0_1} \approxeq M_{0_2}$, $M_{0_1} \approx M_{0_2}$) in the LTSIS $\Gamma_1 \uplus \Gamma_2$.

Because $M_{0_1} \approxeq M_{0_2}$ implies $M_{0_2} \approxeq M_{0_1}$, we have that $\Sigma_1 \boxtimes \Sigma_2$ implies $\Sigma_2 \boxtimes \Sigma_1$, i.e., $\boxtimes$ satisfies the symmetry. Therefore, it is suitable that we use "bisimular" in Definition 9. Obviously, states $p_{1,1} + p_{1,2}$ and $p_{2,1} + p_{2,2} + p_{2,20}$ in Fig. 3 are bisimular. Therefore, the two LPNs in Fig. 1 are bisimular, i.e., they are equivalent by the bisimulation theory. By the analysis in Sect. 1, however, we know that they should not be equivalent. Now, we use secure bisimulation to distinguish them. Places $p_{1,9}$ and $p_{1,16}$ in Fig. 1(a), are insecure because they may be attacked by a Trojan. In Fig. 3(a), therefore, states $p_{1,7} + p_{1,9}$ and $p_{1,15} + p_{1,16}$ are insecure. Only place $p_{2,9}$ is insecure in Fig. 1(b) since only it can be attacked. Therefore, state $p_{2,7} + p_{2,9} + p_{2,20}$ is insecure in Fig. 3(b). There does not exist any secure bisimulation B such that $(p_{1,1} + p_{1,2}, p_{2,1} + p_{2,2} + p_{2,20}) \in B$ because any insecure state in Fig. 3(b) is not securely bisimular to the insecure state $p_{1,15} + p_{1,16}$ in Fig. 3(a). Therefore, the two LPNIPs in Fig. 1 are not securely bisimular, i.e., they are not equivalent.

Figure 4(a), (b), (c) show the LPNIPs corresponding to the LTSISs in Fig. 2(a), (b), (c), respectively. Places $p_{1,2}$, $p_{2,2}$, and $p_{3,2}$ are insecure because these local states can be reached by anyone (legal or illegal users). Notice that for simplification of graphs in Fig. 4, we omit the transitions' names and directly label the related actions' names. The last two LPNIPs are securely bisimular, but neither of them is securely bisimular to the first one.

It seems that LPNIP is unnecessary to define secure bisimulation because LTSIS has done this and an LPNIP must be translated to an LTSIS, but that is not the fact. The examples in Figs. 1 and 4(c) show that LPNIPs are better for the modelling of systems than their related LTSISs. It is easy to prove that $\boxtimes$ (resp. $\bowtie$, $\bowtie$) is an equivalence relation and the proof is omitted for saving space.

Proposition 2. $\boxtimes$ (resp. $\bowtie$, $\bowtie$) is an equivalence relation.

In consequence, $\boxtimes$ can divide all LPNIPs into a set of equivalence classes. All LPNIPs in an equivalence class are securely bisimular. Secure bisimulation can more precisely distinguish two systems especially when they are equivalent from the aspect of functions but not equivalent from the aspect of securities. Certainly, if two systems are not equivalent in functions, then they are not equivalent in securities because there exist no secure bisimulation for them. Other questions we pay attention to are that:

1. Which security policy makes a system securer?
2. Whether securities of a system resulted from different policies are comparable?

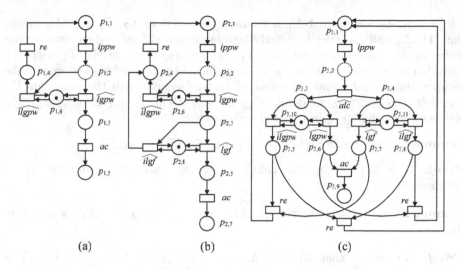

Fig. 4. LPNIPs corresponding to LTSISs in Fig. 2(a), (b), (c), respectively.

5   Secure Levels of LPNIPs

In this section we answer the above two questions. When we define secure bisimulation (resp. weak bisimulation, bisimulation) for two LPNIPs in Definition 9, the binary relation B such that $(M_{0_1}, M_{0_2}) \in B$ is considered over $(Q_{S_1} \cup Q_{U_1} \cup Q_{S_2} \cup Q_{U_2}) \times (Q_{S_1} \cup Q_{U_1} \cup Q_{S_2} \cup Q_{U_2})$. In fact, we only need to consider it over $((Q_{S_1} \cup Q_{U_1}) \times (Q_{S_2} \cup Q_{U_2})) \cup ((Q_{S_2} \cup Q_{U_2}) \times (Q_{S_1} \cup Q_{U_1}))$. Additionally, if $B_i \subseteq ((Q_{S_1} \cup Q_{U_1}) \times (Q_{S_2} \cup Q_{U_2})) \cup ((Q_{S_2} \cup Q_{U_2}) \times (Q_{S_1} \cup Q_{U_1}))$, $i = 1, 2$, are two secure bisimulations (resp. weak bisimulations, bisimulations) such that $(M_{0_1}, M_{0_2}) \in B_i$, then $B_1 \cup B_2$ is also a secure bisimulation (resp. weak bisimulation, bisimulation) such that $(M_{0_1}, M_{0_2}) \in B_1 \cup B_2$. Therefore, when two LPNIPs are securely bisimular (resp. weakly bisimular, bisimular), there exists a *maximum* secure bisimulation (resp. weak bisimulation, bisimulation) B such that $(M_{0_1}, M_{0_2}) \in B$. In what follows, when we say two LPNIPs are securely bisimular (resp. weakly bisimular, bisimular), the related binary relation B is this maximum one.

Definition 10 (Secure Level). *Let $\Sigma_i = (P_{S_i} \cup P_{U_i}, T_i, F_i, M_{0_i}, E_i, \lambda_i)$, $i \in \{1, 2\}$, be two LPNIPs, and $\Gamma_i = (Q_{S_i} \cup Q_{U_i}, Act_i, Tr_i)$, $i \in \{1, 2\}$, be their LTSISs.*

- *Σ_1 is as secure as Σ_2, denoted as $\Sigma_1 =_{SL} \Sigma_2$, if $\Sigma_1 \boxtimes \Sigma_2$.*
- *Σ_1 is securer than Σ_2, denoted as $\Sigma_1 >_{SL} \Sigma_2$, if*
    1. *$\Sigma_1 \boxtimes \Sigma_2$; and*
    2. *for the weak bisimulation B over $\Gamma_1 \uplus \Gamma_2$ such that $(M_{0_1}, M_{0_2}) \in B$, the following two conditions always hold:*
        - *2.1. $\forall(q, q') \in B: q \in Q_{U_1} \Rightarrow q' \in Q_{U_2}$; and*
        - *2.2. $\exists(q, q') \in B: q \in Q_{S_1} \wedge q' \in Q_{U_2}$.*

$\Sigma_1 =_{SL} \Sigma_2$ means that Σ_1 is securely bisimular to Σ_2. $\Sigma_1 >_{SL} \Sigma_2$ means that: (1) Σ_1 and Σ_2 must be weakly bisimular; and (2) only when some secure states of Γ_1 *become insecure* (i.e., Γ_1 reduces its secure level), Γ_1 with the extended set of insecure states is securely bisimular to Γ_2. In other words, the security policy in Σ_1 make the related system securer than the policy in Σ_2. Based on $=_{SL}$ and $>_{SL}$, we define $\geq_{SL}$: $\Sigma_1 \geq_{SL} \Sigma_2$ iff $\Sigma_1 >_{SL} \Sigma_2 \lor \Sigma_1 =_{SL} \Sigma_2$. Now we prove that $\geq_{SL}$ is a partial order.

Lemma 1. $=_{SL}$ *is symmetric, i.e.,* $\Sigma_1 =_{SL} \Sigma_2$ *iff* $\Sigma_2 =_{SL} \Sigma_1$.

Proof: It is derived by the definition of $=_{SL}$ and the symmetry of ⋈ (Proposition 2). □

Lemma 2. $>_{SL}$ *is asymmetric, i.e.,* $(\Sigma_1 >_{SL} \Sigma_2) \land (\Sigma_2 >_{SL} \Sigma_1)$ *is a contradiction.*

Proof: We assume that $\Sigma_1 >_{SL} \Sigma_2$ and $\Sigma_2 >_{SL} \Sigma_1$ both hold. Let $\Gamma_i = (Q_{S_i} \cup Q_{U_i}, Act_i, Tr_i)$ be the LTSIS generated by Σ_i, where $i = 1, 2$. Then, we know by the definition of $>_{SL}$ that for the weak bisimulation B over $\Gamma_1 \uplus \Gamma_2$ such that $(M_{0_1}, M_{0_2}) \in B$, the following three conclusions always hold:

1. $\forall (q, q') \in B: q \in Q_{U_1} \Leftrightarrow q' \in Q_{U_2}$ (because $\Sigma_1 >_{SL} \Sigma_2$ and $\Sigma_2 >_{SL} \Sigma_1$);
2. $\exists (q, q') \in B: q \in Q_{S_1} \land q' \in Q_{U_2}$ (because $\Sigma_1 >_{SL} \Sigma_2$); and
3. $\exists (q, q') \in B: q \in Q_{S_2} \land q' \in Q_{U_1}$ (because $\Sigma_2 >_{SL} \Sigma_1$)

The last two conclusions contradict the first one. Therefore, $>_{SL}$ is asymmetric. □

Proposition 3. *Let* $\mathbb{A}$ *be a set of LPNIPs. Then* $(\mathbb{A}, \geq_{SL})$ *is a partially ordered set.*

Proof: *(Reflexivity)* Since $\Sigma \bowtie \Sigma$ for each $\Sigma \in \mathbb{A}$ (by Proposition 2), we have that $\Sigma =_{SL} \Sigma$. Hence, $\Sigma \geq_{SL} \Sigma$.

(Antisymmetry) We only need to prove that $(\Sigma_1 \geq_{SL} \Sigma_2) \land (\Sigma_2 \geq_{SL} \Sigma_1)$ implies $\Sigma_1 =_{SL} \Sigma_2$, where $\Sigma_1, \Sigma_2 \in \mathbb{A}$. By Lemmas 1 and 2 and the rules of logical operations, it is easy to know that:
$(\Sigma_1 \geq_{SL} \Sigma_2) \land (\Sigma_2 \geq_{SL} \Sigma_1) \Leftrightarrow$
$((\Sigma_1 >_{SL} \Sigma_2) \lor (\Sigma_1 =_{SL} \Sigma_2)) \land ((\Sigma_2 >_{SL} \Sigma_1) \lor (\Sigma_2 =_{SL} \Sigma_1)) \Leftrightarrow$
$((\Sigma_1 >_{SL} \Sigma_2) \land (\Sigma_2 >_{SL} \Sigma_1)) \lor (\Sigma_1 =_{SL} \Sigma_2) \Leftrightarrow$
$False \lor (\Sigma_1 =_{SL} \Sigma_2) \Leftrightarrow$
$\Sigma_1 =_{SL} \Sigma_2$

(Transitivity) We only need to show that $(\Sigma_1 >_{SL} \Sigma_2) \land (\Sigma_2 >_{SL} \Sigma_3)$ implies $\Sigma_1 >_{SL} \Sigma_3$, where $\Sigma_1, \Sigma_2, \Sigma_3 \in \mathbb{A}$. Let $\Gamma_i = (Q_{S_i} \cup Q_{U_i}, Act_i, Tr_i)$ be the LTSIS generated by $\Sigma_i = (P_{S_i} \cup P_{U_i}, T_i, F_i, M_{0_i}, E_i, \lambda_i)$, where $i = 1, 2, 3$. Because $\Sigma_1 \bowtie \Sigma_2$, $\Sigma_2 \bowtie \Sigma_3$, and $\bowtie$ is an equivalence relation (by Proposition 2), we have $\Sigma_1 \bowtie \Sigma_3$. Therefore, Condition 1 of the definition of $>_{SL}$ holds.

Because $\bowtie$ is an equivalence relation, it satisfies the transitivity. Therefore, the weak bisimulation B over $\Gamma_1 \uplus \Gamma_3$ such that $(M_{0_1}, M_{0_3}) \in B$ can be generated

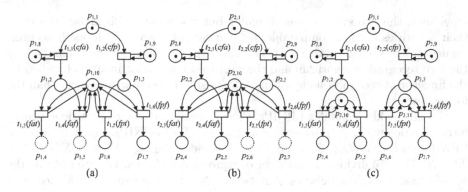

Fig. 5. Not all policies for the same system can compare their secure levels.

by the weak bisimulation B' over $\Gamma_1 \uplus \Gamma_2$ such that $(M_{0_1}, M_{0_2}) \in B'$ and the weak bisimulation B'' over $\Gamma_2 \uplus \Gamma_3$ such that $(M_{0_2}, M_{0_3}) \in B''$. That is, $\forall(q, s) \in B$, $\exists r \in Q_{S_2} \cup Q_{U_2}: (q, r) \in B' \wedge (r, s) \in B''$. Based on this, we can draw the following two conclusions:

$\forall(q, s) \in B$, let $(q, r) \in B'$ and $(r, s) \in B''$. If $q \in Q_{U_1}$, then $r \in Q_{U_2}$ due to $\Sigma_1 >_{SL} \Sigma_2$. Furthermore, $s \in Q_{U_3}$ due to $\Sigma_2 >_{SL} \Sigma_3$. Therefore, Condition 2.1 of the definition of $>_{SL}$ holds.

Since $\Sigma_1 >_{SL} \Sigma_2$, we have that $\exists(q, r) \in B': q \in Q_{S_1} \wedge r \in Q_{U_2}$. Let $(r, s) \in B''$. Then $s \in Q_{U_3}$ due to $\Sigma_2 >_{SL} \Sigma_3 \wedge r \in Q_{U_2}$. Therefore, $(q, s) \in B \wedge q \in Q_{S_1} \wedge s \in Q_{U_3}$. Therefore, Condition 2.2 of the definition of $>_{SL}$ holds.

In summary, $(\mathbb{A}, \geq_{SL})$ is a partially ordered set.   □

From Definition 10, a precondition that the securities of two systems are comparable is that the two systems are weakly bisimular. That is to say, if two systems are not weakly bisimular, then their securities are not comparable in this paper. In fact, what we pay more attention to is a system with different security policies. Now we show that for two different security policies of a system, the securities resulted in by them are not necessarily comparable. We consider the following example as shown in Fig. 5.

The face/fingerprint recognition technology has been quite mature and widely used in the door-lock systems. Algorithms of recognizing face or fingerprint both go to handle a captured image. However, if we use the fingerprint (resp. face) recognition algorithm to recognize an image of face (resp. fingerprint), then the result is inaccurate very much. We assume that there is a door-lock system (as shown in Fig. 5(a)) which may handle both the face images and the fingerprint images, but its kernel algorithm is about the fingerprint recognition. Similarly, another system (as shown in Fig. 5(b)) also do the same thing but its kernel algorithm is about the face recognition. In these figures, action cfa (resp. cfp) represents that a face (resp. fingerprint) image is captured, fat (resp. fpt) means that the captured face (fingerprint) image is recognized, and faf (resp. fpf) means that the captured face (fingerprint) image is not recognized.

Obviously, the two systems are bisimular but not securely bisimular. However, their securities are not comparable, i.e., we cannot assert which one is securer. Figure 5(c) is such a system in which the captured face image is handled by the face recognition algorithm and the captured fingerprint image is handled by the fingerprint recognition algorithm. Obviously, this system is securer than the former two.

For all weakly bisimular LPNIPs, their equivalence classes partitioned by $\bowtie$ form a lattice w.r.t. $\geq_{SL}$. Denote $\mathbb{P}$ as the set of all LPNIPs. Let $\mathbb{A}$ be a set of LPNIPs such that $\forall \Sigma_1, \Sigma_2 \in \mathbb{A}: \Sigma_1 \bowtie \Sigma_2$ and $\forall \Sigma \in \mathbb{A}, \forall \Sigma' \in \mathbb{P}: \Sigma \bowtie \Sigma' \Rightarrow \Sigma' \in \mathbb{A}$. Then $\bowtie$ divides $\mathbb{A}$ into a set of equivalence classes. Denote $\mathcal{C}(\mathbb{A})$ as the set of these equivalence classes. Any two LPNIPs in the same equivalence class has the same secure level since they are securely bisimular. It can be proven that $(\mathcal{C}(\mathbb{A}), \geq_{SL})$ forms a lattice and the proof is omitted for saving space.

Proposition 4. $(\mathcal{C}(\mathbb{A}), \geq_{SL})$ *is a lattice.*

Because $(\mathcal{C}(\mathbb{A}), \geq_{SL})$ is a lattice, it has *maximum* (the securest) and *minimum* (the most insecure). Obviously, the LTSIS in which all states are secure is the securest, and the LTSIS in which all states are insecure is the most insecure. As for how to confirm which places/states are secure or insecure, we need engineers' help.

6   Conclusion

Starting with a real application, this paper proposes a question: how to utilize a formal method to distinguish two systems that are of the same functions but of different security policies? We find that a security policy can influence the interactions between a system and its users. In other words, if two different security policies are independently taken in the same system, then the two systems resulted in by the two policies can yield different interactional behaviors. This is the reason why a good policy can enhance the security of the system. Based on the classic bisimulation theory, we propose the concept of secure bisimulation that can solve the above question. By using secure bisimulation, we present a binary relation $\geq_{SL}$ to compare different security policies. To the best of our knowledge, it is the first time for researchers to utilize a formal method to consider these questions.

However, it is relatively simple/rough to use (in)secure places to distinguish different security policies. Some complex policies maybe cannot be characterize by this way. The reason maybe is that LPNs and LTSs are typically too high-level and abstract for the practical systems, but we still believe that the natures of the problem has been captured via them, i.e.,

1. The determinism and nondeterminism of the internal actions of a system can affect the interacting behaviors between the system and its users [6]; and
2. Some external events that do not belong to a system but can happen in some insecure states of the system can also affect the interacting behaviors.

Therefore, future work focuses on a more generalized method to formally model interactive systems with security policies.

The (weak) bisimulation over LPNs defined in this paper is the same with the *interleaving-bisimulation* defined in [1]. The secure bisimulation is defined on the basis of this interleaving semantic. In fact, other kinds of definitions of bisimulations such as *step-bisimulation* and *process-bisimulation* have been proposed for LPNs to reflect their concurrent behavior equivalency in more details [2,3,7,8,14]. Therefore, another future work may redefine the secure bisimulation on the basis of these complex ones and explore their properties.

Acknowledgement. The authors would like to thank the three reviewers for their helpful comments. This paper is supported in part by the Alexander von Humboldt Foundation and in part by the National Natural Science Foundation of China (Grant Nos. 61202016, 61572360, and 91218301).

References

1. Autant, C., Schnoebelen, P.: Place bisimulations in Petri nets. In: Jensen, K. (ed.) ICALP 1992. LNCS, vol. 616, pp. 45–61. Springer, Heidelberg (1992)
2. Boudol, G., Castellani, I.: On the semantics of concurrency: partial orders and transition systems. In: Ehrig, H., Kowalski, R., Levi, G., Montanari, U. (eds.) TAPSOFT 1987. LNCS, vol. 249, pp. 123–137. Springer, Heidelberg (1987)
3. van Glabbeek, R.J., Vaandrager, F.: Petri net models for algebraic theories of concurrency. In: de Bakker, J.W., Nijman, A.J., Treleaven, P.C. (eds.) PARLE Parallel Architectures and Languages Europe. LNCS, vol. 259, pp. 224–242. Springer, Heidelberg (1987)
4. Hopcroft, J.E., Ullman, J.D.: Introduction to Automata Theory. Languages and Computation. Addison-Wesley, Boston (1979)
5. Milner, R.: Communication and Concurrency. Printice Hall, Upper Saddle River (1989)
6. Milner, R.: Communicating and Mobile Systems: The π-Calculus. Cambridge University Press, Cambridge (1999)
7. Nielsen, M., Thiagarajaa, P.S.: Degrees of non-determinism and concurrency: a Petri net view. In: Joseph, M., Shyamasundar, R. (eds.) Foundations of Software Technology and Theoretical Computer Science. LNCS, vol. 181, pp. 89–117. Springer, Heidelberg (1984)
8. Nielsen, M., Winskel, G.: Bisimulations and Petri nets. Theor. Comput. Sci. **153**, 211–244 (1996)
9. Pao, H.K., Fadlil, J., Lin, H.Y., Chen, K.T.: Trajectory analysis for user verification and recognition. Knowl.-Based Syst. **34**, 81–90 (2012)
10. Peterson, J.: Petri Net Theory and the Modeling of Systems. Prentice Hall, Upper Saddle River (1981)
11. Reisig, W.: Understanding Petri Nets: Modeling Techniques, Analysis Methods, Case Studies. Springer, Heidelberg (2013)
12. Rúa, E.A., Castro, J.L.A.: Online signature verification based on generative models. IEEE Trans. Syst., Man, Cybern. B: Cybern. **42**, 1231–1242 (2012)
13. Shen, C., Cai, Z., Guan, X., Du, Y., Maxion, R.A.: User authentication through mouse dynamics. IEEE Trans. Inf. Forensics Secur. **8**, 16–30 (2013)
14. Vogler, W.: Bisimulation and action refinement. In: Choffrut, C., Jantzen, M. (eds.) STACS 1991. LNCS, vol. 480, pp. 309–321. Springer, Heidelberg (1991)

Privacy Preserving for Network Coding in Smart Grid

Shiming He[1]($\boxtimes$), Weini Zeng[2], and Kun Xie[3,4]

[1] Hunan Provincial Key Laboratory of Intelligent Processing of Big Data
on Transportation, School of Computer and Communication Engineering,
Hunan Province Engineering Research Center of Electric Transportation and Smart
Distributed Network, Changsha University of Science and Technology,
Changsha 410114, China
heshiming_hsm@163.com
[2] The 716th Research Institute, China Shipbuilding Industry Corporation,
Lianyungang 222061, China
[3] College of Computer Science and Electronics Engineering, Hunan University,
Changsha 410082, China
[4] Department of Electrical and Computer Engineering,
State University of New York at Stony Brook, New York, USA
cskxie@gmail.com

Abstract. In smart grid, privacy implications to individuals and their
family is an important issue, due to the fine-grained usage data collection. Wireless communications are considered by many utility companies to obtain information. Network coding is exploited in smart grids,
to enhance network performance in terms of throughput, delay, robustness, and energy consumption. However, Network Coding introduces new
challenge for privacy preserving due to the encoding of packet in forwarder nodes. We propose a distributed privacy preserving scheme for
network coding in smart grid, which considers the converged flows character of smart grid and exploits a homomorphic encryption function to
decrease the complex in forwarder node. The message content of packet is
encrypted and the tag of packet is encrypted by homomorphic encryption
function. Then the forwarder node linear random codes the encrypted
message contents and directly processes the tags cryptotext based on the
homomorphism feature. It offers message content confidentiality privacy
preserving feature, which can efficiently thwart traffic analysis. Extensive
security analysis and performance evaluations demonstrate the validity
and efficiency of the proposed scheme.

Keywords: Privacy preserving · Network coding · Smart grid · Homomorphic encryption function · Traffic analysis

1 Introduction

With the introduction of information and communication technologies, the Smart
Grid (SG) [1] allows for two-way flow of information, automation as well as

© Springer International Publishing Switzerland 2015
G. Wang et al. (Eds.): ICA3PP 2015, Part III, LNCS 9530, pp. 640–654, 2015.
DOI: 10.1007/978-3-319-27137-8_46

distributed intelligence over the grid. Several communication technologies have been proposed [2] in SG. They can be broadly classified in three categories, namely power line communication (PLC), cable communication (copper or optical fiber), and wireless communication (ad-hoc, mesh and cellular architectures). Since cable communication involves the development of a dedicated infrastructure with high capital costs, PLC and wireless communications are considered by many utility companies to be the most promising alternatives [3]. Nevertheless, practical issues pertaining to these technologies are currently delaying the large-scale deployment of smart meters in distribution systems. In particular, PLC techniques may fail to connect every single household (or substation) of the grid due to the strong attenuation of the communication signal [4]. Furthermore, interference is a salient issue for PLC in distribution grids as the spectrum is unregulated [5,6]. As for wireless communication, the main challenges are related with transmission media characteristics, including signal fading, noise, and path loss [7]. In fact, studies of advanced metering infrastructures have highlighted that both technologies suffer a lack of reliability, as the information loss often exceeds 1 % [7,8], even after employing reliable communication methods to improve performance.

To address this bottleneck, researcher has mainly focused on exploiting network coding in smart grid, to enhance network performance in terms of throughput, delay, robustness, and energy consumption [9–14].

The wireless communication strategy relies on accessible transmission mediums and is thus subject to security issues, including potential malicious attacks [15] and provision of privacy guarantees [16]. In smart grid, privacy implications to individuals and their family is an important issue, due to the fine-grained usage data collection. For example, smart metering data could reveal highly accurate real-time home appliance energy load, which may be used to infer the human activities inside the houses. Public outcry about privacy has led to the banning of smart meters in North American cities [17], and derailed a planned mandatory deployment of smart meters in the Netherlands. Where they are still deployed, users must now consent to opting in voluntarily. It is clear that users will not opt in if the privacy implications of doing so remain unclear.

Several technologies have been proposed for privacy preserving, Data Encrypt [18,19], Data Distorting [19,20] and Battery-based Load Hiding (BLH) [20,21]. Data Encrypt is exploit for distributed transmitting and computing. Data Distorting adds noise to the database. In Battery-based Load Hiding (BLH) to hide actual appliance loads, a battery is installed for each household and smartly controlled to store and supply power to the appliances.

However, Network Coding introduces new challenge for privacy preserving due to the encoding of packet in forwarder nodes. The Data Encrypt becomes low efficient, since the forwarder nodes need to decrypt the packet, encode the packet and encrypt the packet again before forwarding it. The privacy preserving scheme [22,23] proposed by us on data aggregation can't work with network coding.

There are several researches [9,10,24,25] focusing on it. Hasen et al. [9,10] introduced the concept of the sub-graphing the network for privacy preserving, and used a subset of the sub-graphs to transfer the data. They eliminated sending the coefficients of the network coding nodes to the receiver for performing the decoding process to save the bandwidth. But it is a central scheme and is not suitable for large scale distributed smart grid. Fan et al. [24,25] proposed a novel privacy preserving scheme against traffic analysis in network coding. With homomorphic encryption operation on Global Encoding Vectors (GEVs), the proposed scheme offers two significant privacy-preserving features, packet flow untraceability and message content confidentiality. It focuses on random linear network coding against traffic analysis, does not consider the converged flows character of smart grid and is not suitable for smart gird with small packets and a large number of nodes. Therefore, the Privacy preserving for Network coding in Smart Grid is still an open problem.

Therefore, in order to solve the problem, we propose a distributed privacy preserving scheme for network coding in smart grid, which considers the converged flows character of smart grid and exploits a homomorphic encryption function to decrease the complex in forwarder node. The message content of packet is encrypted and the tag of packet is encrypted by homomorphic encryption function. Then the forwarder node linear random codes the encrypted message contents and directly processes the tags cryptotext based on the homomorphism feature. It offers message content confidentiality privacy preserving feature, which can efficiently thwart traffic analysis. Extensive security analysis and performance evaluations demonstrate the validity and efficiency of the proposed scheme. We have made following contributions in the proposed scheme.

- With the employment of homomorphic encryption function, the confidentiality of smart meter readings transmitted by network coding is effectively guaranteed, making it difficult for attackers to recover the plain text of smart meter readings. Since only the sink knows the decryption key, the attackers still cannot decrypt the smart meter readings even if some intermediate nodes are compromised. Moreover, the coding/mixing feature of network coding can also be exploited naturally to satisfy the requirements of privacy preservation against traffic analysis.
- Due to the homomorphism of homomorphic encryption function, the forwarder node linear random codes the encrypted message contents and directly processes the tags cryptotext, without knowing the decryption keys or performing expensive decryption operations on each incoming message.
- We have done extensive security analysis and performance evaluations. The security analysis demonstrates that the proposed scheme can not only resist attacks from both inside and outside the network. The performance evaluations on computational complexity demonstrate the efficiency of the proposed scheme.

The rest of this paper is organized as follows. Section 2 states preliminaries about Network coding and Boneh-Goh-Nissim cryptosystem. The System Model is introduced in Sect. 3. Section 4 proposes the scheme. Section 5 discusses the security analysis and performance evaluations. Conclusion is drawn in Sect. 6.

2   Preliminaries

In this section, we briefly recall the ideas of network coding and Boneh-Goh-Nissim cryptosystem [4] which serves as the basis of the proposed scheme.

2.1   Network Coding

The idea behind network coding is that intermediate nodes in the network can mix the packets through algebraic operations, breaking the traditional store-and-forward approach. In particular, random linear network coding (RLNC) provides a fully distributed methodology for network coding, whereby each node in the network selects independently and randomly a set of coefficients and uses them to form linear combinations of the data symbols (or packets) it receives (called also innovative coded packets), as shown in Fig. 1. More recently, tunable sparse network coding was introduced in [26], where the coding is done at different levels of sparsity, i.e., more sparse at the beginning of transmission (coding coefficients mostly zero) and denser towards the end, while keeping the transmitted coded packets innovative with high probability. This scheme reduces the delay and decoding complexity.

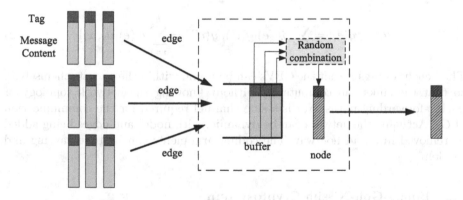

Fig. 1. Random coding

Consider an acyclic network $G(V, E)$, where V is the node set and E is the edge set. Assume that each symbol is an element of a finite field F_q. Consider a network scenario, where a session is comprised of a set of source $S \subseteq V$ and one sink $t \in V$. There are h nodes in source set S where each node send a packet or a symbol to sink t. $x_1, \ldots, x_h$ are the h symbols to be delivered from S to t.

For each outgoing edge e of a node v, let $y(e) \in F_q$ denote the symbol carried on e, which can be computed as a linear combination of the symbols $y(e')$ on the incoming edges e' of node v, i.e., $y(e) = \sum_{e'} \beta_{e'}(e) y(e')$. The coefficient vector $\beta(e) = [\beta_{e'}(e)]$ is called as Local Encoding Vector (LEV).

By induction, the symbol $y(e)$ on any edge $e \in E$ can be computed as a linear combination of the source symbols $x_1, \ldots, x_h$, i.e., $y(e) = \sum_{i=1}^{h} g_i(e) x_i$.

The coefficients form a Global Encoding Vector (GEV, also known as tag) $\boldsymbol{g}(e) = [g_1(e), \ldots, g_h(e)]$, which can be computed recursively as $\boldsymbol{g}(e) = \sum_{e'} \beta_{e'}(e)\boldsymbol{g}(e')$, using the LEVs $\beta(e)$.

Suppose that the sink t receives symbols $y(e_1), \ldots, y(e_h)$, which can be expressed in terms of the source symbols as

$$\begin{bmatrix} y(e_1) \\ \vdots \\ y(e_h) \end{bmatrix} = \begin{bmatrix} g_1(e_1) \cdots g_h(e_1) \\ \vdots \ddots \vdots \\ g_1(e_h) \cdots g_h(e_h) \end{bmatrix} \begin{bmatrix} x_1 \\ \vdots \\ x_h \end{bmatrix} = G_t \begin{bmatrix} x_1 \\ \vdots \\ x_h \end{bmatrix} \tag{1}$$

where G_t is called Global Encoding Matrix (GEM) and the ith row of G_t is the GEV associated with $y(e_i)$. Sink t can recover the h source symbols by inverting the maxtrix G_t and then applying the inverse to $y(e_1), \ldots, y(e_h)$.

In general, each packet can be considered as a vector of symbols $\boldsymbol{y}(e) = [y_1(e), \ldots, y_l(e)]$, where l is the length of packet. By likewise grouping the source symbols into packets $\boldsymbol{x}_i = [x_{i,1}, \ldots, x_{i,l}]$, the above algebraic relationships carry over to packets. To facilitate the decoding at the sinks, each message should be tagged with its GEV $\boldsymbol{g}(e)$, which can be easily achieved by prefixing the ith source packet $\boldsymbol{x}_i$ with the ith unit vector $\boldsymbol{u}_i$. Then, each packet is automatically tagged with the corresponding GEV, since

$$[\boldsymbol{g}(e), \boldsymbol{y}(e)] = \sum_{e'} \beta_{e'}(e)[\boldsymbol{g}(e'), \boldsymbol{y}(e')] = \sum_{i=1}^{h} g_i(e)[\boldsymbol{u}_i, \boldsymbol{x}_i] \tag{2}$$

The benefit of tags is that the GEVs can be found within the packets themselves, so that the sinks can compute G_t without knowing the network topology or packet-forwarding paths. Nor is a side channel required for the communication of G_t. Actually, the network can be dynamic, with nodes and edges being added or removed in an ad hoc way. The coding arguments can be time varying and random.

2.2   Boneh-Goh-Nissim Cryptosystem

The Boneh-Goh-Nissim cryptosystem is a public key encryption scheme that proposed by Boneh, Goh and Nissim in 2005 [27]. It has been widely used in many privacy-preserving applications since it can achieve some nice homomorphic properties.

Given the security parameter $\tau \in Z+$, a bilinear-parameter generation algorithm $F(\tau)$ outputs a tuple $(p, q, G, G1, e)$, where p, q are distinct primes with $|p| = |q| = \tau$, G and $G1$ are two cyclic groups of order $n = pq$, and $e : G \times G \to G1$ is a bilinear map.

The Boneh-Goh-Nissim encryption is comprised of three algorithms: key generation, encryption and decryption as follows.

Key Generation: Given the security parameter $\tau \in Z+$, run $F(\tau)$ to obtain the tuple $(p, q, G, G1, e)$ as described above. Randomly chose two generators $g, x \in G$ and set $k = x^q$. Then k is a random generator of the subgroup of G of order p. The public key is $PK = (n, G, G1, e, g, k)$. The private key is $SK = p$.

Encryption: Given a message $m \in 0, 1, \ldots, T$, where $T << q$ is the bound of the message space, choose a random number $r \in Z_n$. Then the ciphertext can be calculated as $C = g^m \cdot k^r \in G$.

Decryption: Given the private key $SK = p$ and the ciphertext $C \in G$, first compute $C^p = (g^m \cdot k^r)^p = (g^p)^m$. Let $g_p = g^p$, then $C^p = g_p^m$. To recover m, it suffices to compute the discrete logarithm of g_p^m.

Note that when m is a short message, say $m \leq T$ for some small bound T, the decryption takes expected time $O(\sqrt{T})$ using Pollards lambda method [28]. Note that decryption in this system takes polynomial time in the size of the message space T.

The Boneh-Goh-Nissim cryptosystem has some nice homomorphic properties. It is additively homomorphic. For any ciphertexts $C_1, C_2 \in G$ of messages $m_1, m_2 \in 0, 1, \ldots, T$ with random numbers $r_1, r_2 \in Z_n$, it satisfies the following homomorphic property.

$$
\begin{aligned}
E(m_1) \cdot E(m_2) &= (g^{m_1} \cdot k^{r_1}) \cdot (g^{m_2} \cdot k^{r_2}) \\
&= g^{(m_1+m_2)} \cdot k^{(r_1+r_2)} = E(m_1 + m_2)
\end{aligned}
\tag{3}
$$

Further, the following two equation can be easily derived.

$$
E(t \cdot m) = E^t(m)
$$
$$
E(\sum_i t_i \cdot m_i) = \prod_i E^{t_i}(m).
\tag{4}
$$

3 System Model

As shown in Fig. 2, the network is modelled here as a graph represented by the set of nodes. We consider a BS, also called the information sink, in charge of data gathering, coordination, and control of the nodes (secondary substations and households). The BS is aware of the number of online nodes, and the network topology is multi-hop. The terminals are responsible for gathering measurements and forwarding messages to subsystems connected to them. We assume that all the terminals have the same performance capabilities in terms of processing and storage. Moreover, the links between the BS and nodes are noisy and the signal can fade, such that the data transmitted from the terminals to the BS and backward can be lost. The collector obtains the data from smart meter by multi-hop wireless network in smart grid. Smart meter upload its data to the collector at constant frequency, that is, periodically (e.g., every 15 min) conveying one

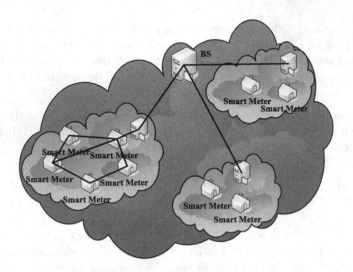

Fig. 2. Smart grid architecture

information packet from each node to the BS. Therefore the flow model in SG is converged, in which there are multiple sources and one destination (BS).

We consider a reasonable clock synchronization (a few seconds drift is acceptable) of the BS and the data senders. The concept of downstream node is used, meaning a node that is closer to the sink than the local node. We intend the information to flow as waves towards the sink and compute the downstream nodes by using a shortest path algorithm.

At the data sink, one data packet from each data sender per data collection period, designated round. On their way to the sink, the packets will be combined with other packets from the same round but different sources.

In particular, random linear network coding (RLNC) provides a fully distributed methodology for network coding, whereby each node in the network selects independently and randomly a set of coefficients and uses them to form linear combinations of the data symbols (or packets) it receives (called also innovative coded packets).

4   Privacy Preserving Scheme for Network Coding

In this section, we propose an scheme named Privacy Preserving scheme for Network Coding (PPNC). There are three steps in PPNC including Sending the packet, Forwarding the packet and Receiving and decoding the packets.

As shown in Algorithm 1 and Fig. 3, due to only one packet sent by each smart meter node per data collection period, each node encrypts the packet data by the public key of the BS. Then, each node set the coefficient of the packet on tag. Simply, the ith value is set to 1 for the node i's packet. In order to protect the information included by the packet, we encrypt the tag by the homomorphic encryption function. Then, the encrypted data and data header are sent.

Algorithm 1. Sending the packet on node i

Input:

    The Public key of node BS, $PubK_{BS}$;

    The plain packet to be sent, x;

    The vector, each value represent one packet, Tag;

    The homomorphic encryption function, HE;

    The encryption function, E;

Output:

    The encrypted packet to be sent, $\bar{x}$;

    The encrypted TAG , $head$;

1: $\bar{x}_i \leftarrow E_{PubK_{BS}}(x_i)$ {Data Encryption}

2: $Tag \leftarrow (0, \cdots, 1, \cdots 0)$ {The i-th value set to one}

3: $head \leftarrow HE_{PubK_{BS}}(Tag)$ {Tag Encryption}

4: $(\bar{x}_i, head) \rightarrow$ downstream node {Sending encrypted data, data header}

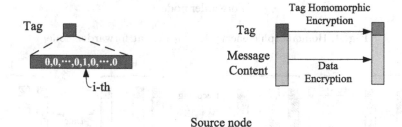

Fig. 3. Set tag and encryption at source node

Algorithm 2. Forwarding the packets on node i

Input:

    The Public key of node BS, $PubK_{BS}$;

    The receiving packet, $\bar{y}$;

    The encrypted Tag of receiving packet, $head$;

    The edge set where the sender of edge is the upstream node of node i, Ein_i;

    The homomorphic encryption function, HE;

Output:

    The coded encrypted packet to be sent, $\bar{y}'$;

    The encrypted Tag of coded packet, $head'$;

1: **for** each edge e in Ein_i **do**

2:    $(\bar{y}(e), head(e))$ {receiving data, data header}

3: **end for**

4: $\bar{y}' \leftarrow \sum\limits_{e \in Ein_i} \beta(e) * \bar{y}(e)$ {Encoding the packet}

5: $head' \leftarrow \prod\limits_{e \in Ein_i} HE_{PubK_{BS}}^{\beta(e)}(head(e))$ {Encoding the Tag}

6: $(\bar{y}', head') \rightarrow$ downstream node {Sending coded data, data header}

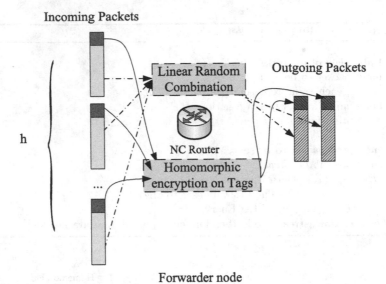

Fig. 4. Homomorphic encryption on tags at forwarder node

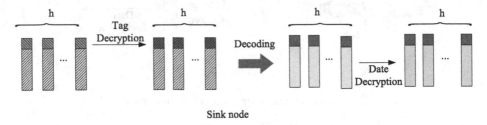

Fig. 5. Decoding and decryption at sink node

As shown in Algorithm 2 and Fig. 4, after receiving packets, the forwarder node need to randomly encodes an new packet and sends it to the downstream node. Firstly, the forwarder node randomly chooses the LEV $\beta(e)$ for receiving packet, that is the coefficient vector. Secondly, according to the LEVs, it linearly encodes the all receiving packets to obtain an new packet $\bar{y}'$. Then, it obtains the encrypted GEV of the new packet by homomorphic encryption function on the encrypted GEVs of receiving packets, as shown in Eq. 5.

$$\prod_{e \in Ein_i} HE_{PubK_{BS}}^{\beta(e)}(head(e)) \tag{5}$$

Finally, it sends the new packet and it's header including the encrypted GEV to the downstream node.

As shown in Algorithm 3 and Fig. 5, when a BS receives the packets, BS (i) utilizes its own private key to decrypt the header to obtain Tag of the packets, (ii) after receiving h independent packets, obtains the reverse value of the transfer matrix G_t, (iii) decodes the receiving packets by transfer matrix and obtains encrypted packets sent by the senders, and (iv) obtains plaint packets by the private key of BS.

5   Security Analyses

In this section, to demonstrate the properties of the proposed scheme we present analysis from privacy and system performance point of views. Then we analyze the computational overhead of our scheme.

5.1   Privacy Performance Analysis

We refer to Dolev-Yao model [29] to design our two adversary models including outside and inside attacker as shown in Fig. 6, in case of the smart grid system.

Outside Attacker. The outside attacker is an external party and is not an entity of the system. An outside attacker can be considered as a global passive eavesdropper who has the ability to observe all network links. The attacker receives all of the packets and examines the tags and message contents entering to a node (smart meter) and departure from the node. Further, even if messages are encrypted in an end-to-end manner, it is still possible for a global outside attacker to trace packets by analyzing and comparing the message ciphertext. The attacker knows the detail information about our proposed privacy mechanism. For instance, the attacker knows public keys of the entire parties and

---

Algorithm 3. Receiving and decoding the packets
___
Input:
    The Private key of node BS, $PrvK_{BS}$;
    The plain packet to be sent, x;
    The matrix of received packets with size of "$1*N$", $\bar{Y}$;
    The matrix of sent packets with size of "$1*N$", $\bar{X}$;
    The transfer matrix , Gt;
    The homomorphic decryption function, HD;
    The decryption function, D;
Output:
    The plain packets , X;
1: $(\bar{y}, head)$\{receiving data, dataheader\}
2: **for** each packet i **do**
3:    $Gt_i \leftarrow HD_{PrvK_{BS}}(head_i)$ \{Tag Decryption\}
4: **end for**
5: $\bar{X} \leftarrow Gt^T \times \bar{Y}$ \{Decoding\}
6: **for** $i = 1 \rightarrow h$ **do**
7:    $x_i \leftarrow D_{PrvK_{BS}}(\bar{x}_i)$ \{Data Decryption\}
8: **end for**
___

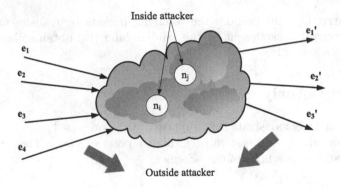

Fig. 6. Attack model: outside attacker and inside attacker.

has the detail knowledge about the network topology. Furthermore, the attacker knows the detail design of our algorithms shown by Algorithms 1–3.

Discussion: Message content correlation used in traffic analysis can be resisted by the mixing feature of network coding. With the assistance of homomorphic encryption function, Tags are kept confidential to eavesdroppers, making it difficult for attackers to perform linear analysis on Tags. In addition, homomorphic encryption function keeps the random coding feature, making the linear analysis on message content almost computationally impossible. Let the number of intercepted packets be w. The computational complexity for attackers to examine if a packet is a linear combination of h messages is $O(h^3 + hl)$ in terms of multiplication, where l is the length of message content. Thus, the computational complexity to analyze the intercepted w packets is $O(C_w^h(h^3 + hl))$,which increases exponentially with w, as shown in Fig. 7 where $h = 5, l = 100$.

For a global outside attacker, it is still possible to trace packets by analyzing and comparing the message ciphertext, even if messages are encrypted in an end-to-end manner and the encrypted message remains the same during its forwarding. In our scheme, the encrypted message is changed after getting through every node, so it's hard to trace the path or to find the source of a message.

Inside Attacker. The inside attacker is an internal party and may compromise several intermediate nodes. The malicious node is already authenticated and receives the system parameters and its own private key, so the inside attacker has these information. The malicious node is under control of the attacker and performs the Algorithm 2. Link-to-link encryption is vulnerable to inside attacker since they may already obtain the decryption keys and reveal message plain text.

Discussion: Having access to a malicious node only improves the attacker situation on modifying its data. The forwarder nodes only mix the packets and do not perform any encryption and decryption. Consequently, his behave is almost same as the previous scenario.

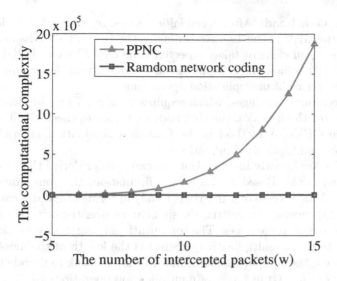

Fig. 7. Privacy enhancement in terms of the computational complexity

5.2 Computational Overhead

The computational overhead of the proposed scheme can be investigated respectively from three aspects, including source node, intermediate node and sink node. Since the computational complexity of the proposed scheme is closely involved with the specific homomorphic encryption algorithm, in the following analysis, we will take the Boneh-Goh-Nissim cryptosystem as the encryption method when necessary. Our scheme can work with all encryption algorithm of the data encryption, therefore we ignore the encryption and decryption of the data in the overhead analysis.

Source Node Overhead: For transmitting the smart meter reading, the source node i needs one encryption operation. According to Boneh-Goh-Nissim cryptosystem, every encryption operation requires 2 exponentiations and 1 multiplication operation. Therefore, the computational complexity is $O(\log n)$ in terms of multiplication operations.

Intermediate Node Overhead: In intermediate nodes, linear transformation on the elements of GEVs can only be performed by manipulating the ciphertext of these elements because intermediate nodes have no knowledge of decryption keys. According to Eq. 5, the computational complexity of producing one element in new GEVs is h exponentiations and $h-1$ multiplications on the ciphertext, which is $O(h * \log n)$ in terms of multiplications together. Thus, the computational complexity is $O(h^2 * \log n)$ for a GEV and $O(h^3 * \log n)$ for a GEM with h GEVs in terms of multiplication operations.

Sink Node Overhead: After receiving an message, the sink can decrypt the elements of the GEV in the Tag. According to the Boneh-Goh-Nissim cryptosystem, decrypting an element takes expected time $O(\sqrt{T})$ using Pollards lambda method [19]. Therefore, the computational complexity of decrypting a GEV is $O(h * \sqrt{T})$ in terms of multiplication operations.

After receiving h messages, which requires $O(h^2 * \sqrt{T})$ multiplication operations to decrypt the h GEVs, the sink node can start to check the linear dependence of the GEVs. A method is the Gaussian elimination algorithm, which requires $O(h^3)$ multiplication operations.

If h GEVs are linearly independent, we can further derive the inverse of the corresponding GEM. Based on Gaussian elimination, the computational complexity to find the inverse of a matrix is $O(h^3)$ in terms of multiplication operations. With the inverse of a matrix, the sink can recover the original messages by decoding the encoded messages. The computational complexity for the recovery is $O(h^2 l)$ in terms of multiplication, where l is the length of the messages.

In summary, the computational complexity for the sink to decode h messages is $O(h^2 * (\sqrt{T} + h + l))$ in terms of multiplication operations.

6   Conclusion

In order to solve the privacy preserving in smart grid with network coding, in this paper, we propose a distributed privacy preserving scheme, which considers the converged flows character of smart grid and exploits a homomorphic encryption function to decrease the complex the in forwarder node. The message content of packet is encrypted and the tag of packet is encrypted by homomorphic encryption function. Then the forwarder node linear random codes the encrypted message contents and directly processes the tags cryptotext based on the homomorphic feature. The scheme offers message content confidentiality privacy preserving feature, which can efficiently thwart traffic analysis. We have done extensive performance evaluations and security analysis, which demonstrates that our scheme not only has good security feature to protect the privacy, but also has low computation.

Acknowledgments. This work was supported by National Natural Science Foundation of China (61303045, 61572184, Key Program 71331001, 71420107027), the Prospective Research Project on Future Networks (Jiangsu Future Networks Innovation Institute) under Grant No. BY2013095-4-06.

References

1. Cohen, F.: The smarter grid. IEEE Secur. Priv. **8**(1), 60–63 (2010)
2. Marihart, D.: Communications technology guidelines for EMS/SCADA systems. IEEE Trans. Power Deliv. **16**(4) (2001)
3. Deconinck, G.: An evaluation of two-way communication means for advanced metering in flanders (Belgium). In: IEEE IIMTC, pp. 1–6 (2008)

4. Gao, Q., Yu, J., Chong, P., So, P., Gunawan, E.: Solutions for the silent node problemin an automaticmeter reading system using powerline communications. IEEE Trans. Power Deliv. **23**, 150–156 (2008)

5. Sivaneasan, B., Gunawan, E., So, P.: Modeling and performance analysis of automatic meter-reading systems using PLC under impulsive noise interference. IEEE Trans. Power Deliv. **25**, 1465–1475 (2010)

6. Galli, S., Scaglione, A., Wang, Z.: For the grid and through the grid: the role of power line communications in the smart grid. In: IEEE, vol. 99, pp. 998–1027 (2011)

7. Gungor, V., Lu, B., Hancke, G.: Opportunities and challenges of wireless sensor networks in smart grid. IEEE Trans. Ind. Electron. **57**, 3557–3564 (2010)

8. Souryal, M., Gentile, C., Griffith, D., Cypher, D., Golmie, N.: A methodology to evaluate wireless technologies for the smart grid. In: IEEE Smart Grid Communication, pp. 356–361 (2010)

9. Nicanfar, H., TalebiFard, P., Alasaad, A., Leung, V.C.: Privacy-preserving scheme in smart grid communication using enhanced network coding. In: ICC, pp. 2022–2026 (2013)

10. Nicanfar, H., TalebiFard, P., Alasaad, A., Leung, V.C.: Enhanced network coding to maintain privacy in smart grid communication. IEEE Trans. Emerg. Top. Comput. **1**(2), 286–296 (2013)

11. Karthick, M., Sivalingam, K.M.: Network coding meets TCP. In: IEEE ANTS, pp. 1–6 (2013)

12. Phulpin, Y., Barros, J., Lucani, D.: Network coding in smart grids. In: IEEE Smart Grid Communication, pp. 1–6 (2011)

13. Rajalingham, G., Ho, Q.D., Le-Ngoc., T.: Random linear network coding for converge-cast smart grid wireless networks. In: IEEE, pp. 208–212 (2014)

14. Prior, R., Lucani, D.E., Phulpin, Y., Nistor, M., Barros, J.: Network coding protocols for smart grid communications. IEEE Trans. Smart Grid **5**(3), 1523–1531 (2014)

15. McDaniel, P., McLaughlin, S.: Security and privacy challenges in the smart grid. IEEE Secur. Priv. **7**(8), 75–77 (2009)

16. Efthymiou, C., Kalogridis, G.: Smart grid privacy via anonymization of smart metering data. In: IEEE Smart Grid Communication, pp. 1–6 (2010)

17. Richardson, I., Thomson, A., Infield, D., Clifford, C.: Domestic electricity use: a high-resolution energy demand model. Energ. Build. **42**, 1878–1887 (2010)

18. Chen, L., Lu, R., Cao, Z., AlHarbi, K., Lin., X.: Mudamultifunctional data aggregation in privacy-preserving smart grid communications. Peer-to-Peer Netw. Appl. **online** (2014)

19. Won, J., Ma, C.Y.T., Yau, D.K.Y., Rao, N.: Proactive fault-tolerant aggregation protocol for privacy-assured smart metering. In: Infocom, pp. 2804–2812 (2014)

20. Zhao, J., Jung, T., Wang, Y., Li., X.Y.: Achieving differential privacy of data disclosure in the smart grid. In: Infocom, pp. 504–512 (2014)

21. Yang, L., Chen, X., Zhang, J., Poor, H.V.: Optimal privacy-preserving energy management for smart meters. In: Infocom, pp. 513–521 (2014)

22. Zeng, W., Lin, Y., He, S., Yu, J.: Data aggregation based on the privacy-preserving element in wireless sensor networks. J. Commun. **33**(10), 16–25 (2012)

23. Zeng, W., Lin, Y., Wang, L., He, S.: Privacy-preserving data aggregation scheme based on the p-function set in wireless sensor networks. Ad hoc Sens. Netw. **21**(1–2), 21–58 (2014)

24. Fan, Y., Jiang, Y., Zhu, H., Shen, X.S.: An efficient privacy-preserving scheme against traffic analysis attacks in network coding. In: Infocom, pp. 2213–2221 (2009)
25. Fan, Y., Jiang, Y., Zhu, H., Shen, X.S.: Network coding based privacy preservation against traffic analysis in multi-hop wireless networks. IEEE Trans. Wirel. Commun. **10**(3), 834–843 (2011)
26. Feizi, S., Lucani, D.E., Mdard, M.: Tunable sparse network coding. In: International Zurich Seminar on Communications (IZS) (2012)
27. Boneh, D., Goh, E., Nissim, K.: Evaluating 2-DNF formulas on ciphertexts. Theory Cryptogr. **3378**, 325–341 (2005)
28. Menezes, A., Oorschot, P., Vanstone, S.: Handbook of Applied Cryptography. CRC Press, Boca Raton (1996)
29. Dolev, D., Yao, A.: On the security of public key protocols. IEEE Trans. Inf. Theory **29**(2), 198–208 (1983)

Verifiable Dynamic Fuzzy Search Over Encrypted Data in Cloud Computing

Xiaoyu Zhu[1], Qin Liu[2], and Guojun Wang[1](✉)

[1] School of Information Science and Engineering, Central South University,
Changsha 410083, China
{zhuxiaoyu,csgjwang}@csu.edu.cn
[2] School of Information Science and Engineering, Hunan University,
Changsha 410082, China
gracelq628@hnu.edu.cn

Abstract. With the increasing popularity of cloud computing, large scale of documents are being outsourced to the cloud. To avoid information leakage, sensitive files usually have to be encrypted before outsourcing. Thus, it is of great importance to enable an encrypted cloud data search service. Considering the huge amount of data users and documents in the cloud, it is necessary to allow typos in the search request, update documents dynamically and return search results in a verifiable way. Existing solutions support only fuzzy keyword search or verifiable dynamic search, not support verifiable dynamic fuzzy search. In this paper, we first present a verifiable dynamic fuzzy search scheme to address this problem, then prove that our proposed scheme is secure. To the best of our knowledge, this is the first work that achieves verifiable dynamic fuzzy search over encrypted cloud data.

Keywords: Cloud computing · Privacy-preserving · Fuzzy search · Verifiable search · Dynamic update

1 Introduction

In recent years, cloud computing has emerged as a paradigm that provides configurable computing resources and elastic storage. Many consumers, companies and organizations that need high storage and computation power tend to outsource their data and services to cloud. In cloud computing, the Cloud Service Provider (CSP) possesses full control of the outsourced data, the data owners require to protect their sensitive data (e.g., medical records, financial transactions, and social network profiles) against the CSP, and therefore all data opt to be encrypted before outsourcing. This in turn makes the effective data utilization, such as search over the encrypted data set, a very challenging problem.

After Song et al. proposed the first work on searchable encryption [1], many novel schemes [2–5] have been proposed with various settings and functionalities. However, almost all such schemes only support exact keyword matching. In practise, the data users may input keywords with some spelling mistakes,

© Springer International Publishing Switzerland 2015
G. Wang et al. (Eds.): ICA3PP 2015, Part III, LNCS 9530, pp. 655–666, 2015.
DOI: 10.1007/978-3-319-27137-8_47

which will result in wrong or no matching. Therefore, it is important to extend the search capability to support fuzzy keyword search over encrypted cloud data. Recently, some schemes proposed methods to solve this problem. Fuzzy keyword search solutions can be divided into two classes: (1) wildcard-based approach [6–8]; (2) using locality sensitive hashing (LSH) functions and Bloom filters [9]. In the wildcard-based approach, a set of fuzzy words similar to the original keyword is generated under the restriction of a certain edit distance. If the keyword is m-letter long and the edit distance is n, the encrypted index is expanded to $O(m^n)$, which results in high storage overhead. In [9], Wang et al. proposed a fuzzy search scheme using LSH and Bloom filters. In their scheme, each keyword is represented as a bigram vector and the file indexes are constructed by using LSH in Bloom filter, which provides efficient fuzzy search with constant size index regardless of the number of keywords associated with the file. However, Wang et al.'s scheme only considered a case such that the server is "honest-but-curious", and they didn't consider the issue in a verifiable way.

Even if cloud server is honest, due to possible virus, trojan horse, or storage corruption, cloud server may return false search results. Furthermore, we consider the server is malicious, which means the cloud server may forge or delete some encrypted files to obtain commercial value. Search result verification is a desirable feature that a robust search system would like to provide to its users. In order to verify search results securely, several approaches have been proposed in recent years [10,11]. When data owners outsource huge amount of data into the cloud, the policy updating becomes an important problem as the data may be dynamically and frequently updated by data owners. In order to solve this problem, Kamara et al. constructed dynamic searchable symmetric encryption (SSE) schemes in [12,13]. Kurosawa et al. extended their verifiable SSE scheme [14] to a verifiable dynamic SSE scheme in [15]. Namely the data users can update (modify, delete and add) documents, and he can detect any cheating behavior of malicious servers. They proved that their scheme is UC-secure, where UC (universal composability) is a very strong notion of security. However, this solution only supports the exact keyword search.

Table 1. Comparison with the previous work.

	Wang et al. [9]	Sun et al. [11]	Kurosawa et al. [15]	This paper
Fuzzy	√	×	×	√
Verifiability	×	√	√	√
Dynamic	×	×	√	√

To date, verifiable dynamic fuzzy search over encrypted data remains a challenging problem. Although fuzzy search and verifiable dynamic search have been implemented separately, a combination of the two does not lead to a secure and verifiable dynamic fuzzy search scheme. Unfortunately, none of these previously known searchable encryption schemes achieve all these properties at the same time. This severely limits the practical value of searchable encryption schemes and decreases their chance of deployment in real-world cloud storage systems. In this paper, we address the challenges of constructing encrypted data search functionalities that support fuzzy keyword search request, result verification and dynamic update. Table 1 shows the comparison with the previous works. In particular, to support fuzzy search and search result verification functionalities, we propose to build the search index based on the LSH and Bloom filter. To implement dynamic update, we adopt RSA accumulator which posses the time stamp functionality as our authentication method. Finally, we demonstrate the security of the proposed schemes.

The contributions of this paper are summarized as follows:

(1) To the best of our knowledge, we propose the first verifiable dynamic fuzzy search scheme, which can not only fulfill the fuzzy search functionality while maintaining privacy, but also can update documents dynamically and support the verifiability of the searching result.
(2) Our scheme provides efficient fuzzy search with constant size index by using locality sensitive hashing and Bloom filter, and it eliminates the need of a predefined dictionary.
(3) We give security analysis to prove our scheme is secure and privacy preserving, which both meets privacy and verifiability requirements.

The rest of the paper is organized as follows. Section 2 presents problem formulation in our work. Following in Sect. 3, we describe the details of our proposed verifiable dynamic fuzzy search scheme. Section 4 presents security analysis. Finally, we draw the conclusion in Sect. 5.

2   Problem Formulation

2.1   System Model

In this paper, the system model is consisted of two entities: the client and the cloud server, as illustrated in Fig. 1. The client outsources a set of documents in an encrypted form, together with a secure searchable index to the cloud server. To search over the encrypted files, the client submits fuzzy search request to the server, then the cloud server returns the search results to the client. The client can dynamically change the files, such as modify, delete or add documents, and the client can detect any cheating behavior of malicious servers.

2.2   Notation

– D: the plaintext documents collection, expressed as $D = \{d_j \mid j = 1, \cdots, n\}$.
– W: the keyword dictionary, expressed as $W = \{w_i \mid i = 1, \cdots, m\}$, each keyword w_i is represented as a Bloom filter.
– I: the file-keyword index, expressed as $m \times n$ binary matrix.
– $\tilde{D}$: the encrypted form of D, expressed as $\tilde{D} = \{\tilde{d}_j \mid j = 1, \cdots, n\}$.

- $\widetilde{W}$: the encrypted form of W, expressed as $\widetilde{W} = \{\widetilde{w}_i \mid i = 1, \cdots, m\}$.
- $\widetilde{I}$: the encrypted form of I, expressed as an $\widetilde{I} = \{\widetilde{I}_i \mid i = 1, \cdots, m\}$.
- γ: a random permutation on $\{1, \cdots, m\}$.
- $Index$: the final searchable index, expressed as an $Index = \{(\widetilde{w}_{r(i)}, \widetilde{I}_{r(i)}) \mid i = 1, \cdots, m\}$.
- $T(w_a)$: the trapdoor of the search request w_a.
- $f_k : \{0,1\}^* \times \{0,1\}^\sigma$: a pseudorandom function, where k is a key.
- $TF = \{tf : \{0,1\}^{3\sigma} \to \{0,1\}^\sigma\}$: two-universal family of functions, where σ is the security parameter.
- $H : \{0,1\}^* \to \{0,1\}^\sigma$: a collision-resistant hash function, where σ is the security parameter.
- $P(H(s))$: a prime $t \in \{0,1\}^{3\sigma}$ such that $tf(t) = H(s)$, and such t is chosen randomly.

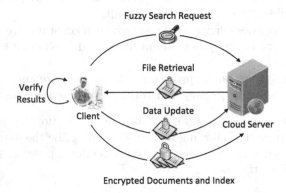

Fig. 1. Architecture of verifiable dynamic fuzzy search scheme

2.3   Preliminaries

Bloom Filter: A Bloom filter is a randomized data structure that supports set membership queries [16]. For a set of n elements, $E = \{e_i \mid 1 \leq i \leq n\}$, a Bloom filter can test whether an element q belongs to E or not. A Bloom filter uses a bit array B of size t, which is set to zeros initially. The Bloom filter uses k independent hash functions from $H = \{h_j \mid 1 \leq j \leq k\}$ to insert an element $e_i \in E$ into the Bloom filter by setting $B[h_j(e_i)] := 1$ for $1 \leq i \leq n$ and $1 \leq j \leq k$. When a query is asked for q, every $B[h_j(q)]$ is checked for $1 \leq j \leq k$. If the bit at any position is zero, then $q \notin E$; otherwise, the Bloom filter gives a positive response. A false positive may happen in a positive response, the false positive rate f is approximately $(1 - e^{-\frac{kn}{t}})^k$. The minimum f is $(1/2)^k$ when $k = \frac{t}{n} \cdot ln2$.

Locality Sensitive Hashing: LSH is an approximation algorithm which uses locality sensitive function families to achieve near neighbour search in high dimensional spaces [17], LSH functions hash similar objects to the same bucket with higher probability than the objects that are dissimilar. Given a distance metric $dist$, e.g. Euclidean distance, $dist(m, n)$ is the distance between the point m and the point n, family of hash functions H is (r_1, r_2, p_1, p_2)-sensitive if any two points m, n and $h \in H$ satisfy:

$$\text{if } dist(m, n) \leq r_1, \text{ then } Pr[h(m) = h(n)] \geq p_1$$
$$\text{if } dist(m, n) \geq r_2, \text{ then } Pr[h(m) = h(n)] \leq p_2$$

2.4 Security Model

Privacy: The cloud server can only access the encrypted files, the secure indexes and the submitted trapdoors. The cloud server can also know and record the search results. We require that the server should not be able to learn any more information.

Verifiability: We assume that the cloud server is malicious as in [14,15], which means that the server may delete some encrypted files to save its storage space or forge erroneous results to save her computation ability. The definition of verifiability means that even if the server is malicious, the client can receive the corresponding files correctly, or he outputs fail in the search phase.

2.5 Design Goals

To enable verifiable dynamic fuzzy keyword search over encrypted cloud data under the aforementioned models, our mechanism is aiming to achieve the following design goals. (1) To provide efficient fuzzy search without predefined keyword dictionary; (2) We propose a scheme to help client ensure the verifiability of the returned search results in the fuzzy keyword search scenario; (3) The client can efficiently update documents.

3   A New Verifiable Dynamic Fuzzy Search Scheme

In this section, we present our verifiable dynamic fuzzy search scheme in cloud computing. We first provide an overview of the scheme, and then describe the detailed description of six algorithms in the proposed scheme.

3.1 Overview

We outline the key ideas of verifiable dynamic fuzzy search scheme over encrypted data in this subsection. We first present the fuzzy search process which is the basis of the whole scheme. For most secure search schemes, index construction is a major process. In order to design a secure index and implement fuzzy search, keywords and trapdoor are all represented as Bloom filters using LSH functions. Then we will introduce how the client can detect the cheating behavior through the verify algorithm. After that, we will describe the details of the data update process.

Fuzzy Search Process: We utilize bigram vector proposed in [9] to represent keywords. Transform a keyword to a 26^2-bit long bigram vector, in which each element represents the contiguous 2 letters appeared in the keyword. For example, the bigram set of keyword security can be constructed as {se,ec,cu,ur,ri,it,ty}. Each element in the vector represents one of the 26^2 possible bigrams. The element is set to 1 if the corresponding bigram exists in the bigram set of a given keyword.

The key to implement fuzzy search is to use LSH functions in transforming the keyword into a Bloom filter. LSH functions will hash inputs with similarity within certain threshold into the same bucket with high probability. For example, a misspelled keyword securite in the search request and a correctly spelled keyword security in the final index will hash into the same output by using LSH functions.

The keyword transformation process is implemented as follows: First extract the keyword dictionary for all documents, then use bigram vector representation to represent each keyword in the dictionary, and after that transform each keyword into a Bloom filter. The search request can be generated into a Bloom filter in the same way as the keyword transformation. The final index is the combination of the encrypted keywords and encrypted file-keyword index. The search can be done by matching the trapdoor and the final index.

Search Result Verification: In this process, we allow the client to verify the searching result. The main idea is to let the cloud server return the authenticators, the client can verify the correctness of the search result by reconstructing the authenticators.

In a malicious model, the server may forge the encrypted data or delete some of them. A naive scheme may use MAC to prevent such active attacks, but this scheme does not work if a malicious server returns $(\widetilde{d}_1, \mathrm{MAC}(\widetilde{d}_1))$ instead of $(\widetilde{d}_2, \mathrm{MAC}(\widetilde{d}_2))$ in the search phase. In order to prevent such attack, scheme [14] proposed a method to verify files and keywords together. However, this method can not modify files efficiently, for example, if the client wants to modify a file which contains m keywords, m authenticators need to be updated. Thus, it is not practical as the files may contain many keywords.

In order to solve this problem, scheme [15] proposed to authenticate files and keywords separately. The file authenticator is represented as $(j, \widetilde{d}_j)$ and the keyword authenticator is $(\widetilde{w}_i, j, [\widetilde{I}_i]_j)$, the modify cost is reduced to $O(1)$ by using this method.

Data Update Process: If the client wants to update $\widetilde{d}_1$ to $\widetilde{d}_1'$, the client only updates the authenticator on $(1, \widetilde{d}_1)$ to $(1, \widetilde{d}_1')$. If the client wants to add a document d_{n+1}, the server updates the encrypted documents and index, and the client updates the authenticators on $(n+1, \widetilde{d}_{n+1})$ and $(\widetilde{w}_i, n+1, [\widetilde{I}_i]_{n+1})$. If the client wants to delete a document $\widetilde{d}_1$, then it updates the authenticator on $(1, \widetilde{d}_1)$ to $(1, delete)$.

In order to verify whether the returned results are acquired from the latest version of outsourced documents or not, we could add time stamp into the authenticators. RSA accumulator [18] is an uniform authenticate method which is adopted in our scheme.

3.2   Scheme Construction

A verifiable dynamic fuzzy search scheme consists of six algorithms (**Keygen, Buildindex, Trapdoor, Search, Verify, Dataupdate**), these algorithms are defined as follows:

Keygen: The system is initialized in this phase.

(1) Our scheme makes use of several basic cryptographic algorithms. A symmetric-key encryption scheme SSE is consisted with three algorithms (SK, Enc, Dec), where algorithm SK is used to generate secret key sk, Enc is an encryption algorithm and Dec is a decryption algorithm. SSE is a CPA-secure encryption scheme.

(2) Let σ be the security parameter, we generate two large primes $x = 2x' + 1$ and $y = 2y' + 1$ such that x' and y' are also primes and $|xy| > 3\sigma$. Let $N = xy$ and $G = \{u \,|\, u = v^2 \bmod N$ for some $v \in Z_N^*\}$. Then G is a cyclic group of size $(x-1)(y-1)/4$, let g be a generator of G.

(3) We use two-universal family of functions $TF = \{tf : \{0,1\}^{3\sigma} \to \{0,1\}^\sigma\}$ and a pseudorandom function $f_k : \{0,1\}^* \times \{0,1\}^\sigma$, we randomly chooses $tf \in TF$, and generate (sk, k_0, k_1, k_2) randomly, where sk is a key of SSE, and k_0, k_1, k_2 are keys of f. We also choose a random permutation γ on $\{1, \cdots, m\}$, where m is the number of the keywords. The client sends (N, g, tf, k_2) to the server and keeps $(x, y, sk, k_0, k_1, \gamma)$ secret.

Buildindex:

(1) For each document $d_j \in D$, $1 \leq j \leq n$, extract all the keywords, the keyword dictionary for all documents is represented as $S = \{s_i \,|\, i = 1, \cdots, m\}$.

(2) The file-keyword index $I = \{I_{i,j}\}$ is a $m \times n$ binary matrix such that

$$I_{i,j} = \begin{cases} 1 \text{ if } s_i \text{ is contained in } d_j \\ 0 \text{ otherwise} \end{cases}$$

Let I_i denotes the ith row of I.

(3) For each keyword $s_i \in S$, transform it into its bigram vector representation, then construct a t-bit Bloom filter w_i to represent the keyword, choose k independent LSH functions from the p-stable LSH family H, insert it into w_i using $h_l \in Y$, $1 \le l \le k$. So the keyword dictionary for D is transformed into $W = \{w_i \mid i = 1, \cdots, m\}$.

(4) For each keyword $w_i \in W$, $1 \le i \le m$, the encrypted form of w_i is $\widetilde{w}_i$

$$\widetilde{w}_i = [f_{k_0}(w_i)]_{1\cdots 128}$$

$$\widetilde{I}_i = I_i \oplus [f_{k_1}(w_i)]_{1\cdots n}$$

Choose γ as a random permutation on $\{1, \cdots, m\}$, the final searchable index is denoted as:

$$Index = \{(\widetilde{w}_{\gamma(i)}, \widetilde{I}_{\gamma(i)}) \mid i = 1, \cdots, m\} \tag{1}$$

For each document $d_j \in D$, $\widetilde{d}_j = Enc_{sk}(d_j)$, the encrypted documents are

$$\widetilde{D} = \{\widetilde{d}_j \mid j = 1, \cdots, n\}$$

Then the client sends $\widetilde{D}$ and $Index$ to the server.

Trapdoor: Transform the search request into its bigram vector representation, then construct a t-bit Bloom filter w_a to represent the keyword, choose k independent LSH functions from the p-stable LSH family H, insert it into w_a using $h_l \in Y$, $1 \le l \le k$. Then encrypt the search request w_a using pseudorandom function f, and output $\widetilde{w}_a$:

$$\widetilde{w}_a = [f_{k_0}(w_a)]_{1\cdots 128}$$

The client also computes the

$$\widetilde{s}_a = [f_{k_1}(w_a)]_{1\cdots n}$$

Then the client sends the trapdoor $T(w_a) = \{\widetilde{w}_a, \widetilde{s}_a\}$ to the server.

Search: Suppose that the client wants to search on a keyword w_a, the server receives $T(w_a)$ from the client, then the server finds $(\widetilde{w}_a, \widetilde{I}_a) \in Index$ by using $\widetilde{w}_a$. She computes

$$I_a = \widetilde{I}_a \oplus \widetilde{s}_a$$

Let $I_a = \{e_j \mid e_1, \cdots, e_n\}$, Then the server returns $\widetilde{D}(w_a) = \{\widetilde{d}_j \mid e_j = 1\}$ to the client.

Verify: The file authenticator is represented as $(j, \widetilde{d}_j)$ and the keyword authenticator is $(\widetilde{w}_i, j, [\widetilde{I}_i]_j)$. The client applies the RSA accumulator to the sets S_D and S_I, and compute their accumulated values V_D and V_I.

$$S_D = \{(j, \widetilde{d}_j) \mid j = 1, \cdots, n\}$$

$$S_I = \{(\widetilde{w}_i, j, [\widetilde{I}_i]_j) \mid i = 1, \cdots, m, j = 1, \cdots, n\}$$

(1) In the *BuildIndex* phase, the client computes the authenticators V_D and V_I

$$V_D = g^{\prod_{j=1}^{n} P(H(j,H(\tilde{d}_j)))} \mod N$$

$$V_I = g^{\prod_{i=1}^{m} \prod_{j=1}^{n} P(H(\tilde{w}_i, j, [\tilde{I}_i]_j))} \mod N$$

The client keeps the secret keys n, V_D and V_I.

(2) In the *Search* phase, the server finds $\tilde{D}(w_a) = \{\tilde{d}_j \,|\, e_j = 1\}$. She next computes

$$C_D = g^{\prod_{e_j = 0} P(H(j, H(\tilde{d}_j)))} \mod N$$

$$C_I = g^{\prod_{i \neq a} \{\prod_{j=1}^{n} P(H(\tilde{w}_i, j, [\tilde{I}_i]_j))\}} \mod N$$

Finally she returns $\{\tilde{D}(w_a), C_D, C_I\}$ to the client.

(3) In the *Verify* phase, the client first computes $x_j = P(H(j, H(\tilde{d}_j)))$ for each $(j, \tilde{d}_j) \in \tilde{D}(w_a)$, and checks if

$$V_D = (C_D)^{\prod_{e_j = 1} x_j} \mod N \tag{2}$$

The client then computes $z_j = P(H(\tilde{w}_a, j, [\tilde{I}_a]_j))$ for $j = 1, \cdots, n$, and checks if

$$V_I = (C_I)^{\prod_{j=1}^{n} z_j} \mod N \tag{3}$$

If all the checks succeed, then the client decrypts all $\tilde{d}_j$ such that $e_j = 1$ and outputs the documents $\{d_j \,|\, e_j = 1\}$. Otherwise he outputs **reject**.

Dataupdate:

(1) Suppose that the client wants to *modify* $\tilde{d}_j$ to $\tilde{d}'_j$. The client sends $(j, \tilde{d}'_j)$ to the server, it computes

$$x'_j = P(H(j, H(\tilde{d}'_j))), V'_D = g^{x_1 \cdots x'_j \cdots x_n} \mod N$$

Then it updates V_D to V'_D.

(2) Suppose that the client wants to *add* a document d_{n+1}. Let

$$I_{i,n+1} = \begin{cases} 1 \text{ if } s_i \text{ is contained in } d_{n+1} \\ 0 \text{ otherwise} \end{cases}$$

The client computes $\tilde{d}_{n+1} = Enc_{sk}(d_{n+1})$, and it computes

$$a_i = [f_{k_1}(w_i)]_{n+1} \oplus I_{i,n+1}$$

for $i = 1, \cdots, m$, where $[f_{k_1}(w_i)]_{n+1}$ denotes the $(n+1)$th bit of $f_{k_1}(w_i)$. Then it sends $\tilde{d}_{n+1}$, $(a_{\gamma(1)}, \cdots, a_{\gamma(m)})$ to the server. The server updates $I_{\gamma(i)}$ to $I'_{\gamma(i)} = I_{\gamma(i)} \| a_{\gamma(i)}$ for $i = 1, \cdots, m$, where $\|$ denotes concatenation.

The client computes

$$V'_D = (V_D)^{P(H(n+1,H(\tilde{d}_{n+1})))} \bmod N$$
$$V'_I = (V_I)^{\prod_{i=1}^{m} P(H(\tilde{w}_i,n+1,a_i))} \bmod N$$

It updates V_D to V'_D, V_I to V'_I, finally it updates n to $n+1$.

(3) Suppose that the client wants to *delete* $\tilde{d}_j$. He first sends $(j, delete)$ to the server. Then apply *modify* to $\tilde{d}'_j = delete$.

4 Security Analysis

Theorem 1. The proposed scheme satisfies privacy.

Proof. In order to prove that the scheme is privacy-preserve, we need to prove that the challenger can only learn the encrypted files, the secure indexes, the submitted trapdoors, and the search results. Suppose that there exists an simulator S, it does the followings:

(1) S receives $|d_1|, \cdots, |d_n|$ and $m = |W|$ from the challenger.
(2) S sends (N, g, tf, k_2) to the challenger and keeps $(x, y, sk, k_0, k_1, \gamma)$.
(3) S computes $\tilde{d}_j = Enc_{sk}(0^{|d_j|})$ for $j = 1, \cdots, n$. S also chooses $\tilde{w}_i \in \{0,1\}^{128}$ and $\tilde{I}_i \in \{0,1\}^n$ randomly for $i = 1, \cdots, m$.
(4) S sends $\tilde{D}' = (\tilde{d}_1, \cdots, \tilde{d}_n)$ and $Index' = \{(\tilde{w}_{\gamma(i)}, \tilde{I}_{\gamma(i)}) \mid i = 1, \cdots, m\}$ to the challenger.
(5) S receives $\tilde{D}(w_a) = \{\tilde{d}_j \mid e_j = 1\}$ from the challenger.
(6) S then computes $\tilde{s}'_a = \tilde{I}_{\gamma(i)} \oplus (e_1, \cdots, e_n)$ and returns $T' = (\tilde{w}_{\gamma(i)}, \tilde{s}'_a)$ to the challenger.

In the search phase, the challenger receives $(\tilde{D}', Index', T')$ from S. In the data update process, the challenger receives $(j, Enc_{sk}(0^{|d'_j|}))$ from S in the modify case, the challenger receives $\tilde{d}'_{n+1}, (a'_{\gamma(1)}, \cdots, a'_{\gamma(m)})$ in the add case, the challenger receives $(j, delete)$ in the delete case.

But as SSE is CPA-secure, $\tilde{D}'$ and $\tilde{D}$, $(j, Enc_{sk}(0^{|d'_j|}))$ and $(j, Enc_{sk}(0^{|d'_j|}))$ are indistinguishable. $Index'$ and $Index$ are indistinguishable because f is a pseudorandom function. $T' = (\tilde{w}_{\gamma(i)}, \tilde{s}'_a)$ and $T(w_a) = (\tilde{w}_a, \tilde{s}_a)$, $(a'_{\gamma(1)}, \cdots, a'_{\gamma(m)})$ and $(a_{\gamma(1)}, \cdots, a_{\gamma(m)})$ are indistinguishable because f is a pseudorandom function and γ is a random permutation. Therefore the challenger cannot learn more information, so the privacy is preserved.

Theorem 2. The proposed scheme satisfies verifiability.

Proof. In order to prove the verifiability, we need to prove that the verification process will fail if the attacker forges wrong authenticators.

Suppose $(\widetilde{D}(w_a), C_D, C_I)$ are correct authenticators. and the attacker forges an invalid $(\widetilde{D}'(w_a), C'_D, C'_I)$ such that $(\widetilde{D}(w_a), C_D, C_I) \neq (\widetilde{D}'(w_a), C'_D, C'_I)$.

There are three possible cases: (1) $\widetilde{D}'(w_a) = \widetilde{D}(w_a)$ and $(C_D, C_I) \neq (C'_D, C'_I)$; (2) $\widetilde{D}'(w_a) \neq \widetilde{D}(w_a)$ and $\{z'_j\} \neq \{z_j\}$; (3) $\widetilde{D}'(w_a) \neq \widetilde{D}(w_a)$ and $\{z'_j\} = \{z_j\}$. We will show that the verification process does not hold with overwhelming probability.

(1) As $(C_D, C_I) \neq (C'_D, C'_I)$, the verification process does not hold with overwhelming probability.
(2) As $\{z'_j\} \neq \{z_j\}$, we can see that the verification of C_I will fail with a negligible probability under strong RSA assumption.
(3) As $\widetilde{D}'(w_a) \neq \widetilde{D}(w_a)$, this means that there exist some $(j, \widetilde{d}_j) \in \widetilde{D}'(w_a)$ and $(j, \widetilde{d}_j) \in \widetilde{D}(w_a)$ such that $\widetilde{d}'_j \neq \widetilde{d}_j$. For such $j, H(j, H(\widetilde{d}'_j)) \neq H(j, H(\widetilde{d}_j))$ because the collision resistance properties of hash function H. Hence the verification of C_D will fail with a negligible probability under strong RSA assumption because $P(H(j, H(\widetilde{d}'_j))) \neq P(H(j, H(\widetilde{d}_j)))$.

Based on the above analysis, the attacker can not forge valid authenticators. Thus our proposed scheme satisfies verifiability.

5 Conclusion

In this paper, we tackled the dynamic fuzzy keyword search problem in the scenario of a malicious server, which may forge or delete encrypted files. We first exploit Bloom filter and locality sensitive hashing to construct search index. In addition, RSA accumulator is used to time stamp the authenticators. We proposed a verifiable dynamic fuzzy search scheme in order to support dynamic fuzzy search and enjoys the verifiability of the searching result. Thorough theoretical security analysis, we demonstrated that our method is private, while correctly realizing the verifiable dynamic fuzzy keyword search.

Acknowledgments. This work is supported in part by the National Natural Science Foundation of China under Grant Numbers 61272151, 61472451 and 61402161, the International Science & Technology Cooperation Program of China under Grant Number 2013DFB10070, the China Hunan Provincial Science & Technology Program under Grant Number 2012GK4106, and the "Mobile Health" Ministry of Education - China Mobile Joint Laboratory (MOE-DST No. [2012]311).

References

1. Song, D.X., Wagner, D., Perrig, A.: Practical techniques for searches on encrypted data. In: Proceedings of the 2000 IEEE Symposium on Security and Privacy (S&P), pp. 44–55. IEEE (2000)
2. Wang, C., Cao, N., Li, J., Ren, K., Lou, W.: Secure ranked keyword search over encrypted cloud data. In: Distributed Computing Systems (ICDCS), pp. 253–262. IEEE (2010)

3. Boneh, D., Di Crescenzo, G., Ostrovsky, R., Persiano, G.: Public key encryption with keyword search. In: Cachin, C., Camenisch, J.L. (eds.) EUROCRYPT 2004. LNCS, vol. 3027, pp. 506–522. Springer, Heidelberg (2004)

4. Curtmola, R., Garay, J., Kamara, S., Ostrovsky, R.: Searchable symmetric encryption: improved definitions and efficient constructions. In: Proceedings of the 13th ACM Conference on Computer and Communications Security, pp. 79–88. ACM (2006)

5. Ning, C., Cong, W., Ming, L., Kui, R., Wenjing, L.: Privacy-preserving multi-keyword ranked search over encrypted cloud data. IEEE Trans. Parallel Distrib. Syst. **25**(1), 222–233 (2011)

6. Li, J., Wang, Q., Wang, C., Cao, N., Ren, K., Lou, W.: Fuzzy keyword search over encrypted data in cloud computing. In: Infocom, pp. 1–5. IEEE (2010)

7. Chuah, M., Hu, W.: Privacy-aware bedtree based solution for fuzzy multi-keyword search over encrypted data. In: Distributed Computing Systems Workshops (ICD-CSW), pp. 273–281. IEEE (2011)

8. Liu, C., Zhu, L., Li, L., Tan, Y.: Fuzzy keyword search on encrypted cloud storage data with small index. In: Cloud Computing and Intelligence Systems (CCIS), pp. 269–273. IEEE (2011)

9. Bing, W., Shucheng, Y., Wenjing, L., Hou, Y.T.: Privacy-preserving multi-keyword fuzzy search over encrypted data in the cloud. In: INFOCOM, pp. 2112–2120. IEEE (2014)

10. Wang, J., Ma, H., Tang, Q., Li, J., Zhu, H., Ma, S., Chen, X.: Efficient verifiable fuzzy keyword search over encrypted data in cloud computing. Comput. Sci. Inf. Syst. **10**(2), 667–684 (2013)

11. Sun, W., Wang, B., Cao, N., Li, M., Lou, W., Hou, Y.T., Li, H.: Verifiable privacy-preserving multi-keyword text search in the cloud supporting similarity-based ranking. IEEE Trans. Parallel Distrib. Syst. **25**(11), 3025–3035 (2014)

12. Kamara, S., Papamanthou, C., Roeder, T.: Dynamic searchable symmetric encryption. In: Proceedings of the 2012 ACM Conference on Computer and Communications Security, pp. 965–976. ACM (2012)

13. Kamara, S., Papamanthou, C.: Parallel and dynamic searchable symmetric encryption. In: Sadeghi, A.-R. (ed.) FC 2013. LNCS, vol. 7859, pp. 258–274. Springer, Heidelberg (2013)

14. Kurosawa, K., Ohtaki, Y.: UC-secure searchable symmetric encryption. In: Keromytis, A.D. (ed.) FC 2012. LNCS, vol. 7397, pp. 285–298. Springer, Heidelberg (2012)

15. Kurosawa, K., Ohtaki, Y.: How to update documents verifiably in searchable symmetric encryption. In: Abdalla, M., Nita-Rotaru, C., Dahab, R. (eds.) CANS 2013. LNCS, vol. 8257, pp. 309–328. Springer, Heidelberg (2013)

16. Bloom, B.H.: Space/time trade-offs in hash coding with allowable errors. Commun. ACM **13**(7), 422–426 (1970)

17. Indyk, P., Motwani, R.: Approximate nearest neighbors: towards removing the curse of dimensionality. In: Proceedings of the Thirtieth Annual ACM Symposium on Theory of Computing, pp. 604–613. ACM (1998)

18. Gennaro, R., Halevi, S., Rabin, T.: Secure hash-and-sign signatures without the random oracle. In: Stern, J. (ed.) EUROCRYPT 1999. LNCS, vol. 1592, pp. 123–139. Springer, Heidelberg (1999)

A Secure and Fine-Grained Query Results Verification Scheme for Private Search Over Encrypted Cloud Data

Hui Yin, Zheng Qin$^{(\boxtimes)}$, Jixin Zhang, Lu Ou, Qin Liu, Yupeng Hu,
and Huigui Rong

College of Computer Science and Electronic Engineering, Hunan University,
Changsha 410082, China
zqin@hnu.edu.cn

Abstract. In a secure query scheme over the encrypted cloud data, an authorized cloud user can obtain data files of interest by submitting encrypted query keywords to the cloud server, which performs a certain secure search algorithm and returns back the corresponding data file set. In practice, the returned query results may be incorrect or incomplete due to possible data corruption, software bugs, or intermediate attackers who maliciously tamper with results; moreover, the cloud server may also intentionally omit some qualified results to save computational resources and communication overhead. Thus, a well-functioning secure query system should provide the query results verification mechanism that allows the data user to verify results. In this paper, we design three varigrained and secure query results verification constructions leveraging the Bloom filter and cryptographic hash functions, for a query result set **R**, by which the data user can verify: (1) the correctness of each data file in **R**, (2) how many qualified data files are not returned by the cloud, and (3) which qualified data files are not returned by the cloud, respectively. Furthermore, our proposed verification mechanism can be very easily integrated into all secure query schemes for cloud computing. Performance evaluation shows that the proposed schemes are practical and efficient.

Keywords: Cloud computing · Privacy-preserving · Query results verification · Secure query · Verification object

1 Introduction

With the rapid development of cloud computing, more and more organizations and individuals are beginning to outsource their private data to cloud for enjoying IT cost savings, quick deployment, excellent computation performance, and on-demand high quality services. But, cloud, as a semi-trusted entity [1], are not fully trusted by its customers usually due to many reasons [2]. Thus, cloud customers are reluctant to outsource their sensitive data to cloud in the form of plaintext for data security. An effective solution is to encrypt data before outsourcing.

© Springer International Publishing Switzerland 2015
G. Wang et al. (Eds.): ICA3PP 2015, Part III, LNCS 9530, pp. 667–681, 2015.
DOI: 10.1007/978-3-319-27137-8_48

However, encrypted data make effective data retrieval and utilization a very challenging task. To solve encrypted data utilization problem, recently, many secure search schemes over the encrypted cloud data have been proposed [6–8,10–13], which aim to improve the query efficiency and retrieval accuracy, enhance query security, and enrich search functionalities such as multi-keyword queries and fuzzy keyword queries, etc. A popular system model of the secure search schemes over encrypted cloud data can be described as follows: a data owner outsources his/her data files and searchable indexes to the cloud server in the encrypted forms; later, an authorized data user submits some encrypted keywords (also called query trapdoor) to the cloud to request data files of interest; upon receiving the query trapdoors, the cloud server performs a certain secure search algorithm on the searchable indexes and returns the corresponding set of encrypted data files.

Under normal circumstances, the cloud server should return back all qualified query results for a given query submitted by the authorized data user. However, in practice, the returned query results may be incorrect or incomplete due to possible data corruption, software bugs, or intermediate attackers who maliciously tamper with query results; moreover, the cloud server may also intentionally omit some qualified results to save computational resources and communication overhead. Thus, a well-functioning secure query system should provide the query results verification mechanism to allow the data user to verify the results returned by the cloud.

Recently, some works [17–19] have studied the query results verification problem in the cloud computing environment. However, these verification schemes can only simply verify the correctness and completeness of the query result set, i.e., if the result set contains all qualified data files, then they simply reply *yes*, otherwise reply *no*. In practice, given a query result set $\mathbf{R}$ which may contain some incorrect results or have been tampered with by attackers partly, the data user needs to verify the correctness of each file in $\mathbf{R}$ (In fact, by this verification operation, the user data can remove incorrect results and retain the correct data files as his/her part results.) or wishes to further check how many or which qualified data files are not returned on earth if the cloud server intentionally omits some query results. In addition, these previous verification techniques are closely related with respective specific secure query schemes.

To allow a data user to more accurately verify his/her query results, in this paper, we design three kinds of privacy-preserving verification constructions (called *Verification Object*) VO-I, VO-II, and VO-III based on the Bloom filter according to the different verification requirements. More specifically, VO-I allows data users to verify the correctness of each data file in a query result set, VO-II allows data users to verify how many qualified data files are not returned by the cloud, and VO-III allows data users to further verify which qualified data files are not returned by the cloud, respectively. Furthermore, our proposed verification scheme can be very easily integrated into all secure query schemes for cloud computing and has nothing to do with the concrete query construction.

2   Related Work

Secure search schemes over the encrypted cloud data allow an authorized cloud data user to search the data owner's outsourced data by submitting some query trapdoors to the cloud server. Many schemes have been proposed to support flexible search operations in the cloud computing environment, however, these schemes do not provide an effective mechanism that allows data users to verify the returned query results.

Researchers have proposed some query results verification schemes [14–16] in the plaintext database scenario. However, these schemes do not consider keyword privacy and are not suitable for secure query scenario. In encrypted data search scenario, in [17], Wang et al. applied hash chain technique to implement a privacy preserving query results verification scheme by embedding the encrypted verification information into their proposed secure searchable index. In [19], Sun et al. used encrypted index tree structure to implement secure query results verification functionality. In this scheme, when the query ends, the cloud server returns query results along with a minimum encrypted index tree, then the data user searches this minimum index tree using the same search algorithm as the cloud server did to finish result verification. Zheng et al. [18] constructed a verifiable secure query scheme over encrypted cloud data based on attribute-based encryption technique (ABE) in the public-key setting. However, these secure verification schemes can only simply check the correctness and completeness of query result set and cannot achieve our proposed verification goals described in Sect. 1 of our paper. Furthermore, these techniques work only under the specific query algorithm and index construction and are not suitable for all secure query schemes for the cloud computing.

In this paper, our objective is to present a secure and privacy-preserving query results verification scheme that achieves our proposed verification requirements and can be very easily integrated into all secure query schemes over encrypted cloud data.

3   Problem Formulation

3.1   System Model

Figure 1 shows the overall system architecture. To guarantee the confidentiality of outsourced data files and enforce the secure query over the encrypted data, generally, the data owner first encrypts the data file set and builds a secure searchable index for data files. In this paper, the data owner also needs to construct the secure *Verification Object* set that allows his/her authorized users to verify their query results. Finally, the data owner outsources the encrypted data file set, the secure searchable indexes, and the secure *Verification Object* set to the cloud server. To search over the encrypted data files, an authorized data user summits a query trapdoor to the cloud server. Upon receiving the query trapdoor, the cloud server performs a secure query algorithm over the searchable indexes and returns matched data files along with a *Verification Object* VO to

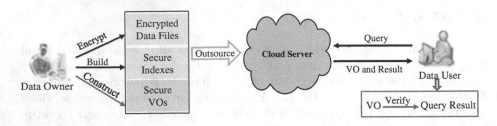

Fig. 1. A system model of secure search and result verification for cloud computing

the data user. The data user verifies query results via VO in client. It is worth emphasizing that, in this paper, we only focus on the query results verification mechanism and the secure query schemes please refer to [6–8,10–13].

3.2 Problem Definition

In this subsection, we further state our proposed problem and define some notations to be used in our paper.

Let $\mathbb{F} = \{F_1, \ldots, F_n\}$ be a set of data files and $\mathbb{W} = \{w_1, \ldots, w_d\}$ be a set of keywords. Generally, for the confidentiality of data, the data owner adopt any semantically secure encryption scheme such as DES or AES to encrypted each $F \in \mathbb{F}$, the ciphertext set of $\mathbb{F}$ can be denoted as $\mathbb{C} = \{C_1, \ldots, C_n\}$. We use w to denote any keyword in $\mathbb{W}$ and $\mathbf{F}(w)$ to denote the set of data files which contain the keyword w and use $\mathbf{C}(w)$ to represent the corresponding ciphertext set of $\mathbf{F}(w)$, $|\mathbf{C}(w)|$ refers to the cardinality of $\mathbf{C}(w)$. Given a query using the keyword $w \in \mathbb{W}$, the cloud server returns the query result set $\mathbf{R}(w)$ to the data user. Theoretically, the two sets $\mathbf{C}(w)$ and $\mathbf{R}(w)$ should be identical. However, the result set $\mathbf{R}$ may be incomplete or contain some incorrect data due to many reasons described in the introduction section. To allow the data user to verify the result set $\mathbf{R}$, our main idea is that the data owner constructs a secure *Verification Object* $\mathrm{OV}(w_i)$ for each set $\mathbf{C}(w_i), 1 \leq i \leq d$. Given a query using a keyword w, the cloud serve returns both the query result set $\mathbf{R}(w)$ and the corresponding *Verification Object* $\mathrm{VO}(w)$. In this paper, we construct three kinds of *Verification Object* VO-I, VO-II, and VO-III to satisfy different verification requirements. In addition, the constructed $\mathrm{VO}(w)$ should be privacy preserving, through which the cloud cannot infer and obtain any useful information, such as the plaintext of the keyword w, the number of the data file contained each set $\mathbf{C}(w)$, the contents of data files, etc.

4   VO Construction and Query Results Verification

To maximize reduce storage cost and communication cost, implement query results verification functions, and achieve privacy guarantee, in this paper, we will utilize the space-efficient probabilistic data structure Bloom filter [3] and the collision-resistant pseudo random function (sometimes called cryptographic hash function) [9] to construct our *verification object*s and make them practical and privacy preserving.

4.1 VO-I Construction and Verification

In this subsection, we propose the first *Verification Object* VO-I, for a query result set $\mathbf{R}(w)$, which allows the data user to verify the correctness of each data file in $\mathbf{R}(w)$.

Construction. Given a set $\mathbf{C}(w)$, $w \in \mathbb{W}$, the data owner first generates an m bit array denoted by $\mathrm{VO}(w)$ representing the Bloom filter. Then, for each encrypted file C in $\mathbf{C}(w)$, he/she computes the Hash Message Authentication Code (HMAC) using a secure and collision-resistant hash function with the key k which is shared by the data owner and the data users, denoted as HMAC(k,C), and then chooses l independent hash functions $h_1, h_2, \ldots, h_l$ with the same range [0, m-1] to hash the value HMAC(k,C), and set $\mathrm{VO}(w)[h_i(\mathrm{HMAC}(k,\mathrm{C}))]$ $(1 \leq i \leq l)$ to be 1. So far, our basic idea is to let the Bloom filter $\mathrm{VO}(w)$ be the *verification object* of the set $\mathbf{C}(w)$; later, we will discuss that how to verify query results via $\mathrm{VO}(w)$. For each $\mathbf{C}(w_i), w_i \in \mathbb{W}, 1 \leq i \leq d$, the data owner repeatedly performs the above same operations respectively to construct the *verification object* set $\mathbf{OV}(\mathbb{W}) = \{\mathrm{OV}(w_i)|w_i \in \mathbb{W}, 1 \leq i \leq d\}$. Here, the HMAC-MD5 [5] is a good implementation for HMAC.

Padding. From the *Verification Object* construction, we can observe that the total number of 1 s contained each array $\mathrm{VO}(w)$ is closely related with the size of the set $\mathbf{C}(w)$. For example, for two different keywords w_i and w_j $(1 \leq i, j \leq d, i \neq j)$, the $\mathrm{VO}(w_i)$ may have less 1 s than $\mathrm{VO}(w_j)$ due to $|\mathbf{C}(w_i)| < |\mathbf{C}(w_j)|$, which brings a certain degree of statistical meaning. The cloud may be able to guess the number of data files that contain the keyword w by statistically analyzing the number of 1 s in the array $\mathrm{VO}(w)$. To eliminate the statical character and avoid revealing the number of distinct data files in $\mathbf{C}(w)$, we let the total number of 1 s in each $\mathrm{VO}(w)$ be equal to a const by doing the following operations. First, the data owner set an upper bound value max. Second, for each $\mathrm{VO}(w)$ in $\mathbf{VO}(\mathbb{W})$, if $\sum_{j=0}^{m-1}\mathrm{VO}(w)[j] < max$, the data owner randomly chooses $max - \sum_{j=0}^{m-1}\mathrm{VO}(w)[j]$ positions of value 0 and sets all these positions to be 1. Now, all VOs in $\mathbf{VO}(\mathbb{W})$ contain the same number of 1 s by the above padding. Figure 2 shows an example of VO-I.

Verification. Now, we discuss how to verify the correctness of query results according to the returned $\mathbf{R}(w)$ and $\mathrm{VO}(w)$ when using the keyword w to query. After receiving $\mathbf{R}(w)$ and $\mathrm{VO}(w)$, the data user takes the following steps to verify the correctness of each encrypted data file C $\in \mathbf{R}(w)$. First, the

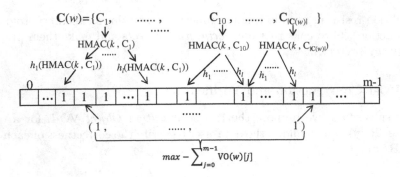

Fig. 2. Example VO-I construction

data user uses the shared key k to compute the Hash Message Authentication Code as HMAC(k,C). Second, he uses the l hash functions $h_1,\ldots,h_l$ to compute $h_1(\text{HMAC}(k,\text{C})),\ldots,h_l(\text{HMAC}(k,\text{C})$ and checks all these positions in VO(w). The data file C is regarded as a correct query result if all l positions $h_1(\text{HMAC}(k,\text{C})),\ldots,h_l(\text{HMAC}(k,\text{C}))$ are 1. Otherwise, the data user can conclude that the data file C is an incorrect query result or may have been tampered with by attackers.

About False Positive. It is worth noticing that our proposed verification method may allow an incorrect query result to pass the correctness checking due to the fact that Bloom filter may yield false positives with a certain probability because of hash collisions. Fortunately, we can adjust the Bloom filter parameters to minimize the false positive rate. More specifically, in this paper, given the bit length of each verification object VO(w) m and the number of data files that are inserted into corresponding VO(w), i.e., $|\mathbf{C}(w)|$, we set the number of hash functions l to be $\frac{m}{|\mathbf{C}(w)|} \times \ln 2$ to minimize the false positive rate to be:

$$1 - (1 - \frac{1}{m})^{l|\mathbf{C}(w)|} \approx (1 - e^{-l|\mathbf{C}(w)|/m})^l = 2^{-l} \approx 0.6185^{m/|\mathbf{C}(w)|}$$

However, the set size $|\mathbf{C}(w_i)|$ is different for different $\mathbf{C}(w_i), w_i \in \mathbb{W}, 1 \leq i \leq d$, to choose the same number of hash functions l for all VOs in $\mathbf{VO}(\mathbb{W})$, we set

$$l = \frac{m}{|\mathbf{C}(w)|_{max}} \times \ln 2$$

where $|\mathbf{C}(w)|_{max}$ is the maximum number of data files containing keyword w, i.e., $|\mathbf{C}(w)|_{max} = \max_{i=1}^{d}|\mathbf{C}(w_i)|, w_i \in \mathbb{W}$. Thus, for any set $\mathbf{C}(w')$ that satisfies $|\mathbf{C}(w')| < |\mathbf{C}(w)|_{max}$, the false positive rate incurred by the corresponding VO(w') is less than $0.6185^{m/|\mathbf{C}(w)|_{max}}$. For example, when $m = 500$ and $|\mathbf{C}(w)|_{max} = 50$, the probability that an incorrect query result may pass user verification is about 8.192×10^{-3}, this is acceptable for data users in practice.

4.2   VO-II Construction and Verification

Obviously, VO-I can only enforces the correctness verification of query result set, the completeness verification of query results still keeps a challenge. In this subsection, we address this problem that data users wish to verify that how many qualified data files are not returned by the cloud when the cloud omits some data files intentionally or maliciously.

Construction. Similarly, we wish to construct an effective *verification object* VO-II based on the Bloom filter and HMAC to be suitable for this application scenario. Intuitively, the VO-II should be able to conserve the information of the number of data files in $\mathbf{C}(w)$, i.e., $|\mathbf{C}(w)|$, and allows the data user to capture the number of data files which are not returned by the cloud according to query result set $\mathbf{R}(w)$. However, the standard Bloom filter does not work well anymore since its each bit cannot record hash collision times when inserting elements using different hash functions. Fortunately, we can achieve the design goal easily by using the counting Bloom filters [4]. The counting Bloom filters use a fixed size counter to substitute a bit to represent each entry. When inserting an element using l hash functions, the corresponding counters are increased by 1. Specifically, the data owner first generates a counting Bloom filter VO(w) with m counters for $\mathbf{C}(w)$. For each encrypted file C in $\mathbf{C}(w)$, he uses a key k to calculate HMAC(k, C), and then uses hash functions $h_1, \ldots, h_l$ to map the value HMAC(k, C) and the corresponding counter VO$(w)[h_i(\mathrm{HMAC}(k, \mathrm{C}))]$ is increased by 1.

Padding. To avoid revealing the number of data files in $\mathbf{C}(w)$ through VO(w), the data owner pads each VO(w) as follows. First, the data owner expands the original m counters to n counters. Second, let $|\mathbf{C}(w)|_{max}$ be the maximum number of data files of all the $\mathbf{C}(w_i), 1 \leq i \leq d$, for each VO$(w)$ in $\mathbf{VO}(\mathbb{W})$, the data owner generates $l \times |\mathbf{C}(w)|_{max} - \sum_{j=0}^{m-1} \mathrm{VO}(w)[j]$ random strings $\{R_1, R_2, \ldots\}$. Finally, he uses an one-way hash function h' with the range $[m, n]$ to compute each random string R and the corresponding VO$(w)[h'(R)]$ is increased by 1. Now, each VO(w) in $\mathbf{VO}(\mathbb{W})$ satisfies:

$$\sum_{j=0}^{n} \mathrm{VO}(w)[j] = l \times |\mathbf{C}(w)|_{max}$$

Figure 3 is an example of VO-II construction.

Verification. The data user can now check how many qualified data files are not returned by the cloud via VO(w) and $\mathbf{R}(w)$ when he uses the keyword w to query. The verification process includes the following three steps. First, the data user removes the incorrect query results from $\mathbf{R}(w)$. In particular, for each result C $\in \mathbf{R}(w)$, the data user uses the shared key k and the l hash functions $h_1, \ldots, h_l$ to calculate $h_1(\mathrm{HMAC}(k, \mathrm{C})), \ldots, h_l(\mathrm{HMAC}(k, \mathrm{C}))$ and then checks all

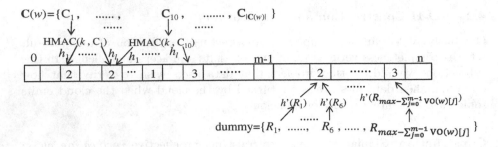

Fig. 3. Example VO-II construction

these counters in $VO(w)$. If one of them is 0, the C is regarded as an incorrect query result and should be removed from $\mathbf{R}(w)$. Second, if $|\mathbf{R}(w)| \neq 0$, for each correct query result C, he calculates $h_1(\text{HMAC}(k, C)), \ldots, h_l(\text{HMAC}(k, C))$ and the corresponding counter $VO(w)[h_i(\text{HMAC}(k, C))](i = 1, 2, \ldots, l)$ is decreased by 1. Finally, the data user calculates the following value:

$$Rem = \frac{(\sum_{j=0}^{m-1} VO(w)[j])}{l}$$

If $Rem = 0$, this indicates that it is a completeness query and the cloud server has returned back all qualified data files; otherwise, the data user can confirm that the cloud have omitted Rem qualified data files in this query.

Storage Space. In addition, the bit length of each counter in VO should be discussed adequately, because the enough large VO will bring heavy storage cost and communication cost, which makes the *verification object* impractical. According to [4], generally, the 4 bits for each counter are sufficient. We give a simple derivation and more detailed analysis please refer to [4]. Theoretically, the probability that the i-th counter has been increased by j times, when inserting the set $\mathbf{C}(w), 1 \leq i \leq m, w \in \mathbb{W}$ using l hash functions, can be denoted:

$$Pr(c(i) = j) = \binom{|\mathbf{C}(w)|l}{j} \left(\frac{1}{m}\right)^j \left(1 - \frac{1}{m}\right)^{|\mathbf{C}(w)|l - j}$$

According to the Stirling's approximation, the probability that any counter is greater or equal j is:

$$Pr(c(i) \geq j) \leq \binom{|\mathbf{C}(w)|l}{j} \left(\frac{1}{m^j}\right) \leq \left(\frac{e|\mathbf{C}(w)|l}{jm}\right)^j$$

To minimize the false positive rate, we set $l = \frac{m}{|\mathbf{C}(w)|} \times \ln 2$ and further simplify the above inequality:

$$pr(c(i) \geq j) \leq m \left(\frac{e \ln 2}{j}\right)^j$$

Hence, if we set the bit length of each counter to be 4, obviously, when $j = 16$, the counter happens overflow and the probability can be calculated as $pr(c(i) \geq 16) \leq 1.37 \times 10^{-15} \times m$. Obviously, the value is infinitesimal and the probability of happening overflow can be ignored for our VO-II.

4.3 VO-III Construction and Verification

In this subsection, we will further improve the construction and enable it to allow the data user to definitely verify which data files are not returned when the cloud server have omitted some qualified query results.

Generally, file identifier is used to exclusively represent a specific data file. Thus, our idea is to construct the VO(w) for set $\mathbf{C}(w)$ based on the counting Bloom filter which stores the file identifiers of all data files in $\mathbf{C}(w)$. However, there is still a key challenge that how to define the identifier of a data file such that the data user can obtain the identifier information of encrypted data file according to returned $\mathbf{R}(w)$ and VO(w). Simply numbering for a data file as its identifier is infeasible, because there is not any association between the identifier and the corresponding encrypted data file such that the data user cannot obtain effective identifier according to encrypted file. To achieve the goal, i.e., the data user should be able to confirm the identifier of a data file from its encrypted version, we define the identifier of a data file F as follows:

$$ID(\text{F}) = PRF(k_1, \text{C})$$

where C is the ciphertext of F, PRF is a collision-resistant pseudo random function, and k_1 is a secret key shared between the data owner and the authorized data users. The PRF defined as $PRF : \{0,1\}^* \times K_1 \to \{0,1\}^s$ where K_1 is the key space. In addition, it is worth emphasizing that the collision-resistant property of the PRF is necessary for generating exclusive identifier for each different data file, i.e., it is computationally infeasible to find two distinct ciphertexts c_1 and c_2 such that $PRF(k_1, c_1) = PRF(k_1, c_2)$.

Construction. We design the OV-III based on the counting Bloom filter, by which the data user can verify which data files are not returned by the cloud server. To record all the encrypted files in $\mathbf{C}(w)$ and their corresponding file identifiers, the VO(w) consists of two arrays a and b. The a array is a counting Bloom filter with m counters and the b is an array of m pointers that each pointer points to a linked list for storing the file identifiers. More specifically, for each encrypted file C in $\mathbf{C}(w)$, the data owner first uses a secret key k to calculate HMAC(k, C), and then applies the l hash functions $h_1, \ldots, h_l$ on HMAC(k, C) to map them to l different positions of a and b arrays. For array a, the $a[h_i(\text{HMAC}(k, \text{C}))](i = 1, 2, \ldots, l)$ is increased by 1. For array b, the data owner generates a node that stores the identifier $PRF(k_1, \text{C})$ of C and appends the node to the linked list that $b[h_i(\text{HMAC}(k, \text{C}))](i = 1, 2, \ldots, l)$ points to.

Obviously, each VO(w) requires l nodes to store the same file identifiers at the l different linked lists for each file C $\in \mathbf{C}(w)$ and thus the whole VO(w) requires

$l \times |\mathbf{C}(w)|$ nodes to store file id information, the huge amount of duplicates lead
to the sharp increment of the storage size of the $\mathrm{VO}(w)$. Intuitively, using only
one node to store the file identifier of C at one linked list is enough for our VO-
III. Hence, we may reduce the $l - 1$ nodes for each C to greatly compress the
size. In fact, it can be easily achieved by the following operations. For each data
file $\mathrm{C} \in \mathbf{C}(w)$, we only choose one position from $h_i(\mathrm{HMAC}(k, \mathrm{C})), i = (1, 2, \ldots, l)$
in the array a, for example the position $a[h_1(\mathrm{HMAC}(k, \mathrm{C})]$, and generate a node
that stores the identifier $PRF(k_1, \mathrm{C})$ of C and append the node to the linked
list that $b[h_1(\mathrm{HMAC}(k, \mathrm{C}))]$ points to. When verifying, the data user performs
one time node delete operation by removing the node that stores $PRF(k_1, \mathrm{C})$
from the linked list that $b[h_1(\mathrm{HMAC}(k, \mathrm{C}))]$ points to.

Padding. Obviously, in the VO-III, the attacker can statistically obtain the
number of data files contained in each $\mathrm{VO}(w)$ by two ways. One is to access
the array a, the other is to accumulate the total number of nodes that store
file identifiers in array b. To hide this information, the padding operation for
$\mathrm{VO}(w)$ is necessary. First, the data owner expands the size of arrays a and
b from m to n. Second, for each $\mathrm{VO}(w)$ in $\mathbf{VO}(\mathbb{W})$, the data owner generates
$l \times |\mathbf{C}(w)|_{max} - \sum_{j=0}^{m-1} \mathrm{VO}(w)[j]$ random strings $\{R_1, R_2, \ldots \ldots\}$. Third, for each
random string R, he computes $h'(R)$, $PRF(k_1, R)$ and generates a node *node*
to store the value $PRF(k_1, R)$; the corresponding counter $a[h'(R)]$ is increased
by 1 and *node* is appended to the linked list that $b[h'(R)]$ points to. Figure 4
shows a simple example. Assume that there are only three data files $\hat{\mathrm{C}}, \tilde{\mathrm{C}}, \bar{\mathrm{C}}$ that
contain a certain keyword w, i.e., $\mathbf{C}(w) = \{\hat{\mathrm{C}}, \tilde{\mathrm{C}}, \bar{\mathrm{C}}\}$, and the data files $\hat{\mathrm{F}}, \tilde{\mathrm{F}}, \bar{\mathrm{F}}$
are corresponding plaintext of $\hat{\mathrm{C}}, \tilde{\mathrm{C}}, \bar{\mathrm{C}}$.

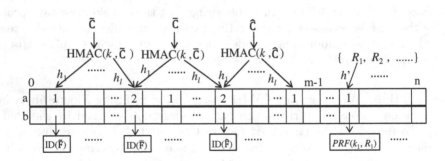

Fig. 4. Example VO-III construction

Verification. An authorized data user can find out which data files are not
returned by the cloud via the following three steps. First, the data user removes
incorrect query results from $\mathbf{R}(w)$ via correctness verification. Second, if $\mathbf{R}(w) \neq$
0, for each correct query result $\mathrm{C} \in \mathbf{R}(w)$, the data user uses the shared secret key
k_1 to calculate the file identifier $\mathrm{ID(F)} = PRF(k_1, \mathrm{C})$, where F is the plaintext

of C, and uses shared secret key k and l hash functions $h_i(i = 1, 2, \ldots, l)$ to calculate $h_i(\text{HMAC}(k, \text{C}))(i = 1, 2, \ldots, l)$. Third, this step includes two operations: (1) for every $1 \leq i \leq l$, the $a[h_i(\text{HMAC}(k, \text{C}))]$ is decreased by 1; (2) for $i = 1$, the data owner delete the node that stores $\text{ID}(\text{F}) = PRF(k_1, \text{C})$ from the linked list that $b[h_1(\text{HMAC}(k, \text{C}))]$ points to. Finally, the data owner checks the array $b[j], (0 \leq j \leq m-1)$, and obtains the identifiers of data files that are not returned by the cloud.

In addition, similar to VO-I and VO-II, the number of hash functions is set $l = \frac{m}{|C(w)|_{max}} \times \ln 2$ to minimize the false positives and the bit length of each counter in the counting Bloom filter is set 4 bits. However, it requires more storage space to store file identifiers and dummy nodes.

5   Securely Obtain the Verification Object

Another important question is that how to obtain the correct *Verification Object* from the set $\mathbf{OV}(\mathbb{W}) = \{\text{OV}(w_i)|w_i \in \mathbb{W}, 1 \leq i \leq d\}$ without leaking any useful information to the cloud server. To obtain the *Verification Object*, a simple way is to use an array to store the keywords and their corresponding *Verification Object*, in which each element consists of two fields, the first field stores the keyword $w \in \mathbb{W}$ and the second field is a pointer that points to the corresponding $\text{VO}(w)$. When the data user wishes the cloud server to return the $\text{VO}(w)$ for the specified keyword w, he submits the keyword w and let the cloud server search on the array. However, the straightforward method compromises the security and privacy of whole secure query system due to the *Verification Object* from two aspects. One is that the query keywords of the data user are leaked (i.e., query privacy); the other is that the cloud server knows the associations between the keywords and *Verification Objects* that allow the cloud to infer some useful information about outsourced data files.

For privacy, we eliminate the two security risks by encrypting keywords using another collision-resistant pseudo random function $\overline{PRF}$ and randomly storing their corresponding *Verification Object* using a hash table T of size v, where $\overline{PRF} : \{0,1\}^* \times K_2 \to [0, v - 1]$ which hashes any string to the range $[0, v - 1]$

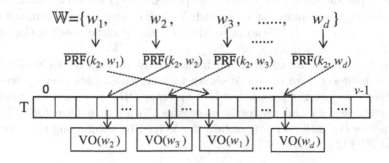

Fig. 5. Representing of *Verification Object* in the cloud server

under a given secret key $k_2 \in K_2$, and K_2 is the key space. More specifically, for each keyword w in $\mathbb{W}$, the data owner computes $\overline{PRF}(k_2, w)$ and uses the element $T[\overline{PRF}(k_2, w)]$ to point to the storage address of the Verification Object $VO(w)$. Figure 5 shows the construction. Suppose that a data user needs to obtain the $VO(w)$ when he uses the keyword w to query, the data user first computes $\overline{PRF}(k_2, w)$ and then submits the value to cloud server; the cloud accesses the hash table T and takes the $VO(w)$ from the position $T[\overline{PRF}(k_2, w)]$. Thus, the cloud sever now cannot gain any plaintext message of the query keyword w as long as the key k_2 is kept secret.

6   Security Analysis

Intuitively, the security of the *Verification Object* aims to capture the notion that an adversary $\mathcal{A}$ cannot deduce a file's contents from its *Verification Object*. Similar to the secure index, a more rigorous security definition is the *Verification Object* indistinguishability, which is defined as that, given two VOs of two different data file set, any probabilistic polynomial time adversary $\mathcal{A}$ (e.g., the cloud server) cannot distinguish which VO is for which data file set with probability non-negligible different from $1/2$.

Essentially, our constructed *Verification Object*s are Bloom filters which do not contain any information of data files and keywords, by which the cloud cannot obtain any useful contents. Moreover, to achieve the indistinguishability, for each data file $C \in \mathbf{C}(w)$, before inserting the C into the Bloom filter $VO(w)$, we first compute the hash message authentication code $HMAC(k, C)$ under the secret key k. Obviously, the cloud server cannot obtain the random value $HMAC(k, C)$ as long as the key k is kept secret and thus cannot determine the l positions representing C in $VO(w)$ using the hash functions $h_1, \ldots, h_l$. Hence, given two sets $\mathbf{C}(w), \mathbf{C}(w')$ with the same cardinality and their *Verification Object*s $VO(w), VO(w')$, the cloud server cannot distinguish which *Verification Object* is for which set with probability non-negligible different from $1/2$. For the VO-III, besides the Bloom filter, it contains data file identifiers which are encrypted adopting the pseudo random function PRF under the key k_1, the indistinguishability of pseudo random function $PRF(k_1, \cdot)$ guarantees semantic security of file identifiers. In addition, to prevent the cloud server from statistically analyzing the number of 1 s in each $VO(w)$ to evaluate the number of the data files in $\mathbf{C}(w)$, each $VO(w)$ is padded by adding some random elements to eliminate the statistical meaning.

At last, in order to allow an authorized data user to securely obtain the *Verification Object* from the cloud server without leaking his query privacy, for each $VO(w)$, we use the pseudo random function $\overline{PRF}$ to encrypt the keyword w under the key k_2 and randomly store the $VO(w)$ to a hash table T while the data user can still correctly obtain the $VO(w)$ by submitting the encrypted keyword $\overline{PRF}(k_2, w)$.

7 Experiment Evaluation

In this paper, we only implement our proposed OV-I, OV-II, and OV-III regardless of secure query schemes.

We perform experiments on the real data set RFC (Request for Comments Database) [20], which contains 7352 text files with the total size 358 M. We adopt Java language to implement all programs that are performed on an Inter Core 2 Duo 2.26 GHZ computer with 3 GB RAM running Windows 7.

To test the time cost of constructing VO-I, VO-II, and VO-III, we extract all data files that contain the keyword *network* from RFC to generate the set $\mathbf{F}(network)$ and use AES to encrypt $\mathbf{F}(network)$ to get the ciphertext set $\mathbf{C}(network)$ which contains 6895 encrypted text files.

We use HMAC-MD5 to compute the Hash Message Authentication Code for each file in $\mathbf{C}(network)$. For the Bloom filter, we set $m = 40000$ and choose the optimal number of hash functions to be $l = \ln 2 \times (40000/6895) = 0.693 \times 5.8013 = 4$. About padding operations, for simplicity, assume that 100 extra elements need to be padded. For VO-II and VO-III we expand the counters of Bloom filter from 40000 to 40499 and pad 100 random elements to $VO(network)$ according to respective padding way.

Table 1 shows the time cost of VO-I, VO-II, and VO-III with the same experimental settings and data. We can observe that the most time-consuming operation is to compute the Hash Message Authentication Code for set $\mathbf{C}(network)$ which contains some large size data files, inserting the Hash Message Authentication into Bloom filters and padding operations do almost not consume time. For VO-III, compared with VO-I and VO-II, a bit more time is required due to creating and appending nodes of data file identifiers.

To test the verification time, for simplicity, we skip the secure query processes and artificially construct a query result set $\mathbf{R}(network)$ by deleting 1800 data files and tampering with 95 data files from the set $\mathbf{C}(network)$. Now, the $\mathbf{R}(network)$ contain 5000 correct data files and 95 incorrect data files.

Table 1. Construction time of VO-I, VO-II, and VO-III

Veification object	HMAC (ms)	Inserting (ms)	Padding (ms)	Total time (ms)
VO-I	24067	15	<1	24082
VO-II	23972	17	<1	23989
VO-III	24104	156	5	24260

Table 2. Verification time and storage space of VO-I, VO-II, and VO-III

Veification object	Verification time (ms)	Storage space (KB)
VO-I	17082	$m/(8 \times 1024)$
VO-II	17087	$4(n + 1)/(8 \times 1024)$
VO-III	17127	$[4(n + 1) + s \times (|\mathbf{C}(w)| + r)]/(8 \times 1024)$

Table 2 shows the verification time cost and storage space of VO-I, VO-II, and VO-III. We can observe the verification time of three *Verification Objects* is very close. In fact, the most time-consuming operation is still to compute the Hash Message Authentication Code for set $\mathbf{R}(network)$. In addition, the VO-I consumes least space storage m bits; VO-II is composed of $n + 1$ counters; Besides containing $n + 1$ counters like VO-II, VO-III also needs to $s \times (|\mathbf{C}|(w) + r)$ bits to represent file identifiers and some random nodes for padding, where r is the number of random nodes.

8   Conclusion

In this paper, we propose three effective verification schemes over encrypted query result set, by which an authorized data user can accurately verify query results returned by the cloud server according to different verification requirements in a privacy-preserving fashion. Our proposed verification constructions can be very easily integrated into all secure query schemes for cloud computing and have nothing to do with concrete secure query schemes. In terms of security, our *Verification Object* does not leak any additional information of outsourced data files and keywords to the cloud server. Performance experiments on the real data set demonstrate the validity and high efficiency of our proposed scheme.

Acknowledgments. The research is supported by the National Natural Science Foundation of China under Grant Nos. 61272546, 61472131, 61402161, 61572181, and 61300218.

References

1. Canetti, R., Feige, U., Goldreich, O., Naor, M.: Adaptively secure multi-part computation. In: Proceedings of the 28th ACM Symposium on Theory of Computing (STOC), pp. 639–648. ACM (1996)
2. Mather, T., Kumaraswamy, S., Latif, S.: Cloud Security and Privacy: An Enterprise Perspective on Risks and Compliance. OReilly Media, Sebastopol (2009)
3. Bloom, B.: Space/time trade-offs in hash coding with allowable errors. Commun. ACM **13**(7), 422–426 (1970)
4. Fan, L., Cao, P., Almeida, J., Broder, A.Z.: Summary cache: a scalable wide area web cache sharing protocol. SIGCOMM Comput. Commun. Rev. **28**(4), 254–265 (1998)
5. Krawczyk, H., Bellare, M., Canetti, R.: HMAC: keyed-hashing for message authentication. RFC 2104 (1997)
6. Li, J.: Fuzzy keyword search over encrypted data in cloud computing. In: Proceedings of INFOCOM Mini-Conference (2010)
7. Wang, C., Cao, N., Li, J., Ren, K., Lou, W.: Secure ranked keyword search over encrypted cloud data. In: ICDCS, pp. 253–262 (2010)
8. Li, M., Yu, S., Cao, N., Lou, W.: Authorized private keyword search over encrypted data in cloud computing. In: Proceedings of the International Conference on Distributed Computing Systems, ICDCS11, pp. 383–392 (2011)

9. Bellare, M., Rogaway, P.: Introduction to Modern Cryptography. Lecture Notes (2001)
10. Cao, N., Wang, C., Li, M., Ren, K., Lou, W.: Privacy-preserving multi-keyword ranked search over encrypted cloud data. In: INFOCOM, pp. 829–837 (2011)
11. Lu, Y.: Privacy-preserving logarithmic-time search on ecnypted data in cloud. In: NDSS (2012)
12. Sun, W., Wang, B., Cao, N., Li, M., Lou, W., Hou, T., Li, H.: Privacy-preserving multi-keyword text search in the cloud supporting similarity-based ranking. In: ASIACCS (2013)
13. Wang, B., Yu, S., Lou, W., Hou, Y.T.: Privacy-preserving multi-keyword fuzzy search over encrypted data in the cloud. In: Proceedings of IEEE INFOCOM, pp. 2112–2120 (2014)
14. Benabbas, S., Gennaro, R., Vahlis, Y.: Verifiable delegation of computation over large datasets. In: Rogaway, P. (ed.) CRYPTO 2011. LNCS, vol. 6841, pp. 111–131. Springer, Heidelberg (2011)
15. Papamanthou, C., Shi, E., Tamassia, R.: Signatures of correct computation. Cryptology ePrint Archive, Report 2011/587. Springer, Berlin (2011). http://eprint.iacr.org/
16. Fiore, D., Gennaro, R.: Publicly verifiable delegation of large polynomials and matrix computations, with applications. In: Proceedings of ACM CCS, pp. 501–512 (2012)
17. Wang, C., Cao, N., Ren, K., Lou, W.: Enabling secure and efficient ranked keyword search over outsourced cloud data. IEEE Trans. Parallel Distrib. Syst. 23(8), 1467–1479 (2012)
18. Zheng, Q.J., Xu, S.H., Ateniese, G.: VABKS: verifiable attribute-based keyword search over outsourced encrypted data. In: Proceedings of IEEE INFOCOM, pp. 522–530 (2014)
19. Sun, W., Wang, B., Cao, N., Li, M., Lou, W., Hou, T., Li, H.: Verifiable privacy-preserving multi-keyword text search in the cloud supporting similarity-based ranking. IEEE Trans. Parallel Distrib. Syst. 25(11), 522–530 (2014)
20. RFC: Request for Comments Database. http://www.ietf.org/rfc.html

PEM4RFID: Privacy Enhancement Model for RFID Systems

Guangquan Xu$^{(\boxtimes)}$, Yuanyuan Ren, Bin Liu, Gaoxu Zhang,
Xiaohong Li, and Zhiyong Feng

School of Computer Science and Technology,
Tianjin University, Tianjin 300350, China
losin@tju.edu.cn

Abstract. With the wider application of radio frequency identification (RFID) technology in various vital systems, more and more privacy threats and security flaws have been emerging. Traditional RFID systems only focus attention on foundational implementation, which lacks privacy protection and effective identity authentication. To solve the privacy protection problem of RFID systems,this paper proposes PEM4RFID privacy enhancement model FOR RFID: a "2 + 2" identity authentication mechanism, which includes a two-factor authentication protocol (TFAP) based on "two-way authentication". Our TFAP adopts "hardware information + AES-ECC encryption" method, and while the "two-way authentication" is based on improved combined public key (CPK). Case study shows that our proposed PEM4RFID has characteristics of untraceability and nonrepeatability of instructions, which realizes a good trade-off between privacy and security in RFID systems.

Keywords: Privacy enhancement model (PEM) · Radio frequency identification (RFID) · Combined public key (CPK) · Two-Factor authentication protocol (TFAP) · Two-way authentication

1 Introduction

Radio frequency identification (RFID) is one of the most important technologies in the 21st century, which is a perfect combination of wireless communication technology and automatic identification technology [1, 2]. RFID can not only achieve non-contact and rapid multi-target recognition, but the recognition effect is almost uninfluenced by many kinds of bad environment. RFID is widely used in all kinds of public systems which are closely related to privacy, such as the second generation ID card of residents, IC card, Railway Tickets, Magnetic card entrance guard system and so on.

With the wider application of RFID technology in various vital systems, more and more privacy threats and security flaws have been emerging. The attacker can identify some security flaws and invade into RFID systems to steal the user's data and sensitive information, which seriously violates the privacy of users and damages the credibility of system provider.

A lot of technologies for RFID security and privacy have been put forward by the researchers at home and abroad, which mainly divided into two broad categories:

© Springer International Publishing Switzerland 2015
G. Wang et al. (Eds.): ICA3PP 2015, Part III, LNCS 9530, pp. 682–694, 2015.
DOI: 10.1007/978-3-319-27137-8_49

physical methods and identity authentication technology based on cryptography system.

As the name implies, physical methods use physical means to stop the information transfer and protect the privacy of RFID systems. These methods mainly include Kill Tag, Active Interference, Faraday Cage and Block Tag [3], whose application would be limited by the cost and the types of tags.

Identity authentication technology based on cryptography system uses the transmission of information to achieve the authentication between Tag, Reader and Backend processing system. With the rapid development of the cryptographic techniques, several of cipher algorithms already can achieve hardware implementation. According to the complexity of the cipher algorithm, the identity authentication technology could be divided into three categories [4]: mature authentication technology adopts sophisticated encryption algorithm such as elliptic curve cryptography (ECC), data encryption standard (DES) and advanced encryption standard (AES) and asymmetric encryption cryptography, etc.; Lightweight information authentication technology adopts the HASH function, redundancy check code, random number generator (RNG) and so on, whose calculation amount is relatively small; Ultra-lightweight information authentication technology adopts equipotential operation of AND, NOT and exclusive or (XOR) for interactive data encryption.

Only in certain conditions, can these techniques achieve data security and privacy protection of RFID systems. That is to say, they almost need improvement.

In order to strengthen identity authentication security and guarantee user's privacy, this paper proposes a privacy enhancement model for RFID Systems (PEM4RFID) based on "2 + 2" authentication mechanism, which includes two-factor authentication protocol (TFAP) and "two-way authentication".

In this paper, we first investigate RFID technology and its security problems, and put forward two-factor authentication protocol (TFAP) based on the "hardware device information + AES-ECC encryption". TFAP could effectively prove user identity legitimacy and avoid the defects of single factor authentication. Next, we introduce the combined public key (CPK) mechanism into RFID systems and put forward the "two-way authentication" on the basis of the original CPK authentication, which effectively prevents RFID systems from the denial of service (DoS) attacks, identity spoofing attacks, and so on. Theoretical analysis shows that "two-way authentication" could achieve the purpose of privacy guarantees and data security. Finally, we propose PEM4RFID based on improved CPK and TFAP. Experimental results show that PEM4RFID successfully strengthens the authentication and privacy guarantees.

The remainder of this paper is organized as follows: Sect. 2 reviews the fundamentals of CPK, Sect. 3 advances the PEM4RFID after introducing TFAP and "two-way authentication", Sect. 4 presents experiments to verify the security performance for our proposed PEM4RFID model, and Sect. 5 summarizes the results and points out the directions for future work.

2 Related Work

2.1 Literature Review

In 1976, Diffie and Hellman [5] published "New Directions in Cryptography" and put forward the public key cryptosystem for the first time, which laid the foundation of public key Cryptography. The algorithm based on mathematical principle separates the encryption key and decryption key. It is extremely difficult to derive the decryption key from the encryption key.

In 1978, Rivest et al [6] put forward RSA cipher system, whose security was based on large integer factorization problem. With the development of computer hardware and high-performance computing (HPC) technology, RSA is no longer safe. RSA not only need more bandwidth, but its encryption efficiency declines.

In this condition, Miller and Koblitz [7, 8] put forward Elliptic Curve Cryptography in 1985, whose security was based on the elliptic curve discrete logarithm problem (ECDLP). ECC requires less network bandwidth, but has strong ability against attack [9]. ECC transplanted the traditional encryption algorithm to the elliptic curve, which achieves key exchange protocol, data encryption and digital signature.

In 1996, public key infrastructure (PKI) began to form, greatly promoted the creation and development of authentication theory. PKI proposed the concept of third party certification for the first time. PKI uses hierarchical certificate authority (CA) authentication centers to release digital certificates, verify the user's identity information and prove its credibility. As PKI expanding the scale of the key management, it requires a great deal of network traffic [10] but has small capacity.

On the basis of PKI, identity based encryption (IBE) was proposed. In 1984, Shamir successfully proves the existence of the key algorithm based on identification. In 2001, IBE algorithm was proposed by Don Boneh and Matthew Franklin [11]. IBE adopts a new private key distribution scheme, undo the CA authentication center, retained the user preferences, and just need online parameter library support. But IBE couldn't adapt to the actual application environment.

In 2006, Nan [12] proposed a more credible certification mechanism: CPK authentication system.

2.2 Basic Knowledge of CPK

CPK is based on Elliptic Curve Cryptosystem [13]. Elliptic curve is a curve defined in a variety of limited domains. That is to say, CPK depends on the elliptic curve group $Ep(a, b)$ based on prime integer fields [14], which is shown in Formula 1.

$$y^2 \equiv \left(x^3 + ax + b\right) \bmod p \tag{1}$$

with curvy parameters a, b, $p \in GF(p)$.

Pick up a basis point G from $Ep(a, b)$.

$$G = (x, y) \tag{2}$$

If $P = (x_1, y_1), Q = (x_2, y_2), P \neq \pm Q$, addition rules of elliptic curve are shown in Formulas 3–5.

$$P + Q = (x_3, y_3) \tag{3}$$

$$x_3 = \left(\frac{y_2 - y_1}{x_2 - x_1}\right)^2 - x_1 - x_2 \tag{4}$$

$$y_3 = \left(\frac{y_2 - y_1}{x_2 - x_1}\right)(x_1 - x_3) - y_1 \tag{5}$$

Multiplication rules of elliptic curve are shown in Formulas 6–8.

$$2P = (x_4, y_4) \tag{6}$$

$$x_4 = \left(\frac{3x_1^2 + a}{2y_1}\right)^2 - 2x_1 \tag{7}$$

$$y_4 = \left(\frac{3x_1^2 + a}{2y_1}\right)(x_1 - x_3) - y_1 \tag{8}$$

In terms of addition and multiplication rules of elliptic curve, a multiple point set, namely generated subgroup S_G, can be calculated based on point G.

$$S_G = (G, 2G, 3G, \ldots, nG) \tag{9}$$

Pick up multiple point kG from S_G, and k is the discrete logarithm of multiple point K.

$$kG = K = (x_k, y_k) \tag{10}$$

Mathematic research shows that K is calculated easily with k and G known [15]. But it is almost impossible to get k with K and G known. This is a classic elliptic curve discrete logarithm problem, which is the origin of ECC.

3 Privacy Enhancement Model

In this paper, we proposed a RFID privacy enhancement model PEM4RFID. In order to protect the privacy of users, PEM4RFID adopts the two-factor authentication protocol (TFAP) based on the "hardware device information + AES-ECC encryption". In addition, TFAP adopts the two-way authentication based on improved CPK to authenticate the identity between Tag, Reader and Backend processing system. Thus, TFAP can effectively prevent the RFID systems from the DoS attacks, identity spoofing attacks, and so on., achieve the purpose of user privacy guarantees and data security. The model structure of PEM4RFID is shown in Fig. 1.

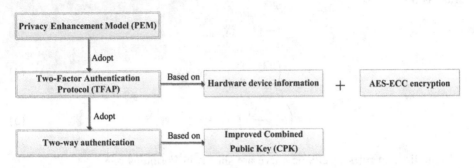

Fig. 1. The model structure of PEM4RFID

3.1   Two-Factor Authentication Protocol

There are many traditional authentication methods, but they simply adopt one of the single factor authentication principles. First, traditional authentication methods usually authenticate the identity of users according to user's information such as the static password. Secondly, these methods use objects users holding to authenticate the identity such as smart card, seal, and so on. Finally, these methods can also make use of unique physical characteristics of user to authenticate the identity such as fingerprint, iris, DNA and other biological characteristics. Because these methods are based on single factor authentication, there will be more or less potential security risks such as seal stolen, static password lost, and so on. These risks will lead to serious damage of user privacy.

In order to solve the potential safety risk, we put forward TFAP, a two-factor authentication protocol of RFID systems. TFAP is based on the "hardware device information + AES-ECC encryption". "Hardware information" means fixed configuration information in CPK chips. A reader or a backend processing system will be configured a chip with unique identification sequence code and key matrix." AES-ECC encryption" means the encryption system combined AES with ECC. In this paper, the AES algorithm is used to encrypt plaintext, ECC algorithm is used to encrypt AES key.

With the combination of "Hardware information" and "AES-ECC encryption", TFAP adopts the chip technology and the encryption technology to implement the functions of RFID systems, such as identity authentication, data encryption, data decryption, and so on. The private keys are only generated in the CPK chips and closely guarded at the hardware level. The private keys are only allowed to be used within the CPK chips. In other words, the private keys will play no part outside the CPK chips. When an attacker attempts to dissect chip and obtain chip data illegally, the chip data will be automatically destroyed. So, the attacker can never get a complete private key [16, 17]. Even if the attacker intercepts the signal of RFID systems illegally, the attacker is still unable to get any information for AES-ECC encryption based on discrete logarithm problem.

Our TFAP protocol algorithm is described as follows.

3.1.1   System Initialization
According to the elliptic curve group $Ep(a, b)$, the secret key management center builds the private key matrix skm and public key matrix PKM.

$$skm = \begin{pmatrix} s_{1,1} & \cdots & s_{1,32} \\ \vdots & \ddots & \vdots \\ s_{32,1} & \cdots & s_{32,32} \end{pmatrix}_{32 \times 32} \tag{11}$$

$$PKM = \begin{pmatrix} (a_{1,1}, b_{1,1}) & \cdots & (a_{1,32}, b_{1,32}) \\ \vdots & \ddots & \vdots \\ (a_{32,1}, b_{32,1}) & \cdots & (a_{32,32}, b_{32,32}) \end{pmatrix}_{32 \times 32} \tag{12}$$

Pick up a basis point G from $Ep(a, b)$.

$$G = (x_0, y_0). \tag{13}$$

3.1.2   User A Sends the Digital Signature to User B
User A selects a random number p, computes digital signature code with unique identification sequence code of CPK chip.

(a)   Compute $pG = (x_p, y_p)$
(b)   Compute $c = (x_p + y_p)^2 \bmod 2^m$
(c)   Compute $s = p^{-1}(h + c * a) \bmod n$
(d)   Send $sign = (s, c)$ to User B.

3.1.3   User B Verifies the Digital Signature of User A
User B receives signals of User A, verifies the digital signature code.

(a)   Compute public key A
(b)   Compute $(x_p', y_p') = s^{-1}hG + s^{-1}cA$
(c)   Compute $c' = (x_p' + y_p')^2 \bmod 2^m$
(d)   If $c = c'$, the verification is successful; else refuse the signature.

3.1.4   User B Sends the Digital Signature to User A
User B selects a random number q, computes digital signature code with unique identification sequence code of CPK chip.

(a)   Compute $qG = (x_q, y_q)$
(b)   Compute $c = (x_q + y_q)^2 \bmod 2^m$

(c) Compute $s = q^{-1}(h + c * b) \bmod n$
(d) Send $sign = (s, c)$ to User A.

3.1.5   User A Verifies the Digital Signature of User B

User A receives signals of User B, verifies the digital signature code.

(a) Compute public key B
(b) Compute $(x'_q, y'_q) = s^{-1}hG + s^{-1}cB$
(c) Compute $c' = (x'_q + y'_q)^2 \bmod 2^m$
(d) If $c = c'$, the verification is successful; else refuse the signature.

After this, the two-way authentication between User A and User B is completed, they can communicate with each other.

3.1.6   User B Encrypts Data

Based on AES-ECC encryption, User B chooses a random number and calculates the value of *key*.

(a) Compute $ENC_A(key) = \beta$,
(b) Compute $E_{key}(data) = code$
(c) Send {code, β} to User A.

3.1.7   User A Decrypts Data

(a) The reader receives {code, β}
(b) Compute $DEC_a(\beta) = key$
(c) $D_{key}(code) = data$.

3.1.8   User A Extracts and Stores Data

User A extracts the decrypted data and then stores the data.

All in all, TFAP guarantees the legitimacy of the user's identity, so the attacker is ultimately difficult to decrypt the signal of RFID systems.

3.2   Two-Way Authentication Based on Improved CPK

CPK authentication is one-way. So, when User A plans to send message to User B, it is only required that User A sends digital signature to User B and User B verifies it [18, 19]. But TFAP proposed in this paper, adopts the two-way authentication to authenticate the identity between Tag, Reader and Backend processing system. Only when both sides authenticate each other successfully, can the data or instructions be encrypted and send.

For example, User A sends message to User B, its working process is shown in Fig. 2.

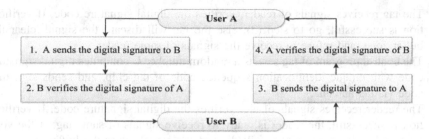

Fig. 2. Two-way authentication between User A and User B

"Two-way authentication" is aimed at insecure channel in the RFID systems to increase the reliability of authentication. Not only can two-way authentication verify the legitimacy of the tags or readers, but it also can effectively prevent the RFID systems from DoS attacks, such as denial of service, identity spoofing attacks, and so on. As a result, Two-way authentication efficiently achieves to ensure privacy guarantees and data security.

3.3 Model Design of PEM4RFID

CPK authentication system is a kind of mature identity authentication system. AES-ECC encryption adopts complex encryption algorithm. As a result of that, PEM4RFID makes use of active tags whose computing power is especially strong. PEM4RFID not only can provide efficient safety protection with TFAP, but also follows the two-way authentication to enhance the privacy of users.

The working principle of PEM4RFID is shown in Fig. 3.

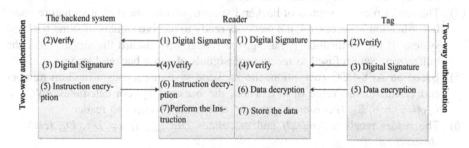

Fig. 3. The working principle of PEM4RFID

Working principles between tags and reader are followed.

(1) The control program of reader selects a random number k, computes digital signature code with unique identification sequence code of CPK chip, and sends signature code via radio frequency interface.

(2) The tag receives signals of reader, verifies the digital signature code. If verification is successful, go to step (3); else the tag will discard the signal, clear the buffer zone, and refuse to receive the signals of same reader.

(3) The control program of tag selects a random number k, computes digital signature code with unique identification sequence code of tag chip, and sends signature code via tag antenna.

(4) The reader receives signals of tag, verifies the digital signature code. If verification is successful, the reader is ready to receive signals of same tag. If the verification is failing, the reader will discard the signal, clear the buffer zone, and refused to receive the signals of same tag.

(5) Based on AES-ECC encryption, the tag chooses a random number and calculates the value of key. Then, the tag calculates $ENC_{READER}(key) = \beta$, $E_{key}(data) = code$, and sends $\{code,\beta\}$ to reader.

(6) The reader receives $\{code,\beta\}$ and calculates $DEC_{reader}(\beta) = key$, $D_{key}(code) = data$.

(7) The reader extracts and stored $data$.

Working principles between the reader and the backend processing system are followed.

(1) The control program of reader selects a random number k, computes digital signature code with unique identification sequence code of CPK chip, and sends signature code to backend processing system via cable channel or wireless channel.

(2) The backend system receives signals of reader, verifies the digital signature code. If verification is successful, go to step (3); else the backend system will discard the signal, clear the buffer zone, and refuse to receive the signals of same reader.

(3) The backend system selects a random number k, computes digital signature code with unique identification sequence code of CPK chip, and sends signature code via cable channel or wireless channel.

(4) The reader receives signals of backend system, verifies the digital signature code. If verification is successful, the reader is ready to receive signals of same backend system. If the verification is failing, the reader will discard the signal, clear the buffer zone, and refused to receive the signals of same backend system.

(5) Based on AES-ECC encryption, the backend system chooses a random number and calculates the value of key. Then, the backend system calculates $ENC_{READER}(key) = \beta$, $E_{key}(Instruction) = code$, and sends $\{code,\beta\}$ to reader.

(6) The reader receives $\{code,\beta\}$ and calculates $DEC_{reader}(\beta) = key$, $D_{key}(code) = Instruction$.

(7) The reader extracts and performs the $Instruction$.

In cryptography, ENC is asymmetric encryption function, and especially means ECC encryption function in this paper. E is symmetric encryption function, and especially means AES encryption function.

DEC is asymmetric decryption function, and especially means ECC decryption function in this paper. D is symmetric decryption function, and especially means AES decryption function.

$READER$ is the public key of reader and $reader$ is the private key.

4   Case Study

4.1   Why Choose AES and ECC

In this paper, the AES algorithm is used to encrypt plaintext, ECC algorithm is used to encrypt AES key.

AES is symmetrical encryption algorithm. Its encryption speed is especially fast, AES is suit for encrypting long plaintext. However, the shortcoming is the key management of AES is complex and unsafe.

ECC is asymmetrical encryption algorithm, which is easy for key management. Therefore, ECC is very suitable for key encryption and digital signature.

AES-ECC encryption synthesizes the advantages of symmetric encryption and asymmetrical encryption, which solves the problem of efficiency and safety in the communication. Although the mixed AES-ECC encryption is divided into two stages, the efficiency is higher than ever before.

4.2   Example

4.2.1   System Initialization

According to the elliptic curve group $E_{541}(116,11)$, the secret key management center builds the private key matrix skm and public key matrix PKM.

$$skm = \begin{pmatrix} 13 & \cdots & 16 \\ \vdots & \ddots & \vdots \\ 35 & \cdots & 26 \end{pmatrix}_{32 \times 32} \tag{14}$$

$$PKM = \begin{pmatrix} (10,508) & \cdots & (506,35) \\ \vdots & \ddots & \vdots \\ (300,204) & \cdots & (55,415) \end{pmatrix}_{32 \times 32} \tag{15}$$

Pick up a basis point G from $E_{541}(116,11)$.

$$G = (257, 290) \tag{16}$$

4.2.2   Digital Signature of Reader

The control program selects a random number $p = 2$, computes digital signature code with unique identification sequence code of CPK chip.

(a) Compute $pG = (x_p, y_p) = (244, 517)$
(b) Compute $c = (x_p + y_p)^2 \bmod 2^m = 9$
(c) Compute $s = p^{-1}(h + c * reader) \bmod n = 26$
(d) Send $sign = (s, c) = (26, 9)$ via radio frequency interface.

4.2.3   Tag Verifies the Digital Signature of Reader

The tag receives signals of reader, verifies the digital signature code.

(a) Compute $(x_p', y_p') = s^{-1}hG + s^{-1}cREADER = (244, 517)$
(b) Compute $c' = (x_p' + y_p')^2 \bmod 2^m = 9$
(c) The verification is successful for $c = c'$.

4.2.4   Digital Signature of Tag

The control program of tag selects a random number q, $q = 3$, computes digital signature code with unique identification sequence code of tag chip.

(a) Compute $qG = (x_q, y_q) = (60, 390)$
(b) Compute $c = (x_q + y_q)^2 \bmod 2^m = 4$
(c) Compute $s = q^{-1}(h + c * tag) \bmod n = 59$
(d) Send $sign = (s, c) = (59, 4)$ via antenna.

4.2.5   Reader Verifies the Digital Signature of Tag

The reader receives signals of tag, verifies the digital signature code.

(a) Compute $(x_q', y_q') = s^{-1}hG + s^{-1}cTAG = (60, 390)$
(b) Compute $c' = (x_q' + y_q')^2 \bmod 2^m = 4$
(c) The verification is successful for $c = c'$.

After this, two-way authentication is completed, the reader and the tag can communicate with each other.

4.2.6   Tag Encrypts Data

Based on AES-ECC encryption, the tag chooses a random number and calculates the value of key. $data = $ 'hello'.

(a) Compute $ENC_{READER}(key) = \beta$, $\beta = (337, 521)$, $key = 13924$
(b) Compute $E_{key}(data) = code$, $code = 83BD4354D5616BDA608C08F41F629E2D$
(c) Send $\{code, \beta\}$ to reader.

4.2.7   Reader Decrypts Data

(a) The reader receives $\{code, \beta\}$
(b) Compute $DEC_{reader}(\beta) = key = 13924$
(c) $D_{key}(code) = data = hello$.

4.2.8   The Reader Extracts and Stores Data

The reader extracts the decrypted data and then stores the data.

4.3   Security Performance Analysis

PEM4RFID adopts the two-way authentication based on improved CPK, which is effective for authentication. If the verification is failing, PEM4RFID will discard the signal, clear the buffer zone, and refused to receive the signals of same origin. There will be buffer overflow in RFID systems. Therefore, this model can effectively prevent direct attack such as DoS attacks.

PEM4RFID adopts the chip technology. The private keys are only generated in the CPK chips and closely guarded at the hardware level. The private keys are only allowed to be used within the CPK chips. In other words, the private keys will play no part outside the CPK chips. When an attacker attempts to dissect chip and obtain chip data illegally, the chip data will be automatically destroyed. So, the attacker can never get a complete private key.

PEM4RFID adopts AES-ECC encryption technology. It is almost impossible to get private key with public key known. This is the classic elliptic curve discrete logarithm problem [19, 20]. Even if the attacker intercepts the signals of RFID systems illegally, the attacker is still unable to get any information from the signals.

PEM4RFID is based on TFAP. Only when verifying signature successfully, can PEM4RFID send encrypted data or instructions. The attacker can neither distinguish different tags nor record the route by eavesdropping communication signals. Therefore, PEM4RFID can effectively prevent RFID systems from identity spoofing attacks or tag tracking attacks.

In addition, PEM4RFID will choose a random number for real-time digital signature and data encryption. So, even sending the same data, PEM4RFID will calculate the different signature or cipher at different time. Therefore, PEM4RFID have nonrepeatability of instructions, which effectively prevent replay attacks or spoofing attacks. The attacker cannot illegally obtain the privacy data of user.

To sum up, PEM4RFID can supply a good trade-off between privacy and data security.

5   Conclusion and Future Work

In this paper, we propose a novel identity authentication mechanism based on "2 + 2" authentication mechanism. First, we put forward two-factor authentication protocol TFAP based on the "hardware device information + AES-ECC encryption". TFAP could effectively prove user's identity legitimacy and avoid the defects of single factor authentication. Next, we introduce the improved CPK into RFID systems and put forward the "two-way authentication", which effectively prevents the RFID systems from the DoS attacks, identity spoofing attacks, and so on. Theoretical analysis shows that "two-way authentication" could achieve a good trade-off between privacy protection and data security.

In this paper, we adopt active tags in RFID systems. However, mobility of active tags is poor and the cost is higher than passive tags. So our future work is to improve the PEM4RFID model to make use of passive tags.

Acknowledgments. This work is supported by the National Natural Science Foundation of China (No. 61340039, 61572355, 61572349) and 985 funds of Tianjin University, Tianjin Research Program of Application Foundation and Advanced Technology under grant No. 15JCYBJC15700 and No. 14JCTPJC00517.

References

1. Roberts, C.M.: Radio frequency identification (RFID). Comput. Secur. **26**, 18–26 (2006)
2. Want, R.: An introduction to RFID technology. IEEE Pervasive Comput. **5**, 25–33 (2006)
3. Miri, A.: Information science reference-imprint: advanced security and privacy for RFID technologies. In: America, p. 342. IGI Global, Hershey (2013)
4. Wang, J.S.: Provable security lightweight service—less RFID security search protocol. J. Hunan Univ. **41**, 117–124 (2013)
5. Diffie, W., Hellman, M.E.: New directions in cryptography. IEEE Trans. Inf. Theory **22**, 644–654 (1976)
6. Rivest, R., Shamir, A., Adleman, M.: A method for obtaining digital signatures and public-key cryptosystems. Commun. ACM **21**, 120–126 (1978)
7. Miller, V.S.: Use of elliptic curves in cryptography. In: Williams, H.C. (ed.) CRYPTO 1985. LNCS, vol. 218, pp. 417–426. Springer, Heidelberg (1986)
8. Koblitz, N.: Elliptic curve cryptosystems. Math. Comput. **48**, 203–209 (1987)
9. Zhang, X.A.: Research of elliptic curve cryptosystems. Commun. Technol. **5**, 208–209, 212 (2009)
10. Peng, D.L., Li, C., Huo, H.: Computer science and information technology: an extended username token-based approach for REST-style web service security authentication. In: Proceedings of IEEE Computer Science and Information Technology Conference, America, pp. 582–586. IEEE (2009)
11. Boneh, D., Franklin, M.: Identity based encryption from weil pairing. In: Kilian, J. (ed.) CRYPTO 2001. LNCS, vol. 2139, pp. 213–229. Springer, Heidelberg (2001)
12. Nan, X.H.: CPK algorithm and identity authentication. China Inf. Secur. **28**, 12–16 (2006)
13. Nan, X.H.: Identity authentication based on CPK, pp. 57–58. National Defense Industry Press, Beijing (2006)
14. Chen, H.P.: Description of CPK several issues. China Inf. Secur. **29**, 47–49 (2007)
15. Jurisic, A., Menezes, A.: Elliptic curves and cryptography. Dr. Dobb's J. 26–36 (1997)
16. Nan, X.H.: CPK combined public key cryptosystem v6.0. Netw. Comput. Secur. **97**(7), 2–4 (2011)
17. Nan, X.H.: CPK combined public key cryptosystem v7.0. Netw. Comput. Secur. **113**, 4–6 (2012)
18. Nan, X.H.: CPK combined public key cryptosystem v8.0. China Inf. Secur. **206**, 12–16 (2012)
19. Nan, X.H., Chen, H.P.: Combined public key system standard. China Inf. Secur. **30**, 21–22 (2008)
20. Johnson, D., Menezes, A.: The elliptic curve digital signature algorithm (ECDSA). Technical report CORR, pp. 99–34, (1999). http://cs.ucsb.edu/~koc/ccs130h/notes/ecdsa-cert.pdf

Improved WOW Adaptive Image Steganography Method

Xin Liao[1,2,3]([✉]), Guoyong Chen[1], Qi Li[1], and Jun Liu[4]

[1] College of Computer Science and Electronic Engineering, Hunan University,
Changsha 410082, China
{xinliao,S1410W0674}@hnu.edu.cn
[2] Institute of Software, Chinese Academy of Sciences, Beijing 100190, China
[3] State Key Laboratory of Information Security, Institute of Information Engineering,
Chinese Academy of Sciences, Beijing 100093, China
[4] State Grid Hunan Electric Power Company, Changsha 410007, China

Abstract. Currently, the most secure adaptive image steganographic methods for spatial domain are to design cost functions to minimize embedding distortion. Wavelet Obtained Weights (WOW) is one of these methods, which can adaptively embed secret message into cover image according to textural complexity. In this paper, an improved WOW adaptive image steganography method is proposed. We apply a binary stochastic matrix to preprocess the cover image to generate a new image firstly, which helps to reduce the probability of locating embedding change positions by stego image. Then, three directional filters are used to weigh the embedding cost of each pixel in the new image and the syndrome-trellis codes are applied to minimize the distortion. Experimental results demonstrate that the proposed method achieves a better performance on resisting the state-of-the-art steganalysis over prior works.

Keywords: Adaptive image steganography · Wavelet obtained weights (WOW) · Embedding positions · Embedding cost · Spatial rich model

1 Introduction

Steganography is a new approach to hide information in stego media and deliver it to receiver without arousing the suspicion of potential attackers [1]. On the contrary, steganalysis is a technique of detecting, extracting and destroying the hiding information in stego image [2]. Both of them are the most active and challenging research subjects [3].

In spatial domain image steganography, the secret messages are usually embedded into cover image by modifying the pixel values. LSB (Least Significant Bit) is the simplest steganography that secret messages are embedded by changing the least significant bit of the pixel value. So far, a lot of enhanced LSB methods have been designed, but they are all regarded as non-adaptive methods, because the image models are not general enough and some marginal or joint image statistics are not preserved in these methods [4]. Therefore, though LSB can easily cheat our human eyes, it is easy to be detected even at a low payload by using some statistical steganalytic methods. In order to improve the security, some adaptive embedding methods have been proposed. The basic idea of these methods

© Springer International Publishing Switzerland 2015
G. Wang et al. (Eds.): ICA3PP 2015, Part III, LNCS 9530, pp. 695–702, 2015.
DOI: 10.1007/978-3-319-27137-8_50

is that secret messages should be embedded into those positions that are difficult to model. In [4], Pevný *et al.* proposed a novel strategy for adaptive steganography. Generally, these adaptive steganography methods firstly build a distortion function to decide the probable embedding change positions, and then combine with the advanced Syndrome-Trellis Codes (STCs) coding technique [5] to minimize the overall distortion of the stego image. Based on this strategy, two modern steganographic methods HUGO [4] and WOW [6] have been proposed. In the HUGO embedding method, the cost for each pixel is computed by a weighted sum of difference between the feature vectors respectively extracted from cover and stego images by Subtractive Pixel Adjacency Matrix (SPAM) features [7]. In contrast to HUGO, WOW uses three directional wavelet filters for obtaining the embedding cost for each pixel. Based on the experimental results in [6], WOW performs better than other methods in spatial domain evaluated by the powerful Spatial Rich Model (SRM) steganalysis [8] which consists of 106 symmetrized sub-models with a total dimension of 34671. In general, most of the modified pixels are at complex textural regions, and this helps WOW to achieve high security against typical steganalytic detectors. In Spatial Rich Model (SRM) steganalysis, features are extracted from the whole stego image and this means that all pixels in an image have the same contribution for detectors. Recently, Tang *et al.* pointed out that most of embedding changes in WOW would be highly concentrated on those complex textural regions and the detector can narrow down those suspicious regions of the stego image [9]. They proposed that only these complex textural regions are used for SRM steganalysis. The experiment results have shown the effectiveness of Tang *et al.*'s steganalysis method.

In this paper, we approach the task of improving WOW adaptive image steganography method to obtain better performance in resisting steganalysis with Tang *et al.*'s strategy. Firstly, the cover image is preprocessed by using a binary stochastic matrix to create a new image. Then, directional wavelet filters are used for obtaining the embedding costs from this new image, and these embedding costs are used for embedding secret messages into the original cover image. The experiment results show that this preprocessing method can scramble possible embedding positions. Since the attacker cannot obtain the preprocessing mode accurately, those suspicious regions cannot be located accurately. The merits of our work are demonstrated experimentally by comparing with WOW and showing an improvement in statistical detectability.

The rest of the paper is structured as follows. The next section briefly reviews WOW embedding method and Tang *et al.*'s adaptive steganalysis method. The improved WOW adaptive image steganography method is presented in Sect. 3. Section 4 presents investigative experiments aimed at comparing the performance among the proposed steganographic methods and some existing ones. Finally, the conclusions and future works are made.

2   Previous Works

In this section, we give a brief overview of WOW embedding method and Tang *et al.*'s adaptive steganalysis.

2.1 WOW Embedding Method

WOW is a secure embedding method in spatial domain. This method works by restricting the embedding changes to textures regions while avoiding smooth edges to improve security.

Firstly, three directional filters are used to obtain the directional residuals for each pixel of the cover image and the embedding suitability of each pixel is computed by using those residuals. Then, these embedding suitabilities are aggregated to get embedding costs. After establishing the distortion function, the STCs are applied to minimize the distortion function and obtain the stego image. In general, pixels in the textural regions have smaller embedding costs and these pixels are more likely to be changed when secret message is embedded by using STCs. In such way, it can achieve high security against typical steganalytic methods. Please see Ref. [6] for more details.

2.2 Tang *et al.*'s Adaptive Steganalysis

All universal steganalytic methods extract features from the whole image, meaning that the contribution for every pixel in an image is assumed the same. However, the secret messages are often embedded by modifying pixels in the textural regions. Therefore, Tang *et al.* proposed a steganalytic method to focus on those textural regions, and feature is extracted only from those textural regions of stego image. That means a small proportion of pixels whose embedding cost values are below a threshold are selected to be used for SRM steganalysis. Experimental results show that this adaptive steganalysis is a great threat to WOW. Please see Ref. [9] for more details.

3 Improved Adaptive Image Steganography Method

WOW method could highly locate at those textural regions, but the detector can also locate at those suspicious regions by the same way. Tang *et al.* pointed out that those suspicious regions of the stego image can be narrowed down and only these complex textural regions are used for steganalysis. Therefore, Tang *et al.*'s method is a great challenge for WOW. From the perspectives of game theory, Tang *et al.*'s method is effective against WOW because the embedding positions can be inferred from the stego image easily. For decreasing the probability of locating the embedding change positions from stego image, we can preprocess the cover image to gain a new image that is similar to the cover image. Cost values are obtained from the new image and these cost values are helped to embed message into the cover image. Because the attacker doesn't know how we have processed the cover image, so they cannot locate at the embedding change positions accurately. The detailed procedures of the proposed method are as follows.

3.1 Embedding Processes

Step 1:   Assume that $\mathbf{X}$ is the cover image and each pixel X_{ij} which is at ij needs to be preprocessed according to the follow equation to obtain the corresponding element Z_{ij}. Then those elements form a new image $\mathbf{Z}$.

$$Z_{ij} = \begin{cases} \lfloor X_{ij}/2 \rfloor & b_{ij} = 0 \\ \lceil X_{ij}/2 \rceil & b_{ij} = 1 \end{cases} \tag{1}$$

Here, $\lfloor c \rfloor$ denotes the largest integer which is not larger than "c", and $\lceil c \rceil$ denotes the smallest integer which is not smaller than "c". b_{ij} is an element of the binary stochastic matrix **B** which is generated by a random function.

Step 2: Three directional filters called Daubechies 8 wavelets (denoted by $\mathbf{K}^{(k)}$, $k = 1, 2, 3$) are used to obtain the LH, HL and HH directional residuals $\mathbf{R}^{(k)}$ of the image **Z**, respectively. The directional residual $\mathbf{R}^{(k)}$ is computed as

$$\mathbf{R}^{(k)} = \mathbf{K}^{(k)} * \mathbf{Z}, \tag{2}$$

where "$*$" is a convolution mirror-padded.

Step 3: The embedding cost ρ_{ij} is computed by

$$\rho_{ij} = \sum_{k=1}^{3} \frac{1}{\left| \mathbf{R}^{(k)} \right| * \left| \mathbf{R}^{(k)} - \mathbf{R}_{ij}^{(k)} \right|}. \tag{3}$$

Step 4: Based on the above embedding cost ρ_{ij} of each pixel, we use the Syndrome-Trellis Codes (STCs) [5] to embed the secret messages into the cover image **X**.

3.2 Extracting Processes

The original STC information extraction algorithm is still effective. What we want to emphasize is that the message can be extracted without original cost values. So it is unnecessary to share binary stochastic matrix **B** with receiver.

4 Experimental Results

In this section, some experiments are carried out and will be shown to demonstrate that the proposed method is better than WOW embedding method. The testing image database in our experiments is BOSSBase (v1.01) [10], which consists of 10000 original images with size of 512×512 pixels. Spatial Rich Model (SRM) [8] and Tang *et al.*'s steganalysis method [9] are used for feature extraction, and the ensemble classifier [11] is applied in the training and testing stages. The ensemble's "out-of-bag" error E_{OOB} is used to quantify the security of these methods.

4.1 Difference of Embedding Changes

In this experiment, we try to compare the differences between our improved WOW method and WOW for these embedding changes. We use Fig. 1(a) as the original cover image, and execute the above two methods to embed the same secret data into cover image when the payload is 0.4 bpp. Figure 1(b, c) show embedding changes of WOW and our improved WOW method, respectively. It can be seen that embedding changes of two methods are distributed mainly over the textured areas. However, Fig. 1(d) shows that there are still some different embedding positions between two methods. Here, red points represent the embedding changes only in our improved WOW (about 4.35 % of the whole changed pixels), while blue points represent the embedding changes only in WOW (about 4.31 % of the whole changed pixels).

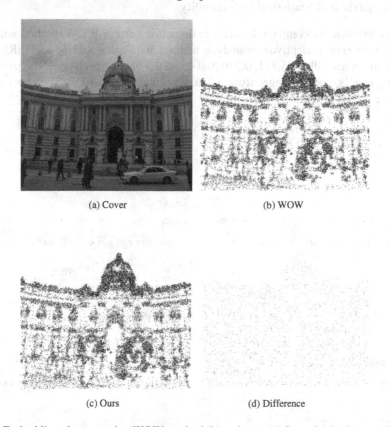

(a) Cover   (b) WOW

(c) Ours   (d) Difference

Fig. 1. Embedding changes using WOW method (b) and ours (c) for a classical grayscale cover image (a), and different embedding changes between two methods (d).

To further demonstrate ours could scramble embedding change positions, we select 1000 images from image database BOSSBase (v1.01) to compare WOW with ours and the secret data are the same under each payload. Table 1 shows the percentages of embedding changes which are only in ours. For example, under the payload 0.2 bpp, average 4.11 % of all embedding change pixels in ours are different embedding change positions between ours and WOW. The experimental results show our method could scramble embedding change positions. Because the procedure of preprocessing is not likely to be obtained, attacker may not locate the embedding change positions accurately from the stego.

Table 1. The average percentage of different embedding changes between ours and WOW

Embedding rate	0.05 bpp	0.1 bpp	0.2 bpp	0.3 bpp	0.4 bpp	0.5 bpp
Differences	3.41 %	3.68 %	4.11 %	4.28 %	4.35 %	4.36 %

4.2 Comparison of Statistical Detectability

In this experiment, we compare the average detection error of WOW method with ours by using Tang *et al.*'s adaptive steganalysis method and Spatial Rich Model (SRM). We fix payload values with 0.05, 0.1, 0.2, 0.3, 0.4 and 0.5 bpp, respectively. The parameter p in Tang *et al.*'s method ranges from 5 % to 95 % with a step 10 %. The experimental results are shown in Fig. 2.

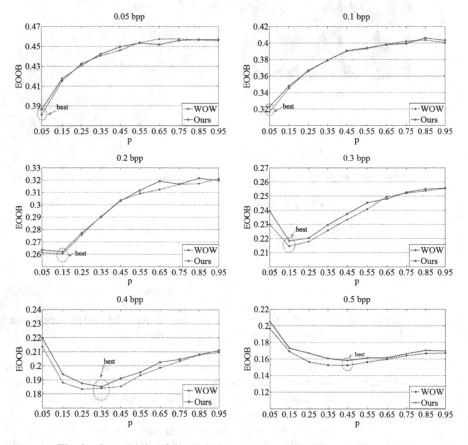

Fig. 2. Comparison of the detection error E_{OOB} with Tang *et al.*'s method

4.2.1 Detection Error with Tang *et al.*'s Method

We compare the detection error E_{OOB} between ours and WOW by using Tang *et al.*'s method. As highlighted in the Fig. 2, the lowest average detection error at the best parameter p has the highest efficiency in Tang *et al.*'s method and the best parameter p is different for different embedding rates. The best parameter p is 0.05 when the payload is 0.05, 0.1 and the best parameter p is 0.15 when the payload is 0.2, 0.3 bpp. The best parameter p is 0.25 and 0.35 when the payload is 0.4 and 0.5 bpp, respectively. It can be seen that all the lowest average detection errors of ours are higher than those of WOW. That is to say, our proposed method works better than WOW at the best parameter p in Tang *et al.*'s method under every payload.

4.2.2 Detection Error with SRM

In this experiment, we compare the detection error E_{OOB} between ours and WOW by using Spatial Rich Model (SRM). The results of our experiment validate that our improved method can obtain the resisting performances approximated to WOW with SRM steganalysis. For example, the detection error E_{OOB} of WOW method is 0.403 and of our method is 0.405 when the payload is 0.1 bpp, and the detection error E_{OOB} of WOW method and of our method is 0.170 and 0.173 when the payload is 0.5 bpp, respectively. That is to say our method doesn't reduce security by using steganalytic method SRM.

From the above, we can draw the conclusion that there are some critical differences between our method and WOW in embedding changes. Though the attacker could guess these textural regions from the stego image which is almost similar to the original cover image, he/she cannot obtain the exact positions in the proposed method due to the procedure of preprocess. Thus, our proposed method performs better than WOW under Tang *et al.'s* method. Moreover, the proposed method can also obtain good performance on resisting SRM steganalysis.

5   Conclusions

In this paper, an improved WOW adaptive image steganography method which is based on scrambling embedding change positions is proposed. The cover image is preprocessed by a binary stochastic matrix to scramble the possible embedding changes firstly, so that the potential attackers cannot locate at these embedding changes regions accurately. Experimental results show that the proposed method is more secure than WOW image steganography method. Furthermore, it remains an open issue to extend the proposed idea to image steganography in frequency domain.

Acknowledgment. This work is supported by National Natural Science Foundation of China (Grant No. 61402162), Hunan Provincial Natural Science Foundation of China (Grant No. 14JJ7024), Specialized Research Fund for the Doctoral Program of Higher Education (Grant No. 20130161120004), China Postdoctoral Science Foundation (Grant No. 2014M560123), Young Teacher Foundation of Hunan University (Grant No. 531107040701).

References

1. Anderson, R.J., Petitcolas, F.A.: On the limits of steganography. IEEE J. Sel. Areas Commun. **16**(4), 474–481 (1998)
2. Petitcolas, F.A., Anderson, R.J., Kuhn, M.G.: Information hiding-a survey. Proc. IEEE **87**(7), 1062–1078 (1999)
3. Wang, H., Wang, S.: Cyber warfare: steganography vs. steganalysis. Commun. ACM **47**(10), 76–82 (2004)
4. Pevný, T., Filler, T., Bas, P.: Using high-dimensional image models to perform highly undetectable steganography. In: Böhme, R., Fong, P.W., Safavi-Naini, R. (eds.) IH 2010. LNCS, vol. 6387, pp. 161–177. Springer, Heidelberg (2010)
5. Filler, T., Judas, J., Fridrich, J.: Minimizing additive distortion in steganography using syndrome-trellis codes. IEEE Trans. Inf. Foren. Secur. **6**(3), 920–935 (2011)
6. Holub, V., Fridrich, J.: Designing steganographic distortion using directional filters. In: 2012 IEEE International Workshop on Information Forensics and Security (WIFS), pp. 234–239 (2012)
7. Pevný, T., Bas, P., Fridrich, J.: Steganalysis by subtractive pixel adjacency matrix. IEEE Trans. Inf. Foren. Secur. **5**(2), 215–224 (2010)
8. Fridrich, J., Kodovský, J.: Rich models for steganalysis of digital images. IEEE Trans. Inf. Foren. Secur. **7**(3), 868–882 (2012)
9. Tang, W., Li, H., Luo, W., Huang, J.: Adaptive steganalysis against WOW embedding algorithm. In: Proceedings of the 2nd ACM Workshop on Information Hiding and Multimedia Security, pp. 91–96 (2014)
10. Bas, P., Filler, T., Pevný, T.: "Break our steganographic system": the ins and outs of organizing BOSS. In: Filler, T., Pevný, T., Craver, S., Ker, A. (eds.) IH 2011. LNCS, vol. 6958, pp. 59–70. Springer, Heidelberg (2011)
11. Kodovský, J., Fridrich, J., Holub, V.: Ensemble classifiers for steganalysis of digital media. IEEE Trans. Inf. Foren. Secur. **7**(2), 432–444 (2012)

CloudS: A Multi-cloud Storage System
with Multi-level Security

Lu Shen, Shifang Feng, Jinjin Sun, Zhongwei Li, Gang Wang$^{(\boxtimes)}$,
and Xiaoguang Liu$^{(\boxtimes)}$

Nankai-Baidu Joint Lab, College of Computer and Control Engineering and College
of Software, Nankai University, Tianjin 300350, China
{shenlu,fengsf,sunjj,lizhongwei,wgzwp,liuxg}@nbjl.nankai.edu.cn

Abstract. With the increase of data quantity, people have begun to
attach importance to cloud storage, however, traditional single cloud
can't ensure the privacy of users' data to a certain extent. To solve the
security issue, we present a multi-cloud storage system called CloudS
which spreads data over multiple cloud storage servers by using a new
kind of XOR-based non-systematic erasure codes - Privacy Protecting
Codes (PPC). For better user experiences and tradeoffs between security
and performance, CloudS provides multiple levels of security by a variety of combinations of compression, encryption and coding schemes. In
addition, we also put forward a novel Parallel Cyclic Encryption (PCE)
scheme to achieve random secret key protection which attains high security and performance. We implement CloudS as a web application which
doesn't require users to perform complicated operations on local.

Keywords: Multi-cloud · Multi-level security · Erasure code · Encryption · Key management

1 Introduction

Cloud storage has become the focus of public attention in recent years. Due to
the ever-growing amount of data and local storage limits, more and more individual and enterprise users have begun to put data in cloud servers. According
to iiMedia Research Group's report [2], only in China, the amount of individual
cloud storage users will reach 450 million in 2015. With the popularity of cloud
storage, many Internet companies have launched their own cloud services such
as Microsoft OneDrive, Amazon S3 and Google Drive. However, cloud storage
security issues are gradually exposed. In 2014, photo leakage occurs to icloud
which is another security incident after Google Docs and Amazon S3 [7,8]. We
summarize potential security hazards of cloud storage as the damage to data
integrity and privacy. For data integrity, network transmission errors, hacker
attacks and faulty operations from server administrators will cause data tampering and loss. For data privacy, both untrusted cloud providers and hacker
attacks will leak out users' data. Besides, the availability of cloud services and
vendor lock-in should be worth attention.

© Springer International Publishing Switzerland 2015
G. Wang et al. (Eds.): ICA3PP 2015, Part III, LNCS 9530, pp. 703–716, 2015.
DOI: 10.1007/978-3-319-27137-8_51

To solve the above problems, many multi-cloud systems whose main idea is data dispersal to multiple cloud servers have appeared such as DepSky [6], RACS [4], HAIL [7]. Existing multi-cloud systems typically use information dispersal algorithms to spread data across multiple storage sites. There are two kinds of common technologies: duplication and erasure codes. Compared by duplication, erasure codes have smaller storage overhead to achieve the same erasure-correcting. Hence, most multi-cloud systems use erasure codes like RAID-5 [13] and RS codes [15,18]. Traditional erasure codes are generally systematic codes which have no confusion and diffusion effects, therefore, they're usually used combined with encryption to reach high-level security, which brings out key management issues. Although non-systematic multi-erasure RS is proposed, it requires relatively complex finite field arithmetic and multi-erasure seems unnecessarily expensive for only a few cloud services. So in this paper, we put forward a new kind of XOR-based non-systematic erasure codes called PPC (Privacy Protecting Code). Although PPC provides relatively weaker protection on users' data compared with modern encryption algorithms, it has pretty high performance and can be combined with other mechanisms to provide multi-level security.

So-called multi-level security, that is, users can choose different security levels for their different data according to their needs. With various types of data uploaded to cloud servers, users' security demands for cloud systems have gradually diversified. Besides, processing a less-confidential file with an overly complex security mechanism will lead to server resource waste and bad user experiences, especially for those devices with a relatively weak computing capability. Therefore, multi-level security is needed to achieve trade-offs between security and performance. Unfortunately, existing multi-cloud systems don't involve this trade-off. So in this paper, we design and implement a multi-cloud system called CloudS which employs different combinations of compression, encryption and coding to achieve multi-level security. As a third party agent, CloudS is allowed to temporarily access user data only when it has got tokens. For better performance and user experiences, we adopt a security authorization mechanism proposed in [22]. In addition, we implement CloudS as a web application, therefore not requiring any complicated operation even installing a software on local, reducing troubles due to changing a computer.

Our Contribution:

- Design and implement a family of XOR-based non-systematic coding schemes called Privacy Protecting Code (PPC).
- Design and implement a variety of combinations of compression, encryption and coding schemes which provides multiple levels of trade-offs between security and performance.
- Implement the secure web-based multi-cloud storage system CloudS with the integration of the above methods.

The rest of this paper is organized as follows. In Sect. 2 we will discuss relevant work about multi-cloud systems and related techniques. Section 3 will introduce the design of CloudS. Section 4 describes PPC codes in detail. Section 5 focuses on the security levels. In Sect. 6 we evaluate the performance of PPC, different security combination schemes and CloudS system. And Sect. 7 concludes this paper and the future work is proposed.

2 Related Work

With the prevalence of cloud storage services and broadband Internet access, data confidentiality, integrity and availability problems in cloud storage raise concern gradually. To address these problems, many multi-cloud storage systems have been proposed to offer integrity and high availability using information dispersal, duplication and erasure codes like MDS [20]. For data confidentiality, Shamir's secret sharing [21] and Rabin's information dispersal [17] are widely used.

In the multi-cloud environment, many well-performance systems appear as well. Depsky, a virtual storage cloud system, addresses availability and confidentiality of data [6]. Similarly, RACS is a proxy that transparently spreads the storage load over many providers with RAID-like techniques to provide high-availability of data stored in the clouds and avoid the costs of vendor lock-in [4]. Aimed at guaranteeing data integrity and availability, HAIL is a distributed cryptographic multi-cloud system [7] which combines proof of retrievability (PORs) [11] and proofs of data possession (PDPs) [5]. ICStore [3] addresses CIRC (confidentiality, integrity, reliability and consistency) by using replication and Shamir's secret sharing. Nevertheless, the above systems don't consider about various security requirements for different data and/or different users. This paper fills that gap by presenting the systematic description of a multi-level security system called CloudS. Meanwhile, we come up with a new XOR-based non-systematic erasure code called PPC Code for data confidentiality and integrity with low storage and computational cost and apply it to CloudS. Compared with systematic erasure codes, PPC is trustworthier in cloud environments that we can still ensure data security even if one cloud server have been attacked.

3 The Framework Design

This section presents the basic model of our system and the architecture of CloudS.

3.1 System Model

Figure 1 shows our system model and there are 3 parts which are users, CloudS agent and public cloud servers provided by different cloud vendors. A user can be abstracted as a single web browser because no codes are executed locally outside the web browser. From another perspective, it doesn't require users to install any plug-ins locally, therefore avoiding inconvenience due to the failure or replacement of local computers. In this model, CloudS works as a third party proxy between users and cloud providers.

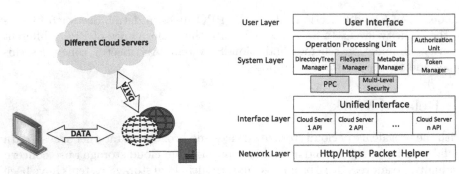

Fig. 1. System model   **Fig. 2.** CloudS architecture

3.2 CloudS Architecture

As presented in Fig. 2, CloudS architecture consists of four layers which are the user layer, the system layer, the interface layer and the network layer.

User Layer: It is used to accept users' requests and submit these requests to the system layer. We can regard the user layer as the "door" of interaction between users and CloudS.

Interface Layer: A multi-cloud system involves different cloud providers, and each provider has its own API. For good scalability, we've designed the interface layer to implement a unified interface.

Network Layer: Data transmission between CloudS and cloud servers is achieved by sending and receiving http/https packet, and the network layer is responsible for the work.

System Layer: The core of CloudS is the system layer. It can be regarded as the "brain" of CloudS and undertakes all computing tasks. It's mainly composed of the operation processing unit, the authorization unit and the token manager unit. As a third party proxy, CloudS can temporarily access to user's data stored in cloud storage only if it has got the user's authorization and holds a string called token. Hence, how to get user's authorization and manage the token is crucial. The authorization unit and the token manager unit are designed for these jobs. The operation processing unit is a data manipulation module. The directory tree manager is designed for directory operation and metadata record directory information.

The filesystem manager is designed to process user data and ensures data security through a series of mechanisms. As mentioned before, security is a vital factor in storage systems but not the only one, so we must consider the tradeoff between security and performance. Here, we assume two different scenes: the user regards cloud services as normal file backup, the other is uploading confidential papers to cloud servers. For the former, users may not require high security and be more likely to pursue the performance of file transfer. For the latter, it's more likely that users pursue high security. Therefore, CloudS provides *different combinations of encryption, compression and coding schemes to satisfy different security levels*. With this mechanism, users can make their choices according to their needs instead of being restricted by system setting, which makes the system more flexible. This mechanism takes full account of user experiences and achieves the trade-offs between performance and security. The filesystem manager takes the security level selected by the user as an input parameter. With this parameter, the filesystem manager adopts the corresponding combination scheme. In addition, *PPC is implmented in this module as the coding scheme*.

4   PPC Design and Implementation

As presented, we propose PPC to meet the tradeoffs between security and performance. In this section, we explain PPC in detail. For convenience, we employ D_i to present the $(i+1)$-th original chunk and P_i for the $(i+1)$-th coding chunk.

4.1   Nomenclature

Before introducing PPC, we first define the terms used in this section.

Chunk [9]: A basic unit of storage holding data and/or coding ('parity') information. This is also referred to as a stripe unit or a strip [10] in traditional storage systems.

Stripe: In our cloud storage model, the user file is split into k chunks and then are encoded into a stripe composed of $n(= k + m)$ chunks. These chunks are spread across n nodes to provide high reliability and availability. From the theoretical view, a stripe is a codeword which is the minimum (and complete) collection of (data and parity) bits that encode and decode together [16].

Node: An independent storage container that stores data and parity chunks. This can be a cloud storage service, a node in peer-to-peer system, and so on.

4.2   Metrics of Privacy Protecting

Privacy Degree. *PPC code has a privacy degree of t, if it can resist any t breaches. That is, given any t out of n parity chunks, we cannot reconstruct any data chunk, and there exists $(t+1)$ parity chunks that can reconstruct some (not necessarily all) data chunks.*

As described before, PPC code is a kind of non-systematic erasure code, so no original data is retained. In other words, we cannot reconstruct any data if we only hold one chunk. Hence, the privacy degree of PPC must be greater than 1. In this paper, we define $PPC(k, n, t)$ which means k original data chunks generating n coding chunks and all original chunks can be recovered when holding at least k coding chunks, achieving $(n - k)$-erasure correcting and t presents privacy degree.

Safe and Unsafe Group. *Let S be a subset of chunks in a stripe. If we cannot reconstruct any data chunk from subset S, we call S a safe group, otherwise an unsafe group.*

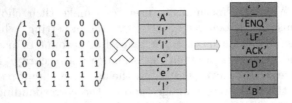

Fig. 3. PPC conversion

Best Case Privacy Degree. *A PPC code has a best case privacy degree of t^{BC} if the size of its biggest safe group in the PPC code is t^{BC}.*

To tell the difference between privacy degree and best case privacy degree, we consider a PPC conversion instance as Fig. 3. It's obvious that the chunk D_4 can be reconstructed by the XOR-sum of P_0, P_2 and P_6 and any data chunk cannot be computed by any pair of parity chunks, so the privacy degree is 2. However, not any three out of those seven parity chunk can reconstruct an original chunk. We can see that the first 5 chunks form a safe group, and any bigger group is unsafe, so its t^{BC} is 5.

S-safe Partible and S-safe Partition. *A PPC code is s-safe partible if its stripe can be split into s safe groups. These groups form an s-safe partition of this PPC code.*

For a distributed storage system, we believe attacks are interrelated in some cases. In other words, attackers will breached relevant multiple nodes simultaneously. In the multi-cloud environment, servers which come from the same country may be regarded as relevant nodes if data security involves the issue of government intervention. In other case, natural disasters will cause all nodes within a region unavailable. The above definition offers a solution to these. For example, if we have four providers from one country and three from another country, we can employ the 2-safe partition $\{\{P_0, P_2, P_4, P_6\},\{P_1, P_3, P_5\}\}$ of $PPC(6,7,2)$ as shown in Fig. 3, so attackers cannot reconstruct original data even if he breaks all the cloud severs belonged to one country.

4.3   Structural Properties of $PPC(k, k+1, t)$

As described before, PPC is a kind of XOR-based (binary) codes, so its encoding and decoding can be achieved by multiplying the generator matrix and original data chunks. Hence, for a $PPC(k, k+1, t)$, we need a $(k+1) \times k$ generator matrix G, and this matrix must have the following properties:

1. *Any k of G's row vectors are linearly independent. In other words, every $k \times k$ square sub-matrix of G is invertible.*

   This property ensures the fault tolerance of PPC. If a coding chunk is unavailable, we delete the corresponding row in G so that the remaining k rows forms a $k \times k$ square matrix. If G satisfies the property, all such a sub-matrix is invertible. We can get the original data chunks by matrix multiplication using the inverse of the sub-matrix and the remaining k coding chunks. But if the property cannot be met, it must exists a chunk that cannot be reconstructed after failure.

2. *Casually choose a row v in G, then $ONES(v) \geq 2$.*

The above property ensures data privacy. We define the function $ONES(v)$ as the weight of the vector v, that is, the number of '1' entries in v. As discussed before, the privacy degree of PPC is greater than 1, we only take use of those generator matrices which are purely composed of row vectors whose weights are greater than or equal to 2.

4.4   Construction of PPC(k, k+1, t)

The key to realizing PPC is finding an optimal generator matrix. We design an algorithm to find optimal matrices which satisfy the structural properties by enumerating valid generator matrices. The algorithm needs an initial $k \times k$ matrix as input and we use r_i to represent the i-th row in the initial matrix. We set r_1 to $\overrightarrow{\mathbf{0}_{k-2}\mathbf{1}_2}$ (($k-2$) '0' followed by two '1'), and set r_m to $\overrightarrow{\mathbf{0}_{k-m-1}\mathbf{1}_2\mathbf{0}_{m-1}}$. If the first k rows are independent, let the $(k+1)$-th row be the XOR-sum of the first k row vectors. We calculate the privacy degree of the new matrix and update the optimal code if the new matrix is a better one. Although the structural properties of generator matrix prune the search space effectively, the enumerating algorithm is still exponential time, and we can find optimal PPC codes in an acceptable time only when $k \leq 9$.

In spite of the above size is appropriate for an end-user of multi-cloud storage systems, we still design and implement two infinite families of $PPC(k, k+1, t)$ codes for large k. The only difference between the two kinds of PPC is the generator matrix, so we only introduce one of them, ShrPPC.

4.5   ShrPPC

To construct a $ShrPPC(k, k+1, t)$ generator matrix, we start with constructing the first $(k-1)$ row vectors by shifting two consecutive set bits right as Formula 1. The i-th row vector $r_i = \overrightarrow{\mathbf{0}_{i-1}\mathbf{1}\mathbf{1}\mathbf{0}_{k-i-1}}$ satisfies $ONES(r_i) \geq 2$. Then, we construct the k-th row vector: If k is even, it is constructed as $\overrightarrow{\mathbf{0}\mathbf{1}_{k-1}}$, otherwise, we set r_k as $\overrightarrow{\mathbf{0}\mathbf{0}\mathbf{1}_{k-2}}$. Finally, we set the last row vector as the XOR-sum of the first k row vectors. When k is even, it is $\overrightarrow{\mathbf{1}_{k-1}\mathbf{0}}$. When k is odd, it is $\overrightarrow{\mathbf{1}\mathbf{0}\mathbf{1}_{k-3}\mathbf{0}}$. Formulas 2 and 3 describe the generator matrices of ShrPPC with even and odd k respectively. It's easy to see that the above two matrices satisfy the second property of generator matrix. Now we will prove they satisfy property 1. First, we transform the first k rows into an upper triangular matrix by performing some elementary matrix transformations. If k is even, we add the $2i$-th row to r_k for all $i \in \{1, 2, ..., \frac{k-2}{2}\}$. And if k is odd, add the $(2i+1)$-th row to r_k for all $i \in \{1, 2, ..., \frac{k-3}{2}\}$. Since the upper triangular matrix is full rank, the first k rows are linearly independent. The $(k+1)$-th row is the XOR-sum of first k rows, so any $k \times k$ sub-matrix of ShrPPC generator matrix is invertible.

$ShrPPC(k, k+1, t)$ provides a good privacy degree of $t = \lfloor \frac{k}{2} \rfloor - 1$, which is very close to the optimal privacy degree of $t = \lfloor \frac{k}{2} \rfloor$, a XOR-based $PPC(k, k+1, t)$ can achieve. For the lack of space, we omit the proof.

4.6   PPC with Higher Security

In the above parts, we introduce PPC whose generator matrix has a minimum row-weight of 2. In other words, each parity chunk is generated by at least two data chunks. It provides high-level performance in most cases, but not all cases. Suppose there are three data chunks, D_0, D_1, D_2, and an attacker has two parity chunks, one of which is $D_0 + D_1$ and the other of which is $D_1 + D_2$. Then he knows the value of $D_0 + D_2$ as well, and it's not complex to guess unencrypted D_0, D_1, and D_2 from this information, even if he's missing other data. Assuming another extreme case that D_0 is a full-zero chunk because of the special file format, it's obvious that the $D_0 + D_1 = D_1$ in this case. In view of these cases, we search optimal generator matrices with larger row-weight using the enumerating algorithm mentioned above. We put the initial matrix of $k \times k$, G, whose first row is $\overrightarrow{\mathbf{0}_{k-3}\mathbf{1}_3}$ and the k-th row is $\overrightarrow{\mathbf{0}_{k-m-2}\mathbf{1}_3\mathbf{0}_{m-1}}$ as input and we have found optimal generator matrices with minimum row-weight larger than or equal to 3 for $k < 9$ (Formula 4 is an example we found using the above method), which means that it becomes much harder for attackers to guess original chunks. In addition, we can resist the above chosen-plaintext attack by means of the combination of PPC and compression and/or encryption.

4.7   Optimal Schedule of PPC Encoding

PPC is a kind of XOR-based code that each coding chunk P is decided by the corresponding row v in the generator matrix G. The greater the weight of v is, the more XOR operations performed in generating P. Suppose G has two vectors of $v_i = \overrightarrow{\mathbf{001}_{k-2}}$ and $v_j = \overrightarrow{\mathbf{0001}_{k-3}}$ and therefore it takes $(2k - 7)$ XOR operations to calculate the two parity chunks P_i and P_j. However, if we calculate P_j first, and then calculate P_i by XORing P_j and D_2, only $(k - 3)$ XOR operations are needed. Since this paper focuses on small-scale multi-cloud systems, we adopt a breadth-first search algorithm [14] to determine the optimal schedule for PPC encoding.

$$
\begin{pmatrix}
1 1 0 \cdots 0 0 \\
0 1 1 \cdots 0 0 \\
0 0 1 \cdots 0 0 \\
\vdots \vdots \vdots \ddots \vdots \vdots \\
0 0 0 \cdots 1 1
\end{pmatrix}
\quad
\begin{pmatrix}
1 1 0 \cdots 0 0 \\
0 1 1 \cdots 0 0 \\
0 0 1 \cdots 0 0 \\
\vdots \vdots \vdots \ddots \vdots \vdots \\
0 0 0 \cdots 1 1 \\
0 1 1 \cdots 1 1 \\
1 1 1 \cdots 1 0
\end{pmatrix}
\quad
\begin{pmatrix}
1 1 0 \cdots 0 0 \\
0 1 1 \cdots 0 0 \\
0 0 1 \cdots 0 0 \\
\vdots \vdots \vdots \ddots \vdots \vdots \\
0 0 0 \cdots 1 1 \\
0 0 1 \cdots 1 1 \\
1 0 1 \cdots 1 0
\end{pmatrix}
\quad
\begin{pmatrix}
0 0 0 1 1 1 \\
0 0 1 1 1 0 \\
0 1 0 0 1 1 \\
0 1 0 1 0 1 \\
0 1 0 1 1 0 \\
1 0 0 0 1 1 \\
1 1 1 0 1 0
\end{pmatrix}
$$
$$
\quad (1) \qquad\qquad (2) \qquad\qquad (3) \qquad\qquad (4)
$$

5 Multi-level Security

For better user experiences, CloudS provides some security levels with different characteristics. From the system perspective, each level logically corresponds to a specific combination scheme of compression, encryption and coding. In CloudS, we implement not only combinations of some existing technologies such as RS, RAID-5, AES [12] and AONT [10], but some new technologies such as PPC and PCE. In this section, we list three new combination schemes and AONT−RS [19] by contrast to introduce different security levels in the system view.

5.1 PCE−PPC

Traditional encryption usually brings key management issues, AONT can be regarded as a better precept to avoid it. The principle of AONT has been amply demonstrated, we don't discuss it any more. Further, AONT−RS, an encryption and dispersal scheme, is proposed in [19] which achieves a pretty high level of security. AONT−RS has another property that it provides partial data the same protection degree as the whole data, e.g., if there're 7 servers used in CloudS, attackers must break 6 servers to retrieve (which is nearly impossible) whether the whole data or a single original byte. In terms of performance, parallel optimization and data extension is difficult in AONT, meanwhile, finite field arithmetic used in RS is relatively complex.

To obtain better performance as well as approximate security, we design a new encryption method called PCE. Figure 4 shows an example of PCE and $ShrPPC(6,7,2)$, after that, we randomly spread the coding chunks to different cloud sites. In PCE, chunk D_i is encrypted into C_i with a unique random secret key k_i in parallel, then we append k_i at the end of $C_{(i+3)mod6}$. It's no doubt that PCE overmatches AONT in performance for its parallel optimization. Besides, PPC after PCE avoids the possible chosen-plaintext attack because we perform PPC on cipher not plaintext. Also, PPC, a kind of binary code, is faster than RS. Using PCE−PPC, attackers must hold $\{C_j, k_{(j-3)mod6}\}$ and $\{C_{(j+3)mod6}, k_j\}$

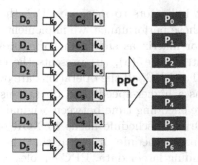

Fig. 4. PCE and PPC

which needs to break 5 cloud servers to decrypt a single chunk D_j, and 6 coding chunks are needed to retrieve all chunks. In a word, PCE–PPC is superior to AONT–RS in terms of performance and achieves the same security as AONT–RS for overall data. Compared with the following schemes containing compression, PCE–PPC provides stable performance without the influence of the repetition rate but more data will be transferred on Internet, thereby satisfying the small-size files with a lower repetition rate.

5.2 Compression–PPC and Compression–PCE–PPC

Considering the time-consuming network transmission process, GZip [1] compression is joint in these two schemes. Compared with AONT–RS, these two schemes have an overwhelming advantage in network transmission. As for security, non-systematic $PPC(k, k + 1, t)$ itself has the effect of data protection, t (greater than 1) coding chunks (means at least two cloud servers) are needed for retrieving only one original chunk, which is very difficult. Meanwhile, chosen-plaintext attack will be remitted since original data patterns will be destroyed after compression. Nonetheless, decompression doesn't need any key, so Compression–PPC has relatively weak security but high speed. We suggest users to adopt Compression–PPC for less-important data. Compression–PCE–PPC is the synthesis of PCE–PPC and Compression–PPC which meets the demands for large confidential data.

6   Evaluation

In this paper, we proposed a family of non-systematic erasure codes named PPC and CloudS with different security schemes to ensure data security in cloud storage environment. Meanwhile, we also concern about their performance. In this section, we will report some performance results. Our prototype is implemented in C++ and the experiments are conducted on Ubuntu 13.04 with Intel i3-350M@2.26 GHz.

6.1   PPC Performance

There're two important indicators to measure PPC, the encoding and decoding speed. To measure those performance, we implement encoders and decoders for PPC which generator matrix as shown in Formula 4 and the single fault-tolerant RS for contrast. Figure 5(a), (b) presents the encoding and decoding speeds of PPC and RS. For PPC, all the operations are over $GF(2)$, it's obvious that XOR operation has a higher-speed than operations over $GF(2^8)$ used by RS. Besides, we compare encoding time between original PPC scheme and optimized PPC schedule. Original schedule needs 15 XOR operations and only 11 are needed in the optimized schedule. It's clear that the optimization becomes more obvious when encoding larger data. PPC enables cloud storage customers to explore trade-offs between a little extra storage cost and data confidentiality and integrity. Therefore, we believe that PPC is practical choice in the multiple clouds environment.

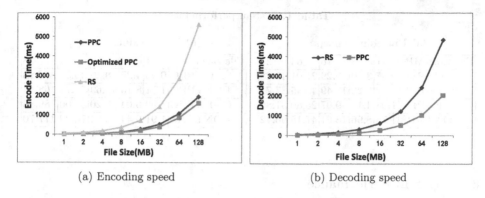

(a) Encoding speed   (b) Decoding speed

Fig. 5. PPC performance

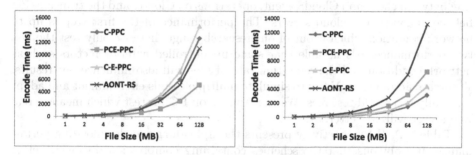

(a) Encoding speed between different secu- (b) Decoding speed between different security schemes   rity schemes

Fig. 6. Security schemes performance

6.2 Performance of Different Security Schemes

In this part, we report scheme performance without network transmission process. We use C–PPC to represent Compression–PPC and C–E–PPC to symbolize the Compression–PCE–PPC. Figure 6(a) presents the encoding speed, two schemes without compression do better because the compression speed is much lower than encryption. PCE–PPC has the greatest performance due to PPC's better capability and parallel optimization using PCE. Figure 6(b) distinguishes the decoding speed between different schemes. Different from the lower compression speed, decompression speed is much faster, schemes with compression perform better. Certainly, PCE–PPC has decent decoding performance after parallel optimization. We can clearly figure that the performance gap of schemes is widening when the data amount increases. Above all, whether for encoding or decoding performance, PCE–PPC indeed excels AONT–RS.

Table 1. System performance

(a) Uploading Time(s).

File Size(MB)	1	8	16	64	128
C−PPC	0.87	3.90	7.29	21.01	45.28
PCE−PPC	1.51	6.23	13.49	43.45	87.71
C−E−PPC	1.08	4.18	9.07	25.80	51.86
AONT−RS	1.78	8.96	16.61	47.15	96.42

(b) Downloading Time(s).

File Size(MB)	1	8	16	64	128
C−PPC	0.98	4.25	8.40	36.38	76.83
PCE−PPC	1.51	8.73	18.69	71.73	168.44
C−E−PPC	1.09	6.04	10.20	39.00	80.83
AONT−RS	1.91	9.44	19.94	75.39	177.70

6.3   System Performance

In CloudS, there're 3 steps in uploading and downloading process: the transmission between client and CloudS agent, operations on CloudS and the transmission between CloudS and cloud servers. The performance of the first step is up to network condition which is out of our research range, here we only test the last two performance. It's notable that some uncontrolled exterior factors such as network condition and the repetition rate of files will also influence our results. We create accounts on Vdisk to simulate multiple clouds environment and adopt randomly generated test files. We run Apache on PC for test which means a real web server will do better.

Table 1(a), (b) respectively presents the uploading and downloading performance. It's obvious that the schemes containing compression do much better due to less data being delivered. C−PPC does the best on account of less data to be transferred and less mechanism being used. PCE−PPC has better performance than AONT−RS on account of PPC's more optimal speeds and parallel optimization using PCE. Certainly, all those schemes are in the range users can accept.

7   Conclusion and Future Work

With the development of cloud storage, the security issues become more and more serious, data integrity and availability is being threatened. We design a new family of erasure code called PPC to guarantee data security. PPC is XOR-based code that results in a low storage computational cost. Simultaneously, for a single-fault-tolerance code, $PPC(k, k + 1, t)$ only need $\frac{(k+1)}{k}$ times extra storage overhead to achieve the trade-offs between storage and fault tolerance. It is important to note that PPC, as a kind of non-systematic code, has a better function of confusion.

With PPC code, we put forward a multi-cloud system called CloudS. Though many multi-cloud systems have appeared in recent years such as RACS and Depsky, they cannot fully adapt to users' different requirements for different files in cloud environment. The single-level security scheme will give rise to a worse user experience and system performance. Specially for the devices with weak computing ability and limited computing resources, redundant and complex security mechanisms will become the bottleneck of the system. In CloudS, we provide several different combination schemes of compression, encryption and coding to achieve multi-level security for better performance and user experiences. At the same time, we implement CloudS as a web application which doesn't require users to do more operation locally.

In our future work, we would like to extend our PPC codes to resist double. In addition, we can still optimize CloudS in terms of performance.

Acknowledgments. This work is partially supported by NSF of China (grant numbers: 61373018, 11301288), Program for New Century Excellent Talents in University (grant number: NCET130301) and the Fundamental Research Funds for the Central Universities (grant number: 65141021).

References

1. Gzip. http://en.wikipedia.org/wiki/Gzip
2. China personal cloud storage industry and users' behavior research. http://www.iimedia.cn/38351.html
3. Dependable storage in the Intercloud. http://domino.research.ibm.com/library/cyberdig.nsf/papers/630549C46339936C852577C200291E78
4. Abu-Libdeh, H., Princehouse, L., Weatherspoon, H.: RACS: a case for cloud storage diversity. In: Proceedings of the 1st ACM Symposium on Cloud Computing, pp. 229–240. ACM, Indianapolis (2010)
5. Ateniese, G., Burns, R., Curtmola, R., Herring, J., Kissner, L., Peterson, Z., Song, D.: Provable data possession at untrusted stores. In: Proceedings of the 14th ACM Conference on Computer and Communications Security, pp. 229–240. ACM, Alexandria (2007)
6. Bessani, A., Correia, M., Quaresma, B., André, F., Sousa, P.: DepSky: dependable and secure storage in a cloud-of-clouds. ACM Trans. Storage (TOS) **9**, 12 (2013)
7. Bowers, K.D., Juels, A., Oprea, A.: HAIL: a high-availability and integrity layer for cloud storage. In: Proceedings of the 16th ACM Conference on Computer and Communications Security, pp. 187–198. ACM, Chicago (2009)
8. Cachin, C., Keidar, I., Shraer, A.: Trusting the cloud. ACM SIGACT News **40**, 81–86 (2009)
9. Ghemawat, S., Gobioff, H., Leung, S.T.: The google file system. In: ACM SIGOPS operating systems review, pp. 29–43. ACM, New York (2003)
10. Hafner, J.L.: WEAVER codes: highly fault tolerant erasure codes for storage systems. In: 4th Conference on File and Storage Technologies, pp. 16–16. USENIX, San Francisco (2005)
11. Juels, A., Kaliski Jr., B.S.: PORs: proofs of retrievability for large files. In: Proceedings of the 14th ACM Conference on Computer and Communications Security, pp. 584–597. ACM, Alexandria (2007)
12. Daemen, J., Rijmen, V.: The Design of Rijndael: AES-The Advanced Encryption Standard. Springer Science and Business Media, Heidelberg (2013)
13. Patterson, D.A., Gibson, G., Katz, R.H.: A case for redundant arrays of inexpensive disks (RAID). ACM (1988)

14. Plank, J.S., Schuman, C.D., Robison, B.D.: Heuristics for optimizing matrix-based erasure codes for fault-tolerant storage systems. In: Proceedings of the 42nd Annual IEEE/IFIP International Conference on Dependable Systems and Networks, pp. 1–12. IEEE/IFIP, Boston (2012)
15. Plank, J.S., et al.: A tutorial on Reed-Solomon coding for fault-tolerance in RAID-like systems. Softw. Prac. Exp. **27**, 995–1012 (1997)
16. Plank, JS, Huang C: Tutorial: erasure coding for storage applications. In: Slides presented at FAST-2013: 11th Usenix Conference on File and Storage Technologies. USENIX, San Jose (2013)
17. Rabin, M.O.: Efficient dispersal of information for security, load balancing, and fault tolerance. J. ACM (JACM) **36**, 335–348 (1989)
18. Rashmi, K., Nakkiran, P., Wang, J., Shah, N.B., Ramchandran, K.: Having your cake and eating it too: jointly optimal erasure codes for I/O, storage, and network-bandwidth. In: Proceedings of the 13th USENIX Conference on File and Storage Technologies, pp. 81–94. USENIX, Santa Clara (2015)
19. Resch, J.K., Plank, J.S.: AONT-RS: blending security and performance in dispersed storage systems. In: Proceedings of the 9th USENIX Conference on File and Storage Technologies. USENIX, San Jose (2011)
20. Singleton, R.: Maximum distance-nary codes. In: IEEE Transactions on Information Theory, pp. 116–118. IEEE (1964)
21. Shamir, A.: How to share a secret. Communications of the ACM. **22**, 612–613 (1979)
22. Sun, J., Xu, M., Feng, S., Li, Z., Wang, G., Liu, X.: Secure store of user authentication tokens in multi-cloud storage system. J. Comput. Inf. Syst. **11**, 1013–1020 (2015)

Crossing – A Highly Available Quorum Protocol for Arbitrary Planar Topologies

Robert Schadek$^{(\boxtimes)}$ and Oliver Theel

Department of Computer Science, Carl von Ossietzky University of Oldenburg,
26111 Oldenburg, Germany
{robert.schadek,theel}@informatik.uni-oldenburg.de

Abstract. Quorums are a powerful concept that can be used to implement highly available services. Quorum protocols use replicas of data to increase service availability. Unfortunately, applying quorum protocols in real-world networks often turns out to be difficult, since efficient quorum protocols depend on a particular topology imposed on the replicas managed by it. To effectuate these protocols, the topology of the real-world network must be identical to the particular topology required by the protocol. Clearly, this is a very strong constraint. In this paper, we present a novel quorum protocol that overcomes this difficulty and works directly on arbitrary planar network topologies. To use the new protocol even on non-planar graphs, we present a method to transform non-planar graphs into planar graphs.

Keywords: Distributed systems · Dependability · High availability · Replication · Quorum protocols · Topologies

1 Introduction

Computer fail from time to time. The idea behind replication is to increase the availability of stored object by installing multiple copies (i.e. replicas) of it. Additionally, replication allows to reduce access costs by accessing local or nearby copies instead of more remotely located ones. A quorum protocol manages those replicas. Quorums have a wide range of applicability. They have been used, for example, for managing data replication and mutual exclusion [1–3]. Nodes are available with a certain probability $p \in [0, 1]$. When used for data replication, each of these nodes hosts a replica of the set of replicas R of the object of interest. If a node is not available, then the hosted replica is also not available. It is a desired property that read and write operations on the replicated data behave as they would do on non-replicated data. This property is formally known as one-copy serializability (1SR) [4]. Managing the replicas on the nodes in a way that the 1SR property is preserved, is the task of the quorum protocol. Quorum protocols usually support read and write operations to manipulate the stored replicated data. For each read and write operation, a set of nodes is identified that executes the operation. Quorum protocols use a set of rules to construct a set of

© Springer International Publishing Switzerland 2015
G. Wang et al. (Eds.): ICA3PP 2015, Part III, LNCS 9530, pp. 717–728, 2015.
DOI: 10.1007/978-3-319-27137-8_52

quorums Q on a static number of nodes N of a distributed system. Generally, a quorum is a subset of N. These sets of quorums are called read quorums (QRs) and write quorums (QWs). A common way for quorum protocols to achieve 1SRs is to construct the QWs in a way that they have at least one replica in common with every other QW:

$$\forall q, q' \in QW, q \neq q' : q \cap q' \neq \emptyset. \tag{1}$$

This way, e.g. locking a QW for writing, prevents every other write operation from locking an additional QW, as a replica has only one write lock. Furthermore, every QR is constructed in a way such that at least one replica of the QR is also part of every QW:

$$\forall q \in QR, q' \in QW : q \cap q' \neq \emptyset. \tag{2}$$

This requirement allows a QR to always read the most recently written data, identified by timestamps or version numbers, as at least one replica of every QR has been part of the last written QW. To prevent data races one possibility is to execute read and write operation mutually exclusive.

The actual physical network topology (PNT) of a, for example data center, a wireless sensor network or any "real life" network, plays no role in any of these considerations.

Some existing quorum protocols use logical network topologies (LNT) for these set operations [5,6]. These structured quorum protocols (SQPs) arrange the nodes in graphs of vertices and edges to decrease the costs of the operations of the quorum protocol. LNTs have been used with great success in quorum protocols. A very prominent and efficient example is the Triangle Lattice (TL) Protocol [5].

If a SQP (having a LNT) is to be used on a PNT, then the two topologies should be identical. This is a very strong requirement, as virtually all PNTs are different and LNTs are often optimized for a specific kind of topology. Therefore, the LNT of the SQP usually must be mapped to the PNT. By "mapping," we mean a bijection from one graph (representing a topology) to another one. This "mapping" can diminish the availability of the operations and increase their costs per operation. A possibility to circumvent such a mapping step is to modify the PNT, but that is not always possible or simply not wanted.

The protocol introduced in this paper does not require any particular a priori LNT. It works directly on the PNT on which it generates an LNT. It does not require a mapping step, which potentially results in an degradation of quorum protocol characteristics. Consequently, the cost and availability analysis for any given PNT in combination with the introduced protocol is precise, compared to those protocols that require a mapping step. The new protocol also can be more efficient than protocols that are agnostic to the PNT in terms of read and write availability and costs per operation. The presented protocol does not require any rearranging of the nodes in the PNT. This is a desired property, as a rearrangement of the elements of the PNT may not be possible.

In this paper we present this new protocol, called the *Crossing Protocol*. We show, how the protocol is applied to planar PNTs, and how non-planar graphs get transformed into a planar graph such that the Crossing Protocol can be applied to them. Additionally, we discuss why the most outer nodes of a graph play a key role for the Crossing Protocol, and we present an efficient algorithm to identify these nodes.

The rest of the paper is structured as follows. Section 2 discusses related work. The system model is presented in Sect. 3. The mapping approach, required by the quorum protocol with dedicated LNTs, is presented in Sect. 4. In Sect. 5, the Crossing Protocol is presented. A short evaluation is given in Sect. 6, followed by an conclusion and ideas for future work in Section 7.

2 Related Work

Quorum protocols can be divided into two categories: unstructured and structured quorum protocols. Unstructured quorum protocols (UQPs) basically only use set operations to guarantee the 1SR property. Examples for UQPs are the *Majority Consensus protocol* [7] and the *Weighted Voting Protocol* [8]. UQPs construct quorums with set operations on the given replicas. This has the advantage that the quorum construction algorithms are usually simple and easy to understand. As the attribute "unstructured" indicates, replicas are not structured in any graph or graph-structure. This can present problems when trying to access the nodes of a quorum mapped to a PNT.

SQPs organize nodes in graphs. Usually, this allows SQPs to exhibit quite high availabilities for the read or write operations and at the same time to limit the costs of these operations. A protocol of this category is the *Grid Protocol* [6]. It has subsequently been generalized to the Triangle Lattice (TL) Protocol [5]. The grid and especially the triangular lattice do not conform well to PNTs as their structure is highly specific and therefore inflexible. The *Crumbling Walls Protocol* [9] is more flexible a protocol, it uses so called *walls* to arrange the managed nodes. These walls consist of rows and columns. Therefore, the Crumbling Walls Protocol is still limited to a specific kind of PNT. In [10], the authors of the Crumbling Walls Protocol even show that a *logarithmic wall* is the only highly available wall. This further diminishes the applicability of the protocol for arbitrary PNTs. In [11], a method has been presented to modify grid-like topologies to balance the availability of read and write operations and their costs to a given requirement. As this method also adds edges to the graph-structure, it is in conflict with our goal to preserve a given PNT. In consequence, the SQPs are limited to the topology they are designed for.

3 System Model

In order to concisely present the Crossing Protocol some definitions are required. A graph-structure $GS = (V, E)$ is defined as a two-tuple with a set of vertices V and a set of edges E. Edges connect vertices. A vertex $v \in V$ is defined as a three-tuple $v = (x, y, i)$, where $x, y \in \mathbb{R}$ are coordinates in a plane and $i \in \mathbb{N}$ is the id of the vertex. The shorthand notation v_i donates a vertex with id i. $|V|$ represents the number of vertices in GS.

An *edge* $e_{i,j} \in E$ is defined as $e_{i,j} := (v_i, v_j)$, where $v_i, v_j \in V$.

A path $\langle v_0, v_1, \ldots, v_n \rangle$ exists in GS iff:

$$\forall i, 0 \le i \le n : \exists v_i \in V \text{ and} \tag{3}$$

$$\forall i, 0 \le i < n : \exists e_{v_i, v_{i+1}} \in E \tag{4}$$

$\mathbb{V}(\langle v_0, v_1, \ldots, v_n \rangle)$ denotes the set of vertices of a path i.e. $\mathbb{V}(\langle v_0, v_1, \ldots, v_n \rangle) = \{v_0, v_1, \ldots, v_n\}$. $\mathbb{E}(\langle v_0, v_1, \ldots, v_n \rangle)$ denotes the set of the edges of a path such that: $\mathbb{E}(\langle v_0, v_1, \ldots, v_n \rangle) = \{e_{0,1} \ldots, e_{n-1,n}\}$.

Two vertices v, v' are called *connected* in a GS if there exists at least one path $\langle v, \ldots, v' \rangle$ in GS denoted by $\diamond_{v,v'}(GS)$. The operator $\models$ is used to state that a given path fulfills a given $\diamond_{v,v'}(GS)$. For instance, a possible path $\diamond_{1,8}(GS)$ for the GS in Fig. 1a is $\langle 1, 14, 8 \rangle$. This fact can be stated by $\diamond_{1,8}(GS) \models \langle 1, 14, 8 \rangle$.

A path $p = \langle v_i, \ldots v_j \rangle \models \diamond_{i,j}(GS)$ is considered to partition GS into two graph-structures $GS_1 = (V_1, E_1), GS_2 = (V_2, E_2)$ iff, given p:

$$\nexists p' : \diamond_{v,v'}(GS) \models p' \wedge p \ne p'$$
$$\wedge\, v \in V_1 \wedge v' \in V_2$$
$$\wedge\, \mathbb{V}(p') \cap \mathbb{V}(p) = \emptyset. \tag{5}$$

This basically states that a path partitions a GS, if there is no path from GS_1 to GS_2 whose vertices do not intersect with the vertices of the partitioning path. For GS_1, GS_2 and p the following is true:

$$V_1 \cup V_2 \cup \mathbb{V}(p) = V \tag{6}$$

$$V_1 \cap V2 \cap \mathbb{V}(p) = \emptyset. \tag{7}$$

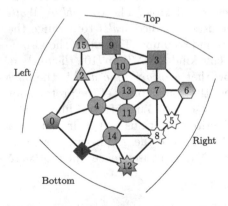

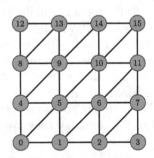

(a) A graph with the Top, Bottom, Left and Right nodes marked in different colors and shapes for easier distinguishing.

(b) A 16 node graph for the Triangle Lattice (TL) Protocol.

Fig. 1. Graphs used by quorum protocols.

As an example for a partitioning path consider the path $\langle 1, 4, 10, 3 \rangle$ in Fig. 1a. It partitions the vertices of the graph in $V_1 = \{0, 2, 9, 15\}$ and $V_2 = \{5, 6, 7, 11, 12, 13, 14\}$. $D = (D_V(GS), D_E(GS))$ is a tuple of two functions displaying the vertices and edges of the graph-structure GS on a two dimensional plane. The resulting graphical representation is called a *graph* G. $D_V(GS)$ displays the vertices of GS as a point each according to their x, y coordinates. An edge $e_{i,j}$ in the graph is represented by $D_E(GS)$ by a set of points between the vertices $v_i, v_j \in G$ such that:

$$\{x \mid x = (v_i.x, v_i.y) + r(v_j.x - v_i.x, v_j.y - v_i.y) \wedge r \in \mathbb{R} \wedge r \in [0, 1]\}, \quad (8)$$

i.e. by a straight line. A graph $G = (V, E)$ is planar iff: $\forall e, e' \in E, e \neq e'$: $D_E(e) \cap D_E(e') = \emptyset$.

4 The Mapping Approach

As presented earlier, existing SQPs are usually limited to a specific LNT, and are therefore not applicable to PNTs in the general case. A generic approach to apply these protocols to any PNT is to map the nodes of a protocol's LNT to the nodes of the PNT. In order to usefully and fairly compare the Crossing Protocol with other protocols, we have to analyze these protocols when they are mapped to an identical PNT.

A mapping is a bijection from one graph to another one. This requires that the number of nodes in the codomain graph is at least equal to the number of the nodes of the original graph. Formally, a mapping $M(G, G')$ from graph $G = (V, E)$ to graph $G' = (V', E')$ is defined as:

$$M(G, G') = \{(v_1, v'_1), \ldots (v_n, v'_n)\} \quad (9)$$
$$\forall (v, v') \in M : v \in V, v' \in V' \quad (10)$$
$$\forall (v, v'), (v, v'') : v' = v'' \quad (11)$$
$$\forall (v', v), (v'', v) : v' = v'' \quad (12)$$

In order to apply SQPs to arbitrary topologies, either their LNT must match the PNT or the nodes of the LNT have to be mapped to the PNT. As it is highly unlikely that the LNT matches the PNT, the mapping often becomes a necessity. As an example, consider the graph in Fig. 1b used by the TL Protocol. To use that LNT on the graph presented in Fig. 1a, it has to be mapped onto it. The mapped TL Protocol obviously has the disadvantage that is not aware of the actual topology used. In order to use the quorums created by the TL Protocol on the PNT shown in Fig. 1a, additional nodes may be required to connect the nodes of the created quorum on the PNT. The Formulas (9)–(12) define that every node v of graph G is uniquely mapped to a node v' of graph G'. The challenge is to find a mapping that requires as few additional nodes as possible to connect the quorums created "for graph G on graph G'". This is best shown by considering a simple example. A hand-optimized mapping from the graph structure GS in Fig. 1b to the graph structure GS' in Fig. 1a is $M(GS, GS') =:$ $\{(0, 12), (1, 8), (2, 5), (3, 6), (4, 14), (5, 11), (6, 7), (7, 3), (8, 0), (9, 2), (10, 10),$ $(11, 9), (12, 1), (13, 13), (14, 4), (15, 15)\}$. If the TL Protocol yields the diagonal consisting of nodes $\{0, 5, 10, 15\}$ as a write quorum and the mapping is as shown, then finding the shortest connecting path between the four nodes is a complex problem. If mapped to the graph in Fig. 1a, with the above given mapping, then the nodes $\{12, 11, 10, 15\}$ have to be connected. None of these nodes of the write quorum are directly connected by an edge of the PNT. Depending on the availability of the additional nodes, the presented write quorum might not even be available. To overcome the discussed shortcomings, we propose the Crossing Protocol.

5   The Crossing Protocol

The idea behind the proposed protocol is to create intersecting paths that cross (or: partitions) a given PNT vertically and/or horizontally. We call these paths *crossings*. The nodes of the crossings are used as quorums in the Crossing Protocol. In this sense quorums must cross the PNT vertically or horizontally. Write quorums have to cross the PNT vertically and horizontally.

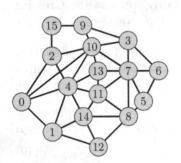

Fig. 2. Non-planar graph

Every vertical crossing must intersect with every horizontal crossing. Therefore, every read quorum has to intersect with every write quorum and every write quorum has to intersect with every other write quorum. In a planar graph, every vertical crossing intersects with every horizontal crossing. This is because a vertical crossing partitions the graph such that the start and end node of a horizontal crossing are not in the same partition. As an example, consider the horizontal crossing $h = \langle 2, 4, 11, 8 \rangle$ in Fig. 1a. There is no way to create a vertical crossing connecting the nodes of top partition $GS1 = \{15, 9, 3, 6, 10, 7, 5, 13\}$ to the nodes of the bottom partition $GS2 = \{0, 1, 12, 14\}$, without using at least one of the nodes of the crossing, i.e.,

$$\nexists p : \diamond_{v,v'} (GS) : v \in GS_1 \wedge v' \in GS_2 \wedge h \cap p = \emptyset. \tag{13}$$

Using the same horizontal crossing for the non-planar graph in Fig. 2 gives a different result. The path $k := \langle 9, 10, 0 \rangle$ connects the two previously defined partitions $GS1$ and $GS2$ without using any of the nodes of the crossing. This is possible, because the $e_{0,10}$ and $e_{2,4}$ introduce non-planarity into the graph. Thereby, disabling the 1SR property.

Crossings are paths that connect specific nodes. These specific nodes are the nodes on the border of the graph. The outer most nodes of the graph make up the border. Furthermore, the border of graph G of a given GS is divided into four subsets, the top set (T), the bottom set (B), the left set (L) and the right set (R). Together, these four sets are called the TBLR sets. The identification of the border nodes and the construction of the TBLR sets are discussed in detail in Sect. 5.1. The TBLR sets are defined as follows: let U be a placeholder for any of the sets T, B, L and R.

$$U \neq \emptyset \tag{14}$$

$$\forall v, v' \in U : \diamond_{v,v'}(GS) \in U \tag{15}$$

$$T \cap L \neq \emptyset \wedge T \cap R \neq \emptyset \tag{16}$$

$$B \cap L \neq \emptyset \wedge B \cap R \neq \emptyset \tag{17}$$

$$T \cap B = \emptyset \wedge L \cap R = \emptyset \tag{18}$$

As an example, consider the topology in Fig. 1a.

Definitions of Read Quorums: The nodes of every vertical or horizontal graph crossing form a read quorum. A vertical read quorum VR for a graph G of a given GS is defined as:

$$\exists v, v' \in VR : v \in T \wedge v' \in B \wedge \diamond_{v,v'}(GS). \tag{19}$$

A horizontal read quorum HR for a given graph G is defined as:

$$\exists v, v' \in VR : v \in L \wedge v' \in R \wedge \diamond_{v,v'}(GS). \tag{20}$$

In order to construct a QR, a path in GS must be found that connects a either a top node to a bottom node or a left node to a right node.

Definition of Write Quorums: A write quorum is defined as:

$$QW := VR \cup HR. \tag{21}$$

This means that every union of a vertical crossing and a horizontal crossing is a valid write quorum.

As seen in the above Formulas (16)–(18), four pairs of border sets intersect and these are called corner sets. The corners are named C_{TL}, C_{TR}, C_{BL}, C_{BR} and are defined as:

$$C_{TL} = T \cap L, \tag{22}$$

$$C_{TR} = T \cap R, \tag{23}$$

$$C_{BL} = B \cap L, \tag{24}$$

$$C_{BR} = B \cap R. \tag{25}$$

These four corners sets can be used to construct a write quorum more easily. Instead of finding a vertical and horizontal crossing separately. In order to create a write quorum, a path must be found that either connects the C_{TL} corner with the C_{BR} corner or a path that connects the C_{BL} corner with the C_{TR} corner.

5.1   Graph Preparation

To use the Crossing Protocol on an arbitrary graph, the graph has to be prepared. The preparation steps are:

1. transforming the graph into a planar graph,
2. selecting border nodes, and
3. dividing the border nodes into the TBLR sets.

1. Transforming a Non-planar Graph into a Planar Graph: The first step is to transform the graph into a planar graph. Non-planarity is an unwanted property. As shown earlier it averts the 1SR property of the Crossing Protocol. Therefore, a non-planar graph must be "made planar" before it can be used by the Crossing Protocol.

There are at least two possible ways to make a graph planar. The first way is to change the coordinates of the vertices in the plane such that no edges intersect. Unfortunately, not all graphs can be transformed into a planar homomorph graph [12]. Additionally, this requires a change of the PNT, we set out to preserve. The second way is to remove edges until the topology is planar. The removal of edges can be achieved without actually physically removing them; they are simply ignored for any operation on the graph. By only removing edges that participate in intersections, the efficiency of this approach can be improved. By removing an edge e we mean removing it from E of the graph-structure. However, removing edges also leads to difficulties: Every removed edge has influence on the number of possible read and write quorums, because these edges can no longer be part of any vertical or horizontal path. Our current strategy is to randomly select one of the intersecting edges for removal. This is repeated until there are no more intersection edges. With a planar graph, we can select the border nodes.

2. Selection of the Border Nodes: To create crossings that partition a graph, the graph must be planar, and the start and end node of the crossing must be on the border of the graph. Considering the invalid horizontal crossing $n = \langle 4, 11, 8 \rangle$ in Fig. 1a, the problem is obvious. The crossing n does not partition the graph. Therefore, vertical crossings e.g. $\langle 0, 2, 15 \rangle$ exist that do not intersect with n and thereby destory the 1SR property of the Crossing Protocol.

We select the border of a graph by traversing the edges of the graph in a specific way. Informally speaking, we traverse the hull by following the leftmost adjacent edge in relation to the current edge, until we reach the starting point. By "leftmost edge," we mean the edge with the highest angle in relation to the current edge (see Fig. 3). The more the edge $e_{1,2}$ turns counterclockwise around node 1 the higher the angle α between $e_{1,2}$ and edge $e_{0,1}$ becomes. Eventually, the angle between the edge $e_{0,1}$ and the edge $e_{1,2}$ becomes $360°$. Considering the edge $e_{0,2}$ in graph in Fig. 1a, the adjacency edges are $e_{2,10}, e_{2,15}$ and the returning edge is $e_{2,0}$.

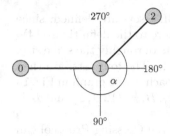

Fig. 3. The angle between two edges

The leftmost, adjacency edge for that edge is edge $e_{2,0}$. The angle between the edge $e_{0,2}$ and $e_{2,0}$ is $360°$. But, we only consider the directly opposite edge if no other adjacency edge is present. Therefore, the leftmost, adjacency edge for the edge $e_{0,2}$ is edge $e_{2,15}$. Form edge $e_{2,15}$, the next leftmost, adjacency edge is edge $e_{15,9}$. When repeating this procedure until the start node is encountered, we get the path $b = \langle 0, 2, 15, 9, 3, 6, 5, 8, 12, 1, 0 \rangle$ (see Fig. 1). The nodes in $\mathbb{V}(b)$ are then the elements of the border of the graph.

So far, it has not been explained how the first edge of the border is obtained. If this edge is not part of the border itself, then the described algorithm will not function correctly. To obtain a correct "starting edge," at least one vertex of the graph must be found that is part of the border. Such a vertex v_l can be identified by selecting the vertex with the smallest x-coordinate. The coordinates of the vertices are given as described in Sect. 3. A horizontal edge is created that leads into the leftmost vertex v_l. This edge e_s is defined as $e_s = (v_{ll}, v_l)$ where v_{ll} is defined as $v_{ll} = (v_l.x - 1, v_l.y)$. Figure 4 shows the construction of the border as well as the placement of the v_{ll}-vertex. The leftmost vertex v_l of the convex hull in Fig. 4 is the vertex with id 0. The edge $e = (v_{ll}, 0)$ is the starting edge for the algorithm in this example. The vertex v_{ll} is not part of the border. To better illustrate the execution order of the algorithm, compare Fig. 4. In Fig. 4, the vertices of the border have a red background and a rectangular shape. There, the edges are numbered correspondingly to the steps of the algorithm.

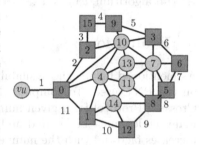

Fig. 4. The border selection process.

The presented approach is different from existing algorithms calculating the border or a specific alpha shape, as it relies on the edges of the graph and not only on the vertices. An example for an algorithms calculating the border of a set of vertices is presented in [13] by Moreira and Santos.

3. Creating the TBLR Sets from the Set of Border Nodes:
Now that the border nodes are selected, the next step is to create the TBLR sets from the border nodes. These sets are needed for defining vertical and horizontal crossings.

The TBLR sets control how many vertical and horizontal crossings can be created. Control over the amount of vertical and horizontal crossings gives control over the amount of read and write quorums that can be created. Having control here is important, since an imbalance in the amount of vertical and horizontal crossings favours QRs as they only need a vertical or an horizontal crossing. QWs are negatively impacted as they need both.

There is quite some freedom in the way how TBLR sets are defined, since the only requirement being that the resulting sets adhere to the definitions (14)–(16). One approach is to divide the border into four sets of roughly the same size, where each set intersects with the next set in one node. The four sets, are then sequentially named T,L,B, and R. Applying this approach to the graph in Fig. 1a results in the sets: $T = \{15, 9, 3, 6\}, R = \{6, 5, 8, 12\}, B = \{12, 1, 0\}$ and $L = \{0, 2, 15\}$.

With a planar graph and the TBLR sets defined, the Crossing Protocol can create QRs and QWs.

5.2   Read and Write Operations

The Crossing Protocol constructs a QR by selecting the nodes of a path from a node of the Top set to a node of the Bottom set or from a node of the Left set to a node of the Right set. The path can change as nodes fail and/or get repaired over time. As mentioned earlier a QW is a union of a vertical and horizontal crossing. Short paths are favorable as they require fewer nodes and therefore decrease the cost of an operation. An algorithm from the literature, like the A^* [14] algorithm, can be used to even find the shortest path.

6   Evaluation

As mentioned before, the availability and cost of the Crossing Protocol depends on the PNT used. To compute the average read and write availability of the Crossing Protocol for a given number of nodes, all possible PNTs having these many nodes must be created and analyzed. But the number of graphs to test increases factorial with the number of nodes.

In order to compare the Crossing Protocol with other protocols, measurement criteria have to be selected first. For quorum protocols, these criteria are the availability of the read and write operations and the costs of these operations. The costs are the average number of nodes required for a read or a write operation under a given average availability of all nodes. The availability measure represents the availability of the read or write operation in relation to the availability of a single node.

Figure 5a, b show a comparison of the read and write availability of the Crossing Protocol (Crossing) on the graph in Fig. 1a, the TL Protocol (Lattice) on the graph in Fig. 1b, and the TL Protocol mapped (Lattice_mapped) to the graph in Fig. 1a, with the earlier shown mapping. The read and write availability of the TL Protocol is exceeding the Crossing Protocol, but only as long as no mapping is used. When doing so, then the Crossing Protocol exceeds the TL Protocol. When comparing average costs per operation, as shown in Figs. 5c, d, the Crossing Protocol is superior to the TL Protocol and especially to the mapped TL Protocol.

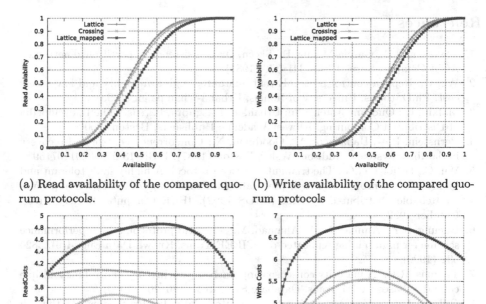

(a) Read availability of the compared quorum protocols.

(b) Write availability of the compared quorum protocols

(c) Read costs of the compared quorum protocols.

(d) Write costs of the compared quorum protocols

Fig. 5. Read availability, and write availability and cost comparison.

7 Conclusion and Future Work

In this paper, the Crossing Protocol was introduced. It has been shown how this new protocol can be applied to arbitrary real-world planar graphs. Furthermore, we have shown how to prepare graphs such that the Crossing Protocol is applicable to them, without impacting the protocol's real-world applicability.

As mentioned in Sect. 5.1, graphs are made planar by removing edges. With a growing number of intersections, the number of possible edge removal combinations grows factorially. Selecting the wrong edge for removal, can lead to a reduction of operation availability or can increase the cost per operation. Therefore, we are developing strategies to remove edges optimally in regards to these two properties.

We are currently evaluating the Crossing Protocol on a extensive set of graphs. The graph generator presented in [15] is used to create this set of graphs.

Acknowledgements. This work has been partially supported by the German Research Foundation (DFG) as part of the Transregional Collaborative Research Center "Automatic Verification and Analysis of Complex Systems" (SFB/TR 14 AVACS).

References

1. Davidson, S.B., García-Molina, H., Skeen, D.: Consistency in partitioned networks. ACM Comput. Surv. **17**(3), 341–370 (1985)
2. Wu, C.: Replica control protocols that guarantee high availability and low access cost. Ph.D. thesis, University of Illinois, Urbana-Champaign (1993)
3. Malkhi, D.: Quorum systems. In: Urban, J., Dasgupta, P. (eds.) The Encyclopedia of Distributed Computing. Kluwer Academic Publishers, Boston (2000)
4. Bernstein, P.A., Hadzilacos, V., Goodman, N.: Concurrency control and recovery in database systems. Addison Wesley, Boston (1987). ISBN-13 978–0201107159
5. Wu, C., Belford, G.G.: The triangular lattice protocol: A highly fault tolerant and highly efficient protocol for replicated data. In: Proceedings of the 11th Symposium on Reliable Distributed Systems (SRDS 1992). IEEE Computer Society Press, October 1992
6. Cheung, S.Y., Ammar, M.H., Ahamad, M.: The grid protocol: a high performance scheme for maintaining replicated data. IEEE Trans. Knowl. Data Eng. **4**(6), 582–592 (1990)
7. Thomas, R.H.: A majority consensus approach to concurrency control for multiple copy databases. ACM Trans. Database Syst. **4**(2), 180–207 (1979)
8. Gifford, D.K.: Weighted voting for replicated data. In: Proceedings of the 7th Symposium on Operating Systems Principles (SOSP 1979), pp. 150–161. ACM Press, December 1979
9. Peleg, D., Wool, A.: Crumbling walls: a class of high availability quorum systems. Technical report CS94-07, Faculty of Mathematical Sciences, Weizmann Institute of Science, Rehovot, Israel, 1 January 1994
10. Peleg, D., Wool, A.: The availability of crumbling wall quorum systems. Discrete Appl. Math. **74**(1), 69–83 (1997)
11. Theel, O., Pagnia-Koch, H.-H.: General design of grid-based data replication schemes using graphs and a few rules. In: Proceedings of the 15th International Conference on Distributed Computing Systems (ICDCS 1995), pp. 395–403. IEEE Computer Society Press, May 1995
12. Boyer, J.M., Myrvold, W.J.: On the cutting edge: simplified o(n) planarity by edge addition. J. Graph Algorithms Appl. **8**, 2004 (2004)
13. Moreira, A., Santos, M.Y.: Concave hull: a k-nearest neighbours approach for the computation of the region occupied by a set of points (2007)
14. Hart, P.E., Nilsson, N.J., Raphael, B.: A formal basis for the heuristic determination of minimum cost paths. IEEE Trans. Syst. Sci. Cybern. **SSC–4**(2), 100–107 (1968)
15. Schadek, R., Theel, O.: A graph suite generator for real world quorum protocol analysis. In: Proceedings of the 2nd Argentinian National Conference on Engineer Informatics and Information Systems (CoNaIISI 2014), San Luis, Argentina, November 2014. Red de Carreras de Ingeniería Informática/Sistemas de Información (RIISIC)

Note on Fast Bridge Fault Test Generation Based on Critical Area

Masayuki Arai[1](✉), Shingo Inuyama[2], and Kazuhiko Iwasaki[3]

[1] College of Industrial Technology, Nihon University, Tokyo, Japan
arai.masayuki@nihon-u.ac.jp
[2] Graduate School of System Design, Tokyo Metropolitan University, Hachioji, Japan
[3] Library and Academic Information Center, Tokyo Metropolitan University, Hachioji, Japan

Abstract. Shrinking feature size and higher integration on semiconductor device manufacturing technology bring a problem of the gap between the defect level estimated at the design stage from the reported one for fabricated devices. As one possible strategy to accurately estimate the defect level, authors have proposed weighted bridge fault coverage estimation. In this study we evaluate the effectiveness of prioritization of target faults based on critical area, aiming to develop fast and compact test pattern set generation. The proposed scheme apply two-step test pattern generation, where test pattern reordering is only applied to the second pattern set which is generated for the residual faults of first small pattern set. The experimental results indicate the proposed scheme can reduce execution time of pattern reordering significantly, while keeping the number of required patterns with the same level as conventional greedy algorithm. We further discuss on test pattern selection algorithm based on only fault detection information, in order to keep the execution time by the linear order with the number of target faults.

Keywords: Weighted fault coverage · Critical area · Bridge fault · Test generation · Greedy algorithm

1 Introduction

Detecting all manufacturing defects by production test is of great difficulty in IC manufacturing process, and thus it is important to predict precisely the incidence of field failure due to overlooked defects, in order to estimate design and manufacturing costs [1–4]. Conventional schemes for field failure rate estimation may include, for example, the following classic formula [2] based on yield Y and production test quality f:

$$DL = 1 - Y(1 - f). \tag{1}$$

The test quality f has usually been represented as fault coverage, or detection probability of modeled faults, where wiring lengths/widths and defect sizes are

© Springer International Publishing Switzerland 2015
G. Wang et al. (Eds.): ICA3PP 2015, Part III, LNCS 9530, pp. 729–740, 2015.
DOI: 10.1007/978-3-319-27137-8_53

not considered. Therefore, gap between defect levels of estimated value based conventional model such as Eq. (1) and actual values for manufacturing devices.

Layout-aware derivation is one of the ways to improve accuracy of estimated fault coverage. We have evaluated effectiveness of weighted fault coverage where incidence rate of each fault is weighted by critical area [5]. We also proposed test pattern reordering based on target fault selection considering critical area and greedy algorithm [6], aiming to achieve higher weighted fault coverage with as smaller number of patterns as possible. While greedy algorithm can quickly improve weighted fault coverage with small number of patterns, it requires unavoidable execution time for reordering. The execution time is proportional to the square to the number of target faults, and thus the results showed inadequateness of application to practical-scale circuits.

In this study we propose fast and compact test pattern set generation, based on prioritization of target faults considering critical area. The proposed scheme apply two-step test pattern generation, where test pattern reordering is only applied to the second pattern set which is generated for the residual faults of first small pattern set. The experimental results indicate the proposed scheme can reduce execution time of pattern reordering significantly, while keeping the number of required patterns with the same level as conventional greedy algorithm. We further discuss on test pattern selection algorithm based on only fault detection information, in order to keep the execution time by the linear order with the number of target faults.

2   Test Pattern Reordering Based on Weighted Fault Coverage

2.1   Weighted Fault Coverage

When a conductive particle exists on a manufactured semiconductor device, it might not cause malfunctions if its size is smaller than minimum line interval; however, it might become a resistive bridge defect if it connects two or more lines. Considering the set of all possible particles that cause defects, the area which is plotted by the central coordinates of such particles is referred to as critical area. The process for calculating critical area for a given defect size r is called as critical area analysis: it can be performed by several commercial tools such as Calibre Yield Analyzer by Mentor Graphics [7].

By adding some constraints on target signal lines for critical area analysis tool, we can calculate the size of critical area for a set of conductive particles which become defects between a given pair of signal lines. In the following we refer to the critical area between two signal lines as bridge defect critical area, and the bridge defect critical area between two signals s_i and s_j for a given defect size r is represented as $A_{bridge}(r, s_i, s_j)$. Figure 1 shows an example of bridge defect critical area. There are three signals A, B, and C, and the area painted gray is the bridge defect critical area between A and B, $A_{bridge}(r, A, B)$. The size of the area (scalar value) might also be implicitly represented by $A_{bridge}(r, A, B)$.

In this study, due to tool constraints, we regard a particle as r by r square one, not circular.

By executing critical area analysis for every pair of two signals s_i and s_j existing in the netlist G, the size of bridge defect critical area $A_{bridge}(r, s_i, s_j)$ under a given defect size r and the layout L. The incident rate of a bridge fault between specific pair of signals is thought to be proportional to the size of its critical area [11]. Therefore, weighted bridge fault coverage for a given defect size r and the test pattern set T, $WFC_{bridge}(r, T)$, can be calculated as

$$WFC_{bridge}(r, T) = \frac{\sum_{i=1}^{t} \sum_{j=i+1}^{n} A_{bridge}(r, s_i, s_j) \cdot D_{bridge}(s_i, s_j, T)}{\sum_{i=1}^{t} \sum_{j=i+1}^{n} A_{bridge}(r, s_i, s_j)}, \quad (2)$$

where $D_{bridge}(s_i, s_j, T)$ is the detection information of the bridge faults, which is 1 if detectable by the test pattern set T and 0 otherwise.

2.2   Greedy-Algorithm-Based Test Pattern Reordering

Aiming to obtain a test pattern set such that achieves higher weighted fault coverage with less number of test patterns, in the previous work we evaluated the effectiveness of reordering by greedy algorithm [6]. Considering suitableness of the scheme to practical-scale device development, we utilized commercial ATPG (automatic test pattern generation) tool to generate test pattern set for the target circuit, and then reordered the patterns using in-house fault simulator, taking critical area of each fault into account.

Let $T = \{t_i : 0 \leq i < n\}$ denote the given test pattern set, where n represents the number of test patterns. First, for every test pattern t_i in T, considering a test pattern set consisting of only t_i, weighted fault coverage $WFC_{bridge}(r, t_i)$ is calculated. Then the test pattern which indicates the highest $WFC_{bridge}(r, t_i)$ is selected as the first pattern t'_0 of reordered set T' and removed from T. Next, for every test pattern t_i in T, the weighted fault coverage for the test pattern set $T' \cup \{t_i\}$ is calculated as $WFC_{bridge}(r, \{t'_0, t_i\})$, and the test pattern t_i with highest $WFC_{bridge}(r, \{t'_0, t_i\})$ is selected as the second pattern. The above selection is repeated until all the patterns are reordered or weighted fault coverage is no more improved. If the weighed fault coverage reaches to the maximum value before all patterns are selected, then the pattern set can be compacted with smaller number of patterns from the original pattern set.

Figure 1 shows experimental results for reordering, where weighted and unweighted fault coverages for original and reordered pattern sets are plotted with given number of the patterns applied. The target circuit is the ISCAS'89 s15850 benchmark circuit. By reordering the patterns weighted fault coverage can be improved at smaller number of patterns. For example, the weighted fault coverage by first 100 patterns was improved from 99.1 to 99.8 %. The number of patterns required to achieve more than 99.9 % of weighted fault coverage was reduced from 204 patterns to 135 patterns. The total number of patterns required to achieve 100 % weighted fault coverage was reduced from 317 to 296.

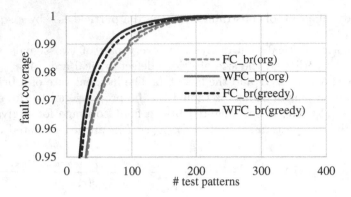

Fig. 1. Weighted and un-weighted fault coverage for original and reordered pattern set (ISCAS'89 s15850).

3   Faster Test Pattern Reordering

3.1   Partitioned Pattern Generation and Window-Based Reordering

In this study we propose a partitioned pattern generation and reordering scheme. While the same fault model of bridging fault is applied to both first and second pattern generation, the first pattern set is generated targeting only a part of faults which have larger critical areas. Then, similarly to the per-model test generation, the second pattern set is generated for the faults which are not detected by the first pattern set, and then reordering is applied only to the second pattern set. The proposed partitioned pattern generation is expected to control the trade-offs between generation time and the number of test patterns.

Figure 2 illustrates the flow of the proposed partitioned pattern generation. First, the target faults are sorted in the descending order of critical areas, and the faults in top k_1 % are selected as the target for the first pattern generation. Next, we execute fault simulation targeting all faults, in order to check whether each non-targeted fault is luckily detectable by the first pattern set. We then generate the second pattern set targeting the undetected faults, and the second pattern set is reordered by greedy algorithm so that weighted fault coverage is improved as less patterns as possible. Note that the reordering assumes that the second pattern set is applied just after the first pattern set, and thus the greedy algorithm selects a pattern which shows highest fault coverage when combined with first pattern set and already-selected second patterns.

For further speed-up, the partitioned pattern generation scheme also introduces search window at reordering of the second pattern set. Figure 3 illustrates the basic idea of window-based reordering. The second patterns are sorted in the descending order of single-pattern weighted fault coverage, and the search of best additional pattern is only performed among the search window consisting of the top k_2 % patterns. After interchanging the best pattern and the pattern at the leftmost position in the window, the window slides one pattern to the right and the search is repeated until window reaches to the end of the second pattern set or coverage reaches to 100 % or other target value.

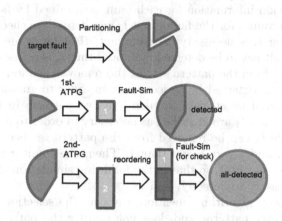

Fig. 2. Flow of partitioned pattern generation and reordering

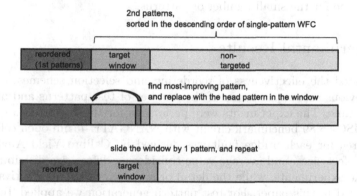

Fig. 3. Window-based speed up of reordering

3.2   Test Pattern Selection Based on Detection Information

Aiming at development of reordering algorithm whose computational complexity is linear order of the number of target faults, we further investigated test pattern selection scheme based on only detection information obtained by fault simulation. The proposed selection scheme executes fault simulation twice and removes redundant patterns from the pattern set.

Figure 4 illustrates the flow of proposed test pattern selection scheme. The first fault simulation is executed where every fault is checked if detectable or not by each pattern. To suppress memory usage, the scheme only counts the detection times for each fault by the pattern set, instead of storing entire detection information according to the pair of a fault and a pattern. For example, a fault f_1 can be detected by the patterns t_1 or t_3, and thus the counter value 2 is stored for f_1 in the end of the simulation. Then the second fault simulation is performed pattern-by-pattern, in the reverse order of first simulation. For a pattern t_i, detection information for each fault is obtained by fault simulation, and then counter values for the faults that t_i can detect are checked in order to determine whether t_i is necessary or redundant. If at least one fault's counter value is 1, this fault has to be detected by t_i, and thus t_i is necessary. Otherwise, t_i can be removed from the pattern set. At the removal, counters corresponding to the faults that is detected by t_i decrement in order to guarantee that every fault can be detected by at least one non-removed pattern. In the example of Fig. 5, patterns t_5 and t_4 are identified as necessary in order to detect f_7 and f_6, respectively, while t_3 can be removed from the pattern set because all counter values for f_1, f_2, and f_4 are larger than 1. Then, the counter values for these three faults decrement by 1, so that in the following simulation the pattern t_1 is identified as necessary to detect f_1 and f_2.

Unlike to greedy algorithms mentioned above, the selection algorithm just removes unnecessary patterns and does not reorder the pattern set. That is, while guaranteeing the detection of all faults that can be detected by the original pattern set, the selection scheme does not contribute to improve the weighted fault coverage for the small number of patterns.

4   Experimental Results

We evaluated the effectiveness of reordering and selection schemes mentioned in the previous section, in terms of the number of test patterns and algorithm execution time. The experiments were performed for the layout data generated based on ISCAS'89 benchmark circuit with NANGATE 45 nm open cell library. Critical area for each bridge fault was derived by Calibre Yield Analyzer for multiple defect sizes, and average value considering defect size distribution was used in the experiments, while the detail of average critical area derivation has been omitted in this paper. For test pattern generation we applied TetraMAX with stuck-at fault model and 4-way bridge fault model. For bridge fault model only the faults which have critical areas were targeted.

4.1   Evaluation of Partitioned Pattern Generation

For partitioned pattern generation scheme, we first evaluated the effectiveness of partitioning on number of patterns and execution time, without applying window-based reordering. Table 1 shows the experimental results for ISCAS'89 s9234 benchmark circuit, where the ratio of the target faults at the first pattern generation, k_1 %, is set in the range of 0–50 %. The tables shows the number of target faults for the given value of k_1, ratio of target faults' critical area among total critical area, the numbers of test patterns in the first, second, and combined pattern set, and execution time for reordering of second pattern set.

	f1	f2	f3	f4	f5	f6	f7
t1	1	1					
t2		1	1		1		
t3	1	1		1			
t4			1		1	1	
t5				1			1
count	2	3	2	2	2	1	1

(a) First fault simulation

	f1	f2	f3	f4	f5	f6	f7
t1							
t2							
~~t3~~	+	+		+			
t4			1		1	1	
t5				1			1
count	2	3	2	2	2	1	1

count	1	2	2	1	2	1	1

(b) Second fault simulation: example of t_3 removal

Fig. 4. Test pattern selection based on fault detection information.

Table 1. Experimental results of numbers of test patterns and execution time for partitioned pattern generation where window-based reordering is not applied (ISCAS'89 s9234 benchmark circuit)

1st stage target fault (k_1)	0 %	1 %	5 %	10 %	50 %
# target faults	0	236	1180	2360	11799
CA of target fault	0.0 %	6.8 %	19.0 %	29.0 %	74.8 %
# 1st pat.	0	42	100	149	268
# 2nd pat.	333	280	221	201	88
# 2nd pat. (reordered)	287	261	214	196	86
# 1st + 2nd pat.	333	322	321	350	356
# 1st + 2nd pat. (reordered)	287	303	314	345	354
Processing time (s)	2044.6	885.8	352.25	210.69	28.213

The circuit under test s9234a has 23597 total target bridge faults which have non-zero critical areas. In the table, the case $k_1 = 0$ represents the results for conventional greedy algorithm, where partitioning is not applied. The conventional greedy algorithm required 2044.6 s of execution time in order to compress the original test pattern set consisting of 333 patterns to 287 patterns. When the proposed partitioned generation is applied targeting top $k_1 = 1\%$ faults at first stage, 42 patterns are generated at the first stage, and then additional 280 patterns are generated at the second stage to detect residual faults, which cannot be detected by the first 42 patterns. The reordering is only applied to these 280 patterns, and the total pattern set is compressed to 303 patterns, which is increased by 5.5 % from conventional scheme. The execution time, however, is significantly reduced to 885.8 s, which is 43 % of the conventional greedy algorithm. As the number of target faults at the first stage increases, the number of second patterns decreases, resulting in reduction of reordering execution time in exchange of increase of the number of combined patterns. When k_1 is larger than 10 % the number of combined patterns was larger than the original test pattern set without reordering.

We then evaluated the effectiveness of window-based reordering. Figure 5 shows the results for s9234a. The window size at the second stage k_2 was in the range of 0–100 %, while the ratio of the first-stage target faults k_1 was fixed as 1 %. The result for the case $k_2 = 100\%$ is equivalent to the result shown as $k_1 = 1\%$ in Table 1, where window-based reordering was not applied. While smaller window size significantly reduces execution time, it does not increase the number of reordered patterns so much. For the case of $k_2 = 1\%$, the execution time was reduced to 3 %, from 885.8 s of $k_2 = 100\%$ to 27 s, while the number of patterns was just increased by 4.

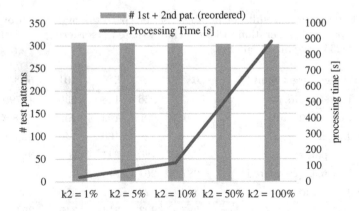

Fig. 5. Experimental results of numbers of test patterns and execution time for partitioned pattern generation with window-based reordering (ISCAS'89 s9234 benchmark circuit)

Table 2 summarizes the results of the numbers of patterns and reordering execution time for 4 benchmark circuits. Except for the case with s1196b, the setting of $k_1 = 1$ and $k_2 = 1\%$ showed less than 10% of execution time from that of greedy algorithm, while the overhead in terms of increased patterns was less than 7%. The table indicates the tendency that the execution time is reduced more significantly with the partitioned generation scheme as the target circuit becomes larger.

4.2   Evaluation of Detection-Information-Based Pattern Selection

We further evaluated the effectiveness of the proposed pattern selection scheme based on detection information. Table 3 shows the experimental results for 4 benchmark circuits. The table shows the number of gates, the number of signal pairs which corresponds to the target faults without considering critical area, the number of target faults having critical area, and the number of selected patterns and execution time when the pattern selection is applied. The table also indicates the number of patterns and execution time with the conventional greedy algorithm, for comparison, which is equivalent to the result shown in Table 2. The results indicate that the proposed selection scheme can reduce the numbers of the patterns further from those with greedy algorithm, by less than half of execution time.

Comparison of Tables 2 and 3 indicates that the selection scheme requires more execution time than partitioned generation. The fault simulation for the reordering becomes faster as the number of pre-selected pattern increases, because already-detected faults can be skipped at the simulation. On the other hand, the simulation for detection-information-based selection can be done with the linear order of the number of the target faults but it has to simulate all faults for all patterns without skipping. Therefore, average execution time of fault simulation for single pattern

Table 2. Numbers of test patterns and execution time with partitioned pattern generation (4 circuits)

Circuit name		s1196b	s1423a	s9234a	s15850a
# pat	ATPG	274	81	333	284
	Greedy	240	71	287	255
	Separation only ($k_1 = 1\%$)	250	71	303	255
	Separation + search window ($k_1 = 1\%$, $k_2 = 1\%$)	279	72	307	259
Processing time (s)	Greedy	50.973	5.067	2044.6	3966.1
	Separation only ($k_1 = 1\%$)	40.102	2.505	885.77	999.39
	Separation + search window ($k_1 = 1\%$, $k_2 = 1\%$)	1.835	0.159	27.353	55.197

Table 3. Numbers of test patterns and execution time with partitioned pattern generation (4 circuits)

Circuit name	s1196b	s1423a	s9234a	s15850a
# gates	561	748	5844	10383
Signal pairs	157080	279378	17073246	35898153
# target faults with CA	8077	3563	23597	53319
# pat (atpg)	274	81	333	284
# pat (greedy)	240	71	287	255
# pat (selection)	235	69	286	253
Processing time (s) (greedy)	50.973	5.067	2044.644	3966.066
Processing time (s) (selection)	3.595	1.675	489.233	1489.655

for selection scheme is always larger than those for partitioned generation, and thus the same tendency may be seen for the total execution time, for smaller circuit.

Figure 6 plots the execution time of the detection-information-based pattern selection scheme and the greedy algorithm as shown in Table 3, where x-axis corresponds to the number of the target faults of each circuit. The execution time of greedy algorithm is proportional to the square of the number of patterns, which linearly corresponds to the number of the faults. Then, as the number of faults increases, the execution time quickly increases for the greedy algorithm. On the other hand, the execution time for pattern selection scheme increases more gently, indicating applicability to practical-scale circuits.

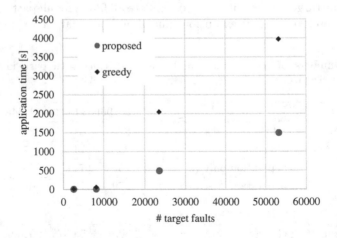

Fig. 6. Numbers of target faults and execution time for greedy algorithm and test pattern selection scheme (s9234a)

Figure 7 shows the growths of weighted fault coverages in s9234a, where x-axis is the number of patterns applied in the pattern set. Three different pattern sets are applied: the original pattern set without reordering, reordered one with greedy algorithm, and the one generated by pattern selection algorithm. While the greedy algorithm reorders the patterns so that the weighted fault coverage can be improved as quick as possible, the selection algorithm just removes redundant patterns and does not reorder the patterns. Therefore, the selection algorithm does not contribute to improve fault coverage quickly, although the total number of patterns can be sometimes reduced from those of greedy algorithm.

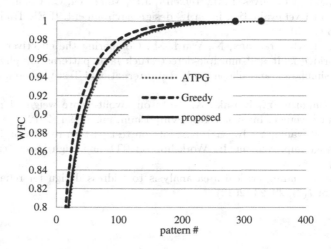

Fig. 7. Weighted fault coverages of original test pattern set, reordered patterns by greedy algorithm, and pattern set generated by test pattern selection scheme (s9234a)

5   Conclusions

In this study we proposed partitioned test pattern generation considering weighted fault coverage, aiming to develop fast and compact test pattern set generation. The proposed scheme firstly generates the test pattern set for small portion of target faults, and then only reorders the second pattern set which is generated for the residual faults of first small pattern set. The experimental results with 1 % of target faults and 1 % of search window indicated the proposed scheme can reduce execution time of pattern reordering significantly by 10 % of greedy algorithm, while keeping the pattern count increments less than 7 %. We also evaluated test pattern selection scheme based on only fault detection information. The proposed selection scheme just execute fault simulation twice for all patterns and faults. We have justified linear-order execution time for the number of target faults. The pattern selection scheme also sometimes achieved generation of even smaller pattern set than those generated by conventional greedy algorithm. Combining partitioned pattern reordering with skipped simulation and pattern selection with linear-order execution time would be a part of our future work.

References

1. International Technology Roadmap for Semiconductors, 2013 edn. (2013)
2. Williams, T.W., Brown, N.C.: Defect level as a function of fault coverage. IEEE Trans. Comput. **C–30**, 987–988 (1981)
3. De Sousa, J.T., Goncalves, F.M., Teixeira, J.P., Marzocca, C., Corsi, F., Williams, T.W.: Defect level evaluation in an IC design environment. IEEE Trans. CAD **15**, 1286–1293 (1996)
4. Goel, S.K., Devta-Prasanna, N., Ward, M.: Comparing the effectiveness of deterministic bridge fault and multiple-detect stuck fault patterns for physical bridge defects: a simulation and silicon study. In: International Test Conference, paper 1.1 (2009)
5. Arai, M., Shimizu, Y., Iwasaki, K.: Note on layout-aware weighted probabilistic bridge fault coverage. In: Asian Test Symposium, pp. 89–94 (2012)
6. Arai, M., Nakayama, Y., Iwasaki, K.: Note on test pattern reordering for weighted fault coverage improvement. In: Workshop on RTL and High Level Testing, paper 4.1 (2013)
7. Ouchi, T.: Extending critical area analysis to address design for reliability. EDA Tech Forum **7**(3), 20–23 (2010)

Joint Redundancy and Inspection-Based Maintenance Optimization for Series-Parallel System

Yuan Yao, Pan He$^{(\boxtimes)}$, Zhihao Zheng, Chun Tan, and Yue Yuan

Chongqing Institute of Green and Intelligent Technology,
Chinese Academy of Sciences, Chongqing 400714, China
{yaoyuan,hepan,zhihao,tanchun,yuanyue}@cigit.ac.cn

Abstract. While researchers have concentrated on the optimization of joint redundancy and maintenance mechanism, maintenance in computing systems is quite different from that in traditional systems. Considering a routine monitoring and inspection mechanisms is conducted to detect component status and trigger repair process, this paper pays attention to the optimization problem of joint redundancy and inspection-based maintenance mechanism. After conducting steady state analysis on subsystems using inspection-based maintenance, shared repair facility and component redundancy, optimization model is built to search appropriate system structure and maintenance policy which maximizes system performance while meeting availability and cost constraints. Due to the complexity of uncertain optimization model, genetic algorithm is used to search optimal solution, using triple-element encoding mechanism and specifically designed operators. Illustrative examples are conducted to show that the optimization model and corresponding solution technique could be used to search optimal system configuration under given constraints and different cost constraints would lead to different optimization result while meeting availability constraints.

Keywords: Reliability optimization · Redundancy · System maintenance · Monitoring · Inspection

1 Introduction

As reliability has become a major concern in most engineering and computing systems, component reliability improvement and the provision of redundant components are often used together to maintain system reliability [1]. Preventive maintenance, which recovers a component from failure or degraded state, could improve the reliability of single component and is often used jointly with component redundancy for multi-performance-state systems [2]. Similar as traditional redundancy, the configuration of preventive maintenance also introduces extra cost to the whole system, so a great majority of researches have concentrated on the optimization of joint mechanism [3, 4]. Existing researches mainly assume that the repair process is taken immediately after component failure or degradation. However, in large distributed computing systems, e.g. cloud based systems, it is difficult to identify failures in various distributed components. Routine monitoring and inspection mechanisms are often conducted to detect component

© Springer International Publishing Switzerland 2015
G. Wang et al. (Eds.): ICA3PP 2015, Part III, LNCS 9530, pp. 741–755, 2015.
DOI: 10.1007/978-3-319-27137-8_54

status and to trigger component repair process [5]. Therefore, the inspection policy plays a key role in the whole system maintenance, but few studies have concentrated on the optimization of joint redundancy and inspection-based maintenance mechanism.

A lot of researches have been taken on the subject of joint traditional fault tolerance mechanism analysis and optimization [11, 12]. For multiple kinds of redundancy strategies, Coit [6], Tavakkoli-Moghaddam et al. [7] and Chambari et al. all [8] studied redundancy optimization problem while simulated annealing algorithm [9] and genetic algorithm [10] were used to get solutions. For maintenance mechanism, Soro et al. evaluated the reliability and performance of multi-state degraded systems with redundancy and imperfect preventive maintenance [2] and then Nourelfath et al. proposed a SP/TG heuristic approach to optimize the joint mechanism in series-parallel systems [3]. Liu et al. considered the deterioration effect after maintenance in this model and conduct optimization using genetic algorithm [4]. The mentioned researches didn't consider monitoring and inspection mechanism for repair process and were not applicable for cloud computing systems. Our previous research conducted a preliminary study on joint optimized redundancy and inspection rate [13]. Due to the computation complexity of state transition analysis, the model was only built for subsystems with two redundant components when inspection used. For systems with k-out-of-n redundancy architecture, Martorell al. analyzed the optimal test interval of a two-component parallel system based on availability analysis [21]. Vaurio developed the optimization on test and maintenance interval time for k-out-of-n system with four components and series systems [22, 23]. Cepin and Mavko also conducted test strategies and maintenance optimization by minimization of risk through simulated annealing [24, 25]. Torres-Echeverria et al. presented an optimization model for the maintenance and test policy design for a system using MooN voting redundancies [26]. In these researches, analytical availability and periodic test cycle analysis are conducted on probabilistic methods, but the working mechanism inside the test or maintenance strategy has not been presented.

The main objective of this paper is to define the optimal system structure and the inspection policy for each component, so that the series-parallel system performance is maximized, subject to the availability and cost budget constraints. The state transition process is first analyzed for subsystems with redundant components and a routine monitoring and inspection mechanism. Because of the recovering effect of maintenance process, the steady state reliability and performance is analyzed from the state transition process. The cost is a combination of redundancy cost and maintenance cost. While original redundancy allocation problem (RAP) has been proven to be NP-hard problem [14], the introduction of inspection-based maintenance strategy even increases the complexity of the optimization problem. Therefore, a genetic algorithm is used to search the optimal solution of redundancy and inspection routine for each subsystem and illustrative examples are presented to explain the analysis and calculation process. The following sections are organized as follows: the problem description and optimization model is listed in the following section and the solution technique is then proposed; illustrate examples are presented with experimental results analysis; conclusions are summarized at last with future work.

2 The Optimization Model

Notations

m	Number of sequential subsystems	A_i	Steady state availability of subsystem i
n_i	Number of redundant components in subsystem i	p_{ri}	Work processing rate of each component in subsystem i
λ_i	Failure rate of each component in subsystem i	P_{ri}	Steady state performance rate of subsystem i
μ_i	Repair rate of each component in subsystem i	q_d	Degradation rate in maintenance state
n_{ri}	Maximal number of components being repaired in parallel in subsystem i	$\mathbf{n}, \boldsymbol{\lambda_m},$ $\mathbf{n_r}$	Corresponding vectors of n_i, λ_{mi}, n_{ri} in all subsystems
q_i	Probability of successful repair for each component in subsystem i	λ_{mi}	Monitoring rate of maintenance mechanism in subsystem i
$\pi_{i,\alpha}$	Steady state probability of state α in subsystem i	$Q_{i,\alpha\beta}$	Transition rate between two states α and β in subsystem i
μ_{si}	Component detection rate for subsystem i	C_{sys}	Overall system redundancy cost
Q_i	The generator matrix of $Q_{i,\alpha\beta}$	M_{sys}	Monitoring and inspection cost per time unit
π_i	Vector of $\pi_{i,\alpha}$	R_{sys}	The repair facility cost
P_{sys}	Average performance rate of the system	A_{sys}	Steady-state system availability

2.1 Problem Description

Assume that there are m sequential subsystems in one system and for subsystem i ($1 \le i \le m$), n_i components are running in parallel or kept as backup. The structure of such series-parallel system is shown in Fig. 1.

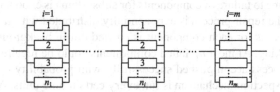

Fig. 1. Structure of general series-parallel system.

Following the fault tolerance mechanism design in researches [5], n_i components are running initially for each subsystem. A routine monitoring and inspection mechanism is used to detect the status of components. When a component fails or degrades, it is replaced by other standby backups instantly. The switched component is repaired or restarted in background and placed as backup components. A brief illustration of the process in each subsystem is shown in Fig. 2.

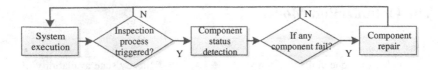

Fig. 2. Illustration of joint redundancy and inspection-based maintenance mechanism.

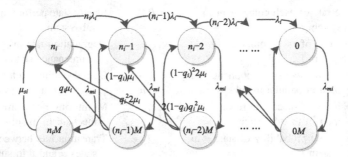

Fig. 3. State transition diagram joint redundancy and inspection-based maintenance.

To illustration the working process of each subsystem, the state transition analysis is conducted on the subsystem with the redundant components. Each subsystem is presented by a multi-state model, shown as Fig. 3, where it is assumed that:

- The working and failure pattern of each component inside one subsystem is the same. In real-world applications, there is more than one type of components inside each subsystem and the failure pattern of these components is not the same. In this case, the patterns of the component with the worst reliability and performance could be used as the common pattern for calculation. Specifically, when a cloud-computing or grid-computing system is chosen for analysis, the same CPU and memory resources would be allocated to each virtual component in one system, it is reasonable to assume that the time-to-failure of each component follows the similar distribution pattern. The time to failure of components for subsystem i is exponentially distributed with rate λ_i. The repair process is exponentially distributed with rate μ_i.
- The repair process for each component is carried out in background as long as the system is working. At most n_{ri} failed components could be repaired in parallel with each repair process accomplished successfully with probability q_i.
- The routine inspection mechanism is run every certain time units. An ideal approach would be to take the time to the next inspection to be uniformly distributed. Since the difference between normal distribution and exponential distribution assumption for routine inspection mechanism is proven to be small [15], the periodical inspection/detection process is approximated to be exponentially distributed with λ_{mi} to reduce model complexity.
- The time used for component status detection is exponentially distributed with rate μ_{si}. It is reasonable to assume that the time is much less than the time of repair process and is not taken into consideration when repair is conducted to avoid state explosion.

In this diagram, state $k_{ij}(1 \leq i{\leq}m, 1 \leq j \leq n_i)$ represents the normal working state of ith subsystem with j active components. State $k_{ij}M$ stands for the corresponding repair and maintenance state from k_{ij}. The performance of these states would be affected by the maintenance process running in the background while only the state of 0 and 0 M are failure states. State transition between states k_{ij} is triggered by the random component failure. State transition from k_{ij} to $k_{ij}M$ is the process waiting for the next inspection. State transition from $k_{ij}M$ back to k_{ij} is the inspection/detection and the repair process. For any state $k_{ij}M$, $n_i - k_{ij}$ components already fail in the system and repairmen process should be taken on these components. While at most n_{ri} failed components could be repaired each time, the probability of only w VM is migrated successfully is denoted by $C_{n_{\min}}^w(q_i)^w(1 - q_i)^{n_{\min}-w}$, where $n_{\min}$ is the minimal value of $n_i - k_{ij}$ and n_{ri}.

The overall state of the whole system is determined by the redundancy, inspection and maintenance policy on each subsystem. So, our main objective is to get the appropriate value of this configuration policy through optimization.

2.2 System Performance Evaluation Model

The reliability of a series-parallel system is determined by the reliability of each subsystem. Before constructing the optimization model for the whole system, the reliability and performance evaluation on top of the state transition diagram of subsystem i is first conducted. Since this kind of system is supposed to be running for a long time, steady state method is used to analyze this diagram as an irreducible CTMC [15].

Let S denotes the set of all states in Fig. 3 $\{0, \ldots n_i, 0\,M, \ldots, n_iM\}$. Let $\pi_{i,\alpha}$ denote the steady state probability of state α $(\alpha \in S)$ in subsystem i and π_i denotes the vector $[\pi_{ni}, \ldots \pi_0, \pi_{ni}M, \ldots, \pi_0M]$. Let $Q_{i,\alpha\beta}$ denotes the transition rate between two states $(\alpha \in S, \beta \in S)$ in subsystem i and Q_i denotes the generator matrix of $Q_{i,\alpha\beta}$. The value of $Q_{i,\alpha\beta}$ is

$$Q_{i,\alpha\beta} = \begin{cases} \alpha\lambda_i, 1 \leq \alpha \leq n_i, \beta = \alpha - 1 \\ \lambda_{mi}, 0 \leq \alpha \leq n_i, \beta = \alpha M \\ \mu_{si}, \alpha = n_iM, \beta = n_i \\ C_w^{\beta-\gamma}q_i^{\beta-\gamma}(1 - q_i)^{w-(\beta-\gamma)}w\mu_i, w = \min\{n_{ri}, n_i - \gamma\}, \alpha = \gamma M, \gamma \leq \beta \leq n_i, 0 \leq \gamma < n_i \\ -w\mu_i, w = \min\{n_{ri}, n_r - \gamma\}, \alpha = \beta = \gamma M, 0 \leq \gamma < n_i \\ -\mu_{si}, \alpha = \beta = n_iM \\ -\alpha\lambda_i - \lambda_{mi}, 0 \leq \alpha \leq n_i, \alpha = \beta \end{cases}$$

$$(1)$$

Considering the Kolmogorov's backward equation [15], the limits value of $\pi_{i,\alpha}$ is calculated as

$$\lim_{t\to\infty} \frac{d\pi_{i,\alpha}(t)}{dt} = \left(\sum_{\beta\in S\ \&\ \beta\neq\alpha} \pi_{i,\beta}Q_{i,\beta\alpha}\right) - \pi_{i,\alpha}Q_{i,\alpha\alpha} = 0 \Rightarrow \begin{cases} \pi_iQ_i = 0 \\ \sum_{\alpha\in S}\pi_{i,\alpha} = 1 \end{cases} \quad (2)$$

which could also be represented in matrix form.

Given the certain system structure, the failure and recover rate of each component, $\pi_{i,\alpha}$ is a function of the number of redundant components n_i, the inspection rate λ_{mi} and the maximum number of parallel repairing components n_{ri}: $\pi_{i,\alpha} = \pi_{i,\alpha}(n_i, \lambda_{mi}, n_{ri})$. Following the steady state analysis pattern, steady state availability A_i is used to describe subsystem reliability and the expected performance rate P_{ri} is used to describe the subsystem performance. Steady state availability A_i is the probability of the subsystem in the working state. Since only states 0 and $0\,M$ are failure states, given the value of n_i, λ_{mi} and n_{ri}, the value of A_i could be calculated as:

$$A_i = \sum_{\alpha \in S \ \& \ \alpha \neq 0,0M} \pi_{i,\alpha} = A_i(n_i, \lambda_{mi}, n_{ri}) \tag{3}$$

The expected performance rate P_{ri} is the average work processing rate performed by all the working components in the subsystem. Let $S_{i,U}$ and $S_{i,M}$ denotes the set of normally working states $\{\pi_{ni}, \ldots \pi_1\}$ and corresponding maintenance states $\{\pi_{ni}M, \ldots, \pi_1M\}$ for subsystem i. In the normally working state $\alpha \in S_{i,U}$. The work processing rate of the subsystem is the sum of processing rate of each working component. In the maintenance state $\beta \in S_{i,M}$, the work processing rate would be degraded due to the inspection and maintenance process running in the background. Assume that the work processing rate for each component is p_{ri} and the degradation rate is q_d. The value of P_{ri} is:

$$P_{ri} = \sum_{\alpha \in S} \pi_{i,\alpha} p_{ri,\alpha} = \sum_{\alpha \in S_{i,U}} \pi_{i,\alpha} \alpha p_{ri} + \sum_{\beta \in S_{i,D}} q_d \pi_{i,\beta} k p_{ri} = P_{ri}(n_i, \lambda_{mi}, n_{ri}), \beta = kM. \tag{4}$$

2.3 Optimization Model Formulation

The main objective of the optimization model is to define the optimal system structure and the maintenance policy for each component, so that the multi-state system performance is maximized, subject to steady state availability and cost budget constraints.

The objective function is evaluated as the average performance rate of the whole system P_{sys}, which is calculated from the performance rate of each subsystem. The working processing time of a series system is the sum of the processing time of each subsystem and the corresponding rate is evaluated as

$$P_{sys} = 1 \bigg/ \sum_{i=1}^{m} (1/P_{ri}(n_i, \lambda_{mi}, n_{ri})) = f(\boldsymbol{n}, \boldsymbol{\lambda_m}, \boldsymbol{n_r}) \tag{5}$$

where $\boldsymbol{n}$, $\boldsymbol{\lambda_m}$, $\boldsymbol{n_r}$ are the corresponding vectors for each parameter in all the subsystem.

The constraint functions include the constraint of reliability, redundancy cost and maintenance cost. The system steady state availability A_{sys} is the probability of the whole system in working state, which is the product of each subsystem's availability:

$$A_{sys} = \prod_{i=1}^{m} A_i(n_i, \lambda_{mi}, n_{ri}) = g(\boldsymbol{n}, \boldsymbol{\lambda_m}, \boldsymbol{n_r}). \tag{6}$$

The overall system redundancy cost C_{sys} is the cost to configure redundant components in each subsystem, which depends on the number of redundant components.

The monitoring and inspection cost is the cost to monitor and detect the status of each subsystem periodically and it is related to the monitoring rate in each subsystem. While the cost is also related to the system running time, M_{sys} stands for the monitoring and inspection cost per time unit. The repair facility cost R_{sys} is the cost used to repair failed components, which is determined by the maximal number of repair facilities prepared for each subsystem. Let c_i denotes the redundancy cost of components in subsystem i, m_{di} stands for the cost for one inspection and detection process and the r_i is the cost of each prepared repair facility. The cost constraint functions are represented as

$$C_{sys} = \sum_{i=1}^{m} c_i n_i, M_{sys} = \sum_{i=1}^{m} m_{di} \lambda_{mi}, R_{sys} = \sum_{i=1}^{m} r_i n_{ri} \tag{7}$$

When redundancy and inspection-based mechanism are both used in one system, it is difficult to choose the configuration settings of each kind of strategy in each subsystem. Based on these objective and constraint functions, the parameter determination problem is cast into an optimization problem. The optimization model is defined as choosing appropriate system configuration parameters n, λ_m, n_r to maximize system work processing rate under the availability and cost constraints:

Max $P_{sys} = f(n, \lambda_m, n_r)$

$s.t. A_{sys} = g(n, \lambda_m, n_r) \geq A_0, C_{sys} = \sum_{i=1}^{m} c_i n_i \leq C_0, M_{sys} = \sum_{i=1}^{m} m_{di} \lambda_{mi} \leq M_0, R_{sys} = \sum_{i=1}^{m} r_i n_{ri} \leq R_0$

$1 \leq n_{ri} \leq n_i \leq n_0, 0 < \lambda_{mi} \leq \lambda_{m0}$

$$\tag{8}$$

A_0, C_0, M_0 and R_0 represents the corresponding constraints value and n_0, λ_{m0} are the value range of configuration parameters.

3 Solution Technique

Although Lagrange multiplier method could be used to solve the optimization problem by calculating partial derivative values, it asks for the closed-form representation of the optimization model. These is no closed-form formula of reliability and performance without certain value of n_i and n_{ri}, thus the proposed model is not a traditional non-linear optimization problem and could not be solved using exact method. So, in this section, a genetic algorithm is used to search the near-optimal solution.

3.1 Genetic Algorithm Framework

Among several kinds of evolutionary algorithms proposed for combinatorial optimization problem, genetic algorithm (GA) conducts a random, yet directed search process wherein solutions evolves according to biological reproduction rules [16]. It is superior to gradient descent technique or random sampling algorithm and has been used in many researches for RAP [17, 18]. The general framework of this algorithm is:

Step I. Initialize population P_0 with N individuals, $P_0 = \{p_1, p_2, ..., p_N\}$. Set offspring population $Q_0=\emptyset$, and generation counter $t=0$.
Step II. While $t<t_{max}$, do the following things:
   1. Use genetic operator to generate Q_t from P_t.
   2. Combine both parent and offspring population to get a new group of population $R_t=P_t\cup Q_t$.
   3. Calculate the fitness value of individuals in R_t according to the objective values and constraints values.
   4. Sort R_t in descending order using fitness value.
   5. Use roulette selection operator to select N individuals in R_t and fill P_{t+1} with them.
   6. Set $t=t+1$ and return to the beginning of Step II.
Step III. Stop the algorithm when it reaches the maximal iteration number.

Following similar framework, the significant parts in genetic algorithm are the solution encoding mechanism, genetic operators and the fitness calculation method. The design of these parts is listed in the following subsections.

3.2   Solution Encoding Mechanism

Each individual in the population set represents a specific solution to the optimization problem. Since there are $3 \times m$ elements to search in the optimization model, a triple-element encoding mechanism is used to represent each solution to the problem [19, 20]. Each solution in our algorithm is represented by a $3 \times m$ matrix. Figure 4 illustrates an example of the encoded solution using this mechanism with $m = 6$.

For the matrix shown in Fig. 4, the first row represents the redundancy of components in each subsystem n, the second row stands for the number of repair facilities for each subsystem n_r while the third row is the inspection and monitoring rate of each subsystem λ_m. Each column of this matrix is the redundancy and inspection-based maintenance configuration of each subsystem. The initialization of a set of these individuals is accomplished by randomly generating values of each element in the matrix. The initial value of n_i or n_{ri} is a random integer which satisfies the condition of $1 \leq n_{ri} \leq n_i \leq n_0$. The initial value of λ_{mi} is real number randomly generate between 0 and λ_{m0}.

	1	2	3	4	5	6
Redundancy 1	2	1	4	4	5	2
Number of repair facility 2	1	1	3	2	3	1
Inspection rate 3	0.1	0.023	0.04	0.2	0.03	0.1

Fig. 4. Example of triple-element encoding mechanism.

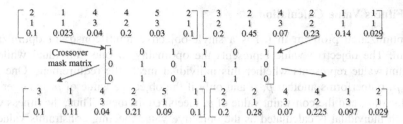

Fig. 5. Crossover operation for triple-element encoded individuals.

3.3 Genetic Operators

In the crossover operation, a $3 \times m$ crossover mask is generated as Fig. 5. There are only 0 and 1 in this mask matrix and this matrix is randomly composed by the two values. For two randomly selected individuals p_x and p_y ($1 \le x, y \le N$), once an element in the mask matrix equals to 1, crossover operation is conducted on the value of elements in the same position of the two solution matrixes. For integer values as n_i or n_{ri} simple swap operation is used in crossover operation. For real values of λ_{mi}, the simulated binary crossover (SBX) operator is used to switch two elements:

$$
p_x.\tilde{\lambda}'_{mi} = \frac{((1-\beta)p_x.\tilde{\lambda}_{mi} + (1+\beta)p_y.\tilde{\lambda}_{mi})}{2}
$$
$$
p_y.\tilde{\lambda}'_{mi} = \frac{((1+\beta)p_x.\tilde{\lambda}_{mi} + (1-\beta)p_y.\tilde{\lambda}_{mi})}{2}, \beta = \begin{cases} (2\alpha)^{\frac{1}{\eta+1}}, 0 \le \alpha < 0.5 \\ \frac{1}{((2(1-\alpha))^{\frac{1}{\eta+1}})}, 0.5 \le \alpha < 1 \end{cases} \tag{9}
$$

where η is the crossover index and $p_x.\tilde{\lambda}_{mi}$ is the normalized value of $p_x.\lambda_{mi}$.

In the mutation operation, similarly, a $3 \times m$ mutation mask is generated with randomly chosen 0 and 1, as Fig. 6. At most two elements could be set to 1 at each row to avoid dramatic change in the mutated individual. For any randomly chosen individual p_x, if any element in mutation mask is 1, the corresponding element at the same position of p_x is changed randomly. The changing process of integer element such as n_i or n_{ri} is similar as the population initialization process. For real numbers λ_{mi}, polynomial mutation operator is used to make changes as:

$$
p_x.\tilde{\lambda}'_{mi} = \begin{cases} p_x.\tilde{\lambda}_{mi} + (2r)^{\frac{1}{\eta_m+1}} - 1, 0 \le r < 0.5 \\ p_x.\tilde{\lambda}_{mi} + 1 - [2(1-r)]^{\frac{1}{\eta_m+1}}, 0.5 \le r < 1 \end{cases} \tag{10}
$$

where η_m denotes the mutation index and $p_x.\tilde{\lambda}_{mi}$ is the normalized value.

$$
\begin{bmatrix} 2 & 1 & 4 & 4 & 5 & 2 \\ 1 & 1 & 3 & 2 & 3 & 1 \\ 0.1 & 0.023 & 0.04 & 0.2 & 0.03 & 0.1 \end{bmatrix}
$$

Mutation mask matrix
$$
\begin{bmatrix} 0 & 0 & 0 & 1 & 0 & 1 \\ 0 & 1 & 0 & 0 & 0 & 0 \\ 0 & 0 & 1 & 0 & 0 & 0 \end{bmatrix}
$$

$$
\begin{bmatrix} 2 & 1 & 4 & 2 & 5 & 3 \\ 1 & 1 & 3 & 2 & 3 & 1 \\ 0.1 & 0.023 & 0.56 & 0.2 & 0.03 & 0.1 \end{bmatrix}
$$

Fig. 6. Mutation operation for triple-element encoded individuals.

3.4   Fitness Value Calculation

The optimization problem in (8) is a single-objective multi-constraint optimization problem. The objective value represents the optimality of one individual while the constraint value represents whether this individual meets the requirement. One individual p_x outperforms another p_y if and only if the objective value of p_x is larger than the value of p_y and the constraint value of p_x meets requirement. Thus, the fitness value I of each individual is calculated as the objective value meeting constraints value:

$$I = \begin{cases} R_{sys}, A_{sys} \geq A_0, C_{sys} \leq C_0, M_{sys} \leq M_0, R_{sys} \leq R_0 \\ 0, else \end{cases} \tag{11}$$

In selection process, a weight value w_x is assigned for each individual so that individuals with larger fitness value will be assigned a higher possibility in selection:

$$w_x = \begin{cases} w_{x-1} + I_x \bigg/ \sum_{y=1}^{N} I_y \\ 0, x = 0 \end{cases} \tag{12}$$

4   Illustrative Examples

In this section, numerical examples are listed to illustrate the optimization of joint redundancy and inspection-based maintenance mechanism and the process of searching near-optimal solutions. System parameters are mainly collected from a cloud-based system used for distributed and parallel processing [27]. Data from 8 series-parallel subsystems in this system are used for analysis. For each subsystem, the failure rate, repair rate, job processing rate of one component are extracted from the operation profiles and presented in Table 1. According to the maintenance schedule, the value of μ_{si} for each component is 30 per hour and the inspection and monitoring cost of each component is set as 1 unit. The repair successful probability q_i is 0.9 and the performance degradation rate is 0.8. The redundancy cost c_i and repair facility cost r_i are estimated and shown in Table 1.

Table 1. Component parameters for example

Subsystem No.	Component feature					Subsystem No.	Component feature				
	λ_i (per hour)	μ_i (per hour)	p_{ri}	c_i	r_i		λ_i (per hour)	μ_i (per hour)	p_{ri}	c_i	r_i
1	0.00499	0.551	2	2	3	5	0.00431	0.782	1	2	4
2	0.00818	0.623	3	2	7	6	0.00567	0.445	3	3	5
3	0.00466	1.13	3	4	5	7	0.0105	1.75	2	3	6
4	0.00683	0.973	2	5	4	8	0.0150	0.237	2	3	4

4.1 Reliability and Performance Analysis

The reliability and performance analysis is first conducted on the first subsystem. The failure rate λ_i and repair rate μ_i is 0.00499 and 0.551 per hour. The inspection and detection rate μ_{si} is 30 per hour. Using only one subsystem, the working processing rate p_{ri} in this experiment is set as 1 unit. First of all, the inspection rate is set as 0.5 per hour and the number of working repair facility is set as 3. The corresponding reliability and performance of this subsystem with redundancy change from 1 to 10 are shown in Fig. 7(a). Then the number of redundant component is set as 5 and inspection rate changes from 0 to 1 per hour. The result of subsystem with different number of repair facilities is included in Fig. 7(b). At last, the number of redundant component is set as 5 and the inspection rate is 0.5 per hour, the result of subsystem with the number of repair facilities changing from 1 to 10 is shown as Fig. 7(c).

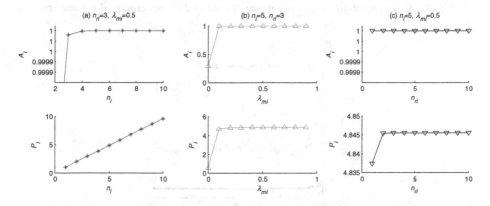

Fig. 7. Subsystem reliability and performance change with different parameters.

It is shown from Fig. 7 that the increase of redundant components and inspection rate has significant impact on the subsystem reliability and performance change. However, with the continuous change of these parameters, the increase trend of both reliability and performance rate declines and converges to 0, except for the performance increase with redundancy increase. The change in the number of repair facility has little impact on both reliability and performance increase. When the number of working repair facilities is larger than then number of redundant components, there is no change in both system metrics. The experiment data shows that three kinds of configuration parameters have total different impact on the overall system.

4.2 Mechanism Optimization

Figure 8 illustrates the overall system reliability and performance change with the configuration parameters change of the first subsystem. The initial redundancy and repair facility for each subsystem is set as 1 and the inspection rate is 0.1 per hour. It is shown that the impact of parameter change on the reliability and performance improvement generally declines dramatically as the parameters increases.

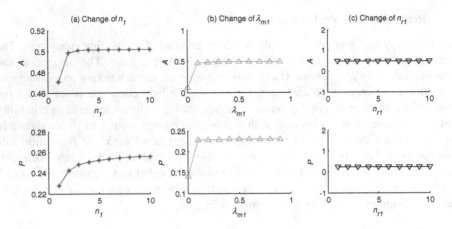

Fig. 8. System reliability and performance change of different groups of parameters.

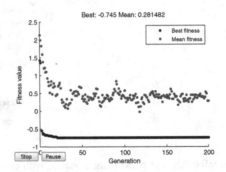

Fig. 9. The mean and best fitness value of each generation.

So in this section, the maximum number of redundant components and repairing facilities in any subsystem is set as 10 and 5 respectively. The maximal inspection rate is set as 1. The maximum generation in the algorithm is set as 200 and the population size is 100. System parameters in Table 1 is used in this experiment for redundancy optimization. Given availability constraint 0.99, redundancy cost 70, repair facilities cost 70 and inspection cost 5, the optimal configuration of redundancy and maintenance policy using the joint mechanism is calculated and the fitness value of each generation is shown in Fig. 9. The fitness value is the negative value of performance rate: $-P_i$. The result in Fig. 9 indicates that the algorithm already converges within 50 generations.

The calculated optimal job performance rate is 0.7448 in this test case and the corresponding configuration parameter for each subsystem is shown in Table 2.

In the following experiments, four kinds of cost constraints are changed to show the different result on joint mechanism optimization. Since GA is a stochastic search algorithm, five trials are performed for each experiment and the best solution is considered as

Table 2. Optimal component configuration result

Subsystem No.	n_i	λ_{mi} (per hour)	n_{ri}	Subsystem No.	n_i	λ_{mi} (per hour)	n_{ri}
1	3	0.4637	3	5	5	0.6065	1
2	3	0.7689	2	6	3	0.5419	2
3	2	0.5878	1	7	3	0.5060	2
4	2	0.8110	2	8	4	0.7092	2

the final solution. First of all, the availability constraint is kept as 0.99 with repair facilities cost as 70 and inspection cost as 5. The result of maximized performance change with near-optimal solution is drawn in Fig. 10(a) while the redundancy cost changes from 60 to 100. Then, using the same availability constraint with redundancy cost as 70 and changing the value of repair facilities cost, the corresponding optimization result for performance rate is shown in Fig. 10(b). Keeping the cost constraints for both redundancy and repair as 70 and changing the value of inspection cost from 1 to 10, Fig. 10(c) shows the optimization result under availability constraint 0.90. Figure 10(d) presents the result for availability constraint change from 0.90 to 0.99.

It is shown in Fig. 10 that given different cost constraint, different system configuration would be get with different performance optimization result. Loosening any kind of cost constraint could all get better result on performance optimization. Specifically, the change of redundancy cost brings significant change on the optimization result while only little change is obtained for the other two kinds of cost constraints change. On the contrary, once the availability constraint could be met under the same cost, different availability constraints generally lead to similar system configuration and performance.

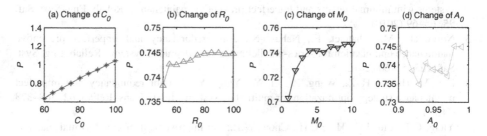

Fig. 10. The change of optimization result with different constraints.

5   Conclusion and Future Work

Aiming at the optimal joint redundancy and inspection-based maintenance configuration problem in series-parallel system, this paper pays attention to the routine monitoring and inspection mechanisms, which helps to detect components status and trigger repair process. Considering the shared repair facilities for different component in each subsystem, a state transition models is first built to analyze the inspection-based maintenance mechanism and Markov chain theory is used to get steady state availability and performance metrics for the system. The optimization problem is built to search the appropriate system structure and maintenance policy maximizing system performance while meeting availability and cost constraints. Due to the complexity of uncertain optimization model, genetic algorithm is used to search optimal solution, built upon triple-element encoding mechanism. Specific genetic operators are designed for the triple-element encoding method and illustrative examples are conducted to explain the calculation and optimization process. Experiment results show that the optimization model and corresponding solution technique could be used to search optimal system configuration under given constraints and different cost constraints would lead to different optimization result while meeting availability constraints. This paper takes a preliminary study on the optimization of joint redundancy and inspection-based maintenance model. The analysis model is simplified on top of several assumptions, such as the exponential distribution time-to-failure. In the future, this model could be modified to be suited for more general failure distributions. Meanwhile, some local search operator could be combined into the genetic algorithm to improve the algorithm efficiency.

Acknowledgments. This work is supported by the National Natural Science Foundation of China (Grant No. 61309005) and the Frontier and Application Basic Research Program of Chongqing (Grant No. cstc2014jcyjA40015).

References

1. Kuo, W., Wan, R.: Recent advances in optimal reliability allocation. IEEE Trans. Syst. Man Cybern. Part A Syst. Hum. **37**, 143–156 (2007)
2. Soro, I.W., Nourelfath, M., Ait-Kadi, D.: Performance evaluation of multi-state degraded systems with minimal repairs and imperfect preventive maintenance. Reliab. Eng. Syst. Saf. **95**, 65–69 (2010)
3. Nourelfath, M., Chatelet, E., Nahas, N.: Joint redundancy and imperfect preventive maintenance optimization for series-parallel multi-state degraded systems. Reliab. Eng. Syst. Saf. **103**, 51–60 (2012)
4. Liu, Y., Huang, H.-Z., Wang, Z., Li, Y., Yang, Y.: A joint redundancy and imperfect maintenance strategy optimization for multi-state systems. IEEE Trans. Reliab. **62**, 368–378 (2013)
5. Yang, C.T., Liu, J.C., Hsu, C.H., Chou, W.L.: On improvement of cloud virtual machine availability with virtualization fault tolerance mechanism. J. Supercomputing **69**, 1103–1122 (2014)
6. Coit, D.W.: Maximization of system reliability with a choice of redundancy strategies. IIE Trans. (Inst. Ind. Eng.) **35**, 535–543 (2003)
7. Tavakkoi-Moghaddam, R., Safari, J., Sassani, F.: Reliability optimization of series-parallel systems with a choice of redundancy strategies using a genetic algorithm. Reliab. Eng. Syst. Saf. **93**, 550–556 (2008)
8. Chambari, A., Rahmati, S.H.A., Najafi, A.A., Karimi, A.: A bi-objective model to optimize reliability and cost of system with a choice of redundancy strategies. Comput. Ind. Eng. **63**, 109–119 (2012)

9. Chambari, A., Najafi, A.A., Rahmati, S.H.A., Karimi, A.: An efficient simulated annealing algorithm for the redundancy allocation problem with a choice of redundancy strategies. Reliab. Eng. Syst. Saf. **119**, 158–164 (2013)

10. Safari, J.: Multi-objective reliability optimization of series-parallel systems with a choice of redundancy strategies. Reliab. Eng. Syst. Saf. **108**, 10–20 (2012)

11. Levitin, G.: Optimal structure of fault-tolerant software systems. Reliab. Eng. Syst. Saf. **89**, 286–295 (2005)

12. Ahmadizar, F., Soltanpanah, H.: Reliability optimization of a series system with multiple-choice and budget constraints using an efficient ant colony approach. Expert Syst. Appl. **38**, 3640–3646 (2011)

13. He, P., Wen, J., Wu, K., Li, P., Ren, H.: Multi-objective service monitoring rate optimization using memetic algorithm. J. Softw. **7**, 990–997 (2012)

14. Chern, M.: On the computational complexity of reliability redundancy allocation in a series system. Oper. Res. Lett. **11**, 309–315 (1992)

15. Trivedi, K.S.: Probability and Statistics with Reliability, Queuing, and Computer Science Applications. Wiley, New York (2001)

16. Srinivas, M., Patnaik, L.M.: Adaptive probabilities of crossover and mutation in genetic algorithms. IEEE Trans. Syst. Man Cybern. **24**, 656–667 (1994)

17. Levitin, G., Lisnianski, A., Ben-Haim, H., Elmakis, D.: Redundancy optimization for series-parallel multi-state systems. IEEE Trans. Reliab. **47**, 165–172 (1998)

18. Tian, Z., Levitin, G., Zuo, M.J.: A joint reliability–redundancy optimization approach for multi-state series–parallel systems. Reliab. Eng. Syst. Saf. **94**, 1568–1576 (2009)

19. Tavakkoli-Moghaddam, R., Safari, J., Sassani, F.: Reliability optimization of series-parallel systems with a choice of redundancy strategies using a genetic algorithm. Reliab. Eng. Syst. Saf. **93**, 550–556 (2008)

20. Ardakan, M.A., Hamadani, A.Z.: Reliability optimization of series-parallel systems with mixed redundancy strategy in subsystems. Reliab. Eng. Syst. Saf. **130**, 132–139 (2014)

21. Martorell, S.A., Serradell, V.G., Samanta, P.K.: Improving allowed outage time and surveillance test interval requirements: a study of their interactions using probabilistic methods. Reliab. Eng. Syst. Saf. **47**, 119–129 (1995)

22. Vaurio, J.K.: The theory and quantification of common cause shock events for redundant standby systems. Reliab. Eng. Syst. Saf. **45**, 315 (1994)

23. Vaurio, J.K.: Optimization of test and maintenance intervals based on risk and cost. Reliab. Eng. Syst. Saf. **49**, 23–36 (1995)

24. Cepin, M., Mavko, B.: Probabilistic safety assessment improves surveillance requirements in technical specifications. Reliab. Eng. Syst. Saf. **56**, 69–77 (1997)

25. Cepin, M.: Optimization of safety equipment outages improves safety. Reliab. Eng. Syst. Saf. **77**, 71–80 (2002)

26. Torres-Echeverria, A.C., Martorell, S., Thompson, H.A.: Multi-objective optimization of design and testing of safety instrumented systems with MooN voting architectures using a genetic algorithm. Reliab. Eng. Syst. Saf. **106**, 45–60 (2012)

27. Yuwen, C., Linhong, X., Jin, Z., Leifeng, L.: Research about mobile AR system based on cloud computing. In: Wireless and Optical Communication Conference (WOCC), 2013 22nd, pp. 355–359 (2013)

Addressing NoC Reliability Through an Efficient Fibonacci-Based Crosstalk Avoidance Codec Design

Zahra Shirmohammadi[1(✉)] and Seyed Ghassem Miremadi[2]

[1] International Campus, Sharif University of Technology, Kish Island, Iran
shirmohammadi@kish.sharif.edu
[2] Department of Computer Engineering,
Sharif University of Technology, Tehran, Iran
miremadi@sharif.edu

Abstract. The reliable transfer in Network on Chips (NoCs) can be threatened by crosstalk fault occurring in wires. Crossstalk fault is due to inter-wire coupling capacitance that based on the patterns of transitions appearing on the wires, significantly limits the reliability of NoCs. Among these transitions, 101 and 010 bit patterns impose the worst crosstalk effects to wires. This work intends to increase the reliability of NoCs against crosstalk faults by applying an improved Fibonacci-based numeral system, called Doubled-Penultimate Fibonacci (DP-Fibo). In the DP-Fibo coding algorithm, code words without '101' and '010' bit patterns are produced to reduce crosstalk faults. Experimental results show that the proposed numerical system: (1) can be utilized in NoC channels with any arbitrary wire width and, (2) can outperform other existing coding mechanism in providing significant reliability improvement and reduction over the area occupation and power consumption of NoCs. Experiments indicated that DP-Fibo provides improvement in area occupation, power-delay product, critical path and power consumptions of codec with respect to the state-of-the-art Fibonacci coding mechanism by 13 %, 22.7 %, 5 % and 25 % respectively.

Keywords: Network on chips · Crosstalk faults · Crosstalk avoidance code · Numerical system

1 Introduction

With marching the *Very Large-Scale Integration* (VLSI) technology into a nanometer regime, designers are able to integrate huge numbers of Processing Elements (PEs) into a single die. These PEs require scalable and performance-efficient communication architecture to transfer packets between them. Network on chip (NoC) has become a promising and revolutionary paradigm for the communication of theses PEs in the recent past years [1, 2]. In NoC, a data packet is broken down into multiple flow control units called flits [3]. These flits are sent and received in the communication channels by means of wires between PEs. During this flit transmission, data reliability can be threatened by serious reliability concerns [4, 6]. One of these reliability concerns is crosstalk fault [5, 6]. Crosstalk fault occurs due to coupling capacitances formed

© Springer International Publishing Switzerland 2015
G. Wang et al. (Eds.): ICA3PP 2015, Part III, LNCS 9530, pp. 756–770, 2015.
DOI: 10.1007/978-3-319-27137-8_55

between adjacent and long wires of NoCs. Unwanted voltage glitches and delays or/and speed up in rising/falling transitions appearing on the victim wire [6] are among the crosstalk effects. These effects can result in reliability degradation, extra power consumption and timing violations in NoCs [7–9]. Crosstalk fault is transition dependent and the strength of crosstalk fault effects depends on the transition patterns appearing on the wires of NoC channels [10]. For example, in a 3-bit NoC channel, bit pattern 101 which follows the 010 bit pattern imposes the worse crosstalk fault effects. These bit patterns are called Triplet Opposite Directions (TODs). In contrast, appearance of bit pattern 111 after a bit pattern 000 is the weakest pattern from the crosstalk fault point of view. To deal with crosstalk faults effects, there have been considerable efforts in different levels of abstraction in the literature [11–14]. At the lowest level of abstraction, physical level mechanisms reduce the coupling capacitance by changing the layering process. Sizing wire width and spacing [11], adding shielding wires [12, 14] and inserting repeaters [13] are among the mechanisms to address crosstalk faults in physical level. But, beside requiring a great knowledge on electric layout, these mechanisms seriously suffer from the area overheads. In transistor level, timing skewing can detract the simultaneous opposite transitions and reduce the crosstalk faults effects [18]. This is done by inserting different time shifts in repeater inserted channel. Problems in adjusting the timing concerns between a sender and a receiver and the area overhead are the main drawbacks of these mechanisms. Coding mechanisms in Register Transfer Level (RTL) are among the efficient mechanisms to increase the reliability of NoCs against crosstalk faults [15–19, 21, 24–32]. Coding mechanisms, beside the reduction of crosstalk fault, are technology-independent and can greatly solve mentioned limitations in physical and transistor level mechanisms [25]. Crosstalk Avoidance Codes (CACs) [25–32] are among the coding mechanisms that can reduce crosstalk fault in NoCs. In CACs, crosstalk fault in data word is prevented in the wires of NoCs by omitting the forbidden pattern transitions and producing code word. Among different kinds of CACs, Forbidden Pattern Frees (FPFs) codes omit TODs completely. In order to apply FPFs practically, efficient codec designs are necessary. One of the challenges of FPFs is the complexity of codec. Numerical systems can be used efficiently to reduce the complexity of the codec modules. A numeral system is a mathematical notation for representing numbers of a given set by symbols in a consistent manner [35]. One of the numerical systems that is proposed recently is Fibonacci numerical system [19]. This numerical system uses the Fibonacci sequence as base in representation of code words. The ambiguity of coding algorithm which leads to representing more than one code word for some input data words and the complex encoder/decoder modules from area occupation, power consumption and timing perspectives are two main drawbacks of Fibonacci numerical system. In this paper, Doubled-Penultimate Fibonacci (DP-Fibo) numerical system is proposed to deal with crosstalk faults. The proposed coding mechanism uses the whole code area and unlike the Fibonacci numerical system does not have ambiguity in producing code words. Simulations using VHDL for different channel widths show that the proposed mechanism can omit TODs and reduce crosstalk fault with lower power consumption and area occupation overheads with respect to Fibonacci coding mechanism. Experiments indicated that DP-Fibo provides reduction by 13 % in area occupation and 22.7 % in power-delay product, 5 % in critical path and 25 % in power consumptions with respect to the state-of-art Fibonacci coding mechanism.

The rest of the paper is organized as following: An overview and background of crosstalk fault is presented in Sect. 2. Section 3 discusses the related work. The FPF codes are introduced in Sect. 4. The proposed Fibonacci-based numerical system is presented in Sect. 5 and evaluated in Sect. 6, finally conclusion remarks are given in Sect. 7.

2 Background and Motivations

According to International Technology Roadmap for Semiconductors (ITRS), the total length of wires on chip will reach to $7000 \frac{m}{cm^2}$ till 2020 [20]. These long and parallel wires are seriously prone to crosstalk fault. Crosstalk fault is the result of coupling capacitance between adjacent and long wires of NoCs. Crosstalk fault has become more important due to technology scaling. With scaling down the technology size, the thickness of wires decreases faster than their width and height. This increases the coupling effects between the than their width and height. This increases the coupling effects between the wires and thus the ratio of the coupling capacitance to the total capacitance (including area and fringe capacitance) increases [16]. With increasing the coupling capacitance, the transitions appearing on the wires of a communication channel can affect other wires more severely than earlier technologies [10, 11]. In the presence of crosstalk faults, the affected wire which is called victim wire encounters the following effects [15, 16]: (1) Unwanted voltage glitches, (2) delays in rising/falling transitions, and (3) speed up in rising/falling transitions [21]. These effects can lead to threatening the reliability of flits, increasing power consumption and reducing the performance of NoC-based systems. Crosstalk can threat the reliability of different kinds of flits transferring in NoC wires. This can lead to corrupting and/or loss of flits. The other effect is timing violation [7, 8]. With technology scaling, gate delay decreases while global wire due to Resistance-Capacitance (RC) delay increases. This delay is increasing in coming years [22]. According to ITRS it is predicted that till 2015, the delay of global wires will reach to 1794×10^2 ps [22]. The delay of wires can be multiples of the RC delay of wires due to crosstalk fault. Also investigations show that 20 %–36 % of total NoC power is dissipated in the wires of NoC channels [16]. As the power consumption of wires dependents on capacitance between wires, tackling the crosstalk fault can reduce the power consumption in wires. Effective capacitance of wires depends on the pattern of transition on the channel. Based on a delay model proposed by Sotiriadis [39] transition patterns over a wire can be classified according to their delays into five classes. Table 1 shows these five classes of transitions, and their patterns. As it is shown in Table 1, transitions of 4C are: $010 \rightarrow 101$ and $101 \rightarrow 010$ (Triplet Opposite Direction (TOD)) that is shown by ↑↓↑ and ↓↑↓ in this paper. Symbols ↑, ↓ and - are used to represent transitions $0 \rightarrow 1, 1 \rightarrow 0$ and no transition respectively. 1C is consists of -↑↑, -↓↓, ↑↑- and ↓↓-. 2C consist of -↑- -↓- transition patterns 3C transition patterns are patterns with a pair of opposite direction transitions which are not 4C patterns. Patterns of -↑↑, -↓↓, ↑↑-, ↓↓- are categorized in this class. 4C transition patterns are patterns with a TOD transitions i.e., ↑↑↑ ↓↓↓ patterns. 4C imposes the maximum delay to the wires and

Table 1. Patterns of transition classes

Transition class	Patterns
0C	↑↑↑ ↓↓↓
1C	− ↑↑ − ↓↓ ↑↑ − ↓↓ −
2C	− ↑ − − ↓ −
3C	− ↑↓ ↑↓ − ↓↑ − ↑↓ −
4C	↑↓↑ ↓↑↓

mitigation of this class not only reduces TOD but also it reduces other classes of transitions. With respect to the importance of TODs, in this paper, a coding mechanism to tackle these kinds of transitions is proposed.

3 Related Work

Crosstalk fault tackling has been extensively explored in the recent past years. Reducing the coupling capacitance by shielding each wire is among the simplest mechanisms to address crosstalk faults. In the active shielding [12], the shield wires have the same transition pattern as the signal wire, while in passive shielding [14], the shield wires, which are statically connected to power or ground, are placed on either sides of the signal wire. Although shielding can reduce the crosstalk faults efficiently, adding additional wires greatly increase wire routing area. Increasing the space and width of wires which results in changing the physical dimension of wires are the other mechanisms proposed in the literature to reduce crosstalk fault. However, these mechanisms impose the area overhead to the chip. In repeater insertion, inverting or non-inverting buffers in each segment of wires can reduce the worst case delay class of 4C to 0C. Beside the area redundancy of repeater insertion, timing adjustment and requiring exact placement of repeaters make repeaters not to be favored by NoC researchers and manufacturers. Eliminating the opposite simultaneous rise and fall transitions by inserting different time shifts in repeater inserted channels with the aim of applying intentionally timing skewing, can also reduce crosstalk fault [18]. Timing concerns between a sender and a receiver and the area overhead are the main drawbacks of this mechanism. As it was mentioned, the main problem of most of the above mentioned crosstalk mitigation mechanisms is the overheads especially area overheads that they impose to NoC-based systems. Using coding mechanisms can efficiently reduce crosstalk fault with much lower area overhead than abovementioned mechanisms [15–19, 21, 24–32]. The basic concept of the coding is to add redundancy to information in order to correct and/or detect and/or preventing crosstalk faults that may occur in the NoCs. The original data as the input to the encoder is referred to as the data word, while the output of the encoder is referred to as the code word. Coding mechanisms that are used to mitigate crosstalk fault can be categorized into Error Detecting/Correcting Codes (EDC/ECC) [15, 17, 21, 26, 29, 31], Crosstalk Avoidance Codes (CAC) [19, 25, 28, 30–32, 34, 35] and Low Power Codes [23]. Boundary Shift Code (BSC) [38], Duplicate-add-parity (DAP) [17], Modified Dual Rail (MDR) [26]. The DAP and BSC use Hamming distance of three by duplicating wires and adding a parity bit to avoid crosstalk in NoCs channels. It should be noted that the hamming distance is defined as the number of bit positions at which the corresponding bits are different. The only difference between BSC and DAP is that in the BSC mechanism, the location of the parity is not fixed like the DAP, and bit places opposite side of the code word in each cycle. In MDR coding, parity bits are duplicated and used in adjacent to the other code word bits to mitigate crosstalk effect. Double Error Correction Coding (CADEC), the Joint Crosstalk Avoidance and Triple-Error-Correction (JTEC) [21] code and Simultaneous Quadruple-Error-Detection code (JTEC-SQED) [21] are the other examples of EDC/ECC with the higher error detection and correction capability. CADEC has Hamming distance of seven that enables up to triple error correction. The JTEC code [21], uses the same algorithm of CADEC but provides more simple decoding algorithm than JTEC. JTEC-SQED can achieve simultaneous triple-error correction and quadruple-error detection to detect all uncorrectable error patterns. JTEC-SQED uses Hsiao SEC–DED where the minimum Hamming distance between code words reaches to four. As EDCs/ECCs cannot detect or correct errors completely and also crosstalk fault is transition-dependent and its arrival is uncertain at a receiver, crosstalk fault can be avoided by preventing transition patterns occurring in wires [37]. CACs have achieved considerable attention in the recent years. In CACs, encoding and decoding is done in such a way that certain transition patterns are avoided. CACs are among the efficient mechanisms to tackle the crosstalk fault in NoC channels. Technology-independence and low power consumption have made CACs popular and attractive for designers in the recent past years [19, 25]. Forbidden Overlap Condition (FOC) Codes [27], Forbidden Transition Condition (FTC) codes [28] Forbidden Pattern Free (FPF) codes [19, 25, 28, 30–32, 34, 35], and One Lambda Codes (OLC) [16] that restrict transition patterns to 3C, 2C and 1C respectively are kinds of these codes. 4C class imposes the worse crosstalk delay to a victim wire. Among CACs, Forbidden Transition Codes (FTC) and Forbidden Pattern Free Codes (FPF) are two types of the most efficient CACs that reduce 4C to 2C. In FTC codes, any transition involving adjacent wires switching in opposite directions is prohibited (i.e., $01 \rightarrow 10$ or $10 \rightarrow 01$ transition); while in FPF codes no $010 \rightarrow 101$ (or $101 \rightarrow 010$) transition exists in two continuous FPF code words. These codes increase the speedup factor of channel by omitting certain transition patterns. The aim of this paper is to propose the efficient numerical-based FPF coding mechanism.

4 Forbidden Patten Free Codes

Forbidden Pattern Free (FPF) codes are efficient types of CACs that reduce crosstalk fault by omitting 010 and 101 transition patterns. As an example 0101001 is not FPF code word while 1100111 is FPF code word. Omitting these transition patterns which are called Triplet Opposite Direction (TOD) leads to restricting the delay to 2C. One of the challenges of FPFs designing is an efficient codec design. Designing an efficient codec plays an important role in providing a tradeoff between reliability improvement and overheads imposed to NoC's router. Mechanisms such as partitioning channel's wires and applying coding separately to each of these partitions; can reduce the encoder and decoder (codec) overheads, but they have the problem of appearing TODs at the boundary between partitions [19, 33]. Numerical systems can overcome the complexity of FPFs [34] especially in wide channels. A numeral system is a mathematical notation for representing numbers of a given set by symbols in a consistent manner [25]. Omitting these transitions is done by providing numerical-based coding mechanism which maps the data word into the code word. Numerical system with the following properties can be used as FPF coding [19]:

(1) The numerical systems should be complete. The numerical system is complete if any data word has at least one code word representation in the numerical system. In other words, for b_i if $b_1 = 1$ for all amount of i we have $b_i \leq 1 + \sum_{j=1}^{i-1} b_j$. Where b_i is base that is used in the numerical system.
(2) The numerical system should be able to encode data word to FPF code word. In a K-bit space, the maximum number of FPF code words is $2f_{k+1}$ [19] where f_{k+1} is $(k+1)^{th}$ sentence of Fibonacci sequence. As an example, in a 6-bit FPF codebook there exist 26 FPF code words.

As numerical system plays an important role in the complexity of the codec modules, selecting an efficient numerical system can efficiently reduce the overhead of codec. One of the numerical systems that is proposed recently is Fibonacci binary numeral system. Fibonacci binary Numeral System (FNS) was first mentioned in the context of CAC designs by Mutyam in [35]. The author proposed a code word generation algorithm for the forbidden pattern free code. However, [35] failed to address the mapping scheme and codec design. Recently, codec design based on a FNS has proposed [19, 26]. These codec designs can effectively solve the complexity problem for FPFs [19]. The main idea behind Fibonacci coding system proposed in [28] is to use the iterative algorithm to replace the 011 by 100 and vice versa. This coding mechanism uses the Fibonacci numerical system as the base to produce FPF codes, e. g for 6-bit space the bases are 8 5 3 2 1 1. Table 2 shows 6-bit codebooks generated by

Table 2. 6bit FPF code word generated by Fibo-CAC [19]

Data word	Fibo-CAC code word 8 5 3 2 1 1	Data word	Fibo-CAC code word 8 5 3 2 1 1
0	0 0 0 0 0 0	13	1 1 0 0 0 0
1	0 0 0 0 0 1	14	1 1 0 0 0 1
2	0 0 0 0 1 1	15	1 1 0 0 1 1
3	0 0 0 1 1 0	16	1 1 1 0 0 0
4	0 0 0 1 1 1	17	1 1 1 0 0 1
5	0 0 1 1 0 0	18	1 1 1 1 0 0
6	0 0 1 1 1 0	19	1 1 1 1 1 0
7	0 0 1 1 1 1	20	1 1 1 1 1 1
8	011000, 100000	21	——
9	011001, 100001	22	——
10	100011, 011100	23	——
11	011110, 100110	24	——
12	011111, 100111	25	——

Fibonacci scheme. However, Fibonacci coding mechanism suffers two main draw-backs: (1) Complex encoder modules (2) the coding algorithm has ambiguity; for example this numerical system has two vector presentations for 12, which are 100111 and 011111. This ambiguity is expiated by adding additional X_n wire in optimal version of coding in [19].

5 Proposed Forbidden Pattern Free Coding Mechanism

As numerical system plays an important role in the complexity of the codec modules, to reduce this complexity, Doubled-Penultimate (DP-Fibo) numerical system is proposed in this paper. The proposed FPF numerical system can omit TODs in code words transmitted in the wires and unlike Fibonacci numerical system does not have ambiguity and uses all of the code word space. DP-Fibo can be applied to any arbitrary channel width. Experimental evaluations show that DP-Fibo provides improvements in the terms of area, power consumption and critical path with respect to similar numerical system.

5.1 Proposed Forbidden Pattern Free Numerical System

Considering $B(k)$ denoting the k bit binary bases vector of the Doubled-Penultimate Fibonacci numerical system with binary string of:

$$B(k) = b_k b_{k-1} b_{k-2} b_{k-3} .... b_2 b_1$$

Where b_1 is the Least Significant Bit (LSB) and b_n is the Most Significant Bit (MSB). In this binary string, b_i for $0 < i \leq k$ is defined as:

$$b_i = \begin{cases} F_i & 1 \leq i \leq K - 2 \\ 2 \times F_{i-1} & i = K - 1 \\ F_i & i = K \end{cases} \tag{1}$$

Where b_i is the base of i'th sentences of numerical system, and F_K is K'th sentence of Fibonacci sequence. According to this definition, DP-Fibo numerical system maps doubled of K − 1'th bit of Fibonacci sequence to penultimate bit position of binary bases vector; in other words, DP-Fibo doubles K − 1'th bit of Fibonacci sequence position. One of the features of DP-Fibo is that it can be applied for any arbitrary widths of wires. For example, in a 6-bit space, the DP-Fibo uses numerical system of 8 10 3 2 1 1 and represents 12 to 100111. Also, the other feature of DP-Fibo is that unlike the Fibo-CAC it has not ambiguity. Table 3 shows all the FPF code words utilizing DP-Fibo numerical system in 6-bit space. In the rest of this paper it is proved that DP-Fibo can produce FPF code words. DP-Fibo numerical system satisfies $b_i \leq 1 + \sum_{j=1}^{i-1} b_j$. So, DP-Fibo is complete. In the rest of this section, we will prove that DP-Fibo meets the required condition for being used as FPF coding; DP-Fibo coding has the following features:

Feature1:   Under   the   DP-Fibo   numerical   system, $10\,b_{k-2}b_{k-3}...b_0b_1$ *and* $01\,b'_{k-2}b'_{k-3}....01\,b'_0b'_1$ vectors are equal.

Proof: according to definition (1), $B_1 = B_2$ and it is clear that the two most significant bits are interchangeable.

Feature2: in k-bit vector $b_kb_{k-1}b_{k-2}b_{k-3}...b_2b_1$ in B_1, DP-Fibo numerical system, if three tandem $b_nb_{n-1}b_{n-2}$ bits have '100' values, this pattern can be replaced by '110' without changing the value

Feature3: in n-bit vector $b_kb_{k-1}b_{k-2}b_{k-3}....b_2b_1$ of DP-Fibo numerical system, all bit patterns, except first two bits, i.e.; '0010',...'1010' can be replaced by patterns '1111'... '1100'.

Proof: replacing '110' with 001 from left to right recursively, the feature 3 is proved.

Feature4: in n-bit vector $b_kb_{k-1}b_{k-2}b_{k-3}...b_2b_1$ of DP-Fibo numerical system, all bit patterns, except first two bits, i.e.; '1101' ... '0101' can be replaced by patterns '0000', ..., '0011', '0011'

Proof: replacing '110' with '001' from left to right recursively, the lemma is proved.

Fibonacci numerical system can represent code words in the range of $[0, f_{k+2} - 1]$ [19]. DP-Fibo, can increase the ability of utilization the code space to the $[0, 2f_{k+1} - 1]$. The main reason is due to the ability of DP-Fibo in avoiding ambiguity in producing code words. DP-Fibo coding mechanism can provide $2f_{k+1} - f_{k+2} = f_{k-1}$ more code words representation than Fibonacci numerical system and thus can use the whole FPF coding space [20]. According to Table 3, all of the 26 data words in the DP-Fibo numerical system, have unique representation and there exist only one code word for each data word, while Fibo-CAC due to its ambiguity, wastes the code space and this leads to not having any representations for 21–25 data words.

Table 3. 6 bit FPF code word generated by DP-Fibo

Data word	DP-Fibo code word	Data word	DP-Fibo code word
	8 10 3 2 1 1		8 10 3 2 1 1
0	0 0 0 0 0 0	13	0 1 1 0 0 1
1	0 0 0 0 0 1	14	0 1 1 0 0 1
2	0 0 0 0 1 1	15	0 1 1 1 0 0
3	0 0 0 1 1 0	16	0 1 1 1 1 0
4	0 0 0 1 1 1	17	0 1 1 1 1 1
5	0 0 1 1 0 0	18	1 1 0 0 0 0
6	0 0 1 1 1 0	19	1 1 0 0 0 1
7	0 0 1 1 1 1	20	1 1 0 0 1 1
8	1 0 0 0 0 0	21	1 1 1 0 0 0
9	1 0 0 0 0 1	22	1 1 1 0 0 1
10	1 0 0 0 1 1	23	1 1 1 1 0 0
11	0 0 01 1 1	24	1 1 1 1 1 0
12	1 0 0 1 1 1	25	1 1 1 1 1 1

> **Input:** code length, data word v ($\leq$ v $\leq \sum_{i=1}^{m} \gamma_i$)
> \\k-1 Stage
>   if v $\geq F_{k+1}$ then
> $d_{k-1} = 1$;
>   else
> $d_{k-1} = 0$;
> $r_{k-1} = v - (2F_{k-1})d_{k-1}$
>   end if
> **MSB**
>   if $r_{k-1} > F_k$ then
> $d_k = 1$;
>   else
> $d_k = 0$;
> $r_k = r_{k-1} - F_k d_k$
>   end if
> \\ **Other Stages**
>   for n=k-3 to 2 do
>   if $r_{n+1} \geq F_{n+1}$
> $d_n = 1$;
>   else if $r_{n+1} < F_n$
> $d_n = 0$;
>   else
> $d_n = d_{n+1}$
> $r_n = r_{n+1} - F_n d_n$
> **end for**

Fig. 1. The algorithm of DP-Fibo

5.2   DP-Fibo Coding Algorithm and Architecture

DP-Fibo coding mechanism uses the algorithm shown in Fig. 1. This algorithm, encodes integer input V, to an equivalent FPF code word $d_k d_{k-1}, \ldots, d_2 d_1$ which in this sequence, k is the width of NoC channel. According to Fig. 1, in each round of this algorithm, d_i and r_i values are calculated where d_i is the i' th bit of the FPF code word and r_i is the remainder of the input value which should be used in the next round i.e., $r_i = v - \sum_{j=1}^{i-1} d_j \times b_j$. This algorithm uses different input role for penultimate bit step, the incoming virtual channel flits is connected to the selected outgoing one. If a free virtual channel in the selected outgoing physical channel becomes free, the header flit is transferred to a next PE. In this situation, other flits in the packet are transferred in a pipelined fashion; but, if the virtual channels are not free, header flit must wait until they become free. Figure 3 shows the architecture of applying DP-Fibo in the NoCs. Figure 3A shows the end to end nature of DP-Fibo. Es/Ds are the encoder and decoder of DP-Fibo that are embedded in the network interface of the NoCs. Also the architecture of each router in the present of DP-Fibo is shown in Fig. 2.

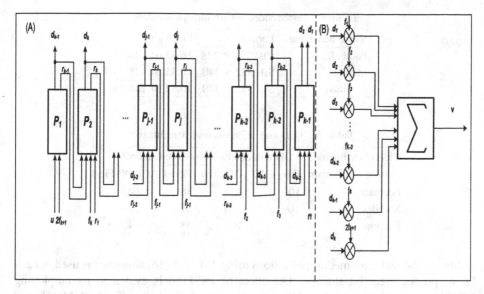

Fig. 2. The architecture of DP-Fibo (A) encoder and (B) decoder used in a K-bit channel

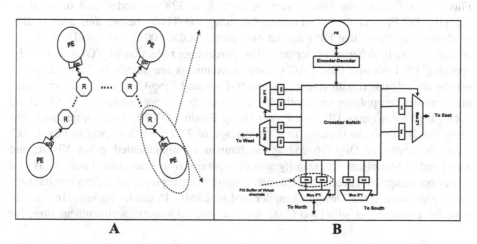

Fig. 3. A General architecture of the proposed approach –B Architecture of router in present of encoder/decoder

6 Experimental Evaluations

The effects of inserting DP-Fibo coding mechanism is evaluated using extensive simulation tools. Coding efficiency, NoC performance and overheads of DP-Fibo codec including critical path, area occupation and power consumption are inspected in the present of DP-Fibo coding mechanism. The efficiency of DP-Fibo coding mechanism on TODs is evaluated on the real multimedia applications. In order to match with

Table 4. Tested video bit streams parameters

Video benchmark	Format	Flit width
Football	CIF 328 × 228	16,32,64,128
Mobile	SIF 352 × 240	16,32,64,128
Foreman	SIF 352 × 240	16,32,64,128

Table 5. TOD and 3C reduction percentage

Video benchmark	TOD reduction%		3C reduction%	
Coding mechanism	Fibo-CAC	DP-Fibo	Fibo-CAC	DP-Fibo
Football	100	100	38	43
Mobile	100	100	37	38
Foreman	100	100	38	40

reality, H.264 real multimedia applications using JM 15.1 [36] simulator is used in each PE to produce real bit streams. The effect of DP-Fibo is evaluated by employing DP-Fibo on three standard video bit stream benchmarks including Football, Mobile and Foreman. The parameters of theses standard video benchmarks are shown in Table 4. Flits with different wire widths varying from 8 to 128 are coded and decoded by applying DP-Fibo coding mechanism. Counting the TODs before and after coding mechanism confirms that DP-Fibo not only omits TODs 100 % but also DP-Fibo can reduce the 3C in different bit streams. The percentage reduction of TODs and 3C by applying DP-Fibo and Fibo-CAC coding mechanisms are shown in Table 5. These results are calculated with respect to the DP-Fibo and Fibo-CAC coding mechanisms after and before applying separately. To measures the energy consumed per switching event, Fig. 4 compares DP-Fibo Power-Delay Product (PDP). This comparison confirms that DP-Fibo can improve PDP by average of 27.2 % with respect to Fibo-CAC. Also, the codec of DP-Fibo coding mechanism is implemented using VHDL and simulated in Modelsim. To quantify area occupation as well as critical path delay and power consumption, encoder and decoder modules of the proposed coding mechanisms are implemented using Design Compiler tool in TSMC 45 nm technology. In order to have fair comparisons with Fibo-CAC mechanisms, the same experiments are done for

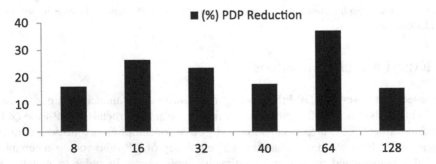

Fig. 4. PDP Improvement of the DP-Fibo with respect to Fibo-CAC

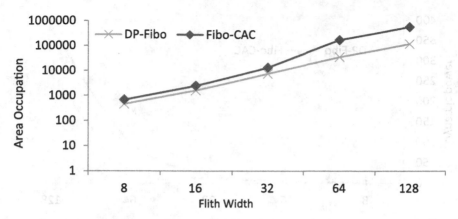

Fig. 5. Area occupation of of DP-Fibo codec with respect to Fibo-CAC codec (μm²)

Table 6. Critical path of codec of DP-Fibo codec in comparison with Fibo-CAC

	Critical path of codec (ns)	
Bus Width	DP-Fibo	Fibo-CAC
8	4.45	4.53
16	13.70	14.23
32	55.89	55.90
64	225.22	230.32
128	803.58	803.64

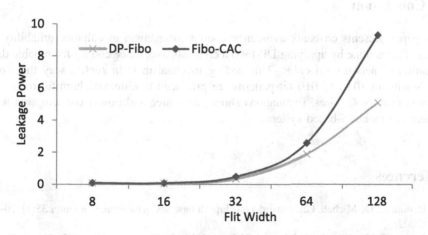

Fig. 6. Leakage power consumption of DP-Fibo codec with respect to Fibo-CAC codec (mw)

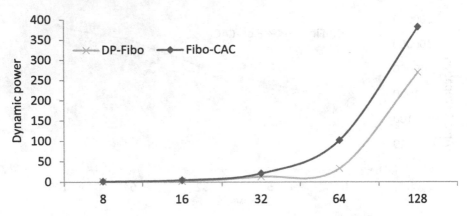

Fig. 7. Dynamic power consumption of DP-Fibo codec with respect to Fibo-CAC codec (mw)

encoder and decoder modules of Fibo-CAC coding mechanism. In practice, bus delay and codec critical path are two important parameters in determining performance of NoCs. Although in low bus widths, results are close, but the efficiency of proposed coding is recognizable with increasing the bus width. Results in Table 6 show that DP-Fibo has improvement of 5 % in critical path delay in comparison with Fibo-CAC. The effect of imposing DP-Fibo codec on the router area occupation is shown in Fig. 5. Results show that we have an average of 13 % decrease in the area occupation of DP-Fibo in comparison with Fibo-CAC. Figures 6 and 7 show the leakage and dynamic power consumptions of DP-Fibo and Fibo-CAC codecs. According to Figs. 6 and 7, DP-Fibo codec can improve an average of 30 % and 25 % less leakage and dynamic power consumptions -CAC.

7   Conclusion

This paper presents crosstalk avoidance coding mechanism to enhance reliability of NoCs. This is done by applying DP-Fibo a crosstalk avoidance coding for reliable data transition of network on chips. This coding mechanism is in such a way that code words without 101 and 010 bit patterns are produced to eliminate harmful transition patterns from NoC wires. Evaluations show lower area and power consumption with respect to Fibonacci-based system.

References

1. Benini, L., De Micheli, G.: Networks on chips: a new SoC paradigm. Computer **35**(1), 70–78 (2002)
2. Kumar, S., Jantsch, A., Soininen, J.P., Forsell, M., Millberg, M., Oberg, J., Tiensyrja, K., Hemani, A.: A network on chip architecture and design methodology. In: IEEE Symposium on VLSI (ISVLSI), pp. 117–122 (2002)

3. Dally, W.J., Towles, B.: Principles and Practices of Interconnection Networks. Morgan Kaufmann, San Mateo (2004)
4. Radetzki, M., Feng, C., Zhao, X., Jantsch, A.: Methods for fault tolerance in network on chip. ACM Comput. Surv. **44**, 1–36 (2013)
5. Kuhlmann, M., Sapatnekar, S.S.: Exact and efficient crosstalk estimation. IEEE Trans. Comput.-Aided Des. Integr. Circ. Syst. **20**(7), 858–866 (2001)
6. Duan, C., Tirumala, A., Khatri, S.P.: Analysis and avoidance of crosstalk in on-chip buses. In: Hot Interconnects (HOTI), pp. 133–138 (2001)
7. Flayyih, W.N., Samsudin, K., Hashim, S.J., Rokhani, F.Z., Ismail, Y.I.: Crosstalk-aware multiple error detection scheme based on two-dimensional parities for energy efficient network on chip. IEEE Trans. Circ. Syst. I **61**(7), 2034–2047 (2014)
8. Frantz, A.P., Kastensmidt, F.L., Carro, L., Cota, E.: Dependable network-on-chip router able to simultaneously tolerate soft errors and crosstalk. In: Proceedings of the International Test Conference (ITC), pp. 1–9 (2006)
9. Bai, X., Dey, S.: High-level crosstalk defect simulation for system-on-chip interconnects. In: Proceedings of VLSI Test Symposium (VTS), pp. 169–175 (2001)
10. Hirose, K., Yasuura, H.: A bus delay reduction technique considering crosstalk. In: Proceedings of Design, Automation and Test in Europe (DATE), pp. 441–445 (2000)
11. Agarwal, K., Sylvester, D., Blaauw, D.: Modeling and analysis of crosstalk noise in coupled RLC interconnects. IEEE Trans. Comput. Aided Des. Integr. Circ. Syst. **25**(5), 892–901 (2005)
12. Zhang E., Friedman, G.: Effect of shield insertion on reducing crosstalk noise between coupled interconnects. In: Proceedings of International Symposium on Circuits and Systems (ISCAS), pp. 23–26, May 2004
13. Akl, C.J., Bayoumi, M.A.: Reducing interconnect delay uncertainty via hybrid polarity repeater insertion. IEEE Trans. Very Large Scale Integr. (VLSI) Syst. **16**(9), 1230–1239 (2008)
14. Kose, S., Salman, E., Friedman, E.G.: Shielding methodologies in the presence of power/ground noise. IEEE Trans. Very Large Scale Integr. (VLSI) Syst. **19**(8), 1458–1468 (2011)
15. Pande, P.P., Ganguly, A., Feero, B., Belzer, B., Grecu, C.: Design of low power and reliable networks on chip through joint crosstalk avoidance and forward error correction coding. In: Proceeding of IEEE International Symposium on Defect and Fault Tolerance in VLSI Systems (DFT), pp. 466–476 (2006)
16. Sridhara, S.R., Shanbhag, N.R.: Coding for reliable on-chip buses: a class of fundamental bounds and practical codes. IEEE Trans. Comput. Aided Des. Integr. Circ. Syst. **26**(5), 977–982 (2007)
17. Sridhara, S.R., Shanbhag, N.R.: Coding for system-on-chip networks: a unified framework. IEEE Trans. Very Large Scale Integr. (VLSI) Syst. **13**(6), 655–667 (2005)
18. Zhang, Y., Huawei, L., Yinghua, M., Xiaowei, L.: Selected transition time adjustment for tolerating crosstalk effects on network-on-chip interconnects. IEEE Trans. Very Large Scale Integr. (VLSI) Syst. **19**(10), 1787–1800 (2011)
19. Duan, C., Calle, V.H.C., Khatri, S.P.: Efficient on-chip crosstalk avoidance codec design. IEEE Trans. Very Large Scale Integr. (VLSI) Syst. **17**(4), 551–560 (2009)
20. International Technology Roadmap for Semiconductors (ITRS), 2005 edn. Technical report (2005). http://public.itrs.net
21. Ganguly, A., Pande, P.P., Belzer, B.: Crosstalk-aware channel coding schemes for energy efficient and reliable interconnects. IEEE Trans. VLSI **17**(11), 1626–1639 (2009)
22. International Technology Roadmap for Semiconductors (ITRS), 2007 edn. Technical report (2007). http://public.itrs.net

23. Stan, M.R., Burleson, W.P.: Bus-invert coding for low-power i/o. IEEE Trans. Very Large Scale Integr. Syst. **3**(1), 49–58 (1995)

24. Shi, F., Wu, X., Yan, Z.: New crosstalk avoidance codes based on a novel pattern classification. IEEE Trans. Very Large Scale Integr. (VLSI) Syst. **21**(10), 1892–1902 (2013)

25. Rossi, D., Nieuwland, A.K., Katoch, A., Metra, C.: Exploiting ECC redundancy to minimize crosstalk impact. IEEE Des. Test Comput. **22**(1), 59–70 (2003)

26. Sridhara, S.R., Ahmed, A., Shanbhag, N.R.: Area and energy-efficient crosstalk avoidance codes for on-chip buses. In: Proceedings of IEEE International Conference on Computer Design (ICCD), pp. 12–17 (2004)

27. Victor, B., Keutzer, K.: Bus encoding to prevent crosstalk delay. In: Proceedings of IEEE/ACM International Conference on Computer Aided Design (ICCAD), pp. 57–63 (2001)

28. Murali, S., Theocharides, T., Vijaykrishnan, N., Irwin, M.J., Benini, L., De Micheli, G.: Analysis of error recovery schemes for networks on chips. IEEE Des. Test Comput. **22**(5), 434–442 (2005)

29. Rossi, D., Metra, C., Nieuwland, A.K., Katoch, A.: New ECC for crosstalk impact minimization. IEEE Des. Test Comput. **22**(4), 340–348 (2005)

30. Ganguly, A., Pande, P.P., Belzer, B., Grecu, C.: Addressing signal integrity in networks on chip interconnects through crosstalk-aware double error correction coding. In: Proceedings of IEEE Computer Society Annual Symposium on VLSI, (ISVLSI), pp. 317–324 (2007)

31. Shirmohammadi, Z., Miremadi, S.G.: S2AP: an efficient numerical-based crosstalk avoidance code for reliable data transfer of NoCs. In: Proceedings of the IEEE International Symposium on Reconfigurable Communication-Centric Systems-on-Chip (ReCoSoC) (2015)

32. Shirmohammadi, Z., Miremadi, S.G.: Crosstalk avoidance coding for reliable data transmission of network on chips. In: Proceedings of the International Symposium on System-on-Chip (SoC), pp. 1–4 (2013)

33. Xuebin, V., Zhiyuan, Y.: Efficient codec designs for crosstalk avoidance codes based on numeral systems. IEEE Trans. Very Large Scale Integr. (VLSI) Syst. **19**(4), 548–558 (2011)

34. Mutyam, M.: Preventing crosstalk delay using fibonacci representation. In: Proceedings of International Conference on of VLSI Design (VLSID 2004), pp. 685–688 (2004)

35. Palesi, M., Fazzino, F., Ascia, G., Catania, V.: Data encoding for low-power in wormhole-switched networks-on-chip. In: Proceedings of Euromicro Conference on Digital System Design, Architectures, Methods and Tools (DSD), pp. 119–126 (2009)

36. H264/AVC JM Reference. http://iphome.hhi.de/suehring/tml/

37. Fu, B., Ampadu, P.: Exploiting parity computation latency for on-chip crosstalk reduction. IEEE Trans. Circ. Syst. **57**(5), 399–403 (2010)

38. Zimmer, H., Jantsch, A.: A fault model notation and error-control scheme for switch-to-switch buses in a network-on-chip. In: Proceedings of International Conference Hardware/Software Codesign and System Synthesis (CODES-ISSS), pp 188–19 (2003)

39. Sotiriadis, P.P., Chandrakasan, A.: Reducing bus delay in submicron technology using coding. In: Proceedings of Asia and South Pacific Design Automation Conference (ASP-DAC), pp. 109–114 (2001)

A Programming Framework for Implementing Fault-Tolerant Mechanism in IoT Applications

Yung-Li Hu[1,2], Yuo-Yu Cho[1], Wei-Bing Su[1], David S.L. Wei[3], Yennun Huang[2], Jiann-Liang Chen[4], Ing-Yi Chen[5], and Sy-Yen Kuo[1(✉)]

[1] Department of Electrical Engineering, National Taiwan University, Taipei 10617, Taiwan
{d99921027,d01921026,r02921092,sykuo}@ntu.edu.tw

[2] Research Center for Information Technology Innovation, Academia Sinica, Taipei 115, Taiwan
yennunhuang@citi.sinica.edu.tw

[3] Department of Computer and Information Sciences, Fordham University, Bronx, NY 10458, USA
wei@dsm.fordham.edu

[4] Department of Electrical Engineering, National Taiwan University of Science and Technology, Taipei 10607, Taiwan
lchen@mail.ntust.edu.tw

[5] Department of Computer Science and Information Engineering, National Taipei University of Technology, Taipei 10608, Taiwan
ichen@ntut.edu.tw

Abstract. Resilience is one of the major issues in Quality of Service (QoS) of IoT applications. Meanwhile, IoT device functions as a small independent computer running on Linux operating system that supports a few high-level programming languages, and has high expandability to allow its expansion with more number of peripherals. Therefore, it enables application developers to construct fault-tolerant programming through software-defined control based on some software fault-tolerant technologies, such as redundancy and diversity, recovery block, and exception handling. In this paper, we propose a programming framework for application developers to effectively and efficiently construct application-level fault-tolerant programming in IoT applications. This framework could assist application developers with programming robust software so that the resilience of IoT applications can be improved.

Keywords: IoT device · Programming framework · Resilience · Robustness · Exception handling

1 Introduction

Embedded devices, when connected via networks or Internet, have extensive applications in various fields. Due to their features of low cost, interaction capabilities, and easy to deploy, there will be more than billions of embedded devices connected to Internet to form a huge scale of Internet of Things (IoT) such that users could be benefited from various services anytime and anywhere. IoT applications, such as smart city, healthcare,

© Springer International Publishing Switzerland 2015
G. Wang et al. (Eds.): ICA3PP 2015, Part III, LNCS 9530, pp. 771–784, 2015.
DOI: 10.1007/978-3-319-27137-8_56

and supply chain management, are becoming key information industry to provide myriad opportunities to produce innovative service model in the future. Because IoT is becoming part of our life, Quality of Service (QoS) for their applications must be carefully addressed by application developers. Resilience is one of the major issues in QoS of IoT applications. There have been some techniques developed for programming sensor networks for improving failure resilience in Wireless Sensor Networks (WSNs) [1]. However, these techniques have been developed to execute on resource-constrained devices but not for more powerful open source hardware, such as Raspberry Pi and Arduino. As such, both of application-level and system-level function design have to be considered to address the issue of fault tolerance. Therefore, application developers need more efforts to program fault-tolerant mechanism.

The mobile or small devices used to constitute IoT are in general called IoT devices. Among various IoT devices, open source hardware (OSH), such as Raspberry Pi and Arduino, if adopted as IoT device, offer several advantages for IoT application developers. Open source hardware functions as a small independent computer running on Linux operating system that supports a few high-level programming languages, such as C, Java, and Python. This way, it enables application developers to program it as needed. Open source hardware has plenty of working memory (e.g. 512 MB on Raspberry Pi Model B+) and is expandable when needed. Open source hardware has high expandability to allow its expansion with more peripherals: adaptation of communication components (e.g. WiFi, Bluetooth, and Zigbee) and various plug-in electronic components (e.g. sensors and electronic circuits). In summary, compared with other traditional embedded devices, using open source hardware in IoT can provide a better programming development environment for application developers to some specific needs. Therefore, regarding IoT devices, we adopt OSH-based devices in our work. Throughout the rest of the paper, by IOT device, we mean OSH-based device or any other programmable device, such as Android.

The research on programming model for sensor networks has recently evolved to the study for IoT programming. Such researches focus on how to propose an application-specific framework for application developers to devise software component in distributed IoT devices using high-level programming languages [2–4]. Various software fault-tolerant technologies, such as redundancy and diversity, recovery block, and exception handling, have been widely employed in large distributed software applications [5]. Since most of the researches on fault-tolerant mechanism in IoT have been focused on wireless network distribution and energy-efficient scheduling, developing application-level fault-tolerant mechanism is still a new challenge for application developers. Comparing with other types of traditional embedded devices, using open source hardware as IoT device has more powerful computational resource with higher expandability that enables application developers to construct fault-tolerant programming through software-defined control. For reducing complexity of resource access control in fault-tolerant programming, some system-level functions, such as communication component control and sensor control, have to conform to a unified framework for application developers to use.

In our work, we propose a programming framework for application developers to effectively and efficiently construct application-level fault-tolerant programming in IoT applications. This framework is supported by a fault-tolerant software architecture that provides some API to reduce complexity in the development of fault-tolerant mechanism. In IoT programming, application developers specify application logic in a task function. Application developers can follow a framework to specify exception handling mechanism in task function which can drive our proposed fault-tolerant software architecture. For recovery to be performed concurrently among the nodes, synchronized state maintenance is a mechanism devised to record operation state change in each node anytime through state table update in the same local WSN. We use a case study to evaluate our framework and it shows that the nodes in experiment scenario are able to execute error recovery concurrently. The contribution of this programming framework is to enable application developers to realize robust software so that the resilience of IoT applications can be reinforced.

The remainder of this paper is organized as follow. Section 2 illustrates proposed programing framework for exception handling. Section 3 illustrates proposed fault-tolerant software architecture using open source hardware. Section 4 gives a case study to evaluate our work and present the experiment results. Section 5 illustrates related works. Finally, Sect. 6 summarizes our work and proposes future research work.

2   Programming Framework for Exception Handling

In the research on IoT programming model, functional method on networked embedded device, such as light control and humidity/temperature monitoring, can be regarded as a task [2–4]. In this paper, we call a program which implements functional method on IoT device as task function. There are quite rich of resources in IoT devices, such as communication, sensor, and actuator components, that can be shared with all tasks executed in the same IoT device and application developers can thus specify application logic in task function with shared resource access. Exception handling is a mechanism which determines error specification and program error process in an application program. When any specified error condition occurs during function execution, error information is packed to an exception message and throws to relative error handling. Many types of high-level programming languages, such as Java and Python, support this mechanism using the style of try and catch blocks in grammar. Therefore, whether functional programming or object-oriented programming is adopted for developing task function on IoT device, exception handling is an efficient way to program error process for task function.

Task function has many operations related to access shared resource in IoT device for application logic, and many application-level errors are caused by shared resource access in IoT device. Therefore, application developers need high complexity to separate error handling of shared resource from application logic in error process, especially on making recovery strategy. For supporting the principle of loosely couple on shared resource access and recovery strategy in error process, we propose a programming framework to specify exception handling mechanism in task function which can effectively and efficiently drive our proposed fault-tolerant software architecture. Our proposed fault-tolerant software architecture is illustrated in Sect. 3. This programming framework for exception handling is formed by four blocks as illustrated as follows:

Declaration of Shared Resource Object: Application developers can import the API ComponentManager to declare the global objects called shared resource objects, which implement access interface of shared resource of IoT device, to program shared resource access in task function. The advantage of this design is to provide shared resource a unified management for configuration through global variable access. It would be easier for application developers to adjust and maintain shared resource utilization for task function operation.

Declaration of Critical State Object: Application developers can import the API Snapshot to declare the global object called critical state object to save several necessary variables, called critical state variables in this paper, for rollback recovery, when errors occur in task function. Like the advantage of declaration of shared resource object, application developers can easily set up what information should be saved for rollback recovery.

Application Logic: Application developers specify functional method with shared resource utilization in application logic block. For protecting available operation, code segment of application logic has to be put in try block for exception handling.

Exception Process: Application developers can specify some error conditions as checked error exceptions, such as connection fail and actuator working fail. For handling error condition under task function execution, exception process can be specified in catch block. ContextLogger and FailureHandler are API which can be used to call specified functions defined in Context Logger and Failure Handler which are in our proposed fault-tolerant software architecture. The illustration of operations on Context Logger and Failure Handler is given in Sect. 3. Application developers use critical state object to save critical state variables, and ContextLogger can be used to make critical state object be logged in Context Logger. The FailureHandler can be used to propagate exception message to Failure Handler, and then drives failure recovery to start. The advantage of this design is to reduce the complexity of programming exception handling, and let fault-tolerant mechanism be handled by application developers as described in our proposed fault-tolerant software architecture. Application developers can then pay more attention on programming functional method in task function and has higher scalability to make suitable recovery strategy.

An example of task function with exception handling in IoT device is presented by pseudo code in Fig. 1. Lines 1–4 import some APIs used to declare shared resource objects and critical state objects. Lines 7–13 declare shared resource objects used to program shared resource access in application logic of task function. Line 16 declares a critical state object to save critical variables in this task function for failure recovery. Lines 24–32 are application logic in this task function allocated in try block. Lines 33–48 are exception process in task function. The operation of task function throws AccessFailException represent as exception e when connection fails or actuator fails. The critical state variables for this example are humidityValue and tempratureValue. Both of them are saved in snapshot, a critical state object, and are logged in Context Logger through calling ContextLogger. Finally, for driving specified fault-tolerant mechanism, exception e is be propagated to Failure Handler through calling FailureHandler.

```
1.    import ComponentManager;
2.    import ContextLogger;
3.    import FailureHandler;
4.    import Snapshot;
5.
6.    // To declare shared resource objects
7.    Humidity humidity = ComponentManager.mount("Humidity");
8.    Temperature temperature =ComponentManager.mount("Temperature");
9.    Sensor sensor _1 = ComponentManager.activate(humidity, frequency_1);
10.   Sensor sensor _2 = ComponentManager.activate(temperature, frequency_2);
11.   WiFi wifi = ComponentManager.connect("WiFi");
12.   Bluetooth blutooth = ComponentManager.connect("Bluetooth");
13.   Connection conn = ComponentManager.activate(wifi);
14.
15.   // To declare critical state objects
16.   Snapshot snapshot = new snapshot();
17.
18.   Function weatherMonitor(){
19.
20.   double humidityValue;
21.   double temperatureValue;
22.
23.   while(true){
24.      try{
25.           //Application logic
26.           humidityValue = sensor _1.getValue();
27.           temperatureValue = sensor_2.getValue();
28.
29.           if((humidityValue > critical_value) {
30.               Message message = new Message("Out of Critical Value");
31.               conn.send(message, node_2);
32.           }
33.      }catch(AccessFailException e){
34.           //Exception process flow
35.           snapshot.save(humidityValue, temperatureValue);
36.           ContextLogger.log(snapshot);
37.           FailuHandler.notify(e);
38.      }
39. }
40. }
```

Fig. 1. Example of task function with exception handling

3   The Fault-Tolerant Software Architecture on IoT Device

The programming framework for application developers to program exception handling mechanism in task function has been illustrated in Sect. 2. Application developers follow this framework to specify exception handling mechanism in task function which drives our proposed fault-tolerant software architecture. This fault-tolerant software architecture that can reduce complexity in the development of fault-tolerant mechanism is illustrated in Fig. 2. The illustration of each software components in this fault-tolerant software architecture design is as follows.

A. Redundancy and Diversity. Redundancy and diversity are key design principles in fault-tolerant computing. Most of IoT devices have high expandability that enables their expansion with more number of peripherals so that application developers can

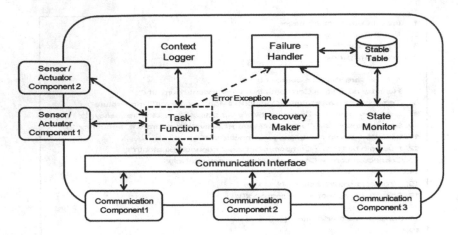

Fig. 2. The fault-tolerant software architecture on IoT device

adopt these principles to specify fault-tolerant programming. Redundancy is realized using various plug-in electronic components (sensors or electronic circuits) to retain available operations once parts of a module are crashed. Diversity is achieved through adaptation of communication components (e.g. WiFi, Bluetooth, and Zigbee, etc.) which can be used to take over the jobs of those failed wireless network connections to guarantee available communications between linked nodes. Every software component used to control communication components implements a unified communication interface for the design of communication adaptation.

B. Context Logger. Context Logger is regarded as a global store object that lets task function record its snapshot which saves several critical state variables during exception handling. Critical state variable stores major information related to objective of task function executed on IoT device in IoT application. If some critical state variables lost when task failure, other tasks requires the computation of these will receive invalid result and causes part of operation lost effectiveness in IoT application even though task was recovered later.

In our proposed programming framework, the exception handling of task function is to throw exception when reaches its error state. Then, the next step is to make snapshot operation to save several critical state variables, and stores them into ContextLogger as log data. In case it is necessary for task function to resume to previous state before error occurrence, critical state variable can be accessed from ContextLogger during task recovering. The benefit of this design can guarantee that the exchange of computation results is valid in IoT application

C. Failure Handler. Failure Handler is responsible for the decision of failure recovery strategy when task function reaches an error state. For fault-tolerant programming, application developers specify several rule patterns in FailureHandler. Every rule pattern expressed as an Event-Condition-Action (ECA) style represents a failure recovery strategy with respect to a specified error condition. When task function throws an exception under error states, it propagates error exception message to

Failure Handler. Every exception is regarded as an event which can trigger a matching recovery strategy. An example of pseudo code of rule pattern is shown in Fig. 3. This example indicates that when AccessFailException representing the connection component is unable to work using task function, the recovery strategy is to select an optimal connection way for each linked nodes by comparing minimal average response time among communication components in a node. The information of average response time in each communication component at a linked node can be obtained from State Table.

```
1.  OnException AccessFailException
2.  when AccessFailException.type equalsTo "connection fail "
3.  Action {
4.      update(nodeID, false);
5.      foreach (node in stateTable){
6.          connectionType = minimum("avgResponseTime");
7.      }
8.      RecoveryMaker.start();
9.  }
```

Fig. 3. An example of rule pattern for failure recovery

For recovery to be performed concurrently among the nodes, we propose a mechanism called synchronized state maintenance to record operational state change of each node in the same local WSN anytime through State Table update. State Table is a data set that records peripheral allocation and operational state of every node in the same local WSN. The data model of state table is presented in Fig. 4. The attributes preResponseTime and avgResponseTime in Communication represent previous response time and average response time in several times at checkpoint with respect to a linked node respectively. Both of them are used to determine what connection way is the best one to take over the failed one. In the example presented in Fig. 3, lines 5–7 perform the selection of the best connection way for replacement on each linked node, which is done by comparing minimal average response time among communication components in a node.

D. State Monitor. State Monitor is responsible for the maintenance of State Table on every IoT device so that every node in the same local WSN can be aware of the latest operational state among them. There are two major works for State Monitor to maintain State Table. First, State Monitor can make measurement of response time on specified checkpoints between each linked nodes, including previous response time and average response time, and save these records into State Table.

Second, State Monitor broadcasts state update message to every node in the same local WSN when there is state change on itself. For example, a node notifies each linked node that its communication way has switched from WiFi to Bluetooth when its WiFi communication just failed. Therefore, maintenance can keep state consistency among the nodes in the same local WSN through the operations of State Monitor.

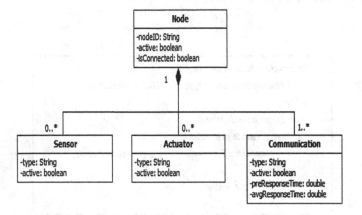

Fig. 4. Data model of state table

E. Recovery Maker. Recovery Maker is called in rule pattern by Failure Handler to adjust parameters of shared resource object such that task function can adaptively select the best alternative component under recovery execution. Recovery Maker can protect shared resource objects' synchronized access and make parameter adjustment be independent of the task function. The benefit of this design is to reduce complexity of shared resource management on IoT device.

4 Experiment Evaluation

4.1 Design of Experimental Case Study

To evaluate our proposed programming framework, we implement a case study to simulate a weather monitoring application. There are eight nodes in the experimental setting. Each node has a sensor component to collect humidity and temperature, and mounts at least two communication components to realize communication diversity. There are three connection ways in this scenario: WiFi, Bluetooth, and Zigbee. Humidity and temperature data are transferred between the nodes. The connection relationship between the nodes and the allocation of communication components are presented in Fig. 5. We simulate scenario that three nodes have communication component fail, i.e. Bluetooth is unable to work on node N2, WiFi is unable to work on node N5, and WiFi is unable to work on node N6. Other nodes were affected due to failed data transmission and did not receive expected data. We adopt the rule pattern presented in Fig. 3 as failure recovery strategy. The initial connection way between the nodes before error occurrence is shown in Fig. 5(a). The connection way between the nodes after failure recovery is showed in Fig. 5(b).

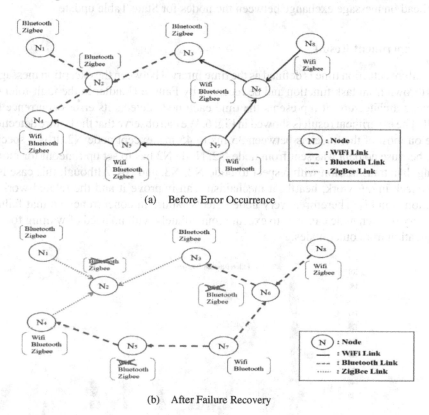

(a)   Before Error Occurrence

(b)   After Failure Recovery

Fig. 5.   Scenario of experimental case study

4.2   Experiment Setup

We implement the case study to evaluate our proposed programming framework using eight nodes. Each node is a Raspberry Pi Model B + which equipped with a Broadcom BCM2835 ARMv6 processor with 700 MHZ and 512 MB SDRAM. Each node mounts a sensor, which can collect humidity and temperature data, and two or three communication components. The allocation of communication components on each node is shown in Fig. 5. The reason why we choice Raspberry Pi to evaluate our proposed framework is its functions as a small independent computer running on Linux operating system that supports a few high-level programming languages, such as Python and Java, and has high expandability to support more number of peripherals [6].

We use python to implement this programming framework, including API of shared objects related to exception handling, task function, and rule pattern for recovery strategy. Our proposed programming framework can be realized using any high-level programming language that supports exception handling. The three experiment objectives to evaluate our work are error detection time, failure recovery time, and message overhead on message exchange between the nodes for State Table update.

4.3   Experiment Result

The failure detection time is defined as the time interval between the exception messages was thrown from task function and be received by Failure Handler in the fault-tolerant software architecture. It represents the time each node detects its error occurrence by itself. The experiment result is showed in Fig. 6. We can observe that the failure detection time on most of the nodes is between 35 ms to 45 ms, except node N2. It is a special case because no data was sent from node N2. Node N2 has to set up timeout for monitoring data transmission with respect to node N2, N3, and N4. Although this case is a bottleneck in our work, heartbeat mechanism can improve it and the related work is mentioned in [7]. Therefore, every node detects failure in concurrency so that failure recovery on each node can start to execute immediately with no need of waiting for the notification from other nodes.

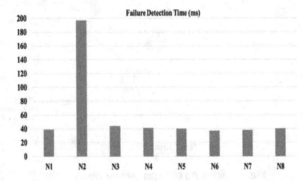

Fig. 6.   Failure detection time on each node

The failure recovery time is defined as the time interval between failure detection time and the time resuming work on each node. The experiment result is showed in Fig. 7. We can observe that the difference of failure recovery time between the nodes is minor, which shows that each node can recover to resume its work by itself concurrently with other nodes. Therefore, we can see that synchronized state maintenance can improve efficiency of recovery execution because Failure Handler can read State Table to know what communication ways are supported by each linked node currently without roll polling. Recovery execution on every node itself in concurrency can improve availability on the application constituted from several nodes.

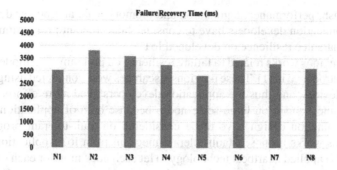

Fig. 7. Failure recovery time on each node

The message overhead on message exchange between the nodes for state table update indicates that the amount of messages that a node has to receive is determined by state update on each linked node due to failure recovery. The experiment results are shown in Fig. 8. The state update messages are received by Nodes N1, N3, N4, N7, and N8 are sent from Nodes N2, N5, and N6 separately, and they show the status of message exchange on communication ways for keeping connection to these nodes. Nodes N2, N5, and N6 just receive two update messages from their neighboring nodes. We can observe that the message overhead on message exchange is proportional to the number of nodes with errors. Therefore, we can see that synchronized state maintenance is a lightweight mechanism to reduce cost of message exchange on failure recovery.

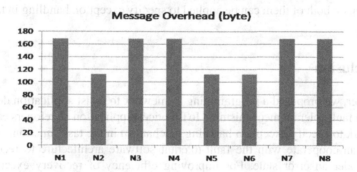

Fig. 8. Message overhead for state table update on each node

5 Related Work

Resilience means that any type of applications can keep its dependability when facing change [8]. The unpredicted change for operational context causes IoT applications operated in an unstable state. Therefore, it is necessary for IoT application to be resilience. There are two types of fault model summarized in [9] related to IoT and its applications. The first type is application context change, such as service binding fail, network disconnection, and context invalidation. The second type is system level error, such as peripheral crash, performance degradation and memory leak, and power degradation. Therefore, application developers have to consider fault-tolerant programming in task function to guarantee resilience on developed IoT.

Several previous works related to failure resilience on programming model of sensor network are introduced in [1]. These previous researches were conducted using resource-constrained devices, and thus the application developers need more efforts to specify fault-tolerant mechanism on large-scale nodes because both of application-level and system-level function design have to be considered on fault-tolerant programming. Some previous works proposed fault-tolerant mechanism in IoT applications [7, 10]. The work in [7] applied heartbeat technology to let each node monitor each other in IoT application, and record resource allocation of every node to realize replication strategy. The work of [10] applied checkpointing technology to realize failure recovery on large-scale IoT application. However, neither of them is on programming perspective for task function.

The research on exception handling is on a programming perspective to realize recovery block in the specified application. Therefore, it is suitable for the design of task function to specify fault-tolerant mechanism. Some previous works applied exception handling to specify fault-tolerant mechanism for application-specific requirements [11, 12]. The work of [11] investigated how to program concurrent exception handling in the scenario of distributed object interaction. The work of [12] was to propose a programming framework for specifying exception handling mechanism with programming context-aware application. The scenario of IoT applications can be regarded as context-aware application based on interaction of distributed objects. Therefore, the contribution on both of them can be applied to specify exception handling in task function.

6   Conclusion

In this paper, we proposed a programming framework to assist application developers to program fault-tolerant mechanism on IoT device. Application developers can follow a framework to specify exception handling mechanism in the task function. Exception handling can cooperate with the fault-tolerant software architecture to recover task function under an error state. For improving efficiency of recovery execution, the synchronized state maintenance mechanism synchronizes state record to maintain consistency on each node in the same local WSN. We used a case study to evaluate this proposed programming framework related to communication strategy under the situation of some failed WiFi or Bluetooth components among the eight nodes. From the experiment results, we observed that failure recovery implemented in this programming framework offers some benefits: concurrently with other nodes, each node could detect different types of error occurrence by itself through exception handling, and could recover by itself depending on the mechanism of node state table with low overhead on message exchanges between nodes.

The programming framework helps application developers with reducing complexity on specifying fault-tolerant mechanism. Some APIs related to exception handling and recovery functionality are specified in the fault-tolerant software architecture so that application developers can program exception handling efficiently and pay more attention on specifying application logic in task function. Because of the declaration of access objects that used for communications and electronic component control are independent of task function in this framework, and high expandability on IoT device, redundancy and diversity can be realized in fault-tolerant programming. Synchronized state maintenance enables recovery to be performed concurrently with low message overhead on every node. State Monitor in the fault-tolerant software architecture can update state table immediately when operation state changes in each node. This way, every node can be aware of component configuration and operation states of each other in the same local WSN. Therefore, every node can select suitable recovery strategy for each linked node with no need of message exchange frequently for state checking between linked nodes.

In summary, our proposed programming framework makes two main contributions: First, based on this framework, application developers can realize fault-tolerant programming efficiently on Raspberry Pi or any other programmable smart device. Second, synchronized state maintenance provides a lightweight and efficient strategy to improve self-healing capability on every node. Therefore, the resilience of IoT applications executed on IoT device can be improved. In the future work, we plan to extend our work to investigate how to construct QoS-aware web service in IoT applications, and explore an automated and lightweight monitoring strategy between distributed nodes in large-scale IoT infrastructure.

Acknowledgments. This study is conducted under the "Big Data Technologies and Applications Project (1/4)" of the Institute for Information Industry which is subsidized by the Ministry of Economic Affairs of the Republic of China. This study is also supported by the Ministry of Science and Technology, Taiwan under Grant NSC 102-2221-E-002-136-MY3.

References

1. Sugihara, R., Gupta, R.K.: Programming models for sensor networks: a survey. ACM Trans. Sensor Netw. **4**(2), 8:1–8:29 (2008)
2. Bakshi, A, Prasanna, V.K., Reich, J., Larner, D.: The abstract task graph: a methodology for architecture-independent programming of networked sensor systems. In: Proceeding of the 2005 Workshop on End to End, Sense-and-Respond Systems, Application and Services, pp. 19–24. USENIX Association (2005)
3. Hong, K, Lillethun, D., Ramachandran, U., Ottenwälder, B., Koldehofe, B.: Mobile fog: a programming model for large-scale applications on the internet of things. In: Proceedings of the Second ACM SIGCOMM Workshop on Mobile Cloud Computing, pp. 15–20. ACM (2013)
4. Vicaire, P.A., Hoque, E., Xie, Z., Stankovic, J.A.: Bundle: a group-based programming abstraction for cyber-physical systems. IEEE Trans. Ind. Inf. **8**(2), 379–392 (2012)
5. Lyu, M.R.: Software Fault Tolerance. Wiley, New York (1995)
6. Vujovic, V., Maksimovic, M.: Raspberry Pi as a wireless sensor node: performance and constraints. In: 37th International Convention on Information and Communication Technology, Electronic and Microelectronics, pp. 1247–1252. IEEE Press (2014)

7. Su, P.H., Shih, C.S., Hsu, J.Y.J., Lin, K.J., Wang, Y.C.: Decentralized fault tolerance mechanism for intelligent IoT/M2M middleware. In: IEEE World Forum on Internet of Things, pp. 45–50. IEEE Press (2014)

8. Laprie, J.C.: From dependability to resilience. In: 38th IEEE/IFIP International Conference on Dependable and Secure Network, pp. G8–G9. IEEE Press (2008)

9. Chetan, S., Ranganathan, A., Campbell, R.: Towards fault-tolerant pervasive computing. IEEE Technol. Soc. Mag. **24**(1), 38–44 (2005)

10. Cherrier, S., Ghamri-Doudane, Y.M., Lohier, S., Roussel, G.: Fault-recovery and coherence in internet of things choreographies. In: IEEE World Forum on Internet of Things, pp. 532–537. IEEE Press (2014)

11. Xu, J., Romanovsky, A., Randell, B.: Concurrent exception handling and resolution in distributed object systems. IEEE Trans. Parallel Distrib. Syst. **11**(10), 1019–1032 (2000)

12. Kulkarni, D., Tripathi, A.: A framework for programming robust context-aware applications. IEEE Trans. Software Eng. **36**(2), 184–197 (2010)

An Agent-Based Framework for Simulating and Analysing Attacks on Cyber Physical Systems

Sridhar Adepu[1](✉), Aditya Mathur[1], Jagadeesh Gunda[2], and Sasa Djokic[2]

[1] Singapore University of Technology and Design, Singapore City 487372, Singapore
{sridhar_adepu, aditya_mathur}@sutd.edu.sg
[2] Institute for Energy Systems, University of Edinburgh, Edinburgh EH9 3JL, UK
J.Gunda@sms.ed.ac.uk, sasa.djokic@ed.ac.uk

Abstract. An agent-based framework is presented to model and analyze physical and cyber attacks on Cyber Physical Systems (CPS). In the first phase of a two phase procedure in the framework, a CPS is modelled using State Condition Graphs (SCGs) representing the structural relations among the cyber and physical components. In the second phase, SCGs are partitioned into separate groups, referred to as *agents*, based on their functional dependency. Each agent is associated with a sensor and an actuator set. The actuator set is further divided into two subsets: active actuator and passive subsets that, respectively, directly or indirectly participate in controlling the environment. Interactions among different agents can be created by assigning an aggregate function to each agent with sensor and actuator sets as the domain of the function and status of the environment as its codomain. A case study was conducted on a segment of a 6-stage Secure Water Treatment (SWaT) system to demonstrate the applicability of the framework. The study reveals promising features of the framework to analyze the steady state response of the system following both cyber and physical attacks.

Keywords: Cyber physical systems · Cyber attacks · Physical attacks · State condition graphs · Agents · Sensor and actuator sets

1 Introduction

Cyber Physical Systems (CPS): These are systems built by integrating computational algorithms and physical components. CPS interact with the physical world and with users, e.g., via Human machine Interface (HMI), engineering work stations, corporate work station, smart phones, etc. CPS are found in diverse areas including public infrastructure such as for electricity, water, and transportation networks, as well as others such as in robotics and health care. Typically, a CPS contains one or more Programmable Logic Controllers (PLCs). Each PLC contains control software for sensing process state, usually partial, and therefrom computing and applying control actions via actuators. The PLCs in a CPS can be viewed as a system that transforms the state of the process (Fig. 1).

© Springer International Publishing Switzerland 2015
G. Wang et al. (Eds.): ICA3PP 2015, Part III, LNCS 9530, pp. 785–798, 2015.
DOI: 10.1007/978-3-319-27137-8_57

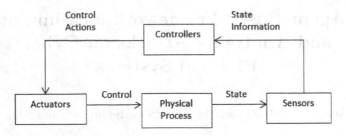

Fig. 1. CPS as a state transformer. In a water treatment system, actuators include pumps and motorised valves, while the sensors include level sensors, pH meters, chlorine sensors, and ORP meters.

Frameworks: Many frameworks, software platforms for modelling and simulation of CPS systems have been proposed. However, there is a lack of an effective unified framework that allows co-design of cyber and physical processes and systematic assessment of a CPS's security in the context of cyber and/or physical attacks. Most existing solutions either do not exhaustively cover the requirements from different domains, or restrict the development environment thus resulting in reduced flexibility of design by enforcing the use of a specific software platform and tightly-coupled tools [1]. To fill this void, an agent-based framework for steady state modelling and analysis is proposed and experimentally evaluated. The proposed framework is generic and applicable to a variety of critical public infrastructure systems due primarily to its simple yet powerful abstraction of a CPS as a collection of sensors and actuators.

Related Work: Previous work in this area can be divided into three groups. *1. Open Research Challenges:* Work in this area has focused mostly on presenting the research challenges, e.g. safety and security against cyber-attacks, that need to be addressed while designing the current and emerging CPS. In [2], the evolution of Industrial Control Systems (ICS) from traditional to emerging CPS with the use of ICT technologies is discussed, including potential vulnerabilities and design challenges. Lee [3] presented the problems associated with the up-to-date computing and networking technologies for full-fledged design of emerging CPS. *2. Framework development for CPS:* In [1], authors present the problems and challenges associated with software development for CPS, and propose to develop a general framework to enable design, modelling and simulation of CPS. In [4], authors propose a multi-view architecture framework that treats models as views of the underlying system structure and uses structural and semantic mappings to ensure consistency and enable system-level verification in a hierarchical and compositional manner. In [5], authors propose to develop a platform-independent and domain-specific modelling language for specifying the design of CPS. *3. Attack modelling and analysis:* Work in this area mainly focused on the identification of vulnerable points in CPS, methods for attack modelling, detection, isolation, and analysis. For example, Kundur et al. [6–8] have developed mathematical models to simulate various cyber-attacks on smart

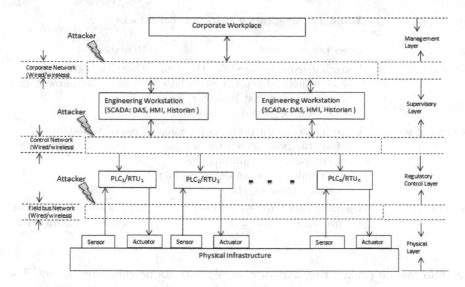

Fig. 2. Architecture of the control portion of a CPS. Note that the actuators, e.g., a pump, also have sensors to indicate their condition.

grids using complex network theory, and validated their models by interfacing with the commercial power system simulators. Pasqualetti et al. [9] proposed mathematical models to detect and identify cyber-attacks in CPS. The work presented in this paper falls under groups 2 and 3 mentioned above.

Contributions: (a) State Condition Graph (SCG) representing the structural relation among various cyber and physical components. (b) An agent-based scalable framework that allows to model a CPS, simulate various cyber and physical attacks assuming that the attacks can be introduced at any level of the system and analyse the system steady state response. (c) Demonstration of the applicability of the agent-based framework on a water treatment plant and analysis of the system response following both cyber and physical attacks.

2   Modeling a CPS

The first step in the proposed methodology is to construct a suitable model of a CPS. A general architecture of a CPS and the modelling procedure based on this architecture, are described next.

2.1   Structure of a CPS

The architecture of the cyber control portion of a typical large scale CPS can be described by hierarchically separated functional layers [2,10] as shown in Fig. 2. Each layer, comprised of specific hardware and software, is intended to perform a set of predefined and coordinated computational tasks by exchanging

Table 1. Classification of basic cyber-attacks

Attack	Description	Remarks
Deception	Unauthorized actor modifies the data and authorized actor receives false data assuming that it is true; e.g., command or false data injection	Loss of integrity of sensor actuator data
Denial of service (DoS)	Unauthorized actor prevents exchange of information, i.e., either delayed or stopped, e.g., jamming the communication channel, impacting routing protocols, etc	Loss of availability of sensor actuator data
Disclosure	Unauthorized actor gain access (listening) to the data	Loss of confidentiality of sensor/actuator data

the information (monitoring and/or control) with its neighbouring layers. The medium of communication among different layers may be wired or wireless. The functions carried out at each layer and communication between each functional layer are described below.

Physical Layer: This layer comprises the physical plant or system to be controlled and is often modelled by differential algebraic equations. The physical layer also consists of sensors and actuators that are used to compute and apply control actions to the physical process by exchanging monitoring and control information with Regulatory Control Layer.

Regulatory Control Layer: This layer mainly comprises of a set of PLCs or Remote Terminal Units (RTUs). In general, a PLC/RTU computes the control actions by applying preprogrammed logic with any associated set point received from the supervisory layer on the information acquired through the sensors and then applies these control actions via actuators to control the process assigned to it. Typically, in any CPS, the overall process is divided into several sub-processes, sometimes referred to as upstream and downstream processes, or main and child processes. At local level, each part of the process is controlled by a specific PLC. At global level, different PLCs exchange the required information via communication networks for coordination among different dependent processes and for the effective control of the entire system or process. As shown in Fig. 2, each PLC communicates with a set of sensors and actuators via a local network. This network is considered to be at Level 0 and is also referred to as the field-bus network [11].

Supervisory Layer: This layer mainly comprises of one or more workstations loaded with SCADA software, mostly desktop applications, and/or hardware: Data Acquisition server, HMI, and data historian. The supervisory layer coordinates activities across all layers by designing and sending appropriate commands, e.g., control set points, to the regulatory layer. It can be viewed as the "brain" of the system. It's primary function is to perform critical data analysis to provide immediate and precise assessment of the situation [10]. As shown in Fig. 2, supervisory layer communicates with regulatory area via control network, and with management layer via corporate network. The control networks and corporate networks may be wired or wireless.

Management Layer: Management layer is a higher level decision-making engine, where the decision-makers take an economic perspective towards the resource allocation problems in control systems [10]. Decision makers access the system information often via web applications. As shown in Fig. 2, the management layer communicates with the supervisory layer via corporate network, which is often wireless.

2.2 Cyber-Attacks Against CPS

Control systems have been at the core of critical infrastructures and industrial plants for many decades, and yet, there have been very few confirmed cases of cyber-attacks [2]. In the past, control systems were generally made up of proprietary software (SCADA, HMI, etc.) and hardware components (PLC, RTU, etc.). In addition, the interconnection between different control systems (i.e. control network) or its components (i.e. field bus network) was mainly provided by dedicated ICT system with proprietary protocols (e.g. Modbus, Profibus, ControlNet, DeviceNet, etc.) which made industrial control systems (ICS) more complex and robust to cyber-attacks. As a consequence of recent efforts for providing efficient communication and interoperability, ICS have evolved from proprietary systems to open architectures such as windows computers for engineering work station, TCP/IP networking, OPC, IEC61850, etc., making CPS much more vulnerable to cyber-attacks [2].

At the physical level, the traditional wired sensor and actuator systems are recently being replaced by smart sensor and actuator systems (i.e. IEDs), which are able to communicate with PLC I/O cards via wireless communication systems. The presence of wireless communications among the CPS infrastructure, makes it even more vulnerable to cyber-attacks. The list of primitive cyber-attacks is given in Table 1. Such attacks could compromise the communication links between sensors and PLCs and among the PLCs. Once one or more links have been compromised, an attacker could use several strategies to send fake state data to one or more PLCs. Unless the defense mechanism of the attacked CPS is highly robust, such attacks could cause an undesirable response from the CPS that in turn may lead to system shutdown and/or device damage. Therefore, it becomes imperative for engineers to understand the response of a CPS to a variety of strategic cyber-attacks and assess the robustness of its defense mechanism.

3 Modelling of CPS and Proposed Framework

3.1 State Condition Graphs

A State Condition Graph (SCG) GS of a CPS S is a pair (N, E), where N is a finite set of nodes and E is a finite set of (possibly) labelled directed edges.

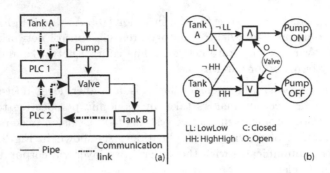

Fig. 3. (a) A subsystem of a CPS S consisting of two tanks, a pump, a valve, and two PLCs controlling the pump and the valve. (b) A portion of the SCG for S depicting the conditions that govern pump operation.

Three types of nodes are considered. A state-node, referred to as *s-node*, denotes the state of an actuator, such as a motorized valve, a tank, a generator, or a tap changing transformer. For an actuator with k states, there are k nodes in the corresponding SCG, each denoting a unique corresponding state. A component node, referred to as a *c-node*, denotes any component of a CPS that could be in two or more states. An operator-node, referred to as *o-node*, denotes a logical operator such as a logical and ($\wedge$), logical or ($\vee$), and logical not ($\sim$). A labelled edge is a triple (n1; l; n2), where n1 and n2 denote, respectively, c-node and s-node, and l the state of the component denoted by n1. n2 denotes the state of an actuator.

Example 1: Consider a system S (Fig. 3(a)), consisting of the following components: a pump, a valve, and two water tanks. PLC 1 controls the pump, while PLC 2 controls the valve. Level sensors at each tank communicate with the PLC as shown. Each tank can be in any of four states: LowLow (LL), Low (L), High (H), and HighHigh (HH). The pump has two states: ON and OFF. The valve that connects pump to Tank B can be in one of two states: O(pen) and C(losed).

Now suppose that the design of S requires the following conditions to govern the pump. The pump is started, i.e., its state changed from OFF to ON, when Tank A is not in state LL, Tank B is not in state HH, and the valve is open (O). The pump state is changed from ON to OFF whenever Tank B is in the HH state, or Tank A is in LL state. Figure 3 shows a partial SCG for S that captures the conditions that govern the pump operation. This partial SCG has two s-nodes labelled Pump ON and Pump OFF, two c-nodes labelled Tank A and Tank B, and two op-nodes labelled $\wedge$ and $\vee$.

3.2 Agent-Based Framework

State Condition Graphs (SCG) are an aid to understanding the structural and functional relation among various nodes of the same process or different processes.

In its current form, SCG based modelling becomes cumbersome when the number of nodes in the system increases. Consequently, it is difficult to simulate cyber and physical attacks across layers of the system and analyse the system response to those attacks. To overcome this difficulty, an agent-based methodology for CPS modelling is proposed. In this an initial study the proposed model is only valid for the steady state modelling and response analysis of the system. The framework is explained in the following stages.

1. **Process or System Partition:** In this step, the overall process of CPS is partitioned into several sub-processes each corresponding to a subsystem. An experienced system operator, or a skilled engineer, with sufficient functional knowledge of the CPS can interactively perform this task given a software tool.
2. **SCG-Based Modelling:** This step models each sub-process, or subsystem, using SCG to capture the structural and functional relationship among various nodes. Here, the nodes represent sensors, actuators, or the physical components, such as transformers, motor-pump sets, generators, and tanks, that need to be monitored and controlled.
3. **Agent Selection:** This step is further divided into the following tasks.
   (a) Identify the critical physical components (or all components, if required) in each sub-process (or subsystem).
   (b) With the help of the SCG's so developed, identify the sensors and actuators associated with each critical component and then define the following two sets: a *sensor set*, which is a group of the associated sensors, and an *actuator set*, which is a group of all the associated actuators.
   (c) **Agent Definition:** An agent is defined as an ordered quadruple, $\varphi = (S,A,C,F)$, where S: sensor set, A: actuator set, C: status of the agent, $\{0,1\}$, F: an aggregated function defined as F: $\{S, A\} \rightarrow$ C. The area that falls under this agent is considered as its environment. The actuator set can be further divided into two sets: *active actuator set*, which directly participates in controlling the environment, and *passive actuator set*, which indirectly participates, i.e., as a sensor, in controlling the environment.
4. **Agent Interaction:** Each agent can sense it's environment through its sensor set and passive actuator set, and can control the environment via its active actuator set. The interaction among different agents, i.e., the ability of an agent to sense, or affect the control of other agent's environment, can be created by assigning an aggregate function to each agent with sensor and actuator sets as the domain of the function, and status of the environment as the codomain of the function.

In general, the values of physical quantities sent by the sensors and received by the actuators may be digital, e.g., 0 represents 0 V and 1 represents 100 V, discrete, e.g., transformer tap positions, analogue, or 4–20 mA DC or 0–110 V AC, or even in a mixed form. In the proposed framework, all digital or analog values received from sensors are converted into digital form, to better represent the actual information flow over the communication network. The bit resolution

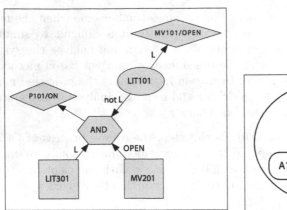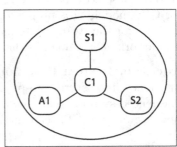

Fig. 4. (a) SCG for P1 stage of SWaT. L: Low level in the tank. (b) An agent-based model for P1 stage with one agent where S1:LIT101, S2:LIT301, A1:MV201, C1:P101

depends on either the magnitude or number of required levels to represent the physical quantity to be measured and controlled. Conversion of analogue and discrete values to digital ones, to represent physical quantities and set theory based approach for function modelling, enables the simulation of various cyber and physical components and subsequently monitoring the system response.

Example 2: Consider the P1-stage of SWaT (Fig. 5), whose SCG is in Fig. 4(a). An agent-based model for this stage considering only the raw water pump P101 as a critical component is shown in Fig. 4(b). As there is only one agent, Fig. 4(b) shows only this one agent. An agent for this subsystem is given below.

Sensor set, S = {LIT101, LIT301}
Actuator Set, A = {MV201}
Status of the motor-pump set, C = {0, 1}
Aggregated function, F: {S,A} → C

where, LIT101 and LIT301 are level sensors, MV201 is a motorized control valve, 0 and 1 represent, respectively, pump status OFF and ON. Each level sensor can be in any of four states: LowLow (LL), LowHigh (LH), HighLow (HL), and

Table 2. Truth table for function mapping

LIT101(S1)	LIT301(S2)	MV201(A1)	P101(C1)
01	01	1	1
10	10	1	1
11	00	1	1
00	11	0	0

HighHigh (HH), which are converted into equivalent digital form. The motorized control valve, MV201, has two states: Open (1) and Closed (0) that represent the actual control valve in SWaT. In general, there is a possibility to operate the control valve from 0 to 100 % with a specified number of steps. The function mapping can be achieved using the truth table as in Table 2.

4 Case Study

The design and analysis approach described in the previous section was used to analyse the response of SWaT to cyber attacks. As is often the case, SWaT was designed and built for correct operation. While the control algorithms in SWaT do account for component failures, they were not designed to detect and defend against cyber and physical attacks aimed at communication or other physical infrastructure. This aspect of SWaT makes it an appropriate testbed to study the effectiveness of the agent-based modelling and analysis framework.

4.1 Architecture of SWaT

SWaT is a testbed for water treatment. In a small footprint producing 5 gallons/h of filtered water, the testbed mimics a large modern water treatment plant found in big cities. It is used to investigate response to cyber-attacks and conduct experiment with novel designs of physics-based and other defense mechanisms. As shown in Fig. 5, SWaT consists of six stages labelled P1 through P6. Each stage is controlled by its own set of dual PLCs (not shown) one serving as a primary and the other as a backup in case of any failure of the primary.

Communications: Each PLC obtains data from sensors associated with the corresponding stage, and controls pumps and valves in its domain. Turning the pumps ON, or opening a valve, causes water to flow either into or out of a tank. Level sensors in each tank inform the PLCs on status of the tank and when to turn a pump ON or OFF. Several other sensors are available to check the physical and chemical properties of water flowing through the six stages. PLCs communicate with each other through a separate network. Communications among sensors, actuators, and PLCs can be via either wired or wireless links; manual switches allow transfer between the wired and wireless modes.

Stages in SWaT: Stage P1 controls the inflow of water to be treated by opening or closing a valve (MV101) that connects the inlet pipe to the raw water tank. Water from the raw water tank is pumped via a chemical dosing station (stage P2) to another UF (Ultrafiltration) feed water tank in stage P3. In stage P3, a UF feed pump sends the water via UF membrane to RO (Reverse Osmosis) feed water tank in stage P4. An RO feed pump sends the water through an ultraviolet dechlorination unit controlled by a PLC in stage P4. This step is necessary to remove any free chlorine from the water prior to passing it through the reverse osmosis unit in stage P5. Sodium bisulphate ($NaHSO_3$) can be added in stage P4 to control the ORP (Oxidation Reduction Potential). In stage P5,

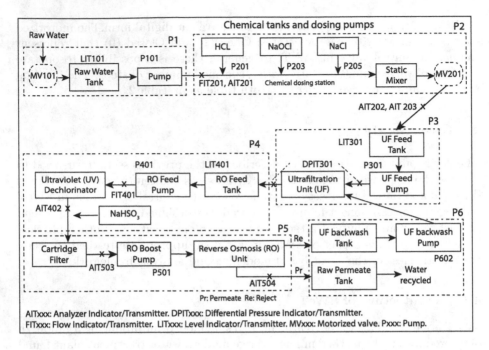

Fig. 5. Physical water treatment process in SWaT and attack points used in the case study. P1 though P6 indicate the six stages in the treatment process. An **x** indicates placement of sensors.

the dechlorinated water is passed through a 2-stage RO filtration unit. The filtered water from the RO unit is stored in the permeate tank and the reject in the UF backwash tank. Stage P6 controls the cleaning of the membranes in the UF unit by turning on or off the UF backwash pump. The backwash cycle is initiated automatically once every 30 min and takes less than a minute to complete. Differential pressure sensors in stage P3 measure the pressure drop across the UF unit. A backwash cycle is also initiated if the pressure drop exceeds 0.4 bar, indicating that the membranes need immediate cleaning. A differential pressure mete (DPIT) installed in stage P3 is used by PLC-3 to obtain the pressure drop.

4.2   Modelling SWaT

The agent-based model was created using executable code embedded in the six PLCs. For attack analysis, this model is implemented for P2 whose SCG is in Fig. 6, and its agent-based model in Fig. 7. A list of components and description is in Table 3. As there are three critical physical components, the agent-based model for this stage has three agents. At the local level, each agent controls its own environment and at the global level, they together control the overall process by exchanging the information (when required). The information

exchange between two agents is automatically achieved provided that the intersection of their function domains is a non-empty set.

4.3   Attack Simulation and Impact Analysis on SWaT

Attack Points in SWaT: For a cyber-attack, the attacker can penetrate the
network from any level (Fig. 2) and create an attack from a sample in Table 4 by
targeting a specific component or communication link. In this case study, decep-
tion attacks and physical attacks were simulated, and the corresponding CPS
responses analysed using the developed framework. The same attacks were also
applied to the CPS to validate the framework. Only the wireless links between
sensors and the corresponding PLCs were considered as the points of cyber-
attacks. A pessimistic approach is taken, implying that all wireless links are

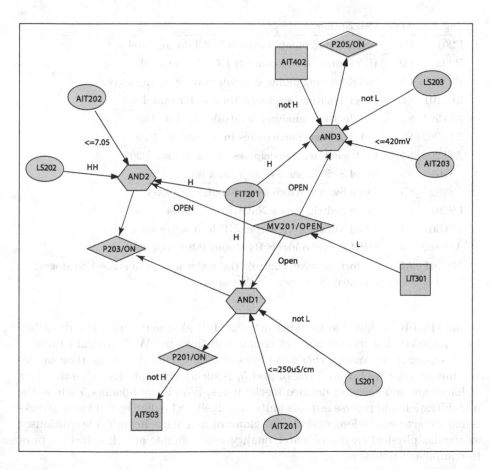

Fig. 6. SCG for stage P2 of SWaT. L and H indicate Low and High, respectively,
states of a tank. Oval: sensors; square: the values collected from other PLCs; diamond:
actuators.

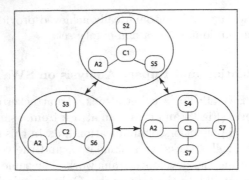

Fig. 7. Agent-based model for stage P2 of SWaT.

Table 3. SWaT components used in the case study

Tag	Type	Description
P201	C1	NaCl dosing pump; controls NaCl dosing level
P203	C2	HCl dosing pump; controls HCl dosing level
P205	C3	NaOCl dosing pump, controls NaOCl dosing level
LIT101	S1	Level Transmitter; senses Raw water tank level
AIT201	S2	Conductivity analyzer; controls NaCl dosing
AIT202	S3	PH Analyzer; participates in controlling P203
AIT203	S4	ORP analyzer; participates in controlling P205
LS201	S5	Level Switch; senses NaCl tank level
LS202	S6	Level Switch, which senses HCL tank level
LS203	S7	Level Switch; senses NaOCL tank level
LIT301	S8	Level Transmitter; senses UF feed water tank level
AIT402	S9	ORP meter: controls P403 and P404 (not shown)
MV201	A2	Motorized valve; controls the water flow from stage-1 to stage-2

C: Physical component, S: Sensor, A: Actuator

assumed to be vulnerable to cyber-attacks. Initial experiments, not described here, revealed that indeed, wireless communications in SWaT are vulnerable.

A summary of various cyber and physical attacks considered and their potential impact on SWaT is in Tables 4 and 5, respectively. Note that due to a lack of hardware and software defence mechanisms, SWaT components, such as the ultrafiltration and reverse osmosis units, are likely to be damaged if these attacks remained active for a long period. The claim of damage is being made cautiously, as regular physical checks of water quality could enable attack detection prior to component damage.

Table 4. Summary of cyber-attacks carried out

Sensor compromised	Actuator affected	Impact
LS201	P201	NaCl dosing level either increased or decreased with respect to the required level
AIT402	P205	NaOCl dosing process be disturbed. The dosing level will be either increased or decreased more than the required level
LIT301	Response-1: MV201	(a) Water flow rate from stage-1 to stage-2 is completely disturbed, as MV201 received fault action from the PLC
	Response-2: MV201, P201, and P205	(b) NaCl and NaOCl dosing will be disturbed. Water flow rate is disturbed

Table 5. Summary of physical attacks carried out

Attacker action	Actuator affected	Impact
Break the UTP or STP cable connection between LS202 and PLC I/O card	P203	HCL dosing will be disturbed due to the change in P203 status
Break the UTP or STP cable connection between MV201 and PLC I/O card.	Response-1: Not applicable	(a) MV201 will be closed as it does not receive any signal from PLC, reducing the water flow rate to zero
	Response-2: P201, P205	(b) HCl, NaCl and NaOCl dosing process disturbed

5 Summary

An agent-based framework is presented for steady state modelling of a CPS. A case study was conducted on a portion of a 6-stage SWaT system to explore the applicability of the framework in the analysis of the system response following a set of cyber and physical attacks. The study reveals promising features of the framework to analyse the steady state response of the system following an attack.

The SCG model captures the conditions required for actuators to be in specific states at any time instant, and after the system reaches a steady state. Thus, the conditions in an SCG must be true regardless of the past, current, or future states of the CPS. Adding attributes of individual CPS components to an SCG will make it more detailed and closer to reality, but will also add to its complexity. SCGs are simpler than a typical dynamic model and will likely make CPS modeling and the attack analysis much easier and quicker than with dynamic models.

Acknowledgments. This work was supported by research grant 9013102373 from the Ministry of Defense and NRF2014-NCR-NCR001-040 from the National Research Foundation, Singapore. Thanks to Kaung Myat Aung for assistance with the design and conduct of experiments.

References

1. Kim, J.E., Mosse, D.: Generic framework for design, modeling and simulation of cyber physical systems. ACM SIGBED Rev. **5**, 1 (2008)
2. Cárdenas, A.A., Amin, S., Sastry, S.: Research challenges for the security of control systems. In: HotSec (2008)
3. Lee, E.A.: Cyber-physical systems-are computing foundations adequate. In: Position Paper for NSF Workshop on Cyber-Physical Systems: Research Motivation, Techniques and Roadmap, vol. 2. Citeseer (2006)
4. Rajhans, A., Bhave, A., Ruchkin, I., Krogh, B.H., Garlan, D., Platzer, A., Schmerl, B.: Supporting heterogeneity in cyber-physical systems architectures. IEEE Trans. Autom. Control **59**, 3178–3193 (2014)
5. Tariq, M.U., Florence, J., Wolf, M.: Design specification of cyber-physical systems: towards a domain-specific modeling language based on simulink, eclipse modeling framework, and giotto. In: Proceedings of the 7th International Workshop on Model-based Architecting, pp. 6–15 (2014)
6. Kundur, D., Feng, X., Liu, S., Zourntos, T., Butler-Purry, K.L.: Towards a framework for cyber attack impact analysis of the electric smart grid. In: First IEEE International Conference on Smart Grid Communications (SmartGridComm), pp. 244–249. IEEE (2010)
7. Liu, S., Mashayekh, S., Kundur, D., Zourntos, T., Butler-Purry, K.: A smart grid vulnerability analysis framework for coordinated variable structure switching attacks. In: Power and Energy Society General Meeting, 2012 IEEE, pp. 1–6. IEEE (2012)
8. Wei, J., Kundur, D.: Two-tier hierarchical cyber-physical security analysis framework for smart grid. In: IEEE Power and Energy Society General Meeting, pp. 1–5. IEEE (2012)
9. Pasqualetti, F., Dörfler, F., Bullo, F.: Attack detection and identification in cyber-physical systems-Part I: Models and fundamental limitations (2012). arXiv preprint arXiv:1202.6144
10. Zhu, Q., Rieger, C., Başar, T.: A hierarchical security architecture for cyber-physical systems. In: 2011 4th International Symposium on Resilient Control Systems (ISRCS), pp. 15–20. IEEE (2011)
11. Stouffer, K., Falco, J., Scarfone, K.: Guide to industrial control systems (ICS) security. Technical report 11, NIST Special Publication (2011)

Author Index

Printed in the United States
By Bookmasters